Collins

— POCKET —

English
Thesaurus

HarperCollins Publishers
Westerhill Road
Bishopbriggs
Glasgow
G64 2QT

Sixth Edition 2012

Reprint 10 9 8 7 6 5 4 3 2 1 0

© HarperCollins Publishers 1992,
2000, 2004, 2005, 2008, 2010, 2012

ISBN 978-0-00-745056-5

Collins® is a registered trademark of
HarperCollins Publishers Limited

www.collinslanguage.com

A catalogue record for this book is
available from the British Library

Typeset by Wordcraft and
Davidson Publishing Solutions,
Glasgow

Printed and bound in Italy by
LEGO SpA, Lavis (Trento)

Acknowledgements
We would like to thank those authors
and publishers who kindly gave
permission for copyright material
to be used in the Collins Corpus.
We would also like to thank Times
Newspapers Ltd for providing
valuable data.

CONTENTS

ABBREVIATIONS USED IN THIS THESAURUS

AD	anno Domini	*meteorol*	meteorology
adj	adjective	*mil*	military
adv	adverb	*n*	noun
anat	anatomy	N	North
archit	architecture	*naut*	nautical
astrol	astrology	NZ	New Zealand
Aust	Australia(n)	*obs*	obsolete
BC	before Christ	*offens*	offensive
biol	biology	*orig*	originally
Brit	British	*photog*	photography
chem	chemistry	*pl*	plural
C of E	Church of England	*prep*	preposition
conj	conjunction	*pron*	pronoun
E	East	*psychol*	psychology
eg	for example	®	trademark
esp	especially	RC	Roman Catholic
etc	et cetera	S	South
fem	feminine	*S Afr*	South Africa(n)
foll	followed	*Scot*	Scottish
geom	geometry	*sing*	singular
hist	history	US	United States
interj	interjection	*usu*	usually
lit	literary	*v*	verb
masc	masculine	W	West
med	medicine	*zool*	zoology

USING THIS THESAURUS

Main Entry Words

Main entry words are printed in blue bold type:

> **altogether**

Parts of Speech

Parts of speech are shown in small capitals. Where a word has several senses for one part of speech, the senses are numbered:

> **altogether** ADVERB 1

Alternatives

The key synonym for each sense is given in bold, with other alternatives given in roman:

> **altogether** ADVERB 1 **absolutely**, quite, completely, totally, perfectly, fully, thoroughly, wholly 2 **completely**, fully, entirely, thoroughly, wholly, in every respect

Opposites

Opposites are indented, with an inequation sign:

> ≠ partially

Related words

Related words are introduced by rightfacing arrows:

> ▷ **RELATED WORD** circle

Word Power

Word Power notes are shown in indented panels:

> ◦ The use of *actress* is now very
> ◦ much in decline, and women
> ◦ who work in the profession
> ◦ invariably prefer to be
> ◦ referred to as *actors*.

Aa

abandon VERB 1 = **leave**, strand, ditch, forsake, run out on, desert, dump 2 = **stop**, give up, halt, pack in (*Brit. informal*), discontinue, leave off ≠ continue 3 = **give up**, yield, surrender, relinquish ≠ keep
▷ NOUN = **recklessness**, wildness ≠ restraint

abandonment NOUN = **desertion**, leaving, forsaking

abbey NOUN = **monastery**, convent, priory, nunnery, friary

abduct VERB = **kidnap**, seize, carry off, snatch (*slang*)

abide VERB = **tolerate**, suffer, accept, bear, endure, put up with, take, stand ▷ PHRASE: **abide by something** = **obey**, follow, agree to, carry out, observe, fulfil, act on, comply with

abiding ADJECTIVE = **enduring**, lasting, continuing, permanent, persistent, everlasting ≠ brief

ability NOUN 1 = **capability**, potential, competence, proficiency ≠ inability 2 = **skill**, talent, expertise, competence, aptitude, proficiency, cleverness

able ADJECTIVE = **capable**, qualified, efficient, accomplished, competent, skilful, proficient ≠ incapable

abnormal ADJECTIVE = **unusual**, different, odd, strange, extraordinary, remarkable, exceptional, peculiar, daggy (*Austral. & N.Z. informal*) ≠ normal

abnormality NOUN 1 = **strangeness**, peculiarity, irregularity, singularity 2 = **anomaly**, oddity, exception, peculiarity, deformity, irregularity

abolish VERB = **do away with**, end, destroy, eliminate, cancel, get rid of, ditch (*slang*), throw out ≠ establish

abolition NOUN = **eradication**, ending, end, destruction, wiping out, elimination, cancellation, termination

abort VERB 1 = **terminate** (*a pregnancy*), miscarry 2 = **stop**, end, finish, check, arrest, halt, cease, axe (*informal*)

abortion NOUN = **termination**, miscarriage, deliberate miscarriage

abound VERB = **be plentiful**, thrive, flourish, be numerous, proliferate, be abundant, be thick on the ground

about PREPOSITION 1 = **regarding**, on, concerning, dealing with, referring to, relating to, as regards 2 = **near**, around, close to, nearby, beside, adjacent to, in the neighbourhood of
▷ ADVERB = **approximately**, around, almost, nearly, approaching, close to, roughly, just about

above PREPOSITION 1 = **over**,

a

upon, beyond, on top of, exceeding, higher than ≠ under **2** = **senior to**, over, ahead of, in charge of, higher than, superior to, more powerful than

abroad ADVERB = **overseas**, out of the country, in foreign lands

abrupt ADJECTIVE **1** = **sudden**, unexpected, rapid, surprising, quick, rash, precipitate ≠ slow **2** = **curt**, brief, short, rude, impatient, terse, gruff, succinct ≠ polite

absence NOUN **1** = **time off**, leave, break, vacation, recess, truancy, absenteeism, nonattendance **2** = **lack**, deficiency, omission, scarcity, want, need, shortage, dearth

absent ADJECTIVE **1** = **away**, missing, gone, elsewhere, unavailable, nonexistent ≠ present **2** = **absent-minded**, blank, vague, distracted, vacant, preoccupied, oblivious, inattentive ≠ alert ▷ PHRASE: **absent yourself** = **stay away**, withdraw, keep away, play truant

absolute ADJECTIVE **1** = **complete**, total, perfect, pure, sheer, utter, outright, thorough **2** = **supreme**, sovereign, unlimited, ultimate, full, unconditional, unrestricted, pre-eminent **3** = **autocratic**, supreme, all-powerful, imperious, domineering, tyrannical

absolutely ADVERB = **completely**, totally, perfectly, fully, entirely, altogether, wholly, utterly ≠ somewhat

absorb VERB **1** = **soak up**, suck up, receive, digest, imbibe **2** = **engross**, involve, engage, fascinate, rivet, captivate

absorbed ADJECTIVE = **engrossed**, lost, involved, gripped, fascinated, caught up, wrapped up, preoccupied

absorbing ADJECTIVE = **fascinating**, interesting, engaging, gripping, compelling, intriguing, enticing, riveting ≠ boring

absorption NOUN **1** = **soaking up**, consumption, digestion, sucking up **2** = **immersion**, involvement, concentration, fascination, preoccupation, intentness

abstract ADJECTIVE = **theoretical**, general, academic, speculative, indefinite, hypothetical, notional, abstruse ≠ actual ▷ NOUN = **summary**, résumé, outline, digest, epitome, rundown, synopsis, précis ≠ expansion ▷ VERB = **extract**, draw, pull, remove, separate, withdraw, isolate, pull out ≠ add

absurd ADJECTIVE = **ridiculous**, crazy (*informal*), silly, foolish, ludicrous, unreasonable, irrational, senseless ≠ sensible

abundance NOUN = **plenty**, bounty, exuberance, profusion, plethora, affluence, fullness, fruitfulness ≠ shortage

abundant ADJECTIVE = **plentiful**, full, rich, liberal, generous, ample, exuberant, teeming ≠ scarce

abuse NOUN 1 = **maltreatment**, damage, injury, hurt, harm, exploitation, manhandling, ill-treatment 2 = **insults**, blame, slights, put-downs, censure, reproach, scolding, defamation 3 = **misuse**, misapplication
▷ VERB 1 = **ill-treat**, damage, hurt, injure, harm, molest, maltreat, knock about or around ≠ care for 2 = **insult**, offend, curse, put down, malign, scold, disparage, castigate ≠ praise

abusive ADJECTIVE 1 = **violent**, rough, cruel, savage, brutal, vicious, destructive, harmful ≠ kind 2 = **insulting**, offensive, rude, degrading, scathing, contemptuous, disparaging, scurrilous ≠ complimentary

academic ADJECTIVE
1 = **scholastic**, educational
2 = **scholarly**, learned, intellectual, literary, erudite, highbrow, studious
3 = **theoretical**, abstract, speculative, hypothetical, impractical, notional, conjectural
▷ NOUN = **scholar**, intellectual, don, master, professor, fellow, lecturer, tutor, acca (Austral. slang)

accelerate VERB 1 = **increase**, grow, advance, extend, expand, raise, swell, enlarge ≠ fall
2 = **expedite**, further, speed up, hasten ≠ delay 3 = **speed up**, advance, quicken, gather momentum ≠ slow down

acceleration NOUN = **hastening**, hurrying, stepping up (informal), speeding up, quickening

accent NOUN = **pronunciation**, tone, articulation, inflection, brogue, intonation, diction, modulation
▷ VERB = **emphasize**, stress, highlight, underline, underscore, accentuate

accept VERB 1 = **receive**, take, gain, pick up, secure, collect, get, obtain 2 = **acknowledge**, believe, allow, admit, approve, recognize, yield, concede

acceptable ADJECTIVE
= **satisfactory**, fair, all right, suitable, sufficient, good enough, adequate, tolerable ≠ unsatisfactory

acceptance NOUN 1 = **accepting**, taking, receiving, obtaining, acquiring, reception, receipt
2 = **acknowledgement**, agreement, approval, recognition, admission, consent, adoption, assent

accepted ADJECTIVE = **agreed**, common, established, traditional, approved, acknowledged, recognized, customary ≠ unconventional

access NOUN 1 = **admission**, entry, passage 2 = **entrance**, road, approach, entry, path, gate, opening, passage

accessible ADJECTIVE = **handy**, near, nearby, at hand, within reach, at your fingertips, reachable, achievable ≠ inaccessible

a

accessory NOUN 1 = **extra**, addition, supplement, attachment, adjunct, appendage 2 = **accomplice**, partner, ally, associate, assistant, helper, colleague, collaborator

accident NOUN 1 = **crash**, smash, wreck, collision 2 = **misfortune**, disaster, tragedy, setback, calamity, mishap, misadventure 3 = **chance**, fortune, luck, fate, hazard, coincidence, fluke, fortuity

accidental ADJECTIVE 1 = **unintentional**, unexpected, incidental, unforeseen, unplanned ≠ deliberate 2 = **chance**, random, casual, unplanned, fortuitous, inadvertent

accidentally ADVERB = **unintentionally**, incidentally, by accident, by chance, inadvertently, unwittingly, randomly, haphazardly ≠ deliberately

acclaim VERB = **praise**, celebrate, honour, cheer, admire, hail, applaud, compliment
▷ NOUN = **praise**, honour, celebration, approval, tribute, applause, kudos, commendation ≠ criticism

accommodate VERB 1 = **house**, put up, take in, lodge, shelter, entertain, cater for 2 = **help**, support, aid, assist, cooperate with, abet, lend a hand to 3 = **adapt**, fit, settle, alter, adjust, modify, comply, reconcile

accommodating ADJECTIVE = **obliging**, willing, kind, friendly, helpful, polite, cooperative, agreeable ≠ unhelpful

accommodation NOUN = **housing**, homes, houses, board, quarters, digs (*Brit. informal*), shelter, lodging(s)

accompaniment NOUN 1 = **backing music**, backing, support, obbligato 2 = **supplement**, extra, addition, companion, accessory, complement, decoration, adjunct

accompany VERB 1 = **go with**, lead, partner, guide, attend, conduct, escort, shepherd 2 = **occur with**, belong to, come with, supplement, go together with, follow

accompanying ADJECTIVE = **additional**, extra, related, associated, attached, attendant, complementary, supplementary

accomplish VERB = **realize**, produce, effect, finish, complete, manage, achieve, perform ≠ fail

accomplished ADJECTIVE = **skilled**, able, professional, expert, masterly, talented, gifted, polished ≠ unskilled

accomplishment NOUN 1 = **achievement**, feat, act, stroke, triumph, coup, exploit, deed 2 = **accomplishing**, finishing, carrying out, conclusion, bringing about, execution, completion, fulfilment

accord NOUN 1 = **treaty**, contract, agreement, arrangement, settlement, pact, deal (*informal*)

2 = **sympathy**, agreement, harmony, unison, rapport, conformity ≠ conflict ▷ **PHRASE**: **accord with something** = **agree with**, match, coincide with, fit with, correspond with, conform with, tally with, harmonize with

accordingly ADVERB
1 = **consequently**, so, thus, therefore, hence, subsequently, in consequence, ergo **2** = **appropriately**, correspondingly, properly, suitably, fitly

account NOUN **1** = **description**, report, story, statement, version, tale, explanation, narrative **2** = **importance**, standing, concern, value, note, worth, weight, honour **3** (*commerce*) = **ledger**, charge, bill, statement, balance, tally, invoice ▷ **VERB** = **consider**, rate, value, judge, estimate, think, count, reckon

accountability NOUN = **responsibility**, liability, culpability, answerability, chargeability

accountable ADJECTIVE = **answerable**, subject, responsible, obliged, liable, amenable, obligated, chargeable

accountant NOUN = **auditor**, book-keeper, bean counter (*informal*)

accumulate VERB = **build up**, increase, be stored, collect, gather, pile up, amass, hoard ≠ disperse

accumulation NOUN
1 = **collection**, increase, stock, store, mass, build-up, pile, stack **2** = **growth**, collection, gathering, build-up

accuracy NOUN = **exactness**, precision, fidelity, authenticity, correctness, closeness, veracity, truthfulness ≠ inaccuracy

accurate ADJECTIVE **1** = **precise**, close, correct, careful, strict, exact, faithful, explicit ≠ inaccurate **2** = **correct**, true, exact, spot-on (*Brit. informal*)

accurately ADVERB **1** = **precisely**, correctly, closely, truly, strictly, exactly, faithfully, to the letter **2** = **exactly**, closely, correctly, precisely, strictly, faithfully, explicitly, scrupulously

accusation NOUN = **charge**, complaint, allegation, indictment, recrimination, denunciation, incrimination

accuse VERB **1** = **point a** *or* **the finger at**, blame for, denounce, hold responsible for, impute blame to ≠ exonerate **2** = **charge with**, indict for, impeach for, censure with, incriminate for ≠ absolve

accustom VERB = **familiarize**, train, discipline, adapt, instruct, school, acquaint, acclimatize

accustomed ADJECTIVE **1** = **used**, trained, familiar, given to, adapted, acquainted, in the habit of, familiarized ≠ unaccustomed **2** = **usual**, established, expected, common, standard, traditional, normal, regular ≠ unusual

ace NOUN 1 (*cards*, *dice*) = **one**, single point 2 (*informal*) = **expert**, star, champion, authority, professional, master, specialist, guru
▷ ADJECTIVE (*informal*) = **great**, brilliant, fine, wonderful, excellent, outstanding, superb, fantastic (*informal*), booshit (*Austral. slang*), exo (*Austral. slang*), sik (*Austral. slang*), ka pai (*N.Z.*), rad (*informal*), phat (*slang*), schmick (*Austral. informal*)

ache VERB = **hurt**, suffer, burn, pain, smart, sting, pound, throb
▷ NOUN = **pain**, discomfort, suffering, hurt, throbbing, irritation, tenderness, pounding

achieve VERB = **accomplish**, fulfil, complete, gain, perform, do, get, carry out

achievement NOUN = **accomplishment**, effort, feat, deed, stroke, triumph, coup, exploit

acid ADJECTIVE 1 = **sour**, tart, pungent, acerbic, acrid, vinegary ≠ sweet 2 = **sharp**, cutting, biting, bitter, harsh, barbed, caustic, vitriolic ≠ kindly

acknowledge VERB 1 = **admit**, own up, allow, accept, reveal, grant, declare, recognize ≠ deny 2 = **greet**, address, notice, recognize, salute, accost ≠ snub 3 = **reply to**, answer, notice, recognize, respond to, react to, retort to ≠ ignore

acquaintance NOUN

1 = **associate**, contact, ally, colleague, comrade ≠ intimate 2 = **relationship**, connection, fellowship, familiarity ≠ unfamiliarity

acquire VERB = **get**, win, buy, receive, gain, earn, secure, collect ≠ lose

acquisition NOUN 1 = **acquiring**, gaining, procurement, attainment 2 = **purchase**, buy, investment, property, gain, prize, asset, possession

acquit VERB = **clear**, free, release, excuse, discharge, liberate, vindicate ≠ find guilty ▷ PHRASE: **acquit yourself** = **behave**, bear yourself, conduct yourself, comport yourself

act VERB 1 = **do something**, perform, function 2 = **perform**, mimic
▷ NOUN 1 = **deed**, action, performance, achievement, undertaking, exploit, feat, accomplishment 2 = **pretence**, show, front, performance, display, attitude, pose, posture 3 = **law**, bill, measure, resolution, decree, statute, ordinance, enactment 4 = **performance**, show, turn, production, routine, presentation, gig (*informal*), sketch

acting NOUN = **performance**, playing, performing, theatre, portrayal, impersonation, characterization, stagecraft
▷ ADJECTIVE = **temporary**, substitute, interim, provisional,

surrogate, stopgap, pro tem

action NOUN 1 = **deed**, act, performance, achievement, exploit, feat, accomplishment **2** = **measure**, act, manoeuvre **3** = **lawsuit**, case, trial, suit, proceeding, dispute, prosecution, litigation **4** = **energy**, activity, spirit, force, vitality, vigour, liveliness, vim **5** = **effect**, working, process, operation, activity, movement, functioning, motion **6** = **battle**, fight, conflict, clash, contest, encounter, combat, engagement

activate VERB = **start**, move, initiate, rouse, mobilize, set in motion, galvanize ≠ stop

active ADJECTIVE 1 = **busy**, involved, occupied, lively, energetic, bustling, on the move, strenuous ≠ sluggish **2** = **energetic**, quick, alert, dynamic, lively, vigorous, animated, forceful ≠ inactive **3** = **in operation**, working, acting, at work, in action, operative, in force, effectual

activist NOUN = **militant**, partisan

activity NOUN 1 = **action**, labour, movement, energy, exercise, spirit, motion, bustle ≠ inaction **2** = **pursuit**, project, scheme, pleasure, interest, hobby, pastime

actor *or* **actress** NOUN = **performer**, player, Thespian, luvvie (*informal*)
- WORD POWER
- The use of *actress* is now very

- much on the decline, and
- women who work in the
- profession invariably prefer to
- be referred to as *actors*.

actual ADJECTIVE = **real**, substantial, concrete, definite, tangible
- WORD POWER
- The words *actual* and *actually*
- are often used when speaking,
- but should only be used
- in writing where they add
- something to the meaning
- of a sentence. For example,
- in the sentence *he actually*
- *rather enjoyed the film*, the word
- *actually* is only needed if there
- was originally some doubt as to
- whether he would enjoy it.

actually ADVERB = **really**, in fact, indeed, truly, literally, genuinely, in reality, in truth

acute ADJECTIVE 1 = **serious**, important, dangerous, critical, crucial, severe, grave, urgent **2** = **sharp**, shooting, powerful, violent, severe, intense, fierce, piercing **3** = **perceptive**, sharp, keen, smart, sensitive, clever, astute, insightful ≠ slow

adamant ADJECTIVE = **determined**, firm, fixed, stubborn, uncompromising, resolute, unbending, obdurate ≠ flexible

adapt VERB 1 = **adjust**, change, alter, modify, accommodate, conform, acclimatize **2** = **convert**, change, transform, alter, modify, tailor, remodel

a

adaptation NOUN
1 = **acclimatization**,
naturalization, familiarization
2 = **conversion**, change,
variation, adjustment,
transformation, modification,
alteration
add VERB 1 = **count up**, total,
reckon, compute, add up, tot up
≠ take away 2 = **include**, attach,
supplement, adjoin, augment,
affix, append
addict NOUN 1 = **junkie** (*informal*),
freak (*informal*), fiend (*informal*)
2 = **fan**, lover, nut (*slang*), follower,
enthusiast, admirer, buff
(*informal*), junkie (*informal*)
addiction NOUN = **dependence**,
habit, obsession, craving,
enslavement *with* **to** = **love of**,
passion for, attachment to
addition NOUN 1 = **extra**,
supplement, increase, gain,
bonus, extension, accessory,
additive 2 = **inclusion**,
adding, increasing, extension,
attachment, insertion,
incorporation, augmentation
≠ removal 3 = **counting
up**, totalling, adding up,
computation, totting up
≠ subtraction ▷ PHRASE: **in
addition to** = **as well as**, along
with, on top of, besides, to boot,
additionally, over and above, to
say nothing of
additional ADJECTIVE = **extra**,
new, other, added, further, fresh,
spare, supplementary
address NOUN 1 = **location**,

home, place, house, point,
position, situation, site
2 (*computing*) = **URL**, website,
addy (*informal*), IP address, web
address
3 = **speech**, talk, lecture,
discourse, sermon, dissertation,
homily, oration
▷ VERB = **speak to**, talk to, greet,
hail, approach, converse with,
korero (*N.Z.*)
adept ADJECTIVE = **skilful**,
able, skilled, expert, practised,
accomplished, versed, proficient
≠ unskilled
▷ NOUN = **expert**, master, genius,
hotshot (*informal*), dab hand (*Brit.
informal*)
adequate ADJECTIVE
1 = **passable**, acceptable, average,
fair, satisfactory, competent,
mediocre, so-so (*informal*)
≠ inadequate 2 = **sufficient**,
enough ≠ insufficient
adhere to VERB = **stick to**, attach
to, cling to, glue to, fix to, fasten
to, hold fast to, paste to
adjacent ADJECTIVE = **adjoining**,
neighbouring, nearby ≠ far away
adjoin VERB = **connect with** *or* **to**,
join, link with, touch on, border on
adjoining ADJECTIVE
= **connecting**, touching,
bordering, neighbouring, next
door, adjacent, abutting
adjourn VERB = **postpone**, delay,
suspend, interrupt, put off, defer,
discontinue ≠ continue
adjust VERB 1 = **adapt**, change,
alter, accustom, conform

2 = **change**, reform, alter, adapt, revise, modify, amend, make conform 3 = **modify**, alter, adapt

adjustable ADJECTIVE = **alterable**, flexible, adaptable, malleable, movable, modifiable

adjustment NOUN
1 = **alteration**, change, tuning, repair, conversion, modifying, adaptation, modification
2 = **acclimatization**, orientation, change, regulation, amendment, adaptation, revision, modification

administer VERB 1 = **manage**, run, control, direct, handle, conduct, command, govern
2 = **dispense**, give, share, provide, apply, assign, allocate, allot
3 = **execute**, give, provide, apply, perform, carry out, impose, implement

administration NOUN
1 = **management**, government, running, control, handling, direction, conduct, application
2 = **directors**, board, executive(s), employers 3 = **government**, leadership, regime

administrative ADJECTIVE
= **managerial**, executive, directing, regulatory, governmental, organizational, supervisory, directorial

administrator NOUN
= **manager**, head, official, director, executive, boss (*informal*), governor, supervisor, baas (*S. African*)

admirable ADJECTIVE

= **praiseworthy**, good, great, fine, wonderful, excellent, brilliant, outstanding, booshit (*Austral. slang*), exo (*Austral. slang*), sik (*Austral. slang*), ka pai (*N.Z.*), rad (*informal*), phat (*slang*), schmick (*Austral. informal*) ≠ deplorable

admiration NOUN = **regard**, wonder, respect, praise, approval, recognition, esteem, appreciation

admire VERB 1 = **respect**, value, prize, honour, praise, appreciate, esteem, approve of ≠ despise
2 = **adore**, like, love, take to, fancy (*Brit. informal*), treasure, cherish, glorify 3 = **marvel at**, look at, appreciate, delight in, wonder at, be amazed by, take pleasure in, gape at

admirer NOUN 1 = **fan**, supporter, follower, enthusiast, partisan, disciple, devotee 2 = **suitor**, lover, boyfriend, sweetheart, beau, wooer

admission NOUN
1 = **admittance**, access, entry, introduction, entrance, acceptance, initiation, entrée
2 = **confession**, declaration, revelation, allowance, disclosure, acknowledgement, unburdening, divulgence

admit VERB 1 = **confess**, confide, own up, come clean (*informal*)
2 = **allow**, agree, accept, reveal, grant, declare, acknowledge, recognize ≠ deny 3 = **let in**, allow, receive, accept, introduce, take in, initiate, give access to ≠ keep out

a

adolescence NOUN =**teens**, youth, minority, boyhood, girlhood

adolescent ADJECTIVE 1 =**young**, junior, teenage, juvenile, youthful, childish, immature, boyish 2 =**teenage**, young, teen (*informal*)
▷ NOUN =**teenager**, girl, boy, kid (*informal*), youth, lad, minor, young man

adopt VERB 1 =**take on**, follow, choose, maintain, assume, take up, engage in, become involved in 2 =**take in**, raise, nurse, mother, rear, foster, bring up, take care of ≠ abandon

adoption NOUN 1 =**fostering**, adopting, taking in 2 =**embracing**, choice, taking up, selection, assumption, endorsement, appropriation, espousal

adore VERB =**love**, honour, admire, worship, esteem, cherish, revere, dote on ≠ hate

adoring ADJECTIVE =**admiring**, loving, devoted, fond, affectionate, doting ≠ hating

adorn VERB =**decorate**, array, embellish, festoon

adrift ADJECTIVE 1 =**drifting**, afloat, unmoored, unanchored 2 =**aimless**, goalless, directionless, purposeless
▷ ADVERB =**wrong**, astray, off course, amiss, off target, wide of the mark

adult NOUN =**grown-up**, mature person, person of mature age, grown *or* grown-up person, man *or* woman
▷ ADJECTIVE 1 =**fully grown**, mature, grown-up, of age, ripe, fully fledged, fully developed, full grown 2 =**pornographic**, blue, dirty, obscene, filthy, indecent, lewd, salacious

advance VERB 1 =**progress**, proceed, come forward, make inroads, make headway ≠ retreat 2 =**accelerate**, speed, promote, hasten, bring forward, crack on (*informal*) 3 =**improve**, rise, develop, pick up, progress, upgrade, prosper, make strides 4 =**suggest**, offer, present, propose, advocate, submit, prescribe, put forward ≠ withhold 5 =**lend**, loan, supply on credit ≠ withhold payment
▷ NOUN 1 =**down payment**, credit, fee, deposit, retainer, prepayment 2 =**attack**, charge, strike, assault, raid, invasion, offensive, onslaught 3 =**improvement**, development, gain, growth, breakthrough, step, headway, inroads
▷ MODIFIER =**prior**, early, beforehand ▷ PHRASE: in advance =**beforehand**, earlier, ahead, previously

advanced ADJECTIVE =**sophisticated**, foremost, modern, revolutionary, up-to-date, higher, leading, recent ≠ backward

advancement NOUN =**promotion**, rise, gain, progress,

improvement, betterment, preferment

advantage NOUN 1 = **benefit**, help, profit, favour ≠ disadvantage 2 = **lead**, sway, dominance, precedence 3 = **superiority**, good

adventure NOUN = **venture**, experience, incident, enterprise, undertaking, exploit, occurrence, caper

adventurous ADJECTIVE = **daring**, enterprising, bold, reckless, intrepid, daredevil ≠ cautious

adversary NOUN = **opponent**, rival, enemy, competitor, foe, contestant, antagonist ≠ ally

adverse ADJECTIVE 1 = **harmful**, damaging, negative, destructive, detrimental, hurtful, injurious, inopportune ≠ beneficial 2 = **unfavourable**, hostile, unlucky 3 = **negative**, opposing, hostile, contrary, dissenting, unsympathetic, ill-disposed

advert NOUN (Brit. informal) = **advertisement**, notice, commercial, ad (informal), announcement, poster, plug (informal), blurb

advertise VERB = **publicize**, promote, plug (informal), announce, inform, hype, notify, tout

advertisement NOUN = **advert** (Brit. informal), notice, commercial, ad (informal), announcement, poster, plug (informal), blurb

advice NOUN = **guidance**, help, opinion, direction, suggestion, instruction, counsel, counselling

advise VERB 1 = **recommend**, suggest, urge, counsel, advocate, caution, prescribe, commend 2 = **notify**, tell, report, announce, warn, declare, inform, acquaint

adviser NOUN = **counsellor**, guide, consultant, aide, guru, mentor, helper, confidant

advisory ADJECTIVE = **advising**, helping, recommending, counselling, consultative

advocate VERB = **recommend**, support, champion, encourage, propose, promote, advise, endorse ≠ oppose ▷ NOUN 1 = **supporter**, spokesman, champion, defender, campaigner, promoter, counsellor, proponent 2 (law) = **lawyer**, attorney, solicitor, counsel, barrister

affair NOUN 1 = **matter**, business, happening, event, activity, incident, episode, topic 2 = **relationship**, romance, intrigue, fling, liaison, flirtation, amour, dalliance

affect[1] VERB 1 = **influence**, concern, alter, change, manipulate, act on, bear upon, impinge upon 2 = **emotionally move**, touch, upset, overcome, stir, disturb, perturb

affect[2] VERB = **put on**, assume, adopt, pretend, imitate, simulate, contrive, aspire to

affected[3] ADJECTIVE = **pretended**,

artificial, contrived, put-on, mannered, unnatural, feigned, insincere ≠ genuine

affection NOUN = **fondness**, liking, feeling, love, care, warmth, attachment, goodwill, aroha (*N.Z.*)

affectionate ADJECTIVE = **fond**, loving, kind, caring, friendly, attached, devoted, tender ≠ cool

affiliate VERB = **associate**, unite, join, link, ally, combine, incorporate, amalgamate

affinity NOUN 1 = **attraction**, liking, leaning, sympathy, inclination, rapport, fondness, partiality, aroha (*N.Z.*) ≠ hostility 2 = **similarity**, relationship, connection, correspondence, analogy, resemblance, closeness, likeness ≠ difference

affirm VERB 1 = **declare**, state, maintain, swear, assert, testify, pronounce, certify ≠ deny 2 = **confirm**, prove, endorse, ratify, verify, validate, bear out, substantiate ≠ refute

affirmative ADJECTIVE = **agreeing**, confirming, positive, approving, consenting, favourable, concurring, assenting ≠ negative

afflict VERB = **torment**, trouble, pain, hurt, distress, plague, grieve, harass

affluent ADJECTIVE = **wealthy**, rich, prosperous, loaded (*slang*), well-off, opulent, well-heeled (*informal*), well-to-do, minted (*Brit. slang*) ≠ poor

afford VERB 1 = **have the money for**, manage, bear, pay for, spare, stand, stretch to 2 = **bear**, stand, sustain, allow yourself 3 = **give**, offer, provide, produce, supply, yield, render

affordable ADJECTIVE = **inexpensive**, cheap, reasonable, moderate, modest, low-cost, economical ≠ expensive

afraid ADJECTIVE 1 = **scared**, frightened, nervous, terrified, shaken, startled, fearful, cowardly ≠ unafraid 2 = **reluctant**, frightened, scared, unwilling, hesitant, loath, disinclined, unenthusiastic 3 = **sorry**, apologetic, regretful, sad, distressed, unhappy ≠ pleased

after PREPOSITION = **at the end of**, following, subsequent to ≠ before
▷ ADVERB = **following**, later, next, succeeding, afterwards, subsequently, thereafter
▷ RELATED WORD: *prefix* post-

aftermath NOUN = **effects**, results, wake, consequences, outcome, sequel, end result, upshot

again ADVERB 1 = **once more**, another time, anew, afresh 2 = **also**, in addition, moreover, besides, furthermore

against PREPOSITION 1 = **beside**, on, up against, in contact with, abutting 2 = **opposed to**, anti (*informal*), hostile to, in opposition to, averse to, opposite to 3 = **in opposition to**, resisting, versus,

counter to, in the opposite
direction of **4** = **in preparation
for**, in case of, in anticipation of,
in expectation of, in provision for
▷ RELATED WORDS: *prefixes* anti-,
contra-, counter-

age NOUN **1** = **years**, days,
generation, lifetime, length of
existence **2** = **old age**, experience,
maturity, seniority, majority,
senility, decline, advancing years
≠ youth **3** = **time**, day(s), period,
generation, era, epoch
▷ VERB **1** = **grow old**, decline,
weather, fade, deteriorate, wither
2 = **mature**, season, condition,
soften, mellow, ripen

aged ADJECTIVE = **old**, getting on,
grey, ancient, antique, elderly,
antiquated ≠ young

agency NOUN **1** = **business**,
company, office, firm,
department, organization,
enterprise, establishment **2**
(*old-fashioned*) = **medium**, means,
activity, vehicle, instrument,
mechanism

agenda NOUN = **programme**, list,
plan, schedule, diary, calendar,
timetable

agent NOUN **1** = **representative**,
rep (*informal*), negotiator,
envoy, surrogate, go-between
2 = **author**, worker, vehicle,
instrument, operator, performer,
catalyst, doer **3** = **force**, means,
power, cause, instrument

aggravate VERB **1** = **make worse**,
exaggerate, intensify, worsen,
exacerbate, magnify, inflame,

increase ≠ improve **2** (*informal*)
= **annoy**, bother, provoke,
irritate, nettle, get on your nerves
(*informal*) ≠ please

aggregate NOUN = **total**, body,
whole, amount, collection, mass,
sum, combination
▷ ADJECTIVE = **collective**,
mixed, combined, collected,
accumulated, composite,
cumulative
▷ VERB = **combine**, mix, collect,
assemble, heap, accumulate, pile,
amass

aggression NOUN **1** = **hostility**,
malice, antagonism,
antipathy, ill will, belligerence,
destructiveness, pugnacity
2 = **attack**, campaign, injury,
assault, raid, invasion, offensive,
onslaught

aggressive ADJECTIVE **1** = **hostile**,
offensive, destructive,
belligerent, unfriendly, contrary,
antagonistic, pugnacious, aggers
(*Austral. slang*), biffo (*Austral.
slang*) ≠ friendly **2** = **forceful**,
powerful, convincing, effective,
enterprising, dynamic, bold,
militant ≠ submissive

agitate VERB **1** = **stir**, beat, shake,
disturb, toss, rouse **2** = **upset**,
worry, trouble, excite, distract,
unnerve, disconcert, fluster
≠ calm

agony NOUN = **suffering**,
pain, distress, misery, torture,
discomfort, torment, hardship

agree VERB **1** = **concur**, be as
one, sympathize, assent, see eye

to eye, be of the same opinion ≠ disagree **2** = **correspond**, match, coincide, tally, conform
▷ **PHRASE**: **agree with someone** = **suit**, get on, befit

agreement NOUN **1** = **treaty**, contract, arrangement, alliance, deal (*informal*), understanding, settlement, bargain **2** = **concurrence**, harmony, compliance, union, agreeing, consent, unison, assent ≠ disagreement
3 = **correspondence**, similarity, consistency, correlation, conformity, compatibility, congruity ≠ difference

agricultural ADJECTIVE = **farming**, country, rural, rustic, agrarian

agriculture NOUN = **farming**, culture, cultivation, husbandry, tillage

ahead ADVERB **1** = **in front**, in advance, towards the front, frontwards **2** = **at an advantage**, in advance, in the lead **3** = **in the lead**, winning, leading, at the head, to the fore, at an advantage **4** = **in front**, before, in advance, in the lead

aid NOUN = **help**, backing, support, benefit, favour, relief, promotion, assistance ≠ hindrance
▷ VERB **1** = **help**, support, serve, sustain, assist, avail, subsidize, be of service to ≠ hinder
2 = **promote**, help, further, forward, encourage, favour, facilitate, pave the way for

aide NOUN = **assistant**, supporter, attendant, helper, right-hand man, second

ailing ADJECTIVE **1** = **weak**, failing, poor, flawed, unstable, unsatisfactory, deficient **2** = **ill**, poorly, sick, weak, crook (*Austral. & N.Z. informal*), unwell, infirm, under the weather (*informal*), indisposed

ailment NOUN = **illness**, disease, complaint, disorder, sickness, affliction, malady, infirmity

aim VERB **1** = **try for**, seek, work for, plan for, strive, set your sights on **2** = **point**
▷ NOUN = **intention**, point, plan, goal, design, target, purpose, desire

air NOUN **1** = **wind**, breeze, draught, gust, zephyr
2 = **atmosphere**, sky, heavens, aerosphere **3** = **tune**, song, theme, melody, strain, lay, aria
4 = **manner**, appearance, look, aspect, atmosphere, mood, impression, aura
▷ VERB **1** = **publicize**, reveal, exhibit, voice, express, display, circulate, make public
2 = **ventilate**, expose, freshen, aerate ▷ **RELATED WORD**: *adjective* **aerial**

airborne ADJECTIVE = **flying**, floating, in the air, hovering, gliding, in flight, on the wing

airing NOUN **1** = **ventilation**, drying, freshening, aeration
2 = **exposure**, display, expression, publicity, vent, utterance,

dissemination

airplane (*U.S. & Canad.*) NOUN
= **plane**, aircraft, jet, aeroplane,
airliner

airs PLURAL NOUN = **affectation**,
arrogance, pretensions,
pomposity, swank (*informal*),
hauteur, haughtiness,
superciliousness

aisle NOUN = **passageway**, path,
lane, passage, corridor, alley,
gangway

alarm NOUN 1 = **fear**, panic,
anxiety, fright, apprehension,
nervousness, consternation,
trepidation ≠ calmness
2 = **danger signal**, warning, bell,
alert, siren, alarm bell, hooter,
distress signal
▷ VERB = **frighten**, scare, panic,
distress, startle, dismay, daunt,
unnerve ≠ calm

alarming ADJECTIVE
= **frightening**, shocking, scaring,
disturbing, distressing, startling,
horrifying, menacing

alcoholic NOUN = **drunkard**,
drinker, drunk, toper, lush (*slang*),
tippler, wino (*informal*), inebriate,
alko or alco (*Austral. slang*)
▷ ADJECTIVE = **intoxicating**, hard,
strong, stiff, brewed, fermented,
distilled

alert ADJECTIVE 1 = **attentive**,
awake, vigilant, watchful, on the
lookout, circumspect, observant,
on guard ≠ careless 2 = **quick-
witted**, bright, sharp
▷ NOUN = **warning**, signal, alarm,
siren ≠ all clear

▷ VERB = **warn**, signal, inform,
alarm, notify, tip off, forewarn
≠ lull

alien NOUN = **foreigner**, incomer,
immigrant, stranger, outsider,
newcomer, asylum seeker
≠ citizen
▷ ADJECTIVE 1 = **foreign**, strange,
imported, unknown, exotic,
unfamiliar 2 = **strange**, new,
foreign, novel, unknown, exotic,
unfamiliar, untried ≠ similar

alienate VERB = **antagonize**,
anger, annoy, offend, irritate,
hassle (*informal*), estrange, hack
off (*informal*)

alienation NOUN
= **estrangement**, setting against,
separation, turning away,
disaffection, remoteness

alight[1] VERB 1 = **get off**, descend,
get down, disembark, dismount
2 = **land**, light, settle, come down,
descend, perch, touch down,
come to rest ≠ take off

alight[2] ADJECTIVE = **lit up**, bright,
brilliant, shining, illuminated,
fiery

align VERB 1 = **ally**, side, join,
associate, affiliate, cooperate,
sympathize 2 = **line up**, order,
range, regulate, straighten, even
up

alike ADJECTIVE = **similar**, close,
the same, parallel, resembling,
identical, corresponding, akin
≠ different
▷ ADVERB = **similarly**,
identically, equally, uniformly,
correspondingly, analogously

≠ differently

alive ADJECTIVE 1 = **living**, breathing, animate, subsisting, existing, functioning, in the land of the living (*informal*) ≠ dead 2 = **in existence**, existing, functioning, active, operative, in force, on-going, prevalent ≠ inoperative 3 = **lively**, active, vital, alert, energetic, animated, agile, perky ≠ dull

all DETERMINER 1 = **the whole amount**, everything, the total, the aggregate, the totality, the sum total, the entirety, the entire amount 2 = **every**, each, every single, every one of, each and every
▷ ADJECTIVE = **complete**, greatest, full, total, perfect, entire, utter
▷ ADVERB = **completely**, totally, fully, entirely, absolutely, altogether, wholly, utterly

allegation NOUN = **claim**, charge, statement, declaration, accusation, assertion, affirmation

allege VERB = **claim**, charge, challenge, state, maintain, declare, assert, uphold ≠ deny

alleged ADJECTIVE = **claimed**, supposed, declared, assumed, so-called, apparent, stated, described

allegiance NOUN = **loyalty**, devotion, fidelity, obedience, constancy, faithfulness ≠ disloyalty

allergic ADJECTIVE = **sensitive**, affected, susceptible, hypersensitive

allergy NOUN = **sensitivity**, reaction, susceptibility, antipathy, hypersensitivity, sensitiveness

alleviate VERB = **ease**, reduce, relieve, moderate, soothe, lessen, lighten, allay

alley NOUN = **passage**, walk, lane, pathway, alleyway, passageway, backstreet

alliance NOUN = **union**, league, association, agreement, marriage, connection, combination, coalition ≠ division

allied ADJECTIVE 1 = **united**, linked, related, combined, integrated, affiliated, cooperating, in league 2 = **connected**, linked, associated

allocate VERB = **assign**, grant, distribute, designate, set aside, earmark, give out, consign

allocation NOUN 1 = **allowance**, share, portion, quota, lot, ration 2 = **assignment**, allowance, allotment

allow VERB 1 = **permit**, approve, enable, sanction, endure, license, tolerate, authorize ≠ prohibit 2 = **let**, permit, sanction, authorize, license, tolerate, consent to, assent to ≠ forbid 3 = **give**, provide, grant, spare, devote, assign, allocate, set aside 4 = **acknowledge**, accept, admit, grant, recognize, yield, concede, confess ▷ PHRASE: **allow for something** = **take into account**, consider, plan for, accommodate, provide for, make provision for, make allowances for, make concessions for

allowance NOUN 1 = **portion**, lot, share, amount, grant, quota, allocation, stint 2 = **pocket money**, grant, fee, payment, ration, handout, remittance 3 = **concession**, discount, reduction, repayment, deduction, rebate

all right ADJECTIVE
1 = **satisfactory**, O.K. or okay (*informal*), average, fair, sufficient, standard, acceptable, good enough ≠ unsatisfactory
2 = **well**, O.K. or okay (*informal*), whole, sound, fit, safe, healthy, unharmed ≠ ill

ally NOUN = **partner**, friend, colleague, associate, mate, comrade, helper, collaborator, cobber (*Austral. & N.Z. old-fashioned, informal*), E hoa (*N.Z.*) ≠ opponent
▷ VERB = **unite with**, associate with, unify, collaborate with, join forces with, band together with

almost ADVERB = **nearly**, about, close to, virtually, practically, roughly, just about, not quite

alone ADJECTIVE 1 = **solitary**, isolated, separate, apart, by yourself, unaccompanied, on your tod (*slang*) ≠ accompanied
2 = **lonely**, abandoned, isolated, solitary, desolate, forsaken, forlorn, destitute
▷ ADVERB 1 = **solely**, only, individually, singly, exclusively, uniquely 2 = **by yourself**, independently, unaccompanied, without help, on your own,

without assistance ≠ with help

aloud ADVERB = **out loud**, clearly, plainly, distinctly, audibly, intelligibly

already ADVERB = **before now**, before, previously, at present, by now, by then, even now, just now

also ADVERB = **and**, too, further, in addition, as well, moreover, besides, furthermore

alter VERB 1 = **modify**, change, reform, vary, transform, adjust, adapt, revise 2 = **change**, turn, vary, transform, adjust, adapt

alternate VERB 1 = **interchange**, change, fluctuate, take turns, oscillate, chop and change
2 = **intersperse**, interchange, exchange, swap, stagger, rotate
▷ ADJECTIVE = **alternating**, interchanging, every other, rotating, every second, sequential

alternative NOUN = **substitute**, choice, other, option, preference, recourse
▷ ADJECTIVE = **different**, other, substitute, alternate

alternatively ADVERB = **or**, instead, otherwise, on the other hand, if not, then again, as an alternative, as another option

although CONJUNCTION = **though**, while, even if, even though, whilst, albeit, despite the fact that, notwithstanding

altogether ADVERB
1 = **absolutely**, quite, completely, totally, perfectly, fully, thoroughly, wholly 2 = **completely**, fully, entirely, thoroughly, wholly, in

every respect ≠ partially **3** = **on the whole**, generally, mostly, in general, collectively, all things considered, on average, for the most part **4** = **in total**, in all, all told, taken together, in sum, everything included

⬤ **WORD POWER**
⬤ The single-word form
⬤ *altogether* should not be used
⬤ as an alternative to *all together*
⬤ because the meanings are very
⬤ distinct. *Altogether* is an adverb
⬤ meaning 'absolutely' or, in a
⬤ different sense, ' in total'. *All*
⬤ *together*, however, means 'all
⬤ at the same time' or 'all in the
⬤ same place'. The distinction
⬤ can be seen in the following
⬤ example: *altogether there were six*
⬤ *or seven families sharing the flat's*
⬤ *facilities* means ' in total', while
⬤ *there were six or seven families all*
⬤ *together in one flat*, means 'all
⬤ crowded in together'.

always ADVERB **1** = **habitually**, regularly, every time, consistently, invariably, perpetually, without exception, customarily ≠ seldom **2** = **forever**, for keeps, eternally, for all time, evermore, till the cows come home (*informal*), till Doomsday **3** = **continually**, constantly, all the time, forever, repeatedly, persistently, perpetually, incessantly

amass VERB = **collect**, gather, assemble, compile, accumulate, pile up, hoard

amateur NOUN = **nonprofessional**, outsider, layman, dilettante, layperson, non-specialist, dabbler

amaze VERB = **astonish**, surprise, shock, stun, alarm, stagger, startle, bewilder

amazement NOUN = **astonishment**, surprise, wonder, shock, confusion, admiration, awe, bewilderment

amazing ADJECTIVE = **astonishing**, surprising, brilliant, stunning, overwhelming, staggering, sensational (*informal*), bewildering

ambassador NOUN = **representative**, minister, agent, deputy, diplomat, envoy, consul, attaché

ambiguity NOUN = **vagueness**, doubt, uncertainty, obscurity, equivocation, dubiousness

ambiguous ADJECTIVE = **unclear**, obscure, vague, dubious, enigmatic, indefinite, inconclusive, indeterminate ≠ clear

ambition NOUN **1** = **goal**, hope, dream, target, aim, wish, purpose, desire **2** = **enterprise**, longing, drive, spirit, desire, passion, enthusiasm, striving

ambitious ADJECTIVE = **enterprising**, spirited, daring, eager, intent, enthusiastic, hopeful, striving ≠ unambitious

ambush VERB = **trap**, attack, surprise, deceive, dupe, ensnare, waylay, bushwhack (*U.S.*)

▷ NOUN = **trap**, snare, lure, waylaying

amend VERB = **change**, improve, reform, fix, correct, repair, edit, alter

amendment NOUN 1 = **addition**, change, adjustment, attachment, adaptation, revision, modification, alteration 2 = **change**, improvement, repair, edit, remedy, correction, revision, modification

amends PLURAL NOUN = **compensation**, redress, reparation, restitution, atonement, recompense

amenity NOUN = **facility**, service, advantage, comfort, convenience

amid or **amidst** PREPOSITION 1 = **during**, among, at a time of, in an atmosphere of 2 = **in the middle of**, among, surrounded by, amongst, in the midst of, in the thick of

ammunition NOUN = **munitions**, rounds, shot, shells, powder, explosives, armaments

amnesty NOUN = **general pardon**, mercy, pardoning, immunity, forgiveness, reprieve, remission, clemency

among or **amongst** PREPOSITION 1 = **in the midst of**, with, together with, in the middle of, amid, surrounded by, amidst, in the thick of 2 = **in the group of**, one of, part of, included in, in the company of, in the class of, in the number of 3 = **between**, to

amount NOUN = **quantity**, measure, size, supply, mass, volume, capacity, extent

▷ PHRASE: **amount to something** 1 = **add up to**, mean, total, equal, constitute, comprise, be equivalent to 2 = **come to**, become, develop into, advance to, progress to, mature into

● WORD POWER
● Although it is common to use a
● plural noun after *amount of*, for
● example in *the amount of people*
● and *the amount of goods*, this
● should be avoided. Preferred
● alternatives would be to use
● *quantity*, as in *the quantity of*
● *people*, or *number*, as in *the*
● *number of goods*.

ample ADJECTIVE 1 = **plenty of**, generous, lavish, abundant, plentiful, expansive, copious, profuse ≠ insufficient 2 = **large**, full, extensive, generous, abundant, bountiful

amply ADVERB = **fully**, completely, richly, generously, abundantly, profusely, copiously ≠ insufficiently

amuse VERB 1 = **entertain**, please, delight, charm, cheer, tickle ≠ bore 2 = **occupy**, interest, involve, engage, entertain, absorb, engross

amusement NOUN 1 = **enjoyment**, entertainment, cheer, mirth, merriment ≠ boredom 2 = **diversion**, fun, pleasure, entertainment 3 = **pastime**, game, sport, joke, entertainment, hobby, recreation, diversion

amusing ADJECTIVE =**funny**,
humorous, comical, droll,
interesting, entertaining, comic,
enjoyable ≠ boring

anaesthetic NOUN =**painkiller**,
narcotic, sedative, opiate,
anodyne, analgesic, soporific
▷ ADJECTIVE =**pain-killing**,
dulling, numbing, sedative,
deadening, anodyne, analgesic,
soporific

analogy NOUN =**similarity**,
relation, comparison, parallel,
correspondence, resemblance,
correlation, likeness

analyse VERB 1 =**examine**,
test, study, research, survey,
investigate, evaluate, inspect
2 =**break down**, separate,
divide, resolve, dissect, think through

analysis NOUN =**examination**,
test, inquiry, investigation,
interpretation, breakdown,
scanning, evaluation

analytic or **analytical** ADJECTIVE
=**rational**, organized, exact,

precise, logical, systematic,
inquiring, investigative

anarchy NOUN =**lawlessness**,
revolution, riot, disorder,
confusion, chaos, disorganization
≠ order

anatomy NOUN 1 =**structure**,
build, make-up, frame,
framework, composition
2 =**examination**, study, division,
inquiry, investigation, analysis,
dissection

ancestor NOUN =**forefather**,
predecessor, precursor,
forerunner, forebear, antecedent,
tupuna or tipuna (N.Z.)
≠ descendant

ancient ADJECTIVE 1 =**classical**,
old, former, past, bygone,
primordial, primeval, olden
2 =**very old**, aged, antique,
archaic, timeworn 3 =**old-
fashioned**, dated, outdated,
obsolete, out of date, unfashionable,
outmoded, passé ≠ up-to-date

and CONJUNCTION 1 =**also**,
including, along with, together

⬤ **AMPHIBIANS**

- axolotl
- brown-striped frog
  (Austral.)
- bullfrog
- caecilian
- cane toad (Austral.)
- congo eel or
  snake
- frog or (Caribbean)
  crapaud

- Goliath frog
- hairy frog
- hyla
- midwife toad
- natterjack
- newt or (dialect or
  archaic) eft
- olm
- Queensland cane
  toad

- salamander
- siren
- toad or (Caribbean)
  crapaud
- tree frog

with, in addition to, as well as
2 = moreover, plus, furthermore
● **WORD POWER**
● The forms *try and do something*
● and *wait and do something*
● should only be used in informal
● or spoken English. In more
● formal writing, use *try to* and
● *wait to*, for example: *we must try*
● *to prevent this happening* (not *try*
● *and prevent*).
anecdote NOUN **= story**, tale,
sketch, short story, yarn, reminiscence,
urban myth, urban legend
angel NOUN **1 = divine**
messenger, cherub, archangel,
seraph **2** (*informal*) **= dear**,
beauty, saint, treasure, darling,
jewel, gem, paragon
anger NOUN **= rage**, outrage,
temper, fury, resentment, wrath,
annoyance, ire ≠ calmness
▷ VERB **= enrage**, outrage, annoy,
infuriate, incense, gall, madden,
exasperate ≠ soothe
angle NOUN **1 = gradient**, bank,
slope, incline, inclination
2 = intersection, point, edge,
corner, bend, elbow, crook, nook
3 = point of view, position,
approach, direction, aspect,
perspective, outlook,
viewpoint
angry ADJECTIVE **= furious**,
cross, mad (*informal*), outraged,
annoyed, infuriated, incensed,
enraged, tooshie (*Austral. slang*),
off the air (*Austral. slang*) ≠ calm
● **WORD POWER**
● Some people feel it is more

● correct to talk about being
● *angry with* someone than
● being *angry at* them. In British
● English, *angry with* is still more
● common than *angry at*, but
● *angry at* is used more commonly
● in American English.
angst NOUN **= anxiety**, worry,
unease, apprehension ≠ peace
of mind
anguish NOUN **= suffering**, pain,
distress, grief, misery, agony,
torment, sorrow
animal NOUN **1 = creature**, beast,
brute **2 = brute**, devil, monster,
savage, beast, bastard (*informal or*
offensive), villain, barbarian
▷ ADJECTIVE **= physical**, gross,
bodily, sensual, carnal, brutish, bestial
▷ *see* **amphibians, animals,**
birds, dinosaurs, fish, insects,
invertebrates, mammals,
reptiles
animate ADJECTIVE **= living**, live,
moving, alive, breathing, alive
and kicking
▷ VERB **= enliven**, excite, inspire,
move, fire, stimulate, energize,
kindle ≠ inhibit
animated ADJECTIVE **= lively**,
spirited, excited, enthusiastic,
passionate, energetic, ebullient,
vivacious ≠ listless
animation NOUN **= liveliness**,
energy, spirit, passion,
enthusiasm, excitement, verve,
zest
announce VERB **= make known**,
tell, report, reveal, declare, advertise,
broadcast, disclose ≠ keep secret

announcement NOUN
1 = **statement**, communication, broadcast, declaration, advertisement, bulletin, communiqué, proclamation
2 = **declaration**, report, reporting, revelation, proclamation

annoy VERB = **irritate**, trouble, anger, bother, disturb, plague, hassle (*informal*), madden, hack you off (*informal*) ≠ soothe

annoying ADJECTIVE = **irritating**, disturbing, troublesome, maddening, exasperating ≠ delightful

annual ADJECTIVE 1 = **once a year**, yearly 2 = **yearlong**, yearly

annually ADVERB 1 = **once a year**, yearly, every year, per year, by the year, every twelve months, per annum 2 = **per year**, yearly, every year, by the year, per annum

anomaly NOUN = **irregularity**, exception, abnormality, inconsistency, eccentricity, oddity, peculiarity, incongruity

anonymous ADJECTIVE
1 = **unnamed**, unknown, unidentified, nameless,

● **ANIMALS**

● animal	collective noun	● animal	collective noun
● antelopes	herd	● crows	murder
● apes	shrewdness	● cubs	litter
● asses	pace *or* herd	● curlews	herd
● badgers	cete	● curs	cowardice
● bears	sloth	● deer	herd
● bees	swarm *or* grist	● dolphins	school
● birds	flock, congregation, flight, *or* volery	● doves	flight *or* dule
		● ducks	paddling *or* team
● bitterns	sedge *or* siege	● dunlins	flight
● boars	sounder	● elk	gang
● bucks	brace *or* lease	● fish	shoal, draught, haul, run, *or* catch
● buffaloes	herd		
● capercailzies	tok	● flies	swarm *or* grist
● cats	clowder	● foxes	skulk
● cattle	drove *or* herd	● geese	gaggle *or* skein
● choughs	chattering	● giraffes	herd
● colts	rag	● gnats	swarm *or* cloud
● coots	covert	● goats	herd *or* tribe
● cranes	herd, sedge, *or* siege	● goldfinches	charm
		● grouse	brood, covey, *or* pack

animal	collective noun		animal	collective noun
gulls	colony		porpoises	school or gam
hares	down or husk		poultry	run
hawks	cast		pups	litter
hens	brood		quails	bevy
herons	sedge or siege		rabbits	nest
herrings	shoal or glean		racehorses	field or string
hounds	pack, mute, or cry		ravens	unkindness
insects	swarm		roes	bevy
kangaroos	troop		rooks	building or clamour
kittens	kindle			
lapwings	desert		ruffs	hill
larks	exaltation		seals	herd or pod
leopards	leap		sheep	flock
lions	pride or troop		sheldrakes	dopping
mallards	sord or sute		snipe	walk or wisp
mares	stud		sparrows	host
martens	richesse		starlings	murmuration
moles	labour		swallows	flight
monkeys	troop		swans	herd or bevy
mules	barren		swifts	flock
nightingales	watch		swine	herd, sounder, or dryft
owls	parliament			
oxen	yoke, drove, team, or herd		teal	bunch, knob, or spring
partridges	covey		whales	school, gam, or run
peacocks	muster		whelps	litter
pheasants	nye or nide		whiting	pod
pigeons	flock or flight		wigeon	bunch, company, knob, or flight
pigs	litter			
plovers	stand or wing		wildfowl	plump, sord, or sute
pochards	flight, rush, bunch, or knob			
ponies	herd		wolves	pack, rout, or herd
			woodcocks	fall

unacknowledged, incognito
≠ identified **2** = **unsigned**,
uncredited, unattributed
≠ signed
answer VERB = **reply**, explain,

respond, resolve, react, return,
retort ≠ ask
▷ NOUN **1** = **reply**, response,
reaction, explanation, comeback,
retort, return, defence ≠ question

ANTS, BEES, AND WASPS

- Amazon ant
- ant or (archaic or dialect) emmet
- army ant or legionary ant
- bee
- blue ant (Austral.)
- bulldog ant, bull ant, or (Austral.) bull Joe
- bumblebee or humblebee
- carpenter bee
- cicada hunter (Austral.)
- cuckoo bee
- digger wasp
- driver ant
- flower wasp (Austral.)
- gall wasp
- honeypot ant or honey ant (Austral.)
- honeybee or hive bee
- horntail or wood wasp
- ichneumon fly or ichneumon wasp
- killer bee
- kootchar (Austral.)
- leafcutter ant
- leafcutter bee
- mason bee
- mason wasp
- minga (Austral.)
- mining bee
- mud dauber
- native bee or sugarbag fly (Austral.)
- Pharaoh ant
- policeman fly (Austral.)
- ruby-tail wasp
- sand wasp
- Sirex wasp (Austral.)
- slave ant
- spider-hunting wasp
- termite or white ant
- velvet ant
- wasp
- wood ant
- yellow jacket (U.S. & Canad.)

2 = **solution**, resolution, explanation **3** = **remedy**, solution

anthem NOUN = **song of praise**, carol, chant, hymn, psalm, paean, chorale, canticle

anthology NOUN = **collection**, selection, treasury, compilation, compendium, miscellany

anticipate VERB **1** = **expect**, predict, prepare for, hope for, envisage, foresee, bank on, foretell **2** = **await**, look forward to, count the hours until

WORD POWER
The Bank of English reveals that the use of *anticipate* and *expect* as synonyms is well established. However, although both words relate to a person's knowledge of something that will happen in the future, there are subtle differences in meaning that should be understood when choosing which word to use. *Anticipate* means that someone foresees an event and has prepared for it, while expect means 'to regard something as probable', but does not necessarily suggest the state of being prepared. Similarly,

using *foresee* as a synonym of *anticipate*, as in *they failed to foresee the vast explosion in commercial revenue which would follow*, is not entirely appropriate.

anticipation NOUN = **expectancy**, expectation, foresight, premonition, prescience, forethought

antics PLURAL NOUN = **clowning**, tricks, mischief, pranks, escapades, playfulness, horseplay, tomfoolery

antique NOUN = **period piece**, relic, bygone, heirloom, collector's item, museum piece
▷ ADJECTIVE = **vintage**, classic, antiquarian, olden

anxiety NOUN = **uneasiness**, concern, worry, doubt, tension, angst, apprehension, misgiving ≠ confidence

anxious ADJECTIVE 1 = **eager**, keen, intent, yearning, impatient, itching, desirous ≠ reluctant 2 = **uneasy**, concerned, worried, troubled, nervous, uncomfortable, tense, fearful ≠ confident

apart ADVERB 1 = **to pieces**, to bits, asunder 2 = **away from each other**, distant from each other 3 = **aside**, away, alone, isolated, to one side, by yourself
▷ PHRASE: **apart from** = **except for**, excepting, other than, excluding, besides, not including, aside from, but

apartment NOUN 1 (*U.S.*) = **flat**, room, suite, penthouse, duplex (*U.S. & Canad.*), crib, bachelor apartment (*Canad.*) 2 = **rooms**, quarters, accommodation, living quarters

apathy NOUN = **lack of interest**, indifference, inertia, coolness, passivity, nonchalance, torpor, unconcern ≠ interest

apiece ADVERB = **each**, individually, separately, for each, to each, respectively, from each ≠ all together

apologize VERB = **say sorry**, express regret, ask forgiveness, make an apology, beg pardon

apology NOUN = **regret**, explanation, excuse, confession ▷ PHRASE: **apology for something** *or* **someone** = **mockery of**, excuse for, imitation of, caricature of, travesty of, poor substitute for

appal VERB = **horrify**, shock, alarm, frighten, outrage, disgust, dishearten, revolt

appalling ADJECTIVE 1 = **horrifying**, shocking, alarming, awful, terrifying, horrible, dreadful, fearful ≠ reassuring 2 = **awful**, dreadful, horrendous

apparatus NOUN 1 = **organization**, system, network, structure, bureaucracy, hierarchy, setup (*informal*), chain of command 2 = **equipment**, tackle, gear, device, tools, mechanism, machinery, appliance

apparent ADJECTIVE 1 = **seeming**, outward, superficial, ostensible ≠ actual 2 = **obvious**, marked, visible, evident, distinct, manifest, noticeable, unmistakable ≠ unclear

apparently ADVERB = **seemingly**, outwardly, ostensibly

appeal VERB 1 = **plead**, ask, request, pray, beg, entreat ≠ refuse ▷ NOUN 1 = **plea**, call, application, request, prayer, petition, overture, entreaty ≠ refusal 2 = **attraction**, charm, fascination, beauty, allure ≠ repulsiveness ▷ PHRASE: **appeal to someone** = **attract**, interest, draw, please, charm, fascinate, tempt, lure

appealing ADJECTIVE = **attractive**, engaging, charming, desirable, alluring, winsome ≠ repellent

appear VERB 1 = **look (like** or **as if)**, seem, occur, look to be, come across as, strike you as 2 = **come into view**, emerge, occur, surface, come out, turn up, be present, show up (*informal*) ≠ disappear

appearance NOUN 1 = **look**, form, figure, looks, manner, expression, demeanour, mien (*literary*) 2 = **arrival**, presence, introduction, emergence 3 = **impression**, air, front, image, illusion, guise, façade, pretence

appease VERB 1 = **pacify**, satisfy, calm, soothe, quiet, placate, mollify, conciliate ≠ anger 2 = **ease**, calm, relieve, soothe,

alleviate, allay

appetite NOUN 1 = **hunger** 2 = **desire**, liking, longing, demand, taste, passion, stomach, hunger ≠ distaste

applaud VERB 1 = **clap**, encourage, praise, cheer, acclaim ≠ boo 2 = **praise**, celebrate, approve, acclaim, compliment, salute, commend, extol ≠ criticize

applause NOUN = **ovation**, praise, cheers, approval, clapping, accolade, big hand

appliance NOUN = **device**, machine, tool, instrument, implement, mechanism, apparatus, gadget

applicable ADJECTIVE = **appropriate**, fitting, useful, suitable, relevant, apt, pertinent ≠ inappropriate

applicant NOUN = **candidate**, claimant, inquirer

application NOUN 1 = **request**, claim, appeal, inquiry, petition, requisition 2 = **effort**, work, industry, trouble, struggle, pains, commitment, hard work 3 = **app** (*informal*), program, package, software, killer application *or* killer app

apply VERB 1 = **request**, appeal, put in, petition, inquire, claim, requisition 2 = **be relevant**, relate, refer, be fitting, be appropriate, fit, pertain, be applicable 3 = **use**, exercise, carry out, employ, implement, practise, exert, enact 4 = **put on**,

work in, cover with, lay on, paint
on, spread on, rub in, smear on
▷ PHRASE: **apply yourself** = **work
hard**, concentrate, try, commit
yourself, buckle down (*informal*),
devote yourself, be diligent,
dedicate yourself

appoint VERB 1 = **assign**, name,
choose, commission, select,
elect, delegate, nominate ≠ fire
2 = **decide**, set, choose, establish,
fix, arrange, assign, designate
≠ cancel

appointed ADJECTIVE 1 = **decided**,
set, chosen, established, fixed,
arranged, assigned, designated
2 = **assigned**, named, chosen,
selected, elected, delegated,
nominated 3 = **equipped**,
provided, supplied, furnished,
fitted out

appointment NOUN
1 = **selection**, naming, election,
choice, nomination, assignment
2 = **job**, office, position, post,
situation, place, employment,
assignment 3 = **meeting**,
interview, date, arrangement,
engagement, fixture, rendezvous,
assignation

appraisal NOUN = **assessment**,
opinion, estimate, judgment,
evaluation, estimation

appreciate VERB 1 = **enjoy**, like,
value, respect, prize, admire,
treasure, rate highly ≠ scorn
2 = **be aware of**, understand,
realize, recognize, perceive,
take account of, be sensitive to,
sympathize with ≠ be unaware of

3 = **be grateful for**, be obliged for,
be thankful for, give thanks for,
be indebted for, be in debt for, be
appreciative of ≠ be ungrateful
for 4 = **increase**, rise, grow, gain,
improve, enhance, soar ≠ fall

appreciation NOUN
1 = **admiration**, enjoyment
2 = **gratitude**, thanks,
recognition, obligation,
acknowledgment, indebtedness,
thankfulness, gratefulness
≠ ingratitude 3 = **awareness**,
understanding, recognition,
perception, sympathy,
consciousness, sensitivity,
realization ≠ ignorance
4 = **increase**, rise, gain, growth,
improvement, escalation,
enhancement ≠ fall

apprehension NOUN
1 = **anxiety**, concern, fear,
worry, alarm, suspicion, dread,
trepidation ≠ confidence
2 = **arrest**, catching, capture,
taking, seizure ≠ release
3 = **awareness**, understanding,
perception, grasp, comprehension
≠ incomprehension

apprentice NOUN = **trainee**,
student, pupil, novice, beginner,
learner, probationer ≠ master

approach VERB 1 = **move
towards**, reach, near, come close,
come near, draw near 2 = **make
a proposal to**, speak to, apply to,
appeal to, proposition, solicit,
sound out, make overtures to
3 = **set about**, tackle, undertake,
embark on, get down to, launch

a

into, begin work on, commence on

▷ NOUN 1 = **advance**, coming, nearing, appearance, arrival, drawing near 2 = **access**, way, drive, road, passage, entrance, avenue, passageway 3 *often plural* = **proposal**, offer, appeal, advance, application, invitation, proposition, overture 4 = **way**, means, style, method, technique, manner

appropriate

ADJECTIVE = **suitable**, fitting, relevant, to the point, apt, pertinent, befitting, well-suited ≠ unsuitable

▷ VERB 1 = **seize**, claim, acquire, confiscate, usurp, impound, commandeer, take possession of ≠ relinquish 2 = **allocate**, allow, budget, devote, assign, designate, set aside, earmark ≠ withhold 3 = **steal**, take, nick (*slang, chiefly Brit.*), pocket, pinch (*informal*), lift (*informal*), embezzle, pilfer

approval NOUN 1 = **consent**, agreement, sanction, blessing, permission, recommendation, endorsement, assent 2 = **favour**, respect, praise, esteem, acclaim, appreciation, admiration, applause ≠ disapproval

approve VERB = **agree to**, allow, pass, recommend, permit, sanction, endorse, authorize ≠ veto ▷ PHRASE: **approve of something** *or* **someone** = **favour**, like, respect, praise, admire, commend, have a good opinion of, regard highly

apt ADJECTIVE 1 = **appropriate**, fitting, suitable, relevant, to the point, pertinent ≠ inappropriate 2 = **inclined**, likely, ready, disposed, prone, liable, given, predisposed 3 = **gifted**, skilled, quick, talented, sharp, capable, smart, clever ≠ slow

● WORD POWER
● Arabic has contributed many
● words to English over the
● ages, particularly in the areas
● of mathematics and science.
● These were adopted into
● English via Latin and French
● with their sounds and spellings
● adapted for the Romance
● languages. For example, *alcohol*
● derives from the Arabic *al-kuhl*
● but these two elements were
● fused together in Medieval
● Latin, entering English in the
● 16th century. The cosmetic
● powder *kohl*, used to darken
● the eyelids, is from the same
● derivation, without *al*, the
● Arabic word for 'the'. Other
● borrowings from Arabic
● describe aspects of Islamic
● religion, such as *muezzin*, *imam*,
● *madrasah*, and *hajj*; food eaten
● in the Middle East, such as
● *kebabs*, *falafel*, *hummus*, and
● *tabbouleh*; and clothes worn in
● Muslim countries, such as the
● *hijab* and *jellaba*. The adoption
● of loan words from other
● languages takes place when
● there is contact between two

- cultures. For this reason, many
- servicemen have introduced
- loan words into English.
- Sometimes, military slang
- remains restricted to army-
- speak, but at other times it
- passes into mainstream usage.
- An example of this is *shufti* (also
- *shufty*) from Arabic *sufti* 'have
- you seen?' We talk about *having*
- *a shufti at something* when we
- want to have a quick look at it.
- It is still chiefly a British slang
- expression, and is now quite
- dated. It is thought to have
- first been used by the RAF in
- the 1920s and was in common
- currency in the British army
- in the Middle East during the
- Second World War.

arbitrary ADJECTIVE = **random**,
chance, subjective, inconsistent,
erratic, personal, whimsical,
capricious ≠ logical

arbitration NOUN = **decision**,
settlement, judgment,
determination, adjudication

arc NOUN = **curve**, bend, bow, arch,
crescent, half-moon

arcade NOUN = **gallery**, cloister,
portico, colonnade

arch¹ NOUN 1 = **archway**, curve,
dome, span, vault 2 = **curve**,
bend, bow, crook, arc, hunch,
sweep, hump
  ▷ VERB = **curve**, bridge, bend,
bow, span, arc

arch² ADJECTIVE = **playful**, sly,
mischievous, saucy, pert, roguish,
frolicsome, waggish

archetypal ADJECTIVE = **typical**,
standard, model, original, classic,
ideal, prototypic *or* prototypical

architect NOUN = **designer**,
planner, draughtsman, master
builder

architecture NOUN 1 = **design**,
planning, building, construction
2 = **construction**, design,
style 3 = **structure**, design,
shape, make-up, construction,
framework, layout, anatomy

archive NOUN = **record office**,
museum, registry, repository
  ▷ PLURAL NOUN = **records**, papers,
accounts, rolls, documents, files,
deeds, chronicles

arctic ADJECTIVE (*informal*)
= **freezing**, cold, frozen, icy, chilly,
glacial, frigid

Arctic ADJECTIVE = **polar**, far-
northern, hyperborean

ardent ADJECTIVE
1 = **enthusiastic**, keen, eager,
avid, zealous ≠ indifferent
2 = **passionate**, intense,
impassioned, lusty, amorous, hot-
blooded ≠ cold

area NOUN 1 = **region**, quarter,
district, zone, neighbourhood,
locality 2 = **part**, section,
sector, portion 3 = **realm**, part,
department, field, province,
sphere, domain

arena NOUN 1 = **ring**, ground,
field, theatre, bowl, pitch,
stadium, enclosure 2 = **scene**,
world, area, stage, field, sector,
territory, province

argue VERB 1 = **quarrel**, fight,

a

row, clash, dispute, disagree, squabble, bicker **2** = **discuss**, debate, dispute **3** = **claim**, reason, challenge, insist, maintain, allege, assert, uphold

argument NOUN **1** = **reason**, case, reasoning, ground(s), defence, logic, polemic, dialectic **2** = **debate**, questioning, claim, discussion, dispute, controversy, plea, assertion **3** = **quarrel**, fight, row, clash, dispute, controversy, disagreement, feud ≠ agreement

arise VERB **1** = **happen**, start, begin, follow, result, develop, emerge, occur **2** (old-fashioned) = **get to your feet**, get up, rise, stand up, spring up, leap up **3** = **get up**, wake up, awaken, get out of bed

aristocrat NOUN = **noble**, lord, lady, peer, patrician, grandee, aristo (informal), peeress

aristocratic ADJECTIVE = **upper-class**, lordly, titled, elite, gentlemanly, noble, patrician, blue-blooded ≠ common

arm¹ NOUN = **upper limb**, limb, appendage

arm² VERB = **equip**, provide, supply, array, furnish, issue with, deck out, accoutre
 ▷ PLURAL NOUN = **weapons**, guns, firearms, weaponry, armaments, ordnance, munitions, instruments of war

 ● WORD POWER
 ● The core meaning of **arm** is a
 ● limb of the human body from
 ● the shoulder to the hand. By

● extension, arm can mean any
● offshoot from a larger area,
● particularly when applied to
● bodies of water, e.g. **an arm**
● **of the North Sea**. This term is
● also used in organisations
● where arm refers to a specific
● branch or division of a larger
● whole, as in **the manufacturing**
● **arm of the company**. Arm has
● also come to mean 'power' or
● 'command', especially in the
● phrase **the (long) arm of the law**.
● It is thought that this phrase
● may derive from a proverb
● found from 16th century
● English: **Kings have long arms**,
● **hands, many ears, and many eyes**
● meaning that royal authority
● was far-reaching. Arms are seen
● as valuable commodities in the
● expressions **(cost) an arm and a**
● **leg** and **(would) give one's right**
● **arm for something**.

armed ADJECTIVE = **carrying weapons**, protected, equipped, primed, fitted out

armour NOUN = **protection**, covering, shield, sheathing, armour plate, chain mail, protective covering

armoured ADJECTIVE = **protected**, mailed, reinforced, toughened, bulletproof, armour-plated, steel-plated, ironclad

army NOUN **1** = **soldiers**, military, troops, armed force, legions, infantry, military force, land force **2** = **vast number**, host, gang, mob, flock, array, legion, swarm

aroma NOUN = **scent**, smell, perfume, fragrance, bouquet, savour, odour, redolence

around PREPOSITION
1 = **approximately**, about, nearly, close to, roughly, just about, in the region of, circa (*of a date*) 2 = **surrounding**, about, enclosing, encompassing, framing, encircling, on all sides of, on every side of
▷ ADVERB 1 = **everywhere**, about, throughout, all over, here and there, on all sides, in all directions, to and fro 2 = **near**, close, nearby, at hand, close at hand

⬤ **WORD POWER**
⬤ In American English, *around* is
⬤ used more often than *round* as
⬤ an adverbial and preposition,
⬤ except in a few fixed phrases
⬤ such as *all year round*. In
⬤ British English, *round* is more
⬤ commonly used as an adverb
⬤ than *around*.

arouse VERB 1 = **stimulate**, encourage, inspire, prompt, spur, provoke, rouse, stir up ≠ quell 2 = **inflame**, move, excite, spur, provoke, stir up, agitate 3 = **awaken**, wake up, rouse, waken

arrange VERB 1 = **plan**, agree, prepare, determine, organize, construct, devise, contrive, jack up (*N.Z. informal*) 2 = **put in order**, group, order, sort, position, line up, organize, classify, jack up (*N.Z. informal*) ≠ disorganize 3 = **adapt**, score, orchestrate, harmonize, instrument

arrangement NOUN 1 *often plural* = **plan**, planning, provision, preparation 2 = **agreement**, contract, settlement, appointment, compromise, deal (*informal*), pact, compact 3 = **display**, system, structure, organization, exhibition, presentation, classification, alignment 4 = **adaptation**, score, version, interpretation, instrumentation, orchestration, harmonization

array NOUN 1 = **arrangement**, show, supply, display, collection, exhibition, line-up, mixture 2 (*poetic*) = **clothing**, dress, clothes, garments, apparel, attire, finery, regalia
▷ VERB 1 = **arrange**, show, group, present, range, display, parade, exhibit 2 = **dress**, clothe, deck, decorate, adorn, festoon, attire

arrest VERB 1 = **capture**, catch, nick (*slang, chiefly Brit.*), seize, detain, apprehend, take prisoner ≠ release 2 = **stop**, end, limit, block, slow, delay, interrupt, suppress ≠ speed up 3 = **fascinate**, hold, occupy, engage, grip, absorb, entrance, intrigue
▷ NOUN 1 = **capture**, bust (*informal*), detention, seizure ≠ release 2 = **stoppage**, suppression, obstruction, blockage, hindrance ≠ acceleration

arresting ADJECTIVE = **striking**,

surprising, engaging, stunning, impressive, outstanding, remarkable, noticeable ≠ unremarkable

arrival NOUN 1 = **appearance**, coming, arriving, entrance, advent, materialization 2 = **coming**, happening, taking place, emergence, occurrence, materialization 3 = **newcomer**, incomer, visitor, caller, entrant

arrive VERB 1 = **come**, appear, turn up, show up (*informal*), draw near ≠ depart 2 = **occur**, happen, take place 3 (*informal*) = **succeed**, make it (*informal*), triumph, do well, thrive, flourish, be successful, make good

arrogance NOUN = **conceit**, pride, swagger, insolence, high-handedness, haughtiness, superciliousness, disdainfulness ≠ modesty

arrogant ADJECTIVE = **conceited**, proud, cocky, overbearing, haughty, scornful, egotistical, disdainful ≠ modest

arrow NOUN 1 = **dart**, flight, bolt, shaft (*archaic*), quarrel 2 = **pointer**, indicator, marker

arsenal NOUN 1 = **store**, supply, stockpile 2 = **armoury**, storehouse, ammunition dump, arms depot, ordnance depot

art NOUN 1 = **artwork**, style of art, fine art, creativity 2 = **skill**, craft, expertise, competence, mastery, ingenuity, virtuosity, cleverness

article NOUN 1 = **feature**, story, paper, piece, item, creation, essay, composition 2 = **thing**, piece, unit, item, object, device, tool, implement 3 = **clause**, point, part, section, item, passage, portion, paragraph

articulate
ADJECTIVE = **expressive**, clear, coherent, fluent, eloquent, lucid ≠ incoherent
▷ VERB 1 = **express**, say, state, word, declare, phrase, communicate, utter 2 = **pronounce**, say, talk, speak, voice, utter, enunciate

artificial ADJECTIVE 1 = **synthetic**, manufactured, plastic, man-made, non-natural 2 = **insincere**, forced, affected, phoney or phony (*informal*), false, contrived, unnatural, feigned ≠ genuine 3 = **fake**, mock, imitation, bogus, simulated, sham, counterfeit ≠ authentic

artillery NOUN = **big guns**, battery, cannon, ordnance, gunnery

artistic ADJECTIVE 1 = **creative**, cultured, original, sophisticated, refined, aesthetic, discerning, eloquent ≠ untalented 2 = **beautiful**, creative, elegant, stylish, aesthetic, tasteful ≠ unattractive

as CONJUNCTION 1 = **when**, while, just as, at the time that 2 = **in the way that**, like, in the manner that 3 = **since**, because, seeing that, considering that, on account of the fact that
▷ PREPOSITION = **in the role of**,

being, under the name of, in the character of

ashamed ADJECTIVE
1 = **embarrassed**, sorry, guilty, distressed, humiliated, self-conscious, red-faced, mortified ≠ proud **2** = **reluctant**, embarrassed

ashore ADVERB = **on land**, on the beach, on the shore, aground, to the shore, on dry land, shorewards, landwards

aside ADVERB = **to one side**, separately, apart, beside, out of the way, on one side, to the side
▷ NOUN = **interpolation**, parenthesis

ask VERB **1** = **inquire**, question, quiz, query, interrogate ≠ answer **2** = **request**, appeal to, plead with, demand, beg **3** = **invite**, bid, summon

asleep ADJECTIVE = **sleeping**, napping, dormant, dozing, slumbering, snoozing (*informal*), fast asleep, sound asleep

aspect NOUN **1** = **feature**, side, factor, angle, characteristic, facet **2** = **position**, view, situation, scene, prospect, point of view, outlook **3** = **appearance**, look, air, condition, quality, bearing, attitude, cast

aspiration NOUN = **aim**, plan, hope, goal, dream, wish, desire, objective

aspire to VERB = **aim for**, desire, hope for, long for, seek out, wish for, dream about, set your heart on

ass NOUN **1** = **donkey**, moke (*slang*) **2** = **fool**, idiot, twit (*informal*, *chiefly Brit.*), oaf, jackass, blockhead, halfwit, numbskull *or* numskull, dorba *or* dorb (*Austral. slang*), bogan (*Austral. slang*)

assassin NOUN = **murderer**, killer, slayer, liquidator, executioner, hit man (*slang*), hatchet man (*slang*)

assassinate VERB = **murder**, kill, eliminate (*slang*), take out (*slang*), terminate, hit (*slang*), slay, liquidate

assault NOUN = **attack**, raid, invasion, charge, offensive, onslaught, foray ≠ defence
▷ VERB = **strike**, attack, beat, knock, bang, slap, smack, thump

assemble VERB **1** = **gather**, meet, collect, rally, come together, muster, congregate ≠ scatter **2** = **bring together**, collect, gather, rally, come together, muster, amass, congregate **3** = **put together**, join, set up, build up, connect, construct, piece together, fabricate ≠ take apart

assembly NOUN **1** = **gathering**, group, meeting, council, conference, crowd, congress, collection, hui (*N.Z.*), runanga (*N.Z.*) **2** = **putting together**, setting up, construction, building up, connecting, piecing together

assert VERB **1** = **state**, argue, maintain, declare, swear, pronounce, affirm, profess ≠ deny **2** = **insist upon**, stress, defend, uphold, put forward, press, stand up for ≠ retract ▷ **PHRASE**: **assert yourself** = **be forceful**, put your foot down (*informal*), put yourself forward, make your presence felt, exert your influence

assertion NOUN 1 = **statement**, claim, declaration, pronouncement 2 = **insistence**, stressing, maintenance

assertive ADJECTIVE = **confident**, positive, aggressive, forceful, emphatic, insistent, feisty (*informal, chiefly U.S. & Canad.*), pushy (*informal*) ≠ meek

assess VERB 1 = **judge**, estimate, analyse, evaluate, rate, value, check out, weigh up 2 = **evaluate**, rate, tax, value, estimate, fix, impose, levy

assessment NOUN 1 = **judgment**, analysis, evaluation, valuation, appraisal, rating, opinion, estimate 2 = **evaluation**, rating, charge, fee, toll, levy, valuation

asset NOUN = **benefit**, help, service, aid, advantage, strength, resource, attraction ≠ disadvantage

assign VERB 1 = **give**, set, grant, allocate, give out, consign, allot, apportion 2 = **select for**, post, commission, elect, appoint, delegate, nominate, name 3 = **attribute**, credit, put down, set down, ascribe, accredit

assignment NOUN = **task**, job, position, post, commission, exercise, responsibility, duty

assist VERB 1 = **help**, support, aid, cooperate with, abet, lend a helping hand to 2 = **facilitate**, help, further, serve, aid, forward, promote, speed up ≠ hinder

assistance NOUN = **help**, backing, support, aid, cooperation, helping hand ≠ hindrance

assistant NOUN = **helper**, ally, colleague, supporter, aide, second, attendant, accomplice

associate VERB 1 = **connect**, link, ally, identify, join, combine, attach, fasten ≠ separate 2 = **socialize**, mix, accompany, mingle, consort, hobnob ≠ avoid ▷ NOUN = **partner**, friend, ally, colleague, mate (*informal*), companion, comrade, affiliate, cobber (*Austral. & N.Z. old-fashioned, informal*), E hoa (*N.Z.*)

association NOUN 1 = **group**, club, society, league, band, set, pack, collection 2 = **connection**, union, joining, pairing, combination, mixture, blend, juxtaposition

assorted ADJECTIVE = **various**, different, mixed, varied, diverse, miscellaneous, sundry, motley ≠ similar

assume VERB 1 = **presume**, think, believe, expect, suppose, imagine, fancy, take for granted ≠ know 2 = **take on**, accept, shoulder, take over, put on, enter upon 3 = **simulate**, affect, adopt, put on, imitate, mimic, feign, impersonate 4 = **take over**, take, appropriate, seize, commandeer ≠ give up

assumed ADJECTIVE = **false**,

made-up, fake, bogus, counterfeit, fictitious, make-believe ≠ real

assumption NOUN
1 = **presumption**, belief, guess, hypothesis, inference, conjecture, surmise, supposition 2 = **taking on**, managing, handling, shouldering, putting on, taking up, takeover, acquisition 3 = **seizure**, taking, takeover, acquisition, appropriation, wresting, confiscation, commandeering

assurance NOUN 1 = **promise**, statement, guarantee, commitment, pledge, vow, declaration, assertion ≠ lie 2 = **confidence**, conviction, certainty, self-confidence, poise, faith, nerve, aplomb ≠ self-doubt

assure VERB 1 = **convince**, encourage, persuade, satisfy, comfort, reassure, hearten, embolden 2 = **make certain**, ensure, confirm, guarantee, secure, make sure, complete, seal 3 = **promise to**, pledge to, vow to, guarantee to, swear to, confirm to, certify to, give your word to

assured ADJECTIVE 1 = **confident**, certain, positive, poised, fearless, self-confident, self-assured, dauntless ≠ self-conscious 2 = **certain**, sure, ensured, confirmed, settled, guaranteed, fixed, secure, nailed-on (*slang*) ≠ doubtful

astonish VERB = **amaze**, surprise, stun, stagger, bewilder, astound, daze, confound

astounding ADJECTIVE = **amazing**, surprising, brilliant, impressive, astonishing, staggering, sensational (*informal*), bewildering

astute ADJECTIVE = **intelligent**, sharp, clever, subtle, shrewd, cunning, canny, perceptive ≠ stupid

asylum NOUN 1 (*old-fashioned*) = **mental hospital**, hospital, institution, psychiatric hospital, madhouse (*informal*) 2 = **refuge**, haven, safety, protection, preserve, shelter, retreat, harbour

athlete NOUN = **sportsperson**, player, runner, competitor, sportsman, contestant, gymnast, sportswoman

athletic ADJECTIVE = **fit**, strong, powerful, healthy, active, trim, strapping, energetic ≠ feeble

athletics PLURAL NOUN = **sports**, games, races, exercises, contests, sporting events, gymnastics, track and field events

atmosphere NOUN 1 = **air**, sky, heavens, aerosphere 2 = **feeling**, character, environment, spirit, surroundings, tone, mood, climate

atom NOUN = **particle**, bit, spot, trace, molecule, dot, speck

atrocity NOUN 1 = **act of cruelty**, crime, horror, evil, outrage, abomination 2 = **cruelty**, horror, brutality, savagery, wickedness, barbarity, viciousness, fiendishness

attach VERB 1 = **affix**, stick, secure, add, join, couple, link, tie ≠ detach 2 = **ascribe**, connect, attribute, assign, associate

attached ADJECTIVE = **spoken for**, married, partnered, engaged, accompanied ▷ PHRASE: **attached to** = **fond of**, devoted to, affectionate towards, full of regard for

attachment NOUN 1 = **fondness**, liking, feeling, relationship, regard, attraction, affection, affinity, aroha (N.Z.) ≠ aversion 2 = **accessory**, fitting, extra, component, extension, supplement, fixture, accoutrement

attack VERB 1 = **assault**, strike (at), mug, ambush, tear into, set upon, lay into (informal) ≠ defend 2 = **invade**, occupy, raid, infringe, storm, encroach 3 = **criticize**, blame, abuse, condemn, knock (informal), put down, slate (informal), have a go (at) (informal) ▷ NOUN 1 = **assault**, charge, campaign, strike, raid, invasion, offensive, blitz ≠ defence 2 = **criticism**, censure, disapproval, abuse, bad press, vilification, denigration, disparagement 3 = **bout**, fit, stroke, seizure, spasm, convulsion, paroxysm

attacker NOUN = **assailant**, assaulter, raider, intruder, invader, aggressor, mugger

attain VERB 1 = **obtain**, get, reach, complete, gain, achieve, acquire, fulfil 2 = **reach**, achieve, acquire, accomplish

attempt VERB = **try**, seek, aim, struggle, venture, undertake, strive, endeavour ▷ NOUN 1 = **try**, go (informal), shot (informal), effort, trial, bid, crack (informal), stab (informal) 2 = **attack**

attend VERB 1 = **be present**, go to, visit, frequent, haunt, appear at, turn up at, patronize ≠ be absent 2 = **pay attention**, listen, hear, mark, note, observe, heed, pay heed ≠ ignore ▷ PHRASE: **attend to something** = **apply yourself to**, concentrate on, look after, take care of, see to, get to work on, devote yourself to, occupy yourself with

attendance NOUN 1 = **presence**, being there, attending, appearance 2 = **turnout**, audience, gate, congregation, house, crowd, throng, number present

attendant NOUN = **assistant**, guard, servant, companion, aide, escort, follower, helper ▷ ADJECTIVE = **accompanying**, related, associated, accessory, consequent, resultant, concomitant

attention NOUN 1 = **thinking**, thought, mind, consideration, scrutiny, heed, deliberation, intentness 2 = **care**, support, concern, treatment, looking after, succour, ministration 3 = **awareness**, regard, notice, recognition, consideration, observation, consciousness ≠ inattention

attic NOUN = **loft**, garret, roof space

attitude NOUN 1 = **opinion**, view, position, approach, mood, perspective, point of view, stance 2 = **position**, bearing, pose, stance, carriage, posture

attract VERB 1 = **allure**, draw, persuade, charm, appeal to, win over, tempt, lure (*informal*) ≠ repel 2 = **pull**, draw, magnetize

attraction NOUN 1 = **appeal**, pull (*informal*), charm, lure, temptation, fascination, allure, magnetism 2 = **pull**, magnetism

attractive ADJECTIVE 1 = **seductive**, charming, tempting, pretty, fair, inviting, lovely, pleasant, hot (*informal*), fit (*Brit. informal*) ≠ unattractive 2 = **appealing**, pleasing, inviting, tempting, irresistible ≠ unappealing

attribute VERB = **ascribe**, credit, refer, trace, assign, charge, allocate, put down ▷ NOUN = **quality**, feature, property, character, element, aspect, characteristic, distinction

audience NOUN 1 = **spectators**, company, crowd, gathering, gallery, assembly, viewers, listeners 2 = **interview**, meeting, hearing, exchange, reception, consultation

aura NOUN = **air**, feeling, quality, atmosphere, tone, mood, ambience

austerity NOUN 1 = **plainness**, simplicity, starkness 2 = **asceticism**, self-discipline, sobriety, puritanism, self-denial

authentic ADJECTIVE 1 = **real**, pure, genuine, valid, undisputed, lawful, bona fide, dinkum (*Austral. & N.Z. informal*), true-to-life ≠ fake 2 = **accurate**, legitimate, authoritative

authenticity NOUN 1 = **genuineness**, purity 2 = **accuracy**, certainty, validity, legitimacy, faithfulness, truthfulness

author NOUN 1 = **writer**, composer, novelist, hack, creator, scribbler, scribe, wordsmith 2 = **creator**, father, producer, designer, founder, architect, inventor, originator

authoritarian ADJECTIVE = **strict**, severe, autocratic, dictatorial, dogmatic, tyrannical, doctrinaire ≠ lenient ▷ NOUN = **disciplinarian**, dictator, tyrant, despot, autocrat, absolutist

authoritative ADJECTIVE 1 = **commanding**, masterly, imposing, assertive, imperious, self-assured ≠ timid 2 = **reliable**, accurate, valid, authentic, definitive, dependable, trustworthy ≠ unreliable

authority NOUN 1 *usually plural* = **powers that be**, government, police, officials, the state, management, administration, the system **2** = **prerogative**, influence, power, control, weight, direction, command, licence, mana (*N.Z.*) **3** = **expert**, specialist, professional, master, guru, virtuoso, connoisseur, fundi (*S. African*) **4** = **command**, power, control, rule, management, direction, mastery

authorize VERB **1** = **empower**, commission, enable, entitle, mandate, accredit, give authority to **2** = **permit**, allow, grant, approve, sanction, license, warrant, consent to ≠ forbid

automatic ADJECTIVE
1 = **mechanical**, automated, mechanized, push-button, self-propelling ≠ done by hand **2** = **involuntary**, natural, unconscious, mechanical, spontaneous, reflex, instinctive, unwilled ≠ conscious

autonomous ADJECTIVE = **self-ruling**, free, independent, sovereign, self-sufficient, self-governing, self-determining

autonomy NOUN
= **independence**, freedom, sovereignty, self-determination, self-government, self-rule, self-sufficiency, home rule, rangatiratanga (*N.Z.*) ≠ dependency

availability NOUN
= **accessibility**, readiness, handiness, attainability

available ADJECTIVE = **accessible**, ready, to hand, handy, at hand, free, to be had, achievable ≠ in use

avalanche NOUN **1** = **snow-slide**, landslide, landslip **2** = **large amount**, barrage, torrent, deluge, inundation

avant-garde ADJECTIVE
= **progressive**, pioneering, experimental, innovative, unconventional, ground-breaking ≠ conservative

avenue NOUN = **street**, way, course, drive, road, approach, route, path

average NOUN = **standard**, normal, usual, par, mode, mean, medium, norm
▷ ADJECTIVE **1** = **usual**, standard, general, normal, regular, ordinary, typical, commonplace ≠ unusual **2** = **mean**, middle, medium, intermediate, median ≠ minimum
▷ VERB = **make on average**, be on average, even out to, do on average, balance out to ▷ PHRASE: **on average** = **usually**, generally, normally, typically, for the most part, as a rule

avert VERB **1** = **ward off**, avoid, prevent, frustrate, fend off, preclude, stave off, forestall **2** = **turn away**, turn aside

avoid VERB **1** = **prevent**, stop, frustrate, hamper, foil, inhibit, avert, thwart **2** = **refrain from**, bypass, dodge, eschew, escape, duck (out of) (*informal*), fight shy of, shirk from **3** = **keep away from**, dodge, shun, evade, steer clear of, bypass

await VERB 1 = **wait for**, expect, look for, look forward to, anticipate, stay for 2 = **be in store for**, wait for, be ready for, lie in wait for, be in readiness for

awake VERB 1 = **wake up**, come to, wake, stir, awaken, rouse 2 = **alert**, stimulate, provoke, revive, arouse, stir up, kindle 3 = **stimulate**, provoke, alert, stir up, kindle
▷ ADJECTIVE 1 = **not sleeping**, sleepless, wide-awake, aware, conscious, aroused, awakened, restless ≠ asleep

award VERB 1 = **present with**, give, grant, hand out, confer, endow, bestow 2 = **grant**, give, confer
▷ NOUN = **prize**, gift, trophy, decoration, grant, bonsela (*S. African*), koha (*N.Z.*)

aware ADJECTIVE = **informed**, enlightened, knowledgeable, learned, expert, versed, up to date, in the picture ≠ ignorant

awareness NOUN ▷ PHRASE: awareness of = **knowledge of**, understanding of, recognition of, perception of, consciousness of, realization of, familiarity with

away ADJECTIVE = **absent**, out, gone, elsewhere, abroad, not here, not present, on vacation
▷ ADVERB 1 = **off**, elsewhere, abroad, hence, from here 2 = **aside**, out of the way, to one side 3 = **at a distance**, far, apart, remote, isolated 4 = **continuously**, repeatedly, relentlessly, incessantly, interminably, unremittingly, uninterruptedly

awe NOUN = **wonder**, fear, respect, reverence, horror, terror, dread, admiration ≠ contempt
▷ VERB = **impress**, amaze, stun, frighten, terrify, astonish, horrify, intimidate

awesome ADJECTIVE = **awe-inspiring**, amazing, stunning, impressive, astonishing, formidable, intimidating, breathtaking

awful ADJECTIVE 1 = **disgusting**, offensive, gross, foul, dreadful, revolting, sickening, frightful, festy (*Austral. slang*), yucko (*Austral. slang*) 2 = **bad**, poor, terrible, appalling, foul, rubbish (*slang*), dreadful, horrendous ≠ wonderful ka pai (*N.Z.*) 3 = **shocking**, dreadful 4 = **unwell**, poorly (*informal*), ill, terrible, sick, crook (*Austral. & N.Z. informal*), unhealthy, off-colour, under the weather (*informal*)

awfully ADVERB 1 (*informal*) = **very**, extremely, terribly, exceptionally, greatly, immensely, exceedingly, dreadfully 2 = **badly**, woefully, dreadfully, disgracefully, wretchedly, unforgivably, reprehensibly

awkward ADJECTIVE
1 = **embarrassing**, difficult, sensitive, delicate, uncomfortable, humiliating, disconcerting, inconvenient, barro (*Austral. slang*)

≠ comfortable **2** = **inconvenient**, difficult, troublesome, cumbersome, unwieldy, unmanageable, clunky (*informal*) ≠ convenient **3** = **clumsy**, lumbering, bumbling, unwieldy, ponderous, ungainly, gauche, gawky, unco (*Austral. slang*) ≠ graceful

axe NOUN = **hatchet**, chopper, tomahawk, cleaver, adze
▷ VERB **1** (*informal*) = **abandon**, end, eliminate, cancel, scrap, cut back, terminate, dispense with **2** (*informal*) = **dismiss**, fire (*informal*), sack (*informal*), remove, get rid of, kennet (*Austral. slang*), jeff (*Austral. slang*) ▷ PHRASE: **the axe** (*informal*) = **the sack** (*informal*), dismissal, the boot (*slang*), termination, the chop (*slang*)

axis NOUN = **pivot**, shaft, axle, spindle, centre line

Bb

baas (*S. African*) NOUN = **master**, chief, ruler, commander, head, overlord, overseer

baby NOUN = **child**, infant, babe, bairn (*Scot. & Northern English*), newborn child, babe in arms, ankle biter (*Austral. slang*), tacker (*Austral. slang*)
▷ ADJECTIVE = **small**, little, minute, tiny, mini, wee, miniature, petite

back NOUN 1 = **spine**, backbone, vertebrae, spinal column, vertebral column 2 = **rear** ≠ front 3 = **reverse**, rear, other side, wrong side, underside, flip side
▷ ADJECTIVE 1 = **rear** ≠ front 2 = **rearmost**, hind, hindmost 3 = **previous**, earlier, former, past, elapsed ≠ future 4 = **tail**, end, rear, posterior
▷ VERB 1 = **support**, help, aid, champion, defend, promote, assist, advocate ≠ oppose 2 = **subsidize**, help, support, sponsor, assist

● **WORD POWER**
● The *back* is the posterior part
● of the human body, extending
● from the neck to the pelvis. It
● is conceived as the part of any
● object opposite the front or to
● the rear, in examples like *the
● back of a car*. It can also mean
● the tail end, e.g. *the back of a
● queue*. The reverse side of an
● object can equally be denoted
● by back, e.g. *the back of a packet*.
● We describe the past and the
● future in terms of backwards
● and forwards. As an adjective,
● back means 'previous' in the
● expression *back catalogue*,
● and, as an adverb, back means
● 'previously' in the expression *a
● few years back*. The back plays an
● important role in supporting
● the human body, therefore
● *backing* is another word for
● support and assistance. We
● cannot see what is going on
● *behind our backs*, therefore this
● expression denotes secrecy and
● even wrongdoing.

backbone NOUN 1 = **spinal column**, spine, vertebrae, vertebral column 2 = **strength of character**, character, resolution, nerve, daring, courage, determination, pluck

backer NOUN 1 = **supporter**, second, angel (*informal*), patron, promoter, subscriber, helper, benefactor 2 = **advocate**, supporter, patron, sponsor, promoter

backfire VERB = **fail**, founder, flop (*informal*), rebound, boomerang, miscarry, misfire

background NOUN 1 = **upbringing**, history, culture, environment,

tradition, circumstances
2 = **experience**, grounding,
education 3 = **circumstances**,
history, conditions, situation,
atmosphere, environment,
framework, ambience

backing NOUN 1 = **support**,
encouragement, endorsement,
moral support 2 = **assistance**,
support, help, aid, sponsorship,
patronage

backlash NOUN = **reaction**,
response, resistance, retaliation,
repercussion, counterblast,
counteraction

backward ADJECTIVE
1 = **underdeveloped**,
undeveloped 2 = **slow**, behind,
retarded, underdeveloped,
subnormal, half-witted,
slow-witted, intellectually
handicapped (*Austral.*)

backwards *or* **backward**
ADVERB = **towards the rear**,
behind you, in reverse, rearwards

bacteria PLURAL NOUN
= **microorganisms**, viruses,
bugs (*slang*), germs, microbes,
pathogens, bacilli

● WORD POWER
● *Bacteria* is a plural noun. It is
● therefore incorrect to talk
● about *a bacteria*, even though
● this is quite commonly heard,
● especially in the media. The
● correct singular is *a bacterium*.

bad ADJECTIVE 1 = **harmful**,
damaging, dangerous,
destructive, unhealthy,
detrimental, hurtful, ruinous

≠ beneficial 2 = **unfavourable**,
distressing, unfortunate, grim,
unpleasant, gloomy, adverse
3 = **inferior**, poor, inadequate,
faulty, unsatisfactory, defective,
imperfect, substandard,
bush-league (*Austral. & N.Z.
informal*), half-pie (*N.Z. informal*),
bodger *or* bodgie (*Austral. slang*)
≠ satisfactory 4 = **incompetent**,
poor, useless, incapable, unfit,
inexpert 5 = **grim**, severe, hard,
tough 6 = **wicked**, criminal, evil,
corrupt, immoral, sinful, depraved
≠ virtuous 7 = **naughty**, defiant,
wayward, mischievous, wicked,
unruly, impish, undisciplined
≠ well-behaved 8 = **rotten**, off,
rank, sour, rancid, mouldy, putrid,
festy (*Austral. slang*)

badge NOUN 1 = **image**, brand,
stamp, identification, crest,
emblem, insignia 2 = **mark**, sign,
token

badger VERB = **pester**, harry,
bother, bug (*informal*), bully,
plague, hound, harass

badly ADVERB 1 = **poorly**,
incorrectly, carelessly,
inadequately, imperfectly, ineptly
≠ well 2 = **severely**, greatly,
deeply, seriously, desperately,
intensely, exceedingly
3 = **unfavourably**, unsuccessfully

baffle VERB = **puzzle**, confuse,
stump, bewilder, confound,
perplex, mystify, flummox
≠ explain

bag NOUN = **sack**, container, sac,
receptacle

▷ **VERB** 1 = **get**, land, score
(*slang*), capture, acquire, procure
2 = **catch**, kill, shoot, capture,
acquire, trap

baggage NOUN = **luggage**,
things, cases, bags, equipment,
gear, suitcases, belongings

baggy ADJECTIVE = **loose**, slack,
bulging, sagging, sloppy, floppy,
roomy, ill-fitting ≠ tight

bail NOUN (*law*) = **security**, bond,
guarantee, pledge, warranty,
surety ▷ **PHRASES**: bail out
= **escape**, withdraw, get away,
retreat, make your getaway, break
free *or* out; **bail something** *or*
someone out (*informal*) = **save**,
help, release, aid, deliver, recover,
rescue, get out

bait NOUN = **lure**, attraction,
incentive, carrot (*informal*),
temptation, snare, inducement,
decoy
▷ **VERB** = **tease**, annoy, irritate,
bother, mock, wind up (*Brit. slang*),
hound, torment

baked ADJECTIVE = **dry**, desert,
seared, scorched, barren, sterile,
arid, torrid

bakkie NOUN (*S. African*) = **truck**,
pick-up, van, lorry, pick-up truck

balance VERB 1 = **stabilize**, level,
steady ≠ overbalance 2 = **weigh**,
consider, compare, estimate,
contrast, assess, evaluate,
set against 3 (*accounting*)
= **calculate**, total, determine,
estimate, settle, count, square,
reckon
▷ NOUN 1 = **equilibrium**,

stability, steadiness, evenness
≠ instability 2 = **stability**,
equanimity, steadiness
3 = **parity**, equity, fairness,
impartiality, equality,
correspondence, equivalence
4 = **remainder**, rest, difference,
surplus, residue 5 = **composure**,
stability, restraint, self-control,
poise, self-discipline, equanimity,
self-restraint

balcony NOUN 1 = **terrace**,
veranda 2 = **upper circle**, gods,
gallery

bald ADJECTIVE 1 = **hairless**,
depilated, baldheaded 2 = **plain**,
direct, frank, straightforward,
blunt, rude, forthright, unadorned

ball NOUN = **sphere**, drop, globe,
pellet, orb, globule, spheroid

balloon VERB = **expand**, rise,
increase, swell, blow up, inflate,
bulge, billow

ballot NOUN = **vote**, election,
voting, poll, polling, referendum,
show of hands

ban VERB 1 = **prohibit**, bar, block,
veto, forbid, boycott, outlaw,
banish ≠ permit 2 = **bar**,
prohibit, exclude, forbid,
disqualify, preclude, debar, declare
ineligible
▷ NOUN = **prohibition**,
restriction, veto, boycott,
embargo, injunction, taboo,
disqualification, rahui (*N.Z.*),
restraining order (*U.S. law*)
≠ permission

band[1] NOUN 1 = **ensemble**, group,
orchestra, combo 2 = **gang**,

company, group, party, team, body, crowd, pack

band² NOUN = **headband**, strip, ribbon

bandage NOUN = **dressing**, plaster, compress, gauze
▷ VERB = **dress**, cover, bind, swathe

bandit NOUN = **robber**, outlaw, raider, plunderer, mugger (*informal*), looter, highwayman, desperado

bang NOUN 1 = **explosion**, pop, clash, crack, blast, slam, discharge, thump 2 = **blow**, knock, stroke, punch, bump, sock (*slang*), smack, thump
▷ VERB 1 = **resound**, boom, explode, thunder, thump, clang 2 = **bump**, knock, elbow, jostle 3 *often with* **on** = **hit**, strike, knock, belt (*informal*), slam, thump, clatter, beat *or* knock seven bells out of (*informal*)
▷ ADVERB = **exactly**, straight, square, squarely, precisely, slap, smack, plumb (*informal*)

banish VERB 1 = **exclude**, ban, dismiss, expel, throw out, eject, evict 2 = **expel**, exile, outlaw, deport ≠ admit 3 = **get rid of**, remove

bank¹ NOUN 1 = **financial institution**, repository, depository 2 = **store**, fund, stock, source, supply, reserve, pool, reservoir
▷ VERB = **deposit**, keep, save

bank² NOUN 1 = **side**, edge, margin, shore, brink 2 = **mound**, banking, rise, hill, mass, pile, heap, ridge, kopje *or* koppie (*S. African*)
▷ VERB = **tilt**, tip, pitch, heel, slope, incline, slant, cant

bank³ NOUN = **row**, group, line, range, series, file, rank, sequence

bankrupt ADJECTIVE = **insolvent**, broke (*informal*), ruined, wiped out (*informal*), impoverished, in the red, destitute, gone bust (*informal*) ≠ solvent

bankruptcy NOUN = **insolvency**, failure, disaster, ruin, liquidation

banner NOUN 1 = **flag**, standard, colours, pennant, ensign, streamer 2 = **placard**

banquet NOUN = **feast**, spread (*informal*), dinner, meal, revel, repast, hakari (*N.Z.*)

bar NOUN 1 = **public house**, pub (*informal, chiefly Brit.*), counter, inn, saloon, tavern, canteen, watering hole (*facetious or slang*), beer parlour (*Canad.*) 2 = **rod**, staff, stick, stake, rail, pole, paling, shaft 3 = **obstacle**, block, barrier, hurdle, hitch, barricade, snag, deterrent ≠ aid
▷ VERB 1 = **lock**, block, secure, attach, bolt, blockade, barricade, fortify 2 = **block**, restrict, restrain, hamper, thwart, hinder, obstruct, impede 3 = **exclude**, ban, forbid, prohibit, keep out of, disallow, shut out of, blackball ≠ admit

barbarian NOUN 1 = **savage**, monster, beast, brute, yahoo, swine, sadist 2 = **lout**, yahoo, bigot, philistine, hoon (*Austral.*

& N.Z.), cougan (*Austral. slang*), scozza (*Austral. slang*), bogan (*Austral. slang*), boor, vulgarian

bare ADJECTIVE 1 = **naked**, nude, stripped, uncovered, undressed, unclothed, unclad, without a stitch on (*informal*) ≠ dressed 2 = **simple**, spare, stark, austere, spartan, unadorned, unembellished, unornamented, bare-bones ≠ adorned 3 = **plain**, simple, basic, obvious, sheer, patent, evident, stark

barely ADVERB = **only just**, just, hardly, scarcely, at a push ≠ completely

bargain NOUN 1 = **good buy**, discount purchase, good deal, steal (*informal*), snip (*informal*), giveaway, cheap purchase 2 = **agreement**, deal (*informal*), promise, contract, arrangement, settlement, pledge, pact ▷ VERB = **negotiate**, deal, contract, mediate, covenant, stipulate, transact, cut a deal

barge NOUN = **canal boat**, lighter, narrow boat, flatboat

bark¹ VERB = **yap**, bay, howl, snarl, growl, yelp, woof ▷ NOUN = **yap**, bay, howl, snarl, growl, yelp, woof

bark² NOUN = **covering**, casing, cover, skin, layer, crust, cortex (*anatomy, botany*), rind

barracks PLURAL NOUN = **camp**, quarters, garrison, encampment, billet

barrage NOUN 1 = **bombardment**, attack, bombing, assault, shelling, battery, volley, blitz 2 = **torrent**, mass, burst, stream, hail, spate, onslaught, deluge

barren ADJECTIVE 1 = **desolate**, empty, desert, waste ≠ fertile 2 (*old-fashioned*) = **infertile**, sterile, childless, unproductive

barricade NOUN = **barrier**, wall, fence, blockade, obstruction, rampart, bulwark, palisade ▷ VERB = **bar**, block, defend, secure, lock, bolt, blockade, fortify

barrier NOUN = **barricade**, wall, bar, fence, boundary, obstacle, blockade, obstruction

base¹ NOUN 1 = **bottom**, floor, lowest part ≠ top 2 = **support**, stand, foot, rest, bed, bottom, foundation, pedestal 3 = **foundation**, institution, organization, establishment, starting point 4 = **centre**, post, station, camp, settlement, headquarters 5 = **home**, house, pad (*slang*), residence 6 = **essence**, source, basis, root, core ▷ VERB 1 = **ground**, found, build, establish, depend, construct, derive, hinge 2 = **place**, set, post, station, establish, locate, install

base² ADJECTIVE = **dishonourable**, evil, disgraceful, shameful, immoral, wicked, sordid, despicable, scungy (*Austral. & N.Z.*) ≠ honourable

bash VERB = **hit**, beat, strike, knock, smash, belt (*informal*), slap, sock (*slang*)

basic ADJECTIVE 1 = **fundamental**,

- **BATS**
- flying fox
- fruit bat
- hammerhead
- horseshoe bat
- kalong
- noctule
- pipistrelle
- serotine
- vampire bat

b

main, essential, primary, vital, principal, cardinal, elementary **2 = vital**, needed, important, key, necessary, essential, primary, crucial **3 = essential**, key, vital, fundamental ≠ secondary **4 = main**, key, essential, primary **5 = plain**, simple, classic, unfussy, unembellished, bare-bones
▷ PLURAL NOUN = **essentials**, principles, fundamentals, nuts and bolts (*informal*), nitty-gritty (*informal*), rudiments, brass tacks (*informal*)

basically ADVERB = **essentially**, mainly, mostly, principally, fundamentally, primarily, at heart, inherently

basis NOUN **1 = arrangement**, way, system, footing, agreement **2 = foundation**, support, base, ground, footing, bottom, groundwork

bask VERB = **lie**, relax, lounge, sprawl, loaf, lie about, swim in, sunbathe, outspan (*S. African*)

bass ADJECTIVE = **deep**, low, resonant, sonorous, low-pitched, deep-toned

batch NOUN = **group**, set, lot, crowd, pack, collection, quantity, bunch

bath NOUN = **wash**, cleaning, shower, soak, cleansing, scrub, scrubbing, douche
▷ VERB = **clean**, wash, shower, soak, cleanse, scrub, bathe, rinse

bathe VERB **1 = swim 2 = wash**, clean, bath, shower, soak, cleanse, scrub, rinse **3 = cleanse**, clean, wash, soak, rinse **4 = cover**, flood, steep, engulf, immerse, overrun, suffuse, wash over

baton NOUN = **stick**, club, staff, pole, rod, crook, cane, mace, mere (*N.Z.*), patu (*N.Z.*)

batter VERB = **beat**, hit, strike, knock, bang, thrash, pound, buffet

battery NOUN = **artillery**, ordnance, gunnery, gun emplacement, cannonry

battle NOUN **1 = fight**, attack, action, struggle, conflict, clash, encounter, combat, biffo (*Austral. slang*), boilover (*Austral.*) ≠ peace **2 = conflict**, campaign, struggle, dispute, contest, crusade **3 = campaign**, drive, movement, push, struggle
▷ VERB **1 = wrestle**, war, fight, argue, dispute, grapple, clamour, lock horns **2 = struggle**, work, labour, strain, strive, toil, go all out (*informal*), give it your best shot (*informal*)

battlefield NOUN = **battleground**, front, field,

● **FAMOUS BATTLES**

● Aboukir *or* Abukir Bay	1798		● Manassas	1861; 1862
● Actium	31 BC		● Marathon	490 BC
● Agincourt	1415		● Marengo	1800
● Alamo	1836		● Marston Moor	1644
● Arnhem	1944		● Missionary Ridge	1863
● Austerlitz	1805		● Navarino	425 BC
● Balaklava *or* Balaclava	1854		● Omdurman	1898
● Bannockburn	1314		● Passchendaele	1917
● Barnet	1471		● Philippi	42 BC
● Bautzen	1813		● Plains of Abraham	1759
● Belleau Wood	1918		● Plassey	1757
● Blenheim	1704		● Plataea	479 BC
● Borodino	1812		● Poltava	1709
● Bosworth Field	1485		● Prestonpans	1745
● Boyne	1690		● Pydna	168 BC
● Cannae	216 BC		● Quatre Bras	1815
● Crécy	1346		● Ramillies	1706
● Culloden	1746		● Roncesvalles	778
● Dien Bien Phu	1954		● Sadowa *or* Sadová	1866
● Edgehill	1642		● Saint-Mihiel	1918
● El Alamein	1942		● Salamis	480 BC
● Falkirk	1298; 1746		● Sedgemoor	1685
● Flodden	1513		● Sempach	1386
● Gettysburg	1863		● Shipka Pass	1877–78
● Guadalcanal	1942-3		● Somme	1916; 1918
● Hastings	1066		● Stamford Bridge	1066
● Imphal	1944		● Tannenberg	1410; 1914
● Inkerman	1854		● Tewkesbury	1471
● Issus	333 BC		● Thermopylae	480 BC
● Jemappes	1792		● Tobruk	1941; 1942
● Jena	1806		● Trafalgar	1805
● Killiecrankie	1689		● Trenton	1776
● Kursk	1943		● Verdun	1916
● Ladysmith	1899–1900		● Vitoria	1813
● Leipzig	1813		● Wagram	1809
● Lepanto	1571		● Waterloo	1815
● Leyte Gulf	1944		● Ypres	1914; 1915; 1917; 1918
● Little Bighorn	1876			
● Lützen	1632		● Zama	202 BC

combat zone, field of battle

batty ADJECTIVE = **crazy**, odd, mad, eccentric, peculiar, daft (*informal*), touched, potty (*Brit. informal*), off the air (*Austral. slang*), porangi (*N.Z.*), daggy (*Austral. & N.Z. informal*)

bay¹ NOUN = **inlet**, sound, gulf, creek, cove, fjord, bight, natural harbour

bay² NOUN = **recess**, opening, corner, niche, compartment, nook, alcove

bay³ VERB = **howl**, cry, roar (*of a hound*), bark, wail, growl, bellow, clamour
▷ NOUN = **cry**, roar (*of a hound*), bark, howl, wail, growl, bellow, clamour

bazaar NOUN 1 = **market**, exchange, fair, marketplace
2 = **fair**, fête, gala, bring-and-buy

be VERB = **be alive**, live, exist, survive, breathe, be present, endure

beach NOUN = **shore**, coast, sands, seaside, water's edge, seashore

beached ADJECTIVE = **stranded**, grounded, abandoned, deserted, wrecked, ashore, marooned, aground

beacon NOUN 1 = **signal**, sign, beam, flare, bonfire
2 = **lighthouse**, watchtower

bead NOUN = **drop**, tear, bubble, pearl, dot, drip, blob, droplet

beam VERB 1 = **smile**, grin
2 = **transmit**, show, air, broadcast,

cable, send out, relay, televise 3 = **radiate**, flash, shine, glow, glitter, glare, gleam
▷ NOUN 1 = **ray**, flash, stream, glow, streak, shaft, gleam, glint
2 = **rafter**, support, timber, spar, plank, girder, joist 3 = **smile**, grin

bear VERB 1 = **carry**, take, move, bring, transfer, conduct, transport, haul ≠ put down
2 = **support**, shoulder, sustain, endure, uphold, withstand ≠ give up 3 = **display**, have, show, hold, carry, possess
4 = **suffer**, experience, go through, sustain, stomach, endure, brook, abide 5 = **bring yourself to**, allow, accept, permit, endure, tolerate 6 = **produce**, generate, yield, bring forth
7 = **give birth to**, produce, deliver, breed, bring forth, beget
8 = **exhibit**, hold, maintain
9 = **conduct**, carry, move, deport
▷ PHRASE: **bear something out** = **support**, prove, confirm, justify, endorse, uphold, substantiate, corroborate

bearer NOUN 1 = **agent**, carrier, courier, herald, envoy, messenger, conveyor, emissary 2 = **carrier**, runner, servant, porter

bearing NOUN 1 *usually with* **on** *or* **upon** = **relevance**, relation, application, connection, import, reference, significance, pertinence ≠ irrelevance

2 = **manner**, attitude, conduct, aspect, behaviour, posture, demeanour, deportment
▷ **PLURAL NOUN** = **way**, course, position, situation, track, aim, direction, location

beast NOUN 1 = **animal**, creature, brute 2 = **brute**, monster, savage, barbarian, fiend, swine, ogre, sadist

beastly ADJECTIVE (*informal*) = **unpleasant**, mean, awful, nasty, rotten, horrid, disagreeable ≠ pleasant

beat VERB 1 = **batter**, hit, strike, knock, pound, smack, thrash, thump 2 = **pound**, strike, hammer, batter, thrash 3 = **throb**, thump, pound, quake, vibrate, pulsate, palpitate 4 = **hit**, strike, bang 5 = **flap**, thrash, flutter, wag 6 = **defeat**, outdo, trounce, overcome, crush, overwhelm, conquer, surpass
▷ NOUN 1 = **throb**, pounding, pulse, thumping, vibration, pulsating, palpitation, pulsation 2 = **route**, way, course, rounds, path, circuit ▷ **PHRASE**: **beat someone up** (*informal*) = **assault**, attack, batter, thrash, set about, set upon, lay into (*informal*), beat the living daylights out of (*informal*)

beaten ADJECTIVE 1 = **stirred**, mixed, whipped, blended, whisked, frothy, foamy
2 = **defeated**, overcome, overwhelmed, cowed, thwarted, vanquished

beautiful ADJECTIVE = **attractive**, pretty, lovely, charming, tempting, pleasant, handsome, fetching, hot (*informal*), fit (*Brit. informal*) ≠ ugly

beauty NOUN 1 = **attractiveness**, charm, grace, glamour, elegance, loveliness, handsomeness, comeliness ≠ ugliness 2 = **good-looker**, lovely (*slang*), belle, stunner (*informal*), beaut (*Austral. & N.Z. slang*)

because CONJUNCTION = **since**, as, in that ▷ **PHRASE**: **because of** = **as a result of**, on account of, by reason of, thanks to, owing to

● **WORD POWER**
● The phrase *on account of* can
● provide a useful alternative
● to *because of* in writing. It
● occurs relatively infrequently
● in spoken language, where it
● is sometimes followed by a
● clause, as in *on account of I don't*
● *do drugs*. However, this use is
● considered nonstandard.

beckon VERB = **gesture**, sign, wave, indicate, signal, nod, motion, summon

become VERB 1 = **come to be**, develop into, be transformed into, grow into, change into, alter to, mature into, ripen into 2 = **suit**, fit, enhance, flatter, embellish, set off

becoming ADJECTIVE
1 = **flattering**, pretty, attractive, enhancing, neat, graceful, tasteful, well-chosen ≠ unflattering 2 = **appropriate**,

seemly, fitting, suitable, proper,
worthy, in keeping, compatible
≠ inappropriate

bed NOUN 1 = **bedstead**, couch,
berth, cot, divan 2 = **plot**, area,
row, strip, patch, ground, land,
garden 3 = **bottom**, ground, floor
4 = **base**, footing, basis, bottom,
foundation, underpinning,
groundwork, bedrock

bee NOUN
▷ see **ants, bees and wasps**

beer parlour NOUN (*Canad.*)
= **tavern**, inn, bar, pub (*informal,
chiefly Brit.*), public house,
beverage room (*Canad.*), hostelry,
alehouse (*archaic*)

before PREPOSITION 1 = **earlier
than**, ahead of, prior to, in
advance of ≠ after 2 = **in front of**,
ahead of, in advance of 3 = **in the
presence of**, in front of 4 = **ahead
of**, in front of, in advance of
▷ ADVERB 1 = **previously**, earlier,

⬤ **BEETLES**
⬤ ambrosia beetle
⬤ Asiatic beetle
⬤ bacon beetle
⬤ bark beetle
⬤ bee beetle
⬤ black beetle *or* (*N.Z.*) kekerengu
  or Māori bug
⬤ blister beetle
⬤ bloody-nosed beetle
⬤ boll weevil
⬤ bombardier beetle
⬤ burying beetle *or* sexton
⬤ cabinet beetle
⬤ cardinal beetle
⬤ carpet beetle *or* (*U.S.*) carpet bug
⬤ chafer
⬤ Christmas beetle *or* king beetle
⬤ click beetle, snapping beetle, *or*
  skipjack
⬤ cockchafer, May beetle, *or* May
  bug
⬤ Colorado beetle *or* potato beetle
⬤ deathwatch beetle
⬤ diving beetle
⬤ dung beetle *or* chafer

⬤ firefly
⬤ flea beetle
⬤ furniture beetle
⬤ glow-worm
⬤ gold beetle *or* goldbug
⬤ goldsmith beetle
⬤ ground beetle
⬤ Japanese beetle
⬤ June bug, June beetle, May bug,
  or May beetle
⬤ ladybird *or* (*U.S. & Canad.*)
  ladybug
⬤ leaf beetle
⬤ leather beetle
⬤ May beetle, cockchafer, *or* June
  bug
⬤ scarab
⬤ scavenger beetle
⬤ snapping beetle
⬤ water beetle
⬤ weevil *or* snout beetle
⬤ weevil, pea weevil, *or* bean
  weevil

sooner, in advance, formerly
≠ after 2 = **in the past**, earlier,
once, previously, formerly,
hitherto, beforehand ▷ **RELATED
WORDS**: *prefixes* ante-, fore-, pre-

beforehand ADVERB = **in
advance**, before, earlier, already,
sooner, ahead, previously, in
anticipation

beg VERB 1 = **implore**, plead
with, beseech, request, petition,
solicit, entreat 2 = **scrounge**,
bum (*informal*), touch (someone)
for (*slang*), cadge, sponge on
(someone) for, freeload (*slang*),
seek charity, solicit charity ≠ give

beggar NOUN = **tramp**, bum
(*informal*), derelict, drifter, down-
and-out, pauper, vagrant, bag lady
(*chiefly U.S.*), derro (*Austral. slang*)

begin VERB 1 = **start**, commence,
proceed ≠ stop 2 = **commence**,
start, initiate, embark on, set
about, instigate, institute, make
a beginning 3 = **start talking**,
start, initiate, commence
4 = **come into existence**, start,
appear, emerge, arise, originate,
come into being 5 = **emerge**,
start, spring, stem, derive,
originate ≠ end

beginner NOUN = **novice**, pupil,
amateur, newcomer, starter,
trainee, apprentice, learner
≠ expert

beginning NOUN 1 = **start**,
opening, birth, origin, outset,
onset, initiation, inauguration
≠ end 2 = **outset**, start, opening,
birth, onset, commencement

3 = **origins**

behave VERB 1 = **act** 2 *often
reflexive* = **be well-behaved**,
mind your manners, keep your
nose clean, act correctly, conduct
yourself properly ≠ misbehave

behaviour NOUN 1 = **conduct**,
ways, actions, bearing, attitude,
manner, manners, demeanour
2 = **action**, performance,
operation, functioning

behind PREPOSITION 1 = **at the
rear of**, at the back of, at the
heels of 2 = **after**, following
3 = **supporting**, for, backing,
on the side of, in agreement
with 4 = **causing**, responsible
for, initiating, at the bottom of,
instigating 5 = **later than**, after
▷ ADVERB 1 = **after**, next,
following, afterwards,
subsequently, in the wake (of)
≠ in advance of 2 = **behind
schedule**, delayed, running
late, behind time ≠ ahead
3 = **overdue**, in debt, in arrears,
behindhand
▷ NOUN (*informal*) = **bottom**, butt
(*U.S. & Canad. informal*), buttocks,
posterior

being NOUN 1 = **individual**,
creature, human being,
living thing 2 = **life**, reality
≠ nonexistence 3 = **soul**, spirit,
substance, creature, essence,
organism, entity

beleaguered ADJECTIVE
1 = **harassed**, troubled, plagued,
hassled (*informal*), badgered,
persecuted, pestered, vexed

b

2 = **besieged**, surrounded, blockaded, beset, encircled, assailed, hemmed in

belief NOUN 1 = **trust**, confidence, conviction ≠ disbelief 2 = **faith**, principles, doctrine, ideology, creed, dogma, tenet, credo 3 = **opinion**, feeling, idea, impression, assessment, notion, judgment, point of view

believe VERB 1 = **think**, judge, suppose, estimate, imagine, assume, gather, reckon 2 = **accept**, trust, credit, depend on, rely on, have faith in, swear by, be certain of ≠ disbelieve

believer NOUN = **follower**, supporter, convert, disciple, devotee, apostle, adherent, zealot ≠ sceptic

bellow VERB = **shout**, cry (out), scream, roar, yell, howl, shriek, bawl
▷ NOUN = **shout**, cry, scream, roar, yell, howl, shriek, bawl

belly NOUN = **stomach**, insides (*informal*), gut, abdomen, tummy, paunch, potbelly, corporation (*informal*), puku (*N.Z.*)

belong VERB = **go with**, fit into, be part of, relate to, be connected with, pertain to

belonging NOUN = **fellowship**, relationship, association, loyalty, acceptance, attachment, inclusion, affinity

belongings PLURAL NOUN = **possessions**, goods, things, effects, property, stuff, gear, paraphernalia

beloved ADJECTIVE = **dear**, loved, valued, prized, admired, treasured, precious, darling

below PREPOSITION 1 = **under**, underneath, lower than 2 = **less than**, lower than 3 = **subordinate to**, subject to, inferior to, lesser than
▷ ADVERB 1 = **lower**, down, under, beneath, underneath 2 = **beneath**, following, at the end, underneath, at the bottom, further on

belt NOUN 1 = **waistband**, band, sash, girdle, girth, cummerbund 2 = **conveyor belt**, band, loop, fan belt, drive belt 3 (*geography*) = **zone**, area, region, section, district, stretch, strip, layer

bemused ADJECTIVE = **puzzled**, confused, baffled, at sea, bewildered, muddled, perplexed, mystified

bench NOUN 1 = **seat**, stall, pew 2 = **worktable**, stand, table, counter, trestle table, workbench
▷ PHRASE: **the bench** = **court**, judges, magistrates, tribunal, judiciary, courtroom

benchmark NOUN = **reference point**, gauge, yardstick, measure, level, standard, model, par

bend VERB = **twist**, turn, wind, lean, hook, bow, curve, arch
▷ NOUN = **curve**, turn, corner, twist, angle, bow, loop, arc

beneath PREPOSITION 1 = **under**, below, underneath, lower than ≠ over 2 = **inferior to**, below 3 = **unworthy of**, unfitting for,

unsuitable for, inappropriate for,
unbefitting
▷ ADVERB = **underneath**, below,
in a lower place ▷ RELATED WORD:
prefix **sub-**

beneficial ADJECTIVE
= **favourable**, useful, valuable,
helpful, profitable, benign,
wholesome, advantageous
≠ harmful

beneficiary NOUN 1 = **recipient**,
receiver, payee 2 = **heir**, inheritor

benefit NOUN 1 = **good**,
help, profit, favour ≠ harm
2 = **advantage**, aid, favour,
assistance
▷ VERB 1 = **profit from**, make the
most of, gain from, do well out of,
reap benefits from, turn to your
advantage 2 = **help**, aid, profit,
improve, enhance, assist, avail
≠ harm

benign ADJECTIVE 1 = **benevolent**,
kind, kindly, warm, friendly,
obliging, sympathetic,
compassionate ≠ unkind
2 (*medical*) = **harmless**, innocent,
innocuous, curable, inoffensive,
remediable ≠ malignant

bent ADJECTIVE 1 = **misshapen**,
twisted, angled, bowed, curved,
arched, crooked, distorted
≠ straight 2 = **stooped**, bowed,
arched, hunched
▷ NOUN = **inclination**, ability,
leaning, tendency, preference,
penchant, propensity, aptitude
▷ PHRASE: **bent on** = **intent on**,
set on, fixed on, predisposed to,
resolved on, insistent on

bequeath VERB 1 = **leave**, will,
give, grant, hand down, endow,
bestow, entrust 2 = **give**, accord,
grant, afford, yield, lend, pass on,
confer

berth NOUN 1 = **bunk**, bed,
hammock, billet 2 (*nautical*)
= **anchorage**, haven, port,
harbour, dock, pier, wharf, quay
▷ VERB (*nautical*) = **anchor**, land,
dock, moor, tie up, drop anchor

beside PREPOSITION = **next to**,
near, close to, neighbouring,
alongside, adjacent to, at the
side of, abreast of ▷ PHRASE:
beside yourself = **distraught**,
desperate, distressed, frantic,
frenzied, demented, unhinged,
overwrought

● WORD POWER
● People occasionally confuse
● *beside* and *besides*. *Besides* is used
● for mentioning something that
● adds to what you have already
● said, for example: *I didn't feel like*
● *going and besides, I had nothing*
● *to wear. Beside* usually means
● *next to or at the side of something*
● *or someone*, for example: *he was*
● *standing beside me* (not *besides*
● *me*).

besides PREPOSITION = **apart
from**, barring, excepting, other
than, excluding, as well (as), in
addition to, over and above
▷ ADVERB = **also**, too, further,
otherwise, in addition, as well,
moreover, furthermore

besiege VERB 1 = **harass**, harry,
plague, hound, hassle (*informal*),

badger, pester **2** = **surround**,
enclose, blockade, encircle, hem
in, shut in, lay siege to

best ADJECTIVE = **finest**, leading,
supreme, principal, foremost,
pre-eminent, unsurpassed, most
accomplished

▷ ADVERB = **most highly**, most
fully, most deeply ▷ PHRASE: **the
best** = **the finest**, the pick, the
flower, the cream, the elite, the
rème de la crème (French)

bestow VERB = **present**, give,
award, grant, commit, hand out,
lavish, impart ≠ obtain

bet VERB = **gamble**, chance, stake,
venture, hazard, speculate, wager,
risk money

▷ NOUN = **gamble**, risk, stake,
venture, speculation, flutter
(informal), punt, wager

betray VERB **1** = **be disloyal to**,
dob in (Austral. slang), double-
cross (informal), stab in the back,
be unfaithful to, inform on or
against **2** = **give away**, reveal,
expose, disclose, uncover, divulge,
unmask, let slip

betrayal NOUN = **disloyalty**,
sell-out (informal), deception,
treason, treachery, trickery,
double-cross (informal), breach of
trust ≠ loyalty

better ADVERB **1** = **to a greater
degree**, more completely,
more thoroughly **2** = **in a
more excellent manner**, more
effectively, more attractively,
more advantageously, more
competently, in a superior way

≠ worse

▷ ADJECTIVE **1** = **well**, stronger,
recovering, cured, fully recovered,
on the mend (informal) ≠ worse
2 = **superior**, finer, higher-quality,
surpassing, preferable, more
desirable ≠ inferior

between PREPOSITION = **amidst**,
among, mid, in the middle of,
betwixt ▷ RELATED WORD: prefix
inter-

 ● WORD POWER
 ● After distribute and words with
 ● a similar meaning, among
 ● should be used rather than
 ● between: share out the sweets
 ● among the children (not between
 ● the children, unless there are
 ● only two children).

beverage NOUN = **drink**, liquid,
liquor, refreshment

beverage room NOUN (Canad.)
= **tavern**, inn, bar, pub (informal,
chiefly Brit.), public house,
beer parlour (Canad.), hostelry,
alehouse (archaic)

beware VERB **1** = **be careful**,
look out, watch out, be wary,
be cautious, take heed, guard
against something **2** = **avoid**,
mind

bewilder VERB = **confound**,
confuse, puzzle, baffle, perplex,
mystify, flummox, bemuse

bewildered ADJECTIVE
= **confused**, puzzled, baffled, at
sea, muddled, perplexed, at a loss,
mystified

beyond PREPOSITION **1** = **on the
other side of 2** = **after**, over,

past, above 3 = **past** 4 = **except for**, but, save, apart from, other than, excluding, besides, aside from 5 = **exceeding**, surpassing, superior to, out of reach of 6 = **outside**, over, above

bias NOUN = **prejudice**, leaning, tendency, inclination, favouritism, partiality ≠ impartiality
▷ VERB = **influence**, colour, weight, prejudice, distort, sway, warp, slant

biased ADJECTIVE = **prejudiced**, weighted, one-sided, partial, distorted, slanted

bid NOUN 1 = **attempt**, try, effort, go (*informal*), shot (*informal*), stab (*informal*), crack (*informal*) 2 = **offer**, price, amount, advance, proposal, sum, tender
▷ VERB 1 = **make an offer**, offer, propose, submit, tender, proffer 2 = **wish**, say, call, tell, greet 3 = **tell**, ask, order, require, direct, command, instruct

bidding NOUN = **order**, request, command, instruction, summons, beck and call

big ADJECTIVE 1 = **large**, great, huge, massive, vast, enormous, substantial, extensive, supersize ≠ small 2 = **important**, significant, urgent, far-reaching ≠ unimportant 3 = **powerful**, important, prominent, dominant, influential, eminent, skookum (*Canad.*) 4 = **grown-up**, adult, grown, mature, elder, full-grown ≠ young 5 = **generous**,

good, noble, gracious, benevolent, altruistic, unselfish, magnanimous

bill¹ NOUN 1 = **charges**, rate, costs, score, account, statement, reckoning, expense 2 = **act of parliament**, measure, proposal, piece of legislation, projected law 3 = **list**, listing, programme, card, schedule, agenda, catalogue, inventory 4 = **advertisement**, notice, poster, leaflet, bulletin, circular, handout, placard
▷ VERB 1 = **charge**, debit, invoice, send a statement to, send an invoice to 2 = **advertise**, post, announce, promote, plug (*informal*), tout, publicize, give advance notice of

bill² NOUN = **beak**, nib, neb (*archaic or dialect*), mandible

bind VERB 1 = **oblige**, make, force, require, engage, compel, constrain, necessitate 2 = **tie**, join, stick, secure, wrap, knot, strap, lash ≠ untie
▷ NOUN (*informal*) = **nuisance**, inconvenience, hassle (*informal*), drag (*informal*), spot (*informal*), difficulty, bore, dilemma, uphill (*S. African*)

binding ADJECTIVE = **compulsory**, necessary, mandatory, obligatory, irrevocable, unalterable, indissoluble ≠ optional

binge NOUN (*informal*) = **bout**, spell, fling, feast, stint, spree, orgy, bender (*informal*)

biography NOUN = **life story**, life, record, account, profile, memoir,

CV, curriculum vitae

bird NOUN = **feathered friend**, fowl, songbird ▷ **RELATED WORDS**: *adjective* **avian**, *male* **cock**, *female* **hen**, *young* **chick**, **fledgeling** or **fledgling**, **nestling**, *collective nouns* **flock**, **flight**, *habitation* **nest**

▷ *see* **birds of prey, seabirds, types of fowl**

bird of prey NOUN

▷ *see* **birds of prey**

birth NOUN 1 = **childbirth**,

● BIRDS

- ● accentor
- ● amokura (N.Z.)
- ● apostle bird or happy family bird (Austral.)
- ● avocet
- ● axebird (Austral.)
- ● banded dotterel (N.Z.)
- ● banded rail (N.Z.)
- ● bee-eater
- ● bellbird or (N.Z.) koromako or makomako
- ● bittern
- ● blackbird
- ● blackcap
- ● black-fronted tern or tara (N.Z.)
- ● black robin (N.Z.)
- ● blue duck, mountain duck, whio or whistling duck (N.Z.)
- ● boobook (Austral.)
- ● brain-fever bird or (Austral.) pallid cuckoo
- ● brambling
- ● brolga, Australian crane, or (Austral.) native companion
- ● brown creeper or pipipi (N.Z.)
- ● brown duck (N.Z.)
- ● brown kiwi (N.Z.)
- ● budgerigar or (Austral.) zebra parrot
- ● bunting
- ● bush wren (N.Z.)

- ● bustard or (Austral.) plain turkey, plains turkey, or wild turkey
- ● button quail or (Austral.) bustard quail
- ● Californian quail (N.Z.)
- ● canary
- ● capercaillie or capercailzie
- ● chaffinch
- ● chicken or (Austral. informal) chook
- ● chiffchaff
- ● chough
- ● chukar
- ● crane
- ● crossbill
- ● crow or (Scot.) corbie
- ● cuckoo
- ● curlew
- ● dipper or water ouzel
- ● diver
- ● dove or (archaic or poetic) culver
- ● dunlin or red-backed sandpiper
- ● egret
- ● fernbird (N.Z.)
- ● fieldfare
- ● finch
- ● firecrest
- ● flamingo
- ● flycatcher
- ● galah or (Austral.) galar or gillar
- ● godwit

- goldcrest
- grebe
- greenshank
- grey-crowned babbler, happy family bird, Happy Jack, or parson bird (*Austral.*)
- grey warbler or riroriro (*N.Z.*)
- grouse
- hen harrier or (*U.S.* & *Canad.*) marsh harrier
- heron
- hoopoe
- jabiru or (*Austral.*) policeman bird
- jackdaw
- jaeger (*U.S.* & *Canad.*)
- jay
- kaka (*N.Z.*)
- kakapo (*N.Z.*)
- kakariki (*N.Z.*)
- karoro or blackbacked gull (*N.Z.*)
- kea (*N.Z.*)
- kingfisher or (*N.Z.*) kotare
- kiwi or apteryx
- knot
- koel or (*Austral.*) black cuckoo or cooee bird
- kokako or blue-wattled crow (*N.Z.*)
- kookaburra, laughing jackass, or (*Austral.*) bushman's clock, settler's clock, goburra, or great brown kingfisher
- kotuku or white heron (*N.Z.*)
- lapwing or green plover
- lark
- linnet
- lorikeet
- lyrebird or (*Austral.*) buln-buln
- magpie or (*Austral.*) piping shrike or piping crow-shrike

- magpie lark or (*Austral.*) mudlark, Murray magpie, mulga, or peewit
- Major Mitchell or Leadbeater's cockatoo
- makomako (*Austral.*)
- martin
- metallic starling or shining starling (*Austral.*)
- miromiro (*N.Z.*)
- mistletoe bird (*Austral.*)
- mohua or bush canary (*N.Z.*)
- New Zealand pigeon or kereru (*N.Z.*)
- nightingale
- nightjar, (*U.S.* & *Canad.*) goatsucker, or (*Austral.*) nighthawk
- noisy miner or (*Austral.*) micky or soldier bird
- nutcracker
- nuthatch
- ouzel or ousel
- paradise duck or putangitangi (*N.Z.*)
- pardalote (*Austral.*)
- partridge
- pheasant
- pigeon
- pipit or (*N.Z.*) pihoihoi
- pipiwharauroa or bronze-winged cuckoo (*N.Z.*)
- pitta (*Austral.*)
- plover
- ptarmigan
- puffin
- quail
- rainbow lorikeet
- raven
- redpoll

b

b

- redshank
- redstart
- redwing
- ringneck parrot, Port Lincoln parrot, or buln-buln (*Austral.*)
- robin or robin redbreast
- roller
- rook
- ruff
- saddlebill or jabiru
- sanderling
- sandpiper
- serin
- shrike or butcherbird
- silver-eye (*Austral.*)
- siskin or (*formerly*) aberdevine
- skylark
- snipe
- sparrow
- spoonbill
- spotted crake or (*Austral.*) water crake
- starling
- stint
- stonechat
- stork
- sulphur-crested cockatoo or white cockatoo

- superb blue wren (*Austral.*)
- superb lyrebird (*Austral.*)
- swallow
- swift
- thrush or (*poetic*) throstle
- tit
- topknot pigeon (*Austral.*)
- tree creeper
- tui or parson bird (*N.Z.*)
- twite
- wagtail
- warbler
- waxwing
- weka, weka rail, Māori hen, or wood hen (*N.Z.*)
- whinchat
- white-eye or (*N.Z.*) blighty, silvereye, tauhou or waxeye
- white-fronted tern or kahawai bird (*N.Z.*)
- whitethroat
- woodcock
- woodlark
- woodpecker
- wren
- yellowhammer
- yellowtail or yellowtail kingfisher (*Austral.*)

delivery, nativity, parturition ≠ **death** 2 = **ancestry**, stock, blood, background, breeding, pedigree, lineage, parentage
▷ **RELATED WORD**: *adjective* **natal**
bit¹ NOUN 1 = **slice**, fragment, crumb, morsel 2 = **piece**, scrap 3 = **jot**, iota 4 = **part**
bit² NOUN = **curb**, check, brake, restraint, snaffle
bite VERB = **nip**, cut, tear, wound,

snap, pierce, pinch, chew
▷ NOUN 1 = **snack**, food, piece, taste, refreshment, mouthful, morsel, titbit 2 = **wound**, sting, pinch, nip, prick
biting ADJECTIVE 1 = **piercing**, cutting, sharp, frozen, harsh, penetrating, arctic, icy
2 = **sarcastic**, cutting, stinging, scathing, acrimonious, incisive, virulent, caustic

bitter ADJECTIVE 1 = **resentful**, angry, offended, sour, sore, acrimonious, sullen, miffed (*informal*) ≠ happy 2 = **freezing**, biting, severe, intense, raw, fierce, chill, stinging ≠ mild 3 = **sour**, sharp, acid, harsh, tart, astringent, acrid, unsweetened ≠ sweet

bitterness NOUN
1 = **resentment**, hostility, indignation, animosity, acrimony, rancour, ill feeling, bad blood
2 = **sourness**, acidity, sharpness, tartness, acerbity

bizarre ADJECTIVE = **strange**, unusual, extraordinary, fantastic, weird, peculiar, eccentric, ludicrous, daggy (*Austral. & N.Z. informal*) ≠ normal

black ADJECTIVE 1 = **dark**, raven, ebony, sable, jet, dusky, pitch-black, swarthy ≠ light 2 = **gloomy**, sad, depressing, grim, bleak, hopeless, dismal, ominous ≠ happy 3 = **terrible**, bad, devastating, tragic, fatal, catastrophic, ruinous, calamitous 4 = **wicked**, bad, evil, corrupt, vicious, immoral, depraved, villainous ≠ good 5 = **angry**, cross, furious, hostile, sour, menacing, moody, resentful ≠ happy

● WORD POWER
● When referring to people with
● dark skin, the adjective black or
● Black is widely used. For people
● of the U.S. whose origins lie
● in Africa, the preferred term
● is African-American. To use 'a
● Black' or 'Blacks' as a noun is
● considered offensive, and it
● is better to talk about a Black
● person and Black people.
● WORD POWER
● *Black* is a colour which has
● nearly no hue due to its
● absorption of light. It has long
● been associated with night-
● time and darkness in Western
● cultures. It is also symbolic
● of death, with the bereaved
● expected to wear black clothes
● to signify mourning in many
● cultures. Some of the senses
● of black include: gloomy as in
● *black despair*; dirty as in *black*
● *with dirt*; terrible as in *Black*
● *Tuesday*; wicked as in *blackest*
● *act*; macabre as in *black comedy*;
● and angry as in *black look*. A
● *black sheep* is a person who is
● a disgrace or an outcast in a
● group, from the proverb 'there
● is a black sheep in every flock'.
● Another phrase involving black
● is *in the black* which means to
● be in credit financially, from
● the practice of marking credit
● items in black ink in a balance
● book. Black is sometimes used
● as a term relating to ethnic
● origin.

blackmail NOUN = **threat**, intimidation, ransom, extortion, hush money (*slang*)
▷ VERB = **threaten**, squeeze, compel, intimidate, coerce, dragoon, extort, hold to ransom

blame VERB 1 = **hold responsible**, accuse, denounce, indict, impeach, incriminate, impute ≠ absolve 2 = **attribute to**, credit to, assign to, put down to, impute to 3 *used in negative constructions* = **criticize**, condemn, censure, reproach, chide, find fault with ≠ praise
▷ NOUN = **responsibility**, liability, accountability, onus, culpability, answerability ≠ praise

bland ADJECTIVE 1 = **dull**, boring, plain, flat, dreary, run-of-the-mill, uninspiring, humdrum ≠ exciting 2 = **tasteless**, insipid, flavourless, thin

blank ADJECTIVE 1 = **unmarked**, white, clear, clean, empty, plain, bare, void ≠ marked 2 = **expressionless**, empty, vague, vacant, deadpan, impassive, poker-faced (*informal*) ≠ expressive
▷ NOUN 1 = **empty space**, space, gap 2 = **void**, vacuum, vacancy, emptiness, nothingness

blanket NOUN 1 = **cover**, rug, coverlet 2 = **covering**, sheet, coat, layer, carpet, cloak, mantle, thickness
▷ VERB = **coat**, cover, hide, mask, conceal, obscure, cloak

blast NOUN 1 = **explosion**, crash, burst, discharge, eruption, detonation 2 = **gust**, rush, storm, breeze, puff, gale, tempest, squall 3 = **blare**, blow, scream, trumpet, wail, resound, clamour, toot
▷ VERB = **blow up**, bomb, destroy, burst, ruin, break up, explode, shatter

blatant ADJECTIVE = **obvious**, clear, plain, evident, glaring, manifest, noticeable, conspicuous ≠ subtle

blaze VERB 1 = **burn**, glow, flare, be on fire, go up in flames, be ablaze, fire, flame 2 = **shine**, flash, beam, glow, flare, glare, gleam, radiate
▷ NOUN 1 = **inferno**, fire, flames, bonfire, combustion, conflagration 2 = **flash**, glow, glitter, flare, glare, gleam, brilliance, radiance

bleach VERB = **lighten**, wash out, blanch, whiten

bleak ADJECTIVE 1 = **dismal**, dark, depressing, grim, discouraging, gloomy, hopeless, dreary ≠ cheerful 2 = **exposed**, empty, bare, barren, desolate, windswept, weather-beaten, unsheltered ≠ sheltered 3 = **stormy**, severe, rough, harsh, tempestuous, intemperate

bleed VERB 1 = **lose blood**, flow, gush, spurt, shed blood 2 = **blend**, run, meet, unite, mix, combine, flow, fuse 3 (*informal*) = **extort**, milk, squeeze, drain, exhaust, fleece

blend VERB 1 = **mix**, join, combine, compound, merge, unite, mingle, amalgamate 2 = **go well**, match, fit, suit, go with, correspond, complement, coordinate 3 = **combine**, mix, link, integrate, merge, unite, amalgamate
▷ NOUN = **mixture**, mix,

combination, compound, brew, union, synthesis, alloy

bless VERB 1 = **sanctify**, dedicate, ordain, exalt, anoint, consecrate, hallow ≠ curse 2 = **endow**, give to, provide for, grant for, favour, grace, bestow to ≠ afflict

blessed ADJECTIVE = **holy**, sacred, divine, adored, revered, hallowed, sanctified, beatified

blessing NOUN 1 = **benefit**, help, service, favour, gift, windfall, kindness, good fortune ≠ disadvantage 2 = **approval**, backing, support, agreement, favour, sanction, permission, leave ≠ disapproval 3 = **benediction**, grace, dedication, thanksgiving, invocation, commendation, consecration, benison ≠ curse

blight NOUN 1 = **curse**, suffering, evil, corruption, pollution, plague, hardship, woe ≠ blessing 2 = **disease**, pest, fungus, mildew, infestation, pestilence, canker ▷ VERB = **frustrate**, destroy, ruin, crush, mar, dash, wreck, spoil, crool or cruel (Austral. slang)

blind ADJECTIVE 1 = **sightless**, unsighted, unseeing, eyeless, visionless ≠ sighted 2 usually followed by **to** = **unaware of**, unconscious of, ignorant of, indifferent to, insensitive to, oblivious of, unconcerned about, inconsiderate of ≠ aware 3 = **unquestioning**, prejudiced, wholesale, indiscriminate, uncritical, unreasoning, undiscriminating

blindly ADVERB 1 = **thoughtlessly**, carelessly, recklessly, indiscriminately, senselessly, heedlessly 2 = **wildly**, aimlessly

blink VERB 1 = **flutter**, wink, bat 2 = **flash**, flicker, wink, shimmer, twinkle, glimmer ▷ PHRASE: **on the blink** (slang) = **not working (properly)**, faulty, defective, playing up, out of action, malfunctioning, out of order

bliss NOUN 1 = **joy**, ecstasy, euphoria, rapture, nirvana, felicity, gladness, blissfulness ≠ misery 2 = **beatitude**, blessedness

blister NOUN = **sore**, boil, swelling, cyst, pimple, carbuncle, pustule

bloc NOUN = **group**, union, league, alliance, coalition, axis

block NOUN 1 = **piece**, bar, mass, brick, lump, chunk, hunk, ingot 2 = **obstruction**, bar, barrier, obstacle, impediment, hindrance ▷ VERB 1 = **obstruct**, close, stop, plug, choke, clog, stop up, bung up (informal) ≠ clear 2 = **obscure**, bar, obstruct 3 = **shut off**, stop, bar, hamper, obstruct

blockade NOUN = **stoppage**, block, barrier, restriction, obstacle, barricade, obstruction, impediment

blog NOUN = **weblog**, microblog, vlog, blook, website, forum, chatroom, column, newsletter, podcast, profile (on a social networking site), webcast, vodcast

bloke NOUN (informal) = **man**, person, individual, character (*informal*), guy (*informal*), fellow, chap

blonde *or* **blond** ADJECTIVE
1 = **fair**, light, flaxen **2** = **fair-haired**, golden-haired, tow-headed

blood NOUN **1** = **lifeblood**, gore, vital fluid **2** = **family**, relations, birth, descent, extraction, ancestry, lineage, kinship

● WORD POWER
● The literal meaning of
● *blood* is that of the red fluid
● circulating in the veins and
● arteries of human beings and
● some animals. Its essential
● role in transporting oxygen
● around the body has led blood
● to represent vitality and
● rejuvenation in phrases such
● as *the lifeblood of the economy*.
● We also associate blood
● with feelings and emotions,
● particularly those of passion
● and temper, when we talk
● about *hot-blooded* people,
● acts being performed *in cold
● blood*, or *bad blood* stirred
● up between people. These
● expressions demonstrate
● that different temperatures
● represent different feelings,
● with anger and passion as
● heat, and indifference and
● cruelty as cold. Blood has
● long been symbolic of family,
● lineage, and race, from the
● expression *flesh and blood* to
● the proverb *blood is thicker than
● water*, meaning that family

● ties take precedence. Blood
● also signifies loss of life from
● *blood-letting* as a therapeutic
● surgical procedure in the past,
● to *bloodshed* which indicates
● murder and death.

bloodshed NOUN = **killing**, murder, massacre, slaughter, slaying, carnage, butchery, blood-letting

bloody ADJECTIVE **1** = **cruel**, fierce, savage, brutal, vicious, ferocious, cut-throat, warlike **2** = **bloodstained**, raw, bleeding, blood-soaked, blood-spattered

bloom NOUN **1** = **flower**, bud, blossom **2** = **prime**, flower, beauty, height, peak, flourishing, heyday, zenith **3** = **glow**, freshness, lustre, radiance ≠ pallor
▷ VERB **1** = **flower**, blossom, open, bud ≠ wither **2** = **grow**, develop, wax **3** = **succeed**, flourish, thrive, prosper, fare well ≠ fail

blossom NOUN = **flower**, bloom, bud, efflorescence, floret
▷ VERB **1** = **bloom**, grow, develop, mature **2** = **succeed**, progress, thrive, flourish, prosper **3** = **flower**, bloom, bud

blow¹ VERB **1** = **move**, carry, drive, sweep, fling, buffet, waft **2** = **be carried**, flutter **3** = **exhale**, breathe, pant, puff **4** = **play**, sound, pipe, trumpet, blare, toot ▷ PHRASES: **blow something up 1** = **explode**, bomb, blast, detonate, blow sky-high **2** = **inflate**, pump up, fill, expand, swell, enlarge, puff up, distend **3** = **magnify**, increase, extend, expand, widen, broaden, amplify; **blow up 1** = **explode**, burst, shatter, erupt, detonate **2** (*informal*) = **lose your temper**, rage, erupt, see red (*informal*), become angry, hit the roof (*informal*), fly off the handle (*informal*), go crook (*Austral. & N.Z. slang*), blow your top

blow² NOUN **1** = **knock**, stroke, punch, bang, sock (*slang*), smack, thump, clout (*informal*) **2** = **setback**, shock, disaster, reverse, disappointment, catastrophe, misfortune, bombshell

bludge VERB (*Austral. & N.Z. informal*) = **slack**, skive (*Brit. informal*), idle, shirk

blue ADJECTIVE **1** = **depressed**, low, sad, unhappy, melancholy, dejected, despondent, downcast ≠ happy **2** = **smutty**, obscene, indecent, lewd, risqué, X-rated (*informal*) ≠ respectable

▷ PLURAL NOUN = **depression**, gloom, melancholy, unhappiness, low spirits, the dumps (*informal*), doldrums

◉ **WORD POWER**

◉ *Blue* has developed many
◉ figurative meanings in English.
◉ The colour of the sky in nature,
◉ blue has come to symbolize
◉ constancy and lack of change,
◉ leading to the phrase *true-blue*,
◉ meaning staunch, as applied
◉ to members of the Scottish
◉ Whig party in the 17th century
◉ and now applied to British
◉ Conservatives. In Australia,
◉ *true blue* means genuine. Blue
◉ denotes right-wing in Britain,
◉ from the choice of this colour
◉ to represent the Conservative
◉ party. It refers to the aristocracy
◉ in the phrase *blue-blood*, but
◉ to manual workers in the
◉ phrase *blue-collar*. Blue-collar
◉ stems from the dress codes
◉ of these industries, where
◉ traditionally shirts had to be
◉ made of a durable material and
◉ non-staining colour. Against
◉ appearances, in Australia *bluey*
◉ is a slang term for someone
◉ with red hair. Though its
◉ origins are not certain, blue

◉ **SHADES OF BLUE**

◉ aqua	◉ navy blue	◉ sky blue
◉ aquamarine	◉ Oxford blue	◉ steel blue
◉ azure	◉ peacock blue	◉ teal
◉ Cambridge blue	◉ perse	◉ turquoise
◉ clear blue	◉ royal blue	◉ ultramarine
◉ cobalt blue	◉ sapphire	
◉ indigo	◉ saxe blue	

b

- has become associated with
- pornography, as in the phrase
- *blue movies*. This may derive
- from so-called 'blue laws'
- which promoted morality in
- the 18th century United States
- by restricting activities such
- as drinking and gaming. Blue
- is also related to depression
- and low spirits, especially
- appearing in the plural form *the*
- *blues*. This is also the name of a
- style of melancholy music.

blue-collar ADJECTIVE = **manual**, industrial, physical, manufacturing, labouring

blueprint NOUN 1 = **scheme**, plan, design, system, programme, proposal, strategy, pattern **2** = **plan**, scheme, pattern, draft, outline, sketch

bluff¹ NOUN = **deception**, fraud, sham, pretence, deceit, bravado, bluster, humbug ▷ VERB = **deceive**, trick, fool, pretend, cheat, con, fake, mislead

bluff² NOUN = **precipice**, bank, peak, cliff, ridge, crag, escarpment, promontory ▷ ADJECTIVE = **hearty**, open, blunt, outspoken, genial, ebullient, jovial, plain-spoken ≠ tactful

blunder NOUN = **mistake**, slip, fault, error, oversight, gaffe, slip-up (*informal*), indiscretion, barry or Barry Crocker (*Austral. slang*) ≠ correctness ▷ VERB 1 = **make a mistake**, blow it (*slang*), err, slip up (*informal*), foul

up, put your foot in it (*informal*) ≠ be correct **2** = **stumble**, fall, reel, stagger, lurch

blunt ADJECTIVE 1 = **frank**, forthright, straightforward, rude, outspoken, bluff, brusque, plain-spoken ≠ tactful **2** = **dull**, rounded, dulled, edgeless, unsharpened ≠ sharp ▷ VERB = **dull**, weaken, soften, numb, dampen, water down, deaden, take the edge off ≠ stimulate

blur NOUN = **haze**, confusion, fog, obscurity, indistinctness ▷ VERB 1 = **become indistinct**, become vague, become hazy, become fuzzy **2** = **obscure**, make indistinct, mask, obfuscate, make vague, make hazy

blush VERB = **turn red**, colour, glow, flush, redden, go red (as a beetroot), turn scarlet ≠ turn pale ▷ NOUN = **reddening**, colour, glow, flush, pink tinge, rosiness, ruddiness, rosy tint

board NOUN 1 = **plank**, panel, timber, slat, piece of timber **2** = **council**, directors, committee, congress, advisers, panel, assembly, trustees **3** = **meals**, provisions, victuals, daily meals ▷ VERB = **get on**, enter, mount, embark ≠ get off

boast VERB 1 = **brag**, crow, vaunt, talk big (*slang*), blow your own trumpet, show off, be proud of, congratulate yourself on, skite (*Austral. & N.Z. informal*) ≠ cover up **2** = **possess**, exhibit

▷ NOUN = **bragging** ≠ disclaimer

bob VERB = **bounce**, duck, hop, oscillate

bodily ADJECTIVE = **physical**, material, actual, substantial, tangible, corporal, carnal, corporeal

body NOUN 1 = **physique**, build, form, figure, shape, frame, constitution 2 = **torso**, trunk 3 = **corpse**, dead body, remains, stiff (*slang*), carcass, cadaver 4 = **organization**, company, group, society, association, band, congress, institution 5 = **main part**, matter, material, mass, substance, bulk, essence 6 = **expanse**, mass ▷ RELATED WORDS: *adjectives* **corporal, physical**

bog NOUN = **marsh**, swamp, slough, wetlands, fen, mire, quagmire, morass, pakihi (*N.Z.*), muskeg (*Canad.*)

bogey NOUN = **bugbear**, bête noire, horror, nightmare, bugaboo

bogus ADJECTIVE = **fake**, false, artificial, forged, imitation, sham, fraudulent, counterfeit ≠ genuine

Bohemian ADJECTIVE *often not cap.* = **unconventional**, alternative, artistic, unorthodox, arty (*informal*), offbeat, left bank, nonconformist ≠ conventional ▷ NOUN *often not cap.* = **nonconformist**, rebel, radical, eccentric, maverick, hippy, dropout, individualist

boil[1] VERB = **simmer**, bubble, foam, seethe, fizz, froth, effervesce

boil[2] NOUN = **pustule**, gathering, swelling, blister, carbuncle

bold ADJECTIVE 1 = **fearless**, enterprising, brave, daring, heroic, adventurous, courageous, audacious ≠ timid 2 = **impudent**, forward, confident, rude, cheeky, feisty (*informal, chiefly U.S. & Canad.*), brazen, shameless, insolent ≠ shy

bolster VERB = **support**, help, boost, strengthen, reinforce, shore up, augment

bolt NOUN 1 = **pin**, rod, peg, rivet 2 = **bar**, catch, lock, latch, fastener, sliding bar ▷ VERB 1 = **lock**, close, bar, secure, fasten, latch 2 = **dash**, fly 3 = **gobble**, stuff, wolf, cram, gorge, devour, gulp, guzzle

bomb NOUN = **explosive**, mine, shell, missile, device, rocket, grenade, torpedo ▷ VERB = **blow up**, attack, destroy, assault, shell, blitz, bombard, torpedo

bombard VERB 1 = **attack**, assault, besiege, beset, assail 2 = **bomb**, shell, blitz, open fire, strafe, fire upon

bombardment NOUN = **bombing**, attack, assault, shelling, blitz, barrage, fusillade

bond NOUN 1 = **tie**, union, coupling, link, association, relation, connection, alliance 2 = **fastening**, tie, chain, cord, shackle, fetter, manacle 3 = **agreement**, word, promise,

contract, guarantee, pledge, obligation, covenant
▷ VERB 1 = **form friendships**, connect 2 = **fix**, hold, bind, connect, glue, stick, paste, fasten, fit (*Brit. informal*)

bonus NOUN 1 = **extra**, prize, gift, reward, premium, dividend 2 = **advantage**, benefit, gain, extra, plus, asset, icing on the cake

book NOUN 1 = **work**, title, volume, publication, tract, tome 2 = **notebook**, album, journal, diary, pad, notepad, exercise book, jotter, e-book *or* ebook, blook
▷ VERB = **reserve**, schedule, engage, organize, charter, arrange for, make reservations ▷ PHRASE: **book in** = **register**, enter

booklet NOUN = **brochure**, leaflet, hand-out, pamphlet, folder, mailshot, handbill

boom NOUN 1 = **expansion**, increase, development, growth, jump, boost, improvement, upsurge ≠ decline 2 = **bang**, crash, clash, blast, burst, explosion, roar, thunder
▷ VERB 1 = **increase**, flourish, grow, develop, expand, strengthen, swell, thrive ≠ fall 2 = **bang**, roll, crash, blast, explode, roar, thunder, rumble

boon NOUN 1 = **benefit**, blessing, godsend, gift 2 (*archaic*) = **gift**, favour

boost VERB = **increase**, develop, raise, expand, add to, heighten, enlarge, amplify ≠ decrease

▷ NOUN 1 = **rise**, increase, jump, addition, improvement, expansion, upsurge, upturn ≠ fall 2 = **encouragement**, help

boot VERB = **kick**, punt, put the boot in(to) (*slang*), drop-kick

border NOUN 1 = **frontier**, line, limit, bounds, boundary, perimeter, borderline 2 = **edge**, margin, verge, rim
▷ VERB = **edge**, bound, decorate, trim, fringe, rim, hem

bore¹ VERB = **drill**, mine, sink, tunnel, pierce, penetrate, burrow, puncture

bore² VERB = **tire**, fatigue, weary, wear out, jade, be tedious, pall on, send to sleep ≠ excite
▷ NOUN = **nuisance**, pain (*informal*), yawn (*informal*), anorak (*informal*)

bored ADJECTIVE = **fed up**, tired, wearied, uninterested, sick and tired (*informal*), listless, brassed off (*Brit. slang*), hoha (*N.Z.*)

boredom NOUN = **tedium**, apathy, weariness, monotony, sameness, ennui, flatness, world-weariness ≠ excitement

boring ADJECTIVE = **uninteresting**, dull, tedious, tiresome, monotonous, flat, humdrum, mind-numbing

borrow VERB 1 = **take on loan**, touch (someone) for (*slang*), scrounge (*informal*), cadge, use temporarily ≠ lend 2 = **steal**, take, copy, adopt, pinch (*informal*)

boss NOUN = **manager**, head, leader, director, chief, master, employer, supervisor, baas (*S. African*), sherang (*Austral. & N.Z.*) ▷ **PHRASE: boss someone around** (*informal*) = **order around**, dominate, bully, oppress, push around (*slang*)

bother VERB 1 = **trouble**, concern, worry, alarm, disturb, disconcert, perturb 2 = **pester**, plague, harass, hassle (*informal*), inconvenience ≠ help
▷ **NOUN** = **trouble**, problem, worry, difficulty, fuss, irritation, hassle (*informal*), nuisance, uphill (*S. African*) ≠ help

bottle shop NOUN (*Austral. & N.Z.*) = **off-licence** (*Brit.*), liquor store (*U.S. & Canad.*), bottle store (*S. African*), package store (*U.S. & Canad.*), offie or offy (*Brit. informal*)

bottle store NOUN (*S. African*) = **off-licence** (*Brit.*), liquor store (*U.S. & Canad.*), bottle shop (*Austral. & N.Z.*), package store (*U.S. & Canad.*), offie or offy (*Brit. informal*)

bottom NOUN 1 = **lowest part**, base, foot, bed, floor, foundation, depths ≠ top 2 = **underside**, sole, underneath, lower side 3 (*informal*) = **buttocks**, behind (*informal*), rear, backside, rump, seat, posterior
▷ **ADJECTIVE** = **lowest**, last ≠ higher

bounce VERB 1 = **rebound**, recoil, ricochet 2 = **bound**, spring, jump, leap, skip, gambol
▷ **NOUN** 1 = **springiness**, give, spring, resilience, elasticity, recoil

2 (*informal*) = **life**, go (*informal*), energy, zip (*informal*), vigour, exuberance, dynamism, vivacity

bound[1] ADJECTIVE 1 = **compelled**, obliged, forced, committed, pledged, constrained, beholden, duty-bound 2 = **tied**, fixed, secured, attached, tied up, fastened, pinioned 3 = **certain**, sure, fated, doomed, destined

bound[2] VERB = **leap**, bob, spring, jump, bounce, skip, vault
▷ **NOUN** = **leap**, bob, spring, jump, bounce, hurdle, skip, vault

bound[3] VERB 1 = **surround**, confine, enclose, encircle, hem in, demarcate 2 = **limit**, restrict, confine, restrain, circumscribe

boundary NOUN 1 = **frontier**, edge, border, barrier, margin, brink 2 = **edges**, limits, fringes, extremities 3 = **dividing line**, borderline

bounds PLURAL NOUN = **boundary**, limit, edge, border, confine, verge, rim, perimeter

bouquet NOUN 1 = **bunch of flowers**, spray, garland, wreath, posy, buttonhole, corsage, nosegay 2 = **aroma**, smell, scent, perfume, fragrance, savour, odour, redolence

bourgeois ADJECTIVE = **middle-class**, traditional, conventional, materialistic, hidebound

bout NOUN 1 = **period**, term, fit, spell, turn, interval 2 = **round**, series, session, cycle, sequence, stint 3 = **fight**, match, competition, struggle, contest,

set-to, encounter, engagement
bow¹ VERB = **bend**, bob, nod, stoop, droop, genuflect
▷ NOUN = **bending**, bob, nod, obeisance, kowtow, genuflection
bow² NOUN (*nautical*) = **prow**, head, stem, fore, beak
bowels PLURAL NOUN 1 = **guts**, insides (*informal*), intestines, innards (*informal*), entrails, viscera, vitals 2 = **depths**, hold, inside, deep, interior, core, belly
bowl¹ NOUN = **basin**, plate, dish, vessel
bowl² VERB = **throw**, hurl, launch, cast, pitch, toss, fling, chuck (*informal*)
box¹ NOUN = **container**, case, chest, trunk, pack, package, carton, casket
▷ VERB = **pack**, package, wrap, encase, bundle up
box² VERB = **fight**, spar, exchange blows
boxer NOUN = **fighter**, pugilist, prizefighter
boy NOUN = **lad**, kid (*informal*), youth, fellow, youngster, schoolboy, junior, stripling
boycott VERB = **embargo**, reject, snub, black ≠ support
boyfriend NOUN = **sweetheart**, man, lover, beloved, admirer, suitor, beau, date
brace VERB 1 = **steady**, support, secure, stabilize 2 = **support**, strengthen, steady, reinforce, bolster, fortify, buttress
▷ NOUN = **support**, stay, prop, bolster, bracket, reinforcement, strut, truss
bracing ADJECTIVE = **refreshing**, fresh, stimulating, crisp, brisk, exhilarating, invigorating ≠ tiring
brain PLURAL NOUN = **intelligence**, understanding, sense, intellect

● **WORD POWER**
● The *brain* controls the nervous
● system and is the seat of
● thought in the human body.
● A brain is a person who is
● intelligent and has great
● intellectual ability; this is
● also expressed in the recent
● coinage *brainiac*. In the plural,
● *brains* refers to intelligence,
● e.g. *He hasn't the brains to do it*.
● If someone is *the brains behind*
● *something*, it has implications
● of masterminding an idea
● or operation. We talk about
● *brainwaves* when an idea comes
● into the brain, and *brainwashing*
● when thought is deliberately
● censored. Both of these words
● show that the physical brain
● is strongly equated with the
● processes of thought in the
● mind.

brake NOUN = **control**, check, curb, restraint, constraint, rein
▷ VERB = **slow**, decelerate, reduce speed
branch NOUN 1 = **bough**, shoot, arm, spray, limb, sprig, offshoot 2 = **office**, department, unit, wing, chapter, bureau 3 = **division**, part, section, subdivision, subsection

4 = **discipline**, section, subdivision

brand NOUN **1** = **trademark**
2 = **label**, mark, sign, stamp, symbol, logo, trademark, marker
▷ VERB **1** = **stigmatize**, mark, expose, denounce, disgrace, discredit, censure **2** = **mark**, burn, label, stamp, scar

brash ADJECTIVE = **bold**, rude, cocky, pushy (*informal*), brazen, impertinent, insolent, impudent ≠ timid

brave ADJECTIVE = **courageous**, daring, bold, heroic, adventurous, fearless, resolute, audacious ≠ timid
▷ VERB = **confront**, face, suffer, tackle, endure, defy, withstand, stand up to ≠ give in to

bravery NOUN = **courage**, nerve, daring, pluck, spirit, fortitude, heroism, mettle ≠ cowardice

brawl NOUN = **fight**, clash, fray, skirmish, scuffle, punch-up (*Brit. informal*), fracas, altercation, biffo (*Austral. slang*)
▷ VERB = **fight**, scrap (*informal*), wrestle, tussle, scuffle

breach NOUN **1** = **nonobservance**, abuse, violation, infringement, trespass, transgression, contravention, infraction ≠ compliance **2** = **opening**, crack, split, gap, rift, rupture, cleft, fissure

bread NOUN **1** = **food**, fare, kai (*N.Z. informal*), nourishment, sustenance **2** (*slang*) = **money**, cash, dough (*slang*)

breadth NOUN **1** = **width**, spread, span, latitude, broadness, wideness **2** = **extent**, range, scale, scope, compass, expanse

break VERB **1** = **shatter**, separate, destroy, crack, snap, smash, crush, fragment ≠ repair **2** = **fracture**, crack, smash **3** = **burst**, split **4** = **disobey**, breach, defy, violate, disregard, flout, infringe, contravene ≠ obey **5** = **stop**, cut, suspend, interrupt, cut short, discontinue **6** = **disturb**, interrupt **7** = **end**, stop, cut, drop, give up, abandon, suspend, interrupt **8** = **weaken**, undermine, tame, subdue, demoralize, dispirit **9** = **be revealed**, be published, be announced, be made public, be proclaimed, be let out **10** = **reveal**, tell, announce, declare, disclose, proclaim, make known **11** = **beat**, top, better, exceed, go beyond, excel, surpass, outstrip
▷ NOUN **1** = **fracture**, opening, tear, hole, split, crack, gap, fissure **2** = **interval**, pause, interlude, intermission **3** = **holiday**, leave, vacation, time off, recess, awayday, schoolie (*Austral.*), acumulated day off or ADO (*Austral.*) **4** (*informal*) = **stroke of luck**, chance, opportunity, advantage, fortune, opening
▷ PHRASES: break off = **stop talking**, pause; break out = **begin**, start, happen, occur, arise, set in, commence, spring

up; **break something off**
= **detach**, separate, divide, cut
off, pull off, sever, part, remove;
break something up = **stop**, end,
suspend, dismantle, terminate,
disband, diffuse; **break up**
1 = **finish**, be suspended, adjourn
2 = **split up**, separate, part,
divorce
breakdown NOUN = **collapse**
break-in NOUN = **burglary**,
robbery, breaking and entering,
home invasion (*Austral.* & *N.Z.*)
breakthrough NOUN
= **development**, advance,
progress, discovery, find,
invention, step forward, leap
forwards
breast NOUN = **bosom**
breath NOUN = **inhalation**,
breathing, pant, gasp, gulp,
wheeze, exhalation, respiration
breathe VERB 1 = **inhale and
exhale**, pant, gasp, puff, gulp,
wheeze, respire, draw in breath
2 = **whisper**, sigh, murmur
breathless ADJECTIVE 1 = **out
of breath**, panting, gasping,
gulping, wheezing, short-winded
2 = **excited**, curious, eager,
enthusiastic, impatient, on
tenterhooks, in suspense
breathtaking ADJECTIVE
= **amazing**, exciting, stunning
(*informal*), impressive, thrilling,
magnificent, astonishing,
sensational
breed NOUN 1 = **variety**, race,
stock, type, species, strain,
pedigree 2 = **kind**, sort, type,

variety, brand, stamp
▷ VERB 1 = **rear**, tend, keep, raise,
maintain, farm, look after, care
for 2 = **reproduce**, multiply,
propagate, procreate, produce
offspring, bear young, bring forth
young 3 = **produce**, cause, create,
generate, bring about, arouse,
give rise to, stir up
breeding NOUN = **refinement**,
culture, taste, manners, polish,
courtesy, sophistication,
cultivation
breeze NOUN = **light wind**, air,
draught, gust, waft, zephyr,
breath of wind, current of air
▷ VERB = **sweep**, move briskly,
pass, sail, hurry, glide, flit
brew VERB 1 = **boil**, make, soak,
steep, stew, infuse (*tea*) 2 = **make**,
ferment 3 = **start**, develop,
gather, foment 4 = **develop**,
form, gather, foment
▷ NOUN = **drink**, preparation,
mixture, blend, liquor, beverage,
infusion, concoction
bribe NOUN = **inducement**, payoff (*informal*), sweetener (*slang*),
kickback (*U.S.*), backhander
(*slang*), enticement, allurement
▷ VERB = **buy off**, reward, pay off
(*informal*), corrupt, suborn, grease
the palm *or* hand of (*slang*)
bribery NOUN = **corruption**,
inducement, buying off, payola
(*informal*), palm-greasing (*slang*)
bridge NOUN = **arch**, span,
viaduct, flyover, overpass
▷ VERB 1 = **span**, cross
2 = **reconcile**, resolve

brief ADJECTIVE = **short**, quick, fleeting, swift, short-lived, momentary, ephemeral, transitory ≠ long
▷ VERB = **inform**, prime, prepare, advise, fill in (*informal*), instruct, put in the picture (*informal*), keep (someone) posted
▷ NOUN = **summary**, résumé, outline, sketch, abstract, digest, epitome, rundown

briefing NOUN 1 = **conference**, priming 2 = **instructions**, information, priming, directions, preparation, guidance, rundown

briefly ADVERB 1 = **quickly**, shortly, hastily, momentarily, hurriedly 2 = **in outline**, in brief, in a nutshell, concisely

brigade NOUN 1 = **corps**, company, force, unit, division, troop, squad, team 2 = **group**, band, squad, organization

bright ADJECTIVE 1 = **vivid**, rich, brilliant, glowing, colourful 2 = **shining**, glowing, dazzling, gleaming, shimmering, radiant, luminous, lustrous 3 (*informal*) = **intelligent**, smart, clever, aware, sharp, enlightened, astute, wide-awake ≠ stupid 4 (*informal*) = **clever**, smart, ingenious 5 = **sunny**, clear, fair, pleasant, lucid, cloudless, unclouded ≠ cloudy

brighten VERB 1 = **light up**, shine, glow, gleam, lighten ≠ dim 2 = **enliven**, animate, make brighter, vitalize 3 = **become brighter**, light up, glow, gleam

brilliance *or* **brilliancy** NOUN 1 = **cleverness**, talent, wisdom, distinction, genius, excellence, greatness, inventiveness ≠ stupidity 2 = **brightness**, intensity, sparkle, dazzle, lustre, radiance, luminosity, vividness ≠ darkness 3 = **splendour**, glamour, grandeur, magnificence, éclat, illustriousness

brilliant ADJECTIVE 1 = **intelligent**, sharp, intellectual, clever, profound, penetrating, inventive, perspicacious ≠ stupid 2 = **expert**, masterly, talented, gifted, accomplished ≠ untalented 3 = **splendid**, famous, celebrated, outstanding, superb, magnificent, glorious, notable 4 = **bright**, shining, intense, sparkling, glittering, dazzling, vivid, radiant ≠ dark

brim NOUN = **rim**, edge, border, lip, margin, verge, brink
▷ VERB 1 = **be full**, spill, well over, run over 2 = **fill**, well over, fill up, overflow

bring VERB 1 = **fetch**, take, carry, bear, transfer, deliver, transport, convey 2 = **take**, guide, conduct, escort 3 = **cause**, produce, create, effect, occasion, result in, contribute to, inflict ▷ PHRASES: **bring someone up** = **rear**, raise, support, train, develop, teach, breed, foster; **bring something about** = **cause**, produce, create, effect, achieve, generate, accomplish, give rise to; **bring something off** = **accomplish**, achieve, perform, succeed, execute, pull off, carry off; **bring something up** = **mention**, raise, introduce, point out, refer to, allude to, broach

brink NOUN = **edge**, limit, border, lip, margin, boundary, skirt, frontier

brisk ADJECTIVE 1 = **quick**, lively, energetic, active, vigorous, bustling, sprightly, spry ≠ slow 2 = **short**, brief, blunt, abrupt, terse, gruff, brusque, monosyllabic

briskly ADVERB = **quickly**, smartly, promptly, rapidly, readily, actively, efficiently, energetically

bristle NOUN = **hair**, spine, thorn, whisker, barb, stubble, prickle ▷ VERB 1 = **stand up**, rise, stand on end 2 = **be angry**, rage, seethe, flare up, bridle, see red

brittle ADJECTIVE = **fragile**, delicate, crisp, crumbling, frail, crumbly, breakable, friable ≠ tough

broad ADJECTIVE 1 = **wide**, large, ample, generous, expansive 2 = **large**, huge, vast, extensive, ample, spacious, expansive, roomy ≠ narrow 3 = **full**, general, comprehensive, complete, wide, sweeping, wide-ranging, thorough 4 = **universal**, general, common, wide, sweeping, worldwide, widespread, wide-ranging 5 = **general**, loose, vague, approximate, indefinite, ill-defined, inexact, unspecific

broadcast NOUN = **transmission**, show, programme, telecast, podcast, vodcast, webcast ▷ VERB 1 = **transmit**, show, air, radio, cable, beam, send out, relay, podcast 2 = **make public**, report, announce, publish, spread, advertise, proclaim, circulate

broaden VERB = **expand**, increase, develop, spread, extend, stretch, swell, supplement ≠ restrict

brochure NOUN = **booklet**, advertisement, leaflet, hand-out, circular, pamphlet, folder, mailshot

broekies PLURAL NOUN (*S. African informal*) = **underpants**, pants, briefs, drawers, knickers, panties, boxer shorts, Y-fronts (*trademark*), underdaks (*Austral. slang*)

broke ADJECTIVE (*informal*) = **penniless**, short, ruined, bust (*informal*), bankrupt, impoverished, in the red, insolvent ≠ rich

broken ADJECTIVE 1 = **interrupted**, incomplete, erratic, intermittent, fragmentary, spasmodic, discontinuous 2 = **imperfect**, halting, hesitating, stammering, disjointed 3 = **smashed**, burst, shattered, fragmented, fractured, severed, ruptured, separated 4 = **defective**, not working, imperfect, out of order, on the blink (*slang*), kaput (*informal*)

broker NOUN = **dealer**, agent, trader, supplier, merchant, negotiator, mediator, intermediary

bronze ADJECTIVE = **reddish-**

brown, copper, tan, rust, chestnut, brownish
▷ see **shades of brown**

brood NOUN 1 = **offspring**, issue, clutch, litter, progeny
2 = **children**, family, nearest and dearest, flesh and blood, ainga (N.Z.)
▷ VERB = **think**, obsess, muse, ponder, agonize, mull over, mope, ruminate

brook NOUN = **stream**, burn (*Scot. & Northern English*), rivulet, beck, watercourse, rill

brother NOUN 1 = **male sibling**
2 = **monk**, cleric, friar, religious
▷ RELATED WORD: *adjective* **fraternal**

brotherly ADJECTIVE = **fraternal**, friendly, neighbourly, sympathetic, affectionate, benevolent, kind, amicable

brown ADJECTIVE 1 = **brunette**, bay, coffee, chocolate, chestnut, hazel, dun, auburn 2 = **tanned**, bronze, tan, sunburnt
▷ VERB = **fry**, cook, grill, sear, sauté

browse VERB 1 = **skim**, scan, glance at, survey, look through, look round, dip into, leaf through
2 = **graze**, eat, feed, nibble

bruise NOUN = **discoloration**, mark, injury, blemish, contusion
▷ VERB 1 = **hurt**, injure, mark
2 = **damage**, mark, mar, discolour

brush¹ NOUN 1 = **broom**, sweeper, besom 2 = **conflict**, clash, confrontation, skirmish, tussle 3 = **encounter**, meeting, confrontation, rendezvous
▷ VERB 1 = **clean**, wash, polish, buff 2 = **touch**, sweep, kiss, stroke, glance, flick, scrape, graze
▷ PHRASES: **brush someone off** (*slang*) = **ignore**, reject, dismiss,

---

SHADES OF BROWN

- amber
- auburn
- bay
- beige
- biscuit
- bisque
- bronze
- buff
- burnt sienna
- burnt umber
- café au lait
- camel
- chestnut
- chocolate
- cinnamon
- cocoa
- coffee
- copper
- dun
- fawn
- ginger
- hazel
- henna
- khaki
- liver
- mahogany
- mocha
- nutbrown
- oxblood
- russet
- rust
- sable
- sepia
- sienna
- tan
- taupe
- tawny
- terracotta
- tortoiseshell
- walnut

snub, disregard, scorn, disdain, spurn; **brush something up** or **brush up on something** = **revise**, study, go over, cram, polish up, read up on, relearn, bone up on (*informal*)

brush² NOUN = **shrubs**, bushes, scrub, undergrowth, thicket, copse, brushwood

brutal ADJECTIVE 1 = **cruel**, savage, vicious, ruthless, callous, sadistic, heartless, inhuman ≠ kind
2 = **harsh**, tough, severe, rough, rude, indifferent, insensitive, callous ≠ sensitive

brutality NOUN = **cruelty**, atrocity, ferocity, savagery, ruthlessness, barbarism, inhumanity, viciousness

bubble NOUN = **air ball**, drop, bead, blister, blob, droplet, globule
▷ VERB 1 = **boil**, seethe 2 = **foam**, fizz, froth, percolate, effervesce
3 = **gurgle**, splash, murmur, trickle, ripple, babble, burble, lap

bubbly ADJECTIVE 1 = **lively**, happy, excited, animated, merry, bouncy, elated, sparky 2 = **frothy**, sparkling, fizzy, effervescent, carbonated, foamy

buckle NOUN = **fastener**, catch, clip, clasp, hasp
▷ VERB 1 = **fasten**, close, secure, hook, clasp 2 = **distort**, bend, warp, crumple, contort
3 = **collapse**, bend, twist, fold, give way, subside, cave in, crumple

bud NOUN = **shoot**, branch, sprout, sprig, offshoot
▷ VERB = **develop**, grow, shoot, sprout, burgeon, burst forth

budding ADJECTIVE = **developing**, beginning, growing, promising, potential, burgeoning, fledgling, embryonic

budge VERB 1 = **move**, stir
2 = **dislodge**, move, push, transfer, shift, stir

budget NOUN = **allowance**, means, funds, income, finances, resources, allocation
▷ VERB = **plan**, estimate, allocate, cost, ration, apportion

buff¹ ADJECTIVE = **fawn**, tan, beige, yellowish, straw-coloured, sand-coloured, yellowish-brown
▷ VERB = **polish**, smooth, brush, shine, rub, wax, brighten, burnish
▷ *see* **shades of brown, shades of yellow**

buff² NOUN (*informal*) = **expert**, fan, addict, enthusiast, admirer, devotee, connoisseur, aficionado, fundi (*S. African*)

buffer NOUN = **safeguard**, screen, shield, cushion, intermediary, bulwark

buffet NOUN 1 = **smorgasbord**
2 = **snack bar**, café, cafeteria, brasserie, refreshment counter

bug NOUN 1 (*informal*) = **illness**, disease, virus, infection, disorder, sickness, ailment, affliction
2 = **fault**, error, defect, flaw, glitch, gremlin
▷ VERB 1 = **tap**, eavesdrop, listen in on 2 (*informal*) = **annoy**, bother, disturb, irritate, hassle

(*informal*), pester, vex, get on your nerves (*informal*)

build VERB = **construct**, make, raise, put up, assemble, erect, fabricate, form ≠ demolish
▷ NOUN = **physique**, form, body, figure, shape, structure, frame

building NOUN = **structure**, house, construction, dwelling, erection, edifice, domicile

build-up NOUN = **increase**, development, growth, expansion, accumulation, enlargement, escalation

bulge VERB 1 = **swell out**, project, expand, stick out, protrude, puff out, distend 2 = **stick out**, stand out, protrude
▷ NOUN 1 = **lump**, swelling, bump, projection, hump, protuberance, protrusion ≠ hollow 2 = **increase**, rise, boost, surge, intensification

bulk NOUN 1 = **size**, volume, dimensions, magnitude, substance, immensity, largeness 2 = **weight**, size, mass, heaviness, poundage 3 = **majority**, mass, most, body, best part, lion's share, better part, preponderance

● **WORD POWER**
● The use of a plural noun after
● *bulk*, when it has the meaning
● 'majority', although common,
● is considered by some to
● be incorrect and should be
● avoided. This usage is most
● commonly encountered,
● according to the Bank of
● English, when referring to

● *funds* and *profits*: *the bulk of our*
● *profits stem from the sale of beer*.
● The synonyms *majority* and
● *most* would work better in this
● context.

bullet NOUN = **projectile**, ball, shot, missile, slug, pellet

bulletin NOUN = **report**, account, statement, message, communication, announcement, dispatch, communiqué

bully NOUN = **persecutor**, tough, oppressor, tormentor, bully boy, browbeater, coercer, ruffian
▷ VERB 1 = **persecute**, intimidate, torment, oppress, pick on, victimize, terrorize, push around (*slang*) 2 = **force**, coerce, browbeat, hector, domineer

bump VERB 1 = **knock**, hit, strike, crash, smash, slam, bang 2 = **jerk**, shake, bounce, rattle, jog, lurch, jolt
▷ NOUN 1 = **knock**, blow, impact, collision, thump 2 = **thud**, crash, knock, bang, smack, thump 3 = **lump**, swelling, bulge, hump, nodule, protuberance, contusion

bumper ADJECTIVE = **exceptional**, excellent, exo (*Austral. slang*), massive, jumbo (*informal*), abundant, whopping (*informal*), bountiful

bunch NOUN 1 (*informal*) = **group**, band, crowd, party, team, gathering, gang, flock 2 = **bouquet**, sheaf 3 = **cluster**, clump ▷ PHRASE: bunch together *or* up = **group**, mass, collect, assemble, cluster, huddle

b

bundle NOUN = **bunch**, group, collection, mass, pile, stack, heap, batch

▷ VERB = **push**, thrust, shove, throw, rush, hurry, jostle, hustle

▷ PHRASE: **bundle someone up** = **wrap up**, swathe

bungle VERB = **mess up**, blow (*slang*), ruin, spoil, blunder, botch, make a mess of, muff, crool *or* cruel (*Austral. slang*) ≠ accomplish

bungling ADJECTIVE = **incompetent**, blundering, clumsy, inept, cack-handed (*informal*), maladroit, ham-fisted (*informal*), unco (*Austral. slang*)

bunk *or* **bunkum** NOUN (*informal*) = **nonsense**, rubbish, garbage (*informal*), hot air (*informal*), twaddle, moonshine, malarkey, baloney (*informal*), hogwash, bizzo (*Austral. slang*), bull's wool (*Austral. & N.Z. slang*), kak (*S. African taboo*)

buoy NOUN = **float**, guide, signal, marker, beacon

buoyant ADJECTIVE = **cheerful**, happy, upbeat (*informal*), carefree, jaunty, chirpy (*informal*), light-hearted ≠ gloomy = **floating**, light

burden NOUN 1 = **trouble**, worry, weight, responsibility, strain, affliction, onus, millstone 2 = **load**, weight, cargo, freight, consignment, encumbrance

▷ VERB = **weigh down**, worry, load, tax, bother, handicap, oppress, inconvenience

bureau NOUN 1 = **agency** 2 = **office**, department, section, branch, station, unit, division, subdivision 3 = **desk**, writing desk

bureaucracy NOUN 1 = **government**, officials, authorities, administration, the system, civil service, corridors of power 2 = **red tape**, regulations, officialdom

bureaucrat NOUN = **official**, officer, administrator, civil servant, public servant, functionary, mandarin

burglar NOUN = **housebreaker**, thief, robber, pilferer, filcher, cat burglar, sneak thief

burglary NOUN = **breaking and entering**, housebreaking, break-in, home invasion (*Austral. & N.Z.*)

burial NOUN = **funeral**, interment, obsequies, entombment, exequies

burn VERB 1 = **be on fire**, blaze, be ablaze, smoke, flame, glow, flare, go up in flames 2 = **set on fire**, light, ignite, kindle, incinerate 3 = **scorch**, toast, sear, char, singe 4 = **be passionate**, be aroused, be inflamed 5 = **seethe**, fume, be angry, simmer, smoulder

burning ADJECTIVE 1 = **intense**, passionate, eager, ardent, fervent, impassioned, vehement ≠ mild 2 = **crucial**, important, pressing, significant, essential, vital, critical, acute

burrow NOUN = **hole**, shelter, tunnel, den, lair, retreat

▷ VERB 1 = **dig**, tunnel, excavate 2 = **delve**, search, probe, ferret, rummage, forage, fossick (*Austral. & N.Z.*)

burst VERB 1 = **explode**, blow
up, break, split, crack, shatter,
puncture, rupture 2 = **rush**, run,
break, break out, erupt, spout,
gush forth 3 = **barge**, charge,
rush, shove
▷ NOUN 1 = **rush**, surge, outbreak,
outburst, spate, gush, torrent,
spurt 2 = **explosion**, crack, blast,
bang, discharge

bury VERB 1 = **inter**, lay to rest,
entomb, consign to the grave,
inhume ≠ dig up 2 = **hide**,
cover, conceal, stash (*informal*),
secrete, stow away ≠ uncover
3 = **sink**, embed, immerse, enfold
4 = **forget**

bush NOUN = **shrub**, plant, hedge,
thicket, shrubbery ▷ PHRASE: **the
bush** = **the wilds**, brush, scrub,
woodland, backwoods, scrubland

business NOUN 1 = **trade**,
selling, industry, manufacturing,
commerce, dealings
2 = **establishment**, company,
firm, concern, organization,
corporation, venture, enterprise
3 = **profession**, work, job,
line, trade, career, function,
employment 4 = **matter**,
issue, subject, point, problem,
responsibility, task, duty
5 = **concern**, affair

businessman NOUN
= **executive**, director, manager,
merchant, capitalist, administrator,
entrepreneur, tycoon

bust¹ NOUN = **bosom**, breasts,
chest, front

bust² (*informal*) VERB 1 = **break**,
smash, split, burst, shatter,
fracture, rupture 2 = **arrest**,
catch, raid ▷ PHRASE: **go bust**
= **go bankrupt**, fail, be ruined,
become insolvent

bustle VERB = **hurry**, rush, fuss,
hasten, scuttle, scurry, scamper
≠ idle
▷ NOUN = **activity**, to-do,
stir, excitement, fuss, flurry,
commotion, ado ≠ inactivity

bustling ADJECTIVE = **busy**, full,
crowded, active, lively, buzzing,
humming, swarming

busy ADJECTIVE 1 = **active**,
industrious, rushed off your
feet ≠ idle 2 = **occupied with**,
working, engaged in, on duty,
employed in, hard at work
≠ unoccupied 3 = **hectic**, full,
exacting, energetic ▷ PHRASE:
busy yourself = **occupy yourself**,
be engrossed, immerse yourself,
involve yourself, absorb yourself,
employ yourself, engage yourself

but CONJUNCTION = **however**, still,
yet, nevertheless
▷ PREPOSITION = **except (for)**,
save, bar, barring, excepting,
excluding, with the exception of
▷ ADVERB = **only**, just, simply,
merely

butcher NOUN = **murderer**, killer,
slaughterer, slayer, destroyer,
executioner, cut-throat,
exterminator
▷ VERB 1 = **slaughter**, prepare,
carve, cut up, dress, cut, clean,
joint 2 = **kill**, slaughter, massacre,
destroy, cut down, assassinate,

slay, liquidate

butt¹ NOUN 1 = **end**, handle, shaft, stock, shank, hilt, haft 2 = **stub**, tip, leftover, fag end (*informal*)

butt² NOUN = **target**, victim, dupe, laughing stock, Aunt Sally

butt³ VERB = **knock**, push, bump, thrust, ram, shove, poke, prod
▷ PHRASE: **butt in** 1 = **interfere**, meddle, intrude, heckle, barge in (*informal*), stick your nose in, put your oar in 2 = **interrupt**, cut in, break in, chip in (*informal*)

butt⁴ NOUN = **cask**, barrel

butterfly NOUN ▷ RELATED WORDS: *young* **caterpillar**, **chrysalis** *or* **chrysalid**, *enthusiast* **lepidopterist**

buy VERB = **purchase**, get, pay for, obtain, acquire, invest in, shop for, procure ≠ sell
▷ NOUN = **purchase**, deal, bargain, acquisition, steal (*informal*), snip (*informal*), giveaway

by PREPOSITION 1 = **through**, through the agency of 2 = **via**, over, by way of 3 = **near**, past, along, close to, closest to,

● **BUTTERFLIES AND MOTHS**
● argus
● bag moth (*N.Z.*)
● brown-tail moth
● cabbage white
● cactoblastis
● cardinal
● carpet moth
● clearwing *or* clearwing moth
● death's-head moth
● ermine moth *or* ermine
● ghost moth
● gipsy moth
● grayling
● hairstreak
● herald moth
● hawk moth, sphinx moth, *or* hummingbird moth
● house moth
● lackey moth
● large white *or* cabbage white
● leopard moth
● magpie moth
● marbled white
● monarch
● orange-tip
● painted lady
● peacock butterfly
● peppered moth
● privet hawk
● processionary moth
● purple emperor
● puss moth
● red admiral
● red underwing
● ringlet
● silver-Y
● skipper
● small white
● snout
● speckled wood
● swallowtail
● swift
● tapestry moth
● tiger (moth)
● umber (moth)
● wax moth, honeycomb moth, *or* bee moth
● white
● white admiral
● winter moth
● yellow underwing

neighbouring, next to, beside
▷ ADVERB = **nearby**, close, handy,
at hand, within reach

bypass VERB 1 = **get round**, avoid
2 = **go round**, circumvent, depart
from, deviate from, pass round,
detour round ≠ cross

Cc

cab NOUN = **taxi**, minicab, taxicab, hackney carriage

cabin NOUN 1 = **room**, berth, quarters, compartment 2 = **hut**, shed, cottage, lodge, shack, chalet, shanty, whare (*N.Z.*)

cabinet NOUN = **cupboard**, case, locker, dresser, closet, press, chiffonier

Cabinet NOUN = **council**, committee, administration, ministry, assembly, board

cad NOUN (*old-fashioned or informal*) = **scoundrel** (*slang*), rat (*informal*), bounder (*Brit. old-fashioned or slang*), rotter (*slang, chiefly Brit.*), heel, wrong 'un (*Austral. slang*)

café NOUN = **snack bar**, restaurant, cafeteria, coffee shop, brasserie, coffee bar, tearoom, lunchroom

cage NOUN = **enclosure**, pen, coop, hutch, pound

cake NOUN = **block**, bar, slab, lump, cube, loaf, mass

calculated ADJECTIVE = **deliberate**, planned, considered, intended, intentional, designed, aimed, purposeful ≠ unplanned

calculating ADJECTIVE = **scheming**, sharp, shrewd, cunning, sly, devious, manipulative, crafty ≠ direct

calculation NOUN 1 = **computation**, working out, reckoning, estimate, forecast, judgment, result, answer 2 = **planning**, intention, deliberation, foresight, contrivance, forethought, premeditation

calibre *or* (*U.S.*) **caliber** NOUN 1 = **worth**, quality, ability, talent, capacity, merit, distinction, stature 2 = **diameter**, bore, gauge, measure

call VERB 1 = **name**, entitle, dub, designate, term, style, label, describe as 2 = **cry**, shout, scream, yell, whoop ≠ whisper 3 = **phone**, telephone, ring (up) (*informal, chiefly Brit.*), video call, Skype (*trademark*) 4 = **hail**, summon 5 = **summon**, gather, rally, assemble, muster, convene ≠ dismiss 6 = **waken**, arouse, rouse
▷ NOUN 1 = **visit** 2 = **request**, order, demand, appeal, notice, command, invitation, plea 3 *used in negative constructions* = **need**, cause, reason, grounds, occasion, excuse, justification 4 = **attraction**, pull (*informal*), appeal, lure, allure, magnetism 5 = **cry**, shout, scream, yell, whoop ≠ whisper ▷ PHRASES: **call for someone** = **fetch**, pick up, collect; **call for something** 1 = **demand**, order, request, insist on, cry out for 2 = **require**, need, involve, demand, occasion, entail, necessitate

calling NOUN = **profession**, trade, career, mission, vocation, life's work

calm ADJECTIVE 1 = **cool**, relaxed, composed, sedate, collected, dispassionate, unemotional, self-possessed, chilled (*informal*) ≠ excited 2 = **still**, quiet, smooth, mild, serene, tranquil, balmy, windless ≠ rough
▷ NOUN 1 = **peacefulness**, peace, serenity 2 = **stillness**, peace, quiet, hush, serenity, tranquillity, repose, peacefulness 3 = **peace**, calmness ≠ disturbance
▷ VERB 1 = **soothe**, quiet, relax, appease, still, allay, assuage, quieten ≠ excite 2 = **placate**, hush, pacify, mollify ≠ aggravate

camouflage NOUN
1 = **protective colouring**
2 = **disguise**, cover, screen, blind, mask, cloak, masquerade, subterfuge
▷ VERB = **disguise**, cover, screen, hide, mask, conceal, obscure, veil ≠ reveal

camp¹ NOUN 1 = **camp site**, tents, encampment, camping ground 2 = **bivouac**, cantonment (*military*)

camp² (*informal*) ADJECTIVE
1 = **effeminate** 2 = **affected**, mannered, artificial, posturing, ostentatious

campaign NOUN 1 = **drive**, appeal, movement, push (*informal*), offensive, crusade
2 = **operation**, drive, attack, movement, push, offensive, expedition, crusade

canal NOUN = **waterway**, channel, passage, conduit, duct, watercourse

cancel VERB 1 = **call off**, drop, forget about 2 = **annul**, abolish, repeal, abort, do away with, revoke, eliminate ▷ PHRASE: **cancel something out** = **counterbalance**, offset, make up for, compensate for, neutralize, nullify, balance out

cancellation NOUN
1 = **abandonment**
2 = **annulment**, abolition, repeal, elimination, revocation

cancer NOUN 1 = **growth**, tumour, malignancy 2 = **evil**, corruption, sickness, pestilence

candidate NOUN = **contender**, competitor, applicant, nominee, entrant, claimant, contestant, runner

cannabis NOUN = **marijuana**, pot (*slang*), dope (*slang*), grass (*slang*), hemp, dagga (*S. African*)

cannon NOUN 1 = **gun**, big gun, field gun, mortar

canon NOUN 1 = **rule**, standard, principle, regulation, formula, criterion, dictate, statute 2 = **list**, index, catalogue, roll

canopy NOUN = **awning**, covering, shade, sunshade

cap VERB 1 (*informal*) = **beat**, top, better, exceed, eclipse, surpass, transcend, outstrip 2 = **top**, crown

capability NOUN = **ability**, means, power, potential, capacity, qualification(s), competence, proficiency ≠ inability

capable ADJECTIVE 1 = **able** ≠ incapable 2 = **accomplished**, qualified, talented, gifted, efficient, competent, proficient ≠ incompetent

capacity NOUN 1 = **ability**, facility, gift, genius, capability, aptitude, aptness, competence *or* competency 2 = **size**, room, range, space, volume, extent, dimensions, scope 3 = **function**, position, role, post, office

cape NOUN = **headland**, point, head, peninsula, promontory

capital NOUN = **money**, funds, investment(s), cash, finances, resources, assets, wealth
▷ ADJECTIVE (*old-fashioned*) = **first-rate**, fine, excellent, superb

capitalism NOUN = **private enterprise**, free enterprise, private ownership, laissez faire *or* laisser faire

capsule NOUN 1 = **pill**, tablet, lozenge 2 (*botany*) = **pod**, case, shell, vessel, sheath, receptacle, seed case

captain NOUN 1 = **leader**, boss, master, skipper, head, chief 2 = **commander**, skipper

captivate VERB = **charm**, attract, fascinate, entrance, enchant, enthral, beguile, allure ≠ repel

captive ADJECTIVE = **confined**, caged, imprisoned, locked up, enslaved, incarcerated, ensnared, subjugated
▷ NOUN = **prisoner**, hostage,

convict, prisoner of war, detainee, internee

captivity NOUN = **confinement**, custody, detention, imprisonment, incarceration, internment

capture VERB = **catch**, arrest, take, bag, secure, seize, collar (*informal*), apprehend ≠ release
▷ NOUN = **arrest**, catching, trapping, imprisonment, seizure, apprehension, taking, taking captive

car NOUN 1 = **vehicle**, motor, wheels (*informal*), auto (*U.S.*), automobile, jalopy (*informal*), motorcar, machine 2 (*U.S. & Canad.*) = **(railway) carriage**, coach, cable car, dining car, sleeping car, buffet car, van

cardinal ADJECTIVE = **principal**, first, leading, chief, main, central, key, essential ≠ secondary

care VERB = **be concerned**, mind, bother, be interested, be bothered, give a damn, concern yourself
▷ NOUN 1 = **custody**, keeping, control, charge, management, protection, supervision, guardianship 2 = **caution**, attention, pains, consideration, heed, prudence, vigilance, forethought ≠ carelessness 3 = **worry**, concern, pressure, trouble, responsibility, stress, anxiety, disquiet ≠ pleasure
▷ PHRASES: **care for someone** 1 = **look after**, mind, tend, attend, nurse, minister to, watch over

2 = **love**, desire, be fond of, want, prize; **care for something** or **someone** = **like**, enjoy, take to, relish, be fond of, be keen on, be partial to 1 = **look after**, mind, watch, protect, tend, nurse, care for, provide for 2 = **deal with**, manage, cope with, see to, handle

career NOUN = **occupation**, calling, employment, pursuit, vocation, livelihood, life's work
▷ VERB = **rush**, race, speed, tear, dash, barrel (along) (*informal, chiefly U.S. & Canad.*), bolt, hurtle

careful ADJECTIVE 1 = **cautious**, scrupulous, circumspect, chary, thoughtful, discreet ≠ careless 2 = **thorough**, full, particular, precise, intensive, in-depth, meticulous, conscientious ≠ casual 3 = **prudent**, sparing, economical, canny, provident, frugal, thrifty

careless ADJECTIVE 1 = **slapdash**, irresponsible, sloppy (*informal*), cavalier, offhand, neglectful, slipshod, lackadaisical ≠ careful 2 = **negligent**, hasty, thoughtless, unthinking, forgetful, absent-minded, remiss ≠ careful 3 = **nonchalant**, casual, offhand, artless, unstudied ≠ careful

caretaker NOUN = **warden**, keeper, porter, superintendent, curator, custodian, watchman, janitor

cargo NOUN = **load**, goods, contents, shipment, freight, merchandise, baggage, consignment

caricature NOUN = **parody**, cartoon, distortion, satire, send-up (*Brit. informal*), travesty, takeoff (*informal*), lampoon
▷ VERB = **parody**, take off (*informal*), mock, distort, ridicule, mimic, send up (*Brit. informal*), lampoon

carnage NOUN = **slaughter**, murder, massacre, holocaust, havoc, bloodshed, shambles, mass murder

carnival NOUN = **festival**, fair, fête, celebration, gala, jubilee, jamboree, revelry

carol NOUN = **song**, hymn, Christmas song

carp VERB = **find fault**, complain, criticize, reproach, quibble, cavil, pick holes, nit-pick (*informal*) ≠ praise

carpenter NOUN = **joiner**, cabinet-maker, woodworker

carriage NOUN 1 = **vehicle**, coach, trap, gig, cab, wagon, hackney, conveyance 2 = **bearing**, posture, gait, deportment, air

carry VERB 1 = **convey**, take, move, bring, bear, transfer, conduct, transport 2 = **transport**, take, transfer 3 = **transmit**, transfer, spread, pass on 4 = **win**, gain, secure, capture, accomplish ▷ PHRASES: **carry on** 1 = **continue**, last, endure, persist, keep going, persevere, crack on (*informal*) 2 (*informal*) = **make a fuss**, misbehave, create (*slang*),

CARNIVORES

- aardwolf
- arctic fox
- badger
- bear
- binturong
- black bear
- bobcat
- brown bear
- caracal or desert lynx
- cat
- catamount, catamountain, or cat-o'-mountain
- cheetah or chetah
- cinnamon bear
- civet
- coyote or prairie wolf
- dhole
- dingo or (Austral.) native dog or warrigal
- dog
- ermine
- fennec
- ferret
- fox
- genet or genette
- giant panda
- grey fox (U.S.)
- grey wolf or timber wolf
- grizzly bear or grizzly
- hyena or hyaena
- ichneumon
- jackal
- jaguar
- jaguarondi, jaguarundi, or (Austral.) eyra
- kinkajou, honey bear, or potto
- Kodiak bear
- laughing hyena or spotted hyena
- leopard or panther
- linsang
- lion
- lynx
- margay
- marten
- meerkat
- mink
- mongoose
- mountain lion
- ocelot
- otter
- otter shrew
- palm civet
- panda
- panther
- pine marten or sweet marten
- polar bear or (N. Canad.) nanook
- polecat
- prairie dog
- puma or cougar
- raccoon, racoon, or coon
- raccoon dog
- ratel
- red fox
- sable
- sea otter
- serval
- silver fox
- skunk
- sloth bear
- snow leopard or ounce
- stoat
- strandwolf
- sun bear
- swift fox or kit fox
- tayra
- teledu
- tiger
- tiger cat
- timber wolf
- weasel
- wolf
- wolverine, glutton, or carcajou

raise Cain; **carry something on** = **engage in**, conduct, carry out, undertake, embark on, enter into; **carry something out** = **perform**, effect, achieve, realize, implement, fulfil, accomplish, execute

carry-on NOUN (*informal, chiefly Brit.*) = **fuss**, disturbance, racket, commotion

carton NOUN = **box**, case, pack, package, container

cartoon NOUN 1 = **drawing**, parody, satire, caricature, comic strip, takeoff (*informal*), lampoon, sketch 2 = **animation**, animated film, animated cartoon

carve VERB 1 = **sculpt**, cut, chip, whittle, chisel, hew, fashion 2 = **etch**, engrave

cascade NOUN = **waterfall**, falls, torrent, flood, shower, fountain, avalanche, deluge
▷ VERB = **flow**, fall, flood, pour, plunge, surge, spill, tumble

case¹ NOUN 1 = **situation**, event, circumstance(s), state, position, condition, context, contingency 2 = **instance**, example, occasion, specimen, occurrence 3 (*law*) = **lawsuit**, trial, suit, proceedings, dispute, action

case² NOUN 1 = **cabinet**, box, chest, holder 2 = **container**, carton, canister, casket, receptacle 3 = **suitcase**, bag, grip, holdall, portmanteau, valise 4 = **crate**, box 5 = **covering**, casing, shell, jacket, envelope, capsule, sheath, wrapper

cash NOUN = **money**, funds, notes, currency, silver, brass (*Northern English dialect*), dough (*slang*), coinage

cast NOUN 1 = **actors**, company, players, characters, troupe, dramatis personae 2 = **type**, sort, kind, style, stamp
▷ VERB 1 = **choose**, name, pick, select, appoint, assign, allot

2 = **bestow**, give, level, direct 3 = **give out**, spread, deposit, shed, distribute, scatter, emit, radiate 4 = **throw**, launch, pitch, toss, thrust, hurl, fling, sling 5 = **mould**, set, found, form, model, shape

caste NOUN = **class**, order, rank, status, stratum, social order

castle NOUN = **fortress**, keep, palace, tower, chateau, stronghold, citadel

casual ADJECTIVE 1 = **careless**, relaxed, unconcerned, blasé, offhand, nonchalant, lackadaisical ≠ serious 2 = **chance**, unexpected, random, accidental, incidental ≠ planned 3 = **informal**, leisure, sporty, non-dressy ≠ formal

casualty NOUN 1 = **fatality**, death, loss, wounded 2 = **victim**, sufferer

cat NOUN = **feline**, pussy (*informal*), moggy (*slang*), puss (*informal*), ballarat (*Austral. informal*), tabby
▷ RELATED WORDS: *adjective* **feline**, *male* **tom**, *female* **queen**, *young* **kitten**

catalogue or (*U.S.*) **catalog** NOUN = **list**, record, schedule, index, register, directory, inventory, gazetteer
▷ VERB = **list**, file, index, register, classify, inventory, tabulate, alphabetize

catastrophe NOUN = **disaster**, tragedy, calamity, cataclysm, trouble, adversity, fiasco

catch VERB 1 = **capture**, arrest,

trap, seize, snare, apprehend,
ensnare, entrap ≠ free **2** = **trap**,
capture, snare, ensnare, entrap
3 = **seize**, get, grab, snatch
4 = **grab**, take, grip, seize, grasp,
clutch, lay hold of ≠ release
5 = **discover**, surprise, find out,
expose, detect, catch in the act,
take unawares **6** = **contract**,
get, develop, suffer from, incur,
succumb to, go down with
≠ escape
▷ **NOUN 1** = **fastener**, clip,
bolt, latch, clasp **2** (informal)
= **drawback**, trick, trap,
disadvantage, hitch, snag,
stumbling block, fly in the
ointment ≠ advantage
▷ **PHRASE**: **catch on 1** (informal)
= **understand**, see, find out, grasp,
see through, comprehend, twig
(Brit. informal), get the picture
2 = **become popular**, take off,
become trendy, come into fashion
catchcry NOUN (Austral.)
= **catchphrase**, slogan, saying,
quotation, motto
catching ADJECTIVE = **infectious**,
contagious, transferable,
communicable, transmittable
≠ non-infectious
category NOUN = **class**, grouping,
heading, sort, department, type,
division, section
cater VERB ▷ **PHRASE**: **cater
for something** or **someone
1** = **provide for**, supply, purvey
2 = **take into account**, consider,
bear in mind, make allowance for,
have regard for

cattle PLURAL NOUN = **cows**,
stock, beasts, livestock, bovines
▷ **RELATED WORDS**: adjective
bovine, collective nouns **drove,
herd**
cause NOUN **1** = **origin**, source,
spring, agent, maker, producer,
root, beginning ≠ result
2 = **reason**, call, need, grounds,
basis, incentive, motive,
motivation **3** = **aim**, movement,
principle, ideal, enterprise
▷ **VERB** = **produce**, create, lead to,
result in, generate, induce, bring
about, give rise to ≠ prevent
caution NOUN **1** = **care**,
discretion, heed, prudence,
vigilance, alertness, forethought,
circumspection ≠ carelessness
2 = **reprimand**, warning,
injunction, admonition
▷ **VERB 1** = **warn**, urge,
advise, alert, tip off, forewarn
2 = **reprimand**, warn, admonish,
give an injunction to
cautious ADJECTIVE = **careful**,
guarded, wary, tentative, prudent,
judicious, circumspect, cagey
(informal) ≠ careless
cavalry NOUN = **horsemen**, horse,
mounted troops ≠ infantrymen
cave NOUN = **hollow**, cavern,
grotto, den, cavity
cavity NOUN = **hollow**, hole, gap,
pit, dent, crater
cease VERB **1** = **stop**, end,
finish, come to an end ≠ start
2 = **discontinue**, end, stop, finish,
conclude, halt, terminate, break
off ≠ begin

celebrate VERB 1 = **rejoice**, party, enjoy yourself, carouse, live it up (*informal*), make merry, put the flags out, kill the fatted calf 2 = **commemorate**, honour, observe, toast, drink to, keep 3 = **perform**, observe, preside over, officiate at, solemnize

celebrated ADJECTIVE = **renowned**, popular, famous, distinguished, well-known, prominent, acclaimed, notable ≠ unknown

celebration NOUN 1 = **party**, festival, gala, jubilee, festivity, revelry, red-letter day, merrymaking 2 = **commemoration**, honouring, remembrance 3 = **performance**, observance, solemnization

celebrity NOUN 1 = **personality**, star, superstar, big name, dignitary, luminary, big shot (*informal*), V.I.P. ≠ nobody 2 = **fame**, reputation, distinction, prestige, prominence, stardom, renown, repute ≠ obscurity

cell NOUN 1 = **room**, chamber, lock-up, compartment, cavity, cubicle, dungeon, stall 2 = **unit**, group, section, core, nucleus, caucus, coterie

cement NOUN 1 = **mortar**, plaster, paste 2 = **sealant**, glue, gum, adhesive
▷ VERB = **stick**, join, bond, attach, seal, glue, plaster, weld

cemetery NOUN = **graveyard**, churchyard, burial ground, necropolis, God's acre

censor VERB = **expurgate**, cut, blue-pencil, bowdlerize

censure VERB = **criticize**, blame, condemn, denounce, rebuke, reprimand, reproach, scold ≠ applaud
▷ NOUN = **disapproval**, criticism, blame, condemnation, rebuke, reprimand, reproach, stick (*slang*) ≠ approval

central ADJECTIVE 1 = **inner**, middle, mid, interior ≠ outer 2 = **main**, chief, key, essential, primary, principal, fundamental, focal ≠ minor

centre NOUN = **middle**, heart, focus, core, nucleus, hub, pivot, kernel ≠ edge ▷ PHRASE: centre on something *or* someone = **focus**, concentrate, cluster, revolve, converge

ceremonial ADJECTIVE = **formal**, public, official, ritual, stately, solemn, liturgical, courtly ≠ informal
▷ NOUN = **ritual**, ceremony, rite, formality, solemnity

ceremony NOUN 1 = **ritual**, service, rite, observance, commemoration, solemnities 2 = **formality**, ceremonial, propriety, decorum

certain ADJECTIVE 1 = **sure**, convinced, positive, confident, satisfied, assured ≠ unsure 2 = **bound**, sure, fated, destined ≠ unlikely 3 = **inevitable**, unavoidable, inescapable 4 = **known**, true, positive, conclusive, unequivocal,

undeniable, irrefutable,
unquestionable, nailed-on (*slang*)
≠ doubtful **5 = fixed**, decided,
established, settled, definite
≠ indefinite

certainly ADVERB = **definitely**,
surely, truly, undoubtedly,
without doubt, undeniably,
indisputably, assuredly

certainty NOUN **1 = confidence**,
trust, faith, conviction, assurance,
sureness, positiveness ≠ doubt
2 = inevitability ≠ uncertainty
3 = fact, truth, reality, sure thing
(*informal*), banker

certificate NOUN = **document**,
licence, warrant, voucher,
diploma, testimonial,
authorization, credential(s)

certify VERB = **confirm**, declare,
guarantee, assure, testify, verify,
validate, attest

chain NOUN **1 = tether**, coupling,
link, bond, shackle, fetter,
manacle **2 = series**, set, train,
string, sequence, succession,
progression
▷ VERB = **bind**, confine, restrain,
handcuff, shackle, tether, fetter,
manacle

chairman *or* **chairwoman**
NOUN **1 = director**, president,
chief, executive, chairperson
2 = master of ceremonies,
spokesman, chair, speaker, MC,
chairperson

● **WORD POWER**
● The general trend of nonsexist
● language is to find a term
● which can apply to both sexes
● equally, as in the use of *actor*
● to refer to both men and
● women. *Chairman* can seem
● inappropriate when applied
● to a woman, while *chairwoman*
● specifies gender, and so, as
● the entry above illustrates, the
● terms *chair* and *chairperson* are
● often preferred as alternatives.

challenge NOUN **1 = dare**,
provocation, wero (*N.Z.*) **2 = test**,
trial, opposition, confrontation,
ultimatum
▷ VERB **1 = dispute**, question,
tackle, confront, defy, object to,
disagree with, take issue with
2 = dare, invite, defy, throw
down the gauntlet **3 = test**
4 = question, interrogate

chamber NOUN **1 = hall**, room
2 = council, assembly, legislature,
legislative body **3 = room**,
bedroom, apartment, enclosure,
cubicle **4 = compartment**

champion NOUN **1 = winner**,
hero, victor, conqueror, title
holder **2 = defender**, guardian,
patron, backer, protector,
upholder
▷ VERB = **support**, back, defend,
promote, advocate, fight for,
uphold, espouse

chance NOUN **1 = probability**,
odds, possibility, prospect,
likelihood ≠ certainty
2 = opportunity, opening,
occasion, time **3 = accident**,
fortune, luck, fate, destiny,
coincidence, providence ≠ design
4 = risk, speculation, gamble,

hazard

▷ VERB = **risk**, try, stake, venture, gamble, hazard, wager

change NOUN 1 = **alteration**, innovation, transformation, modification, mutation, metamorphosis, difference, revolution 2 = **variety**, break (*informal*), departure, variation, novelty, diversion ≠ monotony 3 = **exchange**, trade, conversion, swap, substitution, interchange

▷ VERB 1 = **alter**, reform, transform, adjust, revise, modify, reorganize, restyle ≠ keep 2 = **shift**, vary, transform, alter, modify, mutate ≠ stay 3 = **exchange**, trade, replace, substitute, swap, interchange

channel NOUN 1 = **means**, way, course, approach, medium, route, path, avenue 2 = **strait**, sound, route, passage, canal, waterway 3 = **duct**, artery, groove, gutter, furrow, conduit

▷ VERB = **direct**, guide, conduct, transmit, convey

chant NOUN = **song**, carol, chorus, melody, psalm

▷ VERB = **sing**, chorus, recite, intone, carol

chaos NOUN = **disorder**, confusion, mayhem, anarchy, lawlessness, pandemonium, bedlam, tumult ≠ orderliness

chaotic ADJECTIVE = **disordered**, confused, uncontrolled, anarchic, tumultuous, lawless, riotous, topsy-turvy

chap NOUN (*informal*) = **fellow**, man, person, individual, character, guy (*informal*), bloke (*Brit. informal*)

chapter NOUN 1 = **section**, part, stage, division, episode, topic, segment, instalment 2 = **period**, time, stage, phase

character NOUN 1 = **personality**, nature, attributes, temperament, complexion, disposition 2 = **nature**, kind, quality, calibre 3 = **reputation**, honour, integrity, good name, rectitude 4 = **role**, part, persona 5 = **eccentric**, card (*informal*), original, oddball (*informal*) 6 = **symbol**, mark, sign, letter, figure, device, rune, hieroglyph

characteristic NOUN = **feature**, mark, quality, property, attribute, faculty, trait, quirk

▷ ADJECTIVE = **typical**, special, individual, representative, distinguishing, distinctive, peculiar, singular ≠ rare

characterize VERB = **distinguish**, mark, identify, brand, stamp, typify

charge VERB 1 = **accuse**, indict, impeach, incriminate, arraign ≠ acquit 2 = **attack**, assault, assail ≠ retreat 3 = **rush**, storm, stampede 4 = **fill**, load

▷ NOUN 1 = **price**, rate, cost, amount, payment, expense, toll, expenditure 2 = **accusation**, allegation, indictment, imputation ≠ acquittal 3 = **care**, trust, responsibility, custody, safekeeping 4 = **duty**, office, responsibility, remit **5** = **ward**, pupil, protégé, dependant **6** = **attack**, rush, assault, onset, onslaught, stampede, sortie ≠ retreat

charisma NOUN = **charm**, appeal, personality, attraction, lure, allure, magnetism, force of personality

charismatic ADJECTIVE = **charming**, appealing, attractive, influential, magnetic, enticing, alluring

charitable ADJECTIVE **1** = **benevolent**, liberal, generous, lavish, philanthropic, bountiful, beneficent ≠ mean **2** = **kind**, understanding, forgiving, sympathetic, favourable, tolerant, indulgent, lenient ≠ unkind

charity NOUN **1** = **charitable organization**, fund, movement, trust, endowment **2** = **donations**, help, relief, gift, contributions, assistance, hand-out, philanthropy, koha (N.Z.) ≠ meanness **3** = **kindness**, humanity, goodwill, compassion, generosity, indulgence, altruism, benevolence, aroha (N.Z.) ≠ ill will

charm NOUN **1** = **attraction**, appeal, fascination, allure, magnetism ≠ repulsiveness **2** = **trinket 3** = **talisman**, amulet, fetish **4** = **spell**, magic, enchantment, sorcery, makutu (N.Z.)
▷ VERB **1** = **attract**, delight, fascinate, entrance, win over, enchant, captivate, beguile ≠ repel **2** = **persuade**, seduce, coax, beguile, sweet-talk (informal)

charming ADJECTIVE = **attractive**, pleasing, appealing, fetching, delightful, cute, seductive, captivating ≠ unpleasant

chart NOUN = **table**, diagram, blueprint, graph, plan, map
▷ VERB **1** = **plot**, map out, delineate, sketch, draft, tabulate **2** = **monitor**, follow, record, note, document, register, trace, outline

charter NOUN **1** = **document**, contract, permit, licence, deed, prerogative **2** = **constitution**, laws, rules, code
▷ VERB **1** = **hire**, commission, employ, rent, lease **2** = **authorize**, permit, sanction, entitle, license, empower, give authority

chase VERB **1** = **pursue**, follow, track, hunt, run after, course **2** = **drive away**, drive, expel, hound, send away, send packing, put to flight **3** (informal) = **rush**, run, race, shoot, fly, speed, dash, bolt
▷ NOUN = **pursuit**, race, hunt, hunting

chat VERB = **talk**, gossip, jaw (slang), natter, blather, blether (Scot.)
▷ NOUN = **talk**, tête-à-tête, conversation, gossip, heart-to-heart, natter, blather, blether (Scot.), korero (N.Z.)

chatter VERB = **prattle**, chat, rabbit on (Brit. informal), babble, gab (informal), natter, blather,

schmooze (*slang*)
▷ **NOUN** = **prattle**, chat, gossip, babble, gab (*informal*), natter, blather, blether (*Scot.*)

cheap ADJECTIVE 1 = **inexpensive**, reduced, keen, reasonable, bargain, low-priced, low-cost, cut-price ≠ expensive 2 = **inferior**, poor, worthless, second-rate, shoddy, tawdry, tatty, trashy, bodger *or* bodgie (*Austral. slang*) ≠ good 3 (*informal*) = **despicable**, mean, contemptible, scungy (*Austral. & N.Z.*) ≠ decent

cheat VERB = **deceive**, trick, fool, con (*informal*), mislead, rip off (*slang*), fleece, defraud, scam (*slang*)
▷ **NOUN** = **deceiver**, sharper, shark, charlatan, trickster, con man (*informal*), double-crosser (*informal*), swindler, rorter (*Austral. slang*), rogue trader

check VERB 1 *often with* **out** = **examine**, test, study, look at, research, investigate, monitor, vet ≠ overlook 2 = **stop**, limit, delay, halt, restrain, inhibit, hinder, obstruct ≠ further
▷ **NOUN** 1 = **examination**, test, research, investigation, inspection, scrutiny, once-over (*informal*) 2 = **control**, limitation, restraint, constraint, obstacle, curb, obstruction, stoppage

cheek NOUN (*informal*) = **impudence**, nerve, disrespect, audacity, lip (*slang*), temerity, chutzpah (*U.S. & Canad. informal*), insolence

cheeky ADJECTIVE = **impudent**, rude, forward, insulting, saucy, audacious, pert, disrespectful ≠ respectful

cheer VERB 1 = **applaud**, hail, acclaim, clap ≠ boo 2 = **hearten**, encourage, comfort, uplift, brighten, cheer up, buoy up, gladden ≠ dishearten
▷ **NOUN** = **applause**, ovation
▷ **PHRASES**: **cheer someone up** = **comfort**, encourage, hearten, enliven, gladden, gee up, jolly along (*informal*); **cheer up** = **take heart**, rally, perk up, buck up (*informal*)

cheerful ADJECTIVE 1 = **happy**, optimistic, enthusiastic, jolly, merry, upbeat (*informal*), buoyant, cheery ≠ sad 2 = **pleasant** ≠ gloomy

chemical NOUN = **compound**, drug, substance, synthetic substance, potion

chemist NOUN = **pharmacist**, apothecary (*obsolete*), dispenser

cherish VERB 1 = **cling to**, prize, treasure, hold dear, cleave to ≠ despise 2 = **care for**, love, support, comfort, look after, shelter, nurture, hold dear ≠ neglect 3 = **harbour**, nurse, sustain, foster, entertain

chest NOUN 1 = **breast**, front 2 = **box**, case, trunk, crate, coffer, casket, strongbox ▷ **RELATED WORD**: *adjective* **pectoral**

chew VERB = **munch**, bite, grind, champ, crunch, gnaw, chomp, masticate

chic ADJECTIVE = **stylish**, smart, elegant, fashionable, trendy (*Brit. informal*), schmick (*Austral. informal*) ≠ unfashionable

chief NOUN = **head**, leader, director, manager, boss (*informal*), captain, master, governor, baas (*S. African*), ariki (*N.Z.*), sherang (*Austral. & N.Z.*) ≠ subordinate
▷ ADJECTIVE = **primary**, highest, leading, main, prime, key, premier, supreme ≠ minor

chiefly ADVERB 1 = **especially**, essentially, principally, primarily, above all 2 = **mainly**, largely, usually, mostly, in general, on the whole, predominantly, in the main

child NOUN 1 = **youngster**, baby, kid (*informal*), infant, babe, juvenile, toddler, tot, littlie (*Austral. informal*), ankle-biter (*Austral. slang*), tacker (*Austral. slang*) 2 = **offspring** ▷ RELATED WORDS: *adjective* filial, *prefix* paedo-

childbirth NOUN = **child-bearing**, labour, delivery, lying-in, confinement, parturition

childhood NOUN = **youth**, minority, infancy, schooldays, immaturity, boyhood *or* girlhood

childish ADJECTIVE 1 = **youthful**, young, boyish *or* girlish 2 = **immature**, juvenile, foolish, infantile, puerile ≠ mature

chill VERB 1 = **cool**, refrigerate, freeze 2 = **dishearten**, depress, discourage, dismay, dampen,

deject
▷ NOUN 1 = **coldness**, bite, nip, sharpness, coolness, rawness, crispness, frigidity 2 = **shiver**, frisson
▷ ADJECTIVE = **chilly**, biting, sharp, freezing, raw, bleak, chilly, wintry

chilly ADJECTIVE 1 = **cool**, fresh, sharp, crisp, penetrating, brisk, draughty, nippy ≠ warm 2 = **unfriendly**, hostile, unsympathetic, frigid, unresponsive, unwelcoming ≠ friendly

china¹ NOUN = **pottery**, ceramics, ware, porcelain, crockery, tableware, service

china² NOUN (*Brit. & S. African informal*) = **friend**, pal, mate (*informal*), buddy (*informal*), companion, best friend, intimate, comrade, cobber (*Austral. & N.Z. old-fashioned, informal*), E hoa (*N.Z.*)

● **WORD POWER**
● Some words borrowed into
● English from Chinese have
● further developed in meaning.
● For example, *gung-ho*, which
● literally means 'work together',
● was appropriated as a slogan
● by the U.S. Marines in the
● Second World War. From this
● sense of military co-operation
● arose the idea of militant
● zeal, and nowadays the term
● gung-ho is still used to describe
● those who are all too keen to
● participate in combat. It is also
● used in non-military contexts
● to mean proactive, upbeat,

enthusiastic, and eager,
particularly as an attitude or
approach. It sometimes has the
implication of inflexibility and
aggression, perhaps as a nod
to its military origins. Another
Chinese word which was
originally very specific in its
application is *kowtow*. Literally
'knock the head', it refers to
the former Chinese custom of
touching the forehead to the
ground as an act of deference.
In its extended sense, it means
to behave in an obsequious way
towards someone. Its meaning
has worsened from an act of
submission and deference into
one of servility. It is often found
in statements such as *wouldn't
kowtow to*, *refusal to kowtow*,
too willing to kowtow, showing
the negative associations now
attached to this word.

chip NOUN 1 = **fragment**, shaving,
wafer, sliver, shard 2 = **scratch**,
nick, notch 3 = **counter**, disc,
token
▷ VERB 1 = **nick**, damage, gash
2 = **chisel**, whittle

choice NOUN 1 = **range**,
variety, selection, assortment
2 = **selection**, preference, pick
3 = **option**, say, alternative
▷ ADJECTIVE = **best**, prime, select,
excellent, exclusive, elite, booshit
(*Austral. slang*), exo (*Austral. slang*),
sik (*Austral. slang*), rad (*informal*),
phat (*slang*), schmick (*Austral.
informal*)

choke VERB 1 = **suffocate**, stifle,
smother, overpower, asphyxiate
2 = **strangle**, throttle, asphyxiate
3 = **block**, clog, obstruct, bung,
constrict, congest, stop, bar

choose VERB 1 = **pick**, prefer,
select, elect, adopt, opt for,
designate, settle upon ≠ reject
2 = **wish**, want

chop VERB = **cut**, fell, hack, sever,
cleave, hew, lop

chore NOUN = **task**, job, duty,
burden, hassle (*informal*), errand

chorus NOUN 1 = **refrain**,
response, strain, burden
2 = **choir**, singers, ensemble,
vocalists, choristers ▷ PHRASE:
in chorus = **in unison**, as one, all
together, in concert, in harmony,
in accord, with one voice

christen VERB 1 = **baptize**, name
2 = **name**, call, term, style, title,
dub, designate

Christmas NOUN = **the festive
season**, Noël, Xmas (*informal*),
Yule (*archaic*), Yuletide (*archaic*)

chronicle VERB = **record**, tell,
report, enter, relate, register,
recount, set down
▷ NOUN = **record**, story, history,
account, register, journal, diary,
narrative, blog (*informal*)

chuck VERB 1 (*informal*) = **throw**,
cast, pitch, toss, hurl, fling, sling,
heave 2 *often with* **away** *or* **out**
(*informal*) = **throw out**, dump
(*informal*), scrap, get rid of, ditch
(*slang*), dispose of, dispense with,
jettison 3 (*informal*) = **give up**
or **over**, leave, abandon, cease,

resign from, pack in **4** (*slang*)
= **vomit**, throw up (*informal*), spew,
heave (*slang*), puke (*slang*), barf
(*U.S. slang*), chunder (*slang, chiefly
Austral.*)

chuckle VERB = **laugh**, giggle,
snigger, chortle, titter
▷ NOUN = **laugh**, giggle, snigger,
chortle, titter

chum NOUN (*informal*) = **friend**,
mate (*informal*), pal (*informal*),
companion, comrade, crony,
cobber (*Austral. & N.Z. old-
fashioned*) (*informal*), E hoa (*N.Z.*)

chunk NOUN = **piece**, block, mass,
portion, lump, slab, hunk, nugget

churn VERB **1** = **stir up**, beat,
disturb, swirl, agitate **2** = **swirl**,
toss

cinema NOUN **1** = **pictures**,
movies, picture-house, flicks
(*slang*) **2** = **films**, pictures, movies,
the big screen (*informal*), motion
pictures, the silver screen

circle NOUN **1** = **ring**, disc, hoop,
halo **2** = **group**, company, set,
club, society, clique, coterie
▷ VERB **1** = **go round**, ring,
surround, enclose, envelop,
encircle, circumscribe,
circumnavigate **2** = **wheel**, spiral

circuit NOUN **1** = **course**,
tour, track, route, journey
2 = **racetrack**, course, track,
racecourse **3** = **lap**, tour,
revolution, orbit

circular ADJECTIVE **1** = **round**,
ring-shaped **2** = **circuitous**,
cyclical, orbital
▷ NOUN = **advertisement**, notice,

ad (*informal*), announcement,
advert (*Brit. informal*), press release

circulate VERB **1** = **spread**, issue,
publish, broadcast, distribute,
publicize, disseminate,
promulgate **2** = **flow**, revolve,
rotate, radiate

circulation NOUN
1 = **distribution**, currency,
readership **2** = **bloodstream**,
blood flow **3** = **flow**, circling,
motion, rotation **4** = **spread**,
distribution, transmission,
dissemination

circumstance NOUN **1** *usually
plural* = **situation**, condition,
contingency, state of affairs, lie of
the land **2** *usually plural* = **detail**,
event, particular, respect **3**
usually plural = **situation**, state,
means, position, station, status
4 = **chance**, the times, accident,
fortune, luck, fate, destiny,
providence

cite VERB = **quote**, name, advance,
mention, extract, specify, allude
to, enumerate

citizen NOUN = **inhabitant**,
resident, dweller, denizen,
subject, townsman ▷ RELATED
WORD: *adjective* **civil**

city NOUN = **town**, metropolis,
municipality, conurbation
▷ RELATED WORD: *adjective* **civic**
▷ *see* **capital cities**

civic ADJECTIVE = **public**,
municipal, communal, local

civil ADJECTIVE **1** = **civic**, political,
domestic, municipal ≠ state
2 = **polite**, obliging, courteous,

considerate, affable, well-mannered ≠ rude

civilization NOUN 1 = **society**, people, community, nation, polity 2 = **culture**, development, education, progress, enlightenment, sophistication, advancement, cultivation

civilize VERB = **cultivate**, educate, refine, tame, enlighten, sophisticate

civilized ADJECTIVE 1 = **cultured**, educated, sophisticated, enlightened, humane ≠ primitive 2 = **polite**, mannerly, tolerant, gracious, courteous, well-behaved, well-mannered

claim VERB 1 = **assert**, insist, maintain, allege, uphold, profess 2 = **demand**, call for, ask for, insist on
 ▷ NOUN 1 = **assertion**, statement, allegation, declaration, pretension, affirmation, protestation 2 = **demand**, application, request, petition, call 3 = **right**, title, entitlement

clamour NOUN = **noise**, shouting, racket, outcry, din, uproar, commotion, hubbub

clamp NOUN = **vice**, press, grip, bracket, fastener
 ▷ VERB = **fasten**, fix, secure, brace, make fast

clan NOUN 1 = **family**, group, society, tribe, fraternity, brotherhood, ainga (N.Z.), ngai or ngati (N.Z.) 2 = **group**, set, circle, gang, faction, coterie, cabal

clap VERB = **applaud**, cheer,

acclaim ≠ boo

clarify VERB = **explain**, interpret, illuminate, clear up, simplify, make plain, elucidate, throw or shed light on

clarity NOUN 1 = **clearness**, precision, simplicity, transparency, lucidity, straightforwardness ≠ obscurity 2 = **transparency**, clearness ≠ cloudiness

clash VERB 1 = **conflict**, grapple, wrangle, lock horns, cross swords, war, feud, quarrel 2 = **disagree**, conflict, vary, counter, differ, contradict, diverge, run counter to 3 = **not go**, jar, not match 4 = **crash**, bang, rattle, jar, clatter, jangle, clang, clank
 ▷ NOUN 1 = **conflict**, fight, brush, confrontation, collision, showdown (*informal*), boilover (*Austral.*) 2 = **disagreement**, difference, argument, dispute, dissent, difference of opinion

clasp VERB = **grasp**, hold, press, grip, seize, squeeze, embrace, clutch
 ▷ NOUN 1 = **grasp**, hold, grip, embrace, hug 2 = **fastening**, catch, grip, hook, pin, clip, buckle, brooch

class NOUN 1 = **group**, set, division, rank 2 = **type**, set, sort, kind, category, genre
 ▷ VERB = **classify**, group, rate, rank, brand, label, grade, designate

classic ADJECTIVE 1 = **typical**, standard, model, regular, usual,

ideal, characteristic, definitive, dinki-di (*Austral. informal*) **2 = masterly**, best, finest, world-class, consummate, first-rate ≠ second-rate **3 = lasting**, enduring, abiding, immortal, undying, ageless, deathless
▷ NOUN **= standard**, masterpiece, prototype, paradigm, exemplar, model

classification NOUN
1 = categorization, grading, taxonomy, sorting, analysis, arrangement **2 = class**, grouping, heading, sort, department, type, division, section

classify VERB **= categorize**, sort, rank, arrange, grade, catalogue, pigeonhole, tabulate

classy ADJECTIVE (*informal*) **= high-class**, exclusive, superior, elegant, stylish, posh (*informal, chiefly Brit.*), up-market, top-drawer, schmick (*Austral. informal*)

clause NOUN **= section**, condition, article, chapter, passage, part, paragraph

claw NOUN **1 = nail**, talon
2 = pincer
▷ VERB **= scratch**, tear, dig, rip, scrape, maul, mangulate (*Austral. slang*), lacerate

clean ADJECTIVE **1 = hygienic**, fresh, sterile, pure, purified, antiseptic, sterilized, uncontaminated ≠ contaminated **2 = spotless**, fresh, immaculate, impeccable, flawless, unblemished, unsullied ≠ dirty **3 = moral**, good, pure,

decent, innocent, respectable, upright, honourable ≠ immoral **4 = complete**, final, whole, total, perfect, entire, decisive, thorough
▷ VERB **= cleanse**, wash, scrub, rinse, launder, scour, purify, disinfect ≠ dirty

cleanse VERB **1 = purify**, clear, purge **2 = absolve**, clear, purge, purify **3 = clean**, wash, scrub, rinse, scour

clear ADJECTIVE
1 = comprehensible, explicit, understandable ≠ confused
2 = distinct ≠ indistinct
3 = obvious, plain, apparent, evident, distinct, pronounced, manifest, blatant ≠ ambiguous
4 = certain, sure, convinced, positive, satisfied, resolved, definite, decided ≠ confused
5 = transparent, see-through, translucent, crystalline, glassy, limpid, pellucid ≠ opaque
6 = unobstructed, open, free, empty, unhindered, unimpeded ≠ blocked **7 = bright**, fine, fair, shining, sunny, luminous, cloudless, light ≠ cloudy
8 = untroubled, clean, pure, innocent, immaculate, unblemished, untarnished
▷ VERB **1 = unblock**, free, loosen, extricate, open, disentangle
2 = remove, clean, wipe, cleanse, tidy (up), sweep away
3 = brighten, break up, lighten
4 = pass over, jump, leap, vault, miss **5 = absolve**, acquit, vindicate, exonerate ≠ blame

clear-cut ADJECTIVE
= **straightforward**, specific, plain, precise, black-and-white, explicit, definite, unequivocal

clearly ADVERB 1 = **obviously**, undoubtedly, evidently, distinctly, markedly, overtly, undeniably, beyond doubt 2 = **legibly**, distinctly 3 = **audibly**, distinctly, intelligibly, comprehensibly

clergy NOUN = **priesthood**, ministry, clerics, clergymen, churchmen, the cloth, holy orders

clever ADJECTIVE 1 = **intelligent**, bright, talented, gifted, smart, knowledgeable, quick-witted ≠ stupid 2 = **shrewd**, bright, ingenious, resourceful, canny ≠ unimaginative 3 = **skilful**, talented, gifted ≠ inept

cliché NOUN = **platitude**, stereotype, commonplace, banality, truism, hackneyed phrase

client NOUN = **customer**, consumer, buyer, patron, shopper, patient

cliff NOUN = **rock face**, overhang, crag, precipice, escarpment, scar, bluff

climate NOUN = **weather**, temperature

climax NOUN = **culmination**, top, summit, height, highlight, peak, high point, zenith

climb VERB 1 = **ascend**, scale, mount, go up, clamber, shin up 2 = **clamber**, descend, scramble, dismount 3 = **rise**, go up, soar, ascend, fly up ▷ PHRASE: **climb**

down = **back down**, withdraw, yield, concede, retreat, surrender, give in, cave in (informal)

clinch VERB 1 = **secure**, close, confirm, conclude, seal, sew up (informal), set the seal on 2 = **settle**, decide, determine

cling VERB 1 = **clutch**, grip, embrace, grasp, hug, hold on to, clasp 2 = **stick to**, adhere to

clinical ADJECTIVE = **unemotional**, cold, scientific, objective, detached, analytic, impersonal, dispassionate

clip¹ VERB 1 = **trim**, cut, crop, prune, shorten, shear, snip, pare 2 (informal) = **smack**, strike, knock, punch, thump, clout (informal), cuff, whack
▷ NOUN (informal) = **smack**, strike, knock, punch, thump, clout (informal), cuff, whack

clip² VERB = **attach**, fix, secure, connect, pin, staple, fasten, hold

cloak NOUN 1 = **cape**, coat, wrap, mantle 2 = **covering**, layer, blanket, shroud
▷ VERB 1 = **cover**, coat, wrap, blanket, shroud, envelop 2 = **hide**, cover, screen, mask, disguise, conceal, obscure, veil

clog VERB = **obstruct**, block, jam, hinder, impede, congest

close¹ VERB 1 = **shut**, lock, fasten, secure ≠ open 2 = **shut down**, finish, cease 3 = **wind up**, finish, shut down, terminate 4 = **block up**, bar, seal ≠ open 5 = **end**, finish, complete, conclude, wind up, terminate ≠ begin 6 = **clinch**, confirm, secure, conclude, seal, sew up (*informal*), set the seal on **7** = **come together**, join, connect ≠ separate

▷ **NOUN** = **end**, ending, finish, conclusion, completion, finale, culmination, denouement

close² ADJECTIVE **1** = **near**, neighbouring, nearby, handy, adjacent, adjoining, cheek by jowl ≠ far **2** = **intimate**, loving, familiar, thick (*informal*), attached, devoted, confidential, inseparable ≠ distant **3** = **noticeable**, marked, strong, distinct, pronounced **4** = **careful**, detailed, intense, minute, thorough, rigorous, painstaking **5** = **even**, level, neck and neck, fifty-fifty (*informal*), evenly matched **6** = **imminent**, near, impending, at hand, nigh ≠ far away **7** = **stifling**, oppressive, suffocating, stuffy, humid, sweltering, airless, muggy ≠ airy

closed ADJECTIVE **1** = **shut**, locked, sealed, fastened ≠ open **2** = **shut down**, out of service **3** = **exclusive**, select, restricted **4** = **finished**, over, ended, decided, settled, concluded, resolved, terminated

cloth NOUN = **fabric**, material, textiles

clothe VERB = **dress**, array, robe, drape, swathe, attire, fit out, garb ≠ undress

clothes PLURAL NOUN = **clothing**, wear, dress, gear (*informal*), outfit, costume, wardrobe, garments

clothing NOUN = **clothes**, wear, dress, gear (*informal*), outfit, costume, wardrobe, garments

cloud NOUN = **mist**, haze, vapour, murk, gloom

▷ **VERB 1** = **confuse**, distort, impair, muddle, disorient **2** = **darken**, dim, be overshadowed

clout (*informal*) VERB = **hit**, strike, punch, slap, sock (*slang*), smack, thump, clobber (*slang*)

▷ **NOUN 1** = **thump**, blow, punch, slap, sock (*slang*), wallop (*informal*) **2** = **influence**, power, authority, pull, weight, prestige, mana (*N.Z.*)

clown NOUN **1** = **comedian**, fool, harlequin, jester, buffoon **2** = **joker**, comic, prankster **3** = **fool**, idiot, twit (*informal, chiefly Brit.*), imbecile (*informal*), ignoramus, dolt, blockhead, dorba *or* dorb (*Austral. slang*), bogan (*Austral. slang*)

▷ **VERB** usually with **around** = **play the fool**, mess about, jest, act the fool

club NOUN **1** = **association**, company, group, union, society, lodge, guild, fraternity **2** = **stick**, bat, bludgeon, truncheon, cosh (*Brit.*), cudgel

▷ **VERB** = **beat**, strike, hammer, batter, bash, bludgeon, pummel, cosh (*Brit.*)

clue NOUN = **indication**, lead, sign, evidence, suggestion, trace, hint, suspicion

clump NOUN = **cluster**, group, bunch, bundle

▷ **verb** = **stomp**, thump, lumber, tramp, plod, thud

clumsy ADJECTIVE = **awkward**, lumbering, bumbling, ponderous, ungainly, gauche, gawky, uncoordinated, unco (*Austral. slang*) ≠ skilful

cluster NOUN = **gathering**, group, collection, bunch, knot, clump, assemblage
▷ **verb** = **gather**, group, collect, bunch, assemble, flock, huddle

clutch VERB 1 = **hold**, grip, embrace, grasp, cling to, clasp 2 = **seize**, catch, grab, grasp, snatch
▷ PLURAL NOUN = **power**, hands, control, grip, possession, grasp, custody, sway

clutter NOUN = **untidiness**, mess, disorder, confusion, litter, muddle, disarray, jumble ≠ order
▷ **verb** = **litter**, scatter, strew, mess up ≠ tidy

coach NOUN 1 = **instructor**, teacher, trainer, tutor, handler 2 = **bus**, charabanc
▷ **verb** = **instruct**, train, prepare, exercise, drill, tutor

coalition NOUN = **alliance**, union, association, combination, merger, conjunction, bloc, confederation

coarse ADJECTIVE 1 = **rough**, crude, unfinished, homespun, impure, unrefined, unprocessed, unpolished ≠ smooth 2 = **vulgar**, rude, indecent, improper, earthy, smutty, ribald, indelicate

coast NOUN = **shore**, border, beach, seaside, coastline, seaboard
▷ **verb** = **cruise**, sail, drift, taxi, glide, freewheel

coat NOUN 1 = **fur**, hair, skin, hide, wool, fleece, pelt 2 = **layer**, covering, coating, overlay
▷ **verb** = **cover**, spread, plaster, smear

coax VERB = **persuade**, cajole, talk into, wheedle, sweet-talk (*informal*), prevail upon, entice, allure ≠ bully

cobber NOUN (*Austral. & N.Z. old-fashioned, informal*) = **friend**, pal, mate (*informal*), buddy (*informal*), china (*Brit. & S. African informal*), best friend, intimate, comrade, E hoa (*N.Z.*)

cocktail NOUN = **mixture**, combination, compound, blend, mix

cocky or **cockie** NOUN (*Austral. & N.Z. informal*) = **farmer**, smallholder, crofter (*Scot.*), grazier, agriculturalist, rancher

code NOUN 1 = **principles**, rules, manners, custom, convention, ethics, maxim, etiquette, kawa (*N.Z.*), tikanga (*N.Z.*) 2 = **cipher**, cryptograph

coherent ADJECTIVE 1 = **consistent**, reasoned, organized, rational, logical, meaningful, systematic, orderly ≠ inconsistent 2 = **articulate**, lucid, comprehensible, intelligible ≠ unintelligible

coil VERB 1 = **wind**, twist, curl, loop, spiral, twine 2 = **curl**, wind, twist, snake, loop, twine, wreathe

coin NOUN = **money**, change, cash, silver, copper, specie, kembla (*Austral. slang*)
▷ VERB = **invent**, create, make up, forge, originate, fabricate

coincide VERB 1 = **occur simultaneously**, coexist, synchronize, be concurrent 2 = **agree**, match, accord, square, correspond, tally, concur, harmonize ≠ disagree

coincidence NOUN = **chance**, accident, luck, fluke, stroke of luck, happy accident

cold ADJECTIVE 1 = **chilly**, freezing, bleak, arctic, icy, frosty, wintry, frigid ≠ hot 2 = **distant**, reserved, indifferent, aloof, frigid, undemonstrative, standoffish ≠ emotional 3 = **unfriendly**, indifferent, frigid ≠ friendly
▷ NOUN = **coldness**, chill, frigidity, frostiness, iciness

collaborate VERB 1 = **work together**, team up, join forces, cooperate, play ball (*informal*), participate 2 = **conspire**, cooperate, collude, fraternize

collaboration NOUN
1 = **teamwork**, partnership, cooperation, association, alliance 2 = **conspiring**, cooperation, collusion, fraternization

collaborator NOUN 1 = **co-worker**, partner, colleague, associate, team-mate, confederate 2 = **traitor**, turncoat, quisling, fraternizer

collapse VERB 1 = **fall down**,

fall, give way, subside, cave in, crumple, fall apart at the seams 2 = **fail**, fold, founder, break down, fall through, come to nothing, go belly-up (*informal*)
▷ NOUN 1 = **falling down**, ruin, falling apart, cave-in, disintegration, subsidence 2 = **failure**, slump, breakdown, flop, downfall 3 = **faint**, breakdown, blackout, prostration

collar VERB (*informal*) = **seize**, catch, arrest, grab, capture, nail (*informal*), nab (*informal*), apprehend

colleague NOUN = **fellow worker**, partner, ally, associate, assistant, team-mate, comrade, helper

collect VERB 1 = **gather**, save, assemble, heap, accumulate, amass, stockpile, hoard ≠ scatter 2 = **assemble**, meet, rally, cluster, come together, convene, converge, congregate ≠ disperse

collected ADJECTIVE 1 = **calm**, cool, composed, poised, serene, unperturbed, unruffled, self-possessed, chilled (*informal*) ≠ nervous

collection NOUN
1 = **accumulation**, set, store, mass, pile, heap, stockpile, hoard 2 = **compilation**, accumulation, anthology 3 = **group**, company, crowd, assembly, cluster, assortment 4 = **gathering** 5 = **contribution**, donation, alms 6 = **offering**, offertory

collective ADJECTIVE 1 = **joint**, united, shared, combined,

corporate, unified ≠ individual
2 = **combined**, aggregate,
composite, cumulative
≠ separate

collide VERB **1** = **crash**, clash,
meet head-on, come into
collision **2** = **conflict**, clash, be
incompatible, be at variance

collision NOUN **1** = **crash**, impact,
accident, smash, bump, pile-
up (*informal*), prang (*informal*)
2 = **conflict**, opposition, clash,
encounter, disagreement,
incompatibility

colony NOUN = **settlement**,
territory, province, possession,
dependency, outpost, dominion,
satellite state

colour or (*U.S.*) **color** NOUN
1 = **hue**, tone, shade, tint,
colourway **2** = **paint**, stain, dye,
tint, pigment, colorant
▷ VERB = **blush**, flush, redden
▷ *see* **shades from black to white,
shades of blue, shades of brown,
shades of green, shades of
orange, shades of purple, shades
of red, shades of yellow**

colourful ADJECTIVE **1** = **bright**,
brilliant, psychedelic,
variegated, multicoloured
≠ drab **2** = **interesting**, rich,
graphic, lively, distinctive, vivid,
picturesque ≠ boring

column NOUN **1** = **pillar**, support,
post, shaft, upright, obelisk
2 = **line**, row, file, rank, procession,
cavalcade

coma NOUN = **unconsciousness**,
trance, oblivion, stupor

comb VERB **1** = **untangle**, arrange,
groom, dress **2** = **search**,
hunt through, rake, sift, scour,
rummage, ransack, forage, fossick
(*Austral. & N.Z.*)

combat NOUN = **fight**, war, action,
battle, conflict, engagement,
warfare, skirmish ≠ peace
▷ VERB = **fight**, oppose, resist,
defy, withstand, do battle with
≠ support

combination NOUN **1** = **mixture**,
mix, blend, composite,
amalgamation, coalescence
2 = **association**, union, alliance,
coalition, federation, consortium,
syndicate, confederation

combine VERB **1** = **amalgamate**,
mix, blend, integrate, merge
≠ separate **2** = **join together**,
link, connect, integrate,
merge, amalgamate **3** = **unite**,
associate, team up, get together,
collaborate, join forces, join
together, pool resources ≠ split
up

come VERB **1** = **approach**, near,
advance, move towards, draw
near **2** = **arrive**, turn up (*informal*),
show up (*informal*) **3** = **reach**,
extend **4** = **happen**, fall, occur,
take place, come about, come to
pass **5** = **be available**, be made,
be offered, be produced, be on
offer **6** = **seem**, look, seem to be,
appear to be, give the impression
of being ▷ PHRASES: **come across
someone** = **meet**, encounter,
run into, bump into (*informal*);
come across something = **find**,

discover, notice, unearth, stumble upon, chance upon **VERB = be obtained**, be from, issue, emerge, flow, arise, originate, emanate

comeback NOUN 1 (*informal*) = **return**, revival, rebound, resurgence, rally, recovery, triumph 2 = **response**, reply, retort, retaliation, riposte, rejoinder

comedian NOUN = **comic**, wit, clown, funny man, humorist, wag, joker, jester, dag (*N.Z. informal*)

comedy NOUN 1 = **light entertainment**, soap opera (*slang*), soapie *or* soapy (*Austral.*) ≠ tragedy 2 = **humour**, fun, joking, farce, jesting, hilarity ≠ seriousness

comfort NOUN 1 = **ease**, luxury, wellbeing, opulence 2 = **consolation**, succour, help, support, relief, compensation ≠ annoyance
▷ **VERB = console**, reassure, soothe, hearten, commiserate with ≠ distress

comfortable ADJECTIVE 1 = **pleasant**, homely, relaxing, cosy, agreeable, restful ≠ unpleasant 2 = **at ease**, happy, at home, contented, relaxed, serene ≠ uncomfortable 3 (*informal*) = **well-off**, prosperous, affluent, well-to-do, comfortably-off, in clover (*informal*)

comforting ADJECTIVE = **consoling**, encouraging, cheering, reassuring, soothing, heart-warming ≠ upsetting

comic ADJECTIVE = **funny**, amusing, witty, humorous, farcical, comical, droll, jocular ≠ sad
▷ NOUN = **comedian**, funny man, humorist, wit, clown, wag, jester, dag (*N.Z. informal*), buffoon

coming ADJECTIVE = **approaching**, near, forthcoming, imminent, in store, impending, at hand, nigh
▷ NOUN = **arrival**, approach, advent

command VERB 1 = **order**, tell, charge, demand, require, direct, bid, compel ≠ beg 2 = **have authority over**, lead, head, control, rule, manage, handle, dominate ≠ be subordinate to
▷ NOUN 1 = **order**, demand, instruction, requirement, decree, directive, ultimatum, commandment 2 = **domination**, control, rule, mastery, power, government 3 = **management**, power, control, charge, authority, supervision

commander NOUN = **leader**, chief, officer, boss, head, captain, bass (*S. African*), ruler, sherang (*Austral. & N.Z.*)

commanding ADJECTIVE = **dominant**, controlling, dominating, superior, decisive, advantageous

commemorate VERB = **celebrate**, remember, honour, recognize, salute, pay tribute to, immortalize ≠ ignore

commence VERB 1 = **embark on**, start, open, begin, initiate,

originate, instigate, enter upon
≠ stop 2 = **start**, open, begin, go
ahead ≠ end
commend VERB 1 = **praise**,
acclaim, applaud, compliment,
extol, approve, speak highly
of ≠ criticize 2 = **recommend**,
suggest, approve, advocate,
endorse
comment VERB 1 = **remark**, say,
note, mention, point out, observe,
utter 2 *usually with* **on** = **remark
on**, explain, talk about, discuss,
speak about, say something
about, allude to, elucidate
▷ NOUN 1 = **remark**, statement,
observation 2 = **note**,
explanation, illustration,
commentary, exposition,
annotation, elucidation
commentary NOUN
1 = **narration**, report, review,
explanation, description, voice-
over 2 = **analysis**, notes, review,
critique, treatise
commentator NOUN
1 = **reporter**, special
correspondent, sportscaster
2 = **critic**, interpreter, annotator
commercial ADJECTIVE
1 = **mercantile**, trading
2 = **materialistic**, mercenary,
profit-making
commission VERB = **appoint**,
order, contract, select, engage,
delegate, nominate, authorize
▷ NOUN 1 = **duty**, task, mission,
mandate, errand 2 = **fee**, cut,
percentage, royalties, rake-off
(*slang*) 3 = **committee**, board,

representatives, commissioners,
delegation, deputation
commit VERB 1 = **do**, perform,
carry out, execute, enact,
perpetrate 2 = **put in custody**,
confine, imprison ≠ release
commitment NOUN
1 = **dedication**, loyalty,
devotion ≠ indecisiveness
2 = **responsibility**, tie, duty,
obligation, liability, engagement
common ADJECTIVE 1 = **usual**,
standard, regular, ordinary,
familiar, conventional, routine,
frequent ≠ rare 2 = **popular**,
general, accepted, standard,
routine, widespread, universal,
prevailing 3 = **shared**, collective
4 = **ordinary**, average, typical,
dinki-di (*Austral. informal*)
≠ important 5 = **vulgar**, inferior,
coarse, plebeian ≠ refined
6 = **collective**, public, community,
social, communal ≠ personal
commonplace
ADJECTIVE = **everyday**, common,
ordinary, widespread, mundane,
banal, run-of-the-mill, humdrum
≠ rare
▷ NOUN = **cliché**, platitude,
banality, truism
common sense NOUN = **good
sense**, sound judgment, level-
headedness, prudence, gumption
(*Brit. informal*), horse sense, native
intelligence, wit
communal ADJECTIVE = **public**,
shared, general, joint, collective
≠ private
commune NOUN = **community**,

collective, cooperative, kibbutz

communicate VERB 1 = **contact**, talk, speak, make contact, get in contact, e-mail, text 2 = **make known**, declare, disclose, pass on, proclaim, transmit, convey, impart ≠ keep secret 3 = **pass on**, transfer, spread, transmit

communication NOUN 1 = **contact**, conversation, correspondence, link, relations 2 = **passing on**, circulation, transmission, disclosure, imparting, dissemination, conveyance 3 = **message**, news, report, word, information, statement, announcement, disclosure, e-mail, text

communism NOUN *usually cap.* = **socialism**, Marxism, collectivism, Bolshevism, state socialism

communist NOUN *often cap.* = **socialist**, Red (*informal*), Marxist, Bolshevik, collectivist

community NOUN = **society**, people, public, residents, commonwealth, general public, populace, state

commuter NOUN = **daily traveller**, passenger, suburbanite

compact¹ ADJECTIVE 1 = **closely packed**, solid, thick, dense, compressed, condensed, pressed together ≠ loose 2 = **concise**, brief, to the point, succinct, terse ≠ lengthy
▷ VERB = **pack closely**, stuff, cram, compress, condense, tamp ≠ loosen

compact² NOUN = **agreement**, deal, understanding, contract, bond, arrangement, treaty, bargain

companion NOUN 1 = **friend**, partner, ally, colleague, associate, mate (*informal*), comrade, accomplice, cobber (*Austral. & N.Z. old-fashioned, informal*) 2 = **assistant**, aide, escort, attendant

company NOUN 1 = **business**, firm, association, corporation, partnership, establishment, syndicate, house 2 = **group**, set, community, band, crowd, collection, gathering, assembly 3 = **troop**, unit, squad, team 4 = **companionship**, society, presence, fellowship 5 = **guests**, party, visitors, callers

comparable ADJECTIVE 1 = **equal**, equivalent, on a par, tantamount, a match, proportionate, commensurate, as good ≠ unequal 2 = **similar**, related, alike, corresponding, akin, analogous, of a piece, cognate

comparative ADJECTIVE = **relative**, qualified, by comparison

compare VERB = **contrast**, balance, weigh, set against, juxtapose ▷ PHRASES: **compare to something** = **liken to**, parallel, identify with, equate to, correlate to, mention in the same breath as; **compare with something** = **be as good as**, match, approach, equal, compete with, be on a par with, be the equal of, hold a candle to

comparison NOUN 1 = **contrast**, distinction, differentiation, juxtaposition 2 = **similarity**, analogy, resemblance, correlation, likeness, comparability

compartment NOUN
1 = **section**, carriage, berth
2 = **bay**, booth, locker, niche, cubicle, alcove, pigeonhole, cubbyhole

compass NOUN = **range**, field, area, reach, scope, limit, extent, boundary

compassion NOUN = **sympathy**, understanding, pity, humanity, mercy, sorrow, kindness, tenderness, aroha (N.Z.) ≠ indifference

compassionate ADJECTIVE = **sympathetic**, understanding, pitying, humanitarian, charitable, humane, benevolent, merciful ≠ uncaring

compatible ADJECTIVE
1 = **consistent**, in keeping, congruous ≠ inappropriate
2 = **like-minded**, harmonious, in harmony ≠ incompatible

compel VERB = **force**, make, railroad (informal), oblige, constrain, coerce, impel, dragoon

compelling ADJECTIVE
1 = **convincing**, telling, powerful, forceful, conclusive, weighty, cogent, irrefutable
2 = **fascinating**, gripping, irresistible, enchanting,
enthralling, hypnotic, spellbinding, mesmeric ≠ boring

compensate VERB
1 = **recompense**, repay, refund, reimburse, remunerate, make good 2 = **make amends for**, make up for, atone for, pay for, do penance for, cancel out, make reparation for 3 = **balance**, cancel (out), offset, make up for, redress, counteract, counterbalance

compensation NOUN
1 = **reparation**, damages, recompense, remuneration, restitution, reimbursement
2 = **recompense**, amends, reparation, restitution, atonement

compete VERB 1 = **contend**, fight, vie, challenge, struggle, contest, strive 2 = **take part**, participate, be in the running, be a competitor, be a contestant, play

competence NOUN 1 = **ability**, skill, talent, capacity, expertise, proficiency, capability ≠ incompetence 2 = **fitness**, suitability, adequacy, appropriateness ≠ inadequacy

competent ADJECTIVE 1 = **able**, skilled, capable, proficient ≠ incompetent 2 = **fit**, qualified, suitable, adequate ≠ unqualified

competition NOUN 1 = **rivalry**, opposition, struggle, strife
2 = **opposition**, field, rivals, challengers 3 = **contest**, event, championship, tournament, head-to-head

competitive ADJECTIVE 1 = **cut-throat**, aggressive, fierce, ruthless, relentless, antagonistic, dog-eat-dog 2 = **ambitious**, pushing, opposing, aggressive, vying, contentious, combative

competitor NOUN 1 = **rival**, adversary, antagonist 2 = **contestant**, participant, contender, challenger, entrant, player, opponent

compilation NOUN = **collection**, treasury, accumulation, anthology, assortment, assemblage

compile VERB = **put together**, collect, gather, organize, accumulate, marshal, garner, amass

complacency NOUN = **smugness**, satisfaction, contentment, self-congratulation, self-satisfaction

complacent ADJECTIVE = **smug**, self-satisfied, pleased with yourself, resting on your laurels, contented, satisfied, serene, unconcerned ≠ insecure

complain VERB = **find fault**, moan, grumble, whinge (*informal*), carp, groan, lament, whine, nit-pick (*informal*)

complaint NOUN 1 = **protest**, objection, grievance, charge 2 = **grumble**, criticism, moan, lament, grievance, grouse, gripe (*informal*) 3 = **disorder**, problem, disease, upset, illness, sickness, ailment, affliction

complement VERB = **enhance**, complete, improve, boost, crown, add to, set off, heighten ▷ NOUN 1 = **accompaniment**, companion, accessory, completion, finishing touch, rounding-off, adjunct, supplement 2 = **total**, capacity, quota, aggregate, contingent, entirety

● **WORD POWER**
● This is sometimes confused
● with *compliment* but the two
● words have very different
● meanings. As the synonyms
● show, the verb form of
● *complement* means 'to enhance'
● and 'to complete' something. In
● contrast, common synonyms of
● *compliment* as a verb are *praise*,
● *commend*, and *flatter*.

complementary ADJECTIVE = **matching**, companion, corresponding, compatible, reciprocal, interrelating, interdependent, harmonizing ≠ incompatible

complete ADJECTIVE 1 = **total**, perfect, absolute, utter, outright, thorough, consummate, out-and-out 2 = **whole**, full, entire ≠ partial 3 = **entire**, full, whole, intact, unbroken, faultless ≠ incomplete 4 = **unabridged**, full, entire 5 = **finished**, done, ended, achieved, concluded, fulfilled, accomplished ≠ unfinished ▷ VERB 1 = **perfect**, finish off, round off, crown ≠ spoil 2 = **finish**, conclude, end, close, settle, wrap up (*informal*), finalize ≠ start

completely ADVERB = **totally**, entirely, wholly, utterly, perfectly, fully, absolutely, altogether

completion NOUN = **finishing**, end, close, conclusion, fulfilment, culmination, fruition

complex ADJECTIVE
1 = **compound**, multiple, composite, manifold, heterogeneous, multifarious
2 = **complicated**, difficult, involved, elaborate, tangled, intricate, tortuous, convoluted ≠ simple
▷ NOUN 1 = **structure**, system, scheme, network, organization, aggregate, composite 2 (*informal*) = **obsession**, preoccupation, phobia, fixation, fixed idea, idée fixe (*French*)

● WORD POWER
● Although *complex* and
● *complicated* are close in
● meaning, care should be taken
● when using one as a synonym
● of the other. *Complex* should
● be used to say that something
● consists of several parts rather
● than that it is difficult to
● understand, analyse, or deal
● with, which is what *complicated*
● inherently means. In the
● following real example a clear
● distinction is made between
● the two words: *the British
● benefits system is phenomenally
● complex and is administered by a
● complicated range of agencies*.

complexion NOUN 1 = **skin**, colour, colouring, hue, skin tone, pigmentation 2 = **nature**, character, make-up

complexity NOUN = **complication**, involvement, intricacy, entanglement

complicate VERB = **make difficult**, confuse, muddle, entangle, involve ≠ simplify

complicated ADJECTIVE
1 = **involved**, difficult, puzzling, troublesome, problematic, perplexing ≠ simple
2 = **complex**, involved, elaborate, intricate ≠ understandable 3 (*of an attitude*) = **convoluted**, labyrinthine

complication NOUN
1 = **problem**, difficulty, obstacle, drawback, snag, uphill (*S. African*)
2 = **complexity**, web, confusion, intricacy, entanglement

compliment NOUN = **praise**, honour, tribute, bouquet, flattery, eulogy ≠ criticism
▷ PLURAL NOUN 1 = **greetings**, regards, respects, good wishes, salutation ≠ insult
2 = **congratulations**, praise, commendation
▷ VERB = **praise**, flatter, salute, congratulate, pay tribute to, commend, extol, wax lyrical about ≠ criticize

● WORD POWER
● *Compliment* is sometimes
● confused with *complement*.

complimentary ADJECTIVE
1 = **flattering**, approving,

appreciative, congratulatory, commendatory ≠ critical
2 = **free**, donated, courtesy, honorary, on the house, gratuitous, gratis

comply VERB = **obey**, follow, observe, submit to, conform to, adhere to, abide by, acquiesce with ≠ defy

component NOUN = **part**, piece, unit, item, element, ingredient, constituent

▷ ADJECTIVE = **constituent**, inherent, intrinsic

compose VERB **1** = **put together**, make up, constitute, comprise, make, build, form, fashion ≠ destroy **2** = **create**, write, produce, invent, devise, contrive **3** = **arrange**, make up, construct, put together, order, organize

▷ PHRASE: **compose yourself** = **calm yourself**, control yourself, collect yourself, pull yourself together

composed ADJECTIVE = **calm**, cool, collected, relaxed, poised, at ease, serene, sedate, chilled (*informal*), grounded ≠ agitated

composition NOUN **1** = **design**, structure, make-up, organization, arrangement, formation, layout, configuration **2** = **creation**, work, piece, production, opus, masterpiece **3** = **essay**, exercise, treatise, literary work **4** = **production**, creation, making, fashioning, formation, putting together, compilation, formulation

compound NOUN = **combination**, mixture, blend, composite, fusion, synthesis, alloy, medley ≠ element

▷ ADJECTIVE = **complex**, multiple, composite, intricate ≠ simple

▷ VERB **1** = **intensify**, add to, complicate, worsen, heighten, exacerbate, aggravate, magnify ≠ lessen **2** = **combine**, unite, mix, blend, synthesize, amalgamate, intermingle ≠ divide

comprehend VERB = **understand**, see, take in, perceive, grasp, conceive, make out, fathom ≠ misunderstand

comprehension NOUN = **understanding**, grasp, conception, realization, intelligence, perception, discernment ≠ incomprehension

comprehensive ADJECTIVE = **broad**, full, complete, blanket, thorough, inclusive, exhaustive, all-inclusive ≠ limited

compress VERB **1** = **squeeze**, crush, squash, press **2** = **condense**, contract, concentrate, shorten, abbreviate

comprise VERB **1** = **be composed of**, include, contain, consist of, take in, embrace, encompass **2** = **make up**, form, constitute, compose

● **WORD POWER**
● The use of *of* after *comprise*
● should be avoided: *the library*
● *comprises* (not *comprises*
● *of*) 6,500,000 books and
● manuscripts. *Consist*, however,

● should be followed by *of* when
● used in this way: *Her crew*
● *consisted of children from Devon*
● *and Cornwall.*

compromise NOUN = **give-and-take**, agreement, settlement, accommodation, concession, adjustment, trade-off ≠ disagreement
▷ VERB 1 = **meet halfway**, concede, make concessions, give and take, strike a balance, strike a happy medium, go fifty-fifty (*informal*) ≠ disagree
2 = **undermine**, expose, embarrass, weaken, prejudice, discredit, jeopardize, dishonour ≠ support

compulsive ADJECTIVE
1 = **obsessive**, confirmed, chronic, persistent, addictive, uncontrollable, incurable, inveterate 2 = **fascinating**, gripping, absorbing, compelling, captivating, enthralling, hypnotic, engrossing
3 = **irresistible**, overwhelming, compelling, urgent, neurotic, uncontrollable, driving

compulsory ADJECTIVE
= **obligatory**, forced, required, binding, mandatory, imperative, requisite, de rigueur (*French*) ≠ voluntary

compute VERB = **calculate**, total, count, reckon, figure out, add up, tally, enumerate

computer NOUN = **laptop**, iPad (*trademark*), tablet, PC, MacBook (*trademark*)

comrade NOUN = **companion**, friend, partner, ally, colleague, associate, fellow, co-worker, cobber (*Austral. & N.Z. old-fashioned, informal*)

con (*informal*) VERB = **swindle**, trick, cheat, rip off (*slang*), deceive, defraud, dupe, hoodwink, scam (*slang*)
▷ NOUN = **swindle**, trick, fraud, deception, scam (*slang*), sting (*informal*), fastie (*Austral. slang*)

conceal VERB 1 = **hide**, bury, cover, screen, disguise, obscure, camouflage ≠ reveal 2 = **keep secret**, hide, disguise, mask, suppress, veil ≠ show

concede VERB 1 = **admit**, allow, accept, acknowledge, own, grant, confess ≠ deny 2 = **give up**, yield, hand over, surrender, relinquish, cede ≠ conquer

conceive VERB 1 = **imagine**, envisage, comprehend, visualize, think, believe, suppose, fancy
2 = **think up**, create, design, devise, formulate, contrive

concentrate VERB 1 = **focus your attention**, focus, pay attention, be engrossed, apply yourself ≠ pay no attention
2 = **focus**, centre, converge, bring to bear 3 = **gather**, collect, cluster, accumulate, congregate ≠ scatter

concentrated ADJECTIVE
1 = **condensed**, rich, undiluted, reduced, evaporated, thickened, boiled down 2 = **intense**, hard, deep, intensive, all-out (*informal*)

concentration NOUN

1 = **attention**, application, absorption, single-mindedness, intentness ≠ inattention 2 = **focusing**, centring, consolidation, convergence, bringing to bear, intensification, centralization 3 = **convergence**, collection, mass, cluster, accumulation, aggregation ≠ scattering

concept NOUN = **idea**, view, image, theory, notion, conception, hypothesis, abstraction

conception NOUN 1 = **idea**, plan, design, image, concept, notion 2 = **impregnation**, insemination, fertilization, germination

concern NOUN 1 = **anxiety**, fear, worry, distress, unease, apprehension, misgiving, disquiet 2 = **worry**, care, anxiety 3 = **affair**, issue, matter, consideration 4 = **care**, interest, attentiveness 5 = **business**, job, affair, responsibility, task 6 = **company**, business, firm, organization, corporation, enterprise, establishment 7 = **importance**, interest, bearing, relevance

▷ VERB 1 = **worry**, trouble, bother, disturb, distress, disquiet, perturb, make anxious 2 = **be about**, cover, deal with, go into, relate to, have to do with 3 = **be relevant to**, involve, affect, regard, apply to, bear on, have something to do with, pertain to

concerned ADJECTIVE

1 = **involved**, interested, active, mixed up, implicated, privy to 2 = **worried**, troubled, upset, bothered, disturbed, anxious, distressed, uneasy ≠ indifferent

concerning PREPOSITION = **regarding**, about, re, touching, respecting, relating to, on the subject of, with reference to

concession NOUN

1 = **compromise**, agreement, settlement, accommodation, adjustment, trade-off, give-and-take 2 = **privilege**, right, permit, licence, entitlement, indulgence, prerogative 3 = **reduction**, saving, grant, discount, allowance 4 = **surrender**, yielding, conceding, renunciation, relinquishment

conclude VERB 1 = **decide**, judge, assume, gather, work out, infer, deduce, surmise 2 = **come to an end**, end, close, finish, wind up ≠ begin 3 = **bring to an end**, end, close, finish, complete, wind up, terminate, round off ≠ begin 4 = **accomplish**, effect, bring about, carry out, pull off

conclusion NOUN 1 = **decision**, opinion, conviction, verdict, judgment, deduction, inference 2 = **end**, ending, close, finish, completion, finale, termination, bitter end 3 = **outcome**, result, upshot, consequence, culmination, end result

concrete ADJECTIVE 1 = **specific**, precise, explicit, definite, clear-cut, unequivocal ≠ vague

condemn VERB 1 = **denounce**, damn, criticize, disapprove, censure, reprove, upbraid, blame ≠ approve 2 = **sentence**, convict, damn, doom, pass sentence on ≠ acquit

condemnation NOUN = **denunciation**, blame, censure, disapproval, reproach, stricture, reproof

condition NOUN = **state**, order, shape, nick (*Brit. informal*), trim 2 = **situation**, state, position, status, circumstances 3 = **requirement**, terms, rider, restriction, qualification, limitation, prerequisite, proviso 4 = **health**, shape, fitness, trim, form, kilter, state of health, fettle 5 = **ailment**, problem, complaint, weakness, malady, infirmity ▷ PLURAL NOUN = **circumstances**, situation, environment, surroundings, way of life, milieu ▷ VERB = **train**, teach, adapt, accustom

conditional ADJECTIVE = **dependent**, limited, qualified, contingent, provisional, with reservations ≠ unconditional

condone VERB = **overlook**, excuse, forgive, pardon, turn a blind eye to, look the other way, make allowance for, let pass ≠ condemn

conduct VERB 1 = **carry out**, run, control, manage, direct, handle, organize, administer 2 = **accompany**, lead, escort, guide, steer, convey, usher ▷ NOUN 1 = **management**, running, control, handling, administration, direction, organization, guidance 2 = **behaviour**, ways, bearing, attitude, manners, demeanour, deportment ▷ PHRASE: conduct yourself = **behave yourself**, act, carry yourself, acquit yourself, deport yourself, comport yourself

confer VERB 1 = **discuss**, talk, consult, deliberate, discourse, converse 2 = **grant**, give, present, accord, award, hand out, bestow

conference NOUN = **meeting**, congress, discussion, convention, forum, consultation, seminar, symposium, hui (*N.Z.*)

confess VERB 1 = **admit**, acknowledge, disclose, confide, own up, come clean (*informal*), divulge ≠ cover up 2 = **declare**, allow, reveal, confirm, concede, assert, affirm, profess

confession NOUN = **admission**, revelation, disclosure, acknowledgment, exposure, unbosoming

confidant *or* **confidante** NOUN = **close friend**, familiar, intimate, crony, alter ego, bosom friend

confide VERB = **tell**, admit, reveal, confess, whisper, disclose, impart, divulge

confidence NOUN 1 = **trust**, belief, faith, dependence, reliance, credence ≠ distrust

2 = **self-assurance**, courage, assurance, aplomb, boldness, self-possession, nerve ≠ shyness 3 = **secret** ▷ PHRASE: **in confidence** = **in secrecy**, privately, confidentially, between you and me (and the gatepost), (just) between ourselves

confident ADJECTIVE 1 = **certain**, sure, convinced, positive, secure, satisfied, counting on ≠ unsure 2 = **self-assured**, positive, assured, bold, self-confident, self-reliant, sure of yourself ≠ insecure

confidential ADJECTIVE 1 = **secret**, private, intimate, classified, privy, off the record, hush-hush (*informal*) 2 = **secretive**, low, soft, hushed

confine VERB 1 = **imprison**, enclose, shut up, intern, incarcerate, hem in, keep, cage 2 = **restrict**, limit ▷ PLURAL NOUN = **limits**, bounds, boundaries, compass, precincts, circumference, edge

confirm VERB 1 = **prove**, support, establish, back up, verify, validate, bear out, substantiate 2 = **ratify**, establish, sanction, endorse, authorize 3 = **strengthen**, establish, fix, secure, reinforce, fortify

confirmation NOUN 1 = **proof**, evidence, testimony, verification, ratification, validation, corroboration, authentication ≠ repudiation 2 = **affirmation**, approval, acceptance,
endorsement, ratification, assent, agreement ≠ disapproval

confirmed ADJECTIVE = **long-established**, seasoned, chronic, hardened, habitual, ingrained, inveterate, dyed-in-the-wool

confiscate VERB = **seize**, appropriate, impound, commandeer, sequester ≠ give back

conflict NOUN 1 = **dispute**, difference, opposition, hostility, disagreement, friction, strife, fighting ≠ agreement 2 = **struggle**, battle, clash, strife 3 = **battle**, war, fight, clash, contest, encounter, combat, strife, boilover (*Austral.*) ≠ peace ▷ VERB = **be incompatible**, clash, differ, disagree, collide, be at variance ≠ agree

conflicting ADJECTIVE = **incompatible**, opposing, clashing, contrary, contradictory, inconsistent, paradoxical, discordant ≠ agreeing

conform VERB 1 = **fit in**, follow, adjust, adapt, comply, obey, fall in, toe the line 2 *with* **with** = **fulfil**, meet, match, suit, satisfy, agree with, obey, abide by

confound VERB = **bewilder**, baffle, confuse, astound, perplex, mystify, flummox, dumbfound

confront VERB 1 = **tackle**, deal with, cope with, meet head-on 2 = **trouble**, face, perturb, bedevil 3 = **challenge**, face, oppose, tackle, encounter, defy, stand up to, accost ≠ evade

confrontation NOUN = **conflict**, fight, contest, set-to (*informal*), encounter, showdown (*informal*), head-to-head, boilover (*Austral.*)

confuse VERB 1 = **mix up with**, take for, muddle with 2 = **bewilder**, puzzle, baffle, perplex, mystify, fluster, faze, flummox 3 = **obscure**, cloud, make more difficult

confused ADJECTIVE 1 = **bewildered**, puzzled, baffled, at sea, muddled, perplexed, taken aback, disorientated ≠ enlightened 2 = **disorderly**, disordered, chaotic, mixed up, jumbled, untidy, in disarray, topsy-turvy ≠ tidy

confusing ADJECTIVE = **bewildering**, puzzling, misleading, unclear, baffling, contradictory, perplexing ≠ clear

confusion NOUN 1 = **bewilderment**, doubt, uncertainty ≠ enlightenment 2 = **disorder**, chaos, turmoil, upheaval, muddle, shambles, commotion ≠ order

congestion NOUN = **overcrowding**, crowding, jam, clogging, bottleneck

congratulate VERB = **compliment**, pat on the back, wish joy to

congratulations PLURAL NOUN = **good wishes**, greetings, compliments, best wishes, felicitations
  ▷ INTERJECTION = **good wishes**, greetings, compliments, best wishes, felicitations

congregation NOUN = **parishioners**, brethren, crowd, assembly, flock, fellowship, multitude, throng, flock

congress NOUN 1 = **meeting**, council, conference, assembly, convention, conclave, hui (*N.Z.*), runanga (*N.Z.*) 2 = **legislature**, council, parliament, House of Representatives (*N.Z.*)

conjure VERB = **produce**, generate, bring about, give rise to, make, create, effect, produce as if by magic ▷ PHRASE: **conjure something up** = **bring to mind**, recall, evoke, recreate, recollect, produce as if by magic

connect VERB 1 = **link**, join, couple, attach, fasten, affix, unite ≠ separate 2 = **associate**, join, link, identify, lump together

connected ADJECTIVE = **linked**, united, joined, coupled, related, allied, associated, combined

connection NOUN 1 = **association**, relationship, link, bond, relevance, tie-in 2 = **communication**, alliance, attachment, liaison, affinity, union 3 = **link**, coupling, junction, fastening, tie 4 = **contact**, friend, ally, associate, acquaintance

conquer VERB 1 = **seize**, obtain, acquire, occupy, overrun, annex, win 2 = **defeat**, overcome, overthrow, beat, master, crush, overpower, quell ≠ lose to 3 = **overcome**, beat, defeat, master, overpower

conquest NOUN 1 = **takeover**, coup, invasion, occupation, annexation, subjugation **2** = **defeat**, victory, triumph, overthrow, rout, mastery

conscience NOUN 1 = **principles**, scruples, moral sense, sense of right and wrong, still small voice **2** = **guilt**, shame, regret, remorse, contrition, self-reproach

conscious ADJECTIVE 1 *often with* **of** = **aware of**, alert to, responsive to, sensible of ≠ unaware **2** = **deliberate**, knowing, studied, calculated, self-conscious, intentional, wilful, premeditated ≠ unintentional **3** = **awake**, wide-awake, sentient, alive ≠ asleep

consciousness NOUN = **awareness**, understanding, knowledge, recognition, sensibility, realization, apprehension

consecutive ADJECTIVE = **successive**, running, succeeding, in turn, uninterrupted, sequential, in sequence

consensus NOUN = **agreement**, general agreement, unanimity, common consent, unity, harmony, assent, concord, kotahitanga (*N.Z.*)

- WORD POWER
- The original meaning of the
- word *consensus* is *a collective*
- *opinion*. Because the concept of
- 'opinion' is contained within
- this word, a few people argue
- that the phrase *a consensus*
- *of opinion* is incorrect and
- should be avoided. However,
- this common use of the word
- is unlikely to jar with the
- majority of speakers.

consent NOUN = **agreement**, sanction, approval, go-ahead (*informal*), permission, compliance, assent, acquiescence ≠ refusal ▷ VERB = **agree**, approve, permit, concur, assent, acquiesce ≠ refuse

consequence NOUN 1 = **result**, effect, outcome, repercussion, issue, sequel, end result, upshot **2** = **importance**, concern, moment, value, account, weight, import, significance

consequently ADVERB = **as a result**, thus, therefore, hence, subsequently, accordingly, for that reason, thence

conservation NOUN 1 = **preservation**, saving, protection, maintenance, safeguarding, upkeep, guardianship, safekeeping **2** = **economy**, saving, thrift, husbandry

conservative ADJECTIVE = **traditional**, conventional, cautious, sober, reactionary, die-hard, hidebound ≠ radical ▷ NOUN = **traditionalist**, reactionary, die-hard, stick-in-the-mud (*informal*) ≠ radical

Conservative ADJECTIVE = **Tory**,

Republican (*U.S.*), right-wing
▷ NOUN = **Tory**, Republican (*U.S.*), right-winger

conserve VERB 1 = **save**, husband, take care of, hoard, store up, use sparingly ≠ waste 2 = **protect**, keep, save, preserve

consider VERB 1 = **think**, see, believe, rate, judge, suppose, deem, view as 2 = **think about**, reflect on, weigh, contemplate, deliberate, ponder, meditate, ruminate 3 = **bear in mind**, remember, respect, think about, take into account, reckon with, take into consideration, make allowance for

considerable ADJECTIVE = **large**, goodly, great, marked, substantial, noticeable, plentiful, appreciable ≠ small

considerably ADVERB = **greatly**, very much, significantly, remarkably, substantially, markedly, noticeably, appreciably

consideration NOUN 1 = **thought**, review, analysis, examination, reflection, scrutiny, deliberation 2 = **thoughtfulness**, concern, respect, kindness, tact, considerateness 3 = **factor**, point, issue, concern, element, aspect 4 = **payment**, fee, reward, remuneration, recompense, tip

considering PREPOSITION = **taking into account**, in the light of, bearing in mind, in view of, keeping in mind, taking into consideration

consist VERB ▷ PHRASES: **consist**
in something = **lie in**, involve, reside in, be expressed by, subsist in, be found or contained in; **consist of something** = **be made up of**, include, contain, incorporate, amount to, comprise, be composed of

consistency NOUN 1 = **agreement**, regularity, uniformity, constancy, steadiness, steadfastness, evenness 2 = **texture**, density, thickness, firmness, viscosity, compactness

consistent ADJECTIVE 1 = **steady**, even, regular, stable, constant, persistent, dependable, unchanging ≠ erratic 2 = **compatible**, agreeing, in keeping, harmonious, in harmony, consonant, in accord, congruous ≠ incompatible 3 = **coherent**, logical, compatible, harmonious, consonant ≠ contradictory

consolation NOUN = **comfort**, help, support, relief, cheer, encouragement, solace, succour

console VERB = **comfort**, cheer, soothe, support, encourage, calm, succour, express sympathy for ≠ distress

consolidate VERB 1 = **strengthen**, secure, reinforce, fortify, stabilize 2 = **combine**, unite, join, merge, unify, amalgamate, federate

conspicuous ADJECTIVE = **obvious**, clear, patent, evident, noticeable, blatant, salient ≠ inconspicuous

conspiracy NOUN = **plot**, scheme, intrigue, collusion, machination

conspire VERB 1 = **plot**, scheme, intrigue, manoeuvre, contrive, machinate, plan 2 = **work together**, combine, contribute, cooperate, concur, tend

constant ADJECTIVE
1 = **continuous**, sustained, perpetual, interminable, unrelenting, incessant, ceaseless, nonstop ≠ occasional
2 = **unchanging**, even, fixed, permanent, stable, steady, uniform, invariable ≠ changing
3 = **faithful**, true, devoted, loyal, stalwart, staunch, trustworthy, trusty ≠ undependable

constantly ADVERB
= **continuously**, always, all the time, invariably, continually, endlessly, perpetually, incessantly ≠ occasionally

constituent NOUN 1 = **voter**, elector, member of the electorate 2 = **component**, element, ingredient, part, unit, factor
▷ ADJECTIVE = **component**, basic, essential, integral, elemental

constitute VERB 1 = **represent**, be, consist of, embody, exemplify, be equivalent to 2 = **make up**, form, compose, comprise

constitution NOUN 1 = **state of health**, build, body, frame, physique, physical condition
2 = **structure**, form, nature, make-up, composition, character, disposition

constitutional ADJECTIVE

= **legitimate**, official, legal, chartered, statutory, vested

constrain VERB 1 = **restrict**, confine, curb, restrain, constrict, straiten, check 2 = **force**, bind, compel, oblige, necessitate, coerce, impel, pressurize

constraint NOUN 1 = **restriction**, limitation, curb, rein, deterrent, hindrance, check 2 = **force**, pressure, necessity, restraint, compulsion, coercion

construct VERB 1 = **build**, make, form, create, fashion, shape, manufacture, assemble ≠ demolish 2 = **create**, make, form, compose, put together

construction NOUN 1 = **building**, creation, composition 2 (*formal*) = **interpretation**, reading, explanation, rendering, inference

constructive ADJECTIVE
= **helpful**, positive, useful, practical, valuable, productive ≠ unproductive

consult VERB 1 = **ask**, refer to, turn to, take counsel, pick (someone's) brains, question 2 = **confer**, talk, compare notes 3 = **refer to**, check in, look in

consultant NOUN = **specialist**, adviser, counsellor, authority

consultation NOUN
1 = **discussion**, talk, council, conference, dialogue
2 = **meeting**, interview, session, appointment, examination, deliberation, hearing

consume VERB 1 = **eat**, swallow, devour, put away, gobble (up), eat up **2** = **use up**, spend, waste, absorb, exhaust, squander, dissipate, expend **3** = **destroy**, devastate, demolish, ravage, annihilate, lay waste **4** *often passive* = **obsess**, dominate, absorb, preoccupy, eat up, monopolize, engross

consumer NOUN = **buyer**, customer, user, shopper, purchaser

consumption NOUN **1** = **using up**, use, loss, waste, expenditure, exhaustion, depletion, dissipation **2** (*old-fashioned*) = **tuberculosis**, T.B.

contact NOUN **1** = **communication**, link, association, connection, correspondence **2** = **touch**, contiguity **3** = **connection**, colleague, associate, liaison, acquaintance, confederate ▷ VERB = **get** *or* **be in touch with**, call, reach, approach, write to, speak to, communicate with, e-mail, text

contain VERB **1** = **hold**, incorporate, accommodate, enclose, have capacity for **2** = **include**, consist of, embrace, comprise, embody, comprehend **3** = **restrain**, control, hold in, curb, suppress, hold back, stifle, repress

container NOUN = **holder**, vessel, repository, receptacle

contaminate VERB = **pollute**, infect, stain, corrupt, taint, defile, adulterate, befoul ≠ purify

contamination NOUN = **pollution**, infection, corruption, poisoning, taint, impurity, contagion, defilement

contemplate VERB **1** = **consider**, plan, think of, intend, envisage, foresee **2** = **think about**, consider, ponder, reflect upon, ruminate (upon), muse over, deliberate over **3** = **look at**, examine, inspect, gaze at, eye up, view, study, regard

contemporary ADJECTIVE **1** = **modern**, recent, current, up-to-date, present-day, à la mode, newfangled, present ≠ old-fashioned **2** = **coexisting**, concurrent, contemporaneous ▷ NOUN = **peer**, fellow, equal

● **WORD POWER**
● Since *contemporary* can mean
● either 'of the same period'
● or 'of the present period',
● it is best to avoid it where
● ambiguity might arise, as
● in *a production of Othello in*
● *contemporary dress*. A synonym
● such as *modern* or *present-day*
● would clarify if the sense 'of
● the present period' were being
● used, while a specific term,
● such as *Elizabethan*, would be
● appropriate if the sense 'of the
● same period' were being used.

contempt NOUN = **scorn**, disdain, mockery, derision, disrespect, disregard ≠ respect

contend VERB **1** = **argue**, hold, maintain, allege, assert, affirm **2** = **compete**, fight, struggle, clash, contest, strive, vie, jostle

content¹ NOUN 1 = **subject matter**, material, theme, substance, essence, gist
2 = **amount**, measure, size, load, volume, capacity
▷ PLURAL NOUN = **constituents**, elements, load, ingredients

content² ADJECTIVE = **satisfied**, happy, pleased, contented, comfortable, fulfilled, at ease, gratified
▷ NOUN = **satisfaction**, ease, pleasure, comfort, peace of mind, gratification, contentment
▷ PHRASE: **content yourself with something** = **satisfy yourself with**, be happy with, be satisfied with, be content with

contented ADJECTIVE = **satisfied**, happy, pleased, content, comfortable, glad, thankful, gratified ≠ discontented

contentious ADJECTIVE = **argumentative**, wrangling, bickering, quarrelsome, querulous, cavilling, disputatious, captious

contest NOUN 1 = **competition**, game, match, trial, tournament
2 = **struggle**, fight, battle, conflict, dispute, controversy, combat
▷ VERB 1 = **compete in**, take part in, fight in, go in for, contend for, vie in 2 = **oppose**, question, challenge, argue, debate, dispute, object to, call in or into question

contestant NOUN = **competitor**, candidate, participant, contender, entrant, player

context NOUN
1 = **circumstances**, conditions, situation, ambience 2 = **frame of reference**, background, framework, relation, connection

contingency NOUN = **possibility**, happening, chance, event, incident, accident, emergency, eventuality

continual ADJECTIVE
1 = **constant**, interminable, incessant, unremitting ≠ erratic
2 = **frequent**, regular, repeated, recurrent ≠ occasional

continually ADVERB
1 = **constantly**, always, all the time, forever, incessantly, nonstop, interminably
2 = **repeatedly**, often, frequently, many times, over and over, persistently

continuation NOUN
1 = **continuing**, lasting, carrying on, keeping up, endurance, perpetuation, prolongation
2 = **addition**, extension, supplement, sequel, resumption, postscript

continue VERB 1 = **keep on**, go on, maintain, sustain, carry on, persist in, persevere, stick at ≠ stop 2 = **go on**, progress, proceed, carry on, keep going, crack on (*informal*) 3 = **resume**, return to, take up again, proceed, carry on, recommence, pick up where you left off ≠ stop
4 = **remain**, last, stay, survive, carry on, live on, endure, persist ≠ quit

continuing ADJECTIVE = **lasting**, sustained, enduring, ongoing, in progress

continuity NOUN = **cohesion**, flow, connection, sequence, succession, progression

continuous ADJECTIVE = **constant**, extended, prolonged, unbroken, uninterrupted, unceasing ≠ occasional

contract NOUN = **agreement**, commitment, arrangement, settlement, bargain, pact, covenant
▷ VERB 1 = **agree**, negotiate, pledge, bargain, undertake, come to terms, covenant, make a deal ≠ refuse 2 = **constrict**, confine, tighten, shorten, compress, condense, shrivel 3 = **tighten**, narrow, shorten ≠ stretch 4 = **lessen**, reduce, shrink, diminish, decrease, dwindle ≠ increase 5 = **catch**, get, develop, acquire, incur, be infected with, go down with, be afflicted with ≠ avoid

contraction NOUN
1 = **tightening**, narrowing, shortening, constricting, shrinkage 2 = **abbreviation**, reduction, shortening, compression

contradict VERB 1 = **dispute**, deny, challenge, belie, fly in the face of, be at variance with 2 = **negate**, deny, rebut, controvert ≠ confirm

contradiction NOUN 1 = **conflict**, inconsistency, contravention, incongruity 2 = **negation**, opposite, denial

contradictory ADJECTIVE = **inconsistent**, conflicting, opposed, opposite, contrary, incompatible, paradoxical

contrary ADJECTIVE 1 = **opposite**, different, opposed, clashing, counter, reverse, adverse, contradictory ≠ in agreement 2 = **perverse**, difficult, awkward, intractable, obstinate, stroppy (*Brit. slang*), cantankerous, disobliging ≠ cooperative
▷ NOUN = **opposite**, reverse, converse, antithesis

contrast NOUN = **difference**, opposition, comparison, distinction, foil, disparity, divergence, dissimilarity
▷ VERB 1 = **differentiate**, compare, oppose, distinguish, set in opposition 2 = **differ**, be contrary, be at variance, be dissimilar

contribute VERB = **give**, provide, supply, donate, subscribe, chip in (*informal*), bestow ▷ PHRASE: **contribute to something** = **be partly responsible for**, lead to, be instrumental in, be conducive to, help

contribution NOUN = **gift**, offering, grant, donation, input, subscription, koha (*N.Z.*)

contributor NOUN = **donor**, supporter, patron, subscriber, giver

contrive VERB 1 = **devise**, plan, fabricate, create, design, scheme, manufacture, plot **2** = **manage**, succeed, arrange, manoeuvre

contrived ADJECTIVE = **forced**, planned, laboured, strained, artificial, elaborate, unnatural, overdone ≠ natural

control NOUN **1** = **power**, authority, management, command, guidance, supervision, supremacy, charge **2** = **restraint**, check, regulation, brake, limitation, curb **3** = **self-discipline**, self-restraint, restraint, self-command **4** = **switch**, instrument, button, dial, lever, knob
▷ PLURAL NOUN = **instruments**, dash, dials, console, dashboard, control panel
▷ VERB **1** = **have power over**, manage, direct, handle, command, govern, administer, supervise **2** = **limit**, restrict, curb **3** = **restrain**, limit, check, contain, curb, hold back, subdue, repress

controversial ADJECTIVE = **disputed**, contentious, at issue, debatable, under discussion, open to question, disputable

controversy NOUN = **argument**, debate, row, dispute, quarrel, squabble, wrangling, altercation

convene VERB **1** = **call**, gather, assemble, summon, bring together, convoke **2** = **meet**, gather, assemble, come together, congregate

convenience NOUN **1** = **benefit**, good, advantage **2** = **suitability**, fitness, appropriateness

3 = **usefulness**, utility ≠ uselessness **4** = **accessibility**, availability, nearness
5 = **appliance**, facility, comfort, amenity, labour-saving device, help

convenient ADJECTIVE **1** = **suitable**, fit, handy, satisfactory **2** = **useful**, practical, handy, serviceable, labour-saving ≠ useless **3** = **nearby**, available, accessible, handy, at hand, within reach, close at hand, just round the corner ≠ inaccessible **4** = **appropriate**, timely, suitable, helpful

convention NOUN **1** = **custom**, practice, tradition, code, usage, protocol, etiquette, propriety, kawa (N.Z.), tikanga (N.Z.) **2** = **agreement**, contract, treaty, bargain, pact, protocol **3** = **assembly**, meeting, council, conference, congress, convocation, hui (N.Z.), runanga (N.Z.)

conventional ADJECTIVE **1** = **proper**, conservative, respectable, genteel, conformist **2** = **ordinary**, standard, normal, regular, usual **3** = **traditional**, accepted, orthodox, customary **4** = **unoriginal**, routine, stereotyped, banal, prosaic, run-of-the-mill, hackneyed ≠ unconventional

converge VERB = **come together**, meet, join, combine, gather, merge, coincide, intersect
▷ PHRASE: **converge on**

something = **close in on**, arrive at, move towards, home in on, come together at

conversation NOUN = **talk**, discussion, dialogue, tête-à-tête, conference, chat, gossip, discourse, korero (N.Z.) ▷ **RELATED WORD**: adjective colloquial

conversion NOUN 1 = **change**, transformation, metamorphosis 2 = **adaptation**, reconstruction, modification, alteration, remodelling, reorganization

convert VERB 1 = **change**, turn, transform, alter, transpose 2 = **adapt**, modify, remodel, reorganize, customize, restyle 3 = **reform**, convince, proselytize ▷ NOUN = **neophyte**, disciple, proselyte

convey VERB 1 = **communicate**, impart, reveal, relate, disclose, make known, tell 2 = **carry**, transport, move, bring, bear, conduct, fetch

convict VERB = **find guilty**, sentence, condemn, imprison, pronounce guilty ▷ NOUN = **prisoner**, criminal, lag (slang), felon, jailbird

conviction NOUN 1 = **belief**, view, opinion, principle, faith, persuasion, creed, tenet, kaupapa (N.Z.) 2 = **certainty**, confidence, assurance, firmness, certitude

convince VERB 1 = **assure**, persuade, satisfy, reassure 2 = **persuade**, induce, coax, talk into, prevail upon, bring round to

the idea of

 ● **WORD POWER**
 ● The use of convince to talk
 ● about persuading someone to
 ● do something is considered
 ● by many British speakers to
 ● be wrong or unacceptable. It
 ● would be preferable to use an
 ● alternative such as persuade or
 ● talk into.

convincing ADJECTIVE = **persuasive**, credible, conclusive, telling, powerful, impressive, plausible, cogent ≠ unconvincing

cool ADJECTIVE 1 = **cold**, chilled, refreshing, chilly, nippy ≠ warm 2 = **calm**, collected, relaxed, composed, sedate, self-controlled, unruffled, unemotional, chilled (informal) ≠ agitated 3 = **unfriendly**, distant, indifferent, aloof, lukewarm, offhand, unenthusiastic, unwelcoming ≠ friendly 4 = **unenthusiastic**, indifferent, lukewarm, unwelcoming ▷ VERB 1 = **lose heat**, cool off ≠ warm (up) 2 = **make cool**, freeze, chill, refrigerate, cool off ≠ warm (up) ▷ NOUN 1 = **coldness**, chill, coolness 2 (slang) = **calmness**, control, temper, composure, self-control, poise, self-discipline, self-possession

cooperate VERB = **work together**, collaborate, coordinate, join forces, conspire, pull together, pool resources, combine your efforts ≠ conflict

cooperation NOUN = **teamwork**, unity, collaboration, give-and-take, combined effort, esprit de corps, kotahitanga (*N.Z.*) ≠ opposition

cooperative ADJECTIVE 1 = **shared**, joint, combined, collective, collaborative 2 = **helpful**, obliging, accommodating, supportive, responsive, onside (*informal*)

cope VERB = **manage**, get by (*informal*), struggle through, survive, carry on, make the grade, hold your own ▷ PHRASE: **cope with something** = **deal with**, handle, struggle with, grapple with, wrestle with, contend with, weather

copy NOUN = **reproduction**, duplicate, replica, imitation, forgery, counterfeit, likeness, facsimile ≠ original ▷ VERB 1 = **reproduce**, replicate, duplicate, transcribe, counterfeit ≠ create 2 = **imitate**, act like, emulate, behave like, follow, repeat, mirror, ape

cord NOUN = **rope**, line, string, twine

cordon NOUN = **chain**, line, ring, barrier, picket line ▷ PHRASE: **cordon something off** = **surround**, isolate, close off, fence off, separate, enclose, picket, encircle

core NOUN 1 = **centre** 2 = **heart**, essence, nucleus, kernel, crux, gist, nub, pith

corner NOUN 1 = **angle**, joint,

crook 2 = **bend**, curve 3 = **space**, hideaway, nook, hide-out ▷ VERB 1 = **trap**, catch, run to earth 2 (*a market*) = **monopolize**, take over, dominate, control, hog (*slang*), engross

corporation NOUN 1 = **business**, company, concern, firm, society, association, organization, enterprise 2 = **town council**, council, municipal authorities, civic authorities

corps NOUN = **team**, unit, regiment, detachment, company, band, division, troop

corpse NOUN = **body**, remains, carcass, cadaver, stiff (*slang*)

correct ADJECTIVE 1 = **accurate**, right, true, exact, precise, flawless, faultless, O.K. *or* okay (*informal*) ≠ inaccurate 2 = **right**, standard, appropriate, acceptable, proper, precise 3 = **proper**, seemly, standard, fitting, kosher (*informal*) ≠ inappropriate ▷ VERB 1 = **rectify**, remedy, redress, right, reform, cure, adjust, amend ≠ spoil 2 = **rebuke**, discipline, reprimand, chide, admonish, chastise, chasten, reprove ≠ praise

correction NOUN 1 = **rectification**, improvement, amendment, adjustment, modification, alteration, emendation 2 = **punishment**, discipline, reformation, admonition, chastisement, reproof, castigation

correctly ADVERB = **rightly**, right, perfectly, properly, precisely, accurately

correctness NOUN 1 = **truth**, accuracy, precision, exactitude, exactness, faultlessness 2 = **decorum**, propriety, good manners, civility, good breeding

correspond VERB 1 = **be consistent**, match, agree, accord, fit, square, tally, conform ≠ differ 2 = **communicate**, write, keep in touch, exchange letters, e-mail, text

correspondence NOUN 1 = **communication**, writing, contact 2 = **letters**, post, mail 3 = **relation**, match, agreement, comparison, harmony, coincidence, similarity, correlation

correspondent NOUN 1 = **reporter**, journalist, contributor, hack 2 = **letter writer**, pen friend or pen pal

corresponding ADJECTIVE = **equivalent**, matching, similar, related, complementary, reciprocal, analogous

corridor NOUN = **passage**, alley, aisle, hallway, passageway

corrupt ADJECTIVE 1 = **dishonest**, bent (slang), crooked (informal), fraudulent, unscrupulous, venal, unprincipled ≠ honest 2 = **depraved**, vicious, degenerate, debased, profligate, dissolute 3 = **distorted**, doctored, altered, falsified

▷ VERB 1 = **bribe**, fix (informal), buy off, suborn, grease (someone's) palm (slang) 2 = **deprave**, pervert, subvert, debauch ≠ reform 3 = **distort**, doctor, tamper with

corruption NOUN 1 = **dishonesty**, fraud, bribery, extortion, venality, shady dealings (informal) 2 = **depravity**, vice, evil, perversion, decadence, wickedness, immorality 3 = **distortion**, doctoring, falsification

cosmetic ADJECTIVE = **superficial**, surface, nonessential

cosmic ADJECTIVE 1 = **extraterrestrial**, stellar 2 = **universal**, general, overarching

cosmopolitan ADJECTIVE = **sophisticated**, cultured, refined, cultivated, urbane, well-travelled, worldly-wise ≠ unsophisticated

cost NOUN 1 = **price**, worth, expense, charge, damage (informal), amount, payment, outlay 2 = **loss**, suffering, damage, injury, penalty, hurt, expense, harm

▷ PLURAL NOUN = **expenses**, spending, expenditure, overheads, outgoings, outlay, budget

▷ VERB 1 = **sell at**, come to, set (someone) back (informal), be priced at, command a price of 2 = **lose**, deprive of, cheat of

costly ADJECTIVE 1 = **expensive**, dear, stiff, steep (informal), highly-priced, exorbitant, extortionate ≠ inexpensive 2 = **damaging**, disastrous, harmful, catastrophic, loss-making, ruinous, deleterious

costume NOUN = **outfit**, dress, clothing, uniform, ensemble, livery, apparel, attire

cosy ADJECTIVE 1 = **comfortable**, homely, warm, intimate, snug, comfy (*informal*), sheltered 2 = **snug**, warm, comfortable, sheltered, comfy (*informal*), tucked up 3 = **intimate**, friendly, informal

cottage NOUN = **cabin**, lodge, hut, shack, chalet, whare (*N.Z.*)

cough VERB = **clear your throat**, bark, hack
 ▷ NOUN = **frog** *or* **tickle in your throat**, bark, hack

council NOUN 1 = **committee**, governing body, board 2 = **governing body**, parliament, congress, cabinet, panel, assembly, convention, conference, runanga (*N.Z.*)

counsel NOUN 1 = **advice**, information, warning, direction, suggestion, recommendation, guidance 2 = **legal adviser**, lawyer, attorney, solicitor, advocate, barrister
 ▷ VERB = **advise**, recommend, advocate, warn, urge, instruct, exhort

count VERB 1 *often with* **up** = **add (up)**, total, reckon (up), tot up, calculate, compute, tally, number 2 = **matter**, be important, carry weight, tell, rate, weigh, signify 3 = **consider**, judge, regard, deem, think of, rate, look upon

4 = **include**, number among, take into account *or* consideration
 ▷ NOUN = **calculation**, poll, reckoning, sum, tally, numbering, computation, enumeration
 ▷ PHRASE: **count on** *or* **upon something** *or* **someone** = **depend on**, trust, rely on, bank on, take for granted, lean on, reckon on, take on trust

counter VERB 1 = **oppose**, meet, block, resist, parry, deflect, repel, rebuff 2 = **retaliate**, answer, reply, respond, retort, hit back, rejoin, strike back ≠ yield
 ▷ ADVERB = **opposite to**, against, versus, conversely, in defiance of, at variance with, contrariwise ≠ in accordance with

counterpart NOUN = **opposite number**, equal, twin, equivalent, match, fellow, mate

countless ADJECTIVE = **innumerable**, legion, infinite, myriad, untold, limitless, incalculable, immeasurable ≠ limited

country NOUN 1 = **nation**, state, land, commonwealth, kingdom, realm, people 2 = **people**, community, nation, society, citizens, inhabitants, populace, public 3 = **countryside**, provinces, sticks (*informal*), farmland, outback (*Austral. & N.Z.*), green belt, backwoods, bush (*N.Z. & S. African*) ≠ town

countryside NOUN = **country**, rural areas, outback (*Austral. & N.Z.*), green belt, sticks (*informal*)

county NOUN = **province**, district, shire

coup NOUN = **masterstroke**, feat, stunt, action, exploit, manoeuvre, deed, accomplishment

couple NOUN = **pair**, two, brace, duo, twosome ▷ PHRASE: **couple something to something** = **link to**, connect to, pair with, unite with, join to, hitch to, yoke to

coupon NOUN = **slip**, ticket, certificate, token, voucher, card

courage NOUN = **bravery**, nerve, resolution, daring, pluck, heroism, mettle, gallantry ≠ cowardice

courageous ADJECTIVE = **brave**, daring, bold, gritty, fearless, gallant, intrepid, valiant ≠ cowardly

courier NOUN 1 = **messenger**, runner, carrier, bearer, envoy 2 = **guide**, representative, escort, conductor

course NOUN 1 = **route**, way, line, road, track, direction, path, passage 2 = **procedure**, plan, policy, programme, method, conduct, behaviour, manner 3 = **progression**, order, unfolding, development, movement, progress, flow, sequence 4 = **classes**, programme, schedule, lectures, curriculum 5 = **racecourse**, circuit 6 = **period**, time, duration, term, passing ▷ VERB 1 = **run**, flow, stream, gush, race, speed, surge 2 = **hunt**, follow, chase, pursue ▷ PHRASE:

of course = **naturally**, certainly, obviously, definitely, undoubtedly, needless to say, without a doubt, indubitably

court NOUN 1 = **law court**, bar, bench, tribunal 2 = **palace**, hall, castle, manor 3 = **royal household**, train, suite, attendants, entourage, retinue, cortege ▷ VERB 1 = **cultivate**, seek, flatter, solicit, pander to, curry favour with, fawn upon 2 = **invite**, seek, attract, prompt, provoke, bring about, incite 3 = **woo**, go (out) with, date, take out, run after, walk out with, set your cap at, step out with (*informal*)

courtesy NOUN 1 = **politeness**, good manners, civility, gallantry, graciousness, affability, urbanity 2 = **favour**, kindness, indulgence

courtyard NOUN = **yard**, square, piazza, quadrangle, plaza, enclosure, cloister, quad (*informal*)

cove NOUN = **bay**, sound, inlet, anchorage

covenant NOUN = **promise**, contract, agreement, commitment, arrangement, pledge, pact

cover VERB 1 = **conceal**, hide, mask, disguise, obscure, veil, cloak, shroud ≠ reveal 2 = **clothe**, dress, wrap, envelop ≠ uncover 3 = **overlay**, blanket 4 = **coat**, cake, plaster, smear, envelop, spread, encase, daub 5 = **submerge**, flood, engulf, overrun, wash over 6 = **travel**

over, cross, traverse, pass through *or* over **7** = **protect**, guard, defend, shield **8** = **consider**, deal with, investigate, describe, tell of **9** = **report on**, write about, commentate on, relate, tell of, narrate, write up **10** = **pay for**, fund, provide for, offset, be enough for

▷ NOUN **1** = **protection**, shelter, shield, defence, guard, camouflage, concealment

2 = **insurance**, protection, compensation, indemnity, reimbursement **3** = **covering**, case, top, coating, envelope, lid, canopy, wrapper **4** = **bedclothes**, bedding, sheet, blanket, quilt, duvet, eiderdown **5** = **jacket**, case, wrapper **6** = **disguise**, front, screen, mask, veil, façade, pretext, smoke screen

covering NOUN = **cover**, coating, casing, wrapping, layer, blanket

▷ ADJECTIVE = **explanatory**, accompanying, introductory, descriptive

covet VERB = **long for**, desire, envy, crave, aspire to, yearn for, lust after, set your heart on

coward NOUN = **wimp**, chicken (*slang*), scaredy-cat (*informal*), yellow-belly (*slang*)

cowardly ADJECTIVE = **faint-hearted**, scared, spineless, soft, yellow (*informal*), weak, chicken (*slang*), fearful, sookie (*N.Z.*) ≠ brave

cowboy NOUN = **cowhand**, drover, rancher, stockman, cattleman,

herdsman, gaucho

crack VERB **1** = **break**, split, burst, snap, fracture, splinter **2** = **snap**, ring, crash, burst, explode, pop, detonate **3** (*informal*) = **hit**, clip (*informal*), slap, smack, clout (*informal*), cuff, whack **4** = **break**, cleave **5** = **solve**, work out, resolve, clear up, fathom, decipher, suss (out) (*slang*), get to the bottom of **6** = **break down**, collapse, yield, give in, give way, succumb, lose control, be overcome

▷ NOUN **1** = **break**, chink, gap, fracture, rift, cleft, crevice, fissure **2** = **split**, break, fracture **3** = **snap**, pop, crash, burst, explosion, clap, report **4** (*informal*) = **blow**, slap, smack, clout (*informal*), cuff, whack, clip (*informal*) **5** (*informal*) = **joke**, dig, gag (*informal*), quip, jibe, wisecrack, witticism, funny remark

▷ ADJECTIVE (*slang*) = **first-class**, choice, excellent, ace, elite, superior, world-class, first-rate

crackdown NOUN = **clampdown**, crushing, repression, suppression

cracked ADJECTIVE = **broken**, damaged, split, chipped, flawed, faulty, defective, imperfect

cradle NOUN **1** = **crib**, cot, Moses basket, bassinet **2** = **birthplace**, beginning, source, spring, origin, fount, fountainhead, wellspring

▷ VERB = **hold**, support, rock, nurse, nestle

craft NOUN **1** = **vessel**, boat, ship, plane, aircraft, spacecraft

2 = **occupation**, work, business, trade, employment, pursuit, vocation, handicraft 3 = **skill**, art, ability, technique, know-how (*informal*), expertise, aptitude, artistry

craftsman NOUN = **skilled worker**, artisan, master, maker, wright, technician, smith

cram VERB 1 = **stuff**, force, jam, shove, compress 2 = **pack**, fill, stuff 3 = **squeeze**, press, pack in 4 = **study**, revise, swot, bone up (*informal*), mug up (*slang*)

cramp¹ NOUN = **spasm**, pain, ache, contraction, pang, stitch, convulsion, twinge

cramp² VERB = **restrict**, hamper, inhibit, hinder, handicap, constrain, obstruct, impede

cramped ADJECTIVE = **restricted**, confined, overcrowded, crowded, packed, uncomfortable, closed in, congested ≠ spacious

crash NOUN 1 = **collision**, accident, smash, wreck, prang (*informal*), bump, pile-up (*informal*) 2 = **smash**, clash, boom, bang, thunder, racket, din, clatter 3 = **collapse**, failure, depression, ruin, downfall ▷ VERB 1 = **fall**, plunge, topple, lurch, hurtle, overbalance, fall headlong 2 = **plunge**, hurtle 3 = **collapse**, fail, go under, be ruined, go bust (*informal*), fold up, go to the wall, go belly up (*informal*) ▷ PHRASE: **crash into** = **collide with**, hit, bump into, drive into, plough into

crate NOUN = **container**, case, box, packing case, tea chest

crater NOUN = **hollow**, hole, depression, dip, cavity

crave VERB 1 = **long for**, yearn for, hanker after, want, desire, hope for, lust after 2 (*informal*) = **beg**, ask for, seek, petition, pray for, plead for, solicit, implore

craving NOUN = **longing**, hope, desire, yen (*informal*), hunger, appetite, yearning, thirst

crawl VERB 1 = **creep**, slither, inch, wriggle, writhe, worm your way, advance slowly ≠ run 2 = **grovel**, creep, humble yourself ▷ PHRASE: **crawl to someone** = **fawn on**, toady to

craze NOUN = **fad**, fashion, trend, rage, enthusiasm, vogue, mania, infatuation

crazed ADJECTIVE = **mad**, crazy, raving, insane, lunatic, berko (*Austral. slang*), off the air (*Austral. slang*), porangi (*N.Z.*)

crazy ADJECTIVE 1 (*informal*) = **ridiculous**, absurd, foolish, ludicrous, senseless, preposterous, idiotic, nonsensical, porangi (*N.Z.*) ≠ sensible 2 = **insane**, mad, unbalanced, deranged, nuts (*slang*), crazed, demented, off the air (*Austral. slang*), out of your mind, porangi (*N.Z.*) ≠ sane 3 = **fanatical**, wild (*informal*), mad, devoted, enthusiastic, passionate, infatuated ≠ uninterested

cream NOUN 1 = **lotion**, ointment,

oil, essence, cosmetic, paste, emulsion, salve **2** = **best**, elite, prime, pick, flower, crème de la crème (*French*)
▷ ADJECTIVE = **off-white**, ivory, yellowish-white
▷ *see* **shades from black to white**

creamy ADJECTIVE **1** = **milky**, buttery **2** = **smooth**, soft, velvety, rich

crease NOUN **1** = **fold**, line, ridge, groove, corrugation **2** = **wrinkle**, line, crow's-foot
▷ VERB **1** = **crumple**, rumple, fold, double up, corrugate **2** = **wrinkle**, crumple, screw up

create VERB **1** = **cause**, lead to, occasion, bring about **2** = **make**, produce, invent, compose, devise, originate, formulate, spawn ≠ destroy **3** = **appoint**, make, establish, set up, invest, install, constitute

creation NOUN **1** = **universe**, world, nature, cosmos **2** = **invention**, production, achievement, brainchild (*informal*), concoction, handiwork, pièce de résistance (*French*), magnum opus **3** = **making**, generation, formation, conception, genesis **4** = **setting up**, development, production, institution, foundation, establishment, formation, inception

creative ADJECTIVE = **imaginative**, gifted, artistic, inventive, original, inspired, clever, ingenious

creativity NOUN = **imagination**, inspiration, ingenuity, originality, inventiveness, cleverness

creator NOUN **1** = **maker**, father, author, designer, architect, inventor, originator **2** *usually with cap.* = **God**, Maker

creature NOUN **1** = **living thing**, being, animal, beast, brute **2** = **person**, man, woman, individual, soul, human being, mortal

credentials PLURAL NOUN **1** = **qualifications**, ability, skill, fitness, attribute, capability, eligibility, aptitude **2** = **certification**, document, reference(s), papers, licence, passport, testimonial, authorization

credibility NOUN = **believability**, reliability, plausibility, trustworthiness

credible ADJECTIVE **1** = **believable**, possible, likely, reasonable, probable, plausible, conceivable, imaginable ≠ unbelievable **2** = **reliable**, honest, dependable, trustworthy, sincere, trusty ≠ unreliable

credit NOUN **1** = **praise**, honour, recognition, approval, tribute, acclaim, acknowledgment, kudos **2** = **source of satisfaction** or **pride**, asset, honour, feather in your cap **3** = **prestige**, reputation, standing, position, influence, regard, status, esteem **4** = **belief**, trust, confidence, faith, reliance, credence

▷ VERB = **believe**, rely on, have faith in, trust, accept ▷ PHRASE: **credit someone with something** = **attribute to**, assign to, ascribe to, impute to

creed NOUN = **belief**, principles, doctrine, dogma, credo, catechism, articles of faith

creek NOUN 1 = **inlet**, bay, cove, bight, firth or frith (*Scot.*) 2 (*U.S., Canad., Austral. & N.Z.*) = **stream**, brook, tributary, bayou, rivulet, watercourse, runnel

creep VERB = **sneak**, steal, tiptoe, slink, skulk, approach unnoticed ▷ NOUN (*slang*) = **bootlicker** (*informal*), sneak, sycophant, crawler (*slang*), toady (*informal*) ▷ VERB = **disgust**, frighten, scare, repel, repulse, make your hair stand on end, make you squirm

crescent NOUN = **meniscus**, sickle, new moon

crest NOUN 1 = **top**, summit, peak, ridge, highest point, pinnacle, apex, crown 2 = **tuft**, crown, comb, plume, mane 3 = **emblem**, badge, symbol, insignia, bearings, device

crew NOUN 1 = **(ship's) company**, hands, (ship's) complement 2 = **team**, squad, gang, corps, posse 3 (*informal*) = **crowd**, set, bunch (*informal*), band, pack, gang, mob, horde

crime NOUN 1 = **offence**, violation, trespass, felony, misdemeanour, misdeed, transgression, unlawful act 2 = **lawbreaking**, corruption, illegality, vice, misconduct, wrongdoing

criminal NOUN = **lawbreaker**, convict, offender, crook (*informal*), villain, culprit, sinner, felon, rorter (*Austral. slang*), skelm (*S. African*), rogue trader, perp (*U.S. & Canad. informal*)
▷ ADJECTIVE 1 = **unlawful**, illicit, lawless, wrong, illegal, corrupt, crooked (*informal*), immoral ≠ lawful 2 (*informal*) = **disgraceful**, ridiculous, foolish, senseless, scandalous, preposterous, deplorable

cripple VERB 1 = **disable**, paralyse, lame, maim, incapacitate, weaken, hamstring 2 = **damage**, destroy, ruin, spoil, impair, put paid to, put out of action ≠ help

crippled ADJECTIVE = **disabled**, handicapped, challenged, paralysed, lame, incapacitated

crisis NOUN 1 = **emergency**, plight, predicament, trouble, deep water, meltdown (*informal*), dire straits 2 = **critical point**, climax, height, crunch (*informal*), turning point, culmination, crux, moment of truth, tipping point

crisp ADJECTIVE 1 = **firm**, crunchy, crispy, crumbly, fresh, brittle, unwilted ≠ soft 2 = **bracing**, fresh, refreshing, brisk, invigorating ≠ warm 3 = **clean**, smart, trim, neat, tidy, spruce, well-groomed, well-pressed

criterion NOUN = **standard**, test, rule, measure, principle, gauge, yardstick, touchstone
  ● **WORD POWER**
  ● The word *criteria* is the plural

- of *criterion* and it is incorrect to
- use it as an alternative singular
- form; *these criteria are not valid*
- is correct, and so is *this criterion*
- *is not valid*, but not *this criteria is*
- *not valid*.

critic NOUN 1 = **judge**, authority, expert, analyst, commentator, pundit, reviewer, connoisseur 2 = **fault-finder**, attacker, detractor, knocker (*informal*)

critical ADJECTIVE 1 = **crucial**, decisive, pressing, serious, vital, urgent, all-important, pivotal ≠ unimportant 2 = **grave**, serious, acute, precarious ≠ safe 3 = **disparaging**, disapproving, scathing, derogatory, nit-picking (*informal*), censorious, fault-finding, captious, nit-picky (*informal*) ≠ complimentary 4 = **analytical**, penetrating, discriminating, discerning, perceptive, judicious ≠ undiscriminating

criticism NOUN 1 = **fault-finding**, censure, disapproval, disparagement, stick (*slang*), flak (*informal*), bad press, character assassination 2 = **analysis**, assessment, judgment, commentary, evaluation, appreciation, appraisal, critique

criticize VERB = **find fault with**, censure, disapprove of, knock (*informal*), condemn, carp, put down, slate (*informal*), nit-pick (*informal*) ≠ praise

crook NOUN (*informal*) = **criminal**, rogue, cheat, thief, shark, villain, robber, racketeer, skelm (*S. African*) ▷ ADJECTIVE (*Austral. & N.Z. informal*) = **ill**, sick, poorly (*informal*), unhealthy, seedy (*informal*), unwell, queasy, out of sorts (*informal*) ▷ PHRASE: **go (off) crook** (*Austral. & N.Z. informal*) = **lose your temper**, be furious, rage, go mad, lose it (*informal*), crack up (*informal*), see red (*informal*), blow your top

crooked ADJECTIVE 1 = **bent**, twisted, curved, irregular, warped, out of shape, misshapen ≠ straight 2 = **deformed**, distorted 3 = **at an angle**, uneven, slanting, squint, awry, lopsided, askew, off-centre 4 (*informal*) = **dishonest**, criminal, illegal, corrupt, unlawful, shady (*informal*), fraudulent, bent (*slang*) ≠ honest

crop NOUN = **yield**, produce, gathering, fruits, harvest, vintage, reaping ▷ VERB 1 = **graze**, eat, browse, feed on, nibble 2 = **cut**, trim, clip, prune, shear, snip, pare, lop ▷ PHRASE: **crop up** (*informal*) = **happen**, appear, emerge, occur, arise, turn up, spring up

cross VERB 1 = **go across**, pass over, traverse, cut across, move across, travel across 2 = **span**, bridge, go across, extend over 3 = **intersect**, intertwine, crisscross 4 = **oppose**, interfere with, obstruct, block, resist, impede 5 = **interbreed**, mix, blend, cross-pollinate, crossbreed,

hybridize, cross-fertilize, intercross
▷ **NOUN 1** = **crucifix 2** = **trouble**, worry, trial, load, burden, grief, woe, misfortune **3** = **mixture**, combination, blend, amalgam, amalgamation
▷ **ADJECTIVE** = **angry**, annoyed, put out, grumpy, short, ill-tempered, irascible, tooshie (*Austral. slang*), in a bad mood, hoha (*N.Z.*) ≠ good-humoured
▷ **PHRASE**: **cross something out** or **off** = **strike off** or **out**, eliminate, cancel, delete, blue-pencil, score off or out

crouch VERB = **bend down**, kneel, squat, stoop, bow, duck, hunch

crow VERB = **gloat**, triumph, boast, swagger, brag, exult, blow your own trumpet

crowd NOUN **1** = **multitude**, mass, throng, army, host, pack, mob, swarm **2** = **group**, set, lot, circle, gang, bunch (*informal*), clique **3** = **audience**, spectators, house, gate, attendance
▷ **VERB 1** = **flock**, mass, collect, gather, stream, surge, swarm, throng **2** = **squeeze**, pack, pile, bundle, cram **3** = **congest**, pack, cram

crowded ADJECTIVE = **packed**, full, busy, cramped, swarming, teeming, congested, jam-packed

crown NOUN **1** = **coronet**, tiara, diadem, circlet **2** = **laurel wreath**, trophy, prize, honour, garland, laurels, wreath **3** = **high point**, top, tip, summit, crest, pinnacle, apex
▷ **VERB 1** = **install**, honour, dignify, ordain, inaugurate **2** = **top**, cap, be on top of, surmount **3** = **cap**, finish, complete, perfect, round off, put the finishing touch to, be the climax or culmination of **4** (*slang*) = **strike**, belt (*informal*), bash, hit over the head, box, punch, cuff, biff (*slang*) ▷ **PHRASE**: **the Crown 1** = **monarch**, ruler, sovereign, emperor or empress, king or queen **2** = **monarchy**, sovereignty, royalty

crucial ADJECTIVE **1** (*informal*) = **vital**, important, pressing, essential, urgent, momentous, high-priority **2** = **critical**, central, key, psychological, decisive, pivotal

crude ADJECTIVE **1** = **rough**, basic, makeshift **2** = **simple**, rudimentary, basic, primitive, coarse, clumsy, rough-and-ready **3** = **vulgar**, dirty, rude, obscene, coarse, indecent, tasteless, smutty ≠ tasteful **4** = **unrefined**, natural, raw, unprocessed ≠ processed

crudely ADVERB **1** = **roughly**, basically **2** = **simply**, roughly, basically, coarsely **3** = **vulgarly**, rudely, coarsely, crassly, obscenely, lewdly, impolitely, tastelessly

cruel ADJECTIVE **1** = **brutal**, ruthless, callous, sadistic, inhumane, vicious, monstrous, unkind ≠ kind **2** = **bitter**, ruthless, traumatic, grievous,

unrelenting, merciless, pitiless
cruelly ADVERB 1 = **brutally**,
severely, mercilessly, in cold
blood, callously, monstrously,
sadistically, pitilessly 2 = **bitterly**,
deeply, severely, ruthlessly,
mercilessly, grievously, pitilessly,
traumatically
cruelty NOUN = **brutality**,
ruthlessness, depravity,
inhumanity, barbarity,
callousness, spitefulness,
mercilessness
cruise NOUN = **sail**, voyage, boat
trip, sea trip
▷ VERB 1 = **sail**, coast, voyage
2 = **travel along**, coast, drift, keep
a steady pace
crumb NOUN 1 = **bit**, grain,
fragment, shred, morsel
2 = **morsel**, scrap, shred, snippet,
soupçon (*French*)
crumble VERB 1 = **disintegrate**,
collapse, deteriorate, decay,
fall apart, degenerate, tumble
down, go to pieces 2 = **crush**,
fragment, pulverize, pound, grind,
powder, granulate 3 = **collapse**,
deteriorate, decay, fall apart,
degenerate, go to pieces, go to
wrack and ruin
crumple VERB 1 = **crush**, squash,
screw up, scrumple 2 = **crease**,
wrinkle, rumple, ruffle, pucker
3 = **collapse**, sink, go down, fall
4 = **break down**, fall, collapse,
give way, cave in, go to pieces
5 = **screw up**
crunch VERB = **chomp**, champ,
munch, chew noisily, grind

▷ PHRASE: **the crunch** (*informal*)
= **critical point**, test, crisis,
emergency, crux, moment of truth
crusade NOUN 1 = **campaign**,
drive, movement, cause, push
2 = **holy war**
▷ VERB = **campaign**, fight, push,
struggle, lobby, agitate, work
crush VERB 1 = **squash**, break,
squeeze, compress, press,
pulverize 2 = **crease**, wrinkle,
crumple 3 = **overcome**,
overwhelm, put down, subdue,
overpower, quash, quell, stamp
out 4 = **demoralize**, depress,
devastate, discourage, humble,
put down (*slang*), humiliate,
squash
▷ NOUN = **crowd**, mob, horde,
throng, pack, mass, jam, huddle
crust NOUN = **layer**, covering,
coating, skin, surface, shell
cry VERB 1 = **weep**, sob, shed
tears, blubber, snivel ≠ laugh
2 = **shout**, scream, roar, yell,
howl, call out, exclaim, shriek
≠ whisper
▷ NOUN 1 = **weep**, sob, bawl,
blubber 2 = **shout**, call, scream,
roar, yell, howl, shriek, bellow
3 = **weeping**, sobbing, blubbering,
snivelling ▷ PHRASE: **cry off**
(*informal*) = **back out**, withdraw,
quit, excuse yourself
cuddle VERB 1 = **hug**, embrace,
fondle, cosset 2 = **pet**, hug, bill
and coo ▷ PHRASE: **cuddle up**
= **snuggle**
cue NOUN = **signal**, sign, hint,
prompt, reminder, suggestion

● **CRUSTACEANS**

- barnacle
- crab
- crayfish, crawfish, (U.S.) or (Austral. & N.Z. informal) craw
- freshwater shrimp
- hermit crab
- horseshoe crab or king crab
- king prawn
- koura (N.Z.)
- krill
- land crab
- langoustine
- lobster
- oyster crab
- prawn
- robber crab
- sand shrimp
- scorpion
- sea spider
- shrimp
- soft-shell crab
- spider crab
- spiny lobster, rock lobster, crawfish, or langouste

culminate VERB = **end up**, close, finish, conclude, wind up, climax, come to a head, come to a climax

culprit NOUN = **offender**, criminal, felon, guilty party, wrongdoer, miscreant, evildoer, transgressor, perp (U.S. & Canad. informal)

cult NOUN 1 = **sect**, faction, school, religion, clique, hauhau (N.Z.)
2 = **craze**, fashion, trend, fad
3 = **obsession**, worship, devotion, idolization

cultivate VERB 1 = **farm**, work, plant, tend, till, plough
2 = **develop**, establish, foster
3 = **court**, seek out, run after, dance attendance upon
4 = **improve**, refine

cultural ADJECTIVE 1 = **ethnic**, national, native, folk, racial
2 = **artistic**, educational, aesthetic, enriching, enlightening, civilizing, edifying

culture NOUN 1 = **the arts**
2 = **civilization**, society, customs, way of life 3 = **lifestyle**, habit, way of life, mores
4 = **refinement**, education, enlightenment, sophistication, good taste, urbanity

cultured ADJECTIVE = **refined**, intellectual, educated, sophisticated, enlightened, well-informed, urbane, highbrow ≠ uneducated

cunning ADJECTIVE 1 = **crafty**, sly, devious, artful, sharp, wily, Machiavellian, shifty ≠ frank
2 = **ingenious**, imaginative, sly, devious, artful, Machiavellian
3 = **skilful**, clever ≠ clumsy
▷ NOUN 1 = **craftiness**, guile, trickery, deviousness, artfulness, slyness ≠ candour 2 = **skill**, subtlety, ingenuity, artifice, cleverness ≠ clumsiness

cup NOUN 1 = **mug**, goblet, chalice, teacup, beaker, bowl 2 = **trophy**

cupboard NOUN = **cabinet**, press

curb VERB = **restrain**, control, check, restrict, suppress, inhibit, hinder, retard
▷ NOUN = **restraint**, control, check, brake, limitation, rein, deterrent, bridle

cure VERB 1 = **make better**, correct, heal, relieve, remedy, mend, ease 2 = **restore to health**,

restore, heal **3** = **preserve**,
smoke, dry, salt, pickle
▷ NOUN = **remedy**, treatment,
antidote, panacea, nostrum
curiosity NOUN
1 = **inquisitiveness**, interest,
prying, snooping (*informal*),
nosiness (*informal*) **2** = **oddity**,
wonder, sight, phenomenon,
spectacle, freak, novelty, rarity
curious ADJECTIVE **1** = **inquisitive**,
interested, questioning,
searching, inquiring, meddling,
prying, nosy (*informal*)
≠ uninterested **2** = **strange**,
unusual, bizarre, odd, novel,
rare, extraordinary, unexpected
≠ ordinary
curl NOUN **1** = **ringlet**, lock
2 = **twist**, spiral, coil, kink, whorl
▷ VERB **1** = **crimp**, wave, perm
2 = **twirl**, turn, bend, twist, curve,
loop, spiral, coil **3** = **wind**
curly ADJECTIVE = **wavy**, curled,
curling, fuzzy, frizzy
currency NOUN **1** = **money**,
coinage, legal tender, notes,
coins **2** = **acceptance**, popularity,

circulation, vogue, prevalence
current NOUN **1** = **flow**, course,
undertow, jet, stream, tide,
progression, river **2** = **draught**,
flow, breeze, puff **3** = **mood**,
feeling, spirit, atmosphere, trend,
tendency, undercurrent
▷ ADJECTIVE **1** = **present**,
fashionable, up-to-date,
contemporary, trendy (*Brit.
informal*), topical, present-
day, in fashion ≠ out-of-date
2 = **prevalent**, common,
accepted, popular, widespread,
customary, in circulation
curse VERB **1** = **swear**, cuss
(*informal*), blaspheme, take the
Lord's name in vain **2** = **abuse**,
damn, scold, vilify
▷ NOUN **1** = **oath**, obscenity,
blasphemy, expletive, profanity,
imprecation, swearword
2 = **malediction**, jinx,
anathema, hoodoo (*informal*),
excommunication **3** = **affliction**,
plague, scourge, trouble, torment,
hardship, bane
cursed ADJECTIVE = **under a**

◉ **CRUSTACEANS**
◉ barnacle
◉ crab
◉ crayfish, crawfish,
(*U.S.*) or (*Austral. &
N.Z. informal*) craw
◉ freshwater shrimp
◉ hermit crab
◉ horseshoe crab *or*
king crab

◉ king prawn
◉ koura (*N.Z.*)
◉ krill
◉ land crab
◉ langoustine
◉ lobster
◉ oyster crab
◉ prawn
◉ robber crab

◉ sand shrimp
◉ scorpion
◉ sea spider
◉ shrimp
◉ soft-shell crab
◉ spider crab
◉ spiny lobster, rock
lobster, crawfish, *or*
langouste

curse, damned, doomed, jinxed, bedevilled, accursed, ill-fated

curtail VERB = **reduce**, diminish, decrease, dock, cut back, shorten, lessen, cut short

curtain NOUN = **hanging**, drape (chiefly U.S.), portière

curve NOUN = **bend**, turn, loop, arc, curvature
▷ VERB = **bend**, turn, wind, twist, arch, snake, arc, coil

curved ADJECTIVE = **bent**, rounded, twisted, bowed, arched, serpentine, sinuous

cushion NOUN = **pillow**, pad, bolster, headrest, beanbag, hassock
▷ VERB 1 = **protect** 2 = **soften**, dampen, muffle, mitigate, deaden, suppress, stifle

custody NOUN 1 = **care**, charge, protection, supervision, safekeeping, keeping
2 = **imprisonment**, detention, confinement, incarceration

custom NOUN 1 = **tradition**, practice, convention, ritual, policy, rule, usage, kaupapa (N.Z.) 2 = **habit**, way, practice, procedure, routine, wont
3 = **customers**, business, trade, patronage

customary ADJECTIVE 1 = **usual**, common, accepted, established, traditional, normal, ordinary, conventional ≠ unusual
2 = **accustomed**, regular, usual

customer NOUN = **client**, consumer, regular (informal), buyer, patron, shopper, purchaser

customs PLURAL NOUN = **import charges**, tax, duty, toll, tariff

cut VERB 1 = **slit**, score, slice, slash, pierce, penetrate 2 = **chop**, split, slice, dissect 3 = **carve**, slice 4 = **sever**, cut in two 5 = **shape**, carve, engrave, chisel, form, score, fashion, whittle 6 = **slash**, wound 7 = **clip**, mow, trim, prune, snip, pare, lop 8 = **trim**, shave, snip 9 = **reduce**, lower, slim (down), diminish, slash, decrease, cut back, kennet (Austral. slang), jeff (Austral. slang) ≠ increase 10 = **abridge**, edit, shorten, curtail, condense, abbreviate ≠ extend 11 = **delete**, take out, expurgate 12 = **hurt**, wound, upset, sting, hurt someone's feelings 13 (informal) = **ignore**, avoid, slight, blank (slang), snub, spurn, cold-shoulder, turn your back on ≠ greet 14 = **cross**, bisect
▷ NOUN 1 = **incision**, nick, stroke, slash, slit 2 = **gash**, nick, wound, slash, laceration 3 = **reduction**, fall, lowering, slash, decrease, cutback 4 (informal) = **share**, piece, slice, percentage, portion 5 = **style**, look, fashion, shape

cutback NOUN = **reduction**, cut, retrenchment, economy, decrease, lessening

cute ADJECTIVE = **appealing**, sweet, attractive, engaging, charming, delightful, lovable, winsome

cutting ADJECTIVE = **hurtful**, wounding, bitter, malicious, scathing, acrimonious, barbed, sarcastic ≠ kind

cycle NOUN = **series of events**,
circle, revolution, rotation

cynic NOUN = **sceptic**, doubter,
pessimist, misanthrope,
misanthropist, scoffer

cynical ADJECTIVE 1 = **sceptical**,
mocking, pessimistic, scoffing,
contemptuous, scornful,
distrustful, derisive ≠ trusting
2 = **unbelieving**, sceptical,
disillusioned, pessimistic,
disbelieving, mistrustful
≠ optimistic

cynicism NOUN 1 = **scepticism**,
pessimism, misanthropy
2 = **disbelief**, doubt, scepticism,
mistrust

Dd

dab VERB 1 = **pat**, touch, tap
2 = **apply**, daub, stipple
▷ NOUN 1 = **spot**, bit, drop, pat, smudge, speck 2 = **touch**, stroke, flick

daft (chiefly Brit.) ADJECTIVE
1 = **stupid**, crazy, silly, absurd, foolish, idiotic, witless, crackpot (informal), off the air (Austral. slang)
2 (slang) = **crazy**, mad, touched, nuts (slang), crackers (Brit. slang), insane, demented, deranged, off the air (Austral. slang), porangi (N.Z.)

dag NOUN (N.Z. informal) = **joker**, comic, wag, wit, comedian, clown, humorist, prankster
▷ PHRASE: **rattle your dags** (N.Z. informal) = **hurry up**, get a move on, step on it (informal), get your skates on (informal), make haste

dagga NOUN (S. African) = **cannabis**, marijuana, pot (slang), dope (slang), hash (slang), grass (slang), weed (slang), hemp

daggy (Austral. & N.Z. informal) ADJECTIVE 1 = **untidy**, unkempt, dishevelled, tousled, disordered, messy, ruffled, scruffy, rumpled, bedraggled, ratty (informal), straggly, windblown, disarranged, mussed up (informal)
2 = **eccentric**, odd, strange, bizarre, weird, peculiar, abnormal, queer (informal), irregular, uncommon, quirky, singular, unconventional, idiosyncratic, off-the-wall (slang), outlandish, whimsical, rum (Brit. slang), capricious, anomalous, freakish, aberrant, wacko (slang), outré

daily ADJECTIVE = **everyday**, diurnal, quotidian
▷ ADVERB = **every day**, day by day, once a day

dam NOUN = **barrier**, wall, barrage, obstruction, embankment
▷ VERB = **block up**, restrict, hold back, barricade, obstruct

damage NOUN 1 = **destruction**, harm, loss, injury, suffering, hurt, ruin, devastation ≠ improvement
2 (informal) = **cost**, price, charge, bill, amount, payment, expense, outlay
▷ VERB = **spoil**, hurt, injure, harm, ruin, crush, devastate, wreck ≠ fix
▷ PLURAL NOUN (law) = **compensation**, fine, satisfaction, amends, reparation, restitution, reimbursement, atonement

damaging ADJECTIVE = **harmful**, detrimental, hurtful, ruinous, deleterious, injurious, disadvantageous ≠ helpful

dame NOUN with cap. = **lady**, baroness, dowager, grande dame (French), noblewoman, peeress

damn VERB = **criticize**, condemn, blast, denounce, put down, censure ≠ praise

damned ADJECTIVE (*slang*)
= **infernal**, detestable,
confounded, hateful, loathsome

damp ADJECTIVE = **moist**, wet,
soggy, humid, dank, sopping,
clammy, dewy ≠ dry

▷ NOUN = **moisture**, liquid,
drizzle, dampness, wetness,
dankness ≠ dryness

▷ VERB = **moisten**, wet, soak,
dampen, moisturize ▷ PHRASE:
damp something down = **curb**,
reduce, check, diminish, inhibit,
stifle, allay, pour cold water on

dampen VERB 1 = **reduce**, check,
moderate, dull, restrain, stifle,
lessen 2 = **moisten**, wet, spray,
make damp

dance VERB 1 = **prance**, trip,
hop, skip, sway, whirl, caper,
jig 2 = **caper**, trip, spring, jump,
bound, skip, frolic, cavort

▷ NOUN = **ball**, social, hop
(*informal*), disco, knees-up (*Brit.
informal*), discotheque, B and S
(*Austral. informal*)

dancer NOUN = **ballerina**,
Terpsichorean

danger NOUN 1 = **jeopardy**,
vulnerability 2 = **hazard**, risk,
threat, menace, peril, pitfall

dangerous ADJECTIVE = **perilous**,
risky, hazardous, vulnerable,
insecure, unsafe, precarious,
breakneck ≠ safe

dangerously ADVERB
= **perilously**, alarmingly,
precariously, recklessly, riskily,
hazardously, unsafely

dangle VERB 1 = **hang**, swing,
trail, sway, flap, hang down
2 = **offer**, flourish, brandish,
flaunt

dare VERB 1 = **risk doing**, venture,
presume, make bold (*archaic*),
hazard doing 2 = **challenge**,
provoke, defy, taunt, goad, throw
down the gauntlet

daring ADJECTIVE = **brave**, bold,
adventurous, reckless, fearless,
audacious, intrepid, daredevil
≠ timid

▷ NOUN = **bravery**, nerve
(*informal*), courage, spirit, bottle
(*Brit. slang*), pluck, audacity,
boldness ≠ timidity

dark ADJECTIVE 1 = **dim**, murky,
shady, shadowy, grey, dingy, unlit,
poorly lit 2 = **black**, brunette,
ebony, dark-skinned, sable, dusky,
swarthy ≠ fair 3 = **evil**, foul,
sinister, vile, wicked, infernal
4 = **secret**, hidden, mysterious,
concealed 5 = **gloomy**, sad,
grim, miserable, bleak, dismal,
pessimistic, melancholy
≠ cheerful

▷ NOUN 1 = **darkness**, shadows,
gloom, dusk, obscurity, murk,
dimness, semi-darkness

2 = **night**, twilight, evening, evo
(*Austral. slang*), dusk, night-time,
nightfall

darken VERB 1 = **cloud**, obscure,
dim, overshadow, blacken
≠ brighten 2 = **make dark**,
blacken

darkness NOUN = **dark**, shadows,
shade, gloom, blackness, murk,
duskiness

darling NOUN = **beloved**, love, dear, dearest, angel, treasure, precious, sweetheart
▷ ADJECTIVE = **beloved**, dear, treasured, precious, adored, cherished

dart VERB = **dash**, run, race, shoot, fly, speed, spring, tear

dash VERB 1 = **rush**, run, race, shoot, fly, career, speed, tear ≠ dawdle 2 = **throw**, cast, pitch, slam, toss, hurl, fling, chuck (informal) 3 = **crash**, break, smash, shatter, splinter
▷ NOUN 1 = **rush**, run, race, sprint, dart, spurt, sortie 2 = **drop**, little, bit, shot (informal), touch, spot, trace, hint ≠ lot 3 = **style**, spirit, flair, flourish, verve, panache, élan, brio

dashing ADJECTIVE (old-fashioned) = **stylish**, smart, elegant, flamboyant, sporty, jaunty, showy

data NOUN 1 = **details**, facts, figures, intelligence, statistics (computing) 2 = **information**

date NOUN 1 = **time**, stage, period 2 = **appointment**, meeting, arrangement, commitment, engagement, rendezvous, tryst, assignation 3 = **partner**, escort, friend
▷ VERB 1 = **put a date on**, assign a date to, fix the period of 2 = **become dated**, become old-fashioned ▷ PHRASE: date from or date back to (a time or date) = **come from**, belong to, originate in, exist from, bear a date of

dated ADJECTIVE = **old-fashioned**, outdated, out of date, obsolete, unfashionable, outmoded, passé, old hat ≠ modern

daunting ADJECTIVE = **intimidating**, alarming, frightening, discouraging, unnerving, disconcerting, demoralizing, off-putting (Brit. informal) ≠ reassuring

dawn NOUN 1 = **daybreak**, morning, sunrise, daylight, aurora (poetic), crack of dawn, sunup, cockcrow
2 (literary) = **beginning**, start, birth, rise, origin, emergence, advent, genesis
▷ VERB 1 = **begin**, start, rise, develop, emerge, unfold, originate 2 = **grow light**, break, brighten, lighten ▷ PHRASE: dawn on or upon someone = **hit**, strike, occur to, register (informal), become apparent, come to mind, come into your head

day NOUN 1 = **twenty-four hours** 2 = **daytime**, daylight 3 = **date** 4 = **time**, age, era, period, epoch

daylight NOUN = **sunlight**, sunshine, light of day

daze VERB = **stun**, shock, paralyse, numb, stupefy, benumb
▷ NOUN = **shock**, confusion, distraction, trance, bewilderment, stupor, trancelike state

dazzle VERB 1 = **impress**, amaze, overwhelm, astonish, overpower, bowl over (informal), take your breath away 2 = **blind**, confuse, daze, bedazzle

▷ NOUN = **splendour**, sparkle, glitter, brilliance, magnificence, razzmatazz (*slang*)

dazzling ADJECTIVE = **splendid**, brilliant, stunning, glorious, sparkling, glittering, sensational (*informal*), virtuoso ≠ ordinary

dead ADJECTIVE 1 = **deceased**, departed, late, perished, extinct, defunct, passed away ≠ alive **2** = **boring**, dull, dreary, flat, plain, humdrum, uninteresting **3** = **not working**, useless, inactive, inoperative ≠ working **4** = **numb**, frozen, paralysed, insensitive, inert, deadened, immobilized, unfeeling **5** (*of a centre, silence, or a stop*) = **total**, complete, absolute, utter, outright, thorough, unqualified **6** (*informal*) = **exhausted**, tired, worn out, spent, done in (*informal*), all in (*slang*), drained, knackered (*slang*)

▷ NOUN = **middle**, heart, depth, midst

▷ ADVERB = **exactly**, completely, totally, directly, fully, entirely, absolutely, thoroughly

deadline NOUN = **time limit**, cutoff point, target date *or* time, limit

deadlock NOUN 1 = **impasse**, stalemate, standstill, gridlock, standoff **2** = **tie**, draw, stalemate, impasse, standstill, gridlock, standoff, dead heat

deadly ADJECTIVE 1 = **lethal**, fatal, deathly, dangerous, devastating, mortal, murderous, malignant

2 (*informal*) = **boring**, dull, tedious, flat, monotonous, uninteresting, mind-numbing, wearisome

deaf ADJECTIVE 1 = **hard of hearing**, without hearing, stone deaf **2** = **oblivious**, indifferent, unmoved, unconcerned, unsympathetic, impervious, unhearing

▷ *see* **disabled**

deal NOUN 1 (*informal*) = **agreement**, understanding, contract, arrangement, bargain, transaction, pact **2** = **amount**, quantity, measure, degree, mass, volume, share, portion

▷ PHRASES: **deal in something** = **sell**, trade in, stock, traffic in, buy and sell; **deal something out** = **distribute**, give, share, assign, allocate, dispense, allot, mete out; **deal with something** = **be concerned with**, involve, concern, touch, regard, apply to, bear on, pertain to; **deal with something** *or* **someone** = **handle**, manage, treat, cope with, take care of, see to, attend to, get to grips with

dealer NOUN = **trader**, merchant, supplier, wholesaler, purveyor, tradesman

dear ADJECTIVE 1 = **beloved**, close, valued, favourite, prized, treasured, precious, intimate ≠ hated **2** = **expensive**, costly, high-priced, pricey (*informal*), at a premium, overpriced, exorbitant ≠ cheap

▷ NOUN = **darling**, love, dearest, angel, treasure, precious, beloved, loved one

dearly ADVERB 1 = **very much**, greatly, extremely, profoundly 2 = **at great cost**, at a high price

death NOUN 1 = **dying**, demise, end, passing, departure ≠ birth 2 = **destruction**, finish, ruin, undoing, extinction, downfall ≠ beginning ▷ RELATED WORDS: *adjectives* fatal, lethal, mortal

deathly ADJECTIVE = **deathlike**, white, pale, ghastly, wan, pallid, ashen

debacle *or* **débâcle** NOUN = **disaster**, catastrophe, fiasco

debate NOUN = **discussion**, talk, argument, dispute, analysis, conversation, controversy, dialogue ▷ VERB 1 = **discuss**, question, talk about, argue about, dispute, examine, deliberate 2 = **consider**, reflect, think about, weigh, contemplate, deliberate, ponder, ruminate

debris NOUN = **remains**, bits, waste, ruins, fragments, rubble, wreckage, detritus

debt NOUN = **debit**, commitment, obligation, liability ▷ PHRASE: **in debt** = **owing**, liable, in the red (*informal*), in arrears

debtor NOUN = **borrower**, mortgagor

debut NOUN 1 = **entrance**, beginning, launch, introduction, first appearance 2 = **presentation**, coming out, introduction, first appearance, initiation

decay VERB 1 = **rot**, spoil, crumble, deteriorate, perish, decompose, moulder, go bad 2 = **decline**, diminish, crumble, deteriorate, fall off, dwindle, lessen, wane ≠ grow ▷ NOUN 1 = **rot**, corruption, mould, blight, decomposition, gangrene, canker, caries 2 = **decline**, collapse, deterioration, failing, fading, degeneration ≠ growth

deceased ADJECTIVE = **dead**, late, departed, expired, defunct, lifeless

deceive VERB = **take in**, trick, fool (*informal*), cheat, con (*informal*), mislead, dupe, swindle, scam (*slang*)

decency NOUN 1 = **propriety**, correctness, decorum, respectability, etiquette 2 = **courtesy**, politeness, civility, graciousness, urbanity, courteousness

decent ADJECTIVE 1 = **satisfactory**, fair, all right, reasonable, sufficient, good enough, adequate, ample ≠ unsatisfactory 2 = **proper**, becoming, seemly, fitting, appropriate, suitable, respectable, befitting ≠ improper 3 (*informal*) = **good**, kind, friendly, neighbourly, generous, helpful, obliging, accommodating 4 = **respectable**, pure, proper, modest, chaste, decorous

deception NOUN 1 = **trickery**,

fraud, deceit, cunning, treachery, guile, legerdemain ≠ honesty **2** = **trick**, lie, bluff, hoax, decoy, ruse, subterfuge, fastie (*Austral. slang*)

decide VERB **1** = **make a decision**, make up your mind, reach *or* come to a decision, choose, determine, conclude ≠ hesitate **2** = **resolve**, answer, determine, conclude, clear up, ordain, adjudicate, adjudge **3** = **settle**, determine, resolve

decidedly ADVERB = **definitely**, clearly, positively, distinctly, downright, unequivocally, unmistakably

decision NOUN **1** = **judgment**, finding, ruling, sentence, resolution, conclusion, verdict, decree **2** = **decisiveness**, purpose, resolution, resolve, determination, firmness, forcefulness, strength of mind *or* will

decisive ADJECTIVE **1** = **crucial**, significant, critical, influential, momentous, conclusive, fateful ≠ uncertain **2** = **resolute**, decided, firm, determined, forceful, incisive, trenchant, strong-minded ≠ indecisive

deck VERB = **decorate**, dress, clothe, array, adorn, embellish, festoon, beautify

declaration NOUN
1 = **announcement**, proclamation, decree, notice, notification, edict, pronouncement **2** = **affirmation**,

profession, assertion, revelation, disclosure, acknowledgment, protestation, avowal **3** = **statement**, testimony

declare VERB **1** = **state**, claim, announce, voice, express, maintain, assert, proclaim **2** = **testify**, state, swear, assert, affirm, bear witness, vouch **3** = **make known**, reveal, show, broadcast, confess, communicate, disclose

decline VERB **1** = **fall**, drop, lower, sink, fade, shrink, diminish, decrease ≠ rise **2** = **deteriorate**, weaken, pine, decay, worsen, languish, degenerate, droop ≠ improve **3** = **refuse**, reject, turn down, avoid, spurn, abstain, say 'no' ≠ accept
▷ NOUN **1** = **depression**, recession, slump, falling off, downturn, dwindling, lessening ≠ rise **2** = **deterioration**, failing, weakening, decay, worsening, degeneration ≠ improvement

decor *or* **décor** NOUN = **decoration**, colour scheme, ornamentation, furnishing style

decorate VERB **1** = **adorn**, trim, embroider, ornament, embellish, festoon, beautify, grace **2** = **do up**, paper, paint, wallpaper, renovate (*informal*), furbish **3** = **pin a medal on**, cite, confer an honour on *or* upon

decoration NOUN
1 = **adornment**, trimming, enhancement, elaboration, embellishment, ornamentation,

beautification 2 = **ornament**, trimmings, garnish, frill, bauble 3 = **medal**, award, star, ribbon, badge

decorative ADJECTIVE = **ornamental**, fancy, pretty, attractive, for show, embellishing, showy, beautifying

decrease VERB 1 = **drop**, decline, lessen, lower, shrink, diminish, dwindle, subside 2 = **reduce**, cut, lower, moderate, weaken, diminish, cut down, shorten ≠ increase
▷ NOUN = **lessening**, decline, reduction, loss, falling off, dwindling, contraction, cutback ≠ growth

decree NOUN 1 = **law**, order, ruling, act, command, statute, proclamation, edict 2 = **judgment**, finding, ruling, decision, verdict, arbitration
▷ VERB = **order**, rule, command, demand, proclaim, prescribe, pronounce, ordain

dedicate VERB 1 = **devote**, give, apply, commit, pledge, surrender, give over to 2 = **offer**, address, inscribe

dedicated ADJECTIVE = **committed**, devoted, enthusiastic, single-minded, zealous, purposeful, wholehearted ≠ indifferent

dedication NOUN 1 = **commitment**, loyalty, devotion, allegiance, adherence, single-mindedness, faithfulness, wholeheartedness ≠ indifference

2 = **inscription**, message, address

deduct VERB = **subtract**, remove, take off, take away, reduce by, knock off (*informal*), decrease by ≠ add

deduction NOUN 1 = **conclusion**, finding, verdict, judgment, assumption, inference 2 = **reasoning**, thinking, thought, analysis, logic 3 = **discount**, reduction, cut, concession, decrease, rebate, diminution 4 = **subtraction**, reduction, concession

deed NOUN 1 = **action**, act, performance, achievement, exploit, feat 2 (*law*) = **document**, title, contract

deep ADJECTIVE 1 = **big**, wide, broad, profound, yawning, bottomless, unfathomable ≠ shallow 2 = **intense**, great, serious (*informal*), acute, extreme, grave, profound, heartfelt ≠ superficial = **sound**, profound, unbroken, undisturbed, untroubled 3 *with* **in** = **absorbed in**, lost in, gripped by, preoccupied with, immersed in, engrossed in, rapt by 4 = **dark**, strong, rich, intense, vivid ≠ light 5 = **low**, booming, bass, resonant, sonorous, low-pitched ≠ high 6 = **secret**, hidden, mysterious, obscure, abstract, esoteric, mystifying, arcane
▷ NOUN = **middle**, heart, midst, dead
▷ ADVERB = **far**, a long way, a good way, miles, a great distance

▷ **PHRASE**: **the deep** (*poetic*) = **the ocean**, the sea, the waves, the main, the high seas, the briny (*informal*)

deepen VERB 1 = **intensify**, increase, grow, strengthen, reinforce, escalate, magnify 2 = **dig out**, excavate, scoop out, hollow out

deeply ADVERB = **thoroughly**, completely, seriously, sadly, severely, gravely, profoundly, intensely

de facto ADVERB = **in fact**, really, actually, in effect, in reality ▷ **ADJECTIVE** = **actual**, real, existing

default NOUN 1 = **failure**, neglect, deficiency, lapse, omission, dereliction 2 = **nonpayment**, evasion ▷ **VERB** = **fail to pay**, dodge, evade, neglect

defeat VERB 1 = **beat**, crush, overwhelm, conquer, master, rout, trounce, vanquish ≠ surrender 2 = **frustrate**, foil, thwart, ruin, baffle, confound, balk, get the better of ▷ **NOUN** 1 = **conquest**, beating, overthrow, rout ≠ victory 2 = **frustration**, failure, reverse, setback, thwarting

defect NOUN = **deficiency**, failing, fault, error, flaw, imperfection ▷ **VERB** = **desert**, rebel, quit, revolt, change sides

defence *or* (*U.S.*) **defense** NOUN 1 = **protection**, cover, security, guard, shelter, safeguard,

immunity 2 = **armaments**, weapons 3 = **argument**, explanation, excuse, plea, justification, vindication, rationalization 4 = **plea** (*law*), testimony, denial, alibi, rebuttal ▷ **PLURAL NOUN** = **shield**, barricade, fortification, buttress, rampart, bulwark, fortified pa (*N.Z.*)

defend VERB 1 = **protect**, cover, guard, screen, preserve, look after, shelter, shield 2 = **support**, champion, justify, endorse, uphold, vindicate, stand up for, speak up for

defendant NOUN = **accused**, respondent, prisoner at the bar

defender NOUN 1 = **supporter**, champion, advocate, sponsor, follower 2 = **protector**, guard, guardian, escort, bodyguard

defensive ADJECTIVE 1 = **protective**, watchful, on the defensive, on guard 2 = **oversensitive**, uptight (*informal*)

defer VERB = **postpone**, delay, put off, suspend, shelve, hold over, procrastinate, put on ice (*informal*)

defiance NOUN = **resistance**, opposition, confrontation, contempt, disregard, disobedience, insolence, insubordination ≠ obedience

defiant ADJECTIVE = **resisting**, rebellious, daring, bold, provocative, audacious, antagonistic, insolent ≠ obedient

deficiency NOUN 1 = **lack**, want, deficit, absence, shortage, scarcity, dearth ≠ sufficiency 2 = **failing**, fault, weakness, defect, flaw, drawback, shortcoming, imperfection

deficit NOUN = **shortfall**, shortage, deficiency, loss, arrears

define VERB 1 = **mark out**, outline, limit, bound, delineate, circumscribe, demarcate 2 = **describe**, interpret, characterize, explain, spell out, expound 3 = **establish**, specify, designate

definite ADJECTIVE 1 = **specific**, exact, precise, clear, particular, fixed, black-and-white, cut-and-dried (*informal*) ≠ vague 2 = **clear**, black-and-white, unequivocal, unambiguous, guaranteed, cut-and-dried (*informal*) 3 = **noticeable**, marked, clear, decided, striking, particular, distinct, conspicuous 4 = **certain**, decided, sure, settled, convinced, positive, confident, assured ≠ uncertain

definitely ADVERB = **certainly**, clearly, surely, absolutely, positively, without doubt, unquestionably, undeniably

definition NOUN 1 = **description**, interpretation, explanation, clarification, exposition, elucidation, statement of meaning 2 = **sharpness**, focus, clarity, contrast, precision, distinctness

definitive ADJECTIVE 1 = **final**, convincing, absolute, clinching, decisive, definite, conclusive, irrefutable 2 = **authoritative**, greatest, ultimate, reliable, exhaustive, superlative

deflect VERB = **turn aside**, bend

defy VERB = **resist**, oppose, confront, brave, disregard, stand up to, spurn, flout

degenerate VERB = **decline**, slip, sink, decrease, deteriorate, worsen, decay, lapse ▷ ADJECTIVE = **depraved**, corrupt, low, perverted, immoral, decadent, debauched, dissolute

degrade VERB = **demean**, disgrace, humiliate, shame, humble, discredit, debase, dishonour ≠ ennoble

degree NOUN = **amount**, stage, grade

delay VERB 1 = **put off**, suspend, postpone, shelve, defer, hold over 2 = **hold up**, detain, hold back, hinder, obstruct, impede, bog down, set back ≠ speed (up) ▷ NOUN = **hold-up**, wait, setback, interruption, stoppage, impediment, hindrance

delegate NOUN = **representative**, agent, deputy, ambassador, commissioner, envoy, proxy, legate ▷ VERB 1 = **entrust**, transfer, hand over, give, pass on, assign, consign, devolve 2 = **appoint**, commission, select, contract, engage, nominate, designate, mandate

delegation NOUN

d

1 = **deputation**, envoys, contingent, commission, embassy, legation
2 = **commissioning**, assignment, devolution, committal

delete VERB = **remove**, cancel, erase, strike out, obliterate, efface, cross out, expunge

deliberate ADJECTIVE
1 = **intentional**, meant, planned, intended, conscious, calculated, wilful, purposeful ≠ accidental
2 = **careful**, measured, slow, cautious, thoughtful, circumspect, methodical, unhurried ≠ hurried
▷ VERB = **consider**, think, ponder, discuss, debate, reflect, consult, weigh

deliberately ADVERB
= **intentionally**, on purpose, consciously, knowingly, wilfully, by design, in cold blood, wittingly

deliberation NOUN
1 = **consideration**, thought, reflection, calculation, meditation, forethought, circumspection
2 usually plural = **discussion**, talk, conference, debate, analysis, conversation, dialogue, consultation

delicacy NOUN 1 = **fragility**, flimsiness 2 = **daintiness**, charm, grace, elegance, neatness, prettiness, slenderness, exquisiteness 3 = **difficulty**
4 = **sensitivity**, understanding, consideration, diplomacy, discretion, tact, thoughtfulness,

sensitiveness 5 = **treat**, luxury, savoury, dainty, morsel, titbit
6 = **lightness**, accuracy, precision, elegance, sensibility, purity, subtlety, refinement

delicate ADJECTIVE 1 = **fine**, elegant, exquisite, graceful
2 = **subtle**, fine, delicious, faint, refined, understated, dainty
≠ bright 3 = **fragile**, weak, frail, brittle, tender, flimsy, dainty, breakable 4 = **skilled**, precise, deft 5 = **diplomatic**, sensitive, thoughtful, discreet, considerate, tactful ≠ insensitive

delicious ADJECTIVE = **delectable**, tasty, choice, savoury, dainty, mouthwatering, scrumptious (informal), appetizing, lekker (S. African slang), yummo (Austral. slang) ≠ unpleasant

delight VERB = **please**, satisfy, thrill, charm, cheer, amuse, enchant, gratify ≠ displease
▷ PHRASE: **delight in** or **take a delight in something** or **someone** = **like**, love, enjoy, appreciate, relish, savour, revel in, take pleasure in NOUN = **pleasure**, joy, satisfaction, happiness, ecstasy, enjoyment, bliss, glee ≠ displeasure

delightful ADJECTIVE = **pleasant**, charming, thrilling, enjoyable, enchanting, agreeable, pleasurable, rapturous ≠ unpleasant

deliver VERB 1 = **bring**, carry, bear, transport, distribute, convey,

cart **2** *sometimes with* **over** *or*
up = **hand over**, commit, give
up, yield, surrender, turn over,
relinquish, make over **3** = **give**,
read, present, announce, declare,
utter **4** = **strike**, give, deal,
launch, direct, aim, administer,
inflict **5** = **release**, free, save,
rescue, loose, liberate, ransom,
emancipate

delivery NOUN **1** = **handing
over**, transfer, distribution,
transmission, dispatch,
consignment, conveyance
2 = **consignment**, goods,
shipment, batch **3** = **speech**,
utterance, articulation,
intonation, elocution,
enunciation **4** = **childbirth**,
labour, confinement, parturition

delusion NOUN = **misconception**,
mistaken idea, misapprehension,
fancy, illusion, hallucination,
fallacy, false impression

demand VERB **1** = **request**, ask
(for), order, expect, claim, seek,
insist on, exact **2** = **challenge**,
ask, question, inquire **3** = **require**,
want, need, involve, call for,
entail, necessitate, cry out for
≠ provide
▷ NOUN **1** = **request**, order
2 = **need**, want, call, market,
claim, requirement

demanding ADJECTIVE = **difficult**,
trying, hard, taxing, wearing,
challenging, tough, exacting
≠ easy

demise NOUN **1** = **failure**, end, fall,
defeat, collapse, ruin, breakdown,

overthrow **2** (*euphemistic*)
= **death**, end, dying, passing,
departure, decease

democracy NOUN = **self-
government**, republic,
commonwealth

Democrat NOUN = **left-winger**

democratic ADJECTIVE
= **self-governing**, popular,
representative, autonomous,
populist, egalitarian

demolish VERB **1** = **knock down**,
level, destroy, dismantle, flatten,
tear down, bulldoze, raze ≠ build
2 = **destroy**, wreck, overturn,
overthrow, undo

demolition NOUN = **knocking
down**, levelling, destruction,
explosion, wrecking, tearing
down, bulldozing, razing

demon NOUN **1** = **evil spirit**, devil,
fiend, goblin, ghoul, malignant
spirit, atua (*N.Z.*), wairua (*N.Z.*)
2 = **wizard**, master, ace (*informal*),
fiend

demonstrate VERB **1** = **prove**,
show, indicate, make clear,
manifest, testify to, flag up
2 = **show**, express, display,
indicate, exhibit, manifest, flag up
3 = **march**, protest, rally, object,
parade, picket, remonstrate,
express disapproval, hikoi (*N.Z.*)
4 = **describe**, show, explain,
teach, illustrate

demonstration NOUN
1 = **march**, protest, rally, sit-in,
parade, picket, mass lobby,
hikoi (*N.Z.*) **2** = **display**, show,
performance, explanation,

description, presentation, exposition **3** = **indication**, proof, testimony, confirmation, substantiation **4** = **exhibition**, display, expression, illustration

den NOUN **1** = **lair**, hole, shelter, cave, haunt, cavern, hide-out **2** (*chiefly U.S.*) = **study**, retreat, sanctuary, hideaway, sanctum, cubbyhole

denial NOUN **1** = **negation**, contradiction, dissent, retraction, repudiation ≠ admission **2** = **refusal**, veto, rejection, prohibition, rebuff, repulse

denomination NOUN **1** = **religious group**, belief, sect, persuasion, creed, school, hauhau (*N.Z.*) **2** = **unit**, value, size, grade

denounce VERB **1** = **condemn**, attack, censure, revile, vilify, stigmatize **2** = **report**, dob in (*Austral. slang*)

dense ADJECTIVE **1** = **thick**, heavy, solid, compact, condensed, impenetrable, close-knit ≠ thin **2** = **heavy**, thick, opaque, impenetrable **3** = **stupid** (*informal*), thick, dull, dumb (*informal*), dozy (*Brit. informal*), stolid, dopey (*informal*), moronic ≠ bright

density NOUN **1** = **tightness**, thickness, compactness, impenetrability, denseness **2** = **mass**, bulk, consistency, solidity

dent NOUN = **hollow**, chip, indentation, depression, impression, pit, dip, crater, ding

(*Austral. & N.Z. dated, informal*) ▷ VERB = **make a dent in**, press in, gouge, hollow, push in

deny VERB **1** = **contradict**, disagree with, rebuff, negate, rebut, refute ≠ admit **2** = **renounce**, reject, retract, repudiate, disown, recant, disclaim **3** = **refuse**, forbid, reject, rule out, turn down, prohibit, withhold, preclude ≠ permit

depart VERB **1** = **leave**, go, withdraw, retire, disappear, quit, retreat, exit, rack off (*Austral. & N.Z. slang*) ≠ arrive **2** = **deviate**, vary, differ, stray, veer, swerve, diverge, digress

department NOUN = **section**, office, unit, station, division, branch, bureau, subdivision

departure NOUN **1** = **leaving**, going, retirement, withdrawal, exit, going away, removal, exodus ≠ arrival **2** = **retirement**, going, withdrawal, exit, going away, removal **3** = **shift**, change, difference, variation, innovation, novelty, deviation, divergence

dependent *or* (*U.S. sometimes*) **dependant** ADJECTIVE **1** = **reliant**, vulnerable, helpless, powerless, weak, defenceless ≠ independent **2** = **determined by**, depending on, subject to, influenced by, conditional on, contingent on ▷ PHRASE: **dependent on** *or* **upon** = **reliant on**, relying on

depend on VERB **1** = **be determined by**, be based on, be subject to, hang on, rest on, revolve around, hinge on, be subordinate to **2** = **count on**, turn to, trust in, bank on, lean on, rely upon, reckon on

depict VERB **1** = **illustrate**, portray, picture, paint, outline, draw, sketch, delineate **2** = **describe**, present, represent, outline, characterize

deplete VERB = **use up**, reduce, drain, exhaust, consume, empty, lessen, impoverish ≠ increase

deplore VERB = **disapprove of**, condemn, object to, denounce, censure, abhor, take a dim view of

deploy VERB (*troops or military resources*) = **use**, station, position, arrange, set out, utilize

deployment NOUN (*of troops or military resources*) = **use**, stationing, spread, organization, arrangement, positioning, utilization

deport VERB = **expel**, exile, throw out, oust, banish, expatriate, extradite, evict

depose VERB = **oust**, dismiss, displace, demote, dethrone, remove from office

deposit VERB **1** = **put**, place, lay, drop **2** = **store**, keep, put, bank, lodge, entrust, consign
▷ NOUN **1** = **down payment**, security, stake, pledge, instalment, retainer, part payment **2** = **accumulation**, mass, build-up, layer
3 = **sediment**, grounds, residue, lees, precipitate, silt, dregs

depot NOUN **1** = **arsenal**, warehouse, storehouse, repository, depository **2** (*U.S. & Canad.*) = **bus station**, station, garage, terminus

depreciation NOUN = **devaluation**, fall, drop, depression, slump, deflation

depress VERB **1** = **sadden**, upset, distress, discourage, grieve, oppress, weigh down, make sad ≠ cheer **2** = **lower**, cut, reduce, diminish, decrease, lessen ≠ raise **3** = **devalue**, depreciate, cheapen **4** = **press down**, push, squeeze, lower, flatten, compress, push down

depressed ADJECTIVE **1** = **sad**, blue, unhappy, discouraged, fed up, mournful, dejected, despondent **2** = **poverty-stricken**, poor, deprived, disadvantaged, rundown, impoverished, needy **3** = **lowered**, devalued, weakened, depreciated, cheapened **4** = **sunken**, hollow, recessed, indented, concave

depressing ADJECTIVE = **bleak**, sad, discouraging, gloomy, dismal, harrowing, saddening, dispiriting

depression NOUN **1** = **despair**, misery, sadness, dumps (*informal*), the blues, melancholy, unhappiness, despondency **2** = **recession**, slump, economic decline, stagnation, inactivity, hard *or* bad times **3** = **hollow**, pit, dip, bowl, valley, dent, cavity, indentation

d

deprivation NOUN 1 = **lack**, denial, withdrawal, removal, expropriation, dispossession 2 = **want**, need, hardship, suffering, distress, privation, destitution

deprive VERB = **dispossess**, rob, strip, despoil, bereave

deprived ADJECTIVE = **poor**, disadvantaged, needy, in need, lacking, bereft, destitute, down at heel ≠ prosperous

depth NOUN 1 = **deepness**, drop, measure, extent 2 = **insight**, wisdom, penetration, profundity, discernment, sagacity, astuteness, profoundness ≠ superficiality 3 = **breadth**

deputy NOUN = **substitute**, representative, delegate, lieutenant, proxy, surrogate, second-in-command, legate

derelict ADJECTIVE = **abandoned**, deserted, ruined, neglected, discarded, forsaken, dilapidated ▷ NOUN = **tramp**, outcast, drifter, down-and-out, vagrant, bag lady, derro (*Austral. slang*)

descend VERB 1 = **fall**, drop, sink, go down, plunge, dive, tumble, plummet ≠ rise = **get off** 2 = **go down**, come down, walk down, move down, climb down 3 = **slope**, dip, incline, slant ▷ PHRASE: be descended from = **originate from**, derive from, spring from, proceed from, issue from

descent NOUN 1 = **fall**, drop, plunge, coming down, swoop 2 = **slope**, drop, dip, incline, slant, declivity 3 = **decline**, deterioration, degeneration 4 = **origin**, extraction, ancestry, lineage, family tree, parentage, genealogy, derivation

describe VERB 1 = **relate**, tell, report, explain, express, recount, recite, narrate 2 = **portray**, depict 3 = **trace**, draw, outline, mark out, delineate

description NOUN 1 = **account**, report, explanation, representation, sketch, narrative, portrayal, depiction 2 = **calling**, naming, branding, labelling, dubbing, designation 3 = **kind**, sort, type, order, class, variety, brand, category

desert¹ NOUN = **wilderness**, waste, wilds, wasteland

desert² VERB 1 = **abandon**, leave, quit (*informal*), forsake 2 = **leave**, abandon, strand, maroon, walk out on (*informal*), forsake, jilt, leave stranded ≠ take care of 3 = **abscond**

deserted ADJECTIVE 1 = **empty**, abandoned, desolate, neglected, vacant, derelict, unoccupied 2 = **abandoned**, neglected, forsaken

deserve VERB = **merit**, warrant, be entitled to, have a right to, rate, earn, justify, be worthy of

deserved ADJECTIVE = **well-earned**, fitting, due, earned, justified, merited, proper, warranted

deserving ADJECTIVE = **worthy**,

righteous, commendable,
laudable, praiseworthy,
meritorious, estimable
≠ undeserving

design VERB 1 = **plan**, draw,
draft, trace, outline, devise,
sketch, formulate 2 = **create**,
plan, fashion, propose, invent,
conceive, originate, fabricate
3 = **intend**, mean, plan, aim,
purpose
▷ NOUN 1 = **pattern**, form,
style, shape, organization,
arrangement, construction
2 = **plan**, drawing, model, scheme,
draft, outline, sketch, blueprint
3 = **intention**, end, aim, goal,
target, purpose, object, objective

designate VERB 1 = **name**,
call, term, style, label, entitle,
dub 2 = **choose**, reserve, select,
label, flag, assign, allocate,
set aside 3 = **appoint**, name,
choose, commission, select, elect,
delegate, nominate

designer NOUN 1 = **couturier**
2 = **producer**, architect, deviser,
creator, planner, inventor,
originator

desirable ADJECTIVE
1 = **advantageous**, useful,
valuable, helpful, profitable, of
service, convenient, worthwhile
≠ disadvantageous = **popular**
≠ unpopular 2 = **attractive**,
appealing, pretty, fair, inviting,
lovely, charming, sexy (*informal*)
≠ unattractive

desire VERB = **want**, long for,
crave, hope for, ache for, wish for,

yearn for, thirst for
▷ NOUN 1 = **wish**, want, longing,
hope, urge, aspiration, craving,
thirst 2 = **lust**, passion, libido,
appetite, lasciviousness,
lonesome (*chiefly U.S. & Canad.*)

despair VERB = **lose hope**, give up,
lose heart
▷ NOUN = **despondency**,
depression, misery, gloom,
desperation, anguish,
hopelessness, dejection

despatch ▷ *see* dispatch

desperate ADJECTIVE 1 = **grave**,
pressing, serious, severe, extreme,
urgent, drastic 2 = **last-ditch**,
daring, furious, risky, frantic,
audacious

desperately ADVERB = **gravely**,
badly, seriously, severely,
dangerously, perilously

desperation NOUN 1 = **misery**,
worry, trouble, despair,
agony, anguish, unhappiness,
hopelessness 2 = **recklessness**,
madness, frenzy, impetuosity,
rashness, foolhardiness

despise VERB = **look down on**,
loathe, scorn, detest, revile, abhor
≠ admire

despite PREPOSITION = **in spite of**,
in the face of, regardless of, even
with, notwithstanding, in the
teeth of, undeterred by

destination NOUN = **stop**,
station, haven, resting-place,
terminus, journey's end

destined ADJECTIVE = **fated**,
meant, intended, certain, bound,
doomed, predestined

d

destiny NOUN 1 = **fate**, fortune, lot, portion, doom, nemesis 2 *usually cap.* = **fortune**, chance, karma, providence, kismet, predestination, divine will

destroy VERB 1 = **ruin**, crush, devastate, wreck, shatter, wipe out, demolish, eradicate 2 = **slaughter**, kill

destruction NOUN 1 = **ruin**, havoc, wreckage, demolition, devastation, annihilation 2 slaughter, extermination, eradication

destructive ADJECTIVE = **devastating**, fatal, deadly, lethal, harmful, damaging, catastrophic, ruinous

detach VERB 1 = **separate**, remove, divide, cut off, sever, disconnect, tear off, disengage ≠ attach 2 = **free**, remove, separate, isolate, cut off, disengage

detached ADJECTIVE 1 = **objective**, neutral, impartial, reserved, impersonal, disinterested, unbiased, dispassionate ≠ subjective 2 = **separate**, disconnected, discrete, unconnected, undivided

detachment NOUN 1 = **indifference**, fairness, neutrality, objectivity, impartiality, coolness, remoteness, nonchalance 2 (*military*) = **unit**, party, force, body, squad, patrol, task force

detail NOUN 1 = **point**, fact, feature, particular, respect, factor, element, aspect 2 = **fine point**, particular, nicety, triviality 3 (*military*) = **party**, force, body, duty, squad, assignment, fatigue, detachment
▷ VERB = **list**, relate, catalogue, recount, rehearse, recite, enumerate, itemize

detailed ADJECTIVE = **comprehensive**, full, complete, minute, particular, thorough, exhaustive, all-embracing ≠ brief

detain VERB 1 = **hold**, arrest, confine, restrain, imprison, intern, take prisoner, hold in custody 2 = **delay**, hold up, hamper, hinder, retard, impede, keep back, slow up *or* down

detect VERB 1 = **discover**, find, uncover, track down, unmask 2 = **notice**, see, spot, note, identify, observe, recognize, perceive

detective NOUN = **investigator**, cop (*slang*), private eye, sleuth (*informal*), private investigator, gumshoe (*U.S. slang*)

detention NOUN = **imprisonment**, custody, quarantine, confinement, incarceration ≠ release

deter VERB 1 = **discourage**, inhibit, put off, frighten, intimidate, dissuade, talk out of 2 = **prevent**, stop

deteriorate VERB = **decline**, worsen, degenerate, slump, go downhill ≠ improve

determination NOUN = **resolution**, purpose, resolve,

dedication, fortitude, persistence, tenacity, perseverance
≠ indecision

determine VERB 1 = **affect**, decide, regulate, ordain
2 = **settle**, learn, establish, discover, find out, work out, detect, verify 3 = **decide on**, choose, elect, resolve 4 = **decide**, conclude, resolve, make up your mind

determined ADJECTIVE
= **resolute**, firm, dogged, intent, persistent, persevering, single-minded, tenacious

deterrent NOUN
= **discouragement**, obstacle, curb, restraint, impediment, check, hindrance, disincentive
≠ incentive

devastate VERB = **destroy**, ruin, sack, wreck, demolish, level, ravage, raze

devastation NOUN
= **destruction**, ruin, havoc, demolition, desolation

develop VERB 1 = **grow**, advance, progress, mature, evolve, flourish, ripen 2 = **establish**, set up, promote, generate, undertake, initiate, embark on, cultivate
3 = **form**, establish, breed, generate, originate 4 = **expand**, extend, work out, elaborate, unfold, enlarge, broaden, amplify

development NOUN 1 = **growth**, increase, advance, progress, spread, expansion, evolution, enlargement 2 = **establishment**, forming, generation, institution,

invention, initiation, inauguration, instigation
3 = **event**, happening, result, incident, improvement, evolution, unfolding, occurrence

deviant ADJECTIVE = **perverted**, sick (*informal*), twisted, warped, kinky (*slang*) ≠ normal
▷ NOUN = **pervert**, freak, misfit

device NOUN 1 = **gadget**, machine, tool, instrument, implement, appliance, apparatus, contraption 2 = **ploy**, scheme, plan, trick, manoeuvre, gambit, stratagem, wile

devil NOUN 1 = **evil spirit**, demon, fiend, atua (*N.Z.*), wairua (*N.Z.*)
2 = **brute**, monster, beast, barbarian, fiend, terror, swine, ogre 3 = **person**, individual, soul, creature, thing, beggar
4 = **scamp**, rogue, rascal, scoundrel, scallywag (*informal*), nointer (*Austral. slang*) ▷ PHRASE: **the Devil** = **Satan**, Lucifer, Prince of Darkness, Mephistopheles, Evil One, Beelzebub, Old Nick (*informal*)

devise VERB = **work out**, design, construct, invent, conceive, formulate, contrive, dream up

devoid ADJECTIVE *with of*
= **lacking in**, without, free from, wanting in, bereft of, empty of, deficient in

devote VERB = **dedicate**, give, commit, apply, reserve, pledge, surrender, assign

devoted ADJECTIVE = **dedicated**, committed, true, constant, loyal, faithful, ardent, staunch ≠ disloyal

devotee NOUN = **enthusiast**, fan, supporter, follower, admirer, buff (*informal*), fanatic, adherent

devotion NOUN 1 = **love**, passion, affection, attachment, fondness 2 = **dedication**, commitment, loyalty, allegiance, fidelity, adherence, constancy, faithfulness ≠ indifference 3 = **worship**, reverence, spirituality, holiness, piety, godliness, devoutness ≠ irreverence
▷ PLURAL NOUN = **prayers**, religious observance, church service, divine office

devour VERB 1 = **eat**, consume, swallow, wolf, gulp, gobble, guzzle, polish off (*informal*) 2 = **enjoy**, take in, read compulsively *or* voraciously

devout ADJECTIVE = **religious**, godly, pious, pure, holy, orthodox, saintly, reverent ≠ irreverent

diagnose VERB = **identify**, determine, recognize, distinguish, interpret, pronounce, pinpoint

diagnosis NOUN = **identification**, discovery, recognition, detection

diagram NOUN = **plan**, figure, drawing, chart, representation, sketch, graph

dialogue NOUN 1 = **discussion**, conference, exchange, debate 2 = **conversation**, discussion, communication, discourse

diary NOUN 1 = **journal**, chronicle,

blog (*informal*) 2 = **engagement book**, Filofax (*trademark*), appointment book

dictate VERB = **speak**, say, utter, read out
▷ NOUN 1 = **command**, order, decree, demand, direction, injunction, fiat, edict 2 = **principle**, law, rule, standard, code, criterion, maxim ▷ PHRASE: **dictate to someone** = **order (about)**, direct, lay down the law, pronounce to

dictator NOUN = **absolute ruler**, tyrant, despot, oppressor, autocrat, absolutist, martinet

dictatorship NOUN = **absolute rule**, tyranny, totalitarianism, authoritarianism, despotism, autocracy, absolutism

dictionary NOUN = **wordbook**, vocabulary, glossary, lexicon

die VERB 1 = **pass away**, expire, perish, croak (*slang*), give up the ghost, snuff it (*slang*), peg out (*informal*), kick the bucket (*slang*), cark it (*Austral. & N.Z. slang*) ≠ live 2 = **stop**, fail, halt, break down, run down, stop working, peter out, fizzle out 3 = **dwindle**, decline, sink, fade, diminish, decrease, decay, wither ≠ increase ▷ PHRASE: **be dying for something** = **long for**, want, desire, crave, yearn for, hunger for, pine for, hanker after

diet¹ NOUN 1 = **food**, provisions, fare, rations, kai (*N.Z. informal*), nourishment, sustenance, victuals 2 = **fast**, regime,

abstinence, regimen
▷ **VERB** = **slim**, fast, lose weight, abstain, eat sparingly ≠ overindulge

diet² NOUN *often cap.* = **council**, meeting, parliament, congress, chamber, convention, legislature

differ VERB 1 = **be dissimilar**, contradict, contrast with, vary, belie, depart from, diverge, negate ≠ accord 2 = **disagree**, clash, dispute, dissent ≠ agree

difference NOUN
1 = **dissimilarity**, contrast, variation, change, variety, diversity, alteration, discrepancy ≠ similarity 2 = **remainder**, rest, balance, remains, excess 3 = **disagreement**, conflict, argument, clash, dispute, quarrel, contretemps ≠ agreement

different ADJECTIVE
1 = **dissimilar**, opposed, contrasting, changed, unlike, altered, inconsistent, disparate 2 = **various**, varied, diverse, assorted, miscellaneous, sundry 3 = **unusual**, special, strange, extraordinary, distinctive, peculiar, uncommon, singular

● **WORD POWER**
● On the whole, *different from* is
● preferable to *different to* and
● *different than*, both of which
● are considered unacceptable
● by some people. *Different to* is
● often heard in British English,
● but is thought by some people
● to be incorrect; and *different*
● *than*, though acceptable in

● American English, is often
● regarded as unacceptable in
● British English. This makes
● *different from* the safest option:
● *this result is only slightly different*
● *from that obtained in the U.S.* – or
● you can rephrase the sentence:
● *this result differs only slightly from*
● *that obtained in the U.S.*.

differentiate VERB
1 = **distinguish**, separate, discriminate, contrast, mark off, make a distinction, tell apart, set off *or* apart 2 = **make different**, separate, distinguish, characterize, single out, segregate, individualize, mark off 3 = **become different**, change, convert, transform, alter, adapt, modify

difficult ADJECTIVE 1 = **hard**, tough, taxing, demanding, challenging, exacting, formidable, uphill ≠ easy 2 = **problematical**, involved, complex, complicated, obscure, baffling, intricate, knotty ≠ simple 3 = **troublesome**, demanding, perverse, fussy, fastidious, hard to please, refractory, unaccommodating ≠ cooperative

difficulty NOUN 1 = **problem**, trouble, obstacle, hurdle, dilemma, complication, snag, uphill (*S. African*) 2 = **hardship**, strain, awkwardness, strenuousness, arduousness, laboriousness

dig VERB 1 = **hollow out**, mine, quarry, excavate, scoop out

2 = **delve**, tunnel, burrow **3** = **turn over 4** = **search**, hunt, root, delve, forage, dig down, fossick (*Austral. & N.Z.*) **5** = **poke**, drive, push, stick, punch, stab, thrust, shove

▷ NOUN **1** = **cutting remark**, crack (*slang*), insult, taunt, sneer, jeer, barb, wisecrack (*informal*) **2** = **poke**, thrust, nudge, prod, jab, punch

digest VERB **1** = **ingest**, absorb, incorporate, dissolve, assimilate **2** = **take in**, absorb, grasp, soak up

▷ NOUN = **summary**, résumé, abstract, epitome, synopsis, précis, abridgment

dignity NOUN **1** = **decorum**, gravity, majesty, grandeur, respectability, nobility, solemnity, courtliness **2** = **self-importance**, pride, self-esteem, self-respect

dilemma NOUN = **predicament**, problem, difficulty, spot (*informal*), mess, puzzle, plight, quandary

● WORD POWER

● The use of *dilemma* to refer to a
● problem that seems incapable
● of solution is considered by
● some people to be incorrect. To
● avoid this misuse of the word,
● an appropriate alternative such
● as *predicament* could be used.

dilute VERB **1** = **water down**, thin (out), weaken, adulterate, make thinner, cut (*informal*) ≠ condense **2** = **reduce**, weaken, diminish, temper, decrease, lessen, diffuse, mitigate ≠ intensify

dim ADJECTIVE **1** = **poorly lit**, dark, gloomy, murky, shady, shadowy, dusky, tenebrous **2** = **cloudy**, grey, gloomy, dismal, overcast, leaden ≠ bright **3** = **unclear**, obscured, faint, blurred, fuzzy, shadowy, hazy, bleary ≠ distinct **4** = **stupid** (*informal*), thick, dull, dense, dumb (*informal*), daft (*informal*), dozy (*Brit. informal*), obtuse ≠ bright

▷ VERB **1** = **turn down**, fade, dull **2** = **grow** *or* **become faint**, fade, dull, grow *or* become dim **3** = **darken**, dull, cloud over

dimension NOUN **1** = **aspect**, side, feature, angle, facet **2** = **extent**, size

diminish VERB **1** = **decrease**, decline, lessen, shrink, dwindle, wane, recede, subside ≠ grow **2** = **reduce**, cut, decrease, lessen, lower, curtail ≠ increase

din NOUN = **noise**, row, racket, crash, clamour, clatter, uproar, commotion ≠ silence

dine VERB = **eat**, lunch, feast, sup

dinkum ADJECTIVE (*Austral. & N.Z. informal*) = **genuine**, honest, natural, frank, sincere, candid, upfront (*informal*), artless

dinner NOUN **1** = **meal**, main meal, spread (*informal*), repast **2** = **banquet**, feast, repast, hakari (*N.Z.*)

dip VERB **1** = **plunge**, immerse, bathe, duck, douse, dunk **2** = **drop (down)**, fall, lower, sink, descend, subside **3** = **slope**, drop (down), descend, fall, decline, sink, incline, drop away

▷ NOUN **1** = **plunge**, ducking,

soaking, drenching, immersion, douche **2** = **nod**, drop, lowering, slump, sag **3** = **hollow**, hole, depression, pit, basin, trough, concavity ▷ **PHRASE**: **dip into something** = **sample**, skim, glance at, browse, peruse, surf (*computing*)

diplomacy NOUN
1 = **statesmanship**, statecraft, international negotiation
2 = **tact**, skill, sensitivity, craft, discretion, subtlety, delicacy, finesse ≠ tactlessness

diplomat NOUN = **official**, ambassador, envoy, statesman, consul, attaché, emissary, chargé d'affaires

diplomatic ADJECTIVE
1 = **consular**, official, foreign-office, ambassadorial, foreign-

politic **2** = **tactful**, politic, sensitive, subtle, delicate, polite, discreet, prudent ≠ tactless

dire ADJECTIVE = **desperate**, pressing, critical, terrible, crucial, extreme, awful, urgent

direct VERB **1** = **aim**, point, level, train, focus **2** = **guide**, show, lead, point the way, point in the direction of **3** = **control**, run, manage, lead, guide, handle, conduct, oversee **4** = **order**, command, instruct, charge, demand, require, bid **5** = **address**, send, mail, route, label
▷ ADJECTIVE **1** = **quickest**, shortest **2** = **straight**, through ≠ circuitous **3** = **first-hand**, personal, immediate ≠ indirect **4** = **clear**, specific, plain, absolute, definite, explicit, downright,

● **DINOSAURS**
● allosaur(us)
● ankylosaur(us)
● apatosaur(us)
● atlantosaur(us)
● brachiosaur(us)
● brontosaur(us)
● ceratosaur(us)
● compsognathus
● dimetrodon
● diplodocus
● dolichosaur(us)
● dromiosaur(us)
● elasmosaur(us)
● hadrosaur(us)
● ichthyosaur(us)
● iguanodon or iguanodont

● megalosaur(us)
● mosasaur(us)
● oviraptor
● plesiosaur(us)
● pteranodon
● pterodactyl or pterosaur
● protoceratops
● stegodon or stegodont
● stegosaur(us)
● theropod
● titanosaur(us)
● trachodon
● triceratops
● tyrannosaur(us)
● velociraptor

point-blank ≠ ambiguous
5 = **straightforward**, open,
straight, frank, blunt, honest,
candid, forthright ≠ indirect
6 = **verbatim**, exact, word-for-
word, strict, accurate, faithful,
letter-for-letter
▷ ADVERB = **non-stop**, straight
direction NOUN **1** = **way**, course,
line, road, track, bearing,
route, path **2** = **management**,
control, charge, administration,
leadership, command, guidance,
supervision

directions PLURAL
NOUN = **instructions**, rules,
information, plan, briefing,
regulations, recommendations,
guidelines

directive NOUN = **order**,
ruling, regulation, command,
instruction, decree, mandate,
injunction

directly ADVERB **1** = **straight**,
unswervingly, without deviation,
by the shortest route, in a beeline
2 = **immediately**, promptly, right
away, straightaway **3** = **at once**,
as soon as possible, straightaway,
forthwith **4** = **honestly**, openly,
frankly, plainly, point-blank,
unequivocally, truthfully,
unreservedly

director NOUN = **controller**, head,
leader, manager, chief, executive,
governor, administrator, baas
(*S. African*), sherang (*Austral. &
N.Z.*)

dirt NOUN **1** = **filth**, muck, grime,
dust, mud, impurity, kak (*S. African*

taboo or *slang*) **2** = **soil**, ground,
earth, clay, turf, loam

dirty ADJECTIVE **1** = **filthy**, soiled,
grubby, foul, muddy, polluted,
messy, grimy, festy (*Austral.
slang*) ≠ clean **2** = **dishonest**,
illegal, unfair, cheating, crooked,
fraudulent, treacherous,
unscrupulous ≠ honest
3 = **obscene**, indecent, blue,
offensive, filthy, pornographic,
sleazy, lewd ≠ decent
▷ VERB = **soil**, foul, stain, spoil,
muddy, pollute, blacken, defile
≠ clean

disability NOUN = **handicap**,
affliction, disorder, defect,
impairment, infirmity

disable VERB = **handicap**, cripple,
damage, paralyse, impair,
incapacitate, immobilize,
enfeeble

disabled ADJECTIVE = **differently
abled**, physically challenged,
handicapped, challenged,
weakened, crippled, paralysed,
lame, incapacitated ≠ able-
bodied

● **WORD POWER**
● Referring to people with
● disabilities as *the disabled* can
● cause offence and should be
● avoided. Instead, refer to them
● as people *with disabilities* or
● *who are physically challenged*,
● or, possibly, *disabled people*
● or *differently abled people*.
● In general, the terms used
● for disabilities or medical
● conditions should be avoided

- as collective nouns for people
- who have them – so, for
- example, instead of *the blind*,
- it is preferable to refer to
- *sightless people*, *vision-impaired*
- *people*, or *partially-sighted people*,
- depending on the degree of
- their condition.

disadvantage NOUN
1 = **drawback**, trouble, handicap, nuisance, snag, inconvenience, downside ≠ advantage
2 = **harm**, loss, damage, injury, hurt, prejudice, detriment, disservice ≠ benefit

disagree VERB 1 = **differ (in opinion)**, argue, clash, dispute, dissent, quarrel, take issue with, cross swords ≠ agree 2 = **make ill**, upset, sicken, trouble, hurt, bother, distress, discomfort

disagreement NOUN
= **argument**, row, conflict, clash, dispute, dissent, quarrel, squabble ≠ agreement

disappear VERB 1 = **vanish**, recede, evanesce ≠ appear
2 = **pass**, fade away 3 = **cease**, dissolve, evaporate, perish, die out, pass away, melt away, leave no trace

disappearance NOUN
1 = **vanishing**, going, passing, melting, eclipse, evaporation, evanescence 2 = **flight**, departure
3 = **loss**, losing, mislaying

disappoint VERB = **let down**, dismay, fail, disillusion, dishearten, disenchant, dissatisfy, disgruntle

disappointment NOUN
1 = **regret**, discontent, dissatisfaction, disillusionment, chagrin, disenchantment, dejection, despondency
2 = **letdown**, blow, setback, misfortune, calamity, choker (*informal*) 3 = **frustration**

disapproval NOUN
= **displeasure**, criticism, objection, condemnation, dissatisfaction, censure, reproach, denunciation

disapprove VERB = **condemn**, object to, dislike, deplore, frown on, take exception to, take a dim view of, find unacceptable ≠ approve

disarm VERB 1 = **demilitarize**, disband, demobilize, deactivate
2 = **win over**, persuade

disarmament NOUN = **arms reduction**, demobilization, arms limitation, demilitarization, de-escalation

disarming ADJECTIVE = **charming**, winning, irresistible, persuasive, likable *or* likeable

disarray NOUN 1 = **confusion**, disorder, indiscipline, disunity, disorganization, unruliness ≠ order 2 = **untidiness**, mess, chaos, muddle, clutter, shambles, jumble, hotchpotch ≠ tidiness

disaster NOUN 1 = **catastrophe**, trouble, tragedy, ruin, misfortune, adversity, calamity, cataclysm
2 = **failure**, mess, flop (*informal*), catastrophe, debacle, cock-up (*Brit. slang*), washout (*informal*)

d

disastrous ADJECTIVE
  1 = **terrible**, devastating, tragic, fatal, catastrophic, ruinous, calamitous, cataclysmic
  2 = **unsuccessful**

disbelief NOUN = **scepticism**, doubt, distrust, mistrust, incredulity, unbelief, dubiety ≠ belief

discard VERB = **get rid of**, drop, throw away or out, reject, abandon, dump (informal), dispose of, dispense with ≠ keep

discharge VERB 1 = **release**, free, clear, liberate, pardon, allow to go, set free 2 = **dismiss**, sack (informal), fire (informal), remove, expel, discard, oust, cashier, kennet (Austral. slang), jeff (Austral. slang) 3 = **carry out**, perform, fulfil, accomplish, do, effect, realize, observe 4 = **pay**, meet, clear, settle, square (up), honour, satisfy, relieve 5 = **pour forth**, release, leak, emit, dispense, ooze, exude, give off 6 = **fire**, shoot, set off, explode, let off, detonate, let loose (informal)
  ▷ NOUN 1 = **release**, liberation, clearance, pardon, acquittal
  2 = **dismissal**, notice, removal, the boot (slang), expulsion, the push (slang), marching orders (informal), ejection 3 = **emission**, ooze, secretion, excretion, pus, seepage, suppuration 4 = **firing**, report, shot, blast, burst, explosion, volley, salvo

disciple NOUN 1 = **apostle**
  2 = **follower**, student, supporter, pupil, devotee, apostle, adherent ≠ teacher

discipline NOUN 1 = **control**, authority, regulation, supervision, orderliness, strictness 2 = **self-control**, control, restraint, self-discipline, willpower, self-restraint, orderliness 3 = **training**, practice, exercise, method, regulation, drill, regimen 4 = **field of study**, area, subject, theme, topic, course, curriculum, speciality
  ▷ VERB 1 = **punish**, correct, reprimand, castigate, chastise, chasten, penalize, bring to book
  2 = **train**, educate

disclose VERB 1 = **make known**, reveal, publish, relate, broadcast, confess, communicate, divulge ≠ keep secret 2 = **show**, reveal, expose, unveil, uncover, lay bare, bring to light ≠ hide

disclosure NOUN 1 = **revelation**, announcement, publication, leak, admission, declaration, confession, acknowledgment
  2 = **uncovering**, publication, revelation, divulgence

discomfort NOUN 1 = **pain**, hurt, ache, throbbing, irritation, tenderness, pang, malaise ≠ comfort 2 = **uneasiness**, worry, anxiety, doubt, distress, misgiving, qualms, trepidation ≠ reassurance
  3 = **inconvenience**, trouble, difficulty, bother, hardship, irritation, nuisance, uphill (S. African)

discontent NOUN
= **dissatisfaction**, unhappiness, displeasure, regret, envy, restlessness, uneasiness

discontented ADJECTIVE
= **dissatisfied**, unhappy, fed up, disgruntled, disaffected, vexed, displeased ≠ satisfied

discount VERB 1 = **mark down**, reduce, lower 2 = **disregard**, reject, ignore, overlook, discard, set aside, dispel, pass over
▷ NOUN = **deduction**, cut, reduction, concession, rebate

discourage VERB 1 = **dishearten**, depress, intimidate, overawe, demoralize, put a damper on, dispirit, deject ≠ hearten 2 = **put off**, deter, prevent, dissuade, talk out of ≠ encourage

discourse NOUN
1 = **conversation**, talk, discussion, speech, communication, chat, dialogue
2 = **speech**, essay, lecture, sermon, treatise, dissertation, homily, oration, whaikorero (N.Z.)

discover VERB 1 = **find out**, learn, notice, realize, recognize, perceive, detect, uncover 2 = **find**, come across, uncover, unearth, turn up, dig up, come upon

discovery NOUN 1 = **finding out**, news, revelation, disclosure, realization 2 = **invention**, launch, institution, pioneering, innovation, inauguration
3 = **breakthrough**, find, development, advance, leap, invention, step forward, quantum leap 4 = **finding**, revelation, uncovering, disclosure, detection

discredit VERB 1 = **disgrace**, shame, smear, humiliate, taint, disparage, vilify, slander ≠ honour 2 = **dispute**, question, challenge, deny, reject, discount, distrust, mistrust
▷ NOUN = **disgrace**, scandal, shame, disrepute, stigma, ignominy, dishonour, ill-repute ≠ honour

discreet ADJECTIVE = **tactful**, diplomatic, guarded, careful, cautious, wary, prudent, considerate ≠ tactless

discrepancy NOUN
= **disagreement**, difference, variation, conflict, contradiction, inconsistency, disparity, divergence

discretion NOUN 1 = **tact**, consideration, caution, diplomacy, prudence, wariness, carefulness, judiciousness ≠ tactlessness 2 = **choice**, will, pleasure, preference, inclination, volition

discriminate VERB
= **differentiate**, distinguish, separate, tell the difference, draw a distinction ▷ PHRASE: **discriminate against someone** = **treat differently**, single out, victimize, treat as inferior, show bias against, show prejudice against

discriminating ADJECTIVE
= **discerning**, particular, refined, cultivated, selective, tasteful,

fastidious ≠ undiscriminating
discrimination NOUN
1 = **prejudice**, bias, injustice,
intolerance, bigotry, favouritism,
unfairness 2 = **discernment**,
taste, judgment, perception,
subtlety, refinement
discuss VERB = **talk about**,
consider, debate, examine, argue
about, deliberate about, converse
about, confer about
discussion NOUN 1 = **talk**,
debate, argument, conference,
conversation, dialogue,
consultation, discourse,
korero (N.Z.) 2 = **examination**,
investigation, analysis, scrutiny,
dissection
disdain NOUN = **contempt**, scorn,
arrogance, derision, haughtiness,
superciliousness
  ▷ VERB = **scorn**, reject, slight,
disregard, spurn, deride, look
down on, sneer at
disease NOUN = **illness**, condition,
complaint, infection, disorder,
sickness, ailment, affliction
diseased ADJECTIVE = **unhealthy**,
sick, infected, rotten, ailing,
sickly, unwell, crook (Austral. &
N.Z. informal), unsound
disgrace NOUN 1 = **shame**,
degradation, disrepute, ignominy,
dishonour, infamy, opprobrium,
odium ≠ honour 2 = **scandal**,
stain, stigma, blot, blemish
  ▷ VERB = **shame**, humiliate,
discredit, degrade, taint, sully,
dishonour, bring shame upon
≠ honour

disgraceful ADJECTIVE
= **shameful**, shocking,
scandalous, unworthy,
ignominious, disreputable,
contemptible, dishonourable
disgruntled ADJECTIVE
= **discontented**, dissatisfied,
annoyed, irritated, put out,
grumpy, vexed, displeased, hoha
(N.Z.)
disguise VERB = **hide**, cover,
conceal, screen, mask, suppress,
withhold, veil
  ▷ NOUN = **costume**, mask,
camouflage
disguised ADJECTIVE 1 = **in
disguise**, masked, camouflaged,
undercover, incognito 2 = **false**,
artificial, forged, fake, mock,
imitation, sham, counterfeit
disgust VERB 1 = **sicken**, offend,
revolt, put off, repel, nauseate
≠ delight 2 = **outrage**, shock,
anger, hurt, fury, resentment,
wrath, indignation
disgusting ADJECTIVE
1 = **sickening**, foul, revolting,
gross, repellent, nauseating,
repugnant, loathsome, festy
(Austral. slang), yucko (Austral.
slang) 2 = **appalling**, shocking,
awful, offensive, dreadful,
horrifying
dish NOUN 1 = **bowl**, plate, platter,
salver 2 = **food**, fare, recipe
dishonest ADJECTIVE = **deceitful**,
corrupt, crooked (informal), lying,
bent (slang), false, cheating,
treacherous ≠ honest
disintegrate VERB = **break up**,

crumble, fall apart, separate, shatter, splinter, break apart, go to pieces

dislike VERB = **hate**, object to, loathe, despise, disapprove of, detest, recoil from, take a dim view of ≠ like

▷ NOUN = **hatred**, hostility, disapproval, distaste, animosity, aversion, displeasure, antipathy ≠ liking

dismal ADJECTIVE 1 = **bad**, awful, dreadful, rotten (*informal*), terrible, poor, dire, abysmal 2 = **sad**, gloomy, dark, depressing, discouraging, bleak, dreary, sombre ≠ happy 3 = **gloomy**, depressing, dull, dreary ≠ cheerful

dismantle VERB = **take apart**, strip, demolish, disassemble, take to pieces *or* bits

dismay VERB 1 = **alarm**, frighten, scare, panic, distress, terrify, appal, startle 2 = **disappoint**, upset, discourage, daunt, disillusion, let down, dishearten, dispirit

▷ NOUN 1 = **alarm**, fear, horror, anxiety, dread, apprehension, nervousness, consternation 2 = **disappointment**, frustration, dissatisfaction, disillusionment, chagrin, disenchantment, discouragement

dismiss VERB 1 = **reject**, disregard 2 = **banish**, dispel, discard, set aside, cast out, lay aside, put out of your mind 3 = **sack**, fire (*informal*), remove (*informal*),

axe (*informal*), discharge, lay off, cashier, give notice to, kennet (*Austral. slang*), jeff (*Austral. slang*) 4 = **let go**, free, release, discharge, dissolve, liberate, disperse, send away

dismissal NOUN = **the sack**, removal, notice, the boot (*slang*), expulsion (*informal*), the push (*slang*), marching orders (*informal*)

disobey VERB 1 = **defy**, ignore, rebel, disregard, refuse to obey 2 = **infringe**, defy, refuse to obey, flout, violate, contravene, overstep, transgress

disorder NOUN 1 = **illness**, disease, complaint, condition, sickness, ailment, affliction, malady 2 = **untidiness**, mess, confusion, chaos, muddle, clutter, shambles, disarray 3 = **disturbance**, riot, turmoil, unrest, uproar, commotion, unruliness, biffo (*Austral. slang*)

disorderly ADJECTIVE 1 = **untidy**, confused, chaotic, messy, jumbled, shambolic (*informal*), disorganized, higgledy-piggledy (*informal*) ≠ tidy 2 = **unruly**, disruptive, rowdy, turbulent, tumultuous, lawless, riotous, ungovernable

dispatch *or* **despatch** VERB 1 = **send**, consign 2 = **kill**, murder, destroy, execute, slaughter, assassinate, slay, liquidate 3 = **carry out**, perform, fulfil, effect, finish, achieve, settle, dismiss

▷ NOUN = **message**, news, report,

story, account, communication, bulletin, communiqué

dispel VERB = **drive away**, dismiss, eliminate, expel, disperse, banish, chase away

dispense VERB 1 = **distribute**, assign, allocate, allot, dole out, share out, apportion, deal out **2** = **prepare**, measure, supply, mix **3** = **administer**, operate, carry out, implement, enforce, execute, apply, discharge ▷ PHRASE: **dispense with something** or **someone 1** = **do away with**, give up, cancel, abolish, brush aside, forgo **2** = **do without**, get rid of, dispose of, relinquish

disperse VERB 1 = **scatter**, spread, distribute, strew, diffuse, disseminate, throw about **2** = **break up**, separate, scatter, dissolve, disband ≠ gather **3** = **dissolve**, break up

displace VERB 1 = **replace**, succeed, supersede, oust, usurp, supplant, take the place of **2** = **move**, shift, disturb, budge, misplace

display VERB 1 = **show**, present, exhibit, put on view ≠ conceal **2** = **expose**, show, reveal, exhibit, uncover **3** = **demonstrate**, show, reveal, register, expose, disclose, manifest **4** = **show off**, parade, exhibit, sport (*informal*), flash (*informal*), flourish, brandish, flaunt

▷ NOUN 1 = **proof**, exhibition, demonstration, evidence, expression, illustration, revelation, testimony **2** = **exhibition**, show, demonstration, presentation, array **3** = **ostentation**, show, flourish, fanfare, pomp **4** = **show**, exhibition, parade, spectacle, pageant

disposable ADJECTIVE 1 = **throwaway**, nonreturnable **2** = **available**, expendable, consumable

disposal NOUN = **throwing away**, dumping (*informal*), scrapping, removal, discarding, jettisoning, ejection, riddance ▷ PHRASE: **at your disposal** = **available**, ready, to hand, accessible, handy, at hand, on tap, expendable

dispose VERB = **arrange**, put, place, group, order, distribute, array ▷ PHRASES: **dispose of someone** = **kill**, murder, destroy, execute, slaughter, assassinate, slay, liquidate; **dispose of something 1** = **get rid of**, destroy, dump (*informal*), scrap, discard, unload, jettison, throw out or away **2** = **deal with**, manage, treat, handle, settle, cope with, take care of, see to

disposition NOUN 1 = **character**, nature, spirit, make-up, constitution, temper, temperament **2** = **tendency**, inclination, propensity, habit, leaning, bent, bias, proclivity **3** (*archaic*) = **arrangement**, grouping, ordering, organization, distribution, placement

dispute VERB 1 = **contest**,

question, challenge, deny, doubt, oppose, object to, contradict **2** = **argue**, fight, clash, disagree, fall out (*informal*), quarrel, squabble, bicker
▷ NOUN **1** = **disagreement**, conflict, argument, dissent, altercation **2** = **argument**, row, clash, controversy, contention, feud, quarrel, squabble

disqualify VERB = **ban**, rule out, prohibit, preclude, debar, declare ineligible

disregard VERB **1** = **ignore**, discount, overlook, neglect, pass over, turn a blind eye to, make light of, pay no heed to ≠ pay attention to
▷ NOUN = **ignoring**, neglect, contempt, indifference, negligence, disdain, disrespect

disrupt VERB **1** = **interrupt**, stop, upset, hold up, interfere with, unsettle, obstruct, cut short **2** = **disturb**, upset, confuse, disorder, spoil, disorganize, disarrange

disruption NOUN = **disturbance**, interference, interruption, stoppage

disruptive ADJECTIVE = **disturbing**, upsetting, disorderly, unsettling, troublesome, unruly ≠ well-behaved

dissatisfaction NOUN = **discontent**, frustration, resentment, disappointment, irritation, unhappiness, annoyance, displeasure

dissatisfied ADJECTIVE = **discontented**, frustrated, unhappy, disappointed, fed up, disgruntled, displeased, unsatisfied ≠ satisfied

dissent NOUN = **disagreement**, opposition, protest, resistance, refusal, objection, discord, demur ≠ assent

dissident ADJECTIVE = **dissenting**, disagreeing, nonconformist, heterodox
▷ NOUN = **protester**, rebel, dissenter, demonstrator, agitator

dissolve VERB **1** = **melt**, soften, thaw, liquefy, deliquesce **2** = **end**, suspend, break up, wind up, terminate, discontinue, dismantle, disband

distance NOUN **1** = **space**, length, extent, range, stretch, gap, interval, span **2** = **aloofness**, reserve, detachment, restraint, stiffness, coolness, coldness, standoffishness

distant ADJECTIVE **1** = **far-off**, far, remote, abroad, out-of-the-way, far-flung, faraway, outlying ≠ close **2** = **remote 3** = **reserved**, withdrawn, cool, remote, detached, aloof, unfriendly, reticent ≠ friendly **4** = **faraway**, blank, vague, distracted, vacant, preoccupied, oblivious, absent-minded

distinct ADJECTIVE **1** = **different**, individual, separate, discrete, unconnected ≠ similar **2** = **striking**, dramatic, outstanding, noticeable, well-

d

defined **3** = **definite**, marked, clear, decided, obvious, evident, noticeable, conspicuous ≠ vague

distinction NOUN **1** = **difference**, contrast, variation, differential, discrepancy, disparity, dissimilarity **2** = **excellence**, importance, fame, merit, prominence, greatness, eminence, repute **3** = **feature**, quality, characteristic, mark, individuality, peculiarity, distinctiveness, particularity **4** = **merit**, honour, integrity, excellence, rectitude

distinctive ADJECTIVE = **characteristic**, special, individual, unique, typical, peculiar, singular, idiosyncratic ≠ ordinary

distinctly ADVERB **1** = **definitely**, clearly, obviously, plainly, patently, decidedly, markedly, noticeably **2** = **clearly**, plainly

distinguish VERB **1** = **differentiate**, determine, separate, discriminate, decide, judge, ascertain, tell the difference **2** = **characterize**, mark, separate, single out, set apart **3** = **make out**, recognize, perceive, know, see, tell, pick out, discern

distinguished ADJECTIVE = **eminent**, noted, famous, celebrated, well-known, prominent, esteemed, acclaimed ≠ unknown

distort VERB **1** = **misrepresent**, twist, bias, disguise, pervert, slant, colour, misinterpret **2** = **deform**, bend, twist, warp, buckle, mangle, mangulate (*Austral. slang*), disfigure, contort

distortion NOUN **1** = **misrepresentation**, bias, slant, perversion, falsification **2** = **deformity**, bend, twist, warp, buckle, contortion, malformation, crookedness

distract VERB **1** = **divert**, sidetrack, draw away, turn aside, lead astray, draw or lead away from **2** = **amuse**, occupy, entertain, beguile, engross

distracted ADJECTIVE = **agitated**, troubled, puzzled, at sea, perplexed, flustered, in a flap (*informal*)

distraction NOUN **1** = **disturbance**, interference, diversion, interruption **2** = **entertainment**, recreation, amusement, diversion, pastime

distraught ADJECTIVE = **frantic**, desperate, distressed, distracted, worked-up, agitated, overwrought, out of your mind

distress VERB = **upset**, worry, trouble, disturb, grieve, torment, harass, agitate
▷ NOUN **1** = **suffering**, pain, worry, grief, misery, torment, sorrow, heartache **2** = **need**, trouble, difficulties, poverty, hard times, hardship, misfortune, adversity

distressed ADJECTIVE **1** = **upset**, worried, troubled, distracted, tormented, distraught, agitated, wretched 2 = **poverty-stricken**, poor, impoverished, needy, destitute, indigent, down at heel, straitened

distressing ADJECTIVE = **upsetting**, worrying, disturbing, painful, sad, harrowing, heart-breaking

distribute VERB 1 = **hand out**, pass round 2 = **circulate**, deliver, convey 3 = **share**, deal, allocate, dispense, allot, dole out, apportion

distribution NOUN 1 = **delivery**, mailing, transportation, handling 2 (*economics*) = **sharing**, division, assignment, rationing, allocation, allotment, apportionment 3 = **spread**, organization, arrangement, placement

district NOUN = **area**, region, sector, quarter, parish, neighbourhood, vicinity, locality

distrust VERB = **suspect**, doubt, be wary of, mistrust, disbelieve, be suspicious of ≠ trust
▷ NOUN = **suspicion**, question, doubt, disbelief, scepticism, mistrust, misgiving, wariness ≠ trust

disturb VERB 1 = **interrupt**, trouble, bother, plague, disrupt, interfere with, hassle, inconvenience 2 = **upset**, concern, worry, trouble, alarm, distress, unsettle, unnerve ≠ calm 3 = **muddle**, disorder, mix up, mess up, jumble up, disarrange, muss (*U.S. & Canad.*)

disturbance NOUN 1 = **disorder**, fray, brawl, fracas, commotion, rumpus 2 = **upset**, bother, distraction, intrusion, interruption, annoyance

disturbed ADJECTIVE 1 (*psychiatry*) = **unbalanced**, troubled, disordered, unstable, neurotic, upset, deranged, maladjusted ≠ balanced 2 = **worried**, concerned, troubled, upset, bothered, nervous, anxious, uneasy ≠ calm

disturbing ADJECTIVE = **worrying**, upsetting, alarming, frightening, distressing, startling, unsettling, harrowing

ditch NOUN = **channel**, drain, trench, dyke, furrow, gully, moat, watercourse
▷ VERB 1 (*slang*) = **get rid of**, dump (*informal*), scrap, discard, dispose of, dispense with, jettison, throw out *or* overboard 2 (*slang*) = **leave**, drop, abandon, dump (*informal*), get rid of, forsake

dive VERB 1 = **plunge**, drop, duck, dip, descend, plummet 2 = **go underwater** 3 = **nose-dive**, plunge, crash, swoop, plummet
▷ NOUN = **plunge**, spring, jump, leap, lunge, nose dive

diverse ADJECTIVE 1 = **various**, mixed, varied, assorted, miscellaneous, several, sundry, motley 2 = **different**, unlike, varying, separate, distinct, disparate, discrete, dissimilar

diversify VERB = **vary**, change, expand, spread out, branch out

diversion NOUN 1 = **distraction**,

deviation, digression

2 = **pastime**, game, sport, entertainment, hobby, relaxation, recreation, distraction

3 (*chiefly Brit.*) = **detour**, roundabout way, indirect course

4 (*chiefly Brit.*) = **deviation**, departure, straying, divergence, digression

diversity NOUN **1** = **difference**, multiplicity, heterogeneity, diverseness **2** = **range**, variety, scope, sphere

divert VERB **1** = **redirect**, switch, avert, deflect, deviate, turn aside **2** = **distract**, sidetrack, lead astray, draw *or* lead away from **3** = **entertain**, delight, amuse, please, charm, gratify, beguile, regale

divide VERB **1** = **separate**, split, segregate, bisect ≠ join **2** = **share**, distribute, allocate, dispense, allot, mete, deal out **3** = **split**, break up, come between, estrange, cause to disagree

dividend NOUN = **bonus**, share, cut (*informal*), gain, extra, plus, portion, divvy (*informal*)

divine ADJECTIVE **1** = **heavenly**, spiritual, holy, immortal, supernatural, celestial, angelic, superhuman **2** = **sacred**, religious, holy, spiritual, blessed, revered, hallowed, consecrated **3** (*informal*) = **wonderful**, perfect, beautiful, excellent, lovely, glorious, marvellous, splendid

▷ VERB = **guess**, suppose, perceive, discern, infer, deduce,

apprehend, surmise

division NOUN **1** = **separation**, dividing, splitting up, partition, cutting up **2** = **sharing**, sharing, distribution, assignment, rationing, allocation, allotment, apportionment **3** = **disagreement**, split, rift, rupture, abyss, chasm, variance, discord ≠ unity **4** = **department**, group, branch **5** = **part**, bit, piece, section, class, category, fraction

divorce NOUN = **separation**, split, break-up, parting, split-up, rift, dissolution, annulment

▷ VERB = **separate**, split up, part company, dissolve your marriage

dizzy ADJECTIVE **1** = **giddy**, faint, light-headed, swimming, reeling, shaky, wobbly, off balance **2** = **confused**, dazzled, at sea, bewildered, muddled, bemused, dazed, disorientated

do VERB **1** = **perform**, achieve, carry out, complete, accomplish, execute, pull off **2** = **make**, prepare, fix, arrange, look after, see to, get ready **3** = **solve**, work out, resolve, figure out, decode, decipher, puzzle out **4** = **be adequate**, be sufficient, satisfy, suffice, pass muster, cut the mustard, meet requirements **5** = **produce**, make, create, develop, manufacture, construct, invent, fabricate

▷ NOUN (*informal, chiefly Brit. & N.Z.*) = **party**, gathering, function, event, affair, occasion, celebration, reception ▷ PHRASES:

do away with something
= **get rid of**, remove, eliminate,
abolish, discard, put an end to,
dispense with, discontinue;
do without something or
someone = **manage without**,
give up, dispense with, forgo, kick
(*informal*), abstain from, get along
without

dock¹ NOUN = **port**, haven,
harbour, pier, wharf, quay,
waterfront, anchorage
▷ VERB 1 = **moor**, land, anchor,
put in, tie up, berth, drop anchor
2 (*of a spacecraft*) = **link up**, unite,
join, couple, rendezvous, hook up

dock² VERB 1 = **cut**, reduce,
decrease, diminish, lessen
≠ increase 2 = **deduct**, subtract
3 = **cut off**, crop, clip, shorten,
curtail, cut short

doctor NOUN = **physician**, medic
(*informal*), general practitioner,
medical practitioner, G.P.
▷ VERB 1 = **change**, alter, interfere
with, disguise, pervert, tamper
with, tinker with, misrepresent
2 = **add to**, spike, cut, mix
something with something,
dilute, water down, adulterate

doctrine NOUN = **teaching**,
principle, belief, opinion,
conviction, creed, dogma, tenet,
kaupapa (*N.Z.*)

document NOUN = **paper**,
form, certificate, report, record,
testimonial, authorization
▷ VERB = **support**, certify, verify,
detail, validate, substantiate,
corroborate, authenticate

dodge VERB 1 = **duck**, dart,
swerve, sidestep, shoot, turn
aside 2 = **evade**, avoid, escape,
get away from, elude 3 = **avoid**,
evade, shirk
▷ NOUN = **trick**, scheme, ploy,
trap, device, fraud, manoeuvre,
deception, fastie (*Austral. slang*)

dodgy ADJECTIVE 1 (*Brit., Austral.
& N.Z. informal*) = **nasty**, offensive,
unpleasant, revolting, distasteful,
repellent, obnoxious, repulsive,
shonky (*Austral. & N.Z. informal*)
2 (*Brit., Austral. & N.Z. informal*)
= **risky**, difficult, tricky,
dangerous, delicate, uncertain,
dicey (*informal, chiefly Brit.*),
chancy (*informal*), shonky (*Austral.
& N.Z. informal*)

dog NOUN = **hound**, canine, pooch
(*slang*), cur, man's best friend, kuri
or goorie (*N.Z.*), brak (*S. African*)
▷ VERB 1 = **plague**, follow,
trouble, haunt, hound, torment
2 = **pursue**, follow, track, chase,
trail, hound, stalk ▷ RELATED
WORDS: *adjective* **canine**, *female*
bitch, *young* **pup, puppy**

dogged ADJECTIVE = **determined**,
persistent, stubborn, resolute,
tenacious, steadfast, obstinate,
indefatigable ≠ irresolute

dole NOUN = **share**, grant, gift,
allowance, handout, koha (*N.Z.*)
▷ PHRASE: **dole something out**
= **give out**, distribute, assign,
allocate, hand out, dispense, allot,
apportion

dolphin NOUN ▷ RELATED WORD:
collective noun **school**

d

▷ *see* **whales and dolphins**

domestic ADJECTIVE **1** = **home**, internal, native, indigenous **2** = **household**, home, family, private **3** = **home-loving**, homely, housewifely, stay-at-home, domesticated **4** = **domesticated**, trained, tame, pet, house-trained
▷ NOUN = **servant**, help, maid, daily, char (*informal*), charwoman

dominant ADJECTIVE **1** = **main**, chief, primary, principal, prominent, predominant, pre-eminent ≠ minor **2** = **controlling**, ruling, commanding, supreme, governing, superior, authoritative

dominate VERB **1** = **control**, rule, direct, govern, monopolize, tyrannize, have the whip hand over **2** = **tower above**, overlook, survey, stand over, loom over, stand head and shoulders above

domination NOUN = **control**, power, rule, authority, influence, command, supremacy, ascendancy

don VERB = **put on**, get into, dress in, pull on, change into, get dressed in, clothe yourself in, slip on *or* into

donate VERB = **give**, present, contribute, grant, subscribe, endow, entrust, impart

donation NOUN = **contribution**, gift, subscription, offering, present, grant, hand-out, koha (*N.Z.*)

donor NOUN = **giver**, contributor, benefactor, philanthropist, donator ≠ recipient

doom NOUN = **destruction**, ruin, catastrophe, downfall
▷ VERB = **condemn**, sentence, consign, destine

doomed ADJECTIVE = **hopeless**, condemned, ill-fated, fated, unhappy, unfortunate, cursed, unlucky

door NOUN = **opening**, entry, entrance, exit, doorway

dope NOUN **1** (*slang*) = **drugs**, narcotics, opiates, dadah (*Austral. slang*) **2** (*informal*) = **idiot**, fool, twit (*informal, chiefly Brit.*), dunce, simpleton, dimwit (*informal*), nitwit (*informal*), dumb-ass (*slang*), dorba *or* dorb (*Austral. slang*), bogan (*Austral. slang*)
▷ VERB = **drug**, knock out, sedate, stupefy, anaesthetize, narcotize

dorp NOUN (*S. African*) = **town**, village, settlement, municipality, kainga *or* kaika (*N.Z.*)

dose NOUN **1** (*medical*) = **measure**, amount, allowance, portion, prescription, ration, draught, dosage **2** = **quantity**, measure, supply, portion

dot NOUN = **spot**, point, mark, fleck, jot, speck, speckle ▷ PHRASE: **on the dot** = **on time**, promptly, precisely, exactly (*informal*), to the minute, on the button (*informal*), punctually VERB = **spot**, stud, fleck, speckle

double ADJECTIVE **1** = **matching**, coupled, paired, twin, duplicate, in pairs **2** = **dual**, enigmatic, twofold

▷ **NOUN** = **twin**, lookalike, spitting image, clone, replica, dead ringer (*slang*), Doppelgänger, duplicate
▷ **PHRASE**: **at** *or* **on the double** = **at once**, now, immediately, directly, quickly, promptly, straight away, right away **VERB** 1 = **multiply by two**, duplicate, increase twofold, enlarge, magnify 2 = **fold up** *or* **over** 3 *with* **as** = **function as**, serve as

doubt NOUN 1 = **uncertainty**, confusion, hesitation, suspense, indecision, hesitancy, lack of conviction, irresolution ≠ certainty 2 = **suspicion**, scepticism, distrust, apprehension, mistrust, misgivings, qualms ≠ belief
▷ **VERB** 1 = **be uncertain**, be sceptical, be dubious 2 = **waver**, hesitate, vacillate, fluctuate 3 = **disbelieve**, question, suspect, query, distrust, mistrust, lack confidence in ≠ believe

doubtful ADJECTIVE 1 = **unlikely**, unclear, dubious, questionable, improbable, debatable, equivocal ≠ certain 2 = **unsure**, uncertain, hesitant, suspicious, hesitating, sceptical, tentative, wavering ≠ certain

doubtless ADVERB = **probably**, presumably, most likely

down ADJECTIVE = **depressed**, low, sad, unhappy, discouraged, miserable, fed up, dejected
▷ **VERB** (*informal*) = **swallow**, drink (down), drain, gulp (down), put away (*informal*), toss off

downfall NOUN = **ruin**, fall, destruction, collapse, disgrace, overthrow, undoing, comeuppance (*slang*)

downgrade VERB = **demote**, degrade, take down a peg (*informal*), lower *or* reduce in rank ≠ promote

downright ADJECTIVE = **complete**, absolute, utter, total, plain, outright, unqualified, out-and-out

down-to-earth ADJECTIVE = **sensible**, practical, realistic, matter-of-fact, sane, no-nonsense, unsentimental, plain-spoken, grounded

downward ADJECTIVE = **descending**, declining, heading down, earthward

draft NOUN 1 = **outline**, plan, sketch, version, rough, abstract 2 = **money order**, bill (of exchange), cheque, postal order
▷ **VERB** = **outline**, write, plan, produce, create, design, draw, compose

drag VERB = **pull**, draw, haul, trail, tow, tug, jerk, lug
▷ **NOUN** (*informal*) = **nuisance**, bore, bother, pest, hassle (*informal*), inconvenience, annoyance

drain NOUN 1 = **sewer**, channel, pipe, sink, ditch, trench, conduit, duct 2 = **reduction**, strain, drag, exhaustion, sapping, depletion
▷ **VERB** 1 = **remove**, draw, empty, withdraw, tap, pump, bleed 2 = **empty** 3 = **flow out**, leak,

trickle, ooze, seep, exude, well
out, effuse **4** = **drink up**, swallow,
finish, put away (*informal*), quaff,
gulp down **5** = **exhaust**, wear
out, strain, weaken, fatigue,
debilitate, tire out, enfeeble
6 = **consume**, exhaust, empty, use
up, sap, dissipate

drama NOUN **1** = **play**, show, stage
show, dramatization **2** = **theatre**,
acting, stagecraft, dramaturgy
3 = **excitement**, crisis, spectacle,
turmoil, histrionics
▷ *see* **dramatists**

dramatic ADJECTIVE **1** = **exciting**,
thrilling, tense, sensational,
breathtaking, electrifying,
melodramatic, climactic
2 = **theatrical**, Thespian,
dramaturgical **3** = **expressive**
4 = **powerful**, striking,
impressive, vivid, jaw-dropping
≠ ordinary

drape VERB = **cover**, wrap, fold,
swathe

drastic ADJECTIVE = **extreme**,
strong, radical, desperate, severe,
harsh

draught *or* (*U.S.*) **draft** NOUN
1 = **breeze**, current, movement,
flow, puff, gust, current of air
2 = **drink**

draw VERB **1** = **sketch**, design,
outline, trace, portray, paint,
depict, mark out **2** = **pull**, drag,
haul, tow, tug **3** = **extract**, take,
remove **4** = **deduce**, make,
take, derive, infer **5** = **attract**
6 = **entice**
▷ NOUN **1** = **tie**, deadlock,

stalemate, impasse, dead
heat **2** (*informal*) = **appeal**, pull
(*informal*), charm, attraction,
lure, temptation, fascination,
allure ▷ PHRASE: **draw on** *or* **upon**
something = **make use of**, use,
employ, rely on, exploit, extract,
take from, fall back on

drawback NOUN = **disadvantage**,
difficulty, handicap, deficiency,
flaw, hitch, snag, downside
≠ advantage

drawing NOUN = **picture**,
illustration, representation,
cartoon, sketch, portrayal,
depiction, study

drawn ADJECTIVE = **tense**, worn,
stressed, tired, pinched, haggard

dread VERB = **fear**, shrink from,
cringe at the thought of, quail
from, shudder to think about,
have cold feet about (*informal*),
tremble to think about
▷ NOUN = **fear**, alarm,
horror, terror, dismay, fright,
apprehension, trepidation

dreadful ADJECTIVE **1** = **terrible**,
shocking, awful, appalling,
horrible, fearful, hideous,
atrocious **2** = **serious**, terrible,
awful, horrendous, monstrous,
abysmal **3** = **awful**, terrible,
horrendous, frightful

dream NOUN **1** = **vision**,
illusion, delusion, hallucination
2 = **ambition**, wish, fantasy,
desire, pipe dream **3** = **daydream**
4 = **delight**, pleasure, joy, beauty,
treasure, gem, marvel, pearler
(*Austral. slang*), beaut (*Austral. &*

N.Z. slang)
▷ VERB 1 = **have dreams**, hallucinate 2 = **daydream**, stargaze, build castles in the air or in Spain ▷ PHRASE: **dream of something** or **someone** = **daydream about**, fantasize about

dreamer NOUN = **idealist**, visionary, daydreamer, utopian, escapist, Walter Mitty, fantasist

dreary ADJECTIVE = **dull**, boring, tedious, drab, tiresome, monotonous, humdrum, uneventful ≠ exciting

drench VERB = **soak**, flood, wet, drown, steep, swamp, saturate, inundate

dress NOUN 1 = **frock**, gown, robe 2 = **clothing**, clothes, costume, garments, apparel, attire, garb, togs
▷ VERB 1 = **put on clothes**, don clothes, slip on or into something ≠ undress 2 = **clothe** 3 = **bandage**, treat, plaster, bind up 4 = **arrange**, prepare, get ready

dribble VERB 1 = **run**, drip, trickle, drop, leak, ooze, seep, fall in drops 2 = **drool**, drivel, slaver, slobber

drift VERB 1 = **float**, go (aimlessly), bob, coast, slip, sail, slide, glide 2 = **wander**, stroll, stray, roam, meander, rove, range 3 = **stray**, wander, digress, get off the point 4 = **pile up**, gather, accumulate, amass, bank up
▷ NOUN 1 = **pile**, bank, mass, heap, mound, accumulation

2 = **meaning**, point, gist, direction, import, intention, tendency, significance

drill¹ NOUN 1 = **bit**, borer, gimlet, boring tool 2 = **training**, exercise, discipline, instruction, preparation, repetition 3 (informal) = **practice**
▷ VERB 1 = **bore**, pierce, penetrate, sink in, puncture, perforate 2 = **train**, coach, teach, exercise, discipline, practise, instruct, rehearse

drink VERB 1 = **swallow**, sip, suck, gulp, sup, guzzle, imbibe, quaff 2 = **booze** (informal), tipple, tope, hit the bottle (informal)
▷ NOUN 1 = **glass**, cup, draught 2 = **beverage**, refreshment, potion, liquid 3 = **alcohol**, booze (informal), liquor, spirits, the bottle (informal), hooch or hootch (informal, chiefly U.S. & Canad.)

drip VERB = **drop**, splash, sprinkle, trickle, dribble, exude, plop
▷ NOUN 1 = **drop**, bead, trickle, dribble, droplet, globule, pearl 2 (informal) = **weakling**, wet (Brit. informal), weed (informal), softie (informal), mummy's boy (informal), namby-pamby

drive VERB 1 = **go (by car)**, ride (by car), motor, travel by car 2 = **operate**, manage, direct, guide, handle, steer 3 = **push**, propel 4 = **thrust**, push, hammer, ram 5 = **herd**, urge, impel 6 = **force**, press, prompt, spur, prod, constrain, coerce, goad
▷ NOUN 1 = **run**, ride, trip,

d

journey, spin (*informal*), outing, excursion, jaunt **2** = **initiative**, energy, enterprise, ambition, motivation, zip (*informal*), vigour, get-up-and-go (*informal*) **3** = **campaign**, push (*informal*), crusade, action, effort, appeal **4** (*computing*) = **flash drive**, storage device, key drive, keyring drive, microdrive, pen drive, thumb drive, USB drive, USB key

drop VERB **1** = **fall**, decline, diminish **2** *often with* **away** = **decline**, fall, sink **3** = **plunge**, fall, tumble, descend, plummet **4** = **drip**, trickle, dribble, fall in drops **5** = **sink**, fall, descend **6** = **quit**, give up, axe (*informal*), kick (*informal*), relinquish, discontinue
▷ NOUN **1** = **decrease**, fall, cut, lowering, decline, reduction, slump, fall-off **2** = **droplet**, bead, globule, bubble, pearl, drip **3** = **dash**, shot (*informal*), spot, trace, sip, tot, trickle, mouthful **4** = **fall**, plunge, descent ▷ PHRASES: **drop off 1** = **fall asleep**, nod (off), doze (off), snooze (*informal*), have forty winks (*informal*) **2** = **decrease**, lower, decline, shrink, diminish, dwindle, lessen, subside; **drop out** = **leave**, stop, give up, withdraw, quit, pull out, fall by the wayside

dross = **nonsense**, garbage (*chiefly U.S.*), twaddle, rot, trash, hot air (*informal*), tripe (*informal*), claptrap (*informal*), bizzo (*Austral. slang*), bull's wool (*Austral. & N.Z. slang*)

drought NOUN = **water shortage**, dryness, dry spell, aridity ≠ flood

drove NOUN *often plural* = **herd**, company, crowds, collection, mob, flocks, swarm, horde

drown VERB **1** = **go down**, go under **2** = **drench**, flood, soak, steep, swamp, saturate, engulf, submerge **3** *often with* **out** = **overwhelm**, overcome, wipe out, overpower, obliterate, swallow up

drug NOUN **1** = **medication**, medicine, remedy, physic, medicament **2** = **dope** (*slang*), narcotic (*slang*), stimulant, opiate, dadah (*Austral. slang*)
▷ VERB = **knock out**, dope (*slang*), numb, deaden, stupefy, anaesthetize

drum VERB = **pound**, beat, tap, rap, thrash, tattoo, throb, pulsate

drunk ADJECTIVE = **intoxicated**, plastered (*slang*), drunken, merry (*Brit. informal*), under the influence (*informal*), tipsy, legless (*informal*), inebriated, out to it (*Austral. & N.Z. slang*), babalas (*S. African*)
▷ NOUN = **drunkard**, alcoholic, lush (*slang*), boozer (*informal*), wino (*informal*), inebriate, alko *or* alco (*Austral. slang*)

dry ADJECTIVE **1** = **dehydrated**, dried-up, arid, parched, desiccated ≠ wet **2** = **thirsty**, parched **3** = **sarcastic**, cynical, low-key, sly, sardonic, deadpan, droll, ironical **4** = **dull**, boring, tedious, dreary, tiresome,

monotonous, run-of-the-mill, humdrum ≠ interesting **5** = **plain**, simple, bare, basic, stark, unembellished
▷ VERB **1** = **drain**, make dry **2** *often with* **out** = **dehydrate**, make dry, desiccate, sear, parch, dehumidify ≠ wet ▷ PHRASE: **dry out** *or* **up** = **become dry**, harden, wither, shrivel up, wizen

dual ADJECTIVE = **twofold**, double, twin, matched, paired, duplicate, binary, duplex

dubious ADJECTIVE **1** = **suspect**, suspicious, crooked, dodgy (*Brit., Austral. & N.Z. informal*), questionable, unreliable, fishy (*informal*), disreputable ≠ trustworthy **2** = **unsure**, uncertain, suspicious, hesitating, doubtful, sceptical, tentative, wavering ≠ sure

duck VERB **1** = **bob**, drop, lower, bend, bow, dodge, crouch, stoop **2** (*informal*) = **dodge**, avoid, escape, evade, elude, sidestep, shirk **3** = **dunk**, wet, plunge, dip, submerge, immerse, douse, souse

due ADJECTIVE **1** = **expected**, scheduled **2** = **fitting**, deserved, appropriate, justified, suitable, merited, proper, rightful **3** = **payable**, outstanding, owed, owing, unpaid, in arrears
▷ NOUN = **right(s)**, privilege, deserts, merits, comeuppance (*informal*)
▷ ADVERB = **directly**, dead, straight, exactly, undeviatingly

duel NOUN **1** = **single combat**, affair of honour **2** = **contest**, fight, competition, clash, encounter, engagement, rivalry
▷ VERB = **fight**, struggle, clash, compete, contest, contend, vie with, lock horns

dues PLURAL NOUN = **membership fee**, charges, fee, contribution, levy

duff ADJECTIVE (*Brit., Austral. & N.Z. informal*) = **bad**, poor, useless, inferior, unsatisfactory, defective, imperfect, substandard, bodger *or* bodgie (*Austral. slang*)

dull ADJECTIVE **1** = **boring**, tedious, dreary, flat, plain, monotonous, run-of-the-mill, humdrum ≠ exciting **2** = **lifeless**, indifferent, apathetic, listless, unresponsive, passionless ≠ lively **3** = **cloudy**, dim, gloomy, dismal, overcast, leaden ≠ bright **4** = **blunt**, blunted, unsharpened ≠ sharp
▷ VERB = **relieve**, blunt, lessen, moderate, soften, alleviate, allay, take the edge off

duly ADVERB **1** = **properly**, fittingly, correctly, appropriately, accordingly, suitably, deservedly, rightfully **2** = **on time**, promptly, punctually, at the proper time

dumb ADJECTIVE **1** = **unable to speak**, mute ≠ articulate **2** = **silent**, mute, speechless, tongue-tied, wordless, voiceless, soundless, mum **3** (*informal*) = **stupid**, thick, dull, foolish, dense, unintelligent, asinine, dim-witted (*informal*) ≠ clever

d

dummy NOUN 1 = **model**, figure, mannequin, form, manikin 2 = **imitation**, copy, duplicate, sham, counterfeit, replica 3 (*slang*) = **fool**, idiot, dunce, oaf, simpleton, nitwit (*informal*), blockhead, dumb-ass (*slang*), dorba or dorb (*Austral. slang*), bogan (*Austral. slang*)
▷ MODIFIER = **imitation**, false, fake, artificial, mock, bogus, simulated, sham

dump VERB 1 = **drop**, deposit, throw down, let fall, fling down 2 = **get rid of**, tip, dispose of, unload, jettison, empty out, throw away or out 3 = **scrap**, get rid of, abolish, put an end to, discontinue, jettison, put paid to
▷ NOUN 1 = **rubbish tip**, tip, junkyard, rubbish heap, refuse heap 2 (*informal*) = **pigsty**, hole (*informal*), slum, hovel

dunny NOUN (*Austral. & N.Z. old-fashioned, informal*) = **toilet**, lavatory, bathroom, loo (*Brit. informal*), W.C., bog (*slang*), Gents or Ladies, can (*U.S. & Canad. slang*), bogger (*Austral. slang*), brasco (*Austral. slang*)

duplicate ADJECTIVE = **identical**, matched, matching, twin, corresponding, twofold
▷ NOUN 1 = **copy**, facsimile 2 = **photocopy**, copy, reproduction, replica, carbon copy
▷ VERB 1 = **repeat**, reproduce, copy, clone, replicate 2 = **copy**

durable ADJECTIVE 1 = **hard-wearing**, strong, tough, reliable, resistant, sturdy, long-lasting ≠ fragile 2 = **enduring**, continuing, dependable, unwavering, unfaltering

duration NOUN = **length**, time, period, term, stretch, extent, spell, span, time frame, timeline

dusk NOUN = **twilight**, evening, evo (*Austral. slang*), nightfall, sunset, dark, sundown, eventide, gloaming (*Scot. poetic*) ≠ dawn

dust NOUN 1 = **grime**, grit, powder 2 = **particles**
▷ VERB = **sprinkle**, cover, powder, spread, spray, scatter, sift, dredge

dusty ADJECTIVE = **dirty**, grubby, unclean, unswept

● WORD POWER
● Dutch is a member of the
● western branch of the
● Germanic family of languages,
● as is English. Several compound
● words, whose combination
● of parts contributes a new
● meaning, have been borrowed
● from Dutch into English. The
● word *poppycock*, which came
● into English in the 19th century,
● literally means 'soft excrement',
● which evolved into its modern
● meaning of 'nonsense'. The
● association between words
● for faeces and words meaning
● rubbish has also given us the
● stronger terms 'crap', 'cack',
● and 'bullshit'. Poppycock has
● nothing to do with either
● poppies or cocks, but the
● perception that this was an odd
● mixture may have contributed

- to the meaning of nonsense.
- It is an informal term, often
- used on its own as a mild
- expletive, or in combination
- with *a bunch /load of*. Another
- compound word which has an
- interesting juxtaposition of
- parts is *maelstrom*. From the
- obsolete Dutch 17th century
- *maelstroom* meaning 'whirl-
- stream', it originally denoted an
- authentic strong tidal current
- off the west coast of Norway,
- responsible for shipwrecks.
- This specialized sense, which
- is often capitalized, has been
- superseded by the much more
- common figurative sense
- of maelstrom, meaning a
- turbulent confusion, e.g. *a*
- *maelstrom of emotions*. It is
- quite a literary word, much
- less common in speech than
- in writing. The second part
- 'strom' evokes 'storm' which
- has reinforced the meaning of
- tumult.

duty NOUN 1 = **responsibility**, job, task, work, role, function, obligation, assignment 2 = **tax**, toll, levy, tariff, excise ▷ PHRASE: **on duty** = **at work**, busy, engaged, on active service

dwarf NOUN = **gnome**, midget, Lilliputian, Tom Thumb, pygmy *or* pigmy

  ▷ MODIFIER = **miniature**, small, baby, tiny, diminutive, bonsai, undersized

  ▷ VERB 1 = **tower above** *or*

over, dominate, overlook, stand over, loom over, stand head and shoulders above 2 = **eclipse**, tower above *or* over, put in the shade, diminish

dwell VERB (*formal* or *literary*) = **live**, reside, lodge, abide

dwelling NOUN (*formal* or *literary*) = **home**, house, residence, abode, quarters, lodging, habitation, domicile, whare (*N.Z.*)

dwindle VERB = **lessen**, decline, fade, shrink, diminish, decrease, wane, subside ≠ increase

dye NOUN = **colouring**, colour, pigment, stain, tint, tinge, colorant

  ▷ VERB = **colour**, stain, tint, tinge, pigment

dying ADJECTIVE 1 = **near death**, moribund, in extremis (*Latin*), at death's door, not long for this world 2 = **final**, last, parting, departing 3 = **failing**, declining, foundering, diminishing, decreasing, dwindling, subsiding

dynamic ADJECTIVE = **energetic**, powerful, vital, go-ahead, lively, animated, high-powered, forceful ≠ apathetic

dynasty NOUN = **empire**, house, rule, regime, sovereignty

d

Ee

each ADJECTIVE = **every**, every single

▷ PRONOUN = **every one**, all, each one, each and every one, one and all

▷ ADVERB = **apiece**, individually, for each, to each, respectively, per person, per head, per capita

● WORD POWER
● *Each* is a singular pronoun and
● should be used with a singular
● verb – for example, *each of*
● *the candidates was interviewed*
● *separately* (not *were interviewed*
● *separately*).

eager ADJECTIVE 1 *often with* **to** *or* **for** = **anxious**, keen, hungry, impatient, itching, thirsty ≠ unenthusiastic 2 = **keen**, interested, intense, enthusiastic, passionate, avid (*informal*), fervent ≠ uninterested

ear NOUN = **sensitivity**, taste, discrimination, appreciation

▷ RELATED WORD: *adjectives* **aural**
● WORD POWER
● The *ear* is the organ of hearing
● and balance in humans. In
● the phrase *walls have ears*,
● walls are given the human
● characteristic of a sense of
● hearing. This expression was

● used as a slogan of national
● security in the Second World
● War to discourage indiscreet
● talk along the general
● population. The ability to
● discriminate sounds has led
● to ear meaning sensitivity,
● especially *an ear for music* and
● *an ear for language*. Hearing and
● listening are activities which
● can be selective, therefore ear
● also means paying attention:
● closely in *all ears*; as a conscious
● decision in *lend an ear*; and not
● at all in *turn a deaf ear*. Although
● it might be expected that *ears*
● *of corn* are related to the human
● ear in their resemblance, these
● are actually two different
● words which look the same.

early ADVERB 1 = **in good time**, beforehand, ahead of schedule, in advance, with time to spare ≠ late 2 = **too soon**, before the usual time, prematurely, ahead of time ≠ late

▷ ADJECTIVE 1 = **first**, opening, initial, introductory 2 = **premature**, forward, advanced, untimely, unseasonable ≠ belated 3 = **primitive**, first, earliest, young, original, undeveloped, primordial, primeval ≠ developed

earmark VERB 1 = **set aside**, reserve, label, flag, allocate, designate, mark out 2 = **mark out**, identify, designate

earn VERB 1 = **be paid**, make, get, receive, gain, net, collect, bring in **2** = **deserve**, win, gain, attain, justify, merit, warrant, be entitled to

earnest ADJECTIVE **1** = **serious**, grave, intense, dedicated, sincere, thoughtful, solemn, ardent ≠ frivolous **2** = **determined**, dogged, intent, persistent, persevering, resolute, wholehearted ≠ half-hearted

earnings PLURAL NOUN = **income**, pay, wages, revenue, proceeds, salary, receipts, remuneration

earth NOUN **1** = **world**, planet, globe, sphere, orb, earthly sphere **2** = **ground**, land, dry land, terra firma **3** = **soil**, ground, land, dust, clay, dirt, turf, silt

earthly ADJECTIVE **1** = **worldly**, material, secular, mortal, temporal, human ≠ spiritual **2** = **sensual**, worldly, physical, fleshly, bodily, carnal **3** (informal) = **possible**, likely, practical, feasible, conceivable, imaginable

ease NOUN
1 = **straightforwardness**, simplicity, readiness **2** = **comfort**, luxury, leisure, relaxation, prosperity, affluence, rest, repose ≠ hardship **3** = **peace of mind**, peace, content, quiet, comfort, happiness, serenity, tranquillity ≠ agitation
▷ VERB **1** = **relieve**, calm, soothe, lessen, alleviate, lighten, lower, relax ≠ aggravate **2** often with **off** or **up** = **reduce**, diminish, lessen, slacken **3** = **move carefully**, edge, slip, inch, slide, creep, manoeuvre

easily ADVERB = **without difficulty**, smoothly, readily, comfortably, effortlessly, with ease, straightforwardly

easy ADJECTIVE **1** = **simple**, straightforward, no trouble, not difficult, effortless, painless, uncomplicated, child's play (informal) ≠ hard **2** = **untroubled**, relaxed, peaceful, serene, tranquil, quiet **3** = **carefree**, comfortable, leisurely, trouble-free, untroubled, cushy (informal) ≠ difficult **4** = **tolerant**, soft, mild, laid-back (informal), indulgent, easy-going, lenient, permissive ≠ strict

eat VERB **1** = **consume**, swallow, chew, scoff (slang), devour, munch, tuck into (informal), put away **2** = **have a meal**, lunch, breakfast, dine, snack, feed, graze (informal), have lunch

ebb VERB **1** = **flow back**, go out, withdraw, retreat, wane, recede **2** = **decline**, flag, diminish, decrease, dwindle, lessen, subside, fall away
▷ NOUN = **flowing back**, going out, withdrawal, retreat, wane, low water, low tide, outgoing tide

eccentric ADJECTIVE **1** = **odd**, strange, peculiar, irregular, quirky, unconventional, idiosyncratic, outlandish, daggy (Austral. & N.Z. informal) ≠ normal
▷ NOUN = **crank** (informal), character (informal), oddball (informal), nonconformist, weirdo or weirdie (informal)

echo NOUN **1** = **reverberation**,

ringing, repetition, answer, resonance, resounding **2** = **copy**, reflection, clone, reproduction, imitation, duplicate, double, reiteration

▷ VERB **1** = **reverberate**, repeat, resound, ring, resonate **2** = **recall**, reflect, copy, mirror, resemble, imitate, ape

eclipse NOUN = **obscuring**, covering, blocking, shading, dimming, extinction, darkening, blotting out

▷ VERB **1** = **surpass**, exceed, overshadow, excel, transcend, outdo, outclass, outshine

economic ADJECTIVE
1 = **financial**, industrial, commercial **2** (*Brit.*) = **profitable**, successful, commercial, rewarding, productive, lucrative, worthwhile, viable **3** (*informal*) = **economical**, cheap, reasonable, modest, low-priced, inexpensive

economical ADJECTIVE
1 = **thrifty**, sparing, careful, prudent, provident, frugal, parsimonious, scrimping ≠ extravagant **2** = **efficient**, sparing, cost-effective, money-saving, time-saving ≠ wasteful

economy NOUN **1** = **financial system**, financial state **2** = **thrift**, restraint, prudence, husbandry, frugality, parsimony

ecstasy NOUN = **rapture**, delight, joy, bliss, euphoria, fervour, elation ≠ agony

ecstatic ADJECTIVE = **rapturous**, entranced, joyous, elated, overjoyed, blissful, euphoric, enraptured, stoked (*Austral. & N.Z. informal*)

edge NOUN **1** = **border**, side, limit, outline, boundary, fringe, verge, brink **2** = **verge**, point, brink, threshold **3** = **advantage**, lead, dominance, superiority, upper hand, head start, ascendancy, whip hand **4** = **power**, force, bite, effectiveness, incisiveness, powerful quality **5** = **sharpness**, point, bitterness, keenness

▷ VERB **1** = **inch**, ease, creep, slink, steal, sidle, move slowly **2** = **border**, fringe, hem, pipe

▷ PHRASE: on edge = **tense**, nervous, impatient, irritable, apprehensive, edgy, ill at ease, on tenterhooks, adrenalized

edit VERB = **revise**, improve, correct, polish, adapt, rewrite, condense, redraft

edition NOUN **1** = **printing**, publication **2** = **copy**, impression **3** = **version**, volume, issue **4** = **programme** (*tv, radio*)

educate VERB = **teach**, school, train, develop, improve, inform, discipline, tutor

educated ADJECTIVE **1** = **cultured**, intellectual, learned, sophisticated, refined, cultivated, enlightened, knowledgeable ≠ uncultured **2** = **taught**, schooled, coached, informed, tutored, instructed, nurtured, well-informed ≠ uneducated

education NOUN **1** = **teaching**, schooling, training, development, discipline, instruction, nurture, tuition **2** = **learning**, schooling, cultivation, refinement

educational ADJECTIVE
1 = **academic**, school, learning, teaching, scholastic, pedagogical, pedagogic **2** = **instructive**, useful, cultural, illuminating, enlightening, informative, instructional, edifying

eerie ADJECTIVE = **uncanny**, strange, frightening, ghostly, weird, mysterious, scary (*informal*), sinister

effect NOUN **1** = **result**, consequence, conclusion, outcome, event, end result, upshot **2** = **impression**, feeling, impact, influence **3** = **purpose**, impression, sense, intent, essence, thread, tenor
▷ VERB = **bring about**, produce, complete, achieve, perform, fulfil, accomplish, execute

● WORD POWER
● It is quite common for the
● verb *effect* to be mistakenly
● used where *affect* is intended.
● *Effect* is relatively uncommon
● and rather formal, and is a
● synonym of 'bring about'.
● Conversely, the noun *effect* is
● quite often mistakenly written
● with an initial *a*. The following
● are correct: *the group is still*
● *recovering from the effects of the*
● *recession; they really are powerless*
● *to effect any change*. The next
● two examples are incorrect: *the*
● *full affects of the shutdown won't*

● *be felt for several more days; men*
● *whose lack of hair doesn't effect*
● *their self-esteem.*

effective ADJECTIVE **1** = **efficient**, successful, useful, active, capable, valuable, helpful, adequate ≠ ineffective **2** = **powerful**, strong, convincing, persuasive, telling, impressive, compelling, forceful ≠ weak **3** = **virtual**, essential, practical, implied, implicit, tacit, unacknowledged **4** = **in operation**, official, current, legal, active, in effect, valid, operative ≠ inoperative

effects PLURAL
NOUN = **belongings**, goods, things, property, stuff, gear, possessions, paraphernalia

efficiency NOUN
1 = **effectiveness**, power, economy, productivity, organization, cost-effectiveness, orderliness **2** = **competence**, expertise, capability, professionalism, proficiency, adeptness

efficient ADJECTIVE **1** = **effective**, successful, structured, productive, systematic, streamlined, cost-effective, methodical ≠ inefficient **2** = **competent**, professional, capable, organized, productive, proficient, businesslike, well-organized ≠ incompetent

effort NOUN **1** = **attempt**, try, endeavour, shot (*informal*), bid, essay, go (*informal*), stab (*informal*) **2** = **exertion**, work, trouble, energy, struggle, application, graft, toil

egg NOUN = **ovum**, gamete, germ cell ▷ PHRASE: **egg someone on** = **incite**, push, encourage, urge, prompt, spur, provoke, prod

eject VERB 1 = **throw out**, remove, turn out, expel (*slang*), oust, banish, drive out, evict 2 = **bail out**, escape, get out

elaborate ADJECTIVE 1 = **complicated**, detailed, studied, complex, precise, thorough, intricate, painstaking 2 = **ornate**, involved, complex, fancy, complicated, intricate, baroque, ornamented ≠ plain ▷ VERB 1 = **develop**, flesh out 2 *usually with* **on** *or* **upon** = **expand upon**, extend upon, enlarge on, amplify upon, embellish, flesh out, add detail to ≠ simplify

elastic ADJECTIVE 1 = **flexible**, supple, rubbery, pliable, plastic, springy, pliant, tensile ≠ rigid 2 = **adaptable**, yielding, variable, flexible, accommodating, tolerant, adjustable, supple ≠ inflexible

elbow NOUN = **joint**, angle, curve

elder ADJECTIVE = **older**, first, senior, first-born ▷ NOUN = **older person**, senior

elect VERB 1 = **vote for**, choose, pick, determine, select, appoint, opt for, settle on 2 = **choose**, decide, prefer, select, opt

election NOUN 1 = **vote**, poll, ballot, referendum, franchise, plebiscite, show of hands 2 = **appointment**, picking, choice, selection

electric ADJECTIVE 1 = **electric-powered**, powered, cordless, battery-operated, electrically-charged, mains-operated 2 = **charged**, exciting, stirring, thrilling, stimulating, dynamic, tense, rousing, adrenalized

elegance NOUN = **style**, taste, grace, dignity, sophistication, grandeur, refinement, gracefulness

elegant ADJECTIVE = **stylish**, fine, sophisticated, delicate, handsome, refined, chic, exquisite, schmick (*Austral. informal*) ≠ inelegant

element NOUN 1 = **component**, part, unit, section, factor, principle, aspect, foundation 2 = **group**, faction, clique, set, party, circle 3 = **trace**, suggestion, hint, dash, suspicion, tinge, smattering, soupçon ▷ PLURAL NOUN = **weather conditions**, climate, the weather, wind and rain, atmospheric conditions, powers of nature ▷ PHRASE: **in your element** = **in a situation you enjoy**, in your natural environment, in familiar surroundings

elementary ADJECTIVE = **simple**, clear, easy, plain, straightforward, rudimentary, uncomplicated, undemanding ≠ complicated

elevate VERB 1 = **promote**, raise, advance, upgrade,

exalt, kick upstairs (*informal*),
aggrandize, give advancement to
2 = **increase**, lift, raise, step up,
intensify, move up, hoist, raise
high 3 = **raise**, lift, heighten,
uplift, hoist, lift up, raise up, hike
up

elevated ADJECTIVE 1 = **exalted**,
important, august, grand,
superior, noble, dignified, high-
ranking 2 = **high-minded**, fine,
grand, noble, inflated, dignified,
sublime, lofty ≠ humble
3 = **raised**, high, upraised

elicit VERB 1 = **bring about**, cause,
derive, bring out, evoke, give
rise to, draw out, bring forth
2 = **obtain**, extract, exact, evoke,
wrest, draw out, extort

eligible ADJECTIVE 1 = **entitled**, fit,
qualified, suitable ≠ ineligible
2 = **available**, free, single,
unmarried, unattached

eliminate VERB = **remove**, end,
stop, withdraw, get rid of, abolish,
cut out, dispose of

elite NOUN = **aristocracy**, best,
pick, cream, upper class, nobility,
crème de la crème (*French*), flower
≠ rabble

eloquent ADJECTIVE
1 = **silver-tongued**, moving,
powerful, effective, stirring,
articulate, persuasive, forceful
≠ inarticulate 2 = **expressive**,
telling, pointed, significant, vivid,
meaningful, indicative

elsewhere ADVERB = **in** *or* **to**
another place, away, abroad,
hence (*archaic*), somewhere else,

not here, in other places, in *or* to a
different place

elude VERB 1 = **evade**, escape,
lose, avoid, flee, duck (*informal*),
dodge, get away from 2 = **escape**,
baffle, frustrate, puzzle, stump,
foil, be beyond (someone), thwart

⬤ **WORD POWER**
⬤ *Elude* is sometimes wrongly
⬤ used where *allude* is meant: *he*
⬤ *was alluding* (not *eluding*) *to his*
⬤ *previous visit to the city.*

elusive ADJECTIVE 1 = **difficult**
to catch, tricky, slippery,
difficult to find, evasive, shifty
2 = **indefinable**, fleeting, subtle,
indefinite, transient, intangible,
indescribable, transitory

⬤ **WORD POWER**
⬤ The spelling of *elusive*, as in *a*
⬤ *shy, elusive character*, should be
⬤ noted. This adjective derives
⬤ from the verb *elude*, and should
⬤ not be confused with the rare
⬤ word *illusive* meaning 'not real'
⬤ or 'based on illusion'.

email *or* **e-mail** NOUN = **mail**,
electronic mail, webmail

emanate VERB *often with* **from**
= **flow**, emerge, spring, proceed,
arise, stem, derive, originate

embargo NOUN = **ban**, bar,
restriction, boycott, restraint,
prohibition, moratorium,
stoppage, rahui (*N.Z.*)
▷ VERB = **block**, stop, bar, ban,
restrict, boycott, prohibit,
blacklist

embark VERB = **go aboard**, climb
aboard, board ship, step aboard,

go on board, take ship ≠ get off
▷ PHRASE: **embark on something**
= **begin**, start, launch, enter, take
up, set out, set about, plunge into

embarrass VERB = **shame**,
distress, show up (*informal*),
humiliate, disconcert, fluster,
mortify, discomfit

embarrassed ADJECTIVE
= **ashamed**, shamed,
uncomfortable, awkward,
abashed, humiliated, uneasy,
unsettled

embarrassing ADJECTIVE
= **humiliating**, upsetting,
compromising, delicate,
uncomfortable, awkward,
sensitive, troublesome, barro
(*Austral. slang*)

embarrassment NOUN
1 = **shame**, distress, showing
up (*informal*), humiliation,
discomfort, unease, self-
consciousness, awkwardness
2 = **problem**, difficulty, nuisance,
source of trouble, thorn in your
flesh 3 = **predicament**, problem,
difficulty (*informal*), mess, jam
(*informal*), plight, scrape (*informal*),
pickle (*informal*)

embody VERB 1 = **personify**,
represent, stand for, manifest,
exemplify, symbolize, typify,
actualize 2 *often with* **in**
= **incorporate**, include, contain,
combine, collect, take in,
encompass

embrace VERB 1 = **hug**, hold,
cuddle, seize, squeeze, clasp,
envelop, canoodle (*slang*)

2 = **accept**, support, welcome,
adopt, take up, seize, espouse,
take on board 3 = **include**,
involve, cover, contain, take
in, incorporate, comprise,
encompass
▷ NOUN = **hug**, hold, cuddle,
squeeze, clinch (*slang*), clasp

embroil VERB = **involve**, mix
up, implicate, entangle, mire,
ensnare, enmesh

embryo NOUN 1 = **fetus**, unborn
child, fertilized egg 2 = **germ**,
beginning, source, root, seed,
nucleus, rudiment

emerge VERB 1 = **come out**,
appear, surface, rise, arise,
turn up, spring up, emanate
≠ withdraw 2 = **become
apparent**, come out, become
known, come to light, crop up,
transpire, become evident, come
out in the wash

emergence NOUN 1 = **coming**,
development, arrival, surfacing,
rise, appearance, arising, turning
up 2 = **disclosure**, publishing,
broadcasting, broadcast,
publication, declaration,
revelation, becoming known

emergency NOUN = **crisis**,
danger, difficulty, accident,
disaster, necessity, plight, scrape
(*informal*)
▷ ADJECTIVE 1 = **urgent**, crisis,
immediate 2 = **alternative**,
extra, additional, substitute,
replacement, temporary,
makeshift, stopgap

emigrate VERB = **move abroad**,

move, relocate, migrate, resettle, leave your country

eminent ADJECTIVE = **prominent**, noted, respected, famous, celebrated, distinguished, well-known, esteemed ≠ unknown

emission NOUN = **giving off** *or* **out**, release, shedding, leak, radiation, discharge, transmission, ejaculation

emit VERB 1 = **give off**, release, leak, transmit, discharge, send out, radiate, eject ≠ absorb **2** = **utter**, produce, voice, give out, let out

emotion NOUN 1 = **feeling**, spirit, soul, passion, excitement, sensation, sentiment, fervour **2** = **instinct**, sentiment, sensibility, intuition, tenderness, gut feeling, soft-heartedness

emotional ADJECTIVE
1 = **psychological**, private, personal, hidden, spiritual, inner **2** = **moving**, touching, affecting, stirring, sentimental, poignant, emotive, heart-rending **3** = **emotive**, sensitive, controversial, delicate, contentious, heated, inflammatory, touchy **4** = **passionate**, sentimental, temperamental, excitable, demonstrative, hot-blooded

emphasis NOUN 1 = **importance**, attention, weight, significance, stress, priority, prominence **2** = **stress**, accent, force, weight

emphasize VERB 1 = **highlight**, stress, underline, draw attention

to, dwell on, play up, make a point of, give priority to ≠ minimize **2** = **stress**, accentuate, lay stress on

emphatic ADJECTIVE 1 = **forceful**, positive, definite, vigorous, unmistakable, insistent, unequivocal, vehement ≠ hesitant **2** = **significant**, pronounced, decisive, resounding, conclusive

empire NOUN 1 = **kingdom**, territory, province, federation, commonwealth, realm, domain **2** = **organization**, company, business, firm, concern, corporation, consortium, syndicate ▷ **RELATED WORD**: *adjective* imperial

empirical ADJECTIVE = **first-hand**, direct, observed, practical, actual, experimental, pragmatic, factual ≠ hypothetical

employ VERB 1 = **hire**, commission, appoint, take on, retain, engage, recruit, sign up **2** = **use**, apply, exercise, exert, make use of, utilize, ply, bring to bear **3** = **spend**, fill, occupy, involve, engage, take up, make use of, use up

employed ADJECTIVE
1 = **working**, in work, having a job, in employment, in a job, earning your living ≠ out of work **2** = **busy**, active, occupied, engaged, hard at work, in harness, rushed off your feet ≠ idle

employee *or* (U.S.) **employe** NOUN = **worker**, labourer, workman, staff member, member of staff, hand, wage-earner, white-collar worker

employer NOUN 1 = **boss** (*informal*), manager, head, leader, director, chief, owner, master, baas (*S. African*), sherang (*Austral. & N.Z.*) 2 = **company**, business, firm, organization, establishment, outfit (*informal*)

employment NOUN 1 = **job**, work, position, trade, post, situation, profession, occupation 2 = **taking on**, commissioning, appointing, hire, hiring, retaining, engaging, appointment 3 = **use**, application, exertion, exercise, utilization

empower VERB 1 = **authorize**, allow, commission, qualify, permit, sanction, entitle, delegate 2 = **enable**, equip, emancipate, give means to, enfranchise

empty ADJECTIVE 1 = **bare**, clear, abandoned, deserted, vacant, free, void, desolate ≠ full 2 = **meaningless**, cheap, hollow, vain, idle, futile, insincere 3 = **worthless**, meaningless, hollow, pointless, futile, senseless, fruitless, inane ≠ meaningful
▷ VERB 1 = **clear**, drain, void, unload, pour out, unpack, remove the contents of ≠ fill 2 = **exhaust**, consume the contents of, void, deplete, use up ≠ replenish 3 = **evacuate**, clear, vacate

emulate VERB = **imitate**, follow, copy, mirror, echo, mimic, model yourself on

enable VERB 1 = **allow**, permit, empower, give someone the opportunity, give someone the means ≠ prevent 2 = **authorize**, allow, permit, qualify, sanction, entitle, license, warrant ≠ stop

enact VERB 1 = **establish**, order, command, approve, sanction, proclaim, decree, authorize 2 = **perform**, play, present, stage, represent, put on, portray, depict

enchant VERB = **fascinate**, delight, charm, entrance, dazzle, captivate, enthral, beguile

enclose or **inclose** VERB 1 = **surround**, circle, bound, fence, confine, close in, wall in, encircle 2 = **send with**, include, put in, insert

encompass VERB 1 = **include**, hold, cover, admit, deal with, contain, take in, embrace 2 = **surround**, circle, enclose, close in, envelop, encircle, fence in, ring

encounter VERB 1 = **experience**, meet, face, suffer, have, go through, sustain, endure 2 = **meet**, confront, come across, bump into (*informal*), run across, come upon, chance upon, meet by chance
▷ NOUN 1 = **meeting**, brush, confrontation, rendezvous, chance meeting 2 = **battle**, conflict, clash, contest, run-in (*informal*), confrontation, head-to-head

encourage VERB 1 = **inspire**,

comfort, cheer, reassure, console, hearten, cheer up, embolden ≠ discourage **2 = urge**, persuade, prompt, spur, coax, egg on ≠ dissuade **3 = promote**, back, support, increase, foster, advocate, stimulate, endorse ≠ prevent

encouragement NOUN

1 = inspiration, support, comfort, comforting, cheer, cheering, reassurance, morale boosting **2 = urging**, prompting, stimulus, persuasion, coaxing, egging on, incitement **3 = promotion**, backing, support, endorsement, stimulation, furtherance

end NOUN **1 = close**, ending, finish, expiry, expiration ≠ beginning **2 = conclusion**, ending, climax, completion, finale, culmination, denouement, consummation ≠ start **3 = finish**, close, stop, resolution, conclusion, closure, completion, termination **4 = extremity**, limit, edge, border, extent, extreme, margin, boundary **5 = tip**, point, head, peak, extremity **6 = purpose**, point, reason, goal, target, aim, object, mission **7 = outcome**, resolution, conclusion, destruction, passing on, doom, demise, extinction **9 = remnant**, butt, stub, scrap, fragment, stump, remainder, leftover
▷ VERB **1 = stop**, finish, halt, cease, wind up, terminate, call off, discontinue ≠ start

2 = finish, close, conclude, wind up, culminate, terminate, come to an end, draw to a close ≠ begin
▷ RELATED WORDS: *adjectives* **final, terminal, ultimate**

endanger VERB **= put at risk**, risk, threaten, compromise, jeopardize, imperil, put in danger, expose to danger ≠ save

endearing ADJECTIVE
= attractive, winning, pleasing, appealing, sweet, engaging, charming, pleasant

endeavour (*formal*) VERB **= try**, labour, attempt, aim, struggle, venture, strive, aspire
▷ NOUN **= attempt**, try, effort, trial, bid, venture, enterprise, undertaking

ending NOUN **= finish**, end, close, conclusion, summing up, completion, finale, culmination ≠ start

endless ADJECTIVE **= eternal**, infinite, continual, unlimited, interminable, incessant, boundless, everlasting ≠ temporary

endorse VERB **1 = approve**, back, support, champion, promote, recommend, advocate, uphold **2 = sign**, initial, countersign, sign on the back of

endorsement NOUN **= approval**, backing, support, favour, recommendation, acceptance, agreement, upholding

endow VERB **1 = finance**, fund, pay for, award, confer, bestow, bequeath, donate money to

2 = **imbue**

endowed ADJECTIVE *usually
with* **with** = **provided**, favoured,
graced, blessed, supplied,
furnished

endowment NOUN = **provision**,
funding, award, grant, gift,
contribution, subsidy, donation,
koha (*N.Z.*)

endurance NOUN **1** = **staying
power**, strength, resolution,
determination, patience,
stamina, fortitude, persistence
2 = **permanence**, stability,
continuity, duration, longevity,
durability, continuance

endure VERB **1** = **experience**,
suffer, bear, meet, encounter, cope
with, sustain, undergo **2** = **last**,
continue, remain, stay, stand, go
on, survive, live on

enemy NOUN = **foe**, rival,
opponent, the opposition,
competitor, the other side,
adversary, antagonist ≠ friend

energetic ADJECTIVE **1** = **forceful**,
determined, active, aggressive,
dynamic, vigorous, hard-hitting,
strenuous **2** = **lively**, active,
dynamic, vigorous, animated,
tireless, bouncy, indefatigable
≠ lethargic **3** = **strenuous**,
hard, taxing, demanding, tough,
exhausting, vigorous, arduous

energy NOUN **1** = **strength**,
might, stamina, forcefulness
2 = **liveliness**, drive,
determination, pep, vitality,
vigour, verve, resilience
3 = **power**

enforce VERB **1** = **carry out**,
apply, implement, fulfil, execute,
administer, put into effect, put
into action **2** = **impose**, force,
insist on

engage VERB **1** = **participate in**,
join in, take part in, undertake,
embark on, enter into,
become involved in, set about
2 = **captivate**, catch, arrest, fix,
capture **3** = **occupy**, involve,
draw, grip, absorb, preoccupy,
immerse, engross **4** = **employ**,
appoint, take on, hire, retain,
recruit, enlist, enrol ≠ dismiss
5 = **set going**, apply, trigger,
activate, switch on, energize,
bring into operation **6** (*military*)
= **begin battle with**, attack, take
on, encounter, fall on, battle with,
meet, assail

engaged ADJECTIVE **1** = **occupied**,
working, employed, busy, tied
up **2** = **betrothed**, promised,
pledged, affianced, promised in
marriage ≠ unattached **3** = **in
use**, busy, tied up, unavailable
≠ free

engagement NOUN
1 = **appointment**, meeting,
interview, date, commitment,
arrangement, rendezvous
2 = **betrothal**, marriage contract,
troth (*archaic*), agreement to
marry **3** = **battle**, fight, conflict,
action, struggle, clash, encounter,
combat **4** = **participation**,
joining, taking part, involvement

engaging ADJECTIVE = **charming**,
interesting, pleasing, attractive,

lovely, entertaining, winning,
fetching (*informal*) ≠ unpleasant

engine NOUN = **machine**, motor,
mechanism, generator, dynamo

engineer NOUN 1 = **designer**,
producer, architect, developer,
deviser, creator, planner, inventor
2 = **worker**, specialist, operator,
practitioner, operative, driver,
conductor, technician
▷ VERB 1 = **design**, plan, create,
construct, devise 2 = **bring
about**, plan, effect, set up
(*informal*), scheme, arrange, plot,
mastermind

engraving NOUN = **print**, carving,
etching, inscription, plate,
woodcut, dry point

engulf VERB 1 = **immerse**,
swamp, submerge, overrun,
inundate, envelop, swallow up
2 = **overwhelm**, overcome, crush,
swamp

enhance VERB = **improve**, better,
increase, lift, boost, add to,
strengthen, reinforce ≠ reduce

enjoy VERB 1 = **take pleasure in**
or **from**, like, love, appreciate,
relish, delight in, be pleased with,
be fond of ≠ hate 2 = **have**, use,
own, experience, possess, have
the benefit of, reap the benefits of,
be blessed or favoured with

enjoyable ADJECTIVE
= **pleasurable**, good, great,
fine, nice, satisfying, lovely,
entertaining ≠ unpleasant

enjoyment NOUN 1 = **pleasure**,
liking, fun, delight,
entertainment, joy, happiness,

relish 2 = **benefit**, use, advantage,
favour, possession, blessing

enlarge VERB 1 = **expand**,
increase, extend, add to, build
up, widen, intensify, broaden
≠ reduce 2 = **grow**, increase,
extend, expand, swell, become
bigger, puff up, grow larger
▷ PHRASE: **enlarge on something**
= **expand on**, develop, add to,
fill out, elaborate on, flesh out,
expatiate on, give further details
about

enlighten VERB = **inform**, tell,
teach, advise, counsel, educate,
instruct, illuminate

enlightened ADJECTIVE
= **informed**, aware, reasonable,
educated, sophisticated,
cultivated, open-minded,
knowledgeable ≠ ignorant

enlightenment NOUN
= **understanding**, learning,
education, knowledge,
instruction, awareness, wisdom,
insight

enlist VERB 1 = **join up**, join, enter
(into), register, volunteer, sign
up, enrol 2 = **obtain**, get, gain,
secure, engage, procure

enormous ADJECTIVE = **huge**,
massive, vast, extensive,
tremendous, gross, immense,
gigantic, supersize ≠ tiny

enough ADJECTIVE = **sufficient**,
adequate, ample, abundant, as
much as you need, as much as is
necessary
▷ PRONOUN = **sufficiency**, plenty,
sufficient, abundance, adequacy,

right amount, ample supply
▷ ADVERB = **sufficiently**,
amply, reasonably, adequately,
satisfactorily, abundantly,
tolerably

enquire ▷ see inquire

enquiry ▷ see inquiry

enrage VERB = **anger**, infuriate,
incense, madden, inflame,
exasperate, antagonize, make you
angry ≠ calm

enrich VERB 1 = **enhance**, develop,
improve, boost, supplement,
refine, heighten, augment
2 = **make rich**, make wealthy,
make affluent, make prosperous,
make well-off

enrol or (U.S.) **enroll** VERB
1 = **enlist**, register, be accepted,
be admitted, join up, put your
name down for, sign up or on
2 = **recruit**, take on, enlist

en route ADVERB = **on** or **along
the way**, travelling, on the road,
in transit, on the journey

ensemble NOUN 1 = **group**,
company, band, troupe, cast,
orchestra, chorus 2 = **collection**,
set, body, whole, total, sum,
combination, entity 3 = **outfit**,
suit, get-up (informal), costume

ensue VERB = **follow**, result,
develop, proceed, arise, stem,
derive, issue ≠ come first

ensure VERB 1 = **make certain**,
guarantee, secure, make sure,
confirm, warrant, certify
2 = **protect**, defend, secure,
safeguard, guard, make safe

entail VERB = **involve**, require,

produce, demand, call for,
occasion, need, bring about

enter VERB 1 = **come** or **go
in** or **into**, arrive, set foot in
somewhere, cross the threshold
of somewhere, make an entrance
≠ exit 2 = **penetrate**, get in,
pierce, pass into, perforate
3 = **join**, start work at, begin
work at, enrol in, enlist in ≠ leave
4 = **participate in**, join (in), be
involved in, get involved in, play
a part in, partake in, associate
yourself with, start to be in
5 = **begin**, start, take up, move
into, commence, set out on,
embark upon 6 = **compete in**,
contest, join in, fight, sign up for,
go in for 7 = **record**, note, register,
log, list, write down, take down,
inscribe

enterprise NOUN 1 = **firm**,
company, business, concern,
operation, organization,
establishment, commercial
undertaking 2 = **venture**,
operation, project, adventure,
undertaking, programme,
pursuit, endeavour 3 = **initiative**,
energy, daring, enthusiasm,
imagination, drive, ingenuity,
originality

enterprising ADJECTIVE
= **resourceful**, original, spirited,
daring, bold, enthusiastic,
imaginative, energetic

entertain VERB 1 = **amuse**,
interest, please, delight,
charm, enthral, cheer, regale
2 = **show hospitality to**, receive,

accommodate, treat, put up,
lodge, be host to, have company
of **3** = **consider**, imagine, think
about, contemplate, conceive of,
bear in mind, keep in mind, give
thought to

entertainment NOUN
1 = **enjoyment**, fun, pleasure,
leisure, relaxation, recreation,
enjoyment, amusement
2 = **pastime**, show, sport,
performance, treat, presentation,
leisure activity

enthusiasm NOUN = **keenness**,
interest, passion, motivation,
relish, zeal, zest, fervour

enthusiast NOUN = **fan**,
supporter, lover, follower, addict,
buff (*informal*), fanatic, devotee

enthusiastic ADJECTIVE = **keen**,
committed, eager, passionate,
vigorous, avid, fervent, zealous
≠ apathetic

entice VERB = **lure**, attract, invite,
persuade, tempt, induce, seduce,
lead on

entire ADJECTIVE = **whole**, full,
complete, total

entirely ADVERB = **completely**,
totally, absolutely, fully,
altogether, thoroughly, wholly,
utterly ≠ partly

entitle VERB **1** = **give the right to**,
allow, enable, permit, sanction,
license, authorize, empower
2 = **call**, name, title, term, label,
dub, christen, give the title of

entity NOUN = **thing**, being,
individual, object, substance,
creature, organism

entrance[1] NOUN **1** = **way in**,
opening, door, approach, access,
entry, gate, passage ≠ exit
2 = **appearance**, coming in,
entry, arrival, introduction ≠ exit
3 = **admission**, access, entry,
entrée, admittance, permission to
enter, right of entry

entrance[2] VERB **1** = **enchant**,
delight, charm, fascinate, dazzle,
captivate, enthral, beguile
≠ bore **2** = **mesmerize**, bewitch,
hypnotize, put a spell on, cast a
spell on, put in a trance

entrant NOUN = **competitor**,
player, candidate, entry,
participant, applicant, contender,
contestant

entrenched *or* **intrenched**
ADJECTIVE = **fixed**, set, rooted,
well-established, ingrained, deep-
seated, deep-rooted, unshakeable
or unshakable

entrepreneur NOUN
= **businessman** *or*
businesswoman, tycoon,
executive, industrialist,
speculator, magnate, impresario,
business executive

entrust *or* **intrust** VERB **1** = **give
custody of**, deliver, commit,
delegate, hand over, turn over,
confide **2** *usually with* **with**
= **assign**

entry NOUN **1** = **admission**,
access, entrance, admittance,
entrée, permission to enter, right
of entry **2** = **coming in**, entering,
appearance, arrival, entrance
≠ exit **3** = **introduction**,

presentation, initiation, inauguration, induction, debut, investiture **4** = **record**, listing, account, note, statement, item **5** = **way in**, opening, door, approach, access, gate, passage, entrance

envelope NOUN = **wrapping**, casing, case, covering, cover, jacket, sleeve, wrapper

environment NOUN
1 = **surroundings**, setting, conditions, situation, medium, circumstances, background, atmosphere **2** (*ecology*) = **habitat**, home, surroundings, territory, terrain, locality, natural home

environmental ADJECTIVE = **ecological**, green

environmentalist NOUN = **conservationist**, ecologist, green

envisage VERB **1** = **imagine**, contemplate, conceive (of), visualize, picture, fancy, think up, conceptualize **2** = **foresee**, see, expect, predict, anticipate, envision

envoy NOUN **1** = **ambassador**, diplomat, emissary
2 = **messenger**, agent, representative, delegate, courier, intermediary, emissary

envy NOUN = **covetousness**, resentment, jealousy, bitterness, resentfulness, enviousness (*informal*)
▷ VERB **1** = **be jealous (of)**, resent, begrudge, be envious (of)
2 = **covet**, desire, crave, aspire to, yearn for, hanker after

epidemic NOUN **1** = **outbreak**, plague, growth, spread, scourge, contagion **2** = **spate**, plague, outbreak, wave, rash, eruption, upsurge

episode NOUN **1** = **event**, experience, happening, matter, affair, incident, adventure, occurrence **2** = **instalment**, part, act, scene, section, chapter, passage

equal ADJECTIVE *often with* **to** *or* **with** = **identical**, the same, matching, equivalent, uniform, alike, corresponding ≠ unequal
2 = **fair**, just, impartial, egalitarian, unbiased, even-handed ≠ unfair **3** = **even**, balanced, fifty-fifty (*informal*), evenly matched ≠ uneven
▷ NOUN = **match**, equivalent, twin, counterpart
▷ VERB **1** = **amount to**, make, come to, total, level, parallel, tie with, equate ≠ be unequal to **2** = **be equal to**, match, reach **3** = **be as good as**, match, compare with, equate with, measure up to, be as great as

equality NOUN **1** = **fairness**, equal opportunity, equal treatment, egalitarianism, fair treatment, justness ≠ inequality
2 = **sameness**, balance, identity, similarity, correspondence, parity, likeness, uniformity ≠ disparity

equate VERB **1** = **identify**, associate, connect, compare, relate, mention in the same

breath, think of in connection
with **2 = make equal**, match,
even up

equation NOUN **= equating**,
comparison, parallel,
correspondence

equilibrium NOUN **= stability**,
balance, symmetry, steadiness,
evenness, equipoise

equip VERB **1 = supply**, provide,
stock, arm, array, furnish, fit
out, kit out **2 = prepare**, qualify,
educate, get ready

equipment NOUN **= apparatus**,
stock, supplies, stuff, tackle, gear,
tools, provisions

equitable ADJECTIVE **= even-
handed**, just, fair, reasonable,
proper, honest, impartial,
unbiased

equivalent ADJECTIVE **= equal**,
same, comparable, parallel,
identical, alike, corresponding,
tantamount ≠ different
▷ NOUN **= equal**, counterpart,
twin, parallel, match, opposite
number

era NOUN **= age**, time, period, date,
generation, epoch, day *or* days

eradicate VERB **= wipe out**,
eliminate, remove, destroy, get rid
of, erase, extinguish, obliterate

e-reader *or* **eReader**
NOUN **= electronic book**, e-book
or ebook, book, Kindle (*trademark*)

erotic ADJECTIVE **= sexual**, sexy
(*informal*), crude, explicit, sensual,
seductive, vulgar, voluptuous

erect ADJECTIVE **= upright**,
straight, stiff, vertical, elevated,

perpendicular, pricked-up
≠ bent
▷ VERB **1 = build**, raise, set up,
construct, put up, assemble, put
together ≠ demolish **2 = found**,
establish, form, create, set up,
institute, organize, put up

erode VERB **1 = disintegrate**,
crumble, deteriorate, corrode,
break up, grind down, waste
away, wear down *or* away
2 = destroy, consume, crumble,
eat away, corrode, break up,
grind down, abrade **3 = weaken**,
destroy, undermine, diminish,
impair, lessen, wear away

erosion NOUN **1 = disintegration**,
deterioration, wearing down
or away, grinding down
2 = deterioration, undermining,
destruction, weakening,
attrition, eating away, abrasion,
grinding down

erratic ADJECTIVE
= unpredictable, variable,
unstable, irregular, inconsistent,
uneven, unreliable, wayward
≠ regular

error NOUN **= mistake**, slip,
blunder, oversight, howler
(*informal*), bloomer (*Brit.
informal*), miscalculation,
solecism, barry *or* Barry Crocker
(*Austral. slang*)

erupt VERB **1 = explode**, blow up,
emit lava **2 = gush**, burst out,
pour forth, belch forth, spew forth
or out **3 = start**, break out, began,
explode, flare up, burst out, boil
over **4** (*medical*) **= break out**,

appear, flare up

escalate VERB 1 = **grow**, increase, extend, intensify, expand, surge, mount, heighten ≠ decrease 2 = **increase**, develop, extend, intensify, expand, build up, heighten ≠ lessen

escape VERB 1 = **get away**, flee, take off, fly, bolt, slip away, abscond, make a break for it, do a Skase (*Austral. informal*) 2 = **avoid**, miss, evade, dodge, shun, elude, duck, steer clear of 3 *usually with* **from** = **leak out**, flow out, gush out, emanate, seep out, exude, spill out, pour forth
▷ NOUN 1 = **getaway**, break, flight, break-out 2 = **avoidance**, evasion, circumvention
3 = **relaxation**, recreation, distraction, diversion, pastime
4 = **leak**, emission, outpouring, seepage, issue, emanation

escort NOUN 1 = **guard**, bodyguard, train, convoy, entourage, retinue, cortege
2 = **companion**, partner, attendant, guide, beau, chaperon
▷ VERB = **accompany**, lead, partner, conduct, guide, shepherd, usher, chaperon

especially ADVERB 1 = **notably**, mostly, strikingly, conspicuously, outstandingly 2 = **very**, specially, extremely, remarkably, unusually, exceptionally, markedly, uncommonly

espionage NOUN = **spying**, intelligence, surveillance, counter-intelligence, undercover

work

essay NOUN = **composition**, study, paper, article, piece, assignment, discourse, tract
▷ VERB (*formal*) = **attempt**, try, undertake, endeavour

essence NOUN 1 = **fundamental nature**, nature, being, heart, spirit, soul, core, substance
2 = **concentrate**, spirits, extract, tincture, distillate

essential ADJECTIVE 1 = **vital**, important, needed, necessary, critical, crucial, key, indispensable ≠ unimportant 2 = **fundamental**, main, basic, principal, cardinal, elementary, innate, intrinsic ≠ secondary
▷ NOUN = **prerequisite**, fundamental, necessity, must, basic, sine qua non (*Latin*), rudiment, must-have

establish VERB 1 = **set up**, found, create, institute, constitute, inaugurate 2 = **prove**, confirm, demonstrate, certify, verify, substantiate, corroborate, authenticate 3 = **secure**, form, ground, settle

establishment NOUN
1 = **creation**, founding, setting up, foundation, institution, organization, formation, installation 2 = **organization**, company, business, firm, concern, operation, institution, corporation

Establishment NOUN ▷ PHRASE: the Establishment = **the authorities**, the system, the powers that be, the ruling class

estate NOUN 1 = **lands**, property, area, grounds, domain, manor, holdings, homestead (U.S. & Canad.) 2 (chiefly Brit.) = **area**, centre, park, development, site, zone, plot 3 (law) = **property**, capital, assets, fortune, goods, effects, wealth, possessions

esteem VERB = **respect**, admire, think highly of, love, value, prize, treasure, revere
▷ NOUN = **respect**, regard, honour, admiration, reverence, estimation, veneration

estimate VERB 1 = **calculate roughly**, value, guess, judge, reckon, assess, evaluate, gauge 2 = **think**, believe, consider, rate, judge, hold, rank, reckon
▷ NOUN 1 = **approximate calculation**, guess, assessment, judgment, valuation, guesstimate (informal), rough calculation, ballpark figure (informal)
2 = **assessment**, opinion, belief, appraisal, evaluation, judgment, estimation

estuary NOUN = **inlet**, mouth, creek, firth, fjord

etch VERB 1 = **engrave**, cut, impress, stamp, carve, imprint, inscribe 2 = **corrode**, eat into, burn into

etching NOUN = **print**, carving, engraving, imprint, inscription

eternal ADJECTIVE 1 = **everlasting**, lasting, permanent, enduring, endless, perpetual, timeless, unending ≠ transitory

2 = **interminable**, endless, infinite, continual, immortal, never-ending, everlasting ≠ occasional

eternity NOUN 1 = **the afterlife**, heaven, paradise, the next world, the hereafter 2 = **perpetuity**, immortality, infinity, timelessness, endlessness
3 = **ages**

ethical ADJECTIVE 1 = **moral**, behavioural 2 = **right**, morally acceptable, good, just, fair, responsible, principled ≠ unethical

ethics PLURAL NOUN = **moral code**, standards, principles, morals, conscience, morality, moral values, moral principles, tikanga (N.Z.)

ethnic or **ethnical** ADJECTIVE = **cultural**, national, traditional, native, folk, racial, genetic, indigenous

euphoria NOUN = **elation**, joy, ecstasy, rapture, exhilaration, jubilation ≠ despondency

evacuate VERB 1 = **remove**, clear, withdraw, expel, move out, send to a safe place 2 = **abandon**, leave, clear, desert, quit, withdraw from, pull out of, move out of

evade VERB 1 = **avoid**, escape, dodge, get away from, elude, steer clear of, sidestep, duck ≠ face
2 = **avoid answering**, parry, fend off, fudge, hedge, equivocate

evaluate VERB = **assess**, rate, judge, estimate, reckon, weigh, calculate, gauge

evaporate VERB 1 = **disappear**, vaporize, dematerialize, vanish, dissolve, dry up, fade away, melt away 2 = **dry up**, dry, dehydrate, vaporize, desiccate 3 = **fade away**, disappear, vanish, dissolve, melt away

eve NOUN 1 = **night before**, day before, vigil 2 = **brink**, point, edge, verge, threshold

even ADJECTIVE 1 = **regular**, stable, constant, steady, smooth, uniform, unbroken, uninterrupted ≠ variable 2 = **level**, straight, flat, smooth, true, steady, uniform, parallel ≠ uneven 3 = **equal**, like, matching, similar, identical, comparable ≠ unequal 4 = **equally matched**, level, tied, on a par, neck and neck, fifty-fifty (*informal*), all square ≠ ill-matched 5 = **square**, quits, on the same level, on an equal footing 6 = **calm**, composed, cool, well-balanced, placid, unruffled, imperturbable, even-tempered ≠ excitable

evening NOUN = **dusk** (*archaic*), night, sunset, twilight, sundown, gloaming (*Scot. poetic*), close of day, evo (*Austral. slang*)

event NOUN 1 = **incident**, happening, experience, affair, occasion, proceeding, business, circumstance 2 = **competition**, game, tournament, contest, bout

eventual ADJECTIVE = **final**, overall, concluding, ultimate

eventually ADVERB = **in the end**, finally, one day, after all, some time, ultimately, at the end of the day, when all is said and done

ever ADVERB 1 = **at any time**, at all, in any case, at any point, by any chance, on any occasion, at any period 2 = **always**, for ever, at all times, evermore 3 = **constantly**, continually, perpetually

every ADJECTIVE = **each**, each and every, every single

everybody PRONOUN = **everyone**, each one, the whole world, each person, every person, all and sundry, one and all
  ▷ *see* **everyone**

everyday ADJECTIVE = **ordinary**, common, usual, routine, stock, customary, mundane, run-of-the-mill ≠ unusual

everyone PRONOUN = **everybody**, each one, the whole world, each person, every person, all and sundry, one and all

● **WORD POWER**
● *Everyone* and *everybody* are
● interchangeable, and can be
● used as synonyms of each other
● in any context. Care should be
● taken, however, to distinguish
● between *everyone* as a single
● word and *every one* as two
● words, the latter form correctly
● being used to refer to each
● individual person or thing in
● a particular group: *every one of*
● *them* is wrong.

everything PRONOUN = **all**, the lot, the whole lot, each thing

everywhere ADVERB 1 = **all over**, all around, the world over, high and low, in every nook and cranny, far and wide *or* near, to *or* in every place 2 = **all around**, all over, in every nook and cranny, ubiquitously, far and wide *or* near, to *or* in every place

evidence NOUN 1 = **proof**, grounds, demonstration, confirmation, verification, corroboration, authentication, substantiation 2 = **sign(s)**, suggestion, trace, indication 3 (*law*) = **testimony**, statement, submission, avowal
▷ VERB = **show**, prove, reveal, display, indicate, witness, demonstrate, exhibit

evident ADJECTIVE = **obvious**, clear, plain, apparent, visible, manifest, noticeable, unmistakable ≠ hidden

evidently ADVERB 1 = **obviously**, clearly, plainly, undoubtedly, manifestly, without question, unmistakably 2 = **apparently**, seemingly, outwardly, ostensibly, so it seems, to all appearances

evil ADJECTIVE 1 = **wicked**, bad, malicious, immoral, sinful, malevolent, depraved, villainous 2 = **harmful**, disastrous, destructive, dire, catastrophic, pernicious, ruinous 3 = **demonic**, satanic, diabolical, hellish, devilish, infernal, fiendish 4 = **offensive**, nasty, foul, unpleasant, vile, noxious, disagreeable, pestilential

5 = **unfortunate**, unfavourable, ruinous, calamitous
▷ NOUN 1 = **wickedness**, bad, vice, sin, wrongdoing, depravity, badness, villainy 2 = **harm**, suffering, hurt, woe 3 = **act of cruelty**, crime, ill, horror, outrage, misfortune, mischief, affliction

evoke VERB = **arouse**, cause, induce, awaken, give rise to, stir up, rekindle, summon up ≠ suppress

evolution NOUN 1 (*biology*) = **rise**, development, adaptation, natural selection, Darwinism, survival of the fittest 2 = **development**, growth, advance, progress, working out, expansion, extension, unfolding

evolve VERB 1 = **develop**, metamorphose, adapt yourself 2 = **grow**, develop, advance, progress, mature 3 = **work out**, develop, progress, expand, unfold

exact ADJECTIVE = **accurate**, correct, true, right, specific, precise, definite, faultless ≠ approximate
▷ VERB 1 = **demand**, claim, force, command, extract, compel, extort 2 = **inflict**, apply, administer, mete out, deal out

exacting ADJECTIVE 1 = **demanding**, hard, taxing, difficult, tough ≠ easy 2 = **strict**, severe, harsh, rigorous, stringent

exactly ADVERB 1 = **accurately**, correctly, precisely, faithfully, explicitly, scrupulously, truthfully, unerringly 2 = **precisely**,

e

specifically, bang on (*informal*), to the letter

exaggerate VERB = **overstate**, enlarge, embroider, amplify, embellish, overestimate, overemphasize, pile it on about (*informal*)

examination NOUN 1 (*medical*) = **checkup**, analysis, going-over (*informal*), exploration, health check, check 2 = **exam**, test, research, paper, investigation, practical, assessment, quiz

examine VERB 1 = **inspect**, study, survey, investigate, explore, analyse, scrutinize, peruse 2 (*medical*) = **check**, analyse, check over
3 (*education*) = **test**, question, assess, quiz, evaluate, appraise 4 (*law*) = **question**, quiz, interrogate, cross-examine, grill (*informal*), give the third degree to (*informal*)

example NOUN 1 = **instance**, specimen, case, sample, illustration, particular case, particular instance, typical case 2 = **illustration**, model, ideal, standard, prototype, paradigm, archetype, paragon 3 = **warning**, lesson, caution, deterrent

exceed VERB 1 = **surpass**, better, pass, eclipse, beat, cap (*informal*), top, be over 2 = **go over the limit of**, go beyond, overstep

excel VERB = **be superior**, eclipse, beat, surpass, transcend, outdo, outshine ▷ PHRASE: excel in or at something = **be good at**, shine

at, be proficient in, show talent in, be skilful at, be talented at

excellence NOUN = **high quality**, merit, distinction, goodness, superiority, greatness, supremacy, eminence

excellent ADJECTIVE = **outstanding**, good, great, fine, cool (*informal*), brilliant, very good, superb, booshit (*Austral. slang*), exo (*Austral. slang*), sik (*Austral. slang*), rad (*informal*), phat (*slang*), schmick (*Austral. informal*) ≠ terrible

except PREPOSITION *often with* **for** = **apart from**, but for, saving, barring, excepting, other than, excluding, omitting
▷ VERB = **exclude**, leave out, omit, disregard, pass over

exception NOUN = **special case**, freak, anomaly, inconsistency, deviation, oddity, peculiarity, irregularity

exceptional ADJECTIVE 1 = **remarkable**, special, excellent, extraordinary, outstanding, superior, first-class, marvellous ≠ average 2 = **unusual**, special, odd, strange, extraordinary, unprecedented, peculiar, abnormal ≠ ordinary

excerpt NOUN = **extract**, part, piece, section, selection, passage, fragment, quotation

excess NOUN 1 = **surfeit**, surplus, overload, glut, superabundance, superfluity ≠ shortage 2 = **overindulgence**, extravagance, profligacy, debauchery, dissipation, intemperance, indulgence, prodigality ≠ moderation

excessive ADJECTIVE
1 = **immoderate**, too much, extreme, exaggerated, unreasonable, disproportionate, undue, uncontrolled
2 = **inordinate**, unfair, unreasonable, disproportionate, undue, unwarranted, exorbitant, extortionate

exchange VERB = **interchange**, change, trade, switch, swap, barter, give to each other, give to one another
▷ NOUN 1 = **conversation**, talk, word, discussion, chat, dialogue, natter, powwow
2 = **interchange**, trade, switch, swap, trafficking, swapping, substitution, barter

excite VERB 1 = **thrill**, inspire, stir, provoke, animate, rouse, exhilarate, inflame 2 = **arouse**, provoke, rouse, stir up
3 = **titillate**, thrill, stimulate, turn on (*slang*), arouse, get going (*informal*), electrify

excitement NOUN
= **exhilaration**, action, activity, passion, thrill, animation, furore, agitation

exciting ADJECTIVE
1 = **stimulating**, dramatic, gripping, stirring, thrilling, sensational, rousing, exhilarating ≠ boring 2 = **titillating**, stimulating, arousing, erotic

exclaim VERB = **cry out**, declare, shout, proclaim, yell, utter, call out

exclude VERB 1 = **keep out**, bar, ban, refuse, forbid, boycott, prohibit, disallow ≠ let in
2 = **omit**, reject, eliminate, rule out, miss out, leave out ≠ include
3 = **eliminate**, reject, ignore, rule out, leave out, set aside, omit, pass over

exclusion NOUN 1 = **ban**, bar, veto, boycott, embargo, prohibition, disqualification
2 = **elimination**, missing out, rejection, leaving out, omission

exclusive ADJECTIVE 1 = **select**, fashionable, stylish, restricted, posh (*informal, chiefly Brit.*), chic, high-class, up-market ≠ unrestricted 2 = **sole**, full, whole, complete, total, entire, absolute, undivided ≠ shared
3 = **entire**, full, whole, complete, total, absolute, undivided
4 = **limited**, unique, restricted, confined, peculiar

excursion NOUN = **trip**, tour, journey, outing, expedition, ramble, day trip, jaunt

excuse VERB 1 = **justify**, explain, defend, vindicate, mitigate, apologize for, make excuses for ≠ blame 2 = **forgive**, pardon, overlook, tolerate, acquit, turn a blind eye to, exonerate, make allowances for 3 = **free**, relieve, exempt, release, spare, discharge, let off, absolve ≠ convict
▷ NOUN = **justification**, reason, explanation, defence, grounds,

plea, apology, vindication
≠ accusation

execute VERB 1 = **put to death**, kill, shoot, hang, behead, decapitate, guillotine, electrocute 2 = **carry out**, effect, implement, accomplish, discharge, administer, prosecute, enact 3 = **perform**, carry out, accomplish

execution NOUN 1 = **killing**, hanging, the death penalty, the rope, capital punishment, beheading, the electric chair, the guillotine 2 = **carrying out**, performance, operation, administration, prosecution, enforcement, implementation, accomplishment

executive NOUN
1 = **administrator**, official, director, manager, chairman, managing director, controller, chief executive officer
2 = **administration**, government, directors, management, leadership, hierarchy, directorate
▷ ADJECTIVE = **administrative**, controlling, directing, governing, regulating, decision-making, managerial

exemplify VERB = **show**, represent, display, demonstrate, illustrate, exhibit, embody, serve as an example of

exempt VERB = **grant immunity**, free, excuse, release, spare, relieve, discharge, let off
▷ ADJECTIVE = **immune**, free, excepted, excused, released,

spared, not liable to ≠ liable

exemption NOUN = **immunity**, freedom, relief, exception, discharge, release, dispensation, absolution

exercise VERB 1 = **put to use**, use, apply, employ, exert, utilize, bring to bear, avail yourself of 2 = **train**, work out, practise, keep fit, do exercises
▷ NOUN 1 = **use**, practice, application, operation, discharge, implementation, fulfilment, utilization 2 = **exertion**, training, activity, work, labour, effort, movement, toil 3 (*military*) = **manoeuvre**, campaign, operation, movement, deployment 4 = **task**, problem, lesson, assignment, practice

exert VERB = **apply**, use, exercise, employ, wield, make use of, utilize, bring to bear ▷ PHRASE: **exert yourself** = **make an effort**, work, labour, struggle, strain, strive, endeavour, toil

exhaust VERB 1 = **tire out**, fatigue, drain, weaken, weary, sap, wear out, debilitate 2 = **use up**, spend, consume, waste, go through, run through, deplete, squander

exhausted ADJECTIVE 1 = **worn out**, tired out, drained, spent, bushed (*informal*), done in (*informal*), all in (*slang*), fatigued ≠ invigorated 2 = **used up**, consumed, spent, finished, depleted, dissipated, expended ≠ replenished

e

exhaustion NOUN 1 = **tiredness**, fatigue, weariness, debilitation 2 = **depletion**, emptying, consumption, using up

exhibit VERB 1 = **show**, reveal, display, demonstrate, express, indicate, manifest 2 = **display**, show, set out, parade, unveil, put on view

exhibition NOUN 1 = **show**, display, representation, presentation, spectacle, showcase, exposition 2 = **display**, show, performance, demonstration, revelation

exile NOUN 1 = **banishment**, expulsion, deportation, eviction, expatriation 2 = **expatriate**, refugee, outcast, émigré, deportee
▷ VERB = **banish**, expel, throw out, deport, drive out, eject, expatriate, cast out

exist VERB 1 = **live**, be present, survive, endure, be in existence, be, have breath 2 = **occur**, be present 3 = **survive**, stay alive, make ends meet, subsist, eke out a living, scrape by, scrimp and save, support yourself

existence NOUN 1 = **reality**, being, life, subsistence, actuality 2 = **life**, situation, way of life, life style

existent ADJECTIVE = **in existence**, living, existing, surviving, standing, present, alive, extant

exit NOUN 1 = **way out**, door, gate, outlet, doorway, gateway, escape route ≠ entry 2 = **departure**, withdrawal, retreat, farewell, going, goodbye, exodus, decamping
▷ VERB = **depart**, leave, go out, withdraw, retire, quit, retreat, go away ≠ enter

exodus NOUN = **departure**, withdrawal, retreat, leaving, flight, exit, migration, evacuation

exotic ADJECTIVE 1 = **unusual**, striking, strange, fascinating, mysterious, colourful, glamorous, unfamiliar ≠ ordinary 2 = **foreign**, alien, tropical, external, naturalized

expand VERB 1 = **get bigger**, increase, grow, extend, swell, widen, enlarge, become bigger ≠ contract 2 = **make bigger**, increase, develop, extend, widen, enlarge, broaden, magnify ≠ reduce 3 = **spread (out)**, stretch (out), unfold, unravel, diffuse, unfurl, unroll ▷ PHRASE: **expand on something** = **go into detail about**, embellish, elaborate on, develop, flesh out, expound on, enlarge on, expatiate on

expansion NOUN 1 = **increase**, development, growth, spread, magnification, amplification 2 = **enlargement**, increase, growth, opening out

expatriate ADJECTIVE = **exiled**, refugee, banished, emigrant, émigré, expat
▷ NOUN = **exile**, refugee, emigrant, émigré

e

expect VERB 1 = **think**, believe, suppose, assume, trust, imagine, reckon, presume 2 = **anticipate**, look forward to, predict, envisage, await, hope for, contemplate 3 = **require**, demand, want, call for, ask for, hope for, insist on

expectation NOUN 1 usually plural = **projection**, supposition, assumption, belief, forecast, likelihood, probability, presumption 2 = **anticipation**, hope, promise, excitement, expectancy, apprehension, suspense

expedition NOUN = **journey**, mission, voyage, tour, quest, trek

expel VERB 1 = **throw out**, exclude, ban, dismiss, kick out (informal), ask to leave, turf out (informal), debar ≠ let in 2 = **banish**, exile, deport, evict, force to leave ≠ take in 3 = **drive out**, discharge, force out, let out, eject, issue, spew, belch

expenditure NOUN 1 = **spending**, payment, expense, outgoings, cost, outlay 2 = **consumption**, using, output

expense NOUN = **cost**, charge, expenditure, payment, spending, outlay

expensive ADJECTIVE = **costly**, high-priced, lavish, extravagant, dear, stiff, steep (informal), pricey ≠ cheap

experience NOUN
1 = **knowledge**, practice, skill, contact, expertise, involvement, exposure, participation

2 = **event**, affair, incident, happening, encounter, episode, adventure, occurrence
▷ VERB = **undergo**, feel, face, taste, go through, sample, encounter, endure

experienced ADJECTIVE = **knowledgeable**, skilled, tried, tested, seasoned, expert, veteran, practised ≠ inexperienced

experiment NOUN 1 = **test**, trial, investigation, examination, procedure, demonstration, observation, try-out
2 = **research**, investigation, analysis, observation, research and development, experimentation
▷ VERB = **test**, investigate, trial, research, try, examine, pilot, sample

experimental ADJECTIVE
1 = **test**, trial, pilot, preliminary, provisional, tentative, speculative, exploratory
2 = **innovative**, new, original, radical, creative, ingenious, avant-garde, inventive

expert NOUN = **specialist**, authority, professional, master, genius, guru, pundit, maestro, fundi (S. African) ≠ amateur
▷ ADJECTIVE = **skilful**, experienced, professional, masterly, qualified, talented, outstanding, practised ≠ unskilled

expertise NOUN = **skill**, knowledge, know-how (informal), facility, judgment, mastery, proficiency, adroitness

expire VERB 1 = **become invalid**, end, finish, conclude, close, stop, run out, cease 2 = **die**, depart, perish, kick the bucket (*informal*), depart this life, meet your maker, cark it (*Austral. & N.Z. slang*), pass away *or* on

explain VERB 1 = **make clear** *or* **plain**, describe, teach, define, resolve, clarify, clear up, simplify 2 = **account for**, excuse, justify, give a reason for

explanation NOUN 1 = **reason**, answer, account, excuse, motive, justification, vindication 2 = **description**, report, definition, teaching, interpretation, illustration, clarification, simplification

explicit ADJECTIVE 1 = **clear**, obvious, specific, direct, precise, straightforward, definite, overt ≠ vague 2 = **frank**, specific, graphic, unambiguous, unrestricted, unrestrained, uncensored ≠ indirect

explode VERB 1 = **blow up**, erupt, burst, go off, shatter 2 = **detonate**, set off, discharge, let off 3 = **lose your temper**, rage, erupt, become angry, hit the roof (*informal*), go crook (*Austral. & N.Z. slang*) 4 = **increase**, grow, develop, extend, advance, shoot up, soar, boost 5 = **disprove**, discredit, refute, demolish, repudiate, put paid to, invalidate, debunk

exploit NOUN = **feat**, act, achievement, enterprise, adventure, stunt, deed, accomplishment
▷ VERB 1 = **take advantage of**, abuse, use, manipulate, milk, misuse, ill-treat, play on *or* upon 2 = **make the best use of**, use, make use of, utilize, cash in on (*informal*), capitalize on, use to good advantage, profit by *or* from

exploitation NOUN = **misuse**, abuse, manipulation, using, ill-treatment

exploration NOUN 1 = **expedition**, tour, trip, survey, travel, journey, reconnaissance 2 = **investigation**, research, survey, search, inquiry, analysis, examination, inspection

explore VERB 1 = **travel around**, tour, survey, scout, reconnoitre 2 = **investigate**, consider, research, survey, search, examine, probe, look into

explosion NOUN 1 = **blast**, crack, burst, bang, discharge, report, blowing up, clap 2 = **increase**, rise, development, growth, boost, expansion, enlargement, escalation 3 = **outburst**, fit, storm, attack, surge, flare-up, eruption 4 = **outbreak**, flare-up, eruption, upsurge

explosive ADJECTIVE 1 = **unstable**, dangerous, volatile, hazardous, unsafe, perilous, combustible, inflammable 2 = **fiery**, violent, volatile, stormy, touchy, vehement
▷ NOUN = **bomb**, mine, shell, missile, rocket, grenade, charge,

torpedo

expose VERB 1 = **uncover**, show, reveal, display, exhibit, present, unveil, lay bare ≠ hide 2 = **make vulnerable**, subject, leave open, lay open

exposure NOUN 1 = **hypothermia**, frostbite, extreme cold, intense cold 2 = **uncovering**, showing, display, exhibition, revelation, presentation, unveiling

express VERB 1 = **state**, communicate, convey, articulate, say, word, voice, declare 2 = **show**, indicate, exhibit, demonstrate, reveal, intimate, convey, signify
▷ ADJECTIVE 1 = **explicit**, clear, plain, distinct, definite, unambiguous, categorical 2 = **specific**, exclusive, particular, sole, special, singular, clear-cut, especial 3 = **fast**, direct, rapid, priority, prompt, swift, high-speed, speedy

expression NOUN 1 = **statement**, declaration, announcement, communication, utterance, articulation 2 = **indication**, demonstration, exhibition, display, showing, show, sign, symbol 3 = **look**, countenance, face, air, appearance, aspect 4 = **phrase**, saying, word, term, remark, maxim, idiom, adage

expressive ADJECTIVE = **vivid**, striking, telling, moving, poignant, eloquent ≠ impassive

expulsion NOUN 1 = **ejection**, exclusion, dismissal, removal, eviction, banishment 2 = **discharge**, emission, spewing, secretion, excretion, ejection, seepage, suppuration

exquisite ADJECTIVE 1 = **beautiful**, elegant, graceful, pleasing, attractive, lovely, charming, comely ≠ unattractive 2 = **fine**, beautiful, lovely, elegant, precious, delicate, dainty 3 = **intense**, acute, severe, sharp, keen, extreme

extend VERB 1 = **spread out**, reach, stretch 2 = **stretch**, stretch out, spread out, straighten out 3 = **last**, continue, go on, stretch, carry on 4 = **protrude**, project, stand out, bulge, stick out, hang, overhang, jut out 5 = **widen**, increase, expand, add to, enhance, supplement, enlarge, broaden ≠ reduce 6 = **make longer**, prolong, lengthen, draw out, spin out, drag out ≠ shorten 7 = **offer**, present, confer, stick out, impart, proffer ≠ withdraw

extension NOUN 1 = **annexe**, addition, supplement, appendix, appendage 2 = **lengthening**, extra time, continuation, additional period of time 3 = **development**, expansion, widening, increase, broadening, enlargement, diversification

extensive ADJECTIVE 1 = **large**, considerable, substantial, spacious, wide, broad, expansive ≠ confined 2 = **comprehensive**, complete, wide, pervasive

≠ restricted 3 = **great**, vast, widespread, large-scale, far-reaching, far-flung, voluminous ≠ limited

extent NOUN 1 = **magnitude**, amount, scale, level, stretch, expanse 2 = **size**, area, length, width, breadth

exterior NOUN = **outside**, face, surface, covering, skin, shell, coating, façade
▷ ADJECTIVE = **outer**, outside, external, surface, outward, outermost ≠ inner

external ADJECTIVE 1 = **outer**, outside, surface, outward, exterior, outermost ≠ internal 2 = **foreign**, international, alien, extrinsic ≠ domestic 3 = **outside**, visiting ≠ inside

extinct ADJECTIVE = **dead**, lost, gone, vanished, defunct ≠ living

extinction NOUN = **dying out**, destruction, abolition, oblivion, extermination, annihilation, eradication, obliteration

extra ADJECTIVE 1 = **additional**, more, added, further, supplementary, auxiliary, ancillary ≠ vital 2 = **surplus**, excess, spare, redundant, unused, leftover, superfluous
▷ NOUN = **addition**, bonus, supplement, accessory ≠ necessity
▷ ADVERB 1 = **in addition**, additionally, over and above 2 = **exceptionally**, very, specially, especially, particularly, extremely, remarkably, unusually

extract VERB 1 = **take out**, draw, pull, remove, withdraw, pull out, bring out 2 = **pull out**, remove, take out, draw, uproot, pluck out 3 = **elicit**, obtain, force, draw, derive, glean, coerce
▷ NOUN 1 = **passage**, selection, excerpt, cutting, clipping, quotation, citation 2 = **essence**, solution, concentrate, juice, distillation

● **WORD POWER**
● People sometimes use *extract*
● where *extricate* would be
● better. Although both words
● can refer to a physical act of
● removal from a place, *extract*
● has a more general sense than
● *extricate*. *Extricate* has additional
● overtones of 'difficulty', and
● is most commonly used with
● reference to getting a person
● – particularly *yourself* – out of a
● situation. So, for example, you
● might say *he will find it difficult*
● *to extricate himself* (not *extract*
● *himself*) *from this situation*.

extraordinary ADJECTIVE 1 = **remarkable**, outstanding, amazing, fantastic, astonishing, exceptional, phenomenal, extremely good ≠ unremarkable 2 = **unusual**, strange, remarkable, uncommon ≠ ordinary

extravagant ADJECTIVE 1 = **wasteful**, lavish, prodigal, profligate, spendthrift ≠ economical 2 = **excessive**, outrageous, over the top (*slang*), unreasonable, preposterous

≠ moderate

extreme ADJECTIVE 1 = **great**, highest, supreme, acute, severe, maximum, intense, ultimate ≠ mild 2 = **severe**, radical, strict, harsh, rigid, drastic, uncompromising 3 = **radical**, excessive, fanatical, immoderate ≠ moderate 4 = **farthest**, furthest, far, remotest, far-off, outermost, most distant ≠ nearest
▷ NOUN = **limit**, end, edge, opposite, pole, boundary, antithesis, extremity

extremely ADVERB = **very**, particularly, severely, terribly, unusually, exceptionally, extraordinarily, tremendously

extremist NOUN = **radical**, activist, militant, fanatic, die-hard, bigot, zealot
▷ ADJECTIVE = **extreme**, wild, passionate, frenzied, obsessive, fanatical, fervent, zealous *often with* **over**

eye NOUN 1 = **eyeball**, optic (*informal*), organ of vision, organ of sight 2 *often plural* = **eyesight**, sight, vision, perception, ability to see, power of seeing 3 = **appreciation**, taste, recognition, judgment, discrimination, perception, discernment 4 = **observance**, observation, surveillance, vigil, watch, lookout 5 = **centre**, heart, middle, mid, core, nucleus
▷ VERB = **look at**, view, study, watch, survey, observe, contemplate, check out (*informal*)
▷ **RELATED WORDS**: *adjectives*
ocular, ophthalmic, optic

● **WORD POWER**

● The primary meaning of *eye*
● is that of the organ of sight in
● humans and other animals.
● Sight is perhaps the most
● fundamental sense in humans.
● Eyes are associated with vision
● in descriptions like *prying eyes*
● and *sharp eyes*, and observation
● in *all eyes*, *a watchful eye*, and
● *keeping an eye on someone*.
● When we are attracted to
● someone, eye develops the
● sense 'ogle' in *eye someone up*.
● The ability to discriminate
● with the eyes has led to the
● meaning of appreciation and
● taste, particularly in the visual
● sphere, e.g. *an eye for colour*,
● *design*, *detail*, *quality*, and
● *style*. The physical location
● and shape of the eyes has
● inspired the meaning of
● central in the phrase *the eye*
● *of the storm*, which is applied
● both literally and figuratively.
● Although we understand the
● biblical phrase *eye for an eye*
● to mean retribution, it was
● originally intended as an
● appeal to restrict the degree of
● punishment to fit that of the
● crime. Conversely, when we see
● *eye to eye*, it means agreement,
● and *in the eyes of (the law*,
● *others*, *the world*) it means
● opinion.

Ff

fable NOUN 1 = **legend**, myth, parable, allegory, story, tale 2 = **fiction**, fantasy, myth, invention, yarn (*informal*), fabrication, urban myth, tall story (*informal*) ≠ fact

fabric NOUN 1 = **cloth**, material, stuff, textile, web 2 = **framework**, structure, make-up, organization, frame, foundations, construction, constitution 3 = **structure**, foundations, construction, framework

fabulous ADJECTIVE 1 (*informal*) = **wonderful**, excellent, brilliant, superb, spectacular, fantastic (*informal*), marvellous, sensational (*informal*) ≠ ordinary 2 = **astounding**, amazing, extraordinary, remarkable, incredible, astonishing, unbelievable, breathtaking 3 = **legendary**, imaginary, mythical, fictitious, made-up, fantastic, invented, unreal

façade NOUN 1 = **front**, face, exterior 2 = **show**, front, appearance, mask, exterior, guise, pretence, semblance

face NOUN 1 = **countenance**, features, profile, mug (*slang*), visage 2 = **expression**, look, air, appearance, aspect, countenance 3 = **side**, front, outside, surface, exterior, elevation, vertical surface
▷ VERB 1 *often with* **to**, **towards**, *or* **on** = **look onto**, overlook, be opposite, look out on, front onto 2 = **confront**, meet, encounter, deal with, oppose, tackle, experience, brave

⊛ WORD POWER [f]

⊛ The core sense of *face* is that
⊛ of the front of the head. In
⊛ humans, face can mean facial
⊛ expression, particularly that
⊛ of negative emotion in the
⊛ phrase *make* or *pull a face*. When
⊛ applied to inanimate objects,
⊛ face refers to the functional
⊛ side of an object or the side
⊛ facing front, e.g. *clock face*
⊛ and *cliff face*. There is some
⊛ semantic overlap between the
⊛ terms *façade* and *face*. Both
⊛ can refer to the frontage of a
⊛ building, and equally can refer
⊛ to the outer appearance of a
⊛ person or situation, especially
⊛ the presentation of a deceptive
⊛ image, e.g. *a façade of unity*
⊛ and *on the face of it*. The idea
⊛ of self-image is also present in
⊛ the phrases *lose face* and *save*
⊛ *face*, where face is self-respect.
⊛ The verbal sense of face is
⊛ associated with movement
⊛ forwards or towards the
⊛ front, having the meaning
⊛ of opposite in location in
⊛ *facing south*, and opposing in
⊛ argument in *facing down*.

face up to VERB = **accept**, deal with, tackle, acknowledge, cope with, confront, come to terms with, meet head-on

facilitate VERB = **further**, help, forward, promote, speed up, pave the way for, make easy, expedite ≠ hinder

facility NOUN **1** *often plural* = **amenity**, means, aid, opportunity, advantage, resource, equipment, provision **2** = **opportunity**, possibility, convenience **3** = **ability**, skill, efficiency, fluency, proficiency, dexterity, adroitness **4** = **ease**, fluency, effortlessness ≠ difficulty

fact NOUN **1** = **truth**, reality, certainty, verity ≠ fiction **2** = **event**, happening, act, performance, incident, deed, occurrence, fait accompli (*French*)

faction¹ NOUN **1** = **group**, set, party, gang, bloc, contingent, clique, coterie, public-interest group (*U.S. & Canad.*) **2** = **dissension**, division, conflict, rebellion, disagreement, variance, discord, infighting ≠ agreement

factor NOUN = **element**, part, cause, influence, item, aspect, characteristic, consideration

● **WORD POWER**
● In strict usage, *factor* should
● only be used to refer to
● something which contributes
● to a result. It should not be used
● to refer to a part of something,
● such as a plan or arrangement;
● more appropriate alternatives

● to *factor* in this sense are words
● such as *component* or *element*.

factory NOUN = **works**, plant, mill, workshop, assembly line, shop floor

factual ADJECTIVE = **true**, authentic, real, correct, genuine, exact, precise, dinkum (*Austral. & N.Z. informal*), true-to-life ≠ fictitious

faculty NOUN **1** = **ability**, power, skill, facility, capacity, propensity, aptitude ≠ failing **2** = **department**, school **3** = **teaching staff**, staff, teachers, professors, lecturers (*chiefly U.S.*) **4** = **power**, reason, sense, intelligence, mental ability, physical ability

fad NOUN = **craze**, fashion, trend, rage, vogue, whim, mania

fade VERB **1** = **become pale**, bleach, wash out, discolour, lose colour, decolour **2** = **make pale**, dim, bleach, wash out, blanch, discolour, decolour **3** = **grow dim**, fade away, become less loud **4** *usually with* **away** *or* **out** = **dwindle**, disappear, vanish, melt away, decline, dissolve, wane, die away

fail VERB **1** = **be unsuccessful**, founder, fall, break down, flop (*informal*), fizzle out (*informal*), come unstuck, miscarry ≠ succeed **2** = **disappoint**, abandon, desert, neglect, omit, let down, forsake, be disloyal to **3** = **stop working**, stop, die, break down, stall, cut out, malfunction,

conk out (*informal*) **4** = **wither**, perish, sag, waste away, shrivel up **5** = **go bankrupt**, collapse, fold (*informal*), close down, go under, go bust (*informal*), go out of business, be wound up **6** = **decline**, deteriorate, degenerate **7** = **give out**, dim, peter out, die away, grow dim
▷ **PHRASE**: **without fail** = **without exception**, regularly, constantly, invariably, religiously, unfailingly, conscientiously, like clockwork

failing NOUN = **shortcoming**, fault, weakness, defect, deficiency, flaw, drawback, blemish ≠ strength
▷ **PREPOSITION** = **in the absence of**, lacking, in default of

failure NOUN **1** = **lack of success**, defeat, collapse, breakdown, overthrow, miscarriage, fiasco, downfall ≠ success **2** = **loser**, disappointment, flop (*informal*), write-off, no-hoper (*chiefly Austral.*), dud (*informal*), black sheep, washout (*informal*), dead duck (*slang*) **3** = **bankruptcy**, crash, collapse, ruin, closure, winding up, downfall, going under ≠ prosperity

faint ADJECTIVE **1** = **dim**, low, soft, faded, distant, vague, unclear, muted ≠ clear **2** = **slight**, weak, feeble, unenthusiastic, remote, slim, vague, slender **3** = **dizzy**, giddy, light-headed, weak, exhausted, wobbly, muzzy, woozy (*informal*) ≠ energetic
▷ **VERB** = **pass out**, black out,

lose consciousness, keel over (*informal*), go out, collapse, swoon (*literary*), flake out (*informal*)
▷ **NOUN** = **blackout**, collapse, coma, swoon (*literary*), unconsciousness

faintly ADVERB **1** = **slightly**, rather, a little, somewhat, dimly **2** = **softly**, weakly, feebly, in a whisper, indistinctly, unclearly

fair¹ ADJECTIVE **1** = **unbiased**, impartial, even-handed, unprejudiced, just, reasonable, proper, legitimate ≠ unfair **2** = **respectable**, average, reasonable, decent, acceptable, moderate, adequate, satisfactory **3** = **light**, golden, blonde, blond, yellowish, fair-haired, light-coloured, flaxen-haired **4** = **fine**, clear, dry, bright, pleasant, sunny, cloudless, unclouded **5** = **beautiful**, pretty, attractive, lovely, handsome, good-looking, bonny, comely, fit (*Brit. informal*) ≠ ugly

fair² NOUN **1** = **carnival**, fête, gala, bazaar **2** = **exhibition**, show, festival, mart

fairly ADVERB **1** = **equitably**, objectively, legitimately, honestly, justly, lawfully, without prejudice, dispassionately **2** = **moderately**, rather, quite, somewhat, reasonably, adequately, pretty well, tolerably **3** = **positively**, really, simply, absolutely **4** = **deservedly**, objectively, honestly, justifiably, justly, impartially, equitably, without fear or favour

fairness NOUN = **impartiality**, justice, equity, legitimacy, decency, disinterestedness, rightfulness, equitableness

fairy NOUN = **sprite**, elf, brownie, pixie, puck, imp, leprechaun, peri

fairy tale or **fairy story** NOUN 1 = **folk tale**, romance, traditional story 2 = **lie**, fiction, invention, fabrication, untruth, urban myth, tall story, urban legend

faith NOUN 1 = **confidence**, trust, credit, conviction, assurance, dependence, reliance, credence ≠ distrust 2 = **religion**, church, belief, persuasion, creed, communion, denomination, dogma ≠ agnosticism

faithful ADJECTIVE 1 = **loyal**, true, committed, constant, devoted, dedicated, reliable, staunch ≠ disloyal 2 = **accurate**, close, true, strict, exact, precise

fake VERB 1 = **forge**, copy, reproduce, fabricate, counterfeit, falsify 2 = **sham**, put on, pretend, simulate, feign, go through the motions of
▷ NOUN 1 = **forgery**, copy, fraud, reproduction, dummy, imitation, hoax, counterfeit 2 = **charlatan**, deceiver, sham, quack
▷ ADJECTIVE = **artificial**, false, forged, counterfeit, put-on, pretend (*informal*), mock, imitation ≠ genuine

fall VERB 1 = **drop**, plunge, tumble, plummet, collapse, sink, go down, come down ≠ rise 2 = **decrease**,

drop, decline, go down, slump, diminish, dwindle, lessen ≠ increase 3 = **be overthrown**, surrender, succumb, submit, capitulate, be conquered, pass into enemy hands ≠ triumph 4 = **be killed**, die, perish, meet your end ≠ survive 5 = **occur**, happen, come about, chance, take place, befall, come to pass
▷ NOUN 1 = **drop**, slip, plunge, dive, tumble, descent, plummet, nose dive 2 = **decrease**, drop, lowering, decline, reduction, slump, dip, lessening 3 = **collapse**, defeat, downfall, ruin, destruction, overthrow, submission, capitulation

false ADJECTIVE 1 = **incorrect**, wrong, mistaken, misleading, faulty, inaccurate, invalid, erroneous ≠ correct 2 = **untrue**, fraudulent, trumped up, fallacious, untruthful ≠ true 3 = **artificial**, forged, fake, reproduction, replica, imitation, bogus, simulated ≠ real

falter VERB 1 = **hesitate**, delay, waver, vacillate ≠ persevere 2 = **tumble**, totter 3 = **stutter**, pause, stumble, hesitate, stammer

fame NOUN = **prominence**, glory, celebrity, stardom, reputation, honour, prestige, stature ≠ obscurity

familiar ADJECTIVE 1 = **well-known**, recognized, common, ordinary, routine, frequent, accustomed, customary

≠ unfamiliar 2 = **friendly**, close, dear, intimate, amicable ≠ formal 3 = **relaxed**, easy, friendly, comfortable, intimate, casual, amicable 4 = **disrespectful**, forward, bold, intrusive, presumptuous, impudent, overfamiliar

familiarity NOUN
1 = **acquaintance**, experience, understanding, knowledge, awareness, grasp ≠ unfamiliarity 2 = **friendliness**, intimacy, ease, openness, informality, sociability ≠ formality 3 = **disrespect**, forwardness, overfamiliarity, cheek, presumption, boldness ≠ respect

family NOUN 1 = **relations**, relatives, household, folk (*informal*), kin, nuclear family, next of kin, kith and kin, ainga (*N.Z.*), rellies (*Austral. slang*) 2 = **children**, kids (*informal*), offspring, little ones, littlies (*Austral. informal*) 3 = **ancestors**, house, race, tribe, clan, dynasty, line of descent 4 = **species**, group, class, system, order, network, genre, subdivision

● **WORD POWER**
● Some careful writers insist
● that a singular verb should
● always be used with collective
● nouns such as *government*,
● *team*, *family*, *committee*, and
● *class*, for example: *the class is*
● *doing a project on Vikings*; *the*
● *company is mounting a big sales*
● *campaign*. In British usage,
● however, a plural verb is often
● used with a collective noun,
● especially where the emphasis
● is on a collection of individual
● objects or people rather than
● a group regarded as a unit:
● *the family are all on holiday.*
● The most important thing to
● remember is never to treat
● the same collective noun as
● both singular and plural in the
● same sentence: *the family is well*
● *and sends its best wishes* or *the*
● *family are well and send their best*
● *wishes*, but not *the family is well*
● *and send their best wishes.*

famine NOUN = **hunger**, want, starvation, deprivation, scarcity, dearth

famous ADJECTIVE = **well-known**, celebrated, acclaimed, noted, distinguished, prominent, legendary, renowned ≠ unknown

fan¹ NOUN = **blower**, ventilator, air conditioner
▷ VERB = **blow**, cool, refresh, air-condition, ventilate

fan² NOUN 1 = **supporter**, lover, follower, enthusiast, admirer 2 = **devotee**, buff (*informal*), aficionado

fanatic NOUN = **extremist**, activist, militant, bigot, zealot

fancy ADJECTIVE = **elaborate**, decorative, extravagant, intricate, baroque, ornamental, ornate, embellished ≠ plain
▷ NOUN 1 = **whim**, thought, idea, desire, urge, notion, humour, impulse 2 = **delusion**, dream, vision, fantasy, daydream,

chimera

▷ VERB 1 (*informal*) = **wish for**, want, desire, hope for, long for, crave, yearn for, thirst for 2 (*Brit. informal*) = **be attracted to**, find attractive, lust after, like, take to, be captivated by, have a thing about (*informal*), have eyes for 3 = **suppose**, think, believe, imagine, reckon, conjecture, think likely

fantastic ADJECTIVE 1 (*informal*) = **wonderful**, great, excellent, very good, smashing (*informal*), superb, tremendous (*informal*), magnificent, booshit (*Austral. slang*), exo (*Austral. slang*), sik (*Austral. slang*), rad (*informal*), phat (*slang*), schmick (*Austral. informal*) ≠ ordinary 2 = **strange**, bizarre, grotesque, fanciful, outlandish 3 = **implausible**, unlikely, incredible, absurd, preposterous, cock-and-bull (*informal*)

fantasy *or* **phantasy** NOUN 1 = **daydream**, dream, wish, reverie, flight of fancy, pipe dream 2 = **imagination**, fancy, invention, creativity, originality

far ADVERB 1 = **a long way**, miles, deep, a good way, afar, a great distance 2 = **much**, greatly, very much, extremely, significantly, considerably, decidedly, markedly

▷ ADJECTIVE *often with* **off** = **remote**, distant, far-flung, faraway, out-of-the-way, far-off, outlying, off the beaten track ≠ near

farce NOUN 1 = **comedy**, satire, slapstick, burlesque, buffoonery 2 = **mockery**, joke, nonsense, parody, shambles, sham, travesty

fare NOUN 1 = **charge**, price, ticket price, ticket money 2 = **food**, provisions, board, rations, kai (*N.Z. informal*), nourishment, sustenance, victuals, nutriment

▷ VERB = **get on**, do, manage, make out, prosper, get along

farewell

INTERJECTION = **goodbye**, bye (*informal*), so long, see you, take care, good morning, bye-bye (*informal*), good day, haere ra (*N.Z.*)

▷ NOUN = **goodbye**, parting, departure, leave-taking, adieu, valediction, sendoff (*informal*)

farm NOUN = **smallholding**, ranch (*chiefly U.S. & Canad.*), farmstead, station (*Austral. & N.Z.*), vineyard, plantation, croft (*Scot.*), grange, homestead

▷ VERB = **cultivate**, work, plant, grow crops on, keep animals on

fascinate VERB = **entrance**, absorb, intrigue, rivet, captivate, enthral, beguile, transfix ≠ bore

fascinating ADJECTIVE = **captivating**, engaging, gripping, compelling, intriguing, very interesting, irresistible, enticing ≠ boring

fascination NOUN = **attraction**, pull, magic, charm, lure, allure, magnetism, enchantment

fashion NOUN 1 = **style**, look, trend, rage, custom, mode, vogue, craze 2 = **method**, way, style, manner, mode

▷ **VERB** = **make**, shape, cast, construct, form, create, manufacture, forge

fashionable ADJECTIVE
= **popular**, in fashion, trendy (*Brit. informal*), in (*informal*), modern, with it (*informal*), stylish, chic, schmick (*Austral. informal*), funky ≠ unfashionable

fast[1] ADJECTIVE 1 = **quick**, flying, rapid, fleet, swift, speedy, brisk, hasty ≠ slow 2 = **fixed**, firm, sound, stuck, secure, tight, jammed, fastened ≠ unstable 3 = **dissipated**, wild, exciting, loose, extravagant, reckless, self-indulgent, wanton 4 = **close**, firm, devoted, faithful, steadfast ▷ ADVERB 1 = **quickly**, rapidly, swiftly, hastily, hurriedly, speedily, in haste, at full speed ≠ slowly 2 = **securely**, firmly, tightly, fixedly 3 = **fixedly**, firmly, soundly, deeply, securely, tightly

fast[2] VERB = **go hungry**, abstain, go without food, deny yourself ▷ NOUN = **fasting**, diet, abstinence

fasten VERB 1 = **secure**, close, do up 2 = **tie**, bind, tie up 3 = **fix**, join, link, connect, attach, affix

fat NOUN = **fatness**, flesh, bulk, obesity, flab, blubber, paunch, fatty tissue ▷ ADJECTIVE 1 = **overweight**, large, heavy, plump, stout, obese, tubby, portly ≠ thin 2 = **fatty**, greasy, adipose, oleaginous, oily ≠ lean

fatal ADJECTIVE 1 = **disastrous**, devastating, crippling, catastrophic, ruinous, calamitous, baleful, baneful ≠ minor 2 = **lethal**, deadly, mortal, causing death, final, killing, terminal, malignant ≠ harmless

fate NOUN 1 = **destiny**, chance, fortune, luck, the stars, providence, nemesis, kismet 2 = **fortune**, destiny, lot, portion, cup, horoscope

fated ADJECTIVE = **destined**, doomed, predestined, preordained, foreordained

father NOUN 1 = **daddy** (*informal*), dad (*informal*), male parent, pop (*U.S. informal*), old man (*Brit. informal*), pa (*informal*), papa (*old-fashioned* or *informal*), pater 2 = **founder**, author, maker, architect, creator, inventor, originator, prime mover 3 *often plural* = **forefather**, predecessor, ancestor, forebear, progenitor, tupuna *or* tipuna (*N.Z.*) ▷ VERB = **sire**, parent, conceive, bring to life, beget, procreate, bring into being, give life to ▷ RELATED WORD: *adjective* **paternal**

Father NOUN = **priest**, minister, vicar, parson, pastor, cleric, churchman, padre (*informal*)

fatherly ADJECTIVE = **paternal**, kindly, protective, supportive, benign, affectionate, patriarchal, benevolent

fatigue NOUN = **tiredness**, lethargy, weariness, heaviness, languor, listlessness ≠ freshness

▷ **VERB** = **tire**, exhaust, weaken, weary, drain, wear out, take it out of (*informal*), tire out ≠ refresh

fatty ADJECTIVE = **greasy**, fat, creamy, oily, adipose, oleaginous, suety, rich

faucet NOUN (*U.S. & Canad.*) = **tap**, spout, spigot, stopcock, valve

fault NOUN 1 = **responsibility**, liability, guilt, accountability, culpability 2 = **mistake**, slip, error, blunder, lapse, oversight, indiscretion, howler (*informal*), barry *or* Barry Crocker (*Austral. slang*) 3 = **failing**, weakness, defect, deficiency, flaw, shortcoming, blemish, imperfection ≠ strength

▷ **VERB** = **criticize**, blame, complain, condemn, moan about, censure, hold (someone) responsible, find fault with

▷ **PHRASES**: **find fault with something** *or* **someone** = **criticize**, complain about, whinge about (*informal*), whine about (*informal*), quibble, carp at, take to task, pick holes in, nit-pick (*informal*); **to a fault** = **excessively**, unduly, in the extreme, overmuch, immoderately

faulty ADJECTIVE 1 = **defective**, damaged, malfunctioning, broken, flawed, impaired, imperfect, out of order 2 = **incorrect**, flawed, unsound

favour *or* (*U.S.*) **favor** NOUN 1 = **approval**, goodwill, commendation, approbation ≠ disapproval 2 = **favouritism**, preferential treatment 3 = **support**, backing, aid, assistance, patronage, good opinion 4 = **good turn**, service, benefit, courtesy, kindness, indulgence, boon, good deed ≠ wrong

▷ **VERB** 1 = **prefer**, opt for, like better, incline towards, choose, pick, desire, go for ≠ object to 2 = **indulge**, reward, side with, smile upon 3 = **support**, champion, encourage, approve, advocate, subscribe to, commend, stand up for ≠ oppose 4 = **help**, benefit

favourable *or* (*U.S.*) **favorable** ADJECTIVE 1 = **positive**, encouraging, approving, praising, reassuring, enthusiastic, sympathetic, commending ≠ disapproving 2 = **affirmative**, agreeing, confirming, positive, assenting, corroborative 3 = **advantageous**, promising, encouraging, suitable, helpful, beneficial, auspicious, opportune ≠ disadvantageous

favourite *or* (*U.S.*) **favorite** ADJECTIVE = **preferred**, favoured, best-loved, most-liked, special, choice, dearest, pet

▷ **NOUN** = **darling**, pet, blue-eyed boy (*informal*), beloved, idol, fave (*informal*), teacher's pet, the apple of your eye

fear NOUN 1 = **dread**, horror, panic, terror, fright, alarm, trepidation,

fearfulness 2 = **bugbear**, bête noire, horror, nightmare, anxiety, terror, dread, spectre
▷ **VERB 1** = **be afraid of**, dread, shudder at, be fearful of, tremble at, be terrified by, take fright at, shake in your shoes about 2 = **regret**, feel, suspect, have a feeling, have a hunch, have a sneaking suspicion, have a funny feeling ▷ **PHRASE: fear for something** or **someone** = **worry about**, be anxious about, feel concern for

fearful ADJECTIVE 1 = **scared**, afraid, alarmed, frightened, nervous, terrified, petrified ≠ unafraid 2 = **timid**, afraid, frightened, scared, alarmed, nervous, uneasy, jumpy ≠ brave 3 (*informal*) = **frightful**, terrible, awful, dreadful, horrific, dire, horrendous, gruesome

feasible ADJECTIVE = **practicable**, possible, reasonable, viable, workable, achievable, attainable, likely ≠ impracticable

feast NOUN 1 = **banquet**, repast, spread (*informal*), dinner, treat, hakari (*N.Z.*) 2 = **festival**, holiday, fête, celebration, holy day, red-letter day, religious festival, saint's day
▷ **VERB** = **eat your fill**, wine and dine, overindulge, consume, indulge, gorge, devour, pig out (*slang*)

feat NOUN = **accomplishment**, act, performance, achievement, enterprise, undertaking, exploit, deed

feather NOUN = **plume**

feature NOUN 1 = **aspect**, quality, characteristic, property, factor, trait, hallmark, facet 2 = **article**, report, story, piece, item, column 3 = **highlight**, attraction, speciality, main item 4 = **face**, countenance, physiognomy, lineament
▷ **VERB 1** = **spotlight**, present, emphasize, play up, foreground, give prominence to 2 = **star**, appear, participate, play a part

federation NOUN = **union**, league, association, alliance, combination, coalition, partnership, consortium

fed up ADJECTIVE = **cheesed off**, depressed, bored, tired, discontented, dissatisfied, glum, sick and tired (*informal*), hoha (*N.Z.*)

fee NOUN = **charge**, price, cost, bill, payment, wage, salary, toll

feeble ADJECTIVE 1 = **weak**, frail, debilitated, sickly, puny, weedy (*informal*), infirm, effete ≠ strong 2 = **inadequate**, pathetic, insufficient, lame 3 = **unconvincing**, poor, thin, tame, pathetic, lame, flimsy, paltry ≠ effective

feed VERB 1 = **cater for**, provide for, nourish, provide with food, supply, sustain, cook for, wine and dine 2 = **graze**, eat, browse, pasture 3 = **eat**, drink milk
▷ **NOUN 1** = **food**, fodder, provender, pasturage 2 (*informal*)

= **meal**, spread (*informal*), dinner, lunch, tea, breakfast, feast, supper

feel VERB 1 = **experience**, bear 2 = **touch**, handle, manipulate, finger, stroke, paw, caress, fondle 3 = **be aware of** 4 = **perceive**, detect, discern, experience, notice, observe 5 = **sense**, be aware, be convinced, have a feeling, intuit 6 = **believe**, consider, judge, deem, think, hold ▷ NOUN 1 = **texture**, finish, touch, surface, surface quality 2 = **impression**, feeling, air, sense, quality, atmosphere, mood, aura

feeling NOUN 1 = **emotion**, sentiment 2 = **opinion**, view, attitude, belief, point of view, instinct, inclination 3 = **passion**, emotion, intensity, warmth 4 = **ardour**, love, care, warmth, tenderness, fervour 5 = **sympathy**, understanding, concern, pity, sensitivity, compassion, sorrow, sensibility 6 = **sensation**, sense, impression, awareness 7 = **sense of touch**, perception, sensation 8 = **impression**, idea, sense, notion, suspicion, hunch, inkling, presentiment 9 = **atmosphere**, mood, aura, ambience, feel, air, quality

feisty ADJECTIVE (*informal*) = **fiery**, spirited, bold, plucky, vivacious, (as) game as Ned Kelly (*Austral. slang*)

fell VERB 1 = **cut down**, cut, level, demolish, knock down, hew 2 = **knock down**

fellow NOUN 1 (*old-fashioned*) = **man**, person, individual, character, guy (*informal*), bloke (*Brit. informal*), chap (*informal*) 2 = **associate**, colleague, peer, partner, companion, comrade, crony

fellowship NOUN 1 = **society**, club, league, association, organization, guild, fraternity, brotherhood 2 = **camaraderie**, brotherhood, companionship, sociability

feminine ADJECTIVE = **womanly**, pretty, soft, gentle, tender, delicate, ladylike ≠ masculine

fence NOUN = **barrier**, wall, defence, railings, hedge, barricade, hedgerow, rampart ▷ VERB *with* **in** *or* **off** = **enclose**, surround, bound, protect, pen, confine, encircle

ferocious ADJECTIVE 1 = **fierce**, violent, savage, ravening, predatory, rapacious, wild ≠ gentle 2 = **cruel**, bitter, brutal, vicious, ruthless, bloodthirsty

ferry NOUN = **ferry boat**, boat, ship, passenger boat, packet boat, packet ▷ VERB = **transport**, bring, carry, ship, take, run, shuttle, convey

fertile ADJECTIVE = **productive**, rich, lush, prolific, abundant, plentiful, fruitful, teeming ≠ barren

fertility NOUN = **fruitfulness**, abundance, richness, fecundity, luxuriance, productiveness

fertilizer *or* **fertiliser** NOUN

= **compost**, muck, manure, dung, bone meal, dressing

festival NOUN 1 = **celebration**, fair, carnival, gala, fête, entertainment, jubilee, fiesta 2 = **holy day**, holiday, feast, commemoration, feast day, red-letter day, saint's day, fiesta

festive ADJECTIVE = **celebratory**, happy, merry, jubilant, cheery, joyous, joyful, jovial ≠ mournful

fetch VERB 1 = **bring**, pick up, collect, go and get, get, carry, deliver, transport 2 = **sell for**, make, raise, earn, realize, go for, yield, bring in

fetching ADJECTIVE (informal) = **attractive**, charming, cute, enticing, captivating, alluring, winsome

feud NOUN = **hostility**, row, conflict, argument, disagreement, rivalry, quarrel, vendetta ▷ VERB = **quarrel**, row, clash, dispute, fall out, contend, war, squabble

fever NOUN = **excitement**, frenzy, ferment, agitation, fervour, restlessness, delirium

few ADJECTIVE = **not many**, one or two, scarcely any, rare, meagre, negligible, sporadic, sparse

fiasco NOUN = **flop**, failure, disaster, mess (informal), catastrophe, debacle, cock-up (Brit. slang), washout (informal)

fibre or (U.S.) **fiber** NOUN = **thread**, strand, filament, tendril, pile, texture, wisp

fiction NOUN 1 = **tale**, story, novel, legend, myth, romance, narration, creative writing 2 = **lie**, invention, fabrication, falsehood, untruth, urban myth, tall story, urban legend

fictional ADJECTIVE = **imaginary**, made-up, invented, legendary, unreal, nonexistent

fiddle NOUN 1 (Brit. informal) = **fraud**, racket, scam (slang), fix, swindle 2 (informal) = **violin** ▷ VERB 1 (informal) often with **with** = **fidget**, play, finger, tamper, mess about or around 2 (informal) often with **with** = **tinker**, adjust, interfere, mess about or around 3 (informal) = **cheat**, cook (informal), fix, diddle (informal), wangle (informal)

fiddling ADJECTIVE = **trivial**, small, petty, trifling, insignificant, unimportant, pettifogging, futile

fidelity NOUN 1 = **loyalty**, devotion, allegiance, constancy, faithfulness, dependability, trustworthiness, staunchness ≠ disloyalty 2 = **accuracy**, precision, correspondence, closeness, faithfulness, exactness, scrupulousness ≠ inaccuracy

field NOUN 1 = **meadow**, land, green, lea (poetic), pasture 2 = **speciality**, line, area, department, territory, discipline, province, sphere 3 = **line**, reach, sweep 4 = **competitors**, competition, candidates, runners, applicants, entrants, contestants ▷ VERB 1 (informal) = **deal with**, answer, handle, respond to, reply to, deflect, turn aside **2** (*sport*) = **retrieve**, return, stop, catch, pick up

fierce ADJECTIVE **1** = **ferocious**, wild, dangerous, cruel, savage, brutal, aggressive, menacing, aggers (*Austral. slang*), biffo (*Austral. slang*) ≠ gentle **2** = **intense**, strong, keen, relentless, cut-throat **3** = **stormy**, strong, powerful, violent, intense, raging, furious, howling ≠ tranquil

fiercely ADVERB = **ferociously**, savagely, passionately, furiously, viciously, tooth and nail, tigerishly, with no holds barred

fiery ADJECTIVE **1** = **burning**, flaming, blazing, on fire, ablaze, aflame, afire **2** = **excitable**, fierce, passionate, irritable, impetuous, irascible, hot-headed

fight VERB **1** = **oppose**, campaign against, dispute, contest, resist, defy, contend, withstand **2** = **battle**, combat, do battle **3** = **engage in**, conduct, wage, pursue, carry on
▷ NOUN **1** = **battle**, campaign, movement, struggle **2** = **conflict**, clash, contest, encounter **3** = **brawl**, scrap (*informal*), confrontation, rumble (*U.S. & N.Z. slang*), duel, skirmish, tussle, biffo (*Austral. slang*), boilover (*Austral.*) **4** = **row**, argument, dispute, quarrel, squabble **5** = **resistance**, spirit, pluck, militancy, belligerence, pluckiness

fighter NOUN **1** = **boxer**, wrestler, pugilist, prize fighter **2** = **soldier**, warrior, fighting man, man-at-arms

figure NOUN **1** = **digit**, character, symbol, number, numeral **2** = **shape**, build, body, frame, proportions, physique **3** = **personage**, person, individual, character, personality, celebrity, big name, dignitary **4** = **diagram**, drawing, picture, illustration, representation, sketch **5** = **design**, shape, pattern **6** = **price**, cost, value, amount, total, sum
▷ VERB **1** *usually with* **in** = **feature**, act, appear, contribute to, play a part, be featured **2** = **calculate**, work out, compute, tot up, total, count, reckon, tally ▷ PHRASE:
figure something *or* **someone out** = **understand**, make out, fathom, see, solve, comprehend, make sense of, decipher

figurehead NOUN = **nominal head**, titular head, front man, puppet, mouthpiece

file¹ NOUN **1** = **folder**, case, portfolio, binder **2** = **dossier**, record, information, data, documents, case history, report, case **3** = **line**, row, chain, column, queue, procession
▷ VERB **1** = **arrange**, order, classify, put in place, categorize, pigeonhole, put in order **2** = **register**, record, enter, log, put on record **3** = **march**, troop, parade, walk in line, walk behind

f

one another

file² VERB = **smooth**, shape, polish, rub, scrape, rasp, abrade

fill VERB 1 = **top up**, fill up, make full, become full, brim over 2 = **swell**, expand, become bloated, extend, balloon, fatten 3 = **pack**, crowd, squeeze, cram, throng 4 = **stock**, supply, pack, load 5 = **plug**, close, stop, seal, cork, bung, block up, stop up 6 = **saturate**, charge, pervade, permeate, imbue, impregnate, suffuse 7 = **fulfil**, hold, perform, carry out, occupy, execute, discharge 8 *often with* **up** = **satisfy**, stuff, glut

filling NOUN = **stuffing**, padding, filler, wadding, inside, insides, contents
▷ ADJECTIVE = **satisfying**, heavy, square, substantial, ample

film NOUN 1 = **movie**, picture, flick (*slang*), motion picture 2 = **cinema**, the movies 3 = **layer**, covering, cover, skin, coating, dusting, tissue, membrane
▷ VERB 1 = **photograph**, record, shoot, video, videotape, take 2 = **adapt for the screen**, make into a film

filter NOUN = **sieve**, mesh, gauze, strainer, membrane, riddle, sifter
▷ VERB 1 = **trickle**, seep, percolate, escape, leak, penetrate, ooze, dribble 2 *with* **through** = **purify**, treat, strain, refine, riddle, sift, sieve, winnow

filthy ADJECTIVE 1 = **dirty**, foul, polluted, squalid, slimy, unclean, putrid, festy (*Austral. slang*) 2 = **grimy**, muddy, blackened, grubby, begrimed, festy (*Austral. slang*) 3 = **obscene**, corrupt, indecent, pornographic, lewd, depraved, impure, smutty

final ADJECTIVE 1 = **last**, latest, closing, finishing, concluding, ultimate, terminal ≠ first 2 = **irrevocable**, absolute, definitive, decided, settled, definite, conclusive, irrefutable

finale NOUN = **climax**, ending, close, conclusion, culmination, denouement, last part, epilogue ≠ opening

finally ADVERB 1 = **eventually**, at last, in the end, ultimately, at length, at long last, after a long time 2 = **lastly**, in the end, ultimately 3 = **in conclusion**, lastly, in closing, to conclude, to sum up, in summary

finance NOUN = **economics**, business, money, banking, accounts, investment, commerce
▷ PLURAL NOUN = **resources**, money, funds, capital, cash, affairs, budgeting, assets
▷ VERB = **fund**, back, support, pay for, guarantee, invest in, underwrite, endow

financial ADJECTIVE = **economic**, business, commercial, monetary, fiscal, pecuniary

find VERB 1 = **discover**, uncover, spot, locate, detect, come across, hit upon, put your finger on ≠ lose 2 = **encounter**, meet, recognize 3 = **observe**, learn, note, discover, notice, realize, come up with, perceive

▷ NOUN = **discovery**, catch, asset, bargain, acquisition, good buy

▷ PHRASE: **find something out** = **learn**, discover, realize, observe, perceive, detect, become aware, come to know

fine¹ ADJECTIVE 1 = **excellent**, good, striking, masterly, very good, impressive, outstanding, magnificent ≠ poor 2 = **satisfactory**, good, all right, suitable, acceptable, convenient, fair, O.K. or okay (*informal*) 3 = **thin**, light, narrow, wispy 4 = **delicate**, light, thin, sheer, flimsy, wispy, gossamer, diaphanous ≠ coarse 5 = **stylish**, expensive, elegant, refined, tasteful, quality, schmick (*Austral. informal*) 6 = **exquisite**, delicate, fragile, dainty 7 = **minute**, exact, precise, nice 8 = **keen**, minute, nice, sharp, acute, subtle, precise, hairsplitting 9 = **brilliant**, quick, keen, alert, clever, penetrating, astute 10 = **sunny**, clear, fair, dry, bright, pleasant, clement, balmy ≠ cloudy

fine² NOUN = **penalty**, damages, punishment, forfeit, financial penalty

▷ VERB = **penalize**, charge, punish

finger VERB = **touch**, feel, handle, play with, manipulate, paw (*informal*), maul, toy with

● **WORD POWER**
● The *fingers* are any of the
● digits of the hand, excluding
● the thumb. Their shape and
● function are referred to in many
● of the extended meanings of
● finger. The long and thin shape
● of a finger has come to mean
● a strip or sliver, in *a finger of
● land* and *finger sandwich*. Our
● sense of touch is experienced
● through the fingers, which
● are employed to manipulate
● objects. As a verb, *finger* can
● simply mean to touch, often in
● a restless way, e.g. *He fingered
● the coins in his pocket*. Fingers
● are also used for pointing,
● selection, and identification,
● particularly as a means of
● assigning blame, in the phrase
● *point the finger at* or *finger
● someone to the police*. We pin
● physical objects down with our
● fingers, but can also pin down
● thoughts and memories in our
● minds, e.g. *I couldn't put my
● finger on it*.

finish VERB 1 = **stop**, close, complete, conclude, cease, wrap up (*informal*), terminate, round off ≠ start 2 = **get done**, complete, conclude 3 = **end**, stop, conclude, wind up, terminate 4 = **consume**, dispose of, devour, polish off, eat, get through 5 = **use up**, empty, exhaust 6 = **coat**, polish, stain, texture, wax, varnish, gild, veneer 7 *often with* **off** = **destroy**, defeat, overcome, bring down, ruin, dispose of, rout, put an end to 8 *often with* **off** = **kill**, murder, destroy, massacre, butcher,

slaughter, slay, exterminate
▷ NOUN 1 = **end**, close, conclusion, run-in, completion, finale, culmination, cessation ≠ beginning 2 = **surface**, polish, shine, texture, glaze, veneer, lacquer, lustre

finished ADJECTIVE 1 = **over**, done, through, ended, closed, complete, executed, finalized ≠ begun 2 = **ruined**, done for (*informal*), doomed, through, lost, defeated, wiped out, undone

fire NOUN 1 = **flames**, blaze, combustion, inferno, conflagration, holocaust 2 = **passion**, energy, spirit, enthusiasm, excitement, intensity, sparkle, vitality 3 = **bombardment**, shooting, firing, shelling, hail, volley, barrage, gunfire
▷ VERB 1 = **let off**, shoot, shell, set off, discharge, detonate 2 = **shoot**, explode, discharge, detonate, pull the trigger 3 (*informal*) = **dismiss**, sack (*informal*), get rid of, discharge, lay off, make redundant, cashier, give notice, kennet (*Austral. slang*), jeff (*Austral. slang*) 4 = **inspire**, excite, stir, stimulate, motivate, awaken, animate, rouse

fireworks PLURAL NOUN 1 = **pyrotechnics**, illuminations, feux d'artifice 2 (*informal*) = **trouble**, row, storm, rage, uproar, hysterics

firm¹ ADJECTIVE 1 = **hard**, solid, dense, set, stiff, compacted, rigid, inflexible ≠ soft 2 = **secure**, fixed, rooted, stable, steady, fast, embedded, immovable ≠ unstable 3 = **strong**, close, tight, steady 4 = **strict**, unshakeable, resolute, inflexible, unyielding, unbending 5 = **determined**, resolved, definite, set on, adamant, resolute, inflexible, unyielding ≠ wavering 6 = **definite**, hard, clear, confirmed, settled, fixed, hard-and-fast, cut-and-dried (*informal*)

firm² NOUN = **company**, business, concern, association, organization, corporation, venture, enterprise

firmly ADVERB 1 = **securely**, safely, tightly 2 = **immovably**, securely, steadily, like a rock, unflinchingly, unshakeably 3 = **steadily**, securely, tightly, unflinchingly 4 = **resolutely**, staunchly, steadfastly, definitely, unwaveringly, unchangeably

first ADJECTIVE = **earliest**, initial, opening, introductory, original, maiden, primordial 2 = **top**, best, winning, premier 3 = **elementary**, key, basic, primary, fundamental, cardinal, rudimentary, elemental 4 = **foremost**, highest, greatest, leading, head, ruling, chief, prime
▷ NOUN = **novelty**, innovation, originality, new experience
▷ ADVERB = **to begin with**, firstly, initially, at the beginning, in the first place, beforehand, to start

with, at the outset ▷ **PHRASE**:
from the first = **start**, beginning,
outset, the very beginning,
introduction, starting point,
inception, commencement

fish VERB = **angle**, net, cast, trawl
▷ *see* **sharks**

fit¹ VERB 1 = **adapt**, shape, arrange,
alter, adjust, modify, tweak
(*informal*), customize 2 = **place**,
insert 3 = **suit**, meet, match,
belong to, conform to, correspond
to, accord with, be appropriate to
4 = **equip**, provide, arm, prepare,
fit out, kit out
▷ ADJECTIVE 1 = **appropriate**,
suitable, right, becoming,
seemly, fitting, skilled, correct
≠ inappropriate 2 = **healthy**,
strong, robust, sturdy, well, trim,
strapping, hale ≠ unfit

fit² NOUN 1 (*pathology*) = **seizure**,
attack, bout, spasm, convulsion,
paroxysm 2 = **bout**, burst,
outbreak, outburst, spell

fitness NOUN
1 = **appropriateness**,
competence, readiness, eligibility,
suitability, propriety, aptness
2 = **health**, strength, good health,
vigour, good condition, wellness,
robustness

fitting ADJECTIVE = **appropriate**,
suitable, proper, apt, right,
becoming, seemly, correct
≠ unsuitable
▷ NOUN = **accessory**, part, piece,
unit, component, attachment

fix VERB 1 = **place**, join, stick,
attach, set, position, plant, link

2 *often with* **up** = **decide**, set,
choose, establish, determine,
settle, arrange, arrive at 3 *often
with* **up** = **arrange**, organize, sort
out, see to, make arrangements
for 4 = **repair**, mend, service,
correct, restore, see to, overhaul,
patch up 5 = **focus**, direct at,
fasten on 6 (*informal*) = **rig**, set up
(*informal*), influence, manipulate,
fiddle (*informal*)
▷ NOUN (*informal*) = **mess**,
corner, difficulty, dilemma,
embarrassment, plight, pickle
(*informal*), uphill (*S. African*)
▷ PHRASES: **fix someone up** *often
with* **with** = **provide**, supply, bring
about, lay on, arrange for; **fix
something up** = **arrange**, plan,
settle, fix, organize, sort out,
agree on, make arrangements for

fixed ADJECTIVE 1 = **inflexible**,
set, steady, resolute, unwavering
≠ wavering 2 = **immovable**,
set, established, secure, rooted,
permanent, rigid ≠ mobile
3 = **agreed**, set, planned, decided,
established, settled, arranged,
resolved

fizz VERB 1 = **bubble**, froth, fizzle,
effervesce, produce bubbles
2 = **sputter**, buzz, sparkle, hiss,
crackle *often with* **out**

flag¹ NOUN = **banner**, standard,
colours, pennant, ensign,
streamer, pennon
▷ VERB 1 = **mark**, identify,
indicate, label, pick out, note
2 *often with* **down** = **hail**, stop,
signal, wave down

● FISH

● ahuru (N.Z.)
● alewife
● albacore
● alfonsino
● amberjack
● anabas
● anchovy
● angelfish
● archerfish
● argentine
● aua (N.Z.)
● Australian salmon, native salmon, salmon trout, bay trout or kahawai (N.Z. & Austral.)
● barbel
● barracouta or (Austral.) hake
● barracuda
● barramundi or (Austral.) barra or giant perch
● bass
● beluga
● bib, pout, or whiting pout
● black cod or Māori chief (N.Z.)
● blackfish or (Austral.) nigger
● bleak
● blenny
● blowfish or (Austral.) toado
● blue cod, rock cod, or (N.Z.) rawaru, pakirikiri, or patutuki

● bluefin tuna
● bluefish or snapper
● blue nose (N.Z.)
● bonito or (Austral.) horse mackerel
● bony bream (Austral.)
● bowfin or dogfish
● bream or (Austral.) brim
● brill
● brook trout or speckled trout
● brown trout
● bullhead
● bully or (N.Z.) pakoko, titarakura, or toitoi
● burbot, eelpout, or ling
● butterfish, greenbone, or (N.Z.) koaea or marari
● capelin or caplin
● carp
● catfish
● Chinook salmon, quinnat salmon, or king salmon
● chub
● cisco or lake herring
● clingfish
● coalfish or (Brit.) saithe or coley
● cockabully
● cod or codfish
● coelacanth
● coho or silver salmon

● coley
● conger
● coral trout
● dab
● dace
● dart (Austral.)
● darter
● dory
● dragonet
● eel or (N.Z.) tuna
● eelpout
● electric eel
● fighting fish or betta
● filefish
● flatfish or (N.Z.) flattie
● flathead
● flounder or (N.Z.) patiki
● flying fish
● flying gurnard
● garpike, garfish, gar, or (Austral.) ballahoo
● geelbek
● gemfish or (Austral.) hake
● goby
● golden perch, freshwater bream, Murray perch, or yellow-belly (Austral.)
● goldfish
● gourami
● grayling or (Austral.) yarra herring
● grenadier or rat-tail

f

- groper or grouper
- grunion
- grunt
- gudgeon
- gunnel
- guppy
- gurnard or gurnet
- haddock
- hagfish, hag or blind eel
- hake
- halfbeak
- halibut
- hapuku (Austral. & N.Z.)
- herring
- hogfish
- hoki (N.Z.)
- horse mackerel
- jewelfish
- jewfish or (Austral. informal) jewie
- John Dory
- kelpfish or (Austral. informal) kelpie
- killifish
- kingfish
- kingklip (S. African)
- kokanee
- kokopu (N.Z.)
- lamprey or lamper eel
- leatherjacket
- lemon sole
- ling or (Austral.) beardie
- loach
- luderick or (N.Z.) parore
- lumpfish or

- lumpsucker
- lungfish
- mackerel or (colloquial) shiner
- mangrove Jack (Austral.)
- manta, manta ray, devilfish, or devil ray
- maomao (N.Z.)
- marlin or spearfish
- menhaden
- miller's thumb
- minnow or (Scot.) baggie minnow
- mirror carp
- moki or blue moki (N.Z.)
- molly
- monkfish or (U.S.) goosefish
- moray
- morwong, black perch, or (N.Z.) porae
- mudfish
- mudskipper
- opah, moonfish, or kingfish
- orange roughy (Austral.)
- orfe
- ouananiche
- ox-eye herring (Austral.)
- parore, blackfish, black rockfish or mangrove fish (N.Z.)
- parrotfish

- pearl perch (Austral.)
- perch or (Austral.) redfin
- pickerel
- pike, luce, or jackfish
- pikeperch
- pilchard or (Austral. informal) pillie
- pilot fish
- pipefish or needlefish
- piranha or piraña
- plaice
- pollack or pollock
- pollan
- pompano
- porae (N.Z.)
- porcupine fish or globefish
- porgy or pogy
- pout
- powan or lake herring
- puffer or globefish
- rainbow trout
- ray
- redfin
- redfish
- red mullet or (U.S.) goatfish
- red salmon
- red snapper
- remora
- ribbonfish
- roach
- rock bass
- rockfish or (formerly) rock salmon

- rockling
- rudd
- ruffe, ruff, or pope
- salmon
- sand eel, sand lance, or launce
- sardine
- sauger
- saury or skipper
- sawfish
- scad
- scaldfish
- scorpion fish
- scup or northern porgy
- sea bass
- sea bream
- sea horse
- sea scorpion
- sea snail or snailfish
- sea trout
- Sergeant Baker
- shad
- shanny
- shiner
- Siamese fighting fish
- sild
- silver belly (N.Z.)
- silverfish
- silverside or silversides
- skate
- skipjack or skipjack tuna
- smelt
- smooth hound
- snapper, red bream, or (Austral.) wollomai or wollamai
- snipefish or bellows fish
- snoek
- snook
- sockeye or red salmon
- sole
- Spanish mackerel or Queensland kingfish
- sprat
- steelhead
- stickleback
- stingray
- stonefish
- sturgeon
- sucker
- sunfish
- surgeonfish
- swordfish
- swordtail
- tailor
- tarakihi or terakihi (N.Z.)
- tarpon
- tarwhine
- tautog or blackfish
- tench
- toadfish
- tommy rough or tommy ruff (Austral.)
- trevalla (Austral.)
- trevally, araara or samson fish (Austral. & N.Z.)
- triggerfish
- trout
- trunkfish, boxfish, or cowfish
- tuna or tunny
- turbot
- vendace
- wahoo
- walleye, walleyed pike, or dory
- warehou (N.Z.)
- weever
- whitebait
- whitefish
- whiting
- witch
- wobbegong, wobbygong, or wobegong
- wolffish or catfish
- wrasse
- yellowfin (N.Z.)
- yellow jack

f

flag² VERB = **weaken**, fade, weary, falter, wilt, wane, sag, languish

flagging ADJECTIVE = **weakening**, declining, waning, fading, deteriorating, wearying, faltering, wilting

flair NOUN 1 = **ability**, feel, talent, gift, genius, faculty, mastery,

knack 2 (*informal*) = **style**, taste,
dash, chic, elegance, panache,
discernment, stylishness
flake NOUN = **chip**, scale, layer,
peeling, shaving, wafer, sliver
▷ VERB = **chip**, peel (off), blister
flamboyant ADJECTIVE 1 = **camp**
(*informal*), dashing, theatrical,
swashbuckling 2 = **showy**,
elaborate, extravagant, ornate,
ostentatious 3 = **colourful**,
striking, brilliant, glamorous,
stylish, dazzling, glitzy (*slang*),
showy, bling (*slang*)
flame NOUN 1 = **fire**, light, spark,
glow, blaze, brightness, inferno
2 (*informal*) = **sweetheart**,
partner, lover, girlfriend,
boyfriend, heart-throb (*Brit.*),
beau
▷ VERB = **burn**, flash, shine, glow,
blaze, flare, glare
flank NOUN 1 = **side**, hip, thigh,
loin 2 = **wing**, side, sector, aspect
flap VERB 1 = **flutter**, wave, flail
2 = **beat**, wave, thrash, flutter,
wag, vibrate, shake
▷ NOUN 1 = **flutter**, beating,
waving, shaking, swinging,
swish 2 (*informal*) = **panic**, state
(*informal*), agitation, commotion,
sweat (*informal*), dither (*chiefly
Brit.*), fluster, tizzy (*informal*)
flare VERB 1 = **blaze**, flame, glare,
flicker, burn up 2 = **widen**, spread,
broaden, spread out, dilate, splay
▷ NOUN = **flame**, burst, flash,
blaze, glare, flicker
flash NOUN = **blaze**, burst, spark,
beam, streak, flare, dazzle, glare

▷ VERB 1 = **blaze**, shine, beam,
sparkle, flare, glare, gleam, light
up 2 = **speed**, race, shoot, fly, tear,
dash, whistle, streak 3 (*informal*)
= **show quickly**, display, expose,
exhibit, flourish, show off, flaunt
▷ ADJECTIVE (*informal*)
= **ostentatious**, smart, trendy,
showy, bling (*slang*)
flat¹ ADJECTIVE 1 = **even**, level,
levelled, smooth, horizontal
≠ uneven 2 = **punctured**,
collapsed, burst, blown out,
deflated, empty 3 = **used up**,
finished, empty, drained, expired
4 = **absolute**, firm, positive,
explicit, definite, outright,
downright, unequivocal 5 = **dull**,
dead, empty, boring, depressing,
tedious, lacklustre, tiresome
≠ exciting 6 = **without energy**,
empty, weak, tired, depressed,
drained, weary, worn out
7 = **monotonous**, boring, dull,
tedious, tiresome, unchanging
▷ ADVERB = **completely**, directly,
absolutely, categorically,
precisely, exactly, utterly, outright
▷ PHRASE: **flat out** (*informal*) = **at
full speed**, all out, to the full, hell
for leather (*informal*), as hard as
possible, at full tilt, for all you are
worth
flat² NOUN = **apartment**, rooms,
quarters, digs, suite, penthouse,
living quarters, duplex (*U.S. &
Canad.*), bachelor apartment
(*Canad.*)
flatly ADVERB = **absolutely**,
completely, positively,

categorically, unequivocally, unhesitatingly

flatten VERB 1 *sometimes with* **out** = **level**, squash, compress, trample, iron out, even out, smooth off
2 *sometimes with* **out** = **destroy**, level, ruin, demolish, knock down, pull down, raze, kennet (*Austral. slang*), jeff (*Austral. slang*)

flatter VERB 1 = **praise**, compliment, pander to, sweet-talk (*informal*), wheedle, soft-soap (*informal*), butter up
2 = **suit**, become, enhance, set off, embellish, do something for, show to advantage

flattering ADJECTIVE
1 = **becoming**, kind, effective, enhancing, well-chosen ≠ unflattering 2 = **ingratiating**, complimentary, fawning, fulsome, laudatory, adulatory ≠ uncomplimentary

flavour (*U.S.*) *or* **flavor** NOUN
1 = **taste**, seasoning, flavouring, savour, relish, smack, aroma, zest ≠ blandness 2 = **quality**, feeling, feel, style, character, tone, essence, tinge
▷ VERB = **season**, spice, add flavour to, enrich, infuse, imbue, pep up, leaven

flaw NOUN = **weakness**, failing, defect, weak spot, fault, blemish, imperfection, chink in your armour

flawed ADJECTIVE 1 = **damaged**, defective, imperfect, blemished, faulty 2 = **erroneous**, incorrect,

invalid, wrong, mistaken, false, faulty, unsound

flee VERB = **run away**, escape, bolt, fly, take off (*informal*), depart, run off, take flight

fleet NOUN = **navy**, task force, flotilla, armada

fleeting ADJECTIVE = **momentary**, passing, brief, temporary, short-lived, transient, ephemeral, transitory ≠ lasting

flesh NOUN 1 = **fat**, muscle, tissue, brawn 2 (*informal*) = **fatness**, fat, adipose tissue, corpulence, weight 3 = **meat** 4 = **physical nature**, carnality, human nature, flesh and blood, sinful nature
▷ PHRASE: **your own flesh and blood** = **family**, blood, relations, relatives, kin, kith and kin, blood relations, kinsfolk, ainga (*N.Z.*), rellies (*Austral. slang*)

flexibility NOUN 1 = **elasticity**, pliability, springiness, pliancy, give (*informal*) 2 = **adaptability**, openness, versatility, adjustability 3 = **complaisance**, accommodation, give and take, amenability

flexible ADJECTIVE 1 = **pliable**, plastic, elastic, supple, lithe, springy, pliant, stretchy ≠ rigid
2 = **adaptable**, open, variable, adjustable, discretionary ≠ inflexible

flick VERB 1 = **jerk**, pull, tug, lurch, jolt 2 = **strike**, tap, remove quickly, hit, touch, stroke, flip, whisk ▷ PHRASE: **flick through something** = **browse**, glance at,

f

skim, leaf through, flip through, thumb through, skip through

flicker VERB 1 = **twinkle**, flash, sparkle, flare, shimmer, gutter, glimmer 2 = **flutter**, waver, quiver, vibrate
▷ NOUN 1 = **glimmer**, flash, spark, flare, gleam 2 = **trace**, breath, spark, glimmer, iota

flight¹ NOUN 1 = **journey**, trip, voyage 2 = **aviation**, flying, aeronautics 3 = **flock**, group, unit, cloud, formation, squadron, swarm, flying group

flight² NOUN = **escape**, fleeing, departure, retreat, exit, running away, exodus, getaway

fling VERB = **throw**, toss, hurl, launch, cast, propel, sling, catapult
▷ NOUN = **binge**, good time, bash, party, spree, night on the town, rave-up (*Brit. slang*)

flip VERB 1 = **flick**, switch, snap, slick 2 = **spin**, turn, overturn, turn over, roll over 3 = **toss**, throw, flick, fling, sling
▷ NOUN = **toss**, throw, spin, snap, flick

flirt VERB 1 = **chat up**, lead on (*informal*), make advances at, make eyes at, philander, make sheep's eyes at 2 *usually with* **with** = **toy with**, consider, entertain, play with, dabble in, trifle with, give a thought to, expose yourself to
▷ NOUN = **tease**, philanderer, coquette, heart-breaker

float VERB 1 = **glide**, sail, drift,

move gently, bob, coast, slide, be carried 2 = **be buoyant**, hang, hover ≠ sink 3 = **launch**, offer, sell, set up, promote, get going ≠ dissolve

floating ADJECTIVE
1 = **uncommitted**, wavering, undecided, indecisive, vacillating, sitting on the fence (*informal*), unaffiliated, independent
2 = **free**, wandering, variable, fluctuating, unattached, movable

flock NOUN 1 = **herd**, group, flight, drove, colony, gaggle, skein
2 = **crowd**, company, group, host, collection, mass, gathering, herd
▷ VERB 1 = **stream**, crowd, mass, swarm, throng 2 = **gather**, crowd, mass, collect, assemble, herd, huddle, converge

flog VERB = **beat**, whip, lash, thrash, whack, scourge, hit hard, trounce

flood NOUN 1 = **deluge**, downpour, inundation, tide, overflow, torrent, spate 2 = **torrent**, flow, rush, stream, tide, abundance, glut, profusion 3 = **series**, stream, avalanche, barrage, spate, torrent
4 = **outpouring**, rush, stream, surge, torrent
▷ VERB 1 = **immerse**, swamp, submerge, inundate, drown, cover with water 2 = **pour over**, swamp, run over, overflow, inundate 3 = **engulf**, sweep into, overwhelm, surge into, swarm into, pour into 4 = **saturate**, fill, choke, swamp, glut, oversupply, overfill 5 = **stream**, flow, rush,

pour, surge

floor NOUN 1 = **ground** 2 = **storey**,
level, stage, tier
▷ VERB 1 (*informal*) = **disconcert**,
stump, baffle, confound, throw
(*informal*), defeat, puzzle, bewilder
2 = **knock down**, fell, knock over,
prostrate, deck (*slang*)

flop VERB 1 = **slump**, fall, drop,
collapse, sink 2 = **hang down**,
hang, dangle, sag, droop 3
(*informal*) = **fail**, fold (*informal*),
founder, fall flat, come unstuck,
misfire, go belly-up (*slang*)
≠ succeed
▷ NOUN (*informal*) = **failure**,
disaster, fiasco, debacle, washout
(*informal*), nonstarter ≠ success

floppy ADJECTIVE = **droopy**, soft,
loose, limp, sagging, baggy,
flaccid, pendulous

floral ADJECTIVE = **flowery**, flower-
patterned

flounder VERB 1 = **falter**, struggle,
stall, slow down, run into trouble,
come unstuck (*informal*), be
in difficulties, hit a bad patch
2 = **dither**, struggle, blunder, be
confused, falter, be in the dark, be
out of your depth 3 = **struggle**,
struggle, toss, thrash, stumble,
fumble, grope
● WORD POWER
● *Flounder* is sometimes wrongly
● used where *founder* is meant:
● *the project foundered* (not
● *floundered*) *because of lack of
● funds.*

flourish VERB 1 = **thrive**, increase,
advance, progress, boom,

bloom, blossom, prosper ≠ fail
2 = **succeed**, move ahead, go
places (*informal*) 3 = **grow**, thrive,
flower, succeed, bloom, blossom,
prosper 4 = **wave**, brandish,
display, shake, wield, flaunt
▷ NOUN 1 = **wave**, sweep,
brandish, swish, swing, twirl
2 = **show**, display, parade, fanfare
3 = **curlicue**, sweep, decoration,
swirl, plume, embellishment,
ornamentation

flourishing ADJECTIVE = **thriving**,
successful, blooming, prospering,
rampant, going places, in the pink

flow VERB 1 = **run**, course, rush,
sweep, move, pass, roll, flood
2 = **pour**, move, sweep, flood,
stream 3 = **issue**, follow, result,
emerge, spring, proceed, arise,
derive
▷ NOUN = **stream**, current,
movement, motion, course, flood,
drift, tide

flower NOUN 1 = **bloom**, blossom,
efflorescence 2 = **elite**, best,
prime, finest, pick, choice,
cream, crème de la crème (*French*)
3 = **height**, prime, peak
▷ VERB 1 = **bloom**, open, mature,
flourish, unfold, blossom
2 = **blossom**, grow, develop,
progress, mature, thrive, flourish,
bloom ▷ RELATED WORD: *adjective*
floral

fluctuate VERB 1 = **change**,
swing, vary, alternate, waver, veer,
seesaw 2 = **shift**, oscillate

fluent ADJECTIVE = **effortless**,
natural, articulate, well-versed,

voluble

fluid NOUN = **liquid**, solution, juice, liquor, sap
▷ ADJECTIVE = **liquid**, flowing, watery, molten, melted, runny, liquefied ≠ solid

flurry NOUN 1 = **commotion**, stir, bustle, flutter, excitement, fuss, disturbance, ado 2 = **gust**, shower, gale, swirl, squall, storm

flush¹ VERB 1 = **blush**, colour, glow, redden, turn red, go red 2 = **cleanse**, wash out, rinse out, flood, swill, hose down 3 = **expel**, drive, dislodge
▷ NOUN = **blush**, colour, glow, reddening, redness, rosiness

flush² ADJECTIVE 1 = **level**, even, true, flat, square 2 (*informal*) = **wealthy**, rich, well-off, in the money (*informal*), well-heeled (*informal*), replete, moneyed, minted (*Brit. slang*)

flutter VERB 1 = **beat**, flap, tremble, ripple, waver, quiver, vibrate, palpitate 2 = **flit**
▷ NOUN 1 = **tremor**, tremble, shiver, shudder, palpitation 2 = **vibration**, twitching, quiver 3 = **agitation**, state (*informal*), confusion, excitement, flap (*informal*), dither (*chiefly Brit.*), commotion, fluster

fly VERB 1 = **take wing**, soar, glide, wing, sail, hover, flutter, flit 2 = **pilot**, control, operate, steer, manoeuvre, navigate 3 = **airlift**, send by plane, take by plane, take in an aircraft 4 = **flutter**, wave, float, flap 5 = **display**, show,

flourish, brandish 6 = **rush**, race, shoot, career, speed, tear, dash, hurry 7 = **pass swiftly**, pass, glide, slip away, roll on, flit, elapse, run its course 8 = **leave**, get away, escape, flee, run for it, skedaddle (*informal*), take to your heels

flying ADJECTIVE = **hurried**, brief, rushed, fleeting, short-lived, hasty, transitory

foam NOUN = **froth**, spray, bubbles, lather, suds, spume, head
▷ VERB = **bubble**, boil, fizz, froth, lather, effervesce

focus NOUN 1 = **centre**, focal point, central point 2 = **focal point**, heart, target, hub
▷ VERB 1 *often with* **on** = **concentrate**, centre, spotlight, direct, aim, pinpoint, zoom in 2 = **fix**, train, direct, aim

foe NOUN (*formal or literary*) = **enemy**, rival, opponent, adversary, antagonist ≠ friend

fog NOUN = **mist**, gloom, haze, smog, murk, miasma, peasouper (*informal*)

foil¹ VERB = **thwart**, stop, defeat, disappoint, counter, frustrate, hamper, balk

foil² NOUN = **complement**, relief, contrast, antithesis

fold VERB 1 = **bend**, crease, double over 2 *often with* **up** (*informal*) = **go bankrupt**, fail, crash, collapse, founder, shut down, go under, go bust (*informal*)
▷ NOUN = **crease**, gather, bend, overlap, wrinkle, pleat, ruffle, furrow

folk NOUN 1 = **people**, persons, individuals, men and women, humanity, inhabitants, mankind, mortals 2 *usually plural (informal)* = **family**, parents, relations, relatives, tribe, clan, kin, kindred, ainga (*N.Z.*), rellies (*Austral. slang*)

follow VERB 1 = **accompany**, attend, escort, go behind, tag along behind, come behind 2 = **pursue**, track, dog, hunt, chase, shadow, trail, hound ≠ avoid 3 = **come after**, go after, come next ≠ precede 4 = **result**, issue, develop, spring, flow, proceed, arise, ensue 5 = **obey**, observe, adhere to, stick to, heed, conform to, keep to, pay attention to ≠ ignore 6 = **succeed**, replace, come after, take over from, come next, supersede, supplant, take the place of 7 = **understand**, realize, appreciate, take in, grasp, catch on (*informal*), comprehend, fathom 8 = **keep up with**, support, be interested in, cultivate, be a fan of, keep abreast of

follower NOUN = **supporter**, fan, disciple, devotee, apostle, pupil, adherent, groupie (*slang*) ≠ leader

following ADJECTIVE 1 = **next**, subsequent, successive, ensuing, later, succeeding, consequent 2 = **coming**, about to be mentioned ▷ NOUN = **supporters**, backing, train, fans, suite, clientele, entourage, coterie

folly NOUN = **foolishness**, nonsense, madness, stupidity, indiscretion, lunacy, imprudence, rashness ≠ wisdom

fond ADJECTIVE 1 = **loving**,

◉ **FLIES**
- aphid *or* plant louse
- aphis
- blackfly *or* bean aphid
- blowfly, bluebottle, *or* (*Austral. informal*) blowie
- botfly
- bushfly
- crane fly *or* (*Brit.*) daddy-longlegs
- damselfly
- dragonfly *or* (*colloquial*) devil's darning-needle
- drosophila, fruit fly, *or* vinegar fly
- fly
- fruit fly
- gadfly
- gallfly
- gnat
- green blowfly *or* (*Austral. informal*) blue-arsed fly
- greenfly
- horsefly *or* cleg
- housefly
- hover fly
- lacewing
- mayfly *or* dayfly
- sandfly
- stonefly
- tsetse fly *or* tzetze fly
- warble fly
- whitefly

caring, warm, devoted, tender, adoring, affectionate, indulgent ≠ indifferent **2** = **unrealistic**, empty, naive, vain, foolish, deluded, overoptimistic, delusive ≠ sensible ▷ **PHRASE: fond of 1** = **attached to**, in love with, keen on, attracted to, having a soft spot for, enamoured of **2** = **keen on**, into (*informal*), hooked on, partial to, having a soft spot for, addicted to

fondly ADVERB **1** = **lovingly**, tenderly, affectionately, amorously, dearly, possessively, with affection, indulgently **2** = **unrealistically**, stupidly, vainly, foolishly, naively, credulously

food NOUN = **nourishment**, fare, diet, tucker (*Austral. & N.Z. informal*), rations, nutrition, cuisine, refreshment, nibbles, kai (*N.Z. informal*)

fool NOUN **1** = **simpleton**, idiot, mug (*Brit. slang*), dummy (*slang*), git (*Brit. slang*), twit (*informal, chiefly Brit.*), dunce, imbecile (*informal*), dorba or dorb (*Austral. slang*), bogan (*Austral. slang*) ≠ genius **2** = **dupe**, mug (*Brit. slang*), sucker (*slang*), stooge (*slang*), laughing stock, pushover (*informal*), fall guy (*informal*) **3** = **jester**, clown, harlequin, buffoon, court jester ▷ **VERB** = **deceive**, mislead, delude, trick, take in, con (*informal*), dupe, beguile, scam (*slang*)

foolish ADJECTIVE = **unwise**, silly, absurd, rash, senseless, foolhardy, ill-judged, imprudent ≠ sensible

● **WORD POWER**
● The literal meaning of *foot*
● is the part of the leg below
● the ankle in humans and
● some animals. The function,
● location, and shape of the foot
● have inspired many extended
● meanings. A foot is a unit of
● length in the imperial system,
● originally equal to the length
● of a man's foot. Foot can also
● mean the bottom or base of
● something, from its position at
● the lowest part of the body, e.g.
● *the foot of the hill*, *page*, or *bed*.
● Many phrases with foot involve
● movement, not just the literal
● act of walking *on foot*, but many
● figurative senses to do with
● initiating and deferring your
● actions, as in *drag your feet*.
● The idea of having a physically
● stable and strong position in
● *foothold* or *footing* is also used
● to mean a basis or foundation
● in fact or reality, e.g. *a firm*
● *foothold* and *a solid footing*.

footing NOUN **1** = **basis**, foundation, base position, groundwork **2** = **relationship**, position, basis, standing, rank, status, grade

footpath NOUN (*Austral. & N.Z.*) = **pavement**, sidewalk (*U.S. & Canad.*)

footstep NOUN = **step**, tread, footfall

foray NOUN = **raid**, sally, incursion, inroad, attack, assault, invasion, swoop

forbid VERB = **prohibit**, ban, disallow, exclude, rule out, veto, outlaw, preclude ≠ permit

● WORD POWER
● Traditionally, it has been
● considered more correct to
● talk about *forbidding someone*
● *to do something*, rather than
● *forbidding someone from doing*
● *something*. Recently, however,
● the *from* option has become
● generally more acceptable, so
● that *he was forbidden to come in*
● and *he was forbidden from coming*
● *in* may both now be considered
● correct.

forbidden ADJECTIVE
= **prohibited**, banned, vetoed, outlawed, taboo, out of bounds, proscribed

forbidding ADJECTIVE
= **threatening**, severe, frightening, hostile, menacing, sinister, daunting, ominous ≠ inviting

force NOUN 1 = **compulsion**, pressure, violence, constraint, oppression, coercion, duress, arm-twisting (*informal*) 2 = **power**, might, pressure, energy, strength, momentum, impulse, vigour ≠ weakness 3 = **intensity**, vigour, vehemence, fierceness, emphasis 4 = **army**, unit, company, host, troop, squad, patrol, regiment ▷ VERB 1 = **compel**, make, drive, press, oblige, constrain, coerce,

impel 2 = **push**, thrust, propel 3 = **break open**, blast, wrench, prise, wrest ▷ PHRASE: **in force** 1 = **valid**, working, current, effective, binding, operative, operational, in operation 2 = **in great numbers**, all together, in full strength

forced ADJECTIVE 1 = **compulsory**, enforced, mandatory, obligatory, involuntary, conscripted ≠ voluntary 2 = **false**, affected, strained, wooden, stiff, artificial, contrived, unnatural ≠ natural

forceful ADJECTIVE 1 = **dynamic**, powerful, assertive ≠ weak 2 = **powerful**, strong, convincing, effective, compelling, persuasive, cogent

forecast VERB = **predict**, anticipate, foresee, foretell, divine, prophesy, augur, forewarn ▷ NOUN = **prediction**, prognosis, guess, prophecy, conjecture, forewarning

forefront NOUN = **lead**, centre, front, fore, spearhead, prominence, vanguard, foreground

foreign ADJECTIVE = **alien**, exotic, unknown, strange, imported, remote, external, unfamiliar ≠ native

foreigner NOUN = **alien**, incomer, immigrant, non-native, stranger, settler

foremost ADJECTIVE = **leading**, best, highest, chief, prime, primary, supreme, most important

f

foresee VERB = **predict**, forecast, anticipate, envisage, prophesy, foretell

forever or **for ever** ADVERB 1 = **evermore**, always, ever, for good, for keeps, for all time, in perpetuity, till the cows come home (*informal*) 2 = **constantly**, always, all the time, continually, endlessly, persistently, eternally, perpetually

- **WORD POWER**
- *Forever* and *for ever* can both be
- used to say that something
- is without end. For all other
- meanings, *forever* is the
- preferred form.

forfeit NOUN = **penalty**, fine, damages, forfeiture, loss, mulct
▷ VERB = **relinquish**, lose, give up, surrender, renounce, be deprived of, say goodbye to, be stripped of

forge VERB 1 = **form**, build, create, establish, set up, fashion, shape, frame 2 = **fake**, copy, reproduce, imitate, counterfeit, feign, falsify 3 = **create**, make, work, found, form, model, fashion, shape

forget VERB 1 = **neglect**, overlook, omit, not remember, be remiss, fail to remember 2 = **leave behind**, lose, lose sight of, mislay

forgive VERB = **excuse**, pardon, not hold something against, understand, acquit, condone, let off (*informal*), turn a blind eye to ≠ blame

forgiveness NOUN = **pardon**, mercy, absolution, exoneration, amnesty, acquittal, remission

fork VERB = **branch**, part, separate, split, divide, diverge, subdivide, bifurcate

forked ADJECTIVE = **branching**, split, branched, divided, angled, pronged, zigzag, Y-shaped

form NOUN 1 = **type**, sort, kind, variety, class, style 2 = **shape**, formation, configuration, structure, pattern, appearance 3 = **condition**, health, shape, nick (*informal*), fitness, trim, fettle 4 = **document**, paper, sheet, questionnaire, application 5 = **procedure**, etiquette, use, custom, convention, usage, protocol, wont, kawa (*N.Z.*), tikanga (*N.Z.*) 6 (*education, chiefly Brit.*) = **class**, year, set, rank, grade, stream
▷ VERB 1 = **arrange**, combine, line up, organize, assemble, draw up 2 = **make**, produce, fashion, build, create, shape, construct, forge 3 = **constitute**, make up, compose, comprise 4 = **establish**, start, launch 5 = **take shape**, grow, develop, materialize, rise, appear, come into being, crystallize 6 = **draw up**, devise, formulate, organize 7 = **develop**, pick up, acquire, cultivate, contract

formal ADJECTIVE 1 = **serious**, stiff, detached, official, correct, conventional, remote, precise ≠ informal 2 = **official**, authorized, endorsed, certified, solemn 3 = **ceremonial**, traditional, solemn, ritualistic, dressy **4** = **conventional**, established, traditional

formality NOUN **1** = **correctness**, seriousness, decorum, protocol, etiquette **2** = **convention**, procedure, custom, ritual, rite

format NOUN = **arrangement**, form, style, make-up, look, plan, design, type

formation NOUN
1 = **establishment**, founding, forming, setting up, starting, production, generation, manufacture **2** = **development**, shaping, constitution, moulding, genesis **3** = **arrangement**, grouping, design, structure, pattern, organization, array, configuration

former ADJECTIVE = **previous**, one-time, erstwhile, earlier, prior, sometime, foregoing ≠ current

formerly ADVERB = **previously**, earlier, in the past, at one time, before, lately, once

formidable ADJECTIVE
1 = **impressive**, great, powerful, tremendous, mighty, terrific, awesome, invincible
2 = **intimidating**, threatening, terrifying, menacing, dismaying, fearful, daunting, frightful ≠ encouraging

formula NOUN = **method**, plan, policy, rule, principle, procedure, recipe, blueprint

formulate VERB **1** = **devise**, plan, develop, prepare, work out, invent, forge, draw up
2 = **express**, detail, frame, define, specify, articulate, set down, put into words

fort NOUN = **fortress**, keep, camp, tower, castle, garrison, stronghold, citadel, fortified pa (*N.Z.*) ▷ PHRASE: **hold the fort** (*informal*) = **take responsibility**, cover, stand in, carry on, take over the reins, deputize, keep things on an even keel

forte NOUN = **speciality**, strength, talent, strong point, métier, long suit (*informal*), gift ≠ weak point

forth ADVERB **1** (*formal or old-fashioned*) = **forward**, out, away, ahead, onward, outward **2** = **out**

forthcoming ADJECTIVE
1 = **approaching**, coming, expected, future, imminent, prospective, impending, upcoming **2** = **available**, ready, accessible, at hand, in evidence, obtainable, on tap (*informal*)
3 = **communicative**, open, free, informative, expansive, sociable, chatty, talkative

fortify VERB **1** = **protect**, defend, strengthen, reinforce, support, shore up, augment, buttress
2 = **strengthen**, add alcohol to ≠ dishearten

fortitude NOUN = **courage**, strength, resolution, grit, bravery, backbone, perseverance, valour

fortress NOUN = **castle**, fort, stronghold, citadel, redoubt, fastness, fortified pa (*N.Z.*)

fortunate ADJECTIVE **1** = **lucky**, favoured, jammy (*Brit. slang*), in luck ≠ unfortunate

2 = **providential**, fortuitous, felicitous, timely, helpful, convenient, favourable, advantageous

fortunately ADVERB = **luckily**, happily, as luck would have it, providentially, by good luck, by a happy chance

fortune NOUN **1** = **wealth**, means, property, riches, resources, assets, possessions, treasure ≠ poverty **2** = **luck**, fluke (*informal*), stroke of luck, serendipity, twist of fate, run of luck **3** = **chance**, fate, destiny, providence, the stars, Lady Luck, kismet **4** *often plural* = **destiny**, lot, experiences, history, condition, success, means, adventures

▷ ADJECTIVE **1** = **leading**, first, head, front, advance, foremost **2** = **future**, advanced, premature, prospective **3** = **presumptuous**, familiar, bold, cheeky, brash, pushy (*informal*), brazen, shameless ≠ shy

▷ VERB **1** = **further**, advance, promote, assist, hurry, hasten, expedite **2** = **send on**, send, post, pass on, dispatch, redirect

forwards ADVERB **1** = **forth**, on, ahead, onwards ≠ backward(s) **2** = **on**, onward, onwards

fossick VERB (*Austral. & N.Z.*) = **search**, hunt, explore, ferret, check, forage, rummage

foster VERB **1** = **bring up**, mother, raise, nurse, look after, rear, care for, take care of **2** = **develop**, support, further, encourage, feed, promote, stimulate, uphold ≠ suppress

foul ADJECTIVE **1** = **dirty**, unpleasant, stinking, filthy, grubby, repellent, squalid, repulsive, festy (*Austral. slang*), yucko (*Austral. slang*) ≠ clean **2** = **obscene**, crude, indecent, blue, abusive, coarse, vulgar, lewd **3** = **unfair**, illegal, crooked, shady (*informal*), fraudulent, dishonest, unscrupulous, underhand **4** = **offensive**, bad, wrong, evil, corrupt, disgraceful, shameful, immoral ≠ admirable

▷ VERB = **dirty**, stain, contaminate, pollute, taint, sully, defile, besmirch ≠ clean

found VERB = **establish**, start, set up, begin, create, institute, organize, constitute

foundation NOUN **1** = **basis** **2** *often plural* = **substructure**, underpinning, groundwork, bedrock, base, footing, bottom **3** = **setting up**, institution, instituting, organization, settlement, establishment, initiating, originating

founder[1] NOUN = **initiator**, father, author, architect, creator, beginner, inventor, originator

founder[2] VERB **1** = **fail**, collapse, break down, fall through, be unsuccessful, come unstuck, miscarry, misfire **2** = **sink**, go down, be lost, submerge, capsize, go to the bottom

⬢ WORD POWER

● *Founder* is sometimes wrongly

used where *flounder* is meant: *this unexpected turn of events left him floundering* (not *foundering*).

fountain NOUN 1 = **font**, spring, reservoir, spout, fount, water feature, well 2 = **jet**, stream, spray, gush 3 = **source**, fount, wellspring, cause, origin, derivation, fountainhead

fowl NOUN = **poultry**

foyer NOUN = **entrance hall**, lobby, reception area, vestibule, anteroom, antechamber

fraction NOUN = **percentage**, share, section, slice, portion

fracture NOUN 1 = **break**, split, crack 2 = **cleft**, opening, split, crack, rift, rupture, crevice, fissure ▷ VERB 1 = **break**, crack 2 = **split**, separate, divide, rend, fragment, splinter, rupture

fragile ADJECTIVE 1 = **unstable**, weak, vulnerable, delicate, uncertain, insecure, precarious, flimsy 2 = **fine**, weak, delicate, frail, brittle, flimsy, dainty, easily broken ≠ durable 3 = **unwell**, poorly, weak, delicate, crook (*Austral. & N.Z. informal*), shaky, frail, feeble, sickly

fragment NOUN = **piece**, bit, scrap, particle, portion, shred, speck, sliver ▷ VERB 1 = **break**, shatter, crumble, disintegrate, splinter, come apart, break into pieces, come to pieces ≠ fuse 2 = **break up**, split up

fragrance *or* **fragrancy** NOUN 1 = **scent**, smell, perfume,

bouquet, aroma, sweet smell, sweet odour, redolence ≠ stink 2 = **perfume**, scent, cologne, eau de toilette, eau de Cologne, toilet water, Cologne water

fragrant ADJECTIVE = **aromatic**, perfumed, balmy, redolent, sweet-smelling, sweet-scented, odorous ≠ stinking

frail ADJECTIVE 1 = **feeble**, weak, puny, infirm ≠ strong 2 = **flimsy**, weak, vulnerable, delicate, fragile, insubstantial

frame NOUN 1 = **casing**, framework, structure, shell, construction, skeleton, chassis 2 = **physique**, build, form, body, figure, anatomy, carcass ▷ VERB 1 = **mount**, case, enclose 2 = **surround**, ring, enclose, encompass, envelop, encircle, hem in 3 = **devise**, draft, compose, sketch, put together, draw up, formulate, map out ▷ PHRASE: **frame of mind** = **mood**, state, attitude, humour, temper, outlook, disposition, mind-set

framework NOUN 1 = **system**, plan, order, scheme, arrangement, the bare bones 2 = **structure**, body, frame, foundation, shell, skeleton

frank ADJECTIVE = **candid**, open, direct, straightforward, blunt, sincere, outspoken, honest ≠ secretive

frankly ADVERB 1 = **honestly**, sincerely, in truth, candidly, to tell you the truth, to be frank, to be frank with someone, to be honest

f

● TYPES OF FOWL
● barnacle goose
● brush turkey or scrub turkey
● bufflehead
● Canada goose
● canvasback
● chicken or (Austral. slang) chook
● cock or cockerel
● duck
● eider or eider duck
● gadwall
● goldeneye
● goosander
● goose
● greylag or greylag goose
● hen
● mallard
● mallee fowl or (Austral.) gnow
● mandarin duck
● megapode
● merganser or sawbill
● moorhen
● Muscovy duck or musk duck
● mute swan
● paradise duck
● pintail
● pochard
● redhead
● Rhode Island Red chicken
● scaup or scaup duck
● screamer
● shelduck
● shoveler
● smew
● snow goose
● sultan
● swan
● teal
● trumpeter swan
● turkey
● whooper or whooper swan
● wigeon or widgeon

2 = **openly**, freely, directly, plainly, bluntly, candidly, without reserve

frantic ADJECTIVE 1 = **frenzied**, wild, furious, distracted, distraught, berserk, at the end of your tether, beside yourself, berko (*Austral. slang*) ≠ calm 2 = **hectic**, desperate, frenzied, fraught (*informal*), frenetic

fraternity NOUN
1 = **companionship**, fellowship, brotherhood, kinship, camaraderie 2 = **circle**, company, guild 3 (*U.S. & Canad.*) = **brotherhood**, club, union, society, league, association

fraud NOUN 1 = **deception**, deceit, treachery, swindling, trickery, duplicity, double-dealing, chicanery ≠ honesty 2 = **scam**, deception (*slang*) 3 = **hoax**, trick, con (*informal*), deception, sham, spoof (*informal*), prank, swindle, fastie (*Austral. slang*) 4 (*informal*) = **impostor**, fake, hoaxer, pretender, charlatan, fraudster, swindler, phoney or phony (*informal*)

fraudulent ADJECTIVE = **deceitful**, crooked (*informal*), untrue, sham, treacherous, dishonest, swindling, double-dealing ≠ genuine

fray VERB = **wear thin**, wear, rub, wear out, chafe

freak MODIFIER = **abnormal**, chance, unusual, exceptional, unparalleled
▷ NOUN 1 (*informal*) = **enthusiast**, fan, nut (*slang*), addict, buff

(*informal*), fanatic, devotee, fiend (*informal*) **2** = **aberration**, eccentric, anomaly, oddity, monstrosity, malformation **3** (*informal*) = **weirdo** or **weirdie** (*informal*), eccentric, character (*informal*), oddball (*informal*), nonconformist

free ADJECTIVE

1 = **complimentary**, for free (*informal*), for nothing, unpaid, for love, free of charge, on the house, without charge **2** = **allowed**, permitted, unrestricted, unimpeded, clear, able **3** = **at liberty**, loose, liberated, at large, on the loose ≠ confined **4** = **independent**, unfettered, footloose **5** = **available**, empty, spare, vacant, unused, unoccupied, untaken **6** *often with* **of** or **with** = **generous**, liberal, lavish, unstinting, unsparing ≠ mean

▷ VERB **1** *often with* **of** or **from** = **clear**, disengage, cut loose, release, rescue, extricate
2 = **release**, liberate, let out, set free, deliver, loose, untie, unchain ≠ confine **3** = **disentangle**, extricate, disengage, loose, unravel, disconnect, untangle

freedom NOUN

1 = **independence**, democracy, sovereignty, self-determination, emancipation, autarchy, rangatiratanga (*N.Z.*) **2** = **liberty**, release, discharge, emancipation, deliverance ≠ captivity
3 = **licence**, latitude, free

rein, opportunity, discretion, carte blanche, blank cheque ≠ restriction

freely ADVERB **1** = **abundantly**, liberally, lavishly, extravagantly, copiously, unstintingly, amply **2** = **openly**, frankly, plainly, candidly, unreservedly, straightforwardly, without reserve **3** = **willingly**, readily, voluntarily, spontaneously, without prompting, of your own free will, of your own accord

freeway NOUN (*U.S. & Austral.*) = **motorway** (*Brit.*), autobahn (*German*), autoroute (*French*), autostrada (*Italian*)

freeze VERB **1** = **ice over** or **up**, harden, stiffen, solidify, become solid **2** = **chill 3** = **fix**, hold, limit, hold up **4** = **suspend**, stop, shelve, curb, cut short, discontinue

freezing (*informal*) ADJECTIVE
1 = **icy**, biting, bitter, raw, chill, arctic, frosty, glacial **2** = **frozen**, very cold

freight NOUN **1** = **transportation**, traffic, delivery, carriage, shipment, haulage, conveyance, transport **2** = **cargo**, goods, load, delivery, burden, shipment, merchandise, consignment

French ADJECTIVE = **Gallic**
  ● **WORD POWER**
  ● The number of words which
  ● English has borrowed from
  ● French is considerable. In the
  ● following passage, French
  ● loan words are highlighted
  ● in bold: *Close* to half the

f

general vocabulary of *modern*
English *derives* from either
French or Latin and, of this, a
remarkable amount is *directly*
descended from French. Words
from French *tend* to be longer,
with more *syllables*, and of
a higher *register* than their
English *counterparts*. They also
tend to be *nouns*, *adjectives*,
verbs, and *adverbs* rather than
grammatical words. There
were *several historical periods*
during which the *majority* of
borrowing took *place*. After
the Norman *Conquest*, the
ruling class spoke Anglo-
Norman, a *dialect* of French,
for nearly 300 hundred years.
French was the *language* of
government, law, *administration*,
and *literature*, but words were
also *adopted* into the fields of
medicine, *art*, *and fashion*. A later
period of *influx* was *during* the
Renaissance when *developments*
in *science* and technology,
and a focus on education and
learning, led to a deliberate
attempt to *enrich* the English
language with *foreign* words.
Equally, the French *language*
has borrowed words from
English and the *close* contact
between the two *cultures* has
even *inspired* a *corrupt version* of
French called *Franglais*.

frenzied ADJECTIVE
= **uncontrolled**, wild, crazy,
furious, frantic, frenetic, feverish,
rabid

frenzy NOUN = **fury**, passion,
rage, seizure, hysteria, paroxysm,
derangement ≠ calm

frequent ADJECTIVE = **common**,
repeated, usual, familiar,
everyday, persistent, customary,
recurrent ≠ infrequent
▷ VERB = **visit**, attend, haunt,
be found at, patronize, hang out
at (*informal*), visit often, go to
regularly ≠ keep away

frequently ADVERB = **often**,
commonly, repeatedly,
many times, habitually,
not infrequently, much
≠ infrequently

fresh ADJECTIVE 1 = **additional**,
more, new, other, added, further,
extra, supplementary 2 = **natural**,
unprocessed, unpreserved
≠ preserved 3 = **new**, original,
novel, different, recent, modern,
up-to-date, unorthodox ≠ old
4 = **invigorating**, clean, pure,
crisp, bracing, refreshing, brisk,
unpolluted ≠ stale 5 = **cool**, cold,
refreshing, brisk, chilly, nippy
6 = **lively**, keen, alert, refreshed,
vigorous, energetic, sprightly,
spry ≠ weary 7 (*informal*)
= **cheeky** (*informal*), impertinent,
forward, familiar, audacious,
disrespectful, presumptuous,
insolent ≠ well-mannered

fret VERB = **worry**, brood, agonize,
obsess, lose sleep, upset yourself,
distress yourself

friction NOUN 1 = **conflict**,
hostility, resentment,

disagreement, animosity, discord, bad blood, dissension **2** = **resistance**, rubbing, scraping, grating, rasping, chafing, abrasion **3** = **rubbing**, scraping, grating, rasping, chafing, abrasion

friend NOUN **1** = **companion**, pal, mate (*informal*), buddy (*informal*), best friend, close friend, comrade, chum (*informal*), cobber (*Austral. & N.Z.*), E hoa (*N.Z. old-fashioned or informal*) ≠ foe **2** = **supporter**, ally, associate, sponsor, patron, well-wisher

friendly ADJECTIVE **1** = **amiable**, welcoming, warm, neighbourly, pally (*informal*), helpful, sympathetic, affectionate **2** = **amicable**, warm, familiar, pleasant, intimate, informal, cordial, congenial ≠ unfriendly

friendship NOUN **1** = **attachment**, relationship, bond, link, association, tie **2** = **friendliness**, affection, harmony, goodwill, intimacy, familiarity, rapport, companionship ≠ unfriendliness

fright NOUN **1** = **fear**, shock, alarm, horror, panic, dread, consternation, trepidation ≠ courage **2** = **scare**, start, turn, surprise, shock, jolt, the creeps (*informal*), the willies (*slang*)

frighten VERB = **scare**, shock, alarm, terrify, startle, intimidate, unnerve, petrify ≠ reassure

frightened ADJECTIVE = **afraid**, alarmed, scared, terrified,

shocked, startled, petrified, flustered

frightening ADJECTIVE = **terrifying**, shocking, alarming, startling, horrifying, menacing, scary (*informal*), fearful

fringe NOUN **1** = **border**, edging, edge, trimming, hem, frill, flounce **2** = **edge**, limits, border, margin, outskirts, perimeter, periphery, borderline ▷ MODIFIER = **unofficial**, alternative, radical, innovative, avant-garde, unconventional, unorthodox

frog NOUN ▷ *see* **amphibians**

front NOUN **1** = **head**, start, lead, forefront **2** = **exterior**, face, façade, frontage **3** = **foreground**, fore, forefront, nearest part **4** (*military*) = **front line**, trenches, vanguard, firing line **5** (*informal*) = **disguise**, cover, blind, mask, cover-up, cloak, façade, pretext ▷ ADJECTIVE **1** = **foremost**, at the front ≠ back **2** = **leading**, first, lead, head, foremost, topmost ▷ VERB *often with* **on** *or* **onto** = **face onto**, overlook, look out on, have a view of, look over or onto

frontier NOUN = **border**, limit, edge, boundary, verge, perimeter, borderline, dividing line

frost NOUN = **hoarfrost**, freeze, rime

frown VERB = **glare**, scowl, glower, make a face, look daggers, knit your brows, lour or lower ▷ NOUN = **scowl**, glare, glower, dirty look

frozen ADJECTIVE 1 = **icy**, hard, solid, frosted, arctic, ice-covered, icebound 2 = **chilled**, cold, iced, refrigerated, ice-cold 3 = **ice-cold**, freezing, numb, very cold, frigid, frozen stiff

fruit NOUN 1 (*botany*) = **produce**, crop, yield, harvest 2 *often plural* = **result**, reward, outcome, end result, return, effect, benefit, profit

frustrate VERB = **thwart**, stop, check, block, defeat, disappoint, counter, spoil, crool *or* cruel (*Austral. slang*) ≠ further

frustrated ADJECTIVE = **disappointed**, discouraged, infuriated, exasperated, resentful, embittered, disheartened

frustration NOUN 1 = **annoyance**, disappointment, resentment, irritation, grievance, dissatisfaction, exasperation, vexation 2 = **obstruction**, blocking, foiling, spoiling, thwarting, circumvention

fudge VERB = **misrepresent**, hedge, stall, flannel (*Brit. informal*), equivocate

fuel NOUN = **incitement**, ammunition, provocation, incentive

fugitive NOUN = **runaway**, refugee, deserter, escapee

fulfil *or* (*U.S.*) **fullfil** VERB 1 = **carry out**, perform, complete, achieve, accomplish ≠ neglect 2 = **achieve**, realize, satisfy, attain, consummate, bring to

fruition 3 = **satisfy**, please, content, cheer, refresh, gratify, make happy 4 = **comply with**, meet, fill, satisfy, observe, obey, conform to, answer

fulfilment *or* (*U.S.*) **fullfilment** NOUN = **achievement**, implementation, completion, accomplishment, realization, attainment, consummation

full ADJECTIVE 1 = **filled**, stocked, brimming, replete, complete, loaded, saturated ≠ empty 2 = **satiated**, having had enough, replete 3 = **extensive**, complete, generous, adequate, ample, abundant, plentiful ≠ incomplete 4 = **comprehensive**, complete, exhaustive, all-embracing 5 = **rounded**, strong, rich, powerful, intense, pungent 6 = **plump**, rounded, voluptuous, shapely, well-rounded, buxom, curvaceous 7 = **voluminous**, large, loose, baggy, billowing, puffy, capacious, loose-fitting ≠ tight 8 (*music*) = **rich**, strong, deep, loud, distinct, resonant, sonorous, clear ≠ thin

full-scale ADJECTIVE = **major**, wide-ranging, all-out, sweeping, comprehensive, thorough, in-depth, exhaustive

fully ADVERB 1 = **completely**, totally, perfectly, entirely, altogether, thoroughly, wholly, utterly 2 = **in all respects**, completely, totally, entirely, altogether, thoroughly, wholly

fumble VERB *often with* **for** *or* **with**

= **grope**, flounder, scrabble, feel around

fume VERB = **rage**, seethe, see red (*informal*), storm, rant, smoulder, get hot under the collar (*informal*)
▷ NOUN *often plural* = **smoke**, gas, exhaust, pollution, vapour, smog

fun NOUN 1 = **amusement**, sport, pleasure, entertainment, recreation, enjoyment, merriment, jollity
2 = **enjoyment**, pleasure, mirth ≠ gloom
▷ MODIFIER = **enjoyable**, entertaining, pleasant, amusing, lively, diverting, witty, convivial ▷ PHRASE: **make fun of something** *or* **someone** = **mock**, tease, ridicule, poke fun at, laugh at, mimic, parody, send up (*Brit. informal*)

function NOUN 1 = **purpose**, business, job, use, role, responsibility, task, duty
2 = **reception**, party, affair, gathering, bash (*informal*), social occasion, soiree, do (*informal*)
▷ VERB 1 = **work**, run, operate, perform, go 2 *with* **as** = **act**, operate, perform, behave, do duty, have the role of

functional ADJECTIVE 1 = **practical**, utilitarian, serviceable, hard-wearing, useful 2 = **working**, operative, operational, going, prepared, ready, viable, up and running

fund NOUN = **reserve**, stock, supply, store, collection, pool
▷ VERB = **finance**, back, support,

pay for, subsidize, provide money for, put up the money for

fundamental ADJECTIVE 1 = **central**, key, basic, essential, primary, principal, cardinal ≠ incidental 2 = **basic**, essential, underlying, profound, elementary, rudimentary

fundamentally ADVERB 1 = **basically**, at heart, at bottom 2 = **essentially**, radically, basically, primarily, profoundly, intrinsically

fundi NOUN (*S. African*) = **expert**

funds PLURAL NOUN = **money**, capital, cash, finance, means, savings, resources, assets

funeral NOUN = **burial**, committal, laying to rest, cremation, interment, obsequies, entombment

funny ADJECTIVE 1 = **humorous**, amusing, comical, entertaining, comic, witty, hilarious, riotous ≠ unfunny 2 = **comic**, comical 3 = **peculiar**, odd, strange, unusual, bizarre, curious, weird, mysterious
4 (*informal*) = **ill**, poorly (*informal*), sick, odd, crook (*Austral. & N.Z. informal*), ailing, unhealthy, unwell, off-colour (*informal*)

furious ADJECTIVE 1 = **angry**, raging, fuming, infuriated, incensed, enraged, inflamed, very angry, tooshie (*Austral. slang*) ≠ pleased 2 = **violent**, intense, fierce, savage, turbulent, vehement, unrestrained

furnish VERB 1 = **decorate**, fit

out, stock, equip **2** = **supply**, give,
offer, provide, present, grant,
hand out

furniture NOUN = **household
goods**, furnishings, fittings,
house fittings, goods, things
(*informal*), possessions, appliances

furore or (U.S.) **furor** NOUN
= **commotion**, to-do, stir,
disturbance, outcry, uproar,
hullabaloo

further ADVERB = **in addition**,
moreover, besides, furthermore,
also, to boot, additionally, into
the bargain
▷ ADJECTIVE = **additional**,
more, new, other, extra, fresh,
supplementary
▷ VERB = **promote**, help, develop,
forward, encourage, advance,
work for, assist ≠ hinder

furthermore ADVERB
= **moreover**, further, in addition,
besides, too, as well, to boot,
additionally

furthest ADJECTIVE = **most
distant**, extreme, ultimate,
remotest, furthermost, outmost

fury NOUN **1** = **anger**, passion,
rage, madness, frenzy, wrath,
impetuosity ≠ calmness
2 = **violence**, force, intensity,
severity, ferocity, savagery,
vehemence, fierceness ≠ peace

fuss NOUN **1** = **commotion**, to-do,
bother, stir, excitement, ado,
hue and cry, palaver **2** = **bother**,
trouble, struggle, hassle (*informal*),
nuisance, inconvenience,
hindrance **3** = **complaint**, row,

protest, objection, trouble,
argument, squabble, furore
▷ VERB = **worry**, flap (*informal*),
fret, fidget, take pains, be
agitated, get worked up

futile ADJECTIVE = **useless**,
vain, unsuccessful, pointless,
worthless, fruitless, ineffectual,
unprofitable ≠ useful

future NOUN **1** = **time to come**,
hereafter, what lies ahead
2 = **prospect**, expectation,
outlook
▷ ADJECTIVE = **forthcoming**,
coming, later, approaching,
to come, succeeding, fated,
subsequent ≠ past

fuzzy ADJECTIVE **1** = **frizzy**, fluffy,
woolly, downy **2** = **indistinct**,
blurred, vague, distorted, unclear,
bleary, out of focus, ill-defined
≠ distinct

Gg

gadget NOUN = **device**, thing, appliance, machine, tool, implement, invention, instrument

- **WORD POWER**
- Gaelic is a member of the Celtic
- family of languages whose
- varieties can still be found in
- parts of Scotland (Scottish
- Gaelic), Ireland (Irish Gaelic),
- and the Isle of Man (Manx
- Gaelic). Although Gaelic has
- influenced Scottish and Irish
- English through colourful loan
- words, only a few Gaelic words
- have become assimilated into
- today's Standard English. The
- Irish Gaelic loan word *brogue*,
- referring to a broad gentle-
- sounding dialectal accent, was
- borrowed in the 18th century
- into English. It is not known
- whether it is related to the
- walking shoe of that name. It
- refers first and foremost to the
- accent with which the Irish
- speak English, known as *the*
- *brogue*, but has been applied
- more widely to other British
- regional accents, particularly
- those of Celtic origin. Another
- Irish Gaelic word is *galore*,
- meaning 'to sufficiency' or 'in
- abundance' which came into
- English in the 17th century. It
- is one of a very small group
- of words which are only ever
- used after the noun they
- describe, and this structure is
- typical of some words English
- has borrowed, e.g. There had
- been *opportunities galore* in
- the 1980s. It can be compared
- to the adjective *aplenty*, both
- in its meaning and in its
- grammatical behaviour. Unlike
- 'abundance' which describes
- a surplus which can be good,
- bad, or neutral, 'galore' tends to
- have positive connotations and
- is often used in advertising, e.g.
- *bargains galore*.

gag[1] NOUN = **muzzle**, tie, restraint
▷ VERB 1 = **suppress**, silence, muffle, curb, stifle, muzzle, quieten 2 = **retch**, heave

gag[2] NOUN (*informal*) = **joke**, crack (*slang*), funny (*informal*), quip, pun, jest, wisecrack (*informal*), witticism

gain VERB 1 = **acquire**, get, receive, pick up, secure, collect, gather, obtain 2 = **profit**, get, land, secure, collect, gather, capture, acquire ≠ lose 3 = **put on**, increase in, gather, build up 4 = **attain**, get, reach, get to, secure, obtain, acquire, arrive at
▷ NOUN 1 = **rise**, increase, growth, advance, improvement, upsurge, upturn, upswing 2 = **profit**, return, benefit, advantage, yield, dividend ≠ loss

▷ PLURAL NOUN = **profits**, earnings, revenue, proceeds, winnings, takings ▷ PHRASE: **gain on something** or **someone** = **get nearer to**, close in on, approach, catch up with, narrow the gap on

gala NOUN = **festival**, fête, celebration, carnival, festivity, pageant, jamboree

gale NOUN 1 = **storm**, hurricane, tornado, cyclone, blast, typhoon, tempest, squall 2 (*informal*) = **outburst**, scream, roar, fit, storm, shout, burst, explosion

gall VERB = **annoy**, provoke, irritate, trouble, disturb, madden, exasperate, vex

gallop VERB 1 = **run**, race, career, speed, bolt 2 = **dash**, run, race, career, speed, rush, sprint

gamble NOUN 1 = **risk**, chance, venture, lottery, speculation, uncertainty, leap in the dark ≠ certainty 2 = **bet**, flutter (*informal*), punt (*chiefly Brit.*), wager
▷ VERB 1 *often with* **on** = **take a chance**, speculate, stick your neck out (*informal*) 2 = **risk**, chance, hazard, wager 3 = **bet**, play, game, speculate, punt, wager, have a flutter (*informal*)

game NOUN 1 = **pastime**, sport, activity, entertainment, recreation, distraction, amusement, diversion ≠ job 2 = **match**, meeting, event, competition, tournament, clash, contest, head-to-head 3 = **amusement**, joke,

entertainment, diversion 4 = **wild animals** or **birds**, prey, quarry 5 = **scheme**, plan, design, trick, plot, tactic, manoeuvre, ploy, fastie (*Austral. slang*)
▷ ADJECTIVE 1 = **willing**, prepared, ready, keen, eager, interested, desirous 2 = **brave**, courageous, spirited, daring, persistent, gritty, feisty (*informal, chiefly U.S. & Canad.*), intrepid, plucky, (as) game as Ned Kelly (*Austral. slang*) ≠ cowardly

gang NOUN = **group**, crowd, pack, company, band, bunch, mob

gangster NOUN = **hoodlum** (*chiefly U.S.*), crook (*informal*), bandit, hood (*U.S. slang*), robber, mobster (*U.S. slang*), racketeer, ruffian, tsotsi (*S. African*)

gap NOUN 1 = **opening**, space, hole, break, crack, slot, aperture, cleft 2 = **interval**, pause, interruption, respite, lull, interlude, breathing space, hiatus 3 = **difference**, gulf, contrast, disagreement, discrepancy, inconsistency, disparity, divergence

gape VERB 1 = **stare**, wonder, goggle, gawp (*Brit. slang*), gawk 2 = **open**, split, crack, yawn

gaping ADJECTIVE = **wide**, great, open, broad, vast, yawning, wide open, cavernous

garland NOUN = **wreath**, band, bays, crown, honours, laurels, festoon, chaplet
▷ VERB = **adorn**, crown, deck, festoon, wreathe

garment NOUN *often plural*
= **clothes**, dress, clothing, gear
(*slang*), uniform, outfit, costume,
apparel

garnish NOUN = **decoration**,
embellishment, adornment,
ornamentation, trimming
▷ VERB = **decorate**, adorn,
ornament, embellish, trim ≠ strip

garrison NOUN 1 = **troops**, group,
unit, section, command, armed
force, detachment 2 = **fort**,
fortress, camp, base, post,
station, stronghold, fortification,
fortified pa (*N.Z.*)
▷ VERB = **station**, position, post,
install, assign, put on duty

gas NOUN 1 = **fumes**, vapour 2
(*U.S., Canad. & N.Z.*) = **petrol**,
gasoline

gasp VERB = **pant**, blow, puff,
choke, gulp, catch your breath
▷ NOUN = **pant**, puff, gulp, sharp
intake of breath

gate NOUN = **barrier**, opening,
door, entrance, exit, gateway,
portal

gather VERB 1 = **congregate**,
assemble, collect, meet, mass,
come together, muster, converge
≠ scatter 2 = **assemble**, collect,
bring together, muster, call
together ≠ disperse 3 = **collect**,
assemble, accumulate, mass,
muster, garner, amass, stockpile
4 = **pick**, harvest, pluck, reap,
garner, glean 5 = **build up**,
rise, increase, grow, expand,
swell, intensify, heighten
6 = **understand**, believe, hear,

learn, assume, conclude, presume,
infer 7 = **fold**, tuck, pleat

gathering NOUN = **assembly**,
group, crowd, meeting,
conference, company, congress,
mass, hui (*N.Z.*), runanga (*N.Z.*)

gauge VERB 1 = **measure**,
calculate, evaluate, value,
determine, count, weigh,
compute 2 = **judge**, estimate,
guess, assess, evaluate, rate,
appraise, reckon
▷ NOUN = **meter**, dial, measuring
instrument

gay ADJECTIVE 1 = **homosexual**,
lesbian, queer (*informal* or
derogatory), moffie (*S. African slang*)
2 = **cheerful**, lively, sparkling,
merry, upbeat (*informal*),
buoyant, cheery, carefree ≠ sad
3 = **colourful**, rich, bright,
brilliant, vivid, flamboyant, flashy,
showy ≠ drab
▷ NOUN = **homosexual**, lesbian,
auntie *or* aunty (*Austral. slang*), lily
(*Austral. slang*) ≠ heterosexual

◉ WORD POWER
◉ By far the most common and
◉ up-to-date use of the word
◉ *gay* is in reference to being
◉ homosexual. Other senses
◉ of the word have become
◉ uncommon and dated.

gaze VERB = **stare**, look, view,
watch, regard, gape
▷ NOUN = **stare**, look, fixed look

gazette NOUN = **newspaper**,
paper, journal, periodical, news-
sheet

g'day *or* **gidday** INTERJECTION

(*Austral. & N.Z.*) = **hello**, hi
(*informal*), greetings, how do you
do?, good morning, good evening,
good afternoon, welcome, kia ora
(*N.Z.*)

gear NOUN 1 = **mechanism**,
works, machinery, cogs,
cogwheels, gearwheels
2 = **equipment**, supplies, tackle,
tools, instruments, apparatus,
paraphernalia, accoutrements
3 = **clothing**, wear, dress, clothes,
outfit, costume, garments, togs
▷ VERB *with* **to** *or* **towards**
= **equip**, fit, adjust, adapt

gem NOUN 1 = **precious stone**,
jewel, stone 2 = **treasure**,
prize, jewel, pearl, masterpiece,
humdinger (*slang*), taonga (*N.Z.*)

general ADJECTIVE
1 = **widespread**, accepted,
popular, public, common, broad,
extensive, universal ≠ individual
2 = **overall**, complete, total,
global, comprehensive, blanket,
inclusive, all-embracing
≠ restricted 3 = **universal**,
overall, widespread, collective,
across-the-board ≠ exceptional
4 = **vague**, loose, blanket,
sweeping, unclear, approximate,
woolly, indefinite ≠ specific

generally ADVERB 1 = **usually**,
commonly, typically, normally, on
the whole, by and large, ordinarily,
as a rule ≠ occasionally
2 = **commonly**, widely, publicly,
universally, extensively, popularly,
conventionally, customarily
≠ individually

generate VERB = **produce**,
create, make, cause, give rise to,
engender ≠ end

generation NOUN 1 = **age group**,
peer group 2 = **age**, period, era,
time, lifetime, span, epoch

generic ADJECTIVE = **collective**,
general, common, wide,
comprehensive, universal,
blanket, inclusive ≠ specific

generosity NOUN 1 = **liberality**,
charity, bounty, munificence,
beneficence, largesse *or* largess
2 = **magnanimity**, goodness,
kindness, selflessness, charity,
unselfishness, high-mindedness,
nobleness

generous ADJECTIVE 1 = **liberal**,
lavish, charitable, hospitable,
bountiful, open-handed,
unstinting, beneficent ≠ mean
2 = **magnanimous**, kind, noble,
good, high-minded, unselfish,
big-hearted 3 = **plentiful**, lavish,
ample, abundant, full, rich, liberal,
copious ≠ meagre

genesis NOUN = **beginning**,
origin, start, birth, creation,
formation, inception ≠ end

genius NOUN 1 = **brilliance**,
ability, talent, capacity, gift, bent,
excellence, flair 2 = **master**,
expert, mastermind, maestro,
virtuoso, whiz (*informal*), hotshot
(*informal*), brainbox, fundi
(*S. African*) ≠ dunce

genre NOUN = **type**, group, order,
sort, kind, class, style, species

gentle ADJECTIVE 1 = **kind**,
kindly, tender, mild, humane,

compassionate, meek, placid
≠ unkind **2** = **slow**, easy, slight,
moderate, gradual, imperceptible
3 = **moderate**, light, soft, slight,
mild, soothing ≠ violent

gentlemanly ADJECTIVE
= **chivalrous**, refined, polite, civil,
courteous, gallant, genteel, well-
mannered

genuine ADJECTIVE **1** = **authentic**,
real, actual, true, valid,
legitimate, veritable, bona fide,
dinkum (*Austral. & N.Z. informal*)
≠ counterfeit **2** = **heartfelt**,
sincere, honest, earnest, real,
true, frank, unaffected ≠ affected
3 = **sincere**, honest, frank, candid,
dinkum (*Austral. & N.Z. informal*),
guileless ≠ hypocritical

germ NOUN **1** = **microbe**, virus,
bug (*informal*), bacterium, bacillus,
microorganism **2** = **beginning**,
root, seed, origin, spark, embryo,
rudiment

● **WORD POWER**
● German has provided English
● with some very evocative
● words which have distinct
● meanings from their English
● synonyms. *Schadenfreude*,
● borrowed in the 19th century,
● literally means of 'harm-joy'
● and describes a feeling of
● enjoyment at the misfortunes
● of others. Schadenfreude
● conveys a feeling of
● satisfaction that another
● has got their comeuppance,
● usually without the agency of
● the person experiencing it. It

● is often experienced as a guilty
● pleasure, rather than an open
● gloat and contains elements
● of voyeurism, titillation, and
● shame. It has retained its core
● meaning through the ages,
● precisely because there is no
● other word in English for this
● phenomenon. It is used solidly
● as a noun or noun-modifier,
● and is never used as a verb,
● because of its unwieldly and
● foreign sound. It can be found
● both with a capital (common
● to all nouns in German) or
● without. Another word which
● has no direct equivalent in
● English is *Zeitgeist* which
● entered the language in the
● 19th century. Literally it means
● 'time-spirit' and is loosely
● translated as 'the spirit of the
● times'. It conveys a sense of
● shared outlook in a culture
● at a particular point in time,
● especially when it is reflected
● in the arts or philosophy, and
● can be contrasted with its
● synonyms mood, attitude,
● trend, spirit and outlook.
● Zeitgeists are conceptualized
● in English as transitory and
● even elusive; they are captured
● or caught and pinned down, or
● else, like a wave, you can ride
● or surf them. The tautologous
● 'zeitgeist of our times' shows
● that the original German is
● not always known, though its
● meaning obviously is. The more

g

recent *zeitgeisty* shows that the concept is now being used as an adjective.

gesture NOUN = **sign**, action, signal, motion, indication, gesticulation
▷ VERB = **signal**, sign, wave, indicate, motion, beckon, gesticulate

get VERB 1 = **become**, grow, turn, come to be 2 = **persuade**, convince, induce, influence, entice, incite, impel, prevail upon 3 (*informal*) = **annoy**, upset, anger, disturb, trouble, bug (*informal*), irritate, gall 4 = **obtain**, receive, gain, acquire, win, land, net, pick up 5 = **fetch**, bring, collect 6 = **understand**, follow, catch, see, realize, take in, perceive, grasp 7 = **catch**, develop, contract, succumb to, fall victim to, go down with, come down with 8 = **arrest**, catch, grab, capture, seize, take, nab (*informal*), apprehend ▷ PHRASES: **get at someone** = **criticize**, attack, blame, put down, knock (*informal*), nag, pick on, disparage; **get at something 1 = reach**, touch, grasp, get (a) hold of, stretch to VERB 2 = **find out**, learn, reach, reveal, discover, acquire, detect, uncover 3 = **imply**, mean, suggest, hint, intimate, lead up to, insinuate; **get by = manage**, survive, cope, fare, exist, get along, make do, muddle through; **get something across = communicate**, pass on, transmit, convey, impart, bring home, make known, put over

ghastly ADJECTIVE = **horrible**, shocking, terrible, awful, dreadful, horrendous, hideous, frightful ≠ lovely

ghost NOUN 1 = **spirit**, soul, phantom, spectre, spook (*informal*), apparition, wraith, atua (*N.Z.*), kehua (*N.Z.*), wairua (*N.Z.*) 2 = **trace**, shadow, suggestion, hint, suspicion, glimmer, semblance ▷ RELATED WORD: *adjective* spectral

ghostly ADJECTIVE = **unearthly**, phantom, eerie, supernatural, spooky (*informal*), spectral

giant ADJECTIVE = **huge**, vast, enormous, tremendous, immense, titanic, gigantic, monumental, supersize ≠ tiny
▷ NOUN = **ogre**, monster, titan, colossus

gift NOUN 1 = **donation**, offering, present, contribution, grant, legacy, hand-out, endowment, bonsela (*S. African*), koha (*N.Z.*) 2 = **talent**, ability, capacity, genius, power, capability, flair, knack

gifted ADJECTIVE = **talented**, able, skilled, expert, masterly, brilliant, capable, clever ≠ talentless

gigantic ADJECTIVE = **huge**, large, giant, massive, enormous, tremendous, immense, titanic, supersize ≠ tiny

giggle VERB = **laugh**, chuckle, snigger, chortle, titter, twitter
▷ NOUN = **laugh**, chuckle, snigger,

chortle, titter, twitter

girl NOUN = **female child**, lass, lassie (*informal*), miss, maiden (*archaic*), maid (*archaic*)

give VERB 1 = **perform**, do, carry out, execute 2 = **communicate**, announce, transmit, pronounce, utter, issue 3 = **produce**, make, cause, occasion, engender 4 = **present**, contribute, donate, provide, supply, award, grant, deliver ≠ take 5 = **concede**, allow, grant 6 = **surrender**, yield, devote, hand over, relinquish, part with ▷ PHRASES: **give in** = **admit defeat**, yield, concede, collapse, quit, submit, surrender, succumb; **give something away** = **reveal**, expose, leak, disclose, betray, uncover, let out, divulge; **give something off** *or* **out** = **emit**, produce, release, discharge, send out, throw out, exude; **give something up** = **abandon**, stop, quit, cease, renounce, leave off, desist

glad ADJECTIVE 1 = **happy**, pleased, delighted, contented, gratified, joyful, overjoyed ≠ unhappy 2 (*archaic*) = **pleasing**, happy, cheering, pleasant, cheerful, gratifying

gladly ADVERB 1 = **happily**, cheerfully, gleefully 2 = **willingly**, freely, happily, readily, cheerfully, with pleasure ≠ reluctantly

glamorous ADJECTIVE 1 = **attractive**, elegant, dazzling ≠ unglamorous 2 = **exciting**, glittering, prestigious, glossy, bling (*slang*) ≠ unglamorous

glamour NOUN 1 = **charm**, appeal, beauty, attraction, fascination, allure, enchantment 2 = **excitement**, magic, thrill, romance, prestige, glitz (*slang*)

glance VERB = **peek**, look, view, glimpse, peep ≠ scrutinize ▷ NOUN = **peek**, look, glimpse, peep, dekko (*slang*) ≠ good look

- ◉ WORD POWER
- ◉ Care should be taken not to
- ◉ confuse *glance* and *glimpse*: *he*
- ◉ *caught a glimpse* (not *glance*) *of*
- ◉ *her making her way through the*
- ◉ *crowd; he gave a quick glance* (not
- ◉ *glimpse*) *at his watch. A glance*
- ◉ is a deliberate action, while a
- ◉ *glimpse* seems opportunistic.

glare VERB 1 = **scowl**, frown, glower, look daggers, lour *or* lower 2 = **dazzle**, blaze, flare, flame ▷ NOUN 1 = **scowl**, frown, glower, dirty look, black look, lour *or* lower 2 = **dazzle**, glow, blaze, flame, brilliance

glaring ADJECTIVE = **obvious**, gross, outrageous, manifest, blatant, conspicuous, flagrant, unconcealed ≠ inconspicuous

glaze NOUN = **coat**, finish, polish, shine, gloss, varnish, enamel, lacquer ▷ VERB = **coat**, polish, gloss, varnish, enamel, lacquer

gleam VERB = **shine**, flash, glow, sparkle, glitter, shimmer, glint, glimmer ▷ NOUN 1 = **glimmer**, flash, beam, glow, sparkle 2 = **trace**, suggestion, hint, flicker, glimmer, inkling

glide VERB = **slip**, sail, slide

glimpse NOUN = **look**, sighting, sight, glance, peep, peek
▷ VERB = **catch sight of**, spot, sight, view, spy, espy

glitter VERB = **shine**, flash, sparkle, glare, gleam, shimmer, twinkle, glint
▷ NOUN 1 = **glamour**, show, display, splendour, tinsel, pageantry, gaudiness, showiness
2 = **sparkle**, flash, shine, glare, gleam, sheen, shimmer, brightness

global ADJECTIVE 1 = **worldwide**, world, international, universal
2 = **comprehensive**, general, total, unlimited, exhaustive, all-inclusive ≠ limited

globe NOUN = **planet**, world, earth, sphere, orb

gloom NOUN 1 = **darkness**, dark, shadow, shade, twilight, dusk, obscurity, blackness ≠ light
2 = **depression**, sorrow, woe, melancholy, unhappiness, despondency, dejection, low spirits ≠ happiness

gloomy ADJECTIVE 1 = **dark**, dull, dim, dismal, black, grey, murky, dreary ≠ light 2 = **miserable**, sad, pessimistic, melancholy, glum, dejected, dispirited, downcast ≠ happy 3 = **depressing**, bad, dreary, sombre, dispiriting, disheartening, cheerless

glorious ADJECTIVE 1 = **splendid**, beautiful, brilliant, shining,

superb, gorgeous, dazzling ≠ dull 2 = **delightful**, fine, wonderful, excellent, marvellous, gorgeous 3 = **illustrious**, famous, celebrated, distinguished, honoured, magnificent, renowned, eminent ≠ ordinary

glory NOUN 1 = **honour**, praise, fame, distinction, acclaim, prestige, eminence, renown ≠ shame 2 = **splendour**, majesty, greatness, grandeur, nobility, pomp, magnificence, pageantry
▷ VERB = **triumph**, boast, relish, revel, exult, take delight, pride yourself

gloss¹ NOUN = **shine**, gleam, sheen, polish, brightness, veneer, lustre, patina

gloss² NOUN = **interpretation**, comment, note, explanation, commentary, translation, footnote, elucidation
▷ VERB = **interpret**, explain, comment, translate, annotate, elucidate

glossy ADJECTIVE = **shiny**, polished, shining, glazed, bright, silky, glassy, lustrous ≠ dull

glow NOUN = **light**, gleam, splendour, glimmer, brilliance, brightness, radiance, luminosity ≠ dullness
▷ VERB 1 = **shine**, burn, gleam, brighten, glimmer, smoulder
2 = **be pink**

glowing ADJECTIVE
= **complimentary**, enthusiastic, rave (*informal*), ecstatic, rhapsodic, laudatory, adulatory ≠ scathing

glue NOUN = **adhesive**, cement, gum, paste
  ▷ VERB = **stick**, fix, seal, cement, gum, paste, affix

go VERB 1 = **move**, travel, advance, journey, proceed, pass, set off ≠ stay 2 = **leave**, withdraw, depart, move out, slope off, make tracks 3 = **elapse**, pass, flow, fly by, expire, lapse, slip away 4 = **be given**, be spent, be awarded, be allotted 5 = **function**, work, run, move, operate, perform ≠ fail 6 = **match**, blend, correspond, fit, suit, chime, harmonize 7 = **serve**, help, tend
  ▷ NOUN 1 = **attempt**, try, effort, bid, shot (*informal*), crack (*informal*) 2 = **turn**, shot (*informal*), stint 3 (*informal*) = **energy**, life, drive, spirit, vitality, vigour, verve, force
  ▷ PHRASES: **go off** 1 = **depart**, leave, quit, go away, move out, decamp, slope off, rack off (*Austral.*

& *N.Z. slang*) 2 = **explode**, fire, blow up, detonate, come about 3 (*informal*) = **go bad**, turn, spoil, rot, go stale; **go out** 1 = **see someone**, court, date (*informal, chiefly U.S.*), woo, go steady (*informal*), be romantically involved with, step out with (*informal*) 2 = **be extinguished**, die out, fade out; **go through something** 1 = **suffer**, experience, bear, endure, brave, undergo, tolerate, withstand 2 = **search**, look through, rummage through, rifle through, hunt through, fossick through (*Austral. & N.Z.*), ferret about in 3 = **examine**, check, search, explore, look through

goal NOUN = **aim**, end, target, purpose, object, intention, objective, ambition

god NOUN = **deity**, immortal, divinity, divine being, supreme being, atua (*N.Z.*)

g

● **GODS AND GODDESSES**
● **Greek**

● Aeolus	winds
● Aphrodite	love and beauty
● Apollo	light, youth, and music
● Ares	war
● Artemis	hunting and the moon
● Asclepius	healing
● Athene *or* Pallas Athene	wisdom
● Bacchus	wine
● Boreas	north wind
● Cronos	fertility of the earth
● Demeter	agriculture
● Dionysus	wine
● Eos	dawn
● Eros	love
● Fates	destiny
● Gaea *or* Gaia	the earth
● Graces	charm and beauty
● Hades	underworld
● Hebe	youth and spring
● Hecate	underworld
● Helios	sun
● Hephaestus	fire and metalworking

Hera	queen of the gods
Hermes	messenger of the gods
Horae *or* the Hours	seasons
Hymen	marriage
Hyperion	sun
Hypnos	sleep
Iris	rainbow
Momus	blame and mockery
Morpheus	sleep and dreams
Nemesis	vengeance
Nike	victory
Pan	woods and shepherds
Poseidon	sea and earthquakes
Rhea	fertility
Selene	moon
Uranus	sky
Zephyrus	west wind
Zeus	king of the gods

Roman

Aesculapius	medicine
Apollo	light, youth, and music
Aurora	dawn
Bacchus	wine
Bellona	war
Bona Dea	fertility
Ceres	agriculture

Cupid	love
Cybele	nature
Diana	hunting and the moon
Faunus	forests
Flora	flowers
Janus	doors and beginnings
Juno	queen of the gods
Jupiter *or* Jove	king of the gods
Lares	household
Luna	moon
Mars	war
Mercury	messenger of the gods
Minerva	wisdom
Neptune	sea
Penates	storeroom
Phoebus	sun
Pluto	underworld
Quirinus	war
Saturn	agriculture and vegetation
Sol	sun
Somnus	sleep
Trivia	crossroads
Venus	love
Victoria	victory
Vulcan	fire and metalworking

godly ADJECTIVE = **devout**, religious, holy, righteous, pious, good, saintly, god-fearing

gogga NOUN (*S. African*) = **insect**, bug, creepy-crawly (*Brit. informal*)

golden ADJECTIVE 1 = **yellow**, blonde, blond, flaxen ≠ dark 2 = **successful**, glorious, prosperous, rich, flourishing, halcyon ≠ worst 3 = **promising**, excellent, favourable, opportune ≠ unfavourable

▷ *see* **shades of orange, shades of yellow**

● **WORD POWER**
● Gold is a precious metal
● used as a monetary standard
● and in jewellery; in many
● societies it signifies wealth,
● status, and luxury. The
● colour adjective golden
● has taken on some of the
● positive connotations of the
● substance. The value of gold
● has resulted in the meaning
● 'successful' or 'prosperous'
● in phrases like a *golden age*,
● denoting a thriving period
● in history in a particular
● field. Closely related to
● this, a *golden opportunity*
● is one which is promising
● and advantageous. Gold
● symbolizes winning first
● place in a race, as in a *gold*
● *medal*, which has led people
● to be described as *golden boys*
● or *golden girls* when they are
● prized and popular.

gone ADJECTIVE 1 = **missing**, lost, away, vanished, absent, astray 2 = **past**, over, ended, finished, elapsed

good ADJECTIVE 1 = **excellent**, great, fine, pleasing, acceptable, first-class, splendid, satisfactory, booshit (*Austral. slang*), exo (*Austral. slang*), sik (*Austral. slang*), rad (*informal*), phat (*slang*), schmick (*Austral. informal*) ≠ bad 2 = **proficient**, able, skilled, expert, talented, clever, accomplished, first-class ≠ bad 3 = **beneficial**, useful, helpful, favourable, wholesome, advantageous ≠ harmful 4 = **honourable**, moral, worthy, ethical, upright, admirable, honest, righteous ≠ bad 5 = **well-behaved**, polite, orderly, obedient, dutiful, well-mannered ≠ naughty 6 = **kind**, kindly, friendly, obliging, charitable, humane, benevolent, merciful ≠ unkind 7 = **true**, real, genuine, proper, dinkum (*Austral. & N.Z. informal*) 8 = **full**, complete, extensive ≠ scant 9 = **considerable**, large, substantial, sufficient, adequate, ample 10 = **valid**, convincing, compelling, legitimate, authentic, persuasive, bona fide ≠ invalid 11 = **convenient**, timely, fitting, appropriate, suitable ≠ inconvenient

▷ NOUN 1 = **benefit**, interest, gain, advantage, use, profit, welfare, usefulness ≠ disadvantage 2 = **virtue**, goodness, righteousness, worth, merit, excellence, morality, rectitude ≠ evil ▷ PHRASE: **for good** = **permanently**, finally, for ever, once and for all, irrevocably

goodbye NOUN = **farewell**, parting, leave-taking

▷ INTERJECTION = **farewell**, see you, see you later, ciao (*Italian*), cheerio, adieu, ta-ta, au revoir (*French*), haere ra (*N.Z.*)

goodness NOUN = **virtue**,

g

g

honour, merit, integrity, morality, honesty, righteousness, probity ≠ badness **2** = **excellence**, value, quality, worth, merit, superiority **3** = **nutrition**, benefit, advantage, wholesomeness, salubriousness **4** = **kindness**, charity, humanity, goodwill, mercy, compassion, generosity, friendliness

goods PLURAL NOUN
   1 = **merchandise**, stock, products, stuff, commodities, wares
   2 = **property**, things, effects, gear, possessions, belongings, trappings, paraphernalia

goodwill NOUN = **friendliness**, friendship, benevolence, amity, kindliness

gore¹ NOUN = **blood**, slaughter, bloodshed, carnage, butchery

gore² VERB = **pierce**, wound, transfix, impale

gorge NOUN = **ravine**, canyon, pass, chasm, cleft, fissure, defile, gulch (*U.S. & Canad.*)
   ▷ VERB **1** = **overeat**, devour, gobble, wolf, gulp, guzzle **2** *usually reflexive* = **stuff**, feed, cram, glut

gorgeous ADJECTIVE
   1 = **magnificent**, beautiful, superb, spectacular, splendid, dazzling, sumptuous ≠ shabby **2** (*informal*) = **beautiful**, lovely, stunning (*informal*), elegant, handsome, exquisite, ravishing, hot (*informal*) ≠ dull

gospel NOUN **1** = **doctrine**, news, teachings, message, revelation, creed, credo, tidings **2** = **truth**,

fact, certainty, the last word

gossip NOUN **1** = **idle talk**, scandal, hearsay, tittle-tattle, goss (*informal*), small talk, chitchat, blether, chinwag (*Brit. informal*) **2** = **busybody**, chatterbox (*informal*), chatterer, scandalmonger, gossipmonger, tattletale (*chiefly U.S. & Canad.*)
   ▷ VERB = **chat**, chatter, jaw (*slang*), blether

gourmet NOUN = **connoisseur**, foodie (*informal*), bon vivant (*French*), epicure, gastronome

govern VERB **1** = **rule**, lead, control, command, manage, direct, guide, handle **2** = **restrain**, control, check, master, discipline, regulate, curb, tame

government NOUN
   1 = **administration**, executive, ministry, regime, powers-that-be **2** = **rule**, authority, administration, sovereignty, governance, statecraft

governor NOUN = **leader**, administrator, ruler, head, director, manager, chief, executive, baas (*S. African*)

gown NOUN = **dress**, costume, garment, robe, frock, garb, habit

grab VERB = **snatch**, catch, seize, capture, grip, grasp, clutch, snap up

grace NOUN **1** = **elegance**, poise, ease, polish, refinement, fluency, suppleness, gracefulness ≠ ungainliness **2** = **manners**, decency, etiquette, consideration, propriety, tact, decorum ≠ bad manners **3** = **indulgence**, mercy, pardon, reprieve

4 = **benevolence**, favour, goodness, goodwill, generosity, kindness, kindliness ≠ ill will

5 = **prayer**, thanks, blessing, thanksgiving, benediction

6 = **favour**, regard, respect, approval, approbation, good opinion ≠ disfavour

▷ VERB **1** = **adorn**, enhance, decorate, enrich, set off, ornament, embellish **2** = **honour**, favour, dignify ≠ insult

graceful ADJECTIVE = **elegant**, easy, pleasing, beautiful ≠ inelegant

gracious ADJECTIVE = **courteous**, polite, civil, accommodating, kind, friendly, cordial, well-mannered ≠ ungracious

grade VERB = **classify**, rate, order, class, group, sort, range, rank

▷ NOUN **1** = **class 2** degree **3** = **level**, rank, group, class, stage, category, echelon

gradual ADJECTIVE = **steady**, slow, regular, gentle, progressive, piecemeal, unhurried ≠ sudden

gradually ADVERB = **steadily**, slowly, progressively, gently, step by step, little by little, by degrees, unhurriedly

graduate VERB **1** = **mark off**, grade, proportion, regulate, gauge, calibrate, measure out **2** = **classify**, rank, grade, group, order, sort, arrange

graft NOUN = **shoot**, bud, implant, sprout, splice, scion

▷ VERB = **join**, insert, transplant, implant, splice, affix

graft NOUN (*informal*) = **labour**, work, effort, struggle, sweat, toil, slog, exertion

▷ VERB = **work**, labour, struggle, sweat (*informal*), slave, strive, toil

grain NOUN **1** = **seed**, kernel, grist **2** = **cereal**, corn **3** = **bit**, piece, trace, scrap, particle, fragment, speck, morsel **4** = **texture**, pattern, surface, fibre, weave, nap

grand ADJECTIVE **1** = **impressive**, great, large, magnificent, imposing, splendid, regal, stately ≠ unimposing **2** = **ambitious**, great, grandiose **3** = **superior**, great, dignified, stately

4 = **excellent**, great (*informal*), fine, wonderful, outstanding, smashing (*informal*), first-class, splendid ≠ bad

grandeur NOUN = **splendour**, glory, majesty, nobility, pomp, magnificence, sumptuousness, sublimity

grant NOUN = **award**, allowance, donation, endowment, gift, subsidy, hand-out

▷ VERB **1** = **give**, allow, present, award, permit, assign, allocate, hand out **2** = **accept**, allow, admit, acknowledge, concede

graphic ADJECTIVE **1** = **vivid**, clear, detailed, striking, explicit, expressive ≠ vague **2** = **pictorial**, visual, diagrammatic ≠ impressionistic

grapple VERB **1** = **deal**, tackle, struggle, take on, confront, get to grips, address yourself to 2 = **struggle**, fight, combat, wrestle, battle, clash, tussle, scuffle

grasp VERB 1 = **grip**, hold, catch, grab, seize, snatch, clutch, clinch 2 = **understand**, realize, take in, get, see, catch on, comprehend, catch *or* get the drift of
▷ NOUN 1 = **grip**, hold, possession, embrace, clutches, clasp 2 = **understanding**, knowledge, grip, awareness, mastery, comprehension 3 = **reach**, power, control, scope

grasping ADJECTIVE = **greedy**, acquisitive, rapacious, avaricious, covetous, snoep (*S. African informal*) ≠ generous

grate VERB 1 = **shred**, mince, pulverize 2 = **scrape**, grind, rub, scratch, creak, rasp

grateful ADJECTIVE = **thankful**, obliged, in (someone's) debt, indebted, appreciative, beholden

grating[1] NOUN = **grille**, grid, grate, lattice, trellis, gridiron

grating[2] ADJECTIVE = **irritating**, harsh, annoying, jarring, unpleasant, raucous, strident, discordant ≠ pleasing

gratitude NOUN = **thankfulness**, thanks, recognition, obligation, appreciation, indebtedness, gratefulness ≠ ingratitude

grave[1] NOUN = **tomb**, vault, crypt, mausoleum, sepulchre, pit, burying place

grave[2] ADJECTIVE 1 = **serious**, important, critical, pressing, threatening, dangerous, acute, severe ≠ trifling 2 = **solemn**, sober, sombre, dour, unsmiling ≠ carefree

graveyard NOUN = **cemetery**, churchyard, burial ground, charnel house, necropolis

gravity NOUN 1 = **seriousness**, importance, significance, urgency, severity, acuteness, weightiness, momentousness ≠ triviality 2 = **solemnity**, seriousness, gravitas ≠ frivolity

graze[1] VERB = **feed**, crop, browse, pasture

graze[2] VERB 1 = **scratch**, skin, scrape, chafe, abrade 2 = **touch**, brush, rub, scrape, shave, skim, glance off
▷ NOUN = **scratch**, scrape, abrasion

greasy ADJECTIVE = **fatty**, slippery, oily, slimy, oleaginous

great ADJECTIVE 1 = **large**, big, huge, vast, enormous, immense, gigantic, prodigious, supersize ≠ small 2 = **important**, serious, significant, critical, crucial, momentous ≠ unimportant 3 = **famous**, outstanding, remarkable, prominent, renowned, eminent, illustrious, noteworthy 4 (*informal*) = **excellent**, fine, wonderful, superb, fantastic (*informal*), tremendous (*informal*), marvellous (*informal*), terrific (*informal*), booshit (*Austral. slang*), exo (*Austral. slang*), sik (*Austral. slang*), rad (*informal*), phat (*slang*), schmick (*Austral. informal*) ≠ poor

5 = **very**, really, extremely, exceedingly

greatly ADVERB = **very much**, hugely, vastly, considerably, remarkably, enormously, immensely, tremendously

greatness NOUN **1** = **grandeur**, glory, majesty, splendour, pomp, magnificence **2** = **fame**, glory, celebrity, distinction, eminence, note, renown, illustriousness

greed or **greediness** NOUN
1 = **gluttony**, voracity
2 = **avarice**, longing, desire, hunger, craving, selfishness, acquisitiveness, covetousness ≠ generosity

greedy ADJECTIVE **1** = **gluttonous**, insatiable, voracious, ravenous, piggish **2** = **avaricious**, grasping, selfish, insatiable, acquisitive, rapacious, materialistic, desirous ≠ generous

⊕ WORD POWER
⊕ The period of greatest
⊕ borrowing from Greek
⊕ into English was during
⊕ the Renaissance when the
⊕ classical languages were
⊕ plundered for terms to
⊕ describe new developments
⊕ in science, technology,
⊕ and medicine. Concepts
⊕ from Greek philosophy and
⊕ mythology were brought to
⊕ the English public for the first
⊕ time through translations of
⊕ classical texts. *Nemesis*, a word
⊕ adopted into English in the
⊕ 16th century, was the goddess
⊕ of retribution in classical
⊕ mythology. Both people and
⊕ situations can embody the
⊕ concept of nemesis in today's
⊕ English. A nemesis is an agent
⊕ of retribution, a person who
⊕ avenges a wrongdoing, or
⊕ more loosely, an arch-enemy
⊕ or rival. The coinage *arch-*
⊕ *nemesis* reiterates the latter
⊕ meaning. Nemesis can also
⊕ refer to a situation which is
⊕ inevitable or unavoidable,
⊕ and overlaps semantically
⊕ with the notion of downfall,
⊕ e.g. Spyware may now be
⊕ the nemesis of PCs. Another
⊕ Greek word which came
⊕ into English during the 16th
⊕ century is *nous*. Philosophers
⊕ used *nous* in different senses
⊕ to refer to the mind, the
⊕ intellect, intelligence, or
⊕ reason. Nowadays it means
⊕ common sense, acumen, and
⊕ applied intelligence, and is
⊕ particularly found in British
⊕ English. It is among several
⊕ other slang words for common
⊕ sense, including smarts and
⊕ savvy, and is commonly used in
⊕ collocations like *economic nous*
⊕ and *political nous*.

green ADJECTIVE **1** = **verdant**, leafy, grassy **2** = **ecological**, conservationist, environment-friendly, ozone-friendly, non-polluting **3** = **inexperienced**, new, raw, naive, immature, gullible, untrained, wet behind the ears (*informal*) **4** = **jealous**, grudging, resentful, envious, covetous

▷ NOUN = **lawn**, common, turf, sward

● **WORD POWER**
● *Green* is the colour of plants
● and vegetation and many of
● its extended meanings derive
● from this. If an area is described
● as having green spaces, it
● has parkland, gardens, fields
● and the like. Similarly, *green*
● *belt* is a zone of open country
● surrounding a city which
● is protected from urban
● development. *Green politics* are
● those which concentrate on
● preserving the environment
● and natural resources. Green
● is also the colour of unripe
● fruit and plants, which has
● led to the meanings of youth,
● lack of maturity, and lack of
● experience. When applied to
● human physiology, green is
● the colour of biliousness and
● sickness as in the phrase *green*
● *around the gills*. Jealousy was
● formerly linked with the colour
● yellow, but now is expressed
● in various phrases with green,

● such as Shakespeare's *green-*
● *eyed monster* (jealousy) and
● *green with envy*. One modern
● metaphorical meaning of
● green is in traffic signalling,
● where a *green light* means go.
● The verb *greenlight*, meaning to
● authorize or permit something
● to proceed, shows a recent
● extension of this sense.

greet VERB **1** = **salute**, hail, say hello to, address, accost **2** = **welcome**, meet, receive, karanga (*N.Z.*), mihi (*N.Z.*) **3** = **receive**, take, respond to, react to

greeting NOUN = **welcome**, reception, salute, address, salutation, hongi (*N.Z.*), kia ora (*N.Z.*)

grey ADJECTIVE **1** = **dull**, dark, dim, gloomy, drab **2** = **boring**, dull, anonymous, faceless, colourless, nondescript, characterless **3** = **pale**, wan, pallid, ashen **4** = **ambiguous**, uncertain, neutral, unclear, debatable

▷ *see* **shades from black to white**

● **WORD POWER**
● *Grey* is a neutral tone which
● is intermediate between
● black and white. Because it

● **SHADES OF GREEN**

● apple green	● lime green	● pistachio
● aquamarine	● Lincoln green	● sea green
● avocado	● Nile green	● teal
● emerald green	● olive	● turquoise
● jade	● pea green	

- only reflects a little light, it is
- perceived as a dull colour. By
- extension, it has been used to
- describe many things which
- are dull in colour, such as
- weather conditions, as in a *grey*
- *day*. If human personalities
- are described as grey, it means
- they are boring or colourless.
- The hair of humans and some
- animals turns grey with age –
- this has lead to applications of
- grey meaning older, such as the
- *grey vote*. Grey can also mean
- pale in an unhealthy way when
- used of a person's skin-tone. As
- grey is neither entirely black
- nor white but a combination
- of both, it has developed the
- meaning 'ambiguous', as in the
- phrase *grey area*. Colloquially,
- the brain is referred to as *grey*
- *matter* or as *grey cells* because
- of the greyish colour of the
- physical brain.

grief NOUN = **sadness**, suffering, regret, distress, misery, sorrow, woe, anguish ≠ joy

grievance NOUN = **complaint**, gripe (*informal*), axe to grind

grieve VERB 1 = **mourn**, suffer, weep, lament 2 = **sadden**, hurt, injure, distress, wound, pain, afflict, upset ≠ gladden

grim ADJECTIVE = **terrible**, severe, harsh, forbidding, formidable, sinister

grind VERB 1 = **crush**, mill, powder, grate, pulverize, pound, abrade, granulate 2 = **press**, push, crush,

jam, mash, force down 3 = **grate**, scrape, gnash 4 = **sharpen**, polish, sand, smooth, whet
▷ NOUN 1 = **hard work** (*informal*), labour, sweat (*informal*), chore, toil, drudgery

grip VERB 1 = **grasp**, hold, catch, seize, clutch, clasp, take hold of 2 = **engross**, fascinate, absorb, entrance, hold, compel, rivet, enthral
▷ NOUN 1 = **clasp**, hold, grasp 2 = **control**, rule, influence, command, power, possession, domination, mastery 3 = **hold**, purchase, friction, traction 4 = **understanding**, sense, command, awareness, grasp, appreciation, mastery, comprehension

gripping ADJECTIVE = **fascinating**, exciting, thrilling, entrancing, compelling, riveting, enthralling, engrossing

grit NOUN 1 = **gravel**, sand, dust, pebbles 2 = **courage**, spirit, resolution, determination, guts (*informal*), backbone, fortitude, tenacity
▷ VERB = **clench**, grind, grate, gnash

gritty ADJECTIVE 1 = **rough**, sandy, dusty, rasping, gravelly, granular 2 = **courageous**, dogged, determined, spirited, brave, feisty (*informal*, *chiefly U.S. & Canad.*), resolute, tenacious, plucky, (as) game as Ned Kelly (*Austral. slang*)

groan VERB 1 = **moan**, cry, sigh 2 (*informal*) = **complain**, object,

g

moan, grumble, gripe (*informal*),
carp, lament, whine
▷ **NOUN 1** = **moan**, cry, sigh,
whine **2** (*informal*) = **complaint**,
protest, objection, grumble,
grouse, gripe (*informal*)
groom NOUN **1** = **stableman**,
stableboy, hostler *or* ostler
(*archaic*) **2** = **newly-wed**, husband,
bridegroom, marriage partner
▷ **VERB 1** = **brush**, clean, tend,
rub down, curry **2** = **smarten
up**, clean, tidy, preen, spruce up,
primp **3** = **train**, prime, prepare,
coach, ready, educate, drill,
nurture
groove NOUN = **indentation**, cut,
hollow, channel, trench, flute,
trough, furrow
grope VERB = **feel**, search, fumble,
flounder, fish, scrabble, cast
about, fossick (*Austral. & N.Z.*)
gross ADJECTIVE **1** = **flagrant**,
blatant, rank, sheer, utter,
grievous, heinous, unmitigated
≠ qualified **2** = **vulgar**, offensive,
crude, obscene, coarse, indelicate
≠ decent **3** = **fat**, obese,
overweight, hulking, corpulent
≠ slim **4** = **total**, whole, entire,
aggregate, before tax, before
deductions ≠ net
▷ **VERB** = **earn**, make, take, bring
in, rake in (*informal*)
grotesque ADJECTIVE
1 = **unnatural**, bizarre, strange,
fantastic, distorted, deformed,
outlandish, freakish ≠ natural
2 = **absurd**, preposterous
≠ natural

ground NOUN **1** = **earth**, land, dry
land, terra firma **2** = **arena**, pitch,
stadium, park (*informal*), field,
enclosure
▷ **PLURAL NOUN 1** = **estate**,
land, fields, gardens, territory
2 = **reason**, cause, basis, occasion,
foundation, excuse, motive,
justification **3** = **dregs**, lees,
deposit, sediment
▷ **VERB 1** = **base**, found, establish,
set, settle, fix **2** = **instruct**, train,
teach, initiate, tutor, acquaint
with, familiarize with
group NOUN = **crowd**, party, band,
pack, gang, bunch
▷ **VERB** = **arrange**, order, sort,
class, classify, marshal, bracket
grove NOUN = **wood**, plantation,
covert, thicket, copse, coppice,
spinney
grow VERB **1** = **develop**, get bigger
≠ shrink **2** = **get bigger**, spread,
swell, stretch, expand, enlarge,
multiply **3** = **cultivate**, produce,
raise, farm, breed, nurture,
propagate **4** = **become**, get, turn,
come to be **5** = **originate**, spring,
arise, stem, issue **6** = **improve**,
advance, progress, succeed,
thrive, flourish, prosper
grown-up NOUN = **adult**, man,
woman
▷ **ADJECTIVE** = **mature**, adult, of
age, fully-grown
growth NOUN **1** = **increase**,
development, expansion,
proliferation, enlargement,
multiplication ≠ decline
2 = **progress**, success,

improvement, expansion, advance, prosperity ≠ failure 3 (*medical*) = **tumour**, cancer, swelling, lump, carcinoma (*pathology*), sarcoma (*medical*)

grudge NOUN = **resentment**, bitterness, grievance, dislike, animosity, antipathy, enmity, rancour ≠ goodwill
▷ VERB = **resent**, mind, envy, covet, begrudge ≠ welcome

gruelling ADJECTIVE = **exhausting**, demanding, tiring, taxing, severe, punishing, strenuous, arduous ≠ easy

gruesome ADJECTIVE = **horrific**, shocking, terrible, horrible, grim, ghastly, grisly, macabre ≠ pleasant

grumble VERB 1 = **complain**, moan, gripe (*informal*), whinge (*informal*), carp, whine, grouse, bleat 2 = **rumble**, growl, gurgle
▷ NOUN 1 = **complaint**, protest, objection, moan, grievance, grouse, gripe (*informal*), grouch (*informal*) 2 = **rumble**, growl, gurgle

guarantee VERB 1 = **ensure**, secure, assure, warrant, make certain 2 = **promise**, pledge, undertake
▷ NOUN 1 = **promise**, pledge, assurance, certainty, word of honour 2 = **warranty**, contract, bond

guard VERB = **protect**, defend, secure, mind, preserve, shield, safeguard, watch over
▷ NOUN 1 = **sentry**, warder, warden, custodian, watch, lookout, watchman, sentinel 2 = **shield**, security, defence, screen, protection, safeguard, buffer

guarded ADJECTIVE = **cautious**, reserved, careful, suspicious, wary, prudent, reticent, circumspect

guardian NOUN = **keeper**, champion, defender, guard, warden, curator, protector, custodian

guerrilla NOUN = **freedom fighter**, partisan, underground fighter

guess VERB 1 = **estimate**, predict, work out, speculate, conjecture, postulate, hypothesize ≠ know 2 = **suppose**, think, believe, suspect, judge, imagine, reckon, fancy
▷ NOUN 1 = **estimate**, speculation, judgment, hypothesis, conjecture, shot in the dark ≠ certainty 2 = **supposition**, idea, theory, hypothesis

guest NOUN = **visitor**, company, caller, manu(w)hiri (*N.Z.*)

guidance NOUN = **advice**, direction, leadership, instruction, help, management, teaching, counselling

guide NOUN 1 = **handbook**, manual, guidebook, instructions, catalogue 2 = **directory**, street map 3 = **escort**, leader, usher 4 = **pointer**, sign, landmark, marker, beacon, signpost,

g

guiding light, lodestar **5** = **model**, example, standard, ideal, inspiration, paradigm
▷ **VERB 1** = **lead**, direct, escort, conduct, accompany, shepherd, usher, show the way **2** = **steer**, control, manage, direct, handle, command, manoeuvre **3** = **supervise**, train, teach, influence, advise, counsel, instruct, oversee

guild NOUN = **society**, union, league, association, company, club, order, organization

guilt NOUN **1** = **shame**, regret, remorse, contrition, guilty conscience, self-reproach ≠ pride **2** = **culpability**, blame, responsibility, misconduct, wickedness, sinfulness, guiltiness ≠ innocence

guilty ADJECTIVE **1** = **ashamed**, sorry, rueful, sheepish, contrite, remorseful, regretful, shamefaced ≠ proud **2** = **culpable**, responsible, to blame, offending, erring, at fault, reprehensible, blameworthy ≠ innocent

guise NOUN **1** = **form**, appearance, shape, aspect, mode, semblance **2** = **pretence**, disguise, aspect, semblance

gulch NOUN (*U.S. & Canad.*) = **ravine**, canyon, defile, gorge, gully, pass

gulf NOUN **1** = **bay**, bight, sea inlet **2** = **chasm**, opening, split, gap, separation, void, rift, abyss

gum NOUN = **glue**, adhesive, resin, cement, paste
▷ **VERB** = **stick**, glue, affix, cement, paste

gun NOUN = **firearm**, shooter (*slang*), piece (*slang*), handgun

gunman NOUN = **armed man**, gunslinger (*U.S. slang*)

guru NOUN **1** = **authority**, expert, leader, master, pundit, Svengali, fundi (*S. African*) **2** = **teacher**, mentor, sage, master, tutor

gush VERB **1** = **flow**, run, rush, flood, pour, stream, cascade, spurt **2** = **enthuse**, rave, spout, overstate, effuse
▷ **NOUN** = **stream**, flow, rush, flood, jet, cascade, torrent, spurt

gut NOUN = **paunch** (*informal*), belly, spare tyre (*Brit. slang*), potbelly, puku (*N.Z.*)
▷ **VERB 1** = **disembowel**, clean **2** = **ravage**, empty, clean out, despoil
▷ **ADJECTIVE** = **instinctive**, natural, basic, spontaneous, intuitive, involuntary, heartfelt, unthinking

guts PLURAL NOUN **1** = **intestines**, insides (*informal*), stomach, belly, bowels, innards (*informal*), entrails **2** (*informal*) = **courage**, spirit, nerve, daring, pluck, backbone, bottle (*slang*), audacity

gutter NOUN = **drain**, channel, ditch, trench, trough, conduit, sluice

guy NOUN (*informal*) = **man**, person, fellow, lad, bloke (*Brit. informal*), chap

Gypsy or **Gipsy** NOUN = **traveller**, roamer, wanderer, Bohemian, rover, rambler, nomad, Romany

g

Hh

habit NOUN 1 = **mannerism**, custom, way, practice, characteristic, tendency, quirk, propensity 2 = **addiction**, dependence, compulsion

hack¹ VERB 1 = **cut**, chop, slash, mutilate, mangle, mangulate (*Austral. slang*), hew, lacerate 2 (*a computer, phone etc.*) = **manipulate**, exploit, attack, hijack, access, spoof, bluejack, pharm, bluesnarf, phish, phreak, spear-fish

hack² NOUN = **reporter**, writer, correspondent, journalist, scribbler, contributor

hacker NOUN = **fraudster**, black hat, white hat, cybercriminal, script kiddie, hacktivist (*informal*), intruder

hail³ NOUN 1 = **hailstones**, sleet, hailstorm, frozen rain 2 = **shower**, rain, storm, battery, volley, barrage, bombardment, downpour

hail⁴ VERB 1 = **acclaim**, honour, acknowledge, cheer, applaud ≠ condemn 2 = **salute**, greet, address, welcome, say hello to, halloo ≠ snub 3 = **flag down**, summon, signal to, wave down
▷ PHRASE: **hail from somewhere** = **come from**, be born in, originate in, be a native of, have your roots in

hair NOUN = **locks**, mane, tresses, shock, mop, head of hair
- **WORD POWER**
- *Hair* has long been a focus of
- care and attention for humans,
- even seen as our 'crowning
- glory'. The extended meanings
- and idioms involving hair tend
- to refer either to the physical
- appearance of hair or the
- emotions. A hair describes a
- very small amount or distance
- in the expression *by a hair ('s*
- *breadth)*, meaning 'very close',
- which is also like the phrase *by*
- *a whisker*. Physical fineness of
- hair is also referenced in the
- expression *split hairs* whereby
- petty distinctions are made.
- Other expressions with hair
- allude to emotional states,
- such as *get in your hair* meaning
- 'annoy'. The idea that emotions
- can affect the hair has its
- foundation in fact in that cold,
- fear, and shock cause body hair
- to erect, literally *hair-raising* or
- *making your hair stand on end*. In
- olden times, the elaborate
- hairdressing of ladies and
- gentlemen in public meant that
- they would only *let their hair down*
- in private, thus the meaning of
- relaxing, or becoming
- confidential, developed.

hairy ADJECTIVE 1 = **shaggy**, woolly, furry, stubbly, bushy, unshaven, hirsute 2 (*slang*) = **dangerous**, risky, unpredictable, hazardous, perilous

hale ADJECTIVE (*old-fashioned*)
= **healthy**, well, strong, sound, fit, flourishing, robust, vigorous

half NOUN 1 = **fifty per cent**, equal part
▷ ADJECTIVE = **partial**, limited, moderate, halved
▷ ADVERB = **partially**, partly, in part ▷ RELATED WORDS: *prefixes* **bi-, hemi-, demi-, semi-**

halfway ADVERB = **midway**, to *or* in the middle
▷ ADJECTIVE = **midway**, middle, mid, central, intermediate, equidistant

hall NOUN 1 = **passage**, lobby, corridor, hallway, foyer, entry, passageway, entrance hall
2 = **meeting place**, chamber, auditorium, concert hall, assembly room

hallmark NOUN 1 = **trademark**, sure sign, telltale sign 2 (*Brit.*)
= **mark**, sign, device, stamp, seal, symbol

halt VERB 1 = **stop**, break off, stand still, wait, rest ≠ continue
2 = **come to an end**, stop, cease
3 = **hold back**, end, check, block, curb, terminate, cut short, bring to an end ≠ aid
▷ NOUN = **stop**, end, close, pause, standstill, stoppage ≠ continuation

halting ADJECTIVE = **faltering**, stumbling, awkward, hesitant, laboured, stammering, stuttering

halve VERB 1 = **cut in half**, reduce by fifty per cent, decrease by fifty per cent, lessen by fifty per cent
2 = **split in two**, cut in half, bisect, divide in two, share equally, divide equally

hammer VERB 1 = **hit**, drive, knock, beat, strike, tap, bang
2 (*informal*) = **defeat**, beat, thrash, trounce, run rings around (*informal*), wipe the floor with (*informal*), drub

hamper VERB = **hinder**, handicap, prevent, restrict, frustrate, hamstring, interfere with, obstruct ≠ help

hand NOUN 1 = **palm**, fist, paw (*informal*), mitt (*slang*)
2 = **worker**, employee, labourer, workman, operative, craftsman, artisan, hired man 3 = **round of applause**, clap, ovation, big hand
4 = **writing**, script, handwriting, calligraphy
▷ VERB = **give**, pass, hand over, present to, deliver

⬤ WORD POWER
⬤ The primary meaning of **hand** is
⬤ the part of the body at the end
⬤ of the arm. Other meanings
⬤ of hand make reference to its
⬤ shape, position, and function,
⬤ especially its use in touching
⬤ and moving objects in the
⬤ physical world. The size of
⬤ a hand is still used as a unit
⬤ of measurement in horses.
⬤ The appearance of a hand is
⬤ reflected in a **hand of bananas**
⬤ and pointing **clock hands**.
⬤ The use of a hand for holding
⬤ objects can be seen in a **hand of**
⬤ **cards** and its ability to clap in

the phrase *give a (warm) hand to*. Handwriting can be referred to simply as a hand, e.g. *written in his own hand*. Workers are referred to as *hands*, where the most pertinent part of their body represents the whole, likewise in the phrase *all hands on deck*. The multiple roles of a hand have led to transferred senses of: agency – *have a hand in*, assistance – *lend/give a hand to*, and control – *in hand*. Various gestures of giving are expressed by the phrasal verbs *hand over*, *hand out*, *hand on*, and *hand in*.

handbook NOUN = **guidebook**, guide, manual, instruction book

handcuff VERB = **shackle**, secure, restrain, fetter, manacle
▷ PLURAL NOUN = **shackles**, cuffs (*informal*), fetters, manacles

handful NOUN = **few**, sprinkling, small amount, smattering, small number ≠ a lot

handicap NOUN 1 = **disability**, defect, impairment, physical abnormality 2 = **disadvantage**, barrier, restriction, obstacle, limitation, drawback, stumbling block, impediment ≠ advantage 3 = **advantage**, head start
▷ VERB = **hinder**, limit, restrict, burden, hamstring, hamper, hold back, impede ≠ help

handle NOUN = **grip**, hilt, haft, stock
▷ VERB 1 = **manage**, deal with, tackle, cope with 2 = **deal with**,

manage 3 = **control**, manage, direct, guide, manipulate, manoeuvre 4 = **hold**, feel, touch, pick up, finger, grasp

handsome ADJECTIVE 1 = **good-looking**, attractive, gorgeous, elegant, personable, dishy (*informal, chiefly Brit.*), comely, hot (*informal*), fit (*Brit. informal*) ≠ ugly 2 = **generous**, large, princely, liberal, considerable, lavish, ample, abundant ≠ mean

handy ADJECTIVE 1 = **useful**, practical, helpful, neat, convenient, easy to use, manageable, user-friendly ≠ useless 2 = **convenient**, close, available, nearby, accessible, on hand, at hand, within reach ≠ inconvenient 3 = **skilful**, skilled, expert, adept, deft, proficient, adroit, dexterous ≠ unskilled

hang VERB 1 = **dangle**, swing, suspend 2 = **lower**, suspend, dangle 3 = **lean** 4 = **execute**, lynch, string up (*informal*)
▷ PHRASES: **get the hang of something** = **grasp**, understand, learn, master, comprehend, catch on to, acquire the technique of; **hang back** = **be reluctant**, hesitate, hold back, recoil, demur

hangover NOUN = **aftereffects**, morning after (*informal*)

hang-up NOUN (*informal*) = **preoccupation**, thing (*informal*), problem, block, difficulty, obsession, mania, inhibition

hank NOUN = **coil**, roll, length,

bunch, piece, loop, clump, skein

happen VERB 1 = **occur**, take place, come about, result, develop, transpire (*informal*), come to pass 2 = **chance**, turn out (*informal*)

happening NOUN = **event**, incident, experience, affair, proceeding, episode, occurrence

happily ADVERB 1 = **luckily**, fortunately, providentially, opportunely 2 = **joyfully**, cheerfully, gleefully, blithely, merrily, gaily, joyously
3 = **willingly**, freely, gladly, with pleasure

happiness NOUN = **pleasure**, delight, joy, satisfaction, ecstasy, bliss, contentment, elation ≠ unhappiness

happy ADJECTIVE 1 = **pleased**, delighted, content, thrilled, glad, cheerful, merry, ecstatic, stoked (*Austral. & N.Z. informal*)
2 = **contented**, joyful, blissful ≠ sad 3 = **fortunate**, lucky, timely, favourable, auspicious, propitious, advantageous ≠ unfortunate

harass VERB = **annoy**, trouble, bother, harry, plague, hound, hassle (*informal*), persecute

harassed ADJECTIVE = **hassled**, worried, troubled, strained, under pressure, tormented, distraught (*informal*), vexed

harassment NOUN = **hassle**, trouble, bother, irritation, persecution (*informal*), nuisance, annoyance, pestering

harbour NOUN = **port**, haven, dock, mooring, marina, pier, wharf, anchorage
▷ VERB 1 = **hold**, bear, maintain, nurse, retain, foster, entertain, nurture 2 = **shelter**, protect, hide, shield, provide refuge, give asylum to

hard ADJECTIVE 1 = **tough**, strong, firm, solid, stiff, rigid, resistant, compressed ≠ soft 2 = **difficult**, involved, complicated, puzzling, intricate, perplexing, impenetrable, thorny ≠ easy
3 = **exhausting**, tough, exacting, rigorous, gruelling, strenuous, arduous, laborious ≠ easy
4 = **harsh**, cold, cruel, stern, callous, unkind, unsympathetic, pitiless ≠ kind 5 = **grim**, painful, distressing, harsh, unpleasant, intolerable, grievous, disagreeable
▷ ADVERB 1 = **strenuously**, steadily, persistently, doggedly, diligently, energetically, industriously, untiringly
2 = **intently**, closely, carefully, sharply, keenly 3 = **forcefully**, strongly, heavily, sharply, severely, fiercely, vigorously, intensely ≠ softly

harden VERB 1 = **solidify**, set, freeze, cake, bake, clot, thicken, stiffen 2 = **accustom**, season, toughen, train, inure, habituate

hardened ADJECTIVE 1 = **habitual**, chronic, shameless, inveterate, incorrigible ≠ occasional
2 = **seasoned**, experienced,

accustomed, toughened, inured, habituated ≠ naive

hardly ADVERB 1 = **barely**, only just, scarcely, just, with difficulty, with effort ≠ completely 2 = **only just**, just, barely, scarcely

hardship NOUN = **suffering**, need, difficulty, misfortune, adversity, tribulation, privation ≠ ease

hardy ADJECTIVE = **strong**, tough, robust, sound, rugged, sturdy, stout ≠ frail

hare NOUN ▷ RELATED WORDS: *adjective* **leporine**, *male* **buck**, *female* **doe**, *young* **leveret**, *habitation* **down, husk**

harm VERB 1 = **injure**, hurt, wound, abuse, ill-treat, maltreat ≠ heal 2 = **damage**, hurt, ruin, spoil
▷ NOUN 1 = **injury**, suffering, damage, ill, hurt, distress
2 = **damage**, loss, ill, hurt, misfortune, mischief ≠ good

harmful ADJECTIVE = **damaging**, dangerous, negative, destructive, hazardous, unhealthy, detrimental, hurtful ≠ harmless

harmless ADJECTIVE 1 = **safe**, benign, wholesome, innocuous, nontoxic ≠ dangerous
2 = **inoffensive**, innocent, innocuous, gentle, tame, unobjectionable

harmony NOUN 1 = **accord**, peace, agreement, friendship, sympathy, cooperation, rapport, compatibility ≠ conflict
2 = **tune**, melody, unison, tunefulness, euphony ≠ discord

harness VERB = **exploit**, control, channel, employ, utilize, mobilize
▷ NOUN = **equipment**, tackle, gear, tack

harrowing ADJECTIVE = **distressing**, disturbing, painful, terrifying, traumatic, tormenting, agonizing, nerve-racking

harry VERB = **pester**, bother, plague, harass, hassle (*informal*), badger, chivvy

harsh ADJECTIVE 1 = **severe**, hard, tough, stark, austere, inhospitable, bare-bones
2 = **bleak**, freezing, severe, icy 3 = **cruel**, savage, ruthless, barbarous, pitiless 4 = **hard**, severe, cruel, stern, pitiless ≠ kind 5 = **drastic**, punitive, Draconian 6 = **raucous**, rough, grating, strident, rasping, discordant, guttural, dissonant ≠ soft

harshly ADVERB = **severely**, roughly, cruelly, strictly, sternly, brutally

harvest NOUN 1 = **harvesting**, picking, gathering, collecting, reaping, harvest-time 2 = **crop**, yield, year's growth, produce
▷ VERB = **gather**, pick, collect, bring in, pluck, reap

hassle (*informal*) NOUN = **trouble**, problem, difficulty, bother, grief (*informal*), uphill (*S. African*), inconvenience
▷ VERB = **bother**, bug (*informal*), annoy, hound, harass, badger, pester

hasten VERB = **rush**, race, fly,

speed, dash, hurry (up), scurry, make haste ≠ dawdle

hastily ADVERB 1 = **quickly**, rapidly, promptly, speedily
2 = **hurriedly**, rashly, precipitately, impetuously

hatch VERB 1 = **incubate**, breed, sit on, brood, bring forth
2 = **devise**, design, invent, put together, conceive, brew, formulate, contrive

hate VERB 1 = **detest**, loathe, despise, dislike, abhor, recoil from, not be able to bear ≠ love
2 = **dislike**, detest, shrink from, recoil from, not be able to bear ≠ like 3 = **be unwilling**, regret, be reluctant, hesitate, be sorry, be loath, feel disinclined
▷ NOUN = **dislike**, hostility, hatred, loathing, animosity, aversion, antipathy, enmity ≠ love

hatred NOUN = **hate**, dislike, animosity, aversion, revulsion, antipathy, enmity, repugnance ≠ love

haul VERB = **drag**, draw, pull, heave
▷ NOUN = **yield**, gain, spoils, catch, harvest, loot, takings, booty

haunt VERB = **plague**, trouble, obsess, torment, possess, stay with, recur, prey on
▷ NOUN = **meeting place**, hangout (*informal*), rendezvous, stamping ground

haunted ADJECTIVE
1 = **possessed**, ghostly, cursed, eerie, spooky (*informal*), jinxed
2 = **preoccupied**, worried, troubled, plagued, obsessed, tormented

haunting ADJECTIVE = **evocative**, poignant, unforgettable

have VERB 1 = **own**, keep, possess, hold, retain, boast, be the owner of 2 = **get**, obtain, take, receive, accept, gain, secure, acquire 3 = **suffer**, experience, undergo, sustain, endure, be suffering from 4 = **give birth to**, bear, deliver, bring forth, beget
5 = **experience**, go through, undergo, meet with, come across, run into, be faced with
▷ PHRASES: **have someone on** = **tease**, kid (*informal*), wind up (*Brit. slang*), trick, deceive, take the mickey, pull someone's leg; **have something on** = **wear**, be wearing, be dressed in, be clothed in, be attired in; **have to 1** *with* **to** = **must**, should, be forced, ought, be obliged, be bound, have got to, be compelled 2 = **have got to**, must

haven NOUN = **sanctuary**, shelter, retreat, asylum, refuge, oasis, sanctum

havoc NOUN 1 = **devastation**, damage, destruction, ruin
2 (*informal*) = **disorder**, confusion, chaos, disruption, mayhem, shambles

hazard NOUN = **danger**, risk, threat, problem, menace, peril, jeopardy, pitfall
▷ VERB = **jeopardize**, risk, endanger, threaten, expose, imperil, put in jeopardy ▷ PHRASE:

hazard a guess = guess, conjecture, presume, take a guess

hazardous ADJECTIVE = **dangerous**, risky, difficult, insecure, unsafe, precarious, perilous, dicey (*informal, chiefly Brit.*) ≠ safe

haze NOUN = **mist**, cloud, fog, obscurity, vapour

head NOUN 1 = **skull**, crown, pate, nut (*slang*), loaf (*slang*) 2 = **mind**, reasoning, understanding, thought, sense, brain, brains (*informal*), intelligence 3 = **top**, crown, summit, peak, crest, pinnacle 4 (*informal*) = **head teacher**, principal 5 = **leader**, president, director, manager, chief, boss (*informal*), captain, master, sherang (*Austral. & N.Z.*)
▷ ADJECTIVE = **chief**, main, leading, first, prime, premier, supreme, principal
▷ VERB 1 = **lead**, precede, be the leader of, be or go first, be or go at the front of, lead the way 2 = **top**, lead, crown, cap 3 = **be in charge of**, run, manage, lead, control, direct, guide, command ▷ PHRASES: **go to your head** 1 = **intoxicate** 2 = **make someone conceited**, puff someone up, make someone full of themselves; **head over heels** = **completely**, thoroughly, utterly, intensely, wholeheartedly, uncontrollably

 WORD POWER

 The *head* is the upper or front part of the human body, containing the sensory organs and the brain. Many of its literal or figurative senses refer to a position at the top, at the front, or at the beginning of something. Location is specified in *head of the line*, meaning at the front; *head of the stairs*, meaning at the top; and *head of the river*, meaning at the source. These meanings have been transferred into other fields, with the result that head means leader in *the head of state*, and the forefront in *head of his field*. Conversely, head can also mean end or climax when used in the phrase *come/bring to a head*. In the human body, the head is regarded as the seat of the mind and the intellect, especially when contrasted with the heart, in the phrase *ruled by your heart*, *not your head*. In addition, head can describe an ability or a facility, e.g. *a head for heights* or *a head for figures*.

headache NOUN 1 = **migraine**, head (*informal*), neuralgia 2 = **problem** (*informal*), worry, trouble, bother, nuisance, inconvenience, bane, vexation

heading NOUN = **title**, name, caption, headline, rubric

heady ADJECTIVE 1 = **exciting**, thrilling, stimulating,

exhilarating, intoxicating
2 = **intoxicating**, strong, potent, inebriating

heal VERB **1** *sometimes with* **up**
= **mend**, get better, get well, cure, regenerate, show improvement
2 = **cure**, restore, mend, make better, remedy, make good, make well ≠ injure

health NOUN **1** = **condition**, state, shape, constitution, fettle **2** = **wellbeing**, strength, fitness, vigour, good condition, soundness, robustness, healthiness ≠ illness **3** = **state**, condition, shape

healthy ADJECTIVE **1** = **well**, fit, strong, active, robust, in good shape (*informal*), in the pink, in fine fettle ≠ ill **2** = **wholesome**, beneficial, nourishing, nutritious, salutary, hygienic, salubrious ≠ unwholesome
3 = **invigorating**, beneficial, salutary, salubrious

heap NOUN **1** = **pile**, lot, collection, mass, stack, mound, accumulation, hoard **2** *often plural* (*informal*) = **a lot**, lots (*informal*), plenty, masses, load(s) (*informal*), great deal, tons, stack(s)
▷ VERB *sometimes with* **up** = **pile**, collect, gather, stack, accumulate, amass, hoard ▷ PHRASE: **heap something on someone** = **load with**, confer on, assign to, bestow on, shower upon

hear VERB **1** = **overhear**, catch, detect **2** = **listen to 3** (*law*) = **try**, judge, examine, investigate

4 = **learn**, discover, find out, pick up, gather, ascertain, get wind of (*informal*)

hearing NOUN = **inquiry**, trial, investigation, industrial tribunal

heart NOUN **1** = **emotions**, feelings, love, affection
2 = **nature**, character, soul, constitution, essence, temperament, disposition
3 = **root**, core, centre, nucleus, hub, gist, nitty-gritty (*informal*), nub **4** = **courage**, will, spirit, purpose, bottle (*Brit. informal*), resolution, resolve, stomach
▷ PHRASE: **by heart** = **from** *or* **by memory**, verbatim, word for word, pat, word-perfect, by rote, off by heart, off pat ▷ RELATED WORD: *adjective* **cardiac**

● WORD POWER
● More than any other part of the
● human body, the *heart* has been
● given special significance and
● symbolic power. It is the heart
● which expresses the essential
● character of a human being,
● in phrases such as *at heart*.
● In today's English, the heart
● represents the seat of emotions
● in contrast to the reasoning of
● the head. However, formerly,
● the heart was also considered
● to be the seat of mental
● processes, including the mind
● and memory. This is seen in
● the phrase *by heart*, meaning
● from memory. Nowadays, we
● think of the heart especially
● with reference to love and

compassion in the phrases
heartbreak, *heart-rending*, and
heart-warming. Adding to the
fervour of these emotions, we
have *from the heart* (sincerely);
heart-to-heart (candidly); and
heart and soul (completely).
When we summon emotional
reserves of courage and will,
they come from the heart – we
take heart or *lose heart*. The
heart's role in maintaining
life means it is viewed as the
centre of the body and, by
extension, this can be the hub
of other places, as in *the heart
of the region* or *at the heart of the
company*.

heat VERB *sometimes with* **up**
= **warm (up)**, cook, boil, roast,
reheat, make hot ≠ chill
▷ NOUN 1 = **warmth**, hotness,
temperature ≠ cold 2 = **hot
weather**, warmth, closeness,
high temperature, heatwave,
warm weather, hot climate,
mugginess 3 = **passion**,
excitement, intensity, fury,
fervour, vehemence ≠ calmness
▷ RELATED WORD: *adjectives*
thermal

heated ADJECTIVE
1 = **impassioned**, intense,
spirited, excited, angry, furious,
fierce, lively ≠ calm 2 = **wound
up**, worked up, keyed up, het up
(*informal*)

heaven NOUN 1 = **paradise**,
next world, hereafter, nirvana
(*Buddhism*, *hinduism*), bliss, Zion
(*christianity*), life everlasting,
Elysium *or* Elysian fields (*greek
myth*) 2 (*informal*) = **happiness**,
paradise, ecstasy, bliss, utopia,
rapture, seventh heaven
▷ PHRASE: **the heavens** (*old-
fashioned*) = **sky**, ether, firmament

heavenly ADJECTIVE 1 = **celestial**,
holy, divine, blessed, immortal,
angelic ≠ earthly 2 (*informal*)
= **wonderful**, lovely, delightful,
beautiful, divine (*informal*),
exquisite, sublime, blissful
≠ awful

heavily ADVERB 1 = **excessively**,
to excess, very much, a great
deal, considerably, copiously,
without restraint, immoderately
2 = **densely**, closely, thickly,
compactly 3 = **hard**, clumsily,
awkwardly, weightily

heavy ADJECTIVE 1 = **weighty**,
large, massive, hefty, bulky,
ponderous ≠ light 2 = **intensive**,
severe, serious, concentrated,
fierce, excessive, relentless
3 = **considerable**, large, huge,
substantial, abundant, copious,
profuse ≠ slight

WORD POWER
Many of the words which have
come into English from Hebrew
have their origins in the bible,
and were part of the Jewish
and Christian religions. A
noticeable trend with religious
words is that they spread
into secular language as well.
Two examples are *amen* and
hallelujah. The literal meaning

of amen is 'certainly', and it is used at the end of prayers as a concluding formula. However, it has also passed outside the religious sphere to be used as an expression of agreement to a previous utterance. It is similar in function to 'hear, hear' meaning 'I agree'. Hallelujah, literally 'praise the Lord', is an interjection used by atheists as well as believers as a general exclamation of relief. Another biblical word is *behemoth*, from the Hebrew for 'beasts', which was used in the Old Testament with specific reference but has now become more generalised. The behemoth was a gigantic beast, possibly a hippopotamus. Its modern figurative meaning is that of any huge or monstrous thing. It is often applied to corporations or industries of the modern world in the same way as its synonym 'giant', in expressions like the *software/corporate/ steel/banking behemoth*. It retains the slightly negative connotation of its original meaning of 'beast'.

hectic ADJECTIVE = **frantic**, chaotic, heated, animated, turbulent, frenetic, feverish ≠ peaceful

hedge VERB = **prevaricate**, evade, sidestep, duck, dodge, flannel (*Brit. informal*), equivocate, temporize ▷ **PHRASE**: hedge

against something = **protect**, insure, guard, safeguard, shield, cover

heed VERB = **pay attention to**, listen to, take notice of, follow, consider, note, observe, obey ≠ ignore
▷ NOUN = **thought**, care, mind, attention, regard, respect, notice ≠ disregard

heel NOUN (*slang*) = **swine**, cad (*Brit. informal*), bounder (*Brit. old-fashioned* or *slang*), rotter (*slang*, *chiefly Brit.*), wrong 'un (*Austral. slang*)

hefty (*informal*) ADJECTIVE = **big**, strong, massive, strapping, robust, muscular, burly, hulking ≠ small

height NOUN 1 = **tallness**, stature, highness, loftiness ≠ shortness
2 = **altitude**, measurement, highness, elevation, tallness ≠ depth 3 = **peak**, top, crown, summit, crest, pinnacle, apex ≠ valley 4 = **culmination**, climax, zenith, limit, maximum, ultimate ≠ low point

heighten VERB = **intensify**, increase, add to, improve, strengthen, enhance, sharpen, magnify

heir NOUN = **successor**, beneficiary, inheritor, heiress *fem.* next in line

hell NOUN 1 = **the underworld**, the abyss, Hades (*greek myth*), hellfire, the inferno, fire and brimstone, the nether world, the bad fire (*informal*) 2 (*informal*) = **torment**, suffering, agony, nightmare, misery, ordeal, anguish, wretchedness

hello INTERJECTION = **hi** (informal), greetings, how do you do?, good morning, good evening, good afternoon, welcome, kia ora (N.Z.), gidday or g'day (Austral. & N.Z.)

helm NOUN (nautical) = **tiller**, wheel, rudder

help VERB 1 sometimes with **out** = **aid**, support, assist, cooperate with, abet, lend a hand, succour ≠ hinder 2 = **improve**, ease, relieve, facilitate, alleviate, mitigate, ameliorate ≠ make worse 3 = **assist**, aid, support 4 = **resist**, refrain from, avoid, prevent, keep from
▷ NOUN = **assistance**, aid, support, advice, guidance, cooperation, helping hand ≠ hindrance

helper NOUN = **assistant**, ally, supporter, mate, second, aide, attendant, collaborator

helpful ADJECTIVE
1 = **cooperative**, accommodating, kind, friendly, neighbourly, sympathetic, supportive, considerate 2 = **useful**, practical, profitable, constructive
3 = **beneficial**, advantageous

helping NOUN = **portion**, serving, ration, piece, dollop (informal), plateful

helpless ADJECTIVE = **powerless**, weak, disabled, incapable, challenged, paralysed, impotent, infirm ≠ powerful

hem NOUN 1 = **edge**, border, margin, trimming, fringe
▷ PHRASE: **hem something or someone in** 1 = **surround**, confine, enclose, shut in
2 = **restrict**, confine, beset, circumscribe

hence ADVERB = **therefore**, thus, consequently, for this reason, in consequence, ergo, on that account

herald VERB = **indicate**, promise, usher in, presage, portend, foretoken
▷ NOUN 1 (often literary) = **forerunner**, sign, signal, indication, token, omen, precursor, harbinger
2 = **messenger**, courier, proclaimer, announcer, crier, town crier

herd NOUN = **flock**, crowd, collection, mass, drove, mob, swarm, horde

hereditary ADJECTIVE
1 = **genetic**, inborn, inbred, transmissible, inheritable 2 (law) = **inherited**, passed down, traditional, ancestral

heritage NOUN = **inheritance**, legacy, birthright, tradition, endowment, bequest

hero NOUN 1 = **protagonist**, leading man 2 = **star**, champion, victor, superstar, conqueror
3 = **idol**, favourite, pin-up (slang), fave (informal)

heroic ADJECTIVE = **courageous**, brave, daring, fearless, gallant,

intrepid, valiant, lion-hearted
≠ cowardly

heroine NOUN 1 = **protagonist**,
leading lady, diva, prima donna
2 = **idol**, favourite, pin-up (slang),
fave (informal)

● **WORD POWER**
● Note that the word heroine,
● meaning 'a female hero', has an
● e at the end. The drug heroin is
● spelled without a final e.

hesitate VERB 1 = **waver**, delay,
pause, wait, doubt, falter, dither
(chiefly Brit.), vacillate ≠ be
decisive 2 = **be reluctant**, be
unwilling, shrink from, think
twice, scruple, demur, hang back,
be disinclined ≠ be determined

hesitation NOUN = **reluctance**,
reservation(s), misgiving(s),
ambivalence, qualm(s),
unwillingness, scruple(s),
compunction

hidden ADJECTIVE 1 = **secret**,
veiled, latent 2 = **concealed**,
secret, covert, unseen,
clandestine, secreted, under
wraps

hide¹ VERB 1 = **conceal**, stash
(informal), secrete, put out of sight
≠ display 2 = **go into hiding**,
take cover, keep out of sight, hole
up, lie low, go underground, go
to ground, go to earth 3 = **keep
secret**, suppress, withhold, keep
quiet about, hush up, draw a
veil over, keep dark, keep under
your hat ≠ disclose 4 = **obscure**,
cover, mask, disguise, conceal,
veil, cloak, shroud ≠ reveal

hide² NOUN = **skin**, leather, pelt

hideous ADJECTIVE = **ugly**,
revolting, ghastly, monstrous,
grotesque, gruesome, grisly,
unsightly ≠ beautiful

hiding NOUN (informal) = **beating**,
whipping, thrashing, licking
(informal), spanking, walloping
(informal), drubbing

hierarchy NOUN = **grading**,
ranking, social order, pecking
order, class system, social stratum

high ADJECTIVE 1 = **tall**, towering,
soaring, steep, elevated, lofty
≠ short 2 = **extreme**, great,
acute, severe, extraordinary,
excessive ≠ low 3 = **strong**,
violent, extreme, blustery,
squally, sharp 4 = **important**,
chief, powerful, superior,
eminent, exalted, skookum
(Canad.) ≠ lowly 5 = **high-
pitched**, piercing, shrill,
penetrating, strident, sharp,
acute, piping ≠ deep 6 (informal)
= **intoxicated**, stoned (slang),
tripping (informal)
▷ ADVERB = **way up**, aloft, far up,
to a great height

high-flown ADJECTIVE
= **extravagant**, elaborate,
pretentious, exaggerated,
inflated, lofty, grandiose,
overblown ≠ straightforward

highlight VERB = **emphasize**,
stress, accent, show up,
underline, spotlight, accentuate,
call attention to ≠ play down
▷ NOUN = **high point**, peak,
climax, feature, focus, focal point,

high spot ≠ low point

highly ADVERB = **extremely**, very, greatly, vastly, exceptionally, immensely, tremendously

hijack or **highjack** VERB = **seize**, take over, commandeer, expropriate

hike NOUN = **walk**, march, trek, ramble, tramp, traipse
▷ VERB = **walk**, march, trek, ramble, tramp, back-pack

hilarious ADJECTIVE 1 = **funny**, entertaining, amusing, hysterical, humorous, comical, side-splitting
2 = **merry**, uproarious, rollicking ≠ serious

hill NOUN = **mount**, fell, height, mound, hilltop, tor, knoll, hillock, kopje or koppie (S. African)

hinder VERB = **obstruct**, stop, check, block, delay, frustrate, handicap, interrupt ≠ help

⬤ **WORD POWER**
⬤ Hindi is the official language
⬤ of India, with English
⬤ recognized as an associate
⬤ official language. Before
⬤ independence, India was
⬤ part of the British Empire,
⬤ and contact between the two
⬤ cultures led to the borrowing
⬤ into English of a number of loan
⬤ words. The word *dekko*, literally
⬤ 'look!' in Hindi, entered English
⬤ through British army slang in
⬤ the 19th century. It remains
⬤ restricted to British slang,
⬤ especially in the phrase *take/*
⬤ *have a dekko at*, meaning 'have
⬤ a look'. It can be contrasted

⬤ with a couple of phrases with
⬤ similar meaning – *have a shufti*
⬤ *at* and *do a recce*, which also
⬤ entered English via military
⬤ contact with other cultures
⬤ [See Arabic]. The word *pukka*
⬤ derives from the Hindi word
⬤ for 'firm' or 'mature' and is
⬤ found particularly in Indian
⬤ English and British English.
⬤ It has a range of meaning in
⬤ these two varieties; applied
⬤ to a person it means 'genuine'
⬤ or 'socially acceptable', and
⬤ applied to a thing it means
⬤ 'right' or 'real'. For example, *a*
⬤ *pukka chap*, *a pukka way*, *a pukka*
⬤ *job*. The meaning of *wallah* in
⬤ British English derives from
⬤ a misunderstanding of the
⬤ Hindi word *-wala* which is
⬤ equivalent to the English suffix
⬤ -er, as in teacher, producer. It
⬤ was thought by non-native
⬤ speakers to mean 'man'; this
⬤ has influenced its modern
⬤ meaning in British English
⬤ of a person involved with a
⬤ specified thing, particularly in
⬤ their employment, e.g. *a policy*
⬤ *wallah*, *an company wallah*, *a*
⬤ *personnel wallah*.

hint NOUN 1 = **clue**, suggestion, implication, indication, pointer, allusion, innuendo, intimation 2 = **advice**, help, tip(s), suggestion(s), pointer(s)
3 = **trace**, touch, suggestion, dash, suspicion, tinge, undertone
▷ VERB sometimes with **at**

= **suggest**, indicate, imply, intimate, insinuate

hire VERB 1 = **employ**, commission, take on, engage, appoint, sign up, enlist 2 = **rent**, charter, lease, let, engage
▷ NOUN 1 = **rental**, hiring, rent, lease 2 = **charge**, rental, price, cost, fee

hiss VERB 1 = **whistle**, wheeze, whiz, whirr, sibilate 2 = **jeer**, mock, deride
▷ NOUN = **fizz**, buzz, hissing, fizzing, sibilation

historic ADJECTIVE = **significant**, notable, momentous, famous, extraordinary, outstanding, remarkable, ground-breaking
≠ unimportant

⬤ **WORD POWER**
⬤ Although *historic* and
⬤ *historical* are similarly spelt
⬤ they are very different in
⬤ meaning and should not
⬤ be used interchangeably. A
⬤ distinction is usually made
⬤ between *historic*, which means
⬤ 'important' or 'significant',
⬤ and *historical*, which means
⬤ 'pertaining to history': *a historic
⬤ decision; a historical perspective.*

historical ADJECTIVE
= **factual**, real, documented, actual, authentic, attested
≠ contemporary
▷ *see* **historic**

history NOUN 1 = **the past**, antiquity, yesterday, yesteryear, olden days 2 = **chronicle**, record, story, account, narrative, recital, annals

hit VERB 1 = **strike**, beat, knock, bang, slap, smack, thump, clout (*informal*) 2 = **collide with**, run into, bump into, clash with, smash into, crash against, bang into 3 = **affect**, damage, harm, ruin, devastate, overwhelm, touch, impact on 4 = **reach**, gain, achieve, arrive at, accomplish, attain
▷ NOUN 1 = **shot**, blow 2 = **blow**, knock, stroke, belt (*informal*), rap, slap, smack, clout (*informal*) 3 = **success**, winner, triumph, smash (*informal*), sensation
▷ PHRASES: **hit it off** (*informal*) = **get on (well) with**, click (*slang*), be on good terms, get on like a house on fire (*informal*); **hit on** *or* **upon something** = **think up**, discover, arrive at, invent, stumble on, light upon, strike upon

hitch NOUN = **problem**, catch, difficulty, hold-up, obstacle, drawback, snag, uphill (*S. African*), impediment
▷ VERB 1 (*informal*) = **hitchhike**, thumb a lift 2 = **fasten**, join, attach, couple, tie, connect, harness, tether ▷ PHRASE: **hitch something up** = **pull up**, tug, jerk, yank

hitherto ADVERB (*formal*) = **previously**, so far, until now, thus far, heretofore

hobby NOUN = **pastime**, relaxation, leisure pursuit, diversion, avocation, (leisure) activity

hoist VERB = **raise**, lift, erect, elevate, heave
▷ NOUN = **lift**, crane, elevator, winch

hold VERB 1 = **embrace**, grasp, clutch, hug, squeeze, cradle, clasp, enfold 2 = **restrain** ≠ release 3 = **detain**, confine, imprison, impound ≠ release 4 = **accommodate**, take, contain, seat, have a capacity for 5 = **consider**, think, believe, judge, regard, assume, reckon, deem ≠ deny 6 = **occupy**, have, fill, maintain, retain, possess, hold down (*informal*) 7 = **conduct**, convene, call, run, preside over ≠ cancel
▷ NOUN 1 = **grip**, grasp, clasp 2 = **foothold**, footing 3 = **control**, influence, mastery, mana (*N.Z.*)

holder NOUN 1 = **owner**, bearer, possessor, keeper, proprietor 2 = **case**, cover, container

hold-up NOUN 1 = **robbery**, theft, mugging (*informal*), stick-up (*slang, chiefly U.S.*) 2 = **delay**, wait, hitch, setback, snag, traffic jam, stoppage, bottleneck

hole NOUN 1 = **cavity**, pit, hollow, chamber, cave, cavern 2 = **opening**, crack, tear, gap, breach, vent, puncture, aperture 3 = **burrow**, den, earth, shelter, lair 4 (*informal*) = **hovel**, dump (*informal*), dive (*slang*), slum 5 (*informal*) = **predicament**, spot (*informal*), fix (*informal*), mess, jam (*informal*), dilemma, scrape (*informal*), hot water (*informal*)

holiday NOUN 1 = **vacation**, leave, break, time off, recess, schoolie (*Austral.*), accumulated day off *or* ADO (*Austral.*) 2 = **festival**, fête, celebration, feast, gala

hollow ADJECTIVE 1 = **empty**, vacant, void, unfilled ≠ solid 2 = **worthless**, useless, vain, meaningless, pointless, futile, fruitless ≠ meaningful 3 = **dull**, low, deep, muted, toneless, reverberant ≠ vibrant
▷ NOUN 1 = **cavity**, hole, bowl, depression, pit, basin, crater, trough ≠ mound 2 = **valley**, dale, glen, dell, dingle ≠ hill
▷ VERB *often followed by* **out** = **scoop out**, dig out, excavate, gouge out

holocaust NOUN 1 = **devastation**, destruction, genocide, annihilation, conflagration 2 = **genocide**, massacre, annihilation

holy ADJECTIVE 1 = **sacred**, blessed, hallowed, venerable, consecrated, sacrosanct, sanctified ≠ unsanctified 2 = **devout**, godly, religious, pure, righteous, pious, virtuous, saintly ≠ sinful

homage NOUN = **respect**, honour, worship, devotion, reverence, deference, adulation, adoration ≠ contempt

home NOUN 1 = **dwelling**, house, residence, abode, habitation, pad (*slang*), domicile 2 = **birthplace**, homeland, home town, native land, Godzone (*Austral. informal*)
▷ ADJECTIVE = **domestic**, local,

internal, native ▷ **PHRASES**: **at
home 1** = **in**, present, available
2 = **at ease**, relaxed, comfortable,
content, at peace; **bring
something home to someone**
= **make clear**, emphasize, drive
home, press home, impress upon

homeland NOUN = **native
land**, birthplace, motherland,
fatherland, country of origin,
mother country, Godzone (*Austral.
informal*)

homeless ADJECTIVE = **destitute**,
displaced, dispossessed, down-
and-out

homely ADJECTIVE
1 = **comfortable**, welcoming,
friendly, cosy, homespun
2 = **plain**, simple, ordinary,
modest ≠ elaborate

homicide NOUN = **murder**, killing,
manslaughter, slaying, bloodshed

hone VERB **1** = **improve**, better,
enhance, upgrade, refine,
sharpen, help **2** = **sharpen**, point,
grind, edge, file, polish, whet

● **WORD POWER**
● *Hone* is sometimes wrongly
● used where *home* is meant: *this*
● *device makes it easier to home in*
● *on* (not *hone in on*) *the target*.

honest ADJECTIVE
1 = **trustworthy**, upright,
ethical, honourable, reputable,
truthful, virtuous, law-abiding
≠ dishonest **2** = **open**, direct,
frank, plain, sincere, candid,
forthright, upfront (*informal*)
≠ secretive

honestly ADVERB **1** = **ethically**,

legally, lawfully, honourably, by
fair means **2** = **frankly**, plainly,
candidly, straight (out), truthfully,
to your face, in all sincerity

honesty NOUN **1** = **integrity**,
honour, virtue, morality,
probity, rectitude, truthfulness,
trustworthiness **2** = **frankness**,
openness, sincerity, candour,
bluntness, outspokenness,
straightforwardness

honorary ADJECTIVE = **nominal**,
unofficial, titular, in name *or* title
only

honour NOUN **1** = **integrity**,
morality, honesty, goodness,
fairness, decency, probity,
rectitude ≠ dishonour
2 = **prestige**, credit, reputation,
glory, fame, distinction,
dignity, renown ≠ disgrace
3 = **reputation**, standing,
prestige, image, status,
stature, good name, cachet
4 = **acclaim**, praise, recognition,
compliments, homage, accolades,
commendation ≠ contempt
5 = **privilege**, credit, pleasure,
compliment
▷ VERB **1** = **acclaim**, praise,
decorate, commemorate,
commend **2** = **respect**, value,
esteem, prize, appreciate, adore
≠ scorn **3** = **fulfil**, keep, carry out,
observe, discharge, live up to,
be true to **4** = **pay**, take, accept,
pass, acknowledge ≠ refuse

honourable ADJECTIVE
1 = **principled**, moral, ethical,
fair, upright, honest, virtuous,

trustworthy 2 = **proper**, respectable, virtuous, creditable

hook NOUN = **fastener**, catch, link, peg, clasp
▷ VERB **1** = **fasten**, fix, secure, clasp **2** = **catch**, land, trap, entrap

hooked ADJECTIVE **1** = **bent**, curved, aquiline, hook-shaped **2** (*informal*) = **obsessed**, addicted, taken, devoted, turned on (*slang*), enamoured **3** (*informal*) = **addicted**, dependent, using (*informal*), having a habit

hooligan NOUN = **delinquent**, vandal, hoon (*Austral. & N.Z.*), ruffian, lager lout, yob or yobbo (*Brit. slang*), cougan (*Austral. slang*), scozza (*Austral. slang*), bogan (*Austral. slang*)

hoop NOUN = **ring**, band, loop, wheel, round, girdle, circlet

hop VERB = **jump**, spring, bound, leap, skip, vault, caper
▷ NOUN = **jump**, step, spring, bound, leap, bounce, skip, vault

hope VERB = **believe**, look forward to, cross your fingers
▷ NOUN = **belief**, confidence, expectation, longing, dream, desire, ambition, assumption ≠ despair

hopeful ADJECTIVE **1** = **optimistic**, confident, looking forward to, buoyant, sanguine, expectant ≠ despairing **2** = **promising**, encouraging, bright, reassuring, rosy, heartening, auspicious ≠ unpromising

hopefully ADVERB = **optimistically**, confidently, expectantly, with anticipation

hopeless ADJECTIVE = **impossible**, pointless, futile, useless, vain, no-win, unattainable

horde NOUN = **crowd**, mob, swarm, host, band, pack, drove, gang

horizon NOUN = **skyline**, view, vista

horizontal ADJECTIVE = **level**, flat, parallel

horrible ADJECTIVE **1** (*informal*) = **dreadful**, terrible, awful, nasty, cruel, mean, unpleasant, horrid ≠ wonderful **2** = **terrible**, appalling, terrifying, shocking, grim, dreadful, revolting, ghastly

horrific ADJECTIVE = **horrifying**, shocking, appalling, awful, terrifying, dreadful, horrendous, ghastly

horrify VERB **1** = **terrify**, alarm,

frighten, scare, intimidate, petrify, make your hair stand on end ≠ comfort 2 = **shock**, appal, dismay, sicken, outrage ≠ delight

horror NOUN 1 = **terror**, fear, alarm, panic, dread, fright, consternation, trepidation 2 = **hatred**, disgust, loathing, aversion, revulsion, repugnance, odium, detestation ≠ love

horse NOUN = **nag**, mount, mare, colt, filly, stallion, steed (*archaic* or *literary*), moke (*Austral. slang*), yarraman or yarramin (*Austral.*), gee-gee (*slang*) ▷ **RELATED WORDS**: *adjectives* **equestrian**, **equine**, *male* **stallion**, *female* **mare**, *young* **foal**, **colt**, **filly**

hospitality NOUN = **welcome**, warmth, kindness, friendliness, sociability, conviviality, neighbourliness, cordiality

host¹ or **hostess** NOUN
1 = **master of ceremonies**, proprietor, innkeeper, landlord or landlady 2 = **presenter**, compere (*Brit.*), anchorman or anchorwoman
▷ VERB = **present**, introduce, compere (*Brit.*), front (*informal*)

host² NOUN 1 = **multitude**, lot, load (*informal*), wealth, array, myriad, great quantity, large number 2 = **crowd**, army, pack, drove, mob, herd, legion, swarm

hostage NOUN = **captive**, prisoner, pawn

hostile ADJECTIVE
1 = **antagonistic**, opposed, contrary, ill-disposed

2 = **unfriendly**, belligerent, antagonistic, rancorous, ill-disposed ≠ friendly
3 = **inhospitable**, adverse, uncongenial, unsympathetic, unwelcoming ≠ hospitable

hostility NOUN
1 = **unfriendliness**, hatred, animosity, spite, bitterness, malice, venom, enmity
≠ friendliness 2 = **opposition**, resentment, antipathy, aversion, antagonism, ill feeling, ill-will, animus ≠ approval
▷ PLURAL NOUN = **warfare**, war, fighting, conflict, combat, armed conflict ≠ peace

hot ADJECTIVE 1 = **heated**, boiling, steaming, roasting, searing, scorching, scalding 2 = **warm**, close, stifling, humid, torrid, sultry, sweltering, balmy ≠ cold
3 = **spicy**, pungent, peppery, piquant, biting, sharp ≠ mild
4 = **intense**, passionate, heated, spirited, fierce, lively, animated, ardent 5 = **new**, latest, fresh, recent, up to date, just out, up to the minute, bang up to date (*informal*) ≠ old 6 = **popular**, hip, fashionable, cool, in demand, sought-after, must-see, in vogue ≠ unpopular 7 = **fierce**, intense, strong, keen, competitive, cut-throat 8 = **fiery**, violent, raging, passionate, stormy ≠ calm

hound VERB = **harass**, harry, bother, provoke, annoy, torment, hassle (*informal*), badger
▷ **RELATED WORD**: *collective nouns*

pack

house NOUN 1 = **home**, residence, dwelling, pad (*slang*), homestead, abode, habitation, domicile, whare (*N.Z.*) 2 = **household**, family 3 = **firm**, company, business, organization, outfit (*informal*) 4 = **assembly**, parliament, Commons, legislative body 5 = **dynasty**, tribe, clan
▷ VERB 1 = **accommodate**, quarter, take in, put up, lodge, harbour, billet 2 = **contain**, keep, hold, cover, store, protect, shelter 3 = **take**, accommodate, sleep, provide shelter for, give a bed to
▷ PHRASE: **on the house** = **free**, for free (*informal*), for nothing, free of charge, gratis

household NOUN = **family**, home, house, family circle, ainga (*N.Z.*)

housing NOUN
1 = **accommodation**, homes, houses, dwellings, domiciles
2 = **case**, casing, covering, cover, shell, jacket, holder, container

hover VERB 1 = **float**, fly, hang, drift, flutter 2 = **linger**, loiter, hang about *or* around (*informal*)
3 = **waver**, fluctuate, dither (*chiefly Brit.*), oscillate, vacillate

however ADVERB = **but**, nevertheless, still, though, yet, nonetheless, notwithstanding, anyhow

howl VERB 1 = **bay**, cry 2 = **cry**, scream, roar, weep, yell, wail, shriek, bellow
▷ NOUN 1 = **baying**, cry, bay, bark, barking, yelping 2 = **cry**, scream,

roar, bay, wail, shriek, clamour, bawl

hub NOUN = **centre**, heart, focus, core, middle, focal point, nerve centre

huddle VERB 1 = **curl up**, crouch, hunch up 2 = **crowd**, press, gather, collect, squeeze, cluster, flock, herd
▷ NOUN (*informal*) = **discussion**, conference, meeting, hui (*N.Z.*), powwow, confab (*informal*), korero (*N.Z.*)

hue NOUN = **colour**, tone, shade, dye, tint, tinge

hug VERB = **embrace**, cuddle, squeeze, clasp, enfold, hold close, take in your arms
▷ NOUN = **embrace**, squeeze, bear hug, clinch (*slang*), clasp

huge ADJECTIVE = **enormous**, large, massive, vast, tremendous, immense, gigantic, monumental ≠ tiny

hui NOUN (*N.Z.*) = **meeting**, gathering, assembly, conference, congress, rally, convention, get-together (*informal*)

hull NOUN = **framework**, casing, body, covering, frame

hum VERB 1 = **drone**, buzz, murmur, throb, vibrate, purr, thrum, whir
2 (*informal*) = **be busy**, buzz, bustle, stir, pulse, pulsate

human ADJECTIVE = **mortal**, manlike ≠ nonhuman
▷ NOUN = **human being**, person, individual, creature, mortal, man *or* woman ≠ nonhuman

h

humane ADJECTIVE = **kind**,
compassionate, understanding,
forgiving, tender, sympathetic,
benign, merciful ≠ cruel
humanitarian ADJECTIVE
1 = **compassionate**, charitable,
humane, benevolent, altruistic
2 = **charitable**, philanthropic,
public-spirited
▷ NOUN = **philanthropist**,
benefactor, Good Samaritan,
altruist
humanity NOUN 1 = **the human
race**, man, mankind, people,
mortals, humankind, Homo
sapiens 2 = **human nature**,
mortality 3 = **kindness**, charity,
compassion, sympathy, mercy,
philanthropy, fellow feeling, kind-
heartedness
humble ADJECTIVE 1 = **modest**,
meek, unassuming,
unpretentious, self-effacing,
unostentatious ≠ proud
2 = **lowly**, poor, mean, simple,
ordinary, modest, obscure,
undistinguished ≠ distinguished
▷ VERB = **humiliate**, disgrace,
crush, subdue, chasten, put
(someone) in their place, take
down a peg (*informal*) ≠ exalt
humidity NOUN = **damp**,
moisture, dampness, wetness,
moistness, dankness,
clamminess, mugginess
humiliate VERB = **embarrass**,
shame, humble, crush, put
down, degrade, chasten, mortify
≠ honour
humiliating ADJECTIVE

= **embarrassing**, shaming,
humbling, mortifying, crushing,
degrading, ignominious, barro
(*Austral. slang*)
humiliation NOUN
= **embarrassment**, shame,
disgrace, humbling, put-down,
degradation, indignity, ignominy
humorous ADJECTIVE = **funny**,
comic, amusing, entertaining,
witty, comical, droll, jocular
≠ serious
humour NOUN 1 = **comedy**,
funniness, fun, amusement, funny
side, jocularity, facetiousness,
ludicrousness ≠ seriousness
2 = **mood**, spirits, temper,
disposition, frame of mind
3 = **joking**, comedy, wit, farce,
jesting, wisecracks (*informal*),
witticisms
▷ VERB = **indulge**, accommodate,
go along with, flatter, gratify,
pander to, mollify ≠ oppose
hunch NOUN = **feeling**, idea,
impression, suspicion,
intuition, premonition, inkling,
presentiment
▷ VERB = **crouch**, bend, curve,
arch, draw in
hunger NOUN 1 = **appetite**,
emptiness, hungriness,
ravenousness 2 = **starvation**,
famine, malnutrition,
undernourishment 3 = **desire**,
appetite, craving, ache, lust,
yearning, itch, thirst ▷ PHRASE:
hunger for *or* **after something**
= **want**, desire, crave, long for,
wish for, yearn for, hanker after,

ache for

hungry ADJECTIVE 1 = **starving**, ravenous, famished, starved, empty, voracious, peckish (*informal, chiefly Brit.*) 2 = **eager**, keen, craving, yearning, greedy, avid, desirous, covetous

hunk NOUN = **lump**, piece, chunk, block, mass, wedge, slab, nugget

hunt VERB = **stalk**, track, chase, pursue, trail, hound
▷ NOUN = **search**, hunting, investigation, chase, pursuit, quest ▷ PHRASE: **hunt for something** or **someone** = **search for**, look for, seek for, forage for, scour for, fossick for (*Austral. & N.Z.*), ferret about for

hurdle NOUN 1 = **obstacle**, difficulty, barrier, handicap, hazard, uphill (*S. African*), obstruction, stumbling block 2 = **fence**, barrier, barricade

hurl VERB = **throw**, fling, launch, cast, pitch, toss, propel, sling

hurricane NOUN = **storm**, gale, tornado, cyclone, typhoon, tempest, twister (*U.S. informal*), willy-willy (*Austral.*)

hurried ADJECTIVE 1 = **hasty**, quick, brief, rushed, short, swift, speedy 2 = **rushed**, perfunctory, speedy, hasty, cursory

hurry VERB 1 = **rush**, fly, dash, scurry, scoot ≠ dawdle 2 = **make haste**, rush, get a move on (*informal*), step on it (*informal*), crack on (*informal*)
▷ NOUN = **rush**, haste, speed, urgency, flurry, quickness

≠ slowness

hurt VERB 1 = **injure**, damage, wound, cut, disable, bruise, scrape, impair ≠ heal 2 = **ache**, be sore, be painful, burn, smart, sting, throb, be tender 3 = **harm**, injure, ill-treat, maltreat 4 = **upset**, distress, pain, wound, annoy, grieve, sadden
▷ NOUN = **distress**, suffering, pain, grief, misery, sorrow, heartache, wretchedness ≠ happiness
▷ ADJECTIVE 1 = **injured**, wounded, damaged, harmed, cut, bruised, scarred ≠ healed 2 = **upset**, wounded, crushed, offended, aggrieved, tooshie (*Austral. slang*) ≠ calmed

hurtle VERB = **rush**, charge, race, shoot, fly, speed, tear, crash

husband NOUN = **partner**, spouse, mate, better half (*humorous*)
▷ VERB = **conserve**, budget, save, store, hoard, economize on, use economically ≠ squander

hush VERB = **quieten**, silence, mute, muzzle, shush
▷ NOUN = **quiet**, silence, calm, peace, tranquillity, stillness

hut NOUN 1 = **cabin**, shack, shanty, hovel, whare (*N.Z.*) 2 = **shed**, outhouse, lean-to, lockup

hybrid NOUN 1 = **crossbreed**, cross, mixture, compound, composite, amalgam, mongrel, half-breed 2 = **mixture**, compound, composite, amalgam

hygiene NOUN = **cleanliness**,

h

sanitation, disinfection, sterility

hymn NOUN 1 = **religious song**, song of praise, carol, chant, anthem, psalm, paean 2 = **song of praise**, anthem, paean

hype NOUN = **publicity**, promotion, plugging (*informal*), razzmatazz (*slang*), brouhaha, ballyhoo (*informal*)

hypocrisy NOUN = **insincerity**, pretence, deception, cant, duplicity, deceitfulness ≠ sincerity

hypothesis NOUN = **theory**, premise, proposition, assumption, thesis, postulate, supposition

hysteria NOUN = **frenzy**, panic, madness, agitation, delirium, hysterics

hysterical ADJECTIVE 1 = **frenzied**, frantic, raving, distracted, distraught, crazed, overwrought, berko (*Austral. slang*) ≠ calm 2 (*informal*) = **hilarious**, uproarious, side-splitting, comical ≠ serious

icy ADJECTIVE **1** = **cold**, freezing, bitter, biting, raw, chill, chilly, frosty ≠ hot **2** = **slippery**, glassy, slippy (*informal* or *dialect*), like a sheet of glass **3** = **unfriendly**, cold, distant, aloof, frosty, frigid, unwelcoming ≠ friendly

idea NOUN **1** = **notion**, thought, view, teaching, opinion, belief, conclusion, hypothesis **2** = **understanding**, thought, view, opinion, concept, impression, perception **3** = **intention**, aim, purpose, object, plan, objective

⊕ WORD POWER
⊕ It is usually considered correct
⊕ to say that someone has *the*
⊕ *idea of doing something*, rather
⊕ than *the idea to do something*. For
⊕ example, you would say *he had*
⊕ *the idea of taking a holiday*, not *he*
⊕ *had the idea to take a holiday*.

ideal NOUN **1** = **epitome**, standard, dream, pattern, perfection, last word, paragon, paradigm **2** = **model**, prototype, paradigm ▷ ADJECTIVE = **perfect**, best, model, classic, supreme, ultimate, archetypal, exemplary ≠ imperfect

identical ADJECTIVE = **alike**, matching, twin, duplicate, indistinguishable, interchangeable ≠ different

identification NOUN **1** = **discovery**, recognition, determining, establishment, diagnosis, confirmation, divination **2** = **recognition**, naming, distinguishing, confirmation, pinpointing **3** = **connection**, relationship, association **4** = **understanding**, relationship, involvement, unity, sympathy, empathy, rapport, fellow feeling **5** = **ID**, identity card, proof of identity, photocard, electronic signature

identify VERB **1** = **recognize**, place, name, remember, spot, diagnose, make out, pinpoint **2** = **establish**, spot, confirm, demonstrate, pick out, certify, verify, mark out, flag up ▷ PHRASES: **identify something** *or* **someone with something** *or* **someone** = **equate with**, associate with; **identify with someone** = **relate to**, respond to, feel for, empathize with

identity NOUN = **individuality**, self, character, personality, existence, originality, separateness

idiot NOUN = **fool**, moron, twit (*informal, chiefly Brit.*), chump, imbecile, cretin, simpleton, halfwit, galah (*Austral. & N.Z. informal*), dorba *or* dorb (*Austral. slang*), bogan (*Austral. slang*)

idle ADJECTIVE **1** = **unoccupied**,

unemployed, redundant, inactive
≠ occupied 2 = **unused**, inactive,
out of order, out of service
3 = **lazy**, slow, slack, sluggish, lax,
negligent, inactive, inert ≠ busy
4 = **useless**, vain, pointless,
unsuccessful, ineffective,
worthless, futile, fruitless
≠ useful
▷ **VERB** *often with* **away** = **fritter**,
lounge, potter, loaf, dally, loiter,
dawdle, laze

idol NOUN 1 = **hero**, pin-up,
favourite, pet, darling, beloved
(*slang*), fave (*informal*) 2 = **graven
image**, god, deity

if CONJUNCTION 1 = **provided**,
assuming, given that, providing,
supposing, presuming, on
condition that, as long as
2 = **when**, whenever, every time,
any time

ignite VERB 1 = **catch fire**, burn,
burst into flames, inflame, flare
up, take fire 2 = **set fire to**, light,
set alight, torch, kindle

ignorance NOUN 1 = **lack of
education**, stupidity, foolishness
≠ knowledge 2 *with of*
= **unawareness of**, inexperience
of, unfamiliarity with, innocence
of, unconsciousness of

ignorant ADJECTIVE
1 = **uneducated**, illiterate
≠ educated 2 = **insensitive**, rude,
crass 3 *with* **of** = **uninformed
of**, unaware of, oblivious to,
innocent of, unconscious of,
inexperienced of, uninitiated
about, unenlightened about

≠ informed

ignore VERB 1 = **pay no attention
to**, neglect, disregard, slight,
overlook, scorn, spurn, rebuff
≠ pay attention to 2 = **overlook**,
discount, disregard, reject,
neglect, shrug off, pass over, brush
aside 3 = **snub**, slight, rebuff

ill ADJECTIVE 1 = **unwell**, sick, poorly
(*informal*), diseased, weak, crook
(*Austral. & N.Z. slang*), ailing, frail
≠ healthy 2 = **harmful**, bad,
damaging, evil, foul, unfortunate,
destructive, detrimental
≠ favourable
▷ NOUN = **problem**, trouble,
suffering, worry, injury, hurt,
strain, harm ≠ good
▷ ADVERB 1 = **badly**,
unfortunately, unfavourably,
inauspiciously 2 = **hardly**, barely,
scarcely, just, only just, by no
means, at a push ≠ well

illegal ADJECTIVE = **unlawful**,
banned, forbidden, prohibited,
criminal, outlawed, illicit,
unlicensed ≠ legal

illicit ADJECTIVE 1 = **illegal**,
criminal, prohibited, unlawful,
illegitimate, unlicensed,
unauthorized, felonious ≠ legal
2 = **forbidden**, improper, immoral,
guilty, clandestine, furtive

illness NOUN = **sickness**, disease,
infection, disorder, bug (*informal*),
ailment, affliction, malady

illuminate VERB 1 = **light up**,
brighten ≠ darken 2 = **explain**,
interpret, make clear, clarify,
clear up, enlighten, shed light on,

elucidate ≠ obscure

illuminating ADJECTIVE
= **informative**, revealing, enlightening, helpful, explanatory, instructive ≠ confusing

illusion NOUN 1 = **delusion**, misconception, misapprehension, fancy, fallacy, false impression, false belief 2 = **false impression**, appearance, impression, deception, fallacy ≠ reality 3 = **fantasy**, vision, hallucination, trick, spectre, mirage, daydream, apparition

illustrate VERB 1 = **demonstrate**, emphasize 2 = **explain**, sum up, summarize, bring home, point up, elucidate

illustrated ADJECTIVE = **pictured**, decorated, pictorial

illustration NOUN 1 = **example**, case, instance, sample, specimen, exemplar 2 = **picture**, drawing, painting, image, print, plate, figure, portrait

image NOUN 1 = **thought**, idea, vision, concept, impression, perception, mental picture, conceptualization 2 = **figure of speech** 3 = **reflection**, likeness, mirror image 4 = **figure**, idol, icon, fetish, talisman 5 = **replica**, copy, reproduction, counterpart, clone, facsimile, spitting image (*informal*), Doppelgänger 6 = **picture**, photo, photograph, representation, reproduction, snapshot

imaginary ADJECTIVE = **fictional**, made-up, invented, imagined, unreal, hypothetical, fictitious, illusory ≠ real

imagination NOUN 1 = **creativity**, vision, invention, ingenuity, enterprise, originality, inventiveness, resourcefulness 2 = **mind's eye**, fancy

imaginative ADJECTIVE = **creative**, original, inspired, enterprising, clever, ingenious, inventive ≠ unimaginative

imagine VERB 1 = **envisage**, see, picture, plan, think of, conjure up, envision, visualize 2 = **believe**, think, suppose, assume, suspect, guess (*informal, chiefly U.S. & Canad.*), take it, reckon

imitate VERB 1 = **copy**, follow, repeat, echo, emulate, ape, simulate, mirror 2 = **do an impression of**, mimic, copy

imitation NOUN 1 = **replica**, fake, reproduction, sham, forgery, counterfeiting, likeness, duplication 2 = **copying**, resemblance, mimicry 3 = **impression**, impersonation ▷ ADJECTIVE = **artificial**, mock, reproduction, dummy, synthetic, man-made, simulated, sham ≠ real

immaculate ADJECTIVE 1 = **clean**, spotless, neat, spruce, squeaky-clean, spick-and-span ≠ dirty 2 = **pure**, perfect, impeccable, flawless, faultless, above reproach ≠ corrupt 3 = **perfect**, flawless, impeccable, faultless, unblemished, untarnished, unexceptionable ≠ tainted

immediate ADJECTIVE
1 = **instant**, prompt, instantaneous, quick, on-the-spot, split-second ≠ later
2 = **nearest**, next, direct, close, near ≠ far

immediately ADVERB = **at once**, now, instantly, straight away, directly, promptly, right away, without delay

immense ADJECTIVE = **huge**, great, massive, vast, enormous, extensive, tremendous, very big, supersize ≠ tiny

immerse VERB 1 = **engross**, involve, absorb, busy, occupy, engage 2 = **plunge**, dip, submerge, sink, duck, bathe, douse, dunk

immigrant NOUN = **settler**, incomer, alien, stranger, outsider, newcomer, migrant, emigrant

imminent ADJECTIVE = **near**, coming, close, approaching, gathering, forthcoming, looming, impending ≠ remote

immoral ADJECTIVE = **wicked**, bad, wrong, corrupt, indecent, sinful, unethical, depraved ≠ moral

immortal ADJECTIVE 1 = **timeless**, eternal, everlasting, lasting, traditional, classic, enduring, perennial ≠ ephemeral
2 = **undying**, eternal, imperishable, deathless ≠ mortal
▷ NOUN 1 = **hero**, genius, great
2 = **god**, goddess, deity, divine being, immortal being, atua (N.Z.)

immune ▷ PHRASES: **immune**

from = **exempt from**, free from; **immune to** 1 = **resistant to**, free from, protected from, safe from, not open to, spared from, secure against, invulnerable to
2 = **unaffected by**, invulnerable to

immunity NOUN 1 = **exemption**, amnesty, indemnity, release, freedom, invulnerability 2 with **to** = **resistance**, protection, resilience, inoculation, immunization ≠ susceptibility

impact NOUN 1 = **effect**, influence, consequences, impression, repercussions, ramifications 2 = **collision**, contact, crash, knock, stroke, smash, bump, thump
▷ VERB = **hit**, strike, crash, clash, crush, ram, smack, collide

impair VERB = **worsen**, reduce, damage, injure, harm, undermine, weaken, diminish ≠ improve

impaired ADJECTIVE = **damaged**, flawed, faulty, defective, imperfect, unsound

impasse NOUN = **deadlock**, stalemate, standstill, dead end, standoff

impatient ADJECTIVE 1 = **cross**, annoyed, irritated, prickly, touchy, bad-tempered, intolerant, ill-tempered ≠ easy-going
2 = **eager**, longing, keen, anxious, hungry, enthusiastic, restless, avid ≠ calm

impeccable ADJECTIVE
= **faultless**, perfect, immaculate,

flawless, squeaky-clean, unblemished, unimpeachable, irreproachable ≠ flawed

impending ADJECTIVE = **looming**, coming, approaching, near, forthcoming, imminent, upcoming, in the pipeline

imperative ADJECTIVE = **urgent**, essential, pressing, vital, crucial ≠ unnecessary

imperial ADJECTIVE = **royal**, regal, kingly, queenly, princely, sovereign, majestic, monarchial

impetus NOUN 1 = **incentive**, push, spur, motivation, impulse, stimulus, catalyst, goad 2 = **force**, power, energy, momentum

implant VERB 1 = **insert**, fix, graft 2 = **instil**, infuse, inculcate

implement VERB = **carry out**, effect, carry through, complete, apply, perform, realize, fulfil ≠ hinder
▷ NOUN = **tool**, machine, device, instrument, appliance, apparatus, gadget, utensil

implicate VERB = **incriminate**, involve, embroil, entangle, inculpate ≠ dissociate
▷ PHRASE: **implicate something** or **someone in something** = **involve in**, associate with

implication NOUN
1 = **suggestion**, hint, inference, meaning, significance, presumption, overtone, innuendo
2 = **consequence**, result, development, upshot

implicit ADJECTIVE 1 = **implied**, understood, suggested, hinted

at, taken for granted, unspoken, inferred, tacit ≠ explicit
2 = **inherent**, underlying, intrinsic, latent, ingrained, inbuilt
3 = **absolute**, full, complete, firm, fixed, constant, utter, outright

implied ADJECTIVE = **suggested**, indirect, hinted at, implicit, unspoken, tacit, undeclared, unstated

imply VERB 1 = **suggest**, hint, insinuate, indicate, intimate, signify 2 = **involve**, mean, entail, require, indicate, point to, signify, presuppose

import VERB = **bring in**, buy in, ship in, introduce
▷ NOUN 1 (*formal*) = **significance**, concern, value, weight, consequence, substance, moment, magnitude
2 = **meaning**, implication, significance, sense, intention, substance, drift, thrust

importance NOUN
1 = **significance**, interest, concern, moment, value, weight, import, consequence
2 = **prestige**, standing, status, rule, authority, influence, distinction, esteem, mana (*N.Z.*)

important ADJECTIVE
1 = **significant**, critical, substantial, urgent, serious, far-reaching, momentous, seminal
≠ unimportant 2 = **powerful**, prominent, commanding, dominant, influential, eminent, high-ranking, authoritative, skookum (*Canad.*)

impose ▷ PHRASE: **impose something on** or **upon someone**
1 = **levy**, introduce, charge, establish, fix, institute, decree, ordain 2 = **inflict**, force, enforce, visit, press, apply, thrust, saddle (someone) with

imposing ADJECTIVE
= **impressive**, striking, grand, powerful, commanding, awesome, majestic, dignified ≠ unimposing

imposition NOUN
1 = **application**, introduction, levying 2 = **intrusion**, liberty, presumption

impossible ADJECTIVE 1 = **not possible**, out of the question, impracticable, unfeasible
2 = **unachievable**, out of the question, vain, unthinkable, inconceivable, far-fetched, unworkable, implausible ≠ possible 3 = **absurd**, crazy (informal), ridiculous, outrageous, ludicrous, unreasonable, preposterous, farcical

impotence NOUN
= **powerlessness**, inability, helplessness, weakness, incompetence, paralysis, frailty, incapacity ≠ powerfulness

impoverish VERB 1 = **bankrupt**, ruin, beggar, break 2 = **deplete**, drain, exhaust, diminish, use up, sap, wear out, reduce

impoverished ADJECTIVE = **poor**, needy, destitute, bankrupt, poverty-stricken, impecunious, penurious ≠ rich

impress VERB = **excite**, move, strike, touch, affect, inspire, amaze, overcome ▷ PHRASE: **impress something on** or **upon someone** = **stress**, bring home to, instil in, drum into, knock into, emphasize to, fix in, inculcate in

impression NOUN 1 = **idea**, feeling, thought, sense, view, assessment, judgment, reaction 2 = **effect**, influence, impact 3 = **imitation**, parody, impersonation, send-up (Brit. informal), takeoff (informal)
4 = **mark**, imprint, stamp, outline, hollow, dent, indentation

impressive ADJECTIVE = **grand**, striking, splendid, good, great (informal), fine, powerful, exciting ≠ unimpressive

imprint NOUN = **mark**, impression, stamp, indentation ▷ VERB = **engrave**, print, stamp, impress, etch, emboss

imprison VERB = **jail**, confine, detain, lock up, put away, intern, incarcerate, send down (informal) ≠ free

imprisoned ADJECTIVE = **jailed**, confined, locked up, inside (slang), in jail, captive, behind bars, incarcerated

imprisonment NOUN
= **confinement**, custody, detention, captivity, incarceration

improbable ADJECTIVE
1 = **doubtful**, unlikely, dubious, questionable, fanciful, far-fetched, implausible ≠ probable

2 = **unconvincing**, weak, unbelievable, preposterous ≠ convincing

improper ADJECTIVE
1 = **inappropriate**, unfit, unsuitable, out of place, unwarranted, uncalled-for ≠ appropriate 2 = **indecent**, vulgar, suggestive, unseemly, untoward, risqué, smutty, unbecoming ≠ decent

improve VERB 1 = **enhance**, better, add to, upgrade, touch up, ameliorate ≠ worsen 2 = **get better**, pick up, develop, advance

improvement NOUN
1 = **enhancement**, advancement, betterment 2 = **advance**, development, progress, recovery, upswing

improvise VERB 1 = **devise**, contrive, concoct, throw together 2 = **ad-lib**, invent, busk, wing it (*informal*), play it by ear (*informal*), extemporize, speak off the cuff (*informal*)

impulse NOUN = **urge**, longing, wish, notion, yearning, inclination, itch, whim

inaccurate ADJECTIVE
= **incorrect**, wrong, mistaken, faulty, unreliable, defective, erroneous, unsound ≠ accurate

inadequacy NOUN 1 = **shortage**, poverty, dearth, paucity, insufficiency, meagreness, scantiness 2 = **incompetence**, inability, deficiency, incapacity, ineffectiveness 3 = **shortcoming**, failing, weakness, defect, imperfection

inadequate ADJECTIVE
1 = **insufficient**, meagre, poor, lacking, scant, sparse, sketchy ≠ adequate 2 = **incapable**, incompetent, faulty, deficient, unqualified, not up to scratch (*informal*) ≠ capable

inadvertently ADVERB
= **unintentionally**, accidentally, by accident, mistakenly, unwittingly, by mistake, involuntarily ≠ deliberately

inaugural ADJECTIVE = **first**, opening, initial, maiden, introductory

incarnation NOUN
= **embodiment**, manifestation, epitome, type, personification

incense VERB = **anger**, infuriate, enrage, irritate, madden, inflame, rile (*informal*), make your blood boil (*informal*)

incensed ADJECTIVE = **angry**, furious, fuming, infuriated, enraged, maddened, indignant, irate, tooshie (*Austral. slang*), off the air (*Austral. slang*)

incentive NOUN = **inducement**, encouragement, spur, lure, bait, motivation, carrot (*informal*), stimulus ≠ disincentive

incident NOUN 1 = **disturbance**, scene, clash, disorder, confrontation, brawl, fracas, commotion 2 = **happening**, event, affair, business, fact, matter, occasion, episode
3 = **adventure**, drama, excitement, crisis, spectacle

incidentally ADVERB = **by the way**, in passing, en passant, parenthetically, by the bye

inclination NOUN 1 = **desire**, longing, aspiration, craving, hankering 2 = **tendency**, liking, disposition, penchant, propensity, predisposition, predilection, proclivity ≠ aversion

incline VERB = **predispose**, influence, persuade, prejudice, sway, dispose
▷ NOUN = **slope**, rise, dip, grade, descent, ascent, gradient

inclined ADJECTIVE 1 = **disposed**, given, prone, likely, liable, apt, predisposed 2 = **willing**, minded, disposed

include VERB 1 = **contain**, involve, incorporate, cover, consist of, take in, embrace, comprise ≠ exclude 2 = **count** 3 = **add**, enter, put in, insert

inclusion NOUN = **addition**, incorporation, introduction, insertion ≠ exclusion

inclusive ADJECTIVE = **comprehensive**, general, global, sweeping, blanket, umbrella, across-the-board, all-embracing ≠ limited

income NOUN = **revenue**, earnings, pay, returns, profits, wages, yield, proceeds

incoming ADJECTIVE 1 = **arriving**, landing, approaching, entering, returning, homeward ≠ departing 2 = **new**

incompatible ADJECTIVE = **inconsistent**, conflicting, contradictory, incongruous, unsuited, mismatched ≠ compatible

incompetence NOUN = **ineptitude**, inability, inadequacy, incapacity, ineffectiveness, uselessness, unfitness, incapability

incompetent ADJECTIVE = **inept**, useless, incapable, floundering, bungling, unfit, ineffectual, inexpert ≠ competent

incomplete ADJECTIVE = **unfinished**, partial, wanting, deficient, imperfect, fragmentary, half-pie (*N.Z. informal*) ≠ complete

inconsistency NOUN 1 = **unreliability**, instability, unpredictability, fickleness, unsteadiness 2 = **incompatibility**, discrepancy, disparity, disagreement, variance, divergence, incongruity

inconsistent ADJECTIVE 1 = **changeable**, variable, unpredictable, unstable, erratic, fickle, capricious, unsteady ≠ consistent 2 = **incompatible**, conflicting, at odds, contradictory, incongruous, discordant, out of step, irreconcilable ≠ compatible

inconvenience NOUN = **trouble**, difficulty, bother, fuss, disadvantage, disturbance, disruption, nuisance, uphill (*S. African*)
▷ VERB = **trouble**, bother, disturb, upset, disrupt, put out, discommode

incorporate VERB 1 = **include**, contain, take in, embrace, integrate, encompass, assimilate, comprise of 2 = **integrate**, include, absorb, merge, fuse, assimilate, subsume 3 = **blend**, combine, compound, mingle

incorrect ADJECTIVE = **false**, wrong, mistaken, flawed, faulty, inaccurate, untrue, erroneous ≠ correct

increase VERB 1 = **raise**, extend, boost, expand, develop, advance, strengthen, widen ≠ decrease 2 = **grow**, develop, spread, expand, swell, enlarge, escalate, multiply ≠ shrink
▷ NOUN = **growth**, rise, development, gain, expansion, extension, proliferation, enlargement

increasingly ADVERB = **progressively**, more and more

incredible ADJECTIVE 1 (*informal*) = **amazing**, wonderful, stunning, extraordinary, overwhelming, astonishing, staggering, sensational (*informal*) 2 = **unbelievable**, unthinkable, improbable, inconceivable, preposterous, unconvincing, unimaginable, far-fetched

incumbent NOUN = **holder**, keeper, bearer
▷ ADJECTIVE (*formal*) = **obligatory**, required, necessary, essential, binding, compulsory, mandatory, imperative

incur VERB = **sustain**, experience, suffer, gain, earn, collect, meet

with, provoke

indecent ADJECTIVE 1 = **obscene**, lewd, dirty, inappropriate, rude, crude, filthy, improper ≠ decent 2 = **unbecoming**, unsuitable, vulgar, unseemly, undignified, indecorous ≠ proper

indeed ADVERB 1 = **certainly**, yes, definitely, surely, truly, undoubtedly, without doubt, indisputably 2 = **really**, actually, in fact, certainly, genuinely, in truth, in actuality

indefinitely ADVERB = **endlessly**, continually, for ever, ad infinitum

independence NOUN = **freedom**, liberty, autonomy, sovereignty, self-rule, self-sufficiency, self-reliance, rangatiratanga (*N.Z.*) ≠ subjugation

independent ADJECTIVE 1 = **separate**, unattached, uncontrolled, unconstrained ≠ controlled 2 = **self-sufficient**, free, liberated, self-contained, self-reliant, self-supporting 3 = **self-governing**, free, autonomous, liberated, sovereign, self-determining, nonaligned ≠ subject

independently ADVERB = **separately**, alone, solo, on your own, by yourself, unaided, individually, autonomously

indicate VERB 1 = **show**, suggest, reveal, display, demonstrate, point to, imply, manifest, flag up 2 = **imply**, suggest, hint, intimate, signify, insinuate 3 = **point to**, point out, specify, gesture towards, designate **4** = **register**, show, record, read, express, display, demonstrate

indication NOUN = **sign**, mark, evidence, suggestion, symptom, hint, clue, manifestation

indicator NOUN = **sign**, mark, measure, guide, signal, symbol, meter, gauge

indict VERB = **charge**, accuse, prosecute, summon, impeach, arraign

indictment NOUN = **charge**, allegation, prosecution, accusation, impeachment, summons, arraignment

indifference NOUN = **disregard**, apathy, negligence, detachment, coolness, coldness, nonchalance, aloofness ≠ concern

indifferent ADJECTIVE
1 = **unconcerned**, detached, cold, cool, callous, aloof, unmoved, unsympathetic ≠ concerned
2 = **mediocre**, ordinary, moderate, so-so (*informal*), passable, undistinguished, no great shakes (*informal*), half-pie (*N.Z. informal*) ≠ excellent

indignation NOUN
= **resentment**, anger, rage, exasperation, pique, umbrage

indirect ADJECTIVE **1** = **related**, secondary, subsidiary, incidental, unintended **2** = **circuitous**, roundabout, curving, wandering, rambling, deviant, meandering, tortuous ≠ direct

indispensable ADJECTIVE
= **essential**, necessary, needed,

key, vital, crucial, imperative, requisite ≠ dispensable

individual ADJECTIVE
1 = **separate**, independent, isolated, lone, solitary
≠ collective **2** = **unique**, special, fresh, novel, exclusive, singular, idiosyncratic, unorthodox
≠ conventional
▷ NOUN = **person**, being, human, unit, character, soul, creature

individually ADVERB
= **separately**, independently, singly, one by one, one at a time

induce VERB **1** = **cause**, produce, create, effect, lead to, occasion, generate, bring about ≠ prevent
2 = **persuade**, encourage, influence, convince, urge, prompt, sway, entice ≠ dissuade

indulge VERB **1** = **gratify**, satisfy, feed, give way to, yield to, pander to, gladden **2** = **spoil**, pamper, cosset, humour, give in to, coddle, mollycoddle, overindulge
▷ PHRASE: **indulge yourself**
= **treat yourself**, splash out, spoil yourself, luxuriate in something, overindulge yourself

indulgence NOUN **1** = **luxury**, treat, extravagance, favour, privilege **2** = **gratification**, satisfaction, fulfilment, appeasement, satiation

industrialist NOUN = **capitalist**, tycoon, magnate, manufacturer, captain of industry, big businessman

industry NOUN **1** = **business**, production, manufacturing, trade, commerce **2** = **trade**, world, business, service, line, field, profession, occupation **3** = **diligence**, effort, labour, hard work, trouble, activity, application, endeavour

ineffective ADJECTIVE
1 = **unproductive**, useless, futile, vain, unsuccessful, pointless, fruitless, ineffectual ≠ effective
2 = **inefficient**, useless, poor, powerless, unfit, worthless, inept, impotent

inefficient ADJECTIVE
1 = **wasteful**, uneconomical, profligate **2** = **incompetent**, inept, weak, bungling, ineffectual, disorganized ≠ efficient

inequality NOUN = **disparity**, prejudice, difference, bias, diversity, irregularity, unevenness, disproportion

inevitable ADJECTIVE
= **unavoidable**, inescapable, inexorable, sure, certain, fixed, assured, fated ≠ avoidable

inevitably ADVERB
= **unavoidably**, naturally, necessarily, surely, certainly, as a result, automatically, consequently

inexpensive ADJECTIVE = **cheap**, reasonable, budget, bargain, modest, economical ≠ expensive

inexperienced ADJECTIVE = **new**, green, raw, callow, immature, untried, unpractised, unversed ≠ experienced

infamous ADJECTIVE = **notorious**, ignominious, disreputable, ill-

famed ≠ esteemed

infancy NOUN = **beginnings**, start, birth, roots, seeds, origins, dawn, outset ≠ end

infant NOUN = **baby**, child, babe, toddler, tot, bairn (*Scot.*), littlie (*Austral. informal*), ankle-biter (*Austral. slang*), tacker (*Austral. slang*)

infect VERB **1** = **contaminate**
2 = **pollute**, poison, corrupt, contaminate, taint, defile **3** = **affect**, move, upset, overcome, stir, disturb

infection NOUN = **disease**, condition, complaint, illness, virus, disorder, corruption, poison

infectious ADJECTIVE = **catching**, spreading, contagious, communicable, virulent, transmittable

inferior ADJECTIVE = **lower**, minor, secondary, subsidiary, lesser, humble, subordinate, lowly ≠ superior
▷ NOUN = **underling**, junior, subordinate, lesser, menial, minion

infertility NOUN = **sterility**, barrenness, unproductiveness, infecundity

infiltrate VERB = **penetrate**, pervade, permeate, percolate, filter through to, make inroads into, sneak into (*informal*), insinuate yourself

infinite ADJECTIVE **1** = **vast**, enormous, immense, countless, measureless **2** = **limitless**, endless, unlimited, eternal, never-ending, boundless, everlasting, inexhaustible ≠ finite

inflame VERB = **enrage**, stimulate, provoke, excite, anger, arouse, rouse, infuriate ≠ calm

inflamed ADJECTIVE = **swollen**, sore, red, hot, infected, fevered

inflate VERB 1 = **blow up**, pump up, swell, dilate, distend, bloat, puff up or out ≠ deflate 2 = **increase**, expand, enlarge ≠ diminish 3 = **exaggerate**, embroider, embellish, enlarge, amplify, overstate, overestimate, overemphasize

inflated ADJECTIVE = **exaggerated**, swollen, overblown

inflation NOUN = **increase**, expansion, extension, swelling, escalation, enlargement

inflict VERB = **impose**, administer, visit, apply, deliver, levy, wreak, mete or deal out

influence NOUN 1 = **control**, power, authority, direction, command, domination, supremacy, mastery, mana (N.Z.) 2 = **power**, authority, pull (informal), importance, prestige, clout (informal), leverage 3 = **spell**, hold, power, weight, magic, sway, allure, magnetism ▷ VERB 1 = **affect**, have an effect on, have an impact on, control, concern, direct, guide, bear upon 2 = **persuade**, prompt, urge, induce, entice, coax, incite, instigate

influential ADJECTIVE

1 = **important**, powerful, telling, leading, inspiring, potent, authoritative, weighty ≠ unimportant 2 = **instrumental**, important, significant, crucial

influx NOUN = **arrival**, rush, invasion, incursion, inundation, inrush

inform VERB = **tell**, advise, notify, instruct, enlighten, communicate to, tip someone off ▷ PHRASE: **inform on someone** = **betray**, denounce, shop (slang, chiefly Brit.), give someone away, incriminate, blow the whistle on (informal), grass on (Brit. slang), double-cross (informal), dob someone in (Austral. & N.Z. slang)

informal ADJECTIVE 1 = **natural**, relaxed, casual, familiar, unofficial, laid-back, easy-going, colloquial 2 = **relaxed**, easy, comfortable, simple, natural, casual, cosy, laid-back (informal) ≠ formal 3 = **casual**, comfortable, leisure, everyday, simple 4 = **unofficial**, irregular ≠ official

information NOUN = **facts**, news, report, message, notice, knowledge, data, intelligence, drum (Austral. informal), heads up (U.S. & Canad.)

informative ADJECTIVE = **instructive**, revealing, educational, forthcoming, illuminating, enlightening, chatty, communicative

informed ADJECTIVE = **knowledgeable**, up to date,

enlightened, learned, expert, familiar, versed, in the picture

infuriate VERB = **enrage**, anger, provoke, irritate, incense, madden, exasperate, rile ≠ soothe

infuriating ADJECTIVE = **annoying**, irritating, provoking, galling, maddening, exasperating, vexatious

ingenious ADJECTIVE = **creative**, original, brilliant, clever, bright, shrewd, inventive, crafty ≠ unimaginative

ingredient NOUN = **component**, part, element, feature, piece, unit, item, aspect

inhabit VERB = **live in**, occupy, populate, reside in, dwell in, abide in

inhabitant NOUN = **occupant**, resident, citizen, local, native, tenant, inmate, dweller

inhabited ADJECTIVE = **populated**, peopled, occupied, developed, settled, tenanted, colonized

inhale VERB = **breathe in**, gasp, draw in, suck in, respire ≠ exhale

inherent ADJECTIVE = **intrinsic**, natural, essential, native, fundamental, hereditary, instinctive, innate ≠ extraneous

inherit VERB = **be left**, come into, be willed, succeed to, fall heir to

inheritance NOUN = **legacy**, heritage, bequest, birthright, patrimony

inhibit VERB 1 = **hinder**, check, frustrate, curb, restrain, constrain, obstruct, impede ≠ further 2 = **prevent**, stop, frustrate ≠ allow

inhibited ADJECTIVE = **shy**, reserved, guarded, subdued, repressed, constrained, self-conscious, reticent ≠ uninhibited

initial ADJECTIVE = **opening**, first, earliest, beginning, primary, maiden, introductory, embryonic ≠ final

initially ADVERB = **at first**, first, firstly, originally, primarily, in the beginning, at or in the beginning

initiate VERB 1 = **begin**, start, open, launch, kick off (*informal*), embark on, originate, set about 2 = **introduce**, admit, enlist, enrol, launch, establish, invest, recruit ▷ NOUN = **novice**, member, pupil, convert, amateur, newcomer, beginner, trainee ▷ PHRASE: initiate someone into something = **instruct in**, train in, coach in, acquaint with, drill in, make aware of, teach about, tutor in

initiative NOUN 1 = **advantage**, start, lead, upper hand 2 = **enterprise**, drive, energy, leadership, ambition, daring, enthusiasm, dynamism

inject VERB 1 = **vaccinate**, administer, inoculate 2 = **introduce**, bring in, insert, instil, infuse, breathe

injection NOUN 1 = **vaccination**, shot (*informal*), jab (*informal*), dose, booster, immunization, inoculation 2 = **introduction**, investment, insertion, advancement, dose, infusion

injunction NOUN = **order**, ruling, command, instruction, mandate, precept, exhortation

injure VERB 1 = **hurt**, wound, harm, damage, smash, crush, mar, shatter, mangulate (*Austral. slang*) 2 = **damage**, harm, ruin, wreck, spoil, impair, crool *or* cruel (*Austral. slang*) 3 = **undermine**, damage

injured ADJECTIVE = **hurt**, damaged, wounded, broken, cut, crushed, disabled, challenged, weakened, crook (*Austral. & N.Z. slang*)

injury NOUN 1 = **wound**, cut, damage, trauma (*pathology*), gash, lesion, laceration 2 = **harm**, suffering, damage, ill, hurt, disability, misfortune, affliction 3 = **wrong**, offence, insult, detriment, disservice

injustice NOUN 1 = **unfairness**, discrimination, prejudice, bias, inequality, oppression, intolerance, bigotry ≠ justice 2 = **wrong**, injury, crime, error, offence, sin, misdeed, transgression

inland ADJECTIVE = **interior**, internal, upcountry

inner ADJECTIVE 1 = **inside**, internal, interior, inward ≠ outer 2 = **central**, middle, internal, interior 3 = **hidden**, deep, secret, underlying, obscure, repressed, unrevealed ≠ obvious

innocence NOUN 1 = **naiveté**, simplicity, inexperience, credulity, gullibility, ingenuousness, artlessness, unworldliness ≠ worldliness 2 = **blamelessness**, clean hands, uprightness, irreproachability, guiltlessness ≠ guilt 3 = **chastity**, virtue, purity, modesty, celibacy, continence, maidenhood

innocent ADJECTIVE 1 = **not guilty**, in the clear, blameless, clean, honest, uninvolved, irreproachable, guiltless ≠ guilty 2 = **naive**, open, trusting, simple, childlike, gullible, unsophisticated, unworldly ≠ worldly 3 = **harmless**, innocuous, inoffensive, well-meant, unobjectionable, well-intentioned

innovation NOUN 1 = **change**, revolution, departure, introduction, variation, transformation, upheaval, alteration 2 = **newness**, novelty, originality, freshness, modernization, uniqueness

inquest NOUN = **inquiry**, investigation, probe, inquisition

inquire *or* **enquire** VERB = **ask**, question, query, quiz ▷ PHRASE: **inquire into** = **investigate**, study, examine, research, explore, look into, probe into, make inquiries into

inquiry *or* **enquiry** NOUN 1 = **question**, query, investigation 2 = **investigation**, study, review, survey, examination, probe, inspection, exploration

3 = research, investigation, analysis, inspection, exploration, interrogation

insane ADJECTIVE **1 = mad**, crazy, mentally ill, crazed, demented, deranged, out of your mind, off the air (*Austral. slang*), porangi (*N.Z.*) ≠ sane **2 = stupid**, foolish, daft (*informal*), irresponsible, irrational, senseless, preposterous, impractical ≠ reasonable

insect NOUN **= bug**, creepy-crawly (*Brit. informal*), gogga (*S. African informal*)

▷ *see* **ants, bees and wasps, beetles, butterflies and moths, flies**

insecure ADJECTIVE
1 = unconfident, worried, anxious, afraid, shy, uncertain, unsure, timid ≠ confident
2 = unsafe, exposed, vulnerable, wide-open, unprotected, defenceless, unguarded ≠ safe

insecurity NOUN **= anxiety**, fear, worry, uncertainty ≠ confidence

insert VERB **= put**, place, position, slip, slide, slot, thrust, stick in

inside NOUN **= interior**, contents, core, nucleus
▷ PLURAL NOUN (*informal*)
= stomach, guts, belly, bowels, innards (*informal*), entrails, viscera, vitals
▷ ADJECTIVE **1 = inner**, internal, interior, inward ≠ outside
2 = confidential, private, secret, internal, exclusive, restricted, privileged, classified

▷ ADVERB **= indoors**, in, within, under cover

insight NOUN **1 = understanding**, perception, sense, knowledge, vision, judgment, awareness, grasp **2** *with* **into = understanding**, perception, awareness, experience, description, introduction, observation, judgment

insignificant ADJECTIVE
= unimportant, minor, irrelevant, petty, trivial, meaningless, trifling, paltry ≠ important

insist VERB **1** lay down the law, put your foot down (*informal*)
2 = demand, order, require, command, dictate, entreat
3 = assert, state, maintain, claim, declare, repeat, vow, swear

insistence NOUN **1 = demand**, command, dictate, entreaty, importunity **2 = assertion**, claim, statement, declaration, persistence, pronouncement

inspect VERB **1 = examine**, check, look at, view, survey, look over, scrutinize, go over *or* through
2 = check, examine, investigate, look at, survey, vet, look over, go over *or* through

inspection NOUN
1 = examination, investigation, scrutiny, once-over (*informal*)
2 = check, search, investigation, review, survey, examination, scrutiny, once-over (*informal*)

inspector NOUN **= examiner**, investigator, supervisor, monitor, superintendent, auditor, censor,

- **INSECTS**
- body louse, cootie (*U.S. & N.Z.*), or (*N.Z. slang*) kutu
- bookworm
- caddis worm or caseworm
- cankerworm
- cochineal or cochineal insect
- cockroach
- crab (louse)
- cricket
- earwig, or (*Scot. dialect*) clipshears, or clipshear
- flea
- grasshopper
- katydid
- locust
- louse or (*N.Z.*) kutu
- mantis or praying mantis
- measuring worm, looper, or inchworm
- midge
- mosquito
- nit
- phylloxera
- scale insect
- silkworm
- silverfish
- stick insect or (*U.S. & Canad.*) walking stick
- thrips
- treehopper
- weta (*N.Z.*)
- wireworm
- woodworm

surveyor

inspiration NOUN
1 = **imagination**, creativity, ingenuity, insight, originality, inventiveness, cleverness
2 = **motivation**, example, model, boost, spur, incentive, revelation, stimulus ≠ deterrent
3 = **influence**, spur, stimulus, muse

inspire VERB 1 = **motivate**, stimulate, encourage, influence, spur, animate, enliven, galvanize ≠ discourage 2 = **give rise to**, produce, result in, engender

inspired ADJECTIVE 1 = **brilliant**, wonderful, impressive, outstanding, thrilling, memorable, dazzling, superlative
2 = **stimulated**, uplifted, exhilarated, enthused, elated

inspiring ADJECTIVE = **uplifting**, exciting, moving, stirring, stimulating, rousing, exhilarating, heartening ≠ uninspiring

instability NOUN
1 = **uncertainty**, insecurity, vulnerability, volatility, unpredictability, fluctuation, impermanence, unsteadiness ≠ stability 2 = **imbalance**, variability, unpredictability, unsteadiness, changeableness

install VERB 1 = **set up**, put in, place, position, station, establish, lay, fix 2 = **institute**, establish, introduce, invest, ordain, inaugurate, induct 3 = **settle**, position, plant, establish, lodge, ensconce

installation NOUN 1 = **setting up**, fitting, instalment, placing, positioning, establishment
2 = **appointment**, ordination, inauguration, induction,

investiture
instalment NOUN 1 = **payment**, repayment, part payment 2 = **part**, section, chapter, episode, portion, division

instance NOUN = **example**, case, occurrence, occasion, sample, illustration
▷ VERB = **name**, mention, identify, point out, advance, quote, refer to, point to

instant NOUN 1 = **moment**, second, flash, split second, jiffy (*informal*), trice, twinkling of an eye (*informal*) 2 = **time**, point, hour, moment, stage, occasion, phase, juncture
▷ ADJECTIVE 1 = **immediate**, prompt, instantaneous, direct, quick, on-the-spot, split-second 2 = **ready-made**, fast, convenience, ready-mixed, ready-cooked, precooked

instantly ADVERB = **immediately**, at once, straight away, now, directly, right away, instantaneously, this minute

instead ADVERB = **rather**, alternatively, preferably, in preference, in lieu, on second thoughts ▷ PHRASE: **instead of** = **in place of**, rather than, in preference to, in lieu of, in contrast with

instinct NOUN 1 = **natural inclination**, talent, tendency, faculty, inclination, knack, predisposition, proclivity 2 = **talent**, skill, gift, capacity, bent, genius, faculty, knack

3 = **intuition**, impulse

instinctive ADJECTIVE = **natural**, inborn, automatic, unconscious, inherent, spontaneous, reflex, innate ≠ acquired

instinctively ADVERB = **intuitively**, naturally, automatically, without thinking, involuntarily, by instinct

institute NOUN = **establishment**, body, centre, school, university, society, association, college
▷ VERB = **establish**, start, found, launch, set up, introduce, fix, organize ≠ end

institution NOUN 1 = **establishment**, body, centre, school, university, society, association, college 2 = **custom**, practice, tradition, law, rule, procedure, convention, ritual

institutional ADJECTIVE = **conventional**, accepted, established, formal, routine, orthodox, procedural

instruct VERB 1 = **order**, tell, direct, charge, bid, command, mandate, enjoin 2 = **teach**, school, train, coach, educate, drill, tutor

instruction NOUN 1 = **order**, ruling, command, rule, demand, regulation, dictate, decree 2 = **teaching**, schooling, training, grounding, education, coaching, lesson(s), guidance
▷ PLURAL NOUN = **information**, rules, advice, directions, recommendations, guidance, specifications

instructor NOUN = **teacher**, coach, guide, adviser, trainer, demonstrator, tutor, mentor

instrument NOUN 1 = **tool**, device, implement, mechanism, appliance, apparatus, gadget, contraption (*informal*) 2 = **agent**, means, medium, agency, vehicle, mechanism, organ

instrumental ADJECTIVE = **active**, involved, influential, useful, helpful, contributory

insufficient ADJECTIVE = **inadequate**, scant, meagre, short, sparse, deficient, lacking ≠ ample

insulate VERB = **isolate**, protect, screen, defend, shelter, shield, cut off, cushion

insult VERB = **offend**, abuse, wound, slight, put down, snub, malign, affront ≠ praise
▷ NOUN 1 = **jibe**, slight, put-down, abuse, snub, barb, affront, abusive remark 2 = **offence**, slight, snub, slur, affront, slap in the face (*informal*), kick in the teeth (*informal*), insolence

insulting ADJECTIVE = **offensive**, rude, abusive, degrading, contemptuous, disparaging, scurrilous, insolent ≠ complimentary

insurance NOUN 1 = **assurance**, cover, security, protection, safeguard, indemnity
2 = **protection**, security, guarantee, shelter, safeguard, warranty

insure VERB 1 = **assure**, cover, protect, guarantee, warrant, underwrite, indemnify
2 = **protect**, cover, safeguard

intact ADJECTIVE = **undamaged**, whole, complete, sound, perfect, entire, unscathed, unbroken ≠ damaged

integral ADJECTIVE = **essential**, basic, fundamental, necessary, component, constituent, indispensable, intrinsic ≠ inessential

integrate VERB = **join**, unite, combine, blend, incorporate, merge, fuse, assimilate ≠ separate

integrity NOUN 1 = **honesty**, principle, honour, virtue, goodness, morality, purity, probity ≠ dishonesty 2 = **unity**, unification, cohesion, coherence, wholeness, soundness, completeness

intellect NOUN = **intelligence**, mind, reason, understanding, sense, brains (*informal*), judgment

intellectual
ADJECTIVE = **scholarly**, learned, academic, lettered, intelligent, cerebral, erudite, scholastic ≠ stupid
▷ NOUN = **academic**, expert, genius, thinker, master, mastermind, maestro, highbrow, fundi (*S. African*), acca (*Austral. slang*) ≠ idiot

intelligence NOUN 1 = **intellect**, understanding, brains (*informal*), sense, knowledge, judgment, wit, perception ≠ stupidity

2 = **information**, news, facts, report, findings, knowledge, data, notification, heads up (*U.S. & Canad.*) ≠ misinformation

intelligent ADJECTIVE = **clever**, bright, smart, sharp, enlightened, knowledgeable, well-informed, brainy (*informal*) ≠ stupid

intend VERB = **plan**, mean, aim, propose, purpose, have in mind *or* view

intense ADJECTIVE **1** = **extreme**, great, severe, fierce, deep, powerful, supreme, acute ≠ mild **2** = **fierce**, tough **3** = **passionate**, emotional, fierce, heightened, ardent, fanatical, fervent, heartfelt ≠ indifferent

● **WORD POWER**
● *Intense* is sometimes wrongly
● used where *intensive* is meant:
● *the land is under intensive* (not
● *intense*) *cultivation. Intensely*
● is sometimes wrongly used
● where *intently* is meant: *he*
● *listened intently* (not *intensely*).

intensify VERB **1** = **increase**, raise, add to, strengthen, reinforce, widen, heighten, sharpen ≠ decrease **2** = **escalate**, increase, widen, deepen

intensity NOUN **1** = **force**, strength, fierceness **2** = **passion**, emotion, fervour, force, strength, fanaticism, ardour, vehemence

intensive ADJECTIVE = **concentrated**, thorough, exhaustive, full, demanding, detailed, complete, serious

intent ADJECTIVE = **absorbed**,

intense, fascinated, preoccupied, enthralled, attentive, watchful, engrossed ≠ indifferent
▷ NOUN = **intention**, aim, purpose, meaning, end, plan, goal, design ≠ chance

intention NOUN = **aim**, plan, idea, goal, end, design, target, wish

inter VERB = **bury**, lay to rest, entomb, consign to the grave

intercept VERB = **catch**, stop, block, seize, cut off, interrupt, head off, obstruct

intercourse NOUN **1** = **sexual intercourse**, sex (*informal*), copulation, coitus, carnal knowledge **2** = **contact**, communication, commerce, dealings

interest NOUN **1** *often plural* = **hobby**, activity, pursuit, entertainment, recreation, amusement, preoccupation, diversion **2** *often plural* = **advantage**, good, benefit, profit **3** = **stake**, investment
▷ VERB = **arouse your curiosity**, fascinate, attract, grip, entertain, intrigue, divert, captivate ≠ bore

interested ADJECTIVE **1** = **curious**, attracted, excited, drawn, keen, gripped, fascinated, captivated ≠ uninterested **2** = **involved**, concerned, affected, implicated

interesting ADJECTIVE = **intriguing**, absorbing, appealing, attractive, engaging, gripping, entrancing, stimulating ≠ uninteresting

interface NOUN = **connection**,

link, boundary, border, frontier

interfere VERB = **meddle**, intervene, intrude, butt in, tamper, pry, encroach, stick your oar in (*informal*) ▷ **PHRASE: interfere with something or someone** = **conflict with**, check, clash, handicap, hamper, disrupt, inhibit, thwart

interference NOUN = **intrusion**, intervention, meddling, opposition, conflict, obstruction

interim ADJECTIVE = **temporary**, provisional, makeshift, acting, caretaker, improvised, stopgap

interior NOUN = **inside**, centre, heart, middle, depths, core, nucleus ▷ ADJECTIVE 1 = **inside**, internal, inner ≠ exterior 2 = **mental**, emotional, psychological, private, personal, secret, hidden, spiritual

intermediary NOUN = **mediator**, agent, middleman, broker, go-between

intermediate ADJECTIVE = **middle**, mid, halfway, in-between (*informal*), midway, intervening, transitional, median

internal ADJECTIVE 1 = **domestic**, home, national, local, civic, in-house, intramural 2 = **inner**, inside, interior ≠ external

international ADJECTIVE = **global**, world, worldwide, universal, cosmopolitan, intercontinental

internet NOUN ▷ **PHRASE: the internet** = **the information superhighway**, the net (*informal*), the web (*informal*), the World Wide Web, cyberspace, the cloud, blogosphere, the interweb (*facetious*), blogstream, extranet, podosphere

interpret VERB 1 = **take**, understand, explain, construe 2 = **translate**, transliterate 3 = **explain**, make sense of, decode, decipher, elucidate 4 = **understand**, read, crack, solve, figure out (*informal*), comprehend, decode, deduce 5 = **portray**, present, perform, render, depict, enact, act out

interpretation NOUN 1 = **explanation**, analysis, exposition, elucidation 2 = **performance**, portrayal, presentation, reading, rendition 3 = **reading**, study, review, version, analysis, explanation, examination, evaluation

interrogation NOUN = **questioning**, inquiry, examination, grilling (*informal*), cross-examination, inquisition, third degree (*informal*)

interrupt VERB 1 = **intrude**, disturb, intervene, interfere (with), break in, heckle, butt in, barge in (*informal*) 2 = **suspend**, stop, end, delay, cease, postpone, shelve, put off

interruption NOUN 1 = **disruption**, break, disturbance, hitch, intrusion 2 = **stoppage**, pause, suspension

interval NOUN 1 = **period**, spell, space, stretch, pause, span 2 = **break**, interlude, intermission, rest, gap, pause, respite, lull

3 = **delay**, gap, hold-up, stoppage
4 = **stretch**, space
intervene VERB 1 = **step in**
(*informal*), interfere, mediate,
intrude, intercede, arbitrate, take
a hand (*informal*) 2 = **interrupt**,
involve yourself 3 = **happen**,
occur, take place, follow, arise,
ensue, befall, materialize
intervention NOUN = **mediation**,
interference, intrusion,
arbitration, conciliation, agency
interview NOUN 1 = **meeting**
2 = **audience**, talk, conference,
exchange, dialogue, consultation,
press conference
▷ VERB 1 = **examine**, talk
to 2 = **question**, interrogate,
examine, investigate, pump, grill
(*informal*), quiz, cross-examine
interviewer NOUN = **questioner**,
reporter, investigator, examiner,
interrogator
intimacy NOUN = **familiarity**,
closeness, confidentiality
≠ aloofness
intimate¹ ADJECTIVE 1 = **close**,
dear, loving, near, familiar, thick
(*informal*), devoted, confidential
≠ distant 2 = **private**, personal,
confidential, special, individual,
secret, exclusive ≠ public
3 = **detailed**, minute, full,
deep, particular, immediate,
comprehensive, profound
4 = **cosy**, relaxed, friendly,
informal, harmonious, snug,
comfy (*informal*), warm
▷ NOUN = **friend**, close friend,
crony, cobber (*Austral.* & *N.Z.*

old-fashioned, *informal*), confidant
or confidante, (constant)
companion, E hoa (*N.Z.*)
≠ stranger
intimate² VERB 1 = **suggest**,
indicate, hint, imply, insinuate
2 = **announce**, state, declare,
communicate, make known
intimately ADVERB 1 = **closely**,
personally, warmly, familiarly,
tenderly, affectionately,
confidentially, confidingly
2 = **fully**, very well, thoroughly, in
detail, inside out
intimidate VERB = **frighten**,
pressure, threaten, scare, bully,
plague, hound, daunt
intimidation NOUN = **bullying**,
pressure, threat(s), menaces,
coercion, arm-twisting (*informal*),
browbeating, terrorization
intricate ADJECTIVE
= **complicated**, involved, complex,
fancy, elaborate, tangled,
tortuous, convoluted ≠ simple
intrigue NOUN 1 = **plot**, scheme,
conspiracy, manoeuvre, collusion,
stratagem, chicanery, wile
2 = **affair**, romance, intimacy,
liaison, amour
▷ VERB 1 = **interest**, fascinate,
attract, rivet, titillate 2 = **plot**,
scheme, manoeuvre, conspire,
connive, machinate
intriguing ADJECTIVE
= **interesting**, fascinating,
absorbing, exciting, engaging,
gripping, stimulating, compelling
introduce VERB 1 = **bring in**,
establish, set up, start, found,

launch, institute, pioneer
2 = present, acquaint, make
known, familiarize **3 = suggest**,
air, advance, submit, bring up, put
forward, broach, moot **4 = add**,
insert, inject, throw in (*informal*),
infuse

introduction NOUN **1 = launch**,
institution, pioneering,
inauguration ≠ elimination
2 = opening, prelude, preface,
lead-in, preamble, foreword,
prologue, intro (*informal*)
≠ conclusion

introductory ADJECTIVE
1 = preliminary, first, initial,
inaugural, preparatory
≠ concluding **2 = starting**,
opening, initial

intruder NOUN **= trespasser**,
invader, prowler, interloper,
infiltrator, gate-crasher (*informal*)

intrusion NOUN **1 = interruption**,
interference, infringement,
trespass, encroachment
2 = invasion, breach,
infringement, encroachment,
infraction, usurpation

intuition NOUN **1 = instinct**,
perception, insight, sixth sense
2 = feeling, idea, impression,
suspicion, premonition, inkling,
presentiment

invade VERB **1 = attack**, storm,
assault, capture, occupy, seize,
raid, overwhelm **2 = infest**,
swarm, overrun, ravage, beset,
pervade, permeate

invader NOUN **= attacker**, raider,
plunderer, aggressor, trespasser

invalid¹ NOUN **= patient**, sufferer,
convalescent, valetudinarian
▷ ADJECTIVE **= disabled**,
challenged, ill, sick, ailing, frail,
infirm, bedridden

invalid² ADJECTIVE **1 = null and
void**, void, worthless, inoperative
≠ valid **2 = unfounded**, false,
illogical, irrational, unsound,
fallacious ≠ sound

invaluable ADJECTIVE **= precious**,
valuable, priceless, inestimable,
worth your *or* its weight in gold
≠ worthless

invariably ADVERB **= always**,
regularly, constantly, repeatedly,
consistently, continually,
eternally, habitually

invasion NOUN **1 = attack**,
assault, capture, takeover, raid,
offensive, occupation, conquering
2 = intrusion, breach, violation,
disturbance, disruption,
infringement, encroachment,
infraction

invent VERB **1 = create**, make,
produce, design, discover,
manufacture, devise, conceive
2 = make up, devise, concoct,
forge, fake, fabricate, feign, falsify

invention NOUN **1 = creation**,
machine, device, design,
instrument, discovery,
innovation, gadget
2 = development, design,
production, setting up,
foundation, construction,
creation, discovery **3 = fiction**,
fantasy, lie, yarn, fabrication,
falsehood, untruth **4 = creativity**,

imagination, initiative, enterprise, genius, ingenuity, originality, inventiveness

inventive ADJECTIVE = **creative**, original, innovative, imaginative, inspired, fertile, ingenious, resourceful ≠ uninspired

inventor NOUN = **creator**, maker, author, designer, architect, coiner, originator

inventory NOUN = **list**, record, catalogue, listing, account, roll, file, register

invertebrate NOUN
▷ see **crustaceans, snails, slugs and other gastropods, spiders and other arachnids**

invest VERB 1 = **spend**, expend, advance, venture, put in, devote, lay out, sink in 2 = **empower**, provide, charge, sanction, license, authorize, vest ▷ PHRASE: **invest in something** = **buy**, get, purchase, pay for, obtain, acquire, procure

investigate VERB = **examine**, study, research, go into, explore, look into, inspect, probe into

investigation NOUN = **examination**, study, inquiry, review, search, survey, probe, inspection

investigator NOUN = **examiner**, researcher, monitor, detective, analyser, explorer, scrutinizer, inquirer

---

* **INVERTEBRATES**
* amoeba or (U.S.) ameba
* animalcule or animalculum
* arthropod
* bardy, bardie, or bardi (Austral.)
* bivalve
* blue-ringed octopus (Austral.)
* Bluff oyster (N.Z.)
* box jellyfish or (Austral.) sea wasp
* brachiopod or lamp shell
* brandling
* bryozoan or (colloquial) sea mat
* centipede
* chiton or coat-of-mail shell
* clam
* cone (shell)
* coral
* ctenophore or comb jelly
* cunjevoi or cunje (Austral.)
* cuttlefish or cuttle
* daphnia
* earthworm
* eelworm
* gastropodart
* horseleech
* jellyfish or (Austral. slang) blubber
* kina (N.Z.)
* lancelet or amphioxus
* leech
* lugworm, lug, or lobworm
* millipede, millepede, or milleped
* mollusc
* mussel
* octopus or devilfish
* oyster
* paper nautilus, nautilus, or argonaut
* pearly nautilus, nautilus, or chambered nautilus
* piddock

- pipi or ugari (*Austral.*)
- Portuguese man-of-war or (*Austral.*) bluebottle
- quahog, hard-shell clam, hard-shell, or round clam
- ragworm or (*U.S.*) clamworm
- razor-shell or (*U.S.*) razor clam
- red coral or precious coral
- roundworm
- sandworm or (*Austral.*) pumpworm
- scallop
- sea anemone
- sea cucumber
- sea lily
- sea mouse
- sea squirt
- sea urchin
- seed oyster
- sponge
- squid
- starfish
- tapeworm
- tardigrade or water bear
- teredo or shipworm
- trepang or bêche-de-mer
- tube worm
- tubifex
- tusk shell or tooth shell
- worm

investment NOUN 1 = **investing**, backing, funding, financing, contribution, speculation, transaction, expenditure
2 = **stake**, interest, share, concern, portion, ante (*informal*)
3 = **buy**, asset, acquisition, venture, risk, gamble

invisible ADJECTIVE = **unseen**, imperceptible, indiscernible, unseeable ≠ visible

invitation NOUN = **request**, call, invite (*informal*), summons

invite VERB 1 = **ask** 2 = **request**, look for, bid for, appeal for
3 = **encourage**, attract, cause, court, ask for (*informal*), generate, foster, tempt

inviting ADJECTIVE = **tempting**, appealing, attractive, welcoming, enticing, seductive, alluring, mouthwatering ≠ uninviting

invoke VERB 1 = **apply**, use, implement, initiate, resort to, put into effect 2 = **call upon**, appeal to, pray to, petition, beseech, entreat, supplicate

involve VERB 1 = **entail**, mean, require, occasion, imply, give rise to, necessitate 2 = **concern**, draw in, bear on

involved ADJECTIVE
= **complicated**, complex, intricate, hard, confused, confusing, elaborate, tangled ≠ straightforward

involvement NOUN
= **connection**, interest, association, commitment, attachment

inward ADJECTIVE 1 = **incoming**, entering, inbound, ingoing
2 = **internal**, inner, private, personal, inside, secret, hidden, interior ≠ outward

Ireland NOUN = **Hibernia** (*Latin*)

iron MODIFIER = **ferrous**, ferric
▷ ADJECTIVE = **inflexible**, hard, strong, tough, rigid, adamant, unconditional, steely ≠ weak
▷ PHRASE: **iron something out**
= **settle**, resolve, sort out, get rid

of, reconcile, clear up, put right,
straighten out ▷ **RELATED WORDS**:
adjectives **ferric, ferrous**

ironic *or* **ironical** ADJECTIVE
1 = **sarcastic**, dry, acid, bitter,
mocking, wry, satirical, tongue-
in-cheek 2 = **paradoxical**,
contradictory, puzzling, baffling,
confounding, enigmatic,
incongruous

irony NOUN 1 = **sarcasm**, mockery,
ridicule, satire, cynicism, derision
2 = **paradox**, incongruity

irrational ADJECTIVE = **illogical**,
crazy, absurd, unreasonable,
preposterous, nonsensical
≠ rational

irregular ADJECTIVE 1 = **variable**,
erratic, occasional, random,
casual, shaky, sporadic,
haphazard ≠ steady 2 = **uneven**,
rough, ragged, crooked, jagged,
bumpy, contorted, lopsided
≠ even 3 = **inappropriate**,
unconventional, unethical,
unusual, extraordinary,
exceptional, peculiar, unofficial
4 = **unofficial**, underground,
guerrilla, resistance, partisan,
rogue, paramilitary, mercenary

irrelevant ADJECTIVE
= **unconnected**, unrelated,
unimportant, inappropriate,
peripheral, immaterial,
extraneous, beside the point
≠ relevant

irresistible ADJECTIVE
= **overwhelming**, compelling,
overpowering, urgent, compulsive

irresponsible ADJECTIVE
= **thoughtless**, reckless, careless,
unreliable, untrustworthy,
shiftless, scatterbrained
≠ responsible

irritate VERB 1 = **annoy**, anger,
bother, needle (*informal*), infuriate,
exasperate, nettle, irk ≠ placate
2 = **inflame**, pain, rub, scratch,
scrape, chafe

irritated ADJECTIVE = **annoyed**,
cross, angry, bothered, put out,
exasperated, nettled, vexed,
tooshie (*Austral. slang*), hoha (*N.Z.*)

irritating ADJECTIVE = **annoying**,
trying, infuriating, disturbing,
nagging, troublesome,
maddening, irksome ≠ pleasing

irritation NOUN 1 = **annoyance**,
anger, fury, resentment, gall,
indignation, displeasure,
exasperation ≠ pleasure
2 = **nuisance**, irritant, drag
(*informal*), pain in the neck
(*informal*), thorn in your flesh

island NOUN = **isle**, atoll, islet,
ait *or* eyot (*dialect*), cay *or* key
▷ **RELATED WORD**: *adjective* **insular**

isolate VERB 1 = **separate**, break
up, cut off, detach, split up,
insulate, segregate, disconnect
2 = **quarantine**

isolated ADJECTIVE = **remote**, far,
distant, lonely, out-of-the-way,
hidden, secluded, inaccessible

isolation NOUN = **separation**,
segregation, detachment,
solitude, seclusion, remoteness

issue NOUN 1 = **topic**, point,
matter, problem, question,
subject, theme 2 = **point**,

question, bone of contention
3 = **edition**, printing, copy, publication, number, version
4 = **children**, offspring, babies, kids (*informal*), heirs, descendants, progeny ≠ parent
▷ VERB = **give out**, release, publish, announce, deliver, spread, broadcast, distribute
▷ PHRASE: **take issue with something** *or* **someone** = **disagree with**, question, challenge, oppose, dispute, object to, argue with, take exception to

● **WORD POWER**
● Italian has given English a
● great number of loan words for
● the arts, particularly musical
● terms. Some musical terms,
● which originally referred
● to quite specific parts of a
● musical composition or its
● performers, now can be applied
● more generally. For example,
● *coda* (literally 'tail') and *segue*
● (literally 'follows'), originally
● meant the concluding part of a
● piece of music, and a transition
● from one piece of music to
● another without stopping,
● respectively. Coda now has the
● broader meaning 'concluding
● statement', particularly in
● narratives of people's lives,
● e.g. *He is sanguine about this
● unfortunate coda to his career.*
● In the same fashion, segue is
● now applied to a link between
● two ideas or texts, especially
● in speech-making or news-

● reading, e.g. *He tried to think of
● a segue from Yankee Doodle to
● the New York Yankees.* Another
● group of borrowings, which
● can also now be used outside
● the field of music, relate to
● performers, including *maestro*,
● *diva*, and *prima donna*. In music,
● a maestro (literally 'master') is
● a teacher, conductor, or leading
● musician. This term now more
● broadly refers to a leader in any
● profession or art, e.g. *batting
● maestro*, *fashion maestro*. Diva
● (literally 'goddess') and prima
● donna (literally 'first lady')
● both describe a female lead
● singer. Both have developed
● connotations of women
● who are temperamental and
● demanding. Diva, however,
● still mainly describes women in
● musical professions, whereas
● prima donna is a term often
● used of celebrities.

itch VERB **1** = **prickle**, tickle, tingle **2** = **long**, ache, crave, pine, hunger, lust, yearn, hanker
▷ NOUN **1** = **irritation**, tingling, prickling, itchiness **2** = **desire**, longing, craving, passion, yen (*informal*), hunger, lust, yearning

item NOUN **1** = **article**, thing, object, piece, unit, component
2 = **matter**, point, issue, case, question, concern, detail, subject
3 = **report**, story, piece, account, note, feature, notice, article

itinerary NOUN = **schedule**, programme, route, timetable

Jj

jab VERB = **poke**, dig, punch, thrust, tap, stab, nudge, prod
▷ NOUN = **poke**, dig, punch, thrust, tap, stab, nudge, prod

jacket NOUN = **covering**, casing, case, cover, skin, shell, coat, wrapping

jackpot NOUN = **prize**, winnings, award, reward, bonanza

jail NOUN = **prison**, penitentiary (*U.S.*), confinement, dungeon, nick (*Brit. slang*), slammer (*slang*), reformatory, boob (*Austral. slang*)
▷ VERB = **imprison**, confine, detain, lock up, put away, intern, incarcerate, send down

jam NOUN (*informal*)
= **predicament**, tight spot, situation, trouble, hole (*slang*), fix (*informal*), mess, pinch
▷ VERB 1 = **pack**, force, press, stuff, squeeze, ram, wedge, cram
2 = **crowd**, throng, crush, mass, surge, flock, swarm, congregate
3 = **congest**, block, clog, stick, stall, obstruct

● **WORD POWER**
● A few words of Japanese origin,
● which described concepts or
● things unique to Japanese
● culture, are now used in English
● in a novel and creative way. For
● example, in Japanese myth,
● *kamikaze* was a divine wind
● which saved the Japanese by
● sinking the Mongolian navy.
● In the Second World War, a
● kamikaze was a Japanese pilot
● who flew his plane into an
● enemy ship on a suicide mission.
● Kamikaze is now a metaphor
● for any self-destructive act, as
● in *kamikaze tactics*, *kamikaze*
● *approach*. Another Japanese
● term which has undergone a
● similar meaning development
● is *tsunami*. Literally 'harbour-
● waves', a tsunami is one or
● several large sea waves produced
● by an underwater earthquake
● or volcanic eruption. It is often
● used as a metaphor for a sudden
● increase or large volume of
● either concrete or abstract
● things, e.g. *a tsunami of aid, of*
● *words*, or *of support*. It can be
● compared to flood, deluge, tide,
● wave, and torrent which have
● the same metaphor. Words for
● different religions and faiths
● often develop adjectives which
● describe the particular qualities
● of their believers, e.g. That's not
● very Christian of you. Similarly,
● *Zen*, a branch of Buddhism,
● not only refers to a religion or
● philosophy, but, more loosely, a
● state of calmness or meditation.
● It is sometimes found in phrases
● like *zen-like calm*, with or
● without a capital.

jar¹ NOUN = **pot**, container, drum, vase, jug, pitcher, urn, crock

jar² VERB 1 *usually with* **on**
= **irritate**, annoy, offend, nettle,
irk, grate on, get on your nerves
(*informal*) 2 = **jolt**, rock, shake,
bump, rattle, vibrate, convulse

jargon NOUN = **parlance**, idiom,
usage, argot

jaw PLURAL NOUN = **opening**,
entrance, mouth
▷ VERB (*slang*) = **talk**, chat,
gossip, chatter, spout, natter

jealous ADJECTIVE 1 = **suspicious**,
protective, wary, doubtful,
sceptical, vigilant, watchful,
possessive ≠ trusting
2 = **envious**, grudging, resentful,
green, green with envy, desirous,
covetous ≠ satisfied

jealousy NOUN = **suspicion**,
mistrust, possessiveness, doubt,
spite, resentment, wariness, dubiety

jeer VERB = **mock**, deride, heckle,
barrack, ridicule, taunt, scoff, gibe
≠ cheer
▷ NOUN = **mockery**, abuse,
ridicule, taunt, boo, derision,
gibe, catcall ≠ applause

jeopardy NOUN = **danger**, risk,
peril, vulnerability, insecurity

jerk VERB = **jolt**, bang, bump, lurch
▷ NOUN = **lurch**, movement,
thrust, twitch, jolt

jet NOUN = **stream**, current, spring,
flow, rush, flood, burst, spray
▷ VERB = **fly**, wing, cruise, soar,
zoom

jewel NOUN 1 = **gemstone**, gem,
ornament, sparkler (*informal*),
rock (*slang*) 2 = **treasure**, wonder,
darling, pearl, gem, paragon,

pride and joy, taonga (*N.Z.*)

jewellery NOUN = **jewels**, treasure,
gems, trinkets, ornaments, finery,
regalia, bling (*slang*)

job NOUN 1 = **position**, work,
calling, business, field, career,
employment, profession 2 = **task**,
duty, work, venture, enterprise,
undertaking, assignment, chore

jobless ADJECTIVE = **unemployed**,
redundant, out of work, inactive,
unoccupied, idle

jog VERB 1 = **run**, trot, canter, lope
2 = **nudge**, push, shake, prod
3 = **stimulate**, stir, prod

join VERB 1 = **enrol in**, enter, sign
up for, enlist in 2 = **connect**,
unite, couple, link, combine,
attach, fasten, add ≠ detach

joint ADJECTIVE = **shared**, mutual,
collective, communal, united,
joined, allied, combined
▷ NOUN = **junction**, connection,
brace, bracket, hinge,
intersection, node, nexus

jointly ADVERB = **collectively**,
together, in conjunction, as
one, in common, mutually,
in partnership, in league
≠ separately

joke NOUN 1 = **jest**, gag (*informal*),
wisecrack (*informal*), witticism,
crack (*informal*), quip, pun, one-
liner (*informal*) 2 = **laugh**, jest,
jape 3 = **prank**, trick, practical
joke, lark (*informal*), escapade,
jape 4 = **laughing stock**, clown,
buffoon
▷ VERB = **jest**, kid (*informal*), mock,
tease, taunt, quip, banter, play

the fool

joker NOUN = **comedian**, comic, wit, clown, wag, jester, prankster, buffoon

jolly ADJECTIVE = **happy**, cheerful, merry, upbeat (*informal*), playful, cheery, genial, chirpy (*informal*) ≠ miserable

jolt VERB 1 = **jerk**, push, shake, knock, jar, shove, jog, jostle 2 = **surprise**, stun, disturb, stagger, startle, perturb, discompose ▷ NOUN 1 = **jerk**, start, jump, shake, bump, jar, jog, lurch 2 = **surprise**, blow, shock, setback, bombshell, bolt from the blue

journal NOUN 1 = **magazine**, publication, gazette, periodical 2 = **newspaper**, paper, daily, weekly, monthly 3 = **diary**, record, history, log, notebook, chronicle, annals, yearbook, blog (*informal*)

journalist NOUN = **reporter**, writer, correspondent, newsman *or* newswoman, commentator, broadcaster, hack (*derogatory*), columnist

journey NOUN 1 = **trip**, drive, tour, flight, excursion, trek, expedition, voyage 2 = **progress**, voyage, pilgrimage, odyssey ▷ VERB = **travel**, go, move, tour, progress, proceed, wander, trek, go walkabout (*Austral.*)

joy NOUN = **delight**, pleasure, satisfaction, ecstasy, enjoyment, bliss, glee, rapture ≠ sorrow

jubilee NOUN = **celebration**, holiday, festival, festivity

judge NOUN 1 = **magistrate**, justice, beak (*Brit. slang*), His, Her *or* Your Honour 2 = **referee**, expert, specialist, umpire, umpie (*Austral. slang*), mediator, examiner, connoisseur, assessor 3 = **critic**, assessor, arbiter ▷ VERB 1 = **adjudicate**, referee, umpire, mediate, officiate, arbitrate 2 = **evaluate**, rate, consider, view, value, esteem 3 = **estimate**, guess, assess, calculate, evaluate, gauge ▷ RELATED WORD: *adjective* **judicial**

judgment NOUN 1 = **opinion**, view, estimate, belief, assessment, diagnosis, valuation, appraisal 2 = **verdict**, finding, ruling, decision, sentence, decree, arbitration, adjudication 3 = **sense**, good sense, understanding, discrimination, perception, wisdom, wit, prudence

judicial ADJECTIVE = **legal**, official

jug NOUN = **container**, pitcher, urn, carafe, creamer (*U.S. & Canad.*), vessel, jar, crock

juggle VERB = **manipulate**, change, alter, modify, manoeuvre

juice NOUN 1 = **liquid**, extract, fluid, liquor, sap, nectar 2 = **secretion**

juicy ADJECTIVE 1 = **moist**, lush, succulent 2 = **interesting**, colourful, sensational, vivid, provocative, spicy (*informal*), suggestive, racy

jumble NOUN = **muddle**, mixture, mess, disorder, confusion, clutter, disarray, mishmash ▷ VERB = **mix**, mistake, confuse, disorder, shuffle, muddle, disorganize

jumbo ADJECTIVE = **giant**, large, huge, immense, gigantic, oversized, supersize ≠ tiny

jump VERB 1 = **leap**, spring, bound, bounce, hop, skip 2 = **vault**, hurdle, go over, sail over, hop over 3 = **spring**, bound, bounce 4 = **recoil**, start, jolt, flinch, shake, jerk, quake, shudder 5 = **increase**, rise, climb, escalate, advance, soar, surge, spiral 6 = **miss**, avoid, skip, omit, evade
▷ NOUN 1 = **leap**, spring, skip, bound, hop, vault 2 = **rise**, increase, upswing, advance, upsurge, upturn, increment

jumped-up ADJECTIVE (*informal*) = **conceited**, arrogant, pompous, overbearing, presumptuous, insolent

jumper NOUN = **sweater**, top, jersey, cardigan, woolly, pullover

junior ADJECTIVE 1 = **minor**, lower, secondary, lesser, subordinate, inferior 2 = **younger** ≠ senior

junk NOUN = **rubbish**, refuse, waste, scrap, litter, debris, garbage (*chiefly U.S.*), trash

jurisdiction NOUN 1 = **authority**, power, control, rule, influence, command, mana (*N.Z.*) 2 = **range**, area, field, bounds, province, scope, sphere, compass

just ADVERB 1 = **recently**, lately, only now 2 = **merely**, only, simply, solely 3 = **barely**, hardly, by a whisker, by the skin of your teeth 4 = **exactly**, really, quite, completely, totally, perfectly, entirely, truly
▷ ADJECTIVE 1 = **fair**, good, legitimate, upright, honest, equitable, conscientious, virtuous ≠ unfair 2 = **fitting**, due, correct, deserved, appropriate, justified, decent, merited ≠ inappropriate

🌑 **WORD POWER**
🌑 The expression *just exactly* is
🌑 considered to be poor style
🌑 because, since both words
🌑 mean the same thing, only
🌑 one or the other is needed. Use
🌑 *just* – *it's just what they want* – or
🌑 *exactly* – *it's exactly what they*
🌑 *want*, but not both together.

justice NOUN 1 = **fairness**, equity, integrity, honesty, decency, rightfulness, right ≠ injustice 2 = **justness**, fairness, legitimacy, right, integrity, honesty, legality, rightfulness 3 = **judge**, magistrate, beak (*Brit. slang*), His, Her or Your Honour

justification NOUN = **reason**, grounds, defence, basis, excuse, warrant, rationale, vindication

justify VERB = **explain**, support, warrant, defend, excuse, uphold, vindicate, exonerate

juvenile NOUN = **child**, youth, minor, girl, boy, teenager, infant, adolescent ≠ adult
▷ ADJECTIVE 1 = **young**, junior, adolescent, youthful, immature ≠ adult 2 = **immature**, childish, infantile, puerile, young, youthful, inexperienced, callow

Kk

kai NOUN (*N.Z. informal*) =**food**, grub (*slang*), provisions, fare, tucker (*Austral. & N.Z. informal*), refreshment, foodstuffs

kak (*S. African taboo*) NOUN
1 =**faeces**, excrement, manure, dung, droppings, waste matter
2 =**rubbish**, nonsense, garbage (*informal*), rot, drivel, tripe (*informal*), bizzo (*Austral. slang*), bull's wool (*Austral. & N.Z. slang*)

keen ADJECTIVE 1 =**eager**, intense, enthusiastic, passionate, ardent, avid, fervent, impassioned ≠ unenthusiastic 2 =**earnest**, fierce, intense, vehement, passionate, heightened, ardent, fanatical 3 =**sharp**, incisive, cutting, edged, razor-like ≠ dull 4 =**perceptive**, quick, sharp, acute, smart, wise, clever, shrewd ≠ obtuse 5 =**intense**, strong, fierce, relentless, cut-throat

keep VERB 1 *usually with* **from** =**prevent**, restrain, hinder, keep back 2 =**hold on to**, maintain, retain, save, preserve, nurture, cherish, conserve ≠ lose 3 =**store**, put, place, house, hold, deposit, stack, stow 4 =**carry**, stock, sell, supply, handle 5 =**support**, maintain, sustain, provide for, mind, fund, finance, feed 6 =**raise**, own, maintain, tend, farm, breed, look after, rear 7 =**manage**, run, administer, be in charge (of), direct, handle, supervise 8 =**delay**, detain, hinder, impede, obstruct, set back ≠ release
▷ NOUN 1 =**board**, food, maintenance, living, kai (*N.Z. informal*) 2 =**tower**, castle
▷ PHRASES: **keep something up** 1 =**continue**, make, maintain, carry on, persist in, persevere with 2 =**maintain**, sustain, perpetuate, retain, preserve, prolong; **keep up** =**keep pace**

keeper NOUN =**curator**, guardian, steward, attendant, caretaker, preserver

keeping NOUN =**care**, charge, protection, possession, custody, guardianship, safekeeping
▷ PHRASE: **in keeping with** =**in agreement with**, in harmony with, in accord with, in compliance with, in conformity with, in balance with, in correspondence with, in proportion with

key NOUN 1 =**opener**, door key, latchkey 2 =**answer**
▷ MODIFIER =**essential**, leading, major, main, important, necessary, vital, crucial ≠ minor

kia ora INTERJECTION (*N.Z.*) =**hello**, hi (*informal*), greetings, gidday *or* g'day (*Austral. & N.Z.*), how do you do?, good morning, good evening, good afternoon

kick VERB 1 =**boot**, knock, punt

k

2 (*informal*) = **give up**, break, stop, abandon, quit, cease, eschew, leave off

▷ **NOUN** (*informal*) = **thrill**, buzz (*slang*), tingle, high (*slang*)

▷ **PHRASES**: **kick someone out** (*informal*) = **dismiss**, remove, get rid of, expel, eject, evict, sack (*informal*), kennet (*Austral. slang*), jeff (*Austral. slang*); **kick something off** (*informal*) = **begin**, start, open, commence, initiate, get on the road

kid¹ NOUN (*informal*) = **child**, baby, teenager, youngster, infant, adolescent, juvenile, toddler, littlie (*Austral. informal*), ankle-biter (*Austral. slang*), tacker (*Austral. slang*)

kid² VERB = **tease**, joke, trick, fool, pretend, wind up (*Brit. slang*), hoax, delude

kidnap VERB = **abduct**, capture, seize, snatch (*slang*), hijack, hold to ransom

kill VERB **1** = **slay**, murder, execute, slaughter, destroy, massacre, butcher, cut down **2** (*informal*) = **destroy**, crush, scotch, stop, halt, wreck, shatter, suppress

killer NOUN = **murderer**, slayer, hit man (*slang*), butcher, gunman, assassin, terminator, executioner

killing NOUN = **murder**, massacre, slaughter, dispatch, manslaughter, elimination, slaying, homicide

▷ **ADJECTIVE** (*informal*) = **tiring**, taxing, exhausting, punishing, fatiguing, gruelling, sapping, debilitating ▷ **PHRASE**: **make a killing** (*informal*) = **profit**, gain, clean up (*informal*), be lucky, be successful, make a fortune, strike it rich (*informal*), make a bomb (*slang*)

kind¹ ADJECTIVE = **considerate**, kindly, concerned, friendly, generous, obliging, charitable, benign ≠ unkind

kind² NOUN **1** = **class**, sort, type, variety, brand, category, genre **2** = **sort**, set, type, family, species, breed

 WORD POWER
 It is common in informal
 speech to combine singular
 and plural in sentences like
 *children enjoy those kind of
 stories*. However, this is not
 acceptable in careful writing,
 where the plural must be used
 consistently: *children enjoy those
 kinds of stories*.

kindly ADJECTIVE = **benevolent**, kind, caring, warm, helpful, pleasant, sympathetic, benign ≠ cruel

▷ **ADVERB** = **benevolently**, politely, generously, thoughtfully, tenderly, lovingly, cordially, affectionately ≠ unkindly

kindness NOUN = **goodwill**, understanding, charity, humanity, compassion, generosity, philanthropy, benevolence ≠ malice

king NOUN = **ruler**, monarch, sovereign, leader, lord, Crown, emperor, head of state

kingdom NOUN = **country**, state, nation, territory, realm

kiss VERB 1 = **peck** (*informal*), osculate, neck (*informal*)
2 = **brush**, touch, shave, scrape, graze, glance off, stroke
▷ NOUN = **peck** (*informal*), snog (*Brit. slang*), smacker (*slang*), French kiss, osculation

kit NOUN 1 = **equipment**, materials, tackle, tools, apparatus, paraphernalia
2 = **gear**, things, stuff, equipment, uniform ▷ PHRASE: **kit something** or **someone out** or **up** = **equip**, fit, supply, provide with, arm, stock, costume, furnish

knack NOUN = **skill**, art, ability, facility, talent, gift, capacity, trick ≠ ineptitude

kneel VERB = **genuflect**, stoop

knickers PLURAL NOUN = **underwear**, smalls, briefs, drawers, panties, bloomers

knife NOUN = **blade**, carver, cutter
▷ VERB = **cut**, wound, stab, slash, thrust, pierce, spear, jab

knit VERB 1 = **join**, unite, link, tie, bond, combine, bind, weave
2 = **heal**, unite, join, link, bind, fasten, intertwine 3 = **furrow**, tighten, knot, wrinkle, crease, screw up, pucker, scrunch up

knob NOUN = **ball**, stud, knot, lump, bump, projection, hump, protrusion

knock VERB 1 = **bang**, strike, tap, rap, thump, pummel 2 = **hit**, strike, punch, belt (*informal*), smack, thump, cuff 3 (*informal*)

= **criticize**, condemn, put down, run down, abuse, slate (*informal*), censure, denigrate, nit-pick (*informal*)
▷ NOUN 1 = **knocking**, pounding, beating, tap, bang, banging, rap, thump 2 = **bang**, blow, impact, jar, collision, jolt, smash 3 = **blow**, hit, punch, crack, clip, slap, bash, smack 4 (*informal*) = **setback**, check, defeat, blow, reverse, disappointment, hold-up, hitch ▷ PHRASES: **knock about** or **around** = **wander**, travel, roam, rove, range, drift, stray, ramble, go walkabout (*Austral.*); **knock about** or **around with someone** = **mix with**, associate with, mingle with, consort with, hobnob with, socialize with, accompany; **knock off** (*informal*) = **stop work**, get out, call it a day (*informal*), finish work, clock off, clock out; **knock someone about** or **around** = **hit**, attack, beat, strike, abuse, injure, assault, batter; **knock someone down** = **run over**, hit, run down, knock over, mow down; **knock something down** = **demolish**, destroy, flatten, tear down, level, fell, dismantle, bulldoze, kennet (*Austral. slang*), jeff (*Austral. slang*); **knock something off** (*slang*) = **steal**, take, nick (*slang, chiefly Brit.*), thieve, rob, pinch

knockout NOUN 1 = **killer blow**, coup de grâce (*French*), KO or K.O. (*slang*) 2 (*informal*) = **success**, hit, winner, triumph, smash, sensation, smash hit ≠ failure

k

knot NOUN = **connection**, tie, bond, joint, loop, ligature
▷ VERB = **tie**, secure, bind, loop, tether

know VERB 1 = **have knowledge of**, see, understand, recognize, perceive, be aware of, be conscious of 2 = **be acquainted with**, recognize, be familiar with, be friends with, be friendly with, have knowledge of, have dealings with, socialize with ≠ be unfamiliar with 3 *sometimes with* **about** *or* **of** = **be familiar with**, understand, comprehend, have knowledge of, be acquainted with, feel certain of, have dealings in, be versed in ≠ be ignorant of

know-how NOUN (*informal*) = **expertise**, ability, skill, knowledge, facility, talent, command, capability

knowing ADJECTIVE = **meaningful**, significant, expressive, enigmatic, suggestive

knowledge NOUN
1 = **understanding**, sense, judgment, perception, awareness, insight, grasp, appreciation
2 = **learning**, education, intelligence, instruction, wisdom, scholarship, enlightenment, erudition ≠ ignorance
3 = **acquaintance**, intimacy, familiarity ≠ unfamiliarity

knowledgeable ADJECTIVE
1 = **well-informed**, conversant, au fait (*French*), experienced, aware, familiar, in the know (*informal*), cognizant 2 = **intelligent**, learned, educated, scholarly, erudite

known ADJECTIVE = **famous**, well-known, celebrated, noted, acknowledged, recognized, avowed ≠ unknown

koppie *or* **kopje** NOUN (*S. African*) = **hill**, down (*archaic*), fell, mount, hilltop, knoll, hillock, brae (*Scot.*)

k

Ll

label NOUN = **tag**, ticket, tab, marker, sticker
▷ VERB = **tag**, mark, stamp, ticket, tab

labour NOUN 1 = **workers**, employees, workforce, labourers, hands 2 = **work**, effort, employment, toil, industry 3 = **childbirth**, birth, delivery, parturition
▷ VERB 1 = **work**, toil, strive, work hard, sweat (*informal*), slave, endeavour, slog away (*informal*) ≠ rest 2 = **struggle**, work, strain, work hard, strive, grapple, toil, make an effort 3 = **overemphasize**, stress, elaborate, exaggerate, strain, dwell on, overdo, go on about 4 *usually with* **under** = **be disadvantaged by**, suffer from, be a victim of, be burdened by

Labour Party ADJECTIVE = **left-wing**, Democrat (*U.S.*)

laboured ADJECTIVE = **difficult**, forced, strained, heavy, awkward

labourer NOUN = **worker**, manual worker, hand, blue-collar worker, drudge, navvy (*Brit. informal*)

lace NOUN 1 = **netting**, net, filigree, meshwork, openwork 2 = **cord**, tie, string, lacing, shoelace, bootlace
▷ VERB 1 = **fasten**, tie, tie up, do up, secure, bind, thread 2 = **mix**, drug, doctor, add to, spike, contaminate, fortify, adulterate 3 = **intertwine**, interweave, entwine, twine, interlink

lack NOUN = **shortage**, want, absence, deficiency, need, inadequacy, scarcity, dearth ≠ abundance
▷ VERB = **miss**, want, need, require, not have, be without, be short of, be in need of ≠ have

lad NOUN = **boy**, kid (*informal*), guy (*informal*), youth, fellow, youngster, juvenile, nipper (*informal*)

laden ADJECTIVE = **loaded**, burdened, full, charged, weighed down, encumbered

lady NOUN 1 = **gentlewoman**, duchess, noble, dame, baroness, countess, aristocrat, viscountess 2 = **woman**, female, girl, damsel, charlie (*Austral. slang*), chook (*Austral. slang*), wahine (*N.Z.*)

lag VERB = **hang back**, delay, trail, linger, loiter, straggle, dawdle, tarry

laid-back ADJECTIVE = **relaxed**, calm, casual, easy-going, unflappable (*informal*), unhurried, free and easy, chilled (*informal*) ≠ tense

lake NOUN = **pond**, pool, reservoir, loch (*Scot.*), lagoon, mere, lough (*Irish*), tarn

lame ADJECTIVE 1 = **disabled**, handicapped, crippled, limping, hobbling, game

2 = **unconvincing**, poor, pathetic, inadequate, thin, weak, feeble, unsatisfactory

lament VERB = **bemoan**, grieve, mourn, weep over, complain about, regret, wail about, deplore ▷ NOUN 1 = **complaint**, moan, wailing, lamentation 2 = **dirge**, requiem, elegy, threnody

land NOUN 1 = **ground**, earth, dry land, terra firma 2 = **soil**, ground, earth, clay, dirt, sod, loam 3 = **countryside**, farmland 4 (*law*) = **property**, grounds, estate, real estate, realty, acreage, homestead (*U.S. & Canad.*) 5 = **country**, nation, region, state, district, territory, province, kingdom ▷ VERB 1 = **arrive**, dock, put down, moor, alight, touch down, disembark, come to rest 2 (*informal*) = **gain**, get, win, secure, acquire ▷ PHRASE: **land up** = **end up**, turn up, wind up, finish up, fetch up (*informal*) ▷ RELATED WORD: *adjective* **terrestrial**

landlord NOUN 1 = **owner**, landowner, proprietor, freeholder, lessor, landholder 2 = **innkeeper**, host, hotelier

landmark NOUN 1 = **feature**, spectacle, monument 2 = **milestone**, turning point, watershed, critical point, tipping point

landscape NOUN = **scenery**, country, view, land, scene, prospect, countryside, outlook

landslide NOUN = **landslip**, avalanche, rockfall

lane NOUN = **road**, street, track, path, way, passage, trail, pathway

language NOUN 1 = **tongue**, dialect, vernacular, patois 2 = **speech**, communication, expression, speaking, talk, talking, discourse, parlance

languish VERB 1 = **decline**, fade away, wither away, flag, weaken, wilt ≠ flourish 2 (*literary*) = **waste away**, suffer, rot, be abandoned, be neglected ≠ thrive 3 *often with* **for** = **pine**, long, desire, hunger, yearn, hanker

lap¹ NOUN = **circuit**, tour, leg, stretch, circle, orbit, loop

lap² VERB 1 = **ripple**, wash, splash, swish, gurgle, slosh, purl, plash 2 = **drink**, sip, lick, swallow, gulp, sup ▷ PHRASE: **lap something up** = **relish**, like, enjoy, delight in, savour, revel in, wallow in, accept eagerly

lapse NOUN 1 = **decline**, fall, drop, deterioration 2 = **mistake**, failing, fault, failure, error, slip, negligence, omission 3 = **interval**, break, gap, pause, interruption, lull, breathing space, intermission ▷ VERB 1 = **slip**, fall, decline, sink, drop, slide, deteriorate, degenerate 2 = **end**, stop, run out, expire, terminate

lapsed ADJECTIVE = **expired**, ended, finished, run out, invalid, out of date, discontinued

large ADJECTIVE 1 = **big**, great, huge, heavy, massive, vast, enormous, tall, supersize ≠ small

2 = **massive**, great, big, huge, vast, enormous, considerable, substantial, supersize ≠ small
▷ PHRASES: **at large 1** = **in general**, generally, chiefly, mainly, as a whole, in the main
2 = **free**, on the run, fugitive, at liberty, on the loose, unchained, unconfined; **by and large** = **on the whole**, generally, mostly, in general, all things considered, predominantly, in the main, all in all

largely ADVERB = **mainly**, generally, chiefly, mostly, principally, primarily, predominantly, by and large

large-scale ADJECTIVE = **wide-ranging**, global, sweeping, broad, wide, vast, extensive, wholesale

lash¹ VERB **1** = **pound**, beat, strike, hammer, drum, smack (*dialect*)
2 = **censure**, attack, blast, put down, criticize, slate (*informal, chiefly Brit.*), scold, tear into (*informal*) **3** = **whip**, beat, thrash, birch, flog, scourge
▷ NOUN = **blow**, hit, strike, stroke, stripe, swipe (*informal*)

lash² VERB = **fasten**, tie, secure, bind, strap, make fast

last¹ ADJECTIVE **1** = **most recent**, latest, previous **2** = **hindmost**, final, at the end, remotest, furthest behind, most distant, rearmost ≠ foremost **3** = **final**, closing, concluding, ultimate ≠ first
▷ ADVERB **1** = **in** or **at the end**, after, behind, in the rear, bringing up the rear ▷ PHRASE: **the last word 1** = **final decision**, final say, final statement, conclusive comment **2** = **leading**, finest, cream, supreme, elite, foremost, pre-eminent, unsurpassed

● WORD POWER
● Since *last* can mean either *after*
● *all others* or *most recent*, it is
● better to avoid using this word
● where ambiguity might arise,
● as in *her last novel*. *Final* or *latest*
● should be used as alternatives
● in such contexts to avoid any
● possible confusion.

last² VERB = **continue**, remain, survive, carry on, endure, persist, keep on, abide ≠ end

lasting ADJECTIVE = **continuing**, long-term, permanent, enduring, remaining, abiding, long-standing, perennial ≠ passing

latch NOUN = **fastening**, catch, bar, lock, hook, bolt, hasp
▷ VERB = **fasten**, bar, secure, bolt, make fast

late ADJECTIVE **1** = **overdue**, delayed, last-minute, belated, tardy, behind time, behindhand ≠ early **2** = **dead**, deceased, departed, passed on, former, defunct ≠ alive **3** = **recent**, new, advanced, fresh ≠ old
▷ ADVERB = **behind time**, belatedly, tardily, behindhand, dilatorily ≠ early

lately ADVERB = **recently**, of late, just now, in recent times, not long ago, latterly

later ADVERB = **afterwards**, after,

eventually, in time, subsequently, later on, thereafter, in a while

▷ ADJECTIVE = **subsequent**, next, following, ensuing

latest ADJECTIVE = **up-to-date**, current, fresh, newest, modern, most recent, up-to-the-minute

● **WORD POWER**
● Historically, English borrowed
● its greatest number of words
● from Latin and French. Often
● words of the same root would
● come into English from both
● Latin and French in slightly
● different forms. Some of these
● now exist as synonyms in
● English with fine distinctions.
● This process can be seen with
● *gravitas* and *gravity*. Both
● are derived from an original
● Latin form meaning 'weight':
● gravity came into English via
● French in the 16th century,
● and gravitas was coined from
● Latin in the 20th century.
● There is a significant overlap
● in meaning in that both mean
● 'seriousness', but they are used
● to describe different things.
● Gravitas is used to describe the
● importance and clout attached
● to a person's high status
● or the dignity of pomp and
● ceremony, e.g. he lent gravitas
● to the proceedings. Gravity,
● on the other hand, has a wider
● meaning of seriousness,
● and denotes a situation or
● behaviour, e.g. the gravity
● of their crime. Numerous

● Latin words became legal
● terminology with specialized
● meanings in English. Many
● of these words are still used
● today by lawyers in precise
● technical ways, but have also
● developed a looser meaning
● in general language. For
● example, a *proviso* is a clause in
● a contract making a limitation,
● condition, or exception to
● the rest of the agreement. In
● general language, it also means
● a condition or restriction,
● but not one which is legally
● binding, in the phrase *with the*
● *proviso that*.

latitude NOUN = **scope**, liberty, freedom, play, space, licence, leeway, laxity

latter NOUN = **second**, last, last-mentioned, second-mentioned

▷ ADJECTIVE = **last**, ending, closing, final, concluding

≠ earlier

● **WORD POWER**
● *The latter* should only be used
● to specify the second of two
● items, for example in *if I had to*
● *choose between the hovercraft and*
● *the ferry, I would opt for the latter*.
● Where there are three or more
● items, the last can be referred
● to as *the last-named*, but not *the*
● *latter*.

laugh VERB = **chuckle**, giggle, snigger, cackle, chortle, guffaw, titter, be in stitches

▷ NOUN 1 = **chortle**, giggle, chuckle, snigger, guffaw, titter **2** (*informal*) = **joke**, scream (*informal*), hoot (*informal*), lark, prank **3** (*informal*) = **clown**, character (*informal*), scream (*informal*), entertainer, card (*informal*), joker, hoot (*informal*) ▷ **PHRASE**: **laugh something off** = **disregard**, ignore, dismiss, overlook, shrug off, minimize, brush aside, make light of

laughter NOUN = **amusement**, entertainment, humour, glee, fun, mirth, hilarity, merriment

launch VERB **1** = **propel**, fire, dispatch, discharge, project, send off, set in motion, send into orbit **2** = **begin**, start, open, initiate, introduce, found, set up, originate ▷ **PHRASE**: **launch into something** = **start enthusiastically**, begin, initiate, embark on, instigate, inaugurate, embark upon

laurel NOUN ▷ **PHRASE**: **rest on your laurels** = **sit back**, relax, take it easy, relax your efforts

lavatory NOUN = **toilet**, bathroom, loo (*Brit. informal*), privy, cloakroom (*Brit.*), urinal, latrine, washroom, dunny (*Austral. & N.Z. old-fashioned, informal*), bogger (*Austral. slang*), brasco (*Austral. slang*)

lavish ADJECTIVE **1** = **grand**, magnificent, splendid, abundant, copious, profuse ≠ stingy **2** = **extravagant**, wild, excessive, exaggerated, wasteful, prodigal, unrestrained, immoderate ≠ thrifty **3** = **generous**, free,

liberal, bountiful, open-handed, unstinting, munificent ≠ stingy ▷ **VERB** = **shower**, pour, heap, deluge, dissipate ≠ stint

law NOUN **1** = **constitution**, code, legislation, charter **2** = **statute**, act, bill, rule, order, command, regulation, resolution **3** = **principle**, code, canon, precept, axiom, kaupapa (*N.Z.*) **4** = **the legal profession**, the bar, barristers ▷ **RELATED WORDS**: *adjectives* **legal, judicial**

lawsuit NOUN = **case**, action, trial, suit, proceedings, dispute, prosecution, legal action

lawyer NOUN = **legal adviser**, attorney, solicitor, counsel, advocate, barrister, counsellor, legal representative

lay¹ VERB **1** = **place**, put, set, spread, plant, leave, deposit, put down **2** = **devise**, plan, design, prepare, work out, plot, hatch, contrive **3** = **produce**, bear, deposit **4** = **arrange**, prepare, make, organize, position, set out, devise, put together **5** = **attribute**, assign, allocate, allot, ascribe, impute **6** = **put forward**, offer, present, advance, lodge, submit, bring forward **7** = **bet**, stake, venture, gamble, chance, risk, hazard, wager ▷ **PHRASES**: **lay someone off** = **dismiss**, fire (*informal*), release, sack (*informal*), pay off, discharge, let go, make redundant, kennet (*Austral. slang*), jeff (*Austral. slang*); **lay someone out** (*informal*)

= **knock out**, fell, floor, knock unconscious, knock for six; **lay something out 1** = **arrange**, order, design, display, exhibit, put out, spread out **2** (*informal*) = **spend**, pay, invest, fork out (*slang*), expend, shell out (*informal*), disburse

● **WORD POWER**
● In standard English, the verb *to*
● *lay* (meaning 'to put something
● somewhere') always needs an
● object, for example *the Queen*
● *laid a wreath*. By contrast,
● the verb *to lie* is always used
● without an object, for example
● *he was just lying there*.

lay² ADJECTIVE **1** = **nonclerical**, secular, non-ordained
2 = **nonspecialist**, amateur, unqualified, untrained, inexpert, nonprofessional
layer NOUN = **tier**, level, seam, stratum
layout NOUN = **arrangement**, design, outline, format, plan, formation
lazy ADJECTIVE **1** = **idle**, inactive, indolent, slack, negligent, inert, workshy, slothful ≠ industrious
2 = **lethargic**, languorous, slow-moving, languid, sleepy, sluggish, drowsy, somnolent ≠ quick
leach VERB = **extract**, strain, drain, filter, seep, percolate
lead VERB **1** = **go in front (of)**, head, be in front, be at the head (of), walk in front (of) **2** = **guide**, conduct, steer, escort, precede, usher, pilot, show the way

3 = **connect to**, link, open onto
4 = **be ahead (of)**, be first, exceed, be winning, excel, surpass, come first, transcend **5** = **command**, rule, govern, preside over, head, control, manage, direct **6** = **live**, have, spend, experience, pass, undergo **7** = **result in**, cause, produce, contribute, generate, bring about, bring on, give rise to **8** = **cause**, prompt, persuade, move, draw, influence, motivate, prevail

▷ NOUN **1** = **first place**, winning position, primary position, vanguard **2** = **advantage**, start, edge, margin, winning margin **3** = **example**, direction, leadership, guidance, model, pattern **4** = **clue**, suggestion, hint, indication, pointer, tip-off **5** = **leading role**, principal, protagonist, title role, principal part **6** = **leash**, line, cord, rein, tether
▷ ADJECTIVE = **main**, prime, top, leading, first, head, chief, premier
▷ PHRASES: **lead someone on** = **entice**, tempt, lure, mislead, draw on, seduce, deceive, beguile; **lead up to something** = **introduce**, prepare for, pave the way for
leader NOUN = **principal**, president, head, chief, boss (*informal*), director, manager, chairman, baas (*S. African*), sherang (*Austral.* & *N.Z.*) ≠ follower
leadership NOUN **1** = **authority**,

control, influence, command,
premiership, captaincy,
governance, headship
2 = **guidance**, government,
authority, management,
direction, supervision,
domination, superintendency

leading ADJECTIVE = **principal**,
top, major, main, first, highest,
greatest, chief ≠ minor

leaf NOUN 1 = **frond**, blade,
cotyledon 2 = **page**, sheet,
folio ▷ PHRASE: **leaf through
something** (*a book, magazine, etc*)
= **skim**, glance, scan, browse, look
through, dip into, flick through,
flip through

leaflet NOUN = **booklet**, notice,
brochure, circular, flyer, tract,
pamphlet, handout

leafy ADJECTIVE = **green**, shaded,
shady, verdant

league NOUN 1 = **association**,
union, alliance, coalition, group,
corporation, partnership,
federation 2 = **class**, group, level,
category

leak VERB 1 = **escape**, pass, spill,
release, drip, trickle, ooze, seep
2 = **disclose**, tell, reveal, pass on,
give away, make public, divulge,
let slip
▷ NOUN 1 = **leakage**, discharge,
drip, seepage, percolation
2 = **hole**, opening, crack,
puncture, aperture, chink, crevice,
fissure 3 = **disclosure**, exposé,
exposure, admission, revelation,
uncovering, betrayal, unearthing

lean¹ VERB 1 = **bend**, tip, slope,

incline, tilt, heel, slant 2 = **rest**,
prop, be supported, recline,
repose 3 = **tend**, prefer, favour,
incline, be prone to, be disposed
to ▷ PHRASE: **lean on someone**
= **depend on**, trust, rely on, cling
to, count on, have faith in

lean² ADJECTIVE = **thin**, slim,
slender, skinny, angular, trim,
spare, gaunt ≠ fat

leaning NOUN = **tendency**, bias,
inclination, bent, disposition,
penchant, propensity,
predilection

leap VERB = **jump**, spring, bound,
bounce, hop, skip
▷ NOUN 1 = **jump**, spring, bound,
vault 2 = **rise**, change, increase,
soaring, surge, escalation,
upsurge, upswing ▷ PHRASE: **leap
at something** = **accept eagerly**,
seize on, jump at

learn VERB 1 = **master**, grasp,
pick up, take in, familiarize
yourself with 2 = **discover**, hear,
understand, find out about,
become aware, discern, ascertain,
come to know 3 = **memorize**,
commit to memory, learn by
heart, learn by rote, learn parrot-
fashion, get off pat

learned ADJECTIVE = **scholarly**,
academic, intellectual, versed,
well-informed, erudite, highbrow,
well-read ≠ uneducated

learner NOUN = **student**, novice,
beginner, apprentice, neophyte,
tyro ≠ expert

learning NOUN = **knowledge**,
study, education, scholarship,

enlightenment

lease VERB = **hire**, rent, let, loan, charter, rent out, hire out

least ADJECTIVE = **smallest**, meanest, fewest, lowest, tiniest, minimum, slightest, minimal

leave¹ VERB 1 = **depart from**, withdraw from, go from, escape from, quit, flee, exit, pull out of ≠ arrive 2 = **quit**, give up, get out of, resign from, drop out of 3 = **give up**, abandon, dump (*informal*), drop, surrender, ditch (*informal*), chuck (*informal*), discard ≠ stay with 4 = **entrust**, commit, delegate, refer, hand over, assign, consign, allot 5 = **bequeath**, will, transfer, endow, confer, hand down 6 = **forget**, leave behind, mislay 7 = **cause**, produce, result in, generate, deposit ▷ PHRASE: **leave something** *or* **someone out** = **omit**, exclude, miss out, forget, reject, ignore, overlook, neglect

leave² NOUN 1 = **holiday**, break, vacation, time off, sabbatical, leave of absence, furlough, schoolie (*Austral.*), accumulated day off *or* ADO (*Austral.*) 2 = **permission**, freedom, sanction, liberty, concession, consent, allowance, warrant ≠ refusal 3 = **departure**, parting, withdrawal, goodbye, farewell, retirement, leave-taking, adieu ≠ arrival

lecture NOUN 1 = **talk**, address, speech, lesson, instruction, presentation, discourse, sermon

2 = **telling-off** (*informal*), rebuke, reprimand, talking-to (*informal*), scolding, dressing-down (*informal*), reproof ▷ VERB 1 = **talk**, speak, teach, address, discourse, spout, expound, hold forth 2 = **tell off** (*informal*), berate, scold, reprimand, censure, castigate, admonish, reprove

lees PLURAL NOUN = **sediment**, grounds, deposit, dregs

left ADJECTIVE 1 = **left-hand**, port, larboard (*nautical*) 2 (*of politics*) = **socialist**, radical, left-wing, leftist

left-wing ADJECTIVE = **socialist**, communist, red (*informal*), radical, revolutionary, militant, Bolshevik, Leninist

leg NOUN 1 = **limb**, member, shank, lower limb, pin (*informal*), stump (*informal*) 2 = **support**, prop, brace, upright 3 = **stage**, part, section, stretch, lap, segment, portion ▷ PHRASE: **pull someone's leg** (*informal*) = **tease**, trick, fool, kid (*informal*), wind up (*Brit. slang*), hoax, make fun of, lead up the garden path

● WORD POWER
● The core meaning of *leg* is
● either of the two lower limbs
● of the human body. Their role
● in propping up the body has
● produced the meaning of
● support in other objects like
● *the leg of a chair*. We also talk
● about giving someone *a leg up*
● when they need support and

a boost. The idea of a leg as a structural support is reiterated in the phrases *not have a leg to stand on* and *on one's last legs*. A leg can equally refer to a stage of a journey or race, historically denoting sea journeys, but now with a wider application. Another common meaning of leg is that of movement in *shake a leg* (get moving), *stretch your legs* (go for a walk), and *leg it* (run away). The expression *pull someone's leg*, meaning to tease them, may originate from a Scottish rhyme where a preacher tugged on the leg of a hung criminal to make sure they were dead. Nowadays, pulling someone's leg has a more lighthearted meaning, involving teasing and joking.

legacy NOUN = **bequest**, inheritance, gift, estate, heirloom

legal ADJECTIVE 1 = **judicial**, judiciary, forensic, juridical, jurisdictive 2 = **lawful**, allowed, sanctioned, constitutional, valid, legitimate, authorized, permissible

legend NOUN 1 = **myth**, story, tale, fiction, saga, fable, folk tale, folk story 2 = **celebrity**, star, phenomenon, genius, prodigy, luminary, megastar (*informal*) 3 = **inscription**, title, caption, device, motto, rubric

legendary ADJECTIVE 1 = **famous**, celebrated, well-known, acclaimed, renowned, famed, immortal, illustrious ≠ unknown 2 = **mythical**, fabled, traditional, romantic, fabulous, fictitious, storybook, apocryphal ≠ factual

legion NOUN 1 = **army**, company, force, division, troop, brigade 2 = **multitude**, host, mass, drove, number, horde, myriad, throng

legislation NOUN 1 = **law**, act, ruling, rule, bill, measure, regulation, charter 2 = **lawmaking**, regulation, prescription, enactment

legislative ADJECTIVE = **law-making**, judicial, law-giving

legislator NOUN = **lawmaker**, lawgiver

legislature NOUN = **parliament**, congress, senate, assembly, chamber

legitimate ADJECTIVE 1 = **lawful**, legal, genuine, authentic, authorized, rightful, kosher (*informal*), dinkum (*Austral. & N.Z. informal*), licit ≠ unlawful 2 = **reasonable**, correct, sensible, valid, warranted, logical, justifiable, well-founded ≠ unreasonable
▷ VERB = **legitimize**, allow, permit, sanction, authorize, legalize, pronounce lawful

leisure NOUN = **spare**, free, rest, ease, relaxation, recreation ≠ work

lekker ADJECTIVE (*S. African slang*) = **delicious**, tasty, luscious, palatable, delectable, mouthwatering, scrumptious (*informal*), appetizing, yummo

(Austral. slang)

lemon NOUN ▷ **RELATED WORDS**:
adjectives **citric, citrous**
▷ *see* **shades of yellow**

lend VERB 1 = **loan**, advance, sub
(Brit. informal) 2 = **give**, provide,
add, supply, grant, confer, bestow,
impart ▷ **PHRASE: lend itself to
something** = **be appropriate
for**, suit, be suitable for, be
appropriate to, be serviceable for

length NOUN 1 = **distance**, reach,
measure, extent, span, longitude
2 = **duration**, term, period, space,
stretch, span, expanse 3 = **piece**,
measure, section, segment,
portion ▷ **PHRASE: at length**
1 = **at last**, finally, eventually,
in time, in the end, at long last
2 = **for a long time**, completely,
fully, thoroughly, for hours, in
detail, for ages, in depth

lengthen VERB 1 = **extend**,
continue, increase, stretch,
expand, elongate ≠ shorten
2 = **protract**, extend, prolong,
draw out, spin out, make longer
≠ cut down

lengthy ADJECTIVE 1 = **protracted**,
long, prolonged, tedious, drawn-
out, interminable, long-winded,
long-drawn-out 2 = **very
long**, rambling, interminable,
long-winded, wordy, discursive,
extended ≠ brief

lesbian ADJECTIVE = **homosexual**,
gay, les (slang), sapphic, lesbo
(slang)

less ADJECTIVE = **smaller**, shorter,
not so much

▷ **PREPOSITION** = **minus**, without,
lacking, excepting, subtracting

● **WORD POWER**
● *Less* should not be confused
● with *fewer*. *Less* refers strictly
● only to quantity and not to
● number: *there is less water than*
● *before*. *Fewer* means smaller in
● number: *there are fewer people*
● *than before*.

lessen VERB 1 = **reduce**, lower,
diminish, decrease, ease, narrow,
minimize ≠ increase 2 = **grow
less**, diminish, decrease, contract,
ease, shrink

lesser ADJECTIVE = **lower**,
secondary, subsidiary, inferior,
less important ≠ greater

lesson NOUN 1 = **class**, schooling,
period, teaching, coaching,
session, instruction, lecture
2 = **example**, warning, message,
moral, deterrent 3 = **Bible
reading**, reading, text, Bible
passage, Scripture passage

let VERB 1 = **allow**, permit,
authorize, give the go-ahead,
give permission 2 = **lease**,
hire, rent, rent out, hire out,
sublease ▷ **PHRASES: let on**
(informal) 1 = **reveal**, disclose, say,
tell, admit, give away, divulge,
let slip; **let someone down**
= **disappoint**, fail, abandon,
desert, disillusion, fall short,
leave stranded, leave in the
lurch; **let someone off** (informal)
= **excuse**, release, discharge,
pardon, spare, forgive, exempt,
exonerate; **let something down**

= **deflate**, empty, exhaust, flatten, puncture; **let something off 1** = **fire**, explode, set off, discharge, detonate **2** = **emit**, release, leak, exude, give off; **let something out 1** = **release**, discharge **2** = **emit**, make, produce, give vent to; **let something** or **someone in** = **admit**, include, receive, welcome, greet, take in, incorporate, give access to; **let up** = **stop**, diminish, decrease, subside, relax, ease (up), moderate, lessen

lethal ADJECTIVE = **deadly**, terminal, fatal, dangerous, devastating, destructive, mortal, murderous ≠ harmless

letter NOUN **1** = **message**, line, note, communication, dispatch, missive, epistle, e-mail **2** = **character**, mark, sign, symbol

level NOUN = **position**, standard, degree, grade, standing, stage, rank, status
▷ ADJECTIVE **1** = **equal**, balanced, at the same height **2** = **horizontal**, even, flat, smooth, uniform ≠ slanted **3** = **even**, tied, equal, drawn, neck and neck, all square, level pegging
▷ VERB **1** = **equalize**, balance, even up **2** = **destroy**, devastate, demolish, flatten, knock down, pull down, tear down, bulldoze, kennet (*Austral. slang*), jeff (*Austral. slang*) ≠ build **3** = **direct**, point, turn, train, aim, focus **4** = **flatten**, plane, smooth, even off or out
▷ PHRASE: **on the level** (*informal*)

= **honest**, genuine, straight, fair, square, dinkum (*Austral. & N.Z. informal*), above board

lever NOUN = **handle**, bar
▷ VERB = **prise**, force

leverage NOUN **1** = **influence**, authority, pull (*informal*), weight, clout (*informal*) **2** = **force**, hold, pull, strength, grip, grasp

levy NOUN = **tax**, fee, toll, tariff, duty, excise, exaction
▷ VERB = **impose**, charge, collect, demand, exact

liability NOUN **1** = **disadvantage**, burden, drawback, inconvenience, handicap, nuisance, hindrance, millstone **2** = **responsibility**, accountability, culpability, answerability

liable ADJECTIVE **1** = **likely**, tending, inclined, disposed, prone, apt **2** = **vulnerable**, subject, exposed, prone, susceptible, open, at risk of **3** = **responsible**, accountable, answerable, obligated
● **WORD POWER**
● In the past, it was considered
● incorrect to use *liable* to mean
● 'probable' or 'likely', as in *it's*
● *liable to happen soon*. However,
● this usage is now generally
● considered acceptable.

liaison NOUN **1** = **contact**, communication, connection, interchange **2** = **intermediary**, contact, hook-up **3** = **affair**, romance, intrigue, fling, love affair, amour, entanglement

liar NOUN = **falsifier**, perjurer,

fibber, fabricator

libel NOUN = **defamation**, misrepresentation, denigration, smear, calumny, aspersion
▷ VERB = **defame**, smear, slur, blacken, malign, denigrate, revile, vilify

liberal ADJECTIVE 1 = **tolerant**, open-minded, permissive, indulgent, easy-going, broad-minded ≠ intolerant
2 = **progressive**, radical, reformist, libertarian, forward-looking, free-thinking ≠ conservative 3 = **abundant**, generous, handsome, lavish, ample, rich, plentiful, copious ≠ limited 4 = **generous**, kind, charitable, extravagant, open-hearted, bountiful, magnanimous, open-handed ≠ stingy

liberate VERB = **free**, release, rescue, save, deliver, let out, set free, let loose ≠ imprison

liberty NOUN = **independence**, sovereignty, liberation, autonomy, immunity, self-determination, emancipation, self-government ≠ restraint
▷ PHRASES: **at liberty 1** = **free**, escaped, unlimited, at large, not confined, untied, on the loose, unchained **2** = **able**, free, allowed, permitted, entitled, authorized; **take liberties** or **a liberty** = **not show enough respect**, show disrespect, act presumptuously, behave too familiarly, behave impertinently

licence NOUN 1 = **certificate**, document, permit, charter, warrant 2 = **permission**, the right, authority, leave, sanction, liberty, immunity, entitlement ≠ denial 3 = **freedom**, creativity, latitude, independence, liberty, deviation, leeway, free rein ≠ restraint 4 = **laxity**, excess, indulgence, irresponsibility, licentiousness, immoderation ≠ moderation

license VERB = **permit**, sanction, allow, warrant, authorize, empower, certify, accredit ≠ forbid

lick VERB 1 = **taste**, lap, tongue 2 (*informal*) = **beat**, defeat, overcome, rout, outstrip, outdo, trounce, vanquish 3 (*of a flame*) = **flicker**, touch, flick, dart, ripple, play over
▷ NOUN 1 = **dab**, bit, touch, stroke 2 (*informal*) = **pace**, rate, speed, clip (*informal*)

lie¹ NOUN = **falsehood**, deceit, fabrication, fib, fiction, invention, deception, untruth
▷ VERB = **fib**, fabricate, falsify, prevaricate, not tell the truth, equivocate, dissimulate, tell untruths ▷ PHRASE: **give the lie to something** = **disprove**, expose, discredit, contradict, refute, negate, invalidate, rebut

lie² VERB 1 = **recline**, rest, lounge, sprawl, stretch out, loll, repose 2 = **be placed**, be, rest, exist, be situated 3 = **be situated**, sit, be located, be positioned 4 = **be**

buried, remain, rest, be, be entombed

life NOUN 1 = **being**, existence, vitality, sentience 2 = **existence**, being, lifetime, time, days, span 3 = **way of life**, situation, conduct, behaviour, life style 4 = **liveliness**, energy, spirit, vitality, animation, vigour, verve, zest 5 = **biography**, story, history, profile, confessions, autobiography, memoirs, life story ▷ **RELATED WORDS**: *adjectives* **animate, vital**

lifelong ADJECTIVE = **long-lasting**, enduring, lasting, persistent, long-standing, perennial

lifetime NOUN = **existence**, time, day(s), span

lift VERB 1 = **raise**, pick up, hoist, draw up, elevate, uplift, heave up, upraise ≠ lower 2 = **revoke**, end, remove, withdraw, stop, cancel, terminate, rescind ≠ impose 3 = **disappear**, clear, vanish, disperse, dissipate, rise, be dispelled ▷ NOUN 1 = **boost**, encouragement, stimulus, pick-me-up, fillip, shot in the arm (*informal*), gee-up ≠ blow 2 = **elevator** (*chiefly U.S.*), hoist, paternoster 3 = **ride**, run, drive, hitch (*informal*) ▷ PHRASE: **lift off** = **take off**, be launched, blast off, take to the air

light¹ NOUN 1 = **brightness**, illumination, luminosity, shining, glow, glare, gleam, brilliance ≠ dark 2 = **lamp**, torch, candle, flare, beacon, lantern, taper 3 = **match**, spark, flame, lighter 4 = **aspect**, context, angle, point of view, interpretation, viewpoint, slant, standpoint ▷ ADJECTIVE 1 = **bright**, brilliant, shining, illuminated, luminous, well-lit, lustrous, well-illuminated ≠ dark 2 = **pale**, fair, faded, blonde, blond, bleached, pastel, light-coloured ≠ dark ▷ VERB 1 = **illuminate**, light up, brighten ≠ darken 2 = **ignite**, inflame, kindle, touch off, set alight ≠ put out ▷ PHRASE: **light up 1** = **cheer**, shine, blaze, sparkle, animate, brighten, lighten, irradiate 2 = **shine**, flash, beam, blaze, sparkle, flare, glare, gleam

light² ADJECTIVE 1 = **insubstantial**, thin, slight, portable, buoyant, airy, flimsy, underweight ≠ heavy 2 = **weak**, soft, gentle, moderate, slight, mild, faint, indistinct ≠ strong 3 = **digestible**, modest, frugal ≠ substantial 4 = **insignificant**, small, slight, petty, trivial, trifling, inconsequential, inconsiderable ≠ serious 5 = **light-hearted**, funny, entertaining, amusing, witty, humorous, frivolous, unserious ≠ serious 6 = **nimble**, graceful, deft, agile, sprightly, lithe, limber, lissom ≠ clumsy ▷ PHRASE: **light on** *or* **upon something 1** = **settle**, land, perch, alight 2 = **come across**, find, discover, encounter, stumble on, hit upon, happen upon

lighten³ VERB = **brighten**, illuminate, light up, irradiate, become light

lighten⁴ VERB 1 = **ease**, relieve, alleviate, allay, reduce, lessen, mitigate, assuage ≠ intensify 2 = **cheer**, lift, revive, brighten, perk up, buoy up ≠ depress

lightly ADVERB 1 = **moderately**, thinly, slightly, sparsely, sparingly ≠ heavily 2 = **gently**, softly, slightly, faintly, delicately ≠ forcefully 3 = **carelessly**, breezily, thoughtlessly, flippantly, frivolously, heedlessly ≠ seriously 4 = **easily**, simply, readily, effortlessly, unthinkingly, without thought, flippantly, heedlessly ≠ with difficulty

lightweight ADJECTIVE 1 = **thin**, fine, delicate, sheer, flimsy, gossamer, diaphanous, filmy 2 = **unimportant**, shallow, trivial, insignificant, slight, petty, worthless, trifling ≠ significant

like¹ ADJECTIVE = **similar to**, same as, equivalent to, parallel to, identical to, alike, corresponding to, comparable to ≠ different

● **WORD POWER**
● The use of *like* to mean 'such
● as' was in the past considered
● undesirable in formal
● writing, but has now become
● acceptable, for example in *I*
● *enjoy team sports like football and*
● *rugby*. However, the common
● use of *look like* and *seem like*
● to mean 'look or seem as if' is
● thought by many people to be
● incorrect or nonstandard. You
● might say *it looks as if* (or *as*
● *though*) *he's coming*, but it is still
● wise to avoid *it looks like he's*
● *coming*, particularly in formal or
● written contexts.

like² VERB 1 = **enjoy**, love, delight in, go for, relish, savour, revel in, be fond of ≠ dislike 2 = **admire**, approve of, appreciate, prize, take to, esteem, cherish, hold dear ≠ dislike 3 = **wish**, want, choose, prefer, desire, fancy, care, feel inclined

likelihood NOUN = **probability**, chance, possibility, prospect

likely ADJECTIVE 1 = **inclined**, disposed, prone, liable, tending, apt 2 = **probable**, expected, anticipated, odds-on, on the cards, to be expected 3 = **plausible**, possible, reasonable, credible, feasible, believable

liken VERB = **compare**, match, relate, parallel, equate, set beside

likewise ADVERB = **similarly**, the same, in the same way, in similar fashion, in like manner

liking NOUN = **fondness**, love, taste, weakness, preference, affection, inclination, penchant ≠ dislike

limb NOUN 1 = **part**, member, arm, leg, wing, extremity, appendage 2 = **branch**, spur, projection, offshoot, bough

limelight NOUN = **publicity**, recognition, fame, the spotlight, attention, prominence, stardom, public eye

limit NOUN 1 = **end**, ultimate, deadline, breaking point, extremity 2 = **boundary**, edge, border, frontier, perimeter
▷ VERB = **restrict**, control, check, bound, confine, curb, restrain, ration

limitation NOUN 1 = **restriction**, control, check, curb, restraint, constraint 2 = **weakness**, failing, qualification, reservation, defect, flaw, shortcoming, imperfection

limited ADJECTIVE = **restricted**, controlled, checked, bounded, confined, curbed, constrained, finite ≠ unlimited

limp¹ VERB = **hobble**, stagger, stumble, shuffle, hop, falter, shamble, totter
▷ NOUN = **lameness**, hobble

limp² ADJECTIVE = **floppy**, soft, slack, drooping, flabby, pliable, flaccid ≠ stiff

line NOUN 1 = **stroke**, mark, score, band, scratch, slash, streak, stripe 2 = **wrinkle**, mark, crease, furrow, crow's foot 3 = **row**, queue, rank, file, column, convoy, procession 4 = **string**, cable, wire, rope, thread, cord 5 = **trajectory**, way, course, track, channel, direction, route, path 6 = **boundary**, limit, edge, border, frontier, partition, borderline 7 = **occupation**, work, calling, business, job, area, trade, field
▷ VERB 1 = **border**, edge, bound, fringe 2 = **mark**, crease, furrow,

rule, score ▷ PHRASE: **in line for** = **due for**, shortlisted for, in the running for

lined ADJECTIVE 1 = **wrinkled**, worn, furrowed, wizened 2 = **ruled**, feint

line-up NOUN = **arrangement**, team, row, selection, array

linger VERB = **stay**, remain, stop, wait, delay, hang around, idle, dally

link NOUN 1 = **connection**, relationship, association, tie-up, affinity 2 = **relationship**, association, bond, connection, attachment, affinity 3 = **component**, part, piece, element, constituent
▷ VERB 1 = **associate**, relate, identify, connect, bracket 2 = **connect**, join, unite, couple, tie, bind, attach, fasten ≠ separate

lip NOUN 1 = **edge**, rim, brim, margin, brink 2 (*slang*) = **impudence**, insolence, impertinence, cheek (*informal*), effrontery, backchat (*informal*), brass neck (*informal*)

● **WORD POWER**
● The *lips* are the two fleshy
● folds surrounding the mouth.
● Their physical appearance has
● prompted lip to be applied
● to other structures which
● have an edge or rim, e.g. *lip*
● *of the crater*, *cup*, and **hole**. In
● theatrical circles, the edge
● of the stage is technically
● known as the lip. The lips are

important in the articulation
of speech, so lip in itself can
mean speech, specifically
impudent backchat in *none
of your lip*. The expression
pay lip service means to offer
insincere support which is not
put into practice, stemming
from a sense of service as duty,
for show but not for real. Lips
have developed connotations
of appetite, both for food and
love: we *smack* or *lick our lips* in
anticipation of these things.

liquid NOUN =**fluid**, solution,
juice, sap
▷ ADJECTIVE 1 =**fluid**, running,
flowing, melted, watery, molten,
runny, aqueous 2 (*of an asset*)
=**convertible**, disposable,
negotiable, realizable

liquor NOUN 1 =**alcohol**, drink,
spirits, booze (*informal*), hard stuff
(*informal*), strong drink 2 =**juice**,
stock, liquid, extract, broth

list¹ NOUN =**inventory**, record,
series, roll, index, register,
catalogue, directory
▷ VERB =**itemize**, record, enter,
register, catalogue, enumerate,
note down, tabulate

list² VERB =**lean**, tip, incline, tilt,
heel over, careen
▷ NOUN =**tilt**, leaning, slant, cant

listen VERB 1 =**hear**, attend, pay
attention, lend an ear, prick up
your ears 2 =**pay attention**,
observe, obey, mind, heed, take
notice, take note of, take heed of

literacy NOUN =**education**,
learning, knowledge

literal ADJECTIVE 1 =**exact**, close,
strict, accurate, faithful, verbatim,
word for word 2 =**actual**, real,
true, simple, plain, genuine, bona
fide, unvarnished

literally ADVERB =**exactly**, really,
closely, actually, truly, precisely,
strictly, faithfully

literary ADJECTIVE =**well-read**,
learned, formal, intellectual,
scholarly, erudite, bookish

literate ADJECTIVE =**educated**,
informed, knowledgeable

literature NOUN =**writings**,
letters, compositions, lore,
creative writing
▷ see **Shakespeare**

litigation NOUN =**lawsuit**, case,
action, prosecution

litter NOUN 1 =**rubbish**, refuse,
waste, junk, debris, garbage
(*chiefly U.S.*), trash, muck
2 =**brood**, young, offspring,
progeny
▷ VERB 1 =**clutter**, mess up,
clutter up, be scattered about,
disorder, disarrange, derange,
muss (*U.S. & Canad.*) 2 =**scatter**,
spread, shower, strew

little ADJECTIVE 1 =**small**, minute,
short, tiny, wee, compact,
miniature, diminutive ≠ big
2 =**young**, small, junior, infant,
immature, undeveloped, babyish
▷ ADVERB 1 =**hardly**, barely,
scarcely ≠ much 2 =**rarely**,
seldom, scarcely, not often,
infrequently, hardly ever ≠ always
▷ NOUN =**bit**, touch, spot, trace,

hint, particle, fragment, speck ≠ lot ▷ PHRASE: **a little** = **to a small extent**, slightly, to some extent, to a certain extent, to a small degree

live¹ VERB 1 = **dwell**, board, settle, lodge, occupy, abide, inhabit, reside 2 = **exist**, last, prevail, be, have being, breathe, persist, be alive 3 = **survive**, get along, make a living, make ends meet, subsist, eke out a living, support yourself, maintain yourself 4 = **thrive**, flourish, prosper, have fun, enjoy yourself, live life to the full

live² ADJECTIVE 1 = **living**, alive, breathing, animate 2 = **active**, unexploded 3 = **topical**, important, pressing, current, hot, burning, controversial, prevalent

livelihood NOUN = **occupation**, work, employment, living, job, bread and butter (*informal*)

lively ADJECTIVE 1 = **animated**, spirited, quick, keen, active, alert, dynamic, vigorous ≠ dull 2 = **vivid**, strong, striking, bright, exciting, stimulating, bold, colourful ≠ dull 3 = **enthusiastic**, strong, keen, stimulating, eager, formidable, vigorous, animated

living NOUN = **lifestyle**, ways, situation, conduct, behaviour, customs, lifestyle, way of life ▷ ADJECTIVE 1 = **alive**, existing, moving, active, breathing, animate ≠ dead 2 = **current**, present, active, contemporary, in use, extant ≠ obsolete

lizard NOUN

▷ *see* **reptiles**

load VERB 1 = **fill**, stuff, pack, pile, stack, heap, cram, freight 2 = **make ready**, charge, prime ▷ NOUN 1 = **cargo**, delivery, haul, shipment, batch, freight, consignment 2 = **oppression**, charge, worry, trouble, weight, responsibility, burden, onus ▷ PHRASE: **load someone down** = **burden**, worry, oppress, weigh down, saddle with, encumber, snow under

loaded ADJECTIVE 1 = **tricky**, charged, sensitive, delicate, manipulative, emotive, insidious, artful 2 = **biased**, weighted, rigged, distorted 3 (*slang*) = **rich**, wealthy, affluent, well off, flush (*informal*), well-heeled (*informal*), well-to-do, moneyed, minted (*Brit. slang*)

loaf¹ NOUN 1 = **lump**, block, cake, cube, slab 2 (*slang*) = **head**, mind, sense, common sense, nous (*Brit. slang*), gumption (*Brit. informal*)

loaf² VERB = **idle**, hang around, take it easy, lie around, loiter, laze, lounge around

loan NOUN = **advance**, credit, overdraft ▷ VERB = **lend**, advance, let out

loathe VERB = **hate**, dislike, despise, detest, abhor, abominate

loathing NOUN = **hatred**, hate, disgust, aversion, revulsion, antipathy, repulsion, abhorrence

lobby VERB = **campaign**, press, pressure, push, influence, promote, urge, persuade

▷ NOUN 1 = **pressure group**, group, camp, faction, lobbyists, interest group, special-interest group, ginger group, public-interest group (*U.S.* & *Canad.*)
2 = **corridor**, passage, entrance, porch, hallway, foyer, entrance hall, vestibule

lobola NOUN (*S. African*) = **dowry**, portion, marriage settlement, dot (*archaic*)

local ADJECTIVE 1 = **community**, regional 2 = **confined**, limited, restricted
▷ NOUN = **resident**, native, inhabitant

locate VERB 1 = **find**, discover, detect, come across, track down, pinpoint, unearth, pin down
2 = **place**, put, set, position, seat, site, establish, settle

location NOUN = **place**, point, setting, position, situation, spot, venue, locale

lock¹ VERB 1 = **fasten**, close, secure, shut, bar, seal, bolt
2 = **unite**, join, link, engage, clench, entangle, interlock, entwine 3 = **embrace**, press, grasp, clutch, hug, enclose, clasp, encircle
▷ NOUN = **fastening**, catch, bolt, clasp, padlock ▷ PHRASE: **lock someone up** = **imprison**, jail, confine, cage, detain, shut up, incarcerate, send down (*informal*)

lock² NOUN = **strand**, curl, tuft, tress, ringlet

lodge NOUN 1 = **cabin**, shelter, cottage, hut, chalet, gatehouse
2 = **society**, group, club, section, wing, chapter, branch
▷ VERB 1 = **register**, enter, file, submit, put on record 2 = **stay**, room, board, reside 3 = **stick**, remain, implant, come to rest, imbed

lodging NOUN *often plural* = **accommodation**, rooms, apartments, quarters, digs (*Brit. informal*), shelter, residence, abode, bachelor apartment (*Canad.*)

lofty ADJECTIVE 1 = **noble**, grand, distinguished, renowned, elevated, dignified, illustrious, exalted ≠ humble 2 = **high**, raised, towering, soaring, elevated ≠ low 3 = **haughty**, proud, arrogant, patronizing, condescending, disdainful, supercilious ≠ modest

log NOUN 1 = **stump**, block, branch, chunk, trunk 2 = **record**, account, register, journal, diary, logbook, blog (*informal*)
▷ VERB = **record**, enter, note, register, chart, put down, set down

logic NOUN = **reason**, reasoning, sense, good sense

logical ADJECTIVE 1 = **rational**, clear, reasoned, sound, consistent, valid, coherent, well-organized ≠ illogical
2 = **reasonable**, sensible, natural, wise, plausible ≠ unlikely

lone ADJECTIVE = **solitary**, single, one, only, sole, unaccompanied

loneliness NOUN = **solitude**,

isolation, desolation, seclusion

lonely ADJECTIVE 1 = **solitary**, alone, isolated, abandoned, lone, withdrawn, single, forsaken, lonesome (*chiefly U.S. & Canad.*) ≠ accompanied 2 = **desolate**, deserted, remote, isolated, out-of-the-way, secluded, uninhabited, godforsaken ≠ crowded

lonesome ADJECTIVE (*chiefly U.S. & Canad.*) = **lonely**, gloomy, dreary, desolate, forlorn, friendless, companionless

long¹ ADJECTIVE 1 = **elongated**, extended, stretched, expanded, extensive, lengthy, far-reaching, spread out ≠ short 2 = **prolonged**, sustained, lengthy, lingering, protracted, interminable, spun out, long-drawn-out ≠ brief

long² VERB = **desire**, want, wish, burn, pine, lust, crave, yearn

longing NOUN = **desire**, hope, wish, burning, urge, ambition, hunger, yen (*informal*) ≠ indifference

long-standing ADJECTIVE = **established**, fixed, enduring, abiding, long-lasting, long-established, time-honoured

look VERB 1 = **see**, view, consider, watch, eye, study, survey, examine 2 = **search**, seek, hunt, forage, fossick (*Austral. & N.Z.*) 3 = **consider**, contemplate 4 = **face**, overlook 5 = **hope**, expect, await, anticipate, reckon on 6 = **seem**, appear, look like, strike you as

▷ NOUN 1 = **glimpse**, view, glance, observation, sight, examination, gaze, inspection 2 = **appearance**, bearing, air, style, aspect, manner, expression, impression

▷ PHRASES: **look after something or someone** = **take care of**, mind, protect, tend, guard, nurse, care for, supervise; **look down on or upon someone** = **disdain**, despise, scorn, sneer at, spurn, contemn (*formal*); **look forward to something** = **anticipate**, expect, look for, wait for, await, hope for, long for; **look out for something** = **be careful of**, beware, watch out for, pay attention to, be wary of, keep an eye out for; **look someone up** = **visit**, call on, drop in on (*informal*), look in on; **look something up** = **research**, find, search for, hunt for, track down, seek out; **look up** = **improve**, develop, advance, pick up, progress, get better, shape up (*informal*), perk up; **look up to someone** = **respect**, honour, admire, esteem, revere, defer to, think highly of

lookout NOUN 1 = **watchman**, guard, sentry, sentinel 2 = **watch**, guard, vigil 3 = **watchtower**, post, observatory, observation post 4 (*informal*) = **concern**, business, worry

loom VERB = **appear**, emerge, hover, take shape, threaten, bulk, menace, come into view

loop NOUN = **curve**, ring, circle, twist, curl, spiral, coil, twirl

▷ **VERB** = **twist**, turn, roll, knot, curl, spiral, coil, wind round

loophole NOUN = **let-out**, escape, excuse

loose ADJECTIVE 1 = **free**, detached, insecure, unfettered, unrestricted, untied, unattached, unfastened 2 = **slack**, easy, relaxed, sloppy, loose-fitting ≠ tight 3 (*old-fashioned*) = **promiscuous**, fast, abandoned, immoral, dissipated, profligate, debauched, dissolute ≠ chaste 4 = **vague**, random, inaccurate, rambling, imprecise, ill-defined, indistinct, inexact ≠ precise
▷ **VERB** = **free**, release, liberate, detach, unleash, disconnect, set free, untie ≠ fasten

loosen VERB = **untie**, undo, release, separate, detach, unloose
▷ **PHRASE**: **loosen up** = **relax**, chill (*slang*), soften, unwind, go easy (*informal*), hang loose, outspan (*S. African*), ease up *or* off

loot VERB = **plunder**, rob, raid, sack, rifle, ravage, ransack, pillage
▷ **NOUN** = **plunder**, goods, prize, haul, spoils, booty, swag (*slang*)

lord NOUN 1 = **peer**, nobleman, count, duke, gentleman, earl, noble, baron 2 = **ruler**, leader, chief, master, governor, commander, superior, liege
▷ **PHRASES**: **lord it over someone** = **boss around** *or* **about** (*informal*), order around, threaten, bully, menace, intimidate, hector, bluster; **the Lord** *or* **Our Lord** = **Jesus Christ**, God, Christ, Messiah, Jehovah, the Almighty

lose VERB 1 = **be defeated**, be beaten, lose out, come to grief 2 = **mislay**, drop, forget, be deprived of, lose track of, misplace 3 = **forfeit**, miss, yield, be deprived of, pass up (*informal*)

loser NOUN = **failure**, flop (*informal*), also-ran, no-hoper (*Austral. slang*), dud (*informal*), non-achiever

loss NOUN 1 = **losing**, waste, squandering, forfeiture ≠ gain 2 *sometimes plural* = **deficit**, debt, deficiency, debit, depletion ≠ gain 3 = **damage**, cost, injury, hurt, harm ≠ advantage
▷ **PHRASE**: **at a loss** = **confused**, puzzled, baffled, bewildered, helpless, stumped, perplexed, mystified

lost ADJECTIVE = **missing**, disappeared, vanished, wayward, misplaced, mislaid

lot NOUN 1 = **bunch** (*informal*), group, crowd, crew, set, band, quantity, assortment 2 = **destiny**, situation, circumstances, fortune, chance, accident, fate, doom
▷ **PHRASE**: **a lot** *or* **lots** 1 = **plenty**, scores, masses (*informal*), load(s) (*informal*), wealth, piles (*informal*), a great deal, stack(s) 2 = **often**, regularly, a great deal, frequently, a good deal

lotion NOUN = **cream**, solution, balm, salve, liniment, embrocation

lottery NOUN 1 = **raffle**, draw, lotto (*Brit., N.Z. & S. African*), sweepstake **2** = **gamble**, chance, risk, hazard, toss-up (*informal*)

loud ADJECTIVE **1** = **noisy**, booming, roaring, thundering, forte (*music*), resounding, deafening, thunderous ≠ quiet **2** = **garish**, bold, glaring, flamboyant, brash, flashy, lurid, gaudy ≠ sombre

loudly ADVERB = **noisily**, vigorously, vehemently, vociferously, uproariously, lustily, shrilly, fortissimo (*music*)

lounge VERB = **relax**, loaf, sprawl, lie about, take it easy, loiter, loll, laze, outspan (*S. African*)
  ▷ NOUN = **sitting room**, living room, parlour, drawing room, front room, reception room, television room

love VERB **1** = **adore**, care for, treasure, cherish, prize, worship, be devoted to, dote on ≠ hate **2** = **enjoy**, like, appreciate, relish, delight in, savour, take pleasure in, have a soft spot for ≠ dislike
  ▷ NOUN **1** = **passion**, affection, warmth, attachment, intimacy, devotion, tenderness, adoration, aroha (*N.Z.*) ≠ hatred **2** = **liking**, taste, bent for, weakness for, relish for, enjoyment, devotion to, penchant for **3** = **beloved**, dear, dearest, lover, darling, honey, sweetheart, truelove ≠ enemy **4** = **sympathy**, understanding, pity, humanity, warmth, mercy, sorrow, kindness, aroha (*N.Z.*)
  ▷ PHRASE: **make love** = **have sexual intercourse**, have sex, go to bed, sleep together, do it (*informal*), mate, have sexual relations, have it off (*slang*)

love affair NOUN = **romance**, relationship, affair, intrigue, liaison, amour

lovely ADJECTIVE **1** = **beautiful**, appealing, attractive, charming, pretty, handsome, good-looking, exquisite, fit (*Brit. informal*) ≠ ugly **2** = **wonderful**, pleasing, nice, pleasant, engaging, marvellous, delightful, enjoyable ≠ horrible

lover NOUN = **sweetheart**, beloved, loved one, flame (*informal*), mistress, admirer, suitor, woman friend

loving ADJECTIVE **1** = **affectionate**, dear, devoted, tender, fond, doting, amorous, warm-hearted ≠ cruel **2** = **tender**, kind, caring, warm, gentle, sympathetic, considerate

low ADJECTIVE **1** = **small**, little, short, stunted, squat ≠ tall **2** = **inferior**, bad, poor, inadequate, unsatisfactory, deficient, second-rate, shoddy, half-pie (*N.Z. informal*), bodger or bodgie (*Austral. slang*) **3** = **quiet**, soft, gentle, whispered, muted, subdued, hushed, muffled ≠ loud **4** = **dejected**, depressed, miserable, fed up, moody, gloomy, glum, despondent ≠ happy **5** = **coarse**, common, rough, crude, rude, vulgar, undignified, disreputable **6** = **ill**, weak, frail, stricken, debilitated ≠ strong

lower ADJECTIVE **1** = **subordinate**,

under, smaller, junior, minor, secondary, lesser, inferior **2** = **reduced**, cut, diminished, decreased, lessened, curtailed ≠ increased

▷ VERB **1** = **drop**, sink, depress, let down, submerge, take down, let fall ≠ raise **2** = **lessen**, cut, reduce, diminish, slash, decrease, prune, minimize ≠ increase

low-key ADJECTIVE = **subdued**, quiet, restrained, muted, understated, toned down

loyal ADJECTIVE = **faithful**, true, devoted, dependable, constant, staunch, trustworthy, trusty ≠ disloyal

loyalty NOUN = **faithfulness**, commitment, devotion, allegiance, fidelity, homage, obedience, constancy

luck NOUN **1** = **good fortune**, success, advantage, prosperity, blessing, windfall, godsend, serendipity **2** = **fortune**, lot, stars, chance, accident, fate, destiny, twist of fate

luckily ADVERB = **fortunately**, happily, opportunely

lucky ADJECTIVE = **fortunate**, successful, favoured, charmed, blessed, jammy (*Brit. slang*), serendipitous ≠ unlucky

lucrative ADJECTIVE = **profitable**, rewarding, productive, fruitful, well-paid, advantageous, remunerative

ludicrous ADJECTIVE = **ridiculous**, crazy, absurd, preposterous, silly, laughable, farcical, outlandish

≠ sensible

luggage NOUN = **baggage**, things, cases, bags, gear, suitcases, paraphernalia, impedimenta

lull NOUN = **respite**, pause, quiet, silence, calm, hush, let-up (*informal*)

▷ VERB = **calm**, soothe, subdue, quell, allay, pacify, tranquillize

lumber¹ VERB (*Brit. informal*) = **burden**, land, load, saddle, encumber

▷ NOUN (*Brit.*) = **junk**, refuse, rubbish, trash, clutter, jumble

lumber² VERB = **plod**, shuffle, shamble, trudge, stump, waddle, trundle

lumbering ADJECTIVE = **awkward**, heavy, hulking, ponderous, ungainly

lump NOUN **1** = **piece**, ball, block, mass, chunk, hunk, nugget **2** = **swelling**, growth, bump, tumour, bulge, hump, protrusion

▷ VERB = **group**, throw, mass, combine, collect, pool, consolidate, conglomerate

lunatic NOUN = **madman**, maniac, psychopath, nutcase (*slang*), crazy (*informal*)

▷ ADJECTIVE = **mad**, crazy, insane, irrational, daft, deranged, crackpot (*informal*), crackbrained, off the air (*Austral. slang*)

lunge VERB = **pounce**, charge, dive, leap, plunge, thrust

▷ NOUN = **thrust**, charge, pounce, spring, swing, jab

lurch VERB **1** = **tilt**, roll, pitch, list, rock, lean, heel **2** = **stagger**, reel, stumble, weave, sway, totter

lure VERB = **tempt**, draw, attract,
invite, trick, seduce, entice, allure
▷ NOUN = **temptation**,
attraction, incentive, bait,
carrot (*informal*), inducement,
enticement, allurement

lurk VERB = **hide**, sneak, prowl,
lie in wait, slink, skulk, conceal
yourself

lush ADJECTIVE 1 = **abundant**,
green, flourishing, dense, rank,
verdant 2 = **luxurious**, grand,
elaborate, lavish, extravagant,
sumptuous, plush (*informal*),
ornate

lust NOUN 1 = **lechery**, sensuality,
lewdness, lasciviousness
2 = **desire**, longing, passion,
appetite, craving, greed, thirst
▷ PHRASE: **lust for** *or* **after**
someone *or* **something** = **desire**,
want, crave, yearn for, covet,
hunger for *or* after

luxurious ADJECTIVE
= **sumptuous**, expensive,
comfortable, magnificent,
splendid, lavish, plush (*informal*),
opulent

  ⦾ **WORD POWER**
  ⦾ *Luxurious* is sometimes wrongly
  ⦾ used where *luxuriant* is meant:
  ⦾ *he had a luxuriant* (not *luxurious*)
  ⦾ *moustache; the walls were covered*
  ⦾ *with a luxuriant growth of*
  ⦾ *wisteria*.

luxury NOUN 1 = **opulence**,
splendour, richness,
extravagance, affluence,
hedonism, a bed of roses,

the life of Riley ≠ poverty
2 = **extravagance**, treat, extra,
indulgence, frill ≠ necessity

lyrical ADJECTIVE = **enthusiastic**,
inspired, poetic, impassioned,
effusive, rhapsodic

Mm

machine NOUN 1 = **appliance**, device, apparatus, engine, tool, instrument, mechanism, gadget 2 = **system**, structure, organization, machinery, setup (*informal*)

machinery NOUN = **equipment**, gear, instruments, apparatus, technology, tackle, tools, gadgetry

macho ADJECTIVE = **manly**, masculine, chauvinist, virile

mad ADJECTIVE 1 = **insane**, crazy (*informal*), nuts (*slang*), raving, unstable, psychotic, demented, deranged, off the air (*Austral. slang*) ≠ sane 2 = **foolish**, absurd, wild, stupid, daft (*informal*), irrational, senseless, preposterous ≠ sensible 3 (*informal*) = **angry**, furious, incensed, enraged, livid (*informal*), berserk, berko (*Austral. slang*), tooshie (*Austral. slang*), off the air (*Austral. slang*) ≠ calm 4 *usually with* **about** = **enthusiastic**, wild, crazy (*informal*), ardent, fanatical, avid, impassioned, infatuated ≠ nonchalant 5 = **frenzied**, wild, excited, frenetic, uncontrolled, unrestrained

madden VERB = **infuriate**, irritate, incense, enrage, upset, annoy, inflame, drive you crazy ≠ calm

madly ADVERB 1 (*informal*) = **passionately**, wildly, desperately, intensely, to distraction, devotedly 2 = **foolishly**, wildly, absurdly, ludicrously, irrationally, senselessly 3 = **energetically**, wildly, furiously, excitedly, recklessly, speedily, like mad (*informal*) 4 = **insanely**, frantically, hysterically, crazily, deliriously, distractedly, frenziedly

madness NOUN 1 = **insanity**, mental illness, delusion, mania, dementia, distraction, aberration, psychosis 2 = **foolishness**, nonsense, folly, absurdity, idiocy, wildness, daftness (*informal*), foolhardiness

magazine NOUN = **journal**, publication, supplement, rag (*informal*), issue, glossy (*informal*), pamphlet, periodical

magic NOUN 1 = **sorcery**, wizardry, witchcraft, enchantment, black art, necromancy 2 = **conjuring**, illusion, trickery, sleight of hand, legerdemain, prestidigitation 3 = **charm**, power, glamour, fascination, magnetism, enchantment, allurement ▷ ADJECTIVE = **miraculous**, entrancing, charming, fascinating, marvellous, magical, enchanting, bewitching

magician NOUN 1 = **conjuror**, illusionist, prestidigitator 2 = **sorcerer**, witch, wizard, illusionist, warlock, necromancer, enchanter *or* enchantress

magistrate NOUN = **judge**, justice, justice of the peace, J.P.

magnetic ADJECTIVE = **attractive**, irresistible, seductive, captivating, charming, fascinating, charismatic, hypnotic ≠ repulsive

magnificent ADJECTIVE
1 = **splendid**, impressive, imposing, glorious, gorgeous, majestic, regal, sublime ≠ ordinary 2 = **brilliant**, fine, excellent, outstanding, superb, splendid

magnify VERB 1 = **enlarge**, increase, boost, expand, intensify, blow up (*informal*), heighten, amplify ≠ reduce 2 = **make worse**, exaggerate, intensify, worsen, exacerbate, increase, inflame 3 = **exaggerate**, overstate, inflate, overplay, overemphasize ≠ understate

magnitude NOUN
1 = **importance**, consequence, significance, moment, note, weight, greatness ≠ unimportance 2 = **immensity**, size, extent, enormity, volume, vastness ≠ smallness 3 = **intensity**, amplitude

maid NOUN 1 = **servant**, chambermaid, housemaid, menial, maidservant, female servant, domestic (*archaic*), parlourmaid 2 (*archaic or literary*) = **girl**, maiden, lass, damsel, lassie (*informal*), wench

maiden NOUN (*archaic or literary*) = **girl**, maid, lass, damsel, virgin, lassie (*informal*), wench
  ▷ MODIFIER 1 = **first**, initial, inaugural, introductory 2 = **unmarried**, unwed

mail NOUN = **letters**, post, correspondence
  ▷ VERB 1 = **post**, send, forward, dispatch 2 = **e-mail**, send, forward

main ADJECTIVE = **chief**, leading, head, central, essential, primary, principal, foremost ≠ minor
  ▷ PLURAL NOUN 1 = **pipeline**, channel, pipe, conduit, duct 2 = **cable**, line, electricity supply, mains supply ▷ PHRASE: **in the main** = **on the whole**, generally, mainly, mostly, in general, for the most part

mainly ADVERB = **chiefly**, mostly, largely, principally, primarily, on the whole, predominantly, in the main

mainstream ADJECTIVE = **conventional**, general, established, received, accepted, current, prevailing, orthodox ≠ unconventional

maintain VERB 1 = **continue**, retain, preserve, sustain, carry on, keep up, prolong, perpetuate ≠ end 2 = **assert**, state, claim, insist, declare, contend, profess, avow ≠ disavow 3 = **look after**, care for, take care of, conserve, keep in good condition

maintenance NOUN
1 = **upkeep**, keeping, care,

m

repairs, conservation, nurture, preservation **2 = allowance**, support, keep, alimony
3 = continuation, carrying-on, perpetuation, prolongation

majestic ADJECTIVE **= grand**, magnificent, impressive, superb, splendid, regal, stately, monumental ≠ modest

majesty NOUN **= grandeur**, glory, splendour, magnificence, nobility ≠ triviality

major ADJECTIVE **1 = important**, critical, significant, great, serious, crucial, outstanding, notable
2 = main, higher, greater, bigger, leading, chief, senior, supreme ≠ minor

majority NOUN **1 = most**, mass, bulk, best part, better part, lion's share, preponderance, greater number **2 = adulthood**, maturity, age of consent, seniority, manhood or womanhood

- **WORD POWER**
- *The majority of* should always
- refer to a countable number
- of things or people. If you
- are talking about an amount
- or quantity, rather than a
- countable number, use *most*
- *of*, as in *most of the harvest was*
- *saved* (not *the majority of the*
- *harvest was saved*).

make VERB **1 = produce**, cause, create, effect, lead to, generate, bring about, give rise to
2 = perform, do, effect, carry out, execute **3 = force**, cause, compel, drive, require, oblige, induce,

constrain **4 = create**, build, produce, manufacture, form, fashion, construct, assemble
5 = earn, get, gain, net, win, clear, obtain, bring in **6 = amount to**, total, constitute, add up to, count as, tot up to (*informal*)
▷ NOUN **1 = brand**, sort, style, model, kind, type, variety, marque ▷ PHRASES: **make for something = head for**, aim for, head towards, be bound for; **make it** (*informal*) **= succeed**, prosper, arrive (*informal*), get on, crack it (*informal*); **make off = flee**, clear out (*informal*), bolt, take to your heels, run away *or* off; **make something up = invent**, create, construct, compose, frame, coin, devise, originate; **make up = settle your differences**, bury the hatchet, call it quits, declare a truce, be friends again; **make up for something = compensate for**, make amends for, atone for, balance out, offset, make recompense for; **make up something 1 = form**, account for, constitute, compose, comprise
2 = complete, supply, fill, round off

maker NOUN **= manufacturer**, producer, builder, constructor

makeshift ADJECTIVE **= temporary**, provisional, substitute, expedient, stopgap

make-up NOUN **1 = cosmetics**, paint (*informal*), powder, face (*informal*), greasepaint (*theatre*) **2 = nature**, character, constitution, temperament, disposition **3** = **structure**, organization, arrangement, construction, assembly, constitution, format, composition

making NOUN = **creation**, production, manufacture, construction, assembly, composition, fabrication
▷ PLURAL NOUN = **beginnings**, potential, capacity, ingredients

male ADJECTIVE = **masculine**, manly, macho, virile ≠ female

malicious ADJECTIVE = **spiteful**, malevolent, resentful, vengeful, rancorous, ill-disposed, ill-natured ≠ benevolent

mammal ▷ see bats, carnivores, **marsupials, monkeys, apes and other primates, rodents, sea mammals, whales and dolphins**

- **EXTINCT MAMMALS**
- apeman
- aurochs
- australopithecine
- eohippus
- glyptodont
- mammoth
- mastodon
- megathere
- quagga
- sabre-toothed tiger or cat
- tarpan

mammoth ADJECTIVE = **colossal**, huge, giant, massive, enormous, immense, gigantic, monumental, supersize ≠ tiny

man NOUN **1** = **male**, guy (informal), fellow (informal), gentleman, bloke (Brit. informal), chap (Brit. informal), dude (U.S. informal), geezer (informal) **2** = **human**, human being, person, individual, soul **3** = **mankind**, humanity, people, human race, humankind, Homo sapiens
▷ VERB = **staff**, people, crew, occupy, garrison

mana NOUN (N.Z.) = **authority**, influence, power, might, standing, status, importance, eminence

manage VERB **1** = **be in charge of**, run, handle, direct, conduct, command, administer, supervise **2** = **organize**, use, handle, regulate **3** = **cope**, survive, succeed, carry on, make do, get by (informal), muddle through **4** = **perform**, do, achieve, carry out, undertake, cope with, accomplish, contrive **5** = **control**, handle, manipulate

management NOUN **1** = **administration**, control, running, operation, handling, direction, command, supervision **2** = **directors**, board, executive(s), administration, employers

manager NOUN = **supervisor**, head, director, executive, boss (informal), governor, administrator, organizer, baas (S. African), sherang (Austral. & N.Z.)

m

mandate NOUN = **command**, order, commission, instruction, decree, directive, edict

mandatory ADJECTIVE = **compulsory**, required, binding, obligatory, requisite ≠ optional

manhood NOUN = **manliness**, masculinity, virility

manifest ADJECTIVE = **obvious**, apparent, patent, evident, clear, glaring, noticeable, blatant ≠ concealed
▷ VERB = **display**, show, reveal, express, demonstrate, expose, exhibit ≠ conceal

manifestation NOUN 1 = **sign**, symptom, indication, mark, example, evidence, proof, testimony 2 = **display**, show, exhibition, expression, demonstration

manipulate VERB 1 = **influence**, control, direct, negotiate, exploit, manoeuvre 2 = **work**, use, operate, handle

mankind NOUN = **people**, man, humanity, human race, humankind, Homo sapiens

◉ WORD POWER
◉ Some people object to the use
◉ of *mankind* to refer to all human
◉ beings on the grounds that it
◉ is sexist. A preferable term is
◉ *humankind*, which refers to both
◉ men and women.

manly ADJECTIVE = **virile**, masculine, strong, brave, bold, strapping, vigorous, courageous ≠ effeminate

man-made ADJECTIVE = **artificial**, manufactured, mock, synthetic, ersatz

manner NOUN 1 = **style**, way, fashion, method, custom, mode 2 = **behaviour**, air, bearing, conduct, aspect, demeanour 3 = **type**, form, sort, kind, variety, brand, category
▷ PLURAL NOUN 1 = **conduct**, behaviour, demeanour 2 = **politeness**, courtesy, etiquette, refinement, decorum, p's and q's 3 = **protocol**, customs, social graces

mannered ADJECTIVE = **affected**, artificial, pretentious, stilted, arty-farty (*informal*) ≠ natural

manoeuvre VERB 1 = **scheme**, wangle (*informal*), machinate 2 = **manipulate**, arrange, organize, set up, engineer, fix, orchestrate, contrive
▷ NOUN 1 = **stratagem**, scheme, trick, tactic, intrigue, dodge, ploy, ruse 2 *often plural* = **movement**, operation, exercise, war game

mansion NOUN = **residence**, manor, hall, villa, seat

mantle NOUN 1 = **covering**, screen, curtain, blanket, veil, shroud, canopy, pall 2 (*archaic*) = **cloak**, wrap, cape, hood, shawl

manual ADJECTIVE 1 = **physical**, human 2 = **hand-operated**, hand, non-automatic
▷ NOUN = **handbook**, guide, instructions, bible

manufacture VERB 1 = **make**, build, produce, construct, create, turn out, assemble, put together

2 = **concoct**, make up, invent, devise, fabricate, think up, cook up (*informal*), trump up

▷ NOUN = **making**, production, construction, assembly, creation

manufacturer NOUN = **maker**, producer, builder, creator, industrialist, constructor

many ADJECTIVE = **numerous**, various, countless, abundant, myriad, innumerable, manifold, umpteen (*informal*)

▷ PRONOUN = **a lot**, lots (*informal*), plenty, scores, heaps (*informal*)

mar VERB 1 = **harm**, damage, hurt, spoil, stain, taint, tarnish 2 = **ruin**, spoil, scar, flaw, impair, detract from, deform, blemish ≠ improve

march VERB 1 = **parade**, walk, file, pace, stride, swagger 2 = **walk**, strut, storm, sweep, stride, flounce

▷ NOUN 1 = **walk**, trek, slog, yomp (*Brit. informal*), routemarch 2 = **progress**, development, advance, evolution, progression

margin NOUN = **edge**, side, border, boundary, verge, brink, rim, perimeter

marginal ADJECTIVE
1 = **insignificant**, small, minor, slight, minimal, negligible
2 = **borderline**, bordering, on the edge, peripheral

marijuana NOUN = **cannabis**, pot (*slang*), dope (*slang*), grass (*slang*), hemp, dagga (*S. African*)

marine ADJECTIVE = **nautical**, maritime, naval, seafaring, seagoing

mariner NOUN = **sailor**, seaman, sea dog, seafarer, salt

marital ADJECTIVE = **matrimonial**, nuptial, conjugal, connubial

maritime ADJECTIVE 1 = **nautical**, marine, naval, oceanic, seafaring 2 = **coastal**, seaside, littoral

mark NOUN 1 = **spot**, stain, streak, smudge, line, scratch, scar, blot 2 = **characteristic**, feature, standard, quality, measure, stamp, attribute, criterion 3 = **indication**, sign, symbol, token 4 = **brand**, impression, label, device, flag, symbol, token, emblem 5 = **target**, goal, aim, purpose, object, objective

▷ VERB 1 = **scar**, scratch, stain, streak, blot, smudge, blemish 2 = **label**, identify, brand, flag, stamp, characterize 3 = **grade**, correct, assess, evaluate, appraise 4 = **distinguish**, show, illustrate, exemplify, denote 5 = **observe**, mind, note, notice, attend to, pay attention to, pay heed to

marked ADJECTIVE = **noticeable**, clear, decided, striking, obvious, prominent, patent, distinct ≠ imperceptible

markedly ADVERB = **noticeably**, clearly, obviously, considerably, distinctly, decidedly, strikingly, conspicuously

market NOUN = **fair**, mart, bazaar, souk (*Arabic*)

▷ VERB = **sell**, promote, retail, peddle, vend

maroon VERB = **abandon**, leave,

m

desert, strand, leave high and dry (*informal*)

marriage NOUN = **wedding**, match, nuptials, wedlock, matrimony ▷ **RELATED WORDS**: *adjectives* conjugal, marital, nuptial

marry VERB 1 = **tie the knot** (*informal*), wed, get hitched (*slang*) 2 = **unite**, join, link, bond, ally, merge, knit, unify

marsh NOUN = **swamp**, bog, slough, fen, quagmire, morass, muskeg (*Canad.*)

marshal VERB 1 = **conduct**, take, lead, guide, steer, escort, shepherd, usher 2 = **arrange**, group, order, line up, organize, deploy, array, draw up

martial ADJECTIVE = **military**, belligerent, warlike, bellicose

marvel VERB = **be amazed**, wonder, gape, be awed ▷ NOUN 1 = **wonder**, phenomenon, miracle, portent 2 = **genius**, prodigy

marvellous ADJECTIVE = **excellent**, great (*informal*), wonderful, brilliant, amazing, extraordinary, superb, spectacular, booshit (*Austral. slang*), exo (*Austral. slang*), sik (*Austral. slang*), rad (*informal*), phat (*slang*), schmick (*Austral. informal*) ≠ terrible

masculine ADJECTIVE = **male**, manly, mannish, manlike, virile

mask NOUN = **façade**, disguise, front, cover, screen, veil, guise, camouflage

▷ VERB = **disguise**, hide, conceal, obscure, cover (up), screen, blanket, veil

mass NOUN 1 = **lot**, collection, load, pile, quantity, bunch, stack, heap 2 = **piece**, block, lump, chunk, hunk 3 = **size**, matter, weight, extent, bulk, magnitude, greatness

▷ ADJECTIVE = **large-scale**, general, widespread, extensive, universal, wholesale, indiscriminate

▷ VERB = **gather**, assemble, accumulate, collect, rally, swarm, throng, congregate

massacre NOUN = **slaughter**, murder, holocaust, carnage, extermination, annihilation, butchery, blood bath

▷ VERB = **slaughter**, kill, murder, butcher, wipe out, exterminate, mow down, cut to pieces

massage NOUN = **rub-down**, manipulation

▷ VERB 1 = **rub down**, manipulate, knead

2 = **manipulate**, alter, distort, doctor, cook (*informal*), fix (*informal*), rig, fiddle (*informal*)

massive ADJECTIVE = **huge**, big, enormous, immense, hefty, gigantic, monumental, mammoth, supersize ≠ tiny

master NOUN 1 = **lord**, ruler, commander, chief, director, manager, boss (*informal*), head, baas (*S. African*) ≠ servant

2 = **expert**, maestro, ace (*informal*), genius, wizard,

m

- **MARSUPIALS**
- bandicoot
- Bennett's tree kangaroo or tcharibeena
- bettong
- bilby, rabbit(-eared) bandicoot, long-eared bandicoot, dalgyte, or dalgite
- bobuck or mountain (brushtail) possum
- boodie (rat), burrowing rat-kangaroo, Lesueur's rat-kangaroo, tungoo, or tungo
- boongary or Lumholtz's tree kangaroo
- bridled nail-tail wallaby or merrin
- brush-tail(ed) possum
- burramys or (mountain) pygmy possum
- crest-tailed marsupial mouse, Cannings' little dog, or mulgara
- crescent nail-tail wallaby or wurrung
- cuscus
- dasyurid, dasyure, native cat, marsupial cat, or wild cat
- dibbler
- diprotodon
- dunnart
- fluffy glider or yellow-bellied glider
- flying phalanger, flying squirrel, glider, or pongo
- green ringtail possum or toolah
- hare-wallaby
- honey mouse, honey possum, noolbenger, or tait
- jerboa, jerboa pouched mouse, jerboa kangaroo, or kultarr
- kangaroo or (Austral. informal) roo
- koala (bear) or (Austral.) native bear
- kowari
- larapinta or Darling Downs dunnart
- marlu
- marsupial mole
- marsupial mouse
- munning
- ningaui
- northern native cat or satanellus
- numbat or banded anteater
- opossum or possum
- pademelon or paddymelon
- phalanger
- pitchi-pitchi or wuhl-wuhl
- platypus, duck-billed platypus, or duckbill
- potoroo
- pygmy glider, feather glider, or flying mouse
- quokka
- quoll
- rat kangaroo
- squirrel glider
- sugar glider
- tammar, damar, or dama
- Tasmanian devil or ursine dasyure
- thylacine, Tasmanian wolf, or Tasmanian tiger
- tiger cat or spotted native cat
- tree kangaroo
- tuan, phascogale, or wambenger
- wallaby
- wallaroo, uroo, or biggada
- warabi
- wombat or (Austral.) badger
- yapok
- yallara

m

virtuoso, doyen, past master, fundi (*S. African*) ≠ amateur
3 = **teacher**, tutor, instructor ≠ student
▷ ADJECTIVE = **main**, principal, chief, prime, foremost, predominant ≠ lesser
▷ VERB 1 = **learn**, understand, pick up, grasp, get the hang of (*informal*), know inside out, know backwards 2 = **overcome**, defeat, conquer, tame, triumph over, vanquish ≠ give in to

masterly ADJECTIVE = **skilful**, expert, crack (*informal*), supreme, world-class, consummate, first-rate, masterful

mastermind VERB = **plan**, manage, direct, organize, devise, conceive
▷ NOUN = **organizer**, director, manager, engineer, brain(s) (*informal*), architect, planner

masterpiece NOUN = **classic**, tour de force (*French*), pièce de résistance (*French*), magnum opus (*Latin*), jewel

mastery NOUN
1 = **understanding**, skill, know-how, expertise, prowess, finesse, proficiency, virtuosity
2 = **control**, command, domination, superiority, supremacy, upper hand, ascendancy, mana (*N.Z.*), whip hand

match NOUN 1 = **game**, test, competition, trial, tie, contest, fixture, bout 2 = **marriage**, pairing, alliance, partnership

3 = **equal**, rival, peer, counterpart
▷ VERB 1 = **correspond with**, go with, fit with, harmonize with
2 = **correspond**, agree, accord, square, coincide, tally, conform, match up 3 = **rival**, equal, compete with, compare with, emulate, measure up to

matching ADJECTIVE = **identical**, like, twin, equivalent, corresponding, coordinating ≠ different

mate NOUN 1 (*informal*) = **friend**, pal (*informal*), companion, buddy (*informal*), comrade, chum (*informal*), mucker (*Brit. informal*), crony, cobber (*Austral. & N.Z. old-fashioned, informal*), E hoa (*N.Z.*)
2 = **partner**, lover, companion, spouse, consort, helpmeet, husband *or* wife 3 = **assistant**, subordinate, apprentice, helper, accomplice, sidekick (*informal*)
4 = **colleague**, associate, companion
▷ VERB = **pair**, couple, breed

material NOUN 1 = **substance**, matter, stuff 2 = **cloth**, fabric, textile 3 = **information**, details, facts, notes, evidence, particulars, data, info (*informal*)
▷ ADJECTIVE 1 = **physical**, solid, substantial, concrete, bodily, tangible, palpable, corporeal
2 = **relevant**, important, significant, essential, vital, serious, meaningful, applicable

materially ADVERB
= **significantly**, much, greatly, essentially, seriously, gravely,

substantially ≠ insignificantly

maternal ADJECTIVE = **motherly**, protective, nurturing, maternalistic

maternity NOUN = **motherhood**, parenthood, motherliness

matted ADJECTIVE = **tangled**, knotted, unkempt, knotty, tousled, ratty, uncombed

matter NOUN 1 = **situation**, concern, business, question, event, subject, affair, incident **2** = **substance**, material, body, stuff
▷ VERB = **be important**, make a difference, count, be relevant, make any difference, carry weight, cut any ice (*informal*), be of account

matter-of-fact ADJECTIVE = **unsentimental**, plain, sober, down-to-earth, mundane, prosaic, deadpan, unimaginative

mature VERB = **develop**, grow up, bloom, blossom, come of age, age
▷ ADJECTIVE 1 = **matured**, seasoned, ripe, mellow **2** = **grown-up**, adult, of age, fully fledged, full-grown ≠ immature

maturity NOUN 1 = **adulthood**, puberty, coming of age, pubescence, manhood *or* womanhood ≠ immaturity **2** = **ripeness**

maul VERB 1 = **mangle**, claw, lacerate, tear, mangulate (*Austral. slang*) **2** = **ill-treat**, abuse, batter, molest, manhandle

maverick NOUN = **rebel**, radical, dissenter, individualist, protester, eccentric, heretic, nonconformist ≠ traditionalist
▷ ADJECTIVE = **rebel**, radical, dissenting, individualistic, eccentric, heretical, iconoclastic, nonconformist

maximum ADJECTIVE = **greatest**, highest, supreme, paramount, utmost, most, topmost ≠ minimal
▷ NOUN = **top**, peak, ceiling, utmost, upper limit ≠ minimum

maybe ADVERB = **perhaps**, possibly, perchance (*archaic*)

mayhem NOUN = **chaos**, trouble, violence, disorder, destruction, confusion, havoc, fracas

maze NOUN = **web**, confusion, tangle, labyrinth, imbroglio, complex network

meadow NOUN = **field**, pasture, grassland, lea (*poetic*)

mean¹ VERB 1 = **signify**, indicate, represent, express, stand for, convey, spell out, symbolize **2** = **imply**, suggest, intend, hint at, insinuate **3** = **intend**, want, plan, expect, design, aim, wish, think

● WORD POWER
● In standard British English,
● *mean* should not be followed by
● *for* when expressing intention.
● *I didn't mean this to happen* is
● acceptable, but not *I didn't mean*
● *for this to happen.*

mean² ADJECTIVE 1 = **miserly**, stingy, parsimonious, niggardly, mercenary, penny-pinching, ungenerous, tight-fisted, snoep

(S. African informal) ≠ generous
2 = **dishonourable**, petty,
shameful, shabby, vile, callous,
sordid, despicable, scungy
(Austral. & N.Z.) ≠ honourable

mean³ NOUN = **average**, middle,
balance, norm, midpoint
▷ ADJECTIVE = **average**, middle,
standard

meaning NOUN **1** = **significance**,
message, substance, drift,
connotation, gist **2** = **definition**,
sense

meaningful ADJECTIVE
= **significant**, important,
material, useful, relevant, valid,
worthwhile, purposeful ≠ trivial

meaningless ADJECTIVE
= **nonsensical**, senseless,
inconsequential, inane
≠ worthwhile

means PLURAL NOUN **1** = **method**,
way, process, medium, agency,
instrument, mode **2** = **money**,
funds, capital, income, resources,
fortune, wealth, affluence
▷ PHRASES: **by all means**
= **certainly**, surely, of course,
definitely, doubtlessly; **by no
means** = **in no way**, definitely
not, not in the least, on no
account

meantime or **meanwhile**
ADVERB = **at the same time**,
simultaneously, concurrently

meanwhile or **meantime**
ADVERB = **for now**, in the interim

measure VERB = **quantify**,
determine, assess, weigh,
calculate, evaluate, compute,
gauge
▷ NOUN **1** = **quantity**, share,
amount, allowance, portion,
quota, ration, allotment
2 = **action**, act, step, procedure,
means, control, initiative,
manoeuvre **3** = **gauge**, rule, scale,
metre, ruler, yardstick **4** = **law**,
act, bill, legislation, resolution,
statute

measured ADJECTIVE **1** = **steady**,
even, slow, regular, dignified,
stately, solemn, leisurely
2 = **considered**, reasoned,
studied, calculated, deliberate,
sober, well-thought-out

measurement NOUN
= **calculation**, assessment,
evaluation, valuation,
computation, calibration,
mensuration

meat NOUN = **food**, flesh, kai (N.Z.
informal)

mechanical ADJECTIVE
1 = **automatic**, automated,
mechanized, power-driven,
motor-driven ≠ manual
2 = **unthinking**, routine,
automatic, instinctive,
involuntary, impersonal, cursory,
perfunctory ≠ conscious

mechanism NOUN **1** = **process**,
way, means, system, operation,
agency, method, technique
2 = **machine**, device, tool,
instrument, appliance, apparatus,
contrivance

mediate VERB = **intervene**, step
in (informal), intercede, referee,
umpire, reconcile, arbitrate,

conciliate

mediation NOUN =**arbitration**, intervention, reconciliation, conciliation, intercession

mediator NOUN =**negotiator**, arbitrator, referee, umpire, intermediary, middleman, arbiter, peacemaker

medicine NOUN =**remedy**, drug, cure, prescription, medication, nostrum, medicament

mediocre ADJECTIVE =**second-rate**, average, ordinary, indifferent, middling, pedestrian, inferior, so-so (*informal*), half-pie (*N.Z. informal*) ≠ excellent

meditation NOUN =**reflection**, thought, study, musing, pondering, contemplation, rumination, cogitation

medium ADJECTIVE =**average**, mean, middle, middling, fair, intermediate, midway, mediocre ≠ extraordinary
▷ NOUN 1 =**spiritualist**, seer, clairvoyant, fortune teller, channeller 2 =**middle**, mean, centre, average, compromise, midpoint

meet VERB 1 =**encounter**, come across, run into, happen on, find, contact, confront, bump into (*informal*) ≠ avoid 2 =**gather**, collect, assemble, get together, come together, muster, convene, congregate ≠ disperse 3 =**fulfil**, match (up to), answer, satisfy, discharge, comply with, come up to, conform to ≠ fall short of 4 =**experience**, face, suffer,

bear, go through, encounter, endure, undergo 5 =**converge**, join, cross, touch, connect, come together, link up, intersect ≠ diverge

meeting NOUN 1 =**conference**, gathering, assembly, congress, session, convention, get-together (*informal*), reunion, hui (*N.Z.*) 2 =**encounter**, introduction, confrontation, engagement, rendezvous, tryst, assignation

melancholy ADJECTIVE =**sad**, depressed, miserable, gloomy, glum, mournful, despondent, dispirited ≠ happy
▷ NOUN =**sadness**, depression, misery, gloom, sorrow, unhappiness, despondency, dejection ≠ happiness

mellow ADJECTIVE 1 =**full-flavoured**, rich, sweet, delicate 2 =**ripe**, mature, ripened ≠ unripe
▷ VERB 1 =**relax**, improve, settle, calm, mature, soften, sweeten 2 =**season**, develop, improve, ripen

melody NOUN 1 =**tune**, song, theme, air, music, strain 2 =**tunefulness**, harmony, musicality, euphony, melodiousness

melt VERB 1 =**dissolve**, run, soften, fuse, thaw, defrost, liquefy, unfreeze 2 *often with* **away** =**disappear**, fade, vanish, dissolve, disperse, evaporate, evanesce 3 =**soften**, relax, disarm, mollify

m

member NOUN = **representative**, associate, supporter, fellow, subscriber, comrade, disciple

membership NOUN
1 = **participation**, belonging, fellowship, enrolment
2 = **members**, body, associates, fellows

memoir NOUN = **account**, life, record, journal, essay, biography, narrative, monograph

memoirs PLURAL NOUN = **autobiography**, diary, life story, experiences, memories, journals, recollections, reminiscences

memorable ADJECTIVE = **noteworthy**, celebrated, historic, striking, famous, significant, remarkable, notable ≠ forgettable

memorandum NOUN = **note**, minute, message, communication, reminder, memo, jotting, e-mail

memorial NOUN = **monument**, shrine, plaque, cenotaph
▷ ADJECTIVE = **commemorative**, remembrance, monumental

memory NOUN 1 = **recall**, mind, retention, ability to remember, powers of recall, powers of retention 2 = **recollection**, reminder, reminiscence, impression, echo, remembrance
3 = **commemoration**, respect, honour, recognition, tribute, remembrance, observance

menace NOUN 1 (*informal*) = **nuisance**, plague, pest, annoyance, troublemaker

2 = **threat**, warning, intimidation, ill-omen, ominousness
▷ VERB = **bully**, threaten, intimidate, terrorize, frighten, scare

menacing ADJECTIVE = **threatening**, frightening, forbidding, looming, intimidating, ominous, louring *or* lowering ≠ encouraging

mend VERB 1 = **repair**, fix, restore, renew, patch up, renovate, refit, retouch 2 = **darn**, repair, patch, stitch, sew 3 = **heal**, improve, recover, get better, be all right, be cured, recuperate, pull through 4 = **improve**, reform, correct, revise, amend, rectify, ameliorate, emend ▷ PHRASE: on the mend = **convalescent**, improving, recovering, getting better, recuperating

mental ADJECTIVE 1 = **intellectual**, rational, theoretical, cognitive, brain, conceptual, cerebral 2 (*slang*) = **insane**, mad, disturbed, unstable, mentally ill, psychotic, unbalanced, deranged

mentality NOUN = **attitude**, character, personality, psychology, make-up, outlook, disposition, cast of mind

mentally ADVERB = **psychologically**, intellectually, inwardly

mention VERB = **refer to**, point out, bring up, state, reveal, declare, disclose, intimate
▷ NOUN 1 *often with* of

= **reference**, observation, indication, remark, allusion

2 = **acknowledgment**, recognition, tribute, citation, honourable mention

menu NOUN = **bill of fare**, tariff (*chiefly Brit.*), set menu, table d'hôte (*French*), carte du jour (*French*)

merchandise NOUN = **goods**, produce, stock, products, commodities, wares

merchant NOUN = **tradesman**, dealer, trader, broker, retailer, supplier, seller, salesman

mercy NOUN **1** = **compassion**, pity, forgiveness, grace, kindness, clemency, leniency, forbearance ≠ cruelty **2** = **blessing**, boon, godsend

mere ADJECTIVE **1** = **simple**, nothing more than, common, plain, pure **2** = **bare**, slender, trifling, meagre, just, only, basic, no more than

merge VERB **1** = **combine**, blend, fuse, amalgamate, unite, join, mix, mingle ≠ separate **2** = **join**, unite, combine, fuse ≠ separate **3** = **melt**, blend, mingle

merger NOUN = **union**, fusion, consolidation, amalgamation, combination, coalition, incorporation

merit NOUN = **advantage**, value, quality, worth, strength, asset, virtue, strong point
▷ VERB = **deserve**, warrant, be entitled to, earn, have a right to, be worthy of

merry ADJECTIVE **1** = **cheerful**, happy, carefree, jolly, festive, joyous, convivial, blithe ≠ gloomy **2** (*Brit. informal*) = **tipsy**, happy, mellow, tiddly (*slang, chiefly Brit.*), squiffy (*Brit. informal*)

mesh NOUN = **net**, netting, network, web, tracery
▷ VERB = **engage**, combine, connect, knit, coordinate, interlock, dovetail, harmonize

mess NOUN **1** = **untidiness**, disorder, confusion, chaos, litter, clutter, disarray, jumble **2** = **shambles 3** = **difficulty**, dilemma, plight, hole (*informal*), fix (*informal*), jam (*informal*), muddle, pickle (*informal*), uphill (*S. African*) ▷ PHRASES: mess about *or* around = **potter about**, dabble, amuse yourself, fool about *or* around, muck about *or* around (*informal*), play about *or* around, trifle; **mess something up 1** = **botch**, muck something up (*Brit. slang*), muddle something up **2** = **dirty**, pollute, clutter, disarrange, dishevel; **mess with something or someone** = **interfere with**, play with, fiddle with (*informal*), tamper with, tinker with, meddle with

message NOUN
1 = **communication**, note, bulletin, word, letter, dispatch, memorandum, communiqué, email *or* e-mail, text *or* text message, SMS, IMS, tweet (*on the Twitter website*), mention *or* @mention (*on the Twitter website*) **2** = **point**, meaning,

m

idea, moral, theme, import, purport

messenger NOUN = **courier**, runner, carrier, herald, envoy, go-between, emissary, delivery boy

messy ADJECTIVE
1 = **disorganized**, sloppy (*informal*), untidy 2 = **dirty**
3 = **untidy**, disordered, chaotic, muddled, cluttered, shambolic, disorganized, daggy (*Austral. & N.Z. informal*) ≠ tidy
4 = **dishevelled**, ruffled, untidy, rumpled, bedraggled, tousled, uncombed, daggy (*Austral. & N.Z. informal*) 5 = **confusing**, difficult, complex, confused, tangled, chaotic, tortuous

metaphor NOUN = **figure of speech**, image, symbol, analogy, conceit (*literary*), allegory, trope, figurative expression

method NOUN 1 = **manner**, process, approach, technique, way, system, style, procedure
2 = **orderliness**, planning, order, system, purpose, pattern, organization, regularity

midday NOUN = **noon**, twelve o'clock, noonday

middle NOUN = **centre**, heart, midst, halfway point, midpoint, midsection
▷ ADJECTIVE 1 = **central**, medium, mid, intervening, halfway, intermediate, median
2 = **intermediate**, intervening

middle-class ADJECTIVE
= **bourgeois**, traditional, conventional

middling ADJECTIVE 1 = **mediocre**, all right, indifferent, so-so (*informal*), unremarkable, tolerable, run-of-the-mill, passable, half-pie (*N.Z. informal*)
2 = **moderate**, medium, average, fair, ordinary, modest, adequate

midnight NOUN = **twelve o'clock**, middle of the night, dead of night, the witching hour

midst ▷ PHRASE: **in the midst of** 1 = **during**, in the middle of, amidst 2 = **among**, in the middle of, surrounded by, amidst, in the thick of

midway ADVERB = **halfway**, in the middle of, part-way, equidistant, at the midpoint, betwixt and between

might NOUN = **power**, force, energy, strength, vigour

mighty ADJECTIVE = **powerful**, strong, strapping, robust, vigorous, sturdy, forceful, lusty ≠ weak

migrant NOUN = **wanderer**, immigrant, traveller, rover, nomad, emigrant, itinerant, drifter
▷ ADJECTIVE = **itinerant**, wandering, drifting, roving, travelling, shifting, immigrant, transient

migrate VERB = **move**, travel, journey, wander, trek, voyage, roam, emigrate

migration NOUN = **wandering**, journey, voyage, travel, movement, trek, emigration, roving

m

mild ADJECTIVE 1 = **gentle**, calm, easy-going, meek, placid, docile, peaceable, equable, chilled (*informal*) ≠ harsh 2 = **temperate**, warm, calm, moderate, tranquil, balmy ≠ cold 3 = **bland**, thin, smooth, tasteless, insipid, flavourless

militant ADJECTIVE = **aggressive**, active, vigorous, assertive, combative ≠ peaceful

military ADJECTIVE = **warlike**, armed, soldierly, martial
▷ PHRASE: **the military = the armed forces**, the forces, the services, the army

milk VERB = **exploit**, pump, take advantage of ▷ RELATED WORD: *adjective* **lactic**

mill NOUN 1 = **grinder**, crusher, quern 2 = **factory**, works, plant, workshop, foundry
▷ VERB = **grind**, pound, crush, powder, grate ▷ PHRASE: **mill about** *or* **around = swarm**, crowd, stream, surge, throng

mimic VERB = **imitate**, do (*informal*), take off (*informal*), ape, parody, caricature, impersonate
▷ NOUN = **imitator**, impressionist, copycat (*informal*), impersonator, caricaturist

mince VERB 1 = **cut**, grind, crumble, dice, hash, chop up 2 = **tone down**, spare, moderate, weaken, soften

mincing ADJECTIVE = **affected**, camp (*informal*), precious, pretentious, dainty, sissy, effeminate, foppish

mind NOUN 1 = **memory**, recollection, remembrance, powers of recollection 2 = **intelligence**, reason, reasoning, understanding, sense, brain(s) (*informal*), wits, intellect 3 = **intention**, wish, desire, urge, fancy, leaning, notion, inclination 4 = **sanity**, reason, senses, judgment, wits, marbles (*informal*), rationality, mental balance
▷ VERB 1 = **take offence at**, dislike, care about, object to, resent, disapprove of, be bothered by, be affronted by 2 = **be careful**, watch, take care, be wary, be cautious, be on your guard 3 = **look after**, watch, protect, tend, guard, take care of, attend to, keep an eye on 4 = **pay attention to**, mark, note, listen to, observe, obey, heed, take heed of ▷ RELATED WORD: *adjective* **mental**

mine NOUN 1 = **pit**, deposit, shaft, colliery, excavation 2 = **source**, store, fund, stock, supply, reserve, treasury, wealth
▷ VERB = **dig up**, extract, quarry, unearth, excavate, hew, dig for

miner NOUN = **coalminer**, pitman (*Brit.*), collier (*Brit.*)

mingle VERB 1 = **mix**, combine, blend, merge, unite, join, interweave, intermingle ≠ separate 2 = **associate**, consort, socialize, rub shoulders (*informal*), hobnob, fraternize, hang about *or* around

≠ dissociate

miniature ADJECTIVE = **small**, little, minute, tiny, toy, scaled-down, diminutive, minuscule ≠ giant

minimal ADJECTIVE = **minimum**, smallest, least, slightest, token, nominal, negligible, least possible

minimize VERB 1 = **reduce**, decrease, shrink, diminish, prune, curtail, miniaturize ≠ increase 2 = **play down**, discount, belittle, disparage, decry, underrate, deprecate, make light or little of ≠ praise

minimum ADJECTIVE = **lowest**, smallest, least, slightest, minimal, least possible ≠ maximum
▷ NOUN = **lowest**, least, lowest level, nadir

minister NOUN = **clergyman**, priest, vicar, parson, preacher, pastor, cleric, rector ▷ PHRASE: **minister to** = **attend to**, serve, tend to, take care of, cater to, pander to, administer to

ministry NOUN 1 = **department**, office, bureau, government department 2 = **administration**, council 3 = **the priesthood**, the church, the cloth, holy orders

minor ADJECTIVE = **small**, lesser, slight, petty, trivial, insignificant, unimportant, inconsequential ≠ major

mint VERB = **make**, produce, strike, take, cast, stamp, punch, coin

minute¹ NOUN = **moment**, second, bit, flash, instant, tick (Brit. informal), sec (informal), short time

minute² ADJECTIVE 1 = **small**, little, tiny, miniature, microscopic, diminutive, minuscule, infinitesimal ≠ huge 2 = **precise**, close, detailed, critical, exact, meticulous, exhaustive, painstaking ≠ imprecise

minutes PLURAL NOUN = **record**, notes, proceedings, transactions, transcript, memorandum

miracle NOUN = **wonder**, phenomenon, sensation, marvel, amazing achievement, astonishing feat

miraculous ADJECTIVE = **wonderful**, amazing, extraordinary, incredible, astonishing, unbelievable, phenomenal, astounding ≠ ordinary

mirror NOUN = **looking-glass**, glass (Brit.), reflector
▷ VERB = **reflect**, follow, copy, echo, emulate

miscarriage NOUN = **failure**, error, breakdown, mishap, perversion

misconduct NOUN = **immorality**, wrongdoing, mismanagement, malpractice, impropriety

miserable ADJECTIVE 1 = **sad**, depressed, gloomy, forlorn, dejected, despondent, sorrowful, wretched ≠ happy 2 = **pathetic**, sorry, shameful, despicable, deplorable, lamentable ≠ respectable

misery NOUN 1 = **unhappiness**,

distress, despair, grief, suffering, depression, gloom, torment ≠ happiness 2 (*Brit. informal*) = **moaner**, pessimist, killjoy, spoilsport, prophet of doom, wet blanket (*informal*), sourpuss (*informal*), wowser (*Austral. & N.Z. slang*)

misfortune NOUN 1 *often plural* = **bad luck**, adversity, hard luck, ill luck, infelicity, bad trot (*Austral. slang*) 2 = **mishap**, trouble, disaster, reverse, tragedy, setback, calamity, affliction ≠ good luck

misguided ADJECTIVE = **unwise**, mistaken, misplaced, deluded, ill-advised, imprudent, injudicious

mislead VERB = **deceive**, fool, delude, take someone in (*informal*), misdirect, misinform, hoodwink, misguide

misleading ADJECTIVE = **confusing**, false, ambiguous, deceptive, evasive, disingenuous ≠ straightforward

miss VERB 1 = **fail to notice**, overlook, pass over 2 = **long for**, yearn for, pine for, long to see, ache for, feel the loss of, regret the absence of 3 = **not go to**, skip, cut, omit, be absent from, fail to attend, skive off (*informal*), play truant from, bludge (*Austral. & N.Z. informal*) 4 = **avoid**, beat, escape, skirt, duck, cheat, bypass, dodge ▷ NOUN = **mistake**, failure, error, blunder, omission, oversight

missile NOUN = **projectile**, weapon, shell, rocket

missing ADJECTIVE = **lost**, misplaced, not present, astray, unaccounted for, mislaid

mission NOUN = **task**, job, commission, duty, undertaking, quest, assignment, vocation

missionary NOUN = **evangelist**, preacher, apostle

mist NOUN = **fog**, cloud, steam, spray, film, haze, vapour, smog

mistake NOUN 1 = **error**, blunder, oversight, slip, gaffe (*informal*), miscalculation, faux pas (*French*), barry or Barry Crocker (*Austral. slang*) 2 = **oversight**, error, slip, fault, howler (*informal*), erratum, barry or Barry Crocker (*Austral. slang*) ▷ VERB = **misunderstand**, misinterpret, misjudge, misread, misconstrue, misapprehend ▷ PHRASE: mistake something *or* someone for something *or* someone = **confuse with**, take for, mix up with

mistaken ADJECTIVE 1 = **wrong**, incorrect, misguided, wide of the mark ≠ correct 2 = **inaccurate**, false, faulty, erroneous, unsound ≠ accurate

mistress NOUN = **lover**, girlfriend, concubine, kept woman, paramour

misunderstand VERB 1 = **misinterpret**, misread, mistake, misjudge, misconstrue, misapprehend, be at cross-purposes with 2 = **miss the point**, get the wrong end of the stick

m

misunderstanding
 NOUN = **mistake**, error,
 mix-up, misconception,
 misinterpretation, misjudgment
misuse NOUN 1 = **waste**,
 squandering 2 = **abuse**
 3 = **misapplication**, abuse, illegal
 use, wrong use 4 = **perversion**,
 desecration 5 = **misapplication**
 ▷ VERB 1 = **abuse**, misapply,
 prostitute 2 = **waste**, squander,
 embezzle, misappropriate
mix VERB 1 = **combine**, blend,
 merge, join, cross, fuse,
 mingle, jumble 2 = **socialize**,
 associate, hang out (*informal*),
 mingle, circulate, consort,
 hobnob, fraternize 3 *often with*
 up = **combine**, marry, blend,
 integrate, amalgamate, coalesce,
 meld
 ▷ NOUN = **mixture**, combination,
 blend, fusion, compound,
 assortment, alloy, medley
 ▷ PHRASE: **mix something up**
 1 = **confuse**, scramble, muddle,
 confound 2 = **blend**, beat, mix,
 stir, fold
mixed ADJECTIVE 1 = **varied**,
 diverse, different, differing,
 cosmopolitan, assorted, jumbled,
 disparate ≠ homogeneous
 2 = **combined**, blended, united,
 compound, composite, mingled,
 amalgamated ≠ pure
mixed-up ADJECTIVE = **confused**,
 disturbed, puzzled, bewildered, at
 sea, upset, distraught, muddled
mixture NOUN 1 = **blend**, mix,
 variety, fusion, assortment,

brew, jumble, medley
 2 = **composite**, compound
 3 = **cross**, combination, blend
 4 = **concoction**, compound,
 blend, brew, amalgam
mix-up NOUN = **confusion**,
 mistake, misunderstanding,
 mess, tangle, muddle
moan VERB 1 = **groan**, sigh,
 sob, whine, lament 2 (*informal*)
 = **grumble**, complain, groan,
 whine, carp, grouse, whinge
 (*informal*), bleat
 ▷ NOUN 1 = **groan**, sigh, sob,
 lament, wail, grunt, whine 2
 (*informal*) = **complaint**, protest,
 grumble, whine, grouse, gripe
 (*informal*), grouch (*informal*)
mob NOUN 1 = **crowd**, pack, mass,
 host, drove, flock, swarm, horde
 2 = **gang**, group, set, lot, crew
 (*informal*)
 ▷ VERB = **surround**, besiege,
 jostle, fall on, set upon, crowd
 around, swarm around
mobile ADJECTIVE = **movable**,
 moving, travelling, wandering,
 portable, itinerant, peripatetic
mobilize VERB 1 = **rally**, organize,
 stimulate, excite, prompt,
 marshal, activate, awaken
 2 = **deploy**, prepare, ready, rally,
 assemble, call up, marshal,
 muster
mock VERB = **laugh at**, tease,
 ridicule, taunt, scorn, sneer, scoff,
 deride ≠ respect
 ▷ ADJECTIVE = **imitation**,
 pretended, artificial, fake, false,
 dummy, sham, feigned ≠ genuine

mocking ADJECTIVE = **scornful**, scoffing, satirical, contemptuous, sarcastic, sardonic, disrespectful, disdainful

mode NOUN 1 = **method**, way, system, form, process, style, technique, manner 2 = **fashion**, style, trend, rage, vogue, look, craze

model NOUN 1 = **representation**, image, copy, miniature, dummy, replica, imitation, duplicate
2 = **pattern**, example, standard, original, ideal, prototype, paradigm, archetype 3 = **sitter**, subject, poser
▷ VERB 1 = **show off** (*informal*), wear, display, sport 2 = **shape**, form, design, fashion, carve, mould, sculpt

moderate ADJECTIVE 1 = **mild**, reasonable, controlled, limited, steady, modest, restrained, middle-of-the-road ≠ extreme
2 = **average**, middling, fair, ordinary, indifferent, mediocre, so-so (*informal*), passable, half-pie (*N.Z. informal*)
▷ VERB 1 = **soften**, control, temper, regulate, curb, restrain, subdue, lessen 2 = **lessen**, ease ≠ intensify

modern ADJECTIVE 1 = **current**, contemporary, recent, present-day, latter-day 2 = **up-to-date**, fresh, new, novel, newfangled ≠ old-fashioned

modest ADJECTIVE 1 = **moderate**, small, limited, fair, ordinary, middling, meagre, frugal

2 = **unpretentious**, reserved, retiring, shy, coy, reticent, self-effacing, demure

modesty NOUN = **reserve**, humility, shyness, reticence, timidity, diffidence, coyness, bashfulness ≠ conceit

modification NOUN = **change**, variation, qualification, adjustment, revision, alteration, refinement

modify VERB 1 = **change**, reform, convert, alter, adjust, adapt, revise, remodel 2 = **tone down**, lower, qualify, ease, moderate, temper, soften, restrain

mogul NOUN = **tycoon**, baron, magnate, big shot (*informal*), big noise (*informal*), big hitter (*informal*), heavy hitter (*informal*), V.I.P.

moist ADJECTIVE = **damp**, wet, soggy, humid, clammy, dewy

moisture NOUN = **damp**, water, liquid, dew, wetness

molecule NOUN = **particle**, jot, speck

mom NOUN (*U.S. & Canad.*) = **mum**, mother, ma

moment NOUN 1 = **instant**, second, flash, twinkling, split second, jiffy (*informal*), trice
2 = **time**, point, stage, juncture

momentous ADJECTIVE = **significant**, important, vital, critical, crucial, historic, pivotal, fateful ≠ unimportant

momentum NOUN = **impetus**, force, power, drive, push, energy, strength, thrust

m

monarch NOUN = **ruler**, king or queen, sovereign, tsar, potentate, emperor or empress, prince or princess

monarchy NOUN
 1 = **sovereignty**, autocracy, kingship, royalism, monocracy
 2 = **kingdom**, empire, realm, principality

monastery NOUN = **abbey**, convent, priory, cloister, nunnery, friary

monetary ADJECTIVE = **financial**, money, economic, capital, cash, fiscal, budgetary, pecuniary

money NOUN = **cash**, capital, currency, hard cash, readies (*informal*), riches, silver, coin, kembla (*Austral. slang*)
 ▷ *see* **currencies**

monitor VERB = **check**, follow, watch, survey, observe, keep an eye on, keep track of, keep tabs on
 ▷ NOUN **1** = **guide**, observer, supervisor, invigilator (*Brit.*) **2** = **prefect** (*Brit.*), head girl, head boy, senior boy, senior girl

monk NOUN = **friar**, brother
 ▷ RELATED WORD: *adjective* **monastic**

monkey NOUN **1** = **simian**, ape, primate **2** = **rascal**, horror, devil, rogue, imp, tyke, scallywag, scamp, nointer (*Austral. slang*)
 ▷ RELATED WORD: *adjective* **simian**

monster NOUN **1** = **giant**, mammoth, titan, colossus, monstrosity **2** = **brute**, devil, beast, demon, villain, fiend

monstrous ADJECTIVE

1 = **outrageous**, shocking, foul, intolerable, disgraceful, scandalous, inhuman, diabolical ≠ decent **2** = **huge**, massive, enormous, tremendous, immense, mammoth, colossal, prodigious ≠ tiny **3** = **unnatural**, horrible, hideous, grotesque, gruesome, frightful, freakish, fiendish ≠ normal

monument NOUN = **memorial**, cairn, marker, shrine, tombstone, mausoleum, commemoration, headstone

monumental ADJECTIVE
 = **important**, significant, enormous, historic, memorable, awesome, majestic, unforgettable ≠ unimportant
 ▷ INTENSIFIER (*informal*)
 = **immense**, great, massive, staggering, colossal ≠ tiny

mood NOUN = **state of mind**, spirit, humour, temper, disposition, frame of mind

moody ADJECTIVE **1** = **changeable**, volatile, unpredictable, erratic, fickle, temperamental, impulsive, mercurial ≠ stable **2** = **sulky**, irritable, temperamental, touchy, ill-tempered, tooshie (*Austral. slang*) ≠ cheerful **3** = **gloomy**, sad, sullen, glum, morose ≠ cheerful **4** = **sad**, gloomy, melancholy, sombre

moon NOUN = **satellite**
 ▷ VERB = **idle**, drift, loaf, languish, waste time, daydream, mope
 ▷ RELATED WORD: *adjective* **lunar**

moor¹ NOUN = **moorland**, fell

● **MONKEYS, APES AND OTHER**
  PRIMATES

- baboon
- Barbary ape
- bushbaby *or* galago
- capuchin
- chacma
- chimpanzee *or* chimp
- colobus
- douroucouli
- flying lemur *or* colugo
- gelada
- gibbon
- gorilla
- green monkey
- grivet
- guenon
- guereza
- howler monkey
- indris *or* indri
- langur
- lemur
- loris
- macaque
- mandrill
- mangabey
- marmoset
- mona
- monkey *or* (*archaic*) jackanapes
- orang-outang, orang-utan, *or* orang
- proboscis monkey
- rhesus monkey
- saki
- siamang
- sifaka
- spider monkey
- squirrel monkey
- tamarin
- tarsier
- vervet

(*Brit.*), heath

moor² VERB = **tie up**, secure, anchor, dock, lash, berth, make fast

mop NOUN 1 = **squeegee**, sponge, swab 2 = **mane**, shock, mass, tangle, mat, thatch
  ▷ VERB = **clean**, wash, wipe, sponge, swab

moral ADJECTIVE = **good**, just, right, principled, decent, noble, ethical, honourable ≠ immoral
  ▷ NOUN = **lesson**, meaning, point, message, teaching, import, significance, precept
  ▷ PLURAL NOUN = **morality**, standards, conduct, principles,

behaviour, manners, habits, ethics

morale NOUN = **confidence**, heart, spirit, self-esteem, team spirit, esprit de corps (*French*)

morality NOUN 1 = **virtue**, justice, morals, honour, integrity, goodness, honesty, decency
  2 = **ethics**, conduct, principles, morals, manners, philosophy, mores 3 = **rights and wrongs**, ethics

moratorium NOUN
  = **postponement**, freeze, halt, suspension, standstill

more DETERMINER = **extra**, additional, new, other,

added, further, new-found, supplementary

▷ ADVERB 1 = **to a greater extent**, longer, better, further, some more 2 = **moreover**, also, in addition, besides, furthermore, what's more, on top of that, to boot

moreover ADVERB = **furthermore**, also, further, in addition, too, as well, besides, additionally

morning NOUN 1 = **before noon**, forenoon, morn (*poetic*), a.m. 2 = **dawn**, sunrise, first light, daybreak, break of day

mortal ADJECTIVE 1 = **human**, worldly, passing, fleshly, temporal, transient, ephemeral, perishable 2 = **fatal**, killing, terminal, deadly, destructive, lethal, murderous, death-dealing

▷ NOUN = **human being**, being, man, woman, person, human, individual, earthling

mortality NOUN 1 = **humanity**, transience, impermanence, corporeality, impermanency 2 = **death**, dying, fatality

mostly ADVERB 1 = **mainly**, largely, chiefly, principally, primarily, on the whole, predominantly 2 = **generally**, usually, on the whole, as a rule

moth NOUN ▷ RELATED WORDS: *young* **caterpillar**, *enthusiast* **lepidopterist**

▷ see **butterflies and moths**

mother NOUN = **female parent**, mum (*Brit. informal*), ma (*informal*), mater, dam, mummy (*Brit. informal*), foster mother, biological mother

▷ VERB = **nurture**, raise, protect, tend, nurse, rear, care for, cherish

▷ MODIFIER = **native**, natural, innate, inborn ▷ RELATED WORD: *adjective* **maternal**

motherly ADJECTIVE = **maternal**, loving, caring, comforting, sheltering, protective, affectionate

motif NOUN 1 = **design**, shape, decoration, ornament 2 = **theme**, idea, subject, concept, leitmotif

motion NOUN 1 = **movement**, mobility, travel, progress, flow, locomotion 2 = **proposal**, suggestion, recommendation, proposition, submission

▷ VERB = **gesture**, direct, wave, signal, nod, beckon, gesticulate

motivate VERB 1 = **inspire**, drive, stimulate, move, cause, prompt, stir, induce 2 = **stimulate**, drive, inspire, stir, arouse, galvanize, incentivize

motivation NOUN = **incentive**, inspiration, motive, stimulus, reason, spur, inducement, incitement

motive NOUN = **reason**, ground(s), purpose, object, incentive, inspiration, stimulus, rationale

motto NOUN = **saying**, slogan, maxim, rule, adage, proverb, dictum, precept

mould[1] NOUN 1 = **cast**, shape, pattern 2 = **design**, style, fashion, build, form, kind, shape, pattern

3 = **nature**, character, sort, kind, quality, type, stamp, calibre
▷ **VERB 1** = **shape**, make, work, form, create, model, fashion, construct **2** = **influence**, make, form, control, direct, affect, shape

mould² NOUN = **fungus**, blight, mildew

mound NOUN **1** = **heap**, pile, drift, stack, rick **2** = **hill**, bank, rise, dune, embankment, knoll, hillock, kopje or koppie (S. African)

mount VERB **1** = **increase**, build, grow, swell, intensify, escalate, multiply ≠ decrease
2 = **accumulate**, increase, collect, gather, build up, pile up, amass
3 = **ascend**, scale, climb (up), go up, clamber up ≠ descend **4** = **get (up) on**, jump on, straddle, climb onto, hop on to, bestride, get on the back of ≠ get off **5** = **display**, present, prepare, put on, organize, put on display
▷ NOUN **1** = **horse**, steed (literary)
2 = **backing**, setting, support, stand, base, frame

mountain NOUN **1** = **peak**, mount, horn, ridge, fell (Brit.), berg (S. African), alp, pinnacle
2 = **heap**, mass, masses, pile, a great deal, ton, stack, abundance

mourn VERB **1** often with **for** = **grieve for**, lament, weep for, wail for **2** = **bemoan**, rue, deplore, bewail

mourning NOUN **1** = **grieving**, grief, bereavement, weeping, woe, lamentation **2** = **black**, sackcloth and ashes, widow's

weeds

mouth NOUN **1** = **lips**, jaws, gob (slang, esp. Brit.), maw, cakehole (Brit. slang) **2** = **entrance**, opening, gateway, door, aperture, orifice **3** = **opening 4** = **inlet**, outlet, estuary, firth, outfall, debouchment ▷ **RELATED WORD**: adjective **oral**

WORD POWER

The *mouth* is the opening through which many animals take in food and issue vocal sounds. The entrance or rim of other structures can also be referred to as a mouth, for example a bottle, a tunnel, or the point at which a river meets the sea. The speech of humans is articulated through their mouths, therefore mouth itself means talk, especially empty talk and boasting in *she is all mouth*. Similarly, impassioned talk is implicated in *mouth off*. Mouth is similar to lip and cheek, which all refer to the idea of impudence. The corners of the mouth turn down with displeasure and negative emotion – for this reason we talk about people being *down in the mouth*.

move VERB **1** = **transfer**, change, switch, shift, transpose **2** = **go**, advance, progress, shift, proceed, stir, budge, make a move
3 = **relocate**, leave, remove, quit, migrate, emigrate, decamp, up sticks (Brit. informal) **4** = **drive**,

cause, influence, persuade, shift, inspire, prompt, induce ≠ discourage **5** = **touch**, affect, excite, impress, stir, disquiet **6** = **propose**, suggest, urge, recommend, request, advocate, submit, put forward
▷ NOUN **1** = **action**, step, manoeuvre **2** = **ploy**, action, measure, step, initiative, stroke, tactic, manoeuvre **3** = **transfer**, posting, shift, removal, relocation **4** = **turn**, go, play, chance, shot (*informal*), opportunity

movement NOUN **1** = **group**, party, organization, grouping, front, faction **2** = **campaign**, drive, push, crusade **3** = **move**, action, motion, manoeuvre **4** = **activity**, moving, stirring, bustle **5** = **advance**, progress, flow **6** = **transfer**, transportation, displacement **7** = **development**, change, variation, fluctuation **8** = **progression**, progress **9** (*music*) = **section**, part, division, passage

movie NOUN = **film**, picture, feature, flick (*slang*)

moving ADJECTIVE **1** = **emotional**, touching, affecting, inspiring, stirring, poignant ≠ unemotional **2** = **mobile**, running, active, going, operational, in motion, driving, kinetic ≠ stationary

mow VERB = **cut**, crop, trim, shear, scythe ▷ PHRASE: **mow something** *or* **someone down** = **massacre**, butcher, slaughter, cut down, shoot down, cut to pieces

much ADVERB **1** = **greatly**, a lot, considerably, decidedly, exceedingly, appreciably ≠ hardly **2** = **often**, a lot, routinely, a great deal, many times, habitually, on many occasions, customarily
▷ ADJECTIVE = **great**, a lot of, plenty of, considerable, substantial, piles of (*informal*), ample, abundant, shedful (*slang*) ≠ little
▷ PRONOUN = **a lot**, plenty, a great deal, lots (*informal*), masses (*informal*), loads (*informal*), tons (*informal*), heaps (*informal*) ≠ little

muck NOUN **1** = **dirt**, mud, filth, ooze, sludge, mire, slime, gunge (*informal*), kak (*S. African informal*) **2** = **manure**, dung, ordure

mud NOUN = **dirt**, clay, ooze, silt, sludge, mire, slime

muddle NOUN = **confusion**, mess, disorder, chaos, tangle, mix-up, disarray, predicament
▷ VERB **1** = **jumble**, disorder, scramble, tangle, mix up **2** = **confuse**, bewilder, daze, confound, perplex, disorient, stupefy, befuddle

muddy ADJECTIVE **1** = **boggy**, swampy, marshy, quaggy **2** = **dirty**, soiled, grimy, mucky, mud-caked, bespattered

mug¹ NOUN = **cup**, pot, beaker, tankard

mug² NOUN **1** (*slang*) = **face**, features, countenance, visage **2** (*Brit.*) = **fool**, sucker (*slang*), chump (*informal*), simpleton, easy *or* soft touch (*slang*), dorba *or* dorb (*Austral. slang*), bogan (*Austral. slang*)

▷ VERB (*informal*) = **attack**, assault, beat up, rob, set about *or* upon ▷ PHRASE: **mug up (on) something** = **study**, cram (*informal*), bone up on (*informal*), swot up on (*Brit. informal*)

multiple ADJECTIVE = **many**, several, various, numerous, sundry, manifold, multitudinous

multiply VERB 1 = **increase**, extend, expand, spread, build up, proliferate ≠ decrease 2 = **reproduce**, breed, propagate

multitude NOUN 1 = **great number**, host, army, mass, horde, myriad 2 = **crowd**, host, mass, mob, swarm, horde, throng

mundane ADJECTIVE 1 = **ordinary**, routine, commonplace, banal, everyday, day-to-day, prosaic, humdrum ≠ extraordinary 2 = **earthly**, worldly, secular, mortal, terrestrial, temporal ≠ spiritual

municipal ADJECTIVE = **civic**, public, local, council, district, urban, metropolitan

murder NOUN = **killing**, homicide, massacre, assassination, slaying, bloodshed, carnage, butchery

▷ VERB = **kill**, massacre, slaughter, assassinate, eliminate (*slang*), butcher, slay, bump off (*slang*)

murderer NOUN = **killer**, assassin, slayer, butcher, slaughterer, cut-throat, hit man (*slang*)

murderous ADJECTIVE = **deadly**, savage, brutal, cruel, lethal, ferocious, cut-throat, bloodthirsty

murky ADJECTIVE 1 = **dark**, gloomy, grey, dull, dim, cloudy, misty, overcast ≠ bright 2 = **dark**, cloudy

murmur VERB = **mumble**, whisper, mutter

▷ NOUN = **whisper**, drone, purr

muscle NOUN 1 = **tendon**, sinew 2 = **strength**, might, power, weight, stamina, brawn

▷ PHRASE: **muscle in** (*informal*) = **impose yourself**, encroach, butt in, force your way in

muscular ADJECTIVE = **strong**, powerful, athletic, strapping, robust, vigorous, sturdy, sinewy

muse VERB = **ponder**, consider, reflect, contemplate, deliberate, brood, meditate, mull over

musical ADJECTIVE = **melodious**, lyrical, harmonious, melodic, tuneful, dulcet, sweet-sounding, euphonious ≠ discordant

muskeg NOUN (*Canad.*) = **swamp**, bog, marsh, quagmire, slough, fen, mire, morass, pakihi (*N.Z.*)

muss (*U.S. & Canad.*) VERB = **mess (up)**, disarrange, dishevel, ruffle, rumple, make untidy, tumble

must NOUN = **necessity**, essential, requirement, fundamental, imperative, requisite, prerequisite, sine qua non (*Latin*)

muster VERB 1 = **summon up**, marshal 2 = **rally**, gather, assemble, marshal, mobilize, call together 3 = **assemble**, convene

▷ NOUN = **assembly**, meeting,

● MUSIC

● Instruction	Meaning
● accelerando	with increasing speed
● adagio	slowly
● agitato	in an agitated manner
● allegretto	fairly quickly or briskly
● allegro	quickly, in a brisk, lively manner
● amoroso	lovingly
● andante	at a moderately slow tempo
● andantino	slightly faster than andante
● assai	(in combination) very
● cantabile	in a singing style
● con	(in combination) with
● con amore	lovingly
● con brio	vigorously
● con moto	quickly
● crescendo	gradual increase in loudness
● diminuendo	gradual decrease in loudness
● dolce	gently and sweetly
● doloroso	in a sorrowful manner
● espressivo	expressively
● forte	loud or loudly
● fortissimo	very loud
● furioso	in a frantically rushing manner
● giocoso	merry
● grave	solemn and slow
● grazioso	graceful
● largo	slowly and broadly
● larghetto	slowly and broadly, but less so than largo
● legato	smoothly and connectedly
● leggiero	light
● lento	slowly
● maestoso	majestically
● mezzo	(in combination) moderately
● moderato	at a moderate tempo
● molto	(in combination) very
● non troppo or non tanto	(in combination) not too much
● pianissimo	very quietly
● piano	softly
● più	(in combination) more

m

Instruction	Meaning
● pizzicato	(in music for stringed instruments) to be plucked with the finger
● poco or un poco	(in combination) a little
● pomposo	in a pompous manner
● presto	very fast
● prestissimo	faster than presto
● quasi	(in combination) almost, as if
● rallentando	becoming slower
● rubato	with a flexible tempo
● scherzando	in jocular style
● semplice	simple and unforced
● sforzando	with strong initial attack
● sostenuto	in a smooth and sustained manner
● sotto voce	extremely quiet
● staccato	(of notes) short, clipped, and separate
● strepitoso	noisy
● stringendo	with increasing speed
● tanto	(in combination) too much
● troppo	(in combination) too much
● vivace	in a brisk lively manner

m

collection, gathering, rally, convention, congregation, roundup, hui (N.Z.), runanga (N.Z.)

mutation NOUN **1** = **anomaly**, variation, deviant, freak of nature **2** = **change**, variation, evolution, transformation, modification, alteration, metamorphosis, transfiguration

mute ADJECTIVE **1** = **close-mouthed**, silent **2** = **silent**, dumb, unspoken, tacit, wordless, voiceless, unvoiced **3** = **dumb**, speechless, voiceless

mutter VERB = **grumble**, complain, murmur, rumble, whine, mumble, grouse, bleat

mutual ADJECTIVE = **shared**, common, joint, returned, reciprocal, interchangeable, requited

● **WORD POWER**
● *Mutual* is sometimes used,
● as in *a mutual friend*, to mean
● 'common to or shared by two
● or more people'. This use has
● sometimes been frowned
● on in the past because it
● does not reflect the two-way
● relationship contained in the
● origins of the word, which
● comes from Latin *mutuus*
● meaning 'reciprocal'. However,
● this usage is very common and
● is now generally regarded as
● acceptable.

myriad NOUN = **multitude**, host, army, swarm, horde
▷ ADJECTIVE = **innumerable**, countless, untold, incalculable, immeasurable, multitudinous

mysterious ADJECTIVE
1 = **strange**, puzzling, secret, weird, perplexing, uncanny, mystifying, arcane ≠ clear
2 = **secretive**, enigmatic, evasive, discreet, covert, reticent, furtive, inscrutable

mystery NOUN = **puzzle**, problem, question, secret, riddle, enigma, conundrum, teaser

mystical or **mystic** ADJECTIVE = **supernatural**, mysterious, transcendental, occult, metaphysical, paranormal, inscrutable, otherworldly

myth NOUN 1 = **legend**, story, fiction, saga, fable, allegory, fairy story, folk tale 2 = **illusion**, story, fancy, fantasy, imagination, invention, delusion, superstition

mythology NOUN = **legend**, folklore, tradition, lore

Nn

nab VERB = **catch**, arrest, apprehend, seize, grab, capture, collar (*informal*), snatch

nag[1] VERB = **scold**, harass, badger, pester, worry, plague, hassle (*informal*), upbraid
▷ NOUN = **scold**, complainer, grumbler, virago, shrew, tartar, moaner, harpy

nag[2] NOUN *often derog.* = **horse** (*U.S.*), hack

nagging ADJECTIVE
1 = **continuous**, persistent, continual, niggling, repeated, constant, endless, perpetual
2 = **scolding**, shrewish

nail NOUN 1 = **tack**, spike, rivet, hobnail, brad (*technical*)
2 = **fingernail**, toenail, talon, thumbnail, claw
▷ VERB 1 = **fasten**, fix, secure, attach, pin, hammer, tack 2 (*informal*) = **catch**, arrest, capture, apprehend, trap, snare, ensnare, entrap

naive *or* **naïve** *or* **naïf** ADJECTIVE = **gullible**, trusting, credulous, unsuspicious, green, simple, innocent, callow ≠ worldly

naked ADJECTIVE = **nude**, stripped, exposed, bare, undressed, starkers (*informal*), stark-naked, unclothed ≠ dressed

name NOUN = **title**, nickname, designation, term, handle (*slang*), epithet, sobriquet, moniker *or* monicker (*slang*)
▷ VERB 1 = **call**, christen, baptize, dub, term, style, label, entitle
2 = **nominate**, choose, select, appoint, specify, designate

namely ADVERB = **specifically**, to wit, viz.

nap[1] VERB = **sleep**, rest, drop off (*informal*), doze, kip (*Brit. slang*), snooze (*informal*), nod off (*informal*), catnap
▷ NOUN = **sleep**, rest, kip (*Brit. slang*), siesta, catnap, forty winks (*informal*)

nap[2] NOUN = **pile**, down, fibre, weave, grain

napkin NOUN = **serviette**, cloth

narcotic NOUN = **drug**, anaesthetic, painkiller, sedative, opiate, tranquillizer, anodyne, analgesic
▷ ADJECTIVE = **sedative**, calming, hypnotic, analgesic, soporific, painkilling

narrative NOUN = **story**, report, history, account, statement, tale, chronicle

narrator NOUN = **storyteller**, writer, author, reporter, commentator, chronicler

narrow ADJECTIVE 1 = **thin**, fine, slim, slender, tapering, attenuated ≠ broad 2 = **limited**, restricted, confined, tight, close, meagre, constricted ≠ wide
3 = **insular**, prejudiced, partial, dogmatic, intolerant, narrow-

minded, small-minded, illiberal
≠ broad-minded
▷ VERB 1 *often with* **down**
= **restrict**, limit, reduce, constrict
2 = **get narrower**, taper, shrink,
tighten, constrict

narrowly ADVERB = **just**, barely,
only just, scarcely, by the skin of
your teeth

nasty ADJECTIVE 1 = **unpleasant**,
ugly, disagreeable ≠ pleasant
2 = **spiteful**, mean, offensive,
vicious, unpleasant, vile,
malicious, despicable ≠ pleasant
3 = **disgusting**, unpleasant,
offensive, vile, distasteful,
obnoxious, objectionable,
disagreeable, festy (*Austral. slang*),
yucko (*Austral. slang*) 4 = **serious**,
bad, dangerous, critical, severe,
painful

nation NOUN 1 = **country**, state,
realm 2 = **public**, people, society

national ADJECTIVE = **nationwide**,
public, widespread, countrywide
▷ NOUN = **citizen**, subject,
resident, native, inhabitant

nationalism NOUN = **patriotism**,
loyalty to your country,
chauvinism, jingoism, allegiance

nationality NOUN
1 = **citizenship**, birth 2 = **race**,
nation

nationwide ADJECTIVE
= **national**, general, widespread,
countrywide

native ADJECTIVE = **mother**,
indigenous, vernacular
▷ NOUN *usually with* **of**
= **inhabitant**, national, resident,

citizen, countryman, aborigine
(*often offensive*), dweller

natural ADJECTIVE 1 = **logical**,
valid, legitimate 2 = **normal**,
common, regular, usual, ordinary,
typical, everyday ≠ abnormal
3 = **innate**, native, characteristic,
inherent, instinctive, intuitive,
inborn, essential 4 = **unaffected**,
open, genuine, spontaneous,
unpretentious, unsophisticated,
dinkum (*Austral. & N.Z. informal*),
ingenuous, real ≠ affected
5 = **pure**, plain, organic, whole,
unrefined ≠ processed

naturally ADVERB 1 = **of course**,
certainly 2 = **typically**, simply,
normally, spontaneously

nature NOUN 1 = **creation**,
world, earth, environment,
universe, cosmos, natural
world 2 = **quality**, character,
make-up, constitution, essence,
complexion 3 = **temperament**,
character, personality,
disposition, outlook, mood,
humour, temper 4 = **kind**, sort,
style, type, variety, species,
category, description

naughty ADJECTIVE
1 = **disobedient**, bad,
mischievous, badly behaved,
wayward, wicked, impish,
refractory ≠ good 2 = **obscene**,
vulgar, improper, lewd, risqué,
smutty, ribald ≠ clean

nausea NOUN = **sickness**,
vomiting, retching,
squeamishness, queasiness,
biliousness

n

naval ADJECTIVE = **nautical**, marine, maritime

navigation NOUN = **sailing**, voyaging, seamanship, helmsmanship

navy NOUN = **fleet**, flotilla, armada

near ADJECTIVE 1 = **close**, neighbouring, nearby, adjacent, adjoining ≠ far 2 = **imminent**, forthcoming, approaching, looming, impending, upcoming, nigh, in the offing ≠ far-off

nearby ADJECTIVE = **neighbouring**, adjacent, adjoining

nearly ADVERB 1 = **practically**, almost, virtually, just about, as good as, well-nigh 2 = **almost**, approaching, roughly, just about, approximately

neat ADJECTIVE 1 = **tidy**, trim, orderly, spruce, shipshape, spick-and-span ≠ untidy 2 = **methodical**, tidy, systematic, fastidious ≠ disorganized 3 = **smart**, trim, tidy, spruce, dapper, natty (*informal*), well-groomed, well-turned out 4 = **graceful**, elegant, adept, nimble, adroit, efficient ≠ clumsy 5 = **clever**, efficient, handy, apt, well-judged ≠ inefficient 6 (*chiefly U.S. & Canad. slang*) = **cool**, great (*informal*), excellent, brilliant, superb, fantastic (*informal*), tremendous, fabulous (*informal*), booshit (*Austral. slang*), exo (*Austral. slang*), sik (*Austral. slang*), rad (*informal*), phat (*slang*), schmick (*Austral. informal*)

≠ terrible 7 (*of an alcoholic drink*) = **undiluted**, straight, pure, unmixed

neatly ADVERB 1 = **tidily**, smartly, systematically, methodically, fastidiously 2 = **smartly**, elegantly, tidily, nattily 3 = **gracefully**, expertly, efficiently, adeptly, skilfully, nimbly, adroitly, dexterously 4 = **cleverly**, efficiently

necessarily ADVERB 1 = **automatically**, naturally, definitely, undoubtedly, certainly 2 = **inevitably**, of necessity, unavoidably, incontrovertibly, nolens volens (*Latin*)

necessary ADJECTIVE 1 = **needed**, required, essential, vital, compulsory, mandatory, imperative, indispensable ≠ unnecessary 2 = **inevitable**, certain, unavoidable, inescapable ≠ avoidable

necessity NOUN 1 = **essential**, need, requirement, fundamental, requisite, prerequisite, sine qua non (*Latin*), desideratum (*Latin*), must-have 2 = **inevitability**, certainty 3 = **essential**, need, requirement, fundamental

need VERB 1 = **want**, miss, require, lack, have to have, demand 2 = **require**, want, demand, call for, entail, necessitate 3 = **have to**, be obliged to ▷ NOUN 1 = **requirement**, demand, essential, necessity, requisite, desideratum (*Latin*), must-have 2 = **necessity**,

n

call, demand, obligation
3 = **emergency**, want, necessity, urgency, exigency **4** = **poverty**, deprivation, destitution, penury

needed ADJECTIVE = **necessary**, wanted, required, lacked, called for, desired

needle VERB = **irritate**, provoke, annoy, harass, taunt, nag, goad, rile

needless ADJECTIVE
= **unnecessary**, pointless, gratuitous, useless, unwanted, redundant, superfluous, groundless ≠ essential

needy ADJECTIVE = **poor**, deprived, disadvantaged, impoverished, penniless, destitute, poverty-stricken, underprivileged ≠ wealthy

negative ADJECTIVE
1 = **pessimistic**, cynical, unwilling, gloomy, jaundiced, uncooperative ≠ optimistic
2 = **dissenting**, contradictory, refusing, denying, rejecting, opposing, resisting, contrary ≠ assenting
▷ NOUN = **denial**, no, refusal, rejection, contradiction

neglect VERB **1** = **disregard**, ignore, fail to look after ≠ look after **2** = **shirk**, forget, overlook, omit, evade, pass over, skimp, be remiss in or about **3** = **fail**, forget, omit
▷ NOUN **1** = **negligence**, inattention ≠ care **2** = **shirking**, failure, oversight, carelessness, dereliction, slackness, laxity

neglected ADJECTIVE
1 = **uncared-for**, abandoned, underestimated, disregarded, undervalued, unappreciated
2 = **run down**, derelict, overgrown, uncared-for

negligence NOUN
= **carelessness**, neglect, disregard, dereliction, slackness, inattention, laxity, thoughtlessness

negotiate VERB **1** = **bargain**, deal, discuss, debate, mediate, hold talks, cut a deal, conciliate **2** = **arrange**, work out, bring about, transact **3** = **get round**, clear, pass, cross, get over, get past, surmount

negotiation NOUN
1 = **bargaining**, debate, discussion, transaction, dialogue, mediation, arbitration, wheeling and dealing (*informal*)
2 = **arrangement**, working out, transaction, bringing about

negotiator NOUN = **mediator**, ambassador, diplomat, delegate, intermediary, moderator, honest broker

neighbourhood or (*U.S.*)
neighborhood NOUN
1 = **district**, community, quarter, region, locality, locale
2 = **vicinity**, environs

neighbouring or (*U.S.*)
neighboring ADJECTIVE
= **nearby**, next, near, bordering, surrounding, connecting, adjacent, adjoining ≠ remote

neighbourly or (*U.S.*)

neighborly ADJECTIVE
= **helpful**, kind, friendly, obliging, harmonious, considerate, sociable, hospitable

nerve NOUN 1 = **bravery**, courage, bottle (*Brit. slang*), resolution, daring, guts (*informal*), pluck, grit 2 (*informal*) = **impudence**, cheek (*informal*), audacity, boldness, temerity, insolence, impertinence, brazenness
▷ PLURAL NOUN (*informal*)
= **tension**, stress, strain, anxiety, butterflies (in your stomach) (*informal*), nervousness, cold feet (*informal*), worry ▷ PHRASE:
nerve yourself = **brace yourself**, prepare yourself, steel yourself, fortify yourself, gear yourself up, gee yourself up

● WORD POWER
● The nervous system in the
● human body is its sensory and
● control apparatus, consisting
● of a network of nerve cells.
● In the middle ages, nerve
● fibres and tendons were
● not distinguished, and so
● nerves were associated with
● strength and physical force.
● The expression *nerve yourself*
● comes from this, meaning to
● brace the body and gear up the
● mind. Nerves became symbolic
● of bravery in the expression
● *get up your nerve*, and of fear
● in *lose your nerve*. The flipside
● of courage and motivation is
● arrogance and cheek: we talk
● about people *having some* or *a*

● *nerve*. In modern times, nerves
● are particularly linked to stress,
● irritation, and excitability,
● especially in the phrases *nerve-*
● *racking*, *get on someone's nerves*,
● and *nervous breakdown*.

nervous ADJECTIVE *often with* **of**
= **apprehensive**, anxious, uneasy, edgy, worried, tense, fearful, uptight (*informal*), toey (*Austral. slang*), adrenalized ≠ calm

nest NOUN = **refuge**, retreat, haunt, den, hideaway

nestle VERB *often with* **up** *or* **down**
= **snuggle**, cuddle, huddle, curl up, nuzzle

nestling NOUN = **chick**, fledgling, baby bird

net¹ NOUN = **mesh**, netting, network, web, lattice, openwork
▷ VERB = **catch**, bag, capture, trap, entangle, ensnare, enmesh

net² *or* **nett** ADJECTIVE = **after taxes**, final, clear, take-home
▷ VERB = **earn**, make, clear, gain, realize, bring in, accumulate, reap

network NOUN 1 = **web**, system, arrangement, grid, lattice
2 = **maze**, warren, labyrinth

neurotic ADJECTIVE = **unstable**, nervous, disturbed, abnormal, obsessive, compulsive, manic, unhealthy ≠ rational

neutral ADJECTIVE 1 = **unbiased**, impartial, disinterested, even-handed, uninvolved, nonpartisan, unprejudiced, nonaligned
≠ biased 2 = **expressionless**, dull 3 = **uncontroversial** *or* **noncontroversial**, inoffensive

n

4 = **colourless**

never ADVERB 1 = **at no time**, not once, not ever ≠ always

2 = **under no circumstances**, not at all, on no account, not ever

● WORD POWER
● *Never* is sometimes used in
● informal speech and writing as
● an emphatic form of *not*, with
● simple past tenses of certain
● verbs: *I never said that* – and
● in very informal speech as a
● denial in place of *did not*: *he says*
● *I hit him, but I never*. These uses
● of *never* should be avoided in
● careful writing.

nevertheless ADVERB = **even so**, still, however, yet, regardless, nonetheless, notwithstanding, in spite of that

new ADJECTIVE 1 = **modern**, recent, contemporary, up-to-date, latest, current, original, fresh ≠ old-fashioned 2 = **brand new** 3 = **extra**, more, added, new-found, supplementary 4 = **unfamiliar**, strange 5 = **renewed**, changed, improved, restored, altered, revitalized

newcomer NOUN 1 = **new arrival**, stranger 2 = **beginner**, novice, new arrival, parvenu (*French*), Johnny-come-lately (*informal*)

news NOUN = **information**, latest (*informal*), report, story, exposé, intelligence, rumour, revelation, goss (*informal*)

next ADJECTIVE 1 = **following**, later, succeeding, subsequent

2 = **adjacent**, closest, nearest, neighbouring, adjoining

▷ ADVERB = **afterwards**, then, later, following, subsequently, thereafter

nice ADJECTIVE 1 = **pleasant**, delightful, agreeable, good, attractive, charming, pleasurable, enjoyable ≠ unpleasant 2 = **kind**, helpful, obliging, considerate ≠ unkind 3 = **likable** *or* **likeable**, friendly, engaging, charming, pleasant, agreeable 4 = **polite**, courteous, well-mannered ≠ vulgar 5 = **precise**, fine, careful, strict, subtle, delicate, meticulous, fastidious ≠ vague

nicely ADVERB 1 = **pleasantly**, well, delightfully, attractively, charmingly, agreeably, acceptably, pleasurably ≠ unpleasantly

2 = **kindly**, politely, thoughtfully, amiably, courteously

niche NOUN 1 = **recess**, opening, corner, hollow, nook, alcove

2 = **position**, calling, place, slot (*informal*), vocation, pigeonhole (*informal*)

nick NOUN = **cut**, mark, scratch, chip, scar, notch, dent

▷ VERB 1 (*slang, chiefly Brit.*) = **steal**, pinch (*informal*), swipe (*slang*), pilfer 2 = **cut**, mark, score, chip, scratch, scar, notch, dent

nickname NOUN = **pet name**, label, diminutive, epithet, sobriquet, moniker *or* monicker (*slang*)

night NOUN = **darkness**, dark, night-time ▷ RELATED WORD:

adjective **nocturnal**

nightly ADJECTIVE 1 = **nocturnal**, night-time
▷ ADVERB = **every night**, nights (*informal*), each night, night after night

nightmare NOUN 1 = **bad dream**, hallucination 2 = **ordeal**, trial, hell, horror, torture, torment, tribulation, purgatory

nil NOUN 1 = **nothing**, love, zero 2 = **zero**, nothing, none, naught

nip¹ VERB 1 *with* **along**, **up**, **out**, = **pop**, go, run, rush, dash 2 = **bite** 3 = **pinch**, squeeze, tweak
▷ PHRASE: **nip something in the bud** = **thwart**, check, frustrate

nip² NOUN = **dram**, shot (*informal*), drop, sip, draught, mouthful, snifter (*informal*)

nirvana (*Buddhism, hinduism*) NOUN = **paradise**, peace, joy, bliss, serenity, tranquillity

no SENTENCE SUBSTITUTE = **not at all**, certainly not, of course not, absolutely not, never, no way, nay ≠ yes
▷ NOUN = **refusal**, rejection, denial, negation ≠ consent

noble ADJECTIVE 1 = **worthy**, generous, upright, honourable, virtuous, magnanimous ≠ despicable 2 = **dignified**, great, imposing, impressive, distinguished, splendid, stately ≠ lowly 3 = **aristocratic**, lordly, titled, patrician, blue-blooded, highborn ≠ humble
▷ NOUN = **lord**, peer, aristocrat, nobleman ≠ commoner

nobody PRONOUN = **no-one**
▷ NOUN = **nonentity**, lightweight (*informal*), zero, cipher ≠ celebrity

nod VERB 1 = **incline**, bow 2 = **signal**, indicate, motion, gesture 3 = **salute**, acknowledge
▷ NOUN 1 = **signal**, sign, motion, gesture, indication 2 = **salute**, greeting, acknowledgment

noise NOUN = **sound**, row, racket, clamour, din, uproar, commotion, hubbub ≠ silence

noisy ADJECTIVE 1 = **rowdy**, strident, boisterous, vociferous, uproarious, clamorous ≠ quiet 2 = **loud**, piercing, deafening, tumultuous, ear-splitting, cacophonous, clamorous ≠ quiet

nominal ADJECTIVE 1 = **titular**, formal, purported, in name only, supposed, so-called, theoretical, professed 2 = **token**, small, symbolic, minimal, trivial, trifling, insignificant, inconsiderable

nominate VERB 1 = **propose**, suggest, recommend, put forward 2 = **appoint**, name, choose, select, elect, assign, designate

nomination NOUN 1 = **proposal**, suggestion, recommendation 2 = **appointment**, election, selection, designation, choice

nominee NOUN = **candidate**, applicant, entrant, contestant, aspirant, runner

none PRONOUN 1 = **not any**, nothing, zero, not one, nil 2 = **no-one**, nobody, not one

nonetheless SENTENCE CONNECTOR = **nevertheless**,

n

however, yet, even so, despite that, in spite of that

nonexistent ADJECTIVE = **imaginary**, fictional, mythical, unreal, hypothetical, illusory ≠ real

nonsense NOUN 1 = **rubbish**, hot air (*informal*), twaddle, drivel, tripe (*informal*), gibberish, claptrap (*informal*), double Dutch (*Brit. informal*), bizzo (*Austral. slang*), bull's wool (*Austral. & N.Z. slang*) ≠ sense 2 = **idiocy**, stupidity

nonstop ADJECTIVE = **continuous**, constant, relentless, uninterrupted, endless, unbroken, interminable, incessant ≠ occasional

▷ ADVERB = **continuously**, constantly, endlessly, relentlessly, perpetually, incessantly, ceaselessly, interminably

noon NOUN = **midday**, high noon, noonday, twelve noon, noontide

norm NOUN = **standard**, rule, pattern, average, par, criterion, benchmark, yardstick

normal ADJECTIVE 1 = **usual**, common, standard, average, natural, regular, ordinary, typical ≠ unusual 2 = **sane**, reasonable, rational, well-adjusted, compos mentis (*Latin*), in your right mind, mentally sound

normally ADVERB 1 = **usually**, generally, commonly, regularly, typically, ordinarily, as a rule, habitually 2 = **as usual**, naturally, properly, conventionally, in the usual way

● **WORD POWER**
● English was brought into
● contact with Old Norse
● through Viking invasions
● which took place between the
● 9th century and the Norman
● Conquest. Old Norse was
● closely related to Old English,
● and extensive borrowing took
● place in all areas of language,
● including vocabulary, place
● names, and personal names.
● Unusually, part of the
● grammatical system of English
● was also affected, with the
● Old Norse personal pronouns
● 'they', 'them', and 'their' ousting
● the Old English forms. In
● contrast to loan words from
● Latin and French in English
● which tend to be of a higher
● register with several syllables,
● Norse contributed everyday,
● general words like *leg*, *sky*,
● *skirt*, and *cake*. Some of the
● most common verbs in English
● came from Old Norse, such as
● *get* and *give*. One borrowing
● which describes a unique part
● of Scandinavian culture is *saga*.
● Literally 'narrative', a saga is
● a story written in Iceland in
● the Middle Ages recounting
● the adventures of a hero or
● the history of a family. The
● term is also applied to modern
● literature which has some of
● the characteristics of a saga,
● particularly a novel or series of

novels depicting a family over several generations. Those describing the English middle classes have humorously been tagged *Aga sagas*. Informally, saga can also mean any story stretching over a long period, or the recounting of a long, boring, involved story, e.g. the continuing saga of the leadership contest.

north ADJECTIVE = **northern**, polar, arctic, boreal, northerly
▷ ADVERB = **northward(s)**, in a northerly direction

nose NOUN = **snout**, bill, beak, hooter (*slang*), proboscis
▷ VERB = **ease forward**, push, edge, shove, nudge ▷ RELATED WORD: *adjective* nasal

● WORD POWER
● The literal meaning of *nose* is
● the organ of smell in human
● beings and other animals used
● in the detection and tasting of
● food. This role, and its physical
● shape, have inspired a host
● of extended meanings and
● idioms. Humans are called
● *noses* if they are experts on
● perfume. In this case, the
● meaning is drawn from the
● most relevant body part of the
● person. A *nose* can also mean
● the characteristic fragrance
● of a wine. A human's sense of
● smell can provide clues at a
● level beyond explicit thought.
● Accordingly, nose can mean
● instinct and intuition, e.g.

● *(have) a nose for trouble*. There
● are many phrases involving
● nose, such as *nose around*,
● *nose about*, and *nose out*, all
● of which involve detection
● and investigation. However,
● too much nosing can lead to
● accusations of *nosiness* and
● *poking your nose (where it doesn't
● belong)*. The physical position
● of the nose has led to a verbal
● sense of edging forward in *nose
● your way*. A nose also means
● a winning margin, originally
● from horseracing, where a
● close win is *by a nose*.

nostalgia NOUN = **reminiscence**, longing, pining, yearning, remembrance, homesickness, wistfulness

nostalgic ADJECTIVE = **sentimental**, longing, emotional, homesick, wistful, maudlin, regretful

notable ADJECTIVE
1 = **remarkable**, striking, unusual, extraordinary, outstanding, memorable, uncommon, conspicuous ≠ imperceptible
2 = **prominent**, famous ≠ unknown
▷ NOUN = **celebrity**, big name, dignitary, luminary, personage, V.I.P.

notably ADVERB = **remarkably**, unusually, extraordinarily, noticeably, strikingly, singularly, outstandingly, uncommonly

notch NOUN 1 (*informal*) = **level**, step, degree, grade 2 = **cut**, nick,

n

incision, indentation, mark, score, cleft
▷ **VERB** = **cut**, mark, score, nick, scratch, indent

note NOUN 1 = **message**, letter, communication, memo, memorandum, epistle, e-mail, text 2 = **record**, reminder, memo, memorandum, jotting, minute 3 = **annotation**, comment, remark 4 = **document**, form, record, certificate 5 = **symbol**, mark, sign, indication, token 6 = **tone**, touch, trace, hint, sound
▷ **VERB** 1 = **notice**, see, observe, perceive 2 = **bear in mind**, be aware, take into account 3 = **mention**, record, mark, indicate, register, remark 4 = **write down**, record, scribble, set down, jot down

notebook NOUN = **notepad**, exercise book, journal, diary

noted ADJECTIVE = **famous**, celebrated, distinguished, well-known, prominent, acclaimed, notable, renowned ≠ unknown

nothing PRONOUN 1 = **nought**, zero, nil, not a thing, zilch (slang) 2 = **a trifle** 3 = **void**, emptiness, nothingness, nullity
▷ NOUN (informal) = **nobody**, cipher, nonentity

notice NOUN 1 = **notification**, warning, advice, intimation, news, communication, announcement, instruction, heads up (U.S. & Canad.) 2 = **attention**, interest, note, regard, consideration,

observation, scrutiny, heed ≠ oversight 3 (chiefly Brit.) = **the sack** (informal), dismissal, the boot (slang), the push (slang), marching orders (informal)
▷ **VERB** = **observe**, see, note, spot, distinguish, perceive, detect, discern ≠ overlook

noticeable ADJECTIVE = **obvious**, clear, striking, plain, evident, manifest, conspicuous, perceptible

notify VERB = **inform**, tell, advise, alert to, announce, warn

notion NOUN 1 = **idea**, view, opinion, belief, concept, impression, sentiment, inkling 2 = **whim**, wish, desire, fancy, impulse, inclination, caprice

notorious ADJECTIVE = **infamous**, disreputable, opprobrious

notoriously ADVERB = **infamously**, disreputably

notwithstanding PREPOSITION = **despite**, in spite of, regardless of

nought (archaic or literary) or **naught** or **ought** or **aught** NOUN = **zero**, nothing, nil

nourish VERB 1 = **feed**, supply, sustain, nurture 2 = **encourage**, support, maintain, promote, sustain, foster

nourishing ADJECTIVE = **nutritious**, beneficial, wholesome, nutritive

novel[1] NOUN = **story**, tale, fiction, romance, narrative

novel[2] ADJECTIVE = **new**, different, original, fresh, unusual, innovative, uncommon

≠ ordinary

novelty NOUN 1 = **newness**, originality, freshness, innovation, surprise, uniqueness, strangeness, unfamiliarity 2 = **curiosity**, rarity, oddity, wonder 3 = **trinket**, souvenir, memento, bauble, trifle, knick-knack

novice NOUN = **beginner**, pupil, amateur, newcomer, trainee, apprentice, learner, probationer ≠ expert

now ADVERB 1 = **nowadays**, at the moment 2 = **immediately**, promptly, instantly, at once, straightaway ▷ PHRASE: **now and then** or **again** = **occasionally**, sometimes, from time to time, on and off, intermittently, infrequently, sporadically

nowadays ADVERB = **now**, today, at the moment, in this day and age

nucleus NOUN = **centre**, heart, focus, basis, core, pivot, kernel, nub

nude ADJECTIVE = **naked**, stripped, bare, undressed, stark-naked, disrobed, unclothed, unclad ≠ dressed

nudge VERB 1 = **push**, touch, dig, jog, prod, elbow, shove, poke 2 = **prompt**, influence, persuade, spur, prod, coax ▷ NOUN 1 = **push**, touch, dig, elbow, bump, shove, poke, jog 2 = **prompting**, push, encouragement, prod

nuisance NOUN = **trouble**, problem, trial, drag (informal), bother, pest, irritation, hassle (informal) ≠ benefit

numb ADJECTIVE 1 = **unfeeling**, dead, frozen, paralysed, insensitive, deadened, immobilized, torpid ≠ sensitive 2 = **stupefied**, deadened, unfeeling ▷ VERB 1 = **stun**, knock out, paralyse, daze 2 = **deaden**, freeze, dull, paralyse, immobilize, benumb

number NOUN 1 = **numeral**, figure, character, digit, integer 2 = **amount**, quantity, collection, aggregate ≠ shortage 3 = **crowd**, horde, multitude, throng 4 = **group**, set, band, crowd, gang 5 = **issue**, copy, edition, imprint, printing ▷ VERB 1 = **amount to**, come to, total, add up to 2 = **calculate**, account, reckon, compute, enumerate ≠ guess 3 = **include**, count

numerous ADJECTIVE = **many**, several, countless, lots, abundant, plentiful, innumerable, copious ≠ few

nurse VERB 1 = **look after**, treat, tend, care for, take care of, minister to 2 = **harbour**, have, maintain, preserve, entertain, cherish 3 = **breast-feed**, feed, nurture, nourish, suckle, wet-nurse

nursery NOUN = **crèche**, kindergarten, playgroup, play-centre (N.Z.)

n

nurture NOUN = **upbringing**,
training, education, instruction,
rearing, development
▷ VERB = **bring up**, raise, look
after, rear, care for, develop
≠ neglect

nut NOUN 1 (*slang*) = **madman**,
psycho (*slang*), crank (*informal*),
lunatic, maniac, nutcase (*slang*),
crazy (*informal*) 2 (*slang*) = **head**,
skull

nutrition NOUN = **food**,
nourishment, sustenance,
nutriment

Oo

oath NOUN 1 = **promise**, bond, pledge, vow, word, affirmation, avowal 2 = **swear word**, curse, obscenity, blasphemy, expletive, four-letter word, profanity

obedience NOUN = **compliance**, respect, reverence, observance, subservience, submissiveness, docility ≠ disobedience

obey VERB 1 = **submit to**, surrender (to), give way to, bow to, give in to, yield to, do what you are told by ≠ disobey 2 = **carry out**, follow, implement, act upon, carry through ≠ disregard 3 = **abide by**, keep, follow, comply with, observe, heed, conform to, keep to

object¹ NOUN 1 = **thing**, article, body, item, entity 2 = **purpose**, aim, end, point, plan, idea, goal, design 3 = **target**, victim, focus, recipient

object² VERB 1 *often with* **to** = **protest against**, oppose, argue against, draw the line at, take exception to, cry out against, complain against, expostulate against ≠ accept 2 = **disagree**, demur, remonstrate, express disapproval ≠ agree

objection NOUN = **protest**, opposition, complaint, doubt, dissent, outcry, protestation, scruple ≠ agreement

objective ADJECTIVE 1 = **factual**, real 2 = **unbiased**, detached, fair, open-minded, impartial, impersonal, disinterested, even-handed ≠ subjective
▷ NOUN = **purpose**, aim, goal, end, plan, hope, idea, target

objectively ADVERB = **impartially**, neutrally, fairly, justly, without prejudice, dispassionately, with an open mind, equitably

obligation NOUN 1 = **duty**, compulsion 2 = **task**, job, duty, work, charge, role, function, mission 3 = **responsibility**, duty, liability, accountability, answerability

oblige VERB 1 = **compel**, make, force, require, bind, constrain, necessitate, impel 2 = **help**, assist, benefit, please, humour, accommodate, indulge, gratify ≠ bother

obliged ADJECTIVE 1 = **forced**, required, bound, compelled, duty-bound 2 = **grateful**, in (someone's) debt, thankful, indebted, appreciative, beholden

obliging ADJECTIVE = **accommodating**, kind, helpful, willing, polite, cooperative, agreeable, considerate ≠ unhelpful

obscene ADJECTIVE 1 = **indecent**, dirty, offensive, filthy, improper, immoral, pornographic, lewd ≠ decent 2 = **offensive**, shocking, evil, disgusting, outrageous, revolting, sickening, vile

obscure ADJECTIVE 1 = **unknown**, little-known, humble, unfamiliar, out-of-the-way, lowly, unheard-of, undistinguished ≠ famous 2 = **abstruse**, complex, confusing, mysterious, vague, unclear, ambiguous, enigmatic ≠ straightforward 3 = **unclear**, uncertain, confused, mysterious, doubtful, indeterminate ≠ well-known 4 = **indistinct**, vague, blurred, dark, faint, dim, gloomy, murky ≠ clear
▷ VERB 1 = **obstruct**, hinder 2 = **hide**, screen, mask, disguise, conceal, veil, cloak, camouflage ≠ expose

observation NOUN 1 = **watching**, study, survey, review, investigation, monitoring, examination, inspection 2 = **comment**, thought, note, statement, opinion, remark, explanation, reflection 3 = **remark**, comment, statement, reflection, utterance 4 with **of** = **observance of**, compliance with, honouring of, fulfilment of, carrying out of

observe VERB 1 = **watch**, study, view, look at, check, survey, monitor, keep an eye on (informal) 2 = **notice**, see, note, discover, spot, regard, witness, distinguish 3 = **remark**, say, comment, state, note, reflect, mention, opine 4 = **comply with**, keep, follow, respect, carry out, honour, discharge, obey ≠ disregard

observer NOUN 1 = **witness**, viewer, spectator, looker-on, watcher, onlooker, eyewitness, bystander 2 = **commentator**, reporter, special correspondent 3 = **monitor**, watchdog, supervisor, scrutineer

obsessed ADJECTIVE = **absorbed**, dominated, gripped, haunted, distracted, hung up (slang), preoccupied ≠ indifferent

obsession NOUN = **preoccupation**, thing (informal), complex, hang-up (informal), mania, phobia, fetish, fixation

obsessive ADJECTIVE = **compulsive**, gripping, consuming, haunting, irresistible, neurotic, besetting, uncontrollable

obsolete ADJECTIVE = **outdated**, old, passé, old-fashioned, discarded, extinct, out of date, archaic ≠ up-to-date

obstacle NOUN 1 = **obstruction**, block, barrier, hurdle, snag, impediment, blockage, hindrance 2 = **hindrance**, bar, difficulty, barrier, handicap, hurdle, hitch, drawback, uphill (S. African) ≠ help

obstruct VERB 1 = **block**, close, bar, plug, barricade, stop up, bung up (informal) 2 = **hold up**, stop, check, block, restrict, slow down, hamper, hinder 3 = **impede**, hamper, hold back, thwart, hinder ≠ help 4 = **obscure**, screen, cover

obtain VERB 1 = **get**, gain, acquire,

land, net, pick up, secure, procure
≠ lose **2** = **achieve**, get, gain,
accomplish, attain **3** (*formal*)
= **prevail**, hold, exist, be the case,
abound, predominate, be in force,
be current

obvious ADJECTIVE = **clear**,
plain, apparent, evident,
distinct, manifest, noticeable,
conspicuous ≠ unclear

obviously ADVERB **1** = **clearly**, of
course, without doubt, assuredly
2 = **plainly**, patently, undoubtedly,
evidently, manifestly, markedly,
without doubt, unquestionably

occasion NOUN **1** = **time**,
moment, point, stage, instance,
juncture **2** = **function**, event,
affair, do (*informal*), happening,
experience, gathering,
celebration **3** = **opportunity**,
chance, time, opening, window
4 = **reason**, cause, call, ground(s),
excuse, incentive, motive,
justification
▷ VERB (*formal*) = **cause**, produce,
lead to, inspire, result in,
generate, prompt, provoke

occasional ADJECTIVE
= **infrequent**, odd, rare, irregular,
sporadic, intermittent, few and
far between, periodic ≠ constant

occasionally ADVERB
= **sometimes**, at times, from time
to time, now and then, irregularly,
now and again, periodically, once
in a while ≠ constantly

occult ADJECTIVE = **supernatural**,
magical, mysterious, psychic,
mystical, unearthly, esoteric,

uncanny ▷ PHRASE: **the occult**
= **magic**, witchcraft, sorcery,
wizardry, enchantment, black art,
necromancy

occupant NOUN = **occupier**,
resident, tenant, inmate,
inhabitant, incumbent, dweller,
lessee

occupation NOUN **1** = **job**, calling,
business, line (of work), trade,
career, employment, profession
2 = **hobby**, pastime, diversion,
relaxation, leisure pursuit,
(leisure) activity **3** = **invasion**,
seizure, conquest, incursion,
subjugation **4** = **occupancy**,
residence, holding, control,
possession, tenure, tenancy

occupied ADJECTIVE **1** = **in use**,
taken, full, engaged, unavailable
2 = **inhabited**, peopled, lived-in,
settled, tenanted ≠ uninhabited
3 = **busy**, engaged, employed,
working, active, hard at work,
rushed off your feet

occupy VERB **1** = **inhabit**, own,
live in, dwell in, reside in, abide
in ≠ vacate **2** = **invade**, take over,
capture, seize, conquer, overrun,
annex, colonize ≠ withdraw
3 = **hold**, control, dominate,
possess **4** = **take up**, consume,
tie up, use up, monopolize **5** *often
passive* = **engage**, involve, employ,
divert, preoccupy, engross **6** = **fill**,
take up, cover, fill up, pervade,
permeate, extend over

occur VERB **1** = **happen**, take
place, come about, turn up
(*informal*), crop up (*informal*),

O

transpire (*informal*), befall
2 = **exist**, appear, be found, develop, turn up, be present, manifest itself, present itself

▷ PHRASE: **occur to someone** = **come to mind**, strike someone, dawn on someone, spring to mind, cross someone's mind, enter someone's head, suggest itself to someone

● WORD POWER
● It is usually regarded as
● incorrect to talk of pre-
● arranged events *occurring* or
● *happening*. For this meaning
● a synonym such as *take place*
● would be more appropriate: *the*
● *wedding took place* (not *occurred*
● or *happened*) *in the afternoon*.

occurrence NOUN **1** = **incident**, happening, event, fact, matter, affair, circumstance, episode
2 = **existence**, instance, appearance, manifestation, materialization

odd ADJECTIVE **1** = **peculiar**, strange, unusual, extraordinary, bizarre, offbeat, freakish, daggy (*Austral. & N.Z. informal*)
2 = **unusual**, strange, rare, extraordinary, remarkable, bizarre, peculiar, irregular ≠ normal **3** = **occasional**, various, random, casual, irregular, periodic, sundry, incidental ≠ regular **4** = **spare**, remaining, extra, surplus, solitary, leftover, unmatched, unpaired ≠ matched

odds PLURAL NOUN
1 = **probability**, chances,

likelihood ▷ PHRASES: **at odds 1** = **in conflict**, arguing, quarrelling, at loggerheads, at daggers drawn **2** = **at variance**, conflicting, contrary to, at odds, out of line, out of step, at sixes and sevens (*informal*); **odds and ends** = **scraps**, bits, remains, fragments, debris, remnants, bits and pieces, bric-a-brac

odour or (*U.S.*) **odor** NOUN = **smell**, scent, perfume, fragrance, stink, bouquet, aroma, stench

Odyssey NOUN *often not cap.* = **journey**, tour, trip, quest, trek, expedition, voyage, crusade

off ADVERB **1** = **away**, out, apart, elsewhere, aside, hence, from here
2 = **absent**, gone, unavailable
▷ ADJECTIVE **1** = **cancelled**, abandoned, postponed, shelved
2 = **bad**, rotten, rancid, mouldy, turned, spoiled, sour, decayed

offence or (*U.S.*) **offense** NOUN
1 = **crime**, sin, fault, violation, wrongdoing, trespass, felony, misdemeanour **2** = **outrage**, shock, anger, trouble, bother, resentment, irritation, hassle (*informal*) **3** = **insult**, slight, hurt, outrage, injustice, snub, affront, indignity

offend VERB **1** = **distress**, upset, outrage, wound, slight, insult, annoy, snub ≠ please **2** = **break the law**, sin, err, do wrong, fall, go astray

offended ADJECTIVE = **upset**, hurt, bothered, disturbed, distressed, outraged, stung, put out

o

(informal), tooshie (Austral. slang)

offender NOUN = **criminal**, convict, crook, villain, culprit, sinner, delinquent, felon, perp (U.S. & Canad. informal)

offensive ADJECTIVE 1 = **insulting**, rude, abusive, degrading, contemptuous, disparaging, objectionable, disrespectful ≠ respectful 2 = **disgusting**, gross, foul, unpleasant, revolting, vile, repellent, obnoxious, festy (Austral. slang), yucko (Austral. slang) ≠ pleasant 3 = **attacking**, threatening, aggressive, striking, hostile, invading, combative ≠ defensive
▷ NOUN = **attack**, charge, campaign, strike, push (informal), assault, raid, drive

offer VERB 1 = **provide**, present, furnish, afford ≠ withhold 2 = **volunteer**, come forward, offer your services 3 = **propose**, suggest, advance, submit 4 = **give**, show, bring, provide, render, impart 5 = **put up for sale**, sell 6 = **bid**, submit, propose, tender, proffer
▷ NOUN 1 = **proposal**, suggestion, proposition, submission 2 = **bid**, tender, bidding price

offering NOUN 1 = **contribution**, gift, donation, present, subscription, hand-out 2 = **sacrifice**, tribute, libation, burnt offering

office NOUN 1 = **place of work**, workplace, base, workroom, place of business 2 = **branch**, department, division, section, wing, subdivision, subsection 3 = **post**, place, role, situation, responsibility, function, occupation

officer NOUN 1 = **official**, executive, agent, representative, appointee, functionary, office-holder, office bearer 2 = **police officer**, detective, PC, police constable, police man, police woman

official ADJECTIVE 1 = **authorized**, formal, sanctioned, licensed, proper, legitimate, authentic, certified ≠ unofficial 2 = **formal**, bureaucratic, ceremonial, solemn, ritualistic
▷ NOUN = **officer**, executive, agent, representative, bureaucrat, appointee, functionary, office-holder

offset VERB = **cancel out**, balance, set off, make up for, compensate for, counteract, neutralize, counterbalance

offspring NOUN 1 = **child**, baby, kid (informal), youngster, infant, successor, babe, toddler, littlie (Austral. informal), ankle-biter (Austral. slang), tacker (Austral. slang) ≠ parent 2 = **children**, young, family, issue, stock, heirs, descendants, brood

often ADVERB = **frequently**, generally, commonly, repeatedly, time and again, habitually, not infrequently ≠ never

oil NOUN 1 = **lubricant**, grease, lubrication, fuel oil 2 = **lotion**,

o

cream, balm, salve, liniment,
embrocation, solution
▷ VERB = **lubricate**, grease
oily ADJECTIVE = **greasy**, slimy,
fatty, slippery, oleaginous
O.K. or **okay** SENTENCE
SUBSTITUTE = **all right**, right,
yes, agreed, very good, roger, very
well, ya (*S. African*), righto (*Brit.
informal*), yebo (*S. African informal*)
▷ ADJECTIVE (*informal*) = **all right**,
fine, fitting, in order, permitted,
suitable, acceptable, allowable
≠ unacceptable 2 = **fine**, good,
average, fair, all right, acceptable,
adequate, satisfactory
≠ unsatisfactory 3 = **well**, all
right, safe, sound, healthy,
unharmed, uninjured
▷ VERB = **approve**, allow, agree
to, permit, sanction, endorse,
authorize, rubber-stamp (*informal*)
▷ NOUN = **authorization**,
agreement, sanction, approval,
go-ahead (*informal*), blessing,
permission, consent
old ADJECTIVE 1 = **aged**, elderly,
ancient, mature, venerable,
antiquated, senile, decrepit
≠ young 2 = **former**, earlier,
past, previous, prior, one-time,
erstwhile 3 = **long-standing**,
established, fixed, enduring,
abiding, long-lasting, long-
established, time-honoured
4 = **stale**, worn-out, banal,
threadbare, trite, overused,
timeworn
old-fashioned ADJECTIVE
1 = **out of date**, dated, outdated,

unfashionable, outmoded,
passé, old hat, behind the times
≠ up-to-date 2 = **oldfangled**,
square (*informal*), outdated,
unfashionable, obsolescent
ominous ADJECTIVE
= **threatening**, sinister, grim,
fateful, foreboding, unpromising,
portentous, inauspicious
≠ promising
omission NOUN 1 = **exclusion**,
removal, elimination, deletion,
excision ≠ inclusion 2 = **gap**,
space, exclusion, lacuna
omit VERB 1 = **leave out**, drop,
exclude, eliminate, skip ≠ include
2 = **forget**, overlook, neglect, pass
over, lose sight of
once ADVERB 1 = **on one occasion**,
one time, one single time 2 = **at
one time**, previously, formerly,
long ago, once upon a time
▷ CONJUNCTION 1 = **as
soon as**, when, after, the
moment, immediately, the
instant ▷ PHRASE: at once
1 = **immediately**, now, straight
away, directly, promptly,
instantly, right away, forthwith
2 = **simultaneously**, together, at
the same time, concurrently
one-sided ADJECTIVE 1 = **unequal**,
unfair, uneven, unjust,
unbalanced, lopsided, ill-matched
≠ equal 2 = **biased**, prejudiced,
weighted, unfair, partial,
distorted, partisan, slanted
≠ unbiased
ongoing ADJECTIVE = **in progress**,
developing, progressing, evolving,

o

unfolding, unfinished

onlooker NOUN = **spectator**, witness, observer, viewer, looker-on, watcher, eyewitness, bystander

only ADJECTIVE = **sole**, one, single, individual, exclusive, unique, lone, solitary
▷ ADVERB 1 = **just**, simply, purely, merely 2 = **hardly**, just, barely, only just, scarcely, at a push

onset NOUN = **beginning**, start, birth, outbreak, inception, commencement ≠ end

onslaught NOUN = **attack**, charge, campaign, strike, assault, raid, invasion, offensive ≠ retreat

onwards or **onward** ADVERB = **forward**, on, forwards, ahead, beyond, in front, forth

ooze¹ VERB 1 = **seep**, well, escape, leak, drain, filter, drip, trickle 2 = **emit**, release, leak, drip, dribble, give off, pour forth 3 = **exude**, emit

ooze² NOUN = **mud**, clay, dirt, silt, sludge, mire, slime, alluvium

open ADJECTIVE 1 = **unclosed**, unlocked, ajar, unfastened, yawning ≠ closed 2 = **unsealed**, unstoppered ≠ unopened 3 = **extended**, unfolded, stretched out, unfurled, straightened out, unrolled ≠ shut 4 = **frank**, direct, straightforward, sincere, transparent, honest, candid, truthful ≠ sly 5 = **receptive**, sympathetic, responsive, amenable 6 = **unresolved**, unsettled, undecided,

debatable, moot, arguable 7 = **clear**, passable, unhindered, unimpeded, navigable, unobstructed ≠ obstructed 8 = **available**, to hand, accessible, handy, at your disposal 9 = **general**, public, free, universal, blanket, across-the-board, unrestricted, overarching ≠ restricted 10 = **vacant**, free, available, empty, unoccupied, unfilled
▷ VERB 1 = **unfasten**, unlock ≠ close 2 = **unwrap**, uncover, undo, unravel, untie ≠ wrap 3 = **uncork** 4 = **unfold**, spread (out), expand, unfurl, unroll ≠ fold 5 = **clear**, unblock ≠ block 6 = **undo**, unbutton, unfasten ≠ fasten 7 = **begin business** 8 = **start**, begin, launch, trigger, kick off (informal), initiate, commence, get going ≠ end 9 = **begin**, start, commence ≠ end

open-air MODIFIER = **outdoor**, outside, out-of-door(s), alfresco

opening ADJECTIVE = **first**, earliest, beginning, premier, primary, initial, maiden, inaugural
▷ NOUN 1 = **beginning**, start, launch, dawn, outset, initiation, inception, commencement ≠ ending 2 = **hole**, space, tear, crack, gap, slot, puncture, aperture ≠ blockage 3 = **opportunity**, chance, time, moment, occasion, look-in (informal) 4 = **job**, position, post,

situation, opportunity, vacancy

openly ADVERB = **frankly**, plainly, honestly, overtly, candidly, unreservedly, unhesitatingly, forthrightly ≠ privately

open-minded ADJECTIVE = **unprejudiced**, liberal, balanced, objective, reasonable, tolerant, impartial, receptive ≠ narrow-minded

operate VERB 1 = **manage**, run, direct, handle, supervise, be in charge of 2 = **function**, work, act 3 = **run**, work, use, control, manoeuvre 4 = **work**, go, run, perform, function ≠ break down

operation NOUN = **performance**, action, movement, motion

operational ADJECTIVE = **working**, going, running, ready, functioning, operative, viable, functional ≠ inoperative

operative ADJECTIVE = **in force**, effective, functioning, active, in effect, operational, in operation ≠ inoperative
  ▷ NOUN 1 = **worker**, employee, labourer, workman, artisan 2 (*U.S. & Canad.*) = **spy**, undercover agent, mole, nark (*Brit., Austral. & N.Z. slang*)

operator NOUN = **worker**, driver, mechanic, operative, conductor, technician, handler

opinion NOUN 1 = **belief**, feeling, view, idea, theory, conviction, point of view, sentiment
  2 = **estimation**, view, impression, assessment, judgment, appraisal, considered opinion

opponent NOUN 1 = **adversary**, rival, enemy, competitor, challenger, foe, contestant, antagonist ≠ ally 2 = **opposer**, dissident, objector ≠ supporter

opportunity NOUN = **chance**, opening, time, turn, moment, possibility, occasion, slot

oppose VERB = **be against**, fight (against), block, take on, counter, contest, resist, combat ≠ support

opposed ADJECTIVE 1 *with* **to** = **against**, hostile, adverse, in opposition, averse, antagonistic, (dead) set against 2 = **contrary**, conflicting, clashing, counter, adverse, contradictory, dissentient

opposing ADJECTIVE
  1 = **conflicting**, different, contrasting, opposite, differing, contrary, contradictory, incompatible 2 = **rival**, conflicting, competing, enemy, opposite, hostile

opposite ADJECTIVE = **facing**, other, opposing 2 = **different**, conflicting, contrasted, contrasting, unlike, contrary, dissimilar, divergent ≠ alike
  3 = **rival**, conflicting, opposing, competing
  ▷ PREPOSITION *often with* **to** = **facing**, face to face with, across from, eyeball to eyeball with (*informal*)
  ▷ NOUN = **reverse**, contrary, converse, antithesis, contradiction, inverse, obverse

opposition NOUN 1 = **hostility**,

resistance, resentment, disapproval, obstruction, animosity, antagonism, antipathy ≠ support **2** = **opponent(s)**, competition, rival(s), enemy, competitor(s), other side, challenger(s), foe

oppress VERB **1** = **subjugate**, abuse, suppress, wrong, master, overcome, subdue, persecute ≠ liberate **2** = **depress**, burden, discourage, torment, harass, afflict, sadden, vex

oppression NOUN = **persecution**, control, abuse, injury, injustice, cruelty, domination, repression ≠ justice

oppressive ADJECTIVE
1 = **tyrannical**, severe, harsh, cruel, brutal, authoritarian, unjust, repressive ≠ merciful
2 = **stifling**, close, sticky, stuffy, humid, sultry, airless, muggy

opt VERB = **choose**, decide, prefer, select, elect ≠ reject ▷ PHRASE: **opt for something** *or* **someone** = **choose**, pick, select, adopt, go for, designate, decide on, plump for

optimistic ADJECTIVE **1** = **hopeful**, positive, confident, encouraged, cheerful, rosy, buoyant, sanguine ≠ pessimistic **2** = **encouraging**, promising, bright, good, reassuring, rosy, heartening, auspicious ≠ discouraging

optimum ADJECTIVE = **ideal**, best, highest, finest, perfect, supreme, peak, outstanding ≠ worst

option NOUN = **choice**,

alternative, selection, preference, freedom of choice, power to choose

optional ADJECTIVE = **voluntary**, open, discretionary, possible, extra, elective ≠ compulsory

opus NOUN = **work**, piece, production, creation, composition, work of art, brainchild, oeuvre (*French*)

oral ADJECTIVE = **spoken**, vocal, verbal, unwritten

orbit NOUN **1** = **path**, course, cycle, circle, revolution, rotation, trajectory, sweep **2** = **sphere of influence**, reach, range, influence, province, scope, domain, compass ▷ VERB = **circle**, ring, go round, revolve around, encircle, circumscribe, circumnavigate

orchestrate VERB **1** = **organize**, plan, run, set up, arrange, put together, marshal, coordinate **2** = **score**, set, arrange, adapt

ordain VERB **1** = **appoint**, name, commission, select, invest, nominate, anoint, consecrate **2** (*formal*) = **order**, will, rule, demand, require, direct, command, dictate

ordeal NOUN = **hardship**, trial, difficulty, test, suffering, nightmare, torture, agony ≠ pleasure

order VERB **1** = **command**, instruct, direct, charge, demand, require, bid, compel ≠ forbid **2** = **decree**, rule, demand, prescribe, pronounce, ordain ≠ ban **3** = **request**, ask (for), book,

o

seek, reserve, apply for, solicit, send away for **4** = **arrange**, group, sort, position, line up, organize, catalogue, sort out ≠ disarrange
▷ NOUN **1** = **instruction**, ruling, demand, direction, command, dictate, decree, mandate **2** = **request**, booking, demand, commission, application, reservation, requisition **3** = **sequence**, grouping, series, structure, chain, arrangement, line-up, array **4** = **organization**, system, method, pattern, symmetry, regularity, neatness, tidiness ≠ chaos **5** = **peace**, control, law, quiet, calm, discipline, law and order, tranquillity **6** = **society**, company, group, club, community, association, institute, organization **7** = **class**, set, rank, grade, caste **8** (*biology*) = **kind**, group, class, family, sort, type, variety, category

orderly ADJECTIVE **1** = **well-behaved**, controlled, disciplined, quiet, restrained, law-abiding, peaceable ≠ disorderly **2** = **well-organized**, regular, in order, organized, precise, neat, tidy, systematic ≠ disorganized

ordinary ADJECTIVE **1** = **usual**, standard, normal, common, regular, typical, conventional, routine **2** = **commonplace**, plain, modest, humble, mundane, banal, unremarkable, run-of-the-mill ≠ extraordinary

organ NOUN **1** = **body part**, part of the body, element, biological structure **2** = **newspaper**, medium, voice, vehicle, gazette, mouthpiece

organic ADJECTIVE **1** = **natural**, biological, living, live, animate **2** = **systematic**, ordered, structured, organized, integrated, orderly, methodical

organism NOUN = **creature**, being, thing, body, animal, structure, beast, entity

organization *or* **organisation** NOUN **1** = **group**, company, party, body, association, band, institution, corporation **2** = **management**, running, planning, control, operation, handling, structuring, administration **3** = **structure**, form, pattern, make-up, arrangement, construction, format, formation

organize *or* **organise** VERB **1** = **arrange**, run, plan, prepare, set up, devise, put together, take care of, jack up (*N.Z. informal*) ≠ disrupt **2** = **put in order**, arrange, group, list, file, index, classify, inventory ≠ muddle

orient *or* **orientate** VERB = **adjust**, adapt, alter, accustom, align, familiarize, acclimatize
▷ PHRASE: **orient yourself** = **get your bearings**, establish your location

orientation NOUN **1** = **inclination**, tendency, disposition, predisposition, predilection, proclivity, partiality

2 = **induction**, introduction,
adjustment, settling in,
adaptation, assimilation,
familiarization, acclimatization
3 = **position**, situation, location,
bearings, direction, arrangement,
whereabouts

origin NOUN **1** = **beginning**,
start, birth, launch, foundation,
creation, emergence, onset ≠ end
2 = **root**, source, basis, base, seed,
foundation, nucleus, derivation

original ADJECTIVE **1** = **first**,
earliest, initial **2** = **initial**,
first, starting, opening,
primary, introductory ≠ final
3 = **new**, fresh, novel, unusual,
unprecedented, innovative,
unfamiliar, seminal ≠ unoriginal
4 = **creative**, inspired,
imaginative, artistic, fertile,
ingenious, visionary, inventive
▷ NOUN = **prototype**, master,
pattern ≠ copy

originally ADVERB = **initially**,
first, firstly, at first, primarily, to
begin with, in the beginning

originate VERB **1** = **begin**, start,
emerge, come, happen, rise,
appear, spring ≠ end **2** = **invent**,
create, design, launch, introduce,
institute, generate, pioneer

ornament NOUN **1** = **decoration**,
trimming, accessory, festoon,
trinket, bauble, knick-knack
2 = **embellishment**, decoration,
embroidery, elaboration,
adornment, ornamentation
▷ VERB = **decorate**, adorn, array,
do up (*informal*), embellish,

festoon, beautify, prettify

orthodox ADJECTIVE
1 = **established**, official, accepted,
received, common, traditional,
normal, usual ≠ unorthodox
2 = **conformist**, conservative,
traditional, strict, devout,
observant ≠ nonconformist

orthodoxy NOUN **1** = **doctrine**,
teaching, opinion, principle,
belief, convention, creed, dogma
2 = **conformity**, received wisdom,
traditionalism, conventionality
≠ nonconformity

other DETERMINER **1** = **additional**,
more, further, new, added,
extra, fresh, spare **2** = **different**,
alternative, contrasting, distinct,
diverse, dissimilar, separate,
alternative

otherwise SENTENCE
CONNECTOR = **or else**, or, if not,
or then
▷ ADVERB **1** = **apart from that**, in
other ways, in (all) other respects
2 = **differently**, any other way,
contrarily

ounce NOUN = **shred**, bit, drop,
trace, scrap, grain, fragment,
atom

oust VERB = **expel**, turn out,
dismiss, exclude, exile, throw out,
displace, topple

out ADJECTIVE **1** = **not in**, away,
elsewhere, outside, gone,
abroad, from home, absent
2 = **extinguished**, ended,
finished, dead, exhausted,
expired, used up, at an end
≠ alight **3** = **in bloom**, opening,

o

open, flowering, blooming,
in flower, in full bloom
4 = **available**, on sale, in the
shops, to be had, purchasable
5 = **revealed**, exposed, common
knowledge, public knowledge,
(out) in the open ≠ kept secret
▷ VERB = **expose**

outbreak NOUN **1** = **eruption**,
burst, explosion, epidemic,
rash, outburst, flare-up, upsurge
2 = **onset**, beginning, outset,
opening, dawn, commencement

outburst NOUN **1** = **explosion**,
surge, outbreak, eruption, flare-
up **2** = **fit**, flare-up, eruption,
spasm, outpouring

outcome NOUN = **result**, end,
consequence, conclusion, payoff
(*informal*), upshot

outcry NOUN = **protest**,
complaint, objection, dissent,
outburst, clamour, uproar,
commotion

outdated ADJECTIVE = **old-
fashioned**, dated, obsolete,
out of date, passé, archaic,
unfashionable, antiquated
≠ modern

outdoor ADJECTIVE = **open-air**,
outside, out-of-door(s), alfresco
≠ indoor

outer ADJECTIVE **1** = **external**,
outside, outward, exterior,
exposed, outermost ≠ inner
2 = **surface 3** = **outlying**, distant,
provincial, out-of-the-way,
peripheral, far-flung ≠ central

outfit NOUN **1** = **costume**,
dress, clothes, clothing, suit,

get-up (*informal*), kit, ensemble
2 (*informal*) = **group**, company,
team, party, unit, crowd, squad,
organization

outgoing ADJECTIVE **1** = **leaving**,
former, previous, retiring,
withdrawing, prior, departing,
erstwhile ≠ incoming
2 = **sociable**, open, social, warm,
friendly, expansive, affable,
extrovert ≠ reserved

outgoings PLURAL NOUN
= **expenses**, costs, payments,
expenditure, overheads, outlay

outing NOUN = **journey**, run, trip,
tour, expedition, excursion, spin
(*informal*), jaunt

outlaw NOUN = **bandit**, criminal,
thief, robber, fugitive, outcast,
felon, highwayman
▷ VERB **1** = **ban**, bar, veto, forbid,
exclude, prohibit, disallow,
proscribe ≠ legalise **2** = **banish**,
put a price on (someone's) head

outlet NOUN **1** = **shop**, store,
supermarket, market, boutique,
emporium, hypermarket
2 = **channel**, release, medium,
avenue, vent, conduit **3** = **pipe**,
opening, channel, exit, duct

outline NOUN **1** = **summary**,
review, résumé, rundown,
synopsis, précis, thumbnail
sketch, recapitulation **2** = **shape**,
lines, form, figure, profile,
silhouette, configuration,
contour(s)
▷ VERB **1** = **summarize**, draft,
plan, trace, sketch (in), sum
up, encapsulate, delineate

2 = **silhouette**, etch

outlook NOUN 1 = **attitude**, opinion, position, approach, mood, perspective, point of view, stance 2 = **prospect(s)**, future, expectations, forecast, prediction, probability, prognosis

out of date ADJECTIVE 1 = **old-fashioned**, dated, outdated, obsolete, démodé (*French*), antiquated, outmoded, passé ≠ modern 2 = **invalid**, expired, lapsed, void, null and void

output NOUN = **production**, manufacture, manufacturing, yield, productivity

outrage NOUN = **indignation**, shock, anger, rage, fury, hurt, resentment, scorn
▷ VERB = **offend**, shock, upset, wound, insult, infuriate, incense, madden

outrageous ADJECTIVE
1 = **atrocious**, shocking, terrible, offensive, appalling, cruel, savage, horrifying ≠ mild
2 = **unreasonable**, unfair, steep (*informal*), shocking, extravagant, scandalous, preposterous, unwarranted ≠ reasonable

outright ADJECTIVE 1 = **absolute**, complete, total, perfect, sheer, thorough, unconditional, unqualified 2 = **definite**, clear, certain, flat, absolute, black-and-white, straightforward, unequivocal
▷ ADVERB 1 = **openly**, frankly, plainly, overtly, candidly, unreservedly, unhesitatingly,

forthrightly 2 = **absolutely**, completely, totally, fully, entirely, thoroughly, wholly, utterly

outset NOUN = **beginning**, start, opening, onset, inauguration, inception, commencement, kickoff (*informal*) ≠ finish

outside ADJECTIVE = **external**, outer, exterior, outward, extraneous ≠ inner 2 = **remote**, small, unlikely, slight, slim, distant, faint, marginal
▷ ADVERB = **outdoors**, out of the house, out-of-doors
▷ NOUN = **exterior**, face, front, covering, skin, surface, shell, coating

⊛ **WORD POWER**
⊛ The use of *outside of* and *inside*
⊛ *of*, although fairly common,
⊛ is generally thought to be
⊛ incorrect or nonstandard: *She*
⊛ *waits outside* (not *outside of*) *the*
⊛ *school*.

outsider NOUN = **stranger**, incomer, visitor, newcomer, intruder, interloper, odd one out

outskirts PLURAL NOUN = **edge**, boundary, suburbs, fringe, perimeter, periphery, suburbia, environs

outspan VERB (*S. African*) = **relax**, chill out (*slang, chiefly U.S.*), take it easy, loosen up, put your feet up

outspoken ADJECTIVE
= **forthright**, open, frank, straightforward, blunt, explicit, upfront (*informal*), unequivocal ≠ reserved

outstanding ADJECTIVE

1 = **excellent**, good, great, important, special, fine, brilliant, impressive, booshit (*Austral. slang*), exo (*Austral. slang*), sik (*Austral. slang*), rad (*informal*), phat (*slang*), schmick (*Austral. informal*) ≠ mediocre
2 = **unpaid**, remaining, due, pending, payable, unsettled, uncollected 3 = **undone**, left, omitted, unfinished, unfulfilled, unperformed

outward ADJECTIVE = **apparent**, seeming, surface, ostensible ≠ inward

outwardly ADVERB = **apparently**, externally, seemingly, it seems that, on the surface, it appears that, ostensibly, on the face of it

outweigh VERB = **override**, cancel (out), eclipse, offset, compensate for, supersede, neutralize, counterbalance

oval ADJECTIVE = **elliptical**, egg-shaped, ovoid

ovation NOUN = **applause**, hand, cheers, praise, tribute, acclaim, clapping, accolade ≠ derision

over PREPOSITION 1 = **above**, on top of 2 = **on top of**, on, across, upon 3 = **across**, (looking) onto 4 = **more than**, above, exceeding, in excess of, upwards of 5 = **about**, regarding, relating to, concerning, apropos of
▷ ADVERB 1 = **above**, overhead, in the sky, on high, aloft, up above
2 = **extra**, more, further, beyond, additional, in addition, surplus, in excess

▷ ADJECTIVE = **finished**, done (with), through, ended, closed, past, completed, complete
▷ RELATED WORDS: *prefixes* hyper-, super-

overall ADJECTIVE = **total**, full, whole, general, complete, entire, global, comprehensive
▷ ADVERB = **in general**, generally, mostly, all things considered, on average, on the whole, predominantly, in the main

overcome VERB 1 = **defeat**, beat, conquer, master, overwhelm, subdue, rout, overpower
2 = **conquer**, beat, master, subdue, triumph over, vanquish

overdue ADJECTIVE 1 = **delayed**, belated, late, behind schedule, tardy, unpunctual, behindhand ≠ early 2 = **unpaid**, owing

overflow VERB = **spill over**, well over, run over, pour over, bubble over, brim over
▷ NOUN 1 = **flood**, spilling over 2 = **surplus**, extra, excess, overspill, overabundance, additional people *or* things

overhaul VERB 1 = **check**, service, maintain, examine, restore, tune (up), repair, go over 2 = **overtake**, pass, leave behind, catch up with, get past, outstrip, get ahead of, outdistance
▷ NOUN = **check**, service, examination, going-over (*informal*), inspection, once-over (*informal*), checkup, reconditioning

overhead ADJECTIVE = **raised**,

suspended, elevated, aerial, overhanging

▷ ADVERB = **above**, in the sky, on high, aloft, up above ≠ underneath

overheads PLURAL NOUN = **running costs**, expenses, outgoings, operating costs

overlook VERB 1 = **look over** or **out on**, have a view of 2 = **miss**, forget, neglect, omit, disregard, pass over ≠ notice 3 = **ignore**, excuse, forgive, pardon, disregard, condone, turn a blind eye to, wink at

overpower VERB 1 = **overcome**, master, overwhelm, overthrow, subdue, quell, subjugate, prevail over 2 defeat, crush, triumph over, vanquish 3 = **overwhelm**, overcome, bowl over (*informal*), stagger

override VERB 1 = **outweigh**, eclipse, supersede, take precedence over, prevail over 2 = **overrule**, cancel, overturn, repeal, rescind, annul, nullify, countermand 3 = **ignore**, reject, discount, overlook, disregard, pass over, take no notice of

overrun VERB 1 = **overwhelm**, attack, assault, occupy, raid, invade, penetrate, rout 2 = **spread over**, overwhelm, choke, swamp, infest, inundate, permeate, swarm over 3 = **exceed**, go beyond, surpass, overshoot, run over or on

overshadow VERB 1 = **spoil**, ruin, mar, wreck, blight, crool or cruel

(*Austral. slang*), mess up, put a damper on 2 = **outshine**, eclipse, surpass, dwarf, tower above, leave or put in the shade

overt ADJECTIVE = **open**, obvious, plain, public, manifest, blatant, observable, undisguised ≠ hidden

overtake VERB 1 = **pass**, leave behind, overhaul, catch up with, get past, outdistance, go by or past 2 = **outdo**, top, exceed, eclipse, surpass, outstrip, get the better of, outclass 3 = **befall**, hit, happen to, catch off guard, catch unawares 4 = **engulf**, overwhelm, hit, strike, swamp, envelop, swallow up

overthrow VERB = **defeat**, overcome, conquer, bring down, oust, topple, rout, overpower ≠ uphold

▷ NOUN = **downfall**, fall, defeat, collapse, destruction, ousting, undoing, unseating ≠ preservation

overturn VERB 1 = **tip over**, topple, upturn, capsize, upend, keel over, overbalance 2 = **knock over** or **down**, upturn, tip over, upend 3 = **reverse**, change, cancel, abolish, overthrow, set aside, repeal, quash 4 = **overthrow**, defeat, destroy, overcome, bring down, oust, topple, depose

overweight ADJECTIVE = **fat**, heavy, stout, hefty, plump, bulky, chunky, chubby ≠ underweight

overwhelm VERB 1 = **overcome**,

o

devastate, stagger, bowl over (*informal*), knock (someone) for six (*informal*), sweep (someone) off his *or* her feet, take (someone's) breath away **2** = **destroy**, defeat, overcome, crush, massacre, conquer, wipe out, overthrow

overwhelming ADJECTIVE
1 = **overpowering**, strong, powerful, towering, stunning, crushing, devastating, shattering ≠ negligible **2** = **vast**, huge, massive, enormous, tremendous, immense, very large ≠ insignificant

owe VERB = **be in debt (to)**, be in arrears (to), be overdrawn (by), be obligated *or* indebted (to)

owing ▷ PHRASE: **owing to** = **because of**, thanks to, as a result of, on account of, by reason of

own DETERMINER = **personal**, special, private, individual, particular, exclusive
▷ VERB = **possess**, have, keep, hold, enjoy, retain, be in possession of, have to your name

owner NOUN = **possessor**, holder, proprietor, titleholder, landlord *or* landlady

ownership NOUN = **possession**, occupation, tenure, dominion

Pp

pace NOUN 1 = **speed**, rate, tempo, velocity 2 = **step**, walk, stride, tread, gait 3 = **footstep**, step, stride
▷ VERB = **stride**, walk, pound, patrol, march up and down

pack VERB 1 = **package**, load, store, bundle, stow 2 = **cram**, crowd, press, fill, stuff, jam, ram, compress
▷ NOUN 1 = **packet**, box, package, carton 2 = **bundle**, parcel, load, burden, rucksack, knapsack, back pack, kitbag 3 = **group**, crowd, company, band, troop, gang, bunch, mob ▷ PHRASES:
pack someone off = **send away**, dismiss, send packing (*informal*);
pack something in 1 (*Brit. & N.Z. informal*) = **resign from**, leave, give up, quit (*informal*), chuck (*informal*), jack in (*informal*) 2 = **stop**, give up, kick (*informal*), cease, chuck (*informal*)

package NOUN 1 = **parcel**, box, container, packet, carton 2 = **collection**, lot, unit, combination, compilation
▷ VERB = **pack**, box, parcel (up)

packet NOUN 1 = **container**, box, package, carton 2 = **package**, parcel 3 (*slang*) = **a fortune**, a bomb (*Brit. slang*), a pile

(*informal*), a small fortune, a tidy sum (*informal*), a king's ransom (*informal*), top whack (*informal*)

pact NOUN = **agreement**, alliance, treaty, deal, understanding, bargain, covenant

pad¹ NOUN 1 = **wad**, dressing, pack, padding, compress, wadding 2 = **cushion**, filling, stuffing, pillow, bolster, upholstery 3 = **notepad**, block, notebook, jotter, writing pad 4 (*slang*) = **home**, flat, apartment, place, bachelor apartment (*Canad.*) 5 = **paw**, foot, sole
▷ VERB = **pack**, fill, protect, stuff, cushion

pad² VERB = **sneak**, creep, steal, go barefoot

padding NOUN 1 = **filling**, stuffing, packing, wadding 2 = **waffle** (*informal, chiefly Brit.*), hot air (*informal*), verbiage, wordiness, verbosity

paddle¹ NOUN = **oar**, scull
▷ VERB = **row**, pull, scull

paddle² VERB = **wade**, splash (about), slop

pagan NOUN = **heathen**, infidel, polytheist, idolater
▷ ADJECTIVE = **heathen**, infidel, polytheistic, idolatrous

page¹ NOUN = **folio**, side, leaf, sheet

page² NOUN 1 = **attendant**, pageboy 2 = **servant**, attendant, squire, pageboy
▷ VERB = **call**, summon, send for

pain NOUN 1 = **suffering**, discomfort, hurt, irritation, tenderness, soreness **2** = **ache**, stinging, aching, cramp, throb, throbbing, pang, twinge

3 = **sorrow**, suffering, torture, distress, despair, misery, agony, sadness

▷ **PLURAL NOUN** = **trouble**, effort, care, bother, diligence

▷ **VERB 1** = **distress**, hurt, torture, grieve, torment, sadden, agonize, cut to the quick **2** = **hurt**

painful ADJECTIVE **1** = **sore**, smarting, aching, tender ≠ painless **2** = **distressing**, unpleasant, grievous, distasteful, agonizing, disagreeable ≠ pleasant **3** = **difficult**, arduous, trying, hard, troublesome, laborious ≠ easy

painfully ADVERB = **distressingly**, clearly, sadly, unfortunately, dreadfully

paint NOUN = **colouring**, colour, stain, dye, tint, pigment, emulsion

▷ **VERB 1** = **colour**, cover, coat, stain, whitewash, daub, distemper, apply paint to

2 = **depict**, draw, portray, picture, represent, sketch

pair NOUN **1** = **set 2** = **couple**, brace, duo

▷ **VERB** *often with* **off** = **team**, match (up), join, couple, twin, bracket

- **WORD POWER**
- Like other collective nouns, *pair*
- takes a singular or a plural verb
- according to whether it is seen
- as a unit or as a collection of

two things: *the pair are said to dislike each other; a pair of good shoes is essential.*

pal NOUN (*informal*) = **friend**, companion, mate (*informal*), buddy (*informal*), comrade, chum (*informal*), crony, cobber (*Austral. & N.Z. old-fashioned, informal*), E hoa (*N.Z.*)

pale ADJECTIVE **1** = **light**, soft, faded, subtle, muted, bleached, pastel, light-coloured **2** = **dim**, weak, faint, feeble, thin, wan, watery **3** = **white**, pasty, bleached, wan, colourless, pallid, ashen ≠ rosy-cheeked

▷ **VERB** = **become pale**, blanch, whiten, go white, lose colour

pamper VERB = **spoil**, indulge, pet, cosset, coddle, mollycoddle

pamphlet NOUN = **booklet**, leaflet, brochure, circular, tract

pan¹ NOUN = **pot**, container, saucepan

▷ **VERB 1** (*informal*) = **criticize**, knock, slam (*slang*), censure, tear into (*informal*) **2** = **sift out**, look for, search for

pan² VERB = **move along** *or* **across**, follow, track, sweep

panic NOUN = **fear**, alarm, terror, anxiety, hysteria, fright, trepidation, a flap (*informal*)

▷ **VERB 1** = **go to pieces**, become hysterical, lose your nerve

2 = **alarm**, scare, unnerve

panorama NOUN **1** = **view**, prospect, vista **2** = **survey**, perspective, overview, overall picture

pant VERB = **puff**, blow, breathe, gasp, wheeze, heave

pants PLURAL NOUN 1 (*Brit.*) = **underpants**, briefs, drawers, knickers, panties, boxer shorts, broekies (*S. African*), underdaks (*Austral. slang*) 2 (*U.S.*) = **trousers**, slacks

paper NOUN 1 = **newspaper**, daily, journal, gazette 2 = **essay**, article, treatise, dissertation 3 = **examination**, test, exam 4 = **report**
▷ PLURAL NOUN 1 = **letters**, records, documents, file, diaries, archive, paperwork, dossier 2 = **documents**, records, certificates, identification, deeds, identity papers, I.D. (*informal*)
▷ VERB = **wallpaper**, hang

parade NOUN 1 = **procession**, march, pageant, cavalcade 2 = **show**, display, spectacle
▷ VERB 1 = **march**, process, promenade 2 = **flaunt**, display, exhibit, show off (*informal*) 3 = **strut**, show off (*informal*), swagger, swank

paradigm NOUN = **model**, example, pattern, ideal

paradise NOUN 1 = **heaven**, Promised Land, Happy Valley, Elysian fields 2 = **bliss**, delight, heaven, felicity, utopia

paradox NOUN = **contradiction**, puzzle, anomaly, enigma, oddity

paragraph NOUN = **section**, part, item, passage, clause, subdivision

parallel NOUN 1 = **equivalent**, counterpart, match, equal, twin, analogue ≠ opposite 2 = **similarity**, comparison, analogy, resemblance, likeness ≠ difference
▷ ADJECTIVE 1 = **matching**, corresponding, like, similar, resembling, analogous ≠ different 2 = **equidistant**, alongside, side by side ≠ divergent

paralyse VERB 1 = **disable**, cripple, lame, incapacitate 2 = **freeze**, stun, numb, petrify, halt, immobilize 3 = **immobilize**, freeze, halt, disable, cripple, incapacitate, bring to a standstill

paralysis NOUN 1 = **immobility**, palsy 2 = **standstill**, breakdown, stoppage, halt

parameter NOUN (*informal*) *usually plural* = **limit**, restriction, framework, limitation, specification

paramount ADJECTIVE = **principal**, prime, first, chief, main, primary, supreme, cardinal ≠ secondary

paranoid ADJECTIVE 1 (*informal*) = **suspicious**, worried, nervous, fearful, antsy (*informal*) 2 = **obsessive**, disturbed, manic, neurotic, mentally ill, psychotic, deluded, paranoiac

parasite NOUN = **sponger** (*informal*), leech, hanger-on, scrounger (*informal*), bloodsucker (*informal*), quandong (*Austral. slang*)

parcel NOUN = **package**, case, box, pack, bundle

P

▷ VERB *often with* **up** = **wrap**, pack, package, tie up, do up, gift-wrap, box up, fasten together

pardon VERB = **acquit**, let off (*informal*), exonerate, absolve ≠ punish
▷ NOUN 1 = **forgiveness**, absolution ≠ condemnation
2 = **acquittal**, amnesty, exoneration ≠ punishment
▷ PHRASE: pardon me = **forgive me**, excuse me

parent NOUN = **father** *or* **mother**, sire, progenitor, procreator, old (*Austral. & N.Z. informal*), oldie (*Austral. informal*), patriarch

parish NOUN 1 = **district**, community 2 = **community**, flock, church, congregation

park NOUN 1 = **recreation ground**, garden, playground, pleasure garden, playpark, domain (*N.Z.*), forest park (*N.Z.*) 2 = **parkland**, grounds, estate, lawns, woodland, grassland 3 = **field**, pitch, playing field

parliament NOUN 1 = **assembly**, council, congress, senate, convention, legislature
2 = **sitting**

parliamentary ADJECTIVE = **governmental**, legislative, law-making

parlour *or* (*U.S.*) **parlor** NOUN 1 (*old-fashioned*) = **sitting room**, lounge, living room, drawing room, front room
2 = **establishment**, shop, store, salon

parody NOUN = **takeoff** (*informal*), satire, caricature, send-up (*Brit. informal*), spoof (*informal*), skit, burlesque
▷ VERB = **take off** (*informal*), caricature, send up (*Brit. informal*), burlesque, satirize, do a takeoff of (*informal*)

parrot VERB = **repeat**, echo, imitate, copy, mimic

parry VERB 1 = **evade**, avoid, dodge, sidestep 2 = **ward off**, block, deflect, repel, rebuff, repulse

parson NOUN = **clergyman**, minister, priest, vicar, preacher, pastor, cleric, churchman

part NOUN 1 = **piece**, share, proportion, percentage, bit, section, scrap, portion ≠ entirety
2 *often plural* = **region**, area, district, neighbourhood, quarter, vicinity 3 = **component**, bit, unit, constituent 4 = **branch**, division, office, section, wing, subdivision, subsection 5 = **organ**, member, limb 6 (*theatre*) = **role**, representation, persona, portrayal, depiction, character part 7 (*theatre*) = **lines**, words, script, dialogue 8 = **side**, behalf
▷ VERB 1 = **divide**, separate, break, tear, split, rend, detach, sever ≠ join 2 = **part company**, separate, split up ≠ meet
▷ PHRASE: in good part = **good-naturedly**, well, cheerfully, without offence

partial ADJECTIVE 1 = **incomplete**, unfinished, imperfect, uncompleted ≠ complete

2 = **biased**, prejudiced, discriminatory, partisan, unfair, one-sided, unjust ≠ unbiased

partially ADVERB = **partly**, somewhat, in part, not wholly, fractionally, incompletely

participant NOUN = **participator**, member, player, contributor, stakeholder

participate VERB = **take part**, be involved, perform, join, partake ≠ refrain from

participation NOUN = **taking part**, contribution, involvement, sharing in, joining in, partaking

particle NOUN = **bit**, piece, scrap, grain, shred, mite, jot, speck

particular ADJECTIVE **1** = **specific**, special, exact, precise, distinct, peculiar ≠ general **2** = **special**, exceptional, notable, uncommon, marked, unusual, remarkable, singular **3** = **fussy**, demanding, fastidious, choosy (*informal*), picky (*informal*), finicky, pernickety (*informal*), nit-picky (*informal*) ≠ indiscriminate

▷ NOUN *usually plural* = **detail**, fact, feature, item, circumstance, specification

particularly ADVERB

1 = **specifically**, expressly, explicitly, especially, in particular, distinctly **2** = **especially**, notably, unusually, exceptionally, singularly, uncommonly

parting NOUN **1** = **farewell**, goodbye **2** = **division**, breaking, split, separation, rift, rupture

partisan ADJECTIVE = **prejudiced**, one-sided, biased, partial, sectarian ≠ unbiased

▷ NOUN **1** = **supporter**, devotee, adherent, upholder ≠ opponent

2 = **underground fighter**, guerrilla, freedom fighter, resistance fighter

partition NOUN **1** = **screen**, wall, barrier **2** = **division**, separation, segregation

▷ VERB = **separate**, screen, divide

partly ADVERB = **partially**, somewhat, slightly ≠ completely

● WORD POWER

● *Partly* and *partially* are to some
● extent interchangeable, but
● *partly* should be used when
● referring to a part or parts of
● something: *the building is partly*
● (not *partially*) *made of stone*,
● while *partially* is preferred for
● the meaning *to some extent: his*
● *mother is partially* (not *partly*)
● *sighted*.

partner NOUN **1** = **spouse**, consort, significant other (*U.S. informal*), mate, husband *or* wife **2** = **companion**, ally, colleague, associate, mate, comrade **3** = **associate**, colleague, collaborator

partnership NOUN

1 = **cooperation**, alliance, sharing, union, connection, participation, copartnership **2** = **company**, firm, house, interest, society, cooperative

party NOUN **1** = **faction**, set, side, league, camp, clique, coterie **2** = **get-together** (*informal*),

P

celebration, do (*informal*), gathering, function, reception, festivity, social gathering **3** = **group**, team, band, company, unit, squad, crew, gang

pass VERB **1** = **go by** *or* **past**, overtake, drive past, lap, leave behind, pull ahead of ≠ stop **2** = **go**, move, travel, progress, flow, proceed **3** = **run**, move, stroke **4** = **give**, hand, send, transfer, deliver, convey **5** = **be left**, come, be bequeathed, be inherited by **6** = **kick**, hit, loft, head, lob **7** = **elapse**, progress, go by, lapse, wear on, go past, tick by **8** = **end**, go, cease, blow over **9** = **spend**, fill, occupy, while away **10** = **exceed**, beat, overtake, go beyond, surpass, outstrip, outdo **11** = **be successful in**, qualify (in), succeed (in), graduate (in), get through, do, gain a pass in ≠ fail **12** = **approve**, accept, decree, enact, ratify, ordain, legislate (for) ≠ ban

▷ NOUN **1** = **licence**, ticket, permit, passport, warrant, authorization **2** = **gap**, route, canyon, gorge, ravine ▷ PHRASES: **pass away** (*euphemistic*) = **die**, pass on, expire, pass over, snuff it (*informal*), kick the bucket (*slang*), shuffle off this mortal coil, cark it (*Austral. & N.Z. informal*); **pass out** (*informal*) = **faint**, black out (*informal*), lose consciousness, become unconscious; **pass someone over**; **pass something over** = **disregard**, ignore, not

dwell on; **pass something up** (*informal*) = **miss**, let slip, decline, neglect, forgo, abstain from, give (something) a miss (*informal*)

● WORD POWER
● The past participle of *pass* is
● sometimes wrongly spelt *past*:
● *the time for recriminations has*
● *passed* (not *past*).

passage NOUN **1** = **corridor**, hall, lobby, vestibule **2** = **alley**, way, close (*Brit.*), course, road, channel, route, path **3** = **extract**, reading, piece, section, text, excerpt, quotation **4** = **journey**, crossing, trip, trek, voyage **5** = **safe-conduct**, right to travel, freedom to travel, permission to travel

passenger NOUN = **traveller**, rider, fare, commuter, fare payer

passer-by NOUN = **bystander**, witness, observer, viewer, spectator, looker-on, watcher, onlooker

passing ADJECTIVE
1 = **momentary**, fleeting, short-lived, transient, ephemeral, brief, temporary, transitory
2 = **superficial**, short, quick, glancing, casual, summary, cursory, perfunctory

passion NOUN **1** = **love**, desire, lust, infatuation, ardour
2 = **emotion**, feeling, fire, heat, excitement, intensity, warmth, zeal ≠ indifference **3** = **mania**, enthusiasm, obsession, bug (*informal*), craving, fascination, craze **4** = **rage**, fit, storm, anger, fury, outburst, frenzy, paroxysm

passionate ADJECTIVE
1 = **emotional**, eager, strong, intense, fierce, ardent, fervent, heartfelt ≠ unemotional
2 = **loving**, erotic, hot, ardent, amorous, lustful ≠ cold

passive ADJECTIVE
1 = **submissive**, compliant, receptive, docile, quiescent ≠ spirited 2 = **inactive**, uninvolved ≠ active

past NOUN 1 = **former times**, long ago, days gone by, the olden days ≠ future 2 = **background**, life, history, past life, life story, career to date
▷ ADJECTIVE 1 = **former**, early, previous, ancient, bygone, olden ≠ future 2 = **previous**, former, one-time, ex- 3 = **last**, previous 4 = **over**, done, ended, finished, gone
▷ PREPOSITION 1 = **after**, beyond, later than 2 = **by**, across, in front of
▷ ADVERB = **on**, by, along
◉ WORD POWER
◉ The past participle of *pass* is
◉ sometimes wrongly spelt *past*:
◉ *the time for recrimination has*
◉ *passed* (not *past*).

paste NOUN 1 = **adhesive**, glue, cement, gum 2 = **purée**, pâté, spread
▷ VERB = **stick**, glue, cement, gum

pastel ADJECTIVE = **pale**, light, soft, delicate, muted ≠ bright

pastime NOUN = **activity**, game, entertainment, hobby, recreation, amusement, diversion

pastor NOUN = **clergyman**, minister, priest, vicar, parson, rector, curate, churchman

pastoral ADJECTIVE
1 = **ecclesiastical**, priestly, ministerial, clerical 2 = **rustic**, country, rural, bucolic

pasture NOUN = **grassland**, grass, meadow, grazing

pat VERB = **stroke**, touch, tap, pet, caress, fondle
▷ NOUN = **tap**, stroke, clap

patch NOUN 1 = **spot**, bit, scrap, shred, small piece 2 = **plot**, area, ground, land, tract
3 = **reinforcement**, piece of fabric, piece of cloth, piece of material, piece sewn on
▷ VERB 1 *often with* **up** = **sew (up)**, mend, repair, reinforce, stitch (up)
2 *often with* **up** = **mend**, cover, reinforce

patent NOUN = **copyright**, licence, franchise, registered trademark
▷ ADJECTIVE = **obvious**, apparent, evident, clear, glaring, manifest

path NOUN 1 = **way**, road, walk, track, trail, avenue, footpath, berm (N.Z.) 2 = **route**, way, course, direction 3 = **course**, way, road, route

pathetic ADJECTIVE = **sad**, moving, touching, affecting, distressing, tender, poignant, plaintive ≠ funny

patience NOUN 1 = **forbearance**, tolerance, serenity, restraint, calmness, sufferance ≠ impatience 2 = **endurance**,

P

resignation, submission, fortitude, long-suffering, perseverance, stoicism, constancy

patient NOUN = **sick person**, case, sufferer, invalid

▷ ADJECTIVE 1 = **forbearing**, understanding, forgiving, mild, tolerant, indulgent, lenient, even-tempered ≠ impatient
2 = **long-suffering**, resigned, calm, enduring, philosophical, persevering, stoical, submissive

patriot NOUN = **nationalist**, loyalist, chauvinist

patriotic ADJECTIVE = **nationalistic**, loyal, chauvinistic, jingoistic

patriotism NOUN = **nationalism**, jingoism

patrol VERB = **police**, guard, keep watch (on), inspect, safeguard, keep guard (on)

▷ NOUN = **guard**, watch, watchman, sentinel, patrolman

patron NOUN 1 = **supporter**, friend, champion, sponsor, backer, helper, benefactor, philanthropist
2 = **customer**, client, buyer, frequenter, shopper, habitué

patronage NOUN = **support**, promotion, sponsorship, backing, help, aid, assistance

pattern NOUN 1 = **order**, plan, system, method, sequence
2 = **design**, arrangement, motif, figure, device, decoration
3 = **plan**, design, original, guide, diagram, stencil, template

pause VERB = **stop briefly**, delay, break, wait, rest, halt, cease,

interrupt ≠ continue

▷ NOUN = **stop**, break, interval, rest, gap, halt, respite, lull ≠ continuance

pave VERB = **cover**, floor, surface, concrete, tile

paw (*informal*) VERB = **manhandle**, grab, maul, molest, handle roughly

pay VERB 1 = **reward**, compensate, reimburse, recompense, requite, remunerate 2 = **spend**, give, fork out (*informal*), remit, shell out (*informal*) 3 = **settle** 4 = **bring in**, earn, return, net, yield 5 = **be profitable**, make money, make a return 6 = **benefit**, repay, be worthwhile 7 = **give**, extend, present with, grant, hand out, bestow

▷ NOUN = **wages**, income, payment, earnings, fee, reward, salary, allowance ▷ PHRASES: **pay off** = **succeed**, work, be effective; **pay something off** = **settle**, clear, square, discharge, pay in full

payable ADJECTIVE = **due**, outstanding, owed, owing

payment NOUN 1 = **remittance**, advance, deposit, premium, instalment 2 = **settlement**, paying, discharge, remittance
3 = **wages**, fee, reward, hire, remuneration

peace NOUN 1 = **truce**, ceasefire, treaty, armistice ≠ war
2 = **stillness**, rest, quiet, silence, calm, hush, tranquillity, seclusion
3 = **serenity**, calm, composure, contentment, repose, equanimity,

peacefulness, harmoniousness
4 = **harmony**, accord, agreement, concord

peaceful ADJECTIVE **1** = **at peace**, friendly, harmonious, amicable, nonviolent ≠ hostile **2** = **peace-loving**, conciliatory, peaceable, unwarlike ≠ belligerent
3 = **calm**, still, quiet, tranquil, restful, chilled (*informal*)
≠ agitated **4** = **serene**, placid, undisturbed

peak NOUN **1** = **high point**, crown, climax, culmination, zenith, acme
2 = **point**, top, tip, summit, brow, crest, pinnacle, apex
▷ VERB = **culminate**, climax, come to a head

peasant NOUN = **rustic**, countryman

peck VERB **1** = **pick**, hit, strike, tap, poke, jab, prick **2** = **kiss**, plant a kiss, give someone a smacker, give someone a peck *or* kiss
▷ NOUN = **kiss**, smacker, osculation (*rare*)

peculiar ADJECTIVE **1** = **odd**, strange, unusual, bizarre, funny, extraordinary, curious, weird
≠ ordinary **2** = **special**, particular, unique, characteristic ≠ common

peddle VERB = **sell**, trade, push (*informal*), market, hawk, flog (*slang*)

pedestrian NOUN = **walker**, foot-traveller ≠ driver
▷ ADJECTIVE = **dull**, ordinary, boring, commonplace, mundane, mediocre, banal, prosaic, half-pie (*N.Z. informal*) ≠ exciting

pedigree MODIFIER = **purebred**, thoroughbred, full-blooded
▷ NOUN = **lineage**, family, line, race, stock, blood, breed, descent

peel NOUN = **rind**, skin, peeling
▷ VERB = **skin**, scale, strip, pare, shuck, flake off, take the skin *or* rind off

peep VERB = **peek**, look, eyeball (*slang*), sneak a look, steal a look
▷ NOUN = **look**, glimpse, peek, look-see (*slang*)

peer¹ NOUN **1** = **noble**, lord, aristocrat, nobleman **2** = **equal**, like, fellow, contemporary, compeer

peer² VERB = **squint**, look, spy, gaze, scan, inspect, peep, peek

peg NOUN = **pin**, spike, rivet, skewer, dowel, spigot
▷ VERB = **fasten**, join, fix, secure, attach

pen¹ VERB = **write (down)**, draft, compose, pencil, draw up, scribble, take down, inscribe

pen² NOUN = **enclosure**, pound, fold, cage, coop, hutch, sty
▷ VERB = **enclose**, confine, cage, fence in, coop up, hedge in, shut up *or* in

penalty NOUN = **punishment**, price, fine, handicap, forfeit

pending ADJECTIVE
1 = **undecided**, unsettled, in the balance, undetermined
2 = **forthcoming**, imminent, prospective, impending, in the wind
▷ PREPOSITION = **awaiting**, until, waiting for, till

p

penetrate VERB 1 = **pierce**, enter,
go through, bore, stab, prick
2 = **grasp**, work out, figure out
(*informal*), comprehend, fathom,
decipher, suss (out) (*slang*), get to
the bottom of

penetrating ADJECTIVE 1 = **sharp**,
harsh, piercing, carrying, piping,
loud, strident, shrill ≠ sweet
2 = **pungent** 3 = **piercing**
4 = **intelligent**, quick, sharp,
keen, acute, shrewd, astute,
perceptive ≠ dull 5 = **perceptive**,
sharp, keen ≠ unperceptive

penetration NOUN 1 = **piercing**,
entry, entrance, puncturing,
incision 2 = **entry**, entrance

pension NOUN = **allowance**,
benefit, welfare, annuity,
superannuation

pensioner NOUN = **senior citizen**,
retired person, retiree (*U.S.*), old-
age pensioner, O.A.P.

people PLURAL NOUN 1 = **persons**,
individuals, folk (*informal*), men
and women, humanity, mankind,
mortals, the human race
2 = **nation**, public, community,
subjects, population, residents,
citizens, folk 3 = **race**, tribe
4 = **family**, parents, relations,
relatives, folk, folks (*informal*),
clan, kin, rellies (*Austral. slang*)
▷ VERB = **inhabit**, occupy, settle,
populate, colonize

pepper NOUN = **seasoning**,
flavour, spice
▷ VERB 1 = **pelt**, hit, shower,
blitz, rake, bombard, assail, strafe
2 = **sprinkle**, spot, scatter, dot,

fleck, intersperse, speck, spatter

perceive VERB 1 = **see**, notice,
note, identify, discover,
spot, observe, recognize
2 = **understand**, gather, see,
learn, realize, grasp, comprehend,
suss (out) (*slang*) 3 = **consider**,
believe, judge, suppose, rate,
deem, adjudge

perception NOUN 1 = **awareness**,
understanding, sense,
impression, feeling, idea,
notion, consciousness
2 = **understanding**, intelligence,
observation, discrimination,
insight, sharpness, cleverness,
keenness

perch VERB 1 = **sit**, rest, balance,
settle 2 = **place**, put, rest, balance
3 = **land**, alight, roost
▷ NOUN = **resting place**, post,
branch, pole

perennial ADJECTIVE = **continual**,
lasting, constant, enduring,
persistent, abiding, recurrent,
incessant

perfect ADJECTIVE 1 = **faultless**,
correct, pure, impeccable,
exemplary, flawless, foolproof
≠ deficient 2 = **excellent**,
ideal, supreme, superb,
splendid, sublime, superlative
3 = **immaculate**, impeccable,
flawless, spotless, unblemished
≠ flawed 4 = **complete**, absolute,
sheer, utter, consummate,
unmitigated ≠ partial 5 = **exact**,
true, accurate, precise, correct,
faithful, unerring
▷ VERB = **improve**, develop,

polish, refine ≠ mar

● **WORD POWER**
● For most of its meanings, the
● adjective *perfect* describes
● an absolute state, so that
● something either is or is not
● *perfect*, and cannot be referred
● to in terms of degree – thus,
● one thing should not be
● described as *more perfect* or
● *less perfect* than another thing.
● However, when *perfect* is used
● in the sense of 'excellent in all
● respects', *more* and *most* are
● acceptable, for example *the next
● day the weather was even more
● perfect*.

perfection NOUN = **excellence**,
integrity, superiority, purity,
wholeness, sublimity,
exquisiteness, faultlessness

perfectly ADVERB 1 = **completely**,
totally, absolutely, quite, fully,
altogether, thoroughly, wholly
≠ partially 2 = **flawlessly**, ideally,
wonderfully, superbly, supremely,
impeccably, faultlessly ≠ badly

perform VERB 1 = **do**, achieve,
carry out, complete, fulfil,
accomplish, execute, pull off
2 = **fulfil**, carry out, execute,
discharge 3 = **present**, act (out),
stage, play, produce, represent,
put on, enact 4 = **appear on
stage**, act

performance NOUN
1 = **presentation**, playing, acting
(out), staging, production,
exhibition, rendering, portrayal
2 = **show**, appearance, concert,

gig (*informal*), recital 3 = **work**,
acts, conduct, exploits, feats
4 = **carrying out**, practice,
achievement, execution,
completion, accomplishment,
fulfilment

performer NOUN = **artiste**,
player, Thespian, trouper, actor *or*
actress

perfume NOUN 1 = **fragrance**,
scent 2 = **scent**, smell, fragrance,
bouquet, aroma, odour

perhaps ADVERB = **maybe**,
possibly, it may be, it is possible
(that), conceivably, perchance
(*archaic*), feasibly, happen (*N.
English dialect*)

peril NOUN 1 = **danger**, risk,
threat, hazard, menace, jeopardy,
perilousness 2 *often plural*
= **pitfall**, problem, risk, hazard
≠ safety

perimeter NOUN = **boundary**,
edge, border, bounds, limit,
margin, confines, periphery
≠ centre

period NOUN = **time**, term, season,
space, run, stretch, spell, phase

periodic ADJECTIVE = **recurrent**,
regular, repeated, occasional,
cyclical, sporadic, intermittent

peripheral ADJECTIVE
1 = **secondary**, minor, marginal,
irrelevant, unimportant,
incidental, inessential
2 = **outermost**, outside, external,
outer, exterior

perish VERB 1 = **die**, be killed,
expire, pass away, lose your life,
cark it (*Austral. & N.Z. slang*) 2 = **be**

destroyed, fall, decline, collapse, disappear, vanish **3** = **rot**, waste away, decay, disintegrate, decompose, moulder

perk NOUN (*Brit. informal*) = **bonus**, benefit, extra, plus, fringe benefit, perquisite

permanent ADJECTIVE
1 = **lasting**, constant, enduring, persistent, eternal, abiding, perpetual, everlasting
≠ temporary **2** = **long-term**, established, secure, stable, steady
≠ temporary

permission NOUN
= **authorization**, sanction, licence, approval, leave, go-ahead (*informal*), liberty, consent
≠ prohibition

permit VERB **1** = **allow**, grant, sanction, let, entitle, license, authorize, consent to ≠ forbid
2 = **enable**, let, allow, cause
▷ NOUN = **licence**, pass, document, certificate, passport, visa, warrant, authorization
≠ prohibition

perpetual ADJECTIVE
1 = **everlasting**, permanent, endless, eternal, lasting, perennial, infinite, never-ending
≠ temporary **2** = **continual**, repeated, constant, endless, continuous, persistent, recurrent, never-ending ≠ brief

perpetuate VERB = **maintain**, preserve, keep going, immortalize
≠ end

persecute VERB **1** = **victimize**, torture, torment, oppress,

pick on, ill-treat, maltreat
≠ mollycoddle **2** = **harass**, bother, annoy, tease, hassle (*informal*), badger, pester ≠ leave alone

persist VERB **1** = **continue**, last, remain, carry on, keep up, linger
2 = **persevere**, continue, go on, carry on, keep on, keep going, press on, not give up, crack on (*informal*)

persistence NOUN
= **determination**, resolution, grit, endurance, tenacity, perseverance, doggedness, pertinacity

persistent ADJECTIVE
1 = **continuous**, constant, repeated, endless, perpetual, continual, never-ending, incessant ≠ occasional
2 = **determined**, dogged, steady, stubborn, persevering, tireless, tenacious, steadfast ≠ irresolute

person NOUN **1** = **individual**, being, body, human, soul, creature, mortal, man *or* woman ▷ PHRASE: in person
1 = **personally**, yourself **2** = **in the flesh**, actually, physically, bodily

personal ADJECTIVE **1** = **own**, special, private, individual, particular, peculiar
2 = **individual**, special, particular, exclusive **3** = **private**
4 = **offensive**, nasty, insulting, disparaging, derogatory

personality NOUN **1** = **nature**, character, make-up, identity, temperament, disposition, individuality **2** = **character**, charm, attraction, charisma, magnetism **3** = **celebrity**, star, notable, household name, famous name, personage, megastar (*informal*)

personally ADVERB **1** = **in your opinion**, in your book, for your part, from your own viewpoint, in your own view **2** = **by yourself**, alone, independently, solely, on your own **3** = **individually**, specially, subjectively, individualistically **4** = **privately**, in private, off the record

personnel NOUN = **employees**, people, staff, workers, workforce, human resources, helpers

perspective NOUN **1** = **outlook**, attitude, context, angle, frame of reference **2** = **objectivity**, proportion, relation, relativity, relative importance

persuade VERB **1** = **talk (someone) into**, urge, influence, win (someone) over, induce, sway, entice, coax ≠ dissuade **2** = **cause**, lead, move, influence, motivate, induce, incline, dispose **3** = **convince**, satisfy, assure, cause to believe

persuasion NOUN **1** = **urging**, inducement, wheedling, enticement, cajolery **2** = **belief**, views, opinion, party, school, side, camp, faith

persuasive ADJECTIVE = **convincing**, telling, effective, sound, compelling, influential, valid, credible ≠ unconvincing

pervasive ADJECTIVE

= **widespread**, general, common, extensive, universal, prevalent, ubiquitous, rife

perverse ADJECTIVE **1** = **stubborn**, contrary, dogged, troublesome, rebellious, wayward, intractable, wilful ≠ cooperative **2** = **ill-natured**, cross, surly, fractious, churlish, ill-tempered, stroppy (*Brit. slang*), peevish ≠ good-natured **3** = **abnormal**, unhealthy, improper, deviant

pervert VERB **1** = **distort**, abuse, twist, misuse, warp, misrepresent, falsify **2** = **corrupt**, degrade, deprave, debase, debauch, lead astray
▷ NOUN = **deviant**, degenerate, sicko (*informal*), weirdo or weirdie (*informal*)

pessimistic ADJECTIVE = **gloomy**, dark, despairing, bleak, depressed, cynical, hopeless, glum ≠ optimistic

pest NOUN **1** = **infection**, bug, insect, plague, epidemic, blight, scourge, pestilence, gogga (*S. African informal*) **2** = **nuisance**, trial, pain (*informal*), drag (*informal*), bother, irritation, annoyance, bane

pet ADJECTIVE = **favourite**, favoured, dearest, cherished, fave (*informal*), dear to your heart
▷ NOUN = **favourite**, treasure, darling, jewel, idol
▷ VERB **1** = **fondle**, pat, stroke, caress **2** = **pamper**, spoil, indulge, cosset, baby, dote on, coddle, mollycoddle **3** (*informal*)

p

= **cuddle**, kiss, snog (*Brit. slang*), smooch (*informal*), neck (*informal*), canoodle (*slang*)

petition NOUN 1 = **appeal**, round robin, list of signatures 2 = **entreaty**, appeal, suit, application, request, prayer, plea, solicitation
▷ VERB = **appeal**, plead, ask, pray, beg, solicit, beseech, entreat

petty ADJECTIVE 1 = **trivial**, insignificant, little, small, slight, trifling, negligible, unimportant ≠ important 2 = **small-minded**, mean, shabby, spiteful, ungenerous, mean-minded ≠ broad-minded

phantom NOUN = **spectre**, ghost, spirit, shade (*literary*), spook (*informal*), apparition, wraith

phase NOUN = **stage**, time, point, position, step, development, period, chapter ▷ PHRASES: **phase something in** = **introduce**, incorporate, ease in, start; **phase something out** = **eliminate**, close, remove, withdraw, wind up, run down, terminate

phenomenal ADJECTIVE = **extraordinary**, outstanding, remarkable, fantastic, unusual, marvellous, exceptional, miraculous ≠ unremarkable

phenomenon NOUN 1 = **occurrence**, happening, fact, event, incident, circumstance, episode 2 = **wonder**, sensation, exception, miracle, marvel, prodigy, rarity

● WORD POWER
● Although *phenomena* is often
● treated as a singular, this is not
● grammatically correct. *Phenomenon*
● is the singular form of this word,
● and *phenomena* the plural; so
● *several new phenomena were recorded*
● *in his notes* is correct, but *that is an*
● *interesting phenomena* is not.

philosopher NOUN = **thinker**, theorist, sage, wise man, logician, metaphysician

philosophical or **philosophic** ADJECTIVE 1 = **theoretical**, abstract, wise, rational, logical, thoughtful, sagacious ≠ practical 2 = **stoical**, calm, composed, cool, collected, serene, tranquil, unruffled ≠ emotional

philosophy NOUN 1 = **thought**, knowledge, thinking, reasoning, wisdom, logic, metaphysics 2 = **outlook**, values, principles, convictions, thinking, beliefs, doctrine, ideology

phone NOUN 1 = **telephone**, blower (*informal*), iPhone (*trademark*), Blackberry (*trademark*), camera phone, picture phone, smartphone, crackberry (*facetious*) 2 = **call**, ring (*informal, chiefly Brit.*), tinkle (*Brit. informal*)
▷ VERB = **call**, telephone, ring (up) (*informal, chiefly Brit.*), give someone a call, give someone a ring (*informal, chiefly Brit.*), make a call, give someone a tinkle (*Brit. informal*), get on the blower (*informal*)

photograph NOUN = **picture**, photo (*informal*), shot, print, snap

(*informal*), snapshot, transparency
▷ VERB = **take a picture of**,
record, film, shoot, snap (*informal*),
take (someone's) picture
photographic ADJECTIVE
1 = **pictorial**, visual, graphic,
cinematic, filmic 2 = **accurate**,
exact, precise, faithful, retentive
phrase NOUN = **expression**,
saying, remark, construction,
quotation, maxim, idiom, adage
▷ VERB = **express**, say, word, put,
voice, communicate, convey, put
into words
physical ADJECTIVE 1 = **corporal**,
fleshly, bodily, corporeal
2 = **earthly**, fleshly, mortal,
incarnate 3 = **material**, real,
substantial, natural, solid,
tangible, palpable
physician NOUN = **doctor**, doc
(*informal*), medic (*informal*),
general practitioner, medical
practitioner, doctor of medicine,
G.P., M.D.
pick VERB 1 = **select**, choose,
identify, elect, nominate, specify,
opt for, single out, flag up
≠ reject 2 = **gather**, pull, collect,
take in, harvest, pluck, garner
3 = **provoke**, start, cause, stir up,
incite, instigate 4 = **open**, force,
crack (*informal*), break into, break
open
▷ NOUN 1 = **choice**, decision,
option, selection, preference
2 = **best**, prime, finest, elect, elite,
cream, jewel in the crown, crème
de la crème (*French*) ▷ PHRASES:
pick on someone 1 = **torment**,

bully, bait, tease, get at (*informal*),
badger, persecute, hector
2 = **choose**, select, prefer, elect,
single out, fix on, settle upon;
pick something up 1 = **learn**,
master, acquire, get the hang of
(*informal*), become proficient in
2 = **obtain**, get, find, buy, discover,
purchase, acquire, locate; **pick
something or someone out**
= **identify**, recognize, distinguish,
perceive, discriminate, make
someone or something out, tell
someone or something apart;
**pick something or someone
up 1** = **lift**, raise, gather, take up,
grasp, uplift 2 = **collect**, get, call
for; **pick up 1** = **improve**, recover,
rally, get better, bounce back,
make progress, perk up, turn the
corner 2 = **recover**, improve, rally,
get better, mend, turn the corner,
be on the mend, take a turn for
the better
picket VERB = **blockade**, boycott,
demonstrate outside
▷ NOUN 1 = **demonstration**,
strike, blockade 2 = **protester**,
demonstrator, picketer
3 = **lookout**, watch, guard, patrol,
sentry, sentinel 4 = **stake**, post,
pale, paling, upright, stanchion
pickle VERB = **preserve**, marinade,
steep
▷ NOUN 1 = **chutney**,
relish, piccalilli 2 (*informal*)
= **predicament**, fix (*informal*),
difficulty, bind (*informal*), jam
(*informal*), dilemma, scrape
(*informal*), hot water (*informal*),

P

uphill (*S. African*)

pick-up NOUN = **improvement**, recovery, rise, rally, strengthening, revival, upturn, change for the better

picnic NOUN = **excursion**, barbecue, barbie (*informal*), cookout (*U.S. & Canad.*), alfresco meal, clambake (*U.S. & Canad.*), outdoor meal, outing

picture NOUN 1 = **representation**, drawing, painting, portrait, image, print, illustration, sketch 2 = **photograph**, photo, still, shot, image, print, frame, slide 3 = **film**, movie (*U.S. informal*), flick (*slang*), feature film, motion picture 4 = **idea**, vision, concept, impression, notion, visualization, mental picture, mental image 5 = **description**, impression, explanation, report, account, image, sketch, depiction 6 = **personification**, embodiment, essence, epitome ▷ VERB 1 = **imagine**, see, envision, visualize, conceive of, fantasize about, conjure up an image of 2 = **represent**, show, draw, paint, illustrate, sketch, depict 3 = **show**, photograph, capture on film

picturesque ADJECTIVE 1 = **interesting**, pretty, beautiful, attractive, charming, scenic, quaint ≠ unattractive 2 = **vivid**, striking, graphic, colourful, memorable ≠ dull

piece NOUN 1 = **bit**, slice, part, block, quantity, segment, portion, fragment 2 = **component**, part, section, bit, unit, segment, constituent, module 3 = **item**, report, story, study, review, article 4 = **composition**, work, production, opus 5 = **work of art**, work, creation 6 = **share**, cut (*informal*), slice, percentage, quantity, portion, quota, fraction

pier NOUN 1 = **jetty**, wharf, quay, promenade, landing place 2 = **pillar**, support, post, column, pile, upright, buttress

pierce VERB = **penetrate**, stab, spike, enter, bore, drill, puncture, prick

piercing ADJECTIVE 1 (*of a sound*) = **penetrating**, sharp, loud, shrill, high-pitched, ear-splitting ≠ low 2 = **perceptive**, sharp, keen, alert, penetrating, shrewd, perspicacious, quick-witted ≠ unperceptive 3 = **sharp**, acute, severe, intense, painful, stabbing, excruciating, agonizing 4 (*of weather*) = **cold**, biting, freezing, bitter, arctic, wintry, nippy

pig NOUN 1 = **hog**, sow, boar, swine, porker 2 (*informal*) = **slob**, glutton 3 (*informal*) = **brute**, monster, scoundrel, rogue, swine, rotter, boor

pigment NOUN = **colour**, colouring, paint, stain, dye, tint, tincture

pile¹ NOUN 1 = **heap**, collection, mountain, mass, stack, mound, accumulation, hoard 2 (*informal*) *often plural* = **lot(s)**, mountain(s), load(s) (*informal*), oceans, wealth,

great deal, stack(s), abundance
3 = **mansion**, building, residence, manor, country house, seat, big house, stately home
▷ VERB **1** = **load**, stuff, pack, stack, charge, heap, cram, lade **2** = **crowd**, pack, rush, climb, flood, stream, crush, squeeze
▷ PHRASE: **pile up** = **accumulate**, collect, gather (up), build up, amass

pile² NOUN = **foundation**, support, post, column, beam, upright, pillar

pile³ NOUN = **nap**, fibre, down, hair, fur, plush

pile-up NOUN (informal) = **collision**, crash, accident, smash, smash-up (informal), multiple collision

pilgrim NOUN = **traveller**, wanderer, devotee, wayfarer

pilgrimage NOUN = **journey**, tour, trip, mission, expedition, excursion

pill NOUN = **tablet**, capsule, pellet

pillar NOUN **1** = **support**, post, column, prop, shaft, upright, pier, stanchion **2** = **supporter**, leader, mainstay, leading light (informal), upholder

pilot NOUN **1** = **airman**, flyer, aviator, aeronaut **2** = **helmsman**, navigator, steersman
▷ VERB **1** = **fly**, operate, be at the controls of **2** = **navigate**, drive, direct, guide, handle, conduct, steer **3** = **direct**, conduct, steer
▷ MODIFIER = **trial**, test, model, sample, experimental

pin NOUN **1** = **tack**, nail, needle, safety pin **2** = **peg**, rod, brace, bolt
▷ VERB **1** = **fasten**, stick, attach, join, fix, secure, nail, clip **2** = **hold fast**, hold down, constrain, immobilize, pinion ▷ PHRASES: **pin someone down** = **force**, pressure, compel, put pressure on, pressurize, nail someone down, make someone commit themselves; **pin something down** = **determine**, identify, locate, name, specify, pinpoint

pinch VERB **1** = **nip**, press, squeeze, grasp, compress **2** = **hurt**, crush, squeeze, pain, cramp **3** (Brit. informal) = **steal**, lift (informal), nick (slang, chiefly Brit.), swipe (slang), knock off (slang), pilfer, purloin, filch
▷ NOUN **1** = **nip**, squeeze **2** = **dash**, bit, mite, jot, speck, soupçon (French) **3** = **emergency**, crisis, difficulty, plight, scrape (informal), strait, uphill (S. African), predicament

pine VERB **1** = **waste**, decline, sicken, fade, languish ▷ PHRASE: **pine for something or someone 1** = **long**, ache, crave, yearn, eat your heart out over **2** = **hanker after**, crave, wish for, yearn for, thirst for, hunger for

pink ADJECTIVE = **rosy**, rose, salmon, flushed, reddish, roseate
▷ see **shades of red**
● **WORD POWER**
● The colour *pink* has a number
● of associations in English.
● From the plant of this name,

- cultivated in gardens for its
- fragrant flowers, pink has
- come to mean 'the flower' or
- the best part of something.
- The contraction *in the pink*
- has the sense 'in good health,
- flourishing'. This phrase also
- reflects our perception that
- flushing and glowing skin is
- healthy, whereas pallor of skin
- is not. Other shades of pink are
- associated with hope, promise,
- and optimism in words such
- as *rosy*, *rose-coloured*, and
- *rose-tinted*. Pink has also
- been applied symbolically to
- different political and social
- groups. Part of the political
- spectrum is represented in
- the informal and sometimes
- derogatory epithet *pinko*
- meaning a left-winger, but
- one who is nearer to the centre
- than a red socialist. The use of
- pink to refer to male gay topics
- is now well-established in
- phrases such as *the pink pound*.

pinnacle NOUN 1 = **summit**, top, height, peak 2 = **height**, top, crown, crest, zenith, apex, vertex

pinpoint VERB 1 = **identify**, discover, define, distinguish, put your finger on 2 = **locate**, find, identify, zero in on

pioneer NOUN 1 = **founder**, leader, developer, innovator, trailblazer 2 = **settler**, explorer, colonist
▷ VERB = **develop**, create, establish, start, discover, institute, invent, initiate

pipe NOUN = **tube**, drain, canal, pipeline, line, main, passage, cylinder
▷ VERB = **convey**, channel, conduct ▷ PHRASE: pipe down (*informal*) = **be quiet**, shut up (*informal*), hush, stop talking, quieten down, shush, shut your mouth, hold your tongue

pipeline NOUN = **tube**, passage, pipe, conduit, duct

pirate NOUN = **buccaneer**, raider, marauder, corsair, freebooter
▷ VERB = **copy**, steal, reproduce, bootleg, appropriate, poach, crib (*informal*), plagiarize

pit NOUN 1 = **coal mine**, mine, shaft, colliery, mine shaft
2 = **hole**, depression, hollow, crater, trough, cavity, abyss, chasm
▷ VERB = **scar**, mark, dent, indent, pockmark

pitch NOUN 1 = **sports field**, ground, stadium, arena, park, field of play 2 = **tone**, sound, key, frequency, timbre, modulation
3 = **level**, point, degree, summit, extent, height, intensity, high point 4 = **talk**, patter, spiel (*informal*)
▷ VERB 1 = **throw**, cast, toss, hurl, fling, chuck (*informal*), sling, lob (*informal*) 2 = **fall**, drop, plunge, dive, tumble, topple, plummet, fall headlong 3 = **set up**, raise, settle, put up, erect
4 = **toss (about)**, roll, plunge, lurch ▷ PHRASE: pitch in = **help**, contribute, participate, join in,

cooperate, chip in (*informal*), get
stuck in (*Brit. informal*), lend a
hand

pitfall NOUN *usually plural*
= **danger**, difficulty, peril, catch,
trap, hazard, drawback, snag,
uphill (*S. African*)

pity NOUN 1 = **compassion**,
charity, sympathy, kindness,
fellow feeling ≠ mercilessness
2 = **shame**, sin (*informal*),
misfortune, bummer (*slang*),
crying shame 3 = **mercy**,
kindness, clemency, forbearance
▷ VERB = **feel sorry for**, feel for,
sympathize with, grieve for, weep
for, bleed for, have compassion for

pivotal ADJECTIVE = **crucial**,
central, vital, critical, decisive

place NOUN 1 = **spot**, point,
position, site, area, location,
venue, whereabouts
2 = **region**, quarter, district,
neighbourhood, vicinity,
locality, locale, dorp (*S. African*)
3 = **position**, point, spot, location
4 = **space**, position, seat,
chair 5 = **situation**, position,
circumstances, shoes (*informal*)
6 = **job**, position, post, situation,
office, employment, appointment
7 = **home**, house, room, property,
accommodation, pad (*slang*),
residence, dwelling, bachelor
apartment (*Canad.*) 8 *used in
negative constructions* = **duty**, right,
job, charge, concern, role, affair,
responsibility ▷ PHRASE: **know
one's place** = **know one's rank**,
know one's standing, know one's

position, know one's footing,
know one's station, know one's
status, know one's grade, know
one's niche
▷ VERB 1 = **lay (down)**, put
(down), set (down), stand,
position, rest, station, stick
(*informal*) 2 = **put**, lay, set, invest,
pin 3 = **classify**, class, group,
put, order, sort, rank, arrange
4 = **entrust to**, give to, assign
to, appoint to, allocate to, find a
home for 5 = **identify**, remember,
recognize, pin someone down,
put your finger on, put a name to
▷ PHRASE: **take place** = **happen**,
occur, go on, go down (*U.S. &
Canad.*), arise, come about, crop
up, transpire (*informal*)

plague NOUN 1 = **disease**,
infection, epidemic, pestilence
2 = **infestation**, invasion,
epidemic, influx, host, swarm,
multitude
▷ VERB 1 = **torment**, trouble,
torture 2 = **pester**, trouble,
bother, annoy, tease, harry,
harass, hassle

plain ADJECTIVE 1 = **unadorned**,
simple, basic, severe, bare, stark,
austere, spartan, bare-bones
≠ ornate 2 = **clear**, obvious,
patent, evident, visible, distinct,
understandable, manifest
≠ hidden 3 = **straightforward**,
open, direct, frank, blunt,
outspoken, honest, downright
≠ roundabout 4 = **ugly**,
unattractive, homely
(*U.S. & Canad.*), unlovely,

P

unprepossessing, not beautiful,
no oil painting (*informal*),
ill-favoured ≠ attractive
5 = ordinary, common, simple,
everyday, commonplace,
unaffected, unpretentious
≠ sophisticated
▷ NOUN = **flatland**, plateau,
prairie, grassland, steppe, veld

plan NOUN **1 = scheme**, system,
design, programme, proposal,
strategy, method, suggestion
2 = diagram, map, drawing,
chart, representation, sketch,
blueprint, layout
▷ VERB **1 = devise**, arrange,
scheme, plot, draft, organize,
outline, formulate **2 = intend**,
aim, mean, propose, purpose
3 = design, outline, draw up a
plan of

plane NOUN **1 = aeroplane**,
aircraft, jet, airliner, jumbo
jet **2 = flat surface**, the flat,
horizontal, level surface **3 = level**,
position, stage, condition,
standard, degree, rung, echelon
▷ ADJECTIVE = **level**, even, flat,
regular, smooth, horizontal
▷ VERB = **skim**, sail, skate, glide

plant¹ NOUN = **flower**, bush,
vegetable, herb, weed, shrub
▷ VERB **1 = sow**, scatter,
transplant, implant, put in the
ground **2 = seed**, sow, implant
3 = place, put, set, fix **4 = hide**,
put, place, conceal **5 = place**, put,
establish, found, fix, insert

plant² NOUN **1 = factory**,
works, shop, yard, mill, foundry

2 = machinery, equipment, gear,
apparatus

plaster NOUN **1 = mortar**,
stucco, gypsum, plaster of Paris
2 = bandage, dressing, sticking
plaster, Elastoplast (*trademark*),
adhesive plaster
▷ VERB = **cover**, spread, coat,
smear, overlay, daub

plastic ADJECTIVE = **pliant**, soft,
flexible, supple, pliable, ductile,
mouldable ≠ rigid

plate NOUN **1 = platter**, dish,
dinner plate, salver, trencher
(*archaic*) **2 = helping**, course,
serving, dish, portion, platter,
plateful **3 = layer**, panel, sheet,
slab **4 = illustration**, picture,
photograph, print, engraving,
lithograph
▷ VERB = **coat**, gild, laminate,
cover, overlay

plateau NOUN **1 = upland**, table,
highland, tableland **2 = levelling
off**, level, stage, stability

platform NOUN **1 = stage**, stand,
podium, rostrum, dais, soapbox
2 = policy, programme, principle,
objective(s), manifesto, party line

plausible ADJECTIVE
1 = believable, possible, likely,
reasonable, credible, probable,
persuasive, conceivable
≠ unbelievable **2 = glib**, smooth,
specious, smooth-talking,
smooth-tongued

play VERB **1 = amuse yourself**,
have fun, sport, fool, romp, revel,
trifle, entertain yourself **2 = take
part in**, be involved in, engage

in, participate in, compete in
3 = **compete against**, challenge, take on, oppose, contend against
4 = **perform**, carry out **5** = **act**, portray, represent, perform, act the part of **6** = **perform on**, strum, make music on
▷ NOUN **1** = **amusement**, pleasure, leisure, games, sport, fun, entertainment, relaxation, me-time **2** = **drama**, show, piece, comedy, tragedy, farce, soapie *or* soapie (*Austral. slang*), pantomime
▷ PHRASES: **play on** *or* **upon something** = **take advantage of**, abuse, exploit, impose on, trade on, capitalize on; **play something down** = **minimize**, make light of, gloss over, talk down, underrate, underplay, pooh-pooh (*informal*), soft-pedal (*informal*); **play something up** = **emphasize**, highlight, underline, stress, accentuate; **play up 1** (*Brit. informal*) = **hurt**, be painful, bother you, trouble you, be sore, pain you **2** (*Brit. informal*) = **malfunction**, not work properly, be on the blink (*slang*) **3** (*Brit. informal*) = **be awkward**, misbehave, give trouble, be disobedient, be stroppy (*Brit. slang*)

playboy NOUN = **womanizer**, philanderer, rake, lady-killer (*informal*), roué, ladies' man

player NOUN **1** = **sportsman** *or* **sportswoman**, competitor, participant, contestant
2 = **musician**, artist, performer, virtuoso, instrumentalist

3 = **performer**, entertainer, Thespian, trouper, actor *or* actress

plea NOUN **1** = **appeal**, request, suit, prayer, petition, entreaty, intercession, supplication
2 = **excuse**, defence, explanation, justification

plead VERB = **appeal**, ask, request, beg, petition, implore, beseech, entreat

pleasant ADJECTIVE **1** = **pleasing**, nice, fine, lovely, amusing, delightful, enjoyable, agreeable, lekker (*S. African slang*) ≠ horrible
2 = **friendly**, nice, agreeable, likable *or* likeable, engaging, charming, amiable, genial ≠ disagreeable

please VERB = **delight**, entertain, humour, amuse, suit, satisfy, indulge, gratify ≠ annoy

pleased ADJECTIVE = **happy**, delighted, contented, satisfied, thrilled, glad, gratified, over the moon (*informal*)

pleasing ADJECTIVE **1** = **enjoyable**, satisfying, charming, delightful, gratifying, agreeable, pleasurable ≠ unpleasant
2 = **likable** *or* **likeable**, engaging, charming, delightful, agreeable ≠ disagreeable

pleasure NOUN **1** = **happiness**, delight, satisfaction, enjoyment, bliss, gratification, gladness, delectation ≠ displeasure
2 = **amusement**, joy ≠ duty

pledge NOUN **1** = **promise**, vow, assurance, word, undertaking, warrant, oath, covenant

2 = **guarantee**, security, deposit, bail, collateral, pawn, surety
▷ **VERB** = **promise**, vow, swear, contract, engage, give your word, give your oath

plentiful ADJECTIVE = **abundant**, liberal, generous, lavish, ample, overflowing, copious, bountiful ≠ scarce

plenty NOUN **1** = **abundance**, wealth, prosperity, fertility, profusion, affluence, plenitude, fruitfulness **2** usually with **of** = **lots of** (informal), enough, a great deal of, masses of, piles of (informal), stacks of, heaps of (informal), an abundance of

plight NOUN = **difficulty**, condition, state, situation, trouble, predicament

plot¹ NOUN **1** = **plan**, scheme, intrigue, conspiracy, cabal, stratagem, machination
2 = **story**, action, subject, theme, outline, scenario, narrative, story line
▷ **VERB** **1** = **plan**, scheme, conspire, intrigue, manoeuvre, contrive, collude, machinate
2 = **devise**, design, lay, conceive, hatch, contrive, concoct, cook up (informal) **3** = **chart**, mark, map, locate, calculate, outline

plot² NOUN = **patch**, lot, area, ground, parcel, tract, allotment

plough VERB = **turn over**, dig, till, cultivate ▷ **PHRASE**: **plough through something** = **forge**, cut, drive, press, push, plunge, wade

ploy NOUN = **tactic**, move, trick, device, scheme, manoeuvre, dodge, ruse

pluck VERB **1** = **pull out** or **off**, pick, draw, collect, gather, harvest
2 = **tug**, catch, snatch, clutch, jerk, yank, tweak, pull at **3** = **strum**, pick, finger, twang
▷ **NOUN** = **courage**, nerve, bottle (Brit. slang), guts (informal), grit, bravery, backbone, boldness

plug NOUN **1** = **stopper**, cork, bung, spigot **2** (informal) = **mention**, advertisement, advert (Brit. informal), push, publicity, hype
▷ **VERB** **1** = **seal**, close, stop, fill, block, stuff, pack, cork **2** (informal) = **mention**, push, promote, publicize, advertise, build up, hype ▷ **PHRASE**: **plug away** (informal) = **slog away**, labour, toil away, grind away (informal), peg away, plod away

plum MODIFIER = **choice**, prize, first-class

plumb VERB = **delve into**, explore, probe, go into, penetrate, gauge, unravel, fathom
▷ **ADVERB** = **exactly**, precisely, bang, slap, spot-on (Brit. informal)

plummet VERB **1** = **drop**, fall, crash, nose-dive, descend rapidly
2 = **plunge**, fall, drop, crash, tumble, nose-dive, descend rapidly

plump ADJECTIVE = **chubby**, fat, stout, round, tubby, dumpy, roly-poly, rotund ≠ scrawny

plunder VERB **1** = **loot**, strip, sack, rob, raid, rifle, ransack, pillage

2 = **steal**, rob, take, nick (*informal*), pinch (*informal*), embezzle, pilfer, thieve
▷ NOUN **1** = **pillage 2** = **loot**, spoils, booty, swag (*slang*), ill-gotten gains

plunge VERB **1** = **descend**, fall, drop, crash, pitch, sink, dive, tumble **2** = **hurtle**, charge, career, jump, tear, rush, dive, dash **3** = **submerge**, dip **4** = **throw**, cast, pitch, propel **5** = **fall steeply**, drop, crash (*informal*), slump, plummet, take a nosedive (*informal*)
▷ NOUN **1** = **fall**, crash (*informal*), slump, drop, tumble **2** = **dive**, jump, duck, descent

plus PREPOSITION = **and**, with, added to, coupled with
▷ NOUN (*informal*) = **advantage**, benefit, asset, gain, extra, bonus, good point
▷ ADJECTIVE = **additional**, added, extra, supplementary, add-on

● **WORD POWER**
● When you have a sentence with
● more than one subject linked
● by *and*, this makes the subject
● plural and means it should take
● a plural verb: *the doctor and all*
● *the nurses were* (not *was*) *waiting*
● *for the patient*. However, where
● the subjects are linked by *plus*,
● *together with*, or *along with*, the
● number of the verb remains
● just as it would have been if
● the extra subjects had not
● been mentioned. Therefore you
● would say *the doctor, together*
● *with all the nurses, was* (not *were*)
● *waiting for the patient*.

plush ADJECTIVE = **luxurious**, luxury, lavish, rich, sumptuous, opulent, de luxe

ply VERB = **work at**, follow, exercise, pursue, carry on, practise

pocket NOUN = **pouch**, bag, sack, compartment, receptacle
▷ MODIFIER = **small**, compact, miniature, portable, little
▷ VERB = **steal**, take, lift (*informal*), appropriate, pilfer, purloin, filch

pod NOUN = **shell**, case, hull, husk, shuck

podium NOUN = **platform**, stand, stage, rostrum, dais

poem NOUN = **verse**, song, lyric, rhyme, sonnet, ode, verse composition

poet NOUN = **bard**, rhymer, lyricist, lyric poet, versifier, elegist
▷ *see* **poetry**

poetic ADJECTIVE **1** = **figurative**, creative, lyric, symbolic, lyrical **2** = **lyrical**, lyric, elegiac, metrical

poetry NOUN = **verse**, poems, rhyme, rhyming, verse composition

pogey NOUN (*Canad.*) = **benefits**, the dole (*Brit. & Austral.*), welfare, social security, unemployment benefit, state benefit, allowance

poignant ADJECTIVE = **moving**, touching, sad, bitter, intense, painful, distressing, pathetic

point NOUN **1** = **essence**, meaning, subject, question, heart, import, drift, thrust **2** = **purpose**, aim, object, end, reason, goal, intention, objective **3** = **aspect**, detail, feature, quality, particular, respect, item, characteristic **4** = **place**, area, position, site, spot, location, locality, locale **5** = **moment**, time, stage, period, phase, instant, juncture, moment in time **6** = **stage**, level, position, condition, degree, pitch, circumstance, extent **7** = **end**, tip, sharp end, top, spur, spike, apex, prong **8** = **score**, tally, mark **9** = **pinpoint**, mark, spot, dot, fleck

▷ **VERB 1** *usually followed by* **at** *or* **to** = **aim**, level, train, direct **2** = **face**, look, direct **3** = **indicate**, show, signal, point to, point out, specify, designate, gesture towards

pointed ADJECTIVE **1** = **sharp**, edged, acute, barbed **2** = **cutting**, telling, biting, sharp, keen, acute, penetrating, pertinent

pointer NOUN **1** = **hint**, tip, suggestion, recommendation, caution, piece of information, piece of advice **2** = **indicator**, hand, guide, needle, arrow

pointless ADJECTIVE = **senseless**, meaningless, futile, fruitless, stupid, silly, useless, absurd ≠ worthwhile

poised ADJECTIVE **1** = **ready**, waiting, prepared, standing by, all set **2** = **composed**, calm, together (*informal*), collected, dignified, self-confident, self-possessed ≠ agitated

poison NOUN = **toxin**, venom, bane (*archaic*)

▷ **VERB 1** = **murder**, kill, give someone poison, administer poison to **2** = **contaminate**, foul, infect, spoil, pollute, blight, taint, befoul **3** = **corrupt**, colour, undermine, bias, sour, pervert, warp, taint

poisonous ADJECTIVE **1** = **toxic**, fatal, deadly, lethal, mortal, virulent, noxious, venomous **2** = **evil**, malicious, corrupting, pernicious, baleful

poke VERB **1** = **jab**, push, stick, dig, stab, thrust, shove, nudge **2** = **protrude**, stick, thrust, jut

▷ **NOUN** = **jab**, dig, thrust, nudge, prod

pole NOUN = **rod**, post, support, staff, bar, stick, stake, paling

police NOUN = **the law** (*informal*), police force, constabulary, fuzz (*slang*), boys in blue (*informal*), the Old Bill (*slang*), rozzers (*slang*)

▷ **VERB** = **control**, patrol, guard, watch, protect, regulate

policy NOUN **1** = **procedure**, plan, action, practice, scheme, code, custom **2** = **line**, rules, approach

polish NOUN **1** = **varnish**, wax, glaze, lacquer, japan **2** = **sheen**, finish, glaze, gloss, brightness, lustre **3** = **style**, class (*informal*), finish, breeding, grace, elegance, refinement, finesse

▷ **VERB 1** = **shine**, wax, smooth, rub, buff, brighten, burnish **2** *often with up* = **perfect**, improve, enhance, refine, finish, brush up, touch up

polished ADJECTIVE 1 = **elegant**, sophisticated, refined, polite, cultivated, suave, well-bred ≠ unsophisticated 2 = **accomplished**, professional, masterly, fine, expert, skilful, adept, superlative ≠ amateurish 3 = **shining**, bright, smooth, gleaming, glossy, burnished ≠ dull

polite ADJECTIVE 1 = **mannerly**, civil, courteous, gracious, respectful, well-behaved, complaisant, well-mannered ≠ rude 2 = **refined**, cultured, civilized, polished, sophisticated, elegant, genteel, well-bred ≠ uncultured

politic ADJECTIVE = **wise**, diplomatic, sensible, prudent, advisable, expedient, judicious

political ADJECTIVE = **governmental**, government, state, parliamentary, constitutional, administrative, legislative, ministerial

politician NOUN = **statesman** or **stateswoman**, representative, senator (*U.S.*), congressman (*U.S.*), Member of Parliament, legislator, public servant, congresswoman (*U.S.*)

politics NOUN 1 = **affairs of state**, government, public affairs, civics 2 = **political beliefs**, party politics, political allegiances, political leanings, political sympathies 3 = **political science**, statesmanship, civics, statecraft

poll NOUN 1 = **survey**, figures, count, sampling, returns, ballot, tally, census 2 = **election**, vote, voting, referendum, ballot, plebiscite ▷ VERB 1 = **question**, interview, survey, sample, ballot, canvass 2 = **gain**, return, record, register, tally

pollute VERB 1 = **contaminate**, dirty, poison, soil, foul, infect, spoil, stain ≠ decontaminate 2 = **defile**, corrupt, sully, deprave, debase, profane, desecrate, dishonour ≠ honour

pollution NOUN 1 = **contamination**, dirtying, corruption, taint, foulness, defilement, uncleanness 2 = **waste**, poisons, dirt, impurities

pond NOUN = **pool**, tarn, small lake, fish pond, duck pond, millpond

ponder VERB = **think about**, consider, reflect on, contemplate, deliberate about, muse on, brood on, meditate on

pool[1] NOUN 1 = **swimming pool**, lido, swimming bath(s) (*Brit.*), bathing pool (*archaic*) 2 = **pond**, lake, mere, tarn 3 = **puddle**, drop, patch

pool[2] NOUN 1 = **supply**, reserve, fall-back 2 = **kitty**, bank, fund, stock, store, pot, jackpot, stockpile ▷ VERB = **combine**, share, merge, put together, amalgamate, lump together, join forces on

P

poor ADJECTIVE 1 = **impoverished**, broke (*informal*), hard up (*informal*), short, needy, penniless, destitute, poverty-stricken ≠ rich 2 = **unfortunate**, unlucky, hapless, pitiful, luckless, wretched, ill-starred, pitiable ≠ fortunate 3 = **inferior**, unsatisfactory, mediocre, second-rate, rotten (*informal*), low-grade, below par, substandard, half-pie (*N.Z. informal*), bodger *or* bodgie (*Austral. slang*) ≠ excellent 4 = **meagre**, inadequate, insufficient, lacking, incomplete, scant, deficient, skimpy ≠ ample

poorly ADVERB = **badly**, incompetently, inadequately, unsuccessfully, insufficiently, unsatisfactorily, inexpertly ≠ well
▷ ADJECTIVE (*informal*) = **ill**, sick, unwell, crook (*Austral. & N.Z. informal*), seedy (*informal*), below par, off colour, under the weather (*informal*), feeling rotten (*informal*) ≠ healthy

pop NOUN = **bang**, report, crack, noise, burst, explosion
▷ VERB 1 = **burst**, crack, snap, bang, explode, go off (with a bang) 2 = **put**, insert, push, stick, slip, thrust, tuck, shove

pope NOUN = **Holy Father**, pontiff, His Holiness, Bishop of Rome, Vicar of Christ

popular ADJECTIVE 1 = **well-liked**, liked, in, accepted, favourite, approved, in favour, fashionable ≠ unpopular 2 = **common**, general, prevailing, current, conventional, universal, prevalent ≠ rare

popularity NOUN 1 = **favour**, esteem, acclaim, regard, approval, vogue 2 = **currency**, acceptance, circulation, vogue, prevalence

populate VERB 1 = **inhabit**, people, live in, occupy, reside in, dwell in (*formal*) 2 = **settle**, occupy, pioneer, colonize

population NOUN = **inhabitants**, people, community, society, residents, natives, folk, occupants

pore NOUN = **opening**, hole, outlet, orifice

pornography NOUN = **obscenity**, porn (*informal*), dirt, filth, indecency, smut

port NOUN = **harbour**, haven, anchorage, seaport

portable ADJECTIVE = **light**, compact, convenient, handy, manageable, movable, easily carried

porter[1] NOUN = **baggage attendant**, carrier, bearer, baggage-carrier

porter[2] NOUN (*chiefly Brit.*) = **doorman**, caretaker, janitor, concierge, gatekeeper

portion NOUN 1 = **part**, bit, piece, section, scrap, segment, fragment, chunk 2 = **helping**, serving, piece, plateful 3 = **share**, allowance, lot, measure, quantity, quota, ration, allocation

portrait NOUN 1 = **picture**, painting, image, photograph, representation, likeness
2 = **description**, profile, portrayal,

P

depiction, characterization, thumbnail sketch

portray VERB 1 = **play**, take the role of, act the part of, represent, personate (*rare*) 2 = **describe**, present, depict, evoke, delineate, put in words 3 = **represent**, draw, paint, illustrate, sketch, figure, picture, depict 4 = **characterize**, represent, depict

portrayal NOUN
1 = **performance**, interpretation, characterization 2 = **depiction**, picture, representation, sketch, rendering 3 = **description**, account, representation
4 = **characterization**, representation, depiction

⬤ **WORD POWER**
⬤ Several loan words came into
⬤ English via Portuguese but had
⬤ a different source language.
⬤ For example, *amok* was a
⬤ Malay word meaning 'frenzied'
⬤ which was, in turn, adopted
⬤ by Portuguese explorers to
⬤ describe a Malay in a state
⬤ of murderous frenzy. From
⬤ Portuguese it was borrowed
⬤ into English, and is almost
⬤ always found in the phrase *run
⬤ amok*, though *go amok* is also
⬤ found. Run amok means to run
⬤ about with a desire to do harm
⬤ or kill, e.g. hooligans ran amok
⬤ in the streets. It is similar in
⬤ meaning to 'on the rampage'
⬤ and 'go berserk'. Interestingly,
⬤ berserk, from Icelandic, also
⬤ originally denoted a person in a

⬤ state of murderous rage, in this
⬤ case Norse warriors who would
⬤ *go berserk* on the battlefield.
⬤ Run amok can also be used
⬤ of abstract nouns, e.g. An
⬤ example of political correctness
⬤ run amok – where it means
⬤ spreading wildly or out of
⬤ control. Another word adopted
⬤ from Portuguese is *palaver*,
⬤ from *palavra* meaning 'talk'.
⬤ This origin can still be seen in
⬤ its meaning of talk or chatter
⬤ which is loud or confused, e.g.
⬤ all the media palaver about
⬤ this issue. However, the most
⬤ common meaning of palaver
⬤ is 'fuss' or 'effort', especially of
⬤ a time-consuming activity,
⬤ e.g. the palaver of changing
⬤ your mobile phone network.
⬤ It is close in meaning to its
⬤ synonym 'rigmarole' in this
⬤ sense.

pose VERB 1 = **position yourself**, sit, model, arrange yourself
2 = **put on airs**, posture, show off (*informal*)
▷ NOUN 1 = **posture**, position, bearing, attitude, stance 2 = **act**, façade, air, front, posturing, pretence, mannerism, affectation
▷ PHRASE: **pose as something** *or* **someone** = **impersonate**, pretend to be, profess to be, masquerade as, pass yourself off as

posh (*informal, chiefly Brit.*)
ADJECTIVE 1 = **smart**, grand, stylish, luxurious, classy (*slang*),

⬤ **p**

swish (*informal*, *chiefly Brit.*), up-market, swanky (*informal*), schmick (*Austral. informal*) **2** = **upper-class**, high-class

position NOUN **1** = **location**, place, point, area, post, situation, station, spot **2** = **posture**, attitude, arrangement, pose, stance **3** = **status**, place, standing, footing, station, rank, reputation, importance **4** = **job**, place, post, opening, office, role, situation, duty **5** = **place**, standing, rank, status **6** = **attitude**, view, perspective, point of view, opinion, belief, stance, outlook
▷ VERB = **place**, put, set, stand, arrange, locate, lay out

positive ADJECTIVE **1** = **beneficial**, useful, practical, helpful, progressive, productive, worthwhile, constructive ≠ harmful **2** = **certain**, sure, convinced, confident, satisfied, assured, free from doubt ≠ uncertain **3** = **definite**, real, clear, firm, certain, express, absolute, decisive, nailed-on (*slang*) ≠ inconclusive **4** (*informal*) = **absolute**, complete, perfect, right (*Brit. informal*), real, total, sheer, utter

positively ADVERB **1** = **definitely**, surely, firmly, certainly, absolutely, emphatically, unquestionably, categorically **2** = **really**, completely, simply, plain (*informal*), absolutely, thoroughly, utterly, downright

possess VERB **1** = **own**, have, hold, be in possession of, be the owner of, have in your possession **2** = **be endowed with**, have, enjoy, benefit from, be possessed of, be gifted with **3** = **seize**, hold, control, dominate, occupy, take someone over, have power over, have mastery over

possession NOUN = **ownership**, control, custody, hold, hands, tenure
▷ PLURAL NOUN = **property**, things, effects, estate, assets, belongings, chattels

possibility NOUN **1** = **feasibility**, likelihood, potentiality, practicability, workableness **2** = **likelihood**, chance, risk, odds, prospect, liability, probability **3** *often plural* = **potential**, promise, prospects, talent, capabilities, potentiality

possible ADJECTIVE **1** = **feasible**, viable, workable, achievable, practicable, attainable, doable, realizable ≠ unfeasible **2** = **likely**, potential, anticipated, probable, odds-on, on the cards ≠ improbable **3** = **conceivable**, likely, credible, plausible, hypothetical, imaginable, believable, thinkable ≠ inconceivable **4** = **aspiring**, would-be, promising, hopeful, prospective, wannabe (*informal*)

● **WORD POWER**
● Although it is very common to
● talk about something's being
● *very possible* or *more possible*,

many people object to such uses, claiming that *possible* describes an absolute state, and therefore something can only be either *possible* or *not possible*. If you want to refer to different degrees of probability, a word such as *likely* or *easy* may be more appropriate than *possible*, for example *it is very likely that he will resign* (not *very possible*).

possibly ADVERB = **perhaps**, maybe, perchance (*archaic*)

post¹ NOUN = **support**, stake, pole, column, shaft, upright, pillar, picket
▷ VERB = **put up**, display, affix, pin something up

post² NOUN 1 = **job**, place, office, position, situation, employment, appointment, assignment 2 = **position**, place, base, beat, station
▷ VERB = **station**, assign, put, place, position, situate, put on duty

post³ NOUN 1 = **mail**, collection, delivery, postal service, snail mail (*informal*) 2 = **correspondence**, letters, cards, mail
▷ VERB = **send (off)**, forward, mail, get off, transmit, dispatch, consign ▷ PHRASE: **keep someone posted** = **notify**, brief, advise, inform, report to, keep someone informed, keep someone up to date, apprise

poster NOUN = **notice**, bill, announcement, advertisement, sticker, placard, public notice

postpone VERB = **put off**, delay, suspend, adjourn, shelve, defer, put back, put on the back burner (*informal*) ≠ go ahead with

posture NOUN = **bearing**, set, attitude, stance, carriage, disposition
▷ VERB = **show off** (*informal*), pose, affect, put on airs

pot NOUN = **container**, bowl, pan, vessel, basin, cauldron, skillet

potent ADJECTIVE 1 = **powerful**, commanding, dynamic, dominant, influential, authoritative 2 = **strong**, powerful, mighty, vigorous, forceful ≠ weak

potential ADJECTIVE 1 = **possible**, future, likely, promising, probable 2 = **hidden**, possible, inherent, dormant, latent
▷ NOUN = **ability**, possibilities, capacity, capability, aptitude, wherewithal, potentiality

potter VERB *usually with* **around** *or* **about** = **mess about**, tinker, dabble, footle (*informal*)

pottery NOUN = **ceramics**, terracotta, crockery, earthenware, stoneware

pounce VERB *often followed by* **on** *or* **upon** = **attack**, strike, jump, leap, swoop

pound¹ NOUN = **enclosure**, yard, pen, compound, kennels

pound² VERB 1 *sometimes with* **on** = **beat**, strike, hammer, batter, thrash, thump, clobber (*slang*), pummel 2 = **crush**, powder,

P

pulverize 3 =**pulsate**, beat, pulse, throb, palpitate 4 =**stomp**, tramp, march, thunder (*informal*)

pour VERB 1 =**let flow**, spill, splash, dribble, drizzle, slop (*informal*), slosh (*informal*), decant 2 =**flow**, stream, run, course, rush, emit, cascade, gush 3 =**rain**, pelt (down), teem, bucket down (*informal*) 4 =**stream**, crowd, flood, swarm, gush, throng, teem

- WORD POWER
- The spelling of *pour* (as
- in *she poured cream on her*
- *strudel*) should be carefully
- distinguished from that of *pore*
- *over* or *through* (as in *she pored*
- *over the manuscript*).

pout VERB =**sulk**, glower, look petulant, pull a long face
▷ NOUN =**sullen look**, glower, long face

poverty NOUN 1 =**pennilessness**, want, need, hardship, insolvency, privation, penury, destitution ≠ wealth 2 =**scarcity**, lack, absence, want, deficit, shortage, deficiency, inadequacy ≠ abundance

powder NOUN =**dust**, talc, fine grains, loose particles
▷ VERB =**dust**, cover, scatter, sprinkle, strew, dredge

power NOUN 1 =**control**, authority, influence, command, dominance, domination, mastery, dominion, mana (*N.Z.*) 2 =**ability**, capacity, faculty, property, potential, capability, competence, competency

≠ inability 3 =**authority**, right, licence, privilege, warrant, prerogative, authorization 4 =**strength**, might, energy, muscle, vigour, potency, brawn ≠ weakness 5 =**forcefulness**, force, strength, punch (*informal*), intensity, potency, eloquence, persuasiveness

powerful ADJECTIVE 1 =**influential**, dominant, controlling, commanding, prevailing, authoritative, skookum (*Canad.*) ≠ powerless 2 =**strong**, strapping, mighty, vigorous, potent, energetic, sturdy ≠ weak 3 =**persuasive**, convincing, telling, moving, striking, storming, dramatic, impressive

powerless ADJECTIVE 1 =**defenceless**, vulnerable, dependent, subject, tied, ineffective, unarmed 2 =**weak**, disabled, helpless, incapable, frail, feeble, debilitated, impotent ≠ strong

practical ADJECTIVE 1 =**functional**, realistic, pragmatic ≠ impractical 2 =**empirical**, real, applied, actual, hands-on, in the field, experimental, factual ≠ theoretical 3 =**sensible**, ordinary, realistic, down-to-earth, matter-of-fact, businesslike, hard-headed, grounded ≠ impractical 4 =**feasible**, possible, viable, workable, practicable, doable ≠ impractical

5 = **useful**, ordinary, appropriate, sensible, everyday, functional, utilitarian, serviceable
6 = **skilled**, experienced, efficient, accomplished, proficient ≠ inexperienced

● **WORD POWER**
● A distinction is usually
● made between *practical* and
● *practicable*. *Practical* refers to a
● person, idea, project, etc, as
● being more concerned with
● or relevant to practice than
● theory: *he is a very practical*
● *person*; *the idea had no practical*
● *application*. *Practicable* refers to a
● project or idea as being capable
● of being done or put into
● effect: *the plan was expensive, yet*
● *practicable*.

practically ADVERB **1** = **almost**, nearly, essentially, virtually, basically, fundamentally, all but, just about **2** = **sensibly**, reasonably, matter-of-factly, realistically, rationally, pragmatically

practice NOUN **1** = **custom**, way, system, rule, method, tradition, habit, routine, tikanga (N.Z.) **2** = **training**, study, exercise, preparation, drill, rehearsal, repetition **3** = **profession**, work, business, career, occupation, pursuit, vocation **4** = **business**, company, office, firm, enterprise, partnership, outfit (*informal*) **5** = **use**, experience, action, operation, application, enactment

practise VERB **1** = **rehearse**, study, prepare, perfect, repeat, go through, go over, refine **2** = **do**, train, exercise, drill **3** = **carry out**, follow, apply, perform, observe, engage in **4** = **work at**, pursue, carry on

practised ADJECTIVE = **skilled**, trained, experienced, seasoned, able, expert, accomplished, proficient ≠ inexperienced

pragmatic ADJECTIVE = **practical**, sensible, realistic, down-to-earth, utilitarian, businesslike, hard-headed ≠ idealistic

praise VERB **1** = **acclaim**, approve of, honour, cheer, admire, applaud, compliment, congratulate ≠ criticize **2** = **give thanks to**, bless, worship, adore, glorify, exalt
▷ NOUN **1** = **approval**, acclaim, tribute, compliment, congratulations, eulogy, commendation, approbation ≠ criticism **2** = **thanks**, glory, worship, homage, adoration

pray VERB **1** = **say your prayers**, offer a prayer, recite the rosary **2** = **beg**, ask, plead, petition, request, solicit, implore, beseech

prayer NOUN **1** = **supplication**, devotion **2** = **orison**, litany, invocation, intercession **3** = **plea**, appeal, request, petition, entreaty, supplication

preach VERB **1** *often with* **to** = **deliver a sermon**, address, evangelize, preach a sermon **2** = **urge**, teach, champion,

P

recommend, advise, counsel, advocate, exhort

preacher NOUN = **clergyman**, minister, parson, missionary, evangelist

precarious ADJECTIVE
1 = **insecure**, dangerous, tricky, risky, dodgy (*Brit., Austral. & N.Z. informal*), unsure, hazardous, shaky, shonky (*Austral. & N.Z. informal*) ≠ secure 2 = **dangerous**, shaky, insecure, unsafe, unreliable ≠ stable

precaution NOUN = **safeguard**, insurance, protection, provision, safety measure

precede VERB 1 = **go before**, antedate 2 = **go ahead of**, lead, head, go before 3 = **preface**, introduce, go before

precedent NOUN = **instance**, example, standard, model, pattern, prototype, paradigm, antecedent

precinct NOUN = **area**, quarter, section, sector, district, zone

precious ADJECTIVE 1 = **valuable**, expensive, fine, prized, dear, costly, invaluable, priceless ≠ worthless 2 = **loved**, prized, dear, treasured, darling, beloved, adored, cherished 3 = **affected**, artificial, twee (*Brit. informal*), overrefined, overnice

precipitate VERB 1 = **quicken**, trigger, accelerate, advance, hurry, speed up, bring on, hasten 2 = **throw**, launch, cast, hurl, fling, let fly
▷ ADJECTIVE 1 = **hasty**, rash,

reckless, impulsive, precipitous, impetuous, heedless 2 = **sudden**, quick, brief, rushing, rapid, unexpected, swift, abrupt

precise ADJECTIVE 1 = **exact**, specific, particular, express, correct, absolute, accurate, explicit ≠ vague 2 = **strict**, particular, exact, formal, careful, stiff, rigid, meticulous ≠ inexact

precisely ADVERB 1 = **exactly**, squarely, correctly, absolutely, strictly, accurately, plumb (*informal*), square on 2 = **just so**, yes, absolutely, exactly, quite so, you bet (*informal*), without a doubt, indubitably 3 = **just**, entirely, absolutely, altogether, exactly, in all respects 4 = **word for word**, literally, exactly, to the letter

precision NOUN = **exactness**, care, accuracy, particularity, meticulousness, preciseness

predecessor NOUN 1 = **previous job holder**, precursor, forerunner, antecedent 2 = **ancestor**, forebear, antecedent, forefather, tupuna *or* tipuna (*N.Z.*)

predicament NOUN = **fix** (*informal*), situation, spot (*informal*), hole (*slang*), mess, jam (*informal*), dilemma, pinch

predict VERB = **foretell**, forecast, divine, prophesy, augur, portend

predictable ADJECTIVE = **likely**, expected, sure, certain, anticipated, reliable, foreseeable ≠ unpredictable

prediction NOUN = **prophecy**,

forecast, prognosis, divination, prognostication, augury

predominantly ADVERB
= **mainly**, largely, chiefly, mostly, generally, principally, primarily, for the most part

prefer VERB 1 = **like better**, favour, go for, pick, fancy, opt for, incline towards, be partial to 2 = **choose**, opt for, pick, desire, would rather, would sooner, incline towards

● WORD POWER
● Normally, to (not than) is used
● after prefer and preferable.
● Therefore, you would say
● I prefer skating to skiing, and
● a small income is preferable
● to no income at all. However,
● when expressing a preference
● between two activities stated
● as infinitive verbs, for example
● to skate and to ski, use than, as in
● I prefer to skate than to ski.

preferable ADJECTIVE = **better**, best, chosen, preferred, recommended, favoured, superior, more suitable ≠ undesirable

preferably ADVERB = **ideally**, if possible, rather, sooner, by choice, in or for preference

preference NOUN 1 = **liking**, wish, taste, desire, leaning, bent, bias, inclination 2 = **first choice**, choice, favourite, pick, option, selection 3 = **priority**, first place, precedence, favouritism, favoured treatment

pregnant ADJECTIVE
1 = **expectant**, expecting (informal), with child, in the club

(Brit. slang), big or heavy with child 2 = **meaningful**, pointed, charged, significant, telling, loaded, expressive, eloquent

prejudice NOUN
1 = **discrimination**, injustice, intolerance, bigotry, unfairness, chauvinism, narrow-mindedness
2 = **bias**, preconception, partiality, preconceived notion, prejudgment
▷ VERB 1 = **bias**, influence, colour, poison, distort, slant, predispose
2 = **harm**, damage, hurt, injure, mar, undermine, spoil, impair, crool or cruel (Austral. slang)

prejudiced ADJECTIVE = **biased**, influenced, unfair, one-sided, bigoted, intolerant, opinionated, narrow-minded ≠ unbiased

preliminary ADJECTIVE 1 = **first**, opening, trial, initial, test, pilot, prior, introductory
2 = **qualifying**, eliminating
▷ NOUN = **introduction**, opening, beginning, start, prelude, preface, overture, preamble

prelude NOUN 1 = **introduction**, beginning, start 2 = **overture**, opening, introduction, introductory movement

premature ADJECTIVE 1 = **early**, untimely, before time, unseasonable 2 = **hasty**, rash, too soon, untimely, ill-timed, overhasty

premier NOUN = **head of government**, prime minister, chancellor, chief minister, P.M.
▷ ADJECTIVE = **chief**, leading,

first, highest, head, main, prime, primary

premiere NOUN = **first night**, opening, debut

premise NOUN = **assumption**, proposition, argument, hypothesis, assertion, supposition, presupposition, postulation

premises PLURAL NOUN = **building(s)**, place, office, property, site, establishment

premium NOUN 1 = **fee**, charge, payment, instalment 2 = **surcharge**, extra charge, additional fee *or* charge 3 = **bonus**, reward, prize, perk (*Brit. informal*), bounty, perquisite ▷ PHRASE: **at a premium** = **in great demand**, rare, scarce, in short supply, hard to come by

preoccupation NOUN 1 = **obsession**, fixation, bee in your bonnet 2 = **absorption**, abstraction, daydreaming, immersion, reverie, absent-mindedness, engrossment, woolgathering

preoccupied ADJECTIVE 1 = **absorbed**, lost, wrapped up, immersed, engrossed, rapt 2 = **lost in thought**, distracted, oblivious, absent-minded

preparation NOUN 1 = **groundwork**, preparing, getting ready 2 *usually plural* = **arrangement**, plan, measure, provision 3 = **mixture**, medicine, compound, concoction

prepare VERB 1 = **make** *or* **get**

ready, arrange, jack up (*N.Z. informal*) 2 = **train**, guide, prime, direct, brief, discipline, put someone in the picture 3 = **make**, cook, put together, get, produce, assemble, muster, concoct 4 = **get ready** 5 = **practise**, get ready, train, exercise, warm up, get into shape

prepared ADJECTIVE 1 = **willing**, inclined, disposed 2 = **ready**, set 3 = **fit**, primed, in order, arranged, in readiness

prescribe VERB 1 = **specify**, order, direct, stipulate, write a prescription for 2 = **ordain**, set, order, rule, recommend, dictate, lay down, decree

prescription NOUN 1 = **instruction**, direction, formula, script (*informal*), recipe 2 = **medicine**, drug, treatment, preparation, cure, mixture, dose, remedy

presence NOUN 1 = **being**, existence, residence, attendance, showing up, occupancy, inhabitance 2 = **personality**, bearing, appearance, aspect, air, carriage, aura, poise ▷ PHRASE: **presence of mind** = **level-headedness**, assurance, composure, poise, cool (*slang*), wits, countenance, coolness

present¹ ADJECTIVE 1 = **current**, existing, immediate, contemporary, present-day, existent 2 = **here**, there, near, ready, nearby, at hand ≠ absent 3 = **in existence**, existing,

existent, extant ▷ **PHRASE**: **the
present** = **now**, today, the time
being, here and now, the present
moment

present² NOUN = **gift**, offering,
grant, donation, hand-out,
endowment, boon, gratuity,
bonsela (*S. African*), koha (*N.Z.*)
▷ **VERB 1** = **give**, award, hand over,
grant, hand out, confer, bestow
2 = **put on**, stage, perform,
give, show, render **3** = **launch**,
display, parade, exhibit, unveil
4 = **introduce**, make known,
acquaint someone with

presentation NOUN
1 = **giving**, award, offering,
donation, bestowal, conferral
2 = **appearance**, look, display,
packaging, arrangement, layout
3 = **performance**, production,
show

presently ADVERB **1** = **at present**,
currently, now, today, these days,
nowadays, at the present time, in
this day and age **2** = **soon**, shortly,
directly, before long, momentarily
(*U.S. & Canad.*), by and by, in a jiffy
(*informal*)

preservation NOUN
1 = **upholding**, support,
maintenance **2** = **protection**,
safety, maintenance,
conservation, salvation,
safeguarding, safekeeping

preserve VERB **1** = **maintain**,
keep, continue, sustain, keep up,
prolong, uphold, conserve ≠ end
2 = **protect**, keep, save, maintain,
defend, shelter, shield, care for

≠ attack
▷ NOUN = **area**, department, field,
territory, province, arena, sphere

preside VERB = **officiate**, chair,
moderate, be chairperson

press VERB **1** = **push (down)**,
depress, lean on, press down,
force down **2** = **push**, squeeze,
jam, thrust, ram, wedge, shove
3 = **hug**, squeeze, embrace, clasp,
crush, hold close, fold in your arms
4 = **urge**, beg, petition, exhort,
implore, pressurize, entreat
5 = **plead**, present, lodge, submit,
tender, advance insistently
6 = **steam**, iron, smooth, flatten
7 = **compress**, grind, reduce, mill,
crush, pound, squeeze, tread
8 = **crowd**, push, gather, surge,
flock, herd, swarm, seethe

pressing ADJECTIVE = **urgent**,
serious, vital, crucial, imperative,
important, high-priority,
importunate ≠ unimportant

pressure NOUN **1** = **force**,
crushing, squeezing,
compressing, weight,
compression **2** = **power**,
influence, force, constraint, sway,
compulsion, coercion **3** = **stress**,
demands, strain, heat, load,
burden, urgency, hassle (*informal*),
uphill (*S. African*)

prestige NOUN = **status**,
standing, credit, reputation,
honour, importance, fame,
distinction, mana (*N.Z.*)

prestigious ADJECTIVE
= **celebrated**, respected,
prominent, great, important,

esteemed, notable, renowned ≠ unknown

presumably ADVERB = **it would seem**, probably, apparently, seemingly, on the face of it, in all probability, in all likelihood

presume VERB 1 = **believe**, think, suppose, assume, guess (*informal, chiefly U.S. & Canad.*), take for granted, infer, conjecture 2 = **dare**, venture, go so far as, take the liberty, make so bold as

pretend VERB 1 = **feign**, affect, assume, allege, fake, simulate, profess, sham 2 = **make believe**, suppose, imagine, act, make up

pretty ADJECTIVE = **attractive**, beautiful, lovely, charming, fair, good-looking, bonny, comely, fit (*Brit. informal*) ≠ plain
▷ ADVERB (*informal*) = **fairly**, rather, quite, kind of (*informal*), somewhat, moderately, reasonably

prevail VERB 1 = **win**, succeed, triumph, overcome, overrule, be victorious 2 = **be widespread**, abound, predominate, be current, be prevalent, exist generally

prevailing ADJECTIVE
1 = **widespread**, general, established, popular, common, current, usual, ordinary
2 = **predominating**, ruling, main, existing, principal

prevalent ADJECTIVE = **common**, established, popular, general, current, usual, widespread, universal ≠ rare

prevent VERB = **stop**, avoid, frustrate, hamper, foil, inhibit, avert, thwart ≠ help

prevention NOUN = **elimination**, safeguard, precaution, thwarting, avoidance, deterrence

preview NOUN = **sample**, sneak preview, trailer, taster, foretaste, advance showing

previous ADJECTIVE 1 = **earlier**, former, past, prior, preceding, erstwhile ≠ later 2 = **preceding**, past, prior, foregoing

previously ADVERB = **before**, earlier, once, in the past, formerly, hitherto, beforehand

prey NOUN 1 = **quarry**, game, kill 2 = **victim**, target, mug (*Brit. slang*), dupe, fall guy (*informal*)

price NOUN 1 = **cost**, value, rate, charge, figure, worth, damage (*informal*), amount 2 = **consequences**, penalty, cost, result, toll, forfeit
▷ VERB = **evaluate**, value, estimate, rate, cost, assess

priceless ADJECTIVE = **valuable**, expensive, precious, invaluable, dear, costly ≠ worthless

prick VERB = **pierce**, stab, puncture, punch, lance, jab, perforate
▷ NOUN = **puncture**, hole, wound, perforation, pinhole

prickly ADJECTIVE 1 = **spiny**, barbed, thorny, bristly 2 = **itchy**, sharp, smarting, stinging, crawling, tingling, scratchy

pride NOUN 1 = **satisfaction**, achievement, fulfilment, delight, content, pleasure, joy,

BIRDS OF PREY

- accipiter
- Australian goshawk or chicken hawk
- bald eagle
- barn owl
- buzzard
- caracara
- condor
- duck hawk
- eagle
- eagle-hawk or wedge-tailed eagle
- falcon or (N.Z.) bush-hawk or karearea
- falconet
- golden eagle
- goshawk
- gyrfalcon or gerfalcon
- harrier
- hawk
- hobby
- honey buzzard
- kestrel
- kite
- lammergeier, lammergeyer, bearded vulture, or (archaic) ossifrage
- lanner
- merlin
- mopoke or (N.Z.) ruru
- osprey, fish eagle, or (archaic) ossifrage
- owl
- peregrine falcon
- saker
- screech owl
- sea eagle, erne, or ern
- secretary bird
- snowy owl
- sparrowhawk
- tawny owl
- turkey buzzard or vulture
- vulture

gratification **2 = self-respect**, honour, ego, dignity, self-esteem, self-image, self-worth **3 = conceit**, vanity, arrogance, pretension, hubris, self-importance, egotism, self-love ≠ humility

priest NOUN **= clergyman**, minister, father, divine, vicar, pastor, cleric, curate

primarily ADVERB **1 = chiefly**, largely, generally, mainly, essentially, mostly, principally, fundamentally **2 = at first**, originally, initially, in the first place, in the beginning, first and foremost, at or from the start

primary ADJECTIVE **= chief**, main, first, highest, greatest, prime, principal, cardinal ≠ subordinate

prime ADJECTIVE **= main**, leading, chief, central, major, key, primary, supreme **2 = best**, top, select, highest, quality, choice, excellent, first-class
▷ NOUN **= peak**, flower, bloom, height, heyday, zenith
▷ VERB **1 = inform**, tell, train, coach, brief, fill in (informal), notify, clue in (informal)
2 = prepare, set up, load, equip, get ready, make ready

P

primitive ADJECTIVE 1 = **early**, first, earliest, original, primary, elementary, primordial, primeval ≠ modern 2 = **crude**, simple, rough, rudimentary, unrefined

prince NOUN = **ruler**, lord, monarch, sovereign, crown prince, liege, prince regent, crowned head

princely ADJECTIVE 1 = **substantial**, considerable, large, huge, massive, enormous, sizable or sizeable 2 = **regal**, royal, imperial, noble, sovereign, majestic

princess NOUN = **ruler**, lady, monarch, sovereign, liege, crowned head, crowned princess, dynast

principal ADJECTIVE = **main**, leading, chief, prime, first, key, essential, primary ≠ minor ▷ NOUN 1 = **headmaster** or **headmistress**, head (informal), dean, head teacher, rector, master or mistress 2 = **star**, lead, leader, prima ballerina, leading man or lady, coryphée 3 = **capital**, money, assets, working capital

principally ADVERB = **mainly**, largely, chiefly, especially, mostly, primarily, predominantly

principle NOUN 1 = **morals**, standards, ideals, honour, virtue, ethics, integrity, conscience, kaupapa (N.Z.) 2 = **rule**, law, truth, precept ▷ PHRASE: **in principle 1** = **in general 2** = **in theory**, ideally, on paper, theoretically, in an ideal world, en principe (French)

● **WORD POWER**
● Principle and principal are often
● confused: the principal (not
● principle) reason for his departure;
● the plan was approved in principle
● (not principal).

print VERB 1 = **run off**, publish, copy, reproduce, issue, engrave 2 = **publish**, release, circulate, issue, disseminate 3 = **mark**, impress, stamp, imprint ▷ NOUN 1 = **photograph**, photo, snap 2 = **picture**, plate, etching, engraving, lithograph, woodcut, linocut 3 = **copy**, photo (informal), picture, reproduction, replica

prior ADJECTIVE = **earlier**, previous, former, preceding, foregoing, pre-existing, pre-existent ▷ PHRASE: **prior to** = **before**, preceding, earlier than, in advance of, previous to

priority NOUN 1 = **prime concern** 2 = **precedence**, preference, primacy, predominance 3 = **supremacy**, rank, precedence, seniority, right of way, pre-eminence

prison NOUN = **jail**, confinement, nick (Brit. slang), cooler (slang), jug (slang), dungeon, clink (slang), gaol, boob (Austral. slang)

prisoner NOUN 1 = **convict**, con (slang), lag (slang), jailbird 2 = **captive**, hostage, detainee, internee

privacy NOUN = **seclusion**, isolation, solitude, retirement, retreat

private ADJECTIVE 1 = **exclusive**, individual, privately owned, own, special, reserved ≠ public 2 = **secret**, confidential, covert, unofficial, clandestine, off the record, hush-hush (*informal*) ≠ public 3 = **personal**, individual, secret, intimate, undisclosed, unspoken, innermost, unvoiced 4 = **secluded**, secret, separate, isolated, sequestered ≠ busy 5 = **solitary**, reserved, retiring, withdrawn, discreet, secretive, self-contained, reclusive ≠ sociable

privilege NOUN = **right**, due, advantage, claim, freedom, liberty, concession, entitlement

privileged ADJECTIVE = **special**, advantaged, favoured, honoured, entitled, elite

prize¹ NOUN 1 = **reward**, cup, award, honour, medal, trophy, accolade 2 = **winnings**, haul, jackpot, stakes, purse ▷ MODIFIER = **champion**, best, winning, top, outstanding, award-winning, first-rate

prize² VERB = **value**, treasure, esteem, cherish, hold dear

prize³ or **prise** VERB 1 = **force**, pull, lever 2 = **drag**, force, draw, wring, extort

probability NOUN 1 = **likelihood**, prospect, chance, odds, expectation, liability, likeliness 2 = **chance**, odds, possibility, likelihood

probable ADJECTIVE = **likely**, possible, apparent, reasonable to think, credible, plausible, feasible, presumable ≠ unlikely

probably ADVERB = **likely**, perhaps, maybe, possibly, presumably, most likely, doubtless, perchance (*archaic*)

probation NOUN = **trial period**, trial, apprenticeship

probe VERB 1 *often with* **into** = **examine**, go into, investigate, explore, search, look into, analyze, dissect 2 = **explore**, examine, poke, prod, feel around ▷ NOUN = **investigation**, study, inquiry, analysis, examination, exploration, scrutiny, scrutinization

problem NOUN 1 = **difficulty**, trouble, dispute, plight, obstacle, dilemma, headache (*informal*), complication 2 = **puzzle**, question, riddle, enigma, conundrum, poser

problematic ADJECTIVE = **tricky**, puzzling, doubtful, dubious, debatable, problematical ≠ clear

procedure NOUN = **method**, policy, process, course, system, action, practice, strategy

proceed VERB 1 = **begin**, go ahead 2 = **continue**, go on, progress, carry on, go ahead, press on, crack on (*informal*) ≠ discontinue 3 = **go on**, continue, progress, carry on, go ahead, move on, move forward, press on, crack on (*informal*) ≠ stop 4 = **arise**, come, issue, result, spring, flow, stem, derive

proceeding NOUN = **action**,

P

process, procedure, move, act, step, measure, deed

proceeds PLURAL NOUN = **income**, profit, revenue, returns, products, gain, earnings, yield

process NOUN 1 = **procedure**, means, course, system, action, performance, operation, measure 2 = **development**, growth, progress, movement, advance, evolution, progression 3 = **method**, system, practice, technique, procedure
▷ VERB = **handle**, manage, action, deal with, fulfil

procession NOUN = **parade**, train, march, file, cavalcade, cortege

proclaim VERB 1 = **announce**, declare, advertise, publish, indicate, herald, circulate, profess ≠ keep secret 2 = **pronounce**, announce, declare

prod VERB 1 = **poke**, push, dig, shove, nudge, jab 2 = **prompt**, move, urge, motivate, spur, stimulate, rouse, incite
▷ NOUN 1 = **poke**, push, dig, shove, nudge, jab 2 = **prompt**, signal, cue, reminder, stimulus

prodigy NOUN = **genius**, talent, wizard, mastermind, whizz (*informal*), up-and-comer (*informal*)

produce VERB 1 = **cause**, effect, generate, bring about, give rise to 2 = **make**, create, develop, manufacture, construct, invent, fabricate 3 = **create**, develop, write, turn out, compose, originate, churn out (*informal*)

4 = **yield**, provide, grow, bear, give, supply, afford, render 5 = **bring forth**, bear, deliver, breed, give birth to, beget, bring into the world 6 = **show**, provide, present, advance, demonstrate, offer, come up with, exhibit 7 = **display**, show, present, proffer 8 = **present**, stage, direct, put on, do, show, mount, exhibit
▷ NOUN = **fruit and vegetables**, goods, food, products, crops, yield, harvest, greengrocery (*Brit.*)

producer NOUN 1 = **director**, promoter, impresario 2 = **maker**, manufacturer, builder, creator, fabricator 3 = **grower**, farmer

product NOUN 1 = **goods**, produce, creation, commodity, invention, merchandise, artefact 2 = **result**, consequence, effect, outcome, upshot

production NOUN 1 = **producing**, making, manufacture, manufacturing, construction, formation, fabrication 2 = **creation**, development, fashioning, composition, origination 3 = **management**, administration, direction 4 = **presentation**, staging, mounting

productive ADJECTIVE 1 = **fertile**, rich, prolific, plentiful, fruitful, fecund ≠ barren 2 = **creative**, inventive 3 = **useful**, rewarding, valuable, profitable, effective, worthwhile, beneficial, constructive ≠ useless

productivity NOUN = **output**,

production, capacity, yield, efficiency, work rate

profess VERB 1 = **claim**, allege, pretend, fake, make out, purport, feign 2 = **state**, admit, announce, declare, confess, assert, proclaim, affirm

professed ADJECTIVE
1 = **supposed**, would-be, alleged, so-called, pretended, purported, self-styled, ostensible
2 = **declared**, confirmed, confessed, proclaimed, self-confessed, avowed, self-acknowledged

profession NOUN = **occupation**, calling, business, career, employment, office, position, sphere

professional ADJECTIVE
1 = **qualified**, trained, skilled, white-collar 2 = **expert**, experienced, skilled, masterly, efficient, competent, adept, proficient ≠ amateurish
▷ NOUN = **expert**, master, pro (*informal*), specialist, guru, adept, maestro, virtuoso, fundi (*S. African*)

professor NOUN = **don** (*Brit.*), fellow (*Brit.*), prof (*informal*)

profile NOUN 1 = **outline**, lines, form, figure, silhouette, contour, side view 2 = **biography**, sketch, vignette, characterization, thumbnail sketch

profit NOUN 1 *often plural* = **earnings**, return, revenue, gain, yield, proceeds, receipts, takings ≠ loss 2 = **benefit**, good,

use, value, gain, advantage, advancement ≠ disadvantage
▷ VERB 1 = **make money**, gain, earn 2 = **benefit**, help, serve, gain, promote, be of advantage to

profitable ADJECTIVE 1 = **money-making**, lucrative, paying, commercial, worthwhile, cost-effective, fruitful, remunerative
2 = **beneficial**, useful, rewarding, valuable, productive, worthwhile, fruitful, advantageous ≠ useless

profound ADJECTIVE 1 = **sincere**, acute, intense, great, keen, extreme, heartfelt, deeply felt ≠ insincere 2 = **wise**, learned, deep, penetrating, philosophical, sage, abstruse, sagacious ≠ uninformed

programme NOUN 1 = **schedule**, plan, agenda, timetable, listing, list, line-up, calendar 2 = **course**, curriculum, syllabus 3 = **show**, performance, production, broadcast, episode, presentation, transmission, telecast, podcast

progress NOUN 1 = **development**, growth, advance, gain, improvement, breakthrough, headway ≠ regression
2 = **movement forward**, passage, advancement, course, advance, headway ≠ movement backward
▷ VERB 1 = **move on**, continue, travel, advance, proceed, go forward, make headway, crack on (*informal*) ≠ move back
2 = **develop**, improve, advance, grow, gain ≠ get behind
▷ PHRASE: in progress = **going**

P

on, happening, continuing, being done, occurring, taking place, proceeding, under way

progression NOUN 1 = **progress**, advance, advancement, gain, headway, furtherance, movement forward 2 = **sequence**, course, series, chain, cycle, string, succession

progressive ADJECTIVE
1 = **enlightened**, liberal, modern, advanced, radical, revolutionary, avant-garde, reformist
2 = **growing**, continuing, increasing, developing, advancing, ongoing

prohibit VERB 1 = **forbid**, ban, veto, outlaw, disallow, proscribe, debar ≠ permit 2 = **prevent**, restrict, stop, hamper, hinder, impede ≠ allow

prohibition NOUN = **ban**, boycott, embargo, bar, veto, prevention, exclusion, injunction, restraining order (*U.S. law*)

project NOUN 1 = **scheme**, plan, job, idea, campaign, operation, activity, venture 2 = **assignment**, task, homework, piece of research
▷ VERB 1 = **forecast**, expect, estimate, predict, reckon, calculate, gauge, extrapolate
2 = **stick out**, extend, stand out, bulge, protrude, overhang, jut

projection NOUN = **forecast**, estimate, reckoning, calculation, estimation, computation, extrapolation

proliferation NOUN
= **multiplication**, increase, spread, expansion

prolific ADJECTIVE 1 = **productive**, creative, fertile, inventive, copious 2 = **fruitful**, fertile, abundant, luxuriant, profuse, fecund ≠ unproductive

prolong VERB = **lengthen**, continue, perpetuate, draw out, extend, delay, stretch out, spin out ≠ shorten

prominence NOUN 1 = **fame**, name, reputation, importance, celebrity, distinction, prestige, eminence 2 = **conspicuousness**, markedness

prominent ADJECTIVE
1 = **famous**, leading, top, important, main, distinguished, well-known, notable ≠ unknown
2 = **noticeable**, obvious, outstanding, pronounced, conspicuous, eye-catching, obtrusive ≠ inconspicuous

promise VERB 1 = **guarantee**, pledge, vow, swear, contract, assure, undertake, warrant
2 = **seem likely**, look like, show signs of, augur, betoken
▷ NOUN 1 = **guarantee**, word, bond, vow, commitment, pledge, undertaking, assurance
2 = **potential**, ability, talent, capacity, capability, aptitude

promising ADJECTIVE
1 = **encouraging**, likely, bright, reassuring, hopeful, favourable, rosy, auspicious ≠ unpromising
2 = **talented**, able, gifted, rising

promote VERB 1 = **help**, back, support, aid, forward, encourage,

advance, boost ≠ impede
2 = **advertise**, sell, hype, publicize, push, plug (*informal*)
3 = **raise**, upgrade, elevate, exalt ≠ demote

promotion NOUN 1 = **rise**, upgrading, move up, advancement, elevation, exaltation, preferment
2 = **publicity**, advertising, plugging (*informal*)
3 = **encouragement**, support, boosting, advancement, furtherance

prompt VERB 1 = **cause**, occasion, provoke, give rise to, elicit
2 = **remind**, assist, cue, help out
▷ ADJECTIVE = **immediate**, quick, rapid, instant, timely, early, swift, speedy ≠ slow
▷ ADVERB (*informal*) = **exactly**, sharp, promptly, on the dot, punctually

promptly ADVERB
1 = **immediately**, swiftly, directly, quickly, at once, speedily
2 = **punctually**, on time, spot on (*informal*), bang on (*informal*), on the dot, on the button (*U.S.*), on the nail

prone ADJECTIVE 1 = **liable**, given, subject, inclined, tending, bent, disposed, susceptible ≠ disinclined 2 = **face down**, flat, horizontal, prostrate, recumbent ≠ face up

pronounce VERB 1 = **say**, speak, sound, articulate, enunciate
2 = **declare**, announce, deliver, proclaim, decree, affirm

pronounced ADJECTIVE
= **noticeable**, decided, marked, striking, obvious, evident, distinct, definite ≠ imperceptible

proof NOUN = **evidence**, demonstration, testimony, confirmation, verification, corroboration, authentication, substantiation
▷ ADJECTIVE = **impervious**, strong, resistant, impenetrable, repellent

prop VERB 1 = **lean**, place, set, stand, position, rest, lay, balance
2 *often with* **up** = **support**, sustain, hold up, brace, uphold, bolster, buttress
▷ NOUN 1 = **support**, stay, brace, mainstay, buttress, stanchion
2 = **mainstay**, support, sustainer, anchor, backbone, cornerstone, upholder

propaganda NOUN
= **information**, advertising, promotion, publicity, hype, disinformation

propel VERB 1 = **drive**, launch, force, send, shoot, push, thrust, shove ≠ stop 2 = **impel**, drive, push, prompt, spur, motivate ≠ hold back

proper ADJECTIVE 1 = **real**, actual, genuine, true, bona fide, dinkum (*Austral. & N.Z. informal*) 2 = **correct**, accepted, established, appropriate, right, formal, conventional, precise ≠ improper 3 = **polite**, right, becoming, seemly, fitting, fit, mannerly, suitable ≠ unseemly

P

properly ADVERB 1 = **correctly**, rightly, fittingly, appropriately, accurately, suitably, aptly ≠ incorrectly 2 = **politely**, decently, respectably ≠ badly

property NOUN 1 = **possessions**, goods, effects, holdings, capital, riches, estate, assets 2 = **land**, holding, estate, real estate, freehold 3 = **quality**, feature, characteristic, attribute, trait, hallmark

prophecy NOUN 1 = **prediction**, forecast, prognostication, augury 2 = **second sight**, divination, augury, telling the future, soothsaying

prophet or **prophetess** NOUN = **soothsayer**, forecaster, diviner, oracle, seer, sibyl, prophesier

proportion NOUN 1 = **part**, share, amount, division, percentage, segment, quota, fraction 2 = **relative amount**, relationship, ratio 3 = **balance**, harmony, correspondence, symmetry, concord, congruity ▷ PLURAL NOUN = **dimensions**, size, volume, capacity, extent, expanse

proportional or **proportionate** ADJECTIVE = **correspondent**, corresponding, even, balanced, consistent, compatible, equitable, in proportion ≠ disproportionate

proposal NOUN = **suggestion**, plan, programme, scheme, offer, project, bid, recommendation

propose VERB 1 = **put forward**, present, suggest, advance, submit 2 = **intend**, mean, plan, aim, design, scheme, have in mind 3 = **nominate**, name, present, recommend 4 = **offer marriage**, pop the question (*informal*), ask for someone's hand (in marriage)

proposition NOUN 1 = **task**, problem, activity, job, affair, venture, undertaking 2 = **theory**, idea, argument, concept, thesis, hypothesis, theorem, premiss 3 = **proposal**, plan, suggestion, scheme, bid, recommendation 4 = **advance**, pass (*informal*), proposal, overture, improper suggestion, come-on (*informal*) ▷ VERB = **make a pass at**, solicit, accost, make an improper suggestion to

proprietor or **proprietress** NOUN = **owner**, titleholder, landlord or landlady

prosecute VERB (*law*) = **take someone to court**, try, sue, indict, arraign, put someone on trial, litigate, bring someone to trial

prospect NOUN 1 = **likelihood**, chance, possibility, hope, promise, odds, expectation, probability 2 = **idea**, outlook 3 = **view**, landscape, scene, sight, outlook, spectacle, vista ▷ PLURAL NOUN = **possibilities**, chances, future, potential, expectations, outlook, scope ▷ VERB = **look**, search, seek, dowse

prospective ADJECTIVE

1 = **potential**, possible

2 = **expected**, coming, future, likely, intended, anticipated, forthcoming, imminent

prospectus NOUN = **catalogue**, list, programme, outline, syllabus, synopsis

prosper VERB = **succeed**, advance, progress, thrive, get on, do well, flourish

prosperity NOUN = **success**, riches, plenty, fortune, wealth, luxury, good fortune, affluence ≠ poverty

prosperous ADJECTIVE
1 = **wealthy**, rich, affluent, well-off, well-heeled (*informal*), well-to-do, moneyed, minted (*Brit. slang*) ≠ poor 2 = **successful**, booming, thriving, flourishing, doing well ≠ unsuccessful

prostitute NOUN = **whore**, hooker (*U.S. slang*), pro (*slang*), tart (*informal*), call girl, harlot, streetwalker, loose woman
▷ VERB = **cheapen**, sell out, pervert, degrade, devalue, squander, demean, debase

protagonist NOUN
1 = **supporter**, champion, advocate, exponent 2 = **leading character**, principal, central character, hero *or* heroine

protect VERB = **keep someone safe**, defend, support, save, guard, preserve, look after, shelter ≠ endanger

protection NOUN 1 = **safety**, care, defence, protecting, security, custody, safeguard,

aegis 2 = **safeguard**, cover, guard, shelter, screen, barrier, shield, buffer 3 = **armour**, cover, screen, barrier, shelter, shield

protective ADJECTIVE
1 = **protecting** 2 = **caring**, defensive, motherly, fatherly, maternal, vigilant, watchful, paternal

protector NOUN 1 = **defender**, champion, guard, guardian, patron, bodyguard 2 = **guard**, screen, protection, shield, pad, cushion, buffer

protest VERB 1 = **object**, demonstrate, oppose, complain, disagree, cry out, disapprove, demur 2 = **assert**, insist, maintain, declare, affirm, profess, attest, avow
▷ NOUN 1 = **demonstration**, march, rally, sit-in, demo (*informal*), hikoi (*N.Z.*)
2 = **objection**, complaint, dissent, outcry, protestation, remonstrance

protocol NOUN = **code of behaviour**, manners, conventions, customs, etiquette, propriety, decorum

prototype NOUN = **original**, model, first, example, standard

protracted ADJECTIVE
= **extended**, prolonged, drawn-out, spun out, dragged out, long-drawn-out

proud ADJECTIVE 1 = **satisfied**, pleased, content, thrilled, glad, gratified, joyful, well-pleased ≠ dissatisfied 2 = **conceited**,

P

arrogant, lordly, imperious,
overbearing, haughty, snobbish,
self-satisfied ≠ humble

prove VERB 1 = **turn out**, come
out, end up 2 = **verify**, establish,
determine, show, confirm,
demonstrate, justify, substantiate
≠ disprove

proven ADJECTIVE = **established**,
proved, confirmed, tested,
reliable, definite, verified,
attested

provide VERB 1 = **supply**, give,
distribute, outfit, equip, donate,
furnish, dispense ≠ withhold
2 = **give**, bring, add, produce,
present, serve, afford, yield
▷ PHRASES: **provide for someone**
= **support**, care for, keep,
maintain, sustain, take care of,
fend for; **provide for something**
followed by **for** *or* **against** = **take
precautions against**, plan for,
prepare for, anticipate, plan ahead
for, forearm for

provider NOUN 1 = **supplier**, giver,
source, donor 2 = **breadwinner**,
supporter, earner, wage earner

providing *or* **provided**
CONJUNCTION *often with* **that**
= **on condition that**, if, given that,
as long as

province NOUN = **region**, section,
district, zone, patch, colony,
domain

provincial ADJECTIVE
1 = **regional**, state, local, county,
district, territorial, parochial
2 = **rural**, country, local, rustic,
homespun, hick (*informal, chiefly*

U.S. & Canad.), backwoods
≠ urban 3 = **parochial**, insular,
narrow-minded, unsophisticated,
limited, narrow, small-town
(*chiefly U.S.*), inward-looking
≠ cosmopolitan

provision NOUN 1 = **supplying**,
giving, providing, supply,
delivery, distribution, catering,
presentation 2 = **condition**,
term, requirement, demand, rider,
restriction, qualification, clause
▷ PLURAL NOUN = **food**, supplies,
stores, fare, rations, foodstuff, kai
(*N.Z. informal*), victuals, edibles

provisional ADJECTIVE
1 = **temporary**, interim
≠ permanent 2 = **conditional**,
limited, qualified, contingent,
tentative ≠ definite

provocation NOUN 1 = **cause**,
reason, grounds, motivation,
stimulus, incitement 2 = **offence**,
challenge, insult, taunt, injury,
dare, grievance, annoyance

provocative ADJECTIVE
= **offensive**, provoking, insulting,
stimulating, annoying, galling,
goading

provoke VERB 1 = **anger**,
annoy, irritate, infuriate, hassle
(*informal*), aggravate (*informal*),
incense, enrage ≠ pacify
2 = **rouse**, cause, produce,
promote, occasion, prompt, stir,
induce ≠ curb

prowess NOUN 1 = **skill**, ability,
talent, expertise, genius,
excellence, accomplishment,
mastery ≠ inability 2 = **bravery**,

daring, courage, heroism, mettle, valour, fearlessness, valiance ≠ cowardice

proximity NOUN = **nearness**, closeness

proxy NOUN = **representative**, agent, deputy, substitute, factor, delegate

prudent ADJECTIVE 1 = **cautious**, careful, wary, discreet, vigilant ≠ careless 2 = **wise**, politic, sensible, shrewd, discerning, judicious ≠ unwise 3 = **thrifty**, economical, sparing, careful, canny, provident, frugal, far-sighted ≠ extravagant

prune VERB 1 = **cut**, trim, clip, dock, shape, shorten, snip 2 = **reduce**, cut, cut back, trim, cut down, pare down, make reductions in

psyche NOUN = **soul**, mind, self, spirit, personality, individuality, anima, wairua (*N.Z.*)

psychiatrist NOUN = **psychotherapist**, analyst, therapist, psychologist, shrink (*slang*), psychoanalyst, headshrinker (*slang*)

psychic ADJECTIVE 1 = **supernatural**, mystic, occult 2 = **mystical**, spiritual, magical, other-worldly, paranormal, preternatural 3 = **psychological**, emotional, mental, spiritual, inner, psychiatric, cognitive ▷ NOUN = **clairvoyant**, fortune teller

psychological ADJECTIVE 1 = **mental**, emotional, intellectual, inner, cognitive, cerebral 2 = **imaginary**, psychosomatic, irrational, unreal, all in the mind

psychology NOUN 1 = **behaviourism**, study of personality, science of mind 2 (*informal*) = **way of thinking**, attitude, behaviour, temperament, mentality, thought processes, mental processes, what makes you tick

pub or **public house** NOUN = **tavern**, bar, inn, saloon, beer parlour (*Canad.*), beverage room (*Canad.*)

public NOUN = **people**, society, community, nation, everyone, citizens, electorate, populace ▷ ADJECTIVE 1 = **civic**, government, state, national, local, official, community, social 2 = **general**, popular, national, shared, common, widespread, universal, collective 3 = **open**, accessible, communal, unrestricted ≠ private 4 = **well-known**, leading, important, respected, famous, celebrated, recognized, distinguished 5 = **known**, open, obvious, acknowledged, plain, patent, overt ≠ secret

publication NOUN 1 = **pamphlet**, newspaper, magazine, issue, title, leaflet, brochure, periodical, blog (*informal*) 2 = **announcement**, publishing, broadcasting, reporting, declaration, disclosure, proclamation, notification

p

publicity NOUN 1 = **advertising**, press, promotion, hype, boost, plug (*informal*) 2 = **attention**, exposure, fame, celebrity, fuss, public interest, limelight, notoriety

publish VERB 1 = **put out**, issue, produce, print 2 = **announce**, reveal, spread, advertise, broadcast, disclose, proclaim, circulate

pudding NOUN = **dessert**, afters (*Brit. informal*), sweet, pud (*informal*)

puff VERB 1 = **smoke**, draw, drag (*slang*), suck, inhale, pull at *or* on 2 = **breathe heavily**, pant, exhale, blow, gasp, gulp, wheeze, fight for breath
▷ NOUN 1 = **drag**, pull (*slang*), moke 2 = **blast**, breath, whiff, draught, gust

pull VERB 1 = **draw**, haul, drag, trail, tow, tug, jerk, yank ≠ push 2 = **extract**, pick, remove, gather, take out, pluck, uproot, draw out ≠ insert 3 (*informal*) = **attract**, draw, bring in, tempt, lure, interest, entice, pull in ≠ repel 4 = **strain**, tear, stretch, rip, wrench, dislocate, sprain
▷ NOUN 1 = **tug**, jerk, yank, twitch, heave ≠ shove 2 = **puff**, drag (*slang*), inhalation 3 (*informal*) = **influence**, power, weight, muscle, clout (*informal*), kai (*N.Z. informal*) ▷ PHRASES: **pull out (of)** 1 = **withdraw**, quit 2 = **leave**, abandon, get out, quit, retreat from, depart, evacuate;

pull someone up = **reprimand**, rebuke, admonish, read the riot act to, tell someone off (*informal*), reprove, bawl someone out (*informal*), tear someone off a strip (*Brit. informal*); **pull something off** (*informal*) = **succeed in**, manage, carry out, accomplish; **pull something out** = **produce**, draw, bring out, draw out; **pull up** = **stop**, halt, brake

pulp NOUN 1 = **paste**, mash, mush 2 = **flesh**, meat, soft part
▷ MODIFIER = **cheap**, lurid, trashy, rubbishy
▷ VERB = **crush**, squash, mash, pulverize

pulse NOUN = **beat**, rhythm, vibration, beating, throb, throbbing, pulsation
▷ VERB = **beat**, throb, vibrate, pulsate

pump VERB 1 = **supply**, send, pour, inject 2 = **interrogate**, probe, quiz, cross-examine

punch[1] VERB = **hit**, strike, box, smash, belt (*informal*), sock (*slang*), swipe (*informal*), bop (*informal*)
▷ NOUN 1 = **blow**, hit, sock (*slang*), jab, swipe (*informal*), bop (*informal*), wallop (*informal*) 2 (*informal*) = **effectiveness**, bite, impact, drive, vigour, verve, forcefulness

punch[2] VERB = **pierce**, cut, bore, drill, stamp, puncture, prick, perforate

punctuate VERB = **interrupt**, break, pepper, sprinkle, intersperse

puncture NOUN 1 = **flat tyre**, flat, flattie (*N.Z.*) 2 = **hole**, opening, break, cut, nick, leak, slit
▷ VERB = **pierce**, cut, nick, penetrate, prick, rupture, perforate, bore a hole

punish VERB = **discipline**, correct, castigate, chastise, sentence, chasten, penalize

punishing ADJECTIVE = **hard**, taxing, wearing, tiring, exhausting, gruelling, strenuous, arduous ≠ easy

punishment NOUN
1 = **penalizing**, discipline, correction, retribution, chastening, chastisement
2 = **penalty**, penance

punitive ADJECTIVE = **retaliatory**, in reprisal, retaliative

punt VERB = **bet**, back, stake, gamble, lay, wager
▷ NOUN = **bet**, stake, gamble, wager

punter NOUN 1 = **gambler**, better, backer 2 (*informal*) = **person**, man in the street

pupil NOUN 1 = **student**, schoolboy *or* schoolgirl, schoolchild ≠ teacher
2 = **learner**, novice, beginner, disciple ≠ instructor

puppet NOUN 1 = **marionette**, doll, glove puppet, finger puppet
2 = **pawn**, tool, instrument, mouthpiece, stooge, cat's-paw

purchase VERB = **buy**, pay for, obtain, get, score (*slang*), gain, pick up, acquire ≠ sell
▷ NOUN 1 = **acquisition**, buy,

investment, property, gain, asset, possession 2 = **grip**, hold, support, leverage, foothold

pure ADJECTIVE 1 = **unmixed**, real, simple, natural, straight, genuine, neat, authentic ≠ adulterated 2 = **clean**, wholesome, sanitary, spotless, sterilized, squeaky-clean, untainted, uncontaminated ≠ contaminated 3 = **complete**, total, perfect, absolute, sheer, patent, utter, outright ≠ qualified 4 = **innocent**, modest, good, moral, impeccable, righteous, virtuous, squeaky-clean ≠ corrupt

purely ADVERB = **absolutely**, just, only, completely, simply, entirely, exclusively, merely

purge VERB 1 = **rid**, clear, cleanse, strip, empty, void 2 = **get rid of**, remove, expel, wipe out, eradicate, do away with, exterminate
▷ NOUN = **removal**, elimination, expulsion, eradication, ejection

purity NOUN 1 = **cleanness**, cleanliness, wholesomeness, pureness, faultlessness, immaculateness ≠ impurity
2 = **innocence**, virtue, integrity, honesty, decency, virginity, chastity, chasteness ≠ immorality

purport VERB = **claim**, allege, assert, profess

purpose NOUN 1 = **reason**, point, idea, aim, object, intention 2 = **aim**, end, plan,

p

SHADES OF PURPLE

- amethyst
- aubergine
- burgundy
- claret
- heather
- indigo
- lavender
- lilac
- magenta
- mauve
- mulberry
- plum
- puce
- Tyrian purple
- violet
- wine

hope, goal, wish, desire, object **3** = **determination**, resolve, will, resolution, ambition, persistence, tenacity, firmness ▷ **PHRASE**: **on purpose** = **deliberately**, purposely, intentionally, knowingly, designedly

WORD POWER

The two concepts *purposeful* and *on purpose* should be carefully distinguished. *On purpose* and *purposely* have roughly the same meaning, and imply that a person's action is deliberate, rather than accidental. However, *purposeful* and its related adverb *purposefully* refer to the way that someone acts as being full of purpose or determination.

purposely ADVERB = **deliberately**, expressly, consciously, intentionally, knowingly, with intent, on purpose ≠ accidentally

purse NOUN **1** = **pouch**, wallet, money-bag **2** (*U.S.*) = **handbag**, bag, shoulder bag, pocket book, clutch bag **3** = **funds**, means, money, resources, treasury, wealth, exchequer
  ▷ **VERB** = **pucker**, contract,

tighten, pout, press together

pursue VERB **1** = **engage in**, perform, conduct, carry on, practise **2** = **try for**, seek, desire, search for, aim for, work towards, strive for **3** = **continue**, maintain, carry on, keep on, persist in, proceed in, persevere in **4** = **follow**, track, hunt, chase, dog, shadow, tail (*informal*), hound ≠ flee

pursuit NOUN **1** = **quest**, seeking, search, aim of, aspiration for, striving towards **2** = **pursuing**, seeking, search, hunt, chase, trailing **3** = **occupation**, activity, interest, line, pleasure, hobby, pastime

push VERB **1** = **shove**, force, press, thrust, drive, knock, sweep, plunge ≠ pull **2** = **press**, operate, depress, squeeze, activate, hold down **3** = **make** *or* **force your way**, move, shoulder, inch, squeeze, thrust, elbow, shove **4** = **urge**, encourage, persuade, spur, press, incite, impel ≠ discourage
  ▷ **NOUN 1** = **shove**, thrust, butt, elbow, nudge ≠ pull **2** (*informal*) = **drive**, go (*informal*), energy, initiative, enterprise, ambition,

vitality, vigour ▷ **PHRASE: the push** (*informal, chiefly Brit.*) =**dismissal**, the sack (*informal*), discharge, the boot (*slang*), your cards (*informal*)

put VERB 1 =**place**, leave, set, position, rest, park (*informal*), plant, lay 2 =**express**, state, word, phrase, utter ▷ **PHRASES: put someone off** 1 =**discourage**, intimidate, deter, daunt, dissuade, demoralize, scare off, dishearten 2 =**disconcert**, confuse, unsettle, throw (*informal*), dismay, perturb, faze, discomfit; **put someone up** 1 =**accommodate**, house, board, lodge, quarter, take someone in, billet 2 =**nominate**, put forward, offer, present, propose, recommend, submit; **put something across** *or* **over** =**communicate**, explain, convey, make clear, get across, make yourself understood; **put something off** =**postpone**, delay, defer, adjourn, hold over, put on the back burner (*informal*), take a rain check on (*U.S. & Canad. informal*); **put something up** 1 =**build**, raise, set up, construct, erect, fabricate 2 =**offer**, present, mount, put forward

puzzle VERB =**perplex**, confuse, baffle, stump, bewilder, confound, mystify, faze
▷ **NOUN** 1 =**problem**, riddle, question, conundrum, poser 2 =**mystery**, problem, paradox, enigma, conundrum

puzzling ADJECTIVE =**perplexing**, baffling, bewildering, involved, enigmatic, incomprehensible, mystifying, abstruse ≠ simple

p

Qq

quake VERB = **shake**, tremble, quiver, move, rock, shiver, shudder, vibrate

qualification NOUN 1 = **eligibility**, quality, ability, skill, fitness, attribute, capability, aptitude 2 = **condition**, proviso, requirement, rider, reservation, limitation, modification, caveat

qualified ADJECTIVE 1 = **capable**, trained, experienced, seasoned, able, fit, expert, chartered ≠ untrained 2 = **restricted**, limited, provisional, conditional, reserved, bounded, adjusted, moderated ≠ unconditional

qualify VERB 1 = **certify**, equip, empower, train, prepare, fit, ready, permit ≠ disqualify 2 = **restrict**, limit, reduce, ease, moderate, regulate, diminish, temper

quality NOUN 1 = **standard**, standing, class, condition, rank, grade, merit, classification 2 = **excellence**, status, merit, position, value, worth, distinction, virtue 3 = **characteristic**, feature, attribute, point, side, mark, property, aspect 4 = **nature**, character, make, sort, kind

quantity NOUN 1 = **amount**, lot, total, sum, part, number 2 = **size**, measure, mass, volume, length, capacity, extent, bulk

- WORD POWER
- The use of a plural noun
- after *quantity of*, as in *a large*
- *quantity of bananas*, used to
- be considered incorrect,
- the objection being that
- the word *quantity* should
- only be used to refer to an
- uncountable amount, which
- was grammatically regarded as
- a singular concept. Nowadays,
- however, most people consider
- the use of *quantity* with a plural
- noun to be acceptable.

quarrel NOUN = **disagreement**, fight, row, argument, dispute, controversy, breach, contention, biffo (*Austral. slang*) ≠ accord ▷ VERB = **disagree**, fight, argue, row, clash, dispute, differ, fall out (*informal*) ≠ get on *or* along (with)

quarry NOUN = **prey**, victim, game, goal, aim, prize, objective

quarter NOUN 1 = **district**, region, neighbourhood, place, part, side, area, zone 2 = **mercy**, pity, compassion, charity, sympathy, tolerance, kindness, forgiveness ▷ VERB = **accommodate**, house, lodge, place, board, post, station, billet

quarters PLURAL NOUN = **lodgings**, rooms, chambers, residence, dwelling, barracks, abode, habitation

quash VERB 1 = **annul**, overturn, reverse, cancel, overthrow,

revoke, overrule, rescind
2 = **suppress**, crush, put down,
beat, overthrow, squash, subdue,
repress

queen NOUN **1** = **sovereign**, ruler,
monarch, leader, Crown, princess,
majesty, head of state **2** = **leading
light**, star, favourite, celebrity,
darling, mistress, big name

queer ADJECTIVE **1** = **strange**, odd,
funny, unusual, extraordinary,
curious, weird, peculiar ≠ normal
2 = **faint**, dizzy, giddy, queasy,
light-headed

● **WORD POWER**

● Although the term *queer*
● meaning 'gay' is still considered
● derogatory when used by
● non-gays, it is now being used
● by gay people themselves
● as a positive term in certain
● contexts, such as *queer politics*,
● *queer cinema*. Nevertheless,
● many gay people would not
● wish to have the term applied
● to them, nor would they use it
● of themselves.

query NOUN **1** = **question**, inquiry,
problem **2** = **doubt**, suspicion,
objection
▷ VERB **1** = **question**, challenge,
doubt, suspect, dispute, object to,
distrust, mistrust **2** = **ask**, inquire
or enquire, question

quest NOUN **1** = **search**, hunt,
mission, enterprise, crusade
2 = **expedition**, journey,
adventure

question NOUN **1** = **inquiry**,
enquiry, query, investigation,

examination, interrogation
≠ answer **2** = **difficulty**, problem,
doubt, argument, dispute,
controversy, query, contention
3 = **issue**, point, matter, subject,
problem, debate, proposal, theme
▷ VERB **1** = **interrogate**, cross-
examine, interview, examine,
probe, quiz, ask questions
2 = **dispute**, challenge, doubt,
suspect, oppose, query,
mistrust, disbelieve ≠ accept
▷ PHRASE: **out of the question**
= **impossible**, unthinkable,
inconceivable, not on (*informal*),
hopeless, unimaginable,
unworkable, unattainable

questionable ADJECTIVE
= **dubious**, suspect, doubtful,
controversial, suspicious, dodgy
(*Brit., Austral. & N.Z. informal*),
debatable, moot, shonky (*Austral.
& N.Z. informal*) ≠ indisputable

queue NOUN = **line**, row, file, train,
series, chain, string, column

quick ADJECTIVE **1** = **fast**, swift,
speedy, express, cracking
(*Brit. informal*), smart, rapid,
fleet ≠ slow **2** = **brief**, passing,
hurried, flying, fleeting, summary,
lightning, short-lived ≠ long
3 = **immediate**, instant, prompt,
sudden, abrupt, instantaneous
4 = **excitable**, passionate,
irritable, touchy, irascible, testy
≠ calm **5** = **intelligent**, bright
(*informal*), alert, sharp, acute,
smart, clever, shrewd ≠ stupid

quicken VERB **1** = **speed up**,
hurry, accelerate, hasten, gee up

q

(*informal*) **2** = **stimulate**, inspire, arouse, excite, revive, incite, energize, invigorate

quickly ADVERB **1** = **swiftly**, rapidly, hurriedly, fast, hastily, briskly, apace ≠ slowly
2 = **soon**, speedily, as soon as possible, momentarily (*U.S.*), instantaneously, pronto (*informal*), a.s.a.p. (*informal*)
3 = **immediately**, at once, directly, promptly, abruptly, without delay

quiet ADJECTIVE **1** = **soft**, low, muted, lowered, whispered, faint, suppressed, stifled ≠ loud
2 = **peaceful**, silent, hushed, soundless, noiseless ≠ noisy
3 = **calm**, peaceful, tranquil, mild, serene, placid, restful, chilled (*informal*) ≠ exciting
4 = **still**, calm, peaceful, tranquil ≠ troubled **5** = **undisturbed**, isolated, secluded, private, sequestered, unfrequented ≠ crowded **6** = **silent**
7 = **reserved**, retiring, shy, gentle, mild, sedate, meek ≠ excitable
▷ NOUN = **peace**, rest, tranquillity, ease, silence, solitude, serenity, stillness ≠ noise

quietly ADVERB **1** = **noiselessly**, silently **2** = **softly**, inaudibly, in an undertone, under your breath
3 = **calmly**, serenely, placidly, patiently, mildly **4** = **silently**, mutely

quilt NOUN = **bedspread**, duvet, coverlet, eiderdown, counterpane, doona (*Austral.*), continental quilt

quip NOUN = **joke**, sally, jest, riposte, wisecrack (*informal*), retort, pleasantry, gibe

quirky ADJECTIVE = **odd**, unusual, eccentric, idiosyncratic, peculiar, offbeat

quit VERB **1** = **resign (from)**, leave, retire (from), pull out (of), step down (from) (*informal*), abdicate
2 = **stop**, give up, cease, end, drop, abandon, halt, discontinue ≠ continue **3** = **leave**, depart from, go out of, go away from, pull out from

quite ADVERB **1** = **somewhat**, rather, fairly, reasonably, relatively, moderately
2 = **absolutely**, perfectly, completely, totally, fully, entirely, wholly

quiz NOUN = **examination**, questioning, interrogation, interview, investigation, grilling (*informal*), cross-examination, cross-questioning
▷ VERB = **question**, ask, interrogate, examine, investigate

quota NOUN = **share**, allowance, ration, part, limit, slice, quantity, portion

quotation NOUN **1** = **passage**, quote (*informal*), excerpt, reference, extract, citation **2** (*commerce*) = **estimate**, price, tender, rate, cost, charge, figure, quote (*informal*)

quote VERB **1** = **repeat**, recite, recall **2** = **refer to**, cite, give, name, detail, relate, mention, instance

Rr

race¹ NOUN 1 = **competition**, contest, chase, dash, pursuit 2 = **contest**, competition, rivalry ▷ VERB 1 = **compete against**, run against 2 = **compete**, run, contend, take part in a race 3 = **run**, fly, career, speed, tear, dash, hurry, dart

race² NOUN = **people**, nation, blood, stock, type, folk, tribe

racial ADJECTIVE = **ethnic**, ethnological, national, folk, genetic, tribal, genealogical

rack NOUN = **frame**, stand, structure, framework ▷ VERB = **torture**, torment, afflict, oppress, harrow, crucify, agonize, pain

> ⦿ **WORD POWER**
> ⦿ The use of the spelling *wrack*
> ⦿ rather than *rack* in sentences
> ⦿ such as *she was wracked by grief*
> ⦿ or *the country was wracked by*
> ⦿ *civil war* is very common, but is
> ⦿ thought by many people to be
> ⦿ incorrect.

racket NOUN 1 = **noise**, row, fuss, disturbance, outcry, clamour, din, pandemonium 2 = **fraud**, scheme

radiate VERB 1 = **emit**, spread, send out, pour, shed, scatter 2 = **shine**, be diffused 3 = **show**, display, demonstrate, exhibit, emanate, give off *or* out 4 = **spread out**, diverge, branch out

radical ADJECTIVE 1 = **extreme**, complete, entire, sweeping, severe, thorough, drastic 2 = **revolutionary**, extremist, fanatical 3 = **fundamental**, natural, basic, profound, innate, deep-seated ≠ superficial ▷ NOUN = **extremist**, revolutionary, militant, fanatic ≠ conservative

rage NOUN 1 = **fury**, temper, frenzy, rampage, tantrum, foulie (*Austral. slang*), hissy fit (*informal*), strop (*Brit. informal*) ≠ calmness 2 = **anger**, passion, madness, wrath, ire 3 = **craze**, fashion, enthusiasm, vogue, fad (*informal*), latest thing ▷ VERB = **be furious**, blow up (*informal*), fume, lose it (*informal*), seethe, lose the plot (*informal*), go ballistic (*slang, chiefly U.S.*), lose your temper ≠ stay calm

ragged ADJECTIVE 1 = **tatty**, worn, torn, rundown, shabby, seedy, scruffy, in tatters ≠ smart 2 = **rough**, rugged, unfinished, uneven, jagged, serrated

raid VERB 1 = **steal from**, plunder, pillage, sack 2 = **attack**, invade, assault 3 = **make a search of**, search, bust (*informal*), make a raid on, make a swoop on ▷ NOUN 1 = **attack**, invasion, foray, sortie, incursion, sally, inroad 2 = **bust** (*informal*), swoop

raider NOUN = **attacker**, thief,

robber, plunderer, invader,
marauder
railing NOUN = **fence**, rails, barrier,
paling, balustrade
rain NOUN = **rainfall**, fall, showers,
deluge, drizzle, downpour,
raindrops, cloudburst
▷ VERB 1 = **pour**, pelt (down),
teem, bucket down (*informal*),
drizzle, come down in buckets
(*informal*) 2 = **fall**, shower, be
dropped, sprinkle, be deposited
rainy ADJECTIVE = **wet**, damp,
drizzly, showery ≠ dry
raise VERB 1 = **lift**, elevate, uplift,
heave 2 = **set upright**, lift, elevate
3 = **increase**, intensify, heighten,
advance, boost, strengthen,
enhance, enlarge ≠ reduce
4 = **make louder**, heighten,
amplify, louden 5 = **collect**,
gather, obtain 6 = **cause**, start,
produce, create, occasion,
provoke, originate, engender
7 = **put forward**, suggest,
introduce, advance, broach,
moot 8 = **bring up**, develop, rear,
nurture 9 = **build**, construct, put
up, erect ≠ demolish
rake¹ VERB 1 = **gather**, collect,
remove 2 = **search**, comb, scour,
scrutinize, fossick (*Austral.* & *N.Z.*)
rake² NOUN = **libertine**, playboy,
swinger (*slang*), lecher, roué,
debauchee ≠ puritan
rally NOUN 1 = **gathering**,
convention, meeting, congress,
assembly, hui (*N.Z.*) 2 = **recovery**,
improvement, revival,
recuperation ≠ relapse
▷ VERB 1 = **gather together**,
unite, regroup, reorganize,
reassemble 2 = **recover**, improve,
revive, get better, recuperate
≠ get worse
ram VERB 1 = **hit**, force, drive into,
crash, impact, smash, dash, butt
2 = **cram**, force, stuff, jam, thrust
ramble NOUN = **walk**, tour, stroll,
hike, roaming, roving, saunter
▷ VERB 1 = **walk**, range, wander,
stroll, stray, roam, rove, saunter,
go walkabout (*Austral.*) 2 *often
with* **on** = **babble**, rabbit (on) (*Brit.
informal*), waffle (*informal*, *chiefly
Brit.*), witter on (*informal*)
ramp NOUN = **slope**, incline,
gradient, rise
rampage VERB = **go berserk**,
storm, rage, run riot, run amok
▷ PHRASE: **on the rampage**
= **berserk**, wild, violent, raging,
out of control, amok, riotous,
berko (*Austral. slang*)
rampant ADJECTIVE
1 = **widespread**, prevalent,
rife, uncontrolled, unchecked,
unrestrained, profuse, spreading
like wildfire 2 (*heraldry*)
= **upright**, standing, rearing, erect
random ADJECTIVE 1 = **chance**,
casual, accidental, incidental,
haphazard, fortuitous, hit or
miss, adventitious ≠ planned
2 = **casual** ▷ PHRASE: **at random**
= **haphazardly**, randomly,
arbitrarily, by chance, willy-nilly,
unsystematically
randy ADJECTIVE (*informal*)
= **lustful**, hot, turned-on (*slang*),

aroused, horny (*slang*), amorous, lascivious

range NOUN 1 = **series**, variety, selection, assortment, lot, collection, gamut 2 = **limits**, reach 3 = **scope**, area, bounds, province, orbit, radius
▷ VERB 1 = **vary**, run, reach, extend, stretch 2 = **roam**, wander, rove, ramble, traverse

rank¹ NOUN 1 = **status**, level, position, grade, order, sort, type, division 2 = **class**, caste 3 = **row**, line, file, column, group, range, series, tier
▷ VERB 1 = **order**, dispose
2 = **arrange**, sort, line up, array, align

rank² ADJECTIVE 1 = **absolute**, complete, total, gross, sheer, utter, thorough, blatant 2 = **foul**, bad, offensive, disgusting, revolting, stinking, noxious, rancid, festy (*Austral. slang*)
3 = **abundant**, lush, luxuriant, dense, profuse

ransom NOUN = **payment**, money, price, payoff

rant VERB = **shout**, roar, yell, rave, cry, declaim

rap VERB = **hit**, strike, knock, crack, tap
▷ NOUN 1 = **blow**, knock, crack, tap, clout (*informal*) 2 (*slang*)
= **rebuke**, blame, responsibility, punishment

rape VERB = **sexually assault**, violate, abuse, ravish, force, outrage
▷ NOUN = **sexual assault**,

violation, ravishment, outrage

rapid ADJECTIVE 1 = **sudden**, prompt, speedy, express, swift
≠ gradual 2 = **quick**, fast, hurried, swift, brisk, hasty ≠ slow

rapidly ADVERB = **quickly**, fast, swiftly, briskly, promptly, hastily, hurriedly, speedily

rare ADJECTIVE 1 = **uncommon**, unusual, few, strange, scarce, singular, sparse, infrequent
≠ common 2 = **superb**, great, fine, excellent, superlative, choice, peerless

rarely ADVERB = **seldom**, hardly, hardly ever, infrequently ≠ often
● WORD POWER
● Since the meaning of *rarely* is
● 'hardly ever', the combination
● *rarely ever* is repetitive and
● should be avoided in careful
● writing, even though you may
● sometimes hear this phrase
● used in informal speech.

raring ADJECTIVE ▷ PHRASE:
raring to = **eager to**, impatient to, longing to, ready to, keen to, desperate to, enthusiastic to

rarity NOUN 1 = **curio**, find, treasure, gem, collector's item
2 = **uncommonness**, scarcity, infrequency, unusualness, shortage, strangeness, sparseness

rash¹ ADJECTIVE = **reckless**, hasty, impulsive, imprudent, careless, ill-advised, foolhardy, impetuous
≠ cautious

rash² NOUN 1 = **outbreak of spots**, (skin) eruption 2 = **spate**, series, wave, flood, plague, outbreak

rate NOUN 1 = **speed**, pace, tempo, velocity, frequency 2 = **degree**, standard, scale, proportion, ratio 3 = **charge**, price, cost, fee, figure ▷ VERB 1 = **evaluate**, consider, rank, reckon, value, measure, estimate, count 2 = **deserve**, merit, be entitled to, be worthy of ▷ PHRASE: **at any rate** = **in any case**, anyway, anyhow, at all events

rather ADVERB 1 = **preferably**, sooner, more readily, more willingly 2 = **to some extent**, quite, a little, fairly, relatively, somewhat, moderately, to some degree

● **WORD POWER**
● It is acceptable to use either
● *would rather* or *had rather* in
● sentences such as *I would rather*
● (or *had rather*) *see a film than a*
● *play*. *Had rather*, however, is less
● common than *would rather*, and
● sounds a little old-fashioned
● nowadays.

ratify VERB = **approve**, establish, confirm, sanction, endorse, uphold, authorize, affirm ≠ annul

rating NOUN = **position**, placing, rate, order, class, degree, rank, status

ratio NOUN = **proportion**, rate, relation, percentage, fraction

ration NOUN = **allowance**, quota, allotment, helping, part, share, measure, portion ▷ VERB = **limit**, control, restrict, budget

rational ADJECTIVE = **sensible**, sound, wise, reasonable, intelligent, realistic, logical, sane, grounded ≠ insane

rationale NOUN = **reason**, grounds, theory, principle, philosophy, logic, motivation, raison d'être (*French*)

rattle VERB 1 = **clatter**, bang, jangle 2 = **shake**, jolt, vibrate, bounce, jar 3 (*informal*) = **fluster**, shake, upset, disturb, disconcert, perturb, faze

ravage VERB = **destroy**, ruin, devastate, spoil, demolish, ransack, lay waste, despoil ▷ NOUN *often plural* = **damage**, destruction, devastation, ruin, havoc, ruination, spoliation

rave VERB 1 = **rant**, rage, roar, go mad (*informal*), babble, be delirious 2 (*informal*) = **enthuse**, praise, gush, be mad about (*informal*), be wild about (*informal*)

raving ADJECTIVE = **mad**, wild, crazy, hysterical, insane, irrational, crazed, delirious, berko (*Austral. slang*), off the air (*Austral. slang*)

raw ADJECTIVE 1 = **unrefined**, natural, crude, unprocessed, basic, rough, coarse, unfinished ≠ refined 2 = **uncooked**, natural, fresh ≠ cooked 3 = **inexperienced**, new, green, immature, callow ≠ experienced 4 = **chilly**, biting, cold, freezing, bitter, piercing, parky (*Brit. informal*)

ray NOUN = **beam**, bar, flash, shaft, gleam

re PREPOSITION = **concerning**, about, regarding, with regard to, with reference to, apropos

- WORD POWER
- In contexts such as *re your letter*,
- *your remarks have been noted* or *he*
- *spoke to me re your complaint*, *re* is
- common in business or official
- correspondence. In spoken
- and in general written English
- *with reference to* is preferable in
- the former case and *about* or
- *concerning* in the latter. Even in
- business correspondence, the
- use of *re* is often restricted to
- the letter heading.

reach VERB 1 = **arrive at**, get to, make, attain 2 = **attain**, get to 3 = **touch**, grasp, extend to, stretch to, contact 4 = **contact**, get in touch with, get through to, communicate with, get hold of
▷ NOUN 1 = **grasp**, range, distance, stretch, capacity, extent, extension, scope 2 = **jurisdiction**, power, influence

react VERB = **respond**, act, proceed, behave

reaction NOUN 1 = **response**, answer, reply 2 = **counteraction**, backlash, recoil 3 = **conservatism**, the right

- WORD POWER
- Some people say that *reaction*
- should always refer to an
- instant response to something
- (as in *his reaction was one of*
- *amazement*), and that this word
- should not be used to refer to
- a considered response given in

- the form of a statement (as in
- *the Minister gave his reaction to*
- *the court's decision*). Use *response*
- instead.

reactionary
ADJECTIVE = **conservative**, right-wing ≠ radical
▷ NOUN = **conservative**, die-hard, right-winger ≠ radical

read VERB 1 = **scan**, study, look at, pore over, peruse, follow (~ *a blog or microblog*) 2 = **understand**, interpret, comprehend, construe, decipher, see, discover 3 = **register**, show, record, display

readily ADVERB 1 = **willingly**, freely, quickly, gladly, eagerly ≠ reluctantly 2 = **promptly**, quickly, easily, smoothly, effortlessly, speedily, unhesitatingly ≠ with difficulty

readiness NOUN 1 = **willingness**, eagerness, keenness 2 = **promptness**, facility, ease, dexterity, adroitness

reading NOUN 1 = **perusal**, study, examination, inspection, scrutiny 2 = **learning**, education, knowledge, scholarship, erudition 3 = **recital**, performance, lesson, sermon 4 = **interpretation**, version, impression, grasp

ready ADJECTIVE 1 = **prepared**, set, primed, organized ≠ unprepared 2 = **completed**, arranged 3 = **mature**, ripe, mellow, ripened, seasoned 4 = **willing**, happy, glad, disposed, keen, eager, inclined, prone ≠ reluctant 5 = **prompt**, smart, quick, bright, sharp, keen,

r

alert, clever ≠ slow **6** = **available**, handy, present, near, accessible, convenient ≠ unavailable

real ADJECTIVE **1** = **true**, genuine, sincere, factual, dinkum (*Austral. & N.Z. informal*), unfeigned **2** = **genuine**, authentic, dinkum (*Austral. & N.Z. informal*) ≠ fake **3** = **proper**, true, valid **4** = **true**, actual **5** = **typical**, true, genuine, sincere, dinkum (*Austral. & N.Z. informal*), unfeigned **6** = **complete**, total, perfect, utter, thorough

realistic ADJECTIVE **1** = **practical**, real, sensible, common-sense, down-to-earth, matter-of-fact, level-headed, grounded ≠ impractical **2** = **attainable**, sensible **3** = **lifelike**, true to life, authentic, true, natural, genuine, faithful

reality NOUN **1** = **fact**, truth, realism, validity, verity, actuality **2** = **truth**, fact, actuality

realization NOUN **1** = **awareness**, understanding, recognition, perception, grasp, conception, comprehension, cognizance **2** = **achievement**, accomplishment, fulfilment

realize VERB **1** = **become aware of**, understand, take in, grasp, comprehend, get the message **2** = **fulfil**, achieve, accomplish, make real **3** = **achieve**, do, effect, complete, perform, fulfil, accomplish, carry out *or* through

really ADVERB **1** = **certainly**, genuinely, positively, surely

2 = **truly**, actually, in fact, indeed, in actuality

realm NOUN **1** = **field**, world, area, province, sphere, department, branch, territory **2** = **kingdom**, country, empire, land, domain, dominion

reap VERB **1** = **get**, gain, obtain, acquire, derive **2** = **collect**, gather, bring in, harvest, garner, cut

rear¹ NOUN **1** = **back part**, back ≠ front **2** = **back**, end, tail, rearguard, tail end
▷ MODIFIER = **back**, hind, last, following ≠ front

rear² VERB **1** = **bring up**, raise, educate, train, foster, nurture **2** = **breed**, keep **3** *often with* **up** *or* **over** = **rise**, tower, soar, loom

reason NOUN **1** = **cause**, grounds, purpose, motive, goal, aim, object, intention **2** = **sense**, mind, understanding, judgment, logic, intellect, sanity, rationality ≠ emotion
▷ VERB = **deduce**, conclude, work out, make out, infer, think
▷ PHRASE: **reason with someone** = **persuade**, bring round, urge, win over, prevail upon (*informal*), talk into *or* out of

● WORD POWER
● Many people object to the
● expression *the reason is*
● *because*, on the grounds that
● it is repetitive. It is therefore
● advisable to use either *this is*
● *because* or *the reason is that*.

reasonable ADJECTIVE

1 = **sensible**, sound, practical, wise, logical, sober, plausible, sane, grounded ≠ irrational 2 = **fair**, just, right, moderate, equitable, tenable ≠ unfair 3 = **within reason**, fit, proper ≠ impossible 4 = **low**, cheap, competitive, moderate, modest, inexpensive 5 = **average**, fair, moderate, modest, O.K. or okay (*informal*)

reassure VERB = **encourage**, comfort, hearten, gee up, restore confidence to, put or set your mind at rest

rebate NOUN = **refund**, discount, reduction, bonus, allowance, deduction

rebel NOUN 1 = **revolutionary**, insurgent, secessionist, revolutionist 2 = **nonconformist**, dissenter, heretic, apostate, schismatic
▷ VERB 1 = **revolt**, resist, rise up, mutiny 2 = **defy**, dissent, disobey
▷ MODIFIER = **rebellious**, revolutionary, insurgent, insurrectionary

rebellion NOUN 1 = **resistance**, rising, revolution, revolt, uprising, mutiny 2 = **nonconformity**, defiance, heresy, schism

rebellious ADJECTIVE
1 = **defiant**, difficult, resistant, unmanageable, refractory ≠ obedient 2 = **revolutionary**, rebel, disorderly, unruly, insurgent, disloyal, seditious, mutinous ≠ obedient

rebound VERB 1 = **bounce**,

ricochet, recoil 2 = **misfire**, backfire, recoil, boomerang

rebuff VERB = **reject**, refuse, turn down, cut, slight, snub, spurn, knock back (*slang*) ≠ encourage
▷ NOUN = **rejection**, snub, knock-back, slight, refusal, repulse, cold shoulder, slap in the face (*informal*) ≠ encouragement

rebuke VERB = **scold**, censure, reprimand, castigate, chide, dress down (*informal*), admonish, tell off (*informal*) ≠ praise
▷ NOUN = **scolding**, censure, reprimand, row, dressing down (*informal*), telling-off (*informal*), admonition ≠ praise

recall VERB 1 = **recollect**, remember, evoke, call to mind 2 = **call back** 3 = **annul**, withdraw, cancel, repeal, revoke, retract, countermand
▷ NOUN 1 = **recollection**, memory, remembrance
2 = **annulment**, withdrawal, repeal, cancellation, retraction, rescindment

recede VERB = **fall back**, withdraw, retreat, return, retire, regress

receipt NOUN 1 = **sales slip**, proof of purchase, counterfoil
2 = **receiving**, delivery, reception, acceptance

receive VERB 1 = **get**, accept, be given, pick up, collect, obtain, acquire, take 2 = **experience**, suffer, bear, encounter, sustain, undergo 3 = **greet**, meet, admit, welcome, entertain,

r

accommodate

recent ADJECTIVE = **new**, modern, up-to-date, late, current, fresh, novel, present-day ≠ old

recently ADVERB = **not long ago**, newly, lately, currently, freshly, of late, latterly

reception NOUN 1 = **party**, gathering, get-together, social gathering, function, celebration, festivity, soirée 2 = **response**, reaction, acknowledgment, treatment, welcome, greeting

recess NOUN 1 = **break**, rest, holiday, interval, vacation, respite, intermission, schoolie (*Austral.*) 2 = **alcove**, corner, bay, hollow, niche, nook

recession NOUN = **depression**, drop, decline, slump ≠ boom

recipe NOUN = **directions**, instructions, ingredients

recital NOUN 1 = **performance**, rendering, rehearsal, reading 2 = **account**, telling, statement, relation, narrative 3 = **recitation**

recite VERB = **perform**, deliver, repeat, declaim

reckless ADJECTIVE = **careless**, wild, rash, precipitate, hasty, mindless, headlong, thoughtless ≠ cautious

reckon VERB 1 (*informal*) = **think**, believe, suppose, imagine, assume, guess (*informal, chiefly U.S. & Canad.*) 2 = **consider**, rate, account, judge, regard, count, esteem, deem 3 = **count**, figure, total, calculate, compute, add up, tally, number

reckoning NOUN = **count**, estimate, calculation, addition

reclaim VERB 1 = **retrieve**, regain 2 = **regain**, salvage, recapture

recognition NOUN 1 = **identification**, recollection, discovery, remembrance 2 = **acceptance**, admission, allowance, confession

recognize VERB 1 = **identify**, know, place, remember, spot, notice, recall, recollect 2 = **acknowledge**, allow, accept, admit, grant, concede ≠ ignore 3 = **appreciate**, respect, notice

recollection NOUN = **memory**, recall, impression, remembrance, reminiscence

recommend VERB 1 = **advocate**, suggest, propose, approve, endorse, commend ≠ disapprove of 2 = **put forward**, approve, endorse, commend, praise 3 = **advise**, suggest, advance, propose, counsel, advocate, prescribe, put forward

recommendation NOUN 1 = **advice**, proposal, suggestion, counsel 2 = **commendation**, reference, praise, sanction, approval, endorsement, advocacy, testimonial

reconcile VERB 1 = **resolve**, settle, square, adjust, compose, rectify, put to rights 2 = **reunite**, bring back together, conciliate 3 = **make peace between**, reunite, propitiate

reconciliation NOUN = **reunion**, conciliation, pacification, reconcilement ≠ separation

reconsider VERB = **rethink**, review, revise, think again, reassess

reconstruct VERB 1 = **rebuild**, restore, recreate, remake, renovate, remodel, regenerate 2 = **build up a picture of**, build up, piece together, deduce

record NOUN 1 = **document**, file, register, log, report, account, entry, journal, blog (*informal*) 2 = **evidence**, trace, documentation, testimony, witness 3 = **disc**, single, album, LP, vinyl 4 = **background**, history, performance, career
▷ VERB 1 = **set down**, minute, note, enter, document, register, log, chronicle 2 = **make a recording of**, video, tape, video-tape, tape-record 3 = **register**, show, indicate, give evidence of

recorder NOUN = **chronicler**, archivist, historian, clerk, scribe, diarist

recording NOUN = **record**, video, tape, disc

recount VERB = **tell**, report, describe, relate, repeat, depict, recite, narrate

recover VERB 1 = **get better**, improve, get well, recuperate, heal, revive, mend, convalesce ≠ relapse 2 = **rally** 3 = **save**, rescue, retrieve, salvage, reclaim ≠ abandon 4 = **recoup**, restore, get back, regain, retrieve, reclaim, redeem, recapture ≠ lose

recovery NOUN
1 = **improvement**, healing,

revival, mending, recuperation, convalescence 2 = **retrieval**, repossession, reclamation, restoration

recreation NOUN = **leisure**, play, sport, fun, entertainment, relaxation, enjoyment, amusement, me-time

recruit VERB 1 = **gather**, obtain, engage, procure 2 = **assemble**, raise, levy, muster, mobilize 3 = **enlist**, draft, enrol ≠ dismiss
▷ NOUN = **beginner**, trainee, apprentice, novice, convert, initiate, helper, learner

recur VERB = **happen again**, return, repeat, persist, revert, reappear, come again

recycle VERB = **reprocess**, reuse, salvage, reclaim, save

red NOUN = **crimson**, scarlet, ruby, vermilion, cherry, coral, carmine
▷ ADJECTIVE 1 = **crimson**, scarlet, ruby, vermilion, cherry, coral, carmine 2 = **flushed**, embarrassed, blushing, florid, shamefaced 3 (*of hair*) = **chestnut**, reddish, flame-coloured, sandy, Titian, carroty, ginger ▷ PHRASES: **in the red** (*informal*) = **in debt**, insolvent, in arrears, overdrawn; **see red** (*informal*) = **lose your temper**, lose it (*informal*), go mad (*informal*), crack up (*informal*), lose the plot (*informal*), go ballistic (*slang, chiefly U.S.*), fly off the handle (*informal*), blow your top
● WORD POWER
● The symbolism of *red* can be

r

● **SHADES OF RED**

- auburn
- baby pink
- burgundy
- burnt sienna
- cardinal red
- carmine
- carnation
- carroty
- cerise
- cherry
- chestnut
- cinnabar
- copper *or* coppery
- coral
- crimson
- damask
- flame

- flesh
- foxy
- fuchsia
- ginger
- henna
- liver
- magenta
- maroon
- mulberry
- old rose
- oxblood
- oyster pink
- peach
- pink
- plum
- poppy
- puce

- raspberry
- rose
- roseate
- rosy
- ruby
- russet
- rust
- sandy
- scarlet
- strawberry
- tea rose
- terracotta
- Titian
- vermilion
- wine

seen in the many phrases involving the word. The colour of fire in nature, red has become associated with fiery emotional states in people. Passion is conceptualized in the phrase **red-hot**, meaning very hot, exciting, or passionate, as is anger in the expression **see red**, meaning lose your temper. The colour of blood and the physical effects of flushing have led to the association of red with health in **rose-red** and **ruddy**; virility in **red-blooded**; shame in **red-faced**; and soreness in **red-rimmed**. Through this combination of meanings, red symbolizes danger and risk in a **red light** in traffic, or sex in a **red light**

district in a town. The phrase *in the red*, meaning 'in debt' also has this negative connotation and stems historically from the red ink used to record debits in an account. From the colour of a communist party badge, red means left-wing politics and socialism in the phrase *red army*.

redeem VERB 1 = **reinstate**, absolve, restore to favour
  2 = **make up for**, compensate for, atone for, make amends for
  3 = **buy back**, recover, regain, retrieve, reclaim, repurchase
  4 = **save**, free, deliver, liberate, ransom, emancipate

redemption NOUN
  1 = **compensation**, amends, reparation, atonement

2 = **salvation**, release, rescue, liberation, emancipation, deliverance

redress VERB **1** = **make amends for**, make up for, compensate for **2** = **put right**, balance, correct, adjust, regulate, rectify, even up ▷ NOUN = **amends**, payment, compensation, reparation, atonement, recompense

reduce VERB **1** = **lessen**, cut, lower, moderate, weaken, diminish, decrease, cut down, kennet (*Austral. slang*), jeff (*Austral. slang*) ≠ increase **2** = **degrade**, downgrade, break, humble, bring low ≠ promote

reduced ADJECTIVE = **impoverished**, broke (*informal*), hard up (*informal*), short, needy, penniless, destitute, poverty-stricken

redundancy NOUN **1** = **layoff**, sacking, dismissal **2** = **unemployment**, the sack (*informal*), the axe (*informal*), joblessness

redundant ADJECTIVE = **superfluous**, extra, surplus, unnecessary, unwanted, inessential, supernumerary ≠ essential

reel VERB **1** = **stagger**, rock, roll, pitch, sway, lurch **2** = **whirl**, spin, revolve, swirl

refer VERB **1** = **direct**, point, send, guide ▷ PHRASE: **refer to something** *or* **someone 1** = **allude to**, mention, cite, speak of, bring up **2** = **relate to**,

concern, apply to, pertain to, be relevant to **3** = **consult**, go, apply, turn to, look up

⦿ **WORD POWER**
⦿ It is usually unnecessary to
⦿ add *back* to the verb *refer*, since
⦿ the sense of *back* is already
⦿ contained in the *re-* part of this
⦿ word. For example, you might
⦿ say *This refers to* (not *refers back*
⦿ *to*) *what has already been said.*
⦿ *Refer back* is only considered
⦿ acceptable when used to mean
⦿ 'return a document or question
⦿ to the person it came from for
⦿ further consideration', as in *he*
⦿ *referred the matter back to me.*

referee NOUN = **umpire**, umpie (*Austral. slang*), judge, ref (*informal*), arbiter, arbitrator, adjudicator ▷ VERB = **umpire**, judge, mediate, adjudicate, arbitrate

reference NOUN **1** = **allusion**, note, mention, quotation **2** = **citation 3** = **testimonial**, recommendation, credentials, endorsement, character reference

referendum NOUN = **public vote**, popular vote, plebiscite

refine VERB **1** = **purify**, process, filter, cleanse, clarify, distil **2** = **improve**, perfect, polish, hone

refined ADJECTIVE **1** = **purified**, processed, pure, filtered, clean, clarified, distilled ≠ unrefined **2** = **cultured**, polished, elegant, polite, civilized, well-bred ≠ coarse **3** = **discerning**, fine, sensitive, delicate, precise,

r

discriminating, fastidious

reflect VERB 1 = **show**, reveal, display, indicate, demonstrate, manifest 2 = **throw back**, return, mirror, echo, reproduce 3 *usually followed by on* = **consider**, think, muse, ponder, meditate, ruminate, cogitate, wonder

reflection NOUN 1 = **image**, echo, mirror image 2 = **consideration**, thinking, thought, idea, opinion, observation, musing, meditation

reflective ADJECTIVE = **thoughtful**, contemplative, meditative, pensive

reform NOUN = **improvement**, amendment, rehabilitation, betterment
  ▷ VERB 1 = **improve**, correct, restore, amend, mend, rectify 2 = **mend your ways**, go straight (*informal*), shape up (*informal*), turn over a new leaf, clean up your act (*informal*), pull your socks up (*Brit. informal*)

refrain¹ VERB = **stop**, avoid, cease, renounce, abstain, leave off, desist, forbear

refrain² NOUN = **chorus**, tune, melody

refresh VERB 1 = **revive**, freshen, revitalize, stimulate, brace, enliven, invigorate 2 = **stimulate**, prompt, renew, jog

refreshing ADJECTIVE 1 = **new**, original, novel 2 = **stimulating**, fresh, bracing, invigorating ≠ tiring

refreshment *plural* = **food and drink**, drinks, snacks, titbits, kai

(*N.Z. informal*)

refuge NOUN 1 = **protection**, shelter, asylum 2 = **haven**, retreat, sanctuary, hide-out

refugee NOUN = **exile**, émigré, displaced person, escapee

refund NOUN = **repayment**, reimbursement, return
  ▷ VERB = **repay**, return, restore, pay back, reimburse

refurbish VERB = **renovate**, restore, repair, clean up, overhaul, revamp, mend, do up (*informal*)

refusal NOUN = **rejection**, denial, rebuff, knock-back (*slang*)

refuse¹ VERB 1 = **decline**, reject, turn down, say no to 2 = **deny**, decline, withhold ≠ allow

refuse² NOUN = **rubbish**, waste, junk (*informal*), litter, garbage, trash

regain VERB 1 = **recover**, get back, retrieve, recapture, win back, take back, recoup 2 = **get back to**, return to, reach again

regal ADJECTIVE = **royal**, majestic, kingly *or* queenly, noble, princely, magnificent

regard VERB 1 = **consider**, see, rate, view, judge, think of, esteem, deem 2 = **look at**, view, eye, watch, observe, clock (*Brit. slang*), check out (*informal*), gaze at
  ▷ NOUN 1 = **respect**, esteem, thought, concern, care, consideration 2 = **look**, gaze, scrutiny, stare, glance 3 *plural* = **good wishes**, respects, greetings, compliments, best wishes ▷ PHRASE: **as regards**

r

= **concerning**, regarding, relating to, pertaining to

regarding PREPOSITION
= **concerning**, about, on the subject of, re, respecting, as regards, with reference to, in *or* with regard to

regardless ADVERB = **in spite of everything**, anyway, nevertheless, in any case
▷ ADJECTIVE *with* **of**
= **irrespective of**, heedless of, unmindful of

regime NOUN 1 = **government**, rule, management, leadership, reign 2 = **plan**, course, system, policy, programme, scheme, regimen

region NOUN = **area**, place, part, quarter, section, sector, district, territory

regional ADJECTIVE = **local**, district, provincial, parochial, zonal

register NOUN = **list**, record, roll, file, diary, catalogue, log, archives
▷ VERB 1 = **enrol**, enlist, list, note, enter 2 = **record**, catalogue, chronicle 3 = **indicate**, show 4 = **show**, mark, indicate, manifest 5 = **express**, show, reveal, display, exhibit

regret VERB 1 = **be** *or* **feel sorry about**, rue, deplore, bemoan, repent (of), bewail ≠ be satisfied with 2 = **mourn**, miss, grieve for *or* over
▷ NOUN 1 = **remorse**, compunction, bitterness, repentance, contrition, penitence 2 = **sorrow** ≠ satisfaction

regular ADJECTIVE 1 = **frequent** 2 = **normal**, common, usual, ordinary, typical, routine, customary, habitual ≠ infrequent 3 = **steady**, consistent 4 = **even**, level, balanced, straight, flat, fixed, smooth, uniform ≠ uneven

regulate VERB 1 = **control**, run, rule, manage, direct, guide, handle, govern 2 = **moderate**, control, modulate, fit, tune, adjust

regulation NOUN 1 = **rule**, order, law, dictate, decree, statute, edict, precept 2 = **control**, government, management, direction, supervision

rehearsal NOUN = **practice**, rehearsing, run-through, preparation, drill

rehearse VERB = **practise**, prepare, run through, go over, train, repeat, drill, recite

reign VERB 1 = **be supreme**, prevail, predominate, hold sway 2 = **rule**, govern, be in power, influence, command
▷ NOUN = **rule**, power, control, command, monarchy, dominion

r

- not be confused; note the
- correct spellings in *he gave full*
- *rein to his feelings* (not *reign*); and
- *it will be necessary to rein in public*
- *spending* (not *reign in*).

rein NOUN = **control**, harness, bridle, hold, check, brake, curb, restraint

reinforce VERB 1 = **support**, strengthen, fortify, toughen, stress, prop, supplement, emphasize 2 = **increase**, extend, add to, strengthen, supplement

reinforcement NOUN 1 = **strengthening**, increase, fortification, augmentation 2 = **support**, stay, prop, brace, buttress 3 *plural* = **reserves**, support, auxiliaries, additional *or* fresh troops

reinstate VERB = **restore**, recall, re-establish, return

reiterate VERB (*formal*) = **repeat**, restate, say again, do again

reject VERB 1 = **rebuff**, jilt, turn down, spurn, refuse, say no to, repulse, unfriend (*computing*), unfollow (*computing*) ≠ accept 2 = **deny**, exclude, veto, relinquish, renounce, disallow, forsake, disown ≠ approve 3 = **discard**, decline, eliminate, scrap, jettison, throw away *or* out ≠ accept ▷ NOUN 1 = **castoff**, second, discard ≠ treasure 2 = **failure**, loser, flop

rejection NOUN 1 = **denial**, veto, dismissal, exclusion, disowning, thumbs down, renunciation, repudiation ≠ approval

2 = **rebuff**, refusal, knock-back (*slang*), kick in the teeth (*slang*), brushoff (*slang*) ≠ acceptance

rejoice VERB = **be glad**, celebrate, be happy, glory, be overjoyed, exult ≠ lament

rejoin VERB = **reply**, answer, respond, retort, riposte

relate VERB 1 = **tell**, recount, report, detail, describe, recite, narrate ▷ PHRASE: **relate to something** *or* **someone** 1 = **concern**, refer to, apply to, have to do with, pertain to, be relevant to 2 = **connect with**, associate with, link with, couple with, join with, correlate to

related ADJECTIVE 1 = **associated**, linked, joint, connected, affiliated, akin, interconnected ≠ unconnected 2 = **akin**, kindred ≠ unrelated

relation NOUN 1 = **similarity**, link, bearing, bond, comparison, correlation, connection 2 = **relative**, kin, kinsman *or* kinswoman, rellie (*Austral. slang*) ▷ PLURAL NOUN 1 = **dealings**, relationship, affairs, contact, connections, interaction, intercourse 2 = **family**, relatives, tribe, clan, kin, kindred, kinsmen, kinsfolk, ainga (*N.Z.*), rellie (*Austral. slang*)

relationship NOUN 1 = **association**, bond, connection, affinity, rapport, kinship 2 = **affair**, romance, liaison, amour, intrigue 3 = **connection**, link, parallel, similarity, tie-up, correlation

relative NOUN = **relation**,
kinsman or kinswoman, member
of your or the family, rellie (Austral.
slang)
▷ ADJECTIVE 1 = **comparative**
2 = **corresponding** 3 with **to** = **in
proportion to**, proportionate to

relatively ADVERB
= **comparatively**, rather,
somewhat

relax VERB 1 = **be** or **feel at ease**,
chill out (slang, chiefly U.S.), take it
easy, lighten up (slang), outspan
(S. African) ≠ be alarmed 2 = **calm
down**, calm, unwind 3 = **make
less tense**, rest 4 = **lessen**,
reduce, ease, relieve, weaken,
loosen, let up, slacken ≠ tighten
5 = **moderate**, ease, relieve,
weaken, slacken ≠ tighten up

relaxation NOUN = **leisure**,
rest, fun, pleasure, recreation,
enjoyment, me-time

relay VERB = **broadcast**, carry,
spread, communicate, transmit,
send out

release VERB 1 = **set free**, free,
discharge, liberate, drop, loose,
undo, extricate ≠ imprison
2 = **acquit**, let go, let off,
exonerate, absolve 3 = **issue**,
publish, make public, make
known, launch, distribute, put
out, circulate ≠ withhold
▷ NOUN 1 = **liberation**, freedom,
liberty, discharge, emancipation,
deliverance ≠ imprisonment
2 = **acquittal**, exemption,
absolution, exoneration

3 = **issue**, publication,
proclamation

relegate VERB = **demote**,
degrade, downgrade

relentless ADJECTIVE
1 = **merciless**, fierce, cruel,
ruthless, unrelenting, implacable,
remorseless, pitiless ≠ merciful
2 = **unremitting**, persistent,
unrelenting, incessant, nonstop,
unrelieved

relevant ADJECTIVE = **significant**,
appropriate, related, fitting, to
the point, apt, pertinent, apposite
≠ irrelevant

reliable ADJECTIVE
1 = **dependable**, trustworthy,
sure, sound, true, faithful,
staunch ≠ unreliable 2 = **safe**,
dependable 3 = **definitive**, sound,
dependable, trustworthy

reliance NOUN 1 = **dependency**,
dependence 2 = **trust**,
confidence, belief, faith

relic NOUN = **remnant**, vestige,
memento, trace, fragment,
souvenir, keepsake

relief NOUN 1 = **ease**, release,
comfort, cure, remedy, solace,
deliverance, mitigation 2 = **rest**,
respite, relaxation, break,
breather (informal) 3 = **aid**, help,
support, assistance, succour

relieve VERB 1 = **ease**, soothe,
alleviate, relax, comfort, calm,
cure, soften ≠ intensify 2 = **help**,
support, aid, sustain, assist,
succour

religion NOUN = **belief**, faith,
theology, creed

r

religious ADJECTIVE 1 = **spiritual**, holy, sacred, devotional
2 = **conscientious**, faithful, rigid, meticulous, scrupulous, punctilious

relinquish VERB (formal) = **give up**, leave, drop, abandon, surrender, let go, renounce, forsake

relish VERB 1 = **enjoy**, like, savour, revel in ≠ dislike 2 = **look forward to**, fancy, delight in
▷ NOUN 1 = **enjoyment**, liking, love, taste, fancy, penchant, fondness, gusto ≠ distaste
2 = **condiment**, seasoning, sauce

reluctance NOUN
= **unwillingness**, dislike, loathing, distaste, aversion, disinclination, repugnance

reluctant ADJECTIVE = **unwilling**, hesitant, loath, disinclined, unenthusiastic ≠ willing

● WORD POWER
● *Reticent* is quite commonly
● used nowadays as a synonym
● of *reluctant* and followed by *to*
● and a verb. In careful writing
● it is advisable to avoid this
● use, since many people would
● regard it as mistaken.

rely on VERB 1 = **depend on**, lean on 2 = **be confident of**, bank on, trust, count on, bet on

remain VERB 1 = **stay**, continue, go on, stand, dwell 2 = **stay**

● **RELIGION**

● animism
● Babi or Babism
● Baha'ism
● Buddhism
● Christianity
● Confucianism
● druidism
● heliolatry
● Hinduism or Hindooism
● Islam
● Jainism
● Judaism

● Macumba
● Manichaeism or Manicheism
● Mithraism or Mithraicism
● Orphism
● paganism
● Rastafarianism
● Ryobu Shinto
● Santeria
● Satanism
● Scientology (trademark)

● shamanism
● Shango
● Shembe
● Shinto
● Sikhism
● Taoism
● voodoo or voodooism
● Yezidis
● Zoroastrianism or Zoroastrism

● **Religious festivals**

● Advent
● Al Hijrah
● Ascension Day
● Ash Wednesday

● Baisakhi
● Bodhi Day
● Candlemas
● Chanukah or

Hanukkah
● Ching Ming
● Christmas
● Corpus Christi

r

- Day of Atonement
- Dhammacakka
- Diwali
- Dragon Boat Festival
- Dussehra
- Easter
- Eid ul-Adha *or* Id-ul-Adha
- Eid ul-Fitr *or* Id-ul-Fitr
- Epiphany
- Feast of Tabernacles
- Good Friday
- Guru Nanak's Birthday
- Hirja
- Hola Mohalla
- Holi
- Janamashtami
- Lailat ul-Barah
- Lailat ul-Isra Wal Mi'raj
- Lailat ul-Qadr
- Lent
- Mahashivaratri
- Maundy Thursday
- Michaelmas
- Moon Festival
- Palm Sunday
- Passion Sunday
- Passover
- Pentecost
- Pesach
- Purim
- Quadragesima
- Quinquagesima
- Raksha Bandhan
- Ramadan
- Rama Naumi
- Rogation
- Rosh Hashanah
- Septuagesima
- Sexagesima
- Shavuot
- Shrove Tuesday
- Sukkoth *or* Succoth
- Trinity
- Wesak
- Whitsun
- Winter Festival
- Yom Kippur
- Yuan Tan

behind, wait, delay ≠ go
3 = **continue**, be left, linger
remainder NOUN = **rest**, remains, balance, excess, surplus, remnant, residue, leavings
remains PLURAL NOUN
1 = **remnants**, leftovers, rest, debris, residue, dregs, leavings
2 = **relics 3** = **corpse**, body, carcass, cadaver
remark VERB **1** = **comment**, say, state, reflect, mention, declare, observe, pass comment
2 = **notice**, note, observe, perceive, see, mark, make out, espy
▷ NOUN = **comment**, observation, reflection, statement, utterance
remarkable ADJECTIVE
= **extraordinary**, striking, outstanding, wonderful, rare, unusual, surprising, notable

≠ ordinary
remedy NOUN = **cure**, treatment, medicine, nostrum
▷ VERB = **put right**, rectify, fix, correct, set to rights
remember VERB **1** = **recall**, think back to, recollect, reminisce about, call to mind ≠ forget
2 = **bear in mind**, keep in mind
3 = **look back (on)**, commemorate
remembrance NOUN
1 = **commemoration**, memorial
2 = **souvenir**, token, reminder, monument, memento, keepsake
3 = **memory**, recollection, thought, recall, reminiscence
remind VERB = **jog your memory**, prompt, make you remember
reminiscent ADJECTIVE
= **suggestive**, evocative, similar
remnant NOUN = **remainder**, remains, trace, fragment, end,

r

rest, residue, leftovers

remorse NOUN = **regret**, shame, guilt, grief, sorrow, anguish, repentance, contrition

remote ADJECTIVE 1 = **distant**, far, isolated, out-of-the-way, secluded, inaccessible, in the middle of nowhere ≠ nearby 2 = **far**, distant 3 = **slight**, small, outside, unlikely, slim, faint, doubtful, dubious ≠ strong 4 = **aloof**, cold, reserved, withdrawn, distant, abstracted, detached, uncommunicative ≠ outgoing

removal NOUN 1 = **extraction**, withdrawal, uprooting, eradication, dislodgment, taking away *or* off *or* out 2 = **dismissal**, expulsion, elimination, ejection 3 = **move**, transfer, departure, relocation, flitting (*Scot. & Northern English dialect*)

remove VERB 1 = **take out**, withdraw, extract ≠ insert 2 = **take off** ≠ put on 3 = **erase**, eliminate, take out 4 = **dismiss**, eliminate, get rid of, discharge, abolish, expel, throw out, oust ≠ appoint 5 = **get rid of**, erase, eradicate, expunge 6 = **take away**, detach, displace ≠ put back 7 = **delete**, get rid of, erase, excise 8 = **move**, depart, relocate, flit (*Scot. & Northern English dialect*)

renaissance *or* **renascence** NOUN = **rebirth**, revival, restoration, renewal, resurgence, reappearance, reawakening

rend VERB (*literary*) = **tear**, rip, separate, wrench, rupture

render VERB 1 = **make**, cause to become, leave 2 = **provide**, give, pay, present, supply, submit, tender, hand out 3 = **represent**, portray, depict, do, give, play, act, perform

renew VERB 1 = **recommence**, continue, extend, repeat, resume, reopen, recreate, reaffirm 2 = **reaffirm**, resume, recommence 3 = **replace**, refresh, replenish, restock 4 = **restore**, repair, overhaul, mend, refurbish, renovate, refit, modernize

renounce VERB 1 = **disown**, quit, forsake, recant, forswear, abjure 2 = **disclaim**, deny, give up, relinquish, waive, abjure ≠ assert

renovate VERB = **restore**, repair, refurbish, do up (*informal*), renew, overhaul, refit, modernize

renowned ADJECTIVE = **famous**, noted, celebrated, well-known, distinguished, esteemed, notable, eminent ≠ unknown

rent[1] VERB 1 = **hire**, lease 2 = **let**, lease
  ▷ NOUN = **hire**, rental, lease, fee, payment

rent[2] NOUN 1 = **tear**, split, rip, slash, slit, gash, hole 2 = **opening**, hole

repair VERB 1 = **mend**, fix, restore, heal, patch, renovate, patch up ≠ damage 2 = **put right**, make up for, compensate for, rectify, redress
  ▷ NOUN 1 = **mend**, restoration, overhaul 2 = **darn**, mend, patch

3 = **condition**, state, form, shape (*informal*)

repay VERB = **pay back**, refund, settle up, return, square, compensate, reimburse, recompense

repeal VERB = **abolish**, reverse, revoke, annul, recall, cancel, invalidate, nullify ≠ pass
▷ NOUN = **abolition**, cancellation, annulment, invalidation, rescindment ≠ passing

repeat VERB **1** = **reiterate**, restate **2** = **retell**, echo, replay, reproduce, rerun, reshow
▷ NOUN **1** = **repetition**, echo, reiteration **2** = **rerun**, replay, reshowing

● **WORD POWER**
● Since the sense of *again* is
● already contained within the
● *re-* part of the word *repeat*, it
● is unnecessary to say that
● something is *repeated again*.

repeatedly ADVERB = **over and over**, often, frequently, many times

repel VERB **1** = **drive off**, fight, resist, parry, hold off, rebuff, ward off, repulse ≠ submit to **2** = **disgust**, offend, revolt, sicken, nauseate, gross out (*U.S. slang*) ≠ delight

repertoire NOUN = **range**, list, stock, supply, store, collection, repertory

repetition NOUN **1** = **recurrence**, repeating, echo **2** = **repeating**, replication, restatement, reiteration, tautology

replace VERB **1** = **take the place of**, follow, succeed, oust, take over from, supersede, supplant **2** = **substitute**, change, exchange, switch, swap **3** = **put back**, restore

replacement NOUN
1 = **replacing 2** = **successor**, double, substitute, stand-in, proxy, surrogate, understudy

replica NOUN **1** = **reproduction**, model, copy, imitation, facsimile, carbon copy ≠ original **2** = **duplicate**, copy, carbon copy

replicate VERB = **copy**, reproduce, recreate, mimic, duplicate, reduplicate

reply VERB = **answer**, respond, retort, counter, rejoin, retaliate, reciprocate
▷ NOUN = **answer**, response, reaction, counter, retort, retaliation, counterattack, rejoinder

report VERB **1** = **inform of**, communicate, recount **2** *often with* **on** = **communicate**, tell, state, detail, describe, relate, broadcast, pass on **3** = **present yourself**, come, appear, arrive, turn up
▷ NOUN **1** = **article**, story, piece, write-up **2** = **account**, record, statement, communication, description, narrative **3** *often plural* = **news**, word **4** = **bang**, sound, crack, noise, blast, boom, explosion, discharge **5** = **rumour**, talk, buzz, gossip, goss (*informal*), hearsay

r

reporter NOUN = **journalist**, writer, correspondent, hack (*derogatory*), pressman, journo (*slang*)

represent VERB 1 = **act for**, speak for 2 = **stand for**, serve as 3 = **express**, correspond to, symbolize, mean 4 = **exemplify**, embody, symbolize, typify, personify, epitomize 5 = **depict**, show, describe, picture, illustrate, outline, portray, denote

representation NOUN 1 = **picture**, model, image, portrait, illustration, likeness 2 = **portrayal**, depiction, account, description

representative NOUN 1 = **delegate**, member, agent, deputy, proxy, spokesman *or* spokeswoman 2 = **agent**, salesman, rep, commercial traveller
▷ ADJECTIVE 1 = **typical**, characteristic, archetypal, exemplary ≠ uncharacteristic 2 = **symbolic**

repress VERB 1 = **control**, suppress, hold back, bottle up, check, curb, restrain, inhibit ≠ release 2 = **hold back**, suppress, stifle 3 = **subdue**, abuse, wrong, persecute, quell, subjugate, maltreat ≠ liberate

repression NOUN 1 = **subjugation**, control, constraint, domination, tyranny, despotism 2 = **suppression**, crushing, quashing 3 = **inhibition**, control, restraint, bottling up

reprieve VERB = **grant a stay of execution to**, pardon, let off the hook (*slang*)
▷ NOUN = **stay of execution**, amnesty, pardon, remission, deferment, postponement of punishment

reproduce VERB 1 = **copy**, recreate, replicate, duplicate, match, mirror, echo, imitate 2 = **print**, copy 3 (*biology*) = **breed**, procreate, multiply, spawn, propagate

reproduction NOUN 1 = **copy**, picture, print, replica, imitation, duplicate, facsimile ≠ original 2 (*biology*) = **breeding**, increase, generation, multiplication

Republican ADJECTIVE = **right-wing**, Conservative
▷ NOUN = **right-winger**, Conservative

reputation NOUN = **name**, standing, character, esteem, stature, renown, repute

request VERB 1 = **ask for**, appeal for, put in for, demand, desire 2 = **invite**, entreat 3 = **seek**, ask (for), solicit
▷ NOUN 1 = **appeal**, call, demand, plea, desire, entreaty, suit 2 = **asking**, plea

require VERB 1 = **need**, crave, want, miss, lack, wish, desire 2 = **order**, demand, command, compel, exact, oblige, call upon, insist upon 3 = **ask**
● WORD POWER
● The use of *require to* as in *I require*

● **REPTILES**
● adder
● agama
● agamid
● alligator
● amphisbaena
● anaconda or (*Caribbean*) camoodi
● asp
● bandy-bandy
● black snake or red-bellied black snake
● blind snake
● blue tongue
● boa
● boa constrictor
● box turtle
● brown snake or (*Austral.*) mallee snake
● bull snake or gopher snake
● bushmaster
● carpet snake or python
● cayman or caiman
● chameleon
● chuckwalla
● cobra
● constrictor
● copperhead
● coral snake
● crocodile
● death adder or deaf adder
● diamondback, diamondback terrapin, or diamondback turtle
● diamond snake or diamond python
● elapid
● fer-de-lance
● frill-necked lizard, frilled lizard, bicycle lizard, cycling lizard, or (*Austral. informal*) frillie
● gaboon viper
● garter snake
● gecko
● giant tortoise
● Gila monster
● glass snake
● goanna, bungarra (*Austral.*), or go (*Austral. informal*)
● grass snake
● green turtle
● harlequin snake
● hawksbill or hawksbill turtle
● hognose snake or puff adder
● horned toad or lizard
● horned viper
● iguana
● jew lizard, bearded lizard, or bearded dragon
● king cobra or hamadryad
● king snake
● Komodo dragon or Komodo lizard
● krait
● leatherback or (*Brit.*) leathery turtle
● lizard
● loggerhead or loggerhead turtle
● mamba
● massasauga
● milk snake
● monitor
● mud turtle
● ngarara (*N.Z.*)
● perentie or perenty
● pit viper
● puff adder
● python
● rat snake
● rattlesnake or (*U.S. & Canad. informal*) rattler
● rock snake, rock python, amethystine python, or Schneider python
● saltwater crocodile or (*Austral. informal*) saltie
● sand lizard
● sand viper
● sea snake
● sidewinder
● skink
● slowworm or blindworm
● smooth snake
● snake
● snapping turtle

r

- soft-shelled turtle
- taipan
- terrapin
- tiger snake
- tokay
- tortoise
- tree snake
- tuatara *or* (*technical*) sphenodon (*N.Z.*)
- turtle
- viper
- wall lizard
- water moccasin, moccasin, *or* cottonmouth
- water snake
- whip snake

to see the manager or *you require to complete a special form* is thought by many people to be incorrect. Useful alternatives are: *I need to see the manager* and *you are required to complete a special form*.

requirement NOUN = **necessity**, demand, stipulation, want, need, must, essential, prerequisite

rescue VERB 1 = **save**, get out, release, deliver, recover, liberate ≠ desert 2 = **salvage**, deliver, redeem

▷ NOUN = **saving**, salvage, deliverance, release, recovery, liberation, salvation, redemption

research NOUN = **investigation**, study, analysis, examination, probe, exploration

▷ VERB = **investigate**, study, examine, explore, probe, analyse

resemblance NOUN = **similarity**, correspondence, parallel, likeness, kinship, sameness, similitude ≠ dissimilarity

resemble VERB = **be like**, look like, mirror, parallel, be similar to, bear a resemblance to

resent VERB = **be bitter about**, object to, grudge, begrudge, take exception to, take offence at ≠ be content with

resentment NOUN = **bitterness**, indignation, ill feeling, ill will, grudge, animosity, pique, rancour

reservation NOUN 1 *often plural* = **doubt**, scruples, hesitancy 2 = **reserve**, territory, preserve, sanctuary

reserve VERB 1 = **book**, prearrange, engage 2 = **put by**, secure 3 = **keep**, hold, save, store, retain, set aside, stockpile, hoard

▷ NOUN 1 = **store**, fund, savings, stock, supply, reservoir, hoard, cache 2 = **park**, reservation, preserve, sanctuary, tract, forest park (*N.Z.*) 3 = **shyness**, silence, restraint, constraint, reticence, secretiveness, taciturnity 4 = **reservation**, doubt, delay, uncertainty, indecision, hesitancy, vacillation, irresolution 5 = **substitute**, extra, spare, fall-back, auxiliary

reserved ADJECTIVE 1 = **uncommunicative**, retiring, silent, shy, restrained, secretive, reticent, taciturn ≠ uninhibited 2 = **set aside**, taken, kept, held, booked, retained, engaged, restricted

reservoir NOUN 1 = **lake**, pond, basin 2 = **store**, stock, source, supply, reserves, pool

r

reside VERB (*formal*) = **live**, lodge, dwell, stay, abide ≠ visit

residence NOUN = **home**, house, dwelling, place, flat, lodging, abode, habitation

resident NOUN 1 = **inhabitant**, citizen, local ≠ nonresident **2** = **tenant**, occupant, lodger **3** = **guest**, lodger

residue NOUN = **remainder**, remains, remnant, leftovers, rest, extra, excess, surplus

resign VERB 1 = **quit**, leave, step down (*informal*), vacate, abdicate, give *or* hand in your notice **2** = **give up**, abandon, yield, surrender, relinquish, renounce, forsake, forgo ▷ PHRASE: **resign yourself to something** = **accept**, succumb to, submit to, give in to, yield to, acquiesce to

resignation NOUN 1 = **leaving**, departure, abandonment, abdication **2** = **acceptance**, patience, submission, compliance, endurance, passivity, acquiescence, sufferance ≠ resistance

resigned ADJECTIVE = **stoical**, patient, subdued, long-suffering, compliant, unresisting

resist VERB 1 = **oppose**, combat, defy, stand up to, hinder ≠ accept **2** = **refrain from**, avoid, keep from, forgo, abstain from, forbear ≠ indulge in **3** = **withstand**, be proof against

resistance NOUN 1 = **opposition**, hostility, aversion **2** = **fighting**, fight, battle, struggle, defiance, obstruction, impediment, hindrance

resistant ADJECTIVE 1 = **opposed**, hostile, unwilling, intractable, antagonistic, intransigent **2** = **impervious**, hard, strong, tough, unaffected

resolution NOUN 1 = **declaration** **2** = **decision**, resolve, intention, aim, purpose, determination, intent **3** = **determination**, purpose, resolve, tenacity, perseverance, willpower, firmness, steadfastness

resolve VERB 1 = **work out**, answer, clear up, crack, fathom **2** = **decide**, determine, agree, purpose, intend, fix, conclude ▷ NOUN 1 = **determination**, resolution, willpower, firmness, steadfastness, resoluteness ≠ indecision **2** = **decision**, resolution, objective, purpose, intention

resort NOUN 1 = **holiday centre**, spot, retreat, haunt, tourist centre **2** = **recourse to**, reference to

resound VERB 1 = **echo**, resonate, reverberate, re-echo **2** = **ring**

resounding ADJECTIVE = **echoing**, full, ringing, powerful, booming, reverberating, resonant, sonorous

resource NOUN 1 = **facility** **2** = **means**, course, resort, device, expedient ▷ PLURAL NOUN 1 = **funds**, holdings, money, capital, riches, assets, wealth **2** = **reserves**, supplies, stocks

r

respect VERB 1 = **think highly of**, value, honour, admire, esteem, look up to, defer to, have a good *or* high opinion of 2 = **show consideration for**, honour, observe, heed 3 = **abide by**, follow, observe, comply with, obey, heed, keep to, adhere to ≠ disregard
▷ NOUN 1 = **regard**, honour, recognition, esteem, admiration, estimation ≠ contempt
2 = **consideration**, kindness, deference, tact, thoughtfulness, considerateness 3 = **particular**, way, point, matter, sense, detail, feature, aspect

respectable ADJECTIVE
1 = **honourable**, good, decent, worthy, upright, honest, reputable, estimable ≠ disreputable 2 = **decent**, neat, spruce 3 = **reasonable**, considerable, substantial, fair, ample, appreciable, sizable *or* sizeable ≠ small

respective ADJECTIVE = **specific**, own, individual, particular, relevant

respite NOUN = **pause**, break, rest, relief, halt, interval, recess, lull

respond VERB 1 = **answer**, return, reply, counter, retort, rejoin ≠ remain silent 2 *often with* **to** = **reply to**, answer 3 = **react**, retaliate, reciprocate

response NOUN = **answer**, return, reply, reaction, feedback, retort, counterattack, rejoinder

responsibility NOUN 1 = **duty**, business, job, role, task, accountability, answerability
2 = **fault**, blame, liability, guilt, culpability 3 = **obligation**, duty, liability, charge, care 4 = **authority**, power, importance, mana (*N.Z.*) 5 = **job**, task, function, role 6 = **level-headedness**, rationality, dependability, trustworthiness, conscientiousness, sensibleness

responsible ADJECTIVE 1 = **to blame**, guilty, at fault, culpable
2 = **in charge**, in control, in authority 3 = **accountable**, liable, answerable ≠ unaccountable
4 = **sensible**, reliable, rational, dependable, trustworthy, level-headed ≠ unreliable

responsive ADJECTIVE
= **sensitive**, open, alive, susceptible, receptive, reactive, impressionable ≠ unresponsive

rest¹ VERB 1 = **relax**, take it easy, sit down, be at ease, put your feet up, outspan (*S. African*) ≠ work
2 = **stop**, have a break, break off, take a breather (*informal*), halt, cease ≠ keep going 3 = **place**, repose, sit, lean, prop 4 = **be placed**, sit, lie, be supported, recline
▷ NOUN 1 = **relaxation**, repose, leisure, me-time ≠ work
2 = **pause**, break, stop, halt, interval, respite, lull, interlude
3 = **refreshment**, release, relief, ease, comfort, cure, remedy, solace 4 = **inactivity**
5 = **support**, stand, base, holder,

prop **6** = **calm**, tranquillity, stillness

rest² NOUN = **remainder**, remains, excess, remnants, others, balance, surplus, residue

restaurant NOUN = **café**, diner (*chiefly U.S. & Canad.*), bistro, cafeteria, tearoom, eatery *or* eaterie

restless ADJECTIVE **1** = **unsettled**, nervous, edgy, fidgeting, on edge, restive, jumpy, fidgety ≠ relaxed **2** = **moving**, wandering, unsettled, unstable, roving, transient, nomadic ≠ settled

restoration NOUN
1 = **reinstatement**, return, revival, restitution, re-establishment, replacement ≠ abolition
2 = **repair**, reconstruction, renewal, renovation, revitalization ≠ demolition

restore VERB **1** = **reinstate**, re-establish, reintroduce ≠ abolish **2** = **revive**, build up, strengthen, refresh, revitalize ≠ make worse **3** = **re-establish**, replace, reinstate, give back **4** = **repair**, refurbish, renovate, reconstruct, fix (up), renew, rebuild, mend ≠ demolish **5** = **return**, replace, recover, bring back, send back, hand back

restrain VERB **1** = **hold back**, control, check, contain, restrict, curb, hamper, hinder ≠ encourage **2** = **control**, inhibit

restrained ADJECTIVE
1 = **controlled**, moderate, self-controlled, calm, mild,

undemonstrative ≠ hot-headed
2 = **unobtrusive**, discreet, subdued, tasteful, quiet ≠ garish

restraint NOUN **1** = **limitation**, limit, check, ban, embargo, curb, rein, interdict, restraining order (*U.S. law*) ≠ freedom **2** = **self-control**, self-discipline, self-restraint, self-possession ≠ self-indulgence **3** = **constraint**, limitation, inhibition, control, restriction

restrict VERB **1** = **limit**, regulate, curb, ration ≠ widen **2** = **hamper**, handicap, restrain, inhibit

restriction NOUN **1** = **control**, rule, regulation, curb, restraint, confinement **2** = **limitation**, handicap, inhibition

result NOUN **1** = **consequence**, effect, outcome, end result, product, sequel, upshot ≠ cause **2** = **outcome**, end
▷ VERB *often followed by* **from** = **arise**, follow, issue, happen, appear, develop, spring, derive

resume VERB = **begin again**, continue, go on with, proceed with, carry on, reopen, restart ≠ discontinue

résumé NOUN = **summary**, synopsis, précis, rundown, recapitulation

resumption NOUN
= **continuation**, carrying on, reopening, renewal, restart, resurgence, re-establishment

resurgence NOUN = **revival**, return, renaissance, resurrection,

r

resumption, rebirth, re-emergence

resurrect VERB 1 = **revive**, renew, bring back, reintroduce 2 = **restore to life**, raise from the dead

resurrection NOUN 1 = **revival**, restoration, renewal, resurgence, return, renaissance, rebirth, reappearance ≠ killing off 2 = **raising** or **rising from the dead**, return from the dead ≠ demise

retain VERB 1 = **maintain**, reserve, preserve, keep up, continue to have 2 = **keep**, save ≠ let go

retaliate VERB = **pay someone back**, hit back, strike back, reciprocate, take revenge, get even with (*informal*), get your own back (*informal*) ≠ turn the other cheek

retaliation NOUN = **revenge**, repayment, vengeance, reprisal, an eye for an eye, reciprocation, requital, counterblow

retard VERB = **slow down**, check, arrest, delay, handicap, hinder, impede, set back ≠ speed up

retire VERB 1 = **stop working**, give up work 2 = **withdraw**, leave, exit, go away, depart 3 = **go to bed**, turn in (*informal*), hit the sack (*slang*), hit the hay (*slang*)

retirement NOUN = **withdrawal**, retreat, privacy, solitude, seclusion

retiring ADJECTIVE = **shy**, reserved, quiet, timid, unassuming, self-effacing, bashful, unassertive

≠ outgoing

retort VERB = **reply**, return, answer, respond, counter, come back with, riposte
▷ NOUN = **reply**, answer, response, comeback, riposte, rejoinder

retreat VERB = **withdraw**, back off, draw back, leave, go back, depart, fall back, pull back ≠ advance
▷ NOUN 1 = **flight**, retirement, departure, withdrawal, evacuation ≠ advance 2 = **refuge**, haven, shelter, sanctuary, hideaway, seclusion

retrieve VERB 1 = **get back**, regain, recover, restore, recapture 2 = **redeem**, save, win back, recoup

retrospect NOUN = **hindsight**, review, re-examination ≠ foresight

return VERB 1 = **come back**, go back, retreat, turn back, revert, reappear ≠ depart 2 = **put back**, replace, restore, reinstate ≠ keep 3 = **give back**, repay, refund, pay back, reimburse, recompense ≠ keep 4 = **recur**, repeat, persist, revert, happen again, reappear, come again 5 = **elect**, choose, vote in
▷ NOUN 1 = **reappearance** ≠ departure 2 = **restoration**, reinstatement, re-establishment ≠ removal 3 = **recurrence**, repetition, reappearance, reversion, persistence 4 = **profit**, interest, gain, income, revenue,

yield, proceeds, takings
5 = statement, report, form, list, account, summary

revamp VERB = **renovate**, restore, overhaul, refurbish, do up (*informal*), recondition

reveal VERB **1 = make known**, disclose, give away, make public, tell, announce, proclaim, let out ≠ keep secret **2 = show**, display, exhibit, unveil, uncover, manifest, unearth, unmask ≠ hide

revel VERB = **celebrate**, carouse, live it up (*informal*), make merry
▷ NOUN *often plural*
= **merrymaking**, party, celebration, spree, festivity, carousal

revelation NOUN **1 = disclosure**, news, announcement, publication, leak, confession, divulgence **2 = exhibition**, publication, exposure, unveiling, uncovering, unearthing, proclamation

revenge NOUN = **retaliation**, vengeance, reprisal, retribution, an eye for an eye
▷ VERB = **avenge**, repay, take revenge for, get your own back for (*informal*)

revenue NOUN = **income**, returns, profits, gain, yield, proceeds, receipts, takings ≠ expenditure

revere VERB = **be in awe of**, respect, honour, worship, reverence, exalt, look up to, venerate ≠ despise

reverse VERB **1** (*law*) = **change**, cancel, overturn, overthrow, undo, repeal, quash, revoke ≠ implement **2 = turn round**, turn over, turn upside down, upend **3 = transpose**, change, move, exchange, transfer, switch, shift, alter **4 = go backwards**, retreat, back up, turn back, move backwards, back ≠ go forward
▷ NOUN **1 = opposite**, contrary, converse, inverse **2 = misfortune**, blow, failure, disappointment, setback, hardship, reversal, adversity **3 = back**, rear, other side, wrong side, underside ≠ front
▷ ADJECTIVE = **opposite**, contrary, converse

revert VERB **1 = go back**, return, come back, resume **2 = return**
◉ WORD POWER
◉ Since the concept *back* is
◉ already contained in the
◉ *re-* part of the word *revert*, it
◉ is unnecessary to say that
◉ someone *reverts back* to a
◉ particular type of behaviour.

review NOUN **1 = survey**, study, analysis, examination, scrutiny **2 = critique**, commentary, evaluation, notice, criticism, judgment **3 = inspection**, parade, march past **4 = magazine**, journal, periodical, zine (*informal*)
▷ VERB **1 = reconsider**, revise, rethink, reassess, re-examine, re-evaluate, think over **2 = assess**, study, judge, evaluate, criticize **3 = inspect**, check, survey, examine, vet **4 = look back on**, remember, recall, reflect on,

r

recollect

reviewer NOUN = **critic**, judge, commentator

revise VERB 1 = **change**, review 2 = **edit**, correct, alter, update, amend, rework, redo, emend 3 = **study**, go over, run through, cram (*informal*), swot up on (*Brit. informal*)

revision NOUN 1 = **emendation**, updating, correction 2 = **change**, amendment 3 = **studying**, cramming (*informal*), swotting (*Brit. informal*), homework

revival NOUN 1 = **resurgence** ≠ decline 2 = **reawakening**, renaissance, renewal, resurrection, rebirth, revitalization

revive VERB 1 = **revitalize**, restore, renew, rekindle, invigorate, reanimate 2 = **bring round**, awaken 3 = **come round**, recover 4 = **refresh** ≠ exhaust

revolt NOUN = **uprising**, rising, revolution, rebellion, mutiny, insurrection, insurgency
▷ VERB 1 = **rebel**, rise up, resist, mutiny 2 = **disgust**, sicken, repel, repulse, nauseate, gross out (*U.S. slang*), turn your stomach, make your flesh creep

revolting ADJECTIVE = **disgusting**, foul, horrible, sickening, horrid, repellent, repulsive, nauseating, yucko (*Austral. slang*) ≠ delightful

revolution NOUN 1 = **revolt**, rising, coup, rebellion, uprising, mutiny, insurgency 2 = **transformation**, shift,

innovation, upheaval, reformation, sea change 3 = **rotation**, turn, cycle, circle, spin, lap, circuit, orbit

revolutionary ADJECTIVE 1 = **rebel**, radical, extremist, subversive, insurgent ≠ reactionary 2 = **innovative**, new, different, novel, radical, progressive, drastic, ground-breaking ≠ conventional
▷ NOUN = **rebel**, insurgent, revolutionist ≠ reactionary

revolve VERB 1 = **go round**, circle, orbit 2 = **rotate**, turn, wheel, spin, twist, whirl

reward NOUN 1 = **punishment**, retribution, comeuppance (*slang*), just deserts 2 = **payment**, return, prize, wages, compensation, bonus, premium, repayment ≠ penalty
▷ VERB = **compensate**, pay, repay, recompense, remunerate ≠ penalize

rewarding ADJECTIVE = **satisfying**, fulfilling, valuable, profitable, productive, worthwhile, beneficial, enriching ≠ unrewarding

rhetoric NOUN 1 = **hyperbole**, bombast, wordiness, verbosity, grandiloquence, magniloquence 2 = **oratory**, eloquence, public speaking, speech-making, elocution, declamation, grandiloquence, whaikorero (*N.Z.*)

rhetorical ADJECTIVE = **high-flown**, bombastic, verbose, oratorical, grandiloquent, declamatory, arty-farty (*informal*), magniloquent

rhyme NOUN = **poem**, song, verse, ode

rhythm NOUN 1 = **beat**, swing, accent, pulse, tempo, cadence, lilt 2 = **metre**, time

rich ADJECTIVE 1 = **wealthy**, affluent, well-off, loaded (*slang*), prosperous, well-heeled (*informal*), well-to-do, moneyed, minted (*Brit. slang*) ≠ poor 2 = **well-stocked**, full, productive, ample, abundant, plentiful, copious, well-supplied ≠ scarce 3 = **full-bodied**, sweet, fatty, tasty, creamy, luscious, succulent ≠ bland 4 = **fruitful**, productive, fertile, prolific ≠ barren 5 = **abounding**, luxurious, lush, abundant

riches PLURAL NOUN 1 = **wealth**, assets, plenty, fortune, substance, treasure, affluence, top whack (*informal*) ≠ poverty 2 = **resources**, treasures

richly ADVERB 1 = **elaborately**, lavishly, elegantly, splendidly, exquisitely, expensively, luxuriously, gorgeously 2 = **fully**, well, thoroughly, amply, appropriately, properly, suitably

rid VERB = **free**, clear, deliver, relieve, purge, unburden, make free, disencumber ▷ PHRASE: **get rid of something** *or* **someone** = **dispose of**, throw away *or* out, dump, remove, eliminate, expel, eject

riddle¹ NOUN 1 = **puzzle**, problem, conundrum, poser 2 = **enigma**, question, secret, mystery, puzzle, conundrum, teaser, problem

riddle² VERB 1 = **pierce**, pepper, puncture, perforate, honeycomb 2 = **pervade**, fill, spread through, spoil, pervade, infest, permeate

ride VERB 1 = **control**, handle, manage 2 = **travel**, be carried, go, move ▷ NOUN = **journey**, drive, trip, lift, outing, jaunt

ridicule VERB = **laugh at**, mock, make fun of, sneer at, jeer at, deride, poke fun at, chaff ▷ NOUN = **mockery**, scorn, derision, laughter, jeer, chaff, gibe, raillery

ridiculous ADJECTIVE = **laughable**, stupid, silly, absurd, ludicrous, farcical, comical, risible ≠ sensible

rife ADJECTIVE = **widespread**, rampant, general, common, universal, frequent, prevalent, ubiquitous

rifle VERB = **ransack**, rob, burgle, loot, strip, sack, plunder, pillage

rift NOUN 1 = **breach**, division, split, separation, falling out (*informal*), disagreement, quarrel 2* = **split**, opening, crack, gap, break, fault, flaw, cleft

rig VERB 1 = **fix**, engineer (*informal*), arrange, manipulate, tamper with, gerrymander 2 (*nautical*) = **equip**, fit out, kit out, outfit, supply, furnish ▷ PHRASE: **rig something up** = **set up**, build,

r

construct, put up, arrange, assemble, put together, erect

right ADJECTIVE 1 = **correct**, true, genuine, accurate, exact, precise, valid, factual, dinkum (*Austral. & N.Z. informal*) ≠ wrong 2 = **proper**, done, becoming, seemly, fitting, fit, appropriate, suitable ≠ inappropriate 3 = **just**, good, fair, moral, proper, ethical, honest, equitable ≠ unfair

▷ ADVERB 1 = **correctly**, truly, precisely, exactly, genuinely, accurately ≠ wrongly 2 = **suitably**, fittingly, appropriately, properly, aptly ≠ improperly 3 = **exactly**, squarely, precisely 4 = **directly**, straight, precisely, exactly, unswervingly, without deviation, by the shortest route, in a beeline 5 = **straight**, directly, quickly, promptly, straightaway ≠ indirectly

▷ NOUN 1 = **prerogative**, business, power, claim, authority, due, freedom, licence 2 = **justice**, truth, fairness, legality, righteousness, lawfulness ≠ injustice

▷ VERB = **rectify**, settle, fix, correct, sort out, straighten, redress, put right

right away ADVERB = **immediately**, now, directly, instantly, at once, straightaway, forthwith, pronto (*informal*)

righteous ADJECTIVE = **virtuous**, good, just, fair, moral, pure, ethical, upright ≠ wicked

rigid ADJECTIVE 1 = **strict**, set, fixed, exact, rigorous, stringent ≠ flexible 2 = **inflexible**, uncompromising, unbending 3 = **stiff**, inflexible, inelastic ≠ pliable

rigorous ADJECTIVE = **strict**, hard, demanding, tough, severe, exacting, harsh, stern ≠ soft

rim NOUN 1 = **edge**, lip, brim 2 = **border**, edge, trim 3 = **margin**, border, verge, brink

ring¹ VERB 1 = **phone**, call, telephone, buzz (*informal, chiefly Brit.*) 2 = **chime**, sound, toll, reverberate, clang, peal 3 = **reverberate**

▷ NOUN 1 = **call**, phone call, buzz (*informal, chiefly Brit.*) 2 = **chime**, knell, peal

● **WORD POWER**
● *Rang* is the past tense of the
● verb *ring*, as in *he rang the bell*.
● *Rung* is the past participle, as in
● *he has already rung the bell*, and
● care should be taken not to use
● it as if it were a variant form of
● the past tense.

ring² NOUN 1 = **circle**, round, band, circuit, loop, hoop, halo 2 = **arena**, enclosure, circus, rink 3 = **gang**, group, association, band, circle, mob, syndicate, cartel

▷ VERB = **encircle**, surround, enclose, girdle, gird

rinse VERB = **wash**, clean, dip, splash, cleanse, bathe

▷ NOUN = **wash**, dip, splash, bath

riot NOUN 1 = **disturbance**,

disorder, confusion, turmoil, upheaval, strife, turbulence, lawlessness **2** = **display**, show, splash, extravaganza, profusion **3** = **laugh**, joke, scream (*informal*), hoot (*informal*), lark
▷ **VERB 1** = **rampage**, run riot, go on the rampage ▷ **PHRASE**: **run riot 1** = **rampage**, go wild, be out of control **2** = **grow profusely**, spread like wildfire

rip VERB 1 = **tear**, cut, split, burst, rend, slash, claw, slit **2** = **be torn**, tear, split, burst
▷ **NOUN** = **tear**, cut, hole, split, rent, slash, slit, gash ▷ **PHRASE**: **rip someone off** (*slang*) = **cheat**, rob, con (*informal*), skin (*slang*), fleece, defraud, swindle, scam (*slang*)

ripe ADJECTIVE 1 = **ripened**, seasoned, ready, mature, mellow ≠ unripe **2** = **right**, suitable **3** = **mature 4** = **suitable**, timely, ideal, favourable, auspicious, opportune ≠ unsuitable

rip-off *or* **ripoff NOUN** (*slang*) = **cheat**, con (*informal*), scam (*slang*), con trick (*informal*), fraud, theft, swindle

rise VERB 1 = **get up**, stand up, get to your feet **2** = **arise 3** = **go up**, climb, ascend ≠ descend **4** = **loom**, tower **5** = **get steeper**, ascend, go uphill, slope upwards ≠ drop **6** = **increase**, mount ≠ decrease **7** = **grow**, go up, intensify **8** = **rebel**, revolt, mutiny **9** = **advance**, progress, get on, prosper
▷ **NOUN 1** = **upward slope**, incline, elevation, ascent, kopje *or* koppie (*S. African*) **2** = **increase**, upturn, upswing, upsurge ≠ decrease **3** = **pay increase**, raise (*U.S.*), increment **4** = **advancement**, progress, climb, promotion ▷ **PHRASE**: **give rise to something** = **cause**, produce, effect, result in, bring about

risk NOUN 1 = **danger**, chance, possibility, hazard **2** = **gamble**, chance, speculation, leap in the dark **3** = **peril**, jeopardy
▷ **VERB 1** = **stand a chance of 2** = **dare**, endanger, jeopardise, imperil, venture, gamble, hazard

risky ADJECTIVE = **dangerous**, hazardous, unsafe, perilous, uncertain, dodgy (*Brit., Austral. & N.Z. informal*), dicey (*informal, chiefly Brit.*), chancy (*informal*), shonky (*Austral. & N.Z. informal*) ≠ safe

rite NOUN = **ceremony**, custom, ritual, practice, procedure, observance

ritual NOUN 1 = **ceremony**, rite, observance **2** = **custom**, tradition, routine, convention, practice, procedure, habit, protocol, tikanga (*N.Z.*)
▷ **ADJECTIVE** = **ceremonial**, conventional, routine, customary, habitual

rival NOUN = **opponent**, competitor, contender, contestant, adversary ≠ supporter
▷ **VERB** = **compete with**, match,

r

equal, compare with, come up to, be a match for
▷ MODIFIER = **competing**, conflicting, opposing

rivalry NOUN = **competition**, opposition, conflict, contest, contention

river NOUN 1 = **stream**, brook, creek, waterway, tributary, burn (*Scot.*) 2 = **flow**, rush, flood, spate, torrent

riveting ADJECTIVE = **enthralling**, gripping, fascinating, absorbing, captivating, hypnotic, engrossing, spellbinding

road NOUN 1 = **roadway**, highway, motorway, track, route, path, lane, pathway 2 = **way**, path

roam VERB = **wander**, walk, range, travel, stray, ramble, prowl, rove

roar VERB 1 = **thunder** 2 = **guffaw**, laugh heartily, hoot, split your sides (*informal*) 3 = **cry**, shout, yell, howl, bellow, bawl, bay
▷ NOUN 1 = **guffaw**, hoot 2 = **cry**, shout, yell, howl, outcry, bellow

rob VERB 1 = **steal from**, hold up, mug (*informal*) 2 = **raid**, hold up, loot, plunder, burgle, pillage 3 = **dispossess**, con (*informal*), cheat, defraud 4 = **deprive**, do out of (*informal*)

robber NOUN = **thief**, raider, burglar, looter, fraud, cheat, bandit, plunderer, rogue trader

robbery NOUN 1 = **burglary**, raid, hold-up, rip-off (*slang*), stick-up (*slang, chiefly U.S.*), home invasion (*Austral. & N.Z.*) 2 = **theft**, stealing, mugging (*informal*),

plunder, swindle, pillage, larceny

robe NOUN = **gown**, costume, habit

robot NOUN = **machine**, automaton, android, mechanical man

robust ADJECTIVE = **strong**, tough, powerful, fit, healthy, strapping, hardy, vigorous ≠ weak

rock¹ NOUN = **stone**, boulder

rock² VERB 1 = **sway**, pitch, swing, reel, toss, lurch, roll 2 = **shock**, surprise, shake, stun, astonish, stagger, astound

rocky¹ ADJECTIVE = **rough**, rugged, stony, craggy

rocky² ADJECTIVE = **unstable**, shaky, wobbly, rickety, unsteady

rod NOUN 1 = **stick**, bar, pole, shaft, cane 2 = **staff**, baton, wand

rogue NOUN 1 = **scoundrel**, crook (*informal*), villain, fraud, blackguard, skelm (*S. African*), rorter (*Austral. slang*), wrong 'un (*Austral. slang*) 2 = **scamp**, rascal, scally (*Northwest English dialect*), nointer (*Austral. slang*)

role NOUN 1 = **job**, part, position, post, task, duty, function, capacity 2 = **part**, character, representation, portrayal

roll VERB 1 = **turn**, wheel, spin, go round, revolve, rotate, whirl, swivel 2 = **trundle**, go, move 3 = **flow**, run, course 4 *often with* **up** = **wind**, bind, wrap, swathe, envelop, furl, enfold 5 *often with* **out** = **level**, even, press, smooth, flatten 6 = **toss**, rock, lurch, reel, tumble, sway

RODENTS

- agouti
- beaver
- capybara
- cavy
- chinchilla
- chipmunk
- coypu *or* nutria
- desert rat
- dormouse
- fieldmouse
- flying squirrel
- gerbil, gerbille, *or* jerbil
- gopher *or* pocket gopher
- gopher *or* ground squirrel
- grey squirrel
- groundhog *or* woodchuck
- guinea pig *or* cavy
- hamster
- harvest mouse
- hedgehog
- house mouse
- jerboa
- kangaroo rat
- kiore (*N.Z.*)
- lemming
- Māori rat *or* (*N.Z.*) kiore
- marmot
- mouse
- muskrat *or* musquash
- paca
- pack rat
- porcupine
- rat
- red squirrel *or* chickaree
- spinifex hopping mouse *or* (*Austral.*) dargawarra
- springhaas
- squirrel
- suslik *or* souslik
- viscacha *or* vizcacha
- vole
- water rat
- water vole *or* water rat

▷ NOUN 1 = **rumble**, boom, roar, thunder, reverberation 2 = **register**, record, list, index, census 3 = **turn**, spin, rotation, cycle, wheel, revolution, reel, whirl

romance NOUN 1 = **love affair**, relationship, affair, attachment, liaison, amour 2 = **excitement**, colour, charm, mystery, glamour, fascination 3 = **story**, tale, fantasy, legend, fairy tale, love story, melodrama

romantic ADJECTIVE 1 = **loving**, tender, passionate, fond, sentimental, amorous, icky (*informal*) ≠ unromantic 2 = **idealistic**, unrealistic, impractical, dreamy, starry-eyed ≠ realistic 3 = **exciting**, fascinating, mysterious, colourful, glamorous ≠ unexciting ▷ NOUN = **idealist**, dreamer, sentimentalist

romp VERB = **frolic**, sport, have fun, caper, cavort, frisk, gambol ▷ NOUN = **frolic**, lark (*informal*), caper

room NOUN 1 = **chamber**, office, apartment 2 = **space**, area, capacity, extent, expanse 3 = **opportunity**, scope, leeway, chance, range, occasion, margin

root[1] NOUN 1 = **stem**, tuber, rhizome 2 = **source**, cause, heart, bottom, base, seat, seed, foundation ▷ PLURAL NOUN = **sense of belonging**, origins, heritage,

r

birthplace, home, family, cradle
▷ **PHRASE**: **root something**
or **someone out** = **get rid of**,
remove, eliminate, abolish,
eradicate, do away with, weed
out, exterminate

root² VERB = **dig**, burrow, ferret

rope NOUN = **cord**, line, cable,
strand, hawser ▷ **PHRASES**: **know
the ropes** = **be experienced**,
be knowledgeable, be an old
hand; **rope someone in** or **into
something** (*Brit.*) = **persuade**,
involve, engage, enlist, talk into,
inveigle

rosy ADJECTIVE 1 = **glowing**,
blooming, radiant, ruddy, healthy-
looking ≠ pale **2** = **promising**,
encouraging, bright, optimistic,
hopeful, cheerful, favourable,
auspicious ≠ gloomy **3** = **pink**,
red
▷ *see* **shades of red**

rot VERB 1 = **decay**, spoil,
deteriorate, perish, decompose,
moulder, go bad, putrefy
2 = **crumble 3** = **deteriorate**,
decline, waste away
▷ NOUN 1 = **decay**,
decomposition, corruption,
mould, blight, canker,
putrefaction **2** (*informal*)
= **nonsense**, rubbish, drivel,
twaddle, garbage (*chiefly U.S.*),
trash, tripe (*informal*), claptrap
(*informal*), bizzo (*Austral. slang*),
bull's wool (*Austral. & N.Z. slang*)
▷ **RELATED WORD**: *adjective* **putrid**

rotate VERB 1 = **revolve**, turn,
wheel, spin, reel, go round, swivel,
pivot **2** = **follow in sequence**,
switch, alternate, take turns

rotation NOUN 1 = **revolution**,
turning, turn, wheel,
spin, spinning, reel, orbit
2 = **sequence**, switching, cycle,
succession, alternation

rotten ADJECTIVE 1 = **decaying**,
bad, rank, corrupt, sour, stinking,
perished, festering, festy (*Austral.
slang*) ≠ fresh **2** = **crumbling**,
perished **3** (*informal*)
= **despicable**, mean, base, dirty,
nasty, contemptible **4** (*informal*)
= **inferior**, poor, inadequate, duff
(*Brit. informal*), unsatisfactory,
lousy (*slang*), substandard,
crummy (*slang*), bodger or bodgie
(*Austral. slang*) **5** = **corrupt**,
immoral, crooked (*informal*),
dishonest, dishonourable,
perfidious ≠ honourable

rough ADJECTIVE 1 = **uneven**,
broken, rocky, irregular, jagged,
bumpy, stony, craggy ≠ even
2 = **boisterous**, hard, tough,
arduous **3** = **ungracious**, blunt,
rude, coarse, brusque, uncouth,
impolite, uncivil ≠ refined
4 = **unpleasant**, hard, difficult,
tough, uncomfortable ≠ easy
5 = **approximate**, estimated
≠ exact **6** = **vague**, general,
sketchy, imprecise, inexact
7 = **basic**, crude, unfinished,
incomplete, imperfect,
rudimentary, sketchy, unrefined
≠ complete **8** = **stormy**, wild,
turbulent, choppy, squally ≠ calm
9 = **harsh**, tough, nasty, cruel,

unfeeling ≠ gentle
▷ NOUN = **outline**, draft, mock-up, preliminary sketch ▷ PHRASES: **rough and ready 1** = **makeshift**, crude, provisional, improvised, sketchy, stopgap **2** = **unrefined**, shabby, untidy, unkempt, unpolished, ill-groomed, daggy (*Austral.* & *N.Z. informal*); **rough something out** = **outline**, plan, draft, sketch

round NOUN **1** = **series**, session, cycle, sequence, succession **2** = **stage**, turn, level, period, division, session, lap **3** = **sphere**, ball, band, ring, circle, disc, globe, orb **4** = **course**, tour, circuit, beat, series, schedule, routine
▷ ADJECTIVE **1** = **spherical**, rounded, curved, circular, cylindrical, rotund, globular **2** = **plump**, full, ample, fleshy, rotund, full-fleshed
▷ VERB = **go round**, circle, skirt, flank, bypass, encircle, turn
▷ PHRASE: **round something** *or* **someone up** = **gather**, muster, group, drive, collect, rally, herd, marshal

roundabout ADJECTIVE
1 = **indirect**, devious, tortuous, circuitous, evasive, discursive ≠ direct **2** = **oblique**, implied, indirect, circuitous

roundup NOUN = **muster**, collection, rally, assembly, herding

rouse VERB **1** = **wake up**, call, wake, awaken **2** = **excite**, move, stir, provoke, anger, animate, agitate, inflame **3** = **stimulate**,
provoke, incite

rousing ADJECTIVE = **lively**, moving, spirited, exciting, inspiring, stirring, stimulating ≠ dull

rout VERB = **defeat**, beat, overthrow, thrash, destroy, crush, conquer, wipe the floor with (*informal*)
▷ NOUN = **defeat**, beating, overthrow, thrashing, pasting (*slang*), debacle, drubbing

route NOUN **1** = **way**, course, road, direction, path, journey, itinerary **2** = **beat**, circuit
● WORD POWER
● When adding -*ing* to the
● verb *route* to form the
● present participle, it is more
● conventional, and clearer, to
● keep the final *e* from the end
● of the verb stem: *routeing*. The
● spelling *routing* in this sense is
● also possible, but keeping the
● *e* distinguishes it from *routing*,
● which is the participle formed
● from the verb *rout* meaning 'to
● defeat'.

routine NOUN = **procedure**, programme, order, practice, method, pattern, custom
▷ ADJECTIVE **1** = **usual**, standard, normal, customary, ordinary, typical, everyday, habitual ≠ unusual **2** = **boring**, dull, predictable, tedious, tiresome, humdrum

row¹ NOUN = **line**, bank, range, series, file, string, column ▷ PHRASE: **in a row**

= **consecutively**, running, in turn, one after the other, successively, in sequence

row² NOUN 1 = **quarrel**, dispute, argument, squabble, tiff, trouble, brawl 2 = **disturbance**, noise, racket, uproar, commotion, rumpus, tumult
▷ VERB = **quarrel**, fight, argue, dispute, squabble, wrangle

royal ADJECTIVE 1 = **regal**, kingly, queenly, princely, imperial, sovereign 2 = **splendid**, grand, impressive, magnificent, majestic, stately

rub VERB 1 = **stroke**, massage, caress 2 = **polish**, clean, shine, wipe, scour 3 = **chafe**, scrape, grate, abrade
▷ NOUN 1 = **massage**, caress, kneading 2 = **polish**, stroke, shine, wipe ▷ PHRASE: **rub something out** = **erase**, remove, cancel, wipe out, delete, obliterate, efface

rubbish NOUN 1 = **waste**, refuse, scrap, junk (*informal*), litter, garbage (*chiefly U.S.*), trash, lumber 2 = **nonsense**, garbage (*chiefly U.S.*), twaddle, rot, trash, hot air (*informal*), tripe (*informal*), claptrap (*informal*), bizzo (*Austral. slang*), bull's wool (*Austral. & N.Z. slang*)

rude ADJECTIVE 1 = **impolite**, insulting, cheeky, abusive, disrespectful, impertinent, insolent, impudent ≠ polite 2 = **uncivilized**, rough, coarse, brutish, boorish, uncouth,

loutish, graceless 3 = **vulgar** ≠ refined 4 = **unpleasant**, sharp, sudden, harsh, startling, abrupt 5 = **roughly-made**, simple, rough, raw, crude, primitive, makeshift, artless ≠ well-made

rue VERB (*literary*) = **regret**, mourn, lament, repent, be sorry for, kick yourself for

ruffle VERB 1 = **disarrange**, disorder, mess up, rumple, tousle, dishevel, muss (*U.S. & Canad.*) 2 = **annoy**, upset, irritate, agitate, nettle, fluster, peeve (*informal*) ≠ calm

rugged ADJECTIVE 1 = **rocky**, broken, rough, craggy, difficult, ragged, irregular, uneven ≠ even 2 = **strong-featured**, rough-hewn, weather-beaten ≠ delicate 3 = **well-built**, strong, tough, robust, sturdy 4 (*chiefly U.S. & Canad.*) = **tough**, strong, robust, muscular, sturdy, burly, husky (*informal*), brawny ≠ delicate

ruin VERB 1 = **destroy**, devastate, wreck, defeat, smash, crush, demolish, lay waste, kennet (*Austral. slang*), jeff (*Austral. slang*) ≠ create 2 = **bankrupt**, break, impoverish, beggar, pauperize 3 = **spoil**, damage, mess up, blow (*slang*), screw up (*informal*), botch, make a mess of, crool *or* cruel (*Austral. slang*) ≠ improve
▷ NOUN 1 = **bankruptcy**, insolvency, destitution 2 = **disrepair**, decay, disintegration, ruination, wreckage 3 = **destruction**, fall,

breakdown, defeat, collapse, wreck, undoing, downfall ≠ preservation

rule NOUN 1 = **regulation**, law, direction, guideline, decree 2 = **precept**, principle, canon, maxim, tenet, axiom 3 = **custom**, procedure, practice, routine, tradition, habit, convention 4 = **government**, power, control, authority, command, regime, reign, jurisdiction, mana (*N.Z.*) ▷ VERB 1 = **govern**, control, direct, have power over, command over, have charge of 2 = **reign**, govern, be in power, be in authority 3 = **decree**, decide, judge, settle, pronounce 4 = **be prevalent**, prevail, predominate, be customary, preponderate ▷ PHRASES: **as a rule** = **usually**, generally, mainly, normally, on the whole, ordinarily; **rule someone out** = **exclude**, eliminate, disqualify, ban, reject, dismiss, prohibit, leave out; **rule something out** = **reject**, exclude, eliminate

ruler NOUN 1 = **governor**, leader, lord, commander, controller, monarch, sovereign, head of state 2 = **measure**, rule, yardstick

ruling ADJECTIVE 1 = **governing**, reigning, controlling, commanding 2 = **predominant**, dominant, prevailing, preponderant, chief, main, principal, pre-eminent ≠ minor ▷ NOUN = **decision**, verdict, judgment, decree, adjudication,

pronouncement

rumour NOUN = **story**, news, report, talk, word, whisper, buzz, gossip, goss (*informal*)

run VERB 1 = **race**, rush, dash, hurry, sprint, bolt, gallop, hare (*Brit. informal*) ≠ dawdle 2 = **flee**, escape, take off (*informal*), bolt, beat it (*slang*), leg it (*informal*), take flight, do a runner (*slang*) ≠ stay 3 = **take part**, compete 4 = **continue**, go, stretch, reach, extend, proceed ≠ stop 5 (*chiefly U.S. & Canad.*) = **compete**, stand, contend, be a candidate, put yourself up for, take part 6 = **manage**, lead, direct, be in charge of, head, control, operate, handle 7 = **go**, work, operate, perform, function 8 = **perform**, carry out 9 = **work**, go, operate, function 10 = **pass**, go, move, roll, glide, skim 11 = **flow**, pour, stream, go, leak, spill, discharge, gush 12 = **publish**, feature, display, print 13 = **melt**, dissolve, liquefy, go soft 14 = **smuggle**, traffic in, bootleg ▷ NOUN 1 = **race**, rush, dash, sprint, gallop, jog, spurt 2 = **ride**, drive, trip, spin (*informal*), outing, excursion, jaunt 3 = **sequence**, period, stretch, spell, course, season, series, string 4 = **enclosure**, pen, coop ▷ PHRASES: **run away** VERB = **flee**, escape, bolt, abscond, do a runner (*slang*), make a run for it, scram (*informal*), fly the coop (*U.S. & Canad. informal*), do

r

a Skase (*Austral. informal*); **run into someone** VERB = **meet**, encounter, bump into, run across, come across *or* upon; **run into something 1** = **be beset by**, encounter, come across *or* upon, face, experience **2** = **collide with**, hit, strike; **run out 1** = **be used up**, dry up, give out, fail, finish, be exhausted **2** = **expire**, end, terminate; **run over something 1** = **exceed**, overstep, go over the top of, go over the limit of **2** = **review**, check, go through, go over, run through, rehearse; **run over something** *or* **someone** = **knock down**, hit, run down, knock over; **run something** *or* **someone down 1** = **criticize**, denigrate, belittle, knock (*informal*), rubbish (*informal*), slag (off) (*slang*), disparage, decry **2** = **downsize**, cut, reduce, trim, decrease, cut back, curtail, kennet (*Austral. slang*), jeff (*Austral. slang*) **3** = **knock down**, hit, run into, run over, knock over

rundown *or* **run-down**
ADJECTIVE **1** = **exhausted**, weak, drained, weary, unhealthy, worn-out, debilitated, below par ≠ fit **2** = **dilapidated**, broken-down, shabby, worn-out, seedy, ramshackle, decrepit

runner NOUN **1** = **athlete**, sprinter, jogger **2** = **messenger**, courier, errand boy, dispatch bearer

running NOUN **1** = **management**, control, administration, direction, leadership, organization, supervision
2 = **working**, performance, operation, functioning, maintenance
▷ ADJECTIVE **1** = **continuous**, constant, perpetual, uninterrupted, incessant
2 = **in succession**, unbroken
3 = **flowing**, moving, streaming, coursing

rupture NOUN = **break**, tear, split, crack, rent, burst, breach, fissure
▷ VERB = **break**, separate, tear, split, crack, burst, sever

rural ADJECTIVE **1** = **agricultural**, country **2** = **rustic**, country, pastoral, sylvan ≠ urban

rush VERB **1** = **hurry**, run, race, shoot, fly, career, speed, tear ≠ dawdle **2** = **push**, hurry, press, hustle **3** = **attack**, storm, charge at
▷ NOUN **1** = **dash**, charge, race, scramble, stampede **2** = **hurry**, haste, hustle **3** = **surge**, flow, gush **4** = **attack**, charge, assault, onslaught
▷ ADJECTIVE = **hasty**, fast, quick, hurried, rapid, urgent, swift ≠ leisurely

● **WORD POWER**
● Most Russian words in English
● refer in a restricted way to
● specific political aspects of
● the former Soviet Union,
● e.g. *agit-prop*, *glasnost*, and
● *perestroika*. A couple of Russian
● words which have gained
● wider currency are *refusenik* and
● *intelligentsia*. The intelligentsia

r

- were the educated class in
- pre-revolutionary Russia – this
- label is now applied more
- generally to the intellectual or
- educated section of any society.
- It shares some of the meaning
- of chattering classes in that
- both refer to the educated
- parts of a society. However,
- whereas 'intelligentsia' implies
- an intellectual elite who shape
- their society through political
- activism or the development
- of culture, 'chattering
- classes' is often a derogatory
- description of the educated
- liberal middle-class. Refusenik
- is a term which originally
- denoted a Jew in the Soviet
- Union who was not permitted
- to emigrate to Israel. It now
- also refers to any protester
- against a system or law, by a
- change in meaning from 'one
- who has been refused' to 'one
- who refuses'. The **-nik** suffix is
- an interesting one: by analogy
- with **Sputnik**, the unmanned
- satellites launched by the
- Soviet Union from the 1950s,
- -nik also appeared in other
- English words after that time,
- e.g. **beatnik**. It is the Russian
- equivalent of the English suffix
- -er, added to nouns to mean
- 'the person who performs this
- action' e.g. teacher, writer.

rust NOUN 1 = **corrosion**,
oxidation 2 = **mildew**, must,
mould, rot, blight

▷ VERB = **corrode**, oxidize

rusty ADJECTIVE 1 = **corroded**,
rusted, oxidized, rust-covered
2 = **out of practice**, weak, stale,
unpractised 3 = **reddish-brown**,
chestnut, reddish, russet, coppery,
rust-coloured
▷ see **shades of red**

ruthless ADJECTIVE = **merciless**,
harsh, cruel, brutal, relentless,
callous, heartless, remorseless
≠ merciful

r

Ss

sabotage VERB = **damage**, destroy, wreck, disable, disrupt, subvert, incapacitate, vandalize
▷ NOUN = **damage**, destruction, wrecking

sack¹ NOUN = **bag**, pocket, sac, pouch, receptacle
▷ VERB (*informal*) = **dismiss**, fire (*informal*), axe (*informal*), discharge, kiss off (*slang, chiefly U.S. & Canad.*), give (someone) the push (*informal*), kennet (*Austral. slang*), jeff (*Austral. slang*)
▷ PHRASE: **the sack** (*informal*) = **dismissal**, discharge, the boot (*slang*), the axe (*informal*), the push (*slang*)

sack² VERB = **plunder**, loot, pillage, strip, rob, raid, ruin
▷ NOUN = **plundering**, looting, pillage

sacred ADJECTIVE 1 = **holy**, hallowed, blessed, divine, revered, sanctified ≠ secular
2 = **religious**, holy, ecclesiastical, hallowed ≠ unconsecrated
3 = **inviolable**, protected, sacrosanct, hallowed, inalienable, unalterable

sacrifice VERB 1 = **offer**, offer up, immolate 2 = **give up**, abandon, relinquish, lose, surrender, let go, do without, renounce
▷ NOUN 1 = **offering**, oblation
2 = **surrender**, loss, giving up, rejection, abdication, renunciation, repudiation, forswearing

sad ADJECTIVE 1 = **unhappy**, down, low, blue, depressed, melancholy, mournful, dejected ≠ happy 2 = **tragic**, moving, upsetting, depressing, dismal, pathetic, poignant, harrowing
3 = **deplorable**, bad, sorry, terrible, unfortunate, regrettable, lamentable, wretched ≠ good

sadden VERB = **upset**, depress, distress, grieve, make sad, deject

saddle VERB = **burden**, load, lumber (*Brit. informal*), encumber

sadness NOUN = **unhappiness**, sorrow, grief, depression, the blues, misery, melancholy, poignancy ≠ happiness

safe ADJECTIVE 1 = **protected**, secure, impregnable, out of danger, safe and sound, in safe hands, out of harm's way ≠ endangered 2 = **all right**, intact, unscathed, unhurt, unharmed, undamaged, O.K. or okay (*informal*) 3 = **risk-free**, sound, secure, certain, impregnable
▷ NOUN = **strongbox**, vault, coffer, repository, deposit box, safe-deposit box

safeguard VERB = **protect**, guard, defend, save, preserve, look after, keep safe
▷ NOUN = **protection**, security, defence, guard

S

safely ADVERB =**in safety**, with impunity, without risk, safe and sound

safety NOUN 1 =**security**, protection, safeguards, precautions, safety measures, impregnability ≠ risk
2 =**shelter**, haven, protection, cover, retreat, asylum, refuge, sanctuary

sag VERB 1 =**sink**, bag, droop, fall, slump, dip, give way, hang loosely
2 =**drop**, sink, slump, flop, droop, loll 3 =**decline**, tire, flag, weaken, wilt, wane, droop

saga NOUN 1 =**carry-on** (*informal*), performance (*informal*), pantomime (*informal*) 2 =**epic**, story, tale, narrative, yarn

sage NOUN =**wise man**, philosopher, guru, master, elder, tohunga (*N.Z.*)
▷ ADJECTIVE =**wise**, sensible, judicious, sagacious, sapient

sail NOUN =**sheet**, canvas
▷ VERB 1 =**go by water**, cruise, voyage, ride the waves, go by sea
2 =**set sail**, embark, get under way, put to sea, put off, leave port, hoist sail, cast *or* weigh anchor
3 =**pilot**, steer 4 =**glide**, sweep, float, fly, wing, soar, drift, skim

sailor NOUN =**mariner**, marine, seaman, sea dog, seafarer

sake NOUN =**purpose**, interest, reason, end, aim, objective, motive ▷ PHRASE: **for someone's sake** =**in someone's interests**, to someone's advantage, on someone's account, for the benefit of, for the good of, for the welfare of, out of respect for, out of consideration for

salary NOUN =**pay**, income, wage, fee, payment, wages, earnings, allowance

sale NOUN 1 =**selling**, marketing, dealing, transaction, disposal
2 =**auction**, fair, mart, bazaar

salt NOUN =**seasoning**
▷ ADJECTIVE =**salty**, saline, brackish, briny

salute VERB 1 =**greet**, welcome, acknowledge, address, hail, mihi (*N.Z.*) 2 =**honour**, acknowledge, recognize, pay tribute *or* homage to
▷ NOUN =**greeting**, recognition, salutation, address

salvage VERB =**save**, recover, rescue, get back, retrieve, redeem

salvation NOUN =**saving**, rescue, recovery, salvage, redemption, deliverance ≠ ruin

same ADJECTIVE 1 =**identical**, similar, alike, equal, twin, corresponding, duplicate
≠ different 2 =**the very same**, one and the same, selfsame
3 =**aforementioned**, aforesaid
4 =**unchanged**, consistent, constant, unaltered, invariable, unvarying, changeless ≠ altered

◉ **WORD POWER**
◉ The use of *same* as in *if you send*
◉ *us your order for the materials,*
◉ *we will deliver same tomorrow*
◉ is common in business and
◉ official English. In general
◉ English, however, this use of

S

the word is best avoided, as it may sound rather stilted: *may I borrow your book? I will return it* (not *same*) *tomorrow.*

sample NOUN **1** = **specimen**, example, model, pattern, instance **2** = **cross section**
▷ VERB = **test**, try, experience, taste, inspect

sanction VERB = **permit**, allow, approve, endorse, authorize ≠ forbid
▷ NOUN **1** *often plural* = **ban**, boycott, embargo, exclusion, penalty, coercive measures ≠ permission **2** = **permission**, backing, authority, approval, authorization, O.K. *or* okay (*informal*), stamp *or* seal of approval ≠ ban

sanctuary NOUN **1** = **protection**, shelter, refuge, haven, retreat, asylum **2** = **reserve**, park, preserve, reservation, national park, tract, nature reserve, conservation area

sane ADJECTIVE **1** = **rational**, all there (*informal*), of sound mind, compos mentis (*Latin*), in your right mind, mentally sound ≠ insane **2** = **sensible**, sound, reasonable, balanced, judicious, level-headed, grounded ≠ foolish

● **WORD POWER**
● Most of the words which
● have come into English from
● Sanskrit are connected with
● eastern religions, such as
● *mantra*, *guru*, *karma*, and
● *nirvana*. These words have

● all developed more general
● meanings alongside their
● specialised religious sense.
● For example, mantra, literally
● 'speech', in Hinduism is a
● sacred word or sound which
● aids concentration and carries
● spiritual meaning. In general
● language, mantra means a
● kind of catchphrase or slogan,
● e.g. Right now, his mantra is
● 'make love, not war'. In both
● Hinduism and Buddhism the
● concept of karma means that a
● person's past deeds will decide
● their future reincarnations.
● It has developed a looser
● meaning of 'fate' or 'destiny'
● in general language where
● bad deeds are punished and
● good deeds rewarded by the
● universe. Nirvana, literally
● 'extinction', has similarly
● generated a non-religious
● meaning. In Hinduism and
● Buddhism, nirvana is liberation
● from the cycle of reincarnation.
● In general language it means
● paradise or a state of bliss.
● Although guru refers to a Hindu
● or Sikh religious teacher, it has
● also been used of an expert or
● leader in any field, particularly
● in a mocking way, e.g. the most
● venerable management guru of
● them all.

sap¹ NOUN **1** = **juice**, essence, vital fluid, lifeblood **2** (*slang*) = **fool**, jerk (*slang, chiefly U.S. & Canad.*), idiot, wally (*slang*), twit (*informal*), simpleton, ninny, dorba *or* dorb (*Austral. slang*), bogan (*Austral. slang*)

sap² VERB = **weaken**, drain, undermine, exhaust, deplete

satanic ADJECTIVE = **evil**, demonic, hellish, black, wicked, devilish, infernal, fiendish ≠ godly

satire NOUN 1 = **mockery**, irony, ridicule 2 = **parody**, mockery, caricature, lampoon, burlesque

satisfaction NOUN
1 = **fulfilment**, pleasure, achievement, relish, gratification, pride ≠ dissatisfaction
2 = **contentment**, content, comfort, pleasure, happiness, enjoyment, satiety, repletion ≠ discontent

satisfactory ADJECTIVE = **adequate**, acceptable, good enough, average, fair, all right, sufficient, passable ≠ unsatisfactory

satisfy VERB 1 = **content**, please, indulge, gratify, pander to, assuage, pacify, quench ≠ dissatisfy 2 = **convince**, persuade, assure, reassure ≠ dissuade 3 = **comply with**, meet, fulfil, answer, serve, fill, observe, obey ≠ fail to meet

saturate VERB 1 = **flood**, overwhelm, swamp, overrun 2 = **soak**, steep, drench, imbue, suffuse, wet through, waterlog, souse

saturated ADJECTIVE = **soaked**, soaking (wet), drenched, sodden, dripping, waterlogged, sopping

(wet), wet through

sauce NOUN = **dressing**, dip, relish, condiment

savage ADJECTIVE 1 = **cruel**, brutal, vicious, fierce, harsh, ruthless, ferocious, sadistic ≠ gentle 2 = **wild**, fierce, ferocious, unbroken, feral, untamed, undomesticated ≠ tame 3 = **primitive**, undeveloped, uncultivated, uncivilized 4 = **uncultivated**, rugged, unspoilt, uninhabited, rough, uncivilized ≠ cultivated
▷ NOUN = **lout**, yob (*Brit. slang*), barbarian, yahoo, hoon (*Austral. & N.Z.*), boor, cougan (*Austral. slang*), scozza (*Austral. slang*), bogan (*Austral. slang*)
▷ VERB = **maul**, tear, claw, attack, mangle, lacerate, mangulate (*Austral. slang*)

save VERB 1 = **rescue**, free, release, deliver, recover, get out, liberate, salvage ≠ endanger 2 = **keep**, reserve, set aside, store, collect, gather, hold, hoard ≠ spend 3 = **protect**, keep, guard, preserve, look after, safeguard, salvage, conserve 4 = **put aside**, keep, reserve, collect, retain, set aside, put by

saving NOUN = **economy**, discount, reduction, bargain
▷ PLURAL NOUN = **nest egg**, fund, store, reserves, resources

saviour NOUN = **rescuer**, deliverer, defender, protector, liberator, redeemer, preserver

Saviour NOUN = **Christ**, Jesus, the

Messiah, the Redeemer

savour VERB 1 = **relish**, delight in, revel in, luxuriate in 2 = **enjoy**, appreciate, relish, delight in, revel in, luxuriate in
▷ NOUN = **flavour**, taste, smell, relish, smack, tang, piquancy

say VERB 1 = **state**, declare, remark, announce, maintain, mention, assert, affirm 2 = **speak**, utter, voice, express, pronounce 3 = **suggest**, express, imply, communicate, disclose, give away, convey, divulge 4 = **suppose**, supposing, imagine, assume, presume 5 = **estimate**, suppose, guess, conjecture, surmise
▷ NOUN 1 = **influence**, power, control, authority, weight, clout (*informal*), mana (*N.Z.*) 2 = **chance to speak**, vote, voice

saying NOUN = **proverb**, maxim, adage, dictum, axiom, aphorism

scale¹ NOUN = **flake**, plate, layer, lamina

scale² NOUN 1 = **degree**, size, range, extent, dimensions, scope, magnitude, breadth 2 = **system of measurement**, measuring system 3 = **ranking**, ladder, hierarchy, series, sequence, progression 4 = **ratio**, proportion
▷ VERB = **climb up**, mount, ascend, surmount, clamber up, escalade

scan VERB 1 = **glance over**, skim, look over, eye, check, examine, check out (*informal*), run over, surf (*computing*) 2 = **survey**, search, investigate, sweep, scour, scrutinize

scandal NOUN 1 = **disgrace**, crime, offence, sin, embarrassment, wrongdoing, dishonourable behaviour, discreditable behaviour 2 = **gossip**, goss (*informal*), talk, rumours, dirt, slander, tattle, aspersion 3 = **shame**, disgrace, stigma, infamy, opprobrium 4 = **outrage**, shame, insult, disgrace, injustice, crying shame

scant ADJECTIVE = **inadequate**, meagre, sparse, little, minimal, barely sufficient ≠ adequate

scapegoat NOUN = **fall guy**, whipping boy

scar NOUN 1 = **mark**, injury, wound, blemish 2 = **trauma**, suffering, pain, torture, anguish
▷ VERB = **mark**, disfigure, damage, mar, mutilate, blemish, deface

scarce ADJECTIVE 1 = **in short supply**, insufficient ≠ plentiful 2 = **rare**, few, uncommon, few and far between, infrequent ≠ common

scarcely ADVERB 1 = **hardly**, barely 2 (*often used ironically*) = **by no means**, hardly, definitely not
◉ WORD POWER
◉ Since *scarcely*, *hardly*, and *barely*
◉ already have negative force, it
◉ is unnecessary to use another
◉ negative word with them.
◉ Therefore, say *he had hardly*
◉ *had time to think* (not *he hadn't*
◉ *hardly had time to think*); and

● *there was scarcely any bread left*
● (not *there was scarcely no bread*
● *left*). When *scarcely*, *hardly*, and
● *barely* are used at the beginning
● of a sentence, as in *scarcely had*
● *I arrived*, the following clause
● should start with *when*: *scarcely*
● *had I arrived when I was asked*
● *to chair a meeting*. The word
● *before* can be used in place of
● *when* in this context, but the
● word *than* used in the same
● way is considered incorrect
● by many people, though this
● use is becoming increasingly
● common.

scare VERB = **frighten**, alarm,
terrify, panic, shock, startle,
intimidate, dismay
▷ NOUN 1 = **fright**, shock, start
2 = **panic**, hysteria 3 = **alert**,
warning, alarm

scared ADJECTIVE = **afraid**,
alarmed, frightened, terrified,
shaken, startled, fearful, petrified

scary ADJECTIVE (*informal*)
= **frightening**, alarming,
terrifying, chilling, horrifying,
spooky (*informal*), creepy (*informal*),
spine-chilling

scatter VERB 1 = **throw about**,
spread, sprinkle, strew, shower,
fling, diffuse, disseminate
≠ gather 2 = **disperse**, dispel,
disband, dissipate ≠ assemble

scenario NOUN 1 = **situation**
2 = **story line**, résumé, outline,
summary, synopsis

scene NOUN 1 = **act**, part,
division, episode 2 = **setting**,
set, background, location,
backdrop 3 = **site**, place, setting,
area, position, spot, locality 4
(*informal*) = **world**, business,
environment, arena 5 = **view**,
prospect, panorama, vista,
landscape, outlook 6 = **fuss**, to-
do, row, performance, exhibition,
carry-on (*informal, chiefly Brit.*),
tantrum, commotion, hissy fit
(*informal*)

scenery NOUN 1 = **landscape**,
view, surroundings, terrain,
vista 2 (*theatre*) = **set**, setting,
backdrop, flats, stage set

scenic ADJECTIVE = **picturesque**,
beautiful, spectacular, striking,
panoramic

scent NOUN 1 = **fragrance**, smell,
perfume, bouquet, aroma, odour
2 = **trail**, track, spoor
▷ VERB = **smell**, sense, detect,
sniff, discern, nose out

scented ADJECTIVE = **fragrant**,
perfumed, aromatic, sweet-
smelling, odoriferous

sceptic NOUN 1 = **doubter**, cynic,
disbeliever 2 = **agnostic**, doubter,
unbeliever, doubting Thomas

sceptical ADJECTIVE = **doubtful**,
cynical, dubious, unconvinced,
disbelieving, incredulous,
mistrustful ≠ convinced

scepticism NOUN = **doubt**,
suspicion, disbelief, cynicism,
incredulity

schedule NOUN = **plan**,
programme, agenda, calendar,
timetable
▷ VERB = **plan**, set up, book,

s

scheme | 500

programme, arrange, organize

scheme NOUN 1 = **plan**,
programme, strategy, system,
project, proposal, tactics 2 = **plot**,
ploy, ruse, intrigue, conspiracy,
manoeuvre, subterfuge,
stratagem
▷ VERB = **plot**, plan, intrigue,
manoeuvre, conspire, contrive,
collude, machinate

scheming ADJECTIVE
= **calculating**, cunning, sly, tricky,
wily, artful, conniving, underhand
≠ straightforward

schmick ADJECTIVE 1 (*Austral.*
slang) = **excellent**, outstanding,
good, great, fine, cool (*informal*),
brilliant, very good, superb,
booshit (*Austral. slang*), exo
(*Austral. slang*), sik (*Austral.*
slang), rad (*informal*), phat (*slang*)
≠ terrible 2 = **stylish**, smart, chic,
fashionable, trendy (*Brit. informal*),
modish, dressy (*informal*), voguish
≠ scruffy

scholar NOUN 1 = **intellectual**,
academic, savant, acca (*Austral.*
slang) 2 = **student**, pupil, learner,
schoolboy or schoolgirl

scholarly ADJECTIVE = **learned**,
academic, intellectual, lettered,
erudite, scholastic, bookish
≠ uneducated

scholarship NOUN 1 = **grant**,
award, payment, endowment,
fellowship, bursary 2 = **learning**,
education, knowledge, erudition,
book-learning

school NOUN 1 = **academy**,
college, institution, institute,

seminary 2 = **group**, set, circle,
faction, followers, disciples,
devotees, denomination
▷ VERB = **train**, coach, discipline,
educate, drill, tutor, instruct

science NOUN = **discipline**,
body of knowledge, branch of
knowledge

scientific ADJECTIVE
= **systematic**, accurate, exact,
precise, controlled, mathematical

scientist NOUN = **researcher**,
inventor, boffin (*informal*),
technophile

scoff[1] VERB = **scorn**, mock, laugh
at, ridicule, knock (*informal*),
despise, sneer, jeer

scoff[2] VERB = **gobble (up)**, wolf,
devour, bolt, guzzle, gulp down,
gorge yourself on

scoop VERB = **win**, get, land, gain,
achieve, earn, secure, obtain
▷ NOUN 1 = **ladle**, spoon, dipper
2 = **exclusive**, exposé, revelation,
sensation ▷ PHRASES: **scoop**
something out 1 = take out,
empty, spoon out, bail or bale out
2 = **dig**, shovel, excavate, gouge,
hollow out; **scoop something or**
someone up = gather up, lift,
pick up, take up, sweep up or away

scope NOUN 1 = **opportunity**,
room, freedom, space, liberty,
latitude 2 = **range**, capacity,
reach, area, outlook, orbit, span,
sphere

scorch VERB = **burn**, sear, roast,
wither, shrivel, parch, singe

scorching ADJECTIVE = **burning**,
boiling, baking, flaming, roasting,

searing, fiery, red-hot

score VERB 1 = **gain**, win, achieve, make, get, attain, notch up (*informal*), chalk up (*informal*) 2 (*music*) = **arrange**, set, orchestrate, adapt 3 = **cut**, scratch, mark, slash, scrape, graze, gouge, deface
▷ NOUN 1 = **rating**, mark, grade, percentage 2 = **points**, result, total, outcome 3 = **composition**, soundtrack, arrangement, orchestration 4 = **grievance**, wrong, injury, injustice, grudge
▷ PLURAL NOUN = **lots**, loads, many, millions, hundreds, masses, swarms, multitudes ▷ PHRASE: **score something out** *or* **through** = **cross out**, delete, strike out, cancel, obliterate

scorn NOUN = **contempt**, disdain, mockery, derision, sarcasm, disparagement ≠ respect
▷ VERB = **despise**, reject, disdain, slight, be above, spurn, deride, flout ≠ respect

⬤ **WORD POWER**

⬤ The Scots language has a
⬤ lexicon of highly evocative and
⬤ colourful words, some of which
⬤ have no direct Standard English
⬤ counterparts. Many of these
⬤ remain restricted to Scottish
⬤ dialects, but some have filtered
⬤ through into Standard English,
⬤ though sometimes only as far
⬤ as British English. For example,
⬤ *canny*, originally from the verb
⬤ 'to know', means shrewd or
⬤ knowing, and is related to
⬤ the words cunning and ken. It
⬤ particularly refers to financial
⬤ astuteness in phrases like *canny*
⬤ *with money*, *canny business*
⬤ *sense*. It is a description very
⬤ often applied to someone else,
⬤ rather than oneself, with a
⬤ mixture of awe and mistrust. It
⬤ might be expected that *uncanny*
⬤ would mean the opposite
⬤ of canny, i.e. not shrewd,
⬤ foolish, careless. However,
⬤ in Standard English, this
⬤ meaning has been superseded
⬤ by the senses 'mysterious'
⬤ and 'beyond what is normal',
⬤ e.g. She bore an uncanny
⬤ resemblance to her mother.
⬤ The Scottish word *blether* has
⬤ come into Standard English
⬤ and sits alongside its more
⬤ common English equivalent
⬤ *blather*. From an Old Norse
⬤ word meaning 'nonsense', it
⬤ refers to foolish talk, which
⬤ can be long-winded, gossipy,
⬤ boasting, or inconsequential.
⬤ A blether can be both the
⬤ person doing the chattering
⬤ and the conversation itself. It
⬤ is similar in meaning to natter
⬤ and chinwag, e.g. He always
⬤ enjoyed a wee dram and a good
⬤ blether.

scour¹ VERB = **scrub**, clean, polish, rub, buff, abrade

scour² VERB = **search**, hunt, comb, ransack

scout NOUN = **vanguard**, lookout, precursor, outrider, reconnoitrer,

advance guard
▷ **VERB** = **reconnoitre**, investigate, watch, survey, observe, spy, probe, recce (*slang*)

scramble VERB 1 = **struggle**, climb, crawl, swarm, scrabble 2 = **strive**, rush, contend, vie, run, push, jostle 3 = **jumble**, mix up, muddle, shuffle
▷ **NOUN** 1 = **clamber**, ascent 2 = **race**, competition, struggle, rush, confusion, commotion, melee *or* mêlée

scrap¹ NOUN = **piece**, fragment, bit, grain, particle, portion, part, crumb 2 = **waste**, junk, off cuts
▷ **PLURAL NOUN** = **leftovers**, remains, bits, leavings
▷ **VERB** = **get rid of**, drop, abandon, ditch (*slang*), discard, write off, jettison, throw away *or* out ≠ bring back

scrap² (*informal*) NOUN = **fight**, battle, row, argument, dispute, disagreement, quarrel, squabble, biffo (*Austral. slang*)
▷ **VERB** = **fight**, argue, row, squabble, wrangle

scrape VERB 1 = **rake**, sweep, drag, brush 2 = **grate**, grind, scratch, squeak, rasp 3 = **graze**, skin, scratch, bark, scuff, rub 4 = **clean**, remove, scour
▷ **NOUN** (*informal*)
= **predicament**, difficulty, fix (*informal*), mess, dilemma, plight, tight spot, awkward situation

scratch VERB 1 = **rub**, scrape, claw at 2 = **mark**, cut, score, damage, grate, graze, etch, lacerate

▷ **NOUN** = **mark**, scrape, graze, blemish, gash, laceration, claw mark ▷ **PHRASE**: not up to scratch (*informal*) = **inadequate**, unacceptable, unsatisfactory, insufficient, not up to standard

scream VERB = **cry**, yell, shriek, screech, bawl, howl
▷ **NOUN** = **cry**, yell, howl, shriek, screech, yelp

screen NOUN = **cover**, guard, shade, shelter, shield, partition, cloak, canopy
▷ **VERB** 1 = **broadcast**, show, put on, present, air, cable, beam, transmit 2 = **cover**, hide, conceal, shade, mask, veil, cloak 3 = **investigate**, test, check, examine, scan 4 = **process**, sort, examine, filter, scan, evaluate, gauge, sift 5 = **protect**, guard, shield, defend, shelter

screw NOUN = **nail**, pin, tack, rivet, fastener, spike
▷ **VERB** 1 = **fasten**, fix, attach, bolt, clamp, rivet 2 = **turn**, twist, tighten 3 (*informal*) = **cheat**, do (*slang*), rip (someone) off (*slang*), skin (*slang*), trick, con, sting (*informal*), fleece 4 (*informal*) *often with* **out of** = **squeeze**, wring, extract, wrest ▷ **PHRASE**: screw something up 1 = **contort**, wrinkle, distort, pucker 2 (*informal*) = **bungle**, botch, mess up, spoil, mishandle, make a mess of (*slang*), make a hash of (*informal*), crool *or* cruel (*Austral. slang*)

scribble VERB = **scrawl**, write, jot,

dash off

script NOUN 1 = **text**, lines, words, book, copy, dialogue, libretto 2 = **handwriting**, writing, calligraphy, penmanship
▷ VERB = **write**, draft

scripture NOUN = **The Bible**, The Gospels, The Scriptures, The Good Book, Holy Scripture, Holy Writ, Holy Bible

scrub VERB 1 = **scour**, clean, polish, rub, wash, cleanse, buff 2 (*informal*) = **cancel**, drop, give up, abolish, forget about, call off, delete

scrutiny NOUN = **examination**, study, investigation, search, analysis, inspection, exploration, perusal

sculpture NOUN = **statue**, figure, model, bust, effigy, figurine, statuette
▷ VERB = **carve**, form, model, fashion, shape, mould, sculpt, chisel

sea NOUN 1 = **ocean**, the deep, the waves, main 2 = **mass**, army, host, crowd, mob, abundance, swarm, horde ▷ PHRASE: **at sea** = **bewildered**, lost, confused, puzzled, baffled, perplexed, mystified, flummoxed ▷ RELATED WORDS: *adjectives* **marine, maritime**

S

- **SEA BIRDS**
- albatross *or* (*informal*) gooney bird
- auk
- black-backed gull
- black shag *or* kawau (*N.Z.*)
- blue penguin, korora *or* little blue penguin (*N.Z.*)
- blue shag (*N.Z.*)
- caspian tern *or* taranui (*N.Z.*)
- coot
- cormorant
- fairy penguin, little penguin, *or* (*N.Z.*) korora
- fish hawk
- fulmar
- gannet
- guillemot
- gull *or* (*archaic or dialect*) cob(b)
- herring gull
- kittiwake
- man-of-war bird *or* frigate bird
- oystercatcher
- petrel
- razorbill *or* razor-billed auk
- scoter
- sea eagle, erne, *or* ern
- seagull
- shearwater
- short-tailed shearwater, (Tasmanian) mutton bird, *or* (*N.Z.*) titi
- skua
- storm petrel, stormy petrel, *or* Mother Carey's chicken
- wandering albatross
- white-fronted tern, black cap, kahawai bird, sea swallow *or* tara (*N.Z.*)

seal VERB = **settle**, clinch, conclude, consummate, finalize
▷ NOUN 1 = **sealant**, sealer, adhesive 2 = **authentication**, stamp, confirmation, ratification, insignia, imprimatur
seam NOUN 1 = **joint**, closure 2 = **layer**, vein, stratum, lode

- ● SEA MAMMALS
- ● dugong
- ● elephant seal
- ● harp seal
- ● manatee
- ● sea cow
- ● seal
- ● sea lion
- ● walrus *or* (*archaic*) sea horse

sear VERB = **wither**, burn, scorch, sizzle
search VERB = **examine**, investigate, explore, inspect, comb, scour, ransack, scrutinize, fossick (*Austral.* & *N.Z.*)
▷ NOUN = **hunt**, look, investigation, examination, pursuit, quest, inspection, exploration, Google (*trademark, computing*), googlewhack (*computing, informal*)
▷ PHRASE: **search for something** *or* **someone** = **look for**, hunt for, pursue
searching ADJECTIVE = **keen**, sharp, probing, close, intent, piercing, penetrating, quizzical
≠ superficial
searing ADJECTIVE 1 = **acute**,

intense, shooting, severe, painful, stabbing, piercing, gut-wrenching 2 = **cutting**, biting, bitter, harsh, barbed, hurtful, caustic
season NOUN = **period**, time, term, spell
▷ VERB = **flavour**, salt, spice, enliven, pep up
seasoned ADJECTIVE = **experienced**, veteran, practised, hardened, time-served
≠ inexperienced
seasoning NOUN = **flavouring**, spice, salt and pepper, condiment
seat NOUN 1 = **chair**, bench, stall, stool, pew, settle 2 = **membership**, place, constituency, chair, incumbency 3 = **centre**, place, site, heart, capital, situation, source, hub 4 = **mansion**, house, residence, abode, ancestral hall
▷ VERB 1 = **sit**, place, settle, set, fix, locate, install 2 = **hold**, take, accommodate, sit, contain
second[1] ADJECTIVE 1 = **next**, following, succeeding, subsequent 2 = **additional**, other, further, extra, alternative 3 = **inferior**, secondary, subordinate, lower, lesser
▷ NOUN = **supporter**, assistant, aide, colleague, backer, helper, right-hand man
▷ VERB = **support**, back, endorse, approve, go along with
second[2] NOUN = **moment**, minute, instant, flash, sec (*informal*), jiffy (*informal*), trice
secondary ADJECTIVE 1 = **subordinate**, minor, lesser,

S

lower, inferior, unimportant
≠ main 2 = **resultant**,
contingent, derived, indirect
≠ original

second-hand ADJECTIVE = **used**,
old, hand-me-down (*informal*),
nearly new, preloved (*Austral.
slang*)

secondly ADVERB = **next**, second,
moreover, furthermore, also, in
the second place

secrecy NOUN 1 = **mystery**,
stealth, concealment, furtiveness,
secretiveness, clandestineness,
covertness 2 = **confidentiality**,
privacy 3 = **privacy**, silence,
seclusion

secret ADJECTIVE 1 = **undisclosed**,
unknown, confidential,
underground, undercover,
unrevealed 2 = **concealed**,
hidden, disguised ≠ unconcealed
3 = **undercover**, furtive ≠ open
4 = **secretive**, reserved, close
≠ frank 5 = **mysterious**, cryptic,
abstruse, occult, clandestine,
arcane ≠ straightforward
▷ NOUN = **private affair**
▷ PHRASE: in secret = **secretly**,
surreptitiously, slyly

secretive ADJECTIVE = **reticent**,
reserved, close, deep,
uncommunicative, tight-lipped
≠ open

secretly ADVERB = **in secret**,
privately, surreptitiously, quietly,
covertly, furtively, stealthily,
clandestinely

sect NOUN = **group**, division,
faction, party, camp,

denomination, schism

section NOUN 1 = **part**, piece,
portion, division, slice, passage,
segment, fraction 2 = **district**,
area, region, sector, zone

sector NOUN 1 = **part**, division
2 = **area**, part, region, district,
zone, quarter

secular ADJECTIVE = **worldly**,
lay, earthly, civil, temporal,
nonspiritual ≠ religious

secure VERB 1 = **obtain**, get,
acquire, score (*slang*), gain,
procure ≠ lose 2 = **attach**, stick,
fix, bind, fasten ≠ detach
▷ ADJECTIVE 1 = **safe**, protected,
immune, unassailable
≠ unprotected 2 = **fast**, firm,
fixed, stable, steady, fastened,
immovable ≠ insecure
3 = **confident**, sure, easy, certain,
assured, reassured ≠ uneasy

security NOUN 1 = **precautions**,
defence, safeguards, protection,
safety measures 2 = **assurance**,
confidence, conviction, certainty,
reliance, sureness, positiveness
≠ insecurity 3 = **pledge**,
insurance, guarantee, hostage,
collateral, pawn, gage, surety
4 = **protection**, safety, custody,
refuge, sanctuary, safekeeping
≠ vulnerability

sediment NOUN = **dregs**,
grounds, residue, lees, deposit

seduce VERB 1 = **tempt**, lure,
entice, mislead, deceive, beguile,
lead astray, inveigle 2 = **corrupt**,
deprave, dishonour, debauch,
deflower

S

seductive ADJECTIVE = **tempting**, inviting, attractive, enticing, provocative, alluring, bewitching, hot (*informal*)

see VERB 1 = **perceive**, spot, notice, sight, witness, observe, distinguish, glimpse 2 = **understand**, get, follow, realize, appreciate, grasp, comprehend, fathom 3 = **find out**, learn, discover, determine, verify, ascertain 4 = **consider**, decide, reflect, deliberate, think over 5 = **make sure**, ensure, guarantee, make certain, see to it 6 = **accompany**, show, escort, lead, walk, usher 7 = **speak to**, receive, interview, consult, confer with 8 = **meet**, come across, happen on, bump into, run across, chance on 9 = **go out with**, court, date (*informal, chiefly U.S.*), go steady with (*informal*), step out with (*informal*) ▷ PHRASE: **seeing as** = **since**, as, in view of the fact that, inasmuch as

S

● **WORD POWER**
● It is common to hear *seeing as how*, as in *seeing as how the bus is always late, I don't need to hurry*. However, the use of *how* here is considered incorrect or nonstandard, and should be avoided.

seed NOUN 1 = **grain**, pip, germ, kernel, egg, embryo, spore, ovum 2 = **beginning**, start, germ 3 = **origin**, source, nucleus 4 (*chiefly bible*) = **offspring**, children, descendants, issue,

progeny ▷ PHRASE: **go** *or* **run to seed** = **decline**, deteriorate, degenerate, decay, go downhill (*informal*), let yourself go, go to pot

seek VERB 1 = **look for**, pursue, search for, be after, hunt 2 = **try**, attempt, aim, strive, endeavour, essay, aspire to

seem VERB = **appear**, give the impression of being, look

seep VERB = **ooze**, well, leak, soak, trickle, exude, permeate

seethe VERB 1 = **be furious**, rage, fume, simmer, see red (*informal*), be livid, go ballistic (*slang, chiefly U.S.*) 2 = **boil**, bubble, foam, fizz, froth

segment NOUN = **section**, part, piece, division, slice, portion, wedge

segregate VERB = **set apart**, divide, separate, isolate, discriminate against, dissociate ≠ unite

segregation NOUN = **separation**, discrimination, apartheid, isolation

seize VERB 1 = **grab**, grip, grasp, take, snatch, clutch, snap up, pluck ≠ let go 2 = **take by storm**, take over, acquire, occupy, conquer 3 = **capture**, catch, arrest, apprehend, take captive ≠ release

seizure NOUN 1 = **attack**, fit, spasm, convulsion, paroxysm 2 = **taking**, grabbing, annexation, confiscation, commandeering 3 = **capture**, arrest, apprehension

seldom ADVERB = **rarely**, not

often, infrequently, hardly ever
≠ often
select VERB = **choose**, take, pick,
opt for, decide on, single out,
adopt, settle upon ≠ reject
▷ ADJECTIVE 1 = **choice**, special,
excellent, superior, first-class,
hand-picked, top-notch (*informal*)
≠ ordinary 2 = **exclusive**,
elite, privileged, cliquish
≠ indiscriminate
selection NOUN 1 = **choice**,
choosing, pick, option, preference
2 = **anthology**, collection, medley,
choice
selective ADJECTIVE = **particular**,
discriminating, careful,
discerning, tasteful, fastidious
≠ indiscriminate
selfish ADJECTIVE = **self-
centred**, self-interested, greedy,
ungenerous, egoistic *or* egoistical,
egotistic *or* egoistical ≠ unselfish
sell VERB 1 = **trade**, exchange,
barter ≠ buy 2 = **deal in**, market,
trade in, stock, handle, retail,
peddle, traffic in ≠ buy ▷ PHRASE:
sell out of something = **run out
of**, be out of stock of
seller NOUN = **dealer**, merchant,
vendor, agent, retailer,
supplier, purveyor, salesman *or*
saleswoman
send VERB 1 = **dispatch**, forward,
direct, convey, remit 2 = **propel**,
hurl, fling, shoot, fire, cast, let
fly ▷ PHRASE: **send something**
or **someone up** (*Brit. informal*)
= **mock**, mimic, parody, spoof
(*informal*), imitate, take off

(*informal*), make fun of, lampoon
sendoff NOUN = **farewell**,
departure, leave-taking,
valediction
senior ADJECTIVE 1 = **higher
ranking**, superior ≠ subordinate
2 = **the elder**, major (*Brit.*)
≠ junior
sensation NOUN 1 = **feeling**,
sense, impression, perception,
awareness, consciousness
2 = **excitement**, thrill, stir, furore,
commotion
sensational ADJECTIVE
1 = **amazing**, dramatic, thrilling,
astounding ≠ dull 2 = **shocking**,
exciting, melodramatic, shock-
horror (*facetious*) ≠ unexciting
3 (*informal*) = **excellent**, superb,
mean (*slang*), impressive,
smashing (*informal*), fabulous
(*informal*), marvellous, out of this
world (*informal*), booshit (*Austral.
slang*), exo (*Austral. slang*), sik
(*Austral. slang*), rad (*informal*), phat
(*slang*), schmick (*Austral. informal*),
funky ≠ ordinary
sense NOUN 1 = **faculty**
2 = **feeling**, impression,
perception, awareness,
consciousness, atmosphere, aura
3 = **understanding**, awareness
4 *sometimes plural* = **intelligence**,
reason, understanding,
brains (*informal*), judgment,
wisdom, wit(s), common sense
≠ foolishness 5 = **meaning**,
significance, import, implication,
drift, gist
▷ VERB = **perceive**, feel,

S

understand, pick up, realize, be aware of, discern, get the impression ≠ be unaware of

sensibility NOUN *often plural* = **feelings**, emotions, sentiments, susceptibilities, moral sense

sensible ADJECTIVE 1 = **wise**, practical, prudent, shrewd, judicious ≠ foolish
2 = **intelligent**, practical, rational, sound, realistic, sage, shrewd, down-to-earth, grounded ≠ senseless

sensitive ADJECTIVE
1 = **thoughtful**, kindly, concerned, patient, attentive, tactful, unselfish 2 = **delicate**, tender
3 = **susceptible**, responsive, easily affected 4 = **touchy**, oversensitive, easily upset, easily offended, easily hurt ≠ insensitive 5 = **precise**, fine, acute, keen, responsive ≠ imprecise

sensitivity NOUN
1 = **susceptibility**, responsiveness, receptiveness, sensitiveness 2 = **consideration**, patience, thoughtfulness
3 = **touchiness**, oversensitivity
4 = **responsiveness**, precision, keenness, acuteness

sensual ADJECTIVE 1 = **sexual**, erotic, raunchy (*slang*), lewd, lascivious, lustful, lecherous
2 = **physical**, bodily, voluptuous, animal, luxurious, fleshly, carnal

sentence NOUN 1 = **punishment**, condemnation 2 = **verdict**, order, ruling, decision, judgment, decree

▷ VERB 1 = **condemn**, doom
2 = **convict**, condemn, penalize

sentiment NOUN 1 = **feeling**, idea, view, opinion, attitude, belief, judgment
2 = **sentimentality**, emotion, tenderness, romanticism, sensibility, emotionalism, mawkishness

sentimental ADJECTIVE
= **romantic**, touching, emotional, nostalgic, maudlin, weepy (*informal*), slushy (*informal*), schmaltzy (*slang*) ≠ unsentimental

separate ADJECTIVE
1 = **unconnected**, individual, particular, divided, divorced, isolated, detached, disconnected ≠ connected 2 = **individual**, independent, apart, distinct ≠ joined
▷ VERB 1 = **divide**, detach, disconnect, disjoin ≠ combine
2 = **come apart**, split, come away ≠ connect 3 = **sever**, break apart, split in two, divide in two ≠ join
4 = **split up**, part, divorce, break up, part company, get divorced, be estranged 5 = **distinguish**, mark, single out, set apart ≠ link

separated ADJECTIVE
1 = **estranged**, parted, separate, apart, disunited
2 = **disconnected**, parted, divided, separate, disassociated, disunited, sundered

separately ADVERB 1 = **alone**, apart, not together, severally ≠ together 2 = **individually**, singly

separation NOUN 1 = **division**, break, dissociation, disconnection, disunion 2 = **split-up**, parting, split, divorce, break-up, rift

sequel NOUN 1 = **follow-up**, continuation, development 2 = **consequence**, result, outcome, conclusion, end, upshot

sequence NOUN = **succession**, course, series, order, chain, cycle, arrangement, progression

series NOUN 1 = **sequence**, course, chain, succession, run, set, order, train 2 = **drama**, serial, soap (*informal*), sitcom (*informal*), soap opera, soapie *or* soapie (*Austral. slang*), situation comedy

serious ADJECTIVE 1 = **grave**, bad, critical, dangerous, acute, severe 2 = **important**, crucial, urgent, pressing, worrying, significant, grim, momentous ≠ unimportant 3 = **thoughtful**, detailed, careful, deep, profound, in-depth 4 = **deep**, sophisticated 5 = **solemn**, earnest, grave, sober, staid, humourless, unsmiling ≠ light-hearted 6 = **sincere**, earnest, genuine, honest, in earnest ≠ insincere

seriously ADVERB 1 = **truly**, in earnest, all joking aside 2 = **badly**, severely, gravely, critically, acutely, dangerously

seriousness NOUN 1 = **importance**, gravity, urgency, significance 2 = **solemnity**, gravity, earnestness, gravitas

sermon NOUN = **homily**, address

servant NOUN = **attendant**, domestic, slave, maid, help, retainer, skivvy (*chiefly Brit.*)

serve VERB 1 = **work for**, help, aid, assist, be in the service of 2 = **perform**, do, complete, fulfil, discharge 3 = **be adequate**, do, suffice, suit, satisfy, be acceptable, answer the purpose 4 = **present**, provide, supply, deliver, set out, dish up

service NOUN 1 = **facility**, system, resource, utility, amenity 2 = **ceremony**, worship, rite, observance 3 = **work**, labour, employment, business, office, duty 4 = **check**, maintenance check
▷ VERB = **overhaul**, check, maintain, tune (up), go over, fine tune

session NOUN = **meeting**, hearing, sitting, period, conference, congress, discussion, assembly

set¹ VERB 1 = **put**, place, lay, position, rest, plant, station, stick 2 = **arrange**, decide (upon), settle, establish, determine, fix, schedule, appoint 3 = **assign**, give, allot, prescribe 4 = **harden**, stiffen, solidify, cake, thicken, crystallize, congeal 5 = **go down**, sink, dip, decline, disappear, vanish, subside 6 = **prepare**, lay, spread, arrange, make ready
▷ ADJECTIVE 1 = **established**, planned, decided, agreed, arranged, rigid, definite,

inflexible 2 = **strict**, rigid, stubborn, inflexible ≠ flexible
3 = **conventional**, traditional, stereotyped, unspontaneous
▷ NOUN 1 = **scenery**, setting, scene, stage set 2 = **position**, bearing, attitude, carriage, posture ▷ PHRASES: **set on** or **upon something** = **determined to**, intent on, bent on, resolute about; **set something up** 1 = **arrange**, organize, prepare, prearrange 2 = **establish**, begin, found, institute, initiate 3 = **build**, raise, construct, put up, assemble, put together, erect 4 = **assemble**, put up

set² NOUN 1 = **series**, collection, assortment, batch, compendium, ensemble 2 = **group**, company, crowd, circle, band, gang, faction, clique

setback NOUN = **hold-up**, check, defeat, blow, reverse, disappointment, hitch, misfortune

setting NOUN = **surroundings**, site, location, set, scene, background, context, backdrop

settle VERB 1 = **resolve**, work out, put an end to, straighten out 2 = **pay**, clear, square (up), discharge 3 = **move to**, take up residence in, live in, dwell in, inhabit, reside in, set up home in, put down roots in 4 = **colonize**, populate, people, pioneer 5 = **land**, alight, descend, light, come to rest 6 = **calm**, quiet, relax, relieve, reassure, soothe,

lull, quell ≠ disturb

settlement NOUN
1 = **agreement**, arrangement, working out, conclusion, establishment, confirmation
2 = **payment**, clearing, discharge
3 = **colony**, community, outpost, encampment, kainga or kaika (N.Z.)

settler NOUN = **colonist**, immigrant, pioneer, frontiersman

setup NOUN (informal) = **arrangement**, system, structure, organization, conditions, regime

sever VERB 1 = **cut**, separate, split, part, divide, detach, disconnect, cut in two ≠ join
2 = **discontinue**, terminate, break off, put an end to, dissociate ≠ continue

several ADJECTIVE = **various**, different, diverse, sundry

severe ADJECTIVE 1 = **serious**, critical, terrible, desperate, extreme, awful, drastic, catastrophic 2 = **acute**, intense, violent, piercing, harrowing, unbearable, agonizing, insufferable 3 = **strict**, hard, harsh, cruel, rigid, drastic, oppressive, austere ≠ lenient
4 = **grim**, serious, grave, forbidding, stern, unsmiling, tight-lipped ≠ genial 5 = **plain**, simple, austere, classic, restrained, Spartan, unadorned, unfussy, bare-bones ≠ fancy

severely ADVERB 1 = **seriously**, badly, extremely, gravely, acutely

2 = **strictly**, harshly, sternly, sharply

severity NOUN = **strictness**, harshness, toughness, hardness, sternness, severeness

sew VERB = **stitch**, tack, seam, hem

sex NOUN **1** = **gender 2** (*informal*) = **lovemaking**, sexual relations, copulation, fornication, coitus, coition

sexual ADJECTIVE **1** = **carnal**, erotic, intimate **2** = **sexy**, erotic, sensual, arousing, naughty, provocative, seductive, sensuous

sexuality NOUN = **desire**, lust, eroticism, sensuality, sexiness (*informal*), carnality

sexy ADJECTIVE = **erotic**, sensual, seductive, arousing, naughty, provocative, sensuous, suggestive, hot (*informal*)

shabby ADJECTIVE **1** = **tatty**, worn, ragged, scruffy, tattered, threadbare ≠ smart **2** = **rundown**, seedy, mean, dilapidated **3** = **mean**, low, rotten (*informal*), cheap, dirty, despicable, contemptible, scurvy ≠ fair

shack NOUN = **hut**, cabin, shanty, whare (*N.Z.*)

shade NOUN **1** = **hue**, tone, colour, tint **2** = **shadow 3** = **dash**, trace, hint, suggestion **4** = **nuance**, difference, degree **5** = **screen**, covering, cover, blind, curtain, shield, veil, canopy **6** (*literary*) = **ghost**, spirit, phantom, spectre, apparition, kehua (*N.Z.*)
▷ VERB **1** = **darken**, shadow, cloud, dim **2** = **cover**, protect,

screen, hide, shield, conceal, obscure, veil

shadow NOUN **1** = **silhouette**, shape, outline, profile **2** = **shade**, dimness, darkness, gloom, cover, dusk
▷ VERB **1** = **shade**, screen, shield, darken, overhang **2** = **follow**, tail (*informal*), trail, stalk

shady ADJECTIVE **1** = **shaded**, cool, dim ≠ sunny **2** (*informal*) = **crooked**, dodgy (*Brit., Austral. & N.Z. informal*), unethical, suspect, suspicious, dubious, questionable, shifty, shonky (*Austral. & N.Z. informal*) ≠ honest

shaft NOUN **1** = **tunnel**, hole, passage, burrow, passageway, channel **2** = **handle**, staff, pole, rod, stem, baton, shank **3** = **ray**, beam, gleam

shake VERB **1** = **jiggle**, agitate **2** = **tremble**, shiver, quake, quiver **3** = **rock**, totter **4** = **wave**, wield, flourish, brandish **5** = **upset**, shock, frighten, disturb, distress, rattle (*informal*), unnerve, traumatize
▷ NOUN = **vibration**, trembling, quaking, jerk, shiver, shudder, jolt, tremor

shaky ADJECTIVE **1** = **unstable**, weak, precarious, rickety ≠ stable **2** = **unsteady**, faint, trembling, faltering, quivery **3** = **uncertain**, suspect, dubious, questionable, iffy (*informal*) ≠ reliable

shallow ADJECTIVE = **superficial**, surface, empty, slight, foolish, trivial, meaningless, frivolous

SHAKESPEARE

Characters in Shakespeare	Play
Sir Andrew Aguecheek	Twelfth Night
Antonio	The Merchant of Venice
Antony	Antony and Cleopatra, Julius Caesar
Ariel	The Tempest
Aufidius	Coriolanus
Autolycus	The Winter's Tale
Banquo	Macbeth
Bassanio	The Merchant of Venice
Beatrice	Much Ado About Nothing
Sir Toby Belch	Twelfth Night
Benedick	Much Ado About Nothing
Bolingbroke	Richard II
Bottom	A Midsummer Night's Dream
Brutus	Julius Caesar
Caliban	The Tempest
Casca	Julius Caesar
Cassio	Othello
Cassius	Julius Caesar
Claudio	Much Ado About Nothing, Measure for Measure
Claudius	Hamlet
Cleopatra	Antony and Cleopatra
Cordelia	King Lear
Coriolanus	Coriolanus
Cressida	Troilus and Cressida
Demetrius	A Midsummer Night's Dream
Desdemona	Othello
Dogberry	Much Ado About Nothing
Edmund	King Lear
Enobarbus	Antony and Cleopatra
Falstaff	Henry IV Parts I and II, The Merry Wives of Windsor
Ferdinand	The Tempest
Feste	Twelfth Night
Fluellen	Henry V
Fool	King Lear
Gertrude	Hamlet
Gloucester	King Lear

Characters in Shakespeare	Play
Goneril	King Lear
Guildenstern	Hamlet
Hamlet	Hamlet
Helena	All's Well that Ends Well, A Midsummer Night's Dream
Hermia	A Midsummer Night's Dream
Hero	Much Ado About Nothing
Hotspur	Henry IV Part I
Iago	Othello
Jaques	As You Like It
John of Gaunt	Richard II
Juliet	Romeo and Juliet
Julius Caesar	Julius Caesar
Katharina or Kate	The Taming of the Shrew
Kent	King Lear
Laertes	Hamlet
Lear	King Lear
Lysander	A Midsummer Night's Dream
Macbeth	Macbeth
Lady Macbeth	Macbeth
Macduff	Macbeth
Malcolm	Macbeth
Malvolio	Twelfth Night
Mercutio	Romeo and Juliet
Miranda	The Tempest
Oberon	A Midsummer Night's Dream
Octavius	Antony and Cleopatra
Olivia	Twelfth Night
Ophelia	Hamlet
Orlando	As You Like It
Orsino	Twelfth Night
Othello	Othello
Pandarus	Troilus and Cressida
Perdita	The Winter's Tale
Petruchio	The Taming of the Shrew
Pistol	Henry IV Part II, Henry V, The Merry Wives of Windsor
Polonius	Hamlet
Portia	The Merchant of Venice

S

Characters in Shakespeare — Play

Characters in Shakespeare	Play
Prospero	The Tempest
Puck	A Midsummer Night's Dream
Mistress Quickly	The Merry Wives of Windsor
Regan	King Lear
Romeo	Romeo and Juliet
Rosalind	As You Like It
Rosencrantz	Hamlet
Sebastian	The Tempest, Twelfth Night
Shylock	The Merchant of Venice
Thersites	Troilus and Cressida
Timon	Timon of Athens
Titania	A Midsummer Night's Dream
Touchstone	As You Like It
Troilus	Troilus and Cressida
Tybalt	Romeo and Juliet
Viola	Twelfth Night

Shakespeare's Plays

- All's Well that Ends Well
- Antony and Cleopatra
- As You Like It
- The Comedy of Errors
- Coriolanus
- Cymbeline
- Hamlet
- Henry IV Part I
- Henry IV Part II
- Henry V
- Henry VI Part I
- Henry VI Part II
- Henry VI Part III
- Henry VIII
- Julius Caesar
- King John
- King Lear
- Love's Labour's Lost
- Macbeth
- Measure for Measure
- The Merchant of Venice
- The Merry Wives of Windsor
- A Midsummer Night's Dream
- Much Ado About Nothing
- Othello
- Pericles, Prince of Tyre
- Richard II
- Richard III
- Romeo and Juliet
- The Taming of the Shrew
- The Tempest
- Timon of Athens
- Titus Andronicus
- Troilus and Cressida
- Twelfth Night
- The Two Gentlemen of Verona
- The Winter's Tale

s

≠ deep

sham NOUN = **fraud**, imitation, hoax, pretence, forgery, counterfeit, humbug, impostor ≠ the real thing

▷ ADJECTIVE = **false**, artificial, bogus, pretended, mock, imitation, simulated, counterfeit ≠ real

shambles NOUN 1 = **chaos**, mess, disorder, confusion, muddle, havoc, disarray, madhouse 2 = **mess**, jumble, untidiness

shame NOUN

1 = **embarrassment**, humiliation, ignominy, mortification, abashment ≠ shamelessness

2 = **disgrace**, scandal, discredit, smear, disrepute, reproach, dishonour, infamy ≠ honour

▷ VERB 1 = **embarrass**, disgrace, humiliate, humble, mortify, abash ≠ make proud 2 = **dishonour**, degrade, stain, smear, blot, debase, defile ≠ honour

shameful ADJECTIVE = **disgraceful**, outrageous, scandalous, mean, low, base, wicked, dishonourable ≠ admirable

shape NOUN 1 = **appearance**, form, aspect, guise, likeness, semblance 2 = **form**, profile, outline, lines, build, figure, silhouette, configuration 3 = **pattern**, model, frame, mould 4 = **condition**, state, health, trim, fettle

▷ VERB 1 = **form**, make, produce, create, model, fashion, mould 2 = **mould**, form, make, fashion, model, frame

share NOUN = **part**, portion, quota, ration, lot, due, contribution, allowance

▷ VERB 1 = **divide**, split, distribute, assign 2 = **go halves on**, go fifty-fifty on (*informal*)

sharp ADJECTIVE 1 = **keen**, jagged, serrated ≠ blunt 2 = **quick-**

S

◉ **SHARKS**

◉ angel shark, angelfish, *or* monkfish
◉ basking shark, sailfish *or* (*N.Z.*) reremai
◉ blue pointer, *or* (*N.Z.*) blue shark *or* blue whaler
◉ bronze whaler (*Austral.*)
◉ carpet shark *or* (*Austral.*) wobbegong
◉ dogfish *or* (*Austral.*) dog shark
◉ gummy (shark)
◉ hammerhead

◉ mako
◉ nurse shark
◉ porbeagle *or* mackerel shark
◉ requiem shark
◉ school shark (*Austral.*)
◉ seven-gill shark (*Austral.*)
◉ shovelhead
◉ thrasher *or* thresher shark
◉ tiger shark
◉ tope
◉ whale shark

witted, clever, astute, knowing, quick, bright, alert, penetrating ≠ dim **3** = **cutting**, biting, bitter, harsh, barbed, hurtful, caustic ≠ gentle **4** = **sudden**, marked, abrupt, extreme, distinct ≠ gradual **5** = **clear**, distinct, well-defined, crisp ≠ indistinct **6** = **sour**, tart, pungent, hot, acid, acrid, piquant ≠ bland **7** = **acute**, severe, intense, painful, shooting, stabbing, piercing, gut-wrenching

▷ ADVERB = **promptly**, precisely, exactly, on time, on the dot, punctually ≠ approximately

sharpen VERB = **make sharp**, hone, whet, grind, edge

shatter VERB **1** = **smash**, break, burst, crack, crush, pulverize **2** = **destroy**, ruin, wreck, demolish, torpedo

shattered ADJECTIVE **1** = **devastated**, crushed, gutted (slang) **2** (informal) = **exhausted**, drained, worn out, done in (informal), all in (slang), knackered (slang), tired out, ready to drop

shave VERB **1** = **trim**, crop **2** = **scrape**, trim, shear, pare

shed¹ NOUN = **hut**, shack, outhouse, whare (N.Z.)

shed² VERB **1** = **drop**, spill, scatter **2** = **cast off**, discard, moult, slough off **3** = **give out**, cast, emit, give, radiate

sheen NOUN = **shine**, gleam, gloss, polish, brightness, lustre

sheer ADJECTIVE **1** = **total**, complete, absolute, utter,

pure, downright, out-and-out, unmitigated ≠ moderate **2** = **steep**, abrupt, precipitous ≠ gradual **3** = **fine**, thin, transparent, see-through, gossamer, diaphanous, gauzy ≠ thick

sheet NOUN **1** = **page**, leaf, folio, piece of paper **2** = **plate**, piece, panel, slab **3** = **coat**, film, layer, surface, stratum, veneer, overlay, lamina **4** = **expanse**, area, stretch, sweep, covering, blanket

shell NOUN **1** = **husk**, case, pod **2** = **carapace 3** = **frame**, structure, hull, framework, chassis

▷ VERB = **bomb**, bombard, attack, blitz, strafe ▷ PHRASE: **shell something out** (informal) = **pay out**, fork out (slang), give, hand over

shelter NOUN **1** = **cover**, screen **2** = **protection**, safety, refuge, cover **3** = **refuge**, haven, sanctuary, retreat, asylum

▷ VERB **1** = **take shelter**, hide, seek refuge, take cover **2** = **protect**, shield, harbour, safeguard, cover, hide, guard, defend ≠ endanger

sheltered ADJECTIVE **1** = **screened**, covered, protected, shielded, secluded ≠ exposed **2** = **protected**, screened, shielded, quiet, isolated, secluded, cloistered

shelve VERB = **postpone**, defer, freeze, suspend, put aside, put on ice, put on the back burner (*informal*), take a rain check on (*U.S. & Canad. informal*)

shepherd NOUN = **drover**, stockman, herdsman, grazier
▷ VERB = **guide**, conduct, steer, herd, usher ▷ RELATED WORD: *adjective* **pastoral**

sherang NOUN (*Austral. & N.Z.*) = **boss**, manager, head, leader, director, chief, master, employer, supervisor, baas (*S. African*)

shield NOUN = **protection**, cover, defence, screen, guard, shelter, safeguard
▷ VERB = **protect**, cover, screen, guard, defend, shelter, safeguard

shift VERB 1 = **move**, move around, budge 2 = **remove**, move, displace, relocate, rearrange, reposition
▷ NOUN 1 = **change**, shifting, displacement 2 = **move**, rearrangement

shimmer VERB = **gleam**, twinkle, glisten, scintillate
▷ NOUN = **gleam**, iridescence

shine VERB 1 = **gleam**, flash, beam, glow, sparkle, glitter, glare, radiate 2 = **polish**, buff, burnish, brush 3 = **be outstanding**, stand out, excel, be conspicuous
▷ NOUN 1 = **polish**, gloss, sheen, lustre 2 = **brightness**, light, sparkle, radiance

shining ADJECTIVE = **bright**, brilliant, gleaming, beaming, sparkling, shimmering, radiant, luminous

shiny ADJECTIVE = **bright**, gleaming, glossy, glistening, polished, lustrous

ship NOUN = **vessel**, boat, craft

shiver VERB = **shudder**, shake, tremble, quake, quiver
▷ NOUN = **tremble**, shudder, quiver, trembling, flutter, tremor

shock NOUN 1 = **upset**, blow, trauma, bombshell, turn (*informal*), distress, disturbance 2 = **impact**, blow, clash, collision 3 = **start**, scare, fright, turn, jolt
▷ VERB 1 = **shake**, stun, stagger, jolt, stupefy 2 = **horrify**, appal, disgust, revolt, sicken, nauseate, scandalize

shocking ADJECTIVE 1 (*informal*) = **terrible**, appalling, dreadful, bad, horrendous, ghastly, deplorable, abysmal 2 = **appalling**, outrageous, disgraceful, disgusting, dreadful, horrifying, revolting, sickening ≠ wonderful

shoot VERB 1 = **open fire on**, blast (*slang*), hit, kill, plug (*slang*), bring down 2 = **fire**, launch, discharge, project, hurl, fling, propel, emit 3 = **speed**, race, rush, charge, fly, tear, dash, barrel (along) (*informal, chiefly U.S. & Canad.*)
▷ NOUN = **sprout**, branch, bud, sprig, offshoot

shop NOUN = **store**, supermarket, boutique, emporium, hypermarket, dairy (*N.Z.*)

shore NOUN = **beach**, coast, sands, strand (*poetic*), seashore

short ADJECTIVE 1 = **brief**, fleeting, momentary ≠ long 2 = **concise**, brief, succinct, summary,

compressed, terse, laconic, pithy ≠ lengthy **3** = **small**, little, squat, diminutive, petite, dumpy ≠ tall **4** = **abrupt**, sharp, terse, curt, brusque, impolite, discourteous, uncivil ≠ polite **5** = **scarce**, wanting, low, limited, lacking, scant, deficient ≠ plentiful
▷ **ADVERB** = **abruptly**, suddenly, without warning ≠ gradually

shortage NOUN = **deficiency**, want, lack, scarcity, dearth, paucity, insufficiency ≠ abundance

shortcoming NOUN = **failing**, fault, weakness, defect, flaw, imperfection

shorten VERB **1** = **cut**, reduce, decrease, diminish, lessen, curtail, abbreviate, abridge ≠ increase **2** = **turn up**

shortly ADVERB = **soon**, presently, before long, in a little while

shot NOUN **1** = **discharge**, gunfire, crack, blast, explosion, bang **2** = **ammunition**, bullet, slug, pellet, projectile, lead, ball **3** = **marksman**, shooter, markswoman **4** = **strike**, throw, lob **5** (informal) = **attempt**, go (informal), try, turn, effort, stab (informal), endeavour

shoulder VERB **1** = **bear**, carry, take on, accept, assume, be responsible for **2** = **push**, elbow, shove, jostle, press

shout VERB = **cry (out)**, call (out), yell, scream, roar, bellow, bawl, holler (informal)
▷ **NOUN** = **cry**, call, yell, scream,

roar, bellow ▷ **PHRASE**: **shout someone down** = **drown out**, overwhelm, drown, silence

shove VERB = **push**, thrust, elbow, drive, press, propel, jostle, impel
▷ **NOUN** = **push**, knock, thrust, elbow, bump, nudge, jostle
▷ **PHRASE**: **shove off** (informal) = **go away**, leave, clear off (informal), depart, push off (informal), scram (informal), rack off (Austral. & N.Z. slang)

shovel VERB **1** = **move**, scoop, dredge, load, heap **2** = **stuff**, ladle

show VERB **1** = **indicate**, demonstrate, prove, reveal, display, point out, manifest, testify to, flag up ≠ disprove **2** = **display**, exhibit **3** = **guide**, lead, conduct, accompany, direct, escort **4** = **demonstrate**, describe, explain, teach, illustrate, instruct **5** = **be visible** ≠ be invisible **6** = **express**, display, reveal, indicate, register, demonstrate, manifest ≠ hide **7** (informal) = **turn up**, appear, attend **8** = **broadcast**, transmit, air, beam, relay, televise, put on the air, podcast
▷ **NOUN 1** = **display**, sight, spectacle, array **2** = **exhibition**, fair, display, parade, pageant **3** = **appearance**, display, pose, parade **4** = **pretence**, appearance, illusion, affectation **5** = **programme**, broadcast, presentation, production **6** = **entertainment**, production, presentation ▷ **PHRASES**: **show**

off (*informal*) = **boast**, brag, blow your own trumpet, swagger; **show someone up** (*informal*) = **embarrass**, let down, mortify, put to shame; **show something off** = **exhibit**, display, parade, demonstrate, flaunt; **show something up** = **reveal**, expose, highlight, lay bare

showdown NOUN (*informal*) = **confrontation**, clash, face-off (*slang*)

shower NOUN = **deluge**
▷ VERB 1 = **cover**, dust, spray, sprinkle 2 = **inundate**, heap, lavish, pour, deluge

show-off NOUN (*informal*) = **exhibitionist**, boaster, poseur, braggart, figjam (*Austral. slang*)

shred NOUN 1 = **strip**, bit, piece, scrap, fragment, sliver, tatter 2 = **particle**, trace, scrap, grain, atom, jot, iota

shrewd ADJECTIVE = **astute**, clever, sharp, keen, smart, calculating, intelligent, cunning ≠ naive

shriek VERB = **scream**, cry, yell, screech, squeal
▷ NOUN = **scream**, cry, yell, screech, squeal

shrink VERB = **decrease**, dwindle, lessen, grow *or* get smaller, contract, narrow, diminish, shorten ≠ grow

shroud NOUN 1 = **winding sheet**, grave clothes 2 = **covering**, veil, mantle, screen, pall
▷ VERB = **conceal**, cover, screen, hide, blanket, veil, cloak, envelop

shudder VERB = **shiver**, shake, tremble, quake, quiver, convulse
▷ NOUN = **shiver**, tremor, quiver, spasm

shuffle VERB 1 = **shamble**, stagger, stumble, dodder 2 = **scuffle**, drag, scrape 3 = **rearrange**, jumble, mix, disorder, disarrange

shun VERB = **avoid**, steer clear of, keep away from

shut VERB = **close**, secure, fasten, seal, slam ≠ open
▷ ADJECTIVE = **closed**, fastened, sealed, locked ≠ open ▷ PHRASE: **shut down** = **stop work**, halt work, close down

shuttle VERB = **go back and forth**, commute, go to and fro, alternate

shy ADJECTIVE 1 = **timid**, self-conscious, bashful, retiring, shrinking, coy, self-effacing, diffident ≠ confident 2 = **cautious**, wary, hesitant, suspicious, distrustful, chary ≠ reckless
▷ VERB *sometimes with* **off** *or* **away** = **recoil**, flinch, draw back, start, balk

sick ADJECTIVE 1 = **unwell**, ill, poorly (*informal*), diseased, crook (*Austral. & N.Z. informal*), ailing, under the weather, indisposed ≠ well 2 = **nauseous**, ill, queasy, nauseated 3 (*informal*) = **tired**, bored, fed up, weary, jaded 4 (*informal*) = **morbid**, sadistic, black, macabre, ghoulish

sicken VERB 1 = **disgust**, revolt, nauseate, repel, gross out (*U.S. slang*), turn your stomach 2 = **fall**

S

ill, take sick, ail

sickening ADJECTIVE
= **disgusting**, revolting, offensive, foul, distasteful, repulsive, nauseating, loathsome, yucko (*Austral. slang*) ≠ delightful

sickness NOUN 1 = **illness**, disorder, ailment, disease, complaint, bug (*informal*), affliction, malady 2 = **nausea**, queasiness 3 = **vomiting**

side NOUN 1 = **border**, margin, boundary, verge, flank, rim, perimeter, edge ≠ middle
2 = **face**, surface, facet 3 = **party**, camp, faction, cause 4 = **point of view**, viewpoint, position, opinion, angle, slant, standpoint
5 = **team**, squad, line-up
6 = **aspect**, feature, angle, facet
▷ ADJECTIVE = **subordinate**, minor, secondary, subsidiary, lesser, marginal, incidental, ancillary ≠ main ▷ PHRASE: **side with someone** = **support**, agree with, stand up for, favour, go along with, take the part of, ally yourself with

sidewalk NOUN (*U.S. & Canad.*) = **pavement**, footpath (*Austral. & N.Z.*)

sideways ADVERB 1 = **indirectly**, obliquely 2 = **to the side**, laterally
▷ ADJECTIVE = **sidelong**, oblique

sift VERB 1 = **part**, filter, strain, separate, sieve 2 = **examine**, investigate, go through, research, analyse, work over, scrutinize

sight NOUN 1 = **vision**, eyes, eyesight, seeing, eye

2 = **spectacle**, show, scene, display, exhibition, vista, pageant
3 = **view**, range of vision, visibility
4 (*informal*) = **eyesore**, mess, monstrosity
▷ VERB = **spot**, see, observe, distinguish, perceive, make out, discern, behold ▷ RELATED WORDS: *adjectives* **optical, visual**

sign NOUN 1 = **symbol**, mark, device, logo, badge, emblem
2 = **figure** 3 = **notice**, board, warning, placard 4 = **indication**, evidence, mark, signal, symptom, hint, proof, gesture 5 = **omen**, warning, portent, foreboding, augury, auspice
▷ VERB 1 = **gesture**, indicate, signal, beckon, gesticulate
2 = **autograph**, initial, inscribe

signal NOUN 1 = **flare**, beam, beacon 2 = **cue**, sign, prompting, reminder 3 = **sign**, gesture, indication, mark, note, expression, token
▷ VERB = **gesture**, sign, wave, indicate, motion, beckon, gesticulate

significance NOUN
= **importance**, consequence, moment, weight

significant ADJECTIVE
1 = **important**, serious, material, vital, critical, momentous, weighty, noteworthy
≠ insignificant 2 = **meaningful**, expressive, eloquent, indicative, suggestive ≠ meaningless

signify VERB = **indicate**, mean, suggest, imply, intimate, be a sign of, denote, connote, flag up

silence NOUN 1 = **quiet**, peace, calm, hush, lull, stillness ≠ noise 2 = **reticence**, dumbness, taciturnity, muteness ≠ speech
▷ VERB = **quieten**, still, quiet, cut off, stifle, cut short, muffle, deaden ≠ make louder

silent ADJECTIVE 1 = **mute**, dumb, speechless, wordless, voiceless ≠ noisy 2 = **uncommunicative**, quiet, taciturn 3 = **quiet**, still, hushed, soundless, noiseless, muted ≠ loud

silently ADVERB 1 = **quietly**, in silence, soundlessly, noiselessly, inaudibly, without a sound 2 = **mutely**, in silence, wordlessly

silhouette NOUN = **outline**, form, shape, profile
▷ VERB = **outline**, etch

silly ADJECTIVE 1 = **stupid**, ridiculous, absurd, daft, inane, senseless, idiotic, fatuous ≠ clever 2 = **foolish**, stupid, unwise, rash, irresponsible, thoughtless, imprudent ≠ sensible

⬤ WORD POWER
⬤ Silver is a precious metal
⬤ used in jewellery, coins, and
⬤ cutlery. Its value is referred
⬤ to in the expression *born with*
⬤ *a silver spoon in one's mouth*
⬤ which means coming from a
⬤ wealthy family. However, when
⬤ contrasted with gold, its worth
⬤ is the lesser of the two, and a
⬤ *silver medal* is given as second
⬤ prize in a competition. Silver

⬤ has also been opposed to the
⬤ colour grey in various idioms.
⬤ For example, the expression
⬤ *every cloud has a silver lining*
⬤ means that even dark
⬤ situations can have comforting
⬤ aspects. In addition, silver is
⬤ now used instead of grey to
⬤ refer to older people, e.g. *silver*
⬤ *surfer*, to avoid the negative
⬤ associations of grey. Silver
⬤ also means articulate and
⬤ persuasive in the expression
⬤ *silver-tongued*.

similar ADJECTIVE 1 = **alike**, resembling, comparable ≠ different 2 *with* **to** = **like**, comparable to, analogous to, close to

⬤ WORD POWER
⬤ *As* should not be used after
⬤ *similar* – so *Wilson held a similar*
⬤ *position to Jones* is correct, but
⬤ not *Wilson held a similar position*
⬤ *as Jones*; and *the system is similar*
⬤ *to the one in France* is correct,
⬤ but not *the system is similar as*
⬤ *in France*.

similarity NOUN = **resemblance**, likeness, sameness, agreement, correspondence, analogy, affinity, closeness ≠ difference

simmer VERB 1 = **bubble**, boil gently, seethe 2 = **fume**, seethe, smoulder, rage, be angry
▷ PHRASE: **simmer down** (*informal*) = **calm down**, control yourself, cool off *or* down

simple ADJECTIVE
1 = **uncomplicated**, clear,

S

plain, understandable, lucid, recognizable, comprehensible, intelligible ≠ complicated
2 = **easy**, straightforward, not difficult, effortless, painless, uncomplicated, undemanding
3 = **plain**, natural, classic, unfussy, unembellished, bare-bones ≠ elaborate **4** = **pure**, mere, sheer, unalloyed **5** = **artless**, innocent, naive, natural, sincere, unaffected, childlike, unsophisticated ≠ sophisticated
6 = **unpretentious**, modest, humble, homely, unfussy, unembellished ≠ fancy

simplicity NOUN
1 = **straightforwardness**, ease, clarity, clearness ≠ complexity
2 = **plainness**, restraint, purity, lack of adornment ≠ elaborateness

simplify VERB = **make simpler**, streamline, disentangle, dumb down, reduce to essentials, declutter

simply ADVERB **1** = **just**, only, merely, purely, solely **2** = **totally**, really, completely, absolutely, wholly, utterly **3** = **clearly**, straightforwardly, directly, plainly, intelligibly **4** = **plainly**, naturally, modestly, unpretentiously
5 = **without doubt**, surely, certainly, definitely, beyond question

simulate VERB = **pretend**, act, feign, affect, put on, sham

simultaneous ADJECTIVE = **coinciding**, concurrent,

contemporaneous, coincident, synchronous, happening at the same time

simultaneously ADVERB = **at the same time**, together, concurrently

sin NOUN **1** = **wickedness**, evil, crime, error, transgression, iniquity **2** = **crime**, offence, error, wrongdoing, misdeed, transgression, act of evil, guilt
▷ VERB = **transgress**, offend, lapse, err, go astray, do wrong

sincere ADJECTIVE = **honest**, genuine, real, true, serious, earnest, frank, candid, dinkum (*Austral. & N.Z. informal*) ≠ false

sincerely ADVERB = **honestly**, truly, genuinely, seriously, earnestly, wholeheartedly, in earnest

sincerity NOUN = **honesty**, truth, candour, frankness, seriousness, genuineness

sing VERB **1** = **croon**, carol, chant, warble, yodel, pipe **2** = **trill**, chirp, warble
  ● **WORD POWER**
  ● *Sang* is the past tense of the
  ● verb *sing*, as in *she sang sweetly*.
  ● *Sung* is the past participle, as in
  ● *we have sung our song*, and care
  ● should be taken not to use it as
  ● if it were a variant form of the
  ● past tense.

singer NOUN = **vocalist**, crooner, minstrel, soloist, chorister, balladeer

single ADJECTIVE **1** = **one**, sole, lone, solitary, only, only one

2 = **individual**, separate, distinct
3 = **unmarried**, free, unattached, unwed **4** = **separate**, individual, exclusive, undivided, unshared
5 = **simple**, unmixed, unblended
▷ PHRASE: **single something** or **someone out** = **pick**, choose, select, separate, distinguish, fix on, set apart, pick on or out, flag up

singly ADVERB = **one by one**, individually, one at a time, separately

singular ADJECTIVE **1** = **single**, individual **2** = **remarkable**, outstanding, exceptional, notable, eminent, noteworthy ≠ ordinary **3** = **unusual**, odd, strange, extraordinary, curious, peculiar, eccentric, queer, daggy (*Austral. & N.Z. informal*) ≠ conventional

sinister ADJECTIVE = **threatening**, evil, menacing, dire, ominous, malign, disquieting ≠ reassuring

sink VERB **1** = **go down**, founder, go under, submerge, capsize **2** = **slump**, drop **3** = **fall**, drop, slip, plunge, subside, abate **4** = **drop**, fall **5** = **stoop**, be reduced to, lower yourself **6** = **decline**, fade, fail, flag, weaken, diminish, decrease, deteriorate ≠ improve **7** = **dig**, bore, drill, drive, excavate

sip VERB = **drink**, taste, sample, sup
▷ NOUN = **swallow**, drop, taste, thimbleful

sit VERB **1** = **take a seat**, perch, settle down **2** = **place**, set, put, position, rest, lay, settle,

deposit **3** = **be a member of**, serve on, have a seat on, preside on **4** = **convene**, meet, assemble, officiate

site NOUN **1** = **area**, plot
2 = **location**, place, setting, point, position, situation, spot
▷ VERB = **locate**, put, place, set, position, establish, install, situate

situation NOUN **1** = **position**, state, case, condition, circumstances, equation, plight, state of affairs **2** = **scenario**, state of affairs **3** = **location**, place, setting, position, site, spot

● WORD POWER
● It is common to hear the word
● *situation* used in sentences
● such as *the company is in a crisis*
● *situation*. This use of *situation* is
● considered bad style and the
● word should be left out, since it
● adds nothing to the sentence's
● meaning.

size NOUN = **dimensions**, extent, range, amount, mass, volume, proportions, bulk ▷ PHRASE: **size something** or **someone up** (*informal*) = **assess**, evaluate, appraise, take stock of

sizeable or **sizable** ADJECTIVE = **large**, considerable, substantial, goodly, decent, respectable, largish

sizzle VERB = **hiss**, spit, crackle, fry, frizzle

skeleton NOUN = **bones**, bare bones

sketch NOUN = **drawing**, design, draft, delineation

S

▷ **VERB** = **draw**, outline, represent, draft, depict, delineate, rough out

skilful ADJECTIVE = **expert**, skilled, masterly, able, professional, clever, practised, competent ≠ clumsy

skill NOUN = **expertise**, ability, proficiency, art, technique, facility, talent, craft ≠ clumsiness

skilled ADJECTIVE = **expert**, professional, able, masterly, skilful, proficient ≠ unskilled

skim VERB 1 = **remove**, separate, cream 2 = **glide**, fly, coast, sail, float 3 *usually with* **over** *or* **through** = **scan**, glance, run your eye over

skin NOUN 1 = **hide**, pelt, fell 2 = **peel**, rind, husk, casing, outside, crust 3 = **film**, coating ▷ **VERB** 1 = **peel** 2 = **scrape**, flay

skinny ADJECTIVE = **thin**, lean, scrawny, emaciated, undernourished ≠ fat

skip VERB 1 = **hop**, dance, bob, trip, bounce, caper, prance, frisk 2 = **miss out**, omit, leave out, overlook, pass over, eschew, give (something) a miss

skirt VERB 1 = **border**, edge, flank 2 *often with* **around** *or* **round** = **go round**, circumvent 3 *often with* **around** *or* **round** = **avoid**, evade, steer clear of, circumvent

skookum ADJECTIVE (*Canad.*) = **powerful**, influential, big, dominant, controlling, commanding, supreme, prevailing, authoritative

sky NOUN = **heavens**, firmament,

rangi (*N.Z.*) ▷ **RELATED WORD**: *adjective* **celestial**

slab NOUN = **piece**, slice, lump, chunk, wedge, portion

slack ADJECTIVE 1 = **limp**, relaxed, loose, lax 2 = **loose**, baggy ≠ taut 3 = **slow**, quiet, inactive, dull, sluggish, slow-moving ≠ busy 4 = **negligent**, lazy, lax, idle, inactive, slapdash, neglectful, slipshod ≠ strict ▷ **NOUN** 1 = **surplus**, excess, glut, surfeit, superabundance, superfluity 2 = **room**, excess, leeway, give (*informal*) ▷ **VERB** = **shirk**, idle, dodge, skive (*Brit. slang*), bludge (*Austral. & N.Z. informal*)

slam VERB 1 = **bang**, crash, smash 2 = **throw**, dash, hurl, fling

slant VERB 1 = **slope**, incline, tilt, list, bend, lean, heel, cant 2 = **bias**, colour, twist, angle, distort ▷ **NOUN** 1 = **slope**, incline, tilt, gradient, camber 2 = **bias**, emphasis, prejudice, angle, point of view, one-sidedness

slanting ADJECTIVE = **sloping**, angled, inclined, tilted, tilting, bent, diagonal, oblique

slap VERB = **smack**, beat, clap, cuff, swipe, spank, clobber (*slang*), wallop (*informal*) ▷ **NOUN** = **smack**, blow, cuff, swipe, spank

slash VERB 1 = **cut**, slit, gash, lacerate, score, rend, rip, hack 2 = **reduce**, cut, decrease, drop, lower, moderate, diminish, cut down

▷ NOUN = **cut**, slit, gash, rent, rip, incision, laceration

slate VERB (*informal, chiefly Brit.*) = **criticize**, censure, rebuke, scold, tear into (*informal*)

slaughter VERB 1 = **kill**, murder, massacre, destroy, execute, assassinate 2 = **butcher**, kill, slay, massacre

▷ NOUN = **slaying**, killing, murder, massacre, bloodshed, carnage, butchery

slave NOUN 1 = **servant**, serf, vassal 2 = **drudge**, skivvy (*chiefly Brit.*)

▷ VERB = **toil**, drudge, slog

slavery NOUN = **enslavement**, servitude, subjugation, captivity, bondage ≠ freedom

slay VERB 1 (*archaic or literary*) = **kill**, slaughter, massacre, butcher 2 = **murder**, kill, massacre, slaughter, mow down

sleaze NOUN (*informal*) = **corruption**, fraud, dishonesty, bribery, extortion, venality, unscrupulousness

sleek ADJECTIVE = **glossy**, shiny, lustrous, smooth ≠ shaggy

sleep NOUN = **slumber(s)**, nap, doze, snooze (*informal*), hibernation, siesta, forty winks (*informal*), zizz (*Brit. informal*)

▷ VERB = **slumber**, doze, snooze (*informal*), hibernate, take a nap, catnap, drowse

sleepy ADJECTIVE = **drowsy**, sluggish, lethargic, heavy, dull, inactive ≠ wide-awake

slender ADJECTIVE 1 = **slim**, narrow, slight, lean, willowy ≠ chubby 2 = **faint**, slight, remote, slim, thin, tenuous ≠ strong 3 = **meagre**, little, small, scant, scanty ≠ large

slice NOUN = **piece**, segment, portion, wedge, sliver, helping, share, cut

▷ VERB = **cut**, divide, carve, sever, dissect, bisect

slick ADJECTIVE 1 = **skilful**, deft, adroit, dexterous, professional, polished ≠ clumsy 2 = **glib**, smooth, plausible, polished, specious

▷ VERB = **smooth**, sleek, plaster down

slide VERB = **slip**, slither, glide, skim, coast

slight ADJECTIVE 1 = **small**, minor, insignificant, trivial, feeble, trifling, meagre, unimportant ≠ large 2 = **slim**, small, delicate, spare, fragile, lightly-built ≠ sturdy

▷ VERB = **snub**, insult, ignore, affront, scorn, disdain ≠ compliment

▷ NOUN = **insult**, snub, affront, rebuff, slap in the face (*informal*), (the) cold shoulder ≠ compliment

slightly ADVERB = **a little**, a bit, somewhat

slim ADJECTIVE 1 = **slender**, slight, trim, thin, narrow, lean, svelte, willowy ≠ chubby 2 = **slight**, remote, faint, slender ≠ strong

▷ VERB = **lose weight**, diet ≠ put on weight

S

sling VERB 1 (*informal*) = **throw**, cast, toss, hurl, fling, chuck (*informal*), lob (*informal*), heave 2 = **hang**, suspend

slip VERB 1 = **fall**, skid 2 = **slide**, slither 3 = **sneak**, creep, steal ▷ NOUN = **mistake**, failure, error, blunder, lapse, omission, oversight, barry or Barry Crocker (*Austral. slang*) ▷ PHRASES: **give someone the slip** = **escape from**, get away from, evade, elude, lose (someone), flee, dodge; **slip up** = **make a mistake**, blunder, err, miscalculate

slippery ADJECTIVE 1 = **smooth**, icy, greasy, glassy, slippy (*informal or dialect*), unsafe 2 = **untrustworthy**, tricky, cunning, dishonest, devious, crafty, evasive, shifty

slit VERB = **cut (open)**, rip, slash, knife, pierce, lance, gash ▷ NOUN 1 = **cut**, gash, incision, tear, rent 2 = **opening**, split

slogan NOUN = **catch phrase**, motto, tag-line, catchword, catchcry (*Austral.*)

slope NOUN = **inclination**, rise, incline, tilt, slant, ramp, gradient ▷ VERB = **slant**, incline, drop away, fall, rise, lean, tilt ▷ PHRASE: **slope off** = **slink away**, slip away, creep away

sloping ADJECTIVE = **slanting**, leaning, inclined, oblique

sloppy ADJECTIVE 1 (*informal*) = **careless**, slovenly, slipshod, messy, untidy 2 (*informal*) = **sentimental**, soppy (*Brit.*

informal), slushy (*informal*), gushing, mawkish, icky (*informal*)

slot NOUN 1 = **opening**, hole, groove, vent, slit, aperture 2 (*informal*) = **place**, time, space, opening, position, vacancy ▷ VERB = **fit**, insert

slow ADJECTIVE 1 = **unhurried**, sluggish, leisurely, lazy, ponderous, dawdling, laggard, lackadaisical ≠ quick 2 = **prolonged**, protracted, long-drawn-out, lingering, gradual 3 = **late**, behind, tardy 4 = **stupid**, dim, dense, thick, retarded, dozy (*Brit. informal*), obtuse, braindead (*informal*) ≠ bright ▷ VERB 1 *often with* **down** = **decelerate**, brake 2 *often with* **down** = **delay**, hold up, handicap, retard ≠ speed up

◉ WORD POWER
◉ While not as unkind as *thick*
◉ and *stupid*, words like *slow*
◉ and *backward*, when used to
◉ talk about a person's mental
◉ abilities, are both unhelpful
◉ and likely to cause offence. It is
◉ preferable to say that a person
◉ has *special educational needs* or
◉ *learning difficulties*.

slowly ADVERB = **gradually**, unhurriedly ≠ quickly

slug NOUN ▷ *see* **snails, slugs and other gastropods**

sluggish ADJECTIVE = **inactive**, slow, lethargic, heavy, dull, inert, indolent, torpid ≠ energetic

slum NOUN = **hovel**, ghetto,

shanty

slump VERB 1 = **fall**, sink, plunge, crash, collapse, slip ≠ increase 2 = **sag**, hunch, droop, slouch, loll ▷ NOUN 1 = **fall**, drop, decline, crash, collapse, reverse, downturn, trough ≠ increase 2 = **recession**, depression, stagnation, inactivity, hard or bad times

slur NOUN = **insult**, stain, smear, affront, innuendo, calumny, insinuation, aspersion

sly ADJECTIVE 1 = **roguish**, knowing, arch, mischievous, impish 2 = **cunning**, scheming, devious, secret, clever, subtle, wily, crafty ≠ open ▷ PHRASE: **on the sly** = **secretly**, privately, covertly, surreptitiously, on the quiet

smack VERB 1 = **slap**, hit, strike, clap, cuff, swipe, spank 2 = **drive**, hit, strike ▷ NOUN = **slap**, blow, cuff, swipe, spank ▷ ADVERB (*informal*) = **directly**, right, straight, squarely, precisely, exactly, slap (*informal*)

small ADJECTIVE 1 = **little**, minute, tiny, mini, miniature, minuscule, diminutive, petite ≠ big 2 = **young**, little, junior, wee, juvenile, youthful, immature 3 = **unimportant**, minor, trivial, insignificant, little, petty, trifling, negligible ≠ important 4 = **modest**, humble, unpretentious ≠ grand

smart ADJECTIVE 1 = **chic**, trim, neat, stylish, elegant, spruce, snappy, natty (*informal*), schmick (*Austral. informal*) ≠ scruffy 2 = **clever**, bright, intelligent, quick, sharp, keen, acute, shrewd ≠ stupid 3 = **brisk**, quick, lively, vigorous ▷ VERB = **sting**, burn, hurt

smash VERB 1 = **break**, crush, shatter, crack, demolish, pulverize 2 = **shatter**, break, disintegrate, crack, splinter 3 = **collide**, crash, meet head-on, clash, come into collision 4 = **destroy**, ruin, wreck, trash (*slang*), lay waste ▷ NOUN = **collision**, crash, accident

smashing ADJECTIVE (*informal, chiefly Brit.*) = **excellent**, mean (*slang*), great (*informal*), wonderful, brilliant (*informal*), cracking (*Brit. informal*), superb, fantastic (*informal*), booshit (*Austral. slang*), exo (*Austral. slang*), sik (*Austral. slang*), rad (*informal*), phat (*slang*), schmick (*Austral. informal*) ≠ awful

smear VERB 1 = **spread over**, daub, rub on, cover, coat, bedaub 2 = **slander**, malign, blacken, besmirch 3 = **smudge**, soil, dirty, stain, sully ▷ NOUN 1 = **smudge**, daub, streak, blot, blotch, splotch 2 = **slander**, libel, defamation, calumny

smell NOUN 1 = **odour**, scent, fragrance, perfume, bouquet, aroma 2 = **stink**, stench, pong (*Brit. informal*), fetor ▷ VERB 1 = **stink**, reek, pong (*Brit.*

S

informal) 2 = **sniff**, scent

smile VERB = **grin**, beam, smirk, twinkle, grin from ear to ear
▷ NOUN = **grin**, beam, smirk

smooth ADJECTIVE 1 = **even**, level, flat, plane, flush, horizontal ≠ uneven 2 = **sleek**, polished, shiny, glossy, silky, velvety ≠ rough 3 = **mellow**, pleasant, mild, agreeable 4 = **flowing**, steady, flat, regular, uniform, rhythmic 5 = **easy**, effortless, well-ordered 6 = **suave**, slick, persuasive, urbane, glib, facile, unctuous, smarmy (*Brit. informal*)
▷ VERB 1 = **flatten**, level, press, plane, iron 2 = **ease**, facilitate ≠ hinder

smother VERB 1 = **extinguish**, put out, stifle, snuff 2 = **suffocate**, choke, strangle, stifle 3 = **suppress**, stifle, repress, hide, conceal, muffle

smug ADJECTIVE = **self-satisfied**, superior, complacent, conceited

snack NOUN = **light meal**, bite, refreshment(s)

snag NOUN = **difficulty**, hitch, problem, obstacle, catch,

disadvantage, complication, drawback
▷ VERB = **catch**, tear, rip

snake NOUN = **serpent** ▷ RELATED WORD: *adjective* serpentine
▷ *see* **reptiles**

snap VERB 1 = **break**, crack, separate 2 = **pop**, click, crackle 3 = **speak sharply**, bark, lash out at, jump down (someone's) throat (*informal*) 4 = **bite at**, bite, nip
▷ MODIFIER = **instant**, immediate, sudden, spur-of-the-moment ▷ PHRASE: snap something up = **grab**, seize, take advantage of, pounce upon

snare NOUN = **trap**, net, wire, gin, noose
▷ VERB = **trap**, catch, net, wire, seize, entrap

snatch VERB 1 = **grab**, grip, grasp, clutch 2 = **steal**, take, nick (*slang, chiefly Brit.*), pinch (*informal*), lift (*informal*), pilfer, filch, thieve 3 = **win** 4 = **save**, recover, get out, salvage
▷ NOUN = **bit**, part, fragment, piece, snippet

sneak VERB 1 = **slink**, slip, steal,

S

● **SNAILS, SLUGS AND OTHER GASTROPODS**
● abalone *or* ear shell
● conch
● cowrie *or* cowry
● limpet
● murex
● nudibranch *or* sea slug
● ormer *or* sea-ear

● periwinkle *or* winkle
● slug
● snail
● triton
● wentletrap
● whelk

pad, skulk **2 = slip**, smuggle, spirit
▷ NOUN **= informer**, betrayer,
telltale, Judas, accuser, stool
pigeon, nark (*Brit., Austral. & N.Z.
slang*), fizgig (*Austral. slang*)

sneaking ADJECTIVE **1 = nagging**,
worrying, persistent,
uncomfortable **2 = secret**,
private, hidden, unexpressed,
unvoiced, undivulged

sneer VERB **1 = scorn**, mock,
ridicule, laugh, jeer, disdain, deride
2 = say contemptuously, snigger
▷ NOUN **= scorn**, ridicule,
mockery, derision, jeer, gibe

sniff VERB **1 = breathe in**, inhale
2 = smell, scent **3 = inhale**,
breathe in, suck in, draw in

snub VERB **= insult**, slight, put
down, humiliate, cut (*informal*),
rebuff, cold-shoulder
▷ NOUN **= insult**, put-down,
affront, slap in the face

so SENTENCE CONNECTOR
= therefore, thus, hence,
consequently, then, as a result,
accordingly, thence

soak VERB **1 = steep 2 = wet**,
damp, saturate, drench, moisten,
suffuse, wet through, waterlog
3 = penetrate, permeate, seep
▷ PHRASE: **soak something up**
= absorb, suck up, assimilate

soaking ADJECTIVE **= soaked**,
dripping, saturated, drenched,
sodden, streaming, sopping, wet
through

soar VERB **1 = rise**, increase, grow,
mount, climb, go up, rocket,
escalate **2 = fly**, wing, climb,

ascend ≠ plunge **3 = tower**,
climb, go up

sob VERB **= cry**, weep, howl, shed
tears
▷ NOUN **= cry**, whimper, howl

sober ADJECTIVE **1 = abstinent**,
temperate, abstemious, moderate
≠ drunk **2 = serious**, cool, grave,
reasonable, steady, composed,
rational, solemn, grounded
≠ frivolous **3 = plain**, dark, sombre,
quiet, subdued, drab ≠ bright

so-called ADJECTIVE **= alleged**,
supposed, professed, pretended,
self-styled

social ADJECTIVE **1 = communal**,
community, collective, group,
public, general, common
2 = organized, gregarious
▷ NOUN **= get-together** (*informal*),
party, gathering, function,
reception, social gathering

social network NOUN
= Facebook (*trademark*), Twitter
(*trademark*), Tumblr (*trademark*),
LinkedIn (*trademark*)

society NOUN **1 = the
community**, people, the public,
humanity, civilization, mankind
2 = culture, community,
population **3 = organization**,
group, club, union, league,
association, institute, circle
4 = upper classes, gentry, elite,
high society, beau monde **5**
(*old-fashioned*) **= companionship**,
company, fellowship, friendship

soft ADJECTIVE **1 = velvety**,
smooth, silky, feathery, downy,
fleecy ≠ rough **2 = yielding**,

S

elastic ≠ hard 3 = **soggy**,
swampy, marshy, boggy
4 = **squashy**, sloppy, mushy,
spongy, gelatinous, pulpy
5 = **pliable**, flexible, supple,
malleable, plastic, elastic,
bendable, mouldable 6 = **quiet**,
gentle, murmured, muted,
dulcet, soft-toned ≠ loud
7 = **lenient**, easy-going, lax,
indulgent, permissive, spineless,
overindulgent ≠ harsh
8 = **kind**, tender, sentimental,
compassionate, sensitive, gentle,
tenderhearted, touchy-feely
(*informal*) 9 (*informal*) = **easy**,
comfortable, undemanding,
cushy (*informal*) 10 = **pale**, light,
subdued, pastel, bland, mellow
≠ bright 11 = **dim**, faint, dimmed
≠ bright 12 = **mild**, temperate,
balmy
soften VERB 1 = **melt**, tenderize
2 = **lessen**, moderate, temper,
ease, cushion, subdue, allay,
mitigate
soil¹ NOUN 1 = **earth**, ground, clay,
dust, dirt 2 = **territory**, country,
land
soil² VERB = **dirty**, foul, stain,
pollute, tarnish, sully, defile,
besmirch ≠ clean
soldier NOUN = **fighter**,
serviceman, trooper, warrior,
man-at-arms, squaddie *or*
squaddy (*Brit. slang*)
sole ADJECTIVE = **only**, one, single,
individual, alone, exclusive,
solitary
solely ADVERB = **only**, completely,

entirely, exclusively, alone, merely
solemn ADJECTIVE 1 = **serious**,
earnest, grave, sober, sedate, staid
≠ cheerful 2 = **formal**, grand,
grave, dignified, ceremonial,
stately, momentous ≠ informal
solid ADJECTIVE 1 = **firm**, hard,
compact, dense, concrete
≠ unsubstantial 2 = **strong**,
stable, sturdy, substantial,
unshakable ≠ unstable
3 = **reliable**, dependable,
upstanding, worthy, upright,
trusty ≠ unreliable 4 = **sound**,
real, reliable, good, genuine,
dinkum (*Austral. & N.Z. informal*)
≠ unsound
solidarity NOUN = **unity**,
unification, accord, cohesion,
team spirit, unanimity,
concordance, like-mindedness,
kotahitanga (*N.Z.*)
solitary ADJECTIVE 1 = **unsociable**,
reclusive, unsocial, isolated,
lonely, cloistered, lonesome,
friendless ≠ sociable 2 = **lone**,
alone 3 = **isolated**, remote, out-
of-the-way, hidden, unfrequented
≠ busy
solution NOUN 1 = **answer**, key,
result, explanation 2 (*chemistry*)
= **mixture**, mix, compound, blend,
solvent
solve VERB = **answer**, work out,
resolve, crack, clear up, unravel,
decipher, suss (out) (*slang*)
sombre ADJECTIVE 1 = **gloomy**,
sad, sober, grave, dismal,
mournful, lugubrious, joyless
≠ cheerful 2 = **dark**, dull, gloomy,

sober, drab ≠ bright

somebody NOUN = **celebrity**, name, star, notable, household name, dignitary, luminary, personage ≠ nobody

somehow ADVERB = **one way or another**, come what may, come hell or high water (*informal*), by fair means or foul, by hook or (by) crook, by some means or other

sometimes ADVERB = **occasionally**, at times, now and then ≠ always

song NOUN = **ballad**, air, tune, carol, chant, chorus, anthem, number, waiata (*N.Z.*)

soon ADVERB = **before long**, shortly, in the near future

soothe VERB 1 = **calm**, still, quiet, hush, appease, lull, pacify, mollify ≠ upset 2 = **relieve**, ease, alleviate, assuage ≠ irritate

soothing ADJECTIVE 1 = **calming**, relaxing, peaceful, quiet, calm, restful 2 = **emollient**, palliative

sophisticated ADJECTIVE 1 = **complex**, advanced, complicated, subtle, delicate, elaborate, refined, intricate ≠ simple 2 = **cultured**, refined, cultivated, worldly, cosmopolitan, urbane ≠ unsophisticated

sophistication NOUN = **poise**, worldliness, savoir-faire, urbanity, finesse, worldly wisdom

sore ADJECTIVE 1 = **painful**, smarting, raw, tender, burning, angry, sensitive, irritated 2 = **annoyed**, cross, angry, pained, hurt, upset, stung, irritated,

tooshie (*Austral. slang*), hoha (*N.Z.*) 3 = **annoying**, troublesome 4 = **urgent**, desperate, extreme, dire, pressing, critical, acute

sorrow NOUN 1 = **grief**, sadness, woe, regret, distress, misery, mourning, anguish ≠ joy 2 = **hardship**, trial, tribulation, affliction, trouble, woe, misfortune ≠ good fortune
▷ VERB = **grieve**, mourn, lament, be sad, bemoan, agonize, bewail ≠ rejoice

sorry ADJECTIVE 1 = **regretful**, apologetic, contrite, repentant, remorseful, penitent, shamefaced, conscience-stricken ≠ unapologetic 2 = **sympathetic**, moved, full of pity, compassionate, commiserative ≠ unsympathetic 3 = **wretched**, miserable, pathetic, mean, poor, sad, pitiful, deplorable

sort NOUN = **kind**, type, class, make, order, style, quality, nature
▷ VERB = **arrange**, group, order, rank, divide, grade, classify, categorize

● **WORD POWER**
● It is common in informal
● speech to combine singular
● and plural in sentences like
● *these sort of distinctions are*
● *becoming blurred.* This is not
● acceptable in careful writing,
● where the plural must be used
● consistently: *these sorts of*
● *distinctions are becoming blurred.*

soul NOUN 1 = **spirit**, essence, life, vital force, wairua (*N.Z.*)

2 = **embodiment**, essence, epitome, personification, quintessence, type **3** = **person**, being, individual, body, creature, man *or* woman

sound¹ NOUN **1** = **noise**, din, report, tone, reverberation **2** = **idea**, impression, drift **3** = **cry**, noise, peep, squeak **4** = **tone**, music, note
▷ VERB **1** = **toll**, set off **2** = **resound**, echo, go off, toll, set off, chime, reverberate, clang **3** = **seem**, seem to be, appear to be ▷ RELATED WORDS : *adjectives* **sonic, acoustic**

sound² ADJECTIVE **1** = **fit**, healthy, perfect, intact, unhurt, uninjured, unimpaired ≠ frail **2** = **sturdy**, strong, solid, stable **3** = **sensible**, wise, reasonable, right, correct, proper, valid, rational, grounded ≠ irresponsible **4** = **deep**, unbroken, undisturbed, untroubled ≠ troubled

sour ADJECTIVE **1** = **sharp**, acid, tart, bitter, pungent, acetic ≠ sweet **2** = **rancid**, turned, gone off, curdled, gone bad, off ≠ fresh **3** = **bitter**, tart, acrimonious, embittered, disagreeable, ill-tempered, waspish, ungenerous ≠ good-natured

source NOUN **1** = **cause**, origin, derivation, beginning, author **2** = **informant**, authority **3** = **origin**, fount

souvenir NOUN = **keepsake**, reminder, memento

sovereign ADJECTIVE

1 = **supreme**, ruling, absolute, royal, principal, imperial, kingly *or* queenly **2** = **excellent**, efficient, effectual
▷ NOUN = **monarch**, ruler, king *or* queen, chief, potentate, emperor *or* empress, prince *or* princess

sovereignty NOUN = **supreme power**, domination, supremacy, primacy, kingship, rangatiratanga (*N.Z.*)

sow VERB = **scatter**, plant, seed, implant

space NOUN **1** = **room**, capacity, extent, margin, scope, play, expanse, leeway **2** = **period**, interval, time, while, span, duration, time frame, timeline **3** = **outer space**, the universe, the galaxy, the solar system, the cosmos **4** = **blank**, gap, interval

spacious ADJECTIVE = **roomy**, large, huge, broad, extensive, ample, expansive, capacious ≠ limited

● WORD POWER
● Several Spanish words in
● English have nuances of
● meaning not shared by their
● synonyms. For example,
● *aficionado*, literally 'fond of',
● refers to a person who is
● passionate about a particular
● activity or pastime, e.g. a wine
● aficionado, an aficionado of
● classical music. Some of its
● synonyms have connotations
● of obsession, e.g. addict, buff,
● freak, fiend, and others have
● connotations of expertise, e.g.

S

- connoisseur, expert, whizz.
- Aficionado is perhaps most
- closely related in meaning to
- admirer, devotee, enthusiast,
- and fan. Another Spanish
- word which has no direct
- English equivalent is *peccadillo*.
- From 'pecado' meaning sin, a
- peccadillo is a lapse or minor
- sin. It describes a fault which
- is ethical or moral, rather than
- legal or religious, although
- there is some overlap between
- these categories. It can be
- contrasted with words relating
- to legal offences such as crime,
- offence, and violation, and
- those of religious wrongdoing
- such as sin, trespass, and
- transgression. It shares the
- meaning of misdemeanour,
- lapse, and misbehaviour, e.g.
- Speeding is indulged as the
- peccadillo of the too-busy.
- *Bonanza*, literally 'calm sea', is a
- Spanish word descended from
- Latin *bonus*, meaning 'good'.
- It signifies a source of luck
- and money, which is usually
- sudden and unexpected, e.g.
- cash bonanza, ratings bonanza.
- In comparison, bonus also has
- associations with money in
- the sense of 'dividend' in British
- English. Many of the synonyms
- of bonanza are found almost
- exclusively in the context of
- money, e.g. windfall, jackpot,
- whereas bonanza can refer to
- other types of good fortune.

span NOUN 1 = **period**, term, duration, spell 2 = **extent**, reach, spread, length, distance, stretch
 ▷ VERB = **extend across**, cross, bridge, cover, link, traverse

spar VERB = **argue**, row, squabble, scrap (*informal*), wrangle, bicker

spare ADJECTIVE 1 = **back-up**, reserve, second, extra, additional, auxiliary 2 = **extra**, surplus, leftover, over, free, odd, unwanted, unused ≠ necessary 3 = **free**, leisure, unoccupied 4 = **thin**, lean, meagre, gaunt, wiry ≠ plump
 ▷ VERB 1 = **afford**, give, grant, do without, part with, manage without, let someone have 2 = **have mercy on**, pardon, leave, let off (*informal*), go easy on (*informal*), save (from harm) ≠ show no mercy to

sparing ADJECTIVE = **economical**, frugal, thrifty, saving, careful, prudent ≠ lavish

spark NOUN 1 = **flicker**, flash, gleam, glint, flare 2 = **trace**, hint, scrap, atom, jot, vestige
 ▷ VERB *often with* **off** = **start**, stimulate, provoke, inspire, trigger (off), set off, precipitate

sparkle VERB = **glitter**, flash, shine, gleam, shimmer, twinkle, dance, glint
 ▷ NOUN 1 = **glitter**, flash, gleam, flicker, brilliance, twinkle, glint 2 = **vivacity**, life, spirit, dash, vitality, élan, liveliness

spate NOUN 1 = **flood**, flow, torrent, rush, deluge, outpouring

S

2 = **series**, sequence, course, chain, succession, run, train

speak VERB 1 = **talk**, say something 2 = **articulate**, say, pronounce, utter, tell, state, talk, express 3 = **converse**, talk, chat, discourse, confer, commune, exchange views, korero (*N.Z.*) 4 = **lecture**, address an audience

speaker NOUN = **orator**, public speaker, lecturer, spokesperson, spokesman *or* spokeswoman

spearhead VERB = **lead**, head, pioneer, launch, set off, initiate, set in motion

special ADJECTIVE 1 = **exceptional**, important, significant, particular, unique, unusual, extraordinary, memorable ≠ ordinary 2 = **specific**, particular, distinctive, individual, appropriate, precise ≠ general

specialist NOUN = **expert**, authority, professional, master, consultant, guru, buff (*informal*), connoisseur, fundi (*S. African*)

speciality NOUN = **forte**, métier, specialty, bag (*slang*), pièce de résistance (*French*)

species NOUN = **kind**, sort, type, group, class, variety, breed, category

specific ADJECTIVE 1 = **particular**, special, characteristic, distinguishing ≠ general 2 = **precise**, exact, explicit, definite, express, clear-cut, unequivocal ≠ vague 3 = **peculiar**, appropriate, individual, particular, unique

specification NOUN = **requirement**, detail, particular, stipulation, condition, qualification

specify VERB = **state**, designate, stipulate, name, detail, mention, indicate, define

specimen NOUN 1 = **sample**, example, model, type, pattern, instance, representative, exemplification 2 = **example**, model, type

spectacle NOUN 1 = **show**, display, exhibition, event, performance, extravaganza, pageant 2 = **sight**, wonder, scene, phenomenon, curiosity, marvel

spectacular
ADJECTIVE = **impressive**, striking, dramatic, stunning (*informal*), grand, magnificent, splendid, dazzling ≠ unimpressive
▷ NOUN = **show**, display, spectacle

spectator NOUN = **onlooker**, observer, viewer, looker-on, watcher, bystander ≠ participant

spectre NOUN = **ghost**, spirit, phantom, vision, apparition, wraith, kehua (*N.Z.*)

speculate VERB 1 = **conjecture**, consider, wonder, guess, surmise, theorize, hypothesize 2 = **gamble**, risk, venture, hazard

speculation NOUN 1 = **theory**, opinion, hypothesis, conjecture, guess, surmise, guesswork, supposition 2 = **gamble**, risk, hazard

speculative ADJECTIVE = **hypothetical**, academic,

S

theoretical, notional, conjectural, suppositional

speech NOUN

1 = **communication**, talk, conversation, discussion, dialogue 2 = **diction**, pronunciation, articulation, delivery, fluency, inflection, intonation, elocution
3 = **language**, tongue, jargon, dialect, idiom, parlance, articulation, diction 4 = **talk**, address, lecture, discourse, homily, oration, spiel (*informal*), whaikorero (*N.Z.*)

speed NOUN 1 = **rate**, pace
2 = **swiftness**, rush, hurry, haste, rapidity, quickness ≠ slowness
▷ VERB 1 = **race**, rush, hurry, zoom, career, tear, barrel (along) (*informal, chiefly U.S. & Canad.*), gallop ≠ crawl 2 = **help**, advance, aid, boost, assist, facilitate, expedite ≠ hinder

⬤ **WORD POWER**
⬤ The past tense of *speed up* is
⬤ *speeded up* (not *sped up*), for
⬤ example *I speeded up to overtake*
⬤ *the lorry.* The past participle is
⬤ also *speeded up*, for example
⬤ *I had already speeded up when I*
⬤ *spotted the police car.*

speedy ADJECTIVE = **quick**, fast, rapid, swift, express, immediate, prompt, hurried ≠ slow

spell¹ VERB = **indicate**, mean, signify, point to, imply, augur, portend

spell² NOUN 1 = **incantation**, charm, makutu (*N.Z.*)

2 = **enchantment**, magic, fascination, glamour, allure, bewitchment

spell³ NOUN = **period**, time, term, stretch, course, season, interval, bout

spend VERB 1 = **pay out**, fork out (*slang*), expend, disburse ≠ save
2 = **pass**, fill, occupy, while away
3 = **use up**, waste, squander, empty, drain, exhaust, consume, run through ≠ save

sphere NOUN 1 = **ball**, globe, orb, globule, circle 2 = **field**, department, function, territory, capacity, province, patch, scope

spice NOUN 1 = **seasoning**
2 = **excitement**, zest, colour, pep, zing (*informal*), piquancy

spicy ADJECTIVE 1 = **hot**, seasoned, aromatic, savoury, piquant 2 (*informal*) = **risqué**, racy, ribald, hot (*informal*), suggestive, titillating, indelicate

spider NOUN ▷ RELATED WORD: *fear* **arachnophobia**

spike NOUN = **point**, stake, spine, barb, prong
▷ VERB = **impale**, spit, spear, stick

spill VERB 1 = **tip over**, overturn, capsize, knock over 2 = **shed**, discharge, disgorge 3 = **slop**, flow, pour, run, overflow

spin VERB 1 = **revolve**, turn, rotate, reel, whirl, twirl, gyrate, pirouette
2 = **reel**, swim, whirl
▷ NOUN 1 (*informal*) = **drive**, ride, joy ride (*informal*) 2 = **revolution**, roll, whirl, gyration ▷ PHRASE:
spin something out = **prolong**,

S

- **SPIDERS AND OTHER ARACHNIDS**
- black widow
- chigger, chigoe, *or* (*U.S. & Canad.*) redbug
- chigoe, chigger, jigger, *or* sand flea
- harvestman *or* (*U.S. & Canad.*) daddy-longlegs
- katipo (*N.Z.*)
- mite
- red-back (spider) (*Austral.*)
- spider
- spider mite
- tarantula
- tick
- trap-door spider
- whip scorpion
- wolf spider *or* hunting spider

extend, lengthen, draw out, drag out, delay, amplify

spine NOUN 1 = **backbone**, vertebrae, spinal column, vertebral column 2 = **barb**, spur, needle, spike, ray, quill

- **WORD POWER**
- The *spine* or backbone of a
- human body supports the
- skeleton, and in turn the whole
- body. Various metaphors have
- developed out of this role,
- specifically the notions of
- underpinning and strength.
- The physical appearance of the
- spine as a ridge has inspired
- many analogies, from hills in
- the landscape to the backs of
- books. In sport, players can be
- described as the *spine of their team* if they are considered
- to support the rest. Although
- spine on its own means
- resolution and endurance,
- it is most commonly seen in
- the negative form *spineless*
- meaning lacking courage or
- will. Parallels for most of the
- meanings of spine are found
- in *backbone*, particularly
- the meaning 'courage', as
- in *show some backbone*. The
- perception of fear is sometimes
- experienced as *sending a chill down the spine* in *spine-chilling*
- and *spine-tingling*.

spiral ADJECTIVE = **coiled**, winding, whorled, helical
▷ NOUN = **coil**, helix, corkscrew, whorl

spirit NOUN 1 = **soul**, life 2 = **life force**, vital spark, mauri (*N.Z.*) 3 = **ghost**, phantom, spectre, apparition, atua (*N.Z.*), kehua (*N.Z.*) 4 = **courage**, guts (*informal*), grit, backbone, spunk (*informal*), gameness 5 = **liveliness**, energy, vigour, life, force, fire, enthusiasm, animation 6 = **attitude**, character, temper, outlook, temperament, disposition 7 = **heart**, sense, nature, soul, core, substance, essence, quintessence 8 = **intention**, meaning, purpose, purport, gist 9 = **feeling**, atmosphere, character, tone, mood, tenor, ambience 10 *plural*

S

= **mood**, feelings, morale, temper, disposition, state of mind, frame of mind

spirited ADJECTIVE = **lively**, energetic, animated, active, feisty (*informal*, *chiefly U.S. & Canad.*), vivacious, mettlesome, (as) game as Ned Kelly (*Austral. slang*) ≠ lifeless

spiritual ADJECTIVE
1 = **nonmaterial**, immaterial, incorporeal ≠ material
2 = **sacred**, religious, holy, divine, devotional

spit VERB 1 = **expectorate**
2 = **eject**, throw out
▷ NOUN = **saliva**, dribble, spittle, drool, slaver

spite NOUN = **malice**, malevolence, ill will, hatred, animosity, venom, spleen, spitefulness ≠ kindness
▷ VERB = **annoy**, hurt, injure, harm, vex ≠ benefit ▷ PHRASE: **in spite of** = **despite**, regardless of, notwithstanding, (even) though

splash VERB 1 = **paddle**, plunge, bathe, dabble, wade, wallow
2 = **scatter**, shower, spray, sprinkle, wet, spatter, slop
3 = **spatter**, mark, stain, speck, speckle
▷ NOUN 1 = **dash**, touch, spattering 2 = **spot**, burst, patch, spurt 3 = **blob**, spot, smudge, stain, smear, fleck, speck

splendid ADJECTIVE 1 = **excellent**, wonderful, marvellous, great (*informal*), cracking (*Brit. informal*), fantastic (*informal*), first-class, glorious, booshit (*Austral. slang*),

exo (*Austral. slang*), sik (*Austral. slang*), rad (*informal*), phat (*slang*), schmick (*Austral. informal*)
≠ poor 2 = **magnificent**, grand, impressive, rich, superb, costly, gorgeous, lavish ≠ squalid

splendour NOUN
= **magnificence**, grandeur, show, display, spectacle, richness, nobility, pomp ≠ squalor

splinter NOUN = **sliver**, fragment, chip, flake
▷ VERB = **shatter**, split, fracture, disintegrate

split VERB 1 = **break**, crack, burst, open, give way, come apart, come undone 2 = **cut**, break, crack, snap, chop 3 = **divide**, separate, disunite, disband, cleave
4 = **diverge**, separate, branch, fork, part 5 = **tear**, rend, rip
6 = **share out**, divide, distribute, halve, allocate, partition, allot
▷ NOUN 1 = **division**, breach, rift, rupture, discord, schism, estrangement, dissension
2 = **separation**, break-up, split-up 3 = **crack**, tear, rip, gap, rent, breach, slit, fissure
▷ ADJECTIVE 1 = **divided**
2 = **broken**, cracked, fractured, ruptured, cleft

spoil VERB 1 = **ruin**, destroy, wreck, damage, injure, harm, mar, trash (*slang*), crool or cruel (*Austral. slang*) ≠ improve
2 = **overindulge**, indulge, pamper, cosset, coddle, mollycoddle
≠ deprive 3 = **indulge**, pamper,

S

satisfy, gratify, pander to **4** = **go bad**, turn, go off (*Brit. informal*), rot, decay, decompose, curdle, addle

spoils PLURAL NOUN = **booty**, loot, plunder, prey, swag (*slang*)

spoken ADJECTIVE = **verbal**, voiced, expressed, uttered, oral, said, told, unwritten

spokesperson NOUN = **speaker**, official, spokesman *or* spokeswoman, voice, spin doctor (*informal*), mouthpiece

sponsor VERB = **back**, fund, finance, promote, subsidize, patronize
▷ NOUN = **backer**, patron, promoter

spontaneous ADJECTIVE = **unplanned**, impromptu, unprompted, willing, natural, voluntary, instinctive, impulsive ≠ planned

sport NOUN **1** = **game**, exercise, recreation, play, amusement, diversion, pastime **2** = **fun**, joking, teasing, banter, jest, badinage
▷ VERB (*informal*) = **wear**, display, flaunt, exhibit, flourish, show off, vaunt

sporting ADJECTIVE = **fair**, sportsmanlike, game (*informal*) ≠ unfair

sporty ADJECTIVE = **athletic**, outdoor, energetic

spot NOUN **1** = **mark**, stain, speck, scar, blot, smudge, blemish, speckle **2** = **pimple**, pustule, zit (*slang*) **3** = **place**, site, point,

position, scene, location **4** (*informal*) = **predicament**, trouble, difficulty, mess, plight, hot water (*informal*), quandary, tight spot
▷ VERB **1** = **see**, observe, catch sight of, sight, recognize, detect, make out, discern **2** = **mark**, stain, soil, dirty, fleck, spatter, speckle, splodge

spotlight NOUN = **attention**, limelight, public eye, fame
▷ VERB = **highlight**, draw attention to, accentuate

spotted ADJECTIVE = **speckled**, dotted, flecked, mottled, dappled

spouse NOUN = **partner**, mate, husband *or* wife, consort, significant other (*U.S. informal*)

sprawl VERB = **loll**, slump, lounge, flop, slouch

spray¹ NOUN **1** = **droplets**, fine mist, drizzle **2** = **aerosol**, sprinkler, atomizer
▷ VERB = **scatter**, shower, sprinkle, diffuse

spray² NOUN = **sprig**, floral arrangement, branch, corsage

spread VERB **1** = **open (out)**, extend, stretch, unfold, sprawl, unroll **2** = **extend**, open, stretch **3** = **grow**, increase, expand, widen, escalate, proliferate, multiply, broaden **4** = **circulate**, broadcast, propagate, disseminate, make known ≠ suppress **5** = **diffuse**, cast, shed, radiate
▷ NOUN **1** = **increase**, development, advance, expansion, proliferation,

dissemination, dispersal

2 = **extent**, span, stretch, sweep

spree NOUN = **fling**, binge (*informal*), orgy

spring NOUN = **flexibility**, bounce, resilience, elasticity, buoyancy

▷ VERB 1 = **jump**, bound, leap, bounce, vault 2 *usually followed by* **from** = **originate**, come, derive, start, issue, proceed, arise, stem

▷ RELATED WORD: *adjective* **vernal**

sprinkle VERB = **scatter**, dust, strew, pepper, shower, spray, powder, dredge

sprinkling NOUN = **scattering**, dusting, few, dash, handful, sprinkle

sprint VERB = **run**, race, shoot, tear, dash, dart, hare (*Brit. informal*)

sprout VERB 1 = **germinate**, bud, shoot, spring 2 = **grow**, develop, ripen

spur VERB = **incite**, drive, prompt, urge, stimulate, animate, prod, prick

▷ NOUN = **stimulus**, incentive, impetus, motive, impulse, inducement, incitement

▷ PHRASE: **on the spur of the moment** = **on impulse**, impulsively, on the spot, impromptu, without planning

spurn VERB = **reject**, slight, scorn, rebuff, snub, despise, disdain, repulse ≠ accept

spy NOUN = **undercover agent**, mole, nark (*Brit., Austral. & N.Z. slang*)

▷ VERB = **catch sight of**, spot,

notice, observe, glimpse, espy

squabble VERB = **quarrel**, fight, argue, row, dispute, wrangle, bicker

▷ NOUN = **quarrel**, fight, row, argument, dispute, disagreement, tiff

squad NOUN = **team**, group, band, company, force, troop, crew, gang

squander VERB = **waste**, spend, fritter away, blow (*slang*), misuse, expend, misspend ≠ save

square ADJECTIVE = **fair**, straight, genuine, ethical, honest, on the level (*informal*), kosher (*informal*), dinkum (*Austral. & N.Z. informal*), above board

▷ VERB *often followed by* **with** = **agree**, match, fit, correspond, tally, reconcile

squash VERB 1 = **crush**, press, flatten, mash, smash, distort, pulp, compress 2 = **suppress**, quell, silence, crush, annihilate 3 = **embarrass**, put down, shame, degrade, mortify

squeeze VERB 1 = **press**, crush, squash, pinch 2 = **clutch**, press, grip, crush, pinch, squash, compress, wring 3 = **cram**, press, crowd, force, stuff, pack, jam, ram 4 = **hug**, embrace, cuddle, clasp, enfold

▷ NOUN 1 = **press**, grip, clasp, crush, pinch, squash, wring 2 = **crush**, jam, squash, press, crowd, congestion 3 = **hug**, embrace, clasp

stab VERB = **pierce**, stick, wound, knife, thrust, spear, jab, transfix

S

▷ NOUN 1 (*informal*) = **attempt**, go, try, endeavour 2 = **twinge**, prick, pang, ache

stability NOUN = **firmness**, strength, soundness, solidity, steadiness ≠ instability

stable ADJECTIVE 1 = **secure**, lasting, strong, sound, fast, sure, established, permanent ≠ insecure 2 = **well-balanced**, balanced, sensible, reasonable, rational 3 = **solid**, firm, fixed, substantial, durable, well-made, well-built, immovable ≠ unstable

stack NOUN 1 = **pile**, heap, mountain, mass, load, mound 2 = **lot**, mass, load (*informal*), ton (*informal*), heap (*informal*), great amount
▷ VERB = **pile**, heap up, load, assemble, accumulate, amass

staff NOUN 1 = **workers**, employees, personnel, workforce, team 2 = **stick**, pole, rod, crook, cane, stave, wand, sceptre

stage NOUN = **step**, leg, phase, point, level, period, division, lap

stagger VERB 1 = **totter**, reel, sway, lurch, wobble 2 = **astound**, amaze, stun, shock, shake, overwhelm, astonish, confound

stain NOUN 1 = **mark**, spot, blot, blemish, discoloration, smirch 2 = **stigma**, shame, disgrace, slur, dishonour 3 = **dye**, colour, tint
▷ VERB 1 = **mark**, soil, discolour, dirty, tinge, spot, blot, blemish 2 = **dye**, colour, tint

stake¹ NOUN = **pole**, post, stick, pale, paling, picket, palisade

stake² NOUN 1 = **bet**, ante, wager 2 = **interest**, share, involvement, concern, investment
▷ VERB = **bet**, gamble, wager, chance, risk, venture, hazard

stale ADJECTIVE 1 = **old**, hard, dry, decayed ≠ fresh 2 = **musty**, fusty 3 = **tasteless**, flat, sour 4 = **unoriginal**, banal, trite, stereotyped, worn-out, threadbare, hackneyed, overused ≠ original

stalk VERB = **pursue**, follow, track, hunt, shadow, haunt

stall¹ VERB = **stop dead**, jam, seize up, catch, stick, stop short
▷ NOUN = **stand**, table, counter, booth, kiosk

stall² VERB = **play for time**, delay, hedge, temporize

stalwart ADJECTIVE 1 = **loyal**, faithful, firm, true, dependable, steadfast 2 = **strong**, strapping, sturdy, stout ≠ puny

stamina NOUN = **staying power**, endurance, resilience, force, power, energy, strength

stammer VERB = **stutter**, falter, pause, hesitate, stumble over your words

stamp NOUN = **imprint**, mark, brand, signature, earmark, hallmark
▷ VERB 1 = **print**, mark, impress 2 = **trample**, step, tread, crush 3 = **identify**, mark, brand, label, reveal, show to be, categorize
▷ PHRASE: **stamp something out** = **eliminate**, destroy, eradicate, crush, suppress, put down,

scotch, quell

stance NOUN 1 = **attitude**, stand, position, viewpoint, standpoint 2 = **posture**, carriage, bearing, deportment

stand VERB 1 = **be upright**, be erect, be vertical 2 = **get to your feet**, rise, stand up, straighten up 3 = **be located**, be, sit, be positioned, be situated or located 4 = **be valid**, continue, exist, prevail, remain valid 5 = **put**, place, position, set, mount 6 = **sit**, mellow 7 = **resist**, endure, tolerate, stand up to 8 = **tolerate**, bear, abide, stomach, endure, brook 9 = **take**, bear, handle, endure, put up with (*informal*), countenance
▷ NOUN 1 = **position**, attitude, stance, opinion, determination 2 = **stall**, booth, kiosk, table
▷ PHRASES: **stand by** = **be prepared**, wait; **stand for something** 1 = **represent**, mean, signify, denote, indicate, symbolize, betoken; **stand in for someone** = **be a substitute for**, represent, cover for, take the place of, deputize for; **stand up for something** or **someone** = **support**, champion, defend, uphold, stick up for (*informal*)

standard NOUN 1 = **level**, grade 2 = **criterion**, measure, guideline, example, model, average, norm, gauge 3 *often plural* = **principles**, ideals, morals, ethics 4 = **flag**, banner, ensign
▷ ADJECTIVE 1 = **usual**, normal, customary, average, basic, regular, typical, orthodox ≠ unusual 2 = **accepted**, official, established, approved, recognized, definitive, authoritative ≠ unofficial

stand-in NOUN = **substitute**, deputy, replacement, reserve, surrogate, understudy, locum, stopgap

standing NOUN 1 = **status**, position, footing, rank, reputation, eminence, repute 2 = **duration**, existence, continuance
▷ ADJECTIVE 1 = **permanent**, lasting, fixed, regular 2 = **upright**, erect, vertical

staple ADJECTIVE = **principal**, chief, main, key, basic, fundamental, predominant

star NOUN 1 = **heavenly body**, celestial body 2 = **celebrity**, big name, megastar (*informal*), name, luminary, leading man or lady, hero or heroine, principal, main attraction
▷ VERB = **play the lead**, appear, feature, perform ▷ RELATED WORDS: *adjectives* astral, stellar

stare VERB = **gaze**, look, goggle, watch, gape, eyeball (*slang*), gawp (*Brit. slang*), gawk

stark ADJECTIVE 1 = **plain**, harsh, basic, grim, straightforward, blunt 2 = **sharp**, clear, striking, distinct, clear-cut 3 = **austere**, severe, plain, bare, harsh, bare-bones 4 = **bleak**, grim, barren, hard 5 = **absolute**, pure, sheer,

S

utter, downright, out-and-out, unmitigated
▷ **ADVERB** = **absolutely**, quite, completely, entirely, altogether, wholly, utterly
start VERB 1 = **set about**, begin, proceed, embark upon, take the first step, make a beginning ≠ stop 2 = **begin**, arise, originate, issue, appear, commence ≠ end 3 = **set in motion**, initiate, instigate, open, trigger, originate, get going, kick-start ≠ stop 4 = **establish**, begin, found, create, launch, set up, institute, pioneer ≠ terminate 5 = **start up**, activate, get something going ≠ turn off 6 = **jump**, shy, jerk, flinch, recoil
▷ **NOUN** 1 = **beginning**, outset, opening, birth, foundation, dawn, onset, initiation ≠ end 2 = **jump**, spasm, convulsion
startle VERB = **surprise**, shock, frighten, scare, make (someone) jump
starving ADJECTIVE = **hungry**, starved, ravenous, famished
state NOUN 1 = **country**, nation, land, republic, territory, federation, commonwealth, kingdom 2 = **government**, ministry, administration, executive, regime, powers-that-be 3 = **condition**, shape 4 = **frame of mind**, condition, spirits, attitude, mood, humour 5 = **ceremony**, glory, grandeur, splendour, majesty, pomp 6 = **circumstances**, situation,

position, predicament
▷ **VERB** = **say**, declare, present, voice, express, assert, utter
stately ADJECTIVE = **grand**, majestic, dignified, royal, august, noble, regal, lofty ≠ lowly
statement NOUN 1 = **announcement**, declaration, communication, communiqué, proclamation 2 = **account**, report
station NOUN 1 = **railway station**, stop, stage, halt, terminal, train station, terminus 2 = **headquarters**, base, depot 3 = **position**, rank, status, standing, post, situation 4 = **post**, place, location, position, situation
▷ **VERB** = **assign**, post, locate, set, establish, install
stature NOUN 1 = **height**, build, size 2 = **importance**, standing, prestige, rank, prominence, eminence
status NOUN 1 = **position**, rank, grade 2 = **prestige**, standing, authority, influence, weight, honour, importance, fame, mana (*N.Z.*) 3 = **state of play**, development, progress, condition, evolution
staunch ADJECTIVE = **loyal**, faithful, stalwart, firm, sound, true, trusty, steadfast
stay VERB 1 = **remain**, continue to be, linger, stop, wait, halt, pause, abide ≠ go 2 *often with* **at** = **lodge**, visit, sojourn, put up at, be accommodated at 3 = **continue**, remain, go on,

survive, endure
▷ NOUN 1 = **visit**, stop,
holiday, stopover, sojourn
2 = **postponement**, delay,
suspension, stopping, halt,
deferment

steady ADJECTIVE 1 = **continuous**,
regular, constant, consistent,
persistent, unbroken,
uninterrupted, incessant
≠ irregular 2 = **stable**, fixed,
secure, firm, safe ≠ unstable
3 = **regular**, established
4 = **dependable**, sensible, reliable,
secure, calm, supportive, sober,
level-headed ≠ undependable

steal VERB 1 = **take**, nick (slang,
chiefly Brit.), pinch (informal),
lift (informal), embezzle, pilfer,
misappropriate, purloin 2 = **copy**,
take, appropriate, pinch (informal)
3 = **sneak**, slip, creep, tiptoe, slink

stealth NOUN = **secrecy**,
furtiveness, slyness, sneakiness,
unobtrusiveness, stealthiness,
surreptitiousness

steep¹ ADJECTIVE 1 = **sheer**,
precipitous, abrupt, vertical
≠ gradual 2 = **sharp**, sudden,
abrupt, marked, extreme, distinct
3 (informal) = **high**, exorbitant,
extreme, unreasonable,
overpriced, extortionate
≠ reasonable

steep² VERB = **soak**, immerse,
marinate (cookery), submerge,
drench, moisten, souse

steeped ADJECTIVE = **saturated**,
pervaded, permeated, filled,
infused, imbued, suffused

steer VERB 1 = **drive**, control,
direct, handle, pilot 2 = **direct**,
lead, guide, conduct, escort

stem¹ NOUN = **stalk**, branch, trunk,
shoot, axis ▷ PHRASE: **stem from**
something = **originate from**, be
caused by, derive from, arise from

stem² VERB = **stop**, hold back,
staunch, check, dam, curb

step NOUN 1 = **pace**, stride,
footstep 2 = **footfall** 3 = **move**,
measure, action, means, act,
deed, expedient 4 = **stage**, point,
phase 5 = **level**, rank, degree
▷ VERB = **walk**, pace, tread, move
▷ PHRASES: **step in** (informal)
= **intervene**, take action, become
involved; **step something up**
= **increase**, intensify, raise

stereotype NOUN = **formula**,
pattern
▷ VERB = **categorize**, typecast,
pigeonhole, standardize

sterile ADJECTIVE 1 = **germ-free**,
sterilized, disinfected, aseptic
≠ unhygienic 2 = **barren**,
infertile, unproductive, childless
≠ fertile

sterling ADJECTIVE = **excellent**,
sound, fine, superlative

stern ADJECTIVE 1 = **strict**,
harsh, hard, grim, rigid, austere,
inflexible ≠ lenient 2 = **severe**,
serious, forbidding ≠ friendly

stick¹ NOUN 1 = **twig**, branch
2 = **cane**, staff, pole, rod, crook,
baton 3 (slang) = **abuse**,
criticism, flak (informal), fault-
finding

stick² VERB 1 (informal) = **put**,

place, set, lay, deposit **2** = **poke**,
dig, stab, thrust, pierce,
penetrate, spear, prod **3** = **fasten**,
fix, bind, hold, bond, attach, glue,
paste **4** = **adhere**, cling, become
joined, become welded **5** = **stay**,
remain, linger, persist **6** (*slang*)
= **tolerate**, take, stand, stomach,
abide ▷ **PHRASES**: **stick out**
= **protrude**, stand out, jut out,
show, project, bulge, obtrude;
stick up for someone (*informal*)
= **defend**, support, champion,
stand up for
sticky ADJECTIVE **1** = **adhesive**,
gummed, adherent **2** = **gooey**,
tacky (*informal*), viscous,
glutinous, gummy, icky (*informal*),
gluey, clinging **3** (*informal*)
= **difficult**, awkward, tricky,
embarrassing, nasty, delicate,
unpleasant, barro (*Austral.
slang*) **4** = **humid**, close, sultry,
oppressive, sweltering, clammy,
muggy
stiff ADJECTIVE **1** = **inflexible**,
rigid, unyielding, hard, firm,
tight, solid, tense ≠ flexible
2 = **formal**, constrained, forced,
unnatural, stilted, unrelaxed
≠ informal **3** = **vigorous**, great,
strong **4** = **severe**, strict, harsh,
hard, heavy, extreme, drastic
5 = **difficult**, hard, tough,
exacting, arduous
stifle VERB **1** = **suppress**, repress,
stop, check, silence, restrain,
hush, smother **2** = **restrain**,
suppress, repress, smother
stigma NOUN = **disgrace**, shame,

dishonour, stain, slur, smirch
still ADJECTIVE **1** = **motionless**,
stationary, calm, peaceful, serene,
tranquil, undisturbed, restful
≠ moving **2** = **silent**, quiet,
hushed ≠ noisy
▷ VERB = **quieten**, calm, settle,
quiet, silence, soothe, hush, lull
≠ get louder
▷ SENTENCE
CONNECTOR = **however**, but, yet,
nevertheless, notwithstanding
stimulate VERB = **encourage**,
inspire, prompt, fire, spur,
provoke, arouse, rouse
stimulating ADJECTIVE
= **exciting**, inspiring, stirring,
rousing, provocative, exhilarating
≠ boring
stimulus NOUN = **incentive**,
spur, encouragement, impetus,
inducement, goad, incitement,
fillip
sting VERB **1** = **hurt**, burn, wound
2 = **smart**, burn, pain, hurt, tingle
stink VERB **1** = **reek**, pong (*Brit.
informal*)
▷ NOUN = **stench**, pong (*Brit.
informal*), foul smell, fetor
stint NOUN = **term**, time, turn,
period, share, shift, stretch, spell
▷ VERB = **be mean**, hold back, be
sparing, skimp on, be frugal
stipulate VERB = **specify**,
agree, require, contract, settle,
covenant, insist upon
stir VERB **1** = **mix**, beat, agitate
2 = **stimulate**, move, excite, spur,
provoke, arouse, awaken, rouse
≠ inhibit **3** = **spur**, drive, prompt,

s

stimulate, prod, urge, animate, prick

▷ NOUN = **commotion**, excitement, activity, disorder, fuss, disturbance, bustle, flurry

stock NOUN 1 = **shares**, holdings, securities, investments, bonds, equities 2 = **property**, capital, assets, funds 3 = **goods**, merchandise, wares, range, choice, variety, selection, commodities 4 = **supply**, store, reserve, fund, stockpile, hoard 5 = **livestock**, cattle, beasts, domestic animals

▷ VERB 1 = **sell**, supply, handle, keep, trade in, deal in 2 = **fill**, supply, provide with, equip, furnish, fit out

▷ ADJECTIVE 1 = **hackneyed**, routine, banal, trite, overused 2 = **regular**, usual, ordinary, conventional, customary

stomach NOUN 1 = **belly**, gut (*informal*), abdomen, tummy (*informal*), puku (*N.Z.*) 2 = **tummy**, pot 3 = **inclination**, taste, desire, appetite, relish

▷ VERB = **bear**, take, tolerate, endure, swallow, abide ▷ RELATED WORD: *adjective* gastric

stone NOUN 1 = **masonry**, rock 2 = **rock**, pebble 3 = **pip**, seed, pit, kernel

stoop VERB 1 = **hunch** 2 = **bend**, lean, bow, duck, crouch

▷ NOUN = **slouch**, bad posture, round-shoulderedness

stop VERB 1 = **quit**, cease, refrain, put an end to, discontinue, desist

≠ start 2 = **prevent**, cut short, arrest, restrain, hold back, hinder, repress, impede ≠ facilitate 3 = **end**, conclude, finish, terminate ≠ continue 4 = **cease**, shut down, discontinue, desist ≠ continue 5 = **halt**, pause ≠ keep going 6 = **pause**, wait, rest, take a break, have a breather (*informal*), stop briefly 7 = **stay**, rest, lodge

▷ NOUN 1 = **halt**, standstill 2 = **station**, stage, depot, terminus 3 = **stay**, break, rest

store NOUN 1 = **shop**, outlet, market, mart 2 = **supply**, stock, reserve, fund, quantity, accumulation, stockpile, hoard 3 = **repository**, warehouse, depository, storeroom

▷ VERB 1 *often with* **away** *or* **up** = **put by**, save, hoard, keep, reserve, deposit, garner, stockpile 2 = **put away**, put in storage, put in store 3 = **keep**, hold, preserve, maintain, retain, conserve

storm NOUN 1 = **tempest**, hurricane, gale, blizzard, squall 2 = **outburst**, row, outcry, furore, outbreak, turmoil, disturbance, strife

▷ VERB 1 = **rush**, stamp, flounce, fly 2 = **rage**, rant, thunder, rave, bluster 3 = **attack**, charge, rush, assault, assail

stormy ADJECTIVE 1 = **wild**, rough, raging, turbulent, windy, blustery, inclement, squally 2 = **rough**, wild, turbulent, raging 3 = **angry**, heated, fierce, passionate, fiery,

S

impassioned

story NOUN 1 = **tale**, romance, narrative, history, legend, yarn 2 = **anecdote**, account, tale, report 3 = **report**, news, article, feature, scoop, news item

stout ADJECTIVE 1 = **fat**, big, heavy, overweight, plump, bulky, burly, fleshy ≠ slim 2 = **strong**, strapping, muscular, robust, sturdy, stalwart, brawny, able-bodied ≠ puny 3 = **brave**, bold, courageous, fearless, resolute, gallant, intrepid, valiant ≠ timid

straight ADJECTIVE 1 = **direct** ≠ indirect 2 = **level**, even, right, square, true, smooth, aligned, horizontal ≠ crooked 3 = **frank**, plain, straightforward, blunt, outright, honest, candid, forthright ≠ evasive 4 = **successive**, consecutive, continuous, running, solid, nonstop ≠ discontinuous 5 (slang) = **conventional**, conservative, bourgeois ≠ fashionable 6 = **honest**, just, fair, reliable, respectable, upright, honourable, law-abiding ≠ dishonest 7 = **undiluted**, pure, neat, unadulterated, unmixed 8 = **in order**, organized, arranged, neat, tidy, orderly, shipshape ≠ untidy
▷ ADVERB 1 = **directly**, precisely, exactly, unswervingly, by the shortest route, in a beeline 2 = **immediately**, directly, promptly, instantly, at once, straight away, without delay,

forthwith

straightaway ADVERB = **immediately**, now, at once, directly, instantly, right away

straighten VERB = **neaten**, arrange, tidy (up), order, put in order

straightforward ADJECTIVE 1 (chiefly Brit.) = **simple**, easy, uncomplicated, routine, elementary, easy-peasy (slang) ≠ complicated 2 = **honest**, open, direct, genuine, sincere, candid, truthful, forthright, dinkum (Austral. & N.Z. informal) ≠ devious

strain¹ NOUN 1 = **pressure**, stress, demands, burden 2 = **stress**, anxiety 3 = **worry**, effort, struggle ≠ ease 4 = **burden**, tension 5 = **injury**, wrench, sprain, pull
▷ VERB 1 = **stretch**, tax, overtax 2 = **strive**, struggle, endeavour, labour, go for it (informal), bend over backwards (informal), give it your best shot (informal), knock yourself out (informal) ≠ relax 3 = **sieve**, filter, sift, purify

strain² NOUN 1 = **trace**, suggestion, tendency, streak 2 = **breed**, family, race, blood, descent, extraction, ancestry, lineage

strained ADJECTIVE 1 = **tense**, difficult, awkward, embarrassed, stiff, uneasy ≠ relaxed 2 = **forced**, put on, false, artificial, unnatural ≠ natural

strait NOUN often plural = **channel**, sound, narrows
▷ PLURAL NOUN = **difficulty**,

dilemma, plight, hardship, uphill (*S. African*), predicament, extremity

strand NOUN = **filament**, fibre, thread, string

stranded ADJECTIVE 1 = **beached**, grounded, marooned, ashore, shipwrecked, aground 2 = **helpless**, abandoned, high and dry

strange ADJECTIVE 1 = **odd**, curious, weird, wonderful, extraordinary, bizarre, peculiar, abnormal, daggy (*Austral. & N.Z. informal*) ≠ ordinary 2 = **unfamiliar**, new, unknown, foreign, novel, alien, exotic, untried ≠ familiar

stranger NOUN 1 = **unknown person** 2 = **newcomer**, incomer, foreigner, guest, visitor, alien, outlander

strangle VERB 1 = **throttle**, choke, asphyxiate, strangulate 2 = **suppress**, inhibit, subdue, stifle, repress, overpower, quash, quell

strap NOUN = **tie**, thong, belt
▷ VERB = **fasten**, tie, secure, bind, lash, buckle

strapping ADJECTIVE = **well-built**, big, powerful, robust, sturdy, husky (*informal*), brawny

strategic ADJECTIVE 1 = **tactical**, calculated, deliberate, planned, politic, diplomatic 2 = **crucial**, important, key, vital, critical, decisive, cardinal

strategy NOUN 1 = **policy**, procedure, approach, scheme

2 = **plan**, approach, scheme

stray VERB 1 = **wander**, go astray, drift 2 = **drift**, wander, roam, meander, rove 3 = **digress**, diverge, deviate, get off the point
▷ MODIFIER = **lost**, abandoned, homeless, roaming, vagrant
▷ ADJECTIVE = **random**, chance, accidental

streak NOUN 1 = **band**, line, strip, stroke, layer, slash, vein, stripe 2 = **trace**, touch, element, strain, dash, vein
▷ VERB = **speed**, fly, tear, flash, sprint, dart, zoom, whizz (*informal*)

stream NOUN 1 = **river**, brook, burn (*Scot.*), beck, tributary, bayou, rivulet 2 = **flow**, current, rush, run, course, drift, surge, tide
▷ VERB 1 = **flow**, run, pour, issue, flood, spill, cascade, gush 2 = **rush**, fly, speed, tear, flood, pour

streamlined ADJECTIVE = **efficient**, organized, rationalized, slick, smooth-running

street NOUN = **road**, lane, avenue, terrace, row, roadway

strength NOUN 1 = **might**, muscle, brawn ≠ weakness 2 = **will**, resolution, courage, character, nerve, determination, pluck, stamina 3 = **health**, fitness, vigour 4 = **mainstay** 5 = **toughness**, soundness, robustness, sturdiness 6 = **force**, power, intensity ≠ weakness 7 = **potency**, effectiveness, efficacy 8 = **strong point**, skill, asset, advantage, talent, forte, speciality ≠ failing

strengthen VERB 1 = **fortify**, harden, toughen, consolidate, stiffen, gee up, brace up ≠ weaken 2 = **reinforce**, support, intensify, bolster, buttress 3 = **bolster**, harden, reinforce 4 = **heighten**, intensify 5 = **make stronger**, build up, invigorate, restore, give strength to 6 = **support**, brace, reinforce, consolidate, harden, bolster, augment, buttress 7 = **become stronger**, intensify, gain strength

stress VERB 1 = **emphasize**, underline, dwell on 2 = **place the emphasis on**, emphasize, give emphasis to, lay emphasis upon
▷ NOUN 1 = **emphasis**, significance, force, weight 2 = **strain**, pressure, worry, tension, burden, anxiety, trauma 3 = **accent**, beat, emphasis, accentuation

stretch VERB 1 = **extend**, cover, spread, reach, put forth, unroll 2 = **last**, continue, go on, carry on, reach 3 = **expand** 4 = **pull**, distend, strain, tighten, draw out, elongate
▷ NOUN 1 = **expanse**, area, tract, spread, distance, extent 2 = **period**, time, spell, stint, term, space

strict ADJECTIVE 1 = **severe**, harsh, stern, firm, stringent ≠ easy-going 2 = **stern**, firm, severe, harsh, authoritarian 3 = **exact**,

accurate, precise, close, true, faithful, meticulous, scrupulous 4 = **absolute**, total, utter

strife NOUN = **conflict**, battle, clash, quarrel, friction, discord, dissension

strike NOUN = **walkout**, industrial action, mutiny, revolt
▷ VERB 1 = **walk out**, down tools, revolt, mutiny 2 = **hit**, smack, thump, beat, knock, punch, hammer, slap 3 = **drive**, hit, smack, wallop (*informal*) 4 = **collide with**, hit, run into, bump into 5 = **knock**, smack, thump, beat 6 = **affect**, touch, devastate, overwhelm, leave a mark on 7 = **attack**, assault someone, set upon someone, lay into someone (*informal*) 8 = **occur to**, hit, come to, register (*informal*), dawn on *or* upon 9 = **seem to**, appear to, look to, give the impression to 10 = **move**, touch, hit, affect, overcome, stir, disturb, perturb

striking ADJECTIVE = **impressive**, dramatic, outstanding, noticeable, conspicuous, jaw-dropping ≠ unimpressive

string NOUN 1 = **cord**, twine, fibre 2 = **series**, line, row, file, sequence, succession, procession 3 = **sequence**, run, series, chain, succession

stringent ADJECTIVE = **strict**, tough, rigorous, tight, severe, rigid, inflexible ≠ lax

strip¹ VERB 1 = **undress**, disrobe, unclothe 2 = **plunder**, rob, loot, empty, sack, ransack, pillage, divest

strip² NOUN 1 = **piece**, shred, band, belt 2 = **stretch**, area, tract, expanse, extent

strive VERB = **try**, labour, struggle, attempt, toil, go all out (*informal*), bend over backwards (*informal*), do your best

stroke VERB = **caress**, rub, fondle, pet
▷ NOUN 1 = **apoplexy**, fit, seizure, attack, collapse 2 = **blow**, hit, knock, pat, rap, thump, swipe

stroll VERB = **walk**, ramble, amble, promenade, saunter
▷ NOUN = **walk**, promenade, constitutional, ramble, breath of air

strong ADJECTIVE 1 = **powerful**, muscular, tough, athletic, strapping, hardy, sturdy, burly ≠ weak 2 = **fit**, robust, lusty 3 = **durable**, substantial, sturdy, heavy-duty, well-built, hard-wearing ≠ flimsy 4 = **extreme**, radical, drastic, strict, harsh, rigid, forceful, uncompromising 5 = **decisive**, firm, forceful, decided, determined, resolute, incisive 6 = **persuasive**, convincing, compelling, telling, sound, effective, potent, weighty 7 = **keen**, deep, acute, fervent, zealous, vehement 8 = **intense**, deep, passionate, ardent, fierce, fervent, vehement, fervid 9 = **staunch**, firm, fierce, ardent, enthusiastic, passionate, fervent 10 = **distinct**, marked,

clear, unmistakable ≠ slight 11 = **bright**, brilliant, dazzling, bold ≠ dull

stronghold NOUN 1 = **bastion**, fortress, bulwark 2 = **refuge**, haven, retreat, sanctuary, hide-out

structure NOUN
1 = **arrangement**, form, make-up, design, organization, construction, formation, configuration 2 = **building**, construction, erection, edifice
▷ VERB = **arrange**, organize, design, shape, build up, assemble

struggle VERB 1 = **strive**, labour, toil, work, strain, go all out (*informal*), give it your best shot (*informal*), exert yourself 2 = **fight**, battle, wrestle, grapple, compete, contend
▷ NOUN 1 = **effort**, labour, toil, work, pains, scramble, exertion 2 = **fight**, battle, conflict, clash, contest, brush, combat, tussle, biffo (*Austral. slang*)

strut VERB = **swagger**, parade, peacock, prance

stubborn ADJECTIVE = **obstinate**, dogged, inflexible, persistent, intractable, tenacious, recalcitrant, unyielding ≠ compliant

stuck ADJECTIVE 1 = **fastened**, fast, fixed, joined, glued, cemented 2 (*informal*) = **baffled**, stumped, beaten

student NOUN
1 = **undergraduate**, scholar
2 = **pupil**, scholar, schoolchild,

schoolboy or schoolgirl
3 = **learner**, trainee, apprentice, disciple

studied ADJECTIVE = **planned**, deliberate, conscious, intentional, premeditated ≠ unplanned

studio NOUN = **workshop**, workroom, atelier

study VERB **1** = **learn**, cram (*informal*), swot (up) (*Brit. informal*), read up, mug up (*Brit. slang*)
2 = **examine**, survey, look at, scrutinize **3** = **contemplate**, read, examine, consider, go into, pore over
▷ NOUN **1** = **examination**, investigation, analysis, consideration, inspection, scrutiny, contemplation **2** = **piece of research**, survey, report, review, inquiry, investigation
3 = **learning**, lessons, school work, reading, research, swotting (*Brit. informal*)

stuff NOUN **1** = **things**, gear, possessions, effects, equipment, objects, tackle, kit **2** = **substance**, material, essence, matter
▷ VERB **1** = **shove**, force, push, squeeze, jam, ram **2** = **cram**, fill, pack, crowd

stuffing NOUN = **wadding**, filling, packing

stumble VERB **1** = **trip**, fall, slip, reel, stagger, falter, lurch
2 = **totter**, reel, lurch, wobble
▷ PHRASE: **stumble across** or **on** or **upon something** or **someone** = **discover**, find, come across, chance upon

stump NOUN = **tail end**, end, remnant, remainder
▷ VERB = **baffle**, confuse, puzzle, bewilder, perplex, mystify, flummox, nonplus

stun VERB **1** = **overcome**, shock, confuse, astonish, stagger, bewilder, astound, overpower
2 = **daze**, knock out, stupefy, numb, benumb

stunning ADJECTIVE (*informal*) = **wonderful**, beautiful, impressive, striking, lovely, spectacular, marvellous, splendid ≠ unimpressive

stunt NOUN = **feat**, act, trick, exploit, deed

stunted ADJECTIVE = **undersized**, little, small, tiny, diminutive

stupid ADJECTIVE
1 = **unintelligent**, thick, simple, slow, dim, dense, simple-minded, moronic ≠ intelligent **2** = **silly**, foolish, daft (*informal*), rash, pointless, senseless, idiotic, fatuous ≠ sensible **3** = **senseless**, dazed, groggy, insensate, semiconscious

sturdy ADJECTIVE **1** = **robust**, hardy, powerful, athletic, muscular, lusty, brawny ≠ puny
2 = **substantial**, solid, durable, well-made, well-built ≠ flimsy

style NOUN **1** = **manner**, way, method, approach, technique, mode **2** = **elegance**, taste, chic, flair, polish, sophistication, panache, élan **3** = **design**, form, cut **4** = **type**, sort, kind, variety, category, genre **5** = **fashion**,

trend, mode, vogue, rage
6 = **luxury**, ease, comfort, elegance, grandeur, affluence
▷ VERB 1 = **design**, cut, tailor, fashion, shape, arrange, adapt
2 = **call**, name, term, label, entitle, dub, designate

stylish ADJECTIVE = **smart**, chic, fashionable, trendy (*Brit. informal*), modish, dressy (*informal*), voguish, schmick (*Austral. informal*), funky ≠ scruffy

subdue VERB 1 = **overcome**, defeat, master, break, control, crush, conquer, tame
2 = **moderate**, suppress, soften, mellow, tone down, quieten down ≠ arouse

subdued ADJECTIVE 1 = **quiet**, serious, sad, chastened, dejected, downcast, crestfallen, down in the mouth ≠ lively 2 = **hushed**, soft, quiet, muted ≠ loud

subject NOUN 1 = **topic**, question, issue, matter, point, business, affair, object 2 = **citizen**, resident, native, inhabitant, national
3 = **dependant**, subordinate
▷ ADJECTIVE = **subordinate**, dependent, satellite, inferior, obedient
▷ VERB = **put through**, expose, submit, lay open ▷ PHRASE:
subject to 1 = liable to, open to, exposed to, vulnerable to, prone to, susceptible to 2 = **bound by**
3 = **dependent on**, contingent on, controlled by, conditional on

subjective ADJECTIVE = **personal**, prejudiced, biased, nonobjective ≠ objective

sublime ADJECTIVE = **noble**, glorious, high, great, grand, elevated, lofty, exalted ≠ lowly

submerge VERB 1 = **flood**, swamp, engulf, overflow, inundate, deluge 2 = **immerse**, plunge, duck 3 = **sink**, plunge, go under water 4 = **overwhelm**, swamp, engulf, deluge

submission NOUN 1 = **surrender**, yielding, giving in, cave-in (*informal*), capitulation
2 = **presentation**, handing in, entry, tendering 3 = **compliance**, obedience, meekness, resignation, deference, passivity, docility

submit VERB 1 = **surrender**, yield, give in, agree, endure, tolerate, comply, succumb 2 = **present**, hand in, tender, put forward, table, proffer

subordinate NOUN = **inferior**, junior, assistant, aide, second, attendant ≠ superior
▷ ADJECTIVE = **inferior**, lesser, lower, junior, subject, minor, secondary, dependent ≠ superior

subscribe to VERB 1 = **support**, advocate, endorse 2 = **contribute to**, give to, donate to

subscription NOUN (*chiefly Brit.*) = **membership fee**, dues, annual payment

subsequent ADJECTIVE
= **following**, later, succeeding, after, successive, ensuing ≠ previous

subsequently ADVERB = **later**,

S

afterwards

subside VERB 1 = **decrease**, diminish, lessen, ease, wane, ebb, abate, slacken ≠ increase 2 = **collapse**, sink, cave in, drop, lower, settle

subsidiary NOUN = **branch**, division, section, office, department, wing, subdivision, subsection

▷ ADJECTIVE = **secondary**, lesser, subordinate, minor, supplementary, auxiliary, ancillary ≠ main

subsidy NOUN = **aid**, help, support, grant, assistance, allowance

substance NOUN 1 = **material**, body, stuff, fabric 2 = **importance**, significance, concreteness 3 = **meaning**, main point, gist, import, significance, essence 4 = **wealth**, means, property, assets, resources, estate

substantial ADJECTIVE = **big**, significant, considerable, large, important, ample, sizable or sizeable ≠ small

substitute VERB = **replace**, exchange, swap, change, switch, interchange

▷ NOUN = **replacement**, reserve, surrogate, deputy, sub, proxy, locum

● **WORD POWER**
● Although *substitute* and *replace*
● have the same meaning, the
● structures they are used in are
● different. You replace A *with*
● B, while you substitute B *for*

A. Accordingly, *he replaced the worn tyre with a new one*, and *he substituted a new tyre for the worn one* are both correct ways of saying the same thing.

subtle ADJECTIVE 1 = **faint**, slight, implied, delicate, understated ≠ obvious 2 = **crafty**, cunning, sly, shrewd, ingenious, devious, wily, artful ≠ straightforward 3 = **muted**, soft, subdued, low-key, toned down 4 = **fine**, minute, narrow, tenuous, hair-splitting

subtlety NOUN 1 = **fine point**, refinement, sophistication, delicacy 2 = **skill**, ingenuity, cleverness, deviousness, craftiness, artfulness, slyness, wiliness

subversive
ADJECTIVE = **seditious**, riotous, treasonal
▷ NOUN = **dissident**, terrorist, saboteur, fifth columnist

succeed VERB 1 = **triumph**, win, prevail 2 = **work out**, work, be successful 3 = **make it** (*informal*), do well, be successful, triumph, thrive, flourish, make good, prosper ≠ fail 4 = **take over from**, assume the office of 5 *with* **to** = **take over**, assume, attain, come into, inherit, accede to, come into possession of 6 = **follow**, come after, follow after ≠ precede

success NOUN 1 = **victory**, triumph ≠ failure 2 = **prosperity**, fortune, luck, fame 3 = **hit** (*informal*), winner, smash (*informal*), triumph, sensation ≠ flop (*informal*) **4** = **big name**, star, hit (*informal*), celebrity, sensation, megastar (*informal*) ≠ nobody

successful ADJECTIVE
1 = **triumphant**, victorious, lucky, fortunate **2** = **thriving**, profitable, rewarding, booming, flourishing, fruitful ≠ unprofitable **3** = **top**, prosperous, wealthy

successfully ADVERB = **well**, favourably, with flying colours, victoriously

succession NOUN **1** = **series**, run, sequence, course, order, train, chain, cycle **2** = **taking over**, assumption, inheritance, accession

successive ADJECTIVE = **consecutive**, following, in succession

succumb VERB **1** *often with* **to** = **surrender (to)**, yield (to), submit (to), give in (to), cave in (to) (*informal*), capitulate (to) ≠ beat **2** *with* **to** (*an illness*) = **catch**, fall ill with

suck VERB **1** = **drink**, sip, draw **2** = **take**, draw, pull, extract

sudden ADJECTIVE = **quick**, rapid, unexpected, swift, hurried, abrupt, hasty ≠ gradual

suddenly ADVERB = **abruptly**, all of a sudden, unexpectedly

sue VERB (*law*) = **take (someone) to court**, prosecute, charge, summon, indict

suffer VERB **1** = **be in pain**, hurt, ache **2** = **be affected**, have

trouble with, be afflicted, be troubled with **3** = **undergo**, experience, sustain, bear, go through, endure **4** = **tolerate**, stand, put up with (*informal*), bear, endure

suffering NOUN = **pain**, distress, agony, misery, ordeal, discomfort, torment, hardship

suffice VERB = **be enough**, do, be sufficient, be adequate, serve, meet requirements

sufficient ADJECTIVE = **adequate**, enough, ample, satisfactory ≠ insufficient

suggest VERB **1** = **recommend**, propose, advise, advocate, prescribe **2** = **indicate 3** = **hint at**, imply, intimate **4** = **bring to mind**, evoke

suggestion NOUN
1 = **recommendation**, proposal, proposition, plan, motion
2 = **hint**, insinuation, intimation
3 = **trace**, touch, hint, breath, indication, whisper, intimation

suit NOUN **1** = **outfit**, costume, ensemble, dress, clothing, habit **2** = **lawsuit**, case, trial, proceeding, cause, action, prosecution
▷ VERB **1** = **be acceptable to**, please, satisfy, do, gratify **2** = **agree with**, become, match, go with, harmonize with

suitable ADJECTIVE
1 = **appropriate**, right, fitting, fit, becoming, satisfactory, apt, befitting ≠ inappropriate
2 = **seemly**, fitting, becoming,

S

proper, correct ≠ unseemly
3 = **suited**, appropriate,
in keeping with ≠ out of
keeping **4** = **pertinent**,
relevant, applicable, fitting,
appropriate, to the point, apt
≠ irrelevant **5** = **convenient**,
timely, appropriate, well-timed,
opportune ≠ inopportune
suite NOUN = **rooms**, apartment
sum NOUN **1** = **amount**, quantity,
volume **2** = **calculation**, figures,
arithmetic, mathematics, maths
(*Brit. informal*), tally, math (*U.S.
informal*), arithmetical problem
3 = **total**, aggregate **4** = **totality**,
whole
summarize VERB = **sum
up**, condense, encapsulate,
epitomize, abridge, précis
summary NOUN = **synopsis**,
résumé, précis, review, outline,
rundown, abridgment
summit NOUN **1** = **peak**, top,
tip, pinnacle, apex, head ≠ base
2 = **height**, pinnacle, peak, zenith,
acme ≠ depths
summon VERB **1** = **send for**,
call, bid, invite **2** *often with* **up**
= **gather**, muster, draw on
sumptuous ADJECTIVE
= **luxurious**, grand, superb,
splendid, gorgeous, lavish,
opulent ≠ plain
sunny ADJECTIVE **1** = **bright**, clear,
fine, radiant, sunlit, summery,
unclouded ≠ dull **2** = **cheerful**,
happy, cheery, buoyant, joyful,
light-hearted ≠ gloomy
sunset NOUN = **nightfall**, dusk,

eventide, close of (the) day
superb ADJECTIVE **1** = **splendid**,
excellent, magnificent, fine,
grand, superior, marvellous,
world-class, booshit (*Austral.
slang*), exo (*Austral. slang*), sik
(*Austral. slang*), rad (*informal*), phat
(*slang*), schmick (*Austral. informal*)
≠ inferior **2** = **magnificent**,
superior, marvellous, exquisite,
superlative ≠ terrible
superficial ADJECTIVE
1 = **shallow**, frivolous, empty-
headed, silly, trivial ≠ serious
2 = **hasty**, cursory, perfunctory,
hurried, casual, sketchy, desultory,
slapdash ≠ thorough **3** = **slight**,
surface, external, on the surface,
exterior ≠ profound
superintendent NOUN
= **supervisor**, director, manager,
chief, governor, inspector,
controller, overseer
superior ADJECTIVE **1** = **better**,
higher, greater, grander,
surpassing, unrivalled ≠ inferior
2 = **first-class**, excellent,
first-rate, choice, exclusive,
exceptional, de luxe, booshit
(*Austral. slang*), exo (*Austral.
slang*), sik (*Austral. slang*),
rad (*informal*), phat (*slang*),
schmick (*Austral. informal*)
≠ average **3** = **supercilious**,
patronizing, condescending,
haughty, disdainful, lordly, lofty,
pretentious
▷ NOUN = **boss**, senior, director,
manager, chief (*informal*),
principal, supervisor, baas

(S. African), sherang (Austral. &
N.Z.) ≠ subordinate

superiority NOUN = **supremacy**,
lead, advantage, excellence,
ascendancy, predominance

supernatural ADJECTIVE
= **paranormal**, unearthly,
uncanny, ghostly, psychic, mystic,
miraculous, occult

supervise VERB 1 = **observe**,
guide, monitor, oversee, keep an
eye on 2 = **oversee**, run, manage,
control, direct, handle, look after,
superintend

supervision NOUN
= **superintendence**, direction,
control, charge, care,
management, guidance

supervisor NOUN = **boss**
(informal), manager, chief,
inspector, administrator,
foreman, overseer, baas (S. African)

supplement VERB = **add to**,
reinforce, augment, extend
▷ NOUN 1 = **pull-out**, insert
2 = **appendix**, add-on, postscript
3 = **addition**, extra

supply VERB 1 = **provide**, give,
furnish, produce, stock, grant,
contribute, yield 2 = **furnish**,
provide, equip, endow
▷ NOUN = **store**, fund, stock,
source, reserve, quantity, hoard,
cache

▷ PLURAL NOUN = **provisions**,
necessities, stores, food,
materials, equipment, rations

support VERB 1 = **help**, back,
champion, second, aid, defend,
assist, side with ≠ oppose
2 = **provide for**, maintain, look
after, keep, fund, finance, sustain
≠ live off 3 = **bear out**, confirm,
verify, substantiate, corroborate
≠ refute 4 = **bear**, carry, sustain,
prop (up), reinforce, hold, brace,
buttress
▷ NOUN 1 = **furtherance**,
backing, promotion, assistance,
encouragement 2 = **help**,
loyalty ≠ opposition 3 = **aid**,
help, benefits, relief, assistance
4 = **prop**, post, foundation,
brace, pillar 5 = **supporter**, prop,
mainstay, tower of strength,
second, backer ≠ antagonist
6 = **upkeep**, maintenance, keep,
subsistence, sustenance

supporter NOUN = **follower**,
fan, advocate, friend, champion,
sponsor, patron, helper
≠ opponent

supportive ADJECTIVE = **helpful**,
encouraging, understanding,
sympathetic

suppose VERB 1 = **imagine**,
consider, conjecture, postulate,
hypothesize 2 = **think**, imagine,
expect, assume, guess (informal,
chiefly U.S. & Canad.), presume,
conjecture

supposed ADJECTIVE 1 usually with
to = **meant**, expected, required,
obliged 2 = **presumed**, alleged,

S

professed, accepted, assumed

supposedly ADVERB
= **presumably**, allegedly, ostensibly, theoretically, hypothetically ≠ actually

suppress VERB 1 = **stamp out**, stop, check, crush, conquer, subdue, put an end to, overpower ≠ encourage 2 = **check**, inhibit, subdue, stop, quell 3 = **restrain**, stifle, contain, silence, conceal, curb, repress, smother

suppression NOUN
1 = **elimination**, crushing, check, quashing 2 = **inhibition**, blocking, restraint, smothering

supremacy NOUN = **domination**, sovereignty, sway, mastery, primacy, predominance, supreme power

supreme ADJECTIVE
1 = **paramount** ≠ least 2 = **chief**, leading, principal, highest, head, top, prime, foremost ≠ lowest 3 = **ultimate**, highest, greatest

supremo NOUN (*Brit. informal*)
= **head**, leader, boss (*informal*), director, master, governor, commander, principal, baas (*S. African*)

sure ADJECTIVE 1 = **certain**, positive, decided, convinced, confident, assured, definite ≠ uncertain 2 = **inevitable**, guaranteed, bound, assured, inescapable, nailed-on (*slang*) ≠ unsure 3 = **reliable**, accurate, dependable, undoubted, undeniable, foolproof, infallible, unerring ≠ unreliable

surely ADVERB 1 = **it must be the case that** 2 = **undoubtedly**, certainly, definitely, without doubt, unquestionably, indubitably, doubtlessly

surface NOUN 1 = **covering**, face, exterior, side, top, veneer 2 = **façade**
▷ VERB 1 = **emerge**, come up, come to the surface 2 = **appear**, emerge, arise, come to light, crop up (*informal*), transpire, materialize

surge NOUN 1 = **rush**, flood 2 = **flow**, wave, rush, roller, gush, outpouring 3 = **tide**, swell, billowing 4 = **rush**, wave, storm, torrent, eruption
▷ VERB 1 = **rush**, pour, rise, gush 2 = **roll**, rush, heave 3 = **sweep**, rush, storm

surpass VERB = **outdo**, beat, exceed, eclipse, excel, transcend, outstrip, outshine

surpassing ADJECTIVE = **supreme**, extraordinary, outstanding, exceptional, unrivalled, incomparable, matchless

surplus NOUN = **excess**, surfeit ≠ shortage
▷ ADJECTIVE = **extra**, spare, excess, remaining, odd, superfluous ≠ insufficient

surprise NOUN 1 = **shock**, revelation, jolt, bombshell, eye-opener (*informal*) 2 = **amazement**, astonishment, wonder, incredulity
▷ VERB 1 = **amaze**, astonish, stun, startle, stagger, take aback

s

2 = **catch unawares** *or* **off-guard**, spring upon

surprised ADJECTIVE = **amazed**, astonished, speechless, thunderstruck

surprising ADJECTIVE = **amazing**, remarkable, incredible, astonishing, unusual, extraordinary, unexpected, staggering

surrender VERB 1 = **give in**, yield, submit, give way, succumb, cave in (*informal*), capitulate ≠ resist 2 = **give up**, abandon, relinquish, yield, concede, part with, renounce, waive
▷ NOUN = **submission**, cave-in (*informal*), capitulation, resignation, renunciation, relinquishment

surround VERB = **enclose**, ring, encircle, encompass, envelop, hem in

surrounding ADJECTIVE = **nearby**, neighbouring

surroundings PLURAL NOUN = **environment**, setting, background, location, milieu

surveillance NOUN = **observation**, watch, scrutiny, supervision, inspection

survey NOUN 1 = **poll**, study, research, review, inquiry, investigation 2 = **examination**, inspection, scrutiny 3 = **valuation**, estimate, assessment, appraisal
▷ VERB 1 = **interview**, question, poll, research, investigate 2 = **look over**, view, examine,

observe, contemplate, inspect, eyeball (*slang*), scrutinize 3 = **measure**, estimate, assess, appraise

survive VERB 1 = **remain alive**, last, live on, endure 2 = **continue**, last, live on 3 = **live longer than**, outlive, outlast

susceptible ADJECTIVE 1 = **responsive**, sensitive, receptive, impressionable, suggestible ≠ unresponsive 2 *usually with* **to** = **liable**, inclined, prone, given, subject, vulnerable, disposed ≠ resistant

suspect VERB 1 = **believe**, feel, guess, consider, suppose, speculate ≠ know 2 = **distrust**, doubt, mistrust ≠ trust
▷ ADJECTIVE = **dubious**, doubtful, questionable, iffy (*informal*), shonky (*Austral. & N.Z. informal*) ≠ innocent

suspend VERB 1 = **postpone**, put off, cease, interrupt, shelve, defer, cut short, discontinue ≠ continue 2 = **hang**, attach, dangle

suspension NOUN = **postponement**, break, breaking off, interruption, abeyance, deferment, discontinuation

suspicion NOUN 1 = **distrust**, scepticism, mistrust, doubt, misgiving, qualm, wariness, dubiety 2 = **idea**, notion, hunch, guess, impression 3 = **trace**, touch, hint, suggestion, shade, streak, tinge, soupçon (*French*)

suspicious ADJECTIVE

1 = **distrustful**, sceptical, doubtful, unbelieving, wary ≠ trusting 2 = **suspect**, dubious, questionable, doubtful, dodgy (*Brit., Austral. & N.Z. informal*), fishy (*informal*), shonky (*Austral. & N.Z. informal*) ≠ beyond suspicion

sustain VERB 1 = **maintain**, continue, keep up, prolong, protract 2 = **suffer**, experience, undergo, feel, bear, endure, withstand 3 = **help**, aid, assist 4 = **keep alive**, nourish, provide for 5 = **support**, bear, uphold

sustained ADJECTIVE = **continuous**, constant, steady, prolonged, perpetual, unremitting, nonstop ≠ periodic

swallow VERB 1 = **eat**, consume, devour, swig (*informal*) 2 = **gulp**, drink

swamp NOUN = **bog**, marsh, quagmire, slough, fen, mire, morass, pakihi (*N.Z.*), muskeg (*Canad.*)
▷ VERB 1 = **flood**, engulf, submerge, inundate
2 = **overload**, overwhelm, inundate

swap *or* **swop** VERB = **exchange**, trade, switch, interchange, barter

swarm NOUN = **multitude**, crowd, mass, army, host, flock, herd, horde
▷ VERB 1 = **crowd**, flock, throng, mass, stream 2 = **teem**, crawl, abound, bristle

swath *or* **swathe** NOUN = **area**, section, tract

swathe VERB = **wrap**, drape, envelop, cloak, shroud, bundle up

sway VERB 1 = **move from side to side**, rock, roll, swing, bend, lean 2 = **influence**, affect, guide, persuade, induce
▷ NOUN = **power**, control, influence, authority, clout (*informal*)

swear VERB 1 = **curse**, blaspheme, be foul-mouthed 2 = **vow**, promise, testify, attest 3 = **declare**, assert, affirm

swearing NOUN = **bad language**, cursing, profanity, blasphemy, foul language

sweat NOUN 1 = **perspiration** 2 (*informal*) = **panic**, anxiety, worry, distress, agitation
▷ VERB 1 = **perspire**, glow 2 (*informal*) = **worry**, fret, agonize, torture yourself

sweep VERB 1 = **brush**, clean 2 = **clear**, remove, brush, clean 3 = **sail**, pass, fly, tear, zoom, glide, skim
▷ NOUN 1 = **movement**, move, swing, stroke 2 = **extent**, range, stretch, scope

sweeping ADJECTIVE 1 = **indiscriminate**, blanket, wholesale, exaggerated, overstated, unqualified 2 = **wideranging**, global, comprehensive, wide, broad, extensive, all-inclusive, all-embracing ≠ limited

sweet ADJECTIVE 1 = **sugary**, cloying, saccharine, icky (*informal*) ≠ sour 2 = **fragrant**, aromatic ≠ stinking 3 = **fresh**, clean,

pure **4** = **melodious**, musical, harmonious, mellow, dulcet ≠ harsh **5** = **charming**, kind, agreeable ≠ nasty **6** = **delightful**, appealing, cute, winning, engaging, lovable, likable or likeable ≠ unpleasant
▷ **NOUN 1** (Brit.) usually plural = **confectionery**, candy (U.S.), lolly (Austral. & N.Z.), bonbon **2** (Brit.) = **dessert**, pudding

sweetheart NOUN **1** = **dearest**, beloved, sweet, angel, treasure, honey, dear, sweetie (informal) **2** = **love**, boyfriend or girlfriend, beloved, lover, darling

swell VERB **1** = **increase**, rise, grow, mount, expand, accelerate, escalate, multiply ≠ decrease **2** = **expand**, increase, grow, rise, balloon, enlarge, bulge, dilate ≠ shrink
▷ **NOUN** = **wave**, surge, billow

swelling NOUN = **enlargement**, lump, bump, bulge, inflammation, protuberance, distension

swift ADJECTIVE **1** = **quick**, prompt, rapid **2** = **fast**, quick, rapid, hurried, speedy ≠ slow

swiftly ADVERB **1** = **quickly**, rapidly, speedily **2** = **fast**, promptly, hurriedly

swing VERB **1** = **brandish**, wave, shake, flourish, wield, dangle **2** = **sway**, rock, wave, veer, oscillate **3** usually with **round** = **turn**, swivel, curve, rotate, pivot **4** = **hit out**, strike, swipe, lash out at, slap **5** = **hang**, dangle, suspend

▷ **NOUN 1** = **swaying**, sway **2** = **fluctuation**, change, shift, switch, variation

swirl VERB = **whirl**, churn, spin, twist, eddy

switch NOUN **1** = **control**, button, lever, on/off device **2** = **change**, shift, reversal
▷ **VERB 1** = **change**, shift, divert, deviate **2** = **exchange**, swap, substitute

swollen ADJECTIVE = **enlarged**, bloated, inflamed, puffed up, distended

swoop VERB **1** = **pounce**, attack, charge, rush, descend **2** = **drop**, plunge, dive, sweep, descend, pounce, stoop

symbol NOUN **1** = **metaphor**, image, sign, representation, token **2** = **representation**, sign, figure, mark, image, token, logo, badge

symbolic ADJECTIVE **1** = **representative**, emblematic, allegorical **2** = **representative**, figurative

sympathetic ADJECTIVE **1** = **caring**, kind, understanding, concerned, interested, warm, pitying, supportive ≠ uncaring **2** = **like-minded**, compatible, agreeable, friendly, congenial, companionable ≠ uncongenial

sympathy NOUN **1** = **compassion**, understanding, pity, commiseration, aroha (N.Z.) ≠ indifference **2** = **affinity**, agreement, rapport, fellow feeling ≠ opposition

S

symptom NOUN 1 = **sign**,
mark, indication, warning
2 = **manifestation**, sign,
indication, mark, evidence,
expression, proof, token

synthetic ADJECTIVE = **artificial**,
fake, man-made ≠ real

system NOUN 1 = **arrangement**,
structure, organization, scheme,
classification 2 = **method**,
practice, technique, procedure,
routine

systematic ADJECTIVE
= **methodical**, organized,
efficient, orderly ≠ unmethodical

Tt

table NOUN 1 = **counter**, bench, stand, board, surface, work surface 2 = **list**, chart, tabulation, record, roll, register, diagram, itemization
▷ VERB (*Brit.*) = **submit**, propose, put forward, move, suggest, enter, file, lodge

taboo *or* **tabu**
ADJECTIVE = **forbidden**, banned, prohibited, unacceptable, outlawed, anathema, proscribed, unmentionable ≠ permitted
▷ NOUN = **prohibition**, ban, restriction, anathema, interdict, proscription, tapu (*N.Z.*)

tack NOUN = **nail**, pin, drawing pin
▷ VERB 1 = **fasten**, fix, attach, pin, nail, affix 2 (*Brit.*) = **stitch**, sew, hem, bind, baste ▷ PHRASE: **tack something on to something** = **append**, add, attach, tag

tackle NOUN 1 (*sport*) = **block**, challenge 2 = **rig**, apparatus
▷ VERB 1 = **deal with**, set about, get stuck into (*informal*), come *or* get to grips with 2 = **undertake**, attempt, embark upon, get stuck into (*informal*), have a go *or* stab at (*informal*) 3 (*sport*) = **intercept**, stop, challenge

tactic NOUN = **policy**, approach, move, scheme, plans, method, manoeuvre, ploy

tactical ADJECTIVE = **strategic**, shrewd, smart, diplomatic, cunning ≠ impolitic

tactics PLURAL NOUN = **strategy**, campaigning, manoeuvres, generalship

tag NOUN = **label**, tab, note, ticket, slip, identification, marker, flap
▷ VERB = **label**, mark

tail NOUN 1 = **extremity**, appendage, brush, rear end, hindquarters, hind part 2 (*astronomy*) = **train**, end, trail, tailpiece
▷ VERB (*informal*) = **follow**, track, shadow, trail, stalk ▷ PHRASE: **turn tail** = **run away**, flee, run off, retreat, cut and run, take to your heels

tailor NOUN = **outfitter**, couturier, dressmaker, seamstress, clothier, costumier
▷ VERB = **adapt**, adjust, modify, style, fashion, shape, alter, mould

taint VERB = **spoil**, ruin, contaminate, damage, stain, corrupt, pollute, tarnish ≠ purify

take VERB 1 = **grip**, grab, seize, catch, grasp, clasp, take hold of 2 = **carry**, bring, bear, transport, ferry, haul, convey, fetch ≠ send 3 = **accompany**, lead, bring, guide, conduct, escort, convoy, usher 4 = **remove**, draw, pull, fish, withdraw, extract 5 = **steal**, appropriate, pocket, pinch (*informal*), misappropriate, purloin ≠ return 6 = **capture**, seize, take into custody, lay hold of ≠ release **7** = **tolerate**, stand, bear, stomach, endure, abide, put up with (*informal*), withstand ≠ avoid **8** = **require**, need, involve, demand, call for, entail, necessitate **9** = **understand**, follow, comprehend, get, see, grasp, apprehend **10** = **have room for**, hold, contain, accommodate, accept ▷ PHRASES: **take off 1** = **lift off**, take to the air **2** (*informal*) = **depart**, go, leave, disappear, abscond, decamp, slope off; **take someone for something** (*informal*) = **regard as**, believe to be, consider to be, perceive to be, presume to be; **take someone in** (*informal*) = **deceive**, fool, con (*informal*), trick, cheat, mislead, dupe, swindle, scam (*slang*); **take someone off** (*informal*) = **parody**, imitate, mimic, mock, caricature, send up (*Brit. informal*), lampoon, satirize; **take something in** = **understand**, absorb, grasp, digest, comprehend, assimilate, get the hang of (*informal*); **take something up 1** = **start**, begin, engage in, adopt, become involved in **2** = **occupy**, absorb, consume, use up, cover, fill, waste, squander

takeover NOUN = **merger**, coup, incorporation

tale NOUN = **story**, narrative, anecdote, account, legend, saga, yarn (*informal*), fable

talent NOUN = **ability**, gift, aptitude, capacity, genius, flair, knack

talented ADJECTIVE = **gifted**, able, expert, master, masterly, brilliant, ace (*informal*), consummate

talk VERB **1** = **speak**, chat, chatter, converse, communicate, natter, earbash (*Austral. & N.Z. slang*) **2** = **discuss**, confer, negotiate, parley, confabulate, korero (*N.Z.*) **3** = **inform**, grass (*Brit. slang*), tell all, give the game away, blab, let the cat out of the bag ▷ NOUN = **speech**, lecture, presentation, report, address, discourse, sermon, symposium, whaikorero (*N.Z.*)

talking-to NOUN (*informal*) = **reprimand**, lecture, rebuke, scolding, criticism, reproach, ticking-off (*informal*), dressing-down (*informal*) ≠ praise

tall ADJECTIVE **1** = **lofty**, big, giant, long-legged, lanky, leggy **2** = **high**, towering, soaring, steep, elevated, lofty ≠ short

tally VERB = **agree**, match, accord, fit, square, coincide, correspond, conform ≠ disagree ▷ NOUN = **record**, score, total, count, reckoning, running total

tame ADJECTIVE **1** = **domesticated**, docile, broken, gentle, obedient, amenable, tractable ≠ wild **2** = **submissive**, meek, compliant, subdued, manageable, obedient, docile, unresisting ≠ stubborn **3** = **unexciting**, boring, dull, bland, uninspiring, humdrum, uninteresting, insipid ≠ exciting ▷ VERB **1** = **domesticate**, train, break in, house-train ≠ make fiercer 2 = **subdue**, suppress, master, discipline, humble, conquer, subjugate ≠ arouse

tangible ADJECTIVE = **definite**, real, positive, material, actual, concrete, palpable, perceptible ≠ intangible

tangle NOUN 1 = **knot**, twist, web, jungle, coil, entanglement 2 = **mess**, jam, fix (*informal*), confusion, complication, mix-up, shambles, entanglement
▷ VERB = **twist**, knot, mat, coil, mesh, entangle, interweave, ravel ≠ disentangle ▷ PHRASE: **tangle with someone** = **come into conflict with**, come up against, cross swords with, dispute with, contend with, contest with, lock horns with

tantrum NOUN = **outburst**, temper, hysterics, fit, flare-up, foulie (*Austral. slang*), hissy fit (*informal*), strop (*Brit. informal*)

tap¹ VERB = **knock**, strike, pat, rap, beat, touch, drum
▷ NOUN = **knock**, pat, rap, touch, drumming

tap² NOUN = **valve**, faucet (*U.S. & Canad.*), stopcock
▷ VERB = **listen in on**, monitor, bug (*informal*), spy on, eavesdrop on, wiretap ▷ PHRASE: **on tap** 1 (*informal*) = **available**, ready, standing by, to hand, on hand, at hand, in reserve 2 = **on draught**, cask-conditioned, from barrels, not bottled *or* canned

tape NOUN = **binding**, strip, band, string, ribbon
▷ VERB 1 = **record**, video, tape-record, make a recording of 2 *sometimes with* **up** = **bind**, secure, stick, seal, wrap

target NOUN 1 = **mark**, goal 2 = **goal**, aim, objective, end, mark, object, intention, ambition 3 = **victim**,,butt, prey, scapegoat

tariff NOUN 1 = **tax**, duty, toll, levy, excise 2 = **price list**, schedule

tarnish VERB 1 = **stain**, discolour, darken, blot, blemish ≠ brighten 2 = **damage**, taint, blacken, sully, smirch ≠ enhance
▷ NOUN = **stain**, taint, discoloration, spot, blot, blemish

tart¹ NOUN = **pie**, pastry, pasty, tartlet, patty

tart² ADJECTIVE = **sharp**, acid, sour, bitter, pungent, tangy, piquant, vinegary ≠ sweet

tart³ NOUN (*informal*) = **slut**, prostitute, whore, call girl, trollop, floozy (*slang*), hornbag (*Austral. slang*)

task NOUN = **job**, duty, assignment, exercise, mission, enterprise, undertaking, chore
▷ PHRASE: **take someone to task** = **criticize**, blame, censure, rebuke, reprimand, reproach, scold, tell off (*informal*)

taste NOUN 1 = **flavour**, savour, relish, smack, tang ≠ blandness 2 = **bit**, bite, mouthful, sample, dash, spoonful, morsel, titbit 3 = **liking**, preference, penchant, fondness, partiality, fancy, appetite, inclination ≠ dislike

4 = **refinement**, style, judgment, discrimination, appreciation, elegance, sophistication, discernment ≠ lack of judgment
▷ VERB **1** *often with* **of** = **have a flavour of**, smack of, savour of **2** = **sample**, try, test, sip, savour **3** = **distinguish**, perceive, discern, differentiate **4** = **experience**, know, undergo, partake of, encounter, meet with ≠ miss

tasty ADJECTIVE = **delicious**, luscious, palatable, delectable, savoury, full-flavoured, scrumptious (*informal*), appetizing, lekker (*S. African slang*), yummo (*Austral. slang*) ≠ bland

tattletale NOUN (*chiefly U.S. & Canad.*) = **gossip**, busybody, chatterbox (*informal*), chatterer, bigmouth (*slang*), scandalmonger, gossipmonger

taunt VERB = **jeer**, mock, tease, ridicule, provoke, insult, torment, deride
▷ NOUN = **jeer**, dig, insult, ridicule, teasing, provocation, derision, sarcasm

tavern NOUN = **inn**, bar, pub (*informal, chiefly Brit.*), public house, beer parlour (*Canad.*), beverage room (*Canad.*), hostelry, alehouse (*archaic*)

tax NOUN = **charge**, duty, toll, levy, tariff, excise, tithe
▷ VERB **1** = **charge**, rate, assess **2** = **strain**, stretch, try, test, load, burden, exhaust, weaken

teach VERB **1** = **instruct**, train, coach, inform, educate, drill, tutor, enlighten **2** *often with* **how** = **show**, train

teacher NOUN = **instructor**, coach, tutor, guide, trainer, lecturer, mentor, educator

team NOUN **1** = **side**, squad **2** = **group**, company, set, body, band, gang, line-up, bunch
▷ PHRASE: **team up** = **join**, unite, work together, cooperate, couple, link up, get together, band together

tear VERB **1** = **rip**, split, rend, shred, rupture **2** = **run 3** = **scratch**, cut (open), gash, lacerate, injure, mangle, cut to pieces, cut to ribbons, mangulate (*Austral. slang*) **4** = **pull apart**, claw, lacerate, mutilate, mangle, mangulate (*Austral. slang*) **5** = **rush**, run, charge, race, fly, speed, dash, hurry
▷ NOUN = **hole**, split, rip, rent, snag, rupture

tears PLURAL NOUN = **crying**, weeping, sobbing, wailing, blubbering ▷ PHRASE: **in tears** = **weeping**, crying, sobbing, blubbering

tease VERB **1** = **mock**, provoke, torment, taunt, goad, pull someone's leg (*informal*), make fun of **2** = **tantalize**, lead on, flirt with, titillate

technical ADJECTIVE = **scientific**, technological, skilled, specialist, specialized, hi-tech *or* high-tech

technique NOUN **1** = **method**, way, system, approach, means, style, manner, procedure

2 = **skill**, performance, craft, touch, execution, artistry, craftsmanship, proficiency

tedious ADJECTIVE = **boring**, dull, dreary, monotonous, drab, tiresome, laborious, humdrum ≠ exciting

teenager NOUN = **youth**, minor, adolescent, juvenile, girl, boy

telephone NOUN = **phone**, mobile (phone), handset, dog and bone (*slang*), iPhone (*trademark*), Blackberry (*trademark*), camera phone, picture phone, smartphone, crackberry (*facetious*)
▷ VERB = **call**, phone, ring (*chiefly Brit.*), dial

telescope NOUN = **glass**, scope (*informal*), spyglass
▷ VERB = **shorten**, contract, compress, shrink, condense, abbreviate, abridge ≠ lengthen

television NOUN = **TV**, telly (*Brit. informal*), small screen (*informal*), the box (*Brit. informal*), the tube (*slang*)

tell VERB 1 = **inform**, notify, state to, reveal to, express to, disclose to, proclaim to, divulge, flag up 2 = **describe**, relate, recount, report, portray, depict, chronicle, narrate 3 = **instruct**, order, command, direct, bid 4 = **distinguish**, discriminate, discern, differentiate, identify 5 = **have** *or* **take effect**, register, weigh, count, take its toll, carry weight, make its presence felt ▷ PHRASE: **tell someone off** = **reprimand**, rebuke, scold,

lecture, censure, reproach, berate, chide

telling ADJECTIVE = **effective**, significant, considerable, marked, striking, powerful, impressive, influential ≠ unimportant

temper NOUN 1 = **irritability**, irascibility, passion, resentment, petulance, surliness, hot-headedness ≠ good humour
2 = **frame of mind**, nature, mind, mood, constitution, humour, temperament, disposition
3 = **rage**, fury, bad mood, passion, tantrum, foulie (*Austral. slang*), hissy fit (*informal*), strop (*Brit. informal*) 4 = **self-control**, composure, cool (*slang*), calmness, equanimity ≠ anger
▷ VERB 1 = **moderate**, restrain, tone down, soften, soothe, lessen, mitigate, assuage ≠ intensify
2 = **strengthen**, harden, toughen, anneal ≠ soften

temperament NOUN = **nature**, character, personality, make-up, constitution, bent, humour, temper

temporarily ADVERB = **briefly**, for the time being, momentarily, fleetingly, pro tem

temporary ADJECTIVE
1 = **impermanent**, transitory, brief, fleeting, interim, short-lived, momentary, ephemeral ≠ permanent 2 = **short-term**, acting, interim, supply, stand-in, fill-in, caretaker, provisional

tempt VERB 1 = **attract**, allure
2 = **entice**, lure, lead on, invite, seduce, coax ≠ discourage

t

temptation NOUN
  1 = **enticement**, lure, inducement, pull, seduction, allurement, tantalization 2 = **appeal**, attraction

tempting ADJECTIVE = **inviting**, enticing, seductive, alluring, attractive, mouthwatering, appetizing ≠ uninviting

tenant NOUN = **leaseholder**, resident, renter, occupant, inhabitant, occupier, lodger, boarder

tend¹ VERB = **be inclined**, be liable, have a tendency, be apt, be prone, lean, incline, gravitate

tend² VERB 1 = **take care of**, look after, keep, attend, nurture, watch over ≠ neglect 2 = **maintain**, take care of, nurture, cultivate, manage ≠ neglect

tendency NOUN = **inclination**, leaning, liability, disposition, propensity, susceptibility, proclivity, proneness

tender¹ ADJECTIVE 1 = **gentle**, loving, kind, caring, sympathetic, affectionate, compassionate, considerate ≠ harsh
  2 = **vulnerable**, young, sensitive, raw, youthful, inexperienced, immature, impressionable ≠ experienced 3 = **sensitive**, painful, sore, raw, bruised, inflamed

tender² VERB = **offer**, present, submit, give, propose, volunteer, hand in, put forward
  ▷ NOUN = **offer**, bid, estimate, proposal, submission

tense ADJECTIVE 1 = **strained**, uneasy, stressful, fraught, charged, difficult, worrying, exciting 2 = **nervous**, edgy, strained, anxious, apprehensive, uptight (*informal*), on edge, jumpy, adrenalized ≠ calm 3 = **rigid**, strained, taut, stretched, tight ≠ relaxed
  ▷ VERB = **tighten**, strain, brace, stretch, flex, stiffen ≠ relax

tension NOUN 1 = **strain**, stress, nervousness, pressure, anxiety, unease, apprehension, suspense ≠ calmness 2 = **friction**, hostility, unease, antagonism, antipathy, enmity 3 = **rigidity**, tightness, stiffness, pressure, stress, stretching, tautness

tentative ADJECTIVE
  1 = **unconfirmed**, provisional, indefinite, test, trial, pilot, preliminary, experimental ≠ confirmed 2 = **hesitant**, cautious, uncertain, doubtful, faltering, unsure, timid, undecided ≠ confident

term NOUN 1 = **word**, name, expression, title, label, phrase 2 = **period**, time, spell, while, season, interval, span, duration
  ▷ VERB = **call**, name, label, style, entitle, tag, dub, designate

terminal ADJECTIVE 1 = **fatal**, deadly, lethal, killing, mortal, incurable, inoperable, untreatable 2 = **final**, last, closing, finishing, concluding, ultimate, terminating ≠ initial
  ▷ NOUN = **terminus**, station,

depot, end of the line

terminate VERB 1 = **end**, stop, conclude, finish, complete, discontinue ≠ begin 2 = **cease**, end, close, finish 3 = **abort**, end
▷ PLURAL NOUN 1 = **conditions**, particulars, provisions, provisos, stipulations, qualifications, specifications 2 = **relationship**, standing, footing, relations, status

terrain NOUN = **ground**, country, land, landscape, topography, going

terrestrial ADJECTIVE = **earthly**, worldly, global

terrible ADJECTIVE 1 = **awful**, shocking, terrifying, horrible, dreadful, horrifying, fearful, horrendous 2 (*informal*) = **bad**, awful, dreadful, dire, abysmal, poor, rotten (*informal*) ≠ wonderful 3 = **serious**, desperate, severe, extreme, dangerous, insufferable ≠ mild

terribly ADVERB 1 = **very much**, very, dreadfully, seriously, extremely, desperately, thoroughly, decidedly 2 = **extremely**, very, dreadfully, seriously, desperately, thoroughly, decidedly, awfully (*informal*)

terrific ADJECTIVE 1 (*informal*) = **excellent**, wonderful, brilliant, amazing, outstanding, superb, fantastic (*informal*), magnificent, booshit (*Austral. slang*), exo (*Austral. slang*), sik (*Austral. slang*), ka pai (*N.Z.*), rad (*informal*), phat (*slang*), schmick (*Austral. informal*)

≠ awful 2 = **intense**, great, huge, enormous, tremendous, fearful, gigantic

terrified ADJECTIVE = **frightened**, scared, petrified, alarmed, panic-stricken, horror-struck

terrify VERB = **frighten**, scare, alarm, terrorize

territory NOUN = **district**, area, land, region, country, zone, province, patch

terror NOUN 1 = **fear**, alarm, dread, fright, panic, anxiety 2 = **nightmare**, monster, bogeyman, devil, fiend, bugbear

test VERB 1 = **check**, investigate, assess, research, analyse, experiment with, try out, put something to the test 2 = **examine**, put someone to the test
▷ NOUN 1 = **trial**, research, check, investigation, analysis, assessment, examination, evaluation 2 = **examination**, paper, assessment, evaluation

testament NOUN 1 = **proof**, evidence, testimony, witness, demonstration, tribute 2 (*law*) = **will**, last wishes

testify VERB = **bear witness**, state, swear, certify, assert, affirm, attest, corroborate ≠ disprove

testimony NOUN 1 (*law*) = **evidence**, statement, submission, affidavit, deposition 2 = **proof**, evidence, demonstration, indication, support, manifestation,

t

verification, corroboration
testing ADJECTIVE = **difficult**,
demanding, taxing, challenging,
searching, tough, exacting,
rigorous ≠ undemanding
text NOUN 1 = **contents**, words,
content, wording, body, subject
matter 2 = **words**, wording
3 = **transcript**, script 4 = **text
message**, SMS, MMS, sext
▷ VERB = **text message**, SMS,
MMS, sext
texture NOUN = **feel**, consistency,
structure, surface, tissue, grain
thanks PLURAL NOUN = **gratitude**,
appreciation, credit, recognition,
acknowledgment, gratefulness
▷ PHRASE: **thanks to** = **because
of**, through, due to, as a result of,
owing to
thaw VERB = **melt**, dissolve,
soften, defrost, warm, liquefy,
unfreeze ≠ freeze
theatrical ADJECTIVE
1 = **dramatic**, stage, Thespian
2 = **exaggerated**, dramatic,
melodramatic, histrionic,
affected, mannered, showy,
ostentatious ≠ natural
theft NOUN = **stealing**, robbery,
thieving, fraud, embezzlement,
pilfering, larceny, purloining
theme NOUN 1 = **motif**, leitmotif
2 = **subject**, idea, topic, essence,
subject matter, keynote, gist
theological ADJECTIVE
= **religious**, ecclesiastical,
doctrinal
theoretical or **theoretic**
ADJECTIVE 1 = **abstract**,

speculative ≠ practical
2 = **hypothetical**, academic,
notional, unproven, conjectural
theory NOUN = **belief**, feeling,
speculation, assumption, hunch,
presumption, conjecture, surmise
therapeutic ADJECTIVE
= **beneficial**, healing, restorative,
good, corrective, remedial,
salutary, curative ≠ harmful
therapist NOUN = **psychologist**,
analyst, psychiatrist, shrink
(*informal*), counsellor, healer,
psychotherapist, psychoanalyst
therapy NOUN = **remedy**,
treatment, cure, healing, method
of healing
therefore ADVERB
= **consequently**, so, thus, as a
result, hence, accordingly, thence,
ergo
thesis NOUN 1 = **proposition**,
theory, hypothesis, idea, view,
opinion, proposal, contention
2 = **dissertation**, paper, treatise,
essay, monograph
thick ADJECTIVE 1 = **bulky**, broad,
big, large, fat, solid, substantial,
hefty ≠ thin 2 = **wide**, across,
deep, broad, in extent *or* diameter
3 = **dense**, close, heavy, compact,
impenetrable, lush 4 = **heavy**,
heavyweight, dense, chunky,
bulky, woolly 5 = **opaque**, heavy,
dense, impenetrable 6 = **viscous**,
concentrated, stiff, condensed,
gelatinous, semi-solid, viscid
≠ runny 7 = **crowded**, full,
covered, bursting, bristling,
brimming ≠ empty 8 = **stupid**,

slow, dense, dopey (*informal*), moronic, obtuse, brainless, dumb-ass (*informal*) ≠ clever **9** (*informal*) = **friendly**, close, intimate, familiar, pally (*informal*), devoted, inseparable ≠ unfriendly

thicken VERB = **set**, condense, congeal, clot, jell, coagulate ≠ thin

thief NOUN = **robber**, burglar, stealer, plunderer, shoplifter, embezzler, pickpocket, pilferer

thin ADJECTIVE **1** = **narrow**, fine, attenuated ≠ thick **2** = **slim**, spare, lean, slight, slender, skinny, skeletal, bony ≠ fat **3** = **meagre**, sparse, scanty, poor, scattered, inadequate, insufficient, deficient ≠ plentiful **4** = **fine**, delicate, flimsy, sheer, skimpy, gossamer, diaphanous, filmy ≠ thick **5** = **unconvincing**, inadequate, feeble, poor, weak, superficial, lame, flimsy ≠ convincing **6** = **wispy**, thinning, sparse, scarce, scanty

thing NOUN **1** = **substance**, stuff, being, body, material, fabric, entity **2** (*informal*) = **phobia**, fear, complex, horror, terror, hang-up (*informal*), aversion, neurosis **3** (*informal*) = **obsession**, liking, preoccupation, mania, fetish, fixation, soft spot, predilection **4** *often plural* = **possessions**, stuff, gear, belongings, effects, luggage, clobber (*Brit. slang*), chattels **5** = **equipment**, gear, tool, stuff, tackle, implement, kit, apparatus **6** = **circumstances**, the situation,

the state of affairs, matters, life, affairs

think VERB **1** = **believe**, be of the opinion, be of the view **2** = **judge**, consider, estimate, reckon, deem, regard as **3** = **ponder**, reflect, contemplate, deliberate, meditate, ruminate, cogitate, be lost in thought ▷ PHRASE: **think something up** = **devise**, create, come up with, invent, contrive, visualize, concoct, dream up

thinker NOUN = **philosopher**, intellect (*informal*), wise man, sage, brain (*informal*), theorist, mastermind

thinking NOUN = **reasoning**, idea, view, position, theory, opinion, judgment, conjecture ▷ ADJECTIVE = **thoughtful**, intelligent, reasoning, rational, philosophical, reflective, contemplative, meditative

thirst NOUN **1** = **dryness**, thirstiness, drought **2** = **craving**, appetite, longing, desire, passion, yearning, hankering, keenness ≠ aversion

thorn NOUN = **prickle**, spike, spine, barb

thorough ADJECTIVE **1** = **comprehensive**, full, complete, sweeping, intensive, in-depth, exhaustive ≠ cursory **2** = **careful**, conscientious, painstaking, efficient, meticulous, exhaustive, assiduous ≠ careless **3** = **complete**, total, absolute, utter, perfect, outright,

t

unqualified, out-and-out
≠ partial

thoroughly ADVERB
1 = **carefully**, fully, efficiently, meticulously, painstakingly, scrupulously, assiduously, intensively ≠ carelessly 2 = **fully** 3 = **completely**, quite, totally, perfectly, absolutely, utterly, downright, to the hilt ≠ partly

though CONJUNCTION = **although**, while, even if, even though, notwithstanding
▷ ADVERB = **nevertheless**, still, however, yet, nonetheless, for all that, notwithstanding

thought NOUN 1 = **thinking**, consideration, reflection, deliberation, musing, meditation, rumination, cogitation 2 = **opinion**, view, idea, concept, notion, judgment 3 = **consideration**, study, attention, care, regard, scrutiny, heed 4 = **intention**, plan, idea, design, aim, purpose, object, notion 5 = **hope**, expectation, prospect, aspiration, anticipation

thoughtful ADJECTIVE
1 = **reflective**, pensive, contemplative, meditative, serious, studious, deliberative, ruminative ≠ shallow
2 = **considerate**, kind, caring, kindly, helpful, attentive, unselfish, solicitous ≠ inconsiderate

thrash VERB 1 = **defeat**, beat, crush, slaughter (*informal*), rout, trounce, run rings around

(*informal*), wipe the floor with (*informal*) 2 = **beat**, wallop, whip, belt (*informal*), cane, flog, scourge, spank 3 = **thresh**, flail, jerk, writhe, toss and turn ▷ PHRASE:
thrash something out = **settle**, resolve, discuss, debate, solve, argue out, have out, talk over

thrashing NOUN 1 = **defeat**, beating, hammering (*informal*), hiding (*informal*), rout, trouncing, drubbing 2 = **beating**, hiding (*informal*), belting (*informal*), whipping, flogging

thread NOUN 1 = **strand**, fibre, yarn, filament, line, string, twine 2 = **theme**, train of thought, direction, plot, drift, story line
▷ VERB = **move**, pass, ease, thrust, squeeze through, pick your way

threat NOUN 1 = **danger**, risk, hazard, menace, peril 2 = **threatening remark**, menace 3 = **warning**, foreshadowing, foreboding

threaten VERB 1 = **intimidate**, bully, menace, terrorize, lean on (*slang*), pressurize, browbeat ≠ defend 2 = **endanger**, jeopardize, put at risk, imperil, put in jeopardy, put on the line ≠ protect 3 = **be imminent**, impend

threshold NOUN 1 = **entrance**, doorway, door, doorstep 2 = **start**, beginning, opening, dawn, verge, brink, outset, inception ≠ end 3 = **limit**, margin, starting point, minimum

thrift NOUN = **economy**,

prudence, frugality, saving, parsimony, carefulness, thriftiness ≠ extravagance

thrill NOUN = **pleasure**, kick (*informal*), buzz (*slang*), high, stimulation, tingle, titillation ≠ tedium

▷ VERB = **excite**, stimulate, arouse, move, stir, electrify, titillate, give someone a kick

thrilling ADJECTIVE = **exciting**, gripping, stimulating, stirring, sensational, rousing, riveting, electrifying ≠ boring

thrive VERB = **prosper**, do well, flourish, increase, grow, develop, succeed, get on ≠ decline

thriving ADJECTIVE = **successful**, flourishing, healthy, booming, blooming, prosperous, burgeoning ≠ unsuccessful

throb VERB 1 = **pulsate**, pound, beat, pulse, thump, palpitate 2 = **vibrate**, pulsate, reverberate, shake, judder (*informal*)

▷ NOUN 1 = **pulse**, pounding, beat, thump, thumping, pulsating, palpitation 2 = **vibration**, throbbing, reverberation, judder (*informal*), pulsation

throng NOUN = **crowd**, mob, horde, host, pack, mass, crush, swarm

▷ VERB 1 = **crowd**, flock, congregate, converge, mill around, swarm around ≠ disperse 2 = **pack**, crowd

throttle VERB = **strangle**, choke, garrotte, strangulate

through PREPOSITION 1 = **via**, by way of, by, between, past, from one side to the other of 2 = **because of**, by way of, by means of 3 = **using**, via, by way of, by means of, by virtue of, with the assistance of 4 = **during**, throughout, for the duration of, in

▷ ADJECTIVE = **completed**, done, finished, ended ▷ PHRASE: **through and through** = **completely**, totally, fully, thoroughly, entirely, altogether, wholly, utterly

throughout PREPOSITION 1 = **right through**, everywhere in, during the whole of, through the whole of 2 = **all over**, everywhere in, through the whole of

▷ ADVERB 1 = **from start to finish**, right through 2 = **all through**, right through

throw VERB 1 = **hurl**, toss, fling, send, launch, cast, pitch, chuck (*informal*) 2 = **toss**, fling, chuck (*informal*), cast, hurl, sling 3 (*informal*) = **confuse**, baffle, faze, astonish, confound, disconcert, dumbfound

▷ NOUN = **toss**, pitch, fling, sling, lob (*informal*), heave

thrust VERB = **push**, force, shove, drive, plunge, jam, ram, propel

▷ NOUN 1 = **stab**, pierce, lunge 2 = **push**, shove, poke, prod 3 = **momentum**, impetus, drive

thug NOUN = **ruffian**, hooligan, tough, heavy (*slang*), gangster, bully boy, bruiser (*informal*), tsotsi (*S. African*)

thump NOUN 1 = **blow**, knock,
punch, rap, smack, clout
(*informal*), whack, swipe 2 = **thud**,
crash, bang, clunk, thwack
▷ VERB = **strike**, hit, punch,
pound, beat, knock, smack, clout
(*informal*)

thunder NOUN = **rumble**, crash,
boom, explosion
▷ VERB 1 = **rumble**, crash, boom,
roar, resound, reverberate, peal
2 = **shout**, roar, yell, bark, bellow

thus ADVERB 1 = **in this way**, so,
like this, as follows 2 = **therefore**,
so, hence, consequently,
accordingly, for this reason, ergo,
on that account

thwart VERB = **frustrate**, foil,
prevent, snooker, hinder, obstruct,
outwit, stymie ≠ assist

tick NOUN 1 = **check mark**, mark,
line, stroke, dash 2 = **click**,
tapping, clicking, ticktock 3 (*Brit.
informal*) = **moment**, second,
minute, flash, instant, twinkling,
split second, trice
▷ VERB 1 = **mark**, indicate, check
off 2 = **click**, tap, ticktock

ticket NOUN 1 = **voucher**, pass,
coupon, card, slip, certificate,
token, chit 2 = **label**, tag, marker,
sticker, card, slip, tab, docket

tide NOUN 1 = **current**, flow,
stream, ebb, undertow, tideway
2 = **course**, direction, trend,
movement, tendency, drift

tidy ADJECTIVE 1 = **neat**, orderly,
clean, spruce, well-kept, well-
ordered, shipshape ≠ untidy
2 = **organized**, neat, methodical

3 (*informal*) = **considerable**, large,
substantial, goodly, healthy,
generous, handsome, ample
≠ small
▷ VERB = **neaten**, straighten,
order, clean, groom, spruce up
≠ disorder

tie VERB 1 = **fasten**, bind, join, link,
connect, attach, knot ≠ unfasten
2 = **tether**, secure 3 = **restrict**,
limit, confine, bind, restrain,
hamper, hinder ≠ free 4 = **draw**,
be level, match, equal
▷ NOUN 1 = **fastening**, binding,
link, bond, knot, cord, fetter,
ligature 2 = **bond**, relationship,
connection, commitment, liaison,
allegiance, affiliation 3 = **draw**,
dead heat, deadlock, stalemate

tier NOUN = **row**, bank, layer, line,
level, rank, storey, stratum

tight ADJECTIVE 1 = **close-
fitting**, narrow, cramped,
snug, constricted, close
≠ loose 2 = **secure**, firm, fast,
fixed 3 = **taut**, stretched,
rigid ≠ slack 4 = **close**, even,
well-matched, hard-fought,
evenly-balanced ≠ uneven
5 (*informal*) = **miserly**, mean,
stingy, grasping, parsimonious,
niggardly, tightfisted ≠ generous
6 (*informal*) = **drunk**, intoxicated,
plastered (*slang*), under the
influence (*informal*), tipsy,
paralytic (*informal*), inebriated,
out to it (*Austral. & N.Z. slang*)
≠ sober

tighten VERB = **close**, narrow,
strengthen, squeeze, harden,

constrict ≠ slacken

till¹ VERB = **cultivate**, dig, plough, work

till² NOUN = **cash register**, cash box

tilt VERB = **slant**, tip, slope, list, lean, heel, incline
▷ NOUN 1 = **slope**, angle, inclination, list, pitch, incline, slant, camber 2 (*medieval history*) = **joust**, fight, tournament, lists, combat, duel

timber NOUN 1 = **beams**, boards, planks 2 = **wood**, logs

time NOUN 1 = **period**, term, space, stretch, spell, span, time frame, timeline 2 = **occasion**, point, moment, stage, instance, point in time, juncture 3 = **age**, duration 4 = **tempo**, beat, rhythm, measure
▷ VERB = **schedule**, set, plan, book, programme, set up, fix, arrange

timeless ADJECTIVE = **eternal**, lasting, permanent, enduring, immortal, everlasting, ageless, changeless ≠ temporary

timely ADJECTIVE = **opportune**, appropriate, well-timed, suitable, convenient, judicious, propitious, seasonable ≠ untimely

timetable NOUN 1 = **schedule**, programme, agenda, list, diary, calendar 2 = **syllabus**, course, curriculum, programme, teaching programme

tinge NOUN 1 = **tint**, colour, shade 2 = **trace**, bit, drop, touch, suggestion, dash, sprinkling, smattering
▷ VERB = **tint**, colour

tinker VERB = **meddle**, play, potter, fiddle (*informal*), dabble, mess about

tint NOUN 1 = **shade**, colour, tone, hue 2 = **dye**, wash, rinse, tinge, tincture
▷ VERB = **dye**, colour

tiny ADJECTIVE = **small**, little, minute, slight, miniature, negligible, microscopic, diminutive ≠ huge

tip¹ NOUN 1 = **end**, point, head, extremity, sharp end, nib, prong 2 = **peak**, top, summit, pinnacle, zenith, spire, acme, vertex
▷ VERB = **cap**, top, crown, surmount, finish

tip² NOUN 1 = **gratuity**, gift, reward, present, sweetener (*informal*) 2 = **hint**, suggestion, piece of advice, pointer, heads up (*U.S. & Canad.*)
▷ VERB 1 = **reward**, remunerate, give a tip to, sweeten (*informal*) 2 = **predict**, back, recommend, think of

tip³ VERB 1 = **pour**, drop, empty, dump, drain, discharge, unload, jettison 2 (*Brit.*) = **dump**, empty, unload, pour out
▷ NOUN (*Brit.*) = **dump**, midden, rubbish heap, refuse heap

tire VERB 1 = **exhaust**, drain, fatigue, weary, wear out ≠ refresh 2 = **flag**, become tired, fail

tired ADJECTIVE 1 = **exhausted**, fatigued, weary, flagging, drained, sleepy, worn out,

t

drowsy, tuckered out (*Austral. & N.Z. informal*) ≠ energetic **2** = **bored**, fed up, weary, sick, hoha (*N.Z.*) ≠ enthusiastic about **3** = **hackneyed**, stale, well-worn, old, corny (*slang*), threadbare, trite, clichéd ≠ original

tiring ADJECTIVE = **exhausting**, demanding, wearing, tough, exacting, strenuous, arduous, laborious

title NOUN **1** = **name**, designation, term, handle (*slang*), moniker *or* monicker (*slang*) **2** (*sport*) = **championship**, trophy, bays, crown, honour **3** (*law*) = **ownership**, right, claim, privilege, entitlement, tenure, prerogative, freehold

toast[1] VERB **1** = **brown**, grill, crisp, roast **2** = **warm (up)**, heat (up), thaw, bring back to life

toast[2] NOUN **1** = **tribute**, compliment, salute, health, pledge, salutation **2** = **favourite**, celebrity, darling, talk, pet, focus of attention, hero *or* heroine, blue-eyed boy *or* girl (*Brit. informal*)
▷ VERB = **drink to**, honour, salute, drink (to) the health of

together ADVERB **1** = **collectively**, jointly, as one, with each other, in conjunction, side by side, mutually, in partnership ≠ separately **2** = **at the same time**, simultaneously, concurrently, contemporaneously, at one fell swoop
▷ ADJECTIVE (*informal*) = **self-possessed**, composed, well-balanced, well-adjusted, grounded

toil NOUN = **hard work**, effort, application, sweat, graft (*informal*), slog, exertion, drudgery ≠ idleness
▷ VERB **1** = **labour**, work, struggle, strive, sweat (*informal*), slave, graft (*informal*), slog **2** = **struggle**, trek, slog, trudge, fight your way, footslog

toilet NOUN **1** = **lavatory**, bathroom, loo (*Brit. informal*), privy, cloakroom (*Brit.*), urinal, latrine, washroom, dunny (*Austral. & N.Z. old-fashioned*) (*informal*), bogger (*Austral. slang*), brasco (*Austral. slang*) **2** = **bathroom**, gents *or* ladies (*Brit. informal*), privy, latrine, water closet, ladies' room, W.C.

token NOUN = **symbol**, mark, sign, note, expression, indication, representation, badge
▷ ADJECTIVE = **nominal**, symbolic, minimal, hollow, superficial, perfunctory

tolerance NOUN **1** = **broad-mindedness**, indulgence, forbearance, permissiveness, open-mindedness ≠ intolerance **2** = **endurance**, resistance, stamina, fortitude, resilience, toughness, staying power, hardiness **3** = **resistance**, immunity, resilience, non-susceptibility

tolerant ADJECTIVE = **broad-minded**, understanding, open-minded, catholic, long-suffering, permissive, forbearing, unprejudiced ≠ intolerant

tolerate VERB 1 = **endure**, stand, take, stomach, put up with (*informal*) 2 = **allow**, accept, permit, take, brook, put up with (*informal*), condone ≠ forbid

toll¹ VERB = **ring**, sound, strike, chime, knell, clang, peal
▷ NOUN = **ringing**, chime, knell, clang, peal

toll² NOUN 1 = **charge**, tax, fee, duty, payment, levy, tariff
2 = **damage**, cost, loss, roll, penalty, sum, number, roster
3 = **adverse effects**, price, cost, suffering, damage, penalty, harm

tomb NOUN = **grave**, vault, crypt, mausoleum, sarcophagus, catacomb, sepulchre

tone NOUN 1 = **pitch**, inflection, intonation, timbre, modulation 2 = **volume**, timbre
3 = **character**, style, feel, air, spirit, attitude, manner, mood
4 = **colour**, shade, tint, tinge, hue
▷ VERB = **harmonize**, match, blend, suit, go well with
▷ PHRASE: **tone something down**
1 = **moderate**, temper, soften, restrain, subdue, play down
2 = **reduce**, moderate

tongue NOUN = **language**, speech, dialect, parlance

⬤ **WORD POWER**
⬤ In the human body, the *tongue*
⬤ is the muscular tissue attached
⬤ to the floor of the mouth used
⬤ in chewing and speaking.
⬤ Objects or areas which
⬤ resemble a tongue also employ
⬤ this metaphor, for example *a*
⬤ *tongue of land*. The function of
⬤ the tongue as one of the organs
⬤ creating speech in humans has
⬤ led tongue to mean a language,
⬤ dialect, or idiom. Examples of
⬤ this are *foreign tongue*, *native*
⬤ *tongue*, and *mother tongue*.
⬤ Equally, tongue can refer
⬤ to an individual utterance
⬤ or a manner of speaking, in
⬤ combination with adjectives
⬤ like quick, sharp, sweet, and
⬤ vulgar. A tongue also describes
⬤ a person's ability to speak:
⬤ you can *lose your tongue* or *be*
⬤ *tongue-tied*. The cat can even
⬤ get your tongue!

tonic NOUN = **stimulant**, boost, pick-me-up (*informal*), fillip, shot in the arm (*informal*), restorative

too ADVERB 1 = **also**, as well, further, in addition, moreover, besides, likewise, to boot
2 = **excessively**, very, extremely, overly, unduly, unreasonably, inordinately, immoderately

tool NOUN 1 = **implement**, device, appliance, machine, instrument, gadget, utensil, contraption
2 = **puppet**, creature, pawn, stooge (*slang*), minion, lackey, flunkey, hireling

top NOUN 1 = **peak**, summit, head, crown, height, ridge, brow, crest ≠ bottom 2 = **lid**, cover, cap, plug, stopper, bung 3 = **first place**, head, peak, lead, high point
▷ ADJECTIVE 1 = **highest**,

t

loftiest, furthest up, uppermost
2 = **leading**, best, first, highest,
head, finest, elite, foremost
≠ lowest **3** = **chief**, most
important, principal, most
powerful, highest, head, leading,
main **4** = **prime**, best, select, first-
class, quality, choice, excellent,
premier
▷ **VERB 1** = **lead**, head, be at
the top of, be first in **2** = **cover**,
garnish, finish, crown, cap
3 = **surpass**, better, beat, improve
on, cap, exceed, eclipse, excel
≠ not be as good as

topic NOUN = **subject**, point,
question, issue, matter, theme,
subject matter

topical ADJECTIVE = **current**,
popular, contemporary, up-
to-date, up-to-the-minute,
newsworthy

topple VERB **1** = **fall over**, fall,
collapse, tumble, overturn, totter,
keel over, overbalance **2** = **knock
over 3** = **overthrow**, overturn,
bring down, oust, unseat, bring
low

torment VERB **1** = **torture**,
distress, rack, crucify ≠ comfort
2 = **tease**, annoy, bother, irritate,
harass, hassle (*informal*), pester,
vex
▷ NOUN = **suffering**, distress,
misery, pain, hell, torture, agony,
anguish ≠ bliss

torn ADJECTIVE **1** = **cut**, split, rent,
ripped, ragged, slit, lacerated
2 = **undecided**, uncertain, unsure,
wavering, vacillating, in two
minds (*informal*), irresolute

tornado NOUN = **whirlwind**,
storm, hurricane, gale, cyclone,
typhoon, tempest, squall

torture VERB **1** = **torment**, abuse,
persecute, afflict, scourge, molest,
crucify, mistreat ≠ comfort
2 = **distress**, torment, worry,
trouble, rack, afflict, harrow,
inflict anguish on
▷ NOUN **1** = **ill-treatment**,
abuse, torment, persecution,
maltreatment, harsh treatment
2 = **agony**, suffering, anguish,
distress, torment, heartbreak
≠ bliss

toss VERB **1** = **throw**, pitch, hurl,
fling, launch, cast, flip, sling
2 = **shake 3** = **thrash (about)**,
twitch, wriggle, squirm, writhe
▷ NOUN = **throw**, pitch, lob
(*informal*)

tot NOUN **1** = **infant**, child, baby,
toddler, mite, littlie (*Austral.
informal*), ankle-biter (*Austral.
slang*), tacker (*Austral. slang*)
2 = **measure**, shot (*informal*),
finger, nip, slug, dram, snifter
(*informal*) ▷ PHRASE: **tot
something up** (*chiefly Brit.*) = **add
up**, calculate, total, reckon,
compute, tally, enumerate, count
up

total NOUN = **sum**, entirety, grand
total, whole, aggregate, totality,
full amount, sum total ≠ part
▷ ADJECTIVE = **complete**,
absolute, utter, whole, entire,
undivided, overarching,
thoroughgoing ≠ partial

▷ VERB 1 = **amount to**, make, come to, reach, equal, run to, number, add up to 2 = **add up**, work out, compute, reckon, tot up ≠ subtract

totally ADVERB = **completely**, entirely, absolutely, fully, comprehensively, thoroughly, wholly, utterly ≠ partly

touch VERB 1 = **feel**, handle, finger, stroke, brush, make contact with, caress, fondle 2 = **come into contact**, meet, contact, border, graze, adjoin, be in contact, abut 3 = **tap** 4 = **affect**, influence, inspire, impress 5 = **consume**, take, drink, eat, partake of 6 = **move**, stir, disturb 7 = **match**, rival, equal, compare with, parallel, hold a candle to (*informal*)
▷ NOUN 1 = **contact**, push, stroke, brush, press, tap, poke, nudge 2 = **feeling**, handling, physical contact 3 = **bit**, spot, trace, drop, dash, small amount, jot, smattering 4 = **style**, method, technique, way, manner, trademark ▷ PHRASES: **touch and go** = **risky**, close, near, critical, precarious, nerve-racking; **touch on** *or* **upon something** = **refer to**, cover, raise, deal with, mention, bring in, speak of, hint at

touching ADJECTIVE = **moving**, affecting, sad, stirring, pathetic, poignant, emotive, pitiable

tough ADJECTIVE 1 = **strong** ≠ weak 2 = **hardy**, strong, seasoned, strapping, vigorous, sturdy, stout 3 = **violent**, rough, ruthless, pugnacious, hard-bitten 4 = **strict**, severe, stern, hard, firm, resolute, merciless, unbending ≠ lenient 5 = **hard**, difficult, troublesome, uphill, strenuous, arduous, laborious 6 = **resilient**, hard, resistant, durable, strong, solid, rugged, sturdy ≠ fragile
▷ NOUN = **ruffian**, bully, thug, hooligan, bruiser (*informal*), roughneck (*slang*), tsotsi (*S. African*)

tour NOUN = **journey**, expedition, excursion, trip, outing, jaunt, junket
▷ VERB 1 = **travel round**, travel through, journey round, trek round, go on a trip through 2 = **visit**, explore, go round, inspect, walk round, drive round, sightsee

tourist NOUN = **traveller**, voyager, tripper, globetrotter, holiday-maker, sightseer, excursionist

tournament NOUN = **competition**, meeting, event, series, contest

tow VERB = **drag**, draw, pull, haul, tug, yank, lug

towards PREPOSITION 1 = **in the direction of**, to, for, on the way to, en route for 2 = **regarding**, about, concerning, respecting, in relation to, with regard to, with respect to, apropos

tower NOUN = **column**, pillar, turret, belfry, steeple, obelisk

toxic ADJECTIVE = **poisonous**, deadly, lethal, harmful, pernicious, noxious, septic,

t

pestilential ≠ harmless

toy NOUN = **plaything**, game, doll
▷ PHRASE: **toy with something**
= **play with**, consider, trifle
with, dally with, entertain the
possibility of, amuse yourself
with, think idly of

trace NOUN 1 = **bit**, drop, touch,
shadow, suggestion, hint,
suspicion, tinge 2 = **remnant**,
sign, record, mark, evidence,
indication, vestige 3 = **track**,
trail, footstep, path, footprint,
spoor, footmark
▷ VERB 1 = **search for**, track,
unearth, hunt down 2 = **find**,
track (down), discover, detect,
unearth, hunt down, ferret out,
locate 3 = **outline**, sketch, draw
4 = **copy**, map, draft, outline,
sketch, reproduce, draw over

track NOUN 1 = **path**, way, road,
route, trail, pathway, footpath
2 = **course**, line, path, orbit,
trajectory 3 = **line**, tramline
▷ VERB = **follow**, pursue, chase,
trace, tail (*informal*), shadow, trail,
stalk ▷ PHRASE: **track something
or someone down** = **find**,
discover, trace, unearth, dig up,
hunt down, sniff out, run to earth
or ground

tract¹ NOUN = **area**, region,
district, stretch, territory, extent,
plot, expanse

tract² NOUN = **treatise**, essay,
booklet, pamphlet, dissertation,
monograph, homily

trade NOUN 1 = **commerce**,
business, transactions, dealing,
exchange, traffic, truck, barter
2 = **job**, employment, business,
craft, profession, occupation, line
of work, métier
▷ VERB 1 = **deal**, do business,
traffic, truck, bargain, peddle,
transact, cut a deal 2 = **exchange**,
switch, swap, barter 3 = **operate**,
run, deal, do business

trader NOUN = **dealer**, supplier,
merchant, seller, purveyor

tradition NOUN 1 = **customs**,
institution, ritual, folklore, lore,
tikanga (*N.Z.*) 2 = **established
practice**, custom, convention,
habit, ritual

traditional ADJECTIVE 1 = **old-
fashioned**, old, established,
conventional, usual, accustomed,
customary, time-honoured
≠ revolutionary 2 = **folk**, old

traffic NOUN 1 = **transport**,
vehicles, transportation, freight
2 = **trade**, commerce, business,
exchange, truck, dealings,
peddling
▷ VERB *often with* **in** = **trade**, deal,
exchange, bargain, do business,
peddle, cut a deal, have dealings

tragedy NOUN = **disaster**,
catastrophe, misfortune,
adversity, calamity ≠ fortune

tragic *or* **tragical** ADJECTIVE
1 = **distressing**, sad, appalling,
deadly, unfortunate, disastrous,
dreadful, dire ≠ fortunate
2 = **sad**, miserable, pathetic,
mournful ≠ happy

trail NOUN 1 = **path**, track, route,
way, course, road, pathway,

footpath **2** = **tracks**, path, marks, wake, trace, scent, footprints, spoor **3** = **wake**, stream, tail
▷ VERB **1** = **follow**, track, chase, pursue, dog, hunt, shadow, trace **2** = **drag**, draw, pull, sweep, haul, tow, dangle, droop **3** = **lag**, follow, drift, wander, linger, trudge, plod

train VERB **1** = **instruct**, school, prepare, coach, teach, guide, educate, drill **2** = **exercise**, prepare, work out, practise, do exercise, get into shape **3** = **aim**, point, level, position, direct, focus, sight, zero in
▷ NOUN = **sequence**, series, chain, string, set, cycle, trail, succession

trainer NOUN = **coach**, manager, guide, adviser, tutor, instructor, counsellor, guru

trait NOUN = **characteristic**, feature, quality, attribute, quirk, peculiarity, mannerism, idiosyncrasy

traitor NOUN = **betrayer**, deserter, turncoat, renegade, defector, Judas, quisling, apostate, fizgig (*Austral. slang*) ≠ loyalist

tramp VERB **1** = **trudge**, stump, toil, plod, traipse (*informal*) **2** = **hike**, walk, trek, roam, march, ramble, slog, rove
▷ NOUN **1** = **vagrant**, derelict, drifter, down-and-out, derro (*Austral. slang*) **2** = **tread**, stamp, footstep, footfall **3** = **hike**, march, trek, ramble, slog

trample VERB *often with* **on**, **upon**, *or* **over** = **stamp**, crush, squash, tread, flatten, run over,

walk over

trance NOUN = **daze**, dream, abstraction, rapture, reverie, stupor, unconsciousness

transaction NOUN = **deal**, negotiation, business, enterprise, bargain, undertaking

transcend VERB = **surpass**, exceed, go beyond, rise above, eclipse, excel, outstrip, outdo

transcript NOUN = **copy**, record, manuscript, reproduction, duplicate, transcription

transfer VERB = **move**, transport, shift, relocate, transpose, change, download (*computing*), upload (*computing*)
▷ NOUN = **transference**, move, handover, change, shift, transmission, translation, relocation

transform VERB **1** = **change**, convert, alter, transmute **2** = **make over**, remodel, revolutionize

transformation NOUN **1** = **change**, conversion, alteration, metamorphosis, transmutation **2** = **revolution**, sea change

transit NOUN = **movement**, transfer, transport, passage, crossing, transportation, carriage, conveyance

transition NOUN = **change**, passing, development, shift, conversion, alteration, progression, metamorphosis

transitional ADJECTIVE **1** = **changing**, passing, fluid, intermediate, unsettled,

t

developmental 2 = **temporary**, working, acting, short-term, interim, fill-in, caretaker, provisional

translate VERB = **render**, put, change, convert, interpret, decode, construe, paraphrase

translation NOUN = **interpretation**, version, rendering, rendition, decoding, paraphrase

transmission NOUN 1 = **transfer**, spread, spreading, passing on, circulation, dispatch, relaying, mediation 2 = **broadcasting**, showing, putting out, relaying, sending 3 = **programme**, broadcast, show, production, telecast, podcast

transmit VERB 1 = **broadcast**, televise, relay, air, radio, send out, disseminate, beam out, podcast 2 = **pass on**, carry, spread, send, bear, transfer, hand on, convey

transparent ADJECTIVE 1 = **clear**, sheer, see-through, lucid, translucent, crystalline, limpid, diaphanous ≠ opaque 2 = **obvious**, plain, patent, evident, explicit, manifest, recognizable, unambiguous ≠ uncertain

transplant VERB 1 (*surgery*) = **implant**, transfer, graft 2 = **transfer**, take, bring, carry, remove, transport, shift, convey

transport VERB 1 = **convey**, take, move, bring, send, carry, bear, transfer 2 = **enrapture**, move, delight, entrance, enchant, captivate, ravish 3 = **exile**, banish, deport
▷ NOUN 1 = **vehicle**, transportation, conveyance 2 = **transference**, carrying, delivery, distribution, transportation, shipment, freight, haulage 3 *often plural* = **ecstasy**, delight, heaven, bliss, euphoria, rapture, enchantment, ravishment ≠ despondency

trap NOUN 1 = **snare**, net, gin, pitfall, noose 2 = **ambush**, set-up (*informal*) 3 = **trick**, set-up (*informal*), deception, ploy, ruse, trickery, subterfuge, stratagem
▷ VERB 1 = **catch**, snare, ensnare, entrap, take, corner, bag, lay hold of 2 = **trick**, fool, cheat, lure, seduce, deceive, dupe, beguile 3 = **capture**, catch, arrest, seize, take, secure, collar (*informal*), apprehend

trash NOUN 1 = **nonsense**, rubbish, rot, drivel, twaddle, tripe (*informal*), moonshine, hogwash, kak (*S. African taboo or slang*), bizzo (*Austral. slang*), bull's wool (*Austral. & N.Z. slang*) ≠ sense 2 (*chiefly U.S. & Canad.*) = **litter**, refuse, waste, rubbish, junk (*informal*), garbage, dross

trauma NOUN 1 = **shock**, suffering, pain, torture, ordeal, anguish 2 (*pathology*) = **injury**, damage, hurt, wound, agony

traumatic ADJECTIVE = **shocking**, upsetting, alarming, awful, disturbing, devastating, painful, distressing ≠ calming

t

travel VERB = **go**, journey, move, tour, progress, wander, trek, voyage
▷ NOUN *usually plural* = **journey**, wandering, expedition, globetrotting, tour, trip, voyage, excursion

traveller NOUN = **voyager**, tourist, explorer, globetrotter, holiday-maker, wayfarer

tread VERB = **step**, walk, march, pace, stamp, stride, hike
▷ NOUN = **step**, walk, pace, stride, footstep, gait, footfall

treason NOUN = **disloyalty**, mutiny, treachery, duplicity, sedition, perfidy, lese-majesty, traitorousness ≠ loyalty

treasure NOUN 1 = **riches**, money, gold, fortune, wealth, valuables, jewels, cash 2 = **angel**, darling, jewel, gem, paragon, nonpareil
▷ VERB = **prize**, value, esteem, adore, cherish, revere, hold dear, love

treasury NOUN = **storehouse**, bank, store, vault, hoard, cache, repository

treat VERB 1 = **behave towards**, deal with, handle, act towards, use, consider, serve, manage 2 = **take care of**, minister to, attend to, give medical treatment to, doctor (*informal*), nurse, care for, prescribe medicine for 3 *often with* **to** = **provide**, stand (*informal*), entertain, lay on, regale
▷ NOUN 1 = **entertainment**, party, surprise, gift, celebration, feast, outing, excursion

2 = **pleasure**, delight, joy, thrill, satisfaction, enjoyment, source of pleasure, fun

treatment NOUN 1 = **care**, medical care, nursing, medicine, surgery, therapy, healing, medication 2 = **cure**, remedy, medication, medicine 3 *often with* **of** = **handling**, dealings with, behaviour towards, conduct towards, management, manipulation, action towards

treaty NOUN = **agreement**, pact, contract, alliance, convention, compact, covenant, entente

trek NOUN 1 = **slog**, tramp 2 = **journey**, hike, expedition, safari, march, odyssey
▷ VERB 1 = **journey**, march, hike, tramp, rove, go walkabout (*Austral.*) 2 = **trudge**, traipse (*informal*), footslog, slog

tremble VERB 1 = **shake**, shiver, quake, shudder, quiver, totter 2 = **vibrate**, shake, quake, wobble
▷ NOUN = **shake**, shiver, quake, shudder, wobble, tremor, quiver, vibration

tremendous ADJECTIVE 1 = **huge**, great, enormous, terrific, formidable, immense, gigantic, colossal ≠ tiny 2 (*informal*) = **excellent**, great, wonderful, brilliant, amazing, extraordinary, fantastic (*informal*), marvellous, booshit (*Austral. slang*), exo (*Austral. slang*), sik (*Austral. slang*), rad (*informal*), phat (*slang*), schmick (*Austral. informal*) ≠ terrible

t

trench NOUN = **ditch**, channel, drain, gutter, trough, furrow, excavation

trend NOUN 1 = **tendency**, swing, drift, inclination, current, direction, flow, leaning 2 = **fashion**, craze, fad (*informal*), mode, thing, style, rage, vogue

trendy (*Brit. informal*) ADJECTIVE = **fashionable**, with it (*informal*), stylish, in fashion, in vogue, modish, voguish, schmick (*Austral. informal*), funky

trial NOUN 1 (*law*) = **hearing**, case, court case, inquiry, tribunal, lawsuit, appeal, litigation 2 = **test**, experiment, evaluation, audition, dry run (*informal*), assessment, probation, appraisal 3 = **hardship**, suffering, trouble, distress, ordeal, adversity, affliction, tribulation

tribe NOUN = **race**, people, family, clan, hapu (*N.Z.*), iwi (*N.Z.*)

tribunal NOUN = **hearing**, court, trial

tribute NOUN = **accolade**, testimonial, eulogy, recognition, compliment, commendation, panegyric ≠ criticism

trick NOUN 1 = **joke**, stunt, spoof (*informal*), prank, practical joke, antic, jape, leg-pull (*Brit. informal*) 2 = **deception**, trap, fraud, manoeuvre, ploy, hoax, swindle, ruse, fastie (*Austral. slang*) 3 = **sleight of hand**, stunt, legerdemain 4 = **secret**, skill, knack, hang (*informal*), technique, know-

how (*informal*) 5 = **mannerism**, habit, characteristic, trait, quirk, peculiarity, foible, idiosyncrasy ▷ VERB = **deceive**, trap, take someone in (*informal*), fool, cheat, con (*informal*), kid (*informal*), mislead, scam (*slang*)

trickle VERB = **dribble**, run, drop, stream, drip, ooze, seep, exude ▷ NOUN = **dribble**, drip, seepage, thin stream

tricky ADJECTIVE 1 = **difficult**, sensitive, complicated, delicate, risky, hairy (*informal*), problematic, thorny ≠ simple 2 = **crafty**, scheming, cunning, slippery, sly, devious, wily, artful ≠ open

trifle NOUN = **knick-knack**, toy, plaything, bauble, bagatelle

trifling ADJECTIVE = **insignificant**, trivial, worthless, negligible, unimportant, paltry, measly ≠ significant

trigger VERB = **bring about**, start, cause, produce, generate, prompt, provoke, set off ≠ prevent

trim ADJECTIVE 1 = **neat**, smart, tidy, spruce, dapper, natty (*informal*), well-groomed, shipshape ≠ untidy 2 = **slender**, fit, slim, sleek, streamlined, shapely, svelte, willowy ▷ VERB 1 = **cut**, crop, clip, shave, tidy, prune, pare, even up 2 = **decorate**, dress, array, adorn, ornament, embellish, deck out, beautify ▷ NOUN 1 = **decoration**, edging, border, piping, trimming, frill, embellishment, adornment

2 = **condition**, health, shape (*informal*), fitness, wellness, fettle
3 = **cut**, crop, clipping, shave, pruning, shearing, tidying up

trimming NOUN = **decoration**, edging, border, piping, frill, embellishment, adornment, ornamentation

▷ PLURAL NOUN = **extras**, accessories, ornaments, accompaniments, frills, trappings, paraphernalia

trinity NOUN = **threesome**, trio, triad, triumvirate

trio NOUN = **threesome**, trinity, trilogy, triad, triumvirate

trip NOUN 1 = **journey**, outing, excursion, day out, run, drive, tour, spin (*informal*) 2 = **stumble**, fall, slip, misstep

▷ VERB 1 *often with* **up** = **stumble**, fall, fall over, slip, tumble, topple, stagger, misstep 2 = **skip**, dance, hop, gambol ▷ PHRASE: **trip someone up** = **catch out**, trap, wrongfoot

triple ADJECTIVE 1 = **treble**, three times 2 = **three-way**, threefold, tripartite

▷ VERB = **treble**, increase threefold

triumph NOUN 1 = **success**, victory, accomplishment, achievement, coup, feat, conquest, attainment ≠ failure
2 = **joy**, pride, happiness, rejoicing, elation, jubilation, exultation

▷ VERB 1 *often with* **over** = **succeed**, win, overcome, prevail, prosper, vanquish ≠ fail
2 = **rejoice**, celebrate, glory, revel, gloat, exult, crow

triumphant ADJECTIVE
1 = **victorious**, winning, successful, conquering ≠ defeated 2 = **celebratory**, jubilant, proud, elated, exultant, cock-a-hoop

trivial ADJECTIVE = **unimportant**, small, minor, petty, meaningless, worthless, trifling, insignificant ≠ important

troop NOUN 1 = **group**, company, team, body, unit, band, crowd, squad 2 *plural* = **soldiers**, men, armed forces, servicemen, army, soldiery

▷ VERB = **flock**, march, stream, swarm, throng, traipse (*informal*)

trophy NOUN 1 = **prize**, cup, award, laurels 2 = **souvenir**, spoils, relic, memento, booty, keepsake

tropical ADJECTIVE = **hot**, stifling, steamy, torrid, sultry, sweltering ≠ cold

trot VERB = **run**, jog, scamper, lope, canter

▷ NOUN = **run**, jog, lope, canter

trouble NOUN 1 = **bother**, problems, concern, worry, stress, difficulty (*informal*), anxiety, distress 2 *often plural* = **distress**, problem, worry, pain, anxiety, grief, torment, sorrow ≠ pleasure
3 = **ailment**, disease, failure, complaint, illness, disorder, defect, malfunction 4 = **disorder**, fighting, conflict, bother, unrest,

t

disturbance, to-do (*informal*), furore, biffo (*Austral. slang*), boilover (*Austral.*) ≠ peace
5 = **effort**, work, thought, care, labour, pains, hassle (*informal*), inconvenience ≠ convenience
▷ VERB **1** = **bother**, worry, upset, disturb, distress, plague, pain, sadden ≠ please **2** = **afflict**, hurt, bother, cause discomfort to, pain, grieve **3** = **inconvenience**, disturb, burden, put out, impose upon, incommode ≠ relieve
4 = **take pains**, take the time, make an effort, exert yourself ≠ avoid

troublesome ADJECTIVE
1 = **bothersome**, trying, taxing, demanding, difficult, worrying, annoying, tricky ≠ simple
2 = **disorderly**, violent, turbulent, rebellious, unruly, rowdy, undisciplined, uncooperative ≠ well-behaved

trough NOUN = **manger**, water trough

truce NOUN = **ceasefire**, peace, moratorium, respite, lull, cessation, let-up (*informal*), armistice

true ADJECTIVE **1** = **correct**, right, accurate, precise, factual, truthful, veracious ≠ false
2 = **actual**, real, genuine, proper, authentic, dinkum (*Austral. & N.Z. informal*) **3** = **faithful**, loyal, devoted, dedicated, steady, reliable, staunch, trustworthy ≠ unfaithful **4** = **exact**, perfect, accurate, precise, spot-on (*Brit.*

informal), on target, unerring ≠ inaccurate

truly ADVERB **1** = **genuinely**, correctly, truthfully, rightly, precisely, exactly, legitimately, authentically ≠ falsely **2** = **really**, very, greatly, indeed, extremely **3** = **faithfully**, steadily, sincerely, staunchly, dutifully, loyally, devotedly

trumpet NOUN = **horn**, clarion, bugle
▷ VERB = **proclaim**, advertise, tout (*informal*), announce, broadcast, shout from the rooftops ≠ keep secret

trunk NOUN **1** = **stem**, stalk, bole **2** = **chest**, case, box, crate, coffer, casket **3** = **body**, torso **4** = **snout**, nose, proboscis

trust NOUN = **confidence**, credit, belief, faith, expectation, conviction, assurance, certainty ≠ distrust
▷ VERB **1** = **believe in**, have faith in, depend on, count on, bank on, rely upon ≠ distrust **2** = **entrust**, commit, assign, confide, consign, put into the hands of, allow to look after, hand over **3** = **expect**, hope, suppose, assume, presume, surmise

trustful or **trusting** ADJECTIVE = **unsuspecting**, naive, gullible, unwary, credulous, unsuspicious ≠ suspicious

truth NOUN **1** = **reality**, fact(s), real life **2** = **truthfulness**, fact, accuracy, precision, validity, legitimacy, veracity, genuineness

≠ inaccuracy

try VERB 1 = **attempt**, seek, aim, strive, struggle, endeavour, have a go, make an effort
2 = **experiment with**, try out, put to the test, test, taste, examine, investigate, sample
▷ NOUN = **attempt**, go (*informal*), shot (*informal*), effort, crack (*informal*), stab (*informal*), bash (*informal*), whack (*informal*)

trying ADJECTIVE = **annoying**, hard, taxing, difficult, tough, stressful, exasperating, tiresome ≠ straightforward

tuck VERB = **push**, stick, stuff, slip, ease, insert, pop (*informal*)
▷ NOUN 1 (*Brit. informal*) = **food**, grub (*slang*), kai (*N.Z. informal*), nosh (*slang*) 2 = **fold**, gather, pleat, pinch

tug VERB 1 = **pull**, pluck, jerk, yank, wrench 2 = **drag**, pull, haul, tow, lug, heave, draw
▷ NOUN = **pull**, jerk, yank

tuition NOUN = **training**, schooling, education, teaching, lessons, instruction, tutoring, tutelage

tumble VERB = **fall**, drop, topple, plummet, stumble, flop
▷ NOUN = **fall**, drop, trip, plunge, spill, stumble

tumour NOUN = **growth**, cancer, swelling, lump, carcinoma (*pathology*), sarcoma (*medical*)

tune NOUN 1 = **melody**, air, song, theme, strain(s), jingle, ditty
2 = **harmony**, pitch, euphony
▷ VERB 1 = **tune up**, adjust

2 = **regulate**, adapt, modulate, harmonize, attune, pitch

tunnel NOUN = **passage**, underpass, passageway, subway, channel, hole, shaft
▷ VERB = **dig**, burrow, mine, bore, drill, excavate

turbulent ADJECTIVE = **stormy**, rough, raging, tempestuous, furious, foaming, agitated, tumultuous ≠ calm

turf NOUN 1 = **grass**, sward 2 = **sod**
▷ PHRASE: **the turf** = **horse-racing**, the flat, racing

turmoil NOUN = **confusion**, disorder, chaos, upheaval, disarray, uproar, agitation, commotion ≠ peace

turn VERB 1 *sometimes with* **round** = **change course**, swing round, wheel round, veer, move, switch, shift, swerve 2 = **rotate**, spin, go round (and round), revolve, roll, circle, twist, spiral 3 *with* **into** = **change**, transform, shape, convert, alter, mould, remodel, mutate 4 = **shape**, form, fashion, cast, frame, mould, make 5 = **go bad**, go off (*Brit. informal*), curdle 6 = **make rancid**, spoil, sour, taint
▷ NOUN 1 = **rotation**, cycle, circle, revolution, spin, twist, whirl, swivel 2 = **change of direction**, shift, departure, deviation
3 = **direction**, course, tack, tendency, drift 4 = **opportunity**, go, time, try, chance, crack (*informal*), stint 5 = **deed**, service, act, action, favour, gesture
▷ PHRASES: **turn on someone**

= **attack**, assault, fall on, round on, lash out at, assail, lay into (*informal*), let fly at; **turn someone on** (*slang*) = **arouse**, attract, excite, thrill, stimulate, please, titillate; **turn something down** 1 = **refuse**, decline, reject, spurn, rebuff, repudiate 2 = **lower**, soften, mute, lessen, muffle, quieten; **turn something in** = **hand in**, return, deliver, give up, hand over, submit, surrender, tender; **turn something off** = **switch off**, turn out, put out, stop, cut out, shut down, unplug, flick off; **turn something on** = **switch on**, activate, start, start up, ignite, kick-start; **turn something up** 1 = **find**, reveal, discover, expose, disclose, unearth, dig up 2 = **increase**, raise, boost, enhance, intensify, amplify; **turn up** 1 = **arrive**, come, appear, show up (*informal*), attend, put in an appearance, show your face 2 = **come to light**, show up, pop up, materialize

turning NOUN 1 = **turn-off**, turn, junction, crossroads, side road, exit 2 = **bend**, turn, curve

turning point NOUN = **crossroads**, change, crisis, crux, moment of truth, tipping point

turnout NOUN = **attendance**, crowd, audience, gate, assembly, congregation, number, throng

turnover NOUN 1 = **output**, business, productivity 2 = **movement**, coming and going, change

turtle NOUN
▷ *see* **reptiles**

tutor NOUN = **teacher**, coach, instructor, educator, guide, guardian, lecturer, guru
▷ VERB = **teach**, educate, school, train, coach, guide, drill, instruct

twig NOUN = **branch**, stick, sprig, shoot, spray

twilight NOUN 1 = **dusk**, evening, sunset, early evening, nightfall, sundown, gloaming (*Scot. poetic*), close of day, evo (*Austral. slang*) ≠ dawn 2 = **half-light**, gloom, dimness, semi-darkness

twin NOUN = **double**, counterpart, mate, match, fellow, clone, duplicate, lookalike
▷ VERB = **pair**, match, join, couple, link, yoke

twinkle VERB = **sparkle**, flash, shine, glitter, gleam, blink, flicker, shimmer
▷ NOUN = **sparkle**, flash, spark, gleam, flicker, shimmer, glimmer

twist VERB 1 = **coil**, curl, wind, wrap, screw, twirl 2 = **intertwine** 3 = **distort**, screw up, contort, mangle, mangulate (*Austral. slang*) ≠ straighten
▷ NOUN 1 = **surprise**, change, turn, development, revelation 2 = **development**, emphasis, variation, slant 3 = **wind**, turn, spin, swivel, twirl 4 = **curve**, turn, bend, loop, arc, kink, zigzag, dog-leg

twitch VERB 1 = **jerk**, flutter, jump, squirm 2 = **pull (at)**, tug (at), pluck (at), yank (at)

▷ **NOUN** = **jerk**, tic, spasm, jump, flutter

tycoon NOUN = **magnate**, capitalist, baron, industrialist, financier, fat cat (*slang, chiefly U.S.*), mogul, plutocrat

type NOUN = **kind**, sort, class, variety, group, order, style, species

typical ADJECTIVE 1 = **archetypal**, standard, model, normal, stock, representative, usual, regular ≠ unusual 2 = **characteristic** 3 = **average**, normal, usual, routine, regular, orthodox, predictable, run-of-the-mill

tyranny NOUN = **oppression**, cruelty, dictatorship, authoritarianism, despotism, autocracy, absolutism, high-handedness ≠ liberality

t

Uu

ubiquitous ADJECTIVE = **ever-present**, pervasive, omnipresent, everywhere, universal

ugly ADJECTIVE 1 = **unattractive**, homely (*chiefly U.S.*), plain, unsightly, unlovely, unprepossessing, ill-favoured ≠ beautiful 2 = **unpleasant**, shocking, terrible, nasty, distasteful, horrid, objectionable, disagreeable ≠ pleasant 3 = **bad-tempered**, dangerous, menacing, sinister, baleful

ulcer NOUN = **sore**, abscess, peptic ulcer, gumboil

ultimate ADJECTIVE 1 = **final**, last, end 2 = **supreme**, highest, greatest, paramount, superlative 3 = **worst**, greatest, utmost, extreme 4 = **best**, greatest, supreme, optimum, quintessential

ultimately ADVERB 1 = **finally**, eventually, in the end, after all, at last, sooner or later, in due time 2 = **fundamentally**, essentially, basically, primarily, at heart, deep down

umpire NOUN = **referee**, judge, arbiter, arbitrator, umpie (*Austral. slang*)
 ▷ VERB = **referee**, judge, adjudicate, arbitrate

unable ADJECTIVE *with* **to** = **incapable**, powerless, unfit, impotent, unqualified, ineffectual ≠ able

unanimous ADJECTIVE 1 = **agreed**, united, in agreement, harmonious, like-minded, of the same mind ≠ divided 2 = **united**, common, concerted, solid, consistent, harmonious, undivided, congruent ≠ split

unarmed ADJECTIVE = **defenceless**, helpless, unprotected ≠ armed

unaware ADJECTIVE = **ignorant**, unconscious, oblivious, uninformed, unknowing, not in the loop (*informal*) ≠ aware

unbearable ADJECTIVE = **intolerable**, insufferable, too much (*informal*), unacceptable ≠ tolerable

unborn ADJECTIVE = **expected**, awaited, embryonic

uncertain ADJECTIVE = **unsure**, undecided, vague, unclear, dubious, hazy, irresolute ≠ sure

uncertainty NOUN 1 = **unpredictability**, precariousness, ambiguity, unreliability, fickleness, chanciness, changeableness ≠ predictability 2 = **doubt**, confusion ≠ confidence 3 = **hesitancy**, indecision

uncomfortable ADJECTIVE 1 = **uneasy**, troubled, disturbed, embarrassed, awkward, discomfited ≠ comfortable 2 = **painful**, awkward, rough

uncommon ADJECTIVE 1 = **rare**, unusual, odd, novel, strange, peculiar, scarce, queer ≠ common 2 = **extraordinary**, remarkable, special, outstanding, distinctive, exceptional, notable ≠ ordinary

uncompromising ADJECTIVE = **inflexible**, strict, rigid, firm, tough, inexorable, intransigent, unbending

unconditional ADJECTIVE = **absolute**, full, complete, total, positive, entire, outright, unlimited ≠ qualified

unconscious ADJECTIVE 1 = **senseless**, knocked out, out cold (*informal*), out, stunned, dazed, in a coma, stupefied ≠ awake 2 = **unaware**, ignorant, oblivious, unknowing ≠ aware 3 = **unintentional**, unwitting, inadvertent, accidental ≠ intentional

uncover VERB 1 = **reveal**, expose, disclose, divulge, make known ≠ conceal 2 = **open**, unveil, unwrap, show, strip, expose, bare, lay bare

under PREPOSITION 1 = **below**, beneath, underneath ≠ over 2 = **subordinate to**, subject to, governed by, secondary to ▷ ADVERB = **below**, down, beneath ≠ up

undercover ADJECTIVE = **secret**, covert, private, hidden, concealed ≠ open

underdog NOUN = **weaker party**, little fellow (*informal*), outsider

underestimate VERB

1 = **undervalue**, understate, diminish, play down, minimize, downgrade, miscalculate, trivialize ≠ overestimate 2 = **underrate**, undervalue, belittle ≠ overrate

● WORD POWER
● *Underestimate* is sometimes
● wrongly used where
● *overestimate* is meant: *the*
● *importance of his work cannot*
● *be overestimated* (not *cannot be*
● *underestimated*).

undergo VERB = **experience**, go through, stand, suffer, bear, sustain, endure

underground ADJECTIVE 1 = **subterranean**, basement, lower-level, sunken, covered, buried, subterrestrial 2 = **secret**, covert, hidden, guerrilla, revolutionary, confidential, dissident, closet ▷ PHRASE: **the underground 1** = **the tube** (*Brit.*), the subway, the metro 2 = **the Resistance**, partisans, freedom fighters

underline VERB 1 = **emphasize**, stress, highlight, accentuate ≠ minimize 2 = **underscore**, mark

underlying ADJECTIVE = **fundamental**, basic, prime, primary, elementary, intrinsic

undermine VERB = **weaken**, sabotage, subvert, compromise, disable ≠ reinforce

understand VERB 1 = **comprehend**, get, take in, perceive, grasp, see, follow, realize

u

2 = **believe**, gather, think, see, suppose, notice, assume, fancy

understandable ADJECTIVE
= **reasonable**, natural, justified, expected, inevitable, legitimate, predictable, accountable

understanding NOUN
1 = **perception**, knowledge, grasp, sense, know-how (*informal*), judgment, awareness, appreciation ≠ ignorance
2 = **agreement**, deal, promise, arrangement, accord, contract, bond, pledge ≠ disagreement
3 = **belief**, view, opinion, impression, interpretation, feeling, idea, notion
▷ ADJECTIVE = **sympathetic**, kind, compassionate, considerate, patient, sensitive, tolerant ≠ unsympathetic

undertake VERB = **agree**, promise, contract, guarantee, engage, pledge

undertaking NOUN 1 = **task**, business, operation, project, attempt, effort, affair, venture
2 = **promise**, commitment, pledge, word, vow, assurance

underwear NOUN
= **underclothes**, lingerie, undies (*informal*), undergarments, underthings, broekies (*S. African informal*), underdaks (*Austral. slang*)

underworld NOUN 1 = **criminals**, gangsters, organized crime, gangland (*informal*) 2 = **nether world**, Hades, nether regions

underwrite VERB = **finance**,
back, fund, guarantee, sponsor, insure, ratify, subsidize

undesirable ADJECTIVE
= **unwanted**, unwelcome, disagreeable, objectionable, unacceptable, unsuitable, unattractive, distasteful
≠ desirable

undo VERB 1 = **open**, unfasten, loose, untie, unbutton, disentangle 2 = **reverse**, cancel, offset, neutralize, invalidate, annul 3 = **ruin**, defeat, destroy, wreck, shatter, upset, undermine, overturn

undone ADJECTIVE = **unfinished**, left, neglected, omitted, unfulfilled, unperformed
≠ finished

undoubtedly ADVERB
= **certainly**, definitely, surely, doubtless, without doubt, assuredly

unearth VERB 1 = **discover**, find, reveal, expose, uncover 2 = **dig up**, excavate, exhume, dredge up

unearthly ADJECTIVE = **eerie**, strange, supernatural, ghostly, weird, phantom, uncanny, spooky (*informal*)

uneasy ADJECTIVE 1 = **anxious**, worried, troubled, nervous, disturbed, uncomfortable, edgy, perturbed ≠ relaxed
2 = **precarious**, strained, uncomfortable, tense, awkward, shaky, insecure

unemployed ADJECTIVE = **out of work**, redundant, laid off, jobless, idle ≠ working

u

unfair ADJECTIVE 1 = **biased**, prejudiced, unjust, one-sided, partial, partisan, bigoted 2 = **unscrupulous**, dishonest, unethical, wrongful, unsporting ≠ ethical

unfit ADJECTIVE 1 = **out of shape**, feeble, unhealthy, flabby, in poor condition ≠ healthy 2 = **incapable**, inadequate, incompetent, no good, useless, unqualified ≠ capable 3 = **unsuitable**, inadequate, useless, unsuited ≠ suitable

unfold VERB 1 = **reveal**, tell, present, show, disclose, uncover, divulge, make known 2 = **open**, spread out, undo, expand, unfurl, unwrap, unroll

unfortunate ADJECTIVE 1 = **disastrous**, calamitous, adverse, ill-fated ≠ opportune 2 = **regrettable**, deplorable, lamentable, unsuitable, unbecoming ≠ becoming 3 = **unlucky**, unhappy, doomed, cursed, unsuccessful, hapless, wretched ≠ fortunate

unhappy ADJECTIVE 1 = **sad**, depressed, miserable, blue, melancholy, mournful, dejected, despondent ≠ happy 2 = **unlucky**, unfortunate, hapless, cursed, wretched, ill-fated ≠ fortunate

unhealthy ADJECTIVE 1 = **harmful**, detrimental, unwholesome, insanitary, insalubrious ≠ beneficial 2 = **sick**, sickly, unwell, delicate, crook (*Austral. & N.Z. informal*), ailing, frail, feeble, invalid ≠ well 3 = **weak**, ailing ≠ strong

unification NOUN = **union**, uniting, alliance, coalition, federation, confederation, amalgamation, coalescence

uniform NOUN 1 = **regalia**, suit, livery, colours, habit 2 = **outfit**, dress, costume, attire, gear (*informal*), get-up (*informal*), ensemble, garb ▷ ADJECTIVE 1 = **consistent**, unvarying, similar, even, same, matching, regular, constant ≠ varying 2 = **alike**, similar, like, same, equal

unify VERB = **unite**, join, combine, merge, consolidate, confederate, amalgamate ≠ divide

union NOUN 1 = **joining**, uniting, unification, combination, coalition, merger, mixture, blend 2 = **alliance**, league, association, coalition, federation, confederacy

unique ADJECTIVE 1 = **distinct**, special, exclusive, peculiar, only, single, lone, solitary 2 = **unparalleled**, unmatched, unequalled, matchless, without equal

⬤ WORD POWER
⬤ *Unique* with the meaning 'being
⬤ the only one' or 'having no
⬤ equal' describes an absolute
⬤ state: *a case unique in British law*.
⬤ In this use it cannot therefore
⬤ be qualified; something is
⬤ either *unique* or *not unique*.
⬤ However, *unique* is also very

u

● commonly used in the sense
● of 'remarkable' or 'exceptional',
● particularly in the language
● of advertising, and in this
● meaning it can be used with
● qualifying words such as *rather*,
● *quite*, etc. Since many people
● object to this use, it is best
● avoided in formal and serious
● writing.

unit NOUN 1 = **entity**, whole, item, feature 2 = **section**, company, group, force, detail, division, cell, squad 3 = **measure**, quantity, measurement 4 = **part**, section, segment, class, element, component, constituent, tutorial

unite VERB 1 = **join**, link, combine, couple, blend, merge, unify, fuse ≠ separate 2 = **cooperate**, ally, join forces, band, pool, collaborate ≠ split

unity NOUN 1 = **union**, unification, coalition, federation, integration, confederation, amalgamation 2 = **wholeness**, integrity, oneness, union, entity, singleness ≠ disunity 3 = **agreement**, accord, consensus, harmony, solidarity, unison, assent, concord ≠ disagreement

universal ADJECTIVE
1 = **widespread**, general, common, whole, total, unlimited, overarching 2 = **global**, worldwide, international, pandemic

universally ADVERB = **without exception**, everywhere, always, invariably

universe NOUN = **cosmos**, space, creation, nature, heavens, macrocosm, all existence

unknown ADJECTIVE 1 = **strange**, new, undiscovered, uncharted, unexplored, virgin, remote, alien 2 = **unidentified**, mysterious, anonymous, unnamed, nameless, incognito 3 = **obscure**, humble, unfamiliar ≠ famous

unlike PREPOSITION 1 = **different from**, dissimilar to, distinct from, unequal to ≠ similar to 2 = **contrasted with**, not like, in contradiction to, in contrast with *or* to, as opposed to, differently from, opposite to

unlikely ADJECTIVE
1 = **improbable**, doubtful, remote, slight, faint ≠ probable 2 = **unbelievable**, incredible, implausible, questionable ≠ believable

unload VERB 1 = **empty**, clear, unpack, dump, discharge 2 = **unburden**

unnatural ADJECTIVE
1 = **abnormal**, odd, strange, unusual, extraordinary, perverted, queer, irregular ≠ normal 2 = **false**, forced, artificial, affected, stiff, feigned, stilted, insincere ≠ genuine

unpleasant ADJECTIVE 1 = **nasty**, bad, horrid, distasteful, displeasing, objectionable, disagreeable ≠ nice 2 = **obnoxious**, rude ≠ likable *or* likeable

unravel VERB 1 = **solve**, explain,

work out, resolve, figure out (*informal*) **2 = undo**, separate, disentangle, free, unwind, untangle

unrest NOUN **= discontent**, rebellion, protest, strife, agitation, discord, sedition, dissension ≠ peace

unsettled ADJECTIVE
1 = unstable, shaky, insecure, disorderly, unsteady **2 = restless**, tense, shaken, confused, disturbed, anxious, agitated, flustered, adrenalized
3 = inconstant, changing, variable, uncertain

unstable ADJECTIVE
1 = changeable, volatile, unpredictable, variable, fluctuating, fitful, inconstant ≠ constant **2 = insecure**, shaky, precarious, unsettled, wobbly, tottering, unsteady
3 = unpredictable, irrational, erratic, inconsistent, temperamental, capricious, changeable ≠ level-headed

unthinkable ADJECTIVE
1 = impossible, out of the question, inconceivable, absurd, unreasonable **2 = inconceivable**, incredible, unimaginable

untold ADJECTIVE
1 = indescribable, unthinkable, unimaginable, undreamed of, unutterable, inexpressible
2 = countless, incalculable, innumerable, myriad, numberless, uncountable

untrue ADJECTIVE **1 = false**, lying,

wrong, mistaken, incorrect, inaccurate, dishonest, deceptive ≠ true **2 = unfaithful**, disloyal, deceitful, treacherous, faithless, false, untrustworthy, inconstant ≠ faithful

unusual ADJECTIVE **1 = rare**, odd, strange, extraordinary, different, curious, queer, uncommon ≠ common **2 = extraordinary**, unique, remarkable, exceptional, uncommon, singular, unconventional ≠ average

upbeat ADJECTIVE (*informal*) **= cheerful**, positive, optimistic, encouraging, hopeful, cheery

upbringing NOUN **= education**, training, breeding, rearing, raising

update VERB **= bring up to date**, improve, correct, renew, revise, upgrade, amend, overhaul

upgrade VERB **1 = improve**, better, update, reform, add to, enhance, refurbish, renovate **2 = promote**, raise, advance, boost, move up, elevate, kick upstairs (*informal*), give promotion to ≠ demote

upheaval NOUN **= disturbance**, revolution, disorder, turmoil, disruption

uphill ADJECTIVE **1 = ascending**, rising, upward, mounting, climbing ≠ descending **2 = arduous**, hard, taxing, difficult, tough, exhausting, gruelling, strenuous

uphold VERB **1 = support**, back, defend, aid, champion, maintain,

u

promote, sustain **2** = **confirm**, endorse

uplift VERB = **improve**, better, raise, advance, inspire, refine, edify

▷ NOUN = **improvement**, enlightenment, advancement, refinement, enhancement, enrichment, edification

upper ADJECTIVE **1** = **topmost**, top ≠ bottom **2** = **higher**, high ≠ lower **3** = **superior**, senior, higher-level, greater, top, important, chief, most important ≠ inferior

upper class ADJECTIVE = **aristocratic**, upper-class, noble, high-class, patrician, blue-blooded, highborn

upright ADJECTIVE **1** = **vertical**, straight, standing up, erect, perpendicular, bolt upright ≠ horizontal **2** = **honest**, good, principled, just, ethical, honourable, righteous, conscientious ≠ dishonourable

uprising NOUN = **rebellion**, rising, revolution, revolt, disturbance, mutiny, insurrection, insurgence

uproar NOUN **1** = **commotion**, noise, racket, riot, turmoil, mayhem, din, pandemonium **2** = **protest**, outrage, complaint, objection, fuss, stink (*informal*), outcry, furore

upset ADJECTIVE **1** = **distressed**, shaken, disturbed, worried, troubled, hurt, bothered, unhappy **2** = **sick**, queasy, bad, ill

▷ VERB **1** = **distress**, trouble,

disturb, worry, alarm, bother, grieve, agitate **2** = **tip over**, overturn, capsize, knock over, spill **3** = **mess up**, spoil, disturb, change, confuse, disorder, unsettle, disorganize

▷ NOUN **1** = **distress**, worry, trouble, shock, bother, disturbance, agitation **2** = **reversal**, shake-up (*informal*), defeat **3** = **illness**, complaint, disorder, bug (*informal*), sickness, malady

upside down or **upside-down** ADVERB = **wrong side up**

▷ ADJECTIVE **1** = **inverted**, overturned, upturned **2** (*informal*) = **confused**, disordered, chaotic, muddled, topsy-turvy, higgledy-piggledy (*informal*)

up-to-date ADJECTIVE = **modern**, fashionable, trendy (*Brit. informal*), current, stylish, in vogue, up-to-the-minute ≠ out of date

urban ADJECTIVE = **civic**, city, town, metropolitan, municipal, dorp (*S. African*)

urge VERB **1** = **beg**, exhort, plead, implore, beseech, entreat **2** = **advocate**, recommend, advise, support, counsel ≠ discourage

▷ NOUN = **impulse**, longing, wish, desire, drive, yearning, itch (*informal*), thirst ≠ reluctance

urgency NOUN = **importance**, need, necessity, gravity, pressure, hurry, seriousness, extremity

urgent ADJECTIVE = **crucial**, desperate, pressing, great,

u

important, crying, critical, immediate ≠ unimportant

usage NOUN 1 = **use**, operation, employment, running, control, management, handling
2 = **practice**, method, procedure, habit, regime, custom, routine, convention

use VERB 1 = **employ**, utilize, work, apply, operate, exercise, practise, resort to 2 *sometimes with* **up** = **consume**, exhaust, spend, run through, expend
3 = **take advantage of**, exploit, manipulate
▷ NOUN 1 = **usage**, employment, operation, application
2 = **purpose**, end, reason, object
3 = **good**, point, help, service, value, benefit, profit, advantage

used ADJECTIVE = **second-hand**, cast-off, nearly new, shopsoiled, preloved (*Austral. slang*) ≠ new

used to ADJECTIVE = **accustomed to**, familiar with

useful ADJECTIVE = **helpful**, effective, valuable, practical, profitable, worthwhile, beneficial, fruitful ≠ useless

useless ADJECTIVE 1 = **worthless**, valueless, impractical, fruitless, unproductive, ineffectual, unsuitable ≠ useful
2 = **pointless**, futile, vain ≠ worthwhile 3 (*informal*) = **inept**, no good, hopeless, incompetent, ineffectual

usher VERB = **escort**, lead, direct, guide, conduct
▷ NOUN = **attendant**, guide, doorman, escort, doorkeeper

usual ADJECTIVE = **normal**, customary, regular, general, common, standard, ordinary, typical ≠ unusual

usually ADVERB = **normally**, generally, mainly, commonly, mostly, on the whole, as a rule, habitually

utility NOUN = **usefulness**, benefit, convenience, practicality, efficacy, serviceableness

utilize VERB = **use**, employ, deploy, take advantage of, make use of, put to use, bring into play, avail yourself of

utmost ADJECTIVE 1 = **greatest**, highest, maximum, supreme, paramount, pre-eminent
2 = **farthest**, extreme, last, final
▷ NOUN = **best**, greatest, maximum, highest, hardest

utter¹ VERB = **say**, state, speak, voice, express, deliver, declare, mouth

utter² ADJECTIVE = **absolute**, complete, total, sheer, outright, thorough, downright, unmitigated

utterly ADVERB = **totally**, completely, absolutely, perfectly, fully, entirely, extremely, thoroughly

u

Vv

vacancy NOUN 1 = **opening**, job, post, place, position, role, situation, opportunity 2 = **room**, space, available accommodation, unoccupied room

vacant ADJECTIVE 1 = **empty**, free, available, abandoned, deserted, for sale, on the market, void ≠ occupied 2 = **unfilled**, unoccupied ≠ taken 3 = **blank**, vague, dreamy, empty, abstracted, idle, vacuous, inane ≠ thoughtful

vacuum NOUN 1 = **gap**, lack, absence, space, deficiency, void 2 = **emptiness**, space, void, gap, nothingness, vacuity

vague ADJECTIVE 1 = **unclear**, indefinite, hazy, confused, loose, uncertain, unsure, superficial ≠ clear 2 = **imprecise**, unspecified, generalized, rough, loose, ambiguous, hazy, equivocal 3 = **absent-minded**, distracted, vacant, preoccupied, oblivious, inattentive 4 = **indistinct**, unclear, faint, hazy, indeterminate, nebulous, ill-defined ≠ distinct

vain ADJECTIVE 1 = **futile**, useless, pointless, unsuccessful, idle, worthless, senseless, fruitless ≠ successful 2 = **conceited**, narcissistic, proud, arrogant, swaggering, egotistical, self-important ≠ modest ▷ PHRASE: **in vain** 1 = **useless**, to no avail, unsuccessful, fruitless, vain 2 = **uselessly**, to no avail, unsuccessfully, fruitlessly, vainly, ineffectually

valid ADJECTIVE 1 = **sound**, good, reasonable, telling, convincing, rational, logical, viable ≠ unfounded 2 = **legal**, official, legitimate, genuine, authentic, lawful, bona fide ≠ invalid

validity NOUN 1 = **soundness**, force, power, weight, strength, cogency 2 = **legality**, authority, legitimacy, right, lawfulness

valley NOUN = **hollow**, dale, glen, vale, depression, dell

valuable ADJECTIVE 1 = **useful**, important, profitable, worthwhile, beneficial, helpful ≠ useless 2 = **treasured**, prized, precious 3 = **precious**, expensive, costly, dear, high-priced, priceless, irreplaceable ≠ worthless ▷ PLURAL NOUN = **treasures**, prized possessions, precious items, heirlooms, personal effects, costly articles

value NOUN 1 = **importance**, benefit, worth, merit, point, service, sense, profit ≠ worthlessness 2 = **cost**, price, worth, rate, market price, face value, asking price, selling price ▷ PLURAL NOUN = **principles**, morals, ethics, mores, standards of behaviour, (moral) standards ▷ VERB 1 = **appreciate**, rate, prize,

regard highly, respect, admire, treasure, esteem ≠ undervalue
2 *with* **at** = **evaluate**, price, estimate, rate, cost, assess, set at, appraise

vanish VERB **1** = **disappear**, dissolve, evaporate, fade away, melt away, evanesce ≠ appear
2 = **die out**, disappear, pass away, end, fade, dwindle, cease to exist, become extinct

vanity NOUN = **pride**, arrogance, conceit, narcissism, egotism, conceitedness ≠ modesty

variable ADJECTIVE = **changeable**, unstable, fluctuating, shifting, flexible, uneven, temperamental, unsteady ≠ constant

variant ADJECTIVE = **different**, alternative, modified, divergent
▷ NOUN = **variation**, form, version, development, alternative, adaptation, revision, modification

variation NOUN **1** = **alternative**, variety, modification, departure, innovation, variant **2** = **variety**, change, deviation, difference, diversity, diversion, novelty ≠ uniformity

varied ADJECTIVE = **different**, mixed, various, diverse, assorted, miscellaneous, sundry, motley ≠ unvarying

variety NOUN **1** = **diversity**, change, variation, difference, diversification, heterogeneity, multifariousness ≠ uniformity
2 = **range**, selection, assortment, mix, collection, line-up, mixture,

array **3** = **type**, sort, kind, class, brand, species, breed, strain

various DETERMINER = **different**, assorted, miscellaneous, varied, distinct, diverse, disparate, sundry ≠ similar
▷ ADJECTIVE = **many**, numerous, countless, several, abundant, innumerable, sundry, profuse

● **WORD POWER**
● The use of *different* after
● *various*, which seems to be
● most common in speech, is
● unnecessary and should be
● avoided in serious writing: *the*
● *disease exists in various forms* (not
● *in various different forms*).

varnish NOUN = **lacquer**, polish, glaze, gloss
▷ VERB = **lacquer**, polish, glaze, gloss

vary VERB **1** = **differ**, be different, be dissimilar, disagree, diverge
2 = **change**, shift, swing, alter, fluctuate, oscillate, see-saw
3 = **alternate**

vast ADJECTIVE = **huge**, massive, enormous, great, wide, immense, gigantic, monumental ≠ tiny

vault¹ NOUN **1** = **strongroom**, repository, depository **2** = **crypt**, tomb, catacomb, cellar, mausoleum, charnel house, undercroft

vault² VERB = **jump**, spring, leap, clear, bound, hurdle

veer VERB = **change direction**, turn, swerve, shift, sheer, change course

vehicle NOUN **1** = **conveyance**,

V

machine, motor vehicle
2 = **medium**, means, channel, mechanism, organ, apparatus

veil NOUN **1** = **mask**, cover, shroud, film, curtain, cloak **2** = **screen**, mask, disguise, blind **3** = **film**, cover, curtain, cloak, shroud
▷ VERB = **cover**, screen, hide, mask, shield, disguise, conceal, obscure ≠ reveal

veiled ADJECTIVE = **disguised**, implied, hinted at, covert, masked, concealed, suppressed

vein NOUN **1** = **blood vessel** **2** = **mood**, style, note, tone, mode, temper, tenor **3** = **seam**, layer, stratum, course, current, bed, deposit, streak

velocity NOUN = **speed**, pace, rapidity, quickness, swiftness

vengeance NOUN = **revenge**, retaliation, reprisal, retribution, requital ≠ forgiveness

vent NOUN = **outlet**, opening, aperture, duct, orifice
▷ VERB = **express**, release, voice, air, discharge, utter, emit, pour out ≠ hold back

venture VERB **1** = **go**, travel, journey, set out, wander, stray, plunge into, rove **2** = **dare**, presume, have the courage to, be brave enough, hazard, go out on a limb (*informal*), take the liberty, go so far as **3** = **put forward**, volunteer
▷ NOUN = **undertaking**, project, enterprise, campaign, risk, operation, activity, scheme

verbal ADJECTIVE = **spoken**, oral,

word-of-mouth, unwritten

verdict NOUN = **decision**, finding, judgment, opinion, sentence, conclusion, conviction, adjudication

verge NOUN **1** = **brink**, point, edge, threshold **2** (*Brit.*) = **border**, edge, margin, limit, boundary, threshold, brim ▷ PHRASE: **verge on something** = **come near to**, approach, border on, resemble, incline to, be similar to, touch on, be more or less

verify VERB **1** = **check**, make sure, examine, monitor, inspect **2** = **confirm**, prove, substantiate, support, validate, bear out, corroborate, authenticate ≠ disprove

versatile ADJECTIVE
1 = **adaptable**, flexible, all-round, resourceful, multifaceted ≠ unadaptable **2** = **all-purpose**, variable, adjustable ≠ limited

versed ADJECTIVE *with* **in** = **knowledgeable**, experienced, seasoned, familiar, practised, acquainted, well-informed, proficient ≠ ignorant

version NOUN **1** = **form**, variety, variant, sort, class, design, style, model **2** = **adaptation**, edition, interpretation, form, copy, rendering, reproduction, portrayal **3** = **account**, report, description, record, reading, story, view, understanding

vertical ADJECTIVE = **upright**, sheer, perpendicular, straight (up and down), erect, plumb, on

end, precipitous, vertiginous
≠ horizontal
very ADVERB = **extremely**, highly,
greatly, really, deeply, unusually,
profoundly, decidedly
▷ ADJECTIVE **1** = **exact**, precise,
selfsame **2** = **ideal**

⊛ WORD POWER
⊛ In strict usage, adverbs of
⊛ degree such as *very*, *too*, *quite*,
⊛ *really*, and *extremely* are used
⊛ only to qualify adjectives: *he*
⊛ *is very happy*; *she is too sad*. By
⊛ this rule, these words should
⊛ not be used to qualify past
⊛ participles that follow the verb
⊛ *to be*, since they would then be
⊛ technically qualifying verbs.
⊛ With the exception of certain
⊛ participles, such as *tired* or
⊛ *disappointed*, that have come
⊛ to be regarded as adjectives,
⊛ all other past participles are
⊛ qualified by adverbs such
⊛ as *much*, *greatly*, *seriously*, or
⊛ *excessively*: *he has been much* (not
⊛ *very*) *inconvenienced*; *she has been*
⊛ *excessively* (not *too*) *criticized*.

vessel NOUN **1** = **ship**, boat, craft
2 = **container**, receptacle, can,
bowl, tank, pot, drum, barrel
vest VERB ▷ PHRASES: **vest in**
something *or* **someone** *usually*
passive = **place**, invest, entrust,
settle, confer, endow, bestow,
consign; **vest with something**
usually passive = **endow with**,
entrust with
vet VERB = **check**, examine,
investigate, review, appraise,

scrutinize
veteran NOUN = **old hand**, past
master, warhorse (*informal*), old
stager ≠ novice
▷ MODIFIER = **long-serving**,
seasoned, experienced, old,
established, qualified, mature,
practised
veto NOUN = **ban**, dismissal,
rejection, vetoing, boycott,
embargo, prohibiting, prohibition
≠ ratification
▷ VERB = **ban**, block, reject, rule
out, turn down, forbid, boycott,
prohibit ≠ pass
viable ADJECTIVE = **workable**,
practical, feasible, suitable,
realistic, operational, applicable,
usable ≠ unworkable
vibrant ADJECTIVE **1** = **energetic**,
dynamic, sparkling, vivid,
spirited, storming, alive, vigorous
2 = **vivid**, bright, brilliant, intense,
clear, rich, glowing
vice NOUN **1** = **fault**, failing,
weakness, limitation, defect,
deficiency, flaw, shortcoming
≠ good point **2** = **wickedness**,
evil, corruption, sin, depravity,
immorality, iniquity, turpitude
≠ virtue
vice versa ADVERB = **the other**
way round, conversely, in reverse,
contrariwise
vicious ADJECTIVE **1** = **savage**,
brutal, violent, cruel,
ferocious, barbarous ≠ gentle
2 = **malicious**, vindictive, spiteful,
mean, cruel, venomous
victim NOUN **1** = **casualty**,

V

sufferer, fatality ≠ survivor
2 = **scapegoat**, sacrifice, martyr

victor NOUN = **winner**, champion, conqueror, vanquisher, prizewinner ≠ loser

victorious ADJECTIVE = **winning**, successful, triumphant, first, champion, conquering, vanquishing, prizewinning ≠ losing

victory NOUN = **win**, success, triumph, conquest, walkover (*informal*) ≠ defeat

vie VERB with **with** or **for** = **compete**, struggle, contend, strive

view NOUN **1** *sometimes plural* = **opinion**, belief, feeling, attitude, impression, conviction, point of view, sentiment **2** = **scene**, picture, sight, prospect, perspective, landscape, outlook, spectacle **3** = **vision**, sight, visibility, perspective, eyeshot
▷ VERB = **regard**, see, consider, perceive, treat, estimate, reckon, deem

viewer NOUN = **watcher**, observer, spectator, onlooker

vigorous ADJECTIVE
1 = **strenuous**, energetic, arduous, hard, taxing, active, rigorous **2** = **spirited**, lively, energetic, active, dynamic, animated, forceful, feisty (*informal*) ≠ lethargic **3** = **strong**, powerful, lively, lusty ≠ weak

vigorously ADVERB
1 = **energetically**, hard, forcefully, strongly, strenuously,
lustily **2** = **forcefully**, strongly, vehemently, strenuously

vigour or (*U.S.*) **vigor** NOUN = **energy**, vitality, power, spirit, strength, animation, verve, gusto ≠ weakness

vile ADJECTIVE **1** = **wicked**, evil, corrupt, perverted, degenerate, depraved, nefarious ≠ honourable **2** = **disgusting**, foul, revolting, offensive, nasty, sickening, horrid, repulsive, yucko (*Austral. slang*) ≠ pleasant

villain NOUN **1** = **evildoer**, criminal, rogue, scoundrel, wretch, reprobate, miscreant, blackguard, wrong 'un (*Austral. slang*) **2** = **baddy** (*informal*), antihero ≠ hero

vindicate VERB **1** = **clear**, acquit, exonerate, absolve, let off the hook, exculpate ≠ condemn **2** = **support**, defend, excuse, justify

vintage NOUN (*of a wine*) = **harvest**
▷ ADJECTIVE **1** (*of a wine*) = **high-quality**, best, prime, quality, choice, select, superior **2** = **classic**, old, veteran, historic, heritage, enduring, antique, timeless

violate VERB **1** = **break**, infringe, disobey, transgress, ignore, defy, disregard, flout ≠ obey **2** = **invade**, infringe on, disturb, upset, shatter, disrupt, impinge on, encroach on **3** = **desecrate**, profane, defile, abuse, pollute, deface, dishonour, vandalize

≠ honour 4 = **rape**, molest, sexually assault, ravish, abuse, assault, interfere with, sexually abuse

violation NOUN 1 = **breach**, abuse, infringement, contravention, abuse, trespass, transgression, infraction
2 = **invasion**, intrusion, trespass, breach, disturbance, disruption, interruption, encroachment
3 = **desecration**, sacrilege, defilement, profanation, spoliation 4 = **rape**, sexual assault, molesting, ravishing (*old-fashioned*), abuse, sexual abuse, indecent assault, molestation

violence NOUN 1 = **brutality**, bloodshed, savagery, fighting, terrorism 2 = **force**, power, strength, might, ferocity, forcefulness, powerfulness
3 = **intensity**, force, cruelty, severity, fervour, vehemence

violent ADJECTIVE 1 = **brutal**, aggressive, savage, wild, fierce, bullying, cruel, vicious ≠ gentle
2 = **sharp** 3 = **passionate**, uncontrollable, unrestrained
4 = **fiery**, fierce, passionate

VIP NOUN = **celebrity**, big name, star, somebody, luminary, big hitter (*informal*), heavy hitter (*informal*)

virgin NOUN = **maiden**, girl (*archaic*)
▷ ADJECTIVE = **pure**, chaste, immaculate, virginal, vestal, uncorrupted, undefiled ≠ corrupted

virtual ADJECTIVE = **practical**, essential, in all but name

virtually ADVERB = **practically**, almost, nearly, in effect, in essence, as good as, in all but name

virtue NOUN 1 = **goodness**, integrity, worth, morality, righteousness, probity, rectitude, incorruptibility ≠ vice 2 = **merit**, strength, asset, plus (*informal*), attribute, good point, strong point ≠ failing 3 = **advantage**, benefit, merit, credit, usefulness, efficacy

visible ADJECTIVE = **perceptible**, observable, clear, apparent, evident, manifest, in view, discernible ≠ invisible

vision NOUN 1 = **image**, idea, dream, plans, hopes, prospect, ideal, concept 2 = **hallucination**, illusion, apparition, revelation, delusion, mirage, chimera
3 = **sight**, seeing, eyesight, view, perception 4 = **foresight**, imagination, perception, insight, awareness, inspiration, innovation, creativity

visionary ADJECTIVE
1 = **idealistic**, romantic, unrealistic, utopian, speculative, impractical, unworkable, quixotic ≠ realistic 2 = **prophetic**, mystical, predictive, oracular, sibylline
▷ NOUN 1 = **idealist**, romantic, dreamer, daydreamer ≠ realist
2 = **prophet**, diviner, mystic, seer, soothsayer, sibyl, scryer, spaewife

V

(*Scot.*)

visit VERB 1 = **call on**, drop in on (*informal*), stop by, look up, go see (*U.S.*), swing by (*informal*) 2 = **stay at**, stay with, spend time with 3 = **stay in**, stop by
▷ NOUN 1 = **call**, social call 2 = **trip**, stop, stay, break, tour, holiday, vacation (*informal*), stopover

visitor NOUN = **guest**, caller, company, manu(w)hiri (*N.Z.*)

vista NOUN = **view**, scene, prospect, landscape, panorama, perspective

visual ADJECTIVE 1 = **optical**, optic, ocular 2 = **observable**, visible, perceptible, discernible ≠ imperceptible

vital ADJECTIVE 1 = **essential**, important, necessary, key, basic, significant, critical, crucial ≠ unnecessary 2 = **lively**, vigorous, energetic, spirited, dynamic, animated, vibrant, vivacious ≠ lethargic

vitality NOUN = **energy**, vivacity, life, strength, animation, vigour, exuberance, liveliness ≠ lethargy

vivid ADJECTIVE 1 = **clear**, detailed, realistic, telling, moving, affecting, arresting, powerful ≠ vague 2 = **bright**, brilliant, intense, clear, rich, glowing, colourful ≠ dull

vocabulary NOUN 1 = **language**, words, lexicon 2 = **wordbook**, dictionary, glossary, lexicon

vocal ADJECTIVE 1 = **outspoken**, frank, forthright, strident,

vociferous, articulate, expressive, eloquent ≠ quiet 2 = **spoken**, voiced, uttered, oral, said

vocation NOUN = **profession**, calling, job, trade, career, mission, pursuit

vogue NOUN = **fashion**, trend, craze, style, mode, passing fancy, dernier cri (*French*)

voice NOUN 1 = **tone**, sound, articulation 2 = **utterance** 3 = **opinion**, will, feeling, wish, desire 4 = **say**, view, vote, comment, input
▷ VERB = **express**, declare, air, raise, reveal, mention, mouth, pronounce ▷ RELATED WORD: *adjective* vocal

void ADJECTIVE = **invalid**, null and void, inoperative, useless, ineffective, worthless
▷ NOUN 1 = **gap**, space, lack, hole, emptiness 2 = **emptiness**, space, vacuum, oblivion, blankness, nullity, vacuity
▷ VERB = **invalidate**, nullify, cancel, withdraw, reverse, undo, repeal, quash

volatile ADJECTIVE 1 = **changeable**, shifting, variable, unsettled, unstable, explosive, unreliable, unsteady ≠ stable 2 = **temperamental**, erratic, mercurial, up and down (*informal*), fickle, over-emotional ≠ calm

volley NOUN = **barrage**, blast, burst, shower, hail, bombardment, salvo, fusillade

volume NOUN 1 = **amount**, quantity, level, body, total,

v

measure, degree, mass **2** = **capacity**, size, mass, extent, proportions, dimensions, bulk, measurements **3** = **book**, work, title, opus, publication, manual, tome, treatise **4** = **loudness**, sound, amplification

voluntarily ADVERB = **willingly**, freely, by choice, off your own bat, of your own accord, of your own volition

voluntary ADJECTIVE
1 = **intentional**, deliberate, planned, calculated, wilful ≠ unintentional **2** = **optional**, discretionary, up to the individual, open, unforced, at your discretion, open to choice ≠ obligatory **3** = **unpaid**, free, willing, pro bono (*law*)

volunteer VERB = **offer**, step forward ≠ refuse

vomit VERB **1** = **be sick**, throw up (*informal*), spew, chuck (*Austral. & N.Z. informal*), heave (*slang*), retch **2** *often with* **up** = **bring up**, throw up, regurgitate, emit (*informal*), disgorge, spew out *or* up

vote NOUN = **poll**, election, ballot, referendum, popular vote, plebiscite, straw poll, show of hands
▷ VERB = **cast your vote**

voucher NOUN = **ticket**, token, coupon, pass, slip, chit, chitty (*Brit. informal*), docket

vow NOUN = **promise**, commitment, pledge, oath, profession, avowal
▷ VERB = **promise**, pledge, swear,

commit, engage, affirm, avow, bind yourself

voyage NOUN = **journey**, trip, passage, expedition, crossing, sail, cruise, excursion
▷ VERB = **travel**, journey, tour, cruise, steam, take a trip, go on an expedition

vulgar ADJECTIVE **1** = **tasteless**, common ≠ tasteful **2** = **crude**, rude, coarse, indecent, tasteless, risqué, ribald **3** = **uncouth**, unrefined, impolite, ill-bred ≠ refined

vulnerable ADJECTIVE
1 = **susceptible**, helpless, unprotected, defenceless, exposed, weak, sensitive, tender ≠ immune **2** (*military*) = **exposed**, open, unprotected, defenceless, accessible, wide open, assailable ≠ well-protected

V

Ww

waddle VERB = **shuffle**, totter, toddle, sway, wobble

wade VERB 1 = **paddle**, splash, splash about, slop 2 = **walk through**, cross, ford, travel across

wag VERB 1 = **wave**, shake, waggle, stir, quiver, vibrate, wiggle 2 = **waggle**, wave, shake, flourish, brandish, wobble, wiggle 3 = **shake**, bob, nod
▷ NOUN 1 = **wave**, shake, quiver, vibration, wiggle, waggle 2 = **nod**, bob, shake

wage NOUN *often plural* = **payment**, pay, remuneration, fee, reward, income, allowance, recompense
▷ VERB = **engage in**, conduct, pursue, carry on, undertake, practise, prosecute, proceed with

wail VERB = **cry**, weep, grieve, lament, howl, bawl, yowl
▷ NOUN = **cry**, moan, howl, lament, yowl

wait VERB 1 = **stay**, remain, stop, pause, rest, linger, loiter, tarry ≠ go 2 = **stand by**, hold back, hang fire 3 = **be postponed**, be suspended, be delayed, be put off, be put back, be deferred, be put on hold (*informal*), be shelved
▷ NOUN = **delay**, gap, pause, interval, stay, rest, halt, hold-up

waiter NOUN = **attendant**, server, flunkey, steward, servant

waitress NOUN = **attendant**, server, stewardess, servant

waive VERB 1 = **give up**, relinquish, renounce, forsake, drop, abandon, set aside, dispense with ≠ claim 2 = **disregard**, ignore, discount, overlook, set aside, pass over, dispense with, brush aside

wake¹ VERB 1 = **awake**, stir, awaken, come to, arise, get up, rouse, get out of bed ≠ fall asleep 2 = **awaken**, arouse, rouse, waken 3 = **evoke**, recall, renew, stimulate, revive, induce, arouse, call up
▷ NOUN = **vigil**, watch, funeral, deathwatch, tangi (*N.Z.*)

● WORD POWER
● Both *wake* and its synonym
● *waken* can be used either with
● or without an object: *I woke/*
● *wakened my sister*, and also
● *I woke/wakened (up) at noon.*
● *Wake, wake up,* and occasionally
● *waken,* can also be used in a
● figurative sense, for example
● *seeing him again woke painful*
● *memories*; and *it's time he woke*
● *up to his responsibilities.* The
● verbs *awake* and *awaken* are
● more commonly used in the
● figurative than the literal
● sense, for example *he awoke to*
● *the danger he was in.*

wake² NOUN = **slipstream**, wash, trail, backwash, train, track, waves, path ▷ PHRASE: **in the**

w

wake of = **in the aftermath of**, following, because of, as a result of, on account of, as a consequence of

walk VERB 1 = **stride**, stroll, go, move, step, march, pace, hike 2 = **travel on foot** 3 = **escort**, take, see, show, partner, guide, conduct, accompany
▷ NOUN 1 = **stroll**, hike, ramble, march, trek, trudge, promenade, saunter 2 = **gait**, step, bearing, carriage, tread 3 = **path**, footpath, track, way, road, lane, trail, avenue, berm (N.Z.)
▷ PHRASE: **walk of life** = **area**, calling, business, line, trade, class, field, career

walker NOUN = **hiker**, rambler, wayfarer, pedestrian

wall NOUN 1 = **partition**, screen, barrier, enclosure 2 = **barrier**, obstacle, barricade, obstruction, check, bar, fence, impediment

wallet NOUN = **purse**, pocketbook, pouch, case, holder, money-bag

wander VERB = **roam**, walk, drift, stroll, range, stray, ramble, prowl
▷ NOUN = **excursion**, walk, stroll, cruise, ramble, meander, promenade, mosey (informal)

wanderer NOUN = **traveller**, rover, nomad, drifter, gypsy, explorer, rambler, voyager

wane VERB 1 = **decline**, weaken, diminish, fail, fade, decrease, dwindle, lessen ≠ grow 2 = **diminish**, decrease, dwindle ≠ wax

want VERB 1 = **wish for**, desire, long for, crave, covet, hope for, yearn for, thirst for ≠ have 2 = **need**, demand, require, call for 3 = **should**, need, must, ought 4 = **desire**, long for, crave, wish for, yearn for, thirst for, hanker after, burn for 5 = **lack**, need, require, miss
▷ NOUN 1 = **lack**, need, absence, shortage, deficiency, famine, scarcity, dearth ≠ abundance 2 = **poverty**, hardship, privation, penury, destitution, neediness, pennilessness ≠ wealth 3 = **wish**, will, need, desire, requirement, longing, appetite, craving

wanting ADJECTIVE 1 = **deficient**, poor, inadequate, insufficient, faulty, defective, imperfect, unsound, bodger or bodgie (Austral. slang) ≠ adequate 2 = **lacking**, missing, absent, incomplete, short, shy ≠ complete

war NOUN 1 = **conflict**, drive, attack, fighting, fight, operation, battle, movement ≠ peace 2 = **campaign**, drive, attack, operation, movement, push, mission = offensive
▷ VERB = **fight**, battle, clash, wage war, campaign, combat, do battle, take up arms ≠ make peace

ward NOUN 1 = **room**, department, unit, quarter, division, section, apartment, cubicle 2 = **district**, constituency, area, division, zone, parish, precinct 3 = **dependant**, charge, pupil, minor, protégé
▷ PHRASES: **ward someone**

w

off = **drive off**, resist, fight off, hold off, repel, fend off; **ward something off 1** = **avert**, fend off, stave off, avoid, frustrate, deflect, repel **2** = **parry**, avert, deflect, avoid, repel, turn aside

warden NOUN **1** = **steward**, guardian, administrator, superintendent, caretaker, curator, custodian **2** (*chiefly U.S. & Canad.*) = **jailer**, prison officer, guard, screw (*slang*) **3** (*Brit.*) = **governor**, head, leader, director, manager, chief, executive, commander, baas (*S. African*) **4** = **ranger**, keeper, guardian, protector, custodian, official

wardrobe NOUN **1** = **clothes cupboard**, cupboard, closet (*U.S.*), cabinet **2** = **clothes**, apparel, attire

warehouse NOUN = **store**, depot, storehouse, repository, depository, stockroom

wares PLURAL NOUN = **goods**, produce, stock, products, stuff, commodities, merchandise

warfare NOUN = **war**, fighting, battle, conflict, combat, hostilities, enmity ≠ peace

warm ADJECTIVE **1** = **balmy**, mild, temperate, pleasant, fine, bright, sunny, agreeable ≠ cool **2** = **cosy**, snug, toasty (*informal*), comfortable, homely, comfy (*informal*) **3** = **moderately hot**, heated ≠ cool **4** = **thermal**, winter, thick, chunky, woolly ≠ cool **5** = **mellow**, relaxing, pleasant, agreeable, restful

6 = **affable**, kindly, friendly, affectionate, loving, tender, amicable, cordial ≠ unfriendly **7** = **near**, close, hot, near to the truth
▷ VERB = **warm up**, heat, thaw (out), heat up ≠ cool down
▷ PHRASE: **warm something or someone up** = **heat**, thaw, heat up

warmth NOUN **1** = **heat**, snugness, warmness, comfort, homeliness, hotness ≠ coolness **2** = **affection**, feeling, love, goodwill, kindness, tenderness, cordiality, kindliness ≠ hostility

warn VERB **1** = **notify**, tell, remind, inform, alert, tip off, give notice, make someone aware **2** = **advise**, urge, recommend, counsel, caution, commend, exhort, admonish

warning NOUN **1** = **caution**, information, advice, injunction, notification **2** = **notice**, notification, sign, alarm, announcement, alert, tip-off (*informal*), heads up (*U.S. & Canad.*) **3** = **omen**, sign, forecast, indication, prediction, prophecy, foreboding, portent, rahui (*N.Z.*) **4** = **reprimand**, admonition

warp VERB **1** = **distort**, bend, twist, buckle, deform, disfigure, contort, malform **2** = **become distorted**, bend, twist, contort, become deformed, become misshapen **3** = **pervert**, twist, corrupt, degrade, deprave, debase, debauch, lead astray

▷ **NOUN** = **twist**, bend, defect, flaw, distortion, imperfection, kink, contortion

warrant VERB = **call for**, demand, require, merit, rate, earn, deserve, permit

▷ **NOUN** = **authorization**, permit, licence, permission, authority, sanction

warranty NOUN = **guarantee**, promise, contract, bond, pledge, certificate, assurance, covenant

warrior NOUN = **soldier**, combatant, fighter, gladiator, trooper, man-at-arms

wary ADJECTIVE 1 = **suspicious**, sceptical, guarded, distrustful, chary 2 = **watchful**, careful, alert, cautious, vigilant, circumspect, heedful ≠ careless

wash VERB 1 = **clean**, scrub, sponge, rinse, scour, cleanse 2 = **launder**, clean, rinse, dry-clean 3 = **rinse**, clean, scrub, lather 4 = **bathe**, bath, clean yourself, soak, douse, scrub yourself down 5 = **move**, overcome, touch, upset, stir, disturb, perturb, surge through 6 (informal) used in negative constructions = **be plausible**, stand up, hold up, pass muster, hold water, stick, carry weight, be convincing

▷ **NOUN** 1 = **laundering**, cleaning, clean, cleansing 2 = **bathe**, dip, soak, scrub, rinse 3 = **backwash**, slipstream, path, trail, train, track, waves, aftermath 4 = **splash**, surge, swell, rise and fall, undulation 5 = **coat**, film, covering, layer, coating, overlay

▷ **PHRASES**: wash something away = **erode**, wear something away; **wash something** or **someone away** = **sweep away**, carry off, bear away

wasp NOUN

▷ see **ants, bees and wasps**

waste VERB 1 = **squander**, throw away, blow (slang), lavish, misuse, dissipate, fritter away ≠ save 2 followed by **away** = **wear out**, wither

▷ **NOUN** 1 = **squandering**, misuse, extravagance, frittering away, dissipation, wastefulness, prodigality ≠ saving 2 = **rubbish**, refuse, debris, scrap, litter, garbage, trash, leftovers 3 usually plural = **desert**, wilderness, wasteland

▷ ADJECTIVE 1 = **unwanted**, useless, worthless, unused, leftover, superfluous, unusable, supernumerary ≠ necessary 2 = **uncultivated**, wild, bare, barren, empty, desolate, unproductive, uninhabited ≠ cultivated ▷ **PHRASE**: waste away = **decline**, dwindle, wither, fade, crumble, decay, wane, wear out

● **WORD POWER**

● Waste and wastage are to some
● extent interchangeable, but
● many people think that wastage
● should not be used to refer
● to loss resulting from human
● carelessness, inefficiency, etc:

W.

● *a waste* (not *a wastage*) *of time,*
● *money*, *effort*, etc.

watch VERB 1 = **look at**, observe, regard, eye, see, view, contemplate, eyeball (*slang*) 2 = **spy on**, follow, track, monitor, keep an eye on, stake out, keep tabs on (*informal*), keep watch on 3 = **guard**, keep, mind, protect, tend, look after, shelter, take care of
▷ NOUN 1 = **wristwatch**, timepiece, chronometer 2 = **guard**, surveillance, observation, vigil, lookout

watchdog NOUN 1 = **guardian**, monitor, protector, custodian, scrutineer 2 = **guard dog**

water NOUN 1 = **liquid**, H_2O, wai (*N.Z.*) 2 *often plural* = **sea**, main, waves, ocean, depths, briny
▷ VERB 1 = **sprinkle**, spray, soak, irrigate, hose, dampen, drench, douse, fertigate (*Austral.*) 2 = **get wet**, cry, weep, become wet, exude water ▷ PHRASE: **water something down** = **dilute**, weaken, water, doctor, thin
▷ RELATED WORD: *adjective* **aquatic**

waterfall NOUN = **cascade**, fall, cataract

wave VERB 1 = **signal**, sign, gesture, gesticulate 2 = **guide**, point, direct, indicate, signal, motion, gesture, nod 3 = **brandish**, swing, flourish, wag, shake 4 = **flutter**, flap, stir, shake, swing, wag, oscillate
▷ NOUN 1 = **gesture**, sign,

signal, indication, gesticulation 2 = **ripple**, breaker, swell, ridge, roller, billow 3 = **outbreak**, rash, upsurge, flood, surge, ground swell 4 = **stream**, flood, surge, spate, current, flow, rush, tide

waver VERB 1 = **hesitate**, dither (*chiefly Brit.*), vacillate, falter, fluctuate, seesaw, hum and haw ≠ be decisive 2 = **flicker**, shake, tremble, wobble, quiver, totter

wax VERB 1 = **increase**, grow, develop, expand, swell, enlarge, magnify ≠ wane 2 = **become fuller**, enlarge

way NOUN 1 = **method**, means, system, process, technique, manner, procedure, mode 2 = **manner**, style, fashion, mode 3 *often plural* = **custom**, manner, habit, style, practice, nature, personality, wont, tikanga (*N.Z.*) 4 = **route**, direction, course, road, path 5 = **access**, road, track, channel, route, path, trail, pathway 6 = **journey**, approach, passage 7 = **distance**, length, stretch

wayward ADJECTIVE = **erratic**, unruly, unmanageable, unpredictable, capricious, ungovernable, inconstant ≠ obedient

weak ADJECTIVE 1 = **feeble**, frail, debilitated, fragile, sickly, puny, unsteady, infirm ≠ strong 2 = **slight**, faint, feeble, pathetic, hollow 3 = **fragile**, brittle, flimsy, fine, delicate, frail, dainty, breakable 4 = **unsafe**, exposed, vulnerable, helpless, unprotected, defenceless, unguarded ≠ secure **5** = **unconvincing**, unsatisfactory, lame, flimsy, pathetic ≠ convincing **6** = **tasteless**, thin, diluted, watery, runny, insipid ≠ strong

weaken VERB **1** = **reduce**, undermine, moderate, diminish, lessen, sap ≠ boost **2** = **wane**, diminish, dwindle, lower, flag, fade, lessen ≠ grow **3** = **sap the strength of** ≠ strengthen

weakness NOUN **1** = **frailty**, fatigue, exhaustion, fragility, infirmity, feebleness, decrepitude ≠ strength **2** = **liking**, appetite, penchant, soft spot, passion, inclination, fondness, partiality ≠ aversion **3** = **powerlessness**, vulnerability, meekness, spinelessness, timorousness, cravenness, cowardliness **4** = **inadequacy**, deficiency, transparency, lameness, hollowness, implausibility, flimsiness, unsoundness **5** = **failing**, fault, defect, deficiency, flaw, shortcoming, blemish, imperfection ≠ strong point

wealth NOUN **1** = **riches**, fortune, prosperity, affluence, money, opulence ≠ poverty **2** = **property**, capital, fortune **3** = **abundance**, plenty, richness, profusion, fullness, cornucopia, copiousness ≠ lack

wealthy ADJECTIVE = **rich**, prosperous, affluent, well-off, flush (*informal*), opulent, well-heeled (*informal*), well-to-do, minted (*Brit. slang*) ≠ poor

wear VERB **1** = **be dressed in**, have on, sport (*informal*), put on **2** = **show**, present, bear, display, assume, put on, exhibit **3** = **deteriorate**, fray, wear thin ▷ NOUN **1** = **clothes**, things, dress, gear (*informal*), attire, costume, garments, apparel **2** = **damage**, wear and tear, erosion, deterioration, attrition, corrosion, abrasion ≠ repair ▷ PHRASE: **wear off** = **subside**, disappear, fade, diminish, decrease, dwindle, wane, peter out

wearing ADJECTIVE = **tiresome**, trying, fatiguing, oppressive, exasperating, irksome, wearisome ≠ refreshing

weary ADJECTIVE **1** = **tired**, exhausted, drained, worn out, done in (*informal*), flagging, fatigued, sleepy, clapped out (*Austral. & N.Z. informal*) ≠ energetic **2** = **tiring**, arduous, tiresome, laborious, wearisome ≠ refreshing ▷ VERB = **grow tired**, tire, become bored ≠ invigorate

weather NOUN = **climate**, conditions, temperature, forecast, outlook, meteorological conditions, elements ▷ VERB = **withstand**, stand, survive, overcome, resist, brave, endure, come through ≠ surrender to

w

weave VERB 1 = **knit**, intertwine, plait, braid, entwine, interlace
2 = **zigzag**, wind, crisscross
3 = **create**, tell, recount, narrate, build, relate, make up, spin

web NOUN 1 = **cobweb**, spider's web 2 = **mesh**, lattice 3 = **tangle**, network

wed VERB 1 = **get married to**, be united to ≠ divorce 2 = **get married**, marry, be united, tie the knot (*informal*), take the plunge (*informal*) ≠ divorce 3 = **unite**, combine, join, link, ally, blend, merge, interweave ≠ divide

wedding NOUN = **marriage**, nuptials, wedding ceremony, marriage service, wedding service

wedge VERB = **squeeze**, force, lodge, jam, crowd, stuff, pack, thrust
▷ NOUN = **block**, lump, chunk

weep VERB = **cry**, shed tears, sob, whimper, mourn, lament, blubber, snivel ≠ rejoice

weigh VERB 1 = **have a weight of**, tip the scales at (*informal*)
2 = **consider**, examine, contemplate, evaluate, ponder, think over, reflect upon, meditate upon 3 = **compare**, balance, contrast, juxtapose, place side by side 4 = **matter**, carry weight, count

weight NOUN 1 = **heaviness**, mass, poundage, load, tonnage
2 = **importance**, force, power, value, authority, influence, impact, import, mana (*N.Z.*)
▷ VERB 1 *often with* **down** = **load**

2 = **bias**, load, slant, unbalance

weird ADJECTIVE 1 = **strange**, odd, unusual, bizarre, mysterious, queer, eerie, unnatural ≠ normal
2 = **bizarre**, odd, strange, unusual, queer, unnatural, creepy (*informal*), freakish ≠ ordinary

welcome VERB 1 = **greet**, meet, receive, embrace, hail, karanga (*N.Z.*), mihi (*N.Z.*) ≠ reject
2 = **accept gladly**, appreciate, embrace, approve of, be pleased by, give the thumbs up to (*informal*), be glad about, express pleasure *or* satisfaction at
▷ NOUN = **greeting**, welcoming, reception, acceptance, hail, hospitality, salutation ≠ rejection
▷ ADJECTIVE 1 = **pleasing**, appreciated, acceptable, pleasant, desirable, refreshing, delightful, gratifying ≠ unpleasant
2 = **wanted** ≠ unwanted 3 = **free**

weld VERB 1 = **join**, link, bond, bind, connect, fuse, solder
2 = **unite**, combine, blend, unify, fuse

welfare NOUN 1 = **wellbeing**, good, interest, health, security, benefit, safety, protection
2 = **state benefit**, support, benefits, pensions, dole (*slang*), social security, unemployment benefit, state benefits, pogey (*Canad.*)

well¹ ADVERB 1 = **skilfully**, expertly, adeptly, professionally, correctly, properly, efficiently, adequately ≠ badly 2 = **satisfactorily**, nicely, smoothly, successfully, pleasantly, splendidly, agreeably ≠ badly **3** = **thoroughly**, completely, fully, carefully, effectively, efficiently, rigorously **4** = **intimately**, deeply, fully, profoundly ≠ slightly **5** = **favourably**, highly, kindly, warmly, enthusiastically, approvingly, admiringly, with admiration ≠ unfavourably **6** = **considerably**, easily, very much, significantly, substantially, markedly **7** = **fully**, highly, greatly, amply, very much, thoroughly, considerably, substantially **8** = **possibly**, probably, certainly, reasonably, conceivably, justifiably **9** = **decently**, right, kindly, fittingly, fairly, properly, politely, suitably ≠ unfairly **10** = **prosperously**, comfortably, splendidly, in comfort, in (the lap of) luxury, without hardship ▷ ADJECTIVE **1** = **healthy**, sound, fit, blooming, in fine fettle, in good condition ≠ ill **2** = **satisfactory**, right, fine, pleasing, proper, thriving ≠ unsatisfactory **3** = **advisable**, proper, agreeable ≠ inadvisable

well² NOUN = **hole**, bore, pit, shaft ▷ VERB **1** = **flow**, spring, pour, jet, surge, gush, spurt, spout **2** = **rise**, increase, grow, mount, surge, intensify

wet ADJECTIVE **1** = **damp**, soaking, saturated, moist, watery, soggy, sodden, waterlogged ≠ dry **2** = **rainy**, damp, drizzly, showery, raining, pouring, drizzling,

teeming ≠ sunny **3** (*informal*) = **feeble**, soft, weak, ineffectual, weedy (*informal*), spineless, effete, timorous ▷ VERB = **moisten**, spray, dampen, water, soak, saturate, douse, irrigate, fertigate (*Austral.*) ≠ dry ▷ NOUN **1** = **rain**, drizzle ≠ fine weather **2** = **moisture**, water, liquid, damp, humidity, condensation, dampness, wetness ≠ dryness

whack (*informal*) VERB = **strike**, hit, belt (*informal*), bang, smack, thrash, thump, swipe ▷ NOUN **1** = **blow**, hit, stroke, belt (*informal*), bang, smack, thump, swipe **2** (*informal*) = **share**, part, cut (*informal*), bit, portion, quota **3** (*informal*) = **attempt**, go (*informal*), try, turn, shot (*informal*), crack (*informal*), stab (*informal*), bash (*informal*)

wharf NOUN = **dock**, pier, berth, quay, jetty, landing stage

wheel NOUN = **disc**, ring, hoop ▷ VERB **1** = **push**, trundle, roll **2** = **turn**, swing, spin, revolve, rotate, whirl, swivel **3** = **circle**, go round, twirl, gyrate

whereabouts PLURAL NOUN = **position**, situation, site, location

whiff NOUN = **smell**, hint, scent, sniff, aroma, odour

whim NOUN = **impulse**, caprice, fancy, urge, notion

whine VERB **1** = **cry**, sob, wail, whimper, sniffle, snivel, moan **2** = **complain**, grumble, gripe

w

● **WHALES AND DOLPHINS**
● baleen whale
● beluga
● blue whale *or* sulphur-bottom
● bottlenose dolphin
● bowhead
● humpback whale
● killer whale, grampus, *or* orca
● narwhal

● porpoise
● right whale *or* (*Austral.*) bay whale
● rorqual
● sperm whale *or* cachalot
● toothed whale
● whalebone whale
● white whale

(*informal*), whinge (*informal*), moan, grouse, grizzle (*informal*, *chiefly Brit.*), grouch (*informal*)
▷ **NOUN 1** = **cry**, moan, sob, wail, whimper **2** = **drone**, note, hum **3** = **complaint**, moan, grumble, grouse, gripe (*informal*), whinge (*informal*), grouch (*informal*)

whip NOUN = **lash**, cane, birch, crop, scourge, cat-o'-nine-tails
▷ **VERB 1** = **lash**, cane, flog, beat, strap, thrash, birch, scourge **2** (*informal*) = **dash**, shoot, fly, tear, rush, dive, dart, whisk **3** = **whisk**, beat, mix vigorously, stir vigorously **4** = **incite**, drive, stir, spur, work up, get going, agitate, inflame

whirl VERB **1** = **spin**, turn, twist, rotate, twirl **2** = **rotate**, roll, twist, revolve, swirl, twirl, pirouette **3** = **feel dizzy**, swim, spin, reel, go round
▷ **NOUN 1** = **revolution**, turn, roll, spin, twist, swirl, rotation, twirl **2** = **bustle**, round, series, succession, flurry, merry-go-round **3** = **confusion**, daze, dither (*chiefly Brit.*), giddiness

4 = **tumult**, spin
whisk VERB **1** = **flick**, whip, sweep, brush **2** = **beat**, mix vigorously, stir vigorously, whip, fluff up
▷ **NOUN 1** = **flick**, sweep, brush, whip **2** = **beater**, mixer, blender
whisper VERB **1** = **murmur**, breathe ≠ shout **2** = **rustle**, sigh, hiss, swish
▷ **NOUN 1** = **murmur**, mutter, mumble, undertone **2** (*informal*) = **rumour**, report, gossip, goss (*informal*), innuendo, insinuation **3** = **rustle**, sigh, hiss, swish
white ADJECTIVE = **pale**, wan, pasty, pallid, ashen
▷ *see* **shades from black to white**
● **WORD POWER**
● *White* is a colour which has no
● hue due to the reflection of
● all light. White has long been
● associated in Western cultures
● with cleanliness and, by
● extension, purity and virginity,
● resulting in the expression
● *whiter than white*, meaning
● extremely white, clean, or pure.
● This focus on cleanliness is
● also evident in the expression

- **white-collar**, which denotes
- workers who are in professions
- that traditionally wore a white
- button-down shirt, rather than
- in manual labour. White is
- also associated with illness or
- severe emotional states, with
- the pallor of the face seen as a
- sign of ill-health or discomfort,
- in phrases like **white with**
- **fear**, **shock** or **anger**. White is
- sometimes used as a term
- relating to ethnic origin.

white-collar ADJECTIVE
= **clerical**, professional, salaried, nonmanual

whittle VERB = **carve**, cut, hew, shape, trim, shave, pare ▷ PHRASE: **whittle something away** = **undermine**, reduce, consume, erode, eat away, wear away, cut down, cut, decrease, prune, scale down

whole NOUN = **unit**, ensemble, entirety, totality ≠ part
▷ ADJECTIVE 1 = **complete**, full, total, entire, uncut, undivided, unabridged ≠ partial **2** = **undamaged**, intact, unscathed, unbroken, untouched, unharmed, in one piece ≠ damaged ▷ PHRASE: **on the whole 1** = **all in all**, altogether, all things considered, by and large **2** = **generally**, in general, as a rule, chiefly, mainly, mostly, principally, on average

wholesale
ADJECTIVE = **extensive**, total, mass, sweeping, broad, comprehensive, wide-ranging, blanket ≠ limited
▷ ADVERB = **extensively**, comprehensively, across the board, indiscriminately

wholly ADVERB = **completely**, totally, perfectly, fully, entirely, altogether, thoroughly, utterly ≠ partly

whore NOUN = **prostitute**, tart (*informal*), streetwalker, call girl

wide ADJECTIVE 1 = **spacious**, broad, extensive, roomy, commodious ≠ confined **2** = **baggy**, full, loose, ample, billowing, roomy, voluminous, capacious **3** = **expanded**, dilated, distended ≠ shut **4** = **broad**, extensive, wide-ranging, large, sweeping, vast, immense, expansive ≠ restricted **5** = **extensive**, general, far-reaching, overarching **6** = **large**, broad, vast, immense **7** = **distant**, remote, off course, off target
▷ ADVERB 1 = **fully**, completely ≠ partly **2** = **off target**, astray, off course, off the mark

widen VERB 1 = **broaden**, expand, enlarge, dilate, spread, extend, stretch ≠ narrow **2** = **get wider**, spread, extend, expand, broaden ≠ narrow

widespread ADJECTIVE
= **common**, general, popular, broad, extensive, universal, far-reaching, pervasive ≠ limited

width NOUN = **breadth**, extent, span, scope, diameter, compass, thickness, girth

w

wield VERB 1 = **brandish**, flourish, manipulate, swing, use, manage, handle, employ 2 = **exert**, maintain, exercise, have, possess

wife NOUN = **spouse**, partner, mate, bride, better half (*humorous*), vrou (*S. African*), wahine (*N.Z.*), wifey (*informal*)

wild ADJECTIVE 1 = **untamed**, fierce, savage, ferocious, unbroken, feral, undomesticated, free, warrigal (*Austral. literary*) ≠ tame 2 = **uncultivated**, natural ≠ cultivated 3 = **stormy**, violent, rough, raging, choppy, tempestuous, blustery 4 = **excited**, crazy (*informal*), enthusiastic, raving, hysterical ≠ unenthusiastic 5 = **uncontrolled**, disorderly, turbulent, wayward, unruly, rowdy, unfettered, riotous ≠ calm 6 = **mad** (*informal*), furious, fuming, infuriated, incensed, enraged, very angry, irate, tooshie (*Austral. slang*), off the air (*Austral. slang*) 7 = **uncivilized**, fierce, savage, primitive, ferocious, barbaric, brutish, barbarous ≠ civilized ▷ PHRASE: **the wilds** = **wilderness**, desert, wasteland, middle of nowhere (*informal*), backwoods, back of beyond (*informal*)

wilderness NOUN = **wilds**, desert, wasteland, uncultivated region

will NOUN 1 = **determination**, drive, purpose, commitment, resolution, resolve, spine, backbone 2 = **wish**, mind, desire, intention, fancy, preference, inclination 3 = **choice**, prerogative, volition 4 = **decree**, wish, desire, command, dictate, ordinance 5 = **testament**, bequest(s), last wishes, last will and testament ▷ VERB 1 = **wish**, want, prefer, desire, see fit 2 = **bequeath**, give, leave, transfer, gift, hand on, pass on, confer

willing ADJECTIVE 1 = **inclined**, prepared, consenting, agreeable, compliant, amenable ≠ unwilling 2 = **ready**, game (*informal*) ≠ reluctant

willingly ADVERB = **readily**, freely, gladly, happily, eagerly, voluntarily, cheerfully, by choice ≠ unwillingly

willingness NOUN = **inclination**, will, agreement, wish, consent, volition ≠ reluctance

wilt VERB 1 = **droop**, wither, sag, shrivel 2 = **weaken**, languish, droop 3 = **wane**, flag, fade

win VERB 1 = **be victorious in**, succeed in, prevail in, come first in, be the victor in ≠ lose 2 = **be victorious**, succeed, triumph, overcome, prevail, conquer, come first, sweep the board ≠ lose 3 = **gain**, get, land, achieve, earn, secure, obtain, acquire ≠ forfeit ▷ NOUN = **victory**, success, triumph, conquest ≠ defeat ▷ PHRASE: **win someone over** *or* **round** = **convince**, influence, persuade, convert, sway, prevail upon, bring *or* talk round

wince VERB = **flinch**, start, shrink, cringe, quail, recoil, cower, draw back
▷ NOUN = **flinch**, start, cringe

wind¹ NOUN 1 = **air**, blast, hurricane, breeze, draught, gust, zephyr 2 = **flatulence**, gas 3 = **breath**, puff, respiration 4 = **nonsense**, talk, boasting, hot air, babble, bluster, humbug, twaddle (*informal*), bizzo (*Austral. slang*), bull's wool (*Austral. & N.Z. slang*) ▷ PHRASE: **get wind of something** = **hear about**, learn of, find out about, become aware of, be told about, be informed of, be made aware of, hear tell of

wind² VERB 1 = **meander**, turn, bend, twist, curve, snake, ramble, twist and turn 2 = **wrap**, twist, reel, curl, loop, coil 3 = **coil**, curl, spiral, encircle ▷ PHRASES: **wind someone up** (*informal*) 1 = **irritate**, excite, anger, annoy, exasperate, nettle, work someone up, pique 2 = **tease**, kid (*informal*), have someone on (*informal*), annoy, rag (*informal*), rib (*informal*), josh (*informal*), vex; **wind something up 1 = end**, finish, settle, conclude, tie up, wrap up, finalize 2 = **close down**, close, dissolve, terminate, put something into liquidation; **wind up = end up**, be left, finish up, fetch up (*informal*), land up

windfall NOUN = **godsend**, find, jackpot, bonanza, manna from heaven ≠ misfortune

windy ADJECTIVE = **breezy**, wild, stormy, windswept, blustery, gusty, squally, blowy ≠ calm

wing NOUN = **faction**, group, arm, section, branch
▷ VERB 1 = **fly**, soar, glide, take wing 2 = **wound**, hit, clip

wink VERB 1 = **blink**, bat, flutter 2 = **twinkle**, flash, shine, sparkle, gleam, shimmer, glimmer
▷ NOUN = **blink**, flutter

winner NOUN = **victor**, champion, master, champ (*informal*), conqueror, prizewinner ≠ loser

winning ADJECTIVE 1 = **victorious**, first, top, successful, unbeaten, conquering, triumphant, undefeated 2 = **charming**, pleasing, attractive, engaging, cute, disarming, enchanting, endearing ≠ unpleasant
▷ PLURAL NOUN = **spoils**, profits, gains, prize, proceeds, takings

wipe VERB 1 = **clean**, polish, brush, rub, sponge, mop, swab 2 = **erase**, remove
▷ NOUN = **rub**, brush ▷ PHRASE: **wipe something** *or* **someone out = destroy**, massacre, erase, eradicate, obliterate, annihilate, exterminate, expunge

wisdom NOUN = **understanding**, learning, knowledge, intelligence, judgment, insight, enlightenment, erudition ≠ foolishness

wise ADJECTIVE 1 = **sage**, clever, intelligent, sensible, enlightened, discerning, perceptive, erudite, grounded ≠ foolish 2 = **sensible**, clever, intelligent, prudent,

w

judicious ≠ unwise

wish NOUN = **desire**, want, hope, urge, intention, fancy (*informal*), ambition, yen (*informal*) ≠ aversion
▷ VERB = **want**, feel, choose, please, desire, think fit ▷ PHRASE: **wish for** = **desire**, want, hope for, long for, crave, aspire to, yearn for, hanker for

wit NOUN 1 = **humour**, quips, banter, puns, repartee, wordplay, witticisms, badinage ≠ seriousness 2 = **humorist**, card (*informal*), comedian, wag, joker, dag (*N.Z. informal*) 3 = **cleverness**, sense, brains, wisdom, common sense, intellect, ingenuity, acumen ≠ stupidity

witch NOUN = **enchantress**, magician, hag, crone, sorceress, Wiccan

witchcraft NOUN = **magic**, voodoo, wizardry, black magic, enchantment, occultism, sorcery, Wicca, makutu (*N.Z.*)

withdraw VERB 1 = **remove**, take off, pull out, extract, take away, pull back, draw out, draw back 2 = **take out**, extract, draw out

withdrawal NOUN = **removal**, ending, stopping, taking away, abolition, elimination, cancellation, termination

withdrawn ADJECTIVE = **uncommunicative**, reserved, retiring, distant, shy, taciturn, introverted, unforthcoming ≠ outgoing

wither VERB 1 = **wilt**, decline, decay, disintegrate, perish, shrivel ≠ flourish 2 = **waste**, decline, shrivel 3 = **fade**, decline, perish ≠ increase

withering ADJECTIVE = **scornful**, devastating, humiliating, snubbing, hurtful, mortifying

withhold VERB 1 = **keep secret**, refuse, hide, reserve, retain, conceal, suppress, hold back ≠ reveal 2 = **hold back**, suppress, keep back ≠ release

withstand VERB = **resist**, suffer, bear, oppose, cope with, endure, tolerate, stand up to ≠ give in to

witness NOUN 1 = **observer**, viewer, spectator, looker-on, watcher, onlooker, eyewitness, bystander 2 = **testifier**
▷ VERB 1 = **see**, view, watch, note, notice, observe, perceive 2 = **countersign**, sign, endorse, validate

witty ADJECTIVE = **humorous**, funny, clever, amusing, sparkling, whimsical, droll, piquant ≠ dull

wizard NOUN = **magician**, witch, shaman, sorcerer, occultist, magus, conjuror, warlock, tohunga (*N.Z.*)

wobble VERB 1 = **shake**, rock, sway, tremble, teeter, totter 2 = **tremble**, shake
▷ NOUN 1 = **unsteadiness**, shake, tremble 2 = **unsteadiness**, shake, tremor

woe NOUN 1 = **misery**, distress, grief, agony, gloom, sadness, sorrow, anguish ≠ happiness 2 = **problem**, grief, misery, sorrow

woman NOUN =**lady**, girl, female, sheila (*Austral. & N.Z. informal*), vrou (*S. African*), adult female, charlie (*Austral. slang*), chook (*Austral. slang*), wahine (*N.Z.*) ≠ man

womanly ADJECTIVE
1 =**feminine**, motherly, female, warm, tender, matronly, ladylike 2 =**curvaceous**, ample, voluptuous, shapely, curvy (*informal*), busty (*informal*), buxom, full-figured

wonder VERB 1 =**think**, question, puzzle, speculate, query, ponder, meditate, conjecture 2 =**be amazed**, stare, marvel, be astonished, gape
▷ NOUN 1 =**amazement**, surprise, admiration, awe, fascination, astonishment, bewilderment, wonderment
2 =**phenomenon**, sight, miracle, spectacle, curiosity, marvel, prodigy, rarity

wonderful ADJECTIVE
1 =**excellent**, great (*informal*), brilliant, outstanding, superb, fantastic (*informal*), tremendous, magnificent, booshit (*Austral. slang*), exo (*Austral. slang*), sik (*Austral. slang*), rad (*informal*), phat (*slang*), schmick (*Austral. informal*) ≠ terrible 2 =**remarkable**, amazing, extraordinary, incredible, astonishing, staggering, startling, phenomenal ≠ ordinary

woo VERB 1 =**seek**, cultivate 2 =**court**, pursue

wood NOUN 1 =**timber**, planks, planking, lumber (*U.S.*)
2 =**woodland**, forest, grove, thicket, copse, coppice, bushland 3 =**firewood**, fuel, logs, kindling

wooded ADJECTIVE =**tree-covered**, forested, timbered, sylvan (*poetic*), tree-clad

wooden ADJECTIVE 1 =**made of wood**, timber, woody, ligneous 2 =**expressionless**, lifeless, deadpan, unresponsive

wool NOUN 1 =**fleece**, hair, coat 2 =**yarn**

word NOUN 1 =**term**, name, expression 2 =**chat**, tête-à-tête, talk, discussion, consultation, confab (*informal*), heart-to-heart, powwow (*informal*) 3 =**comment**, remark, utterance 4 =**message**, news, report, information, notice, intelligence, dispatch, communiqué, heads up (*U.S. & Canad.*) 5 =**promise**, guarantee, pledge, vow, assurance, oath 6 =**command**, order, decree, bidding, mandate
▷ VERB =**express**, say, state, put, phrase, utter, couch, formulate
▷ RELATED WORDS: *adjective* **lexical, verbal**

wording NOUN =**phraseology**, words, language, phrasing, terminology

work VERB 1 =**be employed**, be in work 2 =**labour**, sweat, slave, toil, slog (away), drudge, peg away, exert yourself ≠ relax 3 =**function**, go, run, operate, be in working order ≠ be out of

w

order **4** = **succeed**, work out, pay off (*informal*), be successful, be effective, do the trick (*informal*), do the business (*informal*), get results **5** = **cultivate**, farm, dig, till, plough **6** = **operate**, use, move, control, drive, manage, handle, manipulate **7** = **manipulate**, form, fashion, shape, mould, knead

▷ **NOUN 1** = **employment**, business, job, trade, duty, profession, occupation, livelihood ≠ play **2** = **effort**, industry, labour, sweat, toil, exertion, drudgery, elbow grease (*facetious*) ≠ leisure **3** = **task**, jobs, projects, commissions, duties, assignments, chores, yakka (*Austral. & N.Z. informal*) **4** = **handiwork**, doing, act, feat, deed **5** = **creation**, piece, production, opus, achievement, composition, handiwork

▷ **PHRASE**: work out = **solve**, find out, calculate, figure out

worker NOUN = **employee**, hand, labourer, workman, craftsman, artisan, tradesman

workman NOUN = **labourer**, hand, worker, employee, mechanic, operative, craftsman, artisan

works PLURAL NOUN **1** = **factory**, plant, mill, workshop **2** = **writings**, output, canon, oeuvre (*French*) **3** = **mechanism**, workings, parts, action, movement, machinery

workshop NOUN **1** = **factory**,
plant, mill **2** = **workroom**, studio

world NOUN **1** = **earth**, planet, globe **2** = **mankind**, man, everyone, the public, everybody, humanity, humankind **3** = **sphere**, area, field, environment, realm, domain

▷ **PHRASE**: a world of = **a huge amount of**, a mountain of, a wealth of, a great deal of, a good deal of, an abundance of, an enormous amount of, a vast amount of

worldly ADJECTIVE **1** = **earthly**, physical, secular, terrestrial, temporal, profane ≠ spiritual **2** = **materialistic**, grasping, selfish, greedy ≠ nonmaterialistic **3** = **worldly-wise**, knowing, experienced, sophisticated, cosmopolitan, urbane, blasé ≠ naive

worn ADJECTIVE = **ragged**, frayed, shabby, tattered, tatty, threadbare, the worse for wear

worried ADJECTIVE = **anxious**, concerned, troubled, afraid, frightened, nervous, tense, uneasy ≠ unworried

worry VERB **1** = **be anxious**, be concerned, be worried, obsess, brood, fret, agonize, get in a lather (*informal*) ≠ be unconcerned **2** = **trouble**, upset, bother, disturb, annoy, unsettle, pester, vex ≠ soothe

▷ **NOUN 1** = **anxiety**, concern, fear, trouble, unease, apprehension, misgiving, trepidation ≠ peace of mind

w

2 = **problem**, care, trouble, bother, hassle (*informal*)

worsen VERB **1** = **deteriorate**, decline, sink, decay, get worse, degenerate, go downhill (*informal*) ≠ improve **2** = **aggravate**, damage, exacerbate, make worse ≠ improve

worship VERB **1** = **revere**, praise, honour, adore, glorify, exalt, pray to, venerate ≠ dishonour **2** = **love**, adore, idolize, put on a pedestal ≠ despise ▷ NOUN = **reverence**, praise, regard, respect, honour, glory, devotion, adulation

worth NOUN **1** = **value**, price, rate, cost, estimate, valuation ≠ worthlessness **2** = **merit**, value, quality, importance, excellence, goodness, worthiness ≠ unworthiness **3** = **usefulness**, value, quality, importance, excellence, goodness ≠ uselessness

worthless ADJECTIVE **1** = **valueless**, rubbishy, negligible ≠ valuable **2** = **useless**, unimportant, ineffectual, negligible ≠ useful **3** = **good-for-nothing**, vile, despicable, contemptible ≠ honourable

worthwhile ADJECTIVE = **useful**, valuable, helpful, profitable, productive, beneficial, meaningful, constructive ≠ useless

worthy ADJECTIVE = **praiseworthy**, deserving, valuable, worthwhile, admirable, virtuous, creditable, laudable ≠ disreputable

would-be ADJECTIVE = **budding**, self-styled, wannabe (*informal*), unfulfilled, self-appointed

wound NOUN **1** = **injury**, cut, hurt, trauma (*pathology*), gash, lesion, laceration **2** *often plural* = **trauma**, offence, slight, insult ▷ VERB **1** = **injure**, cut, wing, hurt, pierce, gash, lacerate **2** = **offend**, hurt, annoy, sting, mortify, cut to the quick

wrangle VERB = **argue**, fight, row, dispute, disagree, contend, quarrel, squabble ▷ NOUN = **argument**, row, dispute, quarrel, squabble, bickering, tiff, altercation

wrap VERB **1** = **cover**, enclose, shroud, swathe, encase, enfold, bundle up **2** = **pack**, package, parcel (up), tie up, gift-wrap ≠ unpack **3** = **bind**, swathe ≠ unwind ▷ NOUN **1** = **cloak**, cape, stole, mantle, shawl ▷ PHRASE: **wrap something up 1** = **giftwrap**, pack, package, bundle up **2** (*informal*) = **end**, conclude, wind up, terminate, finish off, round off, polish off

wrath NOUN = **anger**, rage, temper, fury, resentment, indignation, ire, displeasure ≠ satisfaction

wreck VERB **1** = **destroy**, break, smash, ruin, devastate, shatter, spoil, demolish, kennet (*Austral. slang*), jeff (*Austral. slang*) ≠ build

w

2 = **spoil**, ruin, devastate, shatter, crool *or* cruel (*Austral. slang*) ≠ save

▷ NOUN 1 = **shipwreck**, hulk 2 (*wreckage*) = **remains**, pieces, ruin, fragments, debris, rubble

wrench VERB 1 = **twist**, force, pull, tear, rip, tug, jerk, yank

2 = **sprain**, strain, rick

▷ NOUN 1 = **twist**, pull, rip, tug, jerk, yank 2 = **sprain**, strain, twist 3 = **blow**, shock, upheaval, pang 4 = **spanner**, adjustable spanner

wrestle VERB = **fight**, battle, struggle, combat, grapple, tussle, scuffle

wrinkle NOUN 1 = **line**, fold, crease, furrow, crow's-foot, corrugation 2 = **crease**, fold, crumple, furrow, crinkle, corrugation

▷ VERB = **crease**, gather, fold, crumple, furrow, rumple, pucker, corrugate ≠ smooth

writ NOUN = **summons**, document, decree, indictment, court order, subpoena, arraignment

write VERB 1 = **record**, scribble, inscribe, set down, jot down

2 = **compose**, draft, pen, draw up 3 = **correspond**, get in touch, keep in touch, write a letter, drop a line, drop a note, e-mail

writer NOUN = **author**, novelist, hack, scribbler, scribe, wordsmith, penpusher

▷ *see* **dramatists, novelists, poets**

writing NOUN = **script**, hand, printing, fist (*informal*), scribble, handwriting, scrawl, calligraphy

wrong ADJECTIVE 1 = **amiss**, faulty, unsatisfactory, not right, defective, awry

2 = **incorrect**, mistaken, false, inaccurate, untrue, erroneous, wide of the mark, fallacious

3 = **inappropriate**, incorrect, unsuitable, unacceptable, undesirable, incongruous, unseemly, unbecoming ≠ correct

4 = **bad**, criminal, illegal, evil, unlawful, immoral, unjust, dishonest ≠ moral 5 = **defective**, faulty, awry, askew

▷ ADVERB 1 = **incorrectly**, badly, wrongly, mistakenly, erroneously, inaccurately ≠ correctly

2 = **amiss**, astray, awry, askew

▷ NOUN = **offence**, injury, crime, error, sin, injustice, misdeed, transgression ≠ good deed

▷ VERB = **mistreat**, abuse, hurt, harm, cheat, take advantage of, oppress, malign ≠ treat well

X-ray NOUN = **radiograph**, x-ray image

Yy

yank VERB = **pull**, tug, jerk, seize, snatch, pluck, hitch, wrench
▷ NOUN = **pull**, tug, jerk, snatch, hitch, wrench, tweak

yarn NOUN 1 = **thread**, fibre, cotton, wool 2 (*informal*) = **story**, tale, anecdote, account, narrative, fable, reminiscence, urban myth

yawning ADJECTIVE = **gaping**, wide, huge, vast, cavernous

yearly ADJECTIVE = **annual**, each year, every year, once a year
▷ ADVERB = **annually**, every year, by the year, once a year, per annum

yearn VERB *often with* **for** = **long**, desire, hunger, ache, crave, covet, itch, hanker after

yell VERB = **scream**, shout, cry out, howl, call out, wail, shriek, screech ≠ whisper
▷ NOUN = **scream**, cry, shout, roar, howl, shriek, whoop, screech

≠ whisper

yellow NOUN = **lemon**, gold, amber
▷ ADJECTIVE
● WORD POWER
● *Yellow* is a colour which is often associated with the sun, warmth, and positivity. Conversely, there are a number of negative connotations associated with this colour to do with ageing, sickness, jealousy, cowardice, and betrayal. Paper yellows with age and plants turn yellow when they are diseased. Some illnesses, such as jaundice, cause yellowing in the skin. Formerly, jealousy was associated with yellow, because of the meaning 'jaundiced, biased in view', though this symbolism has now transferred to the colour green. The most common modern figurative meaning is that of cowardice. The slang term *yellow-belly* was used in the U.S. from the early 20th century to mean cowardly,

● SHADES OF YELLOW

amber	lemon	saffron
buff	maize	straw
canary yellow	mustard	tea rose
champagne	oatmeal	topaz
cinnamon	ochre	tortoiseshell
daffodil	old gold	
gold *or* golden	primrose	

thought to be derived from the yellow underside of some animals and birds. Yellow has also been the colour of betrayal in Christian religious symbolism, with Judas portrayed by painters over the ages wearing a yellow cloak.

yen NOUN = **longing**, desire, craving, yearning, passion, hunger, ache, itch

yet ADVERB 1 = **so far**, until now, up to now, still, as yet, even now, thus far, up till now 2 = **now**, right now, just now, so soon 3 = **still**, in addition, besides, to boot, into the bargain

▷ CONJUNCTION = **nevertheless**, still, however, for all that, notwithstanding, just the same, be that as it may

● WORD POWER

● Yiddish is a language spoken mainly by Jews in Europe and America, and is a mixture of German, Hebrew, and Slavic languages. Yiddish has contributed many distinctive words to English; many of these remain slang words used primarily in the U.S.. A group of loan words from Yiddish and German have a characteristic 'sh' sound at the beginning: *shemozzle*, *schmuck*, *schlep*, *schlock*, *schmaltz*, *schmooze*, *shtick*, *shlub*. *Schmooze*, literally 'chat', means to talk to someone for the purpose of self-promotion, e.g. This

was his chance to schmooze producers, distributors, and agents. Its onomatopoeic quality and similarity to 'ooze', have perhaps given schmooze connotations of insincere flattery, but it can simply mean to hobnob or mingle. Another word which has entered English from Yiddish is *schmaltz*. Literally 'melted fat', it refers to an animal fat used in cookery. It also means excessive sentimentality, especially in the arts, e.g. Finally, a boxing movie that doesn't descend into schmaltz or heroism. The widespread use of this word has also spawned the adjective *schmaltzy*. It is interesting to note that many of the synonyms for sentimental also refer to fatty, sweet, or creamy foodstuffs, e.g. cheesy, gooey, syrupy, saccharine. This food metaphor is often exploited in text: writers talk about drowning in schmaltz, and generous helpings of schmaltz, showing that its double meaning is still known.

yield VERB 1 = **bow**, submit, give in, surrender, succumb, cave in (*informal*), capitulate 2 = **relinquish**, resign, hand over, surrender, turn over, make over, give over, bequeath ≠ retain 3 = **produce**, give, provide, return, supply, bear, net, earn ≠ use up

y

▷ NOUN 1 = **produce**, crop, harvest, output 2 = **profit**, return, income, revenue, earnings, takings ≠ loss ≠ resist

yielding ADJECTIVE 1 = **soft**, pliable, springy, elastic, supple, spongy, unresisting 2 = **submissive**, obedient, compliant, docile, flexible, accommodating, pliant, acquiescent ≠ obstinate

yob *or* **yobbo** NOUN = **thug**, hooligan, lout, hoon (*Austral. & N.Z. slang*), ruffian, roughneck (*slang*), tsotsi (*S. African*), cougan (*Austral. slang*), scozza (*Austral. slang*), bogan (*Austral. slang*)

young ADJECTIVE 1 = **immature**, juvenile, youthful, little, green, junior, infant, adolescent ≠ old 2 = **early**, new, undeveloped, fledgling ≠ advanced ▷ NOUN = **offspring**, baby, litter, family, issue, brood, progeny ≠ parent

youngster NOUN = **youth**, girl, boy, kid (*informal*), lad, teenager, juvenile, lass

youth NOUN 1 = **immaturity**, adolescence, boyhood *or* girlhood, salad days ≠ old age 2 = **boy**, lad, youngster, kid (*informal*), teenager, young man, adolescent, teen (*informal*) ≠ adult

youthful ADJECTIVE = **young**, juvenile, childish, immature, boyish, girlish ≠ elderly

Zz

zeal NOUN = **enthusiasm**, passion, zest, spirit, verve, fervour, eagerness, gusto ≠ apathy

zero NOUN 1 = **nought**, nothing, nil 2 = **rock bottom**, the bottom, an all-time low, a nadir, as low as you can get

zip VERB 1 = **speed**, shoot, fly, flash, zoom, whizz (*informal*) . 2 (~ *data*) = **compress** (*computing*), archive (*computing*) ≠ unzip
▷ NOUN (*informal*) = **energy**, drive, vigour, verve, zest, gusto, liveliness ≠ lethargy

zone NOUN = **area**, region, section, sector, district, territory, belt, sphere

zoom VERB = **speed**, shoot, fly, rush, flash, dash, whizz (*informal*), hurtle

LANGUAGE
FOR LIFE

CONTENTS

INTRODUCTION

A dictionary can tell you what a word means and when it can be used accurately. It cannot, though, give you guidance on how to write clearly and appropriately in a variety of situations. The *Collins Language for Life* has been written to help you express yourself effectively at work and at home. It includes advice on how to structure your writing, and how to adapt tone, style and content to different forms of communication – from letters and emails to social media.

BEFORE YOU START WRITING

It is amazing how much more effective your writing will be with a bit of thinking time beforehand. There are three questions which you should be able to answer about any piece of writing, whether it's an email, text, letter or post:

- **Who am I writing to?** This will determine the style and tone that you use. If you are writing an email to a friend, for instance, then you are likely to use less formal language than if you are writing to apply for a job.

- **What do I want to say?** Make sure that all the information you want to communicate is included, and that it is set out as clearly as possible.

- **Why do I want to say it?** In other words, what do you want to happen as a result of your communication? Whether it's for a job application, to ask someone out on a date, or to offer your condolences for a bereavement, what you want to achieve should be clearly stated.

Once you've answered these questions, writing becomes much easier.

Tone

The tone of your writing expresses your attitude towards the reader. To achieve the tone you want, consider the following questions:

- If you were talking to your reader, what tone would your voice have?

- Is the language you are using too simple (patronising) or too difficult (pompous)?

- What is your relationship to the reader, are they your employer (formal, professional tone) or friend (informal, chatty tone)?

Then read through your writing to make sure it conveys the tone you intended.

Here are some tips for making your writing successful and some common traps to avoid.

👍 Tips:

- **Use plain English.** Aim for concise, simple expression which will make your writing easy to read.

- **Plan.** Think about what you want to say, and how you want to say it. Planning will save you time and make your writing more effective. It needn't take a lot of time but, even if you're writing a text message, it will pay dividends.

- **Vary the length of your sentences.** Short sentences are powerful. Longer sentences can express more complicated thoughts, but try to keep them to a manageable length or else they become tiring to read! Try to stick to the principle of including one main idea in a sentence, and maybe one related point.

- **Use active rather than passive verbs.** It is usually better to use active verbs because it makes your writing simpler and less stuffy to read:
  The programme was watched by an audience of 13 million people (passive)
  13 million people watched the programme (active).
  The verb 'watched' is 'active' in the second example because it is linked to the subject - '13 million people'. The sentence is shorter and clearer as a result.

- **Read your work aloud.** If the sentences work well, it will be easy to read. Check that you have commas where there are natural pauses.

- **Think about register and tone.** Are you using the right level of formality ('register')? Does your writing accurately express your attitude to the subject and the reader ('tone')? How you address a best friend will be different from how you write to a potential employer.

- **Always check your writing before sending it – and then check it again!** You'll be surprised how easy it is to overlook mistakes. Computers have introduced new errors – for instance, did you delete the original passage that you copied and pasted later in the document? If you correct one word in a sentence, make sure the rest of it still makes sense.

> *I wish people would read through what they have written before pressing 'send'. It would save me a lot of time and make their applications more successful.*
>
> (HR manager)

Traps:

- **Jargon.** Specialist words which are understood by a particular group of people, or overly technical language. Don't talk about 'interfacing' with someone, if you simply mean 'talking' to them.

- **Clichés.** Words or phrases that are used too often, and have little meaning. They will annoy your reader and distract from what you are trying to say. Examples include sayings like, '*A different kettle of fish*,' and '*At the end of the day*'.

- **Long sentences.** Avoid sentences longer than 15-20 words – they can be difficult to read, and can usually be divided into clearer statements. If your sentences work well, they will be easy to read.

- **Repeating words.** Using the same word more than once in a sentence can be clumsy, and there is usually an alternative. For instance, '*The date of the English exam is the same date as the French exam*,' sounds better as, '*The English and the French exams are on the same date*.'

- **Long words.** Avoid using long or complex words for the sake of it, they can be replaced by shorter, clearer ones. For example using 'proffer' when you mean 'give' or 'articulate' when you mean 'say'.

- **Redundancy.** Avoid using ten words where two will do: '*I am meeting Sophie later*,' is clearer than, '*Sophie and I are due to hook up together at some point in the day*.' Also avoid **tautology** – saying the same thing twice: '*10 a.m. in the morning*' is either '*10 a.m.*' or '*10 in the morning*.'

- **Ambiguity.** Many words can be understood in more than one way. So, '*Clarice was really cold*' could mean that Clarice was unfriendly or that she was shivering. Put yourself in the reader's place to make sure that the meaning of your statement is clear.

- **Causing offence.** A simple rule to follow is: *treat everyone equally in your writing, regardless of sex, age, race, sexual orientation, or physical difference*. Be aware of current customs and values, and also consider different cultures. This is especially relevant if you are communicating with people around the world.

These are only a few points to consider before you start writing, but if you refer to them regularly, they will help you express yourself clearly and consistently in all your communications.

EMAIL

Emails are the primary form of written communication in many people's lives. Whether at home or at work, we spend a lot of our time sending and receiving them. Email correspondence can feel more like a conversation than an exchange of letters. The tone is generally less formal, and the time between sending your message and getting a reply can be minutes or even seconds. The fact that it is instant can be good and bad. Good because it can be a very efficient way of corresponding; bad if you write quickly and carelessly.

Addressing emails

When addressing emails, the general rule of thumb is that the fewer people you email, the better. There are three address fields to consider, and each serves a different purpose:

- **'To':** this is for the address of the main recipient, or recipients, of the information or request to do something.

- **'CC':** if you are simply informing someone of your actions or requests, put those people in the 'CC' ('Carbon or Courtesy Copy') field.

- **'BCC':** if you are copying someone in but you don't want the other addressees to know you should use the 'BCC' ('Blind Carbon or Courtesy Copy'). This is frequently used for mailing large groups, where you don't want individuals to know who else is receiving the email.

  Bear in mind that if you send an email to one person you are 95 per cent likely to get a reply; if you send it to 10 people the response rate drops to 5 per cent.

  (Linguistics professor)

Greeting and ending

Emails on work-related issues or personal business require a formal style. You can never go wrong with 'Dear Mr Blake' or 'Dear Peter'. If the contact is long-standing and you are on a familiar footing then 'Hi Peter' is acceptable. In initial exchanges of email it is usual to sign off in the same way that you would in a formal letter with 'Yours sincerely' or 'Yours faithfully'. As your correspondence gets onto a slightly less formal footing then 'Kind regards' or 'Best wishes' is fine.

Subject line

You can really help your correspondents by being precise in the subject line. For example if you send out a regular set of minutes by email, don't just write 'Launch Meeting Minutes', add the date so people can quickly find what they are looking for. If your email contains a specific question it is good practice to add 'Q:' followed by the question in the subject line.

Layout

Use a paragraph per point you wish to make, and put headings above each paragraph if there are more than three. If your email is long and will require the reader to scroll down the screen, consider writing it as a Word document and attaching it to an email – long emails are not easy to read and respond to.

Content

Always remember that with email, your writing can be forwarded to anyone with a single mouse click. Be careful that what you write is not defamatory, offensive, or detrimental to you or your business.

> *Never forward without reading the whole email: you never know what indiscretions or traps are in there. Never put anything in an email you don't want the world to know.*

(Local authority manager)

- Restrict the email to a single subject. If you want to email the same person or people about other issues, use separate emails. It makes filing and action points much easier to follow.

- Don't reply straight away to an email that irks you. You will not be able to hide your anger and will not make the situation better. Wait until you have calmed down enough to think through your response and compose a measured reply dealing with the points raised.

- Don't assume that the person you are writing to has the same cultural reference points, sense of humour, or values.

> *I know of people who communicate regularly with colleagues in Italy, where capitalization is used to show something is urgent whereas we read it as shouting.*

(Marketing executive)

Attachments

Email is great for spreading information held in spreadsheets, pdfs and Word documents. But sending large attachments can cause headaches. Most email providers (and certainly most companies) allocate a storage limit to each email address; if an Inbox becomes too full, you cannot receive or send emails. So be considerate when you send anything as an attachment.

Replying

Sometimes you get an email which contains a series of questions. It is perfectly acceptable to reply to each of these questions by adding your comments (sometimes in a different colour or with your initials in square brackets before your answer) in the body of the original email. This saves you typing out the questions or writing replies that incorporate the original question. For example:

From: Asif Iqbal
To: Fiona McManus
SUBJECT: My paintings

Dear Fiona
Thank you very much for your email about the posters I sell. I've put my answers below your questions with [AI] after.

With thanks and all best wishes

Asif
Mobile: 011111 789456
www.asifiqbal.art.gallery.net

Do you have a website?
[AI] Yes. You can see all my work at www.asifiqbal.art.gallery.net
What sizes do the posters come in?
[AI] Anything from A5 to A1. I can also frame them to order – there's a selection of frames on the website.
What range of prices are there?
[AI] Prices start at $AUS 11.95 and can go up to $AUS 75.00
If you don't have a poster I want in stock, can you source it for me?
[AI] Of course, I'd be happy to help in any way. Have a look through the website and If you can't find what you want, just drop me a line and I'll do my best!

Formal email

The rules for writing formal emails are similar to those for formal letters.

- If you are communicating with someone for the first time you should adopt the structure of a formal letter.

- It is usual and proper to use a greeting of some sort when you begin your email. 'Dear' can never be misunderstood and rarely strikes the wrong note. If you are more familiar with the person you are writing to 'Hi' or 'Hello' is fine. If you're writing to close friends then use whichever greeting you are accustomed to in your social circle.

- If you are emailing someone for the first time without being invited to it is always proper to explain at the very start of the email who you are and why you are writing to them.

- Never leave the subject line blank. In most formal or professional correspondence you should aim to keep the email to one subject. Think clearly what the email is about and be as precise as you can. Keep the subject as short as possible as most people's inbox can only display a limited amount of the line.

- If the email is going to be long it is polite to indicate this in the opening few sentences of the email.

- Structure your email so that each point is addressed in a separate paragraph. If you wish, it is entirely acceptable to add a heading to each paragraph. Your reader can then see at a glance the points you are covering.

- In formal emails, texting abbreviations and emoticons should be avoided.

- When you end your email use the same rules as with formal letters, using 'Yours faithfully' or 'Yours sincerely' as appropriate.

> *I avoid using multiple sub-clauses and long sentences and use lists or bullet points rather than block text.*
>
> (Marketing manager)

Informal emails

For emails to friends and family you can be more relaxed in your style and tone.

- 'Hi' or 'Hey' or other informal greetings are appropriate and you can sign off the email with 'See you' or 'lots of love' or other phrases.

- Even when you're writing to a friend remember that email can seem terse and abrupt if there is no greeting or sign-off.

- It is fine to use texting abbreviations and emoticons in informal emails – just make sure the person you're writing to understands them all!

> *I read the email back to myself as though I were reading someone else's email prior to sending.*
>
> (Course co-ordinator)

JOB APPLICATIONS

A covering letter and CV are usually the first things any prospective employer will see of you. If you want to get an interview for a job, it is important that these documents present you in the best possible light. The following sections deal with how to construct and write your covering letter and CV, and provide tips on how to apply for a job online.

Covering letter

The covering letter should convey confidence, enthusiasm, technical knowledge and demonstrate an understanding of what the job entails. It need not be long and it should not be a rehash of the accompanying CV. A short, clear, well-written covering letter can make all the difference between two candidates.

> *Some people think the covering letter is another CV. It's not. A covering letter is a way of introducing yourself to the employer and of providing a persuasive case for reading the CV and then getting an interview.*
> (HR Director)

The covering letter should alert the employer to the key points of a CV and show the match between the candidate and the job being advertised. In general it will consist of three paragraphs or so:

- **First paragraph.** Introduce yourself, say which job you are applying for and where you saw it. You can also include a general statement of why you want to apply for the job and how you feel about the company.

- **Second paragraph.** Provide information about your skills, strengths, qualifications and experience. Give specific examples of why you are the ideal candidate and don't simply restate your CV.

- **Final paragraph.** Conclude the letter expressing your desire to get the job and requesting an interview. You should also say what the best way to contact you is, and if there are any inconvenient dates. Always thank the employer for their time in considering your application.

FAQ

Q. *Should my letter be typed or handwritten?*
A. It should be typed on A4 paper. Only the signature should be handwritten.

Q. *To whom should I address my letter?*
A. If you do not know the name of the person who would deal with your application, call the company to find out their name.

Q. *Is it OK to send out the same letter to all those companies I'm interested in?*
A. No. Try to avoid general letters. Find out as much as you can about the company, and tailor your letter accordingly.

Q. *Should I mention salary in my accompanying letter?*
A. It is usually best not to touch on the subject of salary at this stage, unless requested in the advertisement.

Useful phrases

First of all, identify the job you are applying for:

- I would like to inquire as to whether there are any openings for junior telesales operators in your company.

- I am writing to apply for the post of senior marketing manager.

- I would like to apply for the position of online learning coordinator, as advertised on your website.

- I am writing to apply for the above post, as advertised in the Guardian of 8 August 2009.

Next, give some examples of personal achievements:

- I have gained experience in several major aspects of publishing.

- I co-ordinated the change-over from one accounting system to another.

- I developed designs for a new range of knitwear.

- I have supervised a team of telesales operators on several projects.

- I contributed to the development of our new database software.

Then outline your personal qualities:

- I see myself as systematic and meticulous in my approach to work.

- I am a fair and broad-minded person, with an ability to get on well with people from all walks of life.

- I am hardworking and business minded, and I tend to thrive under pressure.

Explain why you want this job:

- I am now keen to find a post with more responsibility.

- I now wish to find a more permanent full-time position.

- I would like to further my career in the field of production.

- I feel that your company's activities most closely match my own values and interests.

Express your willingness to attend an interview.

Here is an example covering letter:

Mr J Manners
15 Sandybank Drive
Derby
DX27 9LC
Joelmanners@email.com
01245 645201

27 July 2011

Mr H Carson
Personnel Manager
Allied Derby Building Society
HR House
Illingworth Way
DERBY
DX3 9DF

Dear Mr Carson

Customer Services Manager

I am responding to the job advertised in the *Derby Express* and on your website on the 22nd July. I feel the job is just what I have been looking for, and reading the job description, I am sure that I have the right level of experience, aptitude and training. Your company's support and promotion of ethical investment has always impressed and inspired me and I would very much like to contribute to your success. My CV is attached.

For the past three years I have been Senior Customer Services Adviser at Cathedral County Bank, leading a team of seven people. Since I took on the role our positive response rate has risen by 10 per cent and customer satisfaction in the area I look after by 15 per cent. I was voted Employee of the Month three times by my colleagues in the period. While I am very happy in my job, the opportunities for promotion are limited and I do want to take on a more responsible role in my area of expertise.

I would welcome the opportunity to discuss my application further. Email is the best way to contact me and I am available for interview at your convenience. Thank you for taking the time to read my application.

Yours sincerely

Mr Joel Manners

Mr Joel Manners

- Avoid just sending a letter or email with 'Please find my CV attached'. Remember that this application is a two-stage process to try to get an interview. Each step in the process (covering letter and CV) has to make the employer want to take the next step.

- Remember the basics:
  - check all spelling and grammar two or three times
  - make sure you have spelled all names correctly
  - include all contact details
  - include any information that the job advertisement has specifically asked you to provide.

A speculative job application

- When applying for a job on a speculative basis, try to speak to the person responsible for recruitment in the appropriate department beforehand. This way, you will have a specific person to write to, as well as having established a relationship with them.

34 St Dunstan's Way
Vancouver
V6G 7D7

19 July 2011

Ms D Wallis
Youngs Accountancy and Finance
19 Lockwood Road
Vancouver
V9P 8K1

Dear Ms Wallis

post of software development co-ordinator

Thank you very much for taking the time to speak to me yesterday about the possibility of a position as software development co-ordinator with your company.

Please find attached a CV which highlights my prior professional experience, and the qualities which I feel make me suited to this position. You will see that I have a strong interest in, and knowledge of, staff management, and have gained extensive experience in handling large development projects and meeting deadlines.

I see myself as being well-organized and self-motivated, and have excellent communication skills. I am keen to develop my career with Youngs Accountancy and Finance, and so would very much appreciate the opportunity to discuss further my suitability for the post.

Please feel free to contact me, either by email: dgormanl@netserve.com, or by leaving a message on (604) 473 5522. I look forward to speaking to you soon.

Yours sincerely

D Gorman

Deborah Gorman

CV

Your CV exists to give a brief description of who you are, what you have done and what you can do.

> *What a lot of candidates forget is that the purpose of the CV is to get*
> *the interview – not the job. So they give way too much detail and don't*
> *tailor it to the role they are trying to get.*
>
> (HR Director)

- The language should always be 'active'. Avoid passive statements like 'Turnover growth of 25 per cent was achieved in the period,' say instead, 'I increased turnover for the period by 25 per cent.' Active language simplifies your statements and makes them easier to read.

- Use positive adverbs ('efficiently', 'successfully' 'effectively') so that your CV will convey a positive impression to your prospective employer.

CV structure

The most common CV format is called 'reverse chronological', meaning you start with your current job and work backwards. If your earliest jobs have little relevance to your current application, you can simply list the job title, company and the dates you worked there. Summarize your education after the employment section, and then add any additional skills and interests that may be of use to support your application.

You can see a sample CV on the next page:

Helena Shapur

12 Green Lane, Brighton, Sussex BT1 3EY
Email: h.sharpur@email.com
Mobile: 07123 456789

Personal profile

An enthusiastic, self-motivated professional, highly qualified in the field of online team management. My motivation is to use the web to help make the most of all businesses I work for. I have an in-depth understanding of a wide range of web technologies from Java to Flash.

Career summary

2008 - present Development Team Leader, GoGetting.com

I joined the online travel company GoGetting.com as a development officer before being promoted in August 2010 to my current position. Since becoming team leader the site has had a threefold increase in unique visitors thanks to an extensive linking program I developed. As a result of the increased traffic, the company has given me extra responsibility to drive the marketing of the site with selected web partners. I manage a team of seven development officers and am in charge of a budget of £250,000.

2004 - 2008 Web Developer, Toprank Recruitment

Having learned a lot at my first company and really enjoyed the experience of working in web development, I joined this small recruitment start-up specializing in the catering trade. During the time I helped program the site's search engine and learned ASP, Java and SQL.
I was very proud to have seen one key module of the search engine's development through from design to implementation. The module generated five per cent extra revenue for the company while I was there. I learned a lot about effective teamwork in the process.

2002-2004 Junior programmer, Oakhampton Systems

This was a perfect job after graduation. I was part of a small graduate intake whose job was to develop and code account and customer databases. I went on site visits to understand what a client needed and understand the way the business works. I taught myself HTML in this period and designed the company's first website.

Education and qualifications

1998-2001 University of Windsor, BSC Computer Science (2:1)
1991 – 1998 Greenglades School, Windsor
3 A-levels: Mathematics (A*), Physics (A), Chemistry (B)
10 O-levels

Hobbies and interests

Between leaving school and starting university I worked for six months so that I could spend three months doing charity runs for Famine Relief, whom I continue to work for as a volunteer. I run long-distance competitively, enjoy cinema, computer games and chess.

References available on request

> *One of the worst mistakes a candidate can make is to send employers a 6-page 'novel' about their work experience, school qualification and hobbies and pastimes - especially if it is written in size-9 font. Many managers skim read CVs so using short paragraphs and an almost report-like style will mean they are less likely to miss a candidate with relevant skills or experience. This is where editing down and making the CV relate to the job description/advert works to the candidate's advantage.*
>
> (HR Director)

BASIC GRADUATE CV

CV

Name	Kate Maxwell
Date of birth	29.02.85
Address	19, The Poplars, Bristol B10 2JU
Telephone	0117 123 4567
Email	katemaxwell@atlantic.net
Nationality	British

Education

2004–2008	**BA Hons in Modern Languages, University of Exeter** (final grade 2.1)
2002–2004	**Clifton Road Secondary School:** 3 'A' levels – French (A) German (A) History (B)
1997–2002	**Clifton Road Secondary School:** 8 GCSEs including Maths and English

Employment history

2004–2005	**Sales Assistant, Langs Bookshop, Bristol** I was responsible for training and supervising weekend and holiday staff.
2005–2006	**English Assistant, Lycée Benoit, Lyons** I taught conversational English to pupils aged 12-18, preparing the older students for both technical and more academic qualifications. I organized an educational trip to the UK for fourth year pupils.

Positions of responsibility held

2005–2006	**Entertainments Officer for University Student Social Society** I organized and budgeted for entertainment for a student society with over 1000 members.
2004–2007	**Captain of the university women's netball team** I was in charge of training, organizing and motivating the woman's team.

Other skills

Fluent French and German
Extensive knowledge of Microsoft Word, Excel and Access
I hold a clean driving licence

References

on request

Top ten CV tips

1. Adapt your CV to the job or prospective employer.

2. You have 30-60 seconds to attract your reader's attention so lay out your CV clearly - use a plain typeface like Ariel, Trebuchet or Times New Roman – and keep it to the point. It should not be longer than 3 sides.

3. Remember the CV is a means of getting an interview not getting the job.

4. Avoid gimmicks like thumbnail images or pictures – they distract from the words you are writing about yourself.

5. Focus your description of your current and previous experience on achievements and the contribution you have made to organizations. If possible quantify your achievements – 'my actions led to a saving of £xx' or, 'as a result profits were up by x per cent'.

6. Give examples of your skills and qualities – don't just say 'I am a natural leader', write a brief description of when you showed this attribute.

7. Avoid bullet points when describing your current and previous jobs. It's much better to write short paragraphs because you can give examples.

8. Format the document to make sure that the printed version reflects what you see on screen. Try not to waste paper by leaving just two or three sentences at the top of the last page.

9. Use 'active' verbs such as 'achieve', 'lead', 'manage'.

10. Finally carefully proofread your CV and, if you can, ask someone else to look at it as well.

How to send your CV

You can still post your CV if you wish but most HR professionals prefer to receive the document as an attachment to an email. This means that they can share the CV with the relevant staff or store it on their computer for future reference.

Online applications

Sometimes you will be asked to complete an application form online. Here are some tips to do this effectively:

- As for written job applications, you should write in a formal style.

- The online system will probably dictate the particular text format (the font and size of type) – you should take this into account when you draft your answers.

- It is useful to prepare a draft of the application and then transfer the information to the online form.

- Copy and save your answers regularly into a normal document in case the system crashes or you have to break off your application and start again.

- Just because the application is automatically filed online, does not mean you should be any less rigorous in the editing and proofreading you do. If you can print the document out before you submit it, get someone you trust to read it over to look for errors and omissions.

WRITING FORMAL LETTERS

Emails and other digital media are the prevalent forms of communication for most of us today, at work and at home, but there are still occasions when a handwritten or typed letter is more appropriate.

This section lays out the basic structure and the rules which underpin most formal letter writing. Other sections – Domestic Correspondence, Social Communication and Job Applications – look more closely at situations where formal letter writing is used, and give examples of good practice.

As with any written communication, your letter should be in three discernible parts:

- **An introduction.** This is where you introduce yourself, acknowledge any previous correspondence, and briefly state the reason why you are writing. Ideally it should be no longer than a paragraph of three or four sentences.

- **The middle.** This is the section where you expand your argument, provide further details, and raise any questions you have. The middle of the letter should be a series of paragraphs set out in a logical order. Each paragraph should make a clear, separate point. If the letter is long and covers a range of subjects, it may be appropriate to divide the contents by subheadings.

- **The ending, or conclusion.** The final paragraph should set out what you would like to happen as a result of the communication, whether that be a written response, a meeting to discuss the contents of the letter, or a demand for a refund.

Here is an example of a formal letter:

55 Torrance Close
Gorton
NSW 2234

25 August 2011

Mr L Dylan
Terrigan Building Ltd
340 Shorter Street
Terrigan
NSW 2234
Dear Mr Dylan

Estimate for extension to living room, 55 Torrance Close

I am writing to thank you for the written estimate which I received this morning. I have queries about a couple of details in your letter which I would like to be resolved before we proceed any further.

First, can you say exactly when you would propose to begin work on the extension? I realize this depends, to some extent, on how quickly you can finish your current project. I need to know which week work would commence in, however, so that I can make arrangements to store the living room furniture.

Second, can you tell me when you propose to fit the additional plumbing, so that I can arrange to stay with friends while there is no running water? Also, are there any other times when you anticipate that I shall be without water or electricity?

Finally, there is no mention of additional costs for materials? Can I assume, therefore, that these are included in the estimate you have provided for the overall cost of the extension?

Assuming I receive satisfactory answers in writing to these queries, I shall be happy to accept your proposal and go ahead with the project as discussed.

Yours sincerely

Tom Peterson

Tom Peterson

Points to remember:

- **Your address.** This should be written in the top right corner of the letter. Do not write your name here, and don't put commas after each line.

- **The date.** The date should come under your address, also on the right. It is common practice to write the date as 25 August 2011, instead of 25th August 2011.

- **The recipient's address.** Write this under the date, but on the left side of the page. Again, no punctuation is required.

- **The greeting.** If you are writing to a friend then you will use, 'Dear Luke,' for instance. Otherwise it should be 'Dear Mr Dylan.' Note that if you are writing to a woman and do not know whether she prefers to be addressed as 'Dear Mrs Dylan', or 'Dear Miss Dylan', then you should use 'Dear Ms Dylan.' If you do not know the person's name then use, 'Dear Sir or Madam'.

- **Headings.** If you are using a heading, then it should summarize the subject matter of the letter, and appear between the greeting and the first paragraph. Headings should be written in bold but not capital letters.

- **The ending.** If you have used the name of the person in the greeting, then you should end with 'Yours sincerely'. Otherwise end the letter with 'Yours faithfully'. 'Yours...' should always begin with a capital letter.

- **Punctuation.** It is not necessary to include a comma after the greeting or after the ending. Don't put full stops in initials – write 'Mr L H Dylan' instead of 'Mr L.H. Dylan'.

- **Signature.** Write your signature but include your typewritten name underneath.

- **Further contact details.** If you are including your email address or telephone number as contact details, then these should be included underneath your postal address:

> 55 Torrance Close
> Gorton
> NSW 2234
> tpeterson@email.com
> (02) 4254 6398

Once you have written your letter check that:

- You have explained why you are writing in the first paragraph.

- You have made all the points that you wanted to.

- Each sentence is clear, concise and unambiguous.

- You have not included too much information, or any irrelevant details.

- Your language has been courteous and polite, even if you are writing a letter of complaint.

- Check once more for spelling mistakes – it is surprisingly easy to miss them!

DOMESTIC CORRESPONDENCE

This section tackles the range of letters and correspondence that relates to you, your home, your finances and your family. The following points about content, style and tone apply equally whether you're writing a letter, an email, filling in an online form, or if you are speaking to someone on the phone:

- Use formal language.

- Include every detail that will make the letter easier to deal with.

- Lay the letter out clearly – breaking it down so that each paragraph contains a single point.

- Be explicit about what you want to happen next and introduce a timescale where appropriate.

- What you are writing may have legal implications, so take care with the details you include and the language you use.

- Provide as many contact details as you can.

- Write 'Yours sincerely' to end the letter if you know the surname of the person you are writing to. Write 'Yours faithfully' if you do not.

> *When I'm writing to a company, I always try and find out a specific person to address the letter to – or else it can just end up getting lost in the system.*
> (Teacher)

In the following section there is a selection of letters that many of us will have to write at some point:

- Housing problems.

- Money-related correspondence.

- Insurance claims.

- Local authority correspondence.

- School correspondence.

Housing problems

To a landlord concerning outstanding repairs

In the first instance, simply list the repairs required, and ask the landlord to contact you so that a time may be arranged for them to be carried out.

---

56 Kayside Close
Redditch
Worcs.
RD14 7NX

4 April 2011

Dear Mr Fairchild

I am writing to notify you that the following repairs to 56 Kayside Close require attention:

There are several loose tiles on the roof.
The kitchen tap is leaking.
The sealant round the bath needs replacing.

I would appreciate it if you would contact me as soon as possible to arrange a time to have these problems taken care of.
Thank you very much.

Yours sincerely

Matthew Chalmers

Matthew Chalmers

If you do not get a reply in a reasonable amount of time, write again, once more itemizing the repairs, and reminding the recipient how long you have been waiting. This time you might want to give the landlord a deadline, and show that you are aware of your rights in law.

Useful phrases

- Further to my previous correspondence, the following repairs to the above address remain outstanding: ...

- I have been waiting for a considerable amount of time to have these repairs completed.

- By law, a landlord is responsible for providing and maintaining residence in a good state of repair.

- Please contact me immediately so that we may resolve this problem.

- I would be glad if you could see that the matter is resolved as soon as possible.

56 Kayside Close
Hawkes Bay
4230

1 May 2011

Dear Mr Fairchild

I refer to my letter of 4th April 2011 requesting repairs to be completed to 56 Kayside Close. The following items remain outstanding:

There are several loose tiles on the roof.
The kitchen tap is leaking.
The sealant round the bath needs replacing.

I have been waiting for a considerable amount of time to have these repairs completed. I would ask you to take care of this matter within one week of receipt of this letter.

I remind you that by law, a landlord is responsible for providing and maintaining residence in a good state of repair, and for complying with housing and maintenance standards.

Please contact me immediately so that we may resolve this problem.

Yours sincerely

Matthew Chalmers

Matthew Chalmers

Letter to a housing advice centre regarding unfair rent

If your landlord/landlady is trying to put the rent up and you don't agree to the increase, it may be worth negotiating with them. They may agree to a lower rent increase in return rather than having to relet the property. Alternatively, they may agree to increase the rent in stages over a period of time.

> 45 Victoria
> Street
> Headley
> Northants.
> NO3 7FS
>
> 16 April 2011

The Rents Adviser
Headley Housing Advice
4 The Row
Headley
Northants.
NO2 4TY

Dear Sir/Madam

Unfair rent query

I am writing to request your advice on an issue regarding what I consider to be an unfair increase in rent.

My landlord has recently increased my rent from £300 a month to £360 a month. Not only do I find this amount unreasonable, but I am also having difficulty sustaining the payments. Furthermore, there are several outstanding repairs to be attended to in the house.

I would be grateful if you could inform me of my rights, and let me know what, if anything, I can do to challenge this increase.

I look forward to hearing from you.

Yours faithfully

Katherine Gulliver

Katherine Gulliver

Letter to a housing advice centre regarding eviction

Most private tenants can only be evicted if their landlord gets a possession order from the court. If your landlord has evicted you without following the correct procedure this may be illegal.

34 Tadworth
Court
Ducksbury
Berkshire
RD7 4GN

3 June 2011

Dear Sir/Madam

eviction query

I am writing to request advice from you regarding a matter of urgency.

My landlord has just issued me with an eviction notice, due to come into force on 4 July 2011. His justification for this action is that I have not paid my rent for the last two months.

I am a single mother with two young children, and I have been unable to pay the rent due to the fact that my ex-husband has not kept up regular maintenance payments over the last four months.

Could you please inform me of my rights, and advise me on how I should proceed?

I look forward to hearing from you. If you wish to speak to me directly, please call me on 01456 783219.

Thank you in advance.

Yours faithfully

Sally Nettles

Sally Nettles

Money-related correspondence

Letter to a lender advising of difficulty in mortgage payment

If you are having problems with your mortgage repayments, or think you will have problems in the near future, it is always wise to contact the lender and alert them as soon as possible. In your correspondence explain the problem clearly and state that you are keen to keep paying as much as you can. Also show that you can be flexible and are willing to negotiate.

Useful phrases

- I am writing to inform you that I am anticipating having some difficulty in continuing to meet my mortgage payments.

- I am currently finding it hard to meet all my financial commitments.

- My employers went into liquidation two months ago.

- I have recently been made redundant.

- I am suffering from a long-term illness, and am no longer entitled to sickness pay.

- I was wondering if it would be possible to reduce my monthly payments.

- I would like to request that my mortgage payments be reduced from July.

- I am keen to continue paying as much as possible.

- I would be pleased to come into your office and discuss this matter further with you.

- Would it be possible to arrange an interview with you, so that we may come to some sort of arrangement?

- I do hope that you will give sympathetic consideration to my situation, and look forward to hearing from you.

Pembroke Branch Tel. 6689575

15 May 2011

Mr J McVee
Senior Credit Controller
Castle Building Society
17 Martyn Place
Canberra
2602

Dear Mr McVee

request for reduction in mortgage payments

I am writing to inform you that, due to my recent redundancy, I am anticipating having some difficulty in continuing to meet my mortgage payments.

I am making every attempt to find work elsewhere, but if I am unsuccessful, I would like to request that my mortgage payments be temporarily reduced from July, and the terms of my mortgage extended accordingly.

I am keen to continue paying as much as possible, and am currently in consultation with my financial adviser to calculate how much money I can reasonably afford each month.

Would it be possible to arrange an interview with you, so that we may come to some sort of arrangement?

I do hope that you will give sympathetic consideration to my situation, and look forward to hearing from you.

Yours sincerely

Jack Everett

Jack Everett

Insurance claims

Most of us find ourselves having to make a claim to an insurance company at some stage in our lives – whether it be as the result of a car accident, burglary, incident on holiday or some other regrettable occurrence.

The claim can be made verbally, online or in a written statement but whichever form it takes, it is important to consider the kind of language you use and the information that you include.

Ms C Hall
32, Lime Road
Saddleworth
Devon
SD2 8LN
christinehall@email.com
17 June 2011

Ms Ying
Claims Assessor
Admirable Insurance Company
Claims Avenue
Spottington
Hants
SP31 4AQ

My policy number: AIC008997/CH56.

Dear Ms Ying,

I am writing to make an insurance claim, resulting from an accident I was involved in on 16 June 2011. My car is covered by a comprehensive insurance policy which I took out with you some time ago. The policy number is included above.

The incident occurred at approximately 3pm at the junction of New Street and London Road in Saddleworth. The other driver, a Mr Steve Wall, turned right out of New Street and drove into the front passenger side of my vehicle, causing extensive damage to the bodywork and the headlights. I have enclosed a picture of the damage, together with a diagram showing the relative positions of the vehicles, and the direction they were travelling in at the time of the accident.

Mr Wall has admitted liability for the accident. His insurance company's details, together with his policy number, are also enclosed.

As a result of the incident, my car is not roadworthy. I need therefore, to arrange to collect a replacement car from one of your suppliers, which I am entitled to according to the terms of my policy. Can you advise me on the nearest garage and confirm my entitlement? Please let me know if there are any other details you require to process my claim, and also give me an indication of how long it will take to arrange the repair of my vehicle.

Yours sincerely

Ms C Hall

Ms C Hall

- The letter contains all the relevant information – such as dates, policy number, details of the incident – that the company is likely to require.

- In spite of the nature of the incident, the language is restrained – emotional language will not make your claim any more likely to succeed.

- The letter politely requests information from the insurance company which will move the claim on.

Local authority correspondance

Letter to planning authority inquiring whether planning permission is needed

Some minor developments (such as certain extensions to domestic property, or changes in the way a building is used) may not need express planning permission. With buildings that are listed for preservation, it is generally best to consult with the local planning authority before any changes are made.

If you are unsure whether your development requires planning permission, you should contact your local planning authority.

19 Limes Avenue
Cambridge
CB12 4LA
tel: 01356 721673

17 June 2011

The Planning Department
Cambridge District Council
University Road
Cambridge
CB2 7KS

Dear Sir/Madam

Inquiry re. necessity of planning permission

I am writing to inquire as to whether I will need to apply for planning permission for a proposed development I wish to undertake at the above address.

The specifications of the development are as follows:

description:
garage
location:
side of property
use:
car storage
dimensions:
floor surface area: 6m x 3.5m
height: 2.5m

If you require any further information, please do not hesitate to contact me at the telephone number above. I look forward to hearing from you.

Yours faithfully

Harriet Yates

Harriet Yates (Mrs)

Opposing a planning application

If you are making an objection to a planning proposal, check which aspects of the proposal you can object to and what deadlines the local authority have imposed. Comply with these and lay out your letter clearly, keeping the objections succinct and relevant.

Mr Anderson
Director of Planning
Lime Borough Council
Acacia Road
Lessington
County Durham
D5 1AA

Dear Mr Anderson,

Planning application number LBC123456/7A
Address of proposed extension: 77 Birchtree Row, Lessington, County Durham, D2 8LN

I am writing to object to the proposal to build an extension on the above property. There are several reasons for this.

Design
The very modern design of the proposed extension is in unsympathetic contrast to the Victorian style of all the houses in the area.

Privacy
The two-storey extension will affect the privacy of my property. The plans show a window that will look directly into my garden.

Natural light
The extension will block out the natural light I get in my conservatory all-year round.

Appropriateness of use
It is clear from the plans that the owner intends to make and sell drum kits from the property. This will have a significant impact on the local noise levels - the neighbourhood at the moment is very quiet.

I am sure that other local residents will be objecting as well, and I trust you will refuse this application on the basis that it most definitely contravenes your planning regulations.

I would be grateful if you could acknowledge this letter, confirm that it has been logged as an objection to the application within the deadline set by the council, and keep me informed as to the outcome. I can be contacted at the above address or via the email address at the top of this letter.

Yours Sincerely,

Mr C Hopkins

Mr C Hopkins

- The writer has found out the deadline for his objection and complied with it.

- He has found out and addressed the criteria on which the application will be judged.

- The headings highlight the grounds on which he is basing his objection.

Writing to your MP

When writing to your MP keep the letter to a single subject and make it as concise as possible. Remember to say what you want the MP to do as a result of your letter. At all times be courteous – just because you may disagree with his views, does not mean that you should be anything other than respectful in your writing.

Mr R Boscombe
27 Juniper Road
Flickcroft
West Midlands
reg.boscombe@email.com

15 April 2011

Derek Firbanks MP
House of Commons
Westminster
LONDON
SW1A 1AA

Dear Derek Firbanks

I am writing to draw your attention to the imminent closure of the Priory Centre on Sandhurst Road in Flickcroft. I am a parent whose child uses the premises for a theatre group on Saturday mornings. She finds the opportunity to learn about acting and to perform stimulating and great fun. The group also provides invaluable contact with other children from the area and with the community in general.

There are 120 children aged from six to 16 who attend the theatre classes every week – divided into three age bands. Last term my daughter's group staged a production dramatizing the history of the Priory Centre and its place in the local community.

The theatre group is by no means the only one affected. There are some 30 other activities put on for a huge range of people, including for elderly and disabled groups, at weekends and during the week.

The council plans to pass the plans at a meeting in three weeks' time. I, and many others, would be grateful if you could take this matter up with the leader of the council as a matter of urgency. The loss of the centre will create a huge gap in the cultural life of our community.

Please acknowledge this letter as soon as you can and let me know of your progress.

Yours sincerely,

Mr R Boscombe

Mr R Boscombe

- The letter starts with a very specific description of the problem.

- The writer includes his full address so that the MP knows the letter is from a constituent.

- The letter is about one issue which makes it much easier to deal with.

- Including anecdotes or some personal detail will help the MP remember the letter.

- The writer refers to others who are opposed to the closure. Including supporting evidence – be it a petition or the MPs involvement with or voting record on similar issues – will help the cause.

> *When contacting your MP, a short, handwritten or printed letter is most effective. Take the time to edit your letter for brevity and clarity. Try to make a single coherent point.*
>
> (Campaigning website)

Deferring jury service

A letter requesting you to serve on a jury is a serious matter – in the UK if you ignore it you could be prosecuted. If the dates you have been called for are very disruptive to your plans, or circumstances are such that you can't attend, then you should write asking for a deferment. The grounds for deferment will be laid out in the letter you receive.

Mr J Brown
The Moorings
Chettleworth
LINCOLNSHIRE
AG7 0BC
james.brown@email.com
01285 78945613

3 February 2011

Mr R Ball
Jury Central Summoning Bureau
Derby
DA1 9IO

Dear Mr Ball

Thank you for the letter dated January 30th inviting me to serve on a jury from March 27th. I would like to ask if it would be possible to defer this until sometime next year? My wife has recently had a car accident and suffered a serious injury. I have now had to become a full-time carer for her and as a consequence cannot leave the house for an extended period.

I would be very grateful if you could agree to this request, and if you require me to provide you with any further information, please do not hesitate to contact me.

I look forward to receiving your response.

Yours sincerely,

Mr James Brown

Mr James Brown

- It is more effective to provide specific details for your request: it decreases the likelihood of having to give more information and speeds up the process.

- Do not demand that your attendance is deferred.

School correspondence

There are a few occasions when it will be necessary to write, or email, your child's school about health matters, behaviour or other issues. Below are an email, two letters and a hand-written note giving examples of this kind of correspondence.

Explaining a child's absence due to ill health

To: J Chalfont <jchalfont@derwentwaterschool.ed.uk
From: kevin.bond@email.net

Subject: Charlie Bond's absence 1st - 5th March

Dear Mr Chalfont

I am writing to explain why Charlie was absent from school last week (1st to 5th March). He woke up with a very sore throat on Sunday morning. We went to the doctor on Monday and Charlie was diagnosed with laryngitis. He started to feel better on Friday morning and is able to return to school today.

Charlie is worried, as the exams approach, about keeping on top of his work, so I would be very grateful if you could let him know what he has missed and help him catch up.

If you have any concerns, please do email or phone me on the number below.

Yours sincerely

Mr K Bond
kevin.bond@email.net
Tel: 01234 456789

- The letter quickly and clearly summarizes the course of events and includes evidence of the illness by referring to the doctor's diagnosis.

- The parent, having been very clear about the reason for absence, then presents his own concerns and is explicit about what he wants the teacher to do. The letter is useful and effective for the teacher, the parent and the pupil.

Recording concerns about bullying

Mrs J Trewin
'The Glade'
Farm Road
Kettering
XA7 2WR
janetrewin@email.com
01234 5678913

29 January 2011

Ms L Edge
Long Oak Primary School
West End Lane
Kettering
XA5 9LD

Dear Ms Edge

I am writing to follow up on our conversation on the phone two days ago. I'm afraid that Julia is still very upset when she gets home from school. The name-calling and exclusion from playground games seems to have carried on, in spite of the warning you said you gave the other children concerned. In fact, I fear that it may have made the problem worse.

As you can imagine this is causing Julia great distress and it is certainly affecting her desire to come to school and learn. I am very anxious to get this matter resolved with all possible speed, and request a meeting with you and the head of year at your earliest convenience.

Please telephone or email me as soon as you can to arrange this.

Yours sincerely

Mrs J Trewin

Mrs J Trewin

- The letter quickly summarizes the current situation to remind the teacher of the problem.

- The parent suggests a specific course of action and a timetable.

Excusing a child from religious instruction

67 Langley Avenue
Crawley
W. Sussex
RH8 3FX

12 July 2011

Mrs J Wilson
Langley Green Secondary School
Langley Drive
Crawley
RH8 4WA

Dear Mrs Wilson

religious instruction

My son, Aashir, will be attending your school from the beginning of next term, and I am writing to ask that he be excused from religious education classes.

He is being raised in the Muslim faith, and receives his religious instruction outside school.

Thank you very much for your understanding.

Yours sincerely

Mahira Pandit

Mahira Pandit (Mrs)

Non-completion of homework

Dear Mr Mitchell

John was unable to finish his essay that was due to be handed in today, as he was suffering from a severe migraine for most of yesterday evening.

He will make every effort to complete it tonight and hand it in tomorrow.

Thank you for your understanding.

Yours sincerely
Helen Maxwell

LETTERS OF COMPLAINT

Complaining about faulty goods or services is an unpleasant but common experience. Whatever your complaint, there are several points which you should bear in mind when composing a letter or email to increase your chances of receiving a satisfactory response:

- Make sure you are complaining to the right person. It may seem obvious, but if you have paid for something in cash or by credit card, then it is the seller of the goods or services who you should address your complaint to – not the manufacturer.

- Be aware of your rights under the Sales and Supply of Goods Act, the Trades Descriptions Act and related legislation – these decree that goods or services must be found to be 'as described' when sold.

- There are consumer watchdogs and other bodies who can help you if you are given unsatisfactory responses to your complaints. You can also write to your MP or consult a solicitor, but these should be last measures which hopefully won't be necessary.

Useful phrases

- I am writing to express my dissatisfaction with the service I received from your ...

- At the time of booking it was agreed that ...

- However, on our arrival, we discovered that ...

- I recently bought ...(include colour, model and price) in your shop in ...

- When I tried to use this item, I discovered that ...

- I have contacted you by telephone three times and each time you have promised to visit and put the faults right.

- To date these problems have not been resolved.

- Under the terms of your guarantee, I would like to request a full reimbursement of the amount paid.

- I am withholding payment of the above invoice until I have heard your response to the points outlined above.

- Under the Goods and Services Act 1982, I am entitled to expect work to be carried out using due care and skill.

- If I do not hear from you within 14 days, I will have no choice but to take the matter further.

- Because of these faults I now consider you to be in breach of contract.

Letter or email of complaint concerning faulty goods

Mr F Headley
15 High Street
Corton
LANCS
LA12 3SH
fheadley@email.com

17 August 2011

Mr D Bryant
High Fi
3 The Parade
Soulton
LANCS
LA23 8GG

Dear Mr Bryant,

I am writing to complain about the Soundalive 411 headphones which I bought from your company, High Fi in Soulton, on 14 August.

When I plugged the headphones into my compact disc player and listened to music through them, the sound in the left headphone was distorted at even low levels of volume – it was clear to me that they were faulty.

I returned them to your shop, a thirty mile round trip, but the salesperson who I originally dealt with disputed my claim - stating that the item had been sold in a satisfactory state. He suggested that I take up the complaint with you, as the owner of the shop.

The Sale of Goods Act 1979 makes it clear that goods be as described, fit for purpose and of satisfactory quality. I am therefore rejecting the headphones and request that you refund the £89 I paid, as the condition of the goods I received constitutes a breach of contract. I have enclosed a copy of my receipt.

I also require you to confirm whether you will arrange for the headphones to be collected from me at the above address, or will reimburse me for the cost of returning them by post?

I expect to receive a response detailing your proposals to satisfactorily settle my claim within seven days of this date.

Yours sincerely,

Mr F Headley

Mr F Headley

- Although the writer has being treated badly by a member of staff, the tone of the letter is formal. Emotive language is likely to produce a defensive response, whereas a detailed and factual description of the problem is more likely to succeed.

- It is quite reasonable to seek compensation for the cost of returning a faulty item.

- Don't send originals of receipts and other documentary evidence with your complaint – especially if you have paid in cash. They may be the only way you have to prove purchase should you need to take the complaint further.

Letter to a travel agency complaining about a holiday

Customer Services department
Sunkissed Holidays
14 The Waterglades
Hintenbury
GLOS
FL34 7HH

Dear sir or madam

I am writing to complain about the holiday I booked through your company on 5 May this year (REF: BA12303/Maga003).

The booking stated that I would have a room with a balcony with ocean views, and that I would enjoy '5 star luxury' at the Mirabelle Resort, with 'top class international cuisine', and 'a choice of four swimming pools – two of which are reserved for adult use only.' Furthermore, the booking was on an 'all-inclusive basis, guaranteeing bar snacks, soft drinks and local brands of beers, wines and spirits', as and when I requested them.

The reality of my experience was very different. On arrival at the resort, I was allocated a room at the back of the hotel, with a view over a busy street. The noise from the traffic kept me awake at night.

The 'international cuisine' turned out to be a buffet featuring the same options practically every night – mostly fried food, chips and salad.

One of the swimming pools was closed for maintenance for the duration of my stay, and there was no attempt to keep any of the three remaining pools segregated for adult use.

Finally, the availability of drinks and bar snacks was very limited – peanuts were the only snack at the poolside bar, which also only had wine stocked on two days of the fourteen I was at the hotel.

I complained about each of these issues to your firm's representative at the resort – a Mr Stephens – during my first week's holiday. He said he would 'see what he could do'. I didn't hear back from him, and he failed to turn up for the 'rep meeting' in the second week. The hotel staff were unhelpful and told me they could do nothing to rectify any of the problems.

As a result of these issues, my holiday was ruined. I am therefore writing to you seeking compensation from your firm, which has clearly failed to deliver what was contractually agreed. I request that you reply within seven days, stating your proposal to compensate me.

Yours faithfully

Mrs B Pritchard

Mrs B Pritchard

- Use the company's own description of services to compare your experience with.

- Describe each aspect of your complaint concisely; state what you have done about it, and the response that you received from the relevant authority – in this case the holiday rep and the hotel staff.

Letter of complaint to a noisy neighbour

Mr G Barton
7 Chestnut Mansions
Pibble
Cumbria
PW12 3RR
gbarton@email.com

14 October 2011

Ms R Devlin
8 Chestnut Mansions
Pibble
Cumbria
PW12 3RR

Dear Ms Devlin

I am writing to you to formally register my complaint about the excessive noise that has been generated from your flat since you moved in two months ago.

As you know, I have complained in person to you five times in the past month about extremely loud music being played after 11 pm. You have assured me that you will 'not let it happen again,' only for me and my partner to have our sleep ruined the next weekend.

We have no objection to the occasional party or celebration, but your behaviour is inconsiderate and unreasonable. The interruption to our sleep patterns is affecting our concentration at work, and therefore I am giving you notice that if this happens again, without prior notice and agreement from us, I shall instruct my solicitor to begin legal proceedings to restrain you from excessive noise pollution.

Yours sincerely

Mr G Barton

Mr G Barton

- Legal action should only be threatened after attempts to complain less formally have failed. This letter is written after five such attempts.

- Be clear about what you expect to happen as a result of your complaint – how you expect the other party to modify their behaviour in this instance.

- Also spell out what course of action you intend to take should your demands not be met. You must follow through on this course of action, if you don't get a satisfactory response, or you will not be taken seriously in the future.

Letter complaining about shoddy workmanship

If you are dissatisfied with a piece of work which has been carried out for you discuss the problem with the tradesperson first, and give them a chance to put it right. If this doesn't work, put your complaint in writing giving a clear deadline. If you chose a contractor that belongs to a trade association, they may offer a conciliation or arbitration service to settle your dispute.

Keep copies of all letters sent and received and make a note of conversations.

---

77 Bishop Road
Newport
Gwent
NP3 5NQ

31 October 2011

The Customer Services Manager
L. Smart & Co. Contractors
17 Trevellyan Road
Cardiff
CA4 5GT

Dear Sir/Madam

Re: estimate 700003412

I am writing to express my dissatisfaction with the service I received from one of your builders recently.

Before accepting your estimate for the job, I was assured that the work would be completed by 10 October. Three weeks later, the work is still incomplete. Moreover, the work that has been done is defective. The new door that was fitted is not flush with the frame, and the lock is consequently very stiff.

If the work is not completed and the defect rectified within 14 days, I shall consider our contract to be at an end. I shall then instruct another firm to complete the work, and deduct the cost from your original price.

Yours faithfully

Douglas Fairburn

Douglas Fairburn

Complaining to a health authority

If you wish to make a complaint regarding healthcare treatment you have received you should address your letter to the Complaints Manager of the Local Health Authority. Start by giving the name of the doctor, GP or practitioner concerned and then provide a brief background to the case. Explain the problem clearly and if your complaint consists of a catalogue of errors, itemize them clearly and succinctly.

It is one of the NHS's officially stated core principles that it is committed to shaping its services around the needs and preferences of individual patients, their families and carers. You should not be afraid to voice your opinion.

---

7 Oaklands
Horley
RH6 2QT

17 November 2011

The Complaints Manager
East Surrey Local Health Authority
5 Market Street
Redhill
RH1 4GA

Dear Sir

I am writing to express my concern about the treatment that my elderly mother, Mrs Grace Harding, is currently undergoing. Her GP is Dr Middleton at the Longwood Surgery, Horley.

In 2005, my mother was diagnosed as suffering from shingles. Since that time she has experienced continual pain down the sides of her body.

However, she recently received a letter informing her that she would no longer be able to attend the pain clinic. She has been given no explanation as to the reasons for this decision from the health authority or from her doctor.

Since it is one of the NHS's officially stated core principles that it is committed to shaping its services around the needs and preferences of individual patients, I feel that you have a duty to ensure that she enjoys this later period of her life.

I would be glad to hear your comments on this case.

Yours faithfully

G. Glover

Gillian Glover

Complaining about financial services

If you are having problems with a bank you must complain to the firm in question before you can take your complaint to the financial ombudsman. When writing your letter remember to include your customer number of your policy or your account number. Enclose copies of any relevant documents that you believe support your case and always keep a copy of any letters between you and the firm. You may need to refer to them later.

4 Crow Lane
Wagga Wagga
2650

24 October 2011

The Customer Relations Manager
Castle Building Society
Short Street
Wagga Wagga
2650

Dear Sir/Madam

Complaint: savings acc. no. 9450001992

I wish to register my dissatisfaction with the service that I have received from the staff at your Brighton branch.

I opened a savings account, and arranged for a monthly standing order of $200 a month to be made from my current account, held at another bank. However, the last time I asked for a mini-statement, I noticed that there had not been a credit to my savings account for the previous two months, despite the fact that the money had been debited from my current account. Enclosed are copies of both the relevant statements.

I am therefore appealing to you for a thorough investigation into this matter, and look forward to hearing from you.

Yours faithfully

Patrick Horton

Patrick Horton

SOCIAL COMMUNICATION

> *And none will hear the postman's knock*
> *Without a quickening of the heart.*
> *For who can bear to feel himself forgotten?*

(W.H. Auden)

Although seemingly belonging to a different world – predating mobile phones, texts and tablet devices, all of which convey informal messages instantly and very well – there is still a time and a place for a carefully handwritten note or card, or printed invitation.

Types of correspondence in this category include:

- Thank you notes
- Letters of apology
- Letters wishing a speedy recovery
- Letters of condolence
- Invitations

Here are some general points to consider when writing social communications:

Tone

Apart from invitations, the tone of most social communications is informal and friendly:

- Salutations can range from 'Dear' to 'Hi'.

- Language is usually quite conversational, with shortened sentences and contractions ('I'm', 'won't'); more emotive and less factual than in business correspondence.

- Endings are similarly warm – 'Lots of love'; 'Love'; 'Speak/write soon'; or slightly more formal such as 'Best wishes', 'Kind regards' or 'All the best' if you don't know your correspondent quite so well.

Format

Just because it is handwritten doesn't mean that a note shouldn't have a structure. It is still usual to have:

- An introductory line or paragraph, stating the purpose of the letter ('I was sorry to hear about your loss'; 'thank you for the birthday card...').

- A middle section expounding on the subject ('She was a wonderful woman...'; 'The party went really well, all things considered').

- An ending ('I shall hope to speak to you at the memorial service'; 'Let's meet up before another year goes by...').

> *One thing I can't stand? The computer-generated Christmas card – it's so impersonal – "Look, I can do a mail merge on my pc!" If you can't be bothered to handwrite a greetings card, don't bother!*
>
> (Publishing assistant)

Here are some examples of different kinds of social correspondence:

Thank you note for a dinner party

A thank you letter can be as varied as a formal letter: the writer's relationship with the recipient will determine the tone and language used.

Tuesday

Hi Moz,

I'm just popping this note through your letterbox to thank you so much for dinner on Saturday. Nigel and I had a wonderful evening. It was lovely to meet Sharon and Graham at last – you've talked about them so much over the years - and they were delightful company. I hope Ben has found the champagne cork (sorry about that!)

By the way, please, please send me your recipe for the chocolate mousse – it was exquisite, and Nigel talked of nothing else on Sunday.

You must come to ours for dinner soon.

Love to you both and thanks again,

Lizzie.

- Dating and address can be very informal – this is a note between friends, and knowledge of addresses and contact details can be assumed. Note that the writer uses her friend's nickname 'Moz', rather than full name. You wouldn't use this form of address if writing to a colleague, for example.

- The language is casual – contractions like 'you've' and 'I'm' are absolutely fine. "Please, please send me your recipe...' would be out of place in a formal letter, but it works here.

- In social communication you can refer to events without having to be explicit – here there was clearly an 'incident' with a champagne cork which was a shared source of humour.

Writing a letter of apology

If you feel compelled to apologize for your actions and wish to send the person concerned a letter of apology you should start by making it clear that you are saying sorry. State plainly what you are apologizing for and explain your actions or the mistake (as the case may be) as far as you can. Accept responsibility if you are at fault and try to suggest a means by which you can right the wrong. At the end of the letter, reiterate your apology.

Useful phrases

- I am writing to apologize for ...

- I've just realized that ...

- I can't tell you how sorry I am.

- I am sorry that ...

- Due to ..., I was unable to ...

- I know it's no excuse, but ...

- Unfortunately ...

- I hope you will accept ...

- Can I suggest ...?

- Would you agree to ...?

- Again, please accept my apologies (for ...).

- In the meantime, many apologies again.

Letters wishing a speedy recovery

FAQ

Q. *What sort of tone should I use?*
A. It is acceptable to use a fairly informal tone if you know that the person will recover quickly. If the illness is serious, you will need to use a slightly more formal tone.

Q. *Should I send a card or a letter?*
A. For informal wishes, a card is most appropriate. For more formal wishes, or if the illness is serious, you may like to write a letter.

Informal wishes (card)

- Hoping you get well very soon.

- Wishing you a speedy recovery.

- Sorry to hear you're not well. We're thinking of you

Formal wishes (letter)

- I was very sorry to hear of …

- Please accept my sympathies …

- … and best wishes for a speedy recovery.

- It must be an anxious time for you.

- You have our deepest sympathy.

- Is there any way in which we can help?

- If there's anything I can do, please don't hesitate to let me know.

- We hope and trust you will soon be better.

- We are feeling for you.

Formal letter wishing someone a speedy recovery

Upper Steading 17 June, 2011

Dear Mr Grierson

We were very sorry to hear of your wife's sudden illness. Please accept our sympathies and give her our best wishes for a speedy recovery.

It must be a very anxious time for you. If there's anything we can do, please don't hesitate to let us know. In the meantime, we are thinking of you both.

Yours sincerely
Mary Fawkes

If the recipient is unlikely to make a full recovery, it is unwise to suggest that this might be the case.

Letter of condolence

46 Cork Lane
Lamington
Herts

12 May

Dear Stephen

I am writing to say how sorry I was to hear of your loss, and that I am thinking of you at this difficult time. Although I was aware that Helen was ill, I was nevertheless shocked to hear of her passing.

I know she was never happier than when she had met you, and the two of you made a lovely couple. She seemed to light up the life of everyone who met her.

I shall certainly attend the memorial service next Thursday, but if there is anything I can do in the meantime Stephen, please don't hesitate to call me. I'm sure Jo and Max are a great comfort to you at the moment.

Thinking of you all with love and affection.

Fiona

- The main point of difference with a thank you letter, is that the writer should be acutely sensitive to the addressee's feelings, rather than trying to express their own emotions. The references made to the deceased in this letter are mainly in the context of her relationship with the bereaved partner, rather than the writer.

- A handwritten note can be more appropriate than a phone call in situations of grief and loss like this. Writing a letter also gives you more time to think about what you want to say, and how you want to say it.

- Note that the letter, although it is informal in address and tone, still has a discernible structure: the introductory sentence explains the purpose of the letter; the middle paragraph expands on the theme with the writer's memories of the deceased; and the final paragraph acknowledges the future by accepting an invitation and offering support.

> *It really helped to receive letters of support from friends. Even though I didn't feel like talking to anyone at the time, it was good to know that others appreciated Jim, and that people were thinking of me and the kids.*
>
> (Widow)

Invitations

Invitations are frequently made by email or by text these days, but there are occasions when a written or printed invitation is still the prevalent form of communication.

Occasions that might require an invitation include:

- Weddings.

- Birthday parties.

A wedding invitation

Boris and Isabel Andrews
request the pleasure of the company of
Phillip and Sally Bairstow
at the wedding of their daughter Florence
to James Chater
on Saturday June 18 2011
at St Bart's Church, Eggleton at 2pm.

R.S.V.P.
Isabel Andrews, The Gildings, Foxton Lane, Biblington, BB13 5TR
Tel: 01286 5543077.

- The most important feature of an invitation is that it must possess all the necessary information to allow the recipient to respond with an acceptance or a refusal. There is no point sending out wedding invitations to 400 guests without the date on them!

- Social invitations can be informal or formal. Formal invitations – to a wedding or a christening, for example – will usually be printed.

A Birthday invitation

> YIKES!
> I'm (nearly) thirty!
> Help me get over it on Saturday 21 May
> at the Stag, Riddlesway, Broxton.
> There'll be drinking, dancing and a very special quiz
> – how can you refuse?
> Please RSVP as soon as possible,
> so I can sort out some eats for the night.
> See you there,
> Charlie Bright
> cbright@email.com
> 06785 4459881

- This invitation could be sent in the form of an email, handwritten note or printed card.

- The tone is humorous and the language (and punctuation) informal, which suits the occasion.

- The font is also deliberately informal.

- Note the promise of a 'very special quiz,' to intrigue the reader and hopefully persuade them to attend.

- Even with this casual approach, the host has taken care to include all the information which the recipient will need to decide whether they can attend or not.

Replying to invitations

- When replying to invitations, match the style and formality of the invite.

- If you have to decline an invitation, it is good practice to sound apologetic, regretful and explain the reason why you cannot attend.

WRITING SPEECHES

At some point in your life you're going to have to stand up in front of a group of people and make a speech. It could be at a wedding, at work or at a friend's significant birthday party or your own. Whatever the occasion, there are some basic language rules you should follow to make your speech successful and memorable.

Preparation

As with all written work, preparation is the key to writing a good speech. There are some basics you should cover before you start to write:

- **Make sure you know who you're speaking to.** Always keep in mind all of your audience when you start preparing your speech. If the occasion is going to have a mix of people who you know well and some you know less well, then the tone and content will be less intimate than if you are speaking to good friends and family.

- **Decide or establish with the hosts how long your speech should be.** This could depend on the number of other speakers, the length of time the venue has been hired for, or what other entertainment or activities are planned.

- **Start your research early.** For example, if you are making a speech for a colleague's retirement, try and speak to old as well as current workmates so that you have a range of stories and views to draw from.

- **Think about the venue.** Is it likely to be noisy? Are the audience going to be sitting down and comfortable or standing and eager to move? A long, detailed speech in uncomfortable surroundings will quickly lose the audience's attention.

- **Decide on your main theme.** All good speeches have a central idea that the speaker wants to make – it doesn't matter whether the occasion is a eulogy, wedding or a speech to the student union.

Structure and content

When you have covered this ground, you can start to write the speech. There are three main parts to it:

The opening

This is perhaps the most important part of the speech. Work hard to make it effective:

- **Try to grab your audience's attention from the start.** Make a joke, a controversial statement, or do something unexpected and entertaining. The opening sets the tone for the rest of the speech.

- **Give a brief outline of what you are going to say.** This will help the audience anticipate which parts might be of particular interest to them, and give them a rough idea of how far into the speech you are at any one time.

The body

Having got your audience's attention, you now need to develop your themes:

- **The main theme.** Use the main theme as a thread working through the body of the speech. If you are going to spend a little time talking about related but not central themes, tell your audience what you are doing and why.

- **Use anecdotes.** If possible illustrate your themes with anecdotes. If you're saying what a kind person the bride or a colleague is, tell a story that shows this.

- **Use stories from other people.** Include quotes from friends, famous people or colleagues to vary the tone of the speech.

Above all remember that regardless of the precise aim of the speech, your duty is to entertain: you've asked for people's attention, it is your job to reward them.

The finish

Just as with the opening, you need to finish in a way that will make the speech memorable.

- **Recapping.** Before you end your speech, you should signal to the audience that you are winding up by recapping the points you have made and saying what you hope to have achieved.

- **Thanking your audience.** You should always thank them for their time and attention and leave them with a memorable phrase, statistic or story.

> *Remember, the golden rule of public speaking is to be yourself. An audience can tell when you're being natural and when you're not.*
> (Professional public speaker)

Useful phrases for specific occasions

Weddings

Traditionally, at a wedding, there are three main speeches: the bride's father's; the bridegroom's and the best man's. Nowadays the bride often speaks too. The speeches act as a way of saying thank you to different people and as a prelude to a toast by each speaker.

The bride's father

The bride's father proposes the main toast to the bride and groom and gives a general welcome and thank you to everyone for coming along. He should say a few indulgent words about his daughter and new son-in-law before proposing the toast. Useful phrases for the father of the bride include:

- 'On behalf of [name of wife] and myself, I would like to start by saying what a pleasure it is to welcome [groom's parents], [names of close relatives] and you all to this happiest of occasions...'
- 'As father of the bride, it is my great privilege....'
- 'I am honoured on the proudest day of my life to welcome you all to the wedding of...'
- 'It is now my pleasure to propose a toast to the happy couple. Please be upstanding and raise your glasses to the bride and groom [names]'
- 'Ladies and gentlemen, the bride and groom'.

The bridegroom

The bridegroom has the responsibility of responding to the bride's father, thanking people for coming, mentioning people who could not make it, and saying a few words about his bride. His toast should be to the bridesmaids. Some useful phrases include:

- 'I would like to thank you both [bride's father and mother's names] for welcoming me into the family'
- 'I'd like to thank [bride's father's name] for those very kind words...'·
- 'Thank you to our lovely bridesmaids for taking such good care of [bride's name] and getting her here on time...'

The best man

The best man's speech is traditionally a response on behalf of the bridesmaids – a point often overlooked as guests at a wedding wait for the speech billed as the main event! The best man will also toast the bride and groom's parents before proposing the final toast to the happy couple. Some useful phrases include:

- 'Firstly on behalf of the bridesmaid(s) [names], I'd like to thank [groom's name] for his kind words....'

- 'To the bride and groom's parents and those friends and relatives who couldn't make it today....'

- 'it gives me great pleasure to invite you to stand and raise your glasses in a toast to the bride and groom. We wish them every happiness in their life together...'

A eulogy

> *The eulogy is the moment at which the deceased is brought close,*
> *and a time when he or she steps away.*
> *It is at once a greeting and a letting go*
>
> (Andrew Motion, former Poet Laureate)

A eulogy is a speech given at a memorial or funeral service that celebrates a person's life. If you are giving a eulogy the same rules apply as with any speech: know who your audience is and pitch the speech appropriately.

- Try to entertain as much as the circumstances allow: the audience will be on your side and a funny or appropriate anecdote will help release some of the emotions in the room.

- Be careful not to speak for too long – most eulogies are between three and five minutes; ten at the very most.

- Sometimes more than one person speaks in which case you should talk to the other speakers before the service to make sure you are not saying the same things.

- If you are the only person giving a eulogy, take time to gather the thoughts and anecdotes of other people.

Here are some useful questions to ask yourself (and others) when you are preparing to write your speech:

- How did I first meet the deceased?

- Is there a picture in your mind (of an event or occasion) that you associate with them in particular?

- What have others said to you about the deceased?

- What will you miss most about them?

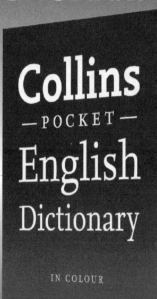

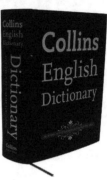

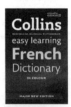

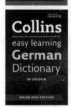